PIMLICO

599

CA

Linda Colley has taught and written history on both sides of the Atlantic. Formerly Richard M. Colgate Professor of History at Yale University and School Professor of History at the London School of Economics, she is now Shelby M. C. Davis 1958 Professor of History at Princeton University. A Fellow of the British Academy, and a regular commentator on current events as well as past cultures, her last book *Britons: Forging the Nation 1707-1837* (1992) won the Wolfson Prize and provoked a major debate on national identities in Britain and elsewhere.

Praise for *Captives*

'*Captives* is an invitation to think again about an old story too often told in the same old way . . . It is a book which should alter the way in which the history not only of the British, but of all the European empires is written.' Anthony Pagden, *London Review of Books*

'Superb . . . coruscating.' Niall Ferguson, *Independent on Sunday*

'This book abounds in fascinating human stories and constantly requires the reader to reconsider accepted dogma.' Philip Ziegler, *Daily Telegraph*

'Brilliantly illuminating.' Christopher Hitchens, *Washington Post*

'Brilliant and original.' Paul Kennedy, *Los Angeles Times*.

'Sublimely well written: cunningly paced, beguilingly fluent, deftly allusive, vividly evocative. It is a major contribution to understanding the paradox of the British: the weak who wangled the earth.' Felipe Fernandez-Armesto, *Literary Review*

'In her reappraisal of what used to be called the first British Empire, Linda Colley mixes genres, turns things around, takes micro-historical stories to the front of the picture in order to fracture the grand narrative . . . In all this, she is a historian of her time; but she is also a completely original intelligence.' Roy Foster, *Financial Times*

'[A] rich, unfailingly inquisitive new book.' John Mullan, *Times Literary Supplement*

'Anyone interested in British history will be happily held prisoner by this learned and eloquent volume.' Michael Gorra, *Boston Globe*

'Linda Colley is a great storyteller and she breathes life into the manuscripts she has discovered by captives in the early days of the Empire.' Martin Bright, *Observer*

'A work of exceptional scholarship, maturity, fairness and originality.' Richard Govender, *New World*

'Dexterous, wonderfully subtle.' Andrew Holgate, *Sunday Times*

'This fine, thought-provoking book – at once readable and educative – is crammed full of . . . telling insights.' Saul David, *Sunday Telegraph*

'Stunningly revisionist . . . Almost every page of *Captives* challenges a settled orthodoxy or opens up a fertile new field for research.' David Armitage, *History Today*

'Endlessly fascinating.' Ian Bell, *Sunday Herald*

CAPTIVES

Britain, Empire and the World, 1600–1850

LINDA COLLEY

PIMLICO

2002 .

Published by Pimlico 2003

2 4 6 8 10 9 7 5 3 1

First published in Great Britain by Jonathan Cape 2002
Pimlico edition 2003

Random House, 20 Vauxhall Bridge Road,
London SW1V 2SA

Random House Australia (Pty) Limited
20 Alfred Street, Milsons Point, Sydney,
New South Wales 2061, Australia

Random House New Zealand Limited
18 Poland Road, Glenfield,
Auckland 10, New Zealand

Random House South Africa (Pty) Limited
Endulini, 5A Jubilee Road, Parktown 2193, South Africa

The Random House Group Limited Reg. No. 954009
www.randomhouse.co.uk

A CIP catalogue record for this book
is available from the British Library

ISBN 0–7126–6528–5

Printed and bound in Great Britain by
Bookmarque Ltd, Croydon, Surrey

In memory of my mother
Marjorie Colley, née Hughes
1920–1998

Contents

Part Two

AMERICA
Captives and Embarrassments

Part Three

INDIA
Captives and Conquest

List of Illustrations

The illustrations in this book form an integral part of the text and have been captioned accordingly. Their full titles and provenance are as follows.

I am most grateful to the libraries, art galleries and private owners listed below for allowing me to reproduce images in their possession. Images with no provenance cited are from my own collection of prints, books and photographs.

Acknowledgements

As befits its subject, this book has been pondered over and written in many different countries and continents, and I have accumulated many debts.

I had long wanted to explore the global context of British history, to move beyond these small islands to a broader vision but, in 1997, two gracious and unlooked for invitations gave me the vital incentive to do so. I was asked to deliver the Trevelyan Lectures at Cambridge University, and the Wiles Lectures at Queen's University, Belfast. Historians traditionally use these occasions to decant the accumulated wisdom of a lifetime. I, however, seized upon them to try out some raw ideas, positions and arguments that none the less proved crucial to the making of this book. I am therefore all the more grateful for the attention, helpful criticisms – and patience – bestowed on me by my Cambridge and Belfast audiences. I am particularly indebted to David Armitage, Chris Bayly, Stephen Conway, Marianne Elliott, Roy Foster, Ian Kershaw, Dominic Lieven, Peter Marshall, Peter Jupp, Terence Ranger and John Walsh, who commented on each Belfast lecture as it was delivered, and in some cases were rewarded only by being sent drafts of this book to read. I hope that the electors to the Trevelyan and Wiles Lectureships will accept my belated thanks for all that their invitations and generosity provoked and made possible.

My second major debt is to friends, former colleagues and students at Yale University. In the sixteen years I had the honour to work there, I was never allowed to forget that Britain and its one-time empire were only episodes in a wider global and temporal drama. Time and time again, I was asked questions, forced to engage in arguments, supplied with booklists, and offered valuable ideas and insights. I am especially grateful to Abbas Amanat, David Bell (now of Johns Hopkins University), John Blum, Jon Butler, David Brion Davis, John Mack Faragher, Maija Jansson, Paul Kennedy, Howard Lamar, John Merriman, Edmund Morgan, Stuart Schwartz, Jonathan Spence, David Underdown, and Robin Winks. I must also thank Alison Richard, Provost of Yale, who granted me leave at a crucial stage in this project, and whose scholarly concern and resilience under fire were a constant inspiration. John Demos however deserves special thanks. It was he, over a New Haven lunch table a long time ago, who first introduced me to captivity narratives. That was the beginning.

The end has been primarily the gift of the Leverhulme Trust of Great Britain which in 1998 awarded me a Senior Research Professorship. This allowed me a span of concentrated time in which to mull over and write up an ambitious topic, and also made it possible for me to visit the various sites discussed in this volume. It was R.H. Tawney who said that historians require a stout pair of boots, and I now understand why. Unless one makes oneself familiar with Britain's own dimensions, and then walks, trains, sails, and explores across those huge regions into which its peoples once intruded, a proper appreciation of the workings, dynamics, and meanings of its one-time empire is not possible. I am therefore most grateful to Barry Supple, former Director of the Leverhulme Trust, and to its other members for their tremendous kindness and generosity. I am also immensely grateful to Tony Giddens and the London School of Economics for giving me such stimulating shelter during the course of my award, and for the opportunity to spend time at London University which brings together so many distinguished scholars. Particular thanks go to Mia Rodriguez-Salgado, Joan-Pau Rubiés, and Patrick O'Brien of the LSE; to David Bindman, Michael Brett, David Feldman, Catherine Hall, Shula Marks, Peter Robb and Miles Taylor; and to the members of the seminar on 'Reconfiguring the British', which has supplied me with so many ideas. I must also thank the British Library and the Paul Mellon Centre of British Art, which – together with the Lewis Walpole Library at Farmington, Connecticut, and the Yale Center for British Art – have supplied wonderful places in which to work, as well as visual images crucial to this book.

As with all big books that take a long time to write, specifying partic- ular individuals and debts in this fashion is in some ways invidious. So many people have contributed to my work over the years. I have indicated particular debts in the end-notes whenever possible, but some who helped me must remain nameless. There was the bus driver in Tangier who lectured me in French on how the English were driven out of his city, as if that event had happened yesterday, rather than in 1684. There was the immaculately polite guide who escorted me around Bangalore, and with whom I argued – ridiculously – over how many sons of Tipu Sultan of Mysore were killed by the British in the 1790s (none in my history books; all of them in hers). And there were year upon year of wonderfully engaged Yale students with whom I discussed sharply varying interpretations of the

American Revolution. This book draws upon stories that individual Britons told in the past in order to relieve their anxieties and apprehensions about engaging in global enterprise, and in due course to make it possible. I have been constantly reminded while writing *Captives* – and have sought throughout to make clear – that other, very different stories exist about the empire that the British once made.

Without the encouragement, wise advice and entrepreneurship of my literary agents, Mike Shaw in London, and Emma Parry and Michael Carlisle in New York, and the enthusiasm, skill and professionalism of my editors, Will Sulkin and Jörg Hensgen at Jonathan Cape and Dan Frank at Pantheon, this book would not have proved possible. Without David Cannadine, I would never have been able to travel so far or complete this journey.

L. J. C.
2002

'When the prison-doors are opened, the real dragon will fly out.'
Ho Chi Minh, *Prison Diary* (Hanoi, 1962)

Two parables exist about the making and meanings of the British empire. In one, a man sets out on an eventful trading voyage, and is ultimately shipwrecked. He finds himself the lone survivor on a desert island, but despair soon gives way to resolution, Protestant faith, and busy ingenuity. By becoming 'an architect, a carpenter, a knife grinder, an astronomer, a baker, a shipwright, a potter, a saddler, a farmer, a tailor', and even 'an umbrella-maker, and a clergyman', he subdues his unpromising environment and renders it fruitful. He encounters a black, and promptly names him and makes him a servant. He uses force and guile to defeat incomers who are hostile, while firmly organising those who defer to his authority: 'How like a king I look'd . . . the whole country was my own mere property . . . [and] my people were perfectly subjected.' This is Daniel Defoe's *Robinson Crusoe* (1719). This is also how the British empire is commonly envisioned.

Empire-making in this parable – as in much of history in fact – involves being a warrior and taking charge. It means seizing land, planting it, and changing it. It means employing guns, technology, trade and the Bible to devastating effect, imposing rule, and subordinating those of a different skin pigmentation or religion. 'The true symbol of the British conquest', declared James Joyce famously, 'is Robinson Crusoe.' Yet if Crusoe seems at one level the archetypal conqueror and coloniser, he is also representative of British imperial experience in a very different sense. Before his shipwreck, Crusoe is captured at sea by Barbary corsairs and becomes 'a miserable slave' in Morocco. He escapes his Muslim owners only to become 'a prisoner locked up with the eternal bars and bolts of the Ocean, in an uninhabited wilderness'. And even as he transforms his desert island into a colony, Crusoe remains uncertain whether to regard his life there as 'my reign, or my captivity, which you please'.[1]

The hero of the second parable about British Empire is left with no doubts on this score. This man sets sail from Bristol, centre of transatlantic commerce and slaving, bound for successive zones of European imperialism: Spanish America, the West Indies, coastal India. He never reaches them. Instead, his voyages are aborted, time and time again, by events and beings beyond his control. First, an apparently puny tribe, the Lilliputians,

1. Britain as global empire: a detail from an 1893 map.

capture him, tie him down and reduce him to their will. Then a people much larger in stature than himself, the Brobdingnags, overwhelm him, sell him like a commodity, turn him into a spectacle, and sexually abuse him. But it is his last captivity that is most devastating. Confined on the island of the Houyhnhnms, creatures utterly unlike himself and far superior, he becomes so caught up in their society that he succumbs to its values. Forced at length to return to Britain, he can barely tolerate the stench of his one-time countrymen or the ugliness, as it now appears to him, of his own family. For this man, overseas venturing brings no conquests, or riches, or easy complacencies: only terror, vulnerability, and repeated captivities, and in the process an alteration of self and a telling of stories. This second

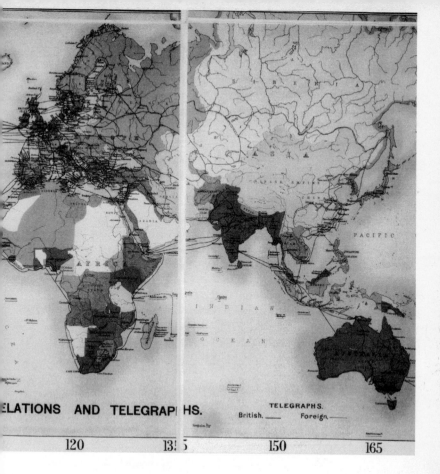

parable about Britain's empire is of course Jonathan Swift's *Gulliver's Travels* (1726), and its subject and themes are also mine.[2]

The primary actors in the pages that follow are those hundreds of thousands of English, Welsh, Scottish and Irish men, women and children who were taken captive in different regions of the extra-European world during the first quarter millennium of British imperial enterprise. The sources I am mining are pre-eminently – though never exclusively – these captives' own extraordinarily rich and virtually unexplored writings and drawings. And my intention throughout is to supply a work both of individual recovery and of imperial revision. As Defoe and Swift recognised, captivity was an integral part of Britain's overseas experience which cannot be

3

properly understood or assessed without it. Nor is it possible to understand this empire's impact on the various non-European peoples it collided and colluded with, unless the full meanings of captivity are uncovered and explored. Captives and captivities were the underbelly of British empire, and they set us free to explore another vision.

Small is vulnerable, small is aggressive

The fundamental reason why their pursuit of empire involved Britons in so many different confinements is contained – but also concealed – in one of the most famous maps ever produced. It shows Britain and Ireland situated close to the centre of the displayed world and coloured red or pink. Around the outer circle of the map are a succession of land masses – Australia, New Zealand, Canada, the Indian subcontinent, large swathes of Africa, assorted Caribbean islands and more – all coloured an identical red or pink to Britain itself. Some late nineteenth- and twentieth-century versions of this map also include the shipping routes and telegraph lines operating between Britain and these various overseas territories, marked out in black or again in red. The visual effect is rather like spokes jutting erratically from the hub of a wheel, or a scarlet spider at the centre of a massive, global web. Britain is made to appear physically connected to the distant lands it claims as its own and that literally take their colour from it.

This map has long since disappeared from the atlases, along with the empire it depicted, but it remains a standard feature of history books and school texts. It is part of our mental furniture even now. And superficially the story behind it is straightforward and unilinear. Before the late sixteenth century, few of the English, and even fewer Scots, Irish and Welsh displayed much interest in the world beyond their own continent. Even in 1630, there were probably little more than 12,000 settlers and traders from these islands clinging to outposts in North America, Guiana, the Caribbean and coastal India: 'a few dispersed men . . . altogether without Government', as one contemporary described some of their number.[3] By the early 1700s, however, the British state and the major trading companies associated with it, claimed authority over more than half a million white settlers, as well as hundreds of thousands of free and enslaved non-whites scattered over four of the five continents of the world. By the 1820s, British dominion had dramatically expanded to encompass a fifth of the population of the globe. A hundred years later, when close to its widest extent in terms of patches of red or pink on the map, the British empire covered in total over fourteen million square miles of the face of the earth.

4

Summarised thus, Britain's expansionist trajectory appears inexorable, and its ultimate if very temporary global hegemony overwhelming. There seems negligible space in this version of events and power relations for white captives: only for the colonial captivity of millions of men and women who in the main were not white. But look again at the famous map of Britain's empire. Like most cartographic exercises, it is not a simple depiction of the lie of the land, but in some respects a lie, or at least a calculated deceit.

The map deceives because it gives the impression that Britain's empire was the only substantial one existing, which was never the case. It deceives, too, because its Mercator projection together with its use of the Greenwich meridian put Britain arbitrarily but not accidentally near the centre of the displayed world. It further deceives by using an identical colour for all of the territories claimed by Britain, thereby making them appear a single, homogeneous unit, which this empire never was in fact. But there is still another sleight of hand involved here that is critical. Because Canada, New Zealand, Australia, the Indian subcontinent, large sectors of Africa, and parts of the Caribbean are coloured the same red or pink in this map as Britain itself, the spectator's eye is adroitly distracted from the smallness of the latter, to the size and global spread of the former. It is the world-wide expanse of this imperial system we are encouraged to focus on and admire, not the relatively tiny islands at its core. Yet in order to under-stand this empire – and its captivities – the proper place to begin is with the smallness of Britain itself. Britons were captured overseas in very large numbers during this period because they were at once uniquely ubiqui-tous intruders, and inherently and sometimes desperately vulnerable.

In terms of geography, Britain's smallness becomes easily manifest if it is compared with today's great powers. The United States is over 3000 miles from sea to shining sea, and – like China – covers more than 3.5 million square miles. The borders of the Russian Federation are still in flux, but it remains close to six million square miles in extent; while India, which Britain sought to govern before 1947, contains some 1.2 million square miles. By contrast, Great Britain and the island of Ireland together make up less than 125,000 square miles. Great Britain itself, which contains England, Wales and Scotland, is smaller than Madagascar. It would fit into the state of Texas twice over with ample room to spare.[4] Of course geo-political size has never been the only or even the prime determinant of global power, and by the standards of present-day giants, *all* of the European states that once presided over maritime empires would appear small. But the scale of the disparity between Britain's massive imperial pretensions on the one hand and its modest domestic size and resources

2. Cut down to size: Britain and Ireland as shown in the Peters projection of the world.

on the other was remarkable. By the early twentieth century, the Dutch empire was perhaps fifty times bigger than the Netherlands, while the French colonies were some eighteen times the size of France itself. Britain's authority, however, was stretched over a global empire 125 times larger than its own islands.[5]

This imperial overstretch was sharpened by another aspect of Britain's smallness: demography. By European standards, much of early modern Britain and Ireland experienced a rapid rate of population growth. Whereas France's population is estimated to have expanded by 79 per cent between 1550 and 1820, and Spain's may have risen by just 56 per cent,

the population of *England* almost trebled over this same period. But it needs remarking that this impressive English population take-off occurred from a very small base, barely three million souls. By 1820, when the British empire contained one in every five beings on the face of the globe, there were still fewer than twelve million men and women living in England itself. This was in marked contrast with Spain, or France, or the various German kingdoms, or the Italian states, which by that stage each averaged some twenty million inhabitants apiece.[6] Political union in 1707 between England and Wales on the one hand, and Scotland on the other, and a further Act of Union with Ireland in 1800, guaranteed London

7

access to additional and indispensable domestic supplies of manpower. None the less, throughout the seventeenth and eighteenth centuries – and occasionally after – Britain's rulers remained uncertain whether their home population was sufficient to generate the armies, navies, settlers, and taxes demanded by large-scale imperial enterprise. Many politicians and commentators convinced themselves indeed that the drain in men and money was too great, and that Britain's population was actually in decline. There was no census here until 1801, in part because of the fear that counting heads might expose an embarrassing demographic deficit to Britain's rivals – and to its colonial subjects.[7]

Britain's limited population and its inhabitants' objections to maintaining large standing armies, provided for a further respect in which this was always an empire challenged at its core by smallness. The size of Britain's own armed forces never remotely kept pace with its global interventions. This was true even at sea. As Daniel Baugh remarks, the very scale of Britain's expanding maritime presence after the seventeenth century itself caused problems. These islands were never able to generate enough seamen by themselves 'to supply the wartime needs of both the navy and the merchant service'. And although by 1700 the Royal Navy was the most powerful in the world, it never possessed sufficient ships both to protect Britain itself from European enemies, and simultaneously to preside in strength over the world's oceans. For most of the quarter millennium covered by this book, the bulk of Britain's fleet was not, and could not be engaged in conquering and coercing the non-European world. Instead, most Royal Navy warships remained in home and European waters monitoring the movements of Dutch, Spanish, and French rivals.[8]

But the pressures on Britain's navy were as nothing to those on its army. Over time, as John Brewer has described, the British became supremely and necessarily adept at recruiting domestic manpower and hiring foreign mercenaries for specific, major wars. But these suddenly swollen legions (which were anyway usually bigger on paper than in the field) were strictly special occasion fare.[9] They could not be afforded, and were never routinely forthcoming for everyday, imperial needs. In 1715, when Britain already claimed authority over some half a million men and women in North America, plus large parts of the West Indies, coastal settlements in India, and vital outposts in the Mediterranean, its army is estimated to have been no bigger than the king of Sardinia's. In 1850, when this book ends, Britain's home-produced army was still conspicuously modest in point of numbers by comparison with that of Russia, or France, or even Prussia. 'At no time', as one military historian writes, '. . . were the land forces available for the peacetime policing and defence of the [British] empire . . .

sufficiently strong for the task'.[10] Even at the height of its imperial power, Britain's military and naval resources would have appeared negligible if set against the bristling overseas garrisons and staggering oceanic naval presence currently possessed by the United States.

These limits in military manpower might not have mattered had Britain commanded throughout the sort of easy and invariable technological supremacy still sometimes attributed to early modern Western empires, but it did not. At sea, to be sure, the major European powers had established a marked lead over other regions of the world by 1600 (though for a long time their wooden ships remained vulnerable on long voyages, and instruments of navigation were crude and sometimes fallible). On land, however, it was a different matter. Part of the excitement and sentimentality with which Britons and other Europeans reacted to Captain James Cook's encounters with Pacific islanders in the 1770s and '80s may well have been due to a gratified recognition that here were societies whose weaponry was indeed indisputably primitive in quality. By contrast, in parts of Africa, in North America, and above all in Asia, British intruders in this period had regularly to confront peoples whose weapons were similar to their own, and occasionally better.[11] The familiar image of ill-provided non-European peoples being casually and terribly mowed down by white imperialists equipped with gatling guns and similar quick-firing weapons belongs in the main to the later nineteenth century and after. For most of the quarter millennium covered by this book, land warfare remained conspicuously low-tech, and there was no necessary gulf between Western and non-Western armaments. As late as 1799, guns, cannon and ammunition together accounted for less than 5 per cent of Britain's land warfare budget. The rest went on horses, carts, uniforms, swords, knives, pikes and soldiers' pay: virtually the same staples of land warfare as in the Ancient World – and in much of the non-European world.[12]

Some might argue that these material factors – Britain's marked limits in terms of geographical size, population, armed forces, and, for a long time, military technology – were of only secondary importance. That manifestly a vast British empire came into being, and therefore that these constraints must have been of less significance than the 'will, self-confidence, even arrogance' that allowed growing numbers of Britons to view the overseas world as a site for action, conquest and exploitation. Yet those living in the seventeenth and eighteenth centuries, and even in the early 1800s, were rarely able to see things this way. There is certainly abundant evidence throughout this period of individual Britons asserting their unbounded superiority to all foreigners, both European and non-European. But as more thoughtful or battle-hardened spirits amongst them acknowledged, where global power relations were concerned, arrogance and jingoism were never enough. Language, culture and complacency had no automatic witchcraft capacity by themselves to magic away more rudimentary deficiencies in terms of numbers and available force. 'The maxim believed by the common people of this country, "That one Englishman is equal to two foreigners" . . . may . . . be useful in some cases,' wrote an experienced imperial soldier and diplomat wearily in 1810, 'but it is . . . devoid of truth.'[13]

As this suggests, alongside routine declarations of Britain's political, religious, economic, and ultimately racial superiority, there were always other voices, sometimes very powerful ones, pointing out that its varieties of domestic smallness were bound to make sustaining a large overseas territorial empire a challenging and chancy business. 'We are a very little spot in the map of the world,' writes the marquis of Halifax in the 1660s, and therefore could make 'a great figure only by trade'. 'We want not the dominion of more countries than we have,' cautions Daniel Defoe in 1707. 'We want nothing but numbers,' laments a British army officer about his country's forces abroad in 1744.[14] Britain's normal 'military establishment', remarks Adam Smith during the war with Revolutionary America that would demonstrate the imperial costs of this, was: '. . . more moderate than that of any European state which can pretend to rival her either in wealth or in power'. 'The extension of our territory and influence has been greater than our means,' observes the future duke of Wellington grimly in 1800.[15] But it was a less senior analyst of military power and empire who summed up the dilemma best. In regard to the size and resources of Britain itself, he wrote in an influential survey published in 1810, its global pretensions resembled 'an oak planted in a flower-pot'.[16] A swollen empire was nonetheless constrained by the smallness in which it was rooted.

There were, to be sure, some respects in which being small – being a flowerpot – actually worked to foster Britain's imperial involvement and success. If emigrants, entrepreneurs and adventurers of all kinds left it in large numbers for other lands (as they still do), if its slavers haggled for chained manpower on the western coasts of Africa, and if its traders ruthlessly invaded other seas and other shores in search of raw materials and new markets, this was in part because the home islands could seem too modest to afford the land, opportunities, manpower, raw materials, and markets that were wanted. Domestic smallness and a lack of self-sufficiency made for continuous British extroversion, not to say global house-breaking, violence and theft. And Britain's compact, physical insularity did more than fuel restlessness and greed, it also provided the means of escape, and the means as well to global commerce and conquest. Nowhere in Britain is more than seventy miles from the sea: and this was a vital advantage in a period when – for a long time – travel by sea was infinitely faster than journeying by land. The sea, the one commodity apart from coal and sheep they had around them in abundance, allowed the British to compensate for sparsity of numbers by sheer mobility and ubiquity.

Britain's compactness facilitated its imperial enterprise in other ways too. The physical smallness of these islands encouraged the rich, powerful and ambitious of England, Wales, Scotland and Ireland to filter into just one extraordinarily large metropolis, London. Magnetised to a conurbation that was at once the site of government and the court, and Britain's biggest port, ship-building centre, money market, and source of print, the different elites of these islands developed, from very early on, a shared avidity for imperial investments, ideas and adventures. This was just one respect in which physical smallness advanced the evolution in Britain of a markedly centralised state, and ultimately a precocious national ideology, with all the cohesion and belligerence that naturally went with these things.[17] The same compactness, together with state-driven political union, also ensured that the island of Great Britain became one of the world's most efficient free-trade areas from very early on, a hive of internal as well as external commercial energy. Even Britain's military vulnerability may have aided in some respects its imperial drive. Self-consciously small, increasingly rich, and confronted with European enemies that were often bigger and militarily more formidable than themselves, the British were frequently on edge, constantly fearful themselves of being invaded, necessarily alert and ready for a fight. A sense of inferiority, suggested Alfred Adler in regard to troubled individuals, breeds aggression and above all an urge to compensate. So arguably it proved with the British as a people.[18]

It is these mixed consequences of Britain's smallness – its cohesiveness, restless extroversion, busy commerce, and aggression on the one hand, and its demographic, military and resource inadequacies on the other – that account in part for the very large numbers of real-life Crusoes and Gullivers seized in regions outside Europe after 1600. Too many small, unarmed merchantmen venturing gamely into hostile or unknown waters, with not enough Royal Navy convoys to protect them, led – as Part One of this book describes – to substantial numbers of Britons being captured at sea. Civilian settlers and traders intruding determinedly but often in very small numbers into lands that other people regarded as their own, or endeavouring to establish themselves there without sufficient or sometimes any British army cover, resulted over the centuries – as Part Two details – in large numbers of captivities and casualties on land. While, throughout this period, under-strength British regiments, dispatched to different regions of the world equipped with weapons of no great sophistication, together with insufficiently manned and poorly supplied colonial cantonments and forts, regularly resulted in sharp imperial reverses, heavy casualties, and high captivity rates, not just among men in uniform, but also among various womenfolk and children.

'The body is a model which can stand for any bounded system,' writes the anthropologist Mary Douglas, and in times of stress the body's 'boundaries can represent any boundaries which are threatened or precarious.'[19] In just such a way, the bodies of English, Welsh, Scottish and Irish men and women, seized in successive captivity crises overseas, mark out the changing boundaries over time of Britain's imperial aggression, and the frontiers of its inhabitants' fears, insecurities, and deficiencies. But these encounters are revealing about far more than just the British themselves. What subsequently happened to these same captive bodies also illumines how those non-European peoples whom the British sought to invade or exploit, sometimes proved able to resist and punish them, and even find their own uses for them.

To this extent, this book uses captive individuals and their tales to investigate and reassess far wider national, imperial and global histories.

People and stories matter

Yet the captives in this book were more than symptomatic and emblematic bodies. All of them participants in first English and subsequently British maritime and imperial enterprise, these were also men, women and children from widely varying social and ethnic backgrounds, of different ages, religious denominations, politics, occupations, education, outlook and even language. How these myriad and miscellaneous individuals reacted to their respective captors was in practice as diverse as how the captor societies involved responded to them. So how can we recover the quality and content of these manifold contacts and confrontations over time?

Like captives from other cultures – like those whom they themselves colonised indeed – Britons seized in the course of overseas enterprise recorded what happened to them in many different ways, not all of them verbal. Some told their tale – or had it told for them – in drawings, or in graveyard inscriptions, in songs, or in sermons. Some scratched evocative and anguished lines and images on coins, or on the walls of places where they were confined. Some even tattooed their reactions on their own entrapped bodies. Captives who were rescued or eventually returned to

Britain might speak rather than write their stories: in order to appease an army court martial, or on the instructions of suspicious magistrates, or to entertain impatient passers-by on busy streets as a means of attracting charity; and these spoken testimonies were occasionally set down on paper by others. But the most complex and comprehensive testimonies of overseas capture, and thus the most valuable as far as this book is concerned, were captivity narratives.

These are substantial accounts usually written in the first person and completely or in part by a one-time captive, but sometimes dictated to others. A mode of writing rather than a genre, captivity narratives commonly describe how a single individual or a group was seized, how the victim/s coped (or not) with the challenges and sufferings that ensued, and how they contrived in the end to escape or were ransomed or released. Such narratives vary widely in length and quality but, at their best, they form the closest approximation we have for the past to the kind of analyses supplied by anthropologists and ethnographers immersed in alien societies today. In Mary Louise Pratt's words:

> The authority of the ethnographer over the 'mere traveller' rests chiefly on the idea that the traveller just passes through, whereas the ethnographer lives with the group under study. But of course this is what captives . . . often do too, living in another culture in every capacity . . . learning indigenous languages and lifeways with a proficiency any ethnographer would envy, and often producing accounts that are indeed full, rich, and accurate by ethnography's own standards. At the same time, the experience of captivity resonates a lot with aspects of the experience of fieldwork – the sense of dependency, lack of control, the vulnerability to being isolated completely or never left alone.[20]

Along with many other sorts of testimonies and evidence, both Western and non-Western, I have drawn extensively in this book on over a hundred printed and manuscript narratives written or dictated by Britons between 1600 and the mid-nineteenth century in response to captivity experiences in the Mediterranean and North African region, in North America, and in South and Central Asia.

By definition, these are subjective, sometimes highly charged writings, and I discuss their authenticity (and what that means) in Chapter Three. But it needs stressing from the start that, while these texts sometimes contain fictional interludes, together of course with a tithe of lies and errors, their overall factual anchorage can usually be tested, and has been tested in these pages throughout.

MADAGASCAR:

OR,

Robert Drury's

JOURNAL

DURING

Fifteen Years Captivity on that ISLAND.

Y Defign, in the enfuing Hiftory, is to give a plain and honeft Narrative of Matters of Fact; I fhall not, therefore, make ufe of any artful Inventions or borrow'd Phrafes to lengthen or embellifh it; nor fhall I offer any other Reflections than what naturally occurr'd from my many uncommon and furprifing Adventures. And,

B

1

3. Robert Drury's narrative.

Consider as an example the captivity narrative of Robert Drury, an English midshipman who was shipwrecked on the southern coast of Madagascar when he was just sixteen, and held for fifteen years there as a slave by the local Antandroy people. When this work, which is over 460 pages long, was published in London in 1729, Drury expressed his anxiety in the preface that, even though it was nothing else but 'a plain and honest narrative of matters of fact', it might be received as just 'such another romance as Robinson Crusoe'. His misgivings proved justified. Even some contemporary readers declined to believe Drury's story; and in 1943 a scholarly monograph 'proved' it to be a literary pastiche written by Daniel

Defoe himself. Libraries worldwide promptly changed their catalogue entries of Drury's work, and the *Encyclopaedia Britannica* downgraded it from respectable anthropological notice to a romantic fiction. Then, in 1991, a marine archaeologist called Mike Parker Pearson went back to Robert Drury's narrative and took it seriously.[21]

His team of archaeologists and ethnographers has now validated the wreck of Drury's ship, a 520-ton East Indiaman called the *Degrave*, lost in 1703 on the return voyage from Bengal to London. They have checked Drury's accounts of early eighteenth-century southern Madagascar's fauna, flora, climate, clothing and cuisine, the details he supplies of river names and mountains, and his descriptions of Antandroy rituals of warfare, circumcision, and death, and of their suspicion of Europeans: 'Every white man is looked on as not less than we think a cannibal.' In addition, Pearson has examined Drury's eight-page lexicon of Malagasy language, its spellings inflected by the seaman's own native Cockney. And the result of all this scholarly detective work? It is clear that Drury or his editor borrowed material from other published works, which was standard practice in the eighteenth century, omitted details, and exaggerated 'quantifications of distance, size and weight'. None the less, Pearson concludes, *Madagascar: or Robert Drury's Journal* is 'not a work of fictional realism nor is it a fancifully embroidered account based on a few authentic pegs'. It is 'a largely accurate historical document', by which is meant not an impeccable source, but a usable and important one.[22] The same is true of most substantial captivity narratives. These are imperfect, idiosyncratic, and sometimes violently slanted texts. They are also astonishingly rich and revealing, both about the British themselves, and about the mixed fortunes and complexities of their dealings with other peoples.

For it is emphatically not the case, as has sometimes been suggested, that captivity narratives were comprehensively 'safe' texts that only corroborated pre-existing and dismissive European viewpoints about other societies. Read scrupulously, indeed, they usefully disrupt the notion that there was ever a single, identifiable British, still less 'European' perspective on the non-European world, any more, of course, than there was on anything else.

In part, this is because their authors were so various. British attitudes to empire have often been reconstructed – and over-homogenised – on the slender basis of testimonies by a few conspicuous actors in positions of power or notoriety: politicians, pro-consuls, generals, colonial governors, monarchs, celebrated authors and intellectuals, merchant princes, industrial magnates, intrepid explorers and the like. Such dominant, confident and predominantly masculine creatures regularly, and necessarily, strut

15

through these pages also. But one of the advantages of investigating captives, and the texts associated with them, is that doing so brings us into contact with the rather different people who always made up the majority of British imperial personnel in fact. Not all captives were obscure individuals, but many of them were. They were minor settlers and farmers, common seamen and private soldiers, junior officers and small traders, itinerants and exiles, convicts and assorted womenfolk. As a result, many of these individuals experienced what one twentieth-century Irish captive called being 'a tiny, insignificant pawn in a global game over which I had no control' in a double sense.[23] At one level, they found themselves at the mercy of non-European captors; but, at another, some of these British captives also felt constrained and subordinated by their own society of origin, and wrote accordingly.

And, irrespective of the social status and sentiments of their authors, captivity narratives were *always* disturbing texts at some level simply by virtue of what they described. For those Britons directly involved, overseas captivity meant not just sudden exposure to danger and extreme vulnerability, but also being dragged across a line of sorts. This might be the line between Christian Europe and bastions of Islam in North Africa and the Ottoman world; or the line between regions of British settlement in North America and more mobile Native American societies. After 1775, the line in question might be that between American territory as British imperialists envisaged it, and as those rebelling against their rule wished to reconfigure it; or it might be the line between regions of encroaching British influence in South or Central Asia, and areas of indigenous power and resistance there. Many of the individuals who feature in this book remained bitterly resentful throughout at being forced to cross into trauma and difference. Some captives, however, chose or were compelled to adjust to their new settings, while others learnt from their experiences to question the very validity of divides between peoples, and the meaning of what they had once regarded as home. Virtually all British captives though were compelled by the nature of their predicament to re-examine – and often question for the first time – conventional wisdoms about nationality, race, religion, allegiance, appropriate modes of behaviour, and the location of power.

These were individuals caught up bodily in zones of imperial contest, forced into protracted encounters where they were at the bottom, and other people who were generally not European, and usually not Christian, or white, had power of life or death over them. What those who survived such encounters wrote, or otherwise recorded about their experiences, proved persistently absorbing and often disquieting to their compatriots back home. 'Autobiographical forms,' remarks James Amelang, 'played a crucial role in circulating information in early modern Europe about the world beyond': and, as far as captives' autobiographies were concerned, this remained true for the British well beyond the early modern period.[24] Until they succeeded in convincing themselves (though never totally and not for long), that global empire was a feasible option for a small people like themselves, all kinds of Britons were drawn to scrutinise, and anguish over the captive's story. We should pay attention to it too.

Re-appraising empire

This book, then, combines the large-scale, panoramic and global, with the small-scale, the individual, and the particular. At one level, it is a macro-narrative of some of the constraints and crises that Britain confronted during the quarter millennium that made it the world's foremost power, and what followed from these both as regards its own peoples, and for other peoples. At another level, this book is an exploration of micro-narratives produced by just some of the very many English, Welsh, Scottish and Irish men and women who got caught and caught out because of this power's amalgam of incessant extroversion and aggression, and frequent and intrinsic vulnerability.

Men and women from these islands were held captive over the centuries in every continent of the world, but I have concentrated on the three vast geographical areas in which London and its rulers took successively the most interest, and sunk the most imperial effort, imagination and expense. Accordingly, Part One of this book focuses on North Africa and the Mediterranean. This region is often left out of the history of English and British commercial and imperial endeavour, yet it witnessed both the most costly (and catastrophically unsuccessful) colonial settlement attempted by the English state in the seventeenth century, and the biggest concentration of British troops overseas before 1750. Part Two is devoted to mainland North America, focusing on those Thirteen Colonies which decolonised so violently after 1775. Part Three belongs to South and Central Asia, and sweeps from British captivities in southern India in the four decades after 1760, to British failures in Afghanistan in the 1840s.

In order to convey changes in power-levels and imperial attitudes over time, I have looked at each of these three regions according to when captivity crises there proved the most dangerous for the British, and provoked the most attention and alarm. Thus Part One stretches from 1600 to the early eighteenth century, a period when English commercial and imperial ambitions in the Mediterranean and North Africa became threatened by, but also dependent upon, local Islamic powers. Part Two examines English and British captivities in North America from the later seventeenth century to the end of the American Revolutionary War in 1783. Throughout these years, captivity crises here – as in the other regions in this book – were linked to much wider issues and anxieties. Captive bodies in America were caught up with clashes between advancing, land-hungry British settlers and angry and retreating indigenous peoples, but also with the tensions and differences emerging between these same assertive white settlers and their fellow Britons on the other side of the Atlantic. Part Three of this book, on South and Central Asia, moves from the mid-eighteenth century into the early Victorian era, a period in which the quality of imperial captivities and domestic reactions to them changed markedly, along with the direction and intensity of Britain's aggression, and the level of its global power.

Since this is a big book that requires readers to travel across several continents as well as through a quarter millennium of time, I have supplied guide-posts. Each of the three sections begins with an orientation chapter, a scene-setting for the captives, captors, countries and cultures involved. Throughout, I have sought to convey both the growing scale of Britain's global reach and its persistent limitations; I have also stressed connectedness, weaving together histories that are often reconstructed only separately. I have ranged impertinently but with purpose over America, Asia, and the Mediterranean world, because patterns of British overseas enterprise in these regions – and patterns of resistance to it – were interconnected. I have sought to consider and complicate the line between aggressors and the invaded, the powerful and the powerless, because it was sometimes crossed and compromised in fact. And I have stressed the linkages between the actions, confinements and writings of English, Welsh, Irish, and Scottish individuals in different parts of the world on the one hand, and events and reactions back in the home islands on the other. This book is written in agreement with those who argue that the segregation of British domestic history from the histories of varieties of Britons overseas cannot stand.

There is another set of connections that I have wanted to stress. I take for granted that the British need to know far more about their impact in the past on different regions of the world, and about how peoples and developments in these same regions have in turn impacted over the centuries on them. But, by the same token, those wanting to understand the histories – and the present – of large parts of Africa, or Asia, or America, or indeed the Caribbean and the Pacific regions, need to reassess the complex roles once played in them by the British, and see the latter clearly for what they actually were, in their real diversity and limited dimensions, as distinct from how they wished to appear then, and from what they are still stereotypically viewed as being now. This book offers a different perspective on Britain's imperial impact and experience, without in any way suggesting that this is the only one that can be adopted. But *Captives* is also concerned to rewrite the British themselves, so that they may be put more accurately in their place in global history.

There is a final point. The people who feature in this book were radically different from men and women today in all kinds of respects, and not least in that – whether European or non-European – many of them tended to take the existence of empire for granted. This was hardly surprising. Britain's maritime empire existed in tandem with, and competed against, the maritime empires of France, Spain, Portugal, Denmark and the Dutch. These Western European seaborne empires coexisted in turn with the great land-based empires of the East. There were the Chinese, Russian and Ottoman empires; and there was the Safavid empire in Persia, and the Mughal empire in India: all of which in 1600 were infinitely more formidable powers than England and its adjacent countries, and all of which continued to expand thereafter for different lengths of time, and with different rates of success. And there were land-based empires within Europe itself: the empire of the Hapsburgs that encompassed Austria and parts of Eastern Europe and Italy, and the empire built up so violently by Napoleon Bonaparte after 1796, that subdued 40 per cent of all Europeans, and threatened for a time to overrun Britain itself.

As this last example suggests, imperialism in this period – and after – was espoused by revolutionary and republican regimes as well as by monarchical, ancien regimes. America's revolution against George III and British rule after 1776 did not lead it to reject empire as such. Its white inhabitants simply continued to invade ever westwards under their own flag, displacing Native Americans and other peoples as they went, intent on constructing what Alexander Hamilton (who had fought against the British) described unabashedly as 'an empire in many respects the most interesting in the world'. The sheer ubiquity of empire in this quarter millennium needs bearing in mind when assessing how the British themselves thought and acted. But the degree to which empire 'has been a way of life for most of the peoples of the world' throughout recorded history also needs bearing in mind and pondering now, in the early twenty-first century.[25]

We are perhaps too ready to believe that, because colonisation by force is no longer a real danger, the substance and tendencies of empire have therefore ceased entirely to exist. This book deals with the relationship between size and power, and with the penalties and paradoxes of the pursuit of global dominance, not just for those encroached upon and invaded, but also for the invaders themselves, the warriors who so easily became captives in one fashion or another. It would be nice to believe that such issues could be safely consigned to the realm of history. It would also be unwise.

Part One

MEDITERRANEAN
Captives and Constraints

ONE

Tangier

Breakers

The strip of sea that brought them to the shores of their new prize and the entrance to the Mediterranean is famously volatile. Even today, crossing or passing through the straits of Gibraltar, the narrowest stretch of water between Europe and Africa, is a slow and turbulent business. However bright the sunshine at embarkation, strong winds and rain can move in swiftly, blotting out coastlines and turning the oil-flecked, ultramarine sea into a choppy slate grey. In bad weather, the trip churns the stomach and can be dangerous. Migrant workers from Morocco and Algeria, their belongings tied up in immaculate brown paper parcels, together with some hardier backpackers will still entrust themselves to the larger, older ferry boats, huddling below deck amidst the cigarette smoke and old coffee stains. But comfortable tourists looking forward to a sea excursion from Gibraltar to Tangier ('Your Day Out In Africa') cancel their bookings in droves, while the smaller, faster hydrofoils linking Tangier with Tarifa and Algeciras in Spain sometimes cease operating. As for amateur craft, they can vanish altogether. Hundreds of men and women still die on this eight-mile stretch of water every year.

It was the unpredictability of its offshore waters, the sudden, violent rainstorms, and the quirks of the landscape that most impressed the English occupation force when it first arrived in Tangier in 1662, yet these things did not make the soldiers, officials and families feel any more at home. The fact that, at a distance and shrouded in mist, the low mountains behind Tangier might almost have passed for those of North Wales, only accentuated the strangeness of the rest: the clarity of the Mediterranean sunlight, the expansive sands, the luminosity of the settlement's white and ochre-coloured buildings, fruits and vegetables most of them had never tasted before, roses that bloomed even in winter. Sir Hugh Cholmley, though, remained undistracted and was immediately busy, for his mission was to regulate the sea itself.

Cholmley was a Yorkshire landowner from a moderately royalist background, a highly intelligent and driven man whose idea of relaxation was

Divers Prospects in and about
TANGIER.
Exactly delineated by W. Hollar; his May:
designer, and by him afterwards
to satisfie the curious, etch'd in Copper
And are to be Sold by John Overton at the
White Horse, without Newgate London

Peterborow Tower

Prospect of y.º North side of Tangier regarding the mayne Sea   from the hill as you come from Whitby or the West, toward the Towne

4. Prospect of Tangier by Wenceslaus Hollar.

pegging away at mathematical puzzles. He was also a gentlemanly capitalist of a kind, as concerned to invest in England's intermittently expanding empire overseas, as he was to diversify his income at home. He developed the alum mines on his family estates at Whitby, married off his daughter to a speculator in Indian diamonds, and, most of all, applied himself mind and muscle to Tangier.[1] Charles II, King of England, Scotland and Ireland, had acquired the settlement along with other colonial booty in 1661, as part of the dowry of his sad, barren Portuguese bride, Catherine of Braganza. One year later, Cholmley signed a contract with the government to build a mole at Tangier at the rate of thirteen shillings for every cubic yard completed. As Cholmley noted down with typical thoroughness, the word 'mole' comes from the French and Latin for a great mass. The idea was to construct a substantial artificial outcrop or breakwater from Tangier's natural shoreline, lined with cannon and other defences, and thereby make the harbour deep enough for the Royal Navy's largest warships, and a safer, more congenial haven for what was expected to become an ever-growing share of the world's trade.[2]

For Tangier was and is a special place. Its now dated reputation for transgressive sexualities and international intrigue masks its extraordinary strategic and geographical significance, but does at least acknowledge the city's role as a meeting-place for different cultures. Adjacent to the point

24

where the continent of Africa comes nearest to Europe, it is bounded on the one side by the Atlantic, while commanding on the other the western entrance to the Mediterranean. So its attractions for its English occupiers were profound and plural. At one level, Tangier offered a base from which they could look to make further commercial and colonial advances into the North African interior. At another, it supplied them with a naval stronghold from which to monitor the fleets of richer and more powerful European rivals, Spain, and above all France. At yet another level, Tangier guarded the entrance of what one contemporary called 'the greatest thoroughfare of commerce in the world', by which he meant not the Atlantic Ocean, but the Mediterranean, at this stage still the most profitable arena by far for English imports and exports.[3] Trade with southern Europe and the eastern Mediterranean seaboard, Turkey and the Levant, had been expanding since before 1600. England shipped its cloth here of course, as well as fresh and salted fish for the Catholic ports, and by the second half of the seventeenth century an ever-growing supply of colonial re-exports, pepper, tobacco, sugar, East Indian silks and calicos. In return, the English looked to the Mediterranean for imports of Levantine silks and dyestuff, for Turkish cotton and Spanish short wool, for Italian wine and Portuguese Madeira, for leather and fine horses from Morocco, and raisins, figs, oranges and olives to diversify the diet of the well-off. Tangier appeared an ideal base and mart for this rich and varied commerce, and one of the first things that London did after 1662 was proclaim it a free port.

On expansionist, strategic, and commercial grounds, then, Tangier seemed to the English an impeccably prudent acquisition that would in due course pay for itself many times over, 'a jewel', as Cholmley put it. Samuel Pepys, writing as a naval administrator and member of the council responsible for the new colony, rather than in his more familiar guise as a man-about-town, confided in his diary that Tangier was 'likely to be the most considerable place the King of England hath in the world'. Catherine of Braganza's other bonus, Bombay, struck him by contrast as no more than 'a poor little island', too distant ever likely to be made properly useful.[4] In seventeenth-century sailing-ship time, Bombay was at least half a year from London; and even England's North American colonies were three months away. Tangier, though, offered proximity as well as seemingly limitless potential. A fast merchantman setting out from London could reach it in well under two weeks. Not surprisingly, then, in the early years of its occupation, the new colony was talked of in official circles 'at a mighty rate as the foundation of a new empire'. It would be easy, urged one supporter in the 1670s, for Charles II so to exploit Tangier as 'to command our northern world, and to give laws to Europe and Africa'.[5]

1. Catharine Fort,
2. The Irish Battery.

Prospect of y⁰ lower part of Tangier,

5. Tangier fortified.

Money was lavished on the colony on a scale appropriate to these ambitions. The Portuguese had allowed the place to decay, and major rebuilding
began almost as soon as the 4000-strong occupation force arrived, many
of the troops veterans of Oliver Cromwell's New Model Army. Long, fortified walls began to coil around the settlement 'one without another, as there
are [skins] to an onion'. The Bohemian engraver turned English court

om the hill West of White-hall ⌇ ⌇ 5 The head Court of Guard,
W: Hollar delin: 4 The Bay,

artist, Wenceslaus Hollar, sketched some of them on an official visit in 1669, together with the newly named towers and fortresses they interlinked, Peterborough Tower, York Castle, Henrietta Fort, Charles Fort, James Fort. Intricate and precise, the last substantial works Hollar ever completed, these drawings suggest something of the scale of the English investment in Tangier, and their confidence at this stage in its permanence.[6] The drawings convey something else as well. Hollar's panoramic views of the new fortifications are clearly designed to impress, yet at the same time he makes Tangier appear familiar and even domestic. A workman and his wife dressed in sombre English fashions trudge homewards arm in arm, their only protection an ambling dog. Carts trundle usefully along well-built roads. And the neatly tiled roofs of the houses inside the city's fortified walls cluster together as reassuringly as if they were located in Hollar's adopted London or his native Prague. Looking at these scenes, there is precious little to indicate that they are set on the northernmost shores of Africa.

Nor did Hollar's employer, Charles II, intend that there should be. Tangier's royal charter, issued in 1668, confined office-holding and voting in the colony to Christians and of course to men. The region's Muslim inhabitants, it insisted, were 'so barbarous and so poor and so continuously embroiled in civil wars, that no near prospect can be imagined to make them apprehended'. In the official mind, Tangier was projected as a substantial colony of settlement with an agenda from the start of expansion, commerce and anglicisation; and initially some roots were put down. By the 1670s, there were almost as many civilian settlers in Tangier as there were soldiers, including over 500 women and children.[7] They lived in a city marked out now with English street names and with its own corporation. Every Sunday, Tangier's mayor, aldermen and common councilmen would put on specially designed scarlet and purple robes and process stickily to its Anglican church, where a pew lined with green velvet cushions awaited the colony's governor and his lady, and a carved and painted image of Charles II's coat of arms was prominently displayed. Through the leaded windows, the more inattentive worshippers could catch a glimpse of an ancient monument inscribed in Arabic still standing firmly in the new Anglican churchyard. But, if their eyes strayed in that direction, it was probably only for an instant, for after the service there were other pursuits to look forward to, especially if you were male. There was Tangier's new bowling-green, where the resident army officers played against the more affluent inhabitants, or the city's growing range of brothels or, for the chaste and studious, a visit to its library from which some unknown settler stole away with the single copy of John Milton's *Paradise Lost*.[8] These colonisers, it seemed, were making themselves at home.

Never before in its history had the English state, as distinct from private investors and trading companies within it, devoted so much effort and thought, and above all so much money to a colonial enterprise outside Europe. The surviving accounts, which are incomplete, suggest that in the 1660s Tangier cost on average over £75,000 every year. Cutting down on its military garrison and establishing a civilian administration failed to

6. Inside colonial Tangier.

7. The bowling green.

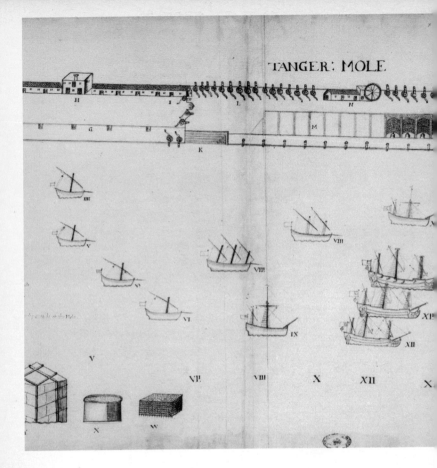

reduce the drain on the Crown. Average annual expenditure on the colony between 1671 and 1681 rose to almost £87,500. Altogether, this North African episode appears to have sucked in close to two million pounds, a substantially greater sum, as Tangier's last governor, Lord Dartmouth, remarked, than Charles II spent on his other overseas outposts, or on all of his garrisons on home territory put together. Over a third of this money went on funding Sir Hugh Cholmley's stupendous mole.[9]

Outwardly at least, the man behaved as though unrelenting energy and technical ingenuity were enough to transform and possess an alien landscape. He removed so many rocks from Tangier's beaches that its city walls began to subside. Undeterred, he blasted out a new quarry to the west of the settlement, and built a road to transport stone from there to

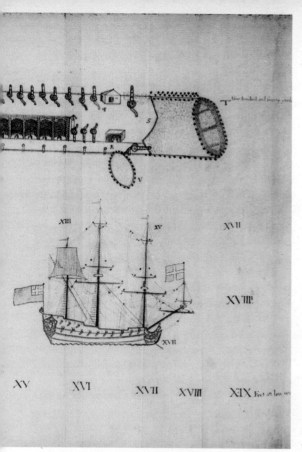

8. Plan of the mole, complete with cannon.

the mole. When the garrison troops, who laboured on the project in their hundreds, still proved insufficient for the task, Cholmley imported skilled workmen from Yorkshire, building them a dormitory town that he named after his native Whitby. Nothing, it seemed, was to get in his way. An uncle summoned to Tangier to assist him sickened and died. His own wife had the temerity to fall pregnant. The family's maids were captured at sea by Barbary corsairs. Yet still Cholmley pressed on. By 1668, in defiance of atrocious weather and at a huge cost in money and lives, Cholmley's mole already extended some 380 yards from the North African shore. By the mid-1670s, it stretched 457 yards out to sea, was 110 feet in width, and rose eighteen foot out of the water. Twenty-six cannon guarded one side, while two batteries of 'great gunnes' protruded from the other.[10]

This was by far the most ambitious engineering work ever carried out up to this point by Englishmen working outside Europe: and in this, as in other respects, Tangier's significance in imperial terms was much greater than itself. Its astonishing mole was the first of those ambitious constructions in stone, brick and iron – bridges, dockyards, railways, roads, dams and canals – which the British subsequently scattered over every part of their overseas empire, means to facilitate trade, transport and control, but also attempts to compensate for their own intrinsic smallness and sparsity of numbers by imposing on the landscape large, enduring monuments in their own technological image. In one draft of his memoirs, Cholmley even compared himself to Nebuchadnezzar, the Babylonian ruler of the Old Testament, who built a mole to subdue the inhabitants of Tyre. A more appropriate analogy, as it turned out, would have been King Canute, except that what was advancing against the English at Tangier was more than just the power of the sea.

Winter gales and fierce coastal currents breached the mole some thirty times during its construction, reducing Cholmley to bouts of despair that he was wasting his youth and energy on an 'endless feeding of the sea with stones'. Not until 1677 was his surveyor, Henry Sheeres, able to inform London that the project had finally been completed. Tangier's mole, all three million cubic foot and 170,000 tons of it, now stood firm in the water, crowed Sheeres unoriginally, 'like a rock'.[11] Just seven years later, the rock shattered into rubble. Forced to evacuate Tangier in 1684, the English exercised the only power left to them and destroyed what they had previously built up at such cost. The intricate houses, the splendid forts, the ringed, defensive walls that Wenceslaus Hollar had found so sketchworthy, and finally Cholmley's engineering triumph, the great mole itself, were all detonated and demolished so as to avoid yielding them up to those Moroccan armies that had always been in wait and watching as the English focused on the dangerous, commerce-laden sea. On Charles II's orders, new-minted coins bearing his engraved image were buried deep in what was left of Tangier: 'which haply, many centuries hence when other memory of it shall be lost, may declare to succeeding ages that [this] place was once a member of the British empire'.

Now, alas, Tangier!
That cost so dear,
In money, lives, and fortunes . . .[12]

It is a strange picture. Men in salt-stained, dust-encrusted uniforms scrambling over smoking ruins, feverishly digging small graves for samples of the king's coinage, as colonial ambition dwindles into the stuff of archaeology. But then the entire Tangier episode appears strange in the light of conventional and current narratives of empire, so much so, that it is usually left out of them altogether. Despite its drama and importance at the time, the unprecedented amounts of state money poured into it, and Cholmley's extraordinary, vanished marine masterwork, only one major book has ever been written about Tangier's rise and fall as seventeenth-century England's most elaborate and expensive extra-European colony. Even this was published before the First World War, and it is suggestive that the E.M.G. Routh whose carefully neutral initials grace the title page of *Tangier: England's Lost Atlantic Outpost* (1912) was a woman, someone who worked outside the then almost entirely male establishment of imperial historians. Routh's solitary and scrupulous investigations have had little impact. The most recent and authoritative survey of England's fledgling empire in the seventeenth century, compiled by a team of American and Irish as well as British scholars, glances at Tangier barely half a dozen times in well over 500 pages.[13] As for Sir Hugh Cholmley, that strange, maniacal imperial projector and builder, his name has long since disappeared from the history books and is absent, too, from *The Dictionary of National Biography*. It is a powerful demonstration of just how effectively Britain's sporadic imperial disasters and retreats were expunged from the historical record and from national and even international memory.

Yet this lost Tangier episode is vital to a proper understanding of Britain's empire in its early modern phase, and a natural starting-point as well from which to explore its varied imperial captivities. Tangier was not a one-off, any more than it was just a cul-de-sac along Britain's uncertain route to temporary global dominion. A post-mortem of this failed colony reveals directions and characteristics that prevailed more widely, and stresses and vulnerabilities that proved persistent.

To begin with, Charles II's monetary and imaginative investment in Tangier is a reminder of the importance of the Mediterranean as a cockpit for contending states and religions, as a place of commerce, and as a site of empire. This point has been largely obscured because the master-narrative of British imperial expansion in the seventeenth and eighteenth centuries has always been the rise of the American colonies and their ultimate revolution, an approach that has been further reinforced by the current primacy of the United States. The fact that Fernand Braudel

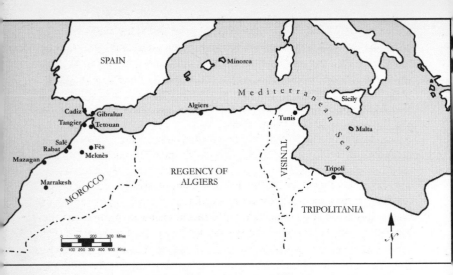

The Mediterranean and North Africa in the early eighteenth century.

ended his superb geo-historical saga of the Mediterranean world in 1598, and suggested – at least initially – that the sea declined abruptly in importance after 1650, has also encouraged historians to concentrate attention thereafter on the Atlantic and on the rise of extra-European commerce and colonies.[14] Yet the Mediterranean remained a major zone of activity for the British and other maritime powers long after the mid-seventeenth century. We have already seen one reason why this was so: the profitability of this zone in commercial terms. In 1700, Southern Europe and the Mediterranean accounted for as much of Britain's trade in terms of value as India and North America did put together; and, even at the end of the eighteenth century, there were probably as many British ships and crews active in the Mediterranean as there were in the Atlantic.[15]

Like other zones of British imperial enterprise, however, the Mediterranean was never just about trade. Here, as elsewhere, empire was also driven by the rivalries and insecurities of the major European powers. An essential part of Tangier's appeal had been that it offered a base from which the Royal Navy could monitor the Spanish fleet at Cadiz and Cartagena, and the French fleet at Toulon. Established at Tangier, with proper resources for ships to re-fit, re-provision and winter over, England hoped to be able to intervene rapidly in the event of either or both of these states massing their fleets for an assault on its colonies or against its

*Handel wrote in
1545* — *I recall it
impact Her* — *H. Butterfield was
on it immediately*

own coastlines. Just how well Tangier functioned as a naval base in fact
has been a matter of debate, but there can be no doubt that it was the
prototype for a succession of similar and more enduring Mediterranean
strongholds – Gibraltar, Minorca, Malta, Cyprus, and the Ionian Islands.
These bases would constitute Britain's empire *inside* Europe, a territorially
modest, often forgotten, but strategically indispensable element of its
global enterprise, which would become even more important once India
and the Suez canal had been seized.

But, in the seventeenth century and after, there were other empires
bordering on, and involved in this sea. As Braudel chronicled with such
magnificent sweep and arresting detail, the early modern Mediterranean
was above all a region where the different states of Western Christendom
confronted and sometimes co-operated with the Ottoman empire and with
Islam. And it was this complex and protracted engagement, between the
Mediterranean ambitions of the Western powers and the forces of the
Crescent, that lay at the heart both of the failure of colonial Tangier, and
of seventeenth- and early eighteenth-century Britain's most significant
captivity fears.

At the time that Sir Hugh Cholmley was constructing his doomed
masterwork at Tangier, the total population of the Ottoman empire may
have been approaching some 30 million souls, as against the 5.5 million
men and women who lived in England and Wales at that point. On paper,
at least, the Ottoman armed forces – the janissaries, provincial militias
and timariots – were well over 150,000 strong, many times as large again
as the armies at the disposal of early modern England's monarchs.[16]
Because of its size, wealth and populousness, the Ottoman empire was a
rich market for overseas traders, but it controlled most of its own inland
trade, just as it generated its own advanced manufactures, paper, glass,
gunpowder, sugar and the like. It also possessed a sophisticated administrative structure that for a long time coped expertly with the demands of
imperial conquest. Within a few years of seizing western Crete from Venice
in the mid-seventeenth century, for instance, the Ottomans had implemented a tax census of the island itemising its property down to the last
beehive. Not until the eighteenth century would the British come close to
matching this degree of fiscal zeal and efficiency even in their own islands,
never mind in their overseas territories.[17] The Ottomans regarded the
Mediterranean as peculiarly their own. They controlled its north-eastern
coastline through Serbia, Albania, Morea and Turkey. They secured access
to its easternmost part through their conquest of Egypt and Syria, and
to the western Mediterranean through their North African provinces,
Tripoli, Tunisia, and Algiers. It was in part from these last three outposts

of Ottoman power and influence that fleets of Muslim corsairs issued into the Mediterranean and the Atlantic, and preyed for centuries on European shipping and exposed shorelines.

The other major North African corsairing power was Morocco. This was not a part of the Ottoman empire, but was culturally influenced by it, and attentive – as all Muslim states were – to the religious significance of its sultan. During the first two-thirds of the seventeenth century, Morocco had been disjointed by civil wars: but then came the Alaouites, the dynasty that rules the country to this day. The second Alaouite sultan, Moulay Ismaïl, was a correspondent of Louis XIV of France, as great, if not an even greater builder, and a mature ruler for almost as long, from 1672 to 1727. Moulay Ismaïl was also a brutally effective centraliser, coming down hard on challenges to his authority from his own population, stamping out Ottoman attempts at interference, and launching successful assaults against many of the small European fortified settlements that had been clinging to the Moroccan coast since the fifteenth century. The Spanish were driven out of Larache, Mamora and Asila. As for English Tangier, it was 'besieged so closely', exulted one Muslim chronicler, 'that the Christians had to flee on their vessels and escape by sea, leaving the place ruined from bottom to top'.[18] This put it too simply, but it was certainly the case that pressure from powerful Moroccan armies, equipped with weapons fully comparable to those of Tangier's English garrison, deterred many families from settling here, undermined the commercial and expansionist dreams of those in residence, and forced on the colony human and defence costs which in the end its masters in London were no longer willing to afford.

The English had always recognised of course that occupying Tangier would bring them into direct contact with Islamic societies, but they had been divided as to the likely consequences of this. Some felt confident that – as with the English East India Company's coastal settlements in Mughal India – proximity to rich, powerful Muslim empires was bound to foster commerce. Moreover, it was thought that if the Royal Navy could only succeed in establishing itself at Tangier, then the danger that North African corsairs presented to English ships and sea-goers would be much reduced. Others however – including Hugh Cholmley – appear to have been nervous from the outset about the threat to the English from Moroccan military power and resistance. When an experienced Scottish soldier, Andrew Rutherford, Lord Teviot, took up the post of governor of Tangier in 1663, he found the garrison's morale already shaken: 'such was the fear they harboured for the Moor'. Teviot's response was energetic and ultimately unwise. He built up the colony's defences, tried to win over and divide local Muslim war leaders, and in May 1664 led a force of 500 elite troops outside Tangier's city walls to prove that Charles II's imperial power in North Africa could stretch beyond them. Teviot and all but nine of his men were promptly wiped out by Moroccan armies.

Subsequent governors of Tangier reacted by constructing still stronger defences, but also by reining in ambition. Initial English projects of using the colony as a point of departure into the North African interior were now tacitly abandoned in favour of simply hanging on. 'We have never sent any to understand their country,' one writer admitted glumly, 'to search into their strength and dependencies, to examine their interest.'[19] Even hanging on came over the years to seem ever more unlikely. By 1680, Moroccan forces were strong enough to seize three of Tangier's forts. Its then governor, Sir Palmes Fairbourne, had offered to surrender one of these – Henrietta Fort – if the men defending it were allowed to go free. The Moroccan commander brushed the offer aside: 'He wanted not stone-walls, but slaves for his master's service, that he could destroy them when he pleased.' Three days later, he did just that. Although eventually driven back, Moroccan armies went on to kill Fairbourne, as well as hundreds of English troops, and seize a further fifty-three men as slaves.[20] Such episodes of bitter defeat, violent deaths, and multiple captivities would be repeated many times in Britain's imperial history.

But this was not the only way in which this brief colonial adventure in Tangier proved both a failure and a portent. For as Moroccan force was exerted, the morale and cohesion of the English frayed and sometimes snapped entirely.

Pressure points

Britons and other Europeans engaged in imperial enterprises outside their own continent are sometimes imagined as monolithic contingents, their solidarity only enhanced by contact and conflict with non-Europeans. This was rarely ever simply and straightforwardly the case; and in Tangier the fracture lines among the colonisers themselves were at once particularly acute, and in some respects extreme versions of tensions that would recur in other imperial locations at other times.[21] The fundamental problem here – as so often – was an insufficiency of manpower. Initially, Tangier's garrison was some 4000 men strong; and there was broad agreement in London that this number should ideally be maintained. In practice, however, there were rarely more than 1500 soldiers in the settlement after 1670, because there was insufficient money available for more, or even to pay the existing ones on time. During the seventeenth century, the English state had become more actively concerned with overseas ventures, and less willing to concede the initiative in such matters to private enterprise. But its ability – as distinct from its desire – to exert and expand control outside its own domestic boundaries, whether in the Mediterranean, or North America and the Caribbean, or Asia, remained a constricted one. In 1670, Charles II would commission a magnificent silver medal from John Roettiers making clear the scale of his imperial aspirations. *Diffusus in Orbe Britannus*, proclaimed its motto: Britons spread throughout the world. Just two years earlier, however, the king had been obliged to give up attempts at direct rule over Bombay. The royal budget could not stretch to Indian adventures at this stage, and neither could the Crown's armed forces. A land attack on Bengal in 1686 in which royal troops participated proved a disaster; and so did a naval campaign against Western India two years later.[22] Set against this context, the fate of Tangier was just another, if more spectacular demonstration of the limits at this stage of the overseas power and personnel of the English state.

Starved of manpower, its garrison's pay always in arrears, hemmed in on the one side by the angry sea, and on the other by superior Moroccan military numbers, Tangier became a prey to festering internal divisions. Many of the garrison troops had fought in the civil wars of the 1640s and '50s for the sake of Parliament and a godly English republic. Sweating now under an alien sun, some of them wondered aloud why they should venture their lives for the sake of a king. 'When I served Oliver Cromwell', one Tangier corporal was heard to complain in 1663, 'I was paid like a man, but now I serve I do not know whom, I am paid like a turd.' Charles II was 'no Englishman' grumbled another Tangier soldier, accurately enough, 'but a Scotchman or a Frenchman'. Both of these men were executed.[23] Some of the settlement's womenfolk also rebelled, mainly it seems out of poverty, boredom and quarrels with neighbours or lovers, but sometimes again for the sake of politics. In June 1664, one Margaret Summerton was found guilty of sedition and of trying to raise a mutiny. She was flogged in front of Tangier's assembled garrison, before disappearing into its prisons and from the archives.[24]

But it was national differences and religious differences that caused the most persistent trouble. On paper, Tangier was an English colony, but like all English, and ultimately British colonies at all times, it contained a medley of nationalities, religions and cultures. There were Dutch, French, Italian, Portuguese and Jewish settlers, as well as fluctuating numbers of Muslim slaves and traders; and there were Welsh and Scottish settlers and soldiers. The main groupings though were the English and Irish, with

9. Demolishing Tangier's mole in 1684, by Dirck Stoop.

Protestants and Catholics well represented in both camps. These religious and national factions constantly jostled against each other, not always in predictable ways. During the siege of 1680, Irish Catholic soldiers and officers defending one of Tangier's forts on behalf of the King of England were obliged to call out instructions to each other in the Gaelic language, so as to avoid being understood by some English Protestant renegades who were serving with the Moroccan forces outside the gates.[25]

As this incident suggests, desertion was a major problem at Tangier. To begin with, a few dozen of the garrison's troops slipped away every year; but much higher numbers defected as the years went on, as pay fell into arrears, and excitement and professionalism faded into boredom and loss of hope. At all times, as the English high command admitted, far more of their men deserted to the Moroccan forces and to Islam, than there were Moroccan defectors willing to try their luck in Tangier as Christian converts.[26] English deserters unlucky enough to be caught by their own side and found guilty were executed, their bodies left hanging from scaffolds until consumed by the sun and carrion birds. Those who managed to convince the courts that their passage beyond Tangier's walls had somehow been innocent, or that they now bitterly repented of their actions, might have their penalty commuted to slavery – and this was the term actually employed in sentencing. They would be put to work without pay on the ceaseless task of repairing fortifications, iron shackles fixed to their wrists and ankles. Thus were English (and Irish, Scottish and Welsh) actors in empire reduced to slavery by their own kind.

It is striking indeed just how much of the language applied to Tangier by its occupiers resonates with images of confinement. For Lord Dartmouth, in his final speech to the colonists before dismissing them in early 1684, the very walls around Tangier which the English had built at such cost, together with the hills behind the settlement, evoked claustrophobic narrowness and irksome restraint. This was in reply to an address from Tangier's settlers thanking Charles II for recalling them 'from danger to security, from imprisonment to liberty, and from banishment to our own native country'.[27] Such complaints may have been partly sour grapes, but other, earlier comments made about the colony by those with direct experience of it strike a very similar note. Tangier was a 'perfect prison' declared some of its early occupiers. And a one-time settler in the colony claimed that the garrison troops viewed it as 'an ill prison, from which they could only hope to be freed by a grave'.[28] For the British, such prison analogies proved to be the colony's most durable cultural legacy. Until the end of the eighteenth century, one of the worst sections of Newgate prison in London was colloquially referred to as Tangier. Airbrushed out of polite histories of the British empire with a thoroughness that misleads to this day, Tangier continued for a while to be remembered at demotic level as a place of confinement and duress, as a site for captivities.

In this respect too, this initially cherished and celebrated colony that came to grief, possesses a much wider imperial relevance. Tangier demonstrates, as would so many later emergencies and disasters, the risks and dangers that England and later Britain could incur in combining overseas territorial ambitions with inadequate military manpower and parsimonious funding. It illustrates how the business of empire sometimes laid real as well as metaphorical chains on the activists directly involved, especially but not uniquely on poor whites. It shows how, when men and women were stranded hundreds of miles from home, and under pressure, discipline and loyalty could fray and fail, and ethnic, religious and political divisions come to the surface. And it demonstrates how, in these circumstances, Welsh, Scottish, English and Irish men and women could become vulnerable to capture, or change sides of their own volition. Tangier was the spectre at the imperial feast, a grim and embarrassing reminder of how difficult, in practical terms, sustaining empire at this early stage could be for Britons, and conversely of just how much effort, adjustment and expense would be required if a greater measure of success was to be achieved in the future. Little wonder, then, that when the rise of British imperial power came finally to be re-imagined as inexorable and inevitable, the story of this particular colony was quietly covered over and left undisturbed.

Which is why disinterring this episode is important. Investigating Tangier, and recognising the degree to which many of its problems were portents of things to come, obliges us to begin approaching the British empire in a more varied, more open-minded, and less over-determined way, and to seek out new things. It reminds us that – for the British – there were paths not taken, interludes of retreat, sporadic failures and significant limits, as well as formidable and indisputable exertions of power, and that those who made this empire were always diverse and sometimes at odds with each other. Investigating Tangier also brings us into contact with the Mediterranean, with its commercial, naval and strategic importance, and with the power and aggression displayed here by the forces of the Crescent, as well as by the states associated with the Cross. All of these elements – trade, naval and strategic imperatives, and the complex relationship between the Western powers and Islam had been closely involved in the rise and fall of colonial Tangier. They also provide the essential context for the British experience of the Mediterranean as a zone of captivity. The sea that enticed them could also entrap.

AFRICA.

10. The frontispiece of John Ogilby's *Africa*.

TWO

The Crescent and the Sea

Barbary

In 1670, John Ogilby published a sumptuous volume entitled simply *Africa*. A Scot, turned London printer and entrepreneur, Ogilby pirated sections of this compendium of real and bogus information from earlier works, while adding material and illustrations of his own. He could easily have chosen to preface it with a view of Tangier, at this stage still an English colony and widely expected to lead to further imperial and commercial gains in North Africa. Instead, he selected a very different and much less complacent frontispiece.

A resplendent black ruler, in leopard-skin cloak and with sceptre in hand, sits enthroned amidst a vision of Africa's people, animals and land-scape. There are large-eyed ostriches, supercilious camels, oddly attenu-ated pyramids, coiling snakes and strange birds; and there is a 'Hottentot' or Khoikhoi woman, whose breasts are so pendulous and elastic that one is stretched back across her own shoulder by a fiercely suckling infant.[1] In this imagined Africa, all is magic, menace and monstrous deviations from European norms. Yet more is on show here than simply the white man's prejudices. In the lower right-hand corner of the engraving, an individual stands gazing up intently at his regal black master. High cheek-boned, mustachioed, broad-shouldered and therefore strong, he wears a turban, the accepted emblem of Islam. Casually, he holds the chains of some fettered, naked slaves. Only these slaves are white; and they are also male. For Ogilby's English readers at the time, the act of opening his book on Africa would have meant being confronted at once with a representation of their own kind in captivity and slavery.

They would have understood the allusion instantly, though by now we have largely forgotten. Throughout the seventeenth century and in the early 1700s, England's (and subsequently Britain's) most widely known and controversial contacts with Islamic cultures were with the so-called Barbary powers, Morocco, Algiers, Tripoli, and Tunisia, the last three all regen-cies or military provinces of the Ottoman empire. Between 1600 and the early 1640s, corsairs operating from these North African territories seized more than 800 English, Scottish, Welsh and Irish trading vessels in the Mediterranean and Atlantic, confiscating their cargoes, and taking their crews and passengers into captivity. Some 12,000 English subjects may have been captured over these decades, and in most cases subsequently enslaved for life in North Africa and elsewhere in the Ottoman empire. Between 1660 and the 1730s, at least another 6000 Britons fell foul of Barbary corsairs. In all, over the course of the seventeenth and eighteenth centuries, there were probably 20,000 or more British captives of Barbary. These represented only a fraction of the total number of European men and women confined in North Africa over this period. There were also French, Neapolitan, Dutch, German, Scandinavian, Portuguese, American and above all Spanish captives and slaves. As late as the 1760s, 1400 Spaniards had to be redeemed from Algiers alone.[2]

Europeans who commented on this trade in humanity at the time – like many who have written on it since – rarely took the trouble to locate it in its full Mediterranean context. They simply branded the men responsible, whether they were Moroccan, Algerian, Tunisian or Tripolitan, as Barbary or Turkish pirates, terrorising the seas, preying on legitimate, peaceful trade, and selling innocent Christians into Muslim slavery. The term 'Barbary' referred originally to the Berbers, North Africa's indigenous people.[3] As the British commonly used it, however, 'Barbary' served as a blanket term for the entire North African region (excluding Egypt), and for all of its diverse peoples, Arabs, Berbers, Moriscos, Ottoman soldiers and officials and more. And the assonance between Barbary as a geographical signifier and the insult 'barbarian' was a gift of which generations of polemicists made abundant and predictable use. 'The sink of trade and stink of slavery,' wrote the clergyman and voyage-writer, Samuel Purchas, of Algiers in the early 1600s:

the cage of unclean birds of prey, the habitation of sea-devils . . . the whip of the Christian world, the wall of the Barbarian; terror of Europe . . . scourge of the islands, den of pirates.[4]

'Pirates', like Barbary, was a convenient and common epithet, but not an accurate one. It put the men who set sail out of Algiers, Morocco, Tunisia or Tripoli to hunt down European shipping on a par with England's own sea-robbers, who were still common enough around its own coastlines in 1600, and active in the Caribbean and other waters for much longer. Greed, need and aggression linked all of these sea-goers, but most North African 'pirates' were not independent agents operating outside of their home communities' laws, so much as a vital and officially recognised part of their revenue-raising machinery. In the regency of Algiers, the biggest threat to English shipping before the 1680s, the governor received a share of the profits on all cargo and captives seized by crews based in his territory. Morocco's rulers also levied taxes on men and merchandise taken by their subjects at sea. Barbary 'pirates' are therefore more properly styled corsairs or privateers; and North African corsair attacks, unlike pirate attacks, were rarely indiscriminate. It was Christian shipping that these corsair fleets targeted, especially ships from countries with which they and their sponsors regarded themselves as being at war.

Not for the last time, Western powers were more ready to condemn aggression on the part of Muslim forces, than acknowledge the parallels existing between it and their own actions. For Europeans practised Mediterranean corsairing too, though not all of them to the same degree. As Peter Earle has described, Malta's sea-going Knights of St John routinely preyed on Muslim vessels, seizing their crews and passengers and selling them in the open market. There were an estimated 10,000 Muslim slaves in Malta in 1720. Those European powers which possessed substantial Mediterranean galley fleets – France, Genoa, Venice, and the Papal States – also drew heavily on slave manpower seized at sea from Ottoman and Moroccan vessels.[5] But it was Spain, so long a meeting-point between the Crescent and the Cross, that was most intricately involved in this Mediterranean slave trade. Most of the Muslims expelled from its shores in successive waves after 1490 had settled along the North African coast. Some of these men and their descendants (the Moriscos) turned to corsairing in order to make a living in what was always a poor area agriculturally, and to act out a holy war of revenge. At least 15,000 Spanish men and women had to be redeemed from North African captivity in the seventeenth century alone; thousands more, snatched in corsairing raids on coastal villages in Andalusia, or from small craft operating off its shores, died before they got the chance to go home. The other side of all this however was Spain's own population of captive Muslims seized in turn from North African vessels. Searching in 1714 for Moroccan slaves to exchange for some of his own enslaved countrymen, a British naval captain remarked unemotionally that 'amongst the several towns situated on the coast of Spain, there may be Moors purchased at very reasonable rates, such as are aged, blind or lame. It's no matter, all will pass so they have life'.[6]

And what of Britain itself? Unlike Spain, France, or some of the Italian states, it possessed no galley fleet for which a pool of captive Muslim labour might have seemed attractive. Moreover, as we shall see, imperial and strategic considerations increasingly made the British more likely to liberate any North Africans they encountered in captivity than enslave them. But this had nothing to do with scruples about Muslim slavery as such. Moroccan slaves were employed in Tangier throughout its time as an English colony; and in periods of open war with one or more of the Barbary powers, the Royal Navy often sold any of their seamen and traders it captured to European states that did employ Muslim slave labour.[7] There are even stray examples of men and women from North Africa falling into the hands of British transatlantic slavers, and ending up labouring on plantations in the American South.

In Abdallah Laroui's words, then, captive-taking and slave-making were emphatically 'a Mediterranean ... phenomenon' in the early modern era, and never exclusively a Muslim one.[8] Frenchmen, Spaniards, Portuguese, Italians, Dutchmen, Britons, and even Americans were all involved in the business, as well as crews operating out of the North African powers. But men and women experiencing captivity and enslavement in this region, or living and sailing in fear of it, rarely adopted a considered, comparative perspective on their plight. Most thought only of their own terrors and, if they moved on from this at all, of fellow sufferers of their own country of origin and religion. This was especially true of the British. By contrast with France, Spain or the Italian states, it was rare for Britain to retain North African or any other Muslim slaves and captives on its own soil, so men and women from these islands were unlikely to view North African corsairing as a natural response to their own state's violence and cruelties. And only a minority of Britons seem to have acknowledged any parallel between their own risk of being captured at sea by North African corsairs, and the much greater threat that British slaving ventures increasingly posed to men and women in West Africa. To most Britons, it is clear, Barbary corsairing and captive-taking were simply monstrous acts, a sort of terrorism. Moreover, Barbary corsairs provoked an altogether different level and quality of anxiety than did the privateers employed by Britain's European enemies. It is unlikely that all of the Barbary powers put together captured more English, Welsh, Scottish and Irish vessels over the centuries than did French privateers operating out of the single port of St Malo, who seized 2000 British ships between 1688 and 1713 alone.[9] But such losses to European privateers were confined to periods of open war and viewed in Britain overwhelmingly in commercial terms. Cargoes and vessels might be lost forever; but people rarely were. By contrast, the Barbary threat was more persistent, much less predictable, and always perceived as involving more than just economic risk and damage.

Barbary corsairing alarmed and angered out of all proportion to its actual extent because it seemed the negation of what England and ultimately Britain and its empire were traditionally about. 'Britons never will be slaves', proclaimed James Thomson's 'Rule Britannia' (1740), but North Africa's corsairs could reduce individual Britons to exactly that servile condition. Barbary corsairing also affronted British Christianity and Protestantism, since slaves and captives in North Africa were believed to be at risk of forcible conversion to Islam or, still worse, of opting voluntarily for that faith if exposed to its influence long enough. Most of all, this mode of captive-taking provoked anxiety because it happened at sea. As David Armitage shows, from the sixteenth century onwards, maritime references were regularly employed by writers and theorists on British national and imperial destiny. Those who wanted the island made up of England, Wales and Scotland to be a single, united state – something not achieved until 1707 – invoked the encircling waves as irresistible proof that God and Nature were in favour of this political arrangement. Quite literally, it was the sea that gave Britain its shape. The sea was also the vehicle of Britain's cherished and totemic commerce, and it was vital as well to British mythologies of empire. This was not simply because this empire rested on the power of the Royal Navy. For generations of publicists and politicians, sea-power was what made British empire distinctive and benevolent. The empires of Ancient Rome and Catholic Spain, they argued, had nourished atrocity, corrupted their makers, and ultimately declined, because of their reliance on military conquest. Britain's empire, by contrast – because it was predominantly maritime – would confer freedom and prosperity, and consequently endure. 'Such as desire Empire & Liberty', wrote Sir William Petty in the 1680s: 'let them encourage the art of ship building'.[10]

At one level, then, Barbary appalled because its corsairs converted the sea from an emblem of commerce, freedom, power and proud British identity, into a source of menace and potential slavery. The corsairs also provoked fear because – like Tangier – they brought Britain into sharp and initially disadvantageous contact with the power and politics of Islam. In contrast with central and eastern Europe and the Iberian peninsula, England, Wales, Scotland and Ireland had never before the seventeenth century been exposed to serious manifestations of Ottoman and Muslim physical force. The onset of major losses to North African sea predators after 1600 was thus experienced with peculiar acuteness. At exactly the same time as the English began encroaching as traders and marginal settlers into one great Muslim empire, Mughal India, they also had to deal with Muslim predators in the Mediterranean and Atlantic, and with the warlike, frontier provinces of the most formidable of all Islamic empires, the Ottomans.

Yet to understand the full imperial significance of this particular captivity panic we have to probe rather more deeply. Instead of approaching the Mediterranean in the past primarily as a site for contest and conflict between the Crescent and the Cross, Fernand Braudel insisted, we should regard this remarkable, inland sea as a stage for more complicated encounters:

> The actors on this stage speak many tongues and do not always understand each other; nor do we, the audience, always realise what is really going on, for the plots and story-lines are complex and not always what they seem.[11]

The Barbary powers threatened commerce and the lives and liberties of unlucky individuals, English, Welsh, Scottish, Irish, and many more: yes, indeed. More profoundly, they were feared and hated over a very long period because their chosen medium of manoeuvre and attack was the sea, and because they were Muslims. Yet, as far as Britain and its empire were concerned, Barbary gradually became something more and something different than just a threat and a focus of hate. So we have to do more than count its victims and explore the kinds of captivity and slaveries it inflicted, important though these were. We also need to explore Barbary's changing relationship with the British state, a small European power that was ever more intent on overseas empire, but always dependent on non-European auxiliaries of different kinds in order to attain it.

Counting

All Barbary captives remain imprisoned in substantial historical ignorance. There is much about them that we cannot know and will never know.[12] When British and other European slave-traders purchased men and women from West Africa and shipped them into bondage across the seas, they usually listed their victims and filled out ledgers of the monetary costs involved. This taste for documentation, for writing up the unspeakable, has allowed historians of the transatlantic slave trade to reach a broad if not a complete consensus about its dimensions over time. No such lists or ledgers exist for the very different, but sometimes no less lethal trade in human beings carried out by North African corsairs, though when the Ottoman archives in Istanbul become better known, a surer statistical base

11. The corsair city of Algiers.

for at least some of these captivities may eventually emerge. But while anything approaching a comprehensive head-count of Barbary captive-taking will always be beyond us, the broad outline of its impact on Britain is clear enough.

Stray English ships and seamen had been captured by Ottoman and Barbary vessels in the sixteenth century, a natural consequence of this country's growing involvement in Mediterranean trade.[13] It was dynastic and diplomatic changes at the start of the following century, however, together with a temporary decline in English naval effectiveness, that raised the risk of capture to an entirely different level. When James VI of Scotland also became James I of England, Wales and Ireland in 1603, he made peace with Spain, and thereby aligned his kingdoms with the prime Christian empire of the period and the state most at odds with the Ottoman empire. Retaliation was swift. By 1616, Algiers alone was estimated to have seized over 450 English vessels, and this was just the beginning.[14] Between the 1610s and '30s, Cornwall and Devon, both sea-going counties heavily involved in trade with southern Europe, lost a fifth of their shipping to North African corsairs. In just one year, 1625, nearly a thousand sailors and fishermen from the major West Country port of Plymouth were seized, most within thirty miles of its shore. Overall, David Hebb calculates, in

49

the two decades before the outbreak of the Civil War in 1642, Barbary corsairs inflicted well over one million pounds of damage on English shipping, a sum that needs to be multiplied more than a hundredfold to gain any sense of its meaning in today's values.[15]

Not all of the 8000 or so English, Welsh, Scottish and Irish captives taken to North Africa during these early decades were seized at sea. At this stage, the Algiers fleet was strong enough to stage occasional raids on England's West Country, on the Channel Islands, and the coast of Ireland. Among nineteen women redeemed from Algiers in 1646 were two, Ellen Hawkins and Joan Brabrook, who had been seized fifteen years before from Baltimore, County Cork; six more of the women brought back that year hailed from Youghall further along the southern Irish coast.[16] It was partly these Barbary depredations – on ships, cargoes, lives, and domestic coastlines – that prompted James I's successor, Charles I, to levy ship money so controversially on his subjects in order to raise additional revenue for his failing navy. By the same token, the massive damage that Barbary corsairs inflicted on lives and commerce after 1603 helps to account for growing popular alienation from and disillusionment with these early Stuart kings. To this extent, the power of the Crescent – so often left out of British history entirely – helped to provoke the civil wars that tore England and its adjacent countries apart after 1642.

In the aftermath of these convulsions, English responses to North African corsairing became more systematic. Parliament levied a duty on imports and exports to raise ransoms for the captives, and the Royal Navy became increasingly formidable, equipped with warships which soon outclassed any available to the North African powers. It is easy to assume, and it sometimes has been assumed, that this burgeoning naval power translated swiftly into suppression of Barbary corsairing. 'And who dares choose, through the broad earth to roam', boasted Daniel Defoe in 1707:

> Shall sail safe under British ships of war;
> Then no damn'd Algerines or corsaire dare
> Attempt our persons, or assault our goods . . .[17]

But this was propaganda designed to persuade Scotland's sea-traders, who were vulnerable to Barbary corsairing, to accede to union with England. In reality, rising British sea-power did not and could not immediately wipe out the threat posed by the corsairs.

I have already drawn an analogy between early modern perceptions of the Barbary corsairs, and Western perceptions of terrorism today. There are other analogies. Barbary corsairing resembled modern terrorism in that it was at once so diffuse and so rooted a phenomenon that even substantial naval and military force for a time won only temporary advantages against it. Indeed, and again like terrorism today, the corsairs were able to turn some of the very sources of Western power to their own advantage. After 1650, the English built up an increasingly powerful navy: but this navy had much more to defend. There were 115,000 tons of English merchant shipping in the 1620s; sixty years later, there were 340,000 tons. These statistics are usually cited as straightforward proof of England's expanding wealth and global reach at this time, yet as Gerald Aylmer pointed out: 'the larger a country's merchant marine and the more far-flung its overseas trading interests, the more potentially vulnerable it is to commerce raiding.'[18] Every additional English ship in the Mediterranean and even the Atlantic increased the corsairs' potential harvest.

This was especially the case since most of these ships were small, with limited crews, and few or no cannon to defend themselves. And it was small ships on which North African corsairs increasingly preyed. A list of twenty-seven vessels from Britain and New England captured by Moroccan corsairs between 1714 and 1719 shows that on average each was crewed by fewer than ten men. A similar pattern emerges in later decades. A British envoy sent to ransom some 150 captives from Morocco in 1734 reported that they came from twelve different ships. Easily the biggest of these had a crew of twenty-five. Far more typical, though, was the *Ann* with its crew of six, or the *John*, captured off Malaga with just eight Scottish seamen aboard.[19] For ships of this type, the only real defence against the corsairs was a naval convoy system, and this was not always available or even practicable. Vessels carrying highly perishable cargoes could not afford to wait for a convoy to assemble. Nor were traders always eager to arrive at a foreign port at the same time as a convoy of their competitors, since this naturally lowered the price their cargo could command. None the less, whenever Britain was at odds with a North African power, there were always shrill appeals to the Admiralty from ports involved in Mediterranean trade. 'Such ships are entirely unprovided for making any defence', wrote Bristol's Merchant Venturers in 1754, when another war with Morocco seemed imminent: 'and must unavoidably fall a prey to our merciless enemies (to the great loss not only of the property but lives of many of His Majesty's subjects) unless your lordships will be pleased to send a sufficient number of ships of war.'[20]

The date of this plea – 1754 – suggests just how long fears of North African corsairs persisted, but calculating the actual number of British and Irish captives of Barbary over time is extremely difficult. The last all-out North African assault on shipping from these islands occurred between

1677 and 1682, when England was at war with the regency of Algiers. This conflict cost the English over £800,000, at least 160 merchant ships (some estimates go as high as 500), and some 3000 captives.[21] It ended with a treaty between England and Algiers in 1682. From now on – as well as paying certain subsidies – the English state bound itself to provide its subjects' vessels with formal passes which Algiers agreed to, and usually did, respect. But this was not the end of British and Irish captivity in North Africa. Instead, the main scene of conflict shifted to Morocco. After 1680, its formidable sultan, Moulay Ismaïl, systematised corsairing as a weapon of state finance. All captives seized by Moroccan corsairs now became the sultan's property, and European states were no longer allowed to redeem nationals on an individual or group basis. Instead, they had to pay for all of their captives detained in Morocco at any given time.

The consequences for British shipping were never as lethal as earlier attacks by Algerian corsairs, but they remained serious for much longer. In 1711, corsairs operating out of Morocco cost Britain £100,000 in lost ships and cargos, and this was a year of formal peace between the two countries. During periods of open war – between 1715 and 1719 for instance – British trading losses were much higher.[22] Since Morocco's rulers were always eager to exchange captives for ransoms, the number of Britons within its borders at any given time was usually limited but regularly replenished. In 1690, Morocco held at least 500 British captives. In 1720, some 300 men and one woman from these islands are known to have been confined there; and in 1759 – after a marked lull in captive-taking – there were over 340 British detainees. Yet, as is true of all such estimates, these figures are mere snapshots of captivity, conveying little of its quality or its real dimensions.

Christian prejudice, fear and ignorance inflated many early assessments of the number of captives in Barbary, but later, more conservative estimates could also err and this time on the downside. As far as England was concerned, many of these apparently more judicious totals were supplied by envoys in North Africa who spoke no Arabic, or derived from petitions by the captives themselves. Thus in 1662, 300 men held in the city of Algiers dispatched a petition to London begging to be redeemed. But these men will have represented only a portion of the total number of English captives held throughout the regency of Algiers at this time, some 1200 according to one estimate.[23] Establishing the number of men and women redeemed from captivity over time is rather easier. Before the outbreak of the Civil War in 1642, barely a quarter of all Britons seized by North African corsairs seem to have got the chance to return home, but after 1650 the English state applied itself more systematically to the business of redemption. Between 1670 and 1734, government records suggest that *at least* 2200 captives were shipped back to Britain.[24] These are individuals whose names and places of origin we can establish with a fair degree of certainty. Yet to say that 2200 men and women returned from North Africa over this sixty-year period is far from saying that this was anywhere near the total of English, Welsh, Scottish and Irish captives seized during this time.

To begin with, this figure of 2200 redeemed captives excludes an incalculable number of Britons and Irishmen who made their own escape from North Africa during this period, as well as those who turned renegade and chose to stay on there. It also excludes an unknown number of Scots, since – before and even after the Treaty of Union in 1707 – the Presbyterian Kirk and prominent individuals north of the border often made their own arrangements to bring local seamen back home. Manifestly, this total of 2200 redeemed captives also leaves out individuals killed in the course of capture. Corsair targets only occasionally made a fight of it, but some encounters were bloody and mortal. James Amos, an Englishman taken captive in Morocco in 1718, was the only survivor from a crew of twenty-seven. The rest of his comrades were blown up along with their ship when they tried to resist the corsairing vessel attacking them.[25] More crucially still, not everyone captured was subsequently redeemed. The treaty with Algiers in 1682 stipulated that its inhabitants were not liable 'against their wills, to set any [slaves] at liberty', and that the English state was under no obligation to ransom its subjects, a let-out clause repeated in later treaties. Such provisions help to explain why England had a reputation in Barbary for being more miserly than other states in its response to its captives. In 1674, the governor of Algiers complained to Charles II that an earlier agreement to redeem his city's English captives had still not been honoured: 'In this condition, your men . . . are neither clearly slaves, nor clearly free . . . in this matter you have taken no care, but have gone on in neglect.'[26]

The English state's meanness on this issue was partly a function of its limited resources at this stage, but it was also simply that: meanness. Before 1700, and especially before 1650, ransoming captives held hundreds of miles away sometimes received low governmental priority. Sporadic official inertia in this connection was in some respects made worse by this culture's Protestantism. Catholic European states vulnerable to Muslim privateering had long ago either organised civic societies to look after the business of ransoming, as Genoa did, or relied like France and Spain on two religious orders which had devoted themselves to Christian captives of Islam since the thirteenth century, the Mercedarians and the Trinitarians.[27] After the

Protestant Reformation, these redemptionist orders were no longer available to assist English subjects held in Ottoman and Barbary captivity. The Church of England, the Presbyterian Kirk in Scotland, and various dissenting churches all played major roles in raising ransoms and publicising the plight of Barbary captives, but they lacked the contacts and linguistic skills of the Catholic redemptionist orders in Continental Europe. Without full-time religious activists working on their behalf, captives from Britain and Ireland sometimes felt bereft. 'All nations is provided for', scrawled a desperate and semi-literate captive to his wife from Morocco in 1716, 'but the poor English has no assistance from their nation.'[28] This man never got home.

This was one example (we will encounter many more) of how the politics of English and British captivity overseas overlapped with the politics of social class back home. As was true of all peoples caught up in it, most British and Irish victims of this Mediterranean trade in captive bodies were poor, labouring men. There were some conspicuous exceptions. The earl of Inchiquin was seized by Algiers corsairs *en route* to Lisbon in 1659, together with his son and heir who lost an eye in the attack. But the majority of captives were, predictably, petty traders, fishermen, soldiers in transit to overseas postings, and above all seamen. 'These are the men who make you rich,' William Sherlock told a congregation assembled in St Paul's cathedral in 1702 to celebrate the return of hundreds of North African captives:

who bring the Indies home to you, and clothe you with all the bravery of the east. These are the men that defend your country in their wooden walls, the great strength and glory of this island.[29]

It was an eloquent summing-up of why Barbary corsairing appeared a particular affront to Britain's essence. Seamen were instruments of Britain's overseas commerce and manned its navy, and these in turn made possible its empire. Yet seamen were the corsairs' pre-eminent victims. They were also overwhelmingly poor men and consequently vulnerable.[30] If seized at sea and held in North Africa, it was extremely unlikely that a common seaman would be able to assemble his own ransom. Unlike prisoners taken in a conventional European war, he could rarely hope to be exchanged for men from the other side. And even if they got to learn of his predicament, his family back in Britain would find it hard to raise money on his behalf. So when the authorities in London were slow to intervene, Barbary captives could be stranded and enslaved in North Africa for many years, and sometimes for ever.

Here is an example. In 1701, five men who had been captured while serving as soldiers in English-occupied Tangier finally returned to their native country from Morocco. The official reporting this noted without comment that they had been 'in slavery for these twenty-four years'.[31] This was an extreme case, but captives from Britain and Ireland often found themselves held in North Africa for five years or more; and, before 1700, ten years was not exceptional. More than anything else, it is the duration of these Barbary captivities that makes the number of men and women eventually redeemed a poor guide to the total captured in the first place. The longer captivity lasted, the more likely it was that those enduring it would cross over and turn renegade or, far more commonly, simply not survive to be freed. In the mid-seventeenth century, one in every five European captives held in Tripoli is known to have died every year. By the eighteenth century, the death-rate among Barbary captives was lower, except in plague years, but it remained substantial. A list of 263 British and colonial American captives in Morocco between 1714 and 1719 shows that fifty-three of these men died over this five-year period: just over 20 per cent of the total number detained. This same list also illustrates how the risk of dying in captivity increased relentlessly along with its duration. Forty-eight of these fifty-three casualties were men and boys whose captivity ordeal had begun in 1716 or earlier.[32]

In many years, plague was the biggest killer of captives and captors alike. Recurrent epidemics reduced the city of Algiers' population from perhaps 100,000 in the early 1600s – about half the size of London's at that time – to some 40,000 by 1800. But, as far as the captives were concerned, major killers also included food poisoning, sudden exposure to a hot climate, shame, despair, and mistreatment. When John Whitehead's boat smashed on Morocco's western coast in February 1691, he and his nine shipmates were seized and marched for weeks on end through Marrakesh to Meknès, a journey of over 200 miles along the foothills of the Middle Atlas mountains. Exhaustion, shock and contaminated water meant that only two of the ten men made it.[33] The trauma involved in being taken by force and reduced to varieties of enslavement in a foreign country, away from friends and family, could also prove lethal. One example of this emerges from the same sample of 263 Anglo-American captives in Morocco just cited. For while, on average, one in five of these men died, among those who had previously been shipmasters, the mortality rate was almost double that: 38 per cent. Shipmasters were generally older than the average crewman, but their previous experience of command may also have made these men particularly sensitive to the terrible loss of status and autonomy involved in captivity. As the Africans whom their countrymen were shipping ever more busily across the Atlantic could have told these British victims, capture and slavery killed through their impact on the mind, not just on the body.

If we factor in those Britons who died during captivity or who were killed while being captured; if we remember that our base figure of 2200 British and Irish redeemed captives between 1670 and 1730 excludes escapees, renegades, many Scots, and those whom the London authorities never knew about, ignored, or were unable to recover; if we remember, too, that this total leaves out English, Welsh, Scottish and Irish seamen who were captured while working or travelling on vessels belonging to foreign states – Spain, Venice, Holland or wherever – and consequently dealt with (or not) by their representatives rather than by Britain: then it seems likely that during this particular sixty-year period well over 5000 Britons and Irishmen spent some of their lives confined in North Africa as captives and slaves. Given that some 12,000 men, women and children from these islands appear to have suffered a similar fate between 1620 and the 1640s, and that another 1200 men were reported captive in Algiers in the early 1660s, it seems almost certain that we should be thinking of a total of at least 20,000 British and Irish captives held in North Africa between the beginning of the seventeenth century and the mid-eighteenth century. How many Britons were held as captives and slaves in addition to this total in other parts of the Ottoman empire after 1600 still remains to be explored.[34]

Britons can be slaves

What did it mean for Britons to be captured and put at risk of enslavement in this fashion, and how were these experiences understood and imagined by their countrymen back home? These questions have never been seriously posed, in part because Britain's notorious role as a dealer in black slaves before 1807 has understandably diverted attention from its own inhabitants' earlier and very different exposure to the threat of slavery. In this, as in other respects, we are not accustomed to scrutinising sources of weakness, fear and failure in rising and ruthless empires, even though they were certainly present, and men and women at the time took their existence for granted.

Moreover, although the Ottoman and North African trade in both white and black slaves existed over a longer period than the transatlantic slave-trade – and was at times comparable in scale – far less is currently known about it, and about the kinds of slavery and forcible confinement operating in these zones over the centuries. Some sites remain of course. If you visit Rabat in Northern Morocco, once a major corsairing centre, you can still enter the medina or old city through the Bab Mellah, and stroll along the narrow and tumultuous Rue des Consuls to one of the places where white captives are known to have been sold, the Souk el Ghezel. But even if you can resist being distracted along the way by the smells of fresh mint, ground spices and new-baked bread, or by displays of goods ranging from tacky, imported toys to jewel-coloured, geometrically patterned carpets, you will still find precious little to see when you finally arrive. The place where unknown numbers of British and other European captives were once stripped, fingered, and haggled over, is now a tree-shaded car park and home to some of Rabat's best wood-carvers, quite lacking in any indicators of its former use.

In contrast to the meagreness of indigenous written and physical evidence, British and other Western sources on Barbary captivities and slaveries are abundant, but shaded with varying degrees of bias. Fear, anger, ignorance and prejudice all worked to distort, and so too did desperation. In the 1670s, the parents and wives of almost a thousand English captives in the regency of Algiers, most of them poor people, dispatched an emotional appeal to the House of Commons:

> The said patrons [Algerian slave-owners] do frequently bugger the said captives, or most of them . . . run iron into their fundaments, rip open their bellies with knives, cut their britches across, and washing them with vinegar and salt, and hot oil, draw them in carts like horses.

Those who drew up this petition can have had little or no direct experience of North Africa or of how the captives were actually faring there. They were merely rehearsing anti-Barbary and anti-Islamic atrocity stories in the frail hope that Parliament might be jolted into ransoming their menfolk. Captives, too, embroidered their sufferings. 'Your petitioners are there to the number of about three thousand in miserable captivity,' wrote some English seamen trapped in Algiers to the House of Commons in 1641:

> Undergoing diverse and most insufferable oppressions as rowing in galleys, drawing in carts, grinding in mills, with diverse such unChristian-like labours . . . suffering much hunger, with many blows on our bare bodies.[35]

There will have been an element of truth to these complaints, but again these men will have wanted to give an unalloyedly negative picture of

12. White slaves being unloaded at Algiers: an English drawing of 1700.

what they were enduring in the hope of persuading Parliament to act. Not until the early eighteenth century, when the threat from Barbary was recognised as receding, did British and other European writings on white captivity and slavery in North Africa become conspicuously more nuanced. In *Robinson Crusoe* (1719), Defoe was careful to distinguish between Barbary captivity in practice and the sensationalist versions on offer in folklore and traditional polemics. His hero falls victim to Moroccan corsairs, and under-goes two years enslavement in Salé in advance of his more lengthy island captivity, but remains throughout phlegmatic: 'the usage I had was not so dreadful as at first I apprehended.'[36]

As this suggests, it is the variety of Barbary captivity experiences, more even than contemporary bias or the paucity of indigenous information, that makes reconstructing them so challenging. At no time – and espe-cially after the early 1720s – were all British captives in North Africa sold into slavery or forced into hard labour. Even those who were experienced markedly diverse fates of widely differing duration. Under Islamic law, to be sure, infidels taken in war, whether on land or sea, and whether white or black, could be enslaved. Certain things followed on from this. All slaves, in whatever system or region of the world, become commodities. Uprooted from where they belong, they are stripped of control over some or all of the most important aspects of their lives. The *Qur'an* recommended that kindness be shown to slaves, but these were still people of inferior status who could be sold, inherited, lent to another owner, or gifted away. Any property they owned was at the disposal of their master or mistress. Both in law and practice, female slaves were at the sexual mercy of their masters, though they were not supposed to be put out to prostitution. British and Irish female victims of Barbary corsairs were always a tiny minority, but – like other European women in this position – many of them before 1720 seem never to have got home. And whether male or female, young or old, black or white, slaves and captives in Islamic regimes, like slaves and captives everywhere, ran the risk of falling into the power of bad owners, guards and supervisors and of suffering sexual and other kinds of abuse.[37]

All this said, both white and black slaves in North Africa lived more diverse lives, and sometimes much freer lives, than the majority of plantation slaves in the Caribbean or American South. Slaves under Islamic law could marry with their owner's permission and own property. There was even a special Arabic term (*ma'dhūn*) for slaves who set up a business, a shop say, or a tavern catering to other Christian captives as well as errant Muslims, and who then handed a percentage of the profits over to their owners. This was the fate of two late seventeenth-century Anglo-Jamaican merchants, a Messrs Nash and Parker. Sailing back from the West Indies to England, their fortunes swollen by exploiting one kind of slave economy, they were captured by Moroccan corsairs and became slaves in their turn in Tetouan. Only in their case, this brought the chance to learn Arabic and local business practices. Once their freedom had been purchased, the two men chose not to return home, but instead set up a trading house in Tetouan which endured into the eighteenth century.[38]

But the most crucial difference between the experiences of white slaves and captives in North Africa, and black plantation slaves across the Atlantic, was that – for the former – deracination and loss of freedom often, though not always, had a temporal limit. After 1650, English, Welsh, Scottish and Irish male captives of Barbary, together with more affluent and protected women detained there, could usually look forward to being ransomed at some point. It bears repeating that such ransoms sometimes took a decade or more to arrive, and consequently arrived too late for those who were unlucky or weak. Nevertheless, the hope of securing them at some point did give owners and employers in North Africa an incentive to keep their British and other European captives alive and moderately healthy. The ransoming system held out the prospect of freedom for captives, and a bounty for their employers. It gave both of them a vested interest in servile survival.

Britons captured by North African powers experienced, then, a wide variety of fates. How they were treated might be influenced by their perceived social class and level of wealth, by their age and gender, and by such skills as they possessed. Those viewed as useful by their captors – such as medical men, boat-builders, fluent linguists and armourers – could be offered all kinds of advancement. In the 1720s, an Anglo-Irishman named Carr, whose brother served in the Royal Navy, was working as Moulay Ismaïls's chief gun-founder in Meknès. 'A very handsome man, very ingenious, and much of a gentleman in his behaviour', this individual had long since buried his captive status, along with his original nationality and religion, in lucrative collaboration, casting 'mortars, shells, cannon etc. as well as can be done in Europe'. Carr's appears to have been a reasonably contented, self-chosen existence, but highly qualified captives of this sort were sometimes excluded from ransoming agreements against their will, precisely because they were too useful to be given up. 'I do keep his accounts and merchandise', complained an unusually well-educated English slave of his Algerian owner in 1646, 'and that keeps me here in misery, when others that are illiterate go off upon easy terms . . . so that my breeding is my undoing.'[39]

The experience of Barbary captivity was also shaped by factors other than the captives' own characteristics and qualifications: by *when* in time they were captured, by *where* exactly they were captured, and by *who* took control of them.

Any moderately healthy European male seized by Barbary corsairs in the first two-thirds of the seventeenth century was at acute risk of becoming a galley slave. Before 1650, Algiers' corsair fleet, for instance, was some seventy vessels strong. Like the galley fleets of France, Spain and the Italian states, it relied on forced labour, with up to twenty-five banks of oars per ship, and three to five men shackled to each oar who might row for more than twenty hours a day. 'Not having so much room as to stretch his legs', remembered the Englishman Francis Knight of his time as a galley slave in the 1630s:

> The stroke regular and punctual, their heads shaved unto the skull, their faces disfigured with disbarbing, their bodies all naked, only a short linen pair of breeches to cover their privities . . . all their bodies pearled with a bloody sweat.[40]

The only blessing of life as a galley slave was that it was often short. Heart-attacks, ruptures, broken limbs, malnutrition and insufficient rations of water to replace what the rowers sweated out were standard occupational hazards. Given levels of intra-state and corsairing violence in the

13. A battle between Barbary corsairs and Royal Navy warships, *c.* 1670s.

Mediterranean, galley slaves also risked being injured or killed by their own kind. When the English naval commander Sir Thomas Allin attacked the Algiers fleet in 1671, his squadron is estimated to have killed, along with large numbers of Muslim seamen, some 400 of their European rowers, chained helplessly to their benches and unable to escape the cannon-fire and the sea.[41]

By 1700, the risk of British and other white slaves being doomed to the oar was shrinking fast, along with the North African galley fleets themselves. But most male Barbary captives, whether sold formally in a slave market or no, could still expect to be exposed to a period of hard, physical labour, particularly if they were of low status or fell under the control of the state. Moulay Ismaïl employed substantial numbers of European captives on his lavish building projects in Meknès and elsewhere. They were used to make and carry bricks, dig foundations and cut marble, build walls, courtyards and arched gateways, and spade those irrigated Andalusian gardens, that remain beautiful to look at now, but would have been back-breaking to establish. The horror stories emerging from all this that were perpetuated in British and Continental European accounts must be exaggerated, but not always or absolutely.[42] A powerful ruler with thousands of slaves at his disposal was likely to be less attentive to their individual welfare than a small private householder with perhaps just one slave in his employ and an eager expectation of securing a ransom at some point. (In the same way Louis XIV, Most Christian King of France, devoted scant attention to the Muslim captives manning his galleys, or indeed to the Huguenot heretics rowing alongside them.) And for Northern European captives in Barbary, hard labour on public works under an overseer's whip could be lethal in a climate for which most of them were utterly unprepared. When the 350-ton London privateering ship *Inspector* was driven aground in Tangier Bay by a storm in January 1746, almost half of its 183-man crew were killed instantly. Of the ninety-six men left alive and sent as captives to the sultan of Morocco, twenty-one had turned Muslim by 1751. In most cases, religious conversion will not have been the prime motive. These men were put to work for long, hot day after long, hot day, repairing fortifications outside the great medieval city of Fès.[43] Changing faiths in the hope this would lead to better treatment must have struck some of them as their only means of self-preservation.

Captivity in Barbary, then, was not a single fate, and neither was enslavement. All men and women seized by North African corsairs, or wrecked on their shores, underwent a measure of terror; and some went on to experience physical and mental suffering, forced labour under the whip, permanent loss of contact with their country of origin, and premature death. But Barbary captivity might be a very different experience from this. It might involve only a brief stay, being reasonably well cared for, followed by a speedy return once a ransom was paid. And even captives confined to North Africa for several years might learn new languages and attitudes, or adjust to Muslim households where they were treated less as slaves than as family members, or convert to Islam out of conviction or in order to marry a cherished Muslim woman, or enter well-paid employment as mercenaries, medical experts, architectural advisers, or armourers.

The diversity of captive experiences is a warning against any simple, monochrome judgement on the quality and significance of this Barbary threat. Suggestions made at the time, and occasionally since, that Barbary corsair assaults and the enslavement of whites that sometimes ensued were comparable to the transatlantic trade in black slaves are, for instance, unsustainable. By 1670 – though probably not before – the number of blacks being shipped out to slavery annually from West Africa by British and other white traders was indisputably in excess of the total number of Europeans seized every year by Barbary and Ottoman corsairs. Moreover, white corsair victims were increasingly allowed a hope of redemption and return, as black slaves shipped across the Atlantic in this period never were. But while it is wrong to draw comparisons between the North African system of seizing and exploiting human beings and the triangular trade in black slaves, it is no less inappropriate to marginalise Barbary depradations and the slave-systems they serviced, or to suggest – as some have done – that Barbary captivities were simply invented or exaggerated by Europeans as a means of vilifying Islam.[44] Barbary corsairs were highly effective predators who succeeded over the centuries in extorting very large amounts of ransom and protection money from virtually all Western European governments. Even a relatively distant and secure state like Denmark devoted about 15 per cent of its profits from Mediterranean trade to paying them off.[45] Such sums would simply not have been forthcoming had the Barbary threat not been judged to be substantial, or had fears of Barbary slavery simply been manufactured.

For early modern Britons, the fear of Barbary was very real. So visceral were these terrors, indeed, that they long outlasted the corsairs' capacity to do serious harm. This inflected the British vision of slavery in ways that have scarcely been acknowledged. It is often suggested that, after 1600, slavery became 'geographically and racially marginalised', a fate that whites in Europe were able to inflict on people of a different skin colour in regions of the world safely distant from their own. A concept 'of *us* – white, English, free', writes Orlando Patterson, grew up alongside a conception of '*them* – black, heathen, slave'.[46] Yet this neat, binary formulation of white, Western slave-traders on the one hand, and black slave victims on the other, gives insufficient attention to Ottoman and North African slave and forced labour systems. For seventeenth- and early eighteenth-century Britons, slavery was never something securely and invariably external to themselves. They knew, all too well, that this fate sometimes befell people like them. Britons *could* be slaves – and were. Moreover, before 1730, men and women in Britain and Ireland were exposed to far more information about white Barbary slavery than about any other variety of slavery. This was partly because so many Barbary captives hailed from London, the centre of Britain's print culture, as well as of its shipping and its trade. So what happened to these people received – as we shall see – extensive newspaper, pamphlet, and ballad coverage, as well as prompting church sermons and appeals for ransom money on a nationwide basis. In the seventeenth and early eighteenth centuries, far more Britons must have met, seen and heard about fellow white countrymen who had undergone, or were still experiencing Barbary slavery, than were in a position to encounter personally the relatively few black slaves resident in their islands at that time.[47] Barbary slavery was able to become a nationwide concern at this point to an extent that was not true of black slavery until much later in the eighteenth century.

Let me be clear what I am arguing here. I am not suggesting that Barbary captivity and slaveries were comparable to black slavery in the

Caribbean and North America. Clearly, they were not. The point is rather that slavery at this early stage was not viewed in Britain as racially restricted. Before 1730, at least, the face of slavery – as far as Britons and other Europeans were concerned – was sometimes white. Public and private language bear this out. References to English, Scottish, Welsh and Irish men and women being enslaved in North Africa were common propaganda currency. 'A great number of our good subjects peaceably following their employment at sea', stated a royal proclamation in the 1690s, were now '. . . slaves in cruel and inhumane bondage . . . driven about by black-a-moors, who are set over them as task-masters' – a reference to Morocco's black slave soldiers who sometimes served as overseers to white captives. Similar vocabulary crops up in official documents not intended to serve a polemical purpose. In 1729, an envoy dispatched to Morocco to ransom British subjects there described his mission in a private memorandum as 'to demand His Majesty's subjects unjustly taken and detained in slavery'.[48] The existence of white slavery involving Britons was taken for granted.

For some, this must only have made acquiescence in black slave-trading easier. The business of slavery – like the business of making empires – was undoubtedly facilitated in the early modern era by widespread recognition that such practices were ubiquitous and had always existed in some form. But awareness that slavery could be racially promiscuous sometimes had very different consequences. It encouraged some writers to question the very connection between slavery and presumed inferiority. If 'some one of this island [Britain] . . . should chance to be snapt by an Algerine, or corsair of Barbary, and there to be set on shore and sold, doth he thereupon become a brute?' enquired an Oxford academic in 1680: 'If not, why should an African?' Like many other anti-slavery arguments, this one faded out for much of the eighteenth century, but resurfaced at its end. 'A negro, although in a state of bondage in his own country, is as feelingly affected at being sold into European slavery', argued a writer in 1806, 'as an Englishman would be at becoming a slave to the Moors or Algerines.'[49]

In the intervening era, it became less common, and less acceptable for British writers to refer in print to the possibility of their own kind being rendered subject in anything approaching the fashion of black slaves. And after the 1730s, slavery became rhetorically established as a polar opposite to Britishness to such a degree that men and women still falling victim to Barbary captivity found it very hard to make sense of their predicament. 'A poor slave, as I am at present in the hands of barbarians', wrote a semi-literate English sailor in servitude in Algiers in 1789, '. . . which is contrary to the laws of Great Briton to have a true Briton a Barberish slave.'[50] 'Contrary to the laws of Great Britain': the certainty is striking. It was also a comparatively recent growth. Back in the seventeenth century, and earlier in the eighteenth century, things had been very different. At that stage, the scale of Barbary captive-taking, together with the rumours, writings and campaigns surrounding it, had meant that neither British nationality nor white skin colour could be viewed as reliable guarantees against the experience of slavery. Britons at that stage had not securely ruled the waves, still less the world. They could be slaves, and some of them were.

Sea raiders and a sea empire

Individual Britons might be forced to stand, then, half-naked in a public space while strangers methodically assessed their flesh and musculature, waiting under a harsh North African sun until an auctioneer sold them; or forced to labour in fear of a whip wielded perhaps by someone who was not white. For their countrymen at the time, these were the most dramatic and obvious respects in which Barbary had the power to turn their world upside down. And, as we have seen, individual liberty was not the only fetish the corsairs outraged. They preyed on commerce, the god of British idolatry; and they attacked at sea, which the British aspired to dominate. In retrospect, however, there is a more significant respect in which Barbary can be viewed as having turned things upside down. After 1600, the islands of Britain and Ireland changed progressively from being marginal European lands into a highly aggressive and supposedly united state avidly pursuing and for a while possessing prime global power. How, then, was Barbary able to attack British trade and seamen so successfully and so profitably for so long? What did it mean that they could get away with what they did?

One reason for the corsairs' continuing menace, and for Britain's failure (along with other European states) to extirpate them once and for all, was the resilience and reputation of the Ottoman empire. As current Ottomanists are now making clear, this empire was emphatically not in serious decline in the seventeenth century, or even, in some respects, for much of the eighteenth century.[51] To be sure, Ottoman armies were turned back from the gates of Vienna in 1683, their terrible advance into Continental Europe halted forever. But the decisiveness of this defeat was much less apparent to men and women at the time, than it has sometimes been to historians since. The Ottomans remained strong enough to seize all of Morea from Venice in 1715, to make good their annexation of

Western Iran in 1727, and to recover Belgrade from Austria in 1739. Not until the disastrous wars with Russia in the 1760s and '70s did they begin to lose substantial portions of their territory.

The British, like other western Europeans, were certainly more attentive by 1700 to signs of incipient Ottoman decay, and they were also aware that Ottoman control over the three North African regencies, Algiers, Tunisia and Tripoli, was slackening. But although the Ottoman empire was now increasingly condescended to in prose, western European governments remained diffident about challenging it in any more substantial fashion, and early modern Britain never seriously contemplated doing so. Unlike the maritime empires of Spain, France, Portugal, the Dutch, and Britain itself, the Ottoman empire was not dispersed over the globe, and thus dependent on sea-power. It was one vast, alarming bloc, a 'jigsaw of interlocking land masses', as Braudel puts it.[52] Its sheer territorial dimensions, like its huge, ill-disciplined armies, and the size of its population, continued to provoke awe, especially in a small, under-populated country like early modern Britain.

This helps to explain why English (and later British) retaliation against the Barbary powers was often sporadic and consciously limited. Behind the corsairs, and their busy, infuriating, expensive sea-raids, Britain continued to discern the enduring shadow of Ottoman grandeur, and held back much of its fire accordingly. Even in 1816, when the Battle of Waterloo had been won and European and global primacy seemed assured, the British government still resisted hawkish suggestions that it should convert a naval assault on Algiers and its corsairs into a full-blown colonising expedition. 'Are the Christian nations to plant colonies along the [North African] coast', enquired a London journalist sarcastically, fully endorsing this official policy of restraint: 'or is it meant to replace the Turk in full and quiet possession of them?' Evidently he, like the men in Whitehall, regarded such a prospect as wholly unrealistic. Even at this stage, the Ottoman sphere of influence still appeared something to be approached with caution, and left in general judiciously alone.[53]

Moreover, and as the fall of Tangier had demonstrated, the North African powers could be formidable in their own right, and not just because of the Ottoman connection. By the late seventeenth century, their corsairing vessels were no match for British and other Western European warships, but this was less decisive than might be expected. As the Pentagon has been repeatedly reminded in the past and may discover again in the future, even the most high-tech weaponry sometimes fails to achieve success in determinedly low-tech conflicts. Late twentieth-century America possessed sufficient nuclear capability to obliterate Vietnam many times

14. The corsair base of Tripoli.

over, but it could not defeat the Vietcong by conventional warfare, any more than it could invade Baghdad during the first Gulf War at an acceptably low cost to itself. By the same token, after 1650 the Royal Navy was increasingly in a position to destroy whole fleets of Barbary corsair ships, had they been foolish enough to meet it in set-piece sea-battles. But this signified little, as the corsairs rarely operated in this fashion. Like stinging insects, their light, rapid vessels were designed to strike at unarmed or lightly armed merchantmen, while being able to flee very speedily at the mere approach of a warship. Barbary corsairs simply refused to play the Western naval game. They had their own.

As a result, there was not much the Royal Navy could do except sporadically bombard the coastal cities from which the corsairs came. Thus in 1655, Admiral Blake attacked Porto Farina, near Tunis, and destroyed several corsair galleys at anchor there. The effects of such bombardments tended however – as in this case – to be localised and temporary, and the risks involved were high. Before the discovery of longitude in the 1760s, which enabled vessels to establish more precisely where they were in relation to the shore, any ship of the line sailing close to the dangerous North African coastline, especially in poor weather, was at risk of smashing there. Immediately before the British warship HMS *Litchfield* hit the Moroccan shore in 1758, *en route* to Gorée in West Africa, its trained navigators reported confidently that the vessel was still 'thirty-five leagues distant from the land'. This dire miscalculation, a comment on the limits of Western technology at this time, cost the lives of 120 men, as well as supplying the sultan of Morocco with 220 lucrative British captives.[54] Nor was Barbary an easy region for Britain to contemplate attacking on land. Algiers always maintained a sizeable army and this, together with its substantial coastal defences, proved strong enough even in 1775 to repel a Spanish invasion force of 300 ships and 22,000 men.[55] Morocco, too, possessed at intervals a much bigger army than Britain disposed of in time of peace. As a Moroccan official remarked evenly to a British envoy in 1718: 'he knew very well by sea the English would be too hard for them, but by land they did not at all fear 'em.' Why should they, when – at this point in time – Britain's standing army was well under 30,000, while Moulay Ismaïl's forces were estimated by some diplomats to exceed 150,000 men?[56]

This military capacity not only worked to keep the British and other Europeans for a long time at bay, but was also directly and indirectly sustained by them. Morocco and Algiers especially made a point of demanding ransoms for their captives in the form of armaments as well as cash, and for a long time they got what they wanted. In 1700, Britain was obliged to provide 100 gun-locks 'each according to the pattern given by the Emperor [of Morocco]', in return for every single captive it wanted back; while in 1721, a British mission to Morocco to recover over 300 captives handed over 1200 barrels of gunpowder and 13,500 gun-locks.[57] If you visit the Bordj Nord, Morocco's military museum in Fès – and it is a fascinating place, ordered with impressive scholarship – you can still see some of these 'donated' Western weapons today. There are rows of early Georgian muskets on show, each bearing the mark of the Tower of London, as well as displays of French, Spanish, Dutch, Portuguese and Italian guns, mortars, and cannon. Some of these were purchased or captured in battle, but many of the armaments on show were supplied to Moroccan sultans at different times by British and other European governments as payment for captured and enslaved nationals.

Here, then, was a trade in arms between Europe and North Africa that was parasitic on, and positively fostered a trade in people. Barbary corsairs seized British and other European ships' crews and passengers. These captives were then exchanged for money and armaments, which in turn helped the North African powers to equip themselves so as to repel military and naval assaults on their shores, and also to maintain their own corsair fleets. It seems an extraordinary system, yet – like so much else that occurred in this vital Mediterranean zone – this trade in arms possesses a wider significance. It demonstrates a point that we will encounter many times in these pages: namely, that until the end of this period, and so far as land warfare was concerned, there was no invariable gulf between the armaments of Western and non-Western powers. Morocco and Algiers were able to secure (and at times manufacture) sufficiently advanced military equipment to keep British and other European forces at bay until the early nineteenth century, just as they were able to counter superior European naval technology by avoiding fighting in the fashion for which that technology was designed. There is another, equally important point. Looked at closely, this trade in men and arms illustrates how Barbary corsairing facilitated communication and barter between different cultures, while seeming only to precipitate conflict between them.

Because so much imperial history is conceptualised in a manichean fashion so as to emphasise opposition and antagonism – whether it be the rise of racial conflict, or the growing divergence between the West and the rest – it is easy to overlook the parallel stories of deals and compromises constantly going on between European and non-European cultures. Yet, as Braudel always insisted, below the surface of its sharp political and religious divisions, the Mediterranean region was characterised by crossings and collaborations between governments as well as individuals.[58] Muslim corsairs preyed on Christian shipping and treated their captives like commodities: yes. Western European powers dealt in Muslim slaves and sporadically bombarded North African cities: yes, again. But, at another level, at least some of the Christian and Islamic societies involved in this Mediterranean cockpit were interdependent. As we shall see later, in 1756 the Moroccan ruler, Sidi Muhammad, would embark on a furious campaign of captive-taking against the British, not in order to sever relations and provoke war, but so as to pressure them into appointing a consul in his country with whom he could do business.[59] By the same token, fierce British propaganda assaults on the Barbary powers, and sporadic naval violence against them, went hand in hand with a persistent logistical and commercial dependence on them. For without the aid of Barbary, Britain could never have maintained its Mediterranean empire.

Just as Tangier, England's earliest, expensive and abortive Mediterranean colony, has been neglected by historians of empire, so there has been a tendency to gloss over Tangier's more durable successors, Gibraltar and Minorca.[60] These were seized from Spain during the War of Spanish Succession, and confirmed in British possession by the Treaty of Utrecht in 1713. They were deemed vital for the same reasons that Tangier had been. They protected and fostered Britain's commercial interests in the Mediterranean, and they provided bases from which this small, expanding but always nervous power could monitor the fleets of its bigger rivals,

France and Spain. Minorca's Port Mahon, which remains a stunning site to visit, is the second largest natural harbour in the world, and France, Spain and Britain fought each other for it repeatedly until the early nineteenth century.

Yet the importance of these places is often passed over now because they fit uneasily into conventional notions of what British empire was about. Far from being commercially profitable, Gibraltar and Minorca – as Adam Smith complained in *The Wealth of Nations* – soaked up British taxpayers' money at a relentless rate. These minute territories offered no raw materials of value, and no land for hungry settlers. They were also white, European colonies, snatched from a Roman Catholic power. For ordinary Britons, this indeed was why they mattered so much. 'Long live the King and let Gibraltar and Minorca stay English for ever,' roared out the crowd as George II processed through London to open Parliament in 1729.[61] Not a word appears to have been said on this occasion about the importance of the American colonies.

Gibraltar and Minorca were also treated with deep seriousness by those in charge of the British state. It was the short-lived French conquest of Minorca in 1756 – in which two hundred ships as well as the future marquis de Sade were involved – which marked for the British the real commencement of the Seven Years War. Admiral Byng, who was made a scapegoat for the island's loss, would be tried and shot to encourage other British naval commanders never to forget the Mediterranean's absolute centrality to British imperial pretensions, sea-power and trade.[62] Gibraltar and Minorca were viewed as equally vital in Britain's subsequent global contest, its lost war with America; and the former even more so when Minorca was lost to Spain. In 1781, the British effectively gave up Yorktown to its besiegers by dispatching a crucial segment of their fleet from its American station to Gibraltar which was also grievously besieged at this time by the French and the Spanish.[63] This decision makes no sense if we adopt present-day perspectives on the absolute centrality of America. It makes perfect sense if we remember how vital the British viewed the Mediterranean in strategic, imperial and commercial terms.

These same imperatives made it indispensable for the British to maintain some kind of constructive engagement with Barbary. Before 1750, more British troops were stationed in Gibraltar and Minorca than in the whole of North America; while British naval vessels regularly docked and reprovisioned here both before and after that date.[64] Without regular supplies from the North African powers – grain, cattle, fish, fresh fruit, and mules for transport – it would have been impossible to feed these British garrisons in Gibraltar and Minorca, or to run these places as provisioning and repair centres for the Royal Navy. As a British official conceded wearily in 1758, as he contemplated paying out yet more substantial ransoms to redeem captives from Morocco:

> It has been found convenient, for the protection and advancement of our navigation and commerce in general, as well as for supplying His Majesty's garrison of Gibraltar, and his fleets when in the Mediterranean, with fresh provisions, to be at peace with these people.[65]

Here, then, was a Protestant empire, Britain, needing to rely on supplies from Islamic societies – in this case the Barbary powers – in order to control territories seized from and inhabited by Catholic Europeans. It is a powerful reminder that, at this time – as since – the polarity between Western states and Islam was often more pronounced on paper and in polemic than it was in terms of substantial politics. It is also a reminder that, for the British, the business of making and maintaining empire always involved dependence on non-whites and non-Christians, and not merely the experience of ruling them.

Thus Barbary which – like the Mediterranean itself – is often left out of the story of early modern British empire, urgently needs incorporating within it, not least because it alerts us to so many paradoxes and limitations to do with power. The protracted assaults of Barbary corsairs, always expensive and sometimes deadly, illustrate how the downside of fast-growing British maritime trade was sometimes increased vulnerability to attack. The difficulties that the Royal Navy experienced in eradicating the corsairs and in bombarding their North African bases indicate some of the restrictions on Western naval power and technology at this time. Then, as now, the possession of advanced firepower did not automatically confer success against opponents who played and fought by different rules, and who were in this case ingenious and resolute as well in maintaining their own military hardware. Barbary captivities, so often treated as the stuff of picturesque, marginal detail, seemed profoundly menacing to seven-teenth- and early eighteenth-century Britons, in part because they suggested that whites as well as blacks might be enslaved. The British state often tolerated these attacks on its trade and its personnel, preferring in the main to pay substantial ransoms rather than declare all-out war, because it continued to be wary of the Ottomans, but also because it had little choice.

For even as they contended with the Barbary powers, the British came increasingly to need them. Britain's relations with these North African societies illustrate some of the contrivances to which a small country was compelled in order to construct a large empire. Charles II's England had not been strong enough to establish a Mediterranean colony at the expense of Muslim North Africa. Tangier had failed, despite all the money, blood and engineering efforts poured into it; and the British would have to wait almost 200 years before establishing another settlement in North Africa itself. None the less, building up a Mediterranean empire did become possible for the British after 1700, but only at the expense of Roman Catholic Europeans, and with North African and Muslim aid. Emphatically not for the last time, its own limited resources required Britain to be dependent on non-European assistance in order to play the imperial game. Like other zones of captivity, then, Barbary challenges, modifies and problematises the story of Britain's empire.

But what of the captives themselves and the tales they told?

THREE

Telling the Tale

Going public

The sea was so vast. The vessels they sailed in were small. Yet still the corsairs tracked them down, by magic and conjuring some sailors believed. It would begin with one or two ships, rarely more, appearing on the horizon. If they flaunted the sign of the Crescent, men straining to identify them knew these were Ottoman vessels, and so possibly from Algiers or Tunisia or Tripoli. Once in range and their identity was clear, the sight of their cannon and heavily armed crews was enough to make most unescorted, civilian ships surrender immediately. But sometimes there was gunfire, splintering timber and killing; and there might also be trickery. In the aftermath of England's treaty with Algiers in 1682, some Moroccan corsairs made a practice of sailing under Algerian colours. They would wait for the approach of a trusting victim, dispatch a boarding party ostensibly to check its sea pass (as the treaty allowed Algiers captains to do), and then suddenly roll out their cannon, overpower the English crew, and fling their futile pass overboard.[1]

This was when terror might be least controllable, the transitional moment when an individual's mundane freedoms and pursuits were overtaken by something utterly different but still largely unknown. Forced below deck on the *John of London* with dozens of other captives in June 1670, his voyage from Lisbon aborted by Moroccan corsairs, a future Anglican clergyman called Adam Elliot found it at first impossible to comprehend what was happening to him. Only when the corsairs adopted a lengthy and circuitous route back to Salé so as to avoid European warships and take more prizes, was Elliot able at last to impose some order on his thoughts: 'There it was that I began to reflect upon my condition, for before the change was so sudden, and the strange uncouth accidents so surprising I had scarce leisure to consider.'[2] Whether seized at sea, as this man was, or on land in other zones of commercial and imperial enterprise, this was usually how individuals began the process of converting their ordeal into a story, desperately trying to make sense of the act of capture itself. If

73

15. *Seapiece: a fight with Barbary corsairs*, by Lorenzo A Castro.

they survived, this initial, unspoken narrative would be supplemented and reshaped many times over. Reshaped, in order to take account of whatever confinement, mistreatment, new employments and encounters followed, as well as all the other shocks and adjustments involved in being forced into a subordinate and vulnerable position in another country and continent.

Captives who managed to return to Britain might communicate these interior narratives of trauma, endurance, and discovery privately to family, lovers, friends or neighbours, almost always censoring in some respects as they went along. Or they might be ordered to tell something of their story more widely by authority figures of some kind: employers, law officers, courts martial, churchmen or politicians. Sometimes, however, they themselves chose to go public about what had happened to them by means of pen and print. Or others did this for them, using their experiences as the stuff of sermons, political speeches, novels, ballads, drawings, travel accounts and other books.

The matter of Barbary, in other words, was never something just external to Britain, or the business only of politicians, diplomats, the Royal Navy, and those traders, seamen and passengers directly involved. Like other captivities in other parts of the world, like empire itself, Barbary corsairing and its victims impacted richly and diversely on British culture at home, in this case influencing images and fears of Islam, and supplying men and women with information on North Africa and the Mediterranean region more broadly. Before examining the imperial impact of all this, it is important to look in more detail at the modes of communication in Britain itself. The captive's tale took many forms and was the work of many voices. Let us begin with the most powerful.

Church and state

One very basic way in which ordinary Britons learnt about Barbary and its captives was through their pockets. In the 1670s, the political economist, Sir William Petty, calculated that it cost at least £60 to redeem each and every detained prisoner in North Africa, and while this was probably an exaggeration, captives were certainly too numerous at the time Petty was writing for the state to be willing or able to ransom them all out of ordinary revenue. Consequently, and until the 1720s, it was the churches that assumed prime responsibility for raising the necessary ransom money. Every Protestant denomination was involved – Quakers, Presbyterians, Huguenots, non-conformists of all kinds – but it was the

Church of England that did most to mobilise and synchronise fund-raising.[3] Anglicans throughout England and Wales had organised collections for mariners captured by 'the Turks' as early as 1579; and there were other major collections in 1624 and 1647. But Church involvement became more important after 1660, when political and public pressure to redeem captives increased. During the next half-century, a committee appointed by the Privy Council, on which a member of the royal family and the current Archbishop of Canterbury and the Bishop of London always served, presided over five nationwide campaigns to raise ransoms to bring home English, Welsh, Scottish and Irish captives of Barbary.

These campaigns were influential in shaping attitudes and enormously successful in raising money. The collection initiated in 1670 'towards the relief of captives taken by the Turks and Moors of Barbary' secured over £21,500 – several million pounds in present-day values – some of this coming as big donations from wealthy individuals, but most from public collections organised at parish and diocesan level. Predictably, it was the regions most heavily involved in Mediterranean trade and consequently vulnerable to corsairing that gave most: the diocese of Exeter, home to the great West Country ports; the diocese of Norfolk, because of the big merchant communities at Norwich, Yarmouth and King's Lynn; and above all London, hub of trade, hub of government. But every region participated in this emergency effort to some degree, even tiny, impoverished St Asaph in Wales, which managed to contribute £113. The collection begun in 1692 achieved less impressive results, perhaps because heavy wartime taxation at this time eroded the capacity and will to give. Just over £8000 trickled in for the captives over a space of five years. Another nationwide collection, initiated in 1700, did capture the public's imagination, despite the coming of the War of Spanish Succession. By 1705, £16,500 had been donated, some of which went the following year on ransoming 190 men from Morocco.[4]

For the captives and those who loved them, this was what mattered most. Public generosity, mobilised by the churches, set individuals free and brought them home – if they managed to survive long enough. But these campaigns were never just about money. Because of how they were organised, virtually every man, woman and child in Britain and Ireland, within reach of some kind of church, was exposed to arguments, assertions and rudimentary information about Muslim North Africa, the Ottoman empire more generally, and commercial and naval activity in the Mediterranean. Not since the crusades, had the power and content of Islam been ventilated in these islands at such a broad and popular level.

The device used for these early disaster appeals was the Charity Brief, a royal warrant authorising collections for a specified charitable object in every place of worship, and frequently by way of house to house visits as well. It was signalled by the King's Printer issuing a special form, about 12,000 copies for each appeal. This set out in highly coloured language why North African captives were such particular objects of Christian and national concern. Bishops, parsons and ministers would then appeal for donations at successive church services, often preceding this with a special sermon. Church wardens and curates would then visit every household within reach, as the 1692 Brief put it: 'to ask and receive from all the parishioners, as well masters and mistresses . . . lodgers, sojourners, or others in their families, their Christian and charitable contributions, and to take the names of all those which shall contribute thereunto'. As the last requirement makes clear, this was closer to being an additional tax than a strictly voluntary donation. Those individuals who remained unnamed were expected and encouraged to feel shamed. Even live-in servants, who generally paid no taxes, were urged on this occasion to give alongside their employers.[5]

Nor was this all. Charity Briefs were authorised not just for collections on behalf of large numbers of people, but also for private initiatives. The five big campaigns to help Barbary captives between 1660 and the early 1700s were thus only the most dramatic demands for mass action on this issue. In addition, there were hundreds of individual appeals, many of them instigated by captives' womenfolk. In 1676, a Brief was issued to help one Joan Bampfield raise a ransom for her son Edward, a captive in Morocco. Four years later, men and women throughout the land were urged in church to help Mary Butland get her husband Ambrose back from Algiers. Every year then, and often several times a year, church-goers would be reminded of how their countrymen were suffering under the yoke of Islam, and exposed to captivity and slavery. In Tavistock, Devon, congregations dipped into their pockets for North African captives on over thirty different occasions between 1660 and 1680.[6] The breadth of the response was sometimes staggering. In 1680, 730 of Tavistock's citizens – a substantial part of the town's adult population – clubbed together to raise over £16 for the captives. As this suggests, most could not give very much, but almost everybody gave something, from Lady Mary Howard who topped the list of donors with ten shillings, down to poor Elizabeth Harris who could only afford a single penny.[7]

Charity Briefs were used to raise funds for all kinds of emergency: flood victims, for instance, or survivors of an outbreak of plague, or a town devastated by fire. But collections on behalf of North African captives seem to have elicited higher levels of generosity and more varied donors than others, and not just because of the element of persuasion and emotional blackmail involved. The enslavement of their own kind – and most of these campaigns made no bones about the fact that Britons were being enslaved – struck men and women right across the social spectrum as peculiarly terrible; just as, when the trade in black slaves came finally and far too belatedly to be perceived as a rectifiable evil, the response in Britain also conspicuously spanned both sexes and all social classes.[8] Fire, plague and flood were acts of God: but captivity and slavery were the acts of men. And since victims of Barbary were held in bondage under the Crescent, their hopes of salvation were seen as being at risk as well as their mortal bodies. 'Above all', thundered the Charity Brief of 1680, the faithful should call to mind 'that accursed tyranny used towards the souls of these miserable wretches . . . who are daily assaulted by these professed enemies of Christ.'[9] Again, there are similarities here with the British abolitionist movement at the end of the eighteenth century. For the latter, too, one of the strongest weapons in its propaganda armoury would be the argument that black slaves were perishing without any opportunity of being introduced to Christianity. As with white Barbary slaves, immortal souls, and not just chained and suffering bodies, were at stake.

Yet some of the multitudes who gave money to free Barbary captives (like many later abolitionists) were moved, more than anything else, by the helplessness and ordinariness of most of the victims involved. Labouring men standing awkwardly at the back of an English, or Welsh, or Irish, or Scottish church, at the easy mercy of landowners or magistrates, could identify all too well with individuals, poor like themselves, who had been suddenly snatched from their work at sea and enslaved. Women, under pressure, coping alone, or grieving for dead children, had little difficulty imagining what it must be like to lose a husband or a son to Barbary, to hope that he was still alive somewhere, but never to be able to communicate with him, or know for certain if he would return. There was a sense in which Barbary captives embodied in a particularly dramatic form the vulnerability of the labouring poor in general. In this respect, as in so many others, the culture of captivity served to interweave the foreign and the domestic, the general and the deeply personal.

More than any other cause at this time, then, Barbary captives were a people's charity. The captives' plight was publicised and addressed by the institution that still possessed, at this stage, unquestionably the strongest pull on mass loyalties and attention, and an unrivalled nationwide organisation, namely the Church. But the issue of how these captivities were to be presented to the public and interpreted was also the business of the secular authorities. Returning captives were greeted with elaborate, public rituals that involved the monarch, politicians, and local dynasts as well as churchmen, and were designed to transform these forlorn representatives of national humiliation into emblems of triumph, self-congratulation and patriotic self-assertion. The men would journey under escort from their port of arrival to the city of London and then, on an appointed day, process through crowded streets to a special service of thanksgiving held at St Paul's cathedral. These ceremonies were carefully choreographed. In the redemption processions held in December 1721 and again in November 1734, the former captives were instructed to wear their 'Moorish' or 'slavish habits', the clothes they still had left from their time in North Africa.[10] This made them more intriguing and pitiable objects to the 'vast multitudes of people that crowded to see them', and so helped attract generous donations on their behalf. But the strangeness of the captives' costume on these occasions also served as a visual reminder of their previous subjection to an alien power and religion, just as its ragged condition could be read as a denunciation of both these things. Now, though, the captives were redeemed. A Christian service, in a Christian church, in the Christian capital of a godly nation would reclaim them as Protestant Britons, and the vestiges of Islamic influence would, surely, be cast off like the ugly rags clinging to their backs.

If these points were not already clear, the sermon at St Paul's cathedral (which was always printed) was explicitly designed to make them so. 'The happy occasion of our present meeting', thundered William Berrington before hundreds of redeemed captives and the rest of his congregation in 1721, was 'to congratulate you . . . upon your return from slavery under the yoke of infidels, to enjoy the liberty of your native country'. 'You are restored to the enjoyment of English air, and English liberty,' he told them, 'free from the despotick rule of your imperious lords.'[11] But not free of obligations. For the aim was at once to reincorporate the captives into the polity and remind them of their duty to it. William Sherlock spelt out the contract succinctly in a Thanksgiving Service in 1702:

> 'Tis not only the charity of private Christians, but the care the government hath taken of you, to which you owe your liberty. And therefore pray consider what it is you owe your country . . . to be loyal to your prince, obedient to government, ready to defend it against all enemies . . . They redeemed you, that you might serve them, not as slaves, but as free-born subjects.

Here, indisputably, was Islam conjured up as usefully defining Other. North African and Ottoman slavery, aggression, and tyranny were invoked so as to throw into even clearer contrast the liberty, benevolence and true religion characterising Britain itself (though not yet, as we shall see, to advocate its global expansion). Free again, yet also subjects again, the captives would rise to their feet in the chill, cavernous cathedral and, clutching their rags to their sunburnt bodies, make ready for the final stage of the ceremony, yet another procession, this time to salute the king of England for his efforts on their behalf. 'His Majesty viewed them from the palace windows', reported a London newspaper on a procession of ransomed captives in 1734, 'and was graciously pleased to order 100 guineas to be distributed amongst them.'[12]

Officially, then, the embarrassment of having large numbers of civilian subjects repeatedly seized by corsairs and held captive in North Africa, and of having to pay substantial ransoms to secure their release, was contained, reinterpreted and put to political use by way of the religious and secular wings of the British state. Yet although these church-run campaigns and public redemption ceremonies were important and carefully orchestrated, they were less spectacular and protracted than comparable events in Continental Europe. This was partly a function of numbers. At no time, except perhaps in the early decades of the seventeenth century, did Britain lose as many captives to North Africa as France, the Italian states, or above all Spain. A more significant difference, however, was the absence in Britain of the Mercedarian and Trinitarian Fathers who played a vital ceremonial and literary role in every Catholic state affected by Muslim privateering.

Their rituals would begin in North Africa itself. Groups of Catholic Fathers from France, or Spain, or Portugal, or Naples, would journey to Tunis, or Meknès, or Algiers, to hand over ransom money collected from the faithful back home. They would arrive in Barbary carrying royal and papal banners, and with the colours of the Trinity much in evidence: white for the Father, blue for the Son, red for the Holy Ghost. They would then assemble their respective countries' captives, dress them in the fresh white robes they had brought with them in order to proclaim their innocence and Christianity, and finally escort them back across the sea to their place of origin. The Fathers would also cut a deal with the captives themselves. Roman Catholics ransomed from Barbary in this fashion were contractually bound to participate in special rituals once they returned home. These might last for a year or longer. In France, for instance, there was not just one elaborate procession and one major church service celebrating the captives' return, as in Britain, but a succession of them. The first took place in the port of re-entry, usually Marseilles. The procession of redeemed captives then followed a traditional route that had evolved over the centuries: Toulon, Avignon, Lyons, and so on to the sacred heart of France, Paris itself. At each and every stopping-off place, there were ceremonies in which local elites participated and ordinary folk watched. Bells rang. Soldiers assembled. Strewn flowers were crushed into scent under milling crowds. Small children struggled protestingly into fancy dress as cherubs and saints. And at the heart of it all were the white-robed captives and their Father-minders, the latter itching to write up and publish accounts of their real and reputed sufferings.[13]

In Britain, it was very different. In this strictly Protestant culture there was simply no provision for year-long spectacles of this kind, occurring both in the capital and the provinces. 'We have no Trinitarian Fathers of Redemption', declared a pamphleteer in 1736, 'to roam up and down, and beg money for the relief of our captive brethren . . . nor any who make it their business to parade with them, when redeemed and brought home, in pompous, solemn, and expensive processions.'[14] As this somewhat perverse piece of Protestant boasting implied, returning British captives of Islam were left far more to their own devices, and not just because of the lack of Redemptionist orders. Relations between the British state and the Barbary powers were, it bears repeating, ambivalent. On the one hand, the former naturally resented Barbary corsair assaults on its reputation, trade and personnel, just as its churches were always anxious in case enforced exposure to Islam polluted Protestant, British subjects. On the other, North Africa and the Ottoman world in general were valued outlets for trade, and the former was an ever more indispensable auxiliary in Britain's Mediterranean empire. Partly for these reasons, governmental orchestration of anti-Barbary sentiment and attentiveness to the captives were on a moderate scale, particularly after the acquisition of Minorca and Gibraltar. The captivity issue could never be allowed to embarrass the entente between Britain, Barbary, and the Ottoman empire.

Official restraint, combined with the lack of busy Redemptionist Fathers, influenced indirectly how the captive's tale was told in Britain. In Catholic cultures, state and the church were more proactive in compiling and disseminating accounts of Barbary captives. In Britain, intervention from above – though present – was less pronounced, while commercial press networks were precociously advanced. In this culture, it was easier to tell the tale through a rich variety of unofficial media. Here, captives were more likely to find, however imperfectly, a voice of their own.

Vincent Jukes was the eldest son of an innkeeper and in the view of most of his neighbours in Myddle, Shropshire, no good. A restless, nimble spirit, he first tested the bounds of rural society by trying his hand at petty burglary, and soon found it expedient to go to sea. This turned out to be a passage to another kind of confinement. In 1636 he and thirty-three other crew members were captured off the coast of Tangier, yet more victims of Algerian corsairs. Except that Jukes was nobody's victim. Sold as a slave in Algiers, he converted to Islam, submitted to circumcision, and adopted local dress, actions that did not automatically make him free, but did confer greater mobility and choice of occupation. He resumed his life as a sailor, working on a corsair ship along with three other renegade Christians and ten Algerians. On one trip, for whatever reason, the four renegades changed sides yet again. According to their own account, they killed some of their Muslim fellow crewmen and managed to lock the rest below deck. One-time captives turned captors, Jukes and his partners sailed to Spain where they sold their stolen vessel – and the surviving Algerians. Richer by £150, Jukes returned to England in 1638, purchased new clothes and a good horse and set off back to Myddle, aching to see its burghers' customary disapproval give way to sour envy at his good fortune. But as he rode through one small market town after another, Jukes experienced himself a kind of theft. He discovered that his Barbary exploits, which he had gossiped about so freely in London's taverns, had already been converted into a ballad which was being sung and distributed in print even as he passed. What Jukes had projected as *his* story was being shaped and disseminated by others over whom he had no control.[15]

The tale of Vincent Jukes went on to inspire a sermon by a London divine and several pirated versions, and was finally written down towards the end of the seventeenth century by Richard Gough, the chronicler of Myddle, whose family had known the man and plainly disliked him. Perhaps because of this, Gough's version is full of holes. He never enquires how Jukes reacted to his brief stay in an Islamic society, or whether motives other than self-interest prompted him to convert, or why exactly such an essentially rootless man should have wanted to return to England. No sooner had Jukes settled back in Myddle, sniffs Gough, than he 'went . . . to sea again, and was heard of no more'. But Gough's account does convey how easily official interpretations of North African (and other) captivities were supplemented and even subverted in Britain by very different versions spread verbally or by print. Those listening to the ballads and sermons spawned by Jukes' adventures, or watching him return, well-mounted and in spanking new clothes, may have felt thrilled to the core by an Englishman's success against superior Barbary numbers and by his bloody-minded determination to return. They may equally well have been struck by the fact that Jukes' stay in an Islamic society and swift abandonment of Christianity when it suited him had apparently done him no harm, and ultimately made him rich.

The ballad of Vincent Jukes is now lost, but scores of other English, Welsh, Scottish and Irish ballads survive celebrating the experiences of Barbary captives. The most famous, the so-called 'Lord Bateman' ballad, appeared in at least 112 different versions between the seventeenth and nineteenth centuries. Here, again, capture by North African corsairs is described not as a source of unalloyed suffering, but as an unlikely and unexpected means of self-betterment, in this case sexual as well as pecuniary. A young man from the North Country goes to sea, is captured by 'Turkish pirates' and flung into prison. There he is visited by the governor's beautiful daughter:

> When she came to the prison strong,
> She boldly ventur'd in,
> How do you like, oh! then she said,
> How do you like to be confin'd . . .

She helps him to escape and, in certain versions of the story, follows him to England, where he abandons his local, Christian fiancée for this 'Turkish' bride, who brings with her a jewelled belt worth more than all the wealth of Northumberland.[16]

At one level these persistently popular verses give a North African twist to the Western world's recurrent Pocahontas fantasy: a European male in peril is rescued by an influential non-European female who promptly falls in love with him and comes over to his society. Yet to read the 'Lord Bateman' ballad only in this fashion is to miss important complexities. In these verses, it is the white man who is initially vulnerable, and the 'Turkish' female who possesses superior power, initiative and wealth. She employs these for the Englishman's benefit, to be sure, but she does not die or get cast aside in the process. Instead, the white man crosses boundaries too, ultimately abandoning a woman of his own kind for her sake. As with the story of that seventeenth-century Shropshire lad, Vincent Jukes, we are a considerable distance in these verses from the public statements on North African corsairing so carefully formulated and advanced by Britain's secular and religious authorities. As evoked in the multiple variations of 'Lord Bateman', captivity in an Islamic power is not a fate worse than death, nor a confrontation with an uncompromising and monolithic Other.

Instead, individual Christians and Muslims break ranks, compromise allegiances, and collaborate for mutual benefit.

Yet while ballads like 'Lord Bateman' obviously differed sharply in tone and emphasis from Church of England sermons, or royal proclamations on Barbary, these media were alike in distorting what being a captive there entailed. Balladeers transmuted the bitterness and hardship of captivity into romance and adventure, while government and clerical propagandists glossed over the complex diplomatic, imperial and commercial ties actually existing between Britain and the North African powers, taking refuge instead in stock and traditional contrasts between the Crescent and the Cross. Rarely did those advancing these equally selective interpretations of Barbary captivity have any personal experience of what it meant, or any first-hand knowledge of North Africa itself. So how could someone like Vincent Jukes retrieve his experiences from the various official and commercial agencies wanting to appropriate and exploit them? How could captives seize control of, and tell their own tales?

Doing so might seem essential. Translating any experience of trauma into one's own words is cathartic. It gives victims back a measure of control. They can tell their side of the story, put themselves at the centre of the plot, and make clear that they still matter.[17] Individuals seized by Barbary, like captives in other regions, seem often to have felt this way, and been eager to tell their version of events, even if only in a brief, unconventional fashion. Forced to build houses in Mustafa Superieur, a suburb of the city of Algiers, an English slave called John Robson wrote his story in the only way available to him. He pressed into the still damp plaster his own name, together with the date: 3 January 1692.[18] This was an act signifying something very different from a builder's usual proud marking of his handiwork. As a slave, Robson would have been renamed by his Muslim owner, stripped of the most obvious emblem of his identity. So impressing on the very stone of Algiers his surname and his *Christian* name, together with the Christian rather than the Islamic date, was an act of defiance and a declaration that what had happened to him had not obliterated what he still considered himself to be.

Captives who returned to Britain might also write their story or cause it to be written in stone. Until destroyed by World War II bombing, a monument in Greenwich, London, read as follows:

> Here lyeth interred ye body of Edward Harris . . . mariner.
> . . . Was 18 years a slave in Barbary,
> And steadfastly kept to ye Church of England,
> . . . died in ye faith of ye said Church, 1797.[19]

One detects in these lines a note of anxiety as well as a testament. Individuals held in an alien society as long as Edward Harris was, might feel on their return home under pressure to tell their version of events. Not just as a form of therapy, but as a means of reassuring friends, relations and neighbours that they were still the same people as before, with the same loyalties, even though this was rarely true in fact. Some one-time Barbary captives were even compelled to tell their story. Since many were labouring men, and returned from North Africa to no money or job, and in some cases to find their families dead or dispersed, descending into vagrancy was a common enough fate. In which case, they might end up telling their tale to a clergyman to obtain charity, or explaining their Barbary past to a bench of sceptical magistrates. Poor John Kay, for instance, experienced virtually his entire adult life as a succession of captivities. He was first bound as an apprentice to a Northumbrian industrialist and landowner, then was swept into the British army. Briefly freed by an outbreak of peace, he went to sea working for a Venetian trader and was promptly captured by Algerian corsairs. This led to three and a half years of slavery in North Africa. In 1724, Kay finally returned to the north of England, only to be snatched up and charged with begging. Justices of the Peace extracted his story from him, putting it into writing as he could not, and making him add his mark at the bottom of the page.[20]

For the illiterate, telling their captivity story through a third party, whether under coercion like John Kay or voluntarily, was the only way to get it recorded. Anyone who takes the trouble to explore seventeenth- and early eighteenth-century local records, especially from maritime counties such as Devon or Cornwall in England, or Fife in Scotland, will find dozens of small narratives like Kay's, tales recounted by one-time Barbary captives but not written down by them.[21] Some of these spoken narratives were probably fakes. It must have been tempting for beggars who were mutilated in some way, and who had perhaps heard ballads or sermons about North African captives, to tell an impressionable church minister or a sympathetic householder that they had lost a leg, or an eye, or teeth, through the cruelties of 'Turkish' pirates. But magistrates were generally cannier. Confronted with impoverished individuals claiming time in Barbary, they wanted names, dates, details of ships and their owners, information about where in North Africa they had been held, even some kind of supporting documentation.

Such assiduity on the part of long-dead officialdom can bequeath extraordinarily valuable insights into the experiences of those normally too poor and unlettered to enter the light of history. This point is neatly made by a captivity tale from the other side. In September 1753, a

Moroccan sailor called Hamet recounted to the Governor of Tetouan his captivity experiences in British America. Sailing southwards from Salé in 1736 with a boatload of corn for what is now Essaouira, he and six comrades were seized by a Portuguese cruiser and taken to Mazagan, one of Portugal's few remaining bases in North Africa. There, he and a friend escaped to a British ship whose captain, a man called Daves, promised to help them. At least this was what the two Moroccans thought he promised, for naturally they neither spoke nor understood English. Daves took them on a sea voyage that lasted months, seemingly always gesturing that they would soon see the shores of England, and return from there to Morocco. But Daves was a part-time slave-trader, and the sea they were crossing was the Atlantic. After landfall in America, Daves sold the two men to an isolated plantation some 150 miles outside Charleston, South Carolina. They worked there fifteen years, grinding corn to feed the plantation's black labour force. Only the accident of their owner's bankruptcy finally freed them. The plantation's seclusion was broken through by the arrival of irate creditors, and by now Hamet and his friend knew enough English to explain who and what they were.[22]

At one level, this is an exceptional story. Muslims as well as Christians living or working in the Mediterranean zone were vulnerable to capture in the early modern era, and to being dragged over the line into varieties of slavery and another society, but the evidence for this is often desperately one-sided. High levels of illiteracy and the lack of a print culture deprived most men and women from North Africa who were captured by western Europeans of any chance of leaving behind durable tales, even if they managed to return home. Yet the picture may turn out to be less bleak than this implies. As North African and Ottoman sources become better known, and as European archives are sieved more imaginatively for non-European material, more stories like Hamet's may emerge, more accounts by illiterate Muslim men and women who lacked print outlets, certainly, but who were sometimes able – like European illiterates – to tell their tales to officials of some kind who did write them down.

And *as a tale*, Hamet's story is more representative than it appears. It demonstrates something that we will see evidence of again and again: the centrality of linguistic capacity to captives' chances of survival. How easily they could be disoriented and entrapped by not understanding the language of their captors (as Hamet and his friend were entrapped by Daves), and conversely how captivity might itself lead to new language skills, and consequently to an enhanced capacity to survive and even prosper. Because they picked up some English during their fifteen years' hard labour on a South Carolina plantation, Hamet and his companion were ultimately able to explain who they were. They could present their case to the colony's governor, James Glen, and convince him to ship them home. Back in Tetouan, the two men could tell their story again, to the local Moroccan governor and to the British envoy, William Petticrew. The latter gave them over £30 in compensation, an enormous sum for two destitute seamen. He did this in part, he wrote, because they 'pretty well understand the English language which corroborates their declaration'.[23]

Petticrew also recompensed the two men in this fashion because of Britain's vital connections with Barbary. Successive treaties between Britain and Morocco after 1721 stipulated that the latter would refrain from capturing and enslaving Britons (an undertaking that occasionally lapsed). In return, Britain undertook not to seize individual Moroccans, and to aid any who were enslaved in Continental Europe and elsewhere and who appealed to its officers for help. Their awareness of these treaty provisions explains why poor Hamet and his friend immediately (and in this case mistakenly) ran to a British vessel for help after evading their Portuguese captors. Normally, though, and for their own reasons, the British did abide by these treaties. Indeed, it is a measure of just how much they wanted to maintain a working relationship with Morocco that first Governor Glen in South Carolina, and then William Petticrew, the British envoy in Tetouan, felt obliged to behave so scrupulously towards two desperately poor seamen, arranging for their passage back from South Carolina to Morocco, and compensating them for their sufferings. Britain at this time was becoming ever more mired in transatlantic slave trading, while Glen presided over, and would have taken for granted, a colonial economy rooted in black slavery. Quite clearly, however, these two particular Africans were recognised at British official level as being strictly off-limits as far as slavery was concerned, and were accordingly helped towards home and freedom.

Another, more broadly applicable point emerges from this selfsame narrative. Telling your own captivity story almost always paid in some way. At the very least, it made you feel better, and it might win you advancement, or help re-establish your credentials as a loyal, put-upon Christian (or Muslim). In addition, those who recounted their captivity experiences often did so with an expectation of receiving money. By telling their story to the right people, Hamet and his friend secured a passage home to Morocco and a substantial cash donation. British captives who succeeded in returning home also frequently obtained charitable hand-outs in return for recounting their hardships. But for the latter, another option was available. They could try to sell their stories in the open market. They could put them into print.

In 1640, an English merchant called Francis Knight wrote that 'none, to my knowledge, hath ever divulged in print, the estate and condition of captives in that place of Algier'. He proceeded to do just this, drawing on the details of his own seven years slavery there, and lending his text cachet by dedicating it to Sir Paul Pindar, a former ambassador to the Ottoman court.[24] Knight was not remotely as pioneering as he thought. Accounts of captivity in Algiers and elsewhere in North Africa, together with narratives of white captivities in the New World, had been circulating in Continental Europe since the sixteenth century. Even in England, the earliest known printed Barbary captivity narrative dates from the 1580s.[25] Yet Knight was correct in sensing that he was offering something distinctive as far as the English print market was concerned. His was a lengthy autobiographical account, which chewed over the multi-facetedness of Barbary captivity, rather than treating it in formulaic terms; and he or his publisher demonstrated a sensitivity to readership, inserting specially drawn illustrations and a preface headed 'To the Reader'.

This kind of complex narrative of captivity, usually printed or at least prepared for publication though not invariably so, flourished in England and later Britain from the 1600s through to the nineteenth century, and continued to appear occasionally after that. As far as Barbary captivity narratives were concerned, it is impossible now to establish exactly how many were produced. Some, particularly very early texts and those that remained unpublished, will not have survived. Others, still in manuscript, almost certainly await discovery; while some printed narratives are anonymous, so it is hard to establish their authenticity. And what, anyway, did authenticity mean in this context?

Readings

Whether in regard to the Mediterranean world, or North America, or India or elsewhere, narratives of the sort written by Francis Knight were at the apex of the culture of captivity in terms of sophistication and auto-biographical appeal, but always modest in point of numbers. Other kinds of printed accounts of captivity – be it newspaper and magazine reports, verses, books and pamphlets by third parties – were far more numerous; while it was still more common for these matters to be described, discussed and analysed orally, in sermons, in testimonies to civil and military courts, in parliamentary speeches, spoken proclamations, sung ballads, and ordinary neighbourhood gossip and private conversation. As far as Barbary is concerned, only fifteen substantial narratives by Britons who were unquestionably captives there, appear to have survived from the seventeenth and eighteenth centuries. These texts reflect quite well, however, some of the broad characteristics of this particular captivity experience.

Two-thirds of them were written by individuals seized before 1720, which is an apt indicator of when the corsairs were at their most dangerous as far as Britain was concerned. Like most Barbary victims, the writers were all under thirty when seized, and they were overwhelmingly male. Only one of these narratives is by a woman, Elizabeth Marsh, the daughter of a ships-carpenter from Portsmouth turned naval dockyard administrator in the Mediterranean, who went on to become a Mrs Crisp.

These accounts also confirm the diversity of Barbary captivities in point of duration, and consequently in quality. A third of the writers were held in North Africa less than a year; another third spent between one and five years there. The rest stayed much longer: one of them, Joseph Pitts, a West Country fisherman, for fifteen years; another, Thomas Pellow, for twenty-three years. Since producing a lengthy narrative usually (though not invariably) demanded a measure of literacy, the proportion of seamen among these authors was lower than among the total number of Britons held in this Mediterranean zone. None the less, six of them, Edward Coxere, Thomas Lurting, Thomas Troughton, James Irving, Thomas Pellow and Joseph Pitts, are known to have worked in the mercantile marine, all but one of them as common seamen. Two others, Adam Elliot and Devereux Spratt were clergymen. Five more, Francis Knight, William Okeley, John Whitehead, Francis Brooks, and Thomas Phelps appear to have been traders and men of business. Only one of the narrators, Lieutenant James Sutherland, was serving with the armed forces when taken. This was emphatically not – as we shall see – because British fighters were averse to becoming writers, even when this involved describing defeat and capture. The scarcity of military and naval testimonies of captivity in North Africa, reflects rather the distinctive imperial politics of the Mediterranean. Britain would find itself with military and naval captives galore as far as North America and India were concerned, because these were zones of conquest, war and occupation. But, between 1600 and 1800 – with the conspicuous exception of the Tangier episode – British soldiers and naval men rarely invaded and operated within North Africa itself. As a result, the overwhelming majority of British captives here were always civilians, more victims than aggressors.

To this extent, then, these fifteen accounts are broadly representative of North African captivity patterns. Their adequacy as descriptions of events and encounters in the non-European world is plainly another matter. 'The teasing gap separating a lived event and its subsequent narration',

1 Hedge Abdacrim, Alcaide or Governor of Tangier. 2 The unhappy British Captives. 3 The City of Mequinez. 4 The Pilot or Director to lead to Slavery. 5 The Guards that Drove the Captives. 6 Heymours like Tents, but made of the Roots of Cain, where the Arbs or Farmers live that supply the Town with Butter, &c. 7 Seede Amera, a Saints House.

16. Thomas Troughton and his fellow captives in Morocco, from a drawing made by one of them.

in Simon Schama's felicitous phrase, was something of which these writers, like other captivity narrators, were painfully aware, and some tried desperately hard to contrive strategies of authentication.[26] As a middle-class woman, terrified that her brief Moroccan captivity had besmirched her reputation, Elizabeth Marsh declined even to raise the possibility of her account being in any way mendacious. She was (or wished to be) a lady: and consequently her veracity was not a matter for dispute even by herself. Instead, she adopted the delicate tactic of subtitling her captivity story 'a narrative of *facts*', which it only partly was. Some male narrators however were willing to tackle the issue head-on. 'Courteous reader,' declared William Okeley in the second edition of his account: 'I do readily agree with thee, that there is no sort of writing more liable to abuse than this of the narrative.' He offered, man of business as he was, to 'pawn his credit, not to wrong the narrative,' but in the end, could only refer those readers who were still sceptical to members of his own family, and ultimately to God: 'This book is Protestant, and hates a lie.'[27]

Some humbler narrators looked to social superiors to bestow legitimacy on their texts. Take Thomas Troughton, a sad, if clearly resilient man who laboured in turn as an apprentice tailor, a plasterer, a common seaman, and then – after five years' captivity in Morocco wore him out – as a failed painter, and died in due course in a Middlesex workhouse. In 1751, he swore to the authenticity of his captivity narrative in front of its printer, and before the Lord Mayor of London himself, Sir Francis Cockayne. He even took twenty-one of his fellow sailors and former comrades in captivity along with him to the Mansion House to 'attest to the accuracy of this account'. Their combined testimonies, which bore the names of the seamen able to write and the marks of those who could not, were inserted as a preface to Troughton's published text (which was still being reprinted in the nineteenth century), in a transparent attempt to reassure and convince readers before they embarked on it.[28]

Yet no matter how they strived, it was impossible for these or any other captivity narrators to prove the truth of all the experiences they laid claim to. The events in question had taken place too far away, amongst people who were unlikely ever to be available as witnesses, and whose perspectives on what had happened would anyway have been very different. Moreover, these accounts were bound to be distorted to some degree, and not just because their writers possessed – as all human beings do – their own preconceptions and prejudices. It was very rare, for instance, for early modern captives of Barbary to have access to pens, paper, or even the time and freedom to write. 'We must needs be very ill qualified to make a history,' remembered one Englishman of his time in Algiers in the 1640s: 'Such a design required leisure, liberty, privacy, retiredness . . . to all which we were perfect strangers.' All this man – William Okeley – could do, was consciously commit to memory a pattern of observations while he was undergoing slavery, which he finally put into print some thirty years later. A few individuals in Okeley's position were able to jot down notes in the margins of a prayer book or a Bible that their captors had allowed them to hold on to, but most narratives from this zone – more so even than from others – were composed from memory, often many years after the event.[29]

Narratives might be further compromised if they were the work of more than just the captives themselves. Since most of those seized by the corsairs were poor and of limited or no education, they often depended on others – friends, patrons, London publishers or whatever – to get into print, and sometimes to aid them with the business of writing itself. 'Till I could prevail with a friend to teach it to speak a little better English, I could not be persuaded to let it walk abroad,' admitted William Okeley of his story: 'the stuff and matter is my own, the trimmings and form is another's.'[30]

In Okeley's case, we can be reasonably sure who these auxiliaries were. A deeply religious man, he was urged to publish his experiences by some Anglican clergymen, and it was probably they who also helped him shape and style his narrative.

As this suggests, it is important to get away from the notion that these and other captivity narratives can usefully be characterised as either truthful or crudely mendacious. We all of us convert life's crowded, untidy experiences into stories in our own minds, re-arranging awkward facts into coherent patterns as we go along, and omitting episodes that seem in retrospect peripheral, discordant, or too embarrassing or painful to bear. Okeley was an intelligent, sensitive man who probably did try conscientiously to relate what he and his advisers saw as the quintessential truth of his six years' captivity. For him and them, however, this involved stressing above all the role of a Protestant God and his Providence. 'When I am tempted to distrust,' wrote Okeley (or his collaborators), 'I may encourage my faith from my own narrative, saying, Remember that God who delivered thee at the sea.' Zeal to testify to God's mercy must have prompted Okeley to cut and paste his memories of North African captivity. As an honest man, he admits indeed that this was what happened:

> I could relate a passage during our captivity in Algiers, that had more of bitterness in it than in all our slavery; and yet they were Christians, not Algerines, Protestants, not Papists, Englishmen, not strangers, that were the cause of it: but I have put a force upon myself, and am resolved not to publish it.[31]

In writing, or letting others write in accordance with this 'force', the desire to bear witness to the omnipotence of a Protestant deity and his merciful interventions in his own Islamic captivity, Okeley pruned and refashioned his experiences, but only so as to bring out what he regarded as their deeper, moral truth.

There is a further respect in which it is inappropriate to look for absolute, unadulterated verisimilitude in these narratives, or read too much into their authors' failure to provide it. As Lennard Davis observes, early modern readers did not expect a published text to be either comprehensively factual or unmitigated fiction to the extent that even in these postmodern times we still tend to do.[32] Authors of travel accounts in particular were well known for muddying the waters. Thus Jonathan Swift's novel *Gulliver's Travels* incorporated maps that were similar in design – right down to their professional-looking scale measurements and ornamental spouting whales – to authentic early eighteenth-century cartography, so his more credulous readers at the time may well have been convinced that Lilliput really was situated just south-west of Sumatra. Conversely, Daniel Defoe's *Tour of the Whole Island of Great Britain* (1724–6) is recognised now as an invaluable source on the social, economic and urban fabric of early Georgian Britain. But the detailed, empirical information it supplies on building practices, market-day customs, the growth of rural industry, and the condition of provincial roads was organised within the framework of a tour on Defoe's part which was a literary invention.[33]

In much the same way, highly factual and invaluable material in Barbary and other captivity narratives is sometimes intercut with fictional or pirated passages. Political, religious, cultural and racial bias is combined with reportage that can be substantially verified; and terrible ignorance is exhibited side by side with rare perceptiveness and serious insights. Like virtually every other source material historians ransack, these are not writings that can be swallowed whole, but they can – and should – be sampled and sieved. For I do not accept the argument that sifting for accuracy in such texts is a fruitless enterprise, or that these and other European writings on encounters with non-Europeans are revealing only about the observers and writers, and never of the observed.[34] No historical source should be automatically discounted on the basis of where its writers come from, or on the grounds of what their presumed ethnic group happens to be. Captivity narratives are fractured, composite sources, but it is inappropriate – indeed it is something of a cop-out – to analyse them textually but not contextually. Too much gets lost along the way.

Consider one of the most remarkable of Barbary narratives, Thomas Pellow's account of his detention in Morocco from 1715 to 1738, first as a captive, then as a renegade and mercenary soldier. Published in London in the early 1740s, its preface describes it as 'truly genuine . . . the real journal of the unhappy sufferer, written by his own hand'. Disproving this bold assertion is a simple enough exercise. Like many publications of the period, *The History of the Long Captivity . . . of Thomas Pellow* contains material pirated from other authors (and it would be pirated in its turn by Thomas Troughton when he came to write his own Barbary story). Pellow's narrative also contains its fair share of embellishments and inventions, particularly with regard to the formidable Moulay Ismaïl, the first sultan he served. Moreover the published text – which is the only version we have – suffered from the attentions of its London editor, whose insertions are pardonable only because they are so jarringly obvious. 'It is much to be regretted', this busy ignoramus interrupts at one point, 'that [Morocco] should go under any other denomination than that of a part of Christendom . . . [but] these digressions are quite out of my way, as well

THE
HISTORY
OF THE
Long Captivity
AND
ADVENTURES
OF
Thomas Pellow,
In SOUTH-BARBARY.

Giving an Account of his being taken by two
Sallee Rovers, and carry'd a Slave to MEQUINEZ,
at Eleven Years of Age : His various *Adventures* in
that Country for the Space of Twenty-three Years :
Escape, and Return Home.

In which is introduced,

A particular Account of the *Manners* and *Customs* of
the MOORS ; the astonishing *Tyranny* and *Cruelty* of their
EMPERORS, and a Relation of all those great *Revolutions*
and *Bloody Wars* which happen'd in the Kingdoms of *Fez*
and *Morocco,* between the Years 1720 and 1736.

Together with a Description of the Cities, Towns, and Pub-
lick Buildings in those Kingdoms ; *Miseries* of the *Christian Slaves* ;
and many other *Curious Particulars.*

Written by HIMSELF.

The Second EDITION.

Printed for R. GOADBY, and sold by W. OWEN, Bookseller,
at *Temple-Bar,* LONDON.

17. Thomas Pellow's narrative.

as a subject far beyond my abilities.'[35] Quite so: because when Pellow's own voice re-emerges, it tells a very different story, and one that would not have been possible without deep and prolonged exposure to Moroccan society.

Magali Morsy's impressive, modern edition of Pellow's tale effectively separates its authorial wheat from its editorial chaff.[36] When Pellow was seized by Moroccan corsairs in 1715, he was just eleven years old, a Cornish schoolboy playing truant and accompanying his uncle on a trading voyage to Genoa. He carefully supplies the dates of his embarkation, capture and arrival in Morocco, and of his belated return to England as an embittered, hardened soldier in his thirties. His account of his time as a renegade, however, employs dates only rarely, and this has sometimes been viewed as proof that Pellow's narrative is little more than a picaresque fiction. Yet to argue thus is to apply Western criteria to the narrative of a man who lived a precarious existence for many years in a non-Western environment. Once Pellow converted to Islam, and joined the ranks of Morocco's 1500-strong army of European renegades, he moved outside the conventions of the Christian calendar, and into indigenous methods of marking the passage of time. His text conveys the changing of the seasons in Morocco by reference to when he was free to hunt game, or when he was allowed to live with the slave woman allocated to him as a wife. Above all, he charts his Moroccan life by reference to the seventeen military campaigns he fought in between 1720 and 1737, and the towns and villages he saw, lived in and sacked as he and his comrades traversed the country again and again harrying the sultan's enemies. For Pellow at this time, the business of tracking time became a spatial and a geographical one, rather than a matter for a watch and a calendar. There are 230 place-names in his narrative, including some unavailable in any other Western source on Morocco at this time.[37]

Thus a characteristic of this narrative that appears at first glance to mark it out as vague and largely fictional – its paucity of Western dating – suggests in fact the degree to which Pellow was caught up in and altered by his other, Moroccan existence. Close analysis of the text reveals indeed the tensions that resulted from his position as a human palimpsest, the original script of his English existence written over by twenty-three years of Moroccan state service, and this version of his life being in turn partially and unconvincingly expunged by re-entry into Britain in 1738. The end of his account relates how, as Morocco became convulsed in civil strife, he finally made the decision to escape, went on the run, and masqueraded for a time as a travelling healer. Pellow describes how he treated some Moroccan peasants who came to him with eye infections by pouring ground red pepper into their open eyes, and comments that their resulting agony moved him not at all: 'Just so (were it in my power) I would use most of the Moors in Barbary.'

Before we shudder at what appears to be a piece of racially motivated nastiness, we should understand what Pellow – or his editor – was trying to do here. Pellow had disowned Christianity and his country, and fought for more than two decades under different, alien banners. Attempting after 1738 to re-enter British society, he naturally sought to use his narrative to prove that in his heart he had never really turned renegade at all. He makes a point, for instance, of including an unlikely episode in which he tells Moulay Ismaïl to his face that he will never marry a black or mulatto slave woman, pleading with him instead 'to give me one of my own colour'. Yet this strenuous and naïve attempt to prove that his prolonged stay in Morocco had never modified his birth identity is compromised by Pellow's account of his red pepper cure. The use of a minute dose of red pepper for eye infections, especially of the inner eyelid, was not an innovative piece of racist cruelty on his part. It was a standard, Moroccan folk remedy for such ailments. An episode which British readers were encouraged to read as anti-Muslim, anti-Moroccan behaviour on Pellow's part, demonstrates in reality the extent to which this one-time Cornishman had assimilated Moroccan folkways.[38] Thomas Pellow had not just been captured by Barbary: he had in the process been changed. Irreversibly so, as it turned out, for he was never able to make a satisfactory life for himself on his return to Britain.

In part, this was because he had been captured so young, when he was only eleven years old, and held in North Africa for so long, well over two decades. As a result, Pellow found himself on his return to 'home' and 'freedom' in eighteenth-century Britain in much the same state of frightened and angry bewilderment that Joan Brady's grandfather seems to have experienced in late nineteenth-century America. The latter, she tells us in her astonishing book *The Theory of War* (1993), was sold as an infant to a mid-western tobacco farmer, and spent virtually all of his childhood and adolescence in what was effectively white slavery. After he escaped from his owner, this man – like Pellow – felt an initial surge of euphoria at the 'sudden freedom, the multiplicity of it, the dazzling, dizzying disorder of it'. But then came panic and fury, as he was forced to realise that freedom by itself could not give him back his past, nor provide for him a present in which he could feel comfortable:

What once fit – what once was life itself – no longer fits, could never be made to fit again. Normality becomes another kind of bondage . . . Like God himself he had to build his world from scratch.[39]

Pellow seems to have undergone a similar shift from wild optimism immediately after his return to England, to feeling desperately and angrily unearthed. His parents failed to recognise him, and for a while his only solace was paying visits to Morocco's ambassador in London who was kind to him. Neither the place nor the date of his death is known.

Pellow's inability to settle back in and make good, may have been due to more, however, than his own alienation. In his absence, not only he, but also his country had been transformed. By the time his captivity narrative appeared, around 1740, Britain had become a first-ranking and increasingly aggressive state inside Europe, and more consciously intent as well on expanding its power outside Europe. This was scarcely a context in which the tale of a Briton who had turned Muslim, foreign mercenary, and defector, was likely to win easy acceptance, still less wide acclaim. As Pellow complained at the end of his narrative, when he finally returned to London in 1738, and with terrible naïvety presented himself at the Navy Office to ask for an interview with the king: 'all I could get from them at the last was the very extraordinary favour of a hammock on board of a man of war.'[40] As far as the British authorities were concerned, Pellow was an embarrassment who might at least have the decency now to get himself killed fighting for the country he had so impertinently (if involuntarily) abandoned.

As this episode suggests, captive-taking by foreign powers was always much more than a matter of individual sufferings and adventures. Then, as now, the capture of one country's nationals by the agents of another was a political issue, a matter for states, governments, diplomats and rulers. As far as Britain was concerned, captivity was also increasingly a matter of empire. Exactly the same points apply to the culture of captivity. As we have seen, this was partly an oral culture, a set of ideas, impressions and images that spread widely across the different social classes by way of sermons, speeches, sung ballads, the spoken accounts of returning captives, and the gossip and stories of those who knew them. Barbary captivity – like other captivity crises – also gave rise to abundant writings, sometimes in manuscript, but often in print. As I have sought to show, some of these texts were highly influential at the time and repay close reading and analysis now. Full-length captivity narratives especially are often moving and gripping sources, because of the intimate details they offer on cross-cultural collisions and collusions in North Africa and other parts of the world. Here are the halting, revealing testimonies of small but not unimportant people caught, sometimes literally, in the cross-fire. But these remarkable micro-narratives – like the rest of the culture of captivity – need to be located as well in a macro-narrative of contending states and empires.

From the very start, individual Barbary captives were caught up in much bigger stories than they themselves can often have been aware. On the one hand, English, Welsh, Scottish and Irish men and women were seized in increasing numbers in the Mediterranean after 1600 because the small, greedy islands from which they came nurtured first commercial and then imperial ambitions in this vital sea among the lands. On the other hand, these captivities also occurred because of the needs and imperatives of the Ottoman empire and its border provinces of Algiers, Tunisia and Tripoli, together with the formidable kingdom of Morocco. There was also a further twist. As Britain's power in the Mediterranean expanded, albeit unevenly and with major reversals on the way, a close relationship evolved between it and some of this region's Muslim powers. As first Gibraltar and then Minorca were seized, Britain became dependent on North African aid to provision and supply these white colonies, and so maintain them against its European enemies. If this tidy arrangement sometimes required that London look the other way when corsairs made sporadic hits against British ships, or strike curious deals to get its people back, or sometimes allow them to die unrevenged, then so be it. Whoever imagined that empire was to be achieved without cost?

In the Mediterranean world, then, as in other zones of British imperial enterprise, the captive's tale needs to be read and interpreted in a wider British and global context. These were never simply stories about individuals under stress, but commentaries on, and by-products of changing power relations over time. There was a particular respect in which this was so in this sector of the world. As we have seen, one result of the large numbers of English, Welsh, Scottish and Irish men and women being captured by Barbary corsairs after 1600 was that Islam came to be invoked and debated in Britain very broadly. The majority of seventeenth- and early eighteenth-century Britons did not approach the Islamic world initially with a view to possible conquests. They began devoting increasing attention to it in large part because the North African powers and the Ottomans, and the captivities they inflicted, allowed them no choice in the matter. Yet, over time, this would change. The great Muslim empires would come to seem less sources of danger to the British than vulnerable. It is this momentous shift over time, and the ways in which captivities can illumine it, that we now need to investigate.

FOUR

Confronting Islam

Dis-orientations

April 1751: it is cold in London this season, especially for the shabby, emaciated men waiting in the wings of Covent Garden Theatre, who hug themselves and stamp their feet as much as their fetters allow. The audience, though, is warm as well as restive. Not every box is occupied, but over a thousand people are packed into the pit and galleries, young men about town, dignified citizens and their wives, merchants and respectable shopkeepers, admiring rustics on their first visit to the capital, the odd army officer lounging in a blaze of scarlet, and – in the cheapest seats – the prostitutes, the servants, and the merely cash-inhibited. The matter of Barbary, as always, is set to play across the social spectrum. Briefly, the sound of the impresario's staff and some discordant and utterly inauthentic music cut through the chatter, then Thomas Troughton and his comrades are prodded on to the stage, caught fast and blinking in the bright candlelight. They know what to do, but find it hard not to be distracted by the particular smell of massed, barely washed Western bodies, and by the powdered faces of the women, eyeing them openly and without a veil. The audience, too, is transfixed. The men standing before them are bone-thin and burnt brown, dressed in rags that seem almost welded to their skins. Suddenly, each of them grasps the iron chains attached to their legs and arms, and rattles the links violently, smashing them down hard against the wood of the stage. Like Marley's ghost, these are spirits back from the dead, with a message of horror and of warning.

The man responsible for this theatrical coup was John Rich, Covent Garden's actor manager. He had sought out Troughton and his former shipmates as soon as they returned to London from almost five years' captivity and hard labour in Morocco, knowing their publicity value and audience appeal were bound for a while to be high. His interest in them may have been prompted by another consideration too. Rich had made his name and fortune staging the most famous musical satire of the century, John Gay's *The Beggar's Opera* (1728), where again the pains of capture and

Turks taking the English.

Selling slaves in Algers

Execution with A batoone.

Turks burning of A Frier er.

Mayork

Divers Cruelties

Makeing the boat & their Escape to May

18. 'Turkish' power and cruelty: the frontispiece to William Okeley's captivity narrative.

imprisonment are much in evidence. Its hero of a kind, Captain Macheath, spends a great deal of this musical drama in shackles and in fear of his life in Newgate prison.[1] It may be that Rich saw in Troughton and his worn-out companions an opportunity to revisit imprisonment and its metaphors. For just as the criminal underworld as evoked in *The Beggar's Opera* was also an attack on corruption in high places, so the spectacle of redeemed but suffering Barbary captives was more than ephemeral sensationalism. Behind the clanking chains, and the men's own eagerness to please and make a little money, was a political statement of sorts. In words, song, and mime, the enthralled habitués of Covent Garden were informed that these were the same loathsome irons and gaping rags in which the men had laboured for so long in Muslim North Africa, enslaved victims – to quote the title of Troughton's captivity narrative – of 'barbarian cruelty'.[2]

Here it was then. As represented in this pantomime version, North African Islamic society stood for tyranny, brutality, poverty and loss of freedom, the reverse and minatory image of Britain's own balanced constitution, commercial prosperity, and individual liberty. The fact that these claims could be rehearsed by a group of confused and hungry amateurs on a chilly London stage only demonstrated how well-primed their audience already was. For what Troughton and his comrades inexpertly acted out had been the stuff of cliché too long for any lack of understanding to be possible. Countless church sermons and royal proclamations whenever money was needed to ransom captives, and the plethora of commercial texts to which this issue gave rise, had all encouraged Britons to view Barbary as a source of aggression and menace, and as their own antithesis and nemesis. An unremarkable middle-class matron called Mary Barber summed it up nicely when dashing off one of her dreadful poems: 'On seeing the Captives, lately redeem'd from Barbary' in 1734:

> See the freed captives hail their native shore,
> And tread the land of LIBERTY once more
> . . . So, Albion, be it ever giv'n to thee,
> To break the bonds, and set the Pris'ners free.[3]

Barbary, in this stock and repeatedly recited view, was explicitly the 'Other', a place of 'inhuman, barbarous Moors'. It was the Other – or so it could seem – because it was not European. 'Wigs, cravats, or neck-cloths, gloves, breeches, nor stockings, they wear none,' one English captive observed conclusively in the 1690s. It was the Other, too, because the majority of its inhabitants were Muslims: 'our greatest enemies, I mean, those barbarous infidels, the Moors'. And it was made Other by its own unfreedom, for which the only compensation available was that it threw into still happier relief Britons' own unique privileges. Native liberty, mused a one-time captive in Morocco, Thomas Phelps, was a 'happiness only valuable by a reflection on captivity and slavery'.[4]

Such perceptions and language have struck some scholars in retrospect as both formative and portentous. For Edward Said famously, in his classic *Orientalism* (1978), these kinds of formulaic denunciations have to be taken seriously and recognised for what they were: 'a set of constraints upon and limitations of [Western] thought'. By consistently resorting to derogatory language of this type – he and others argue – Britons became able to view Islamic cultures over the centuries overwhelmingly in terms of strangeness, backwardness, and political and moral excess. By so projecting a 'settled, clear, unassailably self-evident' divide between 'us' (the West) and 'them' (the non-West), European and above all British imperialism became in due course possible. Because the Islamic world, and other parts of Asia and Africa, had been so thoroughly and persistently debased in cultural terms by the West, it became imaginable, as it would otherwise not have been, to invade and dominate them. Familiar hatreds and contempt bred and permitted expansionism once the other technical, economic and military preconditions were in place. By 1850, the United Kingdom, no more than a puny set of islands in terms of geography, would claim authority over more Muslims than any other state in the world.[5]

This is a powerful and seductive theory which has the great virtue of drawing attention to the minds and myths of those most obviously responsible for making maritime empire, rather than just their material power or short-term actions. For a small people like the British, learning how to think big and act big on the global stage was indeed vital, and required imaginative and intellectual effort, as well as military and economic force. Yet, by definition, concentrating on a persistent and traditional clutch of denunciations and misperceptions is not and cannot be an adequate way of exploring and accounting for change over time. The language and assumptions that the English, Scots, Irish and Welsh had recourse to in regard to North Africa and other Islamic cultures in the nineteenth century were similar in many respects to those their ancestors had deployed in 1600, and can be traced back in part even to classical times. But the power that governments in London exercised in the world was utterly different, and it is this British transition from marginality to global power that has to be investigated and explained. Moreover, as far as Islam and Islamic societies were concerned, language and attitudes were never homogenous or monolithic. The gut reactions to Barbary and Islam that John Rich appealed to so cannily at Covent Garden coexisted in practice with quite different and more varied responses. How, indeed, could it have been otherwise, given the nature of Britain's exposure to Islamic power in the Mediterranean world?

Before the 1750s, as we have seen, this was the sector of the globe where Britain's contacts with Islam were the most extensive, the most intense, and the most well reported among its home population. Up to this point in time, it was the Ottoman empire and North Africa that constituted, for the generality of Britons, the familiar and formidable face of Islam, not Mughal India, which was so much more distant geographically, and where the East India Company's power was still overwhelmingly commercial, rather than military or territorial. Accordingly, before 1750, Islam was more likely to be linked in British minds with aggression against themselves than with their own overseas ambitions. For it bears repeating that, in this Mediterranean zone, it was Britons who were for a long time at risk of being captured and even enslaved by Muslim powers, and not the other way around. Even when British power expanded in this zone in the eighteenth century, it was not at the expense of Islam. It was fellow Europeans and Christians whom the British succeeded in colonising here, not Muslims. Indeed, British empire in the Mediterranean – Gibraltar and Minorca – relied, as we have seen, on the Islamic regimes of North Africa for their basic sustenance. In this contested sea region, Islamic powers were never straightforwardly the 'Other', but rather vital auxiliaries in the business of British empire.

Understood in this way, encounters in the Mediterranean zone make both necessary and possible a more nuanced and more variegated view of relations between the British empire and Islam. They call into question the extent to which Islam was regarded and treated as a uniquely different and degraded 'them', and also the degree to which Britons saw themselves as a unified, superior 'us', possessed of a single, driving aim and interest. The sheer volume and variety of material existing about British–Islamic relations in the Mediterranean also provides for, and positively demands, a no less nuanced treatment of change over time. In the seventeenth century the English state had been bitterly humiliated at Tangier, and forced to pay exorbitant and regular ransoms to Muslim corsairs who preyed on its trade and traded in its people. It was still paying ransoms in the early eighteenth century, and still residually in awe of the Ottomans, a Muslim empire whose rulers regarded all Western Europeans with much the same disdain as did the Ch'ing emperors of China. But by 1750, attitudes and circumstances were alike changing, and we need to examine how and why.

Cosmopolitanism, in the sense of an informed appreciation of rival religious and political systems, and a belief in their equal worth, was not a characteristic of any society anywhere in the early modern world. Popular and polite responses to Islam in Britain were often visceral and derogatory, but this sort of deep-rooted, almost instinctive prejudice was not a monopoly of Europeans, nor did the British themselves deploy it only against non-Europeans. The Muslim peoples of the Mediterranean exhibited a very similar verbal, written and symbolic disdain and contempt for Western Christians. When the new English ambassador to the Ottoman empire, Sir Daniel Harvey, arrived in Istanbul in 1668, he was made to wait a full year for an audience with the sultan, as a stern reminder of the latter's supreme religious and secular importance, and the disparity in grandeur and extent between Harvey's puny kingdom and this huge overland Islamic empire. It is far from clear that the subsequent rise in Western power modulated, at least initially, this traditional sense of Islamic superiority. 'They consider themselves the first people in the world', wrote an astounded British envoy to Morocco as late as 1814, the year before Waterloo, '. . . and contemptuously term all others barbarians.'[6]

Western European Christians and their Muslim neighbours in the Mediterranean were not just alike in often being ignorant, suspicious and contemptuous of each other: they were also equally chauvinist towards their own rival co-religionists. Just as Turks, for instance, looked down on the Egyptian population of the Ottoman empire (often accusing them of a similar indolence and sensuality as Western Europeans regularly attributed to Muslims as a whole), so polite and plebeian Britons frequently derided and despised those of their fellow Europeans who were Roman Catholic:

> What does one find, but want and pride?
> Farces of superstitious folly,
> Decay, distress and melancholy:
> The havoc of despotic power,
> A country rich, its owners poor;
> Unpeopled towns, and lands untilled,
> Bodies unclothed, and mouths unfilled.[7]

Despotism, superstition, backwardness, a timeless poverty: here, it would seem, is unabashed Orientalism, precisely the kind of stereotypical slurs that Britons so often applied to the Islamic world. Except that this particular verse was an English milord's verdict on Italy in the 1730s, and the target could equally well have been Catholic France, or Spain, or Orthodox Russia (or even, in our own day, reputedly bureaucratic Brussels). Then, as now, the British possessed a limited and very durable portmanteau of xenophobic language and assumptions that they drew on and deployed undiscriminatingly, and by no means – as in Lord Hervey's poetic put-down of Italians – invariably with imperial intent.[8] What lay behind these stylised and recycled insults was rather Britain's intense Protestantism, that fostered a sense of special election and grace, together with its conscious-ness of its own smallness and potential vulnerability. Characterising other peoples, whether European or non-European, as morally and politically defective and/or oppressive, while simultaneously vaunting their own achievements and virtues, was – for early modern (and perhaps some modern) Britons – as much a defence mechanism as an expression of serene superiority or considered aggression.

If, then, we are to trace shifting attitudes in Britain towards Islam in the Mediterranean (and anywhere else), we need to look beyond the stan-dard and formulaic language of denunciation, suggestive though it can sometimes be. Contemporary reactions must be explored more broadly and also in some depth, for after 1600 they multiplied rapidly.

One of the paradoxes of Barbary captive-taking was that it not only exacerbated pre-existing hostility to Islam, but also increased the volume and variety of information available about it in Britain, and transformed both the extent and the complexity of Muslim–British contacts. Thus, in the 1630s, Algiers corsairs attacked coastal villages in Western England and Ireland, and Morocco dispatched its first large-scale embassy to London to negotiate ransoms for its English slaves. But this same decade, the 1630s, also saw the establishment of the first ever chairs in Arabic at Oxford and Cambridge Universities, in part so that officials and interpreters could be trained up to deal with Barbary and the Ottoman empire in the future.[9] The 1640s saw both a parliamentary levy on trade to finance Barbary captives' ransoms, and also the first publication of the *Qur'an* in English, a poor translation from a French version, probably by an Alexander Ross. This went through several editions before being entirely superseded in 1734, when the London-based orientalist George Sale (himself 'half a Mussulman' in Edward Gibbon's later opinion) produced a new and remarkable version of the *Qur'an*. And this later publication coincided with a procession through the streets of London of 150 redeemed captives from Morocco, exhibiting their rags and shackles before massive crowds.[10]

This is not to say that Barbary corsairing was the sole cause of this brisk rise in interest in and information about Islam. Growing trade with the Islamic world in the Mediterranean and elsewhere (on which the corsairs sometimes preyed) was an important contributory factor, and so was the scholarly belief that learning more about Islam would enhance understanding about the Bible and Christianity. My point is that – at this stage – it was captivity, commerce and Christian scholarship together, far more than any urge to conquest, that informed British curiosity about and reactions to the matter of Islam.

There was also an element of awe involved, which never entirely went away. By the seventeenth century, the great Islamic empires together probably contained between one third and one quarter of the world's population, and sprawled across the globe on a geographical scale that dwarfed western Europe as a whole, never mind England and its adjacent countries. Here, in the Muslim empires, was a display of daunting territorial reach and military power, in the service of a religion that rivalled Christianity, and resembled it in being monotheistic and international. This explains why, *pace* Nabil Matar, it was rarely the case that 'the Muslim "savage" and the Indian [Native American] "savage" became completely superimposable in English thought and ideology'. To be sure, individuals did occasionally attempt such analogies. When Devereux Spratt (1620–88), an Oxford-educated Anglican minister based in Ireland, compiled a manuscript memoir of his captivity in Algiers, he debated with himself why God permitted his Protestants to suffer so much at the hands of North African Muslims, New England Indians and Irish Catholics. To Spratt, evidently, all of these groupings were alike heathen and malevolent.[11]

But such lack of discrimination was distinctly unusual. Native Americans were seen at this time and for long after as nomadic peoples, with no urge to build in stone or cultivate land over the seasons, and no written records as Europeans understood them. Muslims, by contrast, whether encountered in the Mediterranean, or India, or Persia, were markedly urban (a vital characteristic of civilisation in Western European eyes), highly commercial (ditto), and possessed of an influential written culture. 'That little smattering of knowledge we have', insisted Simon Ockley, Cambridge's Professor of Arabic, in 1717, 'is entirely derived from the East.'[12] Native American religions, insofar as they were recognised at all, appeared polytheistic and parochial. Islam, by contrast, was perceived by most Britons and other Europeans in the early modern era – and after – as inferior to Christianity, but wedded to one God, international, and formidable. As Samuel Johnson put it with characteristic trenchancy: 'There are two objects of curiosity – the Christian world, and the Mahometan world. All the rest may be considered as barbarous.'[13]

It followed that to have some acquaintance with Islam was a constituent part of polite British culture. Even when Arabic and Oriental studies, like so many other subjects, went into decline in the ancient English universities after 1700, this was compensated for to some degree by the greater availability of works on Islam issued by the commercial presses. There was Joseph Pitts' *A True and Faithful Account of the Religion and Manners of the Mohammetans* (1704), a wonderful and lengthy captivity narrative still worth reading, which provided the first authentic English-language account of the *hajj*, the pilgrimage to Mecca. There was a successful English translation of Boulainvilliers' *Life of Mahomet* in 1731, in which the Prophet featured as 'a great man, a great genius, and a great prince'. And there was Sale's seminal translation of the *Qur'an*, three years later, which informed its readers briskly that:

> To be acquainted with the various laws and constitutions of civilized nations, especially of those who flourish in our own time, is, perhaps, the most useful part of knowledge.[14]

The assumptions here are worth underlining. For Sale, writing in the 1730s, Islamic societies were not equal to his own Protestant Christian culture in terms of spiritual revelation, but they were emphatically civilised, and they were no less emphatically flourishing. This was also the view of the foremost Grub Street commentator on Islam in Britain at this time, Joseph Morgan. Morgan – who deserves to be better known – had been a soldier in the British army during the War of Spanish Succession, and was taken prisoner by the Spanish in 1706. His subsequent experience as a prisoner-of-war among fellow Europeans brought him, as captivity so often did, both personal trauma and also an opportunity for reassessing his life and opinions. By Morgan's own account, he was used 'with such hardships and cruelties', that he emerged with a profound sympathy for Spain's traditional enemy, Muslim North Africa. He travelled there for many years, learned Arabic, and used the Spanish he had acquired as a prisoner-of-war to investigate the Moriscos. Once back in London, he wrote and translated a series of books on Islam and the North African powers, all of them informed by the wistful conviction that, if only his countrymen knew more about Islam, their prejudices would be much reduced: 'I am persuaded that were . . . persons to converse unknowingly with Mahometans in a Christian dress, they would look upon them to be just such creatures as themselves.'[15]

Coexisting with the derogatory stereotypes, then, and the fear and hatred provoked by Ottoman power and Barbary corsairing, was a more measured and multi-faceted British discourse on Islam, in which its believers were *not* viewed unambivalently as the 'Other' or wholly different. In part

19. Islam experienced: Joseph Pitts' narrative.

– and as suggested by Morgan's remark that Muslims in Western dress would be indistinguishable – this was because adherents of Islam were not seen as invariably and visibly racially distinct. This was especially true of those Muslims with whom Britons had most contact at this stage: Ottomans and other North Africans.[16] 'They are not a people black like those of Guinea,' Sir Hugh Cholmley reported from Tangier in the 1670s, 'but in features and manners more resembling some of their neighbours, inhabitants of Europe.' A seaman and former captive, John Whitehead, struggled some decades later to supply a more accurately nuanced description, in a way that demonstrates how fluid racial designations still were at this time, and how bound up with analysis in terms of religious allegiance:

As the French, Spaniards and other papists call themselves Roman Catholics, so the subjects of the Emperor of Morocco do all call themselves Moors: though they be of diverse nations, and colours, viz. Moors or Arabians, and Barbarians. These are white, another sort of Arabians that are tawny.[17]

North Africa, as some Britons at least were made aware, was far from being the uniform region suggested by the loaded collective term 'Barbary'. This was particularly true of its coastal cities, where most European captives, envoys and traders were concentrated. Places like Tangier, Salé, Tunis and Algiers were markedly cosmopolitan, arrestingly so by British domestic standards at this time. Their populations included Ottoman janissaries, powerful Jewish communities, sub-Saharan black slaves, sometimes in positions of high authority, and Protestant and Catholic European merchants, bankers, smugglers, drop-outs and renegades aplenty, sometimes prosperous and usually tolerated. One of the aspects of her brief captivity in Morocco in 1756 that Elizabeth Marsh found most disorienting, was that of encountering so many European traders cheerfully cutting deals with her Muslim captors. Badly traumatised by her adventure, she wanted – as the early version of her captivity narrative shows – to make sense of it in retrospect in terms of villainous Muslims on the one hand, and put-upon virtuous Christians on the other. But what she herself had witnessed at first hand kept getting in the way. She describes in one draft how, while being detained in Marrakesh, she encountered a Dutch merchant who was negotiating with the sultan to establish a trading house there. 'The difficulties a Christian is exposed to in that country', she complains almost tearfully, 'were overlooked by him, as matters of no importance or consideration.'[18] Even when the Royal Navy arrived to rescue her, it was only to take her on to British Gibraltar, where again Muslim and Jewish traders normally operated freely. Marsh yearned for strict cultural and religious divisions. She discovered instead, as so many had before her, that this Mediterranean world was often a shared and interdependent one.[19]

This cultural and ethnic diversity, combined with its geographical location and historic connections with the Iberian peninsula, made it difficult for early modern Europeans to situate North Africa securely on their mental maps, and on real ones. Was Barbary African, for instance? And, if so, what did this say about conventional European imaginings of that continent? 'I saw here nothing of that rudeness', wrote one captive revealingly, 'which our people imagine to be in all the parts of Africa.' Or was Barbary – and perhaps the Ottoman empire in general – a kind of rebel sub-section of Europe itself, as some British maps of the continent certainly suggested?[20] In the nineteenth century, it became easier, for those wishing to do so, to advance firm divides between the West and the rest, not just because of the elaboration of racial ideologies, but also because of the pace of technological, scientific and industrial change. The coming of steam power, trains, mass-production, telegraphs, gas-light, efficient plumbing, medical innovation – and of course rapid-firing guns – proved vital, as Michael Adas shows, both to British and Western dominance in the Victorian era in practical terms, and to the ideas sustaining that dominance.[21] Earlier though, and especially before 1750, the characteristics in British and European eyes of efficient and powerful societies were more diffuse and less decisive. Trade and towns were viewed as vital: and these existed in abundance in all Islamic societies. Islamic powers also built and created on a scale that impressed Europeans, far more so and for longer than is sometimes recognised.

It can be hard, for instance, wandering around the imperial city of Meknès in Morocco today, to imagine the grandeur that astounded Western visitors here in the late seventeenth and early eighteenth centuries. Some of the city was destroyed by the Lisbon earthquake of 1755 (a Eurocentric label that ignores the devastation this and connected quakes wreaked in the northerly parts of North Africa). Meknès was also pillaged in the course of successive bouts of civil strife; and much of it is now overgrown and in need of further archaeological recovery. But if you walk through the kilometre-long passage that is the Bab ar-Rouah, the Gate of Winds, or stand in the vast colonnaded space of the Mechouar, you can still obtain a sense of the extraordinary scale of this city-palace complex built by Moulay Ismaïl. This was a project roughly contemporaneous with the building of Versailles by Louis XIV of France, and it was inspired by a comparable regal hubris and territorial ambition. The sultan's palace at Meknès was simply the 'largest he had ever seen', reported an envoy dispatched to redeem Britain's Moroccan captives in the 1720s. Even the stables, which he calculated were three-quarters of a mile long, seemed 'the noblest of the kind perhaps in the world'.[22] Set against this structure in its heyday, Versailles was unduly compact; while William III's extensions to Hampton Court near London would have seemed almost toy-like in comparison.

This, indeed, was a crucial point. To the extent that Islamic societies *did* appear different to Britons at this early stage, it could still be because they seemed bigger, stronger, or richer.

Early modern Britons, like the rest of mankind, had no way of foreseeing the future. Indeed, they were far more likely than we are today to assume that things would continue much as they had done in the past. Self-evidently, they had no way of knowing in 1600, or in 1700, or in 1750, that by 1850 they would rule on paper so many millions of Muslim men and

20. A section of the Mechouar at Meknès.

21. The massive walls of one of Moulay Ismaïl's storehouses.

women. Even at the beginning of the nineteenth century, many Britons felt unable to predict this with any confidence. So when previous generations of English, Welsh, Scottish and Irish men and women contemplated Islamic powers in the Mediterranean and elsewhere, it was rarely with any sense of manifest destiny or expectation of imperial dominance. They could not know that – in due course but briefly – theirs would be an empire on which the sun never set. Instead, they regarded the Islamic presence in the light of what they *did* know: the sheer scale and continuing grandeur of the Ottoman empire, the well-publicised depredations of Barbary corsairs, and the resilience and toughness of the regimes that backed them.

Their vision was also informed by a consciousness of the limitations of their own state. After 1750, the British became increasingly complacent about the calibre of their ostensibly balanced constitution and their political stability. Excesses such as over-mighty monarchs, civil wars, rebellions, mass killings, out-of-control nobilities, and frequent, violent switches of dynasties came – at this later stage – to seem comfortably alien, things that simply did not and could not occur in Britain. Consequently, the political violence, administrative malaise, and dynastic extravagance associated, rightly or wrongly, with many Islamic polities, whether in the Mediterranean or elsewhere, were easily interpreted as evidence of an intrinsic failure in development, and even as a rationalisation of imperial takeover. Since Britain was manifestly so accomplished at governing itself, it increasingly seemed – to its political class at least – that the more places it governed throughout the world, the better it would be for everyone.

But, before 1750, confidence in the stability and supreme desirability of Britain's own political arrangements was less widespread and pronounced: and for good reason. During the 1640s and '50s, Britain and Ireland witnessed lethal civil wars in which hundreds of thousands of people died and a monarch lost his head. In 1688, a change of dynasty was effected by force of arms; and yet another dynastic changeover in 1714 went on to provoke bloody rebellions in protest in 1715 and 1745. Moreover, successive regimes failed to win nationwide acceptance in England, still less in the three countries connected to it, Scotland, Wales and Ireland. As a result of all this, throughout the seventeenth century, and right up to the Jacobite Rising of 1745 and even beyond, despotism, assassination, decadence, court intrigue, corruption and bloody rebellion were unlikely to be viewed as peculiarly characteristic of Islamic regimes, demonstrating their otherness and essential inferiority. To Britons, at this point, such political upheavals and abuses seemed all too familiar, a case of analogy and not difference. 'Are the Algerians the only regicides?' mocked Joseph Morgan gently in 1750, defending their political system:

a king [Charles I] after a solemn trial, has lost his head upon a scaffold
... Remove the ceremony, pomp, and formality, with which these
proceedings were disguised among the Christians, and the act itself will
appear the same with that practised in Barbary.[23]

We come back, in other words, to the fact that the attitudes of Britons to
the outside world – and their capacity for, and interest in empire – can
only be properly assessed when due consideration is also given to the
internal conditions of their own state and their own self-image. British
responses to Islam, and to Islamic powers in the Mediterranean and elsewhere, were never static or uniform. They changed in tandem with shifts
in the intellectual scene, and in the power and reputation of the great
Islamic empires. But they also changed in accordance with the estimates
made by Britons of their own state and of its potential. In this, as in so
many other respects, messages about Islam were mixed and mutating rather
than monolithic. The voices of British men and women who were caught,
and caught up in, this Mediterranean zone are both vocal and varied. It
is time we listened to them – and listened carefully.

Testimonies

Capture, whether in the Mediterranean zone or elsewhere, initially and
unsurprisingly forced victims back on themselves and deepened any pre-
existing prejudices they held. In shock, wounded perhaps, dizzy with the
unaccustomed heat of North Africa, unable in the vast majority of cases
to speak Arabic or Spanish, few men and women seized by Barbary corsairs
can have registered much at first except terror, resentment and bewilderment at the strangeness of it all. When an English seaman briefly held
captive in Tunis in the 1650s, Edward Coxere, tried after his return home
to compose a simple narrative of his experiences, words failed him when
he came to describe his early days as a slave. All he could manage was a
primitive drawing of a large man flourishing a whip and wearing a turban
(the standard European emblem for a Muslim), and a group of small
Englishmen, still in the clothes they were captured in, weighed down with
chains.[24] Here, indeed, was Islam depicted as 'Other' – but also as superior power. Over time, however, Coxere's perceptions became more
nuanced than this cartoon representation suggests, not least because of
the greater religious toleration he, as a Quaker, received from his Muslim
captors, than from the authorities in England. But a crude divide between
Muslim oppressors on the one hand, and forlorn Christians in bondage

on the other, must have been all that most captives of Barbary were at first able to assimilate.

Some chose never to look any deeper. Individuals held only briefly or exposed to unusual harshness might never have the chance to do so; while some clung fast to their preconceptions irrespective of how they were treated or for how long. Devereux Spratt, the Anglican minister, was captured with 120 others in the 1640s by Algiers corsairs off the coast of Youghall, southern Ireland. 'I began to question Providence,' he wrote later, but not for long. An heroic, narrow man, once in the city of Algiers, he began ministering to its other English captives, refusing an early chance to be ransomed because he would not leave their souls untended. His captors allowed Spratt and his white slave congregation freedom of worship. He himself had, as he admits, a 'civil' owner who gave him 'more liberty than ordinary'. This remained the case even after Spratt connived in the daring escape of five other Englishmen. 'I was much suspected', he writes, '. . . but Providence so ordered that I was never questioned.' Yet none of this prompted in him any curiosity about his Muslim captors. He attributed every kindness shown him solely to the omnipotence of his Protestant God: 'God was pleased to guide for me.'[25]

By interpreting any good deed issuing from Algerian Muslims in this fashion, Spratt left himself free to despise them. Early accounts by English colonists seized by Native Americans frequently employ this same tactic of crediting Providence alone with any act of charity extended to them by their captors. In regard to Barbary, however, a 'closed' narrative like Spratt's – closed in the sense of being determinedly incurious about the captors' common humanity – was rare. This was largely because Barbary captivity represented a very different kind of peril. Colonists seized by Native Americans, and subsequently escaping, had an obvious interest even apart from revenge and anger in seeking to dehumanise them. Native Americans were near-neighbours and rivals for the same land, a perpetual, intimate danger. Barbary corsairs, by contrast, were external enemies who threatened British shipping, liberties and lives, but only occasionally and fleetingly British territory. Moreover, Muslims – unlike Native Americans – were rarely regarded as godless or outside of civilisation. British captives of Barbary might, and often did, still hate their captors: but they were also more likely at some point to relax into a measure of detached observation. Once the immediate shock receded, they might begin to look around them and pose questions.

This, however, was when real disorientation often began, as captives were made forcibly aware that they now had to live and labour exposed to another culture's othering that both mirrored and inverted their own.

'Prejudice against unbelievers', as John Hunwick writes, was the 'single great prejudice of Muslim peoples', and since by Islamic law only unbelievers could be enslaved in the first place, anyone held captive or put to hard labour in North Africa was *ipso facto* a creature to be suspected, the infidel, the unclean.[26] James Irving, detained in Morocco for a year along with his crew, was shocked to notice how the local inhabitants 'would never use any vessel that had touched our lips: so great was their detestation & contempt for us'. British and other European captives were also made to recognise that, in the eyes of many of those around them, their physical appearance singled them out and demeaned them. Especially in the less cosmopolitan, inland regions of North Africa, European styles of dress – close to the crotch and legs for men, and to the waist for women – were likely to be viewed as at best strange and ugly, and at worst immoral and obscene. 'She . . . was extremely inquisitive', snaps Elizabeth Marsh of one coolly appraising Moroccan woman, 'curious in examining my dress and person, and . . . highly entertained at the appearance I made.'[27]

There was a more inescapable sense in which British captives found themselves caught fast in a disapproving or ironical Muslim gaze: there was the matter of their skin. Ibn Khaldûn, the great Tunisian scholar of the fourteenth century, wrote in his masterpiece, *Muqaddimah*, of his distaste for the two extremes of skin colour as he saw them, those with black skin, and those whom a cold climate had bleached to whiteness, with their 'blue eyes, freckled skin, and blond hair'. Only people of an intermediate skin-shade, he argued, could claim 'an abundant share of temperance, which is the golden mean'. This kind of prejudice against very dark and very pale skin seems to have persisted in North African societies into at least the nineteenth century, and to have existed at different social levels. Joseph Pitts, the young Exeter seaman who was enslaved in Algiers between 1678 and 1693, was told by one of his captors that pink people of his sort resembled pigs, quintessentially unclean animals.[28]

Captivity in Barbary, then, brought with it a sudden turning of the world upside down and an abrupt education in another society's prejudices, with little or no chance of being able to retaliate. Even British envoys of the Crown visiting North African cities in the seventeenth and eighteenth centuries to negotiate treaties, or redeem captives, had frequently to run the gauntlet of crowds of young local males hurling insults at them as unbelievers, mocking their physical appearance, and firing guns over their heads to make them jump.[29] Individual captives, with no diplomatic status or guards to protect them, were inevitably far more exposed. How they coped depended on those with power over them, but also – often –

on themselves. When William Okeley forgot for a moment the defence-lessness of his new slave status, and insulted his Algerian owner's Muslim faith to his face, he was able both literally and metaphorically to roll with the punches that subsequently rained down on him. 'Well, I learnt from hence two lessons,' he recalled of his beating: 'one, that when the body is a slave, the reason must not expect to be free . . . Second, that it's fair for slaves to enjoy the freedom of their own consciences, without reviling another's religion.'[30]

James Irving, by contrast, never adapted to the strain of submitting to his Moroccan captors. It killed him. His captivity occurred some 150 years after Okeley's, in the early 1790s, by which time Britons of Irving's class possessed a far more inflated sense of national and often racial conceit. The acute shame he experienced derived however as much from what he did as from what he was. An uncompromisingly Protestant Scot, Irving was the captain of a Liverpool-based transatlantic slave-ship and, as his narrative makes clear, possessed a fundamental distaste for those he termed 'black cattle'. To have individuals whom he, at least, viewed as also black-skinned as well as pagan now threaten him with slavery in Morocco was an inversion quite beyond his bearing. The local British consul, who corresponded with him throughout, tried patiently to spell out the facts of his new captive status in words that can only have embittered him further. 'I must beg leave to caution you not to make use of the term infidels, either in your letters or discourse when speaking of the Moors,' Irving was told firmly. 'They look upon the term as the most opprobrious in their language, and *as they have the power in their hands*, it may operate to your prejudice.'[31]

There are two important points to notice about these individual agonies and adjustments. First, they illustrate yet again how the instinct to 'other' seemingly alien individuals and societies in debased terms, which is usually examined only as a Western trait, was not so at all. Britons seized by corsairs from the region they presumed to call 'Barbary' discovered to their dismay that one of the insults most commonly flung at them by their captors was in turn 'barbarian'. Second, while prejudice against those perceived as alien was – and is – ubiquitous, the degree to which different individuals believed in and acted in conformity with such prejudices varied enormously, as of course it still does. Britons taken captive in North Africa did not, in practice, always come 'up against the Orient as a European . . . first, as an individual second'.[32] Just like other human beings, different Britons combined and juggled different identities. For some, like Irving, being dragged across the frontier of an Islamic power did indeed sharpen their sense of themselves as Christian, British, European and white. Others – after they had recovered from the immediate shock – cared about these particular loyalties only some of the time. Still others gave priority to different considerations entirely; while a minority reacted to Barbary captivity by abandoning Christianity, Britishness, and notions of European-ness altogether, or by adjusting their sense of what these allegiances involved. Here, as in other parts of the world, captivity, and the narra-tives emerging from it, never invariably aided the construction or re-inforcement of 'a binary division between captive and captor . . . based on cultural, national, or racial difference'.[33] Captivity and its texts were just as likely to expose and bring to the surface divisions within the victims' own home society, differences of class, education and wealth, differences of precise national origin, and differences of religious outlook.

Devereux Spratt's utter passive resistance to his Algerian context, for instance, stemmed in the main from his intense, professional Protestantism, but also from his sense of himself as a University-educated clergyman and one-time tutor to the English gentry. Most Barbary captives were less programmed and less privileged than this. For them, limited expectations at home might inflect how they reacted to issues of difference in captivity abroad, not least because white captives in North Africa, like black slaves in North America, were sometimes confronted with the phenomenon of the good master. William Okeley wrote of the third Algerian who owned him, a small farmer, that 'I found not only pity and compassion, but love and friendship from my new patron. Had I been his son, I could not have met with more respect, nor been treated with more tenderness.' In his English life, Okeley's trade was deference. He was captured in the 1640s while carrying out a transatlantic mission for Viscount Saye and Sele and Lord Brooke, and would be employed after his escape from Algiers as a steward on a landed estate in Bedfordshire. His published narrative makes clear his sense that serving an aloof patrician who was a fellow Englishman was not necessarily an advance on cheerful household slavery with a good man who just happened to be a North African Muslim:

> There arose a scruple, nay, it amounted to a question, whether to attempt an escape from my [Algerian] patron, one that so dearly loved me . . . For, where could I hope to mend my self? Or better my condition? I might possibly find worse quarter in England . . . Liberty is a good word, but a man cannot buy a meal's meat with a word: And slavery is a hard word, but it breaks no man's back.

In the end, Okeley's decision to run appears to have been based less on revulsion against a new life that was fast becoming comfortably familiar, than on prudential motives that would always weigh with a subordinate man like himself: 'My patron's favour was no freehold . . . He might die, and leave me to another'.[34]

Among Britons who were seized very young, or who remained in North Africa for many years, the pull of the captor society might be stronger still. Joseph Pitts was captured and taken to Algiers in 1678 when he was just fifteen. He remained there until 1693, and converted – he claimed in print only nominally and under pressure – to Islam. Although he finally escaped, after a letter smuggled to him from his father tugged at strings he had thought broken forever, he, too, was open in his published narrative about the kindness of his last Algerian owner who promised to leave him money on his death, and the affection he felt for him. Pitts also confessed to a strong temptation to 'continue a Mussulman'. 'I was', he wrote, 'in a much fairer way for honour and preferment in Algiers, than I could expect ever to have been in England.' How accurate this claim was will never be known, though it seems likely that Pitts himself believed it. On his return to England in the 1690s, in the midst of a major war with France, he was immediately imprisoned and threatened with impressment in the Royal Navy. For a labouring man like this (as we have already seen in Thomas Pellow's case) release from captivity abroad did not necessarily result in a warm sense of liberty recovered and resumed at home. It is suggestive that Pitts' captivity narrative – which was highly successful when it was published in 1704, and reprinted in 1717, 1731 and 1778 – openly and explicitly represented Islamic society as sometimes offering superior opportunities to individual Christians. Pitts writes of at least three fellow English captives known to him who chose to stay in Algiers. One of these was actually ransomed and returned home, but 'came again to Algiers and voluntarily, without the least force used towards him, became a Mohammetan'.[35]

It is in the context of such behaviour that we can understand the many references in Barbary captivity literature to Joseph, the Old Testament figure taken captive into Egypt and enslaved. In 1627, for instance, an English envoy negotiating the redemption of captives from Morocco referred to its ruler as 'a second Pharoah which knew not Joseph', while Devereux Spratt in Algiers 'laboured . . . to remember ye afflictions of Joseph'.[36] These were hostile deployments of the scriptural reference, but men and women familiar with the Bible knew that the lessons of Joseph's tale were mixed. He is enslaved by an alien power, yes. But it is this self-same misfortune that leads to his owner Potiphar, a chief officer of the Pharoah, promoting him to be overseer. Joseph prospers in Egypt and grows powerful, and even has to repel the lustrous advances of his owner's wife: 'God', he boasts, 'hath caused me to be fruitful in the land of my affliction.'[37] As we have seen, ballads like 'Lord Bateman' popularised the notion that British captives of Barbary too might find the site of their affliction productive of worldly opportunity. Some poor whites might flourish under the Crescent, or at least do no worse than at home. The same could even be true of poor blacks.

What may be the only black British Barbary captivity narrative ever written has recently been lost.[38] But, thanks to the work of Marcus Rediker and Peter Linebaugh, we know that blacks formed a persistent minority in both the Royal Navy and in Britain's merchant fleet, and some of these men were certainly captured over the years. Thomas Saphra, a black servant, was seized on the London ship *Philadelphia* in 1716.[39] Three of the eleven crewmen taken captive alongside James Irving in Morocco in 1789 were black, and among the eighty-seven survivors from the *Inspector* ship-wrecked there in 1746, were two black sailors, Thomas Jones and John Armatage. The latter 'turned Moor', and it seems likely that he was absorbed into the *'Abid al-Bukhari*, the black slave army of the Moroccan sultans. This was recruited in the main from the local black slave popu-lation, the *haratin*, but also seems to have drawn on blacks seized from captured European vessels.[40]

Joining the ranks of the *'Abid al-Bukhari* meant exposure to physical danger and brutality, but also the prospect of plunder and promotion. It might even bring the chance to oversee white slaves, a conspicuous demon-stration that Islamic societies could offer opportunities that Western Europe did not. One has only to remember Olaudah Equiano's stunned excite-ment when he visited the Ottoman city of Smyrna in 1768, and observed how white slaves there were 'kept under by the Turks, as the negroes are in the West Indies by the white people'. Equiano seems to have been born to a black slave mother in South Carolina and was subsequently owned by a Royal Naval officer. Free now, but still a servant, he gained from his Ottoman journey not just insight into a very different slave system, but also a sense from witnessing it that power relations between the races might be mutable. Whites, he realised, could be made as vulnerable as he himself had once been. Not all slaves were black; and not all whites were free. For long after this – as he tells us in his own captivity narrative – Equiano cherished the idea of emigrating to the Ottoman empire.[41] In just such a way, some black seamen seized by the North African powers might feel drawn to Muslim society. It sometimes offered individuals like them more options, another world.[42] Here was an extreme version of a much broader and recurrent phenomenon: overseas captivity as a potential gateway to opportunity and a fresh start for those who were disadvan-taged in some way in their home society.

The existence of British-based black captives of Barbary is a reminder that, then as now, the terms 'Briton', 'British', and especially 'English subject' or 'British subject' encompassed a patchwork of people. The quarter millennium covered by this book witnessed a dramatic rise in British national sentiment, but it also saw the British state becoming more composite, and composite in different ways at different stages. One of the more intellectual challenges confronting London in regard to Barbary captive-taking was indeed establishing exactly who it was responsible for redeeming at different times. The flux of Britain's ruling dynasties, state formation, international alliances and imperial acquisitions in the Mediterranean and elsewhere meant that the rules were constantly changing. After the Dutch stadtholder, William of Orange, ousted James II as king of England in 1688, for instance, the Moroccan sultan Moulay Ismaïl agreed that, when it came to ransoming, he would 'look upon the English and Dutch to be united, and in effect to be as one nation'.[43] This arrangement lapsed after William's death; but thereafter French Huguenots, Hanoverians, colonial Americans, and the multi-ethnic inhabitants of Minorca and Gibraltar were all claimed at different times by London as people it had a right and duty to ransom back as 'British subjects' if they were captured by Barbary.[44]

As demonstrated by the troubled internal politics of Tangier's garrison back in the 1660s and 1670s, the view from above of who qualified as an English or British subject could be at odds with the more visceral allegiances of those below. In 1747, British ministers approached the Ironmongers' Company of London, which presided over a lavish charitable fund specifically set up to redeem Barbary captives, for aid in a current ransoming campaign. The Ironmongers' grudging response is a wonderful example of how deep-rooted assumptions about national identity sometimes collided with more flexible and legalistic government notions of what 'Britishness' had practically to involve:

> They further object that in the number of the four score prisoners now detained [in Morocco] there may possibly be some Irishmen . . . and that there must therefore be proof made that they were all Britons before they apply the money.[45]

Quite clearly, as far as these Company members were concerned, the Irish – and no religion is specified in this passage – were not comprehended within the term 'Britons', and many others on the island of Great Britain, at this stage and later, would have concurred in this view.

As this suggests, approaching cross-cultural relationships and conflicts in the past in simple, bloc terms such as West and East, or Europe and non-European, or Britain and Islam glosses over important complexities and vital sub-divisions on all sides, and tends to hobble analysis. As politicians frequently have cause to remark even today, Europe, even western Europe alone, is not a unit and never has been. 'Europeans' did not think alike about Islam or anything else. As far as Britain itself was concerned, we have already seen how its marked territorial smallness helped to foster within it, as a countervailing advantage, a strong, centralised state, and a precocious, though never all-encompassing national unity and ideology. Even so, British unity was a partial and fractured thing, especially before 1750. Most particularly, it was persistently challenged by the divide between Catholic and Protestant, and like its other internal divisions, this complicated its responses to Islam and Islamic powers.

This tension can be seen, working itself out, at an individual level. Shared and fought over by rival states and faiths, the Mediterranean had traditionally always functioned as a frontier region where 'men [and women] passed to and fro, indifferent to . . . states and creeds', pursuing instead their own private, unofficial and sometimes rebellious vision of what they wanted from life.[46] After 1600, and still more after 1700, the volume of such individual crossings declined as states became more efficient at controlling and regulating their subjects, but at no time did they ever entirely cease. Those most likely to cross boundaries and turn renegade here, as far as the British state was concerned, were unsurprisingly the Catholic Irish. For just as some inhabitants of early modern England, Wales and Scotland had little desire to regard Ireland (especially its Catholics) as British: so the Irish (especially, but not exclusively the Catholics) sometimes returned the compliment. Take the case of the Butlers, a dynasty of Irish Catholic merchants who, by the mid-eighteenth century, were well established in Morocco, fluent in Arabic, and 'well acquainted' with the sultan's ministers. They delighted in helping visiting Continental European traders outwit British Protestant ones, and in assisting Spanish intrigues to recover Gibraltar.[47]

Some Catholic Irishmen who crossed over in this Mediterranean zone however did so more than once. From the 1730s, through to the 1750s, successive British envoys in Algiers struggled to determine what to do about a group of twenty-nine Irish Catholic mercenaries who had landed up there. These men had previously served Spain, doubtless at times against Britain. But once sent to the Spanish North African base of Oran – which was as bleak and brutal as garrison life in Tangier had been – these wild geese suddenly discovered the compelling attractions of Britishness. They deserted *en masse*, fled to Algiers where they were promptly enslaved, and appealed for help to the British consul there. Correspondence between him and his London masters about whether these individuals were indeed 'British subjects', and whether or not they – and other Irish mercenaries on the run in North Africa from French or Spanish service – should be ransomed, went on for decades.[48]

But the capacity of religious attachments to blur, rather than simply reinforce the divide between Britain and Islam, was exemplified in more than just the behaviour of disaffected individuals. This was a matter of state and even of theology.

Traditionally, the most persistent enemies of the Ottoman empire and Barbary were the Catholic powers, Spain, Austria, the Italian states, and on occasions France. For the rulers and the inhabitants of a Protestant polity like Britain, this Catholic hostility to the Islamic powers of the Mediterranean could seem a positive argument in the latter's favour. On the well-known principle of the enemy of my enemy is my friend, Elizabeth I sold weapons to the Moroccans in the late sixteenth century to use against the Catholic Portuguese; Charles I sought Moroccan aid against Spain in the 1620s; and, as we have seen, from 1704 onwards Britain relied on Algiers and Morocco to provision Gibraltar and Minorca, and so retain them against His Catholic Majesty of Spain. But there was more behind this Protestant–Islamic entente than just reasons of state or sectarian spite. There were aspects of Islam as a working faith that could seem to Protestants familiar and even congenial. Here, after all, was a religion that banned images from places of worship, that did not treat marriage as a sacrament, and had absolutely no time for monastic orders ('We shall have no Monk-ery,' the Prophet Muhammad is supposed to have declared). More radical Protestants might even relish Islam's contempt for the doctrine of the Trinity.[49]

This helps to explain why Protestant dissenters especially who got caught up in this Mediterranean world of crossings and captivities often adopted a markedly sympathetic perspective on their Muslim captors. Joseph Pitts, whom we have already encountered, used some of his captivity narrative to compare Islam with Roman Catholicism – very much to the former's advantage. He commended Muslims for excluding religious images from their mosques. He remarked on the practical toleration North African regimes extended to other faiths, which seemed to a Presbyterian like himself so much more impressive than the treatment meted out by the Anglican establishment at home. Autodidact as he was, Pitts also noted the zeal with which even some of the poorer Muslims he had known in Algiers studied the *Qur'an*, the primacy they gave to the word. It was a mode of faith and life, he thought, utterly unlike and far superior to 'the poor Romanists . . . [who] live and die in an implicit faith of what they are taught by their priests'.[50] The degree to which Pitts allowed himself to observe and empathise with his Muslim captors rather than judging them emerges most, however, in the tone and the detail of his narrative.

He published it in 1704 to justify the Algerian segment of his life to his Exeter non-conformist neighbours and make 'reparation for my past defection'. Yet, although this was his avowed aim in writing, the memory of how he had once been caught up in and stirred by Muslim North Africa kept impacting on and colouring his prose:

A few days after this [that is, after a twenty days journey on the Red Sea] we came to a place called Rabbock [Rabigh], about four days' sail this side of Mecca; where all the hagges [pilgrims] excepting those of the female sex . . . take off all their clothes, covering themselves with two hirrawems or large white cotton wrappers. One they put about their middle, which reaches down to their ankles; the other they cover the upper part of their body with, except the head. And they wear no other thing on their bodies but these wrappers; only a pair of gimgameea, ie. thin-sol'd shoes, like sandals, the over-leather of which covers only the toes, their insteps being all naked. In this manner, like humble penitents, they go from Rabbock till they come to Mecca to approach the temple; many times enduring the scorching heat of the sun till their very skin is burnt off their backs and arms . . . Yet when any man's health is by such austerities in danger and like to be impaired, they may lawfully put on their clothes, on condition still that, when they come to Mecca, they sacrifice a sheep and give it to the poor . . . During this time . . . they will also be careful to be reconciled and at peace with all such as they had any difference with; accounting it a very shameful and sinful thing to bear the least malice against any.[51]

And so it went on for almost 200 pages, an uneducated working man's evocation of what this wide world so far removed from Exeter had once offered him: the bright sashes of the whores in Egypt, the cheapness of fresh eggs in Cairo, the sweet taste of good camel meat, the whorls of henna that decorated the hands and feet of women. How, on hot North African nights, you could freshen your bed linen by sprinkling it with cold water and wake up baked dry again come morning. And, interspersed among all this, long passages of thick description, like the one quoted above, on the seriousness of Muslim devotion. By the end of his book, Pitts seems to have realised something of its likely effect on British readers, without however wanting to change it. He did his best to extract an

The various gestures of the Mahometans in their prayers to God.

22. Muslim devotion: an illustration in Joseph Pitts' narrative.

orthodox moral of a kind: 'If they [Muslims] are so strict in their false worship, it must need be a reprimand to Christians who are so remiss in the True,' but he also struggled to find some kind of closure that might connect and not thrust apart the Islamic and Christian phases of his life. 'O merciful God,' he ends, '. . . have mercy upon all Jews, Turks, infidels, and heretics . . . and so fetch them home.'[52]

Some two hundred years earlier, an Italian miller called Menocchio had taken a roughly similar line when dragged before the Inquisition, insisting that a merciful God would surely save heretics, Turks and Jews as well as Christians.[53] To a degree, Joseph Pitts was much the same sort of man as Menocchio, a poor, thoughtful, autodidact whose life had been harsh, and who had struggled through to his own conclusions about important things. There was a vital difference however in the respective fates of these two extraordinary plebeians. Menocchio was burnt at the stake as a heretic for his ideas. By contrast, the book in which Pitts set out his personal cosmology was well received and regularly reprinted. In eighteenth-century Britain – and in nineteenth-century Britain – expressing sympathy for elements of Islam, and suggesting that it was a superior faith to Roman Catholicism, did not necessarily set you apart, still less invite fierce persecution. At all social levels, there were Britons who believed – as Pitts did – that the Crescent was far less alien and dangerous than the Cross on a Catholic's rosary.

Transitions?

So when, and to what extent, did all this richness and variety of response begin to change and harden? I have argued that Britain's disdain for Islam and the Eastern, which some have viewed as a vital motor for its subsequent rampant imperialism, was – before 1750 especially – more apparent, noisy, and ritualistic, than profound and formative. Islamic regimes were viciously othered at times, in speech, in texts, in art, and in government pronouncements, but the accusations and language levelled against them were very similar to those used against European Roman Catholic regimes. And hostility towards the Crescent always coexisted with very different trends and tendencies. Islam was certainly rated lower than Protestant Christianity (though not by all Britons), but it was also treated respectfully and even with awe in both polite and popular writings. Muslims' capacity for advanced civilisation was explicitly conceded, and their racial and physical similarities to Europeans often openly canvassed.

As far as relations with the Islamic powers of the Mediterranean were concerned, the British sense of difference and superiority – though present – was frequently offset by other considerations. It was offset by the power of the Ottoman empire, which long overshadowed Britain's own, and by the depredations of the Barbary corsairs. It was offset, too, by the constraints on Britain's military and naval power in this region, and by its need for North African aid to retain its white colonies in this sea among the lands, Gibraltar and Minorca. But, as the multiple testimonies of British actors caught up in the Mediterranean zone document, the sense of difference vis-à-vis Islam was also offset and problematised by divisions within the British state itself. Until Britain could become more assured of its working unity and its own stability – and less conscious of its inhibiting smallness – its capacity for real, as distinct from assumed arrogance towards other regimes, and its capacity for successful imperial aggression had marked limits.

Yet by the 1750s, circumstances were changing. The failure of the 1745–6 Jacobite rebellion marked the end – for well over two hundred years at least – of the spectre of Scotland and its precious manpower breaking away from the British Union. More significantly still, the destruction of Jacobitism ended forever fears of a takeover of the British throne by a Roman Catholic dynasty by force of arms, and this helped to smooth over the fierce divisions between Protestant and Catholic within the British state. These domestic resolutions, and the increased stability and internal cohesion they afforded, helped power the conspicuous take-off in British imperial enterprise in the second half of the eighteenth century. As always, the trajectory of British empire overseas has to be understood in connection with British internal developments, and *vice versa*. In the Mediterranean, as elsewhere, this heightened British power and imperial activism after the mid-eighteenth century showed itself in an increase in soldiers, ships, sieges and battles. Yet as far as the Islamic societies of this region were concerned, Britain's escalating imperial aggression after 1750 remained tempered and qualified in all sorts of ways. Looking through the highly specific but powerful lens offered by captivity and its writings helps to clarify why this was so.

Enter Captain Hyde Parker, RN, young, brave, fundamentally unintelligent and, tellingly, a man in uniform. He was dispatched in the spring of 1756 to negotiate a treaty with Morocco and to recover any British captives remaining there. Sidi Muhammad, the acting ruler and future Sultan, had asked that a British consul fluent in Arabic be based permanently in his country, and expected as well a substantial gift of naval stores. Parker had been instructed to reject both of these Moroccan demands, and was anyway a man tightly corseted in his belief in 'the providence of God and the terror of His Majesty's naval power'. Accordingly, the naval officer removed neither his tricorne hat nor his heavy boots on entering Sidi Muhammad's palace, and made a point of sitting down firmly in the latter's presence, thereby insulting him both as a ruler and as a lineal descendant of the Prophet. Parker and his crew managed to escape the resulting explosion of princely anger, but others of their compatriots did not. Morocco, like the rest of Barbary, had taken few British captives since 1735, bought off in its case by over £60,000 of protection money. Now, Sidi Muhammad reversed this policy of profitable restraint, and by 1758 had secured almost 400 British captives.[54]

This provoked the last substantial cache of British writings about captivity in North Africa, and one of the few full-length Barbary narratives written and published by a woman. Its author was Elizabeth Marsh, the daughter of a British naval dockyard official based in Gibraltar (again, note the heightened presence in the Mediterranean by this stage of agents of a more strongly armed and extrovert British state). Marsh and her fellow passengers were seized off the coast of North Africa by Moroccan corsairs in August 1756, and held captive in Salé and Marrakesh until late that year in retaliation for Captain Hyde Parker's diplomatic deficit. An enthusiastic though strictly amateur writer, Marsh went on to draft several versions of what had happened to her. Initially the plot-line she selected was stark and traditional. She presented herself overwhelmingly as a victim of Islam's historic antipathy and aggression towards the Christian West, even quoting from a popular play about the crusades, John Hughes's *Siege of Damascus*:

> Now in the name of Heav'n, what faith is this
> That stalks gigantick forth thus arm'd with terrors
> As if it meant to ruin, not to save?
> That leads embattel'd legions to the Field,
> And marks its progress out with blood and slaughter.[55]

In the immediate aftermath of her 1756 captivity, Barbary still signified for Marsh – as it had for many other Britons before her – terror, danger, and the alarming shadow of the Crescent.

By the time she came to publish her narrative as *The Female Captive* in 1769, however, her chosen emphasis and mode of writing had both shifted. In this two-volume work, completed more than a decade after her capture, Marsh omitted virtually all references to religious conflict between Christianity and Islam. She left out, too, much of the information she had garnered on North African topography and society, and on the complex inter-relationships that actually existed in Morocco between individual Europeans and Muslims. Traditional prejudice against Islam and close, empirical observation were alike downplayed. Instead, Marsh converted her captive experiences into high drama and romance. She claimed that, from the very beginning of her enforced residence in Morocco, she had trembled for her sexual virtue, and that these fears had reached their culmination in two interviews with Sidi Muhammad himself.

> The Prince was tall, finely shaped, of a good complexion, and appeared to be about five and twenty . . . His figure, all together, was rather agreeable, and his address polite and easy.

This eligible creature ('I was amazed at the elegant figure he made') tried to persuade her to join him in the splendours of his Marrakesh palace. As a result, Marsh wrote, she was forced to lie. She assured Sidi Muhammad that she was married in fact, and that she preferred this equal relationship with a man of her own kind to all the poisoned luxuries of the seraglio. She resisted the prince's subsequent anger as stoutly as his appeals, refused to convert to Islam, and at last obtained her release. 'The Prince, being asked if he would not see the fair Christian before her departure, after a pause, replied, *"No, lest I should be obliged to detain her."*[56]

Elizabeth Marsh was twenty-one and emphatically single when these Marrakesh encounters reportedly occurred, and Sidi Muhammad was indeed about five and twenty. If some version of them really did take place, there may have been a frisson of excitement on his part – and also on hers. It bears repeating, though, that the preliminary drafts of Marsh's narrative, composed soon after her capture, made less of the theme of sexual danger in general, and of these palace show-downs in particular. Nor does any of the considerable official British correspondence on Marsh's confinement in Morocco in 1756 raise the possibility of her virtue being at risk, or of her being swept into a harem. Some female British and Irish captives of Barbary had in the past disappeared into North African private and royal households, but such unfortunates had rarely been women of Marsh's comfortable social status, and there are no known examples of British women of any kind suffering this fate after the 1720s.[57] It seems likely, therefore, that Elizabeth Marsh's belated decision to give prominence in *The Female Captive* to issues of sexual danger and virile, importunate sultans stemmed from something more than just remembered terrors, or even the simple desire to write a quasi-novel and sell copy.

Representing Barbary as a place of sexual threat for captive British women had been unusual up to this point. Indeed, the experiences of British women in North Africa in general had rarely been touched on in any detail. Female captives in the North African powers were of course always very much a minority. None the less, they were sufficiently a presence over the years for dry, government documents regularly to make mention of them. Popular English writings in the seventeenth and earlier eighteenth centuries, by contrast, barely refer to women captives from these islands at all. Elizabeth Marsh's 1769 volumes were the first female Barbary captivity narrative to appear in Britain. There seem to be no popular ballads about British female Barbary captives; and British men's captivity narratives rarely discuss female experiences, even when the writers make it clear that women were taken alongside them. Instead, British captivity literature had traditionally been far more concerned to stress the sexual threat to male captives in Barbary. For every single reference to heterosexual sex I have seen in British discussions of Barbary and Ottoman captivity before 1750, there are at least five to sodomy: and this is true of polite as well as popular literature, public statements and the most private of writings.

The notion found its way into petitions. 'The said [Algerian] patrons' some captives' wives had complained in the 1670s, 'do frequently bugger the said captives, or most of them'. It was the stuff of parliamentary speeches. Algerian captivity, an MP had told the House of Commons in 1614, meant 'children taken, kept for buggery and made Turks'.[58] It informed diplomats' reactions to North African missions. The journal of Thomas Baker, England's consul in Tripoli after 1677, remarks its editor, is obsessed with 'homosexuality, which according to him, was quite acceptable in Tripoli, with homosexual rape . . . openly and violently practised'. Naturally the claim surfaced in captivity narratives. 'They are said to commit sodomy with all creatures,' wrote Francis Knight of his Algerian captors in 1640.[59] But it could equally well be found in more substantial texts, like Paul Rycaut's famous *Present State of the Ottoman Empire* (1668), where the Ottoman world's very need to import Christian captives from without was put down to its own internal failure to reproduce because of 'that abominable vice of sodomy'. And it circulated in all kinds of imaginary literature. Robinson Crusoe himself is kept as a slave by the Moroccan corsair who captures him because he is 'young and nimble, and fit for his business'. Defoe supplies his more sophisticated readers with ample clues as to just what this business is. The corsair's ship, Crusoe tells us, contains a 'cabin, which lay very snug and low, and had in it room for him to lie, with a slave or two'. The *double entendres* fairly jostle each other. William Chetwode's novel *The Voyages and Adventures of Captain Robert Boyle* (1726), reissued a dozen times over the century, dispensed with such wordplay. Sodomy, a Moroccan bluntly informs the properly appalled captive British hero, 'is so common here that 'tis reckon'd only a piece of gallantry'.[60]

For my purposes, it is immaterial how valid such accusations were.[61] Most of those who accused North African and Ottoman males of sodomy were not anyway seriously interested in delineating the sexuality of those they were denouncing. Nor were they using accusations of homosexuality merely as a way of 'othering' Islam and its adherents. Sodomy in the context of writings on Barbary and the Ottoman world before 1750 was rather a metaphor, a particularly acute expression of the fear and insecurity that Britons and other Western Europeans continued to feel in the face of Islamic power and, as they saw it, aggression. The claim sometimes made, that the West eroticised the Islamic world in order to feminise and dominate it, is therefore, as far as this portion of it is concerned, suspect. Indeed the claim can be reversed. Those who accused Muslims of sodomy in the context of discussions of corsairing and captivities were rarely primarily concerned with whether North African and Ottoman males allowed themselves to be sodomised. Rather, the burden of these expressed anxieties, was that captive British and other European males were the potential victims. It was *they* who might be penetrated and invaded. *They* who might be forced into the passive role. Accusing the Barbary powers, and the Ottoman empire in general, of practising sodomy on Christian captives was yet another way in which Britons gave vent to their insecurities and to ancient fears that Islam might in the end use its strength to reduce them to submission.

Only when Ottoman and North African power were broadly recognised as receding, did such accusations of sodomy become thoroughly drowned out by an emphasis instead on the supposed heterosexual lusts of Muslim men and on their harems of docile, scented females. Claiming that Turks, or Moroccans, or Algerians collected and domineered over sexually pliant women, both entrapped Europeans and non-Europeans, was a way also of saying that these peoples were no longer in a position seriously to threaten European males. This is the broader significance of Elizabeth Marsh's strange two-volume captivity narrative. Even more than Captain Hyde Parker's deliberate rudeness to the ruler of Morocco in 1756, it marks an important shift – though only a partial shift – in British perceptions and assumptions. For by the time *The Female Captive* was published, in 1769, global power relations had changed radically, and were still changing fast.

The Seven Years War, which began in the year of Elizabeth Marsh's capture, 1756, and ended in 1763, transformed global politics. Not only did Britain consolidate its position in North America through its conquest of Canada, but for the first time ever it also launched a major and successful military assault on territory governed by Islamic rulers by winning and retaining Bengal. The ghost of the fiasco at Tangier was finally laid, and from now on one of the world's great Islamic empires, Mughal India, would come under serious and escalating British pressure. By the time Elizabeth Marsh published, another Islamic empire was also coming under unparalleled European pressure. The Russo-Turkish Wars, which began in 1768, proved disastrous for the Ottoman empire and confirmed Western Europe's sense that this prime representative of Islam was fast becoming a rusting, antique titan. Confections full of scantily clad harems, Christian damsels in distress, and masterful and strangely attractive Sultans had circulated in Britain as elsewhere in Europe for some time. But, from the 1760s, this sort of 'oriental' literature and art, of which Elizabeth Marsh's *The Female Captive* was a minor example, became conspicuously more prolific, and more easily accepted, because the Islamic world was now seen to be losing much of its power to frighten.[62] References to the threat from Muslim sodomy receded, along with British and European fears of penetration from without. The preferred story-line was now more likely to be that which Mozart selected for his opera about captives, *The Abduction from the Seraglio* (1782), plucky English blondes resisting overweening sultans (had the composer read Miss Marsh?), titillation rather than terror.

In retrospect, then, *The Female Captive*, can be situated on the cusp of what would prove to be a long drawn-out, and never complete, shift away from residual British apprehension and awe of Islam to low regard for, and condescension towards at least some of the states associated with it. In Elizabeth Marsh's strictly amateur production, Morocco is indubitably orientalised, exoticised and downgraded. But all this said, the relationship between British literary and artistic representations of Islam on the one hand, and British coercive power and colonial intent on the other, was not a straightforward one even after 1750, any more than it had been before. It is certainly possible to discern changes in tone in British commentary on Islamic societies in the Mediterranean zone and elsewhere after the 1750s, and of course a quantum leap in British global power. But these shifts were not – repeat not – accompanied by a marked and immediate upsurge in British physical coercion and colonial power in the North African and Ottoman regions.

This point is crisply underlined by the quality of Britain's response to Sidi Muhammad's furious burst of captive-taking after 1756, or rather by the lack of it. No eighteenth-century precursors of gunboats were dispatched to punish the Moroccan ruler and force him back in line, and this was not simply because of the logistical difficulties involved in taking offensive action against the North African coastline. The British simply had no wish to employ force in this direction, and could not afford to do so. William Pitt, soon to be styled 'The Patriot Minister' for his warlike endeavours and public spirit, emphatically did not want to bluster or fight in this part of the Mediterranean world. Instead, he apologised to Sidi Muhammad for Captain Hyde Parker's atrocious manners, and quietly paid out 200,000 Spanish dollars in ransoms for the hundreds of British captives now detained in Morocco. Pitt also climbed down and agreed to station a British consul there. 'We have tested him and conversed with him,' wrote the sultan subsequently of this new official:

> At his appearance in our noble presence he addressed us politely and observed the courtesies incumbent upon him . . . It will not be unknown to you that you were servants of our noble ancestors and it was your

obligation to gladden us before any other nation. But then you fell back
. . . so that we became resentful of you. Despite this we have pardoned
you for the negligence emanating from you . . . and have returned to
peace with you.[63]

Sidi Muhammad dispatched this official communication to the elderly
George II in 1760, when British legions (and large numbers of non-British
auxiliaries) were conquering Canada, driving into Bengal, and helping
themselves to Caribbean islands like so many sugar lumps. Yet Britain's
monarch and its first minister still allowed themselves to be lectured to in
these unabashed terms by the ruler of Morocco, meekly complied with
his wishes, and paid up for the captives he had seized in a unilateral show
of force.

Nor was this at all surprising in the light of the distinctive politics and
practices of the Mediterranean zone, and the nature and familiar limitations of British power here. Britain's perceptions of Islam may have been
shifting by this stage, but it still relied on North African aid to hold its
vital Mediterranean colonies, Gibraltar and Minorca. Indeed, the temporary loss to France in 1756 of Minorca, made maintaining Gibraltar
even more essential. Neither Hyde Parker's stupidity, nor Sidi
Muhammad's retaliatory captive-taking, could be allowed to disrupt this
essential arrangement, especially since the British knew full well that if
they broke with the Barbary powers, the latter might commit themselves
entirely to France, the other prime contender for Mediterranean power.
North Africa could not be invaded, and neither could it be ignored. It
had to be negotiated with, and if need be appeased. After the 1750s, as
before, the British continued to do both.

This situation continued into the nineteenth century, and not simply
because of Britain's enduring need for supplies for its white Mediterranean
empire and ever-expanding Mediterranean fleet. Edward Said and others
are entirely right to stress the importance of investigating the minds and
myths of empire-makers, and not just their weaponry and economic
muscle. None the less, material factors did matter, and were bound to
matter; and in this zone the British capacity to deploy force, as well as its
will to do so, remained circumscribed. The most dramatic proof of this
lies, paradoxically, in an act of British aggression. In 1816, the Royal Navy
bombarded the city of Algiers from the sea in an attempt to put an end
to corsairing and white slavery. Large parts of the city were devastated,
but the corsairs soon returned to work, while Britain's naval casualties in
this action – as a proportion of the men involved – were heavier than at
the Battle of Trafalgar fighting the French and the Spanish. Britons might

23. Algiers, with its coastal defences and slaves: a British plan of 1776.

choose (or not) to effeminise and belittle the Islamic, but – as in this case – doing so did not necessarily help them to invade or defeat it. The British government understood this very well. It pointedly refused to listen to siren voices at home and abroad urging it to convert this naval assault on Algiers into full-scale military occupation and colonisation. But the enduring constraints on the British sense of the possible in this zone are perhaps best evoked by a single remark. The Turks, wrote a Major Lowe worriedly in 1801, were 'invariably men of large stature who appeared to look down on us'.[64] In the Mediterranean, at the start of the nineteenth century, the Crescent and its powerful rays could still seem far from eclipsed to a people even now conscious of their own modest, indigenous size.

Here, in North Africa, and still more in the Ottoman heartland, were boundaries which Britain, even at its most vigorous and vainglorious, was reluctant to cross, and ill-equipped to cross, a sector of the Islamic world which – for all its physical proximity to western Europe – refused for a long time to buckle. Here, too, writ large in this Mediterranean zone, but often passing unnoticed, are persistent reminders of the compromises and collusions that imperial appetite necessarily imposed on the British, a small people who could therefore be caught and caught out. There would be many other reminders of this combination of marked British aggression and inherent British vulnerability, in many other places.

For it is time to leave this sea between the lands and between competing faiths, and look instead across an ocean.

Much of this has been long forgotten.

Part Two

AMERICA
Captives and Embarrassments

FIVE

Different Americans, Different Britons

Looking beyond the Atlantic

The Native American crouching as if in ambush before the west front of St Paul's cathedral in London gazes stone-faced at the passers-by. Most are too intent on tourism or worship to glance in her direction, yet over the centuries the assemblage of statues of which she is a part has provoked individuals to anger and violence. In 1743, a reputed lunatic rudely divested Queen Anne of her orb and sceptre. In 1769, the sculptures were attacked again by a seaman from India, who interpreted them as an affront to his mother. Still more assaults followed, and in the 1880s the battered originals were replaced by the dim replicas existing today. Even they can arouse fury. The figure of Britannia was recently decapitated, while America has lost her bow, though her quiver of arrows remains. Behind some of these mutilations, in the more distant as in the recent past, may have been a half-conscious recognition that more is present here than just a jumble of royal and allegorical images, weighed down by fusty symbolism and the efforts of a second-rate sculptor. For this is quintessentially a monument about British power, and its extension by force and guile over other peoples.

The work of a Londoner called Francis Bird, the initial version was unveiled in readiness for a royal service of thanksgiving for the Treaty of Utrecht in 1713, the formal end of Britain's involvement in the War of Spanish Succession.[1] Imperially, there was a lot for its rulers, politicians and merchants to feel thankful for. The eleven-year-long conflict had gained them Minorca and Gibraltar in the Mediterranean, the right to ship black slaves to Spanish America, and additional territory in North America, Hudson Bay, Nova Scotia, and Newfoundland.[2] All this will have been in Bird's mind as he designed this, the first ever outdoor monument to connect Britain's monarchy explicitly with its extra-European empire. A somewhat stiff figure of Queen Anne, a deeply religious woman, whose back – as the wits commented at the time – is none the less turned uncompromisingly towards Christopher Wren's ecclesiastical masterpiece, surmounts four baroque statues each commemorating one of the

24. Francis Bird's Indian, Queen Anne statue, St Paul's Cathedral.

dominions claimed by her. There is Britannia. There is Hibernia or Ireland who is equipped with a harp. France is represented here too, since on paper it was still part of the British monarchy's inheritance. The fourth figure symbolises America. She is also what white people in Bird's era and long after commonly referred to as an Indian.

As such, she conveys ambivalence but also something more. Bird has given her the same classical features as her sister statues, but has also placed beneath one of her feet the severed head of a white male captive. Bare-breasted, such costume as she possesses is wildly inaccurate. Hers is the feathered skirt and straight-up feathered headdress once characteristic of the Tupinamba Indians of Brazil. Possessed of the notion that all Indians, whether South or North American, must somehow look the same, European artists had been portraying them in this fashion since Portugal's conquests in the New World in the sixteenth century. But it is this figure's inclusion and role in Bird's design that are striking and deserving of notice. Superficially, she is merely subordinate, trapped underfoot by a victorious British monarch. Yet she is also indispensable, for without her sculptural support, the figure of Anne could not remain standing in its elevated position.

25. The severed head of a captive: detail from Francis Bird's Indian.

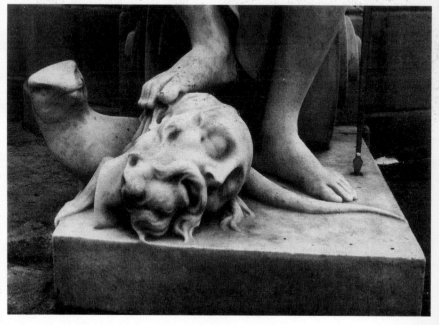

And while Bird's vision of a Native American was distorted by ignorance and prejudice, in one sense at least he got it absolutely right. From the beginnings of settlement through to the Revolution of 1776 and beyond, the people called Indians were integral to how men and women in early modern Britain perceived that part of their empire that was America.

This essential fact has not always been evident from the history books. Until recently, most writers on Britain's empire in North America – particularly on the British side of the Atlantic – tended to leave out indigenous peoples altogether. Even now, the latter are often ghettoised.[3] They may be allocated a token chapter or two, but they can still appear marginal to the famous and familiar saga of how English, and ultimately Welsh, Scottish and Irish emigrants established themselves successfully on the eastern coastline of North America from the early 1600s onwards; and of how these incoming peoples continued for one and three-quarter centuries to share a monarch, language, secular culture, political ideologies, Protestantism, and abundant trade with their counterparts back in Britain, only for the majority of them to go their separate ways after 1775 in a revolution which also partook to some degree of a civil war. Yet different groups of Native Americans were tightly enmeshed within, and crucial to, the evolution of this story throughout, and so were different kinds of captivity.

This latter point, too, is usually missing from the history books. There has been a long tradition in the United States of scholarly and popular interest in the capture of whites over the centuries by Native Americans (though only recently a recognition of the degree to which whites in colonial America and the young Republic also captured and enslaved Indians), and this has been immeasurably deepened by the emergence of a more anthropologically, archaeologically and politically sensitive New Indian History.[4] But even this new work has tended to remain determinedly inward-looking. Indian captivities are still overwhelmingly scanned for the light they can throw on the evolution of *American* national identities and cultures, while the narratives produced by one-time captive whites are still normally approached as a uniquely American mode of writing.

It should now be clear that they were not. The 400,000 or so men and women from Scotland, Ireland, Wales and above all England who crossed the Atlantic in the course of the seventeenth century, almost certainly took with them – along with so much else – a knowledge of the kinds of stories related by and about those of their countrymen who were captured by the powers of Barbary and Islam. These stories of capture by the forces of the Crescent were then adapted to a new American environment and to very different dangers. The very first account of an Englishman held captive by Native Americans to become a publishing success in London, John Smith's famous description of his seizure in Virginia by the forces of Powhatan, and of his subsequent 'rescue' by Powhatan's daughter Pocahontas, was indeed the work of a man previously captured while fighting against Ottoman armies and sold as a slave in Constantinople.[5] As this suggests, Indian captivities in early modern America, and the stories they gave rise to, need examining through more than just a parochial and national lens. Above all, they need situating in a transatlantic and in an imperial context.

Throughout the seventeenth century, and for most of the eighteenth century, white captive bodies in North America were, among many other things, emblems of Britain's imperial ordeal as well as symptoms of the limits of its imperial reach, its besetting, anxiety-making smallness. In the American colonies, as in other zones of Britain's imperial enterprise, the bodies of its people held captive and in terror focused attention on and prompted discussion about much broader constraints, embarrassments and fears. This was the case despite the fact that the initial captors involved in this zone of imperial enterprise – Native Americans – were in some respects peoples in retreat, rolled back and diminished by the spread of British empire, even as they seemed to threaten it.

Taking captive

To begin with, relations between English incomers in mainland North America and its indigenous peoples were complex, mutually uncomprehending, but by no means automatically hostile.[6] The earliest settlers in Virginia and New England were necessarily highly dependent on local Indians for food and for advice on how to grow it, for trade, and for guidance on survival techniques in a new land. They were also initially small in number by comparison with their Indian neighbours. The famous story (at least in the United States) of Tomocomo, Pocahontas's brother-in-law, accompanying her to England in 1616, and bringing with him a 'long stick, whereon by notches he did think to have kept the number of all the men he could see', may be more than just a condescending fiction. As Tomocomo would have known, whites in Virginia at this time were still painfully thin on the ground. There would have been no way for people like him to foresee that the original homeland of these sparse, disruptive and hairy intruders would be any more populous, nor could English settlers themselves have foreseen at this stage that their numbers would burgeon at the rapid rate that they later did. Even in 1630, there were probably fewer than 10,000 English men and women scattered along the eastern shores of North America.[7]

Since they themselves were initially so small in number, and Native Americans had to be taken seriously, the English reacted to them as they nearly always did to overseas peoples. They did not simply 'other' them, but rather looked for and invented points of similarity and contact. They scanned Native American faces and bodies, and saw them – not as red or even tawny at this stage – but as almost as pale-skinned as themselves. They took note of the rituals and ornate possessions surrounding sachems or chiefs, and concluded that these individuals must be 'kings' or 'queens' or aristocratic hunter-warriors. That such wilderness patricians were surrounded by multitudes of lesser, unruly folk seemed only to mirror still further the scheme of things that the English were used to back home. 'You may save your labour if you please', wrote the poet Michael Drayton from London to a friend in Virginia in 1622:

> To write me ought of your savages,
> As savage slaves be in Great Britain here,
> As any one that you can shew me there.[8]

Because Indians were deemed rudely similar, and Indian chiefs incontestably more important than England's own impoverished multitudes, this emphatically did not mean that Indian modes of society and culture were viewed as being – in their current state – of equal worth. The perception of them as heathens, as stateless, and as nomadic precluded that. 'Bestow small crowns or coronets', the King of England, Charles II, was advised in 1677 in relation to some Indian 'kings' who needed wooing: '. . . to be made of thin silver plate, gilt, and adorned with false stones'.[9] The calibration of human significance in terms of glitter is precise. Indians, even their leaders, were not, in this view, people deserving of gold, silver and precious jewels. They could properly be fobbed off with plate, gilt and paste. Yet, for all that, these individuals were still to be crowned: still to be brought at some level within the English and European system of doing things. For their own self-interested reasons, but also sometimes for other reasons, this would always be the strategy favoured by governments in London and by the generality of royal officials in North America. As far as the men and women from Britain who settled here were concerned, however, an initial desire to improve and in some measure to incorporate the Indian easily came to be at odds with other imperatives, and was increasingly overborne by them. The urge to redeem and bring civility to the Indian retreated – albeit unevenly and at different rates in different regions of America – before the settlers' swiftly growing numbers and appetite for land. It faded too before the convenient discovery that Indians were people who could be surprisingly easy to kill.

Historians sometimes claim that, as relations began to sour, English settlers employed unusually lethal styles of warfare against Native Americans because they viewed them as inferior.[10] In fact, the intensity of these struggles proved deadly – and initially impossible for Indians to comprehend – precisely because the English made use of the same brutal strategies in North America as they and other Europeans routinely deployed against each other in their home continent. Thus Captain John Underhill's infamous massacre of Pequot men, women and children near the Mystic River, Connecticut, in 1637 has often been cited as exemplifying the settlers' peculiar bloodthirstiness in the face of Indian opponents. But this act of slaughter needs setting against the contemporaneous Thirty Years War in Europe, which annihilated perhaps a third of the population of the German states, including vast numbers of non-combatants. By the same token, what became a widespread practice of seizing defeated Indians, and selling them as slaves to the West Indies, represented an extension to North America of a penalty often employed against rebels within England itself. Oliver Cromwell enslaved hundreds of defeated Scots in the 1650s, dispatching them, too, to the West Indies. Those English West Country supporters of Monmouth's rebellion in 1685 who were not summarily executed experienced a similar fate. What was distinctive about English settler assaults on Native Americans as time went on was less the degree of violence employed, than the fact that it was not confined – as usually in Europe – to discrete periods of open, declared warfare or rebellion. There was another, far more conclusive characteristic of cross-cultural warfare here. English and other European emigrants to North America had unknowingly brought with them invincible storm troops, their own teeming microbes.

The full extent of the destruction these caused will never be known with any precision. There is no consensus even about the scale of North America's pre-contact indigenous population. Estimates range between two and eighteen million.[11] It is clear too that in some regions, the invisible immigrants of smallpox, diphtheria, influenza, cholera, measles and the like, against which Indians possessed no immunity, had only a blunted or very belated effect. In others, however, Indian communities exposed to these diseases – as well as to white settler violence – experienced mortality rates as high as 70, even 90 per cent. Nine out of every ten New England Indians seem to have died from the effects of European diseases in just the dozen years between 1608 and 1620; the 10,000 Indians still alive in *each* of the Carolinas in 1685 had been pared down to only 8000 in total by 1715.[12] English, Scottish, Welsh and Irish incomers quickly came to recognise, although they did not comprehend why, that death and disease haunted

Indian settlements, while ever more impressive rates of fecundity, far higher than in the islands they had left behind them, came to grace their own.

The quality of the challenge posed to incoming whites by indigenous peoples in America – and consequently the quality of captivity panics here – was therefore very different from that in the other geographical zones explored in this book. In the Mediterranean region, and in South Asia, early modern Britons confronted societies that were partly urbanised like their own, and frequently far more populous and demographically buoyant. In these areas, large-scale English and British settlement either proved impossible (as at Tangier), or was never viewed as a feasible option in the first place (as in India). Accordingly, in the Mediterranean and Asia, the British intruded mainly as traders, soldiers, sailors, administrators and the like, but their overall numbers remained limited, often perilously so. In North America (as in Britain's Pacific colonies much later), it was altogether different. On the one hand, the English came here from the start with the definite intention of settling, and high birth-rates as well as migration subsequently boosted their numbers to more than 260,000 by 1700, and over a million by 1750. On the other hand, North America's own first peoples proved an ever more diminishing asset. None of this prevented various Indian groupings from launching attacks on the English, or from taking them captive, however, for it was often precisely these acute pressures on their numbers and increasing white incursions into their lands that impelled them to action.

Native Americans could not stem the flood of white incomers who multiplied at such a staggering rate, but they did strike back as well as try to secure some advantage from them. The potential for Indian anger to express itself in large-scale violence appeared early. In 1622, local Indians almost succeeded in wiping out the white settlement in Virginia. The conflict known as King Philip's or Metacom's war in southern New England (1675–6) eventually resulted in the destruction of effective Algonquian resistance to white expansion here, but in the process, about 10 per cent of the white colonists involved were killed, and an estimated 12,000 buildings and 8000 cattle were destroyed. In terms of mortality rates as a proportion of population, this was the most lethal war in American history.[13] The Yamasee War in South Carolina in 1715 was at times almost as intense. It forced a sixth of the colony's white males to take up arms, and killed about 7 per cent of the province's 6000 European inhabitants. In addition to these fierce, set-piece conflicts, there was also a perennial, even a daily risk of skirmish, ambush and slaughter for whites, and of course for Indians, in more exposed settlements. 'Every week, some or other is taken captive or killed,' complained the Lieutenant Governor of New Hampshire to London in 1724: 'so that your Lordships may judge how we are wasting.'[14]

To Britons on both sides of the Atlantic, but particularly to those directly affected, the forms of Indian violence easily seemed anarchic and mindlessly cruel, the mark of the savage. Cruel it was, as war always is: but it was less mindless than a message written in blood and flame and destruction of the nature of Indian grievances. When Indians slaughtered and maimed the white man's cattle, horses and pigs, they were also attacking his animal husbandry practices which consumed so much land, and stole pasturage from the wild animals they depended on for food.[15] When they stripped white captives naked and forced them to cover their genitals with pages ripped out of the Bible, they were making clear their opinion of Christianity, and of the white clergymen who sought to impose it on Indian bodies and souls. And when they raided colonial settlements, and systematically killed babies and infant children, as they sometimes did, this was perhaps a conscious strike at these invaders' capacity to reproduce themselves so abundantly, and in revenge for their own lost children.[16] In the same way, Indian captive-taking was rarely a random business, though it was never as overwhelmingly money-oriented as Barbary corsairing gradually came to be.

Indians did sometimes make use of British and other captives to extort ransoms. They also sold them on occasions for cash or kind to representatives of rival empires in America, to the French or Spanish.[17] But white captives might also be employed as slaves. Or they might – particularly if they were adult males taken in combat – be tortured to death, sometimes over many days, in order to appease the spirits of their captors' own dead or their grieving womenfolk. This was the fate of Thomas Nairne, a British Indian agent in Carolina. A man who had lived with the Chickasaws for several years and admired them, he was captured on the first day of the Yamasee war in 1715 and burnt at the stake, very slowly.[18] By contrast, some captives, particularly women and the healthy and malleable young, were adopted by and absorbed into Indian communities as a way of compensating for the losses they had sustained from disease and war. An awareness that white children could become targets for adoption in this way lies behind the most anguished passages in Jonathan Dickenson's *God's Protecting Providence, Man's Surest Help and Defence* (1700), one of the very few American captivity narratives to be a runaway publishing success in Britain before 1750.

Dickenson, his wife Mary, and their six-month-old baby son, were shipwrecked off the coast of Florida in 1696 while on a voyage from Jamaica to Pennsylvania. Together with the rest of the survivors, they were seized by a party of local Indians, and to the Dickensons' initial horror one of the women (whom they decided must be a chief's wife) insisted on holding and suckling their child, and 'viewing and feeling it from top to toe'. This happened first on 25 September. By the time another week had passed, the Dickensons had shifted to feeling profound relief whenever this same woman took an identical interest in their child, because:

> Its mother's milk was almost gone . . . And our child, which had been at death's door, from the time of its birth, until we were cast away, began now to be cheerful and have an appetite to food.

After another week had passed, the couple were actually 'begging' the woman (whose name we never learn) to feed their baby. By now, they themselves were having to subsist on the 'gills and guts of fish . . . and the water they [the Indians] boiled their fish in', and Mrs Dickenson was too malnourished, and too fatigued and frightened with the effort of keeping up with her captors, to be able to produce any milk of her own.[19]

Yet, in the days immediately before they were rescued by some Spanish soldiers based at St Augustine, the Dickensons' attitude to this woman who was bestowing such charity on them shifted once again. They continued to draw comfort from the restored health of their child, chubby and contented now on its borrowed milk, but only up to a point:

> One thing did seem more grievous to me and my wife, than any other thing; which was, that if it should so happen, that we should be put to death, we feared that our child would be kept alive, and bred up as one of those people: when these thoughts did arise, it wounded us deep.

What if the woman who so eagerly suckled their child were to become in time and in name its mother, and the child itself were to be reborn, as it were, as an Indian: no longer a Christian, no longer English, and no longer theirs? As this private captivity crisis suggests, whites who were seized in North America had to confront the possibility – to a greater degree than in the other zones of empire examined in this book – that they or their children might be coerced or coaxed into becoming something else.

To be sure, Indians sometimes made a point of selling Anglophone captives to those other Europeans who were contending for America, to the French authorities in Canada, or the Spanish in Florida, New Mexico, and Pensacola: but to ardent Protestants this fate could seem just as alarming as enforced or self-willed residence among Indians. Having been purchased from their captors, and brought to St Augustine late in 1696, the Dickensons encountered there a man called William Carr, a native of Ely in East Anglia. He had been shipwrecked in Florida *en route* to South Carolina back in the 1660s, lived as a captive among the local Indians for some years, and was then sold to the Spanish. Carr himself appeared contented enough with his situation. He had long since converted to Catholicism, married a Spanish woman, produced seven children, and was now gainfully employed as an interpreter, making full use of the many languages his disparate life had allowed him to acquire. But the Dickensons still shuddered whenever they saw him. What of Carr's English, Protestant soul? What of that?[20]

Ascertaining precisely how many English, Welsh, Scottish and Irish settlers, soldiers, and officials were made captives by Indians in North America during the colonial period is no easier than calculating the exact total of British captives of Barbary. But, once again, the numbers were substantial, and they remained so throughout. We know something of what happened, for instance, to over 1600 New Englanders who were seized by Indians and taken to New France between the mid-seventeenth century and 1763.[21] Fewer than half of these people seem to have returned home. Almost one in ten of the males involved, and close to a third of the females, opted or were compelled to stay with their Indian captors, or more commonly with the French. Of those aged between seven and fifteen when captured, almost 50 per cent remained in their new surroundings. In many cases however, the ultimate fate of captives, and even their existence, went unreported, especially if they were taken from isolated farmsteads, or while travelling alone, or if they disappeared in the course of battle. Only by surveying a mixture of newspaper reports, archives, and captivity narratives has one historian been able to calculate that some 2700 whites were seized in Indian raids on the frontiers of Pennsylvania, Maryland and Virginia alone between 1755 and 1765.[22] This kind of heroic body-count has not been attempted for all of Britain's American colonies, and would not anyway be possible for much of the colonial period.

There is a sense also in which it scarcely matters, because those who had to contend with these captivity panics had no accurate grasp of the total numbers that were involved either. What mattered to them, as so often with such panics, was a dimensionless fear. 'Think upon the miserable captives now in the hands of that brutish adversary,' thundered Boston's most prominent clergyman, Cotton Mather, in 1691:

> *Captives* that are every minute looking when they shall be roasted alive, to make a sport and a feast, for the most execrable cannibals; *Captives*, that must endure the most bitter frost and cold, without rags enough to cover their nakedness; *Captives*, that have scarce a bit of meat allow'd them to put into their mouths, but what a dog would hardly meddle with; *Captives*, that must see their nearest relations butchered before their eyes, and yet be afraid of letting those eyes drop a tear.

Or as one female victim of sudden Indian attack and subsequent captivity put it, less rhetorically but more movingly: 'I can remember the time, when I used to sleep quietly . . . but now it is other ways.'[23] Here was yet another aspect of the imperial ordeal.

Except that, in a crucial respect, these captivities in North America challenged the British in a unique and distinctive way. Here – as in other zones of imperial invasion and enterprise – captives taken from their ranks acted as catalysts of wider anxieties. But white captivities in North America also functioned over the years as a sword dividing the different varieties of British.

Before 1776, the majority of white inhabitants of what became Britain's Thirteen Colonies in America did not view themselves exclusively or even primarily as Americans. In their own minds, they were English, and ultimately Britons, free subjects of the monarch in London, albeit subjects on another shore. As Cotton Mather insisted, New England was also 'a part of the English nation'.[24] Consequently, when men and women from amongst them were seized by Native Americans, American colonists viewed these emergencies in more than just local terms. To them, Indian captivity also seemed an affront to their identity as Englishmen and, in due course, as Britons. But, on the other side of the Atlantic, in Britain itself, it could be otherwise. Many of *its* inhabitants came – for a variety of reasons – to perceive Native Americans, and the dangers posed by them, differently from the colonists and to differing degrees.

Early American captivity narratives usually make abundantly clear their writers' sense of being part of a wider imperial whole. Consider the most famous of them, *The Sovereignty and Goodness of God . . . being a Narrative of the Captivity and Restoration of Mrs. Mary Rowlandson*, published both in Cambridge, Massachusetts, and in London in 1682, but probably written before 1678.[25] Rowlandson was taken captive in the early morning of 10 February 1676, in the course of Metacom's War. Three of her children were also seized, as were nineteen other inhabitants of the small town of Lancaster in Massachusetts. Because of the absurd convention whereby writings by men and women who left Britain for imperial locations drop out of the canon of 'English' literature, Rowlandson's account of her subsequent experiences living as a captive for three months among different groups of New England Indians, Nipmucs, Narragansetts and Wampanoags, remains little known within Britain. Yet, at one level, this is a narrative that is fixated on the bonds of Englishness. Rowlandson had been born in Somerset in the early 1630s, and her family, who were farmers, took part in the 'Great Migration' of English settlers to New England that decade. So did the family of the man who ultimately became her husband, Joseph Rowlandson, who was Puritan minister of Lancaster. For Mary

Rowlandson, though, 'England' was far more than just a shadowy, infant memory, a name for a now distant land. As she tells us repeatedly in her narrative, England, together with her Protestant God, were the totems to which she clung fast throughout her ordeal.

On the first night of her captive journey, weary with scrambling along with 'one poor wounded babe' in her arms (the child would shortly perish), she begged to be allowed to sleep in a farm that had been deserted in terror by its former English occupants. 'What', she claims her Native American captors replied, 'will you love English men still?', for their aim was to wean her from such attachments and make her one of them. All she could do in the days that followed was look for signposts to who she was in the landscape she was gradually being forced to abandon. She saw a place where 'English cattle' had been, and this was a 'comfort to me, such as it was'. When she came across an 'English path' – for settlers like her marked and organised the land in distinctive ways – she yearned to lie down and die there, almost as if she were another Eve reluctant to be driven out of Eden. And when a company of thirty horsemen suddenly appeared on the horizon, and rode towards the line of bedraggled prisoners 'in English apparel, with hats, white neckcloths, and sashes about their waists', her heart skipped with relief and delight, only to sink again. They turned out to be yet more New England Indians, got up in purchased or pillaged items of English Puritan costume.[26] It was the first of many lessons on the possible unreliability of markers of identity.

The ways in which references to England – and ultimately to Britain – served early American colonists as anchors amidst the shipwrecks of Indian captivity emerge from many other narratives. The printed account of John Gyles, who had been seized when he was just nine years old by Maliseet warriors in what is now Maine in 1689, begins with an almost elegiac reminder of his settlement's roots: 'Our people went to their labour, some in one field to their English hay, the others to another field of English corn.' He goes on to describe how his mother, who was also captured, murmured to him in what was almost their last meeting:

O, my child! How joyful and pleasant it would be, if we were going to Old England, to see your uncle Chalker, and other friends there.[27]

Forced, as were most individuals taken captive in North America, not into a confined space, but to undertake a long journey on foot across rough country, this woman's reaction was at once to comfort and torture herself. She travelled in her imagination, not through forest and undergrowth, but across the wide ocean itself to what once had been. In reality, there would be no such journey of return. Instead, what lay before mother and son was the tramp to French Canada, final separation and, for John Gyles himself, a six-year captivity with different Indian groups, and a further three years' service with a French master.

The extreme pathos of many of these early American captivity narratives was partly calculated. Describing in detail touching last interviews, the death agonies of captured infants, storms of women's grief, and the torments of memory, helped to lend colour and attract readers, especially in early colonial America where home-produced fiction and drama were still rare. The pathos of these captivity narratives also worked to sharpen the line between Anglo settlers and Native Americans, as Mary Rowlandson at least seems to have understood and wanted. But this marked sentiment was also a function of a distinctive facet of these North American captivities. As far as the British were concerned, Barbary captivity was a fate usually befalling working individuals and men. To a lesser degree, the same would also be true of pre-1850 British captivities in South Asia. But the various North American provinces were not places of work and warfare merely: they were settlement colonies. So captivity here regularly engulfed whole families, all age-groups, and large numbers of women as well as men. This influenced both the content and the style of the narratives that emerged from them. Mary Rowlandson's was not the first captivity narrative to be a publishing success in the Anglophone world, nor even the first Anglo account of Indian captivity. But it was the first narrative by a settler to become an American bestseller. As such, it influenced how later writers in North America, both female and male, expected to tell their captive stories. American-produced captivity narratives are arguably more feminised, and certainly more domestic and personal, than the generality of their North African and Asian counterparts.[28]

But the frequent, haunting allusions in these early American texts to things English or British were informed by more than private sentiment. For early settlers, as Jill Lepore argues, the idea of the 3000 miles now separating them from England was both liberating and worrying.[29] How, they wondered, were they to preserve their Englishness now that their original homeland was so distant, and other, very different and increasingly despised peoples were so perilously near? How were they to guard against the wilderness changing and corrupting what they were in essence? The experience and even the idea of captivity brought such insecurities quickly to the surface, because – as we have seen – it could lead to assimilation into Native American societies, or into rival, Catholic empires. 'I dreaded going to Canada, to the French, for fear lest I should be overcome by them, to yield to their religion,' wrote Hannah Swarton. She was captured by Abenaki Indians at Casco Bay, Maine, in May 1690, and held for over five years before being redeemed. Her husband, a native of Jersey and an English army veteran, was killed, as was her eldest son; two more of her children were never recovered from the Indians. It was in this context that insisting on her Englishness in her printed narrative appeared crucial. It testified to any doubters, and also to herself, that she had successfully preserved her national and religious identity. 'Came in two men', she recalled of one of her captive days in Canada, 'and one of them spake to me in English: I am glad to see you Countrywoman! This was exceedingly reviving, to hear the voice of an English man,' and so it was.[30]

Early American captivity narrators, then, dwelt on transatlantic ties. Out of loyalty, but also so as to reassure themselves and others, they insisted on their enduring Englishness, and all that this implied, and ultimately on their Britishness. So how were these particular captives' voices heard and reacted to within Britain itself? The answer, before 1750, is only intermittently.

This point can be easily made by looking at the publication histories of the narratives themselves. The first American edition of Mary Rowlandson's story sold out so quickly, and individual copies were passed around between so many people, that today no complete version survives, only a few stained and dog-eared pages. American-based printers brought out two more editions of the text in 1682, and yet another in 1720. But on the other side of the Atlantic the market was far less avid. The 1682 London edition of Rowlandson's tale appears to have been the only one published in Britain before 1900.

A similar pattern emerges in regard to other American captivity narratives. Some, such as John Gyles's belated publication of his experiences, which was published in Boston in 1736, were never issued in Britain at all. Others, such as the story of Elizabeth Hanson, who was captured in 1724 and held for five months, were published soon after the event in America, but had to wait until the second half of the century for a British edition, in this case until 1760. Such American captivity stories as did appear in London, or in provincial English, Scottish or Irish editions before 1750 were rarely commercial successes. In Boston in 1706, Cotton Mather published a highly influential omnibus of captive stories emerging from the colonists' involvement in what they called Queen Anne's War: *Good Fetched out of Evil: A Collection of Memorables relating to our Captives.* It sold 1000 copies in a week, this in a city of some 15,000 people. Again, its circulation was much wider than the sum of its purchasers. Individual copies of the work passed from hand to hand to such an extent that only four now survive. Yet this American bestseller seems never to have been issued in Britain at all.[31] Britons in the home country did have an opportunity to consult another of the prolific

Mather's collections of captivity stories, *Magnalia Christi Americana*, published in London in seven parts in 1702. But, as its format and latinate title suggest, this was an expensive book, take-up was slender, and no new edition ever proved necessary.[32]

In the early modern world, even more than now, publishers were not driven primarily by charity or idealism. Unless writers or subscribers could summon up sufficient resources to fund publication themselves, books were printed only if it was anticipated that they would sell. Manifestly, then, before 1750, printers and publishers in Britain reached the commercial decision that there was only limited domestic demand for tales of settler captivity at the hands of Native Americans, even though Britons in America and Britons at home were ostensibly one, united imperial people.

Why was this, and what does it tell us about the British empire in America at this stage?

Divisions

British domestic interest in and awareness of American captivity panics in the seventeenth and early eighteenth centuries were not limited because the colonial authorities themselves were unconcerned. As the superabundant archives of the Council (later the Board) of Trade and Plantations make clear, London regularly received information from officials and informants about the fate of North American captives, though such news only travelled as fast as a sailing ship could cross the Atlantic. Take the case of the famous attack on Deerfield. This settlement, which was situated on the furthest reaches of Massachusetts' north-western frontier, a short distance from the Connecticut River, had already been hit by Indians half a dozen times in the 1690s alone. But, on 29 February 1704, Abenaki warriors and their allies swept in again and killed forty-eight of Deerfield's 300 inhabitants, and captured 112 men, women and children. The news naturally took several months to reach London, and was not formally announced to Parliament until November. Ministers immediately authorised the dispatch of more firearms so that settlers and 'friendly Indians' in Massachusetts would be better able to defend themselves. When the Treaty of Utrecht was negotiated with France in 1712–13, British diplomats took care to include clauses demanding the return of all American colonists held captive in Canada, including any Deerfield victims still detained there. As late as 1721, British envoys in Paris were still putting pressure on French officials to organise the redemption of those few Deerfield captives who remained with Indian communities in Canada.[33]

In other words, politicians in London did all it was possible to do *indirectly and at an ocean's distance*. They read and digested the reports of the Deerfield 'massacre' dispatched by colonial officials and tormented eye-witnesses ('I shall give you an account of two young men who suffered the cruellest death that ever was thought of').[34] They shipped extra weapons over to America for the settlers to use. Their diplomats did what they could to put pressure on other European capitals to effect captive releases. But British-based politicians had neither the power nor the will at this stage to do much more. Nor was the bulk of their home population in a position to learn much about Deerfield, or the warfare in North America of which it formed only one incident. The major captivity narrative emerging from this disaster was a classic of its kind, *The Redeemed Captive Returning to Zion* written by John Williams, Minister of Deerfield. He lost his wife and two children in the 1704 attack and its aftermath, and subsequently had to wrestle with the grief and embarrassment of having another of his daughters, Eunice, both marry an Indian and turn Roman Catholic. Williams's 25,000-word story was published in Boston in 1707, and reprinted in America half a dozen times over the course of the century. It seems never to have been issued in Britain.

Some of the reasons for this limited British awareness of – and hence limited emotional involvement in – captivity panics in North America are clear enough. As John Elliott famously demonstrated, although the Spanish, Portuguese, French and English invasions of the Americas in the sixteenth and seventeenth centuries are in retrospect seminal episodes in global history, at the time many ordinary Europeans back home remained largely indifferent to these events. Even by the early eighteenth century, when Britain had evolved one of the most vibrant print cultures in the world, readers within its boundaries still found it easier and more to their taste to acquire books and in-depth newspaper reportage about domestic matters and about other European states, than copious, well-informed printed material about the colonies across the Atlantic.[35] Specific crises in North America could, to be sure, fire up British interest for a while. King Philip's War, for instance, led to the publication of at least fourteen narratives in London between 1675 and 1682, all of which had something to say about captivities; while the official broadsheet, the *London Gazette*, also printed several articles about the New England colonists' real and reputed sufferings. But, for most of the time, London's newspaper and book press devoted little sustained coverage to settler experiences in America, as distinct from details of transatlantic trade; while provincial publishers rarely tackled the subject before the 1740s.[36]

Uneven British coverage of American captivities prior to 1750 also reflected the fact that the mechanisms for responding to them differed significantly from those set up to cope with Barbary captive-taking. In the latter case, redemption money was raised time and time again by way of nationwide collections supervised by the churches, and this had the effect of informing English, Welsh, Scottish and Irish church-goers, whether they were literate or no, of the details of these captives' plight. Moreover, such collections occurred on both sides of the Atlantic. American colonial sailors and traders operating in the Mediterranean and Atlantic were regularly among the corsairs' victims. Cotton Mather, who built much of his ruthlessly successful clerical and publishing career on the backs of multifarious captives, devoted at least two sermons to the threat that Barbary and Islam represented to seamen in England and New England both.[37] Barbary captivity, in other words, was perceived and treated as an ordeal that Britons on both sides of the Atlantic had in common.

Indian captive-taking in North America was very different. Obviously, it never directly endangered men and women on the other side of the Atlantic. Nor did Indians always look to ransom their captives. When they did, the necessary cash seems generally to have been raised by the colonists themselves. The £20 needed to ransom Mary Rowlandson, for instance, came from a group of prosperous and devout Bostonians. There must have been some occasions when English, Welsh, Scottish and Irish individuals with kin in the colonies (and also Britain's dissenting churches), dispatched gifts in money and kind across the Atlantic to aid particular captives and their families. But no officially sponsored nationwide collection was ever organised in Britain or Ireland on behalf of settler victims of Native American captive-taking. Religious allegiances may have contributed to this failure. It was the Anglican Church that played the dominant role in synchronising relief for the Barbary captives, but most British settlers and captives in North America were not Anglicans, but Protestant dissenters. It seems very possible that one explanation for the limited take-up of early American captivity narratives within Britain itself was that – to mainstream Anglicans – the Puritan religiosity informing so many of these texts appeared alien and even uncongenial.[38]

Back in the early seventeenth century, an obscure Anglican clergymen had laboured to explain to his English provincial congregation why it was their duty to devote thought and charity to the victims of Barbary, confined and suffering so far from home. 'As for poor prisoners and captives', he told them:

> they (good souls) cannot come to us . . . Therefore it is our duty to visit them, either in person, if we may have access, or by provision, if we can send to them, or by prayers and supplications . . . *Make their bondage*

your thraldom, their suffering, your own smarting. Have a fellow-feeling with them, as being members of the same body.[39]

White settlers in British North America, and the inhabitants of the small islands three thousand miles away on the other side of the Atlantic, were by law and history members of the same imperial body, but before the mid-eighteenth century the captivities of the former did not – remotely as much as might have been expected – nurture fellow-feeling among the latter. This was not so much because men and women in Britain did not care, as because many of them never got to know, and could not properly understand.

Yet there was more behind the markedly different responses to Indian captivities on the two sides of the Atlantic than all this. There was also the matter of limited British imperial power, and – as always – limited British numbers.

From the very beginning, the role of the state in England's North American empire had been slender and enabling rather than interventionist. From Elizabeth I onwards, successive monarchs had authorised private investors to take the risk of establishing colonial outposts in America, and individual proprietors to claim title (on dubious legal grounds) to vast tracts of land there, and for a long time this was all. In some contrast to the Spanish monarchy's hands-on colonial policy in South America, England's rulers, in David Armitage's words, led 'from behind and allowed private enterprise to bear the burdens of conquest and settlement'.[40] One aspect of this cheap and indirect version of empire, was that London displayed only erratic enthusiasm for substantial military investment in its transatlantic colonies. The immediate consequences of this are writ large in early American captivity narratives. Contained within them are implicit (and sometimes explicit) criticisms of the imperial authorities' failure to defend settlers adequately against the threat of Indian and other attacks. Thus the preface to Mary Rowlandson's narrative attributes the Indians descending with such 'mighty force and fury upon Lancaster' to its 'not being garrisoned as it might'; while John Gyles reported that the Pemaquid settlement, in modern Maine, from which he was snatched in 1689, was defended only by an obsolete fort with just three cannon at its disposal and outworks barely nine foot high.[41] More dispassionate observers could be equally damning. When Colonel William Romer, the Crown's chief military engineer, toured New Jersey at the start of the eighteenth century, he found it 'without any forts, or places of defence'; such fortifications as existed in Pennsylvania and North and South Carolina appeared to his trained eyes scarcely more impressive.[42]

But Romer's survey of American defences signalled an important,

New France and the British Mainland Colonies in North America.

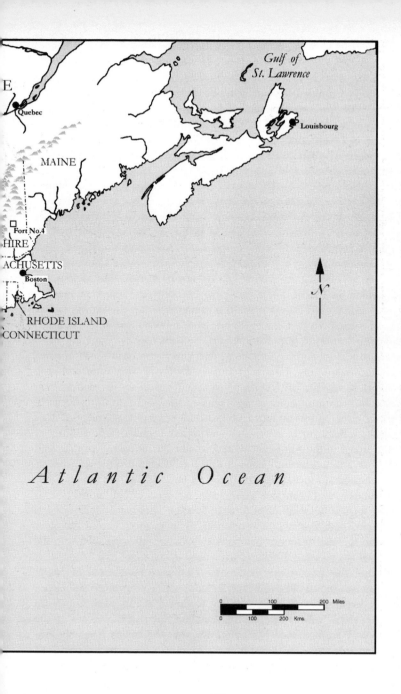

Gulf of
St. Lawrence

E

Quebec

Louisbourg

MAINE

Fort No.4

HIRE

ACHUSETTS

Boston

RHODE ISLAND

CONNECTICUT

N

Atlantic Ocean

| 0 | 100 | 200 Miles |
| 0 | 100 | 200 Kms. |

though partial, shift in imperial policy. England's 'Glorious' Revolution of 1688 replaced a Catholic king, James II, with the Protestant William III and his wife Mary; it also inaugurated a series of Anglo-French wars which increasingly exploded beyond Europe's own battlefields into these rival powers' extra-European colonies. As far as Anglo settlers in North America were concerned, the so-called King William's War (1689–97), would be followed by Queen Anne's War (1702–13), King George I's War (1722–4), King George II's War (1740–48); and then by two more conflicts, that were fought out between 1756 and 1763, and 1775 to 1783, on an altogether different and larger scale. These serial contests between Britain and France and their respective allies progressively transformed the quality and seriousness of warfare in North America – and also intensified the threat of captivity there. They also transformed British official attentiveness to its American colonies, but in one conspicuous respect only slowly.

Beyond doubt, there was growing acceptance that, as the Commissioners of Trade and Plantations reported to William III in 1701: 'His Majesty has a dominion [in America] of a very large extent, which, at present, requires a more special care.'[43] In practice, this meant more fact-finding missions of the sort carried out by Colonel Romer, more subsidies and arms exports to colonial governors to help them defend themselves against the French and their Indian allies, and very occasional direct interventions in North America by British state forces. Thus in 1711, over fifty Royal Navy ships and 8000 men joined varieties of American colonial troops in an invasion attempt against French Canada, an expensive venture that failed dismally. Indicatively, however, even this rare initiative was based on Britain's sea-power, not on its land forces. Before 1750, there was no attempt to maintain large numbers of British troops in the American colonies to take the offensive – or to defend them from attack. The distribution of British army units over the years underlines the point. In 1726, a year of peace on both sides of the Atlantic, only one battalion of British foot soldiers was stationed in North America, as against seven in Minorca and Gibraltar. By 1742, when war with France was threatening both Britain and its colonists, the number of Crown battalions stationed in North America had risen to two, but this contrasted with the ten battalions guarding Britain's Mediterranean colonies.[44]

Behind this persistently constrained military investment in North America was the traditional British Achilles heel: a worrying insufficiency of manpower. Britain's army was just too small at this stage to play an effective global role. Thus in 1715, Carolina, then in the throes of the Yamassee War, petitioned Parliament for aid. The colony had only 'two thousand able men, and [was] in great want of arms', and believed itself confronted by an Indian confederation of 12,000 men, who were receiving assistance from both the French and the Spanish. London promptly dispatched arms and ammunition to the colonists, but not troops. Britain's army had been substantially demobilised after the Treaty of Utrecht in 1713, and what remained of it was now facing a Jacobite rising in the home islands. There were simply no British troops to spare for overseas ventures.[45] And there was another twist to the perennial problem of insufficient imperial cannon fodder. Rising Anglo-French antagonism after 1689 created for Britain a conflict of interest which for a long time it proved unable to resolve. On the one hand, its colonists in America and elsewhere were now threatened by French power and demanded more aid. On the other, Britain itself was now being repeatedly challenged by superior French legions *inside* Europe, and was often at acute risk of invasion. As a result, its already stretched land forces rarely had any slack to spare for military adventures in other continents.

Before 1750, British governments had little choice but to accept that, in any conflict between national and imperial imperatives, the former had to come first. They could not afford to denude themselves of large numbers of men for the sake of imperial commitments lest they themselves be invaded by the French and their Spanish allies. This was why, quite apart from the zone's intrinsic commercial and strategic importance, so many British army battalions were stationed in the Mediterranean at this stage, while so few were sent to America. Such troops as it possessed had to be where they could be ready to defend Britain in Europe, not dispersed across the Atlantic to defend those other Britons living there against Indian and French attack. The Secretary at War, Henry Fox, spelt out this policy in 1748, when it was finally beginning to change:

> In the wars . . . both in King William's and Queen Anne's time, we did nothing but what we were obliged to do for our own safety . . . Our ministers were reduced to the fatal necessity, that they must either neglect the war at land, or that at sea and in America, they must neglect the latter to take care of the former. And the reason is very plain: because our conquests at sea, or in America, would in the end signify nothing if, while we were busied about them, the French should make themselves masters of the continent of Europe.[46]

In North America, as elsewhere, the quality and the course of empire were determined, and sometimes distorted, by Britain's intrinsic smallness. Smallness – in this case, a paucity of military and official investment in the colonies – would come to matter crucially in the shaping of events and opinion on both sides of the Atlantic.

It mattered first and foremost because it nurtured division. After 1689, Anglo settlers in North America found themselves drawn into a succession of major wars with French forces in New France. There had been ample cause for many of them to fear Indian attacks before. But, now, particular Indian groupings acted as auxiliaries of the French (and sometimes also the Spanish) and were armed, supplied and incited by them. Captivities marked the escalating level of danger. New England lost at least 300 captives – and of course many dead – in each of the first three Anglo-French contests.[47] In the colonists' eyes, these were wars that sucked them in because of their connection to Britain. Hence the names they gave them: King William's War, Queen Anne's War, and so forth. The heightened risk these conflicts involved them in of fighting, dying, and being captured, stemmed – as the colonists saw it – from their position as subjects of the monarch over the water. Yet, before 1750, the king's horses and the king's men only rarely came to help them in their trouble. Instead, they had to help themselves. After King Philip's War ended in 1676, one historian writes, the colonists 'rejoiced that victory had been achieved without help from England, interpreting this as an affirmation of their longstanding autonomy within the Empire'. Such reactions became more pronounced after 1689. Part of the price the British state paid for being small – for having a modestly sized peacetime army that was unable, before 1750, to play a sustained role across the Atlantic – was increasingly self-reliant and uppity settlers in North America.[48]

The fact that their own troops were for so long uninvolved across the Atlantic also shaped attitudes among men and women in Britain itself, and helps to account for the restricted interest they initially displayed in tales of Indian captivity. As far as Britons at home were concerned, Native American attacks before 1750 almost exclusively affected colonists, people who increasingly were born in America, and who were unlikely ever to spend time in Britain itself. By contrast, since so few British-based soldiers were sent to America at this stage, *their* level of contact with Indians and risk of being killed or captured by them was naturally minimal. For these men and their friends and families, as for Britain's seamen, it was Europe, and the Islamic powers situated close to it, that were the primary zones of danger before the mid-eighteenth century – not North America. It is suggestive in this context that the British and their American settlers called these post-1689 wars that involved them both by different names. The latter, as we have seen, named them after the reigning British monarch, thereby affirming their ties across the Atlantic. People in Britain, by contrast, came to label these wars by reference to the European world that still dominated their thinking. For them, what happened between 1701 and 1713 was not Queen Anne's War, but the War of Spanish Succession; while the conflict which American colonists called George II's War, would become the War of Austrian Succession. For Britons at home at this stage, Europe and its environs remained the essential cockpit and testing ground; Europe was what had to matter most.

By mid-century, this was beginning to change. And once troops from Britain and their families began crossing the Atlantic in substantial numbers, after the outbreak of the Seven Years War in 1756, the metropolitan market for tales of Indian captivity, as for other information about North America, would sky-rocket. With large numbers of their own kind now flooding over to America – not to settle, but to fight and hopefully live to conquer and return – this vast territory and all its complex dangers came to seem to Britons at home infinitely more real and absorbing.

Yet, for all that it was now ending, the disparity that had for so long persisted between their experience of warfare, and that of their North American colonists had left an indelible mark, not least on this imperial but divided people's perceptions of the Indian. As far as the colonists were concerned, direct experience of danger from Indians in the case of some, a gut fear and dislike of Indians in many more, plus mass exposure to highly emotive captivity texts and sermons, encouraged a widespread though by no means universal belief that there was 'no such thing as a good Indian'. On the British side of the Atlantic, things were different. Overwhelmingly preoccupied for so long with European enemies, and substantially ignorant of Indians – as of much else about the land across the Atlantic – many Britons at home held understandably to a wider spectrum of attitudes.

Artefacts and images help to illustrate the difference. After 'King' Philip or Metacom was shot to death near his home in Mount Hope in August 1676, his ornaments and treasure were dispatched to the King of England in London. What the New Englanders kept for themselves was Philip's body. They hacked it to pieces, hung the joints on trees, and put the head on permanent display at Plymouth colony. Many years later, Cotton Mather – for once not busy penning sermons on captives – grabbed the Wampanoag leader's jaw bone 'from the blasphemous exposed skull of that Leviathan' and bore it away as a trophy.[49] Here, in Mather's gloating snatch of a macabre souvenir, was a hatred born out of fear, a hatred unsated even by the enemy's defeat and death. Here, too, was the disparity in transatlantic perspectives neatly displayed. To London went Philip's belt and gorge and emblems of rank, clean and elegant evidence of Indian artisanal skills and of the warrior's own distinction. Colonial New Englanders, by contrast, savoured the man's decaying carcass and admired his grisly skull. Let me be clear: both London and its politicians and merchants, and English settlers in America, contributed in their own ways to Philip's War, to his defeat, and to the gradual destruction of the way of life he represented. My point is that there were necessarily differences in how Britons on the two sides of the Atlantic tended to perceive these things.

Visual sources reinforce the point. Look, for instance, at the woodcut embellishing one of the many eighteenth-century American editions of Mary Rowlandson's captivity narrative. Its crude, over-exposed quality only makes it more effective as an image of horror. Transfixed lines of flame erupt from the roofs of the houses in Lancaster. Our heroine, Mary Rowlandson, rushes out of the burning buildings, arms raised, face frozen and contorted in a howl of terror almost as audible as Edvard Munch's *Scream*. Converging on her, half-hidden by the stylised undergrowth, are strange, skull-like faces with jagged hair. These are the monstrous instruments of pandemonium; these – as far as many settlers were concerned – were the faces of the Indian. Britons safe and snug at home were simply not in a position to see things in this fashion, or even in many cases to imagine them, any more of course than they were in a position to see what was being done by their settlers to the Indians themselves. The representations of Indians they were exposed to were usually of a very different kind.

Consider the most circulated images of Indians in Britain in the first half of the eighteenth century, those emerging from the famous visit of four Indian 'kings' to the court of Queen Anne in 1710. They were not kings of course, but young men linked to the powerful Iroquois confederacy – the loose union of Mohawk, Seneca, Onondaga, Cayuga and Oneida Indians – that dominated much of what is now upper New York state, the Lake Ontario region and the St Lawrence. They had been brought to London because the British were eager to secure Iroquois aid for their projected (and, as it turned out, abortive) invasion of French Canada. While in London, the men were feted, made much of – and abundantly painted and engraved. It is striking that most of their London hosts had no idea what the 'authentic' appearance of these men actually was (any more than Francis Bird knew what costume his imaginary Indian female should be sculpted in). It is striking too that the theatrical costumier who was ordered to outfit the four 'kings' in readiness for their presentation to the Queen supplied each of them with a turban and a pair of slippers. Naturally enough, given what we have seen of Britain's dangers and concentrated involvement in the Mediterranean, this Londoner's stereotypical non-European was not an Indian at all, but a Muslim, a Turk. Most striking of all, though, is how official Britain determined to see and commemorate these four visiting Native Americans.[50]

26. Mary Rowlandson runs out of her burning house, pursued by Indians: American woodcut.

The most remarkable surviving portraits of them are by John Verelst, who was commissioned by Queen Anne herself. They are remarkable, first, because in some respects they are so individualised. Verelst did not paint archetypal savages, even noble ones. He painted the Iroquois as comely, well-built dignitaries, each with different physiognomies and tattoo markings. Only in one sense are they standardised. The men are posed after the fashion which early modern European artists reserved for patrician males from their own continent, with one arrogant arm akimbo, one leg extended, and with tokens displaying their military prowess and rank. Thus the 'Emperor of the Six Nations' (as the British chose to call him) is accompanied by a wolf, which serves here as the equivalent of his heraldic beast, and a wampum belt, a sign of communication and statecraft. The 'King of the Maquas' is pictured by Verelst as a mighty hunter, while the 'King of the River Nation' is a warrior, with a European sword in a scabbard buckled to his waist and a brocaded cloak falling in folds to the forest floor. Twenty years later, in 1730, seven Cherokee 'chiefs' brought to London on a political mission would be portrayed by another artist in very similar fashion, posed in the grand manner against the background of a landscaped park 'just as if they were members of the English nobility or at least the landed gentry'.[51]

Comparing images such as these, which circulated widely in Britain, against American images like the woodcut of Mary Rowlandson's terror is to some degree unfair. White attitudes to, and relations with Indians in colonial America were at no time ever monolithic or unvaryingly hostile. By the same token, perceptions of Indians in Britain could be brutal and uncompromising, especially amongst those with close ties to the colonists. Thus Daniel Defoe, a Protestant dissenter who was deeply sympathetic to his co-religionists on the other side of the Atlantic, poured scorn on the Iroquois visit to London in 1710. 'When they took any prisoners', he raged: 'they always scalp'd them, which many of our poor *English* people have felt.'[52] None the less, the different emphases of these images reflected a real difference of experience, and also different imperatives. It was not simply that people in Britain – unlike their colonists in America – were immune to danger from Indians, and immune as well to personal hunger for their land. At the same time, British governments were also increasingly coming to see particular groups of Indians as positively useful. It was no accident that Verelst's portraits of the four Iroquois 'kings' were put on display at Kensington Palace right next to a room full of portraits of Royal Navy admirals. To the rulers of the British state, desperate as always for additional manpower, Indian warriors seemed less an unmitigated menace than potential armed auxiliaries in the business of empire. As one imperial official put it cheerfully – writing in this case of the Cherokees, Creeks and Chocktaws – 'while they are our friends, they are the cheapest and strongest barrier for the protection of our settlements'.[53] Gripped and confined by their own smallness, the British in their imperial phase sought out allies, all kinds of allies, everywhere. They could not afford to do otherwise.

Here were tensions then between the different Britons inhabiting the two sides of the Atlantic, and also between different Americans. These

Tee Yee Neen Ho Ga Row · Emperor of the Six Nations

27. Tee Yee Neen Ho Ga Row, Emperor of the Six Nations, by John Verelst.

28. Sa Ga Yeath Qua Pieth Ton, King of the Maquas, by John Verelst.

did not initially detract from the close linkages that existed between Britons on both sides of the Atlantic in other respects: indeed, it bears repeating that the emergence of the captivity narrative in British mainland North America was itself an indication of just how much its inhabitants continued to draw inspiration from, and share cultural forms with, their point of origin. But captivity panics in North America, and the texts that emerged from them, also illustrated the differences that nestled and grated within these transatlantic connections – differences of religion, differences of knowledge and of experience and, of course, massive differences of geography, uneased at this stage by anything more than sailing-power. Despite its enthusiastic advances into the extra-European world, early modern Britain remained pre-eminently a European power. Rival European powers were what it necessarily had to measure itself against; and before 1750 this meant that its modest armies and resources, its official minds, and its inhabitants' attention were concentrated – though never exclusively so – on events and conflicts within Europe and its immediate environs.

Because they were limited in number, dependent psychologically and in many other ways on the 'mother country', and threatened by French power in Canada and to a lesser extent by the Spanish in the South, Britain's American colonists tended to view these European rivalries as involving them as well. Yet geography progressively served to differentiate their outlook too. Sharply threatened in some cases by the actions and existence of Native Americans, and threatened still more widely in their imaginations, they yearned progressively for these peoples' lands, and for their disappearance. The politicians sitting tight and safe in London might be inclined to view Native Americans as potential, subaltern manpower, a palliative for their own besetting smallness of military numbers, but Britain's white settlers in America were more likely to see them as obstacles, peoples to be feared, or despised, and – as time went on – impatiently swept aside.

As the scale of imperial warfare widened after 1750, so would these divisions and differences between Britons at home and British colonists in America. And at the heart of these tensions, would be the battered figure of the Indian, and the figure of the captive.

SIX

War and a New World

Confrontations

29 August 1754: Number 4, New Hampshire. It is so new this place, it has a number, not a name. The sparse white inhabitants, who trickle in on horseback, by cart, and via the Connecticut River, are scattershot in isolated homesteads, and heavily dependent for trade on the local Indians. Most of the time, however, they see no one, neither of their own kind nor of any other. Yet on this high summer evening, at least, Susanna Johnson feels at ease with the harshness of her life. Her husband James has just returned from a long journey, bringing with him some of their far-flung neighbours, a supply of water melons, and bottles of what they call flip, but what Britons back home are more likely by now to style egg-nog. She cuts herself a wedge of the fruit, savouring its coolness against her taut belly, but barely touches the viscous, yellow alcohol. Like all the women of her family, like most of the women that she knows indeed, she falls pregnant easily. This is the last month of her sixth pregnancy, and there will be eight more pregnancies to follow. Enforcedly temperate and dazed with the heat, she enjoys the unaccustomed company while remaining all the while detached within herself. By the time they retire, the Johnsons and their three surviving children to their beds, and the guests to chairs or blankets on the floor, she is probably the only sober adult of the party. She is also too swollen for heavy slumber, and so is the first of them to hear.

When, just before dawn, the rustling outside gives way to a violent pounding, James Johnson too is jerked into wakefulness. Cursing, he pulls on his nightshirt and pads unsteadily but unworriedly towards the door. It is another settler come to join the merry-making, he thinks, but arrived too late. Or a guest has gone out to relieve himself, and is too drunk to find his way back. It is none of these things. The door is forced open: and he sees at once that these are Abenaki warriors, Indians who fight in alliance with the French. There are only twelve of them, but they are armed and alert, whereas Johnson and the other male settlers are neither.

The sounds of struggle and of voices they cannot understand propel the rest of the family out of their beds. At first, Susanna is too shocked to take in the invaders or what their coming may signify. Instead, she stares at the exposed nudity of her three terrified children, and shrieks at them for violating Protestant modesty. Only then does she think to look down: 'On viewing myself, I found that I too was naked.'

An Abenaki busy ransacking the house tosses her a skirt which she has been obliged to lay aside many months ago. She fastens it tremblingly around herself, and then she, James, the children, her younger sister, and two male settlers are driven shoeless and barely clothed into the open, into 'a wilderness where we must sojourn as long as the children of Israel did, for ought we knew'. They have gone barely a mile, before she collapses, winded, to the ground. One of her captors raises his knife – but only so as to slit her too-tight waistband. As a woman who can clearly breed, and who will soon give birth to another captive, she is too valuable to kill, as long as she does not delay them too often or too long. When her new daughter is born a few days later, a child who will become her favourite and whom she determines then and there to name 'Captive', there is no wait for post-partum recovery. Nine days later, travelling in a pallet made for her by the Abenaki, but also at times on the back of a horse (until they slaughter it for food), Susanna, the baby called Captive Johnson, and the rest, arrive with their Indian escort at the east bay of Lake Champlain, New France. They have journeyed over a hundred miles into a different empire and utterly different lives.[1]

Yet although the threads of the Johnsons' previous existence have been severed, never to be properly mended, in some respects what happens to them now follows long-established patterns and precedents.

Ever since 1689, hot and cold war between the French and the British had led the former's colonial authorities in New France to sponsor Indian raids for loot, captives, and destruction against the latter's American colonists, and especially against New Englanders. Susanna Johnson's narrative reveals the extent to which, by the 1750s, this kind of captive-taking possessed, for all its violence, an almost routine quality. When Susanna and her children entered the Abenaki village of St François late in 1754, they were not made to run the gauntlet between two rows of Indians, or undergo any other harsh initiation ceremony: its inhabitants merely lined up and gave them each a purely token pat. She discovered too that the senior chief who became her master at St François was himself a fore-runner and a countryman of sorts, the son of two New Englanders who had been part of a previous generation of white captives. As suggested by this man's progress from birth as an English colonial Protestant to adulthood as a high status Roman Catholic Abenaki warrior, it was entirely predictable that the Johnsons' captivity would have its greatest transforming impact not on Susanna or James but on their children. The younger the victim, the greater – always – the potential pliancy and adaptability. The baby, Captive Johnson, would learn French as her first language, and subsequently refuse for a long time to acquire English, while their eleven-year-old son spent almost four years on his own in an Abenaki village, lost his English altogether, and forgot what his father looked like. All this naturally grieved the Johnsons, making them feel bereft of their own children, but historically it was nothing new or remarkable.

But another aspect of Susanna's own captivity emphatically was. When Britain declared war on France in May 1756, the formal beginning of what became known as the Seven Years War, the treatment meted out to the Johnsons changed abruptly. The couple, together with the girls and Susanna's sister were transferred from their alarming but sometimes congenial Abenaki surroundings to a prison in Quebec. It was from this city, on 20 July 1757, that the female Johnsons boarded a cartel ship that bore them across the Atlantic to Plymouth, England: and this sea passage from captivity in North America to the imperial metropolis was something new. During the seventeenth and early eighteenth centuries, men and women in Britain had learnt about colonial captivities in North America only indirectly, intermittently, and with limited interest. Capture by Barbary corsairs, and the perils of Islam and the Mediterranean, they knew about, understood after a fashion, and feared in their gut: but this was not true, to anything like the same degree, of this other, very different species of captive-taking. Now, in the 1750s, British aloofness and widespread ignorance in this regard substantially altered. The Johnson women were only some of a great many colonial captives who found themselves – because of the circumstances of the Seven Years War – brought to Britain as a prelude to returning to their respective American homes. These men and women were now able to spend time in Britain itself and communicate their experiences to its inhabitants face to face. 'I received much attention,' Susanna remembered complacently of her six-month stay in Britain, 'and had to gratify many inquisitive friends with the history of my sufferings.'

She recorded something else about this British episode of her life. When she, her sister and the girls finally boarded the Royal Navy vessel in Portsmouth that would take them back across the Atlantic, its captain initially misinterpreted their strange and shabby appearance, and 'swore we were women of ill fame, who wished to follow the army' to America.[2] As this suggests, it was not just a case now of some American colonists being able to come to Britain and tell their tales of captivity; British-born soldiers were simultaneously being dispatched to fight in America in unprecedented numbers. Between 1757 and 1761, Parliament provided – at least on paper – for a British force of 30,000 men in North America, which would be joined at times by some 20,000 armed colonists. A minority of these British regulars and the family members accompanying them would themselves go on to experience captivity at the hands of Native Americans and the French; and all would contribute to a quantum rise in British knowledge about America and its inhabitants. Here were multiple transatlantic crossings and confrontations of a new type all brought about by the onset of seismic imperial warfare.

The war proved transforming as far as the British were concerned in the obvious sense that it was successful on a scale never previously experienced. They wrenched Florida from the Spanish, and Canada from the French, as well as Cape Breton Island, strategic key to control of the Gulf of St Lawrence, plus new territories in the Caribbean and West Africa, Grenada, Tobago, St Vincent and Senegal, and their first major administrative enclave in India, the rich province of Bengal. By the time the war officially ended in 1763, the British empire – as Britons now began calling *all* the lands they laid claim to in a way not customary before – was five times larger than it had been a century earlier.[3] More broadly, the war fostered a shift in attitudes in Britain and throughout the West. Before 1750, the major European powers and their overseas settlers had rarely viewed empire as something of which people of their sort, Christian, Western, and white, were uniquely capable. The persistence of the great Muslim empires, and the vast, impenetrable expanse of the Chinese empire, had prevented that. After 1760, however, both the Ottoman and the Mughal empires came to be viewed in the West as weakening as never before, while commentary on China also became less awed and respectful. It was as if the extraordinary global range of the Seven Years War, and the radical transformations it effected, revealed to Western states in a new way just what their fleets, manpower and precocious national cohesion might accomplish – if only they so willed. Adam Smith, emphatically no knee-jerk enthusiast for empire, none the less conveyed something of this heightened sense of Western omnipotence and arrogance. 'In ancient times the opulent and civilized found it difficult to defend themselves against the poor and barbarous nations,' he wrote, but 'in modern times the poor and barbarous find it difficult to defend themselves against the opulent and civilized.' The whole world, 'the great map of mankind' as Edmund Burke styled it, lay open and exposed to European appetites as never before – or so it now sometimes appeared.[4]

In the light of these territorial and attitudinal shifts, one might have expected issues of captivity and confinement to recede rapidly from British consciousness, yet this was not the case. Unprecedented British military involvement in North America brought with it a fresh spate of profoundly disturbing captivities, and a new burden of imperial knowledge. It was now, in the era of the Seven Years War, that the British learnt at first hand the sheer physical extent and complexity of the lands they and their settlers had so casually accumulated. It was now that they were made to realise how varied the peoples of North America were, and the degree to which their own white settlers were more than simply mirrors of themselves. And it was now that they came to understand far more vividly than before that, for all their dwindling numbers, Native Americans could still be highly dangerous as well as potentially useful, and had necessarily to be taken seriously.

The individual captivities Britons experienced in this conflict contributed in all sorts of ways to this fast learning curve about America, but it was the enhanced sense they evolved of their *collective* constraints and challenges in America that proved more important. In the wake of an astonishingly successful global war, the British were left with an inflated commitment to an imperial mission, with a far more informed sense of the dimensions and workings of their rich and populous transatlantic empire, but with a heightened awareness too of the problems it posed in the light of their own inescapable limitations.

Into the wilderness

Many Britons at home embarked on the transatlantic phase of the Seven Years War with a belief comfortably rooted in ignorance that Native Americans were by now finished business, or just simply finished. A government MP waxed typically dismissive when discussing French and British rivalry in North America in 1755: 'Here is a contest between two equals,' he informed the House of Commons suavely, 'about a country where both claim an undivided right . . . I think it is allowed on all hands that the natives have no right at all.'[5] In this strictly armchair view of things, America mattered much less in terms of its own complexities, than as one more theatre for the all-important and protracted duel for primacy between Europe's two most aggressive and competitive states.

In one very practical respect, however, such Eurocentricism actually worked to improve Britain's understanding of its American colonists and the captivities sometimes inflicted on them. After 1756, Britain and France committed themselves to successive treaties whereby all prisoners-of-war 'of whatever sort, wherever' were to be exchanged or ransomed 'in whatever part of the world the belligerent or auxiliary armies of the two nations may be'.[6] Here was an explicit recognition that Anglo-French conflict now spanned the continents in a new way, and an expression too on the part of these powers of a far greater degree of global hubris. All prisoners in this war, whether in Europe or outside it, were now declared to be potentially the business of Britain and France, and not just their respective nationals. As far as British North America was concerned, what this meant was that colonists seized by the French or their Indian allies, like Susanna Johnson, now became London's responsibility, and were often transported to Britain at some stage in the course of their release. In just two months, October and November 1758, over sixty American colonists captured in this fashion were shipped from New France to England, where they were fed and clothed for several months before finally being transported home. Captivity narratives published by colonials during the war regularly refer to these unprecedented transatlantic redemptions. Thus Jean Lowry, who was captured by Indians at Rocky-Spring, Pennsylvania, in April 1756, and lost her husband in the process, described how she was held in New France, then shipped from Quebec to Dartmouth, England, in the autumn of 1758, before being sent back to New York the following year.[7]

It was not unusual by this stage for individual American colonists to pay visits to what most still regarded as the mother-country, but those who did so were generally prosperous males: Southern gentlemen on their version of the Grand Tour, candidates for ordination, well-heeled merchants and lobbyists and the like. The influx into Britain during this war of substantial numbers of miscellaneous colonists (and some blacks) caught up in and damaged by the conflict was a very different phenomenon which has never been investigated.[8] It must have resulted in the oral transmission of abundant though selective information about different kinds of Native Americans and about North American life in general; indeed we know from Susanna Johnson's narrative that it did. But this was only one aspect of an explosion in Britain at this time of information about America. In addition, there were the official and informal letters flooding back to Britain from colonists, and from British soldiers, officials and families dispatched to America for the duration of the war. And, most of all, there was an outburst of print.

It was now that the British began to read about the lands and peoples they laid claim to across the Atlantic as never before. At one level, this was because there was so much more available for them to read. One in five of all works published in Britain about North America between 1640 and 1760 appeared in the last decade of this timespan, the 1750s.[9] To these discrete volumes was added the more widely scanned information now on offer about America in the London and provincial press. As John Brewer long ago pointed out, the middle of the eighteenth century witnessed a quickening in the size and complexity of Britain's press network. More newspapers were sold – an expansion of about 30 per cent over the 1750s alone. More titles were issued – the slaving port of Liverpool, for instance, acquired its first ever newspaper during the Seven Years War, because of the intense local interest it aroused. And this proliferation of different papers and magazines meant in turn that particularly arresting stories and news items could be reprinted many times over and transmitted far beyond the bounds of London and the major cities.[10] Yet the increase in the *volume* of American and other information was only part, and not the most interesting part of the story. There was also a qualitative change in the kinds of information on offer.

Before 1756, most of what British newspapers and magazines printed about America had been brief, factual and overwhelmingly commercial, often little more than a record of incoming and outgoing transatlantic vessels at specific ports. But as the war advanced, far more attention was devoted in papers, pamphlets and books to the American interior, to issues other than trade, and to human interest stories, understandably so, since individual Britons and different varieties of Americans were now encountering each other at a hitherto unknown rate and degree of intensity. 'The scene of action is now in America', wrote a young and very serious Arthur Young in 1758, desperately keen to kick-start his career as a writer and pundit:

> To understand perfectly what the advantage or disadvantage of any place being taken on either side, is to us, it is necessary not only to know the latitude and longitude of such a place (which is frequently the best part of the accounts some authors give) but its situation with regard to its neighbourhood; what nations of Indians it lies near to; whether those Indians are best affected to us, or our enemies; what French forts or settlements are nearest, and their distance; if they can be known, which is not always the case in that uninhabited and extensive country.

Literate and patriotic Britons now came to accept that in regard to North America they had seriously to raise their game, and broaden and deepen their knowledge. A greater emphasis on accounts of captivity and on Native American encounters generally were an integral part of this wider reportage and yearning to know. Captivity narratives written by or about

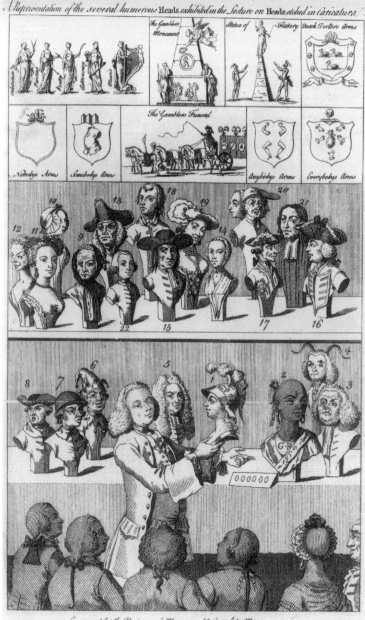

The Gamblers Monument

Statue of Flattery

Quack Doctors Arms

The Gamblers Funeral

Nobodys Arms

Somebodys Arms

Anybodys Arms

Everybodys Arms

Engraved for the Universal Museum & Complete Mag:

29. Learning Empire: a post-war British public lecture on physiognomy makes room for a loyal Native American.

colonists, and originally published in America, came now to stand a far better chance of being reprinted in Britain or extracted in its press.[11] And, for the first time on any significant scale, detailed accounts of captivity and other sufferings at the hands of Indians were written and published by individuals who were active in America on account of the war, but based in Britain and intent on returning there.

By colonial American standards, some of these pioneering British texts about Indian captivities were markedly elementary in quality. When Mary Rowlandson and her clerical mentors put together the first, famous full-length colonial captivity narrative in the 1670s, they had made clear how precious and totemic Englishness remained for them, but they also revealed – perhaps unconsciously – the degree to which New Englanders like themselves were already familiar with some of the material circumstances of Native American life. Words like 'canoe', 'wigwam', 'sagamore', and 'squaw' appear in Rowlandson's captivity story, *The Sovereignty and Goodness of God*, without any explanations being provided, because for her original Massachusetts readers none were required. Well before 1700, British colonists in America were adjusting to, and assimilating information about their new environment and its plural peoples, in a way that was neither possible nor necessary for men and women living in Britain itself.[12] This experiential and knowledge gap between the colonies and the mother-country was far wider by the 1750s. Consequently, British-based writers on captivity and other contacts with Indians during the Seven Years War, who had their own compatriots in mind as an audience, sometimes felt obliged to devote space to very rudimentary information.

Some, like Peter Williamson, whom we will encounter at length later, sought out British analogies so as to make his Indian experiences better understood. A tomahawk, he wrote, was 'something like our plasterer's hammers'. While Henry Grace, a deeply miserable English soldier, who was seized and used as a slave for over five years by various Indian groupings in Nova Scotia and New France, padded out his bitter, self-published narrative with descriptions of snow shoes and wigwams ('a kind of hut made with the bark of birch trees . . . There is always a place left in the middle at top to let out the smoke') that would have seemed superfluous to most American colonists, but not necessarily so to his immediate audience in Basingstoke, England. Even John Rutherfurd, a Yorkshire-born Scot who wrote his remarkable account of captivity at the hands of the Chippewas late in the war, when British knowledge about America had expanded dramatically, still thought it appropriate to interrupt his story with carefully observed explanations of scalps or breech-clouts:

a piece of blue cloth about a yard and a half long and a foot broad which they pass through betwixt their legs, bringing each end under a belt which is round the middle for that purpose.[13]

As always, then, British and colonial American treatments of Indian captivities were characterised by significant differences. But not in all respects. Most of these new British captivity narratives, like most colonial accounts, lingered on the pornography of real or invented Indian violence, in part because such lurid passages attracted readers even as they allowed them to feel properly repelled. Thomas Morris's account of his brief captivity with the Miamis as a British infantry captain in the early 1760s was generally curious and sympathetic. He made a point, for instance, of advocating intermarriage between whites and the 'innocent, much-abused, and once happy people' he called Indians. None the less, Morris still devoted space to the variety and duration of Indian torture techniques:

> The usual modes of torturing prisoners are applying hot stones to the soles of the feet, running hot needles into the eyes, which latter cruelty is generally performed by the women, and shooting arrows and running and pulling them out of the sufferer in order to shoot them again.

'These modes of torture I should not have mentioned', he confessed artlessly, 'if the gentleman who advised me to publish my journal had not thought it necessary.'[14] The main reason why writings by Britons began devoting more space to Indian violence was not however reader titillation. It was rather that people of their own sort were now being exposed to this violence in a new way. Indians no longer just endangered British colonists living 3000 miles away. Because of the way this war was being fought, some Indian peoples were a threat to Britain's own armed forces, and a formidable one.

Some of the reasons why this was so were all too familiar. Initially, many of the British troops dispatched to America were deficient in local knowledge, deficient in training and proper equipment, and above all, and with dismal predictability, deficient in numbers. The destruction of General Edward Braddock and his forces at Monongahela, Western Pennsylvania, in July 1755, is conventionally attributed to the Yorkshireman's personal arrogance and unwillingness to adapt to wilderness fighting. These failings did not help. But the French-led force of Huron, Shawnee, Ottawa and Algonquin warriors was able to slaughter 1000 of the British (including Braddock himself and three-quarters of his officers) in large part because his troops consisted of the unwanted leftovers of several British and Irish battalions, plus some poor-quality American recruits, while the maps he brought with him turned out to be grossly inaccurate.[15] By the same token, the Fall of Oswego, a major fort and trading post on Lake Ontario, in August 1756 – one of the biggest British military disasters in North America that year – owed less to individual incompetence than to insufficent numbers and resources. The mixed French and Indian force that overwhelmed Oswego consisted of over 3000 men. Against this, the British had less than 1500 soldiers and only 'poor [and] pittyful' fortifications.[16]

In other words, at the start of this ultimately very successful war the British were forced to pay in defeats, high casualty rates and captivities for the sort of American empire they had chosen to run – or rather not run – up to this point. French colonisers in North America had long been aware of their demographic inferiority to British settlers here, and had endeavoured to compensate for this with a high level of military preparedness. New France was an armed society, with its own military nobility and culture. There were close links between its extensive militia and the French regular army. Its secular and religious officials devoted constant attention and imagination to nurturing military alliances with local indigenous peoples; while French government investment in the defence of New France rose from some 300,000 livres in 1712, to over 500,000 livres in the 1730s, to millions of livres every year from the 1740s onwards.[17]

Before the Seven Years War, Britain behaved very differently. Possessed of a much smaller domestic population, revenue base and army than France, it had never fortified its colonies in America to the same degree, or maintained large numbers of regular troops here, or exhibited a sustained interest in wooing indigenous allies, or devoted much time or trouble to training up its colonists in the military arts.[18] Yet it needs stressing that even when the British and their American colonists did begin to get their military act together in 1758–9, and finally learnt how to exploit the potential of their combined numbers against the arms and allies of New France, different groups of Native Americans continued to be able to inflict periodic defeats on British regular troops. In 1760, the Cherokees defeated a large British force commanded by Archibald Montgomery and captured Fort Loudoun in the Allegheny Mountains; and between April and June 1763, the confederation of Ottawa, Chippewa, Delaware, Huron, Seneca, Shawnee and other Native American groupings involved in Pontiac's War managed to capture most of the poorly defended British posts in the Great Lakes–Ohio region.

So British-based commentators explored Native American violence more emotionally and at greater length after 1756 in large part because they had been given ample cause to fear it, and because for them this was something new. It is clear, indeed, that some British troops dispatched to North America, already disoriented by their transatlantic crossing, froze into 'a sort of torpor and insensibility' when confronted for the first time by hostile Indians, an enemy of a kind nothing in Europe had prepared them for. The way that Braddock's doomed infantry continued to stand for hours in line together in 1755 while their French and Indian opponents picked them off, instead of scattering for cover into the woods, is usually put down to their ignorance of guerrilla tactics. But these raw recruits may well have found their only, final comfort in huddling together in this fashion, and feared separating in the face of an enemy they did not understand and most of the time could barely see. The few British survivors testified that rarely more than five Indian warriors had been visible during the battle, so adept were the latter at camouflage, and so thick were the surrounding woods.[19] When hostile Native Americans did come into view, it might be still more alarming. Confronted by his soon-to-be Chippewa captors, 'naked, and painted black and red', John Rutherfurd, who had only arrived in America the year before, and was just eighteen, simply gave up 'all hope of being saved, and became in a manner resigned to the worst'. And if war-paint failed to petrify – which was its purpose – inexperienced regulars trained to regard advancing in tight-lipped silence as a mark of military professionalism might still be unmanned by the howls and screams Indians made as they attacked. 'The Indian war cry is represented as too dreadful to be endured', reported Samuel Johnson to his British readers in 1758:

> as a sound that will force the bravest veteran to drop his weapon, and desert his rank; that will deafen his ear, and chill his breast; that will neither suffer him to hear orders or to feel shame, or retain any sensibility but the dread of death.[20]

Yet, in this kind of warfare, death might seem preferable to captivity. It was probably the exception rather than the rule for adult white males seized by Indians during this war to be nurtured throughout a long captivity and live to be freed and tell their tales. Even in the waves of Indian raids on civilian settlers in Pennsylvania, Maryland and Virginia in the late 1750s and early '60s, which resulted in some 3000 captives, white males are estimated to have been nineteen times more likely to be slaughtered than their female counterparts. Men in uniform seized in battle could fare worse. Only twenty captives were taken by Indians from amongst the remnants of Braddock's force at Monongahela. Eight of these were female and allowed to live, because women and girls were deemed fertile, useful and unthreatening. Twelve were soldiers, and these men were tortured to death, to test their courage and appease the dead and bereaved among the Indians themselves. 'They stripped him quite naked', Henry Grace reported being told of one of these victims:

> and tying him to a tree, made two large fires on each side of him and perfectly roasted him alive, while they danced round him, paying no regard to his lamentations . . . one of the young Indians ran in between the two fires and cut off his private parts, and put them into his mouth to stop him crying.[21]

It was not just the extreme physicality of this sort of violence that horrified and alienated, the blood, the body parts, the ingenious mutilations, the deliberate prolongation of excruciating, unmanning pain. For Britons who devoted any thought to it, the sense that all this constituted a kind of language which they themselves could not understand might be just as unnerving. When Colonel John Littlehales was captured at Oswego in 1756 and taken to Montreal, it is likely that neither he, nor his regular army comrades captured alongside him, understood why seventy Abenakis promptly seized upon him there, dragged him along the city's walls, made him dance, and 'afterwards beat him with sticks . . . swearing in Indian, calling him a rascal, a son of a bitch, a dog, and a scoundrel, which lasted for about one hour'. It is only possible for us to decode this behaviour because for once there was a witness present who had some access to all the different cultures involved. Richard Williams had been a drummer with the 51st Regiment at Oswego, but was captured by Indians from La Galette in 1755 and taken to New France. By the time he came to witness Littlehales' ordeal, Williams had already passed successfully through his own. He wore a carved stick through the bridge of his nose, his ears were ritually cut, 'he could paint himself so as not to be known from an Indian', and he had acquired the languages of his different captors. So he was able to ask Littlehales' Indian tormentors 'why they used him . . . and none of the rest of the [British] officers in that manner'. They told him it was 'because Littlehales was a coward and behaved ill, otherwise they would not have beat him'. Littlehales had indeed visibly lost his nerve in the siege in which he was captured, but the significant point is that neither he, nor his comrades, were probably able – as Williams was – to connect this personal failure as a warrior with the protracted and vicious beatings afterwards inflicted on him. Instead, this assault will almost certainly have been interpreted by those Britons witnessing it as one more proof of innate and thoroughly arbitrary indigenous savagery.[22]

The belief that Indian violence was at once hideously cruel and unpredictable, explains why some British troops (including men who had faced other enemies with equanimity) deserted rather than do battle with them, or simply resigned themselves helplessly to death in the face of their attack. This was what happened at Fort William Henry, near the southern end of Lake George, on 9 August 1757, in one of the most controversial episodes of the war. The British garrison had already offered their surrender, and this had been formally accepted by their French opponents, but the British and colonial troops involved were then subsequently attacked by a large band of pro-French Indians and, as one observer reported, some of 'the English were seized with such an unaccountable stupor, that they submitted to the tomahawk without resistance'. Once again, this was a case of men being thrown off balance by a gulf between military cultures. According to western European (but not Indian) conventions, having surrendered, their lives should have been sacrosanct. When this turned out not to be the case, some did not know how to react and so failed to react at all. But, in addition, some of the 180 or so British soldiers and camp followers killed on this occasion may well have given themselves up to a quick death out of fear that the alternatives were bound to be worse. As it happened, at least half of all the white male captives seized at Fort William Henry seem to have survived, while forty more chose to stay with their Indian captors. But to submit to Indian captivity on the offchance that it would lead to these happier results required nerve as well as a level of experience that British troops new to America were often naturally without.[23]

Such wartime incidents, and the accounts of them dispatched back across the Atlantic, served at one level to bring Britons at home into greater harmony with the attitudes towards Native Americans displayed by many of their colonists. The romanticism with which many Britons had earlier viewed Native Americans – their sense that these peoples were potentially useful, assimilable, wild, noble savages of the woodlands – shuddered and sometimes shattered irretrievably under the shock of actual contact and conflict. For dramatic proof of this, one has only to compare John Verelst's flattering and chivalric images of the four Indian 'kings' who visited Queen Anne in 1710 with George Townshend's sketches of Ottawa and Algonquin warriors made while he and they were engaged in the military campaign against Quebec in 1759.

Townshend was the son of an English peer, an army general, and an amateur artist, who enjoyed producing vicious caricatures of white males of his own social class and nationality, so one should not read too much into the negativity of these drawings. In some ways, indeed, he represents his Indian subjects more accurately than Verelst attempted to do. A keen and increasingly expert collector of Indian artefacts, as his income allowed him to be, Townshend would even take an Indian boy child back home with him to his family's great house of Rainham in Norfolk, one more object to be displayed and scrutinised. So he was careful how he drew his subjects and their material life, just as he took pains to convey their physical impressiveness, their tallness, which (normally shorter) British males regularly commented on, the strength of their limbs, and their evident stamina and agility. But it is the particular scenes of Indian life Townshend selected to record, and the titles he gave his drawings, that are most revealing. There is 'An Indian dress'd for war with a scalp', as well as 'An Indian pursuing a wounded enemy with his Tomahawk', and 'An Indian of ye Outawas Tribe & his Family going to war', and several more images of a similar sort. But nowhere in any of these sketches is there evidence of warm humanity or humour on the Indians' part, or of empathy as distinct from fascination on Townshend's. Here are Indians, and Indians in this case acting alongside the British remember, represented as unalloyed creatures of menace, raw, single-minded hunters, utterly beyond civility and sentiment. Emphatically the Other.[24]

Those Britons who came to regard Native Americans in this light were not reacting simply to wartime events across the Atlantic. Part of western Europeans' heightened conceit about themselves at this stage stemmed from a sense that they were coming to conduct war more humanely, as well of course as on a much larger scale.[25] Captives played a vital part in these self-serving ideas as in so much else. By 1757, there were already more than 13,000 French prisoners-of-war being held in Britain and Ireland, and by 1762 over 26,000 Frenchmen were detained there. Never before, had Britons at home been able to see so many defeated and helpless foreign enemies detained on their own shores; and printed accounts of these prisoners and their sufferings, and civic subscriptions on their behalf increased with every year of the war. In 1759, there were charitable collections on behalf of the French prisoners in London, Edinburgh, Dublin and many other major towns. Thousands of pounds were raised, and mountains of shoes, clothes and medicines donated for their comfort. The pamphlet issued to commemorate this nationwide benevolence was prefaced by Samuel Johnson himself, and copies were 'deposited in the British Museum, and in the several universities of the British Empire'. Here was to be proof, preserved in print for all time, that Britain was not merely victorious globally – as by 1759 it very evidently was – but humane in its conduct of war, impressively merciful, quintessentially civilised. Britons, as one journalist glowed, felt 'for their captives as men, and cannot but pity enemies in distress'. Naturally, the French thought exactly the

An Indian who has wounded
his Enemy & pursues with his
Tomahawk to scalp him

30. Watercolour of an Ottawa warrior, by George Townshend.

31. Trumpeting British military mercy: Benjamin West's *General Johnson saving a wounded French officer from the tomahawk of a North American Indian.*

same about themselves, and organised similar charitable collections for British prisoners of war held on their soil.[26]

It is in the light of this more proactive concern on both sides of the Channel on behalf of (overwhelmingly white) captives that one must understand some of the emphases in Emeric de Vattel's *The Law of Nations* (1758), which became one the most influential Enlightenment texts about property, war and empire. In his sections on war, Vattel, a Swiss jurist, drew an absolute distinction between 'unlawful war for havoc and pillage' ('almost all the expeditions' of the Barbary corsairs, he remarked pointedly, came into this category), and 'the humanity with which most nations in Europe carry on wars at present'. It was unjust, Vattel argued, indeed it was savage to kill prisoners-of-war. The lustre of victory should not be tarnished 'by inhuman and brutal actions'. Consequently, he declared: 'We extol, we love the English and French at hearing the accounts of the treatment [they have] given to prisoners of war.'[27] At the same time as it was accelerating in global scope and aggressiveness, European warfare was coming to be presented more explicitly as distinctively humane and generous, especially in regard to the treatment of captives. And in this respect, Vattel put into systematic, intellectual prose what many military professionals already instinctively took for granted.

In the same year as the publication of Vattel's masterwork, 1758, Britain's commander-in-chief in America, General James Abercromby, assured his French opposite number, the marquis de Montcalm, that he wanted 'to carry on the war in this country with the same humanity and generosity it is in Europe, and ought to be everywhere'. Tellingly, Abercromby cited behaviour towards captives as the vital test of these civilised qualities: 'the good treatment of these persons that the state of war . . . throws into our hands'.[28] Here was an approach to the conduct of war that – on the face of it – situated America's indigenous peoples firmly outside the charmed circle of those from whom humanity was to be expected, and excluded them as well from those to whom humanity was due. Indians, as Britons now had much better cause to know, did not invariably exhibit pity to enemies in distress. They were known to torture and occasionally cannibalise prisoners-of-war, and more generally indulged in public and ritual assaults on the human body in a manner that Europeans were coming (unevenly) to have qualms about. They sometimes killed those who had already laid down their weapons and were defenceless; just as they sometimes attacked helpless women and children. Indians, wrote General Jeffrey Amherst, his pen dipped in loathing, were 'the only brutes and cowards in the creation . . . known to exercise their cruelties upon the [female] sex, and to scalp and mangle the poor sick soldiers'. Indians, agreed another British general, were 'assassins, not soldiers, therefore they have no quarter'.[29] In this straightforwardly manichean and vengeful vision, Native Americans were fair game. They could have no respectable part in Britain's fast expanding empire, or be drawn into civilisation as Europeans conceived of it. Their conduct towards the white captives in their hands proved them barbarians, predators and monsters, beyond understanding, and beyond the line.

Yet it needs stressing that this was by no means the only British vision of Native Americans fostered by the Seven Years War.

Because this conflict was followed, barely a dozen years later, by the outbreak of the American Revolution, it can be tempting – especially for American historians – to represent the British military and political classes as already in the 1750s and '60s hardening into uniformly ruthless and intransigent imperialists. Examples of British arrogance and impatient authority in North America are looked for and lingered on, in part because of the retrospective knowledge that massive and successful resistance to them was just around the corner. Exaggerating the degree to which British soldiers and administrators were invariably antipathetic to Indians is one aspect of this. Thus Jeffrey Amherst (who indisputably *was* an Indian-hater) has been described by one scholar as summing 'up British military attitudes toward the Indians', while another has claimed that the British were 'trapped within their understanding of the Indians as childlike, violent creatures'.[30] Many of them were of course; but some were not. At the one extreme, to be sure, there were the likes of Amherst, a man who certainly advocated genocide against Indians, even if the jury remains out on whether he actually implemented it. But at the other extreme, there were British Indian experts like John Stuart, a fellow army officer and no less committed imperialist than Amherst, who married a mixed-blood Cherokee, who befriended Chief Attakullakulla and was rescued by him during the Seven Years War, and who is on record as regarding Native American violence as no more outrageous than the level of street crime in London or Paris.[31] Between the utterly disparate ideas and behaviour of these two equally atypical individuals, there existed many different gradations of British response to Indians at official and military level.

Among ordinary Britons at home, attitudes were even more mixed and shifting. Some of them emerged from the war convinced that Native Americans were irredeemably bestial, cruel to captives and cruel in essence. But other Britons recognised – on the basis of what they read in letters or print – that their own regular troops in America (like French and colonial troops there) sometimes behaved not much differently. British soldiers, too, as private wartime correspondence and the Anglo-American press made abundantly clear, regularly scalped wounded and dying enemies, and were guilty at times of killing women and children, and wallowing in slaughter.[32] So, if Indians were bestial in their conduct of war, then, so, at times, were Britons from both sides of the Atlantic. The increased flow into Britain of information about North America complicated perceptions

Hendrick the Sachem, or Chief of the Mohawks.
Etched from an Original Drawing.

Published according to the Act March 8, 1756. by T. Jefferys at Charing Cross.

32 and 33. Different ways of seeing: two British portraits of an Iroquois ally, Hendrick, during the Seven Years War.

The brave old Hendrick the great SACHEM or Chief of the Mohawk Indians one of the Six Nations now in Alliance with & subject to the King of Great Britain.
Sold by R. Wilkinson & C. Bowles.

187

of Native Americans in another respect. British officials in America regularly reported back to London that Indian violence was frequently the result of provocation on the part of white colonists and their inroads into indigenous lands. As a letter in a London newspaper put it in 1763: 'if we search into the beginning of some of the late Indian wars, we shall find they have taken rise from some of our colonists over-reaching them in their treaties, and getting possession of the hunting and fishing grounds, without which they [the Indians] cannot possibly subsist.'[33]

So, while at one level this war encouraged Britons at home to view Indians as brutal villains, at another it made it easier for the latter to be seen as misunderstood victims. One can see these contradictory impulses in English and Scottish novels published in the aftermath of the war, which gave far more space than before to Indians and Indian captivities. Tobias Smollett's *Expedition of Humphry Clinker*, written in the late 1760s, has the veteran and raconteur, Lieutenant Obadiah Lismahago, at once testifying to comic-strip Indian tortures ('an old lady, with a sharp knife, scooped out one of his eyes, and put a burning coal in the socket'), and recounting his fruitful marriage to a 'squaw'. Indians, Lismahago concludes, 'worship two contending principles; one the fountain of all good, the other the source of evil'. The soldier taken captive in Henry Mackenzie's *Man of the World* (1773) is no less riven. He is cruelly tortured by the Cherokees, but subsequently becomes entranced by their society: 'Scarce any inducement could have tempted me to leave.'[34] But this complex vision of the Indian, at once repelled and admiring, was conveyed most richly – and propagated – by the captivity narratives themselves. Superficially straightforward and ephemeral, they turn out on closer reading, as these sources invariably do, to be anything but.

Consider the narratives – the plural is important – of Peter Williamson. He has been described as 'one of the greatest liars who ever lived', but is much better regarded as someone who repeatedly re-invented himself and his life-story in response to a brief but eventful encounter with Indians, and a longer, enforced encounter with North America.[35] He was born to a family of small farmers in the village of Aboyne, Aberdeenshire, in 1730 and kidnapped by some unscrupulous traders while on a visit to Aberdeen when he was about twelve years old. As happened to many young, poor and unprotected Britons in the seventeenth and eighteenth centuries, he was then shipped across the Atlantic, and sold into indentured servitude. This was Williamson's first experience of captivity. His second occurred in 1754, when he had finished his time in service, and was established as a farmer himself in Berkshire county, Pennsylvania. Early in October that year, his house was raided by Indians, Delawares he claimed, who held on to him until he escaped in January 1755. He was then swept into the colonial forces and the Seven Years War, fighting against the French and their Indian allies, until being captured a final time at Oswego. A Royal Navy vessel shipped him home late in 1756, and it was then that his writing career began.

The initial version of *French and Indian Cruelty exemplified in the life . . . of Peter Williamson* was published a year later in York. From the very beginning, it was a substantial text – over 100 pages – and in some respects conventional enough. There was the usual quota of 'terrible and shocking' Indian cruelties, though Williamson described his reactions to these with a vividness that was not usual. On one of the first nights of his Indian captivity, he wrote, his Delaware captors tied him up, lit a fire, and then brought red hot coals and sticks close to his face. When he wept in terror, they only brought the kindling closer still, 'telling me my face was wet, and that they would dry it for me'. This first version of Williamson's multiple captivities also included enough details to convince me, at least, that he really did live at one stage in close proximity to Native American peoples. There are obvious inventions, and naïve exaggerations designed to inflate his own importance, but there is also a core of close, accurate observation and original insight. He described, for instance, how the Delawares were now dependent on certain Western consumer goods, but systematically worked at adapting them: 'The better sort have shirts of the finest linen they can get, and to those some wear ruffles; but these they never put on till they have painted them of various colours.' It was not these earnest anthropological gobbets however that made *French and Indian Cruelty* a bestseller in Britain for over a century, nor even its tantalising references to 'various and complicated' Indian atrocities.[36] What did was Williamson's genius for gauging changes over time in the British public mood, and for making the leap from narrative to polemic.

These gifts appeared to the full in the extended 1762 edition of his narrative. As the title *French and Indian Cruelty* suggests, from the very beginning Williamson stressed that brutality – like captivity – was not a uniquely Indian practice. He condemned the French for hiring and inciting indigenous mercenaries. He criticised Anglo traders for cheating Indians and selling them alcohol; and he attacked Aberdeen's merchant community for conniving in white slavery and selling vulnerable youths like himself into bondage across the Atlantic. By spreading blame across various national and ethnic groups in this fashion, Williamson effectively liberated the Indians in his text from the usual exceptionalist stereotypes. As he treated them, they were not out-of-the-ordinary monsters, any more than they were romantic, woodland nobles. They were violent, imperfect beings contending against other, different beings who were themselves often violent and imperfect. What Williamson added to this in the 1762 edition of his captivity narrative was political and imperial advocacy. North America's Indians, he now insisted, had been 'treated as a people of whom an advantage might be taken'. Yet unless 'some method' was taken 'to draw them into our interest', Britain's empire here would always remain an unstable one:

> Our late transactions in America testify, that the friendship of the Indians is to be desired, and the only way to maintain a friendly correspondence with them, is by making such propositions to them as will secure their liberties, and be agreeable to their expectations; and not only by keeping these propositions inviolable as well in time of war, but also renewing our treaties with them from time to time . . . They are very proud and love to be esteemed.[37]

French and Indian Cruelty reached, and went on reaching a very wide audience in Britain, though suggestively it was not published in America before independence. By the early 1800s, the text had passed through several London editions, half a dozen Edinburgh editions, and there were separate editions as well – sometimes more than one – issued in York, Dublin, Glasgow, Leith, Liverpool, Stirling, Aberdeen and other towns. If there was a popular British classic about Native Americans in this period, this was certainly it. Yet what did it mean exactly that Peter Williamson chose to write about his captivity and America's indigenous peoples in the ways that he did, and was able to achieve such a wide readership in Britain for so long?

As regards Peter Williamson's own motives, the answer seems clear. To an almost over-determined degree, he was exactly the sort of individual who might have been predicted to view captivity at the hands of non-Europeans in an open-minded and exploratory fashion. He was poor. He was alienated. And he was from the geographical peripheries of Britain, a Northern Scot. As we have seen in the Mediterranean world, and will see again in regard to India, low-status, marginal, and/or alienated whites of Williamson's type frequently did react more flexibly when forced across cultural and political boundaries in this way. Neither Britain nor white colonial America had done Williamson many favours in life, so why not empathise with Native Americans who were also put upon by various whites? By the end of his extraordinary life, by which time he had successively run a coffee-house in Edinburgh (decorated with 'Indian' antiques and costumes), invented agricultural machinery, and set himself up as a publisher, Williamson had persuaded himself that his Delaware captors had actually reared him from childhood, and endowed him with a special wisdom and philosophy.

It was this Native American upbringing, he assured his readers in his last autobiographical work, in 1789, that had made him what he was, a

PETER · WILLIAMSON
In the Drefs of a Delaware Indian.
1 Tomohawk.   5 Powderhorn.
2 Scalping Knife.   6 Indian Canoe.
3 Shot Bag.   7 Bush Lighting.
4 Purse & Belt of Wampum. 8 War Dance.

34. Peter Williamson as a Delaware warrior: frontispiece of the 1762 edition of his
narrative.

fully natural man, capable of rising by his own efforts in defiance of European hierarchies. He conceded that 'had I the education of Voltaire, Pope, or Addison', he might have chronicled his experiences in a more polished manner. But his education had been different, and acquired in a distant and less corrupted school:

> The reader will be here asking, what school I was brought up at? I shall only tell them, that the extent of it was upwards of four thousand miles, and the height thereof as high as the heavens, governed by Indians of many nations; and regular education is no where taught among them, but handed down from one generation to another, and their records are kept, marked with tomahawks on the outside of trees, and can be distinguished by themselves for centuries back.

When Williamson was finally laid to rest in Edinburgh in 1799, it was in a costume he had brought back with him from North America (or so he told his family), the moccasins, fringed leggings, blanket and feathered headdress of the Delaware warrior.[38]

Viewed in this way, Peter Williamson was essentially a rebel and an idealist of a distinct but recognisable type. He was not a conscious disciple of Rousseau, a gentleman embracing the forest and the furred while preserving all the while the comforts of his study, but something rawer and more plebeian. Williamson's ultimate heir as far as his own island was concerned would be Archie Belaney (1888–1938), a very ordinary Englishman who emigrated to Canada in 1906, and re-invented himself there as Wa-Sha-Quon-Asin, He-who-flies-by-night, or, as he came universally to be known, 'Grey Owl'. Belaney became an expert trapper and riverman, adopted buckskins and moccasins, and lived with a succession of authentically indigenous women. He also published bestsellers about his idyllic life in the Canadian wilderness, and drew vast crowds to public lectures on both sides of the Atlantic in which he passed on 'Indian' wisdoms (some of them excellent and far ahead of their time) on man's duty to protect wildlife and the environment.[39] Yet, while Williamson was clearly a man of a similar stamp to Belaney, it would be wrong and inadequate to interpret his captivity stories and their remarkable British success merely in this sort of individual, idiosyncratic light. Williamson and his texts should rather be seen as particularly picturesque examples of a much wider recognition in Britain in the wake of the Seven Years War that Native American societies were complex, possessed of valuable qualities as well as evils, and that whites held captive in them might find the experience attractive and even alluring.

It is striking that the best captivity narrative written by a Briton about

North America at this time makes all of these points, even though the author was of a far more assured social status than Williamson, and shared none of his romanticism. John Rutherfurd was born in Yorkshire in 1746, but had Scottish gentry connections. In 1762, he crossed the Atlantic to join a trading consortium set up in Detroit by his uncle, a former British army officer. Once there, Rutherfurd, who was an ambitious, intelligent, self-regarding man, began learning French as well as several Indian languages so as to equip himself to join in the commercial exploitation of Britain's brand new Canadian empire.[40] Then, in May 1763, he agreed to join a party of British army officers mapping the lakes and rivers between Detroit and Michilimackinac, and as a result got caught in the outbreak of Pontiac's rebellion, the extraordinary attempt by a confederation of Native American peoples, Ottawa, Chippewa, Delaware, Kickapoo, Miami, Seneca and more, to drive the British and their settlers back east of the Appalachians.

What followed horrified Rutherfurd while also entangling him, yet he was able throughout to recognise some of the nuances both of his captors' behaviour and his own. Ambushed by Chippewas, some of the British officers in the party resisted and were promptly killed and scalped, including a Captain Charles Robertson, a friend of Rutherfurd's. Robertson's corpse was subsequently hacked apart and its joints roasted over a fire. 'Small pieces' were then put on a stick and offered to Rutherfurd with the spoken inducement that 'Englishmen's flesh was very good to eat'. As he tells it, Rutherfurd succeeded in controlling himself in this crisis; and we can believe this more easily because he freely admits that, at the moment of capture, he froze in terror and made no effort to save either himself or his friends. Still a civilian at this stage, Rutherfurd did not know how to fight, and he did not want to die. So he used his brain, as well as the new languages he had recently acquired. He also drew on the greater reserves of knowledge about Native Americans that the war had allowed Britons like himself to acquire. He recognised that what appeared to be raw cannibalism on the part of his captors, was in fact a 'religious ceremony' of sorts, and that collops of his former friend were being offered him not as a gratuitous atrocity, but as a test. Rutherfurd was a healthy, personable, eighteen-year-old male. What he was being given in fact – apart from the prospect of a singularly grisly meal – was the chance to submit to an ordeal and become in time a Chippewa warrior himself.

Keeping his head, he assured the Indian in charge of him, a man he called Peewash, that:

I would obey him in everything he desired me, and even in that if he insisted, but that it was very disagreeable to me, and that this was the only command I would make the least hesitation to obey him in, and begged he would not insist upon it. Thus, by a seeming readiness to obey him I avoided eating the body of my friend; and I believe by showing a desire to please him rather gained upon his affections.

Rutherfurd was subsequently stripped of his British clothes and given a blanket and breech-clout. His head was shaved 'leaving only a small tuft of hair upon the crown and two small locks' which were plaited with silver brooches, and he was instructed how to paint his face. But these were only the externals. He also had to submit to hard labour, cutting wood, planting maize, skinning animals, and doing chores for Peewash's formidable wife. Only when he had shown he was both tractable and useful, did the next stage of his initiation begin. As Rutherfurd describes it (and of course his understanding of what he witnessed will have been limited), there was a feast in which a dog was consumed but he himself was not allowed to eat. Another dog was ritually drowned; and then he and his sponsors visited an Indian burial ground on an island, and every member of the party planted a few grains of maize around the grave of one of Peewash's dead sons. Then Peewash killed a bear, and this time Rutherfurd was allowed to join the feast.

The following dawn, they all returned to sit around the same grave, burnt some of the fat of the bear upon a fire, and Peewash made a long speech 'during which he often pointed to the grave and to me alternately, and at every pause we joined in a sort of chorus':

> This, I was told, was to appease the spirit of the deceased, who might be offended at my being adopted in his place, for he then told me I was as much their son as if I had sucked these breasts (showing me those of his wife), telling me at the same time to look upon the boys [Peewash's three surviving blood sons, Mayance, Quido and Quidabin in Rutherfurd's transliteration] as my brothers, and that my name should be no more Saganash, or Englishman, but Addick, which signified a white elk.[41]

Thus did John Rutherfurd, more Scot than Englishman in fact, come by way of captivity to be ritually re-born – as Peter Williamson had so wistfully yearned to be – as something else entirely, as an Indian, as one of them.

Except that this particular crossing was never consolidated. In August 1763, Rutherfurd managed to escape and promptly joined the 42nd Regiment, the Black Watch, throwing himself into fighting Indians and ultimately rebel Americans. Yet the fact that he was never properly absorbed into Indian society, and unlike Williamson had never wanted to be, made the narrative he wrote the year after his escape more revealing in some respects than not. It meant that he was detached enough to be able to analyse in retrospect the degree to which he had – and had not – been accepted by the Chippewas. Rutherfurd recognised that Peewash and his wife wanted him not out of sentiment primarily, which they could not afford, but for the sake of his labour, and the ransom they might obtain for him if times became desperate. And he was aware that many of the other Chippewas had found his white skin risible for all its paint, and regarded him as an apprentice at best. Few of them called him Addick after his re-naming ceremony, he noted. Instead, they referred to him by Peewash's own name, making clear that he, Rutherfurd, was still a lesser, dependent being, a menial on probation who had yet to prove himself.

Yet for all of Rutherfurd's intelligence, and his determination to prise open while rejecting this Indian interlude in his life (for why else did he abandon trade and join the British army, but to wreak vengeance and demonstrate that his birth identity remained intact?), his text reveals rather more than he wanted. After he has described his initiation ceremony, he ceases to refer to Peewash, his wife and sons by their Chippewa names. Instead, he calls them 'my father', 'my mother' and 'my family'. Despite all his efforts, something ineradicable had happened to Rutherfurd on that lost burial island, which he did not wish to acknowledge but could not entirely shake off. Moreover, his captivity narrative is littered with references to other whites who had come by choice or accident into the orbit of Indian societies and been partly or wholly assimilated. There was Sir Robert Davers, an English baronet no less, who was captured alongside Rutherfurd and killed, but who had previously lived for two years with the Hurons, 'adopting their native dress and manners' in the hope that this would free him from his family's curse of melancholy. There was Ensign Pauli, a British army officer captured in Pontiac's War, who, Rutherfurd recorded, promptly got himself involved in a love relationship with a Chippewa woman. And then there was an unnamed Virginian, who had married an Indian woman, and whom Rutherfurd encountered acting as an interpreter for Pontiac himself. This narrative, in other words, contains ample evidence of hate, violence, and prejudice on both sides of the Anglo-Indian divide. But it also documents how this division still remained permeable to the extent that it was regularly broken through by individuals from different backgrounds.[42]

By the 1760s, this permeability had come to be widely recognised both among agents of the British state, and among Britons in general. During the Seven Years War, as Peter Way remarks, desertions from among the lower ranks of British regiments based in North America to various indigenous communities proved so numerous that any redcoat discovered living alongside Indians and claiming to have been captured, risked being court martialled unless he could somehow prove that he really had been forced to cross the culture line against his will. At every stage of their wartime and post-war advance through the American continent, senior British officers found themselves having to claw back white 'captives', who were often nothing of the kind. Jeffrey Amherst was predictably appalled when he occupied Montreal, and found 'British subjects' living contentedly among the local Indians and coming 'into town in their Indian dresses'.[43] More experienced and relaxed officers simply took the fact that such things happened for granted, and routinely inserted demands that stray whites be returned in any treaty negotiated with Indians. 'That any English who are prisoners, or deserters . . . shall be delivered up immediately' required a British treaty with the Hurons in 1764. Indians should not 'shelter wicked & runaway men', the Creek and Choctaw were reminded the following year, but 'deliver up all deserters, whether blacks or whites'.[44]

In the eyes of most imperial administrators, British soldiers and colonists who lived alongside Native Americans, whether out of choice or as an end-result of captivity, were to be deplored. Such interminglings affronted British national, religious, and racial pride, now much enhanced by successful global war. But, in addition, they compromised imperial stability at a strictly practical level. Britain's army in North America, especially after 1763, was simply too small for its soldiers to be allowed to drift away into wilderness entanglements with impunity. And civilian colonists who became 'white indians' might be just as troublesome. The British did not want (though they often had to put up with it anyway) bands of armed colonists attacking Indian settlements or invading Indian land on the pretext that they were only seeking to recover white captives. Much better if imperial officials could nip these problems in the bud, and recover all 'white Indians' in a systematic fashion by way of treaties and negotiation.

As far as ordinary Britons at home were concerned, however, the much greater awareness, bequeathed to them by the Seven Years War and its writings, that individual whites sometimes *chose* to live with Native Americans and were made welcome by them, proved a revelation. For such conjunctures confirmed that Indians were not simply monstrous others. Some Indians at least were manifestly capable of inspiring intense loyalty and attachment among individual whites, and of feeling affection for them in return. Thoughtful and sentimental Britons pondered what had happened when Colonel Bouquet, a Swiss-born British officer and doughty Indian fighter, had come among the Seneca and Delaware late in 1764 and forced them to yield up their white 'captives'. Some of the white children thus 'liberated' had to be dragged screaming from their

35. *The Indians delivering up the English captives to Colonel Bouquet* by Benjamin West.

adoptive Indian parents, to be reunited with blood parents they no longer recognised, and whose language they no longer spoke. But it was how the Indians involved had themselves reacted to these violent, imperially imposed separations that provoked most comment in Britain:

> The Indians too, as if wholly forgetting their usual savageness, bore a capital part in heightening this most affecting scene. They delivered up their beloved captives with the utmost reluctance; shed torrents of tears

over them, recommended them to the care and protection of the commanding officers.[45]

'*As if wholly forgetting their usual savageness*': these words from an account of Bouquet's mission written by a Pennsylvanian Anglican, and published in London in 1766 by the king's geographer himself, alert us both to an important softening of attitude, and to its limits. In the wake of the Seven Years War, and as suggested by the popularity of works like this and Peter Williamson's narrative, some Britons came to view Native Americans as more sinned against than sinning, and even to regard them as better than Europeans in the sense of being freer, more natural, and more generous even. It was still very rare however for Native Americans to be regarded or represented as rational equals to whites. None the less, the resonance in Britain of ideas and writings of this kind was still significant. For if Indians could indeed 'forget' their savageness and deal in recognisable human sentiment in their relations with captives and others, then here was impressive proof that 'savagery' was not innate, and that the 'savages' themselves were capable of change and improvement. And if Indians could indeed change and improve, then a secure and protected space must surely be found for them in Britain's American empire:

> These qualities in [Indian] savages challenge our just esteem. They should make us charitably consider their barbarities as the effects of wrong education, and false notions of bravery and heroism; while we should look on their virtues as sure marks that nature has made them fit subjects of cultivation as well as us; and that we are called by our superior advantages to yield them all the help we can in this way.[46]

For pragmatic as well as humanitarian reasons, this was a point of view that Britain's post-war imperial establishment was increasingly coming to favour.

The spoils of victory, the toils of insular constraints

For, as was always the case, the captive's story was about much more than individuals. Shifting British attitudes towards captives and captivities – in this case whites in North America and the Native Americans who seized them – were intimately bound up with shifting British attitudes towards, and anxieties about empire, in this case empire in America. The ambivalence so clearly exhibited by Britons in their discussions and imaginings of Native Americans in the wake of the Seven Years War was a function of more thoroughgoing uncertainties about their American empire as a whole. The war had been an unparalleled British success here as elsewhere, but extraordinary victories gave rise almost immediately to new challenges and misgivings.

These were partly a product of British America's now greatly inflated size. After 1763, British dominion stretched formally from the frozen Labrador beaches of the far North to the wetlands of Florida in the South, penetrated inland some 200 miles, and included a much wider range of peoples, religions and culture than before 1756. Even while the war was still being fought, British officials and soldiers newly arrived in North America had been startled by the vast size of the terrain and the heterogeneity of its inhabitants. They had been forced to recognise, as we have seen, the variety and potential danger of Native American peoples, as well as how useful some of them could be as military auxiliaries. Mobilising men to fight in America had also taught the British the scale of its black population, larger as a proportion of the Thirteen Colonies' total number of inhabitants at this time than blacks are as a proportion of the population of the United States now. Britain 'did not look to colour, size, or age provided they are able bodied . . . and know the use of a gun', its commander-in-chief in America informed New Yorkers in 1756, and no other attitude had been feasible given the British authorities' usual desperate need for manpower, and the fact that blacks made up a fifth of this city's population.[47]

Now that the war was won, and Canada, Louisiana, and Florida were part of their empire, British officials in America also had to deal with an accession of substantial numbers of new, non-Anglophone white subjects who were Catholics, not Protestants, as well as with these regions' respective indigenous peoples.[48] Here, then, was one dimension of Britain's postwar imperial challenge. British mainland North America was far bigger than before, and demonstrably far less British. Even the Thirteen Colonies, which had been in existence before the Seven Years War, were now increasingly seen in London as heterogenous in terms of peoples, cultures and interests. The wartime presence of so many British soldiers and officials in the Thirteen Colonies, and the increased flow of information about them, not only made Britons more aware of their non-white populations, but also more sensitive to the degree to which their white colonists here were both similar to, and different from themselves. It is surely suggestive that, after 1763, the British seem regularly to have referred to their white American colonists as 'Americans' – a decade or more before white Americans themselves began habitually doing so. Those white men and women on the other side of the Atlantic who had once been carelessly assumed to be identical to Britons at home, now came to be perceived by many, though not by all Britons, as already distinctive, and potentially different.[49]

And this in turn made another of Britain's post-1763 imperial challenges profoundly troubling. During the war, British imperial officials in the Thirteen Colonies had tried, for military and administrative purposes, to count the number of their white and non-white populations. As they soon discovered, there were now a lot of the former as well as the latter to count. The high fertility levels of successive generations of settler women like Susanna Johnson had helped drive the colonies' white population from some 55,000 in 1650, to 265,000 in 1700, to 1.2 million in 1750. In just a hundred years, Anglo colonists in North America had risen from being a hundredth of *England's* own current population, to being a fifth of its current population; and, by 1770, the ratio of American colonists to English men and women had shrunk yet again, to a mere one to three.[50] This faster rate of American demographic growth after 1750 was influenced, like so much else, by the Seven Years War. Once the British proved victorious, and French ambitions in the continent came to an end, migration to America from across the Atlantic accelerated. Between 1760 and 1776, some 55,000 Protestant Irish, 40,000 Scots, and 30,000 inhabitants of England and Wales left their homes for America, a territory about which they and their countrymen were now so much better informed. The majority of these transatlantic emigrants, as the politicians in London took trouble to establish, were young men under thirty, the very age and sex cohort upon which the agriculture, industry, army and navy of Britain itself most depended.[51]

What usually lay behind Britain's recurrent panics about its imperial enterprise thus came after 1763 to rankle and provoke enormous anxiety yet again: the smallness of its own size, resources and population. How was Britain, whose population was known to be growing far less quickly than that of its American colonies, to retain authority over the latter in the future? 'In twenty or thirty years', predicted one expert in 1767 (with an expert's usual capacity for getting things wrong) 'there will be as many people in them [the American colonies], if not more, than are in England.' As it was, this same writer warned, Britain's population was 'a very insufficient number to manage and conduct all the affairs of this nation, both at home and abroad; to people and secure all the British dominions'. If large numbers of its young men were to be regularly lost through emigration to the American colonies, how indeed was Britain to maintain its own national prosperity and defend itself in war, never mind keep hold of its vastly extended empire? 'We know, sir', George Grenville had warned the House of Commons even before the war:

that Spain . . . [has] been almost dispeopled, by too much encouraging their people to remove to their settlements in America; and therefore, however useful such settlements may be to this kingdom, this should be a warning to us not to allow them to dispeople their mother country.[52]

Britons' increased tendency after the war to see the American colonists as people who were subtly different from themselves made such concerns still more disturbing. In the past, Britons had felt able to rejoice unstintingly at their American colonists' evident fertility and profusion, viewing this as an automatic accession as well to their own strength and power. Now some Britons felt less confident that the rapidly rising numbers of their colonists across the Atlantic, what Benjamin Franklin called 'the American multiplication table', would always and necessarily redound to their own national and imperial advantage. 'If they should continue to double and double', wrote Samuel Johnson darkly, in a draft pamphlet on the American colonists in 1775, 'their own hemisphere would not contain them.' The prospect was so terrifying that Johnson scratched these lines out of his manuscript before submitting it to the printers.[53]

But what most concerned the authorities in Britain was less the thought of Americans assuming in time an all-powerful, imperial sway of their own – which still seemed very distant – than the strictly practical question of how their white colonists and the other peoples of British mainland North America were to be effectively governed, controlled, and kept tranquil in the immediate future. During the war, British army and civilian officials in North America had come to the conclusion that it was ceaseless settler intrusions into Native American lands that were often responsible for provoking Indian violence. The outbreak of Pontiac's Rising in 1763, in which Britons like John Rutherfurd and Thomas Morris and many others were captured, and large numbers of British troops were killed, further underlined to the men in London just how imperative it was to keep colonial settlers and Native Americans cordoned off from each other, mutually secure from each other, and alike peaceful and obedient to the Crown. It was in the hope of achieving this that the British sought after 1763 – so contentiously as far as their colonists were concerned – to maintain an army of 10,000 British troops in North America. A permanent and sizeable force of regular army troops, London optimistically believed, would be able to hold the line between the rising numbers of land-hungry white colonists, and those angry, eroded and retreating Indian peoples, who were still capable of being immensely dangerous and expensive to subdue.[54]

But since American colonists understandably refused to be taxed in order that they could be better policed, this army of 10,000 British regulars never materialised. By the early 1770s, Britain had fewer than 4500 men in uniform to enforce its rule over the immense expanses of Canada, the Thirteen Colonies, Florida and the western frontier, because its own standing army was as ever limited, and its domestic taxpayers could not and would not subsidise any more men in time of peace.[55] As was so often the case, Britain's own varieties of smallness compromised and qualified its imperial practice and pretensions.

All this said, one should not exaggerate the degree to which British empire in America was under unbearable pressure at this stage, any more than one should over-emphasise the extent of post-war British angst. There were many men and women on both sides of the Atlantic in the 1760s and early '70s who rejoiced unstintingly in the British empire's unprecedented global reach and riches, who continued to regard each other as Protestant brethren and fellow Britons, and who believed that this transatlantic union based on commerce, religion, and a single monarch would and should always be maintained. But there were also other Britons, on both sides of the Atlantic, who were more presciently aware that victory on a previously unimaginable scale in the Seven Years War had brought with it stunning territorial gains, administrative and military burdens, and popular expectations that would be very hard to sustain, and that in North America British imperial power was already coming under extreme strain, and even in some respects retreating.

And this was perhaps the ultimate reason why post-war British reactions and references to Native Americans were sometimes conspicuously sympathetic, and why texts like Peter Williamson's later, nuanced captivity narratives won so much sustained popularity. Paradoxically, but not as paradoxically as it appeared, Britons at home and the retreating indigenous peoples of North America now possessed certain things in common. Just like the British empire, Native Americans faced mounting pressures. And, just as some Britons at home now felt anxious about the size of their population, and threatened by the rising numbers and restlessness of their white colonists in America, so with far more cause did Native Americans. British imperialists and their one-time indigenous victims thus found themselves, in the wake of the Seven Years War, coming sometimes strangely together in the face of a common challenge: those growing ranks of white American colonists who were growing increasingly impatient by now both of the claims of Native Americans, and of the claims of George III, Parliament, and imperial power. In the coming crisis, neither Native Americans nor the British empire would escape.

SEVEN

Revolutions

Mistaken identities

Friday, September 22, 1780: His second captivity is destined to be short.

It is already night when he is rowed ashore, and the trees lining the western banks of the Hudson River are almost as swallowed up in darkness as his own glittering jacket, concealed beneath his cloak. He rides, unseeing and unseen, to the pre-arranged site near Haverstraw, but the encounter goes on for too long. The American, who is perhaps no longer an American, has put him at risk already by refusing to meet on board the British warship moored discreetly down river. Now, he is obliged to thrash out details of pensions, promotions and proper safeguards until suddenly it is dawn. Tense with fatigue, and sensitive to every sudden sound, the unregarding birds, small mammals rustling the undergrowth, a single cannon shot he cannot place, he lets himself be persuaded to ride to a nearby house and shelter there until it is night again. His refuge is within sight, when suddenly, at far too short a distance, he hears the sentry's voice, and understands. He, John André, aide-de-camp of Henry Clinton, His Majesty's commander-in-chief in America, has closed a deal with a leading Revolutionary general called Benedict Arnold, to defect and deliver up West Point to the British. But, in the process, he himself has been drawn across a crucial boundary. For him, the safe house is not safe at all. It is behind American lines.

He does his best: though, by now, his judgement and nerves are under extreme strain. He replaces the gold-embroidered jacket of a senior British staff-officer with a plain, crimson greatcoat lent him by his Loyalist host, stuffs Arnold's secret instructions into the feet of his white, silk stockings, and sets off that Saturday morning to find a road back to New York and his headquarters. Arnold has given him a pass, and since the American's defection is still some days away, this proves sufficient to take him safely past two sets of sentries and into neutral territory once more. It is perhaps the surge of relief he experiences at this point that undoes him. The three Revolutionary militiamen, in homespun, mud-spattered civilian dress, have been combing the woods for deserters from their own ranks, and they are initially as uncertain of the stranger's identity as he is of theirs. True, his accent is distinctive, and his beard stubble and ill-fitting coat seem at odds with his poise and physical arrogance, but these are troubled, makeshift times, and nobody looks or behaves any more in predictable ways. They are alert enough however to parry the man's anxious, supremely ill-judged question. 'Of which party are you?' asks John André. 'Yours', they reply. At which point, he lets himself relax, and tells them he is a British army officer in need of help. With these words, he puts the rope around his neck.

They hanged him as a spy at Tappan, near the boundary between New York state and New Jersey, on 2 October, five hundred American soldiers keeping back the crowds of men, women and children, who wept and moaned and watched as his body swayed for a full half hour before it was cut down. The sentimental mythologies which sprang up almost immediately around André and his fate lasted much longer, especially in the new United States. Throughout the nineteenth century and after, American

36. John André's pen-and-ink self-portrait the day before his execution.

collectors bid against each other for locks of the dead man's hair, for one of the sketches he completed during his final captivity, for chairs he had sat on, and for books he had owned. Any portrait of a young, handsome, but unknown redcoat officer was virtually certain to be relabelled 'Major John André', so his image was perpetually shifting and multiplying.

This American cult around an executed, twenty-nine-year-old British army major was not as odd as it seems. John André had, after all, lost out in every sense. West Point did not surrender in the Revolutionary War, whereas George III's legions in America ultimately did. So to his admirers, André could appear wrong but unfailingly romantic, a useful foil to his nemesis Benedict Arnold who seemed merely repulsive and renegade, the Judas Iscariot of a great revolution. And André himself had been so charming, so different seemingly from the stereotypes of British arrogance and imperial thuggery. Part French, part Swiss, multi-lingual, a keen artist, a keeper of diaries, a devotee – like so many British army officers – of amateur theatricals, he had possessed as well startlingly good looks and a happy, easy manner that enchanted his own sex as well as women. For all that he was decidedly mercantile in background and flamboyantly cosmopolitan in outlook, the stiff, titled upper reaches of the British army parted and gave way before André's personal appeal like a red sea. And on his last day, he did nothing wrong but die. He cheerfully consumed the breakfast George Washington sent him from his own table. He walked to the place of execution arm-in-arm with two young American officers who had become instantly his friends, and bowed to those other, more senior officers who had sentenced him to hang. The sight of the scaffold and the rope made him stumble and look down for a moment (he had hoped to be shot as a soldier), but he made himself recover. The sound of the American drums, he remarked before stepping lightly on the cart that would transport him to eternity, was more musical than he could ever have imagined.[1]

Yet such details, which drew tears from spectators at the time and nourished his posthumous reputation, can obscure what André was and what he believed. Cultivated, glamorous, sensitive and brave he undoubtedly was, but he was also an ambitious, experienced imperial warrior who fought and schemed out of deep patriotic conviction. As he wrote to a British army friend before his execution: 'I could not think an attempt to put an end to a *civil war* . . . a crime.' Just as Washington, for all his chivalry, never doubted that his graceful British captive must hang, so André, for all his pleasantness to his American captors, never doubted for a moment that they and their kind were rebels wantonly disrupting the good governance and interwoven destiny of the transatlantic empire he served. We

The Unfortunate DEATH of MAJOR ANDRÉ

(Adjutant General to the English Army) at Head Quarters, in New York, Oct. 2. 1780,
who was found within the American Lines in the character of a Spy.

37. The execution of John André.

must also consider that beneath the impeccable manners lay probably a desire for revenge. For André had been captured before. He had surrendered with hundreds more of his comrades at Fort St John, Canada, in November 1775, and was held for months on parole in Lancaster and Carlisle, small, backwoods settlements in Pennsylvania, where the more republican inhabitants sometimes pelted him in the streets, intercepted his letters, threatened him with jail and worse, and 'meant to humiliate us and exalt themselves'.[2] Here was one context where all of André's charm and accomplishments counted for little. Personally contributing to a coup that would strip the Revolutionaries of West Point, in the same year that had seen them soundly defeated at Charleston and Camden, must have appeared a singularly attractive mode of retribution. And what better way to wipe out memories of his own captive mortifications than to entrap and bring over the line Benedict Arnold, the man chiefly responsible for capturing thousands of British troops at the Battle of Saratoga back in 1777?

In this imperial set-piece drama, as in so many others, issues of captivity played a critical part. As far as the British were concerned, captivities of different kinds proved crucial throughout the American Revolutionary War, for distinctive as well as for more customary reasons. It bears repeating that the British had never succeeded in forging a consensus on how to view their American colonists. For a substantial minority of Britons, the people across the Atlantic were always too distant to arouse much interest at all. And while awareness of North America had certainly increased dramatically in Britain with the onset of the Seven Years War, this had not led to unanimity of response. To some, the white inhabitants of the Thirteen Colonies who had contributed so much to victory after 1756 seemed more than ever extensions of themselves on another shore, fellow Protestants and freedom-loving Britons. But, for others in Britain, white settlers in America were first and foremost colonists, people to be governed benevolently but also firmly, just as other North American groupings – Francophone Canadians or Native Americans – were to be governed.

War between Britain and the one-time Thirteen Colonies after 1775 both stemmed from, and also exacerbated these fundamental disagreements and uncertainties. John André gave himself away and was destroyed, because – when it mattered most – he failed to identify Americans correctly, to distinguish those who were his enemies from those who were his friends. In much the same way, vacillation and division over how to *see* the peoples across the Atlantic meant that Britons in this conflict proved unable either to legitimise their own captive-taking effectively, or to agree among themselves over who was to be considered captive from among their own ranks.

Out of these persistent embarrassments was bred a propaganda and political defeat to match the military one.

Who is to count?

At the most straightforward level, the American War of Independence saw tens of thousands of soldiers and seamen on the British side being taken prisoner. The fundamental reasons for this were the by-now familiar ones: Britain was too small, too under-populated, with too restricted a standing army to conduct successful, large-scale land warfare on imperial or any other territory over a protracted period, unless it enjoyed the active support of very large numbers of the local inhabitants, or other, substantial allies. This point needs stressing because, as Stephen Conway remarks, 'the image of a near invincible British military machine' is often summoned up in relation to this conflict 'consciously or sub-consciously . . . to magnify the achievements of the amateurish Americans'.[3] Witness Mel Gibson's film *The Patriot*, with its ranks of red-coated automata, commanded by glittering, malign British officers, confronting scruffy, ill-supplied but sternly virtuous American citizen soldiers. This is the potent legend of American revolution: the battlefield reality was something else.

To be sure, Britain appeared initially a mighty Goliath set against the Revolutionaries' alert but anorexic David, a supremely aggressive state that had transformed the balance of global power in the Seven Years War: but that had been a very different conflict. The British had fought it with the aid of powerful allies in Europe, crucially Prussia, which effectively tied down substantial sectors of their enemies' armed forces in that continent. As far as North America was concerned, the British had also secured the aid eventually of some 20,000 colonial troops, and extensive civilian support among their colonists as well. Even so, it had still taken them several years to beat back France's much smaller colonial forces and move decisively into Canada.

In 1775, the situation was very different and far more dangerous. The major European powers were either hostile to Britain from the outset, like France, or neutral, like Russia. Many American colonists were openly in arms against it, and far more remained glumly uncommitted; while Britain's own armed forces were not what they had been back in the *annus mirabilis* of 1759, when nothing, it seemed, could stand against them. For reasons of economy, the Royal Navy had been run down after 1763, while in reality, as distinct from on paper, the army at the outbreak of this new war could muster less than 36,000 men. The British government's best chance to contain and crush what it regarded as a rebellion was to do so ruthlessly and rapidly, but in the vital first two years of this American war, London raised fewer than 18,000 extra troops. These numbers can still seem impressive when compared with Washington's forces at this time, but distance and geography also need taking into account. Revolutionary troops were on home ground, though not always among friends. By contrast, almost everything the British army in America consumed, wore or shot with had to be shipped 3000 miles across the ocean, or requisitioned from the local inhabitants, and thereby risk alienating them further.[4]

Then there was the sheer scale of this conflict, which for the British was bigger than any previous war they had ever fought. Americans tend naturally to focus only on what happened in the Thirteen Colonies, the germ of what became a new nation and (eventually) a new empire. But these comprised only half of the twenty-six colonies contained within Britain's Atlantic empire at this time, which also included Canada, Nova Scotia, the Floridas, islands in the Caribbean, and unofficial settlements in the Bay of Honduras and the Mosquito Shore. Most of the inhabitants in *these* regions did not revolt in 1775, but almost all of these territories witnessed battles or skirmishes of some kind; and all of them sucked in British troops and auxiliaries, rendering them vulnerable to capture, disease or death.[5] The situation worsened immeasurably after 1778 when France formally entered the war on the Revolutionaries' side, followed by Spain in 1779 and the Dutch in 1780. This not only amplified the military and – above all – the naval resources available to the Americans, but also ensured that the conflict spread to other continents. Every Dutch, Spanish or French colony, and every British possession in the Mediterranean, Africa and India, now became fair game for fighting, fresh sites for death and capture. By 1780, the land forces at Britain's command exceeded 100,000 men, but the geographical range of the war by this stage had widened to such a degree that less than 30 per cent of these troops were available to fight in North America itself.[6] This seeming Goliath haemorrhaged at every joint.

The scale and nature of this war go some way towards explaining why the number of British captives seized during it was at once very large and peculiarly open to dispute. From the very beginning, significant numbers of British combatants and civilians were captured both on land and at sea. At least 250 troops were seized alongside John André in just the single engagement at Fort St John in November 1775. Two years later, the chief American commissary of prisoners, Elias Boudinot, calculated that the British held almost 6500 American prisoners, but that his side had some 10,000 British troops under various kinds of duress.[7] In 1780, in the wake of the battles of Charleston and Camden, the advantage in terms of prisoners-of-war held swung strongly in favour of the British, but Yorktown, and other, less spectacular defeats, changed this decisively. In May 1782, General Clinton grimly informed the authorities in London that the enemy now controlled some 12,000 British prisoners-of-war 'to our 500'.[8]

Yet such figures were little more than rough estimates of certain categories of prisoner. As the British War Office admitted, at this time, it simply did not possess:

> the means of ascertaining the number of men lost by captivity, having no account of what the whole number of prisoners taken in any one year may be, or of the prisoners that may have been exchanged in the course of it.

The Revolutionary American authorities were even less capable of maintaining precise and comprehensive records of captives taken, in part because British prisoners in America were never concentrated in a few, easily-surveyed detention camps and centres, but were widely, even haphazardly scattered. The 2500-odd British soldiers taken at Saratoga, for instance, were subsequently split up between nine of the one-time Thirteen Colonies, and thirty different settlements.[9] Given this scatter-shot distribution, it was hard for officials, however conscientious they were, to keep track of how many men died or escaped during the course of imprisonment, or of how many changed sides, whether by attaching themselves to the American Continental army or local militias, or by marrying a local woman and melting quietly into the community.

Such prisoner totals as were bandied about were also selective in other ways. Estimates of British captives by army men, like those cited above, usually omitted the thousands of Royal Navy prisoners and British merchant seamen and passengers captured at sea by American privateers. David Sproat, the British Commissary responsible for naval prisoners, claimed after the war that, by 1779, 'British seamen lay (much neglected) . . . in almost every gaol in America', and that he himself had supervised exchanges for over 7700 of them.[10] These men represented only a fraction of the total number of Britons captured at sea during this conflict. Once France, Spain and the Dutch entered the war, their navies and privateer fleets also joined in the work of captive-taking, while American privateers operating in the Atlantic and the Channel became able to unload any British captives they seized in French, Spanish or Dutch ports, instead of having to go to the trouble of sailing home with them. In 1779, Benjamin Franklin claimed that there were now more Britons held as

38. Loyalists rescue a British prisoner of war in America. Conditions were usually much harsher than this.

prisoners-of-war in France, than there were countrymen of his in jail in Britain. This may have been no more than a propaganda ploy, a transparent attempt to encourage British ministers to concentrate their minds on future prisoner exchanges. Or it may have been a well-informed guess on Franklin's part. The British themselves calculated that, by the end of the war, at least 2000 of their seamen were imprisoned in Spain, many of them brought there by American privateers.[11]

It seems likely therefore that, in certain peak years in the American Revolutionary War, the number of British soldiers and naval and merchant seamen held captive was in excess of 20,000, particularly since we need to add to the total number of POWs held in America and Europe, men taken in connected battles in the West Indies, in Latin America, in coastal Africa and – as we shall see in a later chapter – in India. Global war resulted in a global pattern of captivities. Yet neither this, nor the poor quality of contemporary record-keeping, is the main obstacle to reconstructing what captivity in this lost imperial war signified for the British. The more intractable and distinctive challenge has to do with definitions.

Who, in this conflict, is to be included in an estimate of 'British captives'? Whom exactly do we count? History is still written overwhelmingly from the viewpoint of the victors, so most accounts of this war conform to the assertions contained in the Declaration of Independence. This means that, after 1775, the main combatants are customarily labelled either as British and pro-British, or as American and pro-American, as though these were distinct, understood and agreed upon polarities at the time. Yet this imposes a degree of clarity and homogeneity on allegiances in this war, and on individual captives, which was often conspicuously absent.

Consider some of the women involved. In 1775, they made up about an eighth of the personnel clustered in the various British army camps in North America. By the end of war, the proportion of women to soldiers in these units was nearer one to four. Inevitably, in the course of battle or in ambushes while on the march, some of these female camp followers and army wives were seized by Revolutionary troops, just as others were raped and/or killed. Just under a quarter of the 'British' taken prisoners alongside André in Canada in 1775 are known to have been women and children. Hundreds more women were seized after the British surrender at Saratoga. 'Such a sordid set of creatures', wrote one genteel female witness who watched appalled as they tramped past in the wake of their captive menfolk:

> great numbers of women, who seemed to be the beasts of burthen, having a bushel basket on their back, by which they were bent double, the contents seemed to be pots and kettles, various sorts of furniture, children peeping thro' gridirons and other utensils, some very young infants who were born on the road, the women bare feet [sic], cloathed in dirty rags, such effluvia filled the air . . . had they not been smoking at the time, I should have been apprehensive of being contaminated.[12]

Here was a very different face of British armed imperialism. As the war went on, a growing proportion of these women, who were indispensable to the army in terms of the nursing, cooking and laundrywork they provided, were actually American-born. This is why their prominence in British army encampments rose so markedly throughout the duration of the war. Many were refugees who had lost parents, husbands or other providers in the course of the fighting, and attached themselves to a passing British regiment in return for a share of rations and a modicum of shelter and companionship. Some had simply formed close attachments to particular British soldiers while their regiment was encamped nearby, and subsequently joined them on the march, perhaps coming to regard themselves as common-law wives. These armed 'invaders' spoke, after all, the same language as the women themselves, and shared similar customs and cultural references, so 'fraternization with the enemy' was scarcely an adequate description of what was going on here. The question arises then: how are women like this who were taken captive, to be classified? Should they be counted as Britons, like the men they catered to? Or should they be viewed as Americans captured by their own side? Almost certainly, many of those involved would have found neither definition appropriate to the complexities and raw imperatives of their position.

Nor is it easy to categorise some of Britain's male auxiliaries in this war. Like their opponents, the British themselves normally drew a distinction between their own regular forces, and those Hessians and other Germans who were hired to fight alongside them, who made up about a third of 'British' troops in North America by 1778. When a Revolutionary soldier called Joshua Pilsberry made his own head-count of the men who surrendered at Saratoga in October 1777, he, too, was very clear on this point, but also unconsciously eloquent about his own lingering confusions. There were 2242 'British Prisoners' among General Burgoyne's defeated army, he calculated; and, in addition, there were also 2390 'Foreigners'. For Pilsberry, evidently, the British, though incontestably the enemy, were not yet foreign.[13] The British themselves also distinguished between the European troops in their service on the one hand, and their Native American allies on the other. They drew even clearer distinctions, on paper and in their minds, between their various white supporters in America and the black slaves that flocked to their armies in such vast numbers in the Southern colonies. American Loyalists, however, were (and are) much harder to categorise.

Naturally enough, in the eyes of zealous Revolutionaries, Loyalists were traitors aiding and abetting a dangerous enemy, friends of corruption, oppression and unfreedom. In December 1777, Congress ruled that any individuals who voluntarily sided with the British in any way were to be confined and dealt with by their respective states, thereby treating them as criminals rather than as prisoners-of-war, and opening the way for significant numbers of Loyalists to be incarcerated, often for many years, deprived of their property, driven into exile, and in some cases tortured and even lynched. As in France after 1789, revolution in America was propagated at grassroots level in part through vigilantism and varieties of terror. John Maguire, a resident of Lancaster, Pennsylvania, took the risk of hiding some escaping British POWs in his own house, and found himself subsequently 'discovered, imprisoned and is now ruined'. Other men and women fell foul of local Revolutionary committees for uttering the wrong words in the wrong places, or for failing to celebrate the right victories unambiguously enough, or simply because they were suspected or disliked by their neighbours.[14]

Naturally enough, in their own eyes, Loyalists were not traitors at all, but very much the opposite. They viewed themselves as adhering faithfully to the allegiance in which they had been born, and many regarded themselves not merely as British subjects, but quite simply as British. So, once again the question arises: how are men and women of this type to be classified? Certainly, if every North American Loyalist who spent some time in prison or in other forms of confinement between 1775 and 1783 is to be included, the total number of Britons taken captive during this conflict would easily reach 50,000, and perhaps even approach 100,000 souls.

There was a further complexity, a further sense in which the ostensibly clear terms 'American' and 'British' proved slippery and contested in practice. By 1779, some 2000 American Revolutionary POWs were being held in different sites throughout Britain and Ireland, but overwhelmingly on the southern coast of England, most of them men taken at sea by the Royal Navy or by British privateers.[15] This was nothing new in that large numbers of POWs had been confined in Britain before. And it was nothing new either for such men to attract sympathy from the locals. During the Seven Years War – as we have seen – there had been public subscriptions to buy comforts for the thousands of French POWs who were confined in Britain, and after 1775 similar collections were organised to aid these new American prisoners. What *was* novel was the degree of uncertainty about how the latter were to be seen. Allan Ramsay, the Scottish artist, put it in a nutshell when he wrote in 1777 that war with the one-time Thirteen Colonies was neither a dispute with a clearly foreign enemy, nor one with a purely domestic opponent. Instead, he argued, there had 'lately started up to view in America a new class of men, who will be found upon examination to belong to neither of these two classes; who, for that reason, give great perplexity'.[16]

Were these ragged, angry men, confined in different English, Welsh, Scottish and Irish coastal towns, who spoke the same language as the British troops and jailers guarding them, simply enemy POWs? Or were they, too, captive Britons of a kind? Or were they perhaps something else besides? To anti-war Whigs and radicals in Britain, the answer was clear. For them, Revolutionary POWs, whether held in North America or in Britain itself, were martyrs in the cause of liberty, victims of George III's oppression, and above all fellow-Britons. But many other Britons viewed their American captives and opponents more ambivalently and more

The Commissioners interview with CONGRESS.

39. *The Commissioners Interview with Congress*: a British print of 1778.

accurately. They perceived them as different from former enemies, to be sure, but they remained uncertain as to what these people were, or just how far they were like or unlike themselves.

This was a dilemma that British cartoonists of the time ventilated without being able to resolve. For much of the eighteenth century, American colonists had been represented in British graphic art in the guise of Indians. This was clearly inappropriate after 1775, since Native Americans were progressively Britain's allies in the war. How, then, to represent the 'disloyal' American white? It is striking how often during the Revolutionary War British artists resorted to different kinds of costume to demarcate these people without ever reaching a satisfactory and universally accepted stereotype. So Revolutionary Americans are shown in British wartime prints wearing absurd, ill-fitting uniforms that look like something borrowed out of a particularly cobwebbed attic. Or the revolutionary purity of the governor of Massachusetts, John Hancock, is at once trumpeted and slyly mocked by picturing him in strange, fur-trimmed garments, with bare, muscular legs as against Lord North's foppish brocade, silken hose and Garter ribbon. Or members of Congress are displayed in the shade of a clearly alien palm tree, gazing disapprovingly at the effete, stick-like earl of Carlisle, who unavailingly offers them a peace, their heads and bodies swathed in fashions that are unquestionably their own. Here, in such images, were glimmers of a growing British awareness that some Americans at least were inventing themselves anew. Yet, at the same time, it is suggestive that American difference in these prints remains largely confined to dress, to that which is put on, but can also be taken off again.

The fact that so much of this conflict had to do with issues of identity and allegiance – with how 'Americans' and 'Britons' were to see each other – meant that men and women taken captive in the course of it became invested, more even than was usual, with a significance greater than themselves. It was not simply that the large numbers of captives seized, like the rising toll of deaths, injuries and taxes, marked out over the years just how dangerous and expensive this war was becoming, though this was certainly the case with regard to both of the main protagonists. In this American war, to a unique degree, the question of how captives from the other side were to be seen and treated fed into and focused much wider debates about where the boundaries of nation and empire were to be situated.

In part, this was due to the combatants' shared literary inheritance. Both the British at home, and British colonists in North America, had evolved their own traditions of narrating and wrestling with captivity. The former had become accustomed to employing such narratives to mull over their national and imperial strengths and weaknesses, and the differences and degree of overlap between themselves and various enemies. In this imperial war, however, the significance of captivity tales was a special one, because the main protagonists shared a common language and a common obsession with print. As a result, men and women in Britain were not merely exposed to accounts of their own soldiers' and supporters' experiences of suffering and capture, but frequently as well to accounts written and printed by Americans attacking Britain's role as an aggressor and captor. In these unique circumstances, the business of writing and arguing about captivity became itself an aspect of war and a Revolutionary manoeuvre.

Catching the lion in the net

On 1 June 1781, a man called William Widger had a dream. A semi-literate Revolutionary privateersman from Marblehead, Massachusetts, Widger had been captured by the Royal Navy in 1779 with the rest of the crew of the brig *Phoenix*, brought back to England, and lodged with other American POWs in Mill Prison in Plymouth. As a place of confinement, this was more ramshackle than ruthless, with a low death-rate by the standards of the day, and a high number of escapees, and Widger seems to have experienced little difficulty in keeping and concealing a prison diary. It was in the pages of this that he set down and attempted to make sense of his vision. Transported instantly in sleep across the thousands of miles that separated him from America, he had imagined himself walking again along a familiar road in Marblehead, though – as is often the way with dreams – he had somehow understood even at the time that this was only an illusion, and that he was engaging with shadows. A one-time neighbour named Sylvester Stephens suddenly materialised out of the mists to greet him, and for a while they had seemed to talk:

I said to him: 'Tis damd hard now I have got so near home and can't git there'. I thought he asked me: 'What the matter was?' I sayes: 'Why you see I am this side of the way.'

In Widger's dream, the wide Atlantic Ocean narrowed drastically to a single dusty New England street, to one side of which he was bound fast. Unable to reach out and make contact with his place of origin for real, it was as if he could still discern tantalizing images of it. In his grimy Plymouth jail, he seemed 'so near home', and yet was not there.[17]

The Unconscious can select its symbolism with dazzling aptness: and Widger's night-time imaginings caught very well the sense that many POWs on both sides of this conflict seem to have experienced, that they were at once divorced from their familiar surroundings and existence, yet because of the peculiar circumstances of this war, not entirely so. Whether British or American, they had to deal with opponents whose skin colour and clothing was often the same as their own, and who might well speak the same language, worship the same Protestant God, react and think for much of the time in very similar ways. So the imaginary wall that normally descends in war brutally separating one side from the other proved in this one sometimes markedly unstable. Men and women would glance at those who were in name and fact their enemies, and find themselves staring at a mirror.

Virtually every captivity narrative that survives from this war contains such ambiguous and equivocal epiphanies. For Thomas Hughes, English army officer and old Etonian, the moment came in Bennington, Vermont, late in 1777. Captured at Ticonderoga that year, and marched along at gunpoint, he was suddenly crowded around by the town's inhabitants, and recognised in their faces a degree of shock that may have registered too on his own features. They 'appear'd surpris'd', he wrote, 'to find us like themselves'.[18] For John Blatchford, a cabin boy on the Revolutionary vessel *Hancock*, who was captured at sea and brought to Portsmouth, the sense of boundaries between enemies giving way occurred amidst the bric-à-brac of an English parlour. He was ushered in:

> To satisfy the curiosity of some ladies, who had never seen a Yankee, as they called me. I went in, and they seemed greatly surprised to see me look like an Englishman; they said they were sure I was no Yankee, but like themselves.

Charles Herbert, a fellow Revolutionary sailor confined in another English seaport, recorded a very similar exchange in his captivity narrative. In his case, it was some curious Royal Navy seamen's wives who pointed out the obvious. 'What sort of people are they?' these women asked, before catching sight of the American prisoners for the first time. 'Are they white?'

> Upon being pointed to where some of them stood, 'Why!' exclaimed they, 'they look like our people, and they talk English!'[19]

Such moments of mutual recognition, between enemies who spoke and looked the same, must have occurred in this war often enough. Yet some of those describing such encounters in retrospect almost certainly did so with an ulterior purpose. Passages, like the ones quoted above, in which captive Revolutionary warriors brought back to Britain are judged by onlookers there to be 'just like themselves', are often followed in American captivity narratives by an incident or a conversation showing that in fact the reverse was true. Thus Charles Herbert's posthumous and heavily edited narrative follows the account of the British seamen's wives' seeming recognition of American POWs as being 'like our people' with an anecdote making clear that this was not the case at all. Herbert (or his editor) describes how he subsequently got hold of a list of rations kept by his British guards in Forton Prison, marked with the words 'For the Rebel Prisoners'. Herbert – we are told – immediately 'scratched out the word "rebel" and wrote "American"' instead. The captivity ordeal, in this version, muddies Herbert's patriot identity only to proclaim it more vigorously than ever.[20] The hardships of detention on enemy territory serve to reveal what he and his comrades truly are – free and independent Americans – as distinct from what they only appear to be. As this example suggests, writings on captivity in the American Revolutionary War carry a particularly heavy freight of conscious political intent. For both main protagonists, but especially for the Revolutionaries, writing and acting out captivity became an integral part of the war of ideas.

As far as the British were concerned, it appeared imperative from the outset to signal exactly what they viewed captive Americans as being. Not until 1782, when all was lost, would the Westminster Parliament grant these men the formal status of 'prisoners-of-war'. Doing so earlier would have been to concede that they were agents of a sovereign enemy state. Instead, the line officially taken was that American prisoners were 'the King's misguided subjects'. Since Britain was a humane state, the official argument went, these men would not be exposed to the savage penalties conventionally visited on rebels. None the less, rebels was precisely what they were.[21] Other ways were sought to treat Revolutionary captives in such a manner as to deny American claims to independence. General Gage initially refused to accommodate his commissioned American prisoners separately from American private soldiers in order to make clear that he recognised no army ranks approved of by George Washington, only those granted by order of King George III. As more and more British prisoners, including officers, were taken by the Americans and placed at their mercy, this particular piece of gesture politics was abandoned, but language was deployed to make analogous points throughout the war. In 1777, Sir William Howe, then British commander-in-chief in North America, advised an underling how an imminent exchange of prisoners was to be conducted:

> One caution I beg leave to add: which is, that neither His Majesty's name on your part, or the Congress on the other, be permitted to appear in any of your transactions, as the agreement must be supposed to subsist between Mr Washington and myself.

Congress's authority over the self-proclaimed United States was not to be formally admitted in British official dealings, any more than was George Washington's right to his army title now that he was leading a rebellion.[22]

From the viewpoint of today, these can easily seem the futile niceties of a bunch of imperial fogeys seriously out of touch with reality. But of course in 1777 neither Howe nor the rest of the world could know that Washington's cause would eventually triumph. What members of the British political and military elites did know, all too well, was that any verbal slip on their part would be gleefully exploited by an enemy that shared the same language and the same delight in printed propaganda. Revolutionary elites were just as concerned not to make any slip that might appear to admit George III's authority over them, and just as calculating about words and gestures. In virtually every exchange of prisoners negotiated, the Americans made use of the formula 'officer for officer, soldier for soldier, citizen for citizen'.[23] Insisting that it was citizens who were being exchanged was one more way of proclaiming that they, as well as the British, possessed their own sovereign state. There were some respects, however, in which American Revolutionaries exploited captivity issues very differently from their British opponents. They were far more unabashed about doing so, and they were infinitely more successful.

One reason for this was Congress's resolution on 10 July 1776 that any cruelties committed by British forces or their allies in North America would be viewed as being done on George III's instructions. This gave Revolutionaries the strongest possible incentive to assemble, broadcast, and, if necessary, manufacture as much evidence of British wartime atrocities as they could possibly manage. There was often plenty of such evidence genuinely available. British as well as American sources make it clear that, on many occasions during this lost imperial war, individual Redcoats raped helpless women, sometimes with their officers' approval, wantonly destroyed civilian property, routinely killed the wounded on the field of battle, arbitrarily imprisoned known and suspected Revolutionary supporters, and sometimes tortured and strung them up.[24] American prisoners-of-war could also run the gauntlet of casual and sometimes deliberate British cruelty. It has become a cliché of patriotic American textbooks that some 11,500 captive Americans were allowed to die in the dank, microbe-infested holds of British prison ships moored in New York harbour: and this number was memorialised in stone when such bones as could be recovered were given formal interment in the city in 1808. In fact, the total number of American POWs who died on these rotting hulks will never be known. The British themselves kept no records; and the figure of 11,500 (11,644 to be precise) seems to have been invented by a New York newspaper in 1783, and to have been faithfully repeated ever since.[25]

But many American prisoners of the British did undoubtedly perish, in New York and elsewhere, of smallpox, of malnutrition, of dysentery, of neglect, of despair, and occasionally of the actions of sadists. There is however an obvious point that is generally forgotten. As is always the case in war, atrocities and sufferings were never the monopoly of one side. Considerable numbers of British soldiers and sailors, together with Loyalist troops and civilians and, still more, pro-British blacks and Native Americans, also found themselves on the receiving end of rape, pillage, torture, arbitrary arrest, lynchings, and casual slaughter; and this side's prisoners-of-war, too, died in very large numbers. For every British villain, like Provost Marshal Cunningham, who – allegedly – embezzled food, fuel and medicines intended for the relief of American POWs in New York, there was a Revolutionary villain like Colonel Henley who – allegedly – used British POWs in Cambridge, Massachusetts, for bayonet practice.[26] For every American Revolutionary sweating and sickening in the dank holds of British prison hulks in New York, there was a captive British naval or merchant seaman sweating and sickening in equally insalubrious American prison ships moored at Boston or off the coast of Connecticut. No one has ever troubled to find out how many of the latter perished while in American hands, but whether offshore or on land the lives of British POWs and Loyalist prisoners seem often to have been nasty, brutish and short. 'The poor wretches under my care are almost all sick and dead', scribbled an (in this case humane) American prison official in 1778.[27] As is the way with conflicts that shade into civil war, the fact that so many of those involved in the Revolutionary War had much in common, usually did less to restrain cruelty than make instances of it even nastier.

Take the case of Captain Joseph Huddy, one of the great Revolutionary *causes célèbres* of the dog-days of war in 1782. Huddy had been a prisoner of the British in New York, but was scheduled to be exchanged along with two of his comrades. Instead, the Loyalist corps appointed to escort the three men to the place of hand-over, stopped on the way, strung Huddy up, and hung a placard around the corpse's neck: 'Up goes Huddy for Philip White', an executed Loyalist. This, understandably, provoked a furious letter from George Washington to the British commander-in-chief, threatening retaliation against British POWs if the murderers of an unarmed American captive were not immediately apprehended and handed over. The papers and testimonies that General Clinton wearily assembled on this case offer depressing evidence not just of one famous atrocity, but of many, now forgotten atrocities. The pro-Revolutionary inhabitants of Monmouth County, where Huddy had been based, testified to his patriot qualities. But Monmouth County Loyalists told, predictably enough, a different story, a story – as the placard around Huddy's stretched and broken neck suggested – of serial outrages followed by bitter retaliation. Huddy and his vigilantes, they claimed, had snatched a local Loyalist from his bed, and hanged him. They had dug up the corpses of other Loyalists from their graves and made sport with them. They had broken a Loyalist captive's legs, put out his eyes, and then bid the man run away. But the most poignant testimony, which Clinton must have tossed aside in disgust, told a different story again. Yes, this Loyalist witness agreed, terrible acts had indeed been committed against his fellow sympathisers in Monmouth County, and the ringleader may have been Huddy. But he was not sure.[28]

If all this sounds drearily familiar, it is. Similar sagas of multiple atrocities, of mistaken identities having lethal consequences, of terrible violence against the helpless on the one side breeding the same against the innocent on the other, are acted out regularly in our own time in a dozen trouble-spots around the world. The American Revolutionary War has been dignified in retrospect because of the ideals associated with it and the good that ultimately emerged from it, but at the time it was just like any other protracted war – filthy, unfair, and indiscriminately deadly for large numbers of combatants and innocent civilians alike. So an obvious question arises. Since suffering and cruelty – like captives – were never the preserve of just one side in this war, why were American Revolutionaries able to make so much better capital out of these things than their opponents? When Thomas Anburey, a British officer who was captured at Saratoga and held for several years in various prison camps in America, published his two-volume captivity narrative in London in 1791, he did so – he wrote in its preface – because he was angry that so many appeared to view 'the favourers of [American] Independence as possessed of every amiable qualification, and those who espoused the rights of the Mother Country, as destitute of common feeling, and humanity itself'.[29] Anburey's exasperation was understandable, but his words were also effectively an admission that Britain had lost not just the Thirteen American colonies, but also the propaganda war.

In part, this was because the Revolutionaries tried harder – since they knew they had to. Right from the beginning, they kept the pressure on. Of course, in virtually every war known to history, each side has routinely accused its opponents of atrocities while claiming superior humanity and morality for itself. This said, however, American Revolutionaries consistently 'emphasized the enemy's cruelty and vindictiveness', especially towards prisoners, 'in a way [that was] altogether unusual in eighteenth-century wars'. They did so at many different levels, but always with an eye to print. Congress passed resolution after resolution condemning real and invented British cruelties, knowing that its words would feature in every sympathetic newspaper in North America and beyond.[30] Any official communication with the British was tailored in the same way. Thus after Yorktown, American treatment of some of the 8000 British prisoners seized there shocked the French auxiliary troops present. None the less, Washington's letter to the hapless Lord Cornwallis, which was broadcast around the world, was utterly uncompromising, referring pointedly to: 'the benevolent treatment of prisoners which is invariably observed by Americans'.[31]

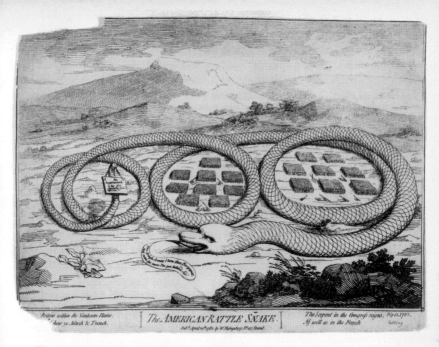

Prison within the Yankeen Plains, how ye March & French.

The AMERICAN RATTLE SNAKE.

Pub.d April 12.1782. by W. Humphrey N.o 227 Strand.

The Serpent in the Congress reigns, B.9.15.1782. As well as in the French. Gillray.

40. The American rattle snake capturing the British in its coils at Saratoga and Yorktown: a brilliant early print by James Gillray.

Along with this careful and calculated use of language by Revolutionary elites, there were hundreds of stories of suffering and captivity at the hands of the British contributed by ordinary men and occasionally women. Thus, in June 1777, the *Boston Gazette* devoted its front page to the tale of Philip Jones, taken captive, shot and bayoneted in the leg, it was claimed, by an arrogant British army colonel. This captivity story – which may or may not have been accurate – was subsequently reprinted in several Connecticut papers. Prison narratives, lists of American POWs, and affidavits from simple people caught and brutalised by the British enemy, became such standard Revolutionary newspaper fare in successive years that James Rivington, editor of the main Loyalist journal, the *New York Gazette*, attempted a spoof. In 1781, he printed a mock advertisement of a new book: *A New and Complete System of Cruelty: Containing a Variety of Modern Improvements in the Art. Embellished with an Elegant Frontispiece representing the Inside of a Prison Ship.* This was mildly amusing: but, again, a tacit acknowledgement that the Revolutionaries had achieved a propaganda walk-over.[32]

The British did sometimes publish their own captivity stories, their own tales of atrocities suffered and of soldiers and supporters brutally confined, but they were hampered in so doing in all kinds of ways. To begin with, they were disadvantaged – in this as in so many other respects – by operating at such a vast distance from their home base and without significant European allies. A Revolutionary soldier, sailor or citizen who was captured or mistreated in North America by the British, or wanted to seem so, was always likely to be within reach of a sympathetic printing press. With far fewer Loyalist papers in America than Revolutionary ones, and with London's print industry 3000 miles away, British and Loyalist victims found it far less easy to get their stories promptly into print.[33] Moreover, tales of Revolutionary captives enjoyed an international currency which equivalent British stories simply could not secure. Benjamin Franklin and other Americans resident in Europe made sure that a steady stream of appropriate material was fed to the French, Spanish, Dutch, and other European press networks. This included the British wartime press, which was far less rigorously censored than newspapers in Revolutionary America. In 1777, for instance, Franklin had an exchange of letters with the British Lord Stormont on the supposed treatment of American POWs in England. Doctored extracts of this correspondence were promptly leaked to the *London Chronicle*, an opposition journal opposed to the war.[34] This incessant print patter of tiny facts – and falsehoods – steadily wore away British resolve and British reputation.

Yet there was far more to the Revolutionaries' advantage than this. Telling tales of captivity catered to American imperatives in this war in ways that simply did not apply as far as the British were concerned. For the latter, complaining in luxuriant detail in print how one-time American colonists had inflicted defeat, imprisonment, and cruelties on their own soldiers, sailors and Loyalist supporters savoured too much of humiliation. 'Every gazette of Europe and America', chortled the anti-war radical John Wilkes to the House of Commons in 1778, 'has published the disgrace of our arms at Saratoga, the ignominious terms of the Convention.' But the British authorities themselves had no desire whatsoever to publish the stories of the thousands of prisoners taken from their army under the terms of the Convention, even though the treatment accorded these men was sometimes very harsh. Indeed, to this day, British historians have yet to investigate the multiple experiences of these prisoners.[35] Such things were simply not supposed to happen to the soldiers of a mighty empire at the hands of its own colonists. For American Revolutionaries, however, it was different. For them – as for Indian and Irish Nationalists much later – captives seized from their ranks were not grim emblems of humiliation, but exemplary figures. The sufferings and confinements of American POWs seemed almost providentially supplied as emblems in miniature of the chains and abuses inflicted on the Thirteen Colonies as a whole by monstrous British villains. For Revolutionaries, in other words, captives were useful, not least because they provided a means to stiffen the line between what was now being invented as America and what was now proclaimed to be foreign.

As we have seen, by its very nature, the American Revolutionary War had been characterised at the start by uncertain identities. The harsh divide between 'Us' and 'Them' that usually obtains in wars was conspicuously lacking in this one, and both main protagonists experienced instead frequent, jarring reminders of what they had in common. For the British, this was a problem throughout, but initially it was also a profound problem for their opponents. As was true in France after 1789, and in Russia after 1917, the outbreak of revolution in America was not remotely the act of a united people, but the work of substantial numbers of activists who had then to persuade and if necessary coerce the rest of their countrymen into thinking like they did. This was bound to be a challenge. Committed Loyalists, it is estimated, comprised at least one fifth of the white population of the one-time Thirteen Colonies, and may have come close at times to making up a third.[36] Moreover, and as the reactions of Joshua Pilsberry to the British captives at Saratoga demonstrated, even among the ranks of the Revolutionaries themselves there were many who found it hard to regard Great Britain unambiguously as a foreign power. This was why Congress and Revolutionary activists devoted so much energy throughout the war to making capital out of captivity stories and other real and invented British atrocities. They needed to construct a firm, unyielding wall between themselves and their opponents, to persuade their own supporters, as well as the uncommitted and as many Loyalists as they could, that the British were cruel *and therefore alien*.

The most famous captivity narrative published during the war illustrates this strategy very clearly. At one level, Ethan Allen was a tough and violent man, a natural democrat and as superbly bloody-minded as only Vermonters can be. Before the war, he had functioned, in the words of one American historian, as 'a frontier ruffian', employing his band of vigilantes, the Green Mountain boys, to enforce supporters' land-claims and drive out rivals in those north-eastern stretches of New York colony that went on to become Vermont. But Allen was also a born actor who understood the potential of words as a means to reinvent himself and to fashion the world anew. As he remarked: 'One story is good till another is told.' When the Revolution came, he duly penned his own kind of story as a means of obliterating the old. Convinced that Canada was destined to form part of what he unabashedly styled 'the American empire', he joined the Revolutionary invasion of it in 1775 and was captured at Montreal. Had the British been prescient, they would either have shot him or let him go. Instead, they held on to him for over two years, sometimes in appalling conditions and sometimes in circumstances that allowed him a remarkable degree of licence.[37] Few such nuances informed Allen's subsequent narrative of his captivity experiences, which went through eight editions in two years, and was extracted in countless American, Continental European and British newspapers, and referred to approvingly in Parliament by Edmund Burke.

Allen's purpose in writing was twofold. He wanted to demonise the British as a 'haughty and cruel nation', and to show simultaneously how superior American virtue could defeat them. He accused Britain's leaders of nothing less than genocide: 'a premeditated and systematical plan . . . to destroy the youths of our land'. American POWs, he insisted, were routinely brutalised, killed outright, or deliberately infected with the smallpox. He, however, had defiantly held his own. Imprisoned for a while in Falmouth, England, he had resolved 'to keep up my spirits and behave in a daring soldier-like manner, that I might exhibit a good example of American fortitude'. He described how he had lectured his hapless guards and any Britons foolish enough to visit him in jail on the principles of the Revolution and on the futility of any attempts to repress it: 'Consider you are but an island! And that your power has been continued longer than the exercise of your humanity.' The bravura was tremendous and the apparent lack of fear or uncertainty was immensely cheering to wavering Revolutionaries and immensely effective.[38]

For political reasons, the British simply could not counter this kind of assault. It was not just that imperial conceit made them more reluctant than their opponents to admit to the thousands of prisoners taken from among their own supporters, and to the atrocities sometimes inflicted on them. Their real problem ran deeper. They could not properly retaliate in kind to Revolutionary atrocity accusations because of the nature of their war aims. Allen and his sort were out to alienate as many Americans as possible from Britain so that they would reject it utterly and commit themselves instead to independence. By contrast, the British military and political elites did not – and could not – want to stir up a thoroughgoing hate campaign against Americans, because their whole purpose in fighting this war was to keep as many of the latter as possible contained within the empire. As was so often the case, the British found themselves hog-tied by the numbers game. They knew, just as well as Allen, that they were 'but an island', and that therefore they could never retain their vast American empire by military means alone. They did not have sufficient manpower; they would never have sufficient manpower. They needed, as always in their imperial projects, the support at some level of substantial numbers of the people they sought to rule.

It was this consideration that sapped the British propaganda effort in this war of much of its potential force, just as it also hobbled their military strategy. British commanders and politicians were never able to make up their minds whether to seek to conciliate and go softly softly with those whom they deemed American rebels, or let loose the dogs of war against them as against any other enemy. By the same token, even on those occasions when the British lashed out in writing or print against their opponents, they often tried simultaneously to win them over. In August 1776, one month after the Declaration of Independence, Howe wrote sternly to Washington about a future exchange of POWs, but ended with a revealing appeal:

> I cannot close this letter without expressing the deepest concern that the unhappy state of the colonies, so different from what I had the honor of experiencing in the course of the last war, deprives me of the pleasure I should otherwise have had in a more personal communication.[39]

Engaged in launching his legions against American Revolutionaries, Howe sought simultaneously to appeal to his and their common cultural and political inheritance. Paradoxically, but not as paradoxically as it seems, he yearned for the Americans to love him and all that he stood for. Increasingly, the Revolutionaries experienced no such inner conflict. They did not care whether the British loved them or no. They did not want their love. They wanted to be free.

Blackening the empire, building empires anew

The bitterness of captivity, then, simultaneously linked the main protagonists in this conflict and drove them further apart. Thousands of American Revolutionaries spent some or all of this war in torment, in limbo, incarcerated; and so, too, did thousands of supporters of the British empire. But it was the former who derived by far the greatest political capital from all of this. The real and rumoured sufferings of confined individuals from among their ranks gave Revolutionaries useful and easily understood metaphors for those wider assaults on liberty they attributed to George

III and his ministers, while accusations of cruelty to captive Americans served to 'other' the British and mobilise support for a new republican nation. Yet while Britain secured far less propaganda advantage from its own individual captive supporters in this war, it remained dogged throughout by its more fundamental and collective brand of confinement, its deficiency of numbers, its irredeemable native smallness. The strategies it adopted in order to address this widened still further the divide between Britain and its former white colonists.

Just how is suggested by the tale of a captive and slaughtered virgin, a war propagandist's dream. In July 1777, Jane McCrea, who was in her early twenties and from Fort Edward, New York, left home under escort bound for Canada and her fiancé, one David Jones, a Loyalist officer who was serving there under Britain's General Burgoyne. What exactly happened on her brutally truncated journey will never be known for sure. According to one version, McCrea's party was ambushed in error by Native Americans in British military service and she was shot. Other sources suggest that it was two Algonquians from amongst the escort party itself who seized the woman, and that she was killed when they quarrelled over who was to take charge of her and of any subsequent ransom. What is rather more certain is that on 'the morning of her intended marriage' (or so Burke mournfully informed the House of Commons), a search party discovered McCrea's scalped and – according to some reports – naked body. After that, mere facts became of no importance whatsoever.[40]

In the ensuing propaganda storm, all that mattered was that an innocent civilian had been killed and mutilated by Indians in British pay. Moreover, McCrea had been from a largely Loyalist family and engaged to another Loyalist fighting manfully in support of the Crown. Her fate, insisted Revolutionary propagandists, offered terrible proof that British inhumanity threatened all of America's inhabitants, irrespective of their politics. Most crucially, McCrea had been a woman, and a white woman. Or as the American General, Horatio Gates, phrased it in a widely distributed public letter to Burgoyne: 'a young lady, lovely to the sight, of virtuous character and amiable disposition'.[41] In John Vanderlyn's painting, completed many years after the event, Jane McCrea is white-skinned to the point of pallor, clothed in blue, the colour of the Virgin's robes, and forced to her knees by two very brown and muscular Indians. One drags her head backwards by the long, unravelling black hair of which she had been naïvely proud. The other seizes her bare, outstretched arm, and raises his tomahawk. The woman's terror and pleas for mercy are plainly ineffectual; and the sinewy menace of her half-naked tormentors, together with the disarray of her own clothing, suggests that death is not the only

41. *The Murder of Jane McCrea* by John Vanderlyn.

violation intended for this captive. The Revolutionary press was careful to insist, with what degree of accuracy we do not know, that McCrea's body was found stripped.

At one level, this was another, particularly dramatic example of the highly successful Revolutionary propaganda tactic already touched on: a deliberate linking of British forces and auxiliaries with lurid instances of atrocity so as to de-nature them and make them into a thoroughly foreign enemy:

> Oh cruel savages! What hearts of steel!
> O cruel *Britons*! Who no pity feel!
> Where did they get the knife, the cruel blade?
> From *Britain* it was sent, where it was made.
> The tom'hawk and the murdering knife were sent
> To barb'rous savages for this intent.
> Yes, they were sent, e'en from the *British throne*.

Yet, as these lines by a pedestrian patriot poet suggest, the British were not just 'othered' on this occasion through being associated with acts of cruelty. In this and many other instances, Revolutionaries sought to blacken the British empire by conflating its cause with those who were not white. A great deal of McCrea propaganda not only reported that the Native Americans reputedly responsible were in British pay, but also collapsed the divide between them and the British themselves:

> Some *British* troops, combin'd with *Indian* bands,
> With swords, with knives and tom'hawks in their hands.
> They gave a shout and pass'd along the wood
> Like beasts of prey, in quest of human blood.[42]

New British imperial threat in this version became old Indian threat writ large and in very similar terms.

This idea, as John Adams put it, that George III was nothing less than a 'sceptred savage', that British imperialists were so vicious as no longer authentically to be white, also cropped up in American wartime captivity narratives.[43] John Dodge, whose story was published in Philadelphia in 1779, and reissued the following year, made a point of stressing the friendship and affinity between his British military captors and their indigenous allies: 'those British barbarians, who, on the first yell of the savages, flew to meet and hug them to their breasts'. 'The British', remembered another one-time American captive, '[furnished] the Indians with firearms, ammunition, the tomahawk and scalping-knife, to assist them against the whites of

America.' A similar point was made, indeed, courtesy of the most famous American captivity narrative of them all, Mary Rowlandson's. Her story, *The Sovereignty and Goodness of God*, that other tale of a lone white woman grievously beset by Indians, had been out of print in North America between 1720 and 1770. But in the 1770s, the decade of the Revolution, Rowlandson's story went through seven different American editions, some of which contained markedly novel illustrations. Traditionally, and if illustrated at all, Rowlandson's tale had been accompanied by an image of Indians surrounding and setting fire to her vulnerable cabin, reducing her and her neighbours to stark terror. In the 1770s, this familiar representational style shifted. Instead, Rowlandson was re-imagined as a plucky lady armed with a gun defending her home against lines of identical stick men who appeared to be wearing uniform jackets. Redcoats (and was this not perhaps an interesting choice of insult by American Revolutionaries?) were now being rendered stand-ins for those indigenous peoples who, by this time, were increasingly referred to as red-skinned.[44]

Nor was this all. To reinforce the argument that the British were so 'othered' by their misdeeds as no longer to be regarded as civilised and therefore white, some Revolutionary writers linked them with blacks as well as with Native Americans. The circumstances of the war made this very easy to do. Ebenezer Fletcher, who fought in the Continental army and was captured at Ticonderoga in 1777, dwelt on the poly-ethnic quality of the British army camp in which he was confined at one stage. 'Indians often came and abused us with their language,' he wrote, and what was worse: 'An old negro came and took my fife, which I considered as the greatest insult I had received while with the enemy.' The encounter with the imperial forces experienced by Benjamin Gilbert, a Quaker captured by pro-British Indians in 1780, was even more rich and strange. Taken under guard to Canada, he encountered there French guerrillas fighting on behalf of George III, pro-British Mohawks whom he rather admired, and various blacks:

These negroes had escaped from confinement, and were on their way to Niagara, when first discovered by the Indians. Being challenged by them, [they] answered *'They were for the King'*, upon which they immediately received them into protection.[45]

They were for the King. As this suggests, the stereotypical view of British forces in the American Revolutionary War – homogeneous phalanxes of white, disciplined males in scarlet coats – is markedly inadequate. British army units in North America after 1775 sucked in Loyalists from different backgrounds and in a medley of uniforms, large numbers of Germans and other European immigrants, and a great many accompanying women. In addition, and of necessity, they operated over the years in alliance with substantial though always shifting numbers of people who were not white. To a degree, this was also true of their opponents. At least 5000 free blacks are known to have fought in the Revolutionary ranks, as did some indigenous warriors, like the Stockbridge Indians of Massachusetts.[46] But there was no comparison between the two sides in point of numbers of non-white auxiliaries. Initially, many Native Americans tried to remain neutral, but as Colin Calloway writes: 'in time and in general, most Indian peoples' who did commit themselves to fighting 'came round to siding with the British'. As for blacks, perhaps as many as 25,000 slaves in South Carolina fled their owners to seek refuge with British armies during the war. So did three-quarters of Georgia's black population and, if Thomas Jefferson was right, 30,000 slaves from Virginia, including many of his own. Blacks in the more northerly states often moved in the same partisan direction.[47]

In so far as the British exercised any control over all this, the immediate reason for their seeking out and accepting such conspicuously large numbers of non-white auxiliaries was straightforward enough: as ever, they had little choice. One of their propagandists wearily spelt it out:

> So small is the ordinary establishment of the British army, that there has never been a war . . . within the memory of us or our fathers, where foreign troops have not been employed.

Small was not beautiful. As far as imperial power under pressure was concerned, small was always desperate. The British had no choice but to mobilise support in America promiscuously: 'Since force is become necessary . . . it would make little difference, whether the instrument be a German or a Calmuck, a Russian or a Mohawk.' Yet, by so reasoning, by fighting in collusion with and in proximity to so many Native Americans and black slaves on the run, the British also made it easier for white American Revolutionaries to represent them as altogether alien in tendency, as un-white. Thus the McCrea incident was a propaganda disaster not simply because a young, helpless Loyalist female was (apparently) killed by Indians in British pay, but also because General Burgoyne was unable to take drastic retaliatory action against those responsible. All he could do was insist, probably correctly, that there had been 'no premeditated barbarity' on the part of the Indians involved.[48] But he was in no position to execute the supposed culprits, as Revolutionary propagandists demanded, even had he wanted to, because he desperately needed to retain the support of his Native American allies. As was so often the case, their own manpower limits – that fundamental captivity that never let them go – compelled the British into a kind of military multi-culturalism.

Yet, by itself, this is an insufficient explanation for the marked diversity of 'British' ranks in this war, because it tells us nothing about the motives of those Native Americans and free and unfree blacks who aligned them- selves, for a time, with the forces of empire. Ideas and commitment in this conflict were never the monopoly of whites, any more than they were the exclusive preserve of Whigs. For some blacks, as for some Native Americans, joining the British after 1775 represented more than just a response to presents, bribes and varieties of coercion, and also more than simply a matter of not having anywhere else to go. Some made the choice, as Benjamin Gilbert's black guards did, to fight 'for the King'. Why?

We can dismiss right away any notion that the bulk of British-born offi- cials and military men operating in North America were any less racist, in the modern sense of the term, than the majority of white American colonists who resisted their rule. Clearly they were not. As Thomas Jefferson trenchantly pointed out, it was at one level grossly hypocritical for a British imperialist like Lord Dunmore to proclaim 'Liberty to Slaves' in the American South, as he did in 1775, when it had been British slave-traders who had been responsible for shipping the majority of blacks into servi- tude there in the first place.[49] By the same token, Britain left its black and indigenous wartime allies in North America entirely out of the peace terms it negotiated with white Americans and with fellow European powers in 1783, though it did provide a post-war refuge for some of these now desper- ately exposed peoples in Canada, Africa, and elsewhere.

Admitting the evident limits of the British imperial authorities' solici- tude for subaltern peoples in this case, however, only makes the original question the more pressing. Britain's own military and demographic reasons for seeking non-white support in the American Revolutionary War are clear enough, but why were its forces able to secure such support so abundantly if, in the end, unavailingly? Answering this takes us again to the very heart of this conflict which, as John André discovered, was always about different and shifting constructions of identity.

Behind all the many and different motives for Britain and its white colonists in America going to war after 1775 were two rival interpretations of what the empire involved. The interpretation favoured by most of those opting for Revolution, and by most of their supporters within Britain itself, was that the transatlantic empire was in essence no less – and no more – than 'two branches of the British nation' as Edmund Burke called it. Those holding this view believed that white British colonists in North America

233

should enjoy the same rights, freedoms and privileges as Britons claimed at home (without however paying the same taxes). They also expected London to give them clearly preferential treatment to that bestowed on any other peoples in imperial North America, be they French Canadians, or Native Americans, or blacks. Hence the fury of James Otis, a Boston lawyer, when he discovered that, in the minds of some in Britain, all the inhabitants of imperial North America seemed much the same. The colonies, he wrote in 1764, were not settled 'as the common people of England foolishly imagine with a compound mongrel mixture of English, Indian and Negro, but with freeborn British white subjects'.[50] Implicit in Otis's words was an assumption that the only people who really mattered in America were its Anglo population and that other groupings were and should remain politically invisible. White, Protestant, Anglo-American colonists did not want to be first among equals. They wanted to be special, fellow and equal Britons on another shore.

For their own reasons, the British imperial authorities could not take such an exclusionist view. As we have seen, over the eighteenth century, and especially after the 1750s, they had evolved a more hybrid construction of their American empire. The growing scale and range of their conquests throughout the world forced this shift of policy and perception on them, but so too did considerations of self-interest and self-preservation. Britain's governing elites recognised, all too well, their state's territorial and demographic limits and the constraints on power and reach that followed from this. Consequently, absolutely to privilege and give free rein to its own fast-multiplying and persistently expanding British settlers in North America appeared unwise, possibly dangerous, and – to some in London – unjust. Far better to play the standard imperial game of divide and rule. Far better to extend a measure of protection and rewards to all the various different groupings in British North America, so that they might remain loyal and continue to coexist and balance each other. Hence London's attempt to seal off the American West from land-hungry white settlers after 1763 and so offer some protection to Native Americans, and hence the Quebec Act extending the legal privileges and territorial range of predominantly Catholic and Francophone Canada in 1774. To London, these initiatives represented both a pragmatic recognition of the diversity contained within its now vast American empire, and also a means of guarding against one particular set of potentially over-mighty subjects. To those American colonists who viewed themselves as fellow Britons, however, such policies savoured of betrayal.

It is against this background that we need to position those thousands of non-Anglos who chose to throw in their lot with the British empire after 1775. Only royal government, a British imperial agent had told the Creeks and Cherokee on the eve of the Revolution, could preserve Indian lands from acquisitive colonial frontiersmen; and many Native Americans decided that he and his kind were right, for what other options did they have? As for black slaves in America's South, the happy idea that Britain might – just – confer on them freedom as well as small-time favours, seems to have been nourished by news of the so-called Somerset legal decision in London in 1772. This was widely interpreted, on both sides of the Atlantic, as affirming that slavery was illegal on British soil. Hence, one historian writes, with some exaggeration, the 'almost universal belief in slave society that a British victory' in the Revolutionary war would lead to 'the eradication of slavery in America'.[51]

In other words, blacks and Native Americans sided with Britain in this conflict not just for the sake of bribes or because there appeared to be little alternative, but in some cases out of a measure of hope, realistic or no. Nor was it just blacks and Indians who decided that rule from distant

42. Strangely-dressed American revolutionaries trample on a black: a British print of 1778.

A VIEW IN AMERICA IN 1778

London woud be better for their sectional interests than a new independent America dominated by a highly self-conscious, fast-multiplying white Protestant majority. So, too – for broadly similar reasons – did other nervous minority groupings. Dutch and German immigrants who spoke only their cradle tongue and not English, French-speaking Huguenots in New Rochelle, Gaelic-speaking Highland Scottish settlers: all of these people, almost without exception, opted staunchly for the Loyalist side after 1775.[52] In many ways, support for Britain in the American Revolution was made up of a coalition of different minorities. This was one reason why it lost, but it was also one more demonstration of how empire, so often assumed now to be *necessarily* racist in operation and ethos, could sometimes be conspicuously poly-ethnic in quality and policy, because it had to be.

Many of these poly-ethnic American-based supporters of the British empire refused to hang around and risk the consequences of defeat. The number of people who fled the new United States after 1782, for Canada, for Britain, for the West Indies, and in some cases for Africa, was five times greater than the number of men and women who abandoned France after its revolution in 1789. As far as the miscellaneous whites involved in this exodus were concerned, such trepidation proved quite needless. For people like them, the new America would come to offer a degree of egalitarianism and opportunity that no other society in the world could or can match. Yet for a long time this wonderful, unprecedented American abundance would be paid for by others. Incomparably free and conspicuously idealistic, the new United States would also be firmly exclusionist and aggressively expansionist, an empire indeed, as Revolutionaries like Ethan Allen had prophesied. The fact that so many blacks and so many Native Americans had sided with the British during the Revolutionary war only made it easier for the new Republic to define citizenship in a way that excluded both of these groups completely.

The half-century after the American Revolution would be a critical era for empire globally, with massive transformations occurring in all of the major European maritime imperial powers, France, Spain, Portugal, Holland, and above all Britain. This self-same period – the 1780s to the 1830s – would also be a seminal era for land-based, contiguous empires. Some, like China and Ottoman Turkey, would weaken desperately; others, like the Russian empire, and the new American empire would be immeasurably strengthened. What he wanted, Thomas Jefferson would remark with regard to America's indigenous inhabitants, was 'the termination of their history', by which he meant an end to Native American land-holding patterns and migratory customs, so that successive generations of white farmers and families could migrate triumphantly ever westwards. And so in time it came to pass.[53]

For the British, the imperial consequences of the lost Revolutionary War were both traumatic and formative. What was involved was not a 'Fall of the First British Empire' (a truly Americo-centric coinage) because the empire had always been bigger than the Thirteen Colonies. Defeat in this war was rather a matter of bitter humiliation and of persistent anxieties being – apparently – proved right. Those who had argued that Britain was simply too small to sustain a substantial overseas empire successfully had, it seemed, been amply vindicated. And to a degree, this was a lesson that the British never forgot. Never again would they attempt to tax a major overseas colony directly from Westminster. Never again would they risk a really protracted full-scale war on several fronts – as distinct from long guerrilla campaigns – in the desperate hope of keeping hold of a segment of their empire determined to be free. To this extent, one might even argue that successful American Revolution in the eighteenth century helps to explain why the British submitted to such rapid decolonisation in the twentieth century. They had been taught by bitter experience to recognise their logistical and warlike limits.

In other respects, too, the American Revolution offered lessons on the strains and pains of empire. It showed the men in London, what Australia and New Zealand would only confirm in the nineteenth century: the extreme difficulties involved in an imperial power like Britain holding a balance between its land-hungry white settlers on the one hand, and half-way decent treatment of indigenous peoples on the other. The Revolution also illustrated the perils that empire could represent to national identity. In this conflict, for all sorts of reasons, the British had found themselves divided, their customary solidarities compromised, while their opponents had proved able to forge a much clearer sense of purpose and mission. The only way for the British to compensate for their smallness on the global stage was to be conspicuously coherent. In this imperial conflict, national and political coherence at home had faltered with disastrous consequences.

Yet for a while all these various failures would be recovered from to an astonishing degree, and so would the persistent fear of overseas disaster and embarrassments, of being too small to accomplish and consolidate great things. It was in 1821 that a British mission arrived at the site on the boundary between New York and New Jersey where some forty years earlier John André's body had been hurriedly buried. Excavating the remains so as to carry them back to his empty tomb at Westminster Abbey proved more difficult than was anticipated. André's skull had come apart from his fractured neck joints, and the roots of a nearby peach tree had wound themselves around it 'like a net'.[54] The small and subdued gathering of army men and officials staring down at this sad relic of imperial failure and ultimate confinement were not unduly dismayed however, for by now Britain's empire was growing at a more spectacular rate than ever before, albeit in different directions. And in this new imperial incarnation, the British would succeed in resolving the challenges of different kinds of captivity for much longer than their past experiences in the Mediterranean and America had given them any right to expect. It is time to turn east, and examine India.

Part Three

INDIA
Captives and Conquest

EIGHT

Another Passage to India

Sarah's story

London, 1801. It is barely twenty years since the hanging of Major John André, but the men sitting listening in this quiet backstreet room inhabit a world that is already utterly changed from his, and they know it. The speaker before them is as hardened a military and imperial actor as André was himself, but in more than just the obvious respect is otherwise a very different human being. We are in another country, and besides, this wench is determined to stay alive. Her name is Sarah Shade, and the story she tells is of India. Life has taught her how to read, and how to speak several languages, but not how to write, so her tale has to be reconstructed solely from memory. Accordingly, she stumbles over dates and the precise ordering of events; but she cannot afford to falter or give up. This is a year of high food prices and unemployment in Britain, as well as global war, so it is vital that she secures the attention and aid of these cautious, charitable gentlemen. All too familiar with tales of misery from the labouring poor, and wary of fraudsters seeking to extract money, the directors of the benevolent foundation are fortunately able to recognise gold when they hear it. Sarah's experiences are teased out from her at length, polished and amended as seems fit, and then published as a pamphlet in the hope that it will sell well enough to provide for her and her latest husband. This is the genesis of the first, reasonably authentic account by an English working-class woman of what it was like to attempt conquest in India and to be captured there.[1]

This is not the kind of text, or the sort of individual, with which conventional imperial histories – or even post-colonial histories – normally concern themselves. Looked at superficially, Shade seems indeed a purely idiosyncratic figure, inevitably marginalised in the broader scheme of things by virtue of her gender as well as her poverty. A worker for British imperial power in India, and therefore not even a conventional victim, she none the less possessed in her own right no power, no glamour, and no capacity for heroic endeavour; and may even have been unaware of the wider significance of the events in which she was caught up. The word 'empire' does not figure at all in the *Narrative of the Life of Sarah Shade*. Yet, for all this, Shade and her story are representative and repay close attention.

She herself was representative in that most Britons who worked in India from the 1740s to the winning of Independence in 1947, were in some respects exactly like her: lower-class and attached to the army. And – for all the peculiarities of its transmission – the tale she told derived from and draws attention to a major shift in British national mood and imperial direction at this time. Shade was not the first plebeian Englishwoman to testify in print to Indian adventures. The credit for that belongs to a Hannah Snell, whose ghost-written memoir *The Female Soldier* was a runaway publishing success in 1750. As her publisher told it, Snell had adopted male costume after being deserted by her husband. She joined the British army as a marine, and by 1748 was in an East India Company fort on India's southern (Coromandel) coast, subsequently taking part in a British assault on the French stronghold of Pondicherry. Wounded in the groin – where else? – Snell was none the less able to keep her identity secret until the regiment's return to England allowed her to dictate her tale at leisure. At the time, it seems to have been widely believed. Chelsea Hospital even awarded her an out-pension as a wounded veteran of imperial warfare. Yet it remains doubtful whether Snell's published Indian adventure contains more than a kernel of accuracy.[2] Certainly, reading it side by side with the *Narrative of the Life of Sarah Shade* is to experience an immediate sense both of disparity and of rapid change over time. It is not just that Hannah Snell's tale is probably bogus in the main, while the details of Sarah Shade's Indian life can be substantially verified in the archives.[3] These two accounts of semi-literate, impoverished women were also separated by a period of fifty years during which the pattern of global empire and of Britain's relations with India underwent a revolution.

In *The Female Soldier*, the Indian subcontinent, and the small European forces contending in the 1740s for a place on its southern shores, are little more than an exotic backdrop to a traditional tale of a bold, lower-class female driven into adventure and transvestism by lost love. Composed half a century later, Shade's narrative is utterly different. Her text is saturated with allusions to more than twenty years' exposure to southern India and Bengal. There are references to Indian cuisine, wild-life, scenery, shipping, languages, and Anglo-Indian sexual relations; and there are Indian place-names galore that Shade seems to have pronounced with facility to her cold, London auditors, and they have sometimes mistranscribed. Back in 1750, Hannah Snell's publishers had relied on episodes of cross-dressing and female transgression to sell her story. But for the men writing down

HANNAH SNELL,
the Female Soldier,
Who went by the Name of James Gray.

43. Hannah Snell as imperial warrior.

Sarah Shade's tale in 1801, it was its information on India that mattered, and understandably so. Now that the richest and oldest sector of Britain's empire in North America had broken away, political and public attention was shifting ever more markedly towards the Indian subcontinent. In the words of William Pitt the Younger, prime minister at the time that Shade's adventures were published: India's importance for the British 'had increased in proportion to the losses sustained by the dismemberment of other great possessions'.[4]

Sarah Shade and the story she related, then, emerged from and appealed to a sharper British awareness of India and appetite for it. Shade also typified the quality of British imperialism at this stage in a more intimate fashion. Not just her published story, but even her own body was a text of empire. While in India, she had been wounded twice in the face. A musket ball had passed through the calf of her right leg; and a sabre had slashed her right arm: 'the marks of which wounds are visible upon her'. Nor was this all. Shade had been scarred as well by powerful claws. She bore the marks of the tiger. She was thus, in her own riven and spoilt flesh, a fit representative of an extraordinarily violent phase of British overseas activity, both in India, and in every continent of the world. The geographical scope of warfare, and the rate at which Britain gained and lost territory in the course of it, had been increasing since the 1750s. From the 1780s, though, the global span of violence became even more pronounced, the stakes became higher, and the possible penalties for losing much greater. In the American Revolution, Spain, the Dutch, and above all France, had intervened to strip Britain of its Thirteen Colonies, and of other territory in the Caribbean, the Mediterranean, and Africa. By the time Sarah Shade dictated her story, at the start of the nineteenth century, Britain and France were caught up in a still bigger conflict that started formally in 1793 and lasted with scarcely a break until 1815. For much of this time, the British were at risk not merely of losing the war, but also of being invaded by Napoleon Bonaparte's numerically superior armies, and deprived of some or all of their overseas territories, a point often forgotten in conventional accounts of the relentless 'rise' of British empire. Britain, judged an experienced army officer in 1810, was 'menaced with destruction by a much superior force', and its 'empire of the seas' was unlikely to last for very much longer. Even now, the British had no way of knowing that unmatched global dominion would briefly be theirs.[5]

British aggression and expansion in India were bound up with the escalation in global warfare after the 1750s, but they also partook of this period's extreme uncertainty, anxiety and conspicuous vicissitudes. At the time, the 'swing to the east', as this shift towards India is often styled, seemed a far more close run and nervous thing than it came to appear in comfortable retrospect. How could it have been otherwise, given the besetting British dilemma: an excess of overseas ambition married to a serious deficiency of domestic size? In the context of India's geographical scale and its vast, indigenous population, Britain's smallness appeared particularly painful and exposed. The challenge for the latter, as always, was to find or manufacture ways around this: and doing so was difficult and fraught with risk. Sarah's mutilated body, like her narrative, evokes the high levels of violence and fear that swept over large parts of the subcontinent and its peoples at this time, and that also sometimes daunted and engulfed the British themselves.

Accompanying this woman on her strange but not atypical passage to and through India is, then, a way of exploring the quality of early British imperial activism in a place that always seemed too large, too crammed with life. It is a means, too, of establishing the essential background to British captivity panics in the subcontinent. Sarah's is a tale of the sea and of the East India Company, and of the constraints and collusions imposed by woefully limited British numbers. It is a tale of aggression and desperate improvisations, and – in the end – a tale of tigers.

Limits

As many of her compatriots would do, Sarah embarked for India because of very limited options at home and in the hope of making her fortune or at least making out. Born to an artisan family in Herefordshire in 1746, and christened Sarah Wall, she was orphaned in her early teens. By her own account, she then 'led the life of a slave' as an agricultural servant, before escaping to work in a button-manufacturer's in Birmingham. It was there that her stepfather, John Bolton, who may also have been her lover, caught up with her and made his proposal. 'Having lost her parents', he told her, 'and being, in short, very comely withal, she would do well to proceed [with him] to India'. And so they did.

It was on 20 January 1769 that they set sail for Madras on the three-decker East Indiaman, the *New Devonshire*. Its log-book, immaculately kept by Captain Matthew Hoare, confirms their embarkation at London, and shows that Sarah masqueraded for the trip as John Bolton's wife.[6] East India Company ships' logs of this sort are rich, still under-used sources that convey very powerfully the range, industry and audacity of 'the grandest society of merchants in the universe'. They document the intricacy of these ships' loading, the co-ordination, book-keeping and organisation required to stock a massive vessel like the *New Devonshire*, over several weeks and from different London dockyards, with the cargo, cannon, gunpowder, army and navy recruits, livestock and provisions needed for a protracted voyage in often dangerous waters. They demonstrate, too, the level of skill and hardship that was involved in navigating these heavily loaded, complex vessels from Britain to India and then on to China, a trip that in the 1760s still lasted close to a year, and for which an ordinary seaman got paid just £22.[7]

British marine artists loved painting East Indiamen. Obvious emblems of national reach and riches, they are represented in literally hundreds of canvases, sailing low in the water as they bring their precious commodities home, or setting out in convoy to keep privateers at bay, their red and white striped Company flags (which must surely have influenced the design of the Stars and Stripes), snapping and fluttering as the huge, drenched sails catch the breeze. Yet, looked at from another angle, these images convey not simply Britain's maritime and commercial reach, but also the quality and the limits of its power. The British delighted in pictures of the sea because – for two centuries or so – their merchant and naval vessels predominated there. Like the Dutch, however, they also relished marine art, because the sea afforded them a global ubiquity that compensated, but never entirely made up for, the restrictions inherent in their own constricted geography and demographic size. By means of the sea and ships, these puny people could and did go everywhere. Ships cannot operate on dry land, however; so after landfall things for the British were always very different, and usually far more difficult. This was emphatically the case as far as the East India Company was concerned.

The Company had been founded by a charter from Elizabeth I in 1600 and granted a monopoly on English trade with Asia. At this stage, neither the Crown, nor the Company's governor and twenty-four London-based directors, were in a position seriously to envisage an eastern empire. They aimed rather at making the English effective bit-players in one of the richest, most advanced, and most competitive manufacturing and commercial sectors in the world. The eight or so ships that the Company sent out every year during the first century of its existence concentrated initially on aromatic spices from the Indonesian archipelago, the cloves, nutmeg, pepper, cinnamon bark and cardamon that made unrefrigerated food and unwashed bodies more tolerable. But, by the second half of the seventeenth century, the Company had begun its work of transforming English lifestyles and consumer habits, importing an expanding range of fine Indian textiles, as well as coffee from Mokha in Yemen, and tea and porcelain from China. As far as the Indian subcontinent was concerned, the

44. English East Indiaman, by Paul Monamy, *c.* 1720.

Company came to operate out of three main coastal bases. The oldest and most southerly was Madras (now Chennai), established in 1639 and with an Indian population by 1700 of some 100,000 souls. On the western coastline was Bombay, acquired in 1661 along with Tangier as part of Catherine of Braganza's dowry. And to the north-east was Calcutta, founded in 1690 to take advantage of Bengal's expert weavers and trade along the Ganges and Jumna rivers. By way of this magic triangle – Madras, Bombay and Calcutta – the East India Company gradually became Britain's single biggest commercial enterprise, and secured a greater share of India's export business than the rival Dutch, Danish, Portuguese and French trading companies.[8]

But it continued for a long time to view its role and rationale mainly in private and commercial terms. Again, this is a point that can be made effectively through contemporary art. In 1731, the Company's directors commissioned George Lambert and Samuel Scott to paint six canvases for the walls of its newly-rebuilt headquarters in Leadenhall Street, London. The resulting works convey very well the Company's restricted image of itself at this time, and the limitations too of its vision of India. Two of the six Company bases chosen for commemoration were actually situated outside the subcontinent, on the Cape of South Africa (then under Dutch control), and at St Helena in the south Atlantic. As this suggests, at this stage, the Company saw itself as an intercontinental trader, rather than as having a unique commitment to India. Even the four Indian locations selected – Bombay, Madras, Calcutta, and Tellicherry on the Malabar coast – were represented from the perspective of the sea, from without. To be sure, Scott and Lambert were careful to foreground the incontestable sources of the Company's reach and power. Here, in their canvases, are the great masted East Indiamen, cannons booming, pennants flying, lying at anchor before the walls of Fort St George, Madras, and the Company's warehouse in Bombay. But these are still emphatically marine and coastal views. The Indian interior does not feature in them, and neither does the Indian population: for, even by the early decades of the eighteenth century, the East India Company possessed in regard to these minimal power and only intermittent interest.[9]

By the time of Sarah's passage to India in 1769, however, circumstances had changed: and, however unconsciously, she would participate in and witness still more violent and radical alterations. Behind all the changes lay the fluctuating fortunes of three different imperial systems. On the one hand, as the eighteenth century progressed, the power and grip of India's own Mughal emperors waned disastrously; on the other, the same Anglo-French competition that was responsible for convulsions and captivities in North America at this time also began impacting on the subcontinent.

After 1744, French and British traders on the Coromandel coast began recruiting small numbers of sepoys (indigenous soldiers), and raising extra levies of men from their respective home states, most of them paid for by the companies themselves, but some of them regular troops. This proved a dress-rehearsal for more extensive Anglo-French warfare in parts of India after 1750, and more ruthless interventions in local struggles and politics. In June 1756, the new young Nawab of Bengal, Siraj-ud-Daulah, seized

45. Bombay, by George Lambert and Samuel Scott.

the East India Company's settlement at Calcutta. The response was immediate and savage. A one-time Company civil servant at Madras turned soldier, Robert Clive, first recaptured Calcutta, and then destroyed Siraj-ud-Daulah at the battle of Plassey in June 1757. Subsequent skirmishes undermined the French and their indigenous allies, and culminated in a major Company victory at Buxar in northern India in 1764. The following year, Clive, by this stage Governor and Commander-in-Chief of the East India Company's forces, received the *diwani*, or land revenue rights, to Bengal, Bihar and Orissa as a (reluctant) grant from the Mughal emperor, Shah Alam II. A trading company once confined to the margins of India and of Mughal regard thus became responsible for some twenty million Indians, and also – and crucially – for the subcontinent's richest province. From now on, the Company had much less need to ship bullion from Britain in order to pay for the textiles, spices and saltpetre it had traditionally sought out in India. Instead, Indian land revenues could now be used to pay for the Company's purchases. Over time, these same revenues also came to pay for ever larger armies of Company soldiers and bureaucrats.[10]

Yet, even after securing the *diwani*, the East India Company's administrative power remained confined to Bengal and adjacent areas of Hyderabad, to the Northern Sarkars, and to its long-established coastal

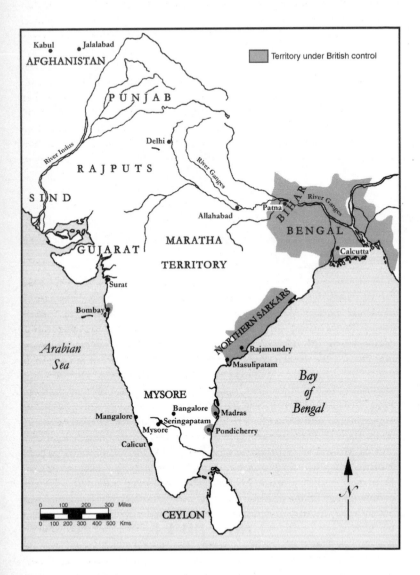

India after the battle of Buxar in 1764.

settlements at Bombay and Madras, while its British personnel continued to be perilously few.[11] Virtually the whole of Sarah's Indian career was shaped by just one aspect of this sparsity of British numbers. On her voyage out from England in 1769, she found herself 'the only woman on board' sailing with 185 men, most of them Company troops. A one-way passage from Britain to India at this time cost at least £30 (well over a thousand pounds in today's values), and the Company disliked laying out such sums on the wives of soldiers and menials. Moreover, Sarah was no wife. Three weeks into the voyage, 'in a fit of inebriety', her stepfather tried to exploit her rarity value by selling her to one of the soldiers on board. When the ship's captain halted the deal, the two men fought him in their fury and frustration. On Sarah's arrival at Madras, she was immediately taken under the protection and into the bed of a Company lieutenant who refused for a long time to release her to one of his subordinates, Sergeant John Cuff, who won her in the end by marrying her. As soon as Cuff died in southern India in the 1780s, she was immediately snapped up in marriage by an army corporal fighting there. One notes her pitiless descent through the ranks of the army as age, war, and the Indian sun stole away with her good looks.

Yet the sexual feeding-frenzy that Sarah Shade so spectacularly provoked in India had much less to do with whatever personal attractions she may have possessed, than with just one aspect of the crucial deficiency there in British numbers. Neither at this nor at any other time was the subcontinent viewed by the Company or London's politicians as a potential settlement colony. The rate at which British women arrived there increased after 1750, but even by comparison with the very limited numbers of their countrymen, they remained a tiny minority. The official intention was never that substantial numbers of Britons should settle there and reproduce themselves by sexual congress with their own kind. This was just as well since, in the eighteenth century and after, many who made the passage to India did not survive long enough to reproduce themselves at all. Of the 645 white male civilians who worked for the East India Company in Bengal between 1707 and 1775 (just 645!), close to 60 per cent are known to have died there, often in the early years of their appointment. Even at the end of the century, one in four British soldiers stationed in India perished every year.[12] Edmund Burke's famous accusation that India's indigenous inhabitants scarcely knew what it was like to see a grey-haired Briton was thus both partisan polemic and perversely accurate. Only a minority of high-level Company servants were able to do what Burke accused them all of doing: make vast, illicit profits in the subcontinent and return triumphantly to Britain as millionaire nabobs. The majority of Britons in India at this stage made limited fortunes or nothing at all, and simply did not survive long enough to go home. As a tour around the oldest Anglican church in India, St Mary's at Madras, demonstrates, one of the favoured epitaphs for memorials and gravestones of Britons perishing in India was necessarily: 'Wisdom is the grey hair unto men'. For many of those arriving in the subcontinent from Britain before and even after 1820, this was the only variety of grey hair that they had any chance of acquiring.[13]

Because their numbers in the Indian subcontinent were so modest and subject to severe attrition, the British always understood at some level that they could never satisfactorily and durably capture it, and that on their own they could not even try. India was too far away from their own islands. It was too big and too complex; and above all it was much too populous. India, calculated a Scottish politician and former military man in 1788, contained 'eleven times as many people' as Britain and Ireland put together, and this was probably an underestimate.[14] Even at the start of the eighteenth century, India's population may already have reached 180 million, which meant that then, as now, it contained a fifth of all the inhabitants of the globe. By contrast, the combined population of Britain and Ireland in the 1780s was under thirteen million souls. Of course, there is an obvious respect in which such a comparison between British and Indian population totals misleads. As Benjamin Disraeli remarked, eighteenth- and nineteenth-century Britons were nervously prone to imagining India as one mighty, unmanageable unit, but it was not one unit at all.[15] India at this stage was still a geographical expression, a collocation of states, kingdoms and sects, further subdivided by hundreds of thousands of intensely localist village communities. This in the end proved vital for British success. At their peak, the Mughal emperors had shown a capacity to tax efficiently, maintain stability, and monopolise force, and some of the successor states emerging in their wake proved highly sophisticated and resilient. But the subcontinent as a whole lacked impersonal, unifying state apparatus or national ideology. By contrast, the East India Company was increasingly bound up with a British state that was able to become precociously centralised and increasingly nationalistic in large part because it was also small and compact in territorial extent.

But for all this – for all the commercial success and financial muscle of the East India Company, for all its access through the British state to naval power on a scale that Indian rulers could only dream of, and for all its busy and highly successful exploitation of religious, cultural and political divisions within the subcontinent – the huge disparity in numbers between the British in India on the one hand, and its indigenous population on the other, meant that the former were of necessity always dependent upon the latter. As Om Prakash and K.N. Chaudhuri have shown, the East India Company – like its European rivals – only established itself to begin with through the aid of Indian bankers and shipping, by leasing land for its initially modest fortifications from Indian rulers, and by working closely with local merchants in the various regional economies, Gujaratis in the western Indian Ocean, Chettiyar and Muslim traders in the south. As late as the 1740s, close to half of the ships servicing the Company's base at Madras were still Indian-owned; and, when Siraj-ud-Daulah moved against Calcutta in 1756, almost all of its white inhabitants were in hock to Indian moneylenders.[16] The shift to military conquest over the next half-century only gave rise to fresh forms of British dependence. The Company increasingly relied on local rulers, agents and landowners to raise men and taxes, and employed a growing array of Indian informants, spies, suppliers, clerks and administrators of all kinds. Most of all, it was obliged to recruit from the same huge labour market of armed peasants that had traditionally served the Mughal emperors. In C.A. Bayly's words, these conquerors would always be 'strictly limited in what they could achieve, for to a great extent the British empire in India remained an empire run and garrisoned by Indians'.[17]

This dependence on those they increasingly strove to rule influenced both how Britons in India experienced captivity, and how the Company and its employees were regarded by their countrymen back home. In the Mediterranean region, and in North America, capture by non-Europeans usually signified, for the British settlers, soldiers, voyagers and traders involved, a sudden, traumatic exposure to alien customs, alien cultures, alien food, alien language and alien dress, and occasionally to cross-racial sex. In India, however, Britons were so thinly distributed and so dependent on the local population, that those who stayed here more than a short time usually had some experience of these things anyway. Indian food, languages and dress, and often Indian sexual partners, were things with which most Britons in the subcontinent before 1820 (especially male Britons) had at least some familiarity. Consequently, captivity here was often less of a cultural shock than in other zones of overseas enterprise, especially when the victims involved were poor whites.

The woman who became Sarah Shade is a case in point. When captured alongside her first husband, Sergeant Cuff, and imprisoned at Bangalore for eleven months by the forces of Haidar Ali, ruler of Mysore, she was able to derive comfort from more than just the companionship of her army spouse. She was aided too by the degree to which by this stage – the early 1780s – she had of necessity become assimilated. One of her Indian guards at Bangalore turned out to be a defector from the East

India Company's Madras army, and he 'interested himself for her on account of [her] speaking his language, and understanding cookery', by which was meant of course southern Indian cookery. This anecdote may seem too good to be true, but I suspect that there was some substance to it. Certainly we know that when Sarah returned to London and was widowed for a second time, in the mid-1790s, she kept herself going for some years by making vegetable curries and other Indian dishes. She would cook these meals to order and at a price for a network of 'different East India families' living in the capital, people, who – like her – had returned to what was nominally their home country, yet found themselves home-sick for the vast subcontinent they had left.

This points to another respect in which the meanings of British captivity in India were distinctive. In the eyes of many of their compatriots at home, *all* Britons who spent substantial time in India were at risk of becoming captive there in a fundamental, if not in a literal sense. Since Britons in India were so sparse, and dependent on the local population in so many ways, fears were regularly expressed back home – particularly at this early stage – that they would be taken over by their Indian surroundings, become entrapped by indigenous habits and values, cease to be authentically British, and go native.

As suggested by the enthusiasm for Sarah's curries among white veterans of the East India Company back in London in the 1790s, these anxieties were not entirely misplaced. But those who gave voice to them, believed that Britons in India were at risk of being suborned in far more serious ways than through their palates and taste buds. They accused the nabobs (and it is suggestive of course that this corruption of *nawab*, meaning a Muslim ruler, was applied to wealthy Britons returning from India) of succumbing to – and exacerbating – endemic Indian corruption and despotism, and of bringing these evils back home. 'They find themselves exotics, and that they have all along been considered as such,' complained one retired East India Company official of the reaction he and his kind encountered back in Britain:

The honest, free-hearted Indian [and note the use of this term by a British Company servant about himself!] is ever considered as worse than a heathen and despising all religions – in short one of those miscreant delinquents, the produce of whose rapine and violence has poisoned and extirpated every genuine virtue of their native country.[18]

This was in 1797. In earlier decades, expressions of hostility within Britain to the East India Company's white employees, both civil and military, were still more pronounced and pervasive. This helps to explain why the published captivity narrative took so long to emerge as far as India was concerned. Before the 1740s, Britons there had rarely seemed dangerous or profitable enough for it to be worth indigenous regimes' bothering to capture them. But, even after this – when captivity for the British did become far more of a risk – printed captivity narratives from this zone of imperial enterprise remained for some time rare.[19] In part, I am sure, this was because, to those on the home front, Britons in India still seemed a long way away, the agents of a greedy, grasping Company rather than of the nation at large, alien in terms of their reputed behaviour, and altogether unworthy of much sympathy. If Britons in India sometimes suffered, Britons at home had no great desire – and would not have until the late 1780s – to read about or identify with their sufferings.

The seeming conspicuous exception to this, John Zephaniah Holwell's *A Genuine Narrative of the deaths . . . in the Black Hole* (1758), only serves to make the point more strongly. When Siraj-ud-Daulah seized Calcutta in June 1756, Holwell, a Dubliner by birth and a senior East India Company official, was imprisoned overnight along with, he claimed, 145 others in an eighteen-foot square punishment cell. By the morning, he tells us, all but twenty-three of them had suffocated, died of dehydration, or been trampled to death by fellow captives frantic to reach the only window, their only chance of air. The real body-count was probably closer to fifty people, not all of whom were British. Yet while Holwell clearly exaggerated what had happened so as to demonise Siraj-ud-Daulah, and revenge the damage done to his career and the death of several of his friends, this in itself was scarcely surprising. Much more striking was the limited impact that Holwell's narrative of the 'Black Hole', and the event itself, had at the time back in Britain. The Victorians would in due course convert 'the Black Hole of Calcutta' into a poignant foundation myth of British India: 'that great crime', as the future Lord Macaulay called it in 1840, 'memorable for its singular atrocity'. Holwell's British contemporaries reacted differently, and in many cases not at all. Extracts from his captivity narrative were, to be sure, reprinted in the English, Scottish and Irish newspaper and periodical press in 1758, but no new edition of it appeared in the English language after that year. Nor do British printmakers or painters seem to have devoted imagination to this episode before the nineteenth century. A monument to the 'victims' was only erected in Calcutta because Holwell commissioned and paid for it himself. It was quickly allowed to crumble into dust, and not replaced until Lord Curzon, Viceroy of India, intervened in the early 1900s.[20]

Some of the reasons why this emotive piece of partly bogus imperial history was neglected for so long have already been touched on. British public sympathy for, and patriotic indentification with the East India Company and its agents were limited at this stage, and remained so for some decades longer. 'I think the East India Company are greatly to blame for provoking the Moors' was how one British officer reacted to Calcutta's fall in 1756. By contrast, Holwell's vilification of Siraj-ud-Daulah was not generally accepted at this time. In 1772, a Parliamentary enquiry was firmly told by one witness that 'he did not believe the nabob had any intention of a massacre when he confined the English in the Black Hole'.[21] Even a careful reading of Holwell's own narrative reveals how removed we are at this point from a careful wrapping of the Company and its works in India in the Union Jack. Few of the Black Hole's victims are presented in heroic terms. Instead, they are described as desperately stripping off and sucking sweat from their clothes, or drinking their own urine until its concentrated acidity revolts them. We learn, too, how – as the night and the heat wore on, and oxygen became used up – those captives who were still living trampled on the dead and dying out of a sheer animal instinct to get to the one window and survive. 'All regards of compassion and affection were lost,' a British writer recalled with disgust in the early nineteenth century, 'no one would recede or give way for the relief of another.' This was not obviously the stuff of stirring imperial adventure, and nor was the immediate background to this episode. When Siraj-ud-Daulah's forces swept into Calcutta in 1756, there were just seventy Company soldiers to oppose them; there were no more than 500 British troops – perhaps less – in the whole of Bengal.[22]

The India in which Sarah arrived in the 1760s, then, was altered more in prospect than in substance. True, European powers had now succeeded, for the first time ever in global history, in disrupting the political order in India, and an armed, mercantile company from Britain was now entrenched in one of its richest regions, Bengal, governing ostensibly as a vassal of the Mughal emperor. But the degree to which the East India Company was able to penetrate the Indian interior at this stage – or that anybody expected it to do so – remained very limited, and so did British domestic interest in and sympathy with such a project. Most of all, and more conspicuously even than in other zones of overseas enterprise, British manpower in India was markedly circumscribed and highly vulnerable. In order to expand their power here, the British would require a quantum leap in military force and available personnel. During the course of Sarah's career in India, they learnt how to acquire it. The price was paid in money, but also in terrible violence, warfare, and captivities.

Almost all of Sarah's life in India, from the late 1760s to the 1790s, was spent in armed camps, or tramping after a succession of uniformed males in one military campaign after another. As the subtitle of her narrative put it: hers was a saga of a woman 'traversing that country in company with THE ARMY [sic], at the sieges of Pondicherry, Vellore, Negapatam', and more. Sustaining this rate of warfare in India required a more dramatic and distinctive augmentation in manpower than the British had ever previously experienced. Back in 1744, a year of war, the East India Company had employed only about 2500 European soldiers in Calcutta, Madras and Bombay combined. By 1765, there were 17,000 Company troops in Bengal alone, and this was just the beginning. In 1778, British army and Company forces in the subcontinent comprised – at least on paper – 67,000 men. When Sarah left India, in the 1790s, the total was in excess of 100,000. By 1815, the Company's armies in India had risen to a quarter of a million.[23]

The connections between this military build-up and the expansion of the Company's territorial reach in India are well known. At one level, sudden, shattering reverses like the loss of Calcutta became much less likely. Enhanced military power made it far easier for the Company to hang on to such territory as it had already secured. At another level, exploitation became easier. The sword proved a powerful argument when extracting land revenues and taxes, or squeezing protection money or treaties out of individual Indian rulers. At another level still, this expanding, turbulent army took the Company much further into the Indian interior than the politicians and directors in London ideally wanted to go. In the half-century after the battle of Plassey in 1757, debates in Parliament, and the reams of correspondence between India House in London and its civilian and military servants in India are full of variations on the theme of 'conquest is by no means our desire', but they got it anyway.[24] Yet escalating military might and violence did not make comprehensive British empire in India a foregone conclusion. In at least four respects, the East India Company's position after 1757 was more vulnerable than the rapidly expanding size of its armies appears to suggest.

To begin with, there were the enduring challenges of the subcontinent's distance from Britain and its population and geographical extent. One indicator of the degree to which Indian history remains 'othered' even today, is the reluctance to apply to it the sort of logic that is customarily employed in analyses of British power in North America. It is a commonplace that the British will to defeat revolution in America was tested by the sheer scale of its terrain, the buoyancy of its population, and the logistical difficulties of transporting war materiel 3000 miles across the Atlantic. Yet the British in India often viewed themselves as facing similar difficulties. Here, too, it could seem that – while occasional, brilliant victories were more than possible – these by themselves would never be enough. That indigenous opponents would simply withdraw temporarily, tap into inexhaustible reserves of local manpower, and regroup to fight another day, with French aid, and with weaponry increasingly comparable to the Company's own. 'We drive Hyder from the field', wrote a British army officer despairingly of a campaign against the southern Indian kingdom of Mysore that would shortly steal his life:

> but we can neither take his artillery, nor prevent his retreat. Every man we lose on these occasions is valuable to us, and though he should lose ten for one, it is a matter of no consequence to him.[25]

As this suggests, while one challenge confronting the British was always the overwhelming scale of India and its population, a second was their own, incurable limits. After 1756, the Company's forces seemed ever more impressive on paper, but maintaining adequate and effective *European* armies in the field was another matter. Even getting sufficient white soldiers to India in the first place was difficult. Company recruiters in Britain were no more popular than their regular army counterparts, and especially in summer when agricultural jobs were plentiful, plebeian volunteers were sparse. The globalisation of war in the six decades after Plassey made them far more so. In 1776, as war with America began sucking in British manpower, the Company calculated that its artillery in India, an indispensable part of its armoury, was at least 700 men short. In 1794, by which time Britain was at war with Revolutionary France, the number of unfilled vacancies in the Company's European regiments was estimated to be as large again as the number of its European infantrymen actually serving in the field.[26]

Men successfully recruited in Britain still had to survive the passage to India. Before 1790, mortality rates among white troops on East Indiamen and transport ships sometimes compared unfavourably with that of chained blacks on transatlantic slave-ships. In 1760, thirty-three of the fifty-three officers and men sailing to India on board the *Osterly* died before arrival; a third of the men on the *Pondicherry* in 1782 perished just on the stretch of voyage between the Cape of Good Hope and Johanna Island, the latter a familiar stop-over *en route* to Madras. Sometimes whole ships, with all their men and would-be memsahibs, were lost to rough seas, as happened to the East Indiaman *Halsewell* in 1786.[27] Those Company troops

46. *The Loss of an East Indiaman* by J.M.W. Turner.

who did survive the voyage out and make landfall still had to contend thereafter with persistent germ warfare, especially dysentery, waterborne cholera, and malaria. At all times, some 20 per cent of the Company's European troops in India are estimated to have been out of action because of illness. It was a commonplace among Company surgeons that a European soldier wounded in India was six times less likely to recover than a sepoy in a similar situation, because the former's immune system was more undermined by recurrent illness, made worse in many cases by too much drink.

The logic of all this was clear to the Company from early on, and created its third perennial problem. If it was ever to control substantial tracts of India, the bulk of its manpower would have to be Indian. The stupendous rise in 'British' forces in India after the 1750s was therefore something of an optical illusion. Both the Company and the British state dispatched more European males to the subcontinent after this point, but the rise in Company army size chiefly signified a growing British dependence on Indians. Even at Plassey, more than twice as many Indians as Europeans fought on the 'British' side. During the next half-century, the disparity between white and

SEAPOYS.
of the 3 Battalion at Bombay

47. East India company sepoys at Bombay.

Indian troops in the Company's pay became far more pronounced. In 1767, just 13 per cent of the Company's rank-and-file troops in the Coromandel region were classified as European: though in reality their numbers included Americans and Caribbean blacks, as well as Germans, Swiss, Portuguese, French and varieties of Britons. Ten years later, the Company employed just over 10,000 white soldiers in India. These men were outnumbered seven to one by the Company's sepoys.[28]

The incidence of disease among whites made these already stark disparities still more so, as did the isolation of some of the Company's outposts. At Fort Victoria, 60 miles south of Bombay, 160 Company sepoys, plus their Indian officers, were nominally supervised in the 1770s by just three white Company officials, none of whom was a military man. In some Company bases, there appear at intervals to have been no whites at all. In the 1780s, a British officer recorded stumbling into a 'British' fort in the south of India where there were no Britons left. Its sepoys had continued to be provisioned by the Company, and so had simply continued to man their post. They all assembled to have a look at him, not having 'seen a European for many years'.[29] This was an extreme case that points however to an enduring phenomenon. Estimates of so-called British military strength in India need always to take account of the fact that most of it was not British at all.

By the onset of the Victorian age, this system of exercising imperial rule overwhelmingly through the bodies, swords and guns of some of the ruled was broadly, though not universally taken for granted. Earlier, however, its intrinsic insecurity and audacity alarmed and even terrified. 'It will be allowed', wrote a Company army officer frankly in 1769: 'that it is a dangerous measure to place our chief dependence upon the very inhabitants of the country we mean to keep in subjection', and similar arguments were regularly advanced in Parliamentary debates and in correspondence between India House and its agents.[30] In part, such nervousness simply reflected the fact that, as far as the Company was concerned, a large-scale sepoy system was still something new, and no one could yet be confident it would endure, as distinct from melting away or turning against its paymasters. But some British officials were also fearful that sufficient cash might not always be forthcoming to pay and provision this ever-expanding Indian mercenary army.

This helps to explain why the Company's directors in London opposed what they perceived as irresponsible expansionism by elements in its army. Warfare in India was expensive in itself, but it also devastated local trade, agriculture, and tax-payers. And how were the Company's sepoys possibly to be paid for, if profits from Indian commerce, agriculture and land began drying up? As it was, a shortage of provisions triggered large-scale sepoy desertions from the Company's armies during the First Mysore War in 1768, and disruptions in supplies of food and cash contributed to serious sepoy mutinies in the early 1780s. To John Zephaniah Holwell and others, it seemed that the spiral of violence after Plassey could only end by swallowing up the East India Company itself:

New *temporary* victories stimulate and push us on to grasp at new acquisitions of territory; these call for a large increase of military force to defend them; and thus we shall go on, grasping and expending, until we cram our hands so full that they become cramped and numbed, and we shall be obliged to quit.[31]

There was a fourth and final respect in which the Company's expanding armies could seem counterproductive, and dangerous to the British themselves as well as to Indians. The East India Company never operated in a vacuum. In the half century after Plassey, it was one, alien, expanding power amidst other contending Indian powers. South Asian scholars now accept that the contraction of Mughal political and military authority in India after 1720 by no means resulted in general fragmentation and disorder. Powerful successor states emerged in certain regions, that sometimes exhibited a greater capacity and will to modernise than had the Mughal emperors. As far as military change was concerned, these renovated Indian states never relied solely on European models. In some, such as the Maratha Confederation, the shift away from feudal armies to greater military centralisation was already apparent in the seventeenth century; while Persian and Afghan invasions in the early eighteenth century, and conflict between the different Indian kingdoms, also helped to power military change in the subcontinent.[32] None the less, and as had been the case since the 1500s, European technologies, tactics, and mercenaries were systematically copied and adopted by some Indian rulers. The growing military machine sponsored in India by the East India Company helped to bring into being – and had to contend against – other very large armies, supplied with comparable weaponry and equipment.

It is easy enough to detect in post-Plassey, post-Buxar British writings a growing recognition of these changes. Ritualistic and reassuring remarks on innate Indian passivity and ductility are ever more intermixed, especially in confidential writings and high-level missives, with acknowledgements that the Indian scene was becoming more militarily dynamic and dangerous in fact. 'Every year brought with it an increase of military knowledge to the black powers,' wrote an East India Company colonel of his Mysore campaigns in the late 1760s.[33] 'The Indians have less terror of our arms,' conceded the British governor of Madras in 1781, 'we less contempt for their opposition.' 'The mass of the [British] people are . . . uninformed in regard to the changes that have taken place among the warlike tribes of India,' wrote a veteran looking back on the struggles of the early 1800s, '. . . which, *combined with their natural courage* and their numerical superiority, has rendered our conflicts with them sanguinary in the extreme.'[34]

Euphoric British assumptions, in the immediate aftermath of Plassey and Buxar, that fighting and winning in India were always going to be a pushover, thus gave way to more realistic and grimmer appraisals of Indian warfare. Again, Sarah Shade's narrative makes the point. Utterly lacking in any kind of triumphalism, it is not just a testimony to over two decades of British imperial advance in India, but also a story of pathos, loss and mixed military fortunes. Shade herself, as we have seen, was taken captive in Mysore and wounded several times. She also lost two husbands, and – in the span of a week – saw 'sixteen officers' wives being widowed' in the British regiment she marched alongside. The essential context of her narrative – and what makes it an arresting read even now – was both expanding British power in India, and British fears and recurrent reversals there. This is also the essential background to the rise in British captivity experiences in India, and to yet another rich seam of captivity writings.

Apprehension and astonishment in the face of the huge risks involved in what they were doing, can be seen among Britons at home, as well as in India, and were expressed indirectly as well as explicitly. From the 1750s onwards, tigers stalk the British imagination. Sarah herself was mauled by a tiger in the early years of her marriage to John Cuff. Her arms were permanently scarified by its claws. She had another confrontation with the animal, when she witnessed one devouring the pregnant Indian companion of a Company army officer. (Or was this perhaps an addition by her ghost-writers worried at what was known about levels of cross-racial sex in the Company's legions?) Building on the horror of these fierce encounters, Sarah's publishers inserted a special appendix in her captivity narrative describing the wild animals of India, of which the tiger, they insisted, was by far the worst:

A tiger is one of the most ferocious animals that Nature has produced; stately and majestic in appearance, yet cowardly and artfully cunning in his actions; never openly facing his prey, but springing upon it from ambush.

The tensions in this description are interesting and suggestive. The tiger, in this version, is at once a magnificent beast and lacking in courage, both dangerous and devious. Most of all, it is unpredictable, as India itself seemed unpredictable. By this stage, anthropomorphic tiger references of this sort had become common in British literature and art. Before the battle of Plassey, however, Britons had known little of tigers outside of wildly inaccurate images in ancient bestiaries and books of heraldry. It was the conquest of Bengal that brought these animals to their notice.

48. George Stubbs' tigress.

Company officials working there encountered them in the wild, in princely zoos, and on tiger-shoots. A few managed to export live examples back to Britain. The duke of Cumberland was given several of the beasts in the 1750s; and in 1762 Robert Clive, now governor of Bengal, presented a tigress to the duke of Marlborough. This was the animal that George Stubbs painted three times over. More even than his canvases of leopards and cheetahs, Stubbs's *Portrait of the Royal Tiger* (1769) became a much reproduced image.[35] There were good and bad copies, engravings, polygraphs, even versions in needlework. Stubbs's tiger also established an artistic fashion. In subsequent decades, James Ward, James Northcote and other artists also painted tiger canvases; while the north country artist Thomas Bewick and the young Edwin Landseer produced wonderful engravings of the beast in books ranging from fine art albums to children's literature.[36]

It was not simply a case, however, of the East India Company's conquests familiarising Britons back home with the subcontinent's most impressive animal. To a degree that was deeply revealing, the tiger became synonymous in British minds with India itself, and an image through which shifting ideas and apprehensions of the subcontinent could be expressed.

49. *Fight between a Lion and a Tiger* by James Ward.

'The tiger is peculiar to Asia', wrote Bewick, '[but] the greatest number are met with in India.'[37]

Tigers seemed appropriate metaphors at various levels. They were massive, magnificent and regal, just as India itself was vast, costly, and a land of multitudinous princes. Sleek and deadly, they were also, as Edmund Burke wrote in the very year of Plassey, creatures of the sublime:

> Look at . . . [an] animal of prodigious strength, and what is your idea before reflection? *Is it that this strength will be subservient to you? . . . No: the emotion you feel is, lest this enormous strength should be employed to the purposes of rapine and destruction* . . . The sublime . . . comes upon us in the gloomy forest, and in the howling wilderness, in the form of . . . the tiger, the panther, or rhinoceros.

As this suggests, for the British, the tiger evoked India most tellingly at this stage because it was dangerous, beyond knowing, and beyond control.

50. A tiger devours a British soldier: wood and clockwork effigy made for Tipu Sultan of Mysore.

Stubbs painted his tigress recumbent and relaxed, but its immense musculature is easily apparent beneath the beautiful, striped pelt, and the lustrous
eyes – which do not engage with the viewer – are entirely unhuman. As
Judy Egerton puts it, we are left in no doubt that this superb beast possesses
the power to 'spring to attack with one lithe and supremely co-ordinated
bound'.[38]

The currency of tiger images after 1750 must be seen as one more
expression of British wonder and uncertainty in the face of their own
increasingly violent but still unpredictable involvement with the Indian
subcontinent. It was an image both of obsession and fear. It was not long
in fact before writers and artists began to play with the conceit of using
encounters between a lion and a tiger to comment on the wider
British–Indian encounter. One thinks of Stubbs's *Lion and Dead Tiger*, or
of James Ward's vicious *Fight between a Lion and a Tiger*, both painted at
times of sharp imperial conflict in India. As the nineteenth century
advanced, imaginary animal contests of this sort became something of a
source of complacency. 'The unanimous voice of ages', remarked Landseer
in his *Twenty Engravings of Lions, Tigers, Panthers and Leopards* (1823),
pronounced the lion 'to be the King of beasts'.[39] India and its tiger, it
appeared, had been safely vanquished by a leonine Britannia. Hence,
surely, the large numbers of Victorian British males who had themselves
painted and later photographed with their feet firmly planted on the skin
or the carcass of a dead tiger. What for Mughal princes had been an
emblem of rule, a tiger caught and killed in the hunt or kept behind bars,

became for the British an emblem of imperial supremacy over India. Before the early 1800s, however, this sense of confident, animal dominion in regard to the subcontinent was rare, because the tiger was still able to catch them unawares. 'They attack all sorts of animals, even the lion,' mused Thomas Pennant in his *History of Quadrupeds* in 1781, a year of terrible British defeats and captivities in southern India 'and it has been known that both have perished in their combats.'[40]

The tiger then was already established in British minds as an emblem for India *before* the reign of Tipu Sultan (1782–99), the Mysore ruler who employed tiger-symbolism for his own religious and ritual purposes in a systematic fashion, and who became the villain of a major British captivity panic in the 1780s and '90s, a captor indeed for several months of Sarah Shade herself. There was a sense in which, for the British, Tipu's tiger-ornamented court, the stylised tiger stripes on the uniforms of his soldiers, and the exquisite, jewelled tiger-heads snarling from the rings on his fingers and the pommel of his sword, only brought into focus more longstanding and inchoate fears that advancing into India was fraught with danger, that they were riding the tiger in fact. And tiger and lion imagery had another, less acknowledged significance for the British.

51. A tiger-headed Mysore cannon at Madras.

If India often seemed to them a large, fierce, untameable, unknowable beast, then by the same token the British themselves appeared ever more dangerous, and ever more remorseless to the peoples of the subcontinent, and to many others across the entire globe. The half-century after the Battle of Buxar in 1764, that won them Bengal, would witness unprecedented levels of British military violence, much of it carried out – as in India – by *condottieri* of a sort, hard men with swords and guns and ships, fiercely on the make, and often operating substantially out of reach of London and its control. They would fall upon and tear out whole chunks of the world, like ravenous beasts unleashed:

'This I seize', says the lion, 'because I have got teeth; this, because I wear a mane on my neck; this, because I have claws; and this last morsel, not because I have either truth, reason, or justice to support me and justify my taking it, but because I am a lion.'[41]

Savage beasts preoccupied the British, then, even before their armies, with Sarah Shade trudging gamely in their wake, marched on to face the tiger-mouthed cannon of Mysore.

NINE

The Tiger and the Sword

Mysore and its meanings

10 September 1780. Pollilur: ten miles north-west of the temple town of Kanchipuram, and just several days' hard marching from Madras. It is imperial nightmare time. There are no Gatling guns to jam, and the one remaining British colonel still has some time to live, but the square of redcoats around him is diminishing in front of our eyes. Outside it, the stragglers are already being picked off, speared through the neck, or decapitated with vicious, curving sabres as they try to run. There is no refuge inside the square either. The men still have their muskets, but the ammunition wagon has just exploded, and soon they will be fighting with swords, pikes, bare hands. Converging on them from all sides is wave upon wave of Mysore cavalry, glittering in scarlet, and blue, and green. Colonel William Baillie lies wounded in a palanquin, sweats into his thick, braid-encrusted uniform, and gnaws at his fingernails in anguish. By contrast, Tipu Sultan Fath Ali Khan, eldest son and soon-to-be successor of Haidar Ali of Mysore, is in control and simply dressed in a silk tunic patterned with tiger stripes. He surveys the slaughter from his war elephant, savours the scent of a rose, and ponders how many of the British to kill, how many to capture.

Yet the thirty-foot-long mural of Pollilur that glows still from the walls of Tipu's elegant wooden summer palace just outside Seringapatam is more than a commemoration of Mysore victory. Looked at closely, this piece of courtly propaganda by an unknown artist in the service of Tipu is also a meditation on warrior masculinity and its absence. Without exception, Tipu and his turbaned armies are shown all sporting beards or moustaches. Even their French allies fighting alongside them bristle with facial hair. But their British opponents have been portrayed very differently. In reality, some of Baillie's men would have struggled and died that day wearing tartan kilts and motley colours.[1] Here, though, his white soldiers all appear in uniform jackets of red, a colour associated with blood, fertility and power, but also in India with eunuchs and with women. Baillie's men

52. The Battle of Pollilur: detail from an 1820 copy by an unknown Indian artist.

are also conspicuously and invariably clean-shaven. Neatly side-burned, with doe-like eyes, raised eyebrows, and pretty pink lips, they have been painted to look like girls, or at least creatures who are not fully male. This was not an atypical form of mockery in the subcontinent at this stage. The British were 'worse than women', another Indian ruler wrote in 1780, sly, fox-like traders who had been foolish enough to challenge tigers. And now the time for their destruction was come.[2]

British reactions at the time were not very different. When news of Pollilur, and other military reversals against Mysore's legions, reached London in 1781, it provoked 'universal consternation'. In rival European capitals, and in Revolutionary America, there was both astonishment and *schadenfreude*. This, after all, was the year of Yorktown, and the end of all of Britain's hopes of retaining the oldest, richest sector of its transatlantic empire. Now it seemed that Britain's newer, eastern empire was also coming under acute pressure. 'India and America are alike escaping,' predicted

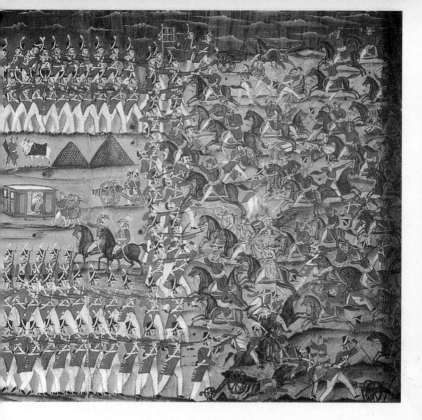

Horace Walpole, an anti-imperial English Whig. This was over-euphoric: but it was the case, as the prime minister, Lord North, admitted, that defeat at Pollilur: 'had engaged the attention of the world . . . and had given rise to so much public clamour and uneasiness'.[3] And although some subsequent successes in southern India allowed this phase of conflict between the East India Company and Mysore to end in a draw, imperial confidence had been severely dented, and remained so for some time. In 1784, Parliament passed new legislation regulating the affairs of the Company, and explicitly renouncing any prospect of future British expansion in India: 'schemes of conquest and extent of dominion . . . [were] repugnant to the wish, the honour and the policy of this nation.' Doubts about the feasibility – and desirability – of further advances in the subcontinent were still in evidence when war with Mysore resumed in 1790. Political prints published in London at that time predicted almost without exception that British forces would be defeated and humiliated there.[4]

53. A Victorian photograph of the original mural of Pollilur at the Darya Daulat, Bagh Seringapatam

The root cause of this mood of imperial recessional was at one level all too obvious: the lost war in America, and the ensuing global repercussions and domestic soul-searching. 'In Europe we have lost Minorca', catalogued one Member of Parliament drearily:

In America thirteen provinces, and the two Pensacolas; in the West Indies, Tobago; and some settlements in Africa . . . In India . . . we have yielded up Chandanagore and all the French settlements in Bengal – We have yielded Pondicherry – Carical – and every settlement we had conquered from the French upon the coasts of Coromandel and Malabar.[5]

In retrospect, it seems clear that Britain's expulsion from the Thirteen Colonies allowed it to concentrate with more devastating effect on imperial projects in India and elsewhere. But most Britons at the time failed to anticipate that this would be the case. Instead, some of them interpreted these reverses in different parts of the globe as conclusive proof that their country was simply too small to engage in large-scale, territorial empire with any hope of durable success. Even those who did not take such a catastrophic view seem to have felt uneasy about post-American War prospects in India itself.

As we have seen, right from the start, the sheer extent of the subcontinent, and especially the scale of its population, had worked to daunt and disturb as well as attract and excite. Pollilur and other military failures inevitably reinforced anxiety that the British presence in India could never be anything more than 'a precarious dominion of a few over millions' which must by definition be short-lived. The experience of major military defeats here, unprecedented since 1700, also deepened pre-existing doubts about Britons in India in another respect. A parliamentary enquiry into these failures, which filled six, substantial volumes, together with investigations into the conduct of the former governor of Bengal, Warren Hastings, revealed levels of East India Company corruption and incompetence that some had previously suspected, but that had never before been so well or publicly documented.[6] Longstanding concerns about India's corrupting effects on the Britons exposed to it – and *vice versa* – seemed now to be fully vindicated. At least some of the pessimism in the 1780s about Britain's imperial prospects in general, and about its Indian enterprise in particular, stemmed from a sense that its civil and military agents had shown themselves unworthy, or at best irredeemably inept. They did not deserve to succeed. Moreover, succeeding in India might not any more be possible.

War with Mysore and its allies confirmed that some of the Indian successor states were evolving into major military players. Haidar Ali, a highly able though illiterate warlord, had usurped the throne of Mysore in 1761, and worked hard from the beginning of his makeshift reign at the modernisation of its armies. Tipu Sultan, who succeeded him in 1782, went further and converted Mysore into a formidable fiscal-military state.[7] The results were manifest on the battlefield. In its first extended confrontation with Mysore in 1767–9, the East India Company had come close to losing Madras and been forced to sue for peace. By 1780, the year of Pollilur, Mysore's war machine was bigger still, its fiscal, commercial and territorial resources stronger. Its intelligence networks were impressive. Its fortifications were generally agreed to be better than the Company's own, as were its supply chains. Its cavalry was easily superior. Two-thirds of Mysore's weaponry was European in manufacture; but it also possessed its own armouries, foundries and war technologies.[8] And its land forces outnumbered those at the disposal of the Company's Madras Presidency.

Haidar Ali commanded 90,000 men, one Company officer claimed in the early 1780s; 150,000 men ventured another British commentator; 200,000 reported a third. All these estimates are in fact suspect, but they suggest the level of British alarm at the scale and danger of Mysore's armies.[9] This was deepened by the fact that, in this second major conflict with Mysore, Britain came close to losing control of the sea. As had been true of Algiers and Morocco in an earlier period, Mysore under Haidar Ali and Tipu Sultan was an Islamic polity (although with a majority Hindu population) with little cause to fear European land forces on their own. Only substantial armies better ordered than in this conflict, effectively combined with sea-power, could render the British lethal here. 'I can defeat them on land,' Haidar is supposed to have remarked, 'but I cannot swallow the sea.'[10] But the French might: and, at one stage, seemed on the verge of doing so.

Even in the 1760s, Haidar had made adept and purposeful use of French and other European mercenaries, engineers, artisans, interpreters and doctors.[11] In the wars of 1779–84, he and Tipu had access to a formal French alliance. Busy undermining British imperial power in America, France was unable to supply Mysore with the men and finance both powers ideally would have liked. But over a quarter of France's war fleet, some twenty capital ships in all, were dispatched to patrol the Coromandel coast. Had this force under Admiral de Suffren succeeded not just in engaging the British, but also in stopping supplies of men, money, information, and provisions from reaching Madras, the Company's southern stronghold, it might well have fallen. Had this happened, the Company's sepoy legions in southern India would have gone unpaid and unfed, and surely have melted away. As it was, there were mutinies among the Company's sepoys in the early 1780s, as well as defections to Mysore.[12]

French sponsorship of Indian resistance, which persisted even after 1800, was one reason why Mysore and its Muslim warlords provoked such persistent British concern. Of course, France was hardly in a position by itself now to replace the British as prime European power in India; and the triangular Mysore state only dominated the southern part of the subcontinent. In 1791, Tipu's dominions extended for some 92,500 square miles, slightly smaller in extent than the Company's fiscal and agrarian base of Bengal.[13] But, even more than Haidar, Tipu showed himself adept at mobilising large numbers of peasant soldiers, at fostering trade, and raising money. If he were to have the additional aid of French warships and artillery, then his future success against the British came within the bounds of possibility. And this in turn might have a domino effect on other Indian powers. As both leading Company administrators and politicians in London realised, the smallness of the British presence in India meant that ultimately its power rested less on capital, or on force simply, than on opinion and imagination, on an *idea* of invulnerability sustained by sporadic bouts of efficient and successful violence on its part. The British had to be seen to win in India, because – bluntly – they could not

54. The British square at bay at Pollilur.

afford to be seen often to be losing. A senior Company army officer spelt it out in a speech to the House of Commons in 1781. The British purchase on India, he told them, was 'more imaginary than real, to hold that vast territory in subjection with such a disparity of numbers'. Defeats like Pollilur were therefore doubly dangerous because they resulted in a loss of face: 'I fear they [the Indians] will soon find out that we are but men like themselves, or very little better.' And, once that happened, what would happen to the British in India?[14] A powerful, expansionist Mysore, allied to Britain's prime European rival France, was therefore not just menacing in itself. In the aftermath of traumatic defeat in America, it also raised the spectre of a wider melt-down of British reputation – and therefore authority – in India as a whole.

And there was a particular, grating respect in which Mysore undermined Britain's imperial prestige. It captured large numbers of its warriors, some of whom it persuaded to change sides.

Just how many British captives were taken by Mysore in its successive wars with the Company will never be known. Pollilur alone resulted in over 200 Britons being seized (some 3000 'British' troops, white and Indian, were killed there). But there were many other defeats and skirmishes productive of captives. In 1782, for instance, the French handed over to Haidar 400 British sailors and more than sixty Royal Navy officers that their naval vessels had captured at sea. Many British captives in Mysore (there were far greater numbers of Company sepoy captives) did not survive to be freed, dying from disease, harsh treatment, or because they were already severely wounded when taken. But we know that over 1300 British troops and at least 2000 Company sepoys remained alive to be handed over when peace was signed in 1784. We also know that an additional 400 British-born captives stayed on in Mysore until the 1790s, some of them voluntarily as Muslim converts.[15]

In comparison with more recent captivity panics in Asia, with the 130,000 British soldiers seized by Japan after the fall of Singapore in 1942 for instance, these Mysore captives seem conspicuously modest in point of numbers. But they must be viewed in the light both of the smallness of the British-born military presence in India at this stage – no more than 10,000 men – and of earlier complacent notions that such paltry numbers of whites, plus a few regiments of Indian auxiliaries, were all that was necessary to carve a swathe through the subcontinent. At Plassey in 1757, the 'British' force of 600 white troops and 2400 Eurasian and Indian soldiers had routed a force some fifteen times larger in number. More dramatically than anything else could have done, the number of white as well as Indian captives seized by Mysore after 1779 – at least one in five of all Britons in arms in the subcontinent – signalled that the days of clear European supremacy in India in terms of military technology, tactics and discipline were well and truly over. As one captive British officer wrote in 1784 of his comrades seized by Mysore: 'Such a force as this twenty years ago would have marched through all India.'[16] But no longer. In Britain, too, the number of Mysore captives was of less importance than what their existence was viewed as signifying. A belief that Mysore was somehow 'teeming with British captives' had an impact similar to post-Vietnam American anxieties about the fate of unknown but wildly inflated numbers of GIs captured by the Vietcong or missing in action. In both cases, the real and rumoured scale of captivity deepened the humiliation of an unsatisfactory imperial war and fostered hatred and apprehension of an insidious, too efficient non-Western enemy.[17]

But there is another important twist to this particular captivity panic, and it can be appreciated by looking again at the mural of Pollilur on the walls of Tipu's Darya Daulat palace at Seringapatam. As we have seen, this was Mysore propaganda as well as wonderfully vigorous art. Yet in spite of himself, the unknown Indian artist responsible for painting it hints at British strengths, even as he celebrates their near-annihilation and strives to un-man them. *In extremis*, the British square – at least in this version – remains conspicuous in its solidarity and almost eerily regimented. The spate of manuscript and published writings on British captivities in Mysore, that started in the early 1780s and continued into the nineteenth century, is revealing about British imperial anxieties in the wake of massive global defeats, and uncertainties about India in particular. But these same texts also document the evolution of a tougher, profoundly military imperial style, and the emergence too of a more self-conscious and confident national and imperial culture within Britain itself. Out of unprecedented British defeat, first in America and now in India, would come something very different and infinitely more dangerous.

Fighters as writers

Mysore captivities spanned barely four decades in all; those we know most about barely two. Yet because many of the Britons detained there were highly literate, and – in contrast with most Barbary and Native American captives – substantial numbers of them had little to do with their time but endure, the captivity texts they produced were abundant and diverse in content and form. There is one characteristic, however, that distinguishes them. Most of the writers were men-at-arms.

At least two women produced Mysore captivity narratives, Sarah Shade whom we encountered in the last chapter, and Eliza Fay, a barrister's wife who was seized with nine other Europeans while journeying through Calicut in 1779. And there were male civilian narrators, like Henry Becher, a trader held captive in Mysore between 1790 and 1792, whose story became the first ever English-language text published in Bombay. Almost certainly, too, many more captivity narratives emerged from these wars than have survived. The Mysore authorities periodically searched prisons and prisoners for concealed paper and books; and captives themselves sometimes destroyed writings to prevent their discovery. Sometimes writers perished along with their texts. In July 1791, British troops invading a fort near Seringapatam, uncovered a 'little journal' in a storehouse there. The Indian storekeepers told them that the document had belonged to a British seaman called Hamilton, captured some nine years before and detained in Mysore because of his carpentry skills. Hamilton had recently been executed as punishment for his countrymen's renewed invasion; and the secret diary he had maintained so painstakingly during nine years of living as a Mysore artisan appears not to have survived either.[18]

But even if the Mysore captivity archive had been preserved intact, as far as the Britons involved were concerned, it seems likely that the same point would still have held true. The vast majority of writers there were men, and men who fought and killed for a living.

Historians of Britain have been less ready than some of their Continental European counterparts to integrate men of the sword into broad cultural and intellectual history. Military and naval historians still concentrate on their subjects' administrative, social and warlike roles; while historians of literature and ideas often write as if in tacit agreement with Aldous Huxley's view that military intelligence is a contradiction in terms.[19] Only rarely are men (or women) in uniform examined in tandem with civilians as creatures who argue, think, write about and react to the societies that contain them both. Yet, as Michel Foucault acknowledged, the 'men of the camps' (and, he might have added, men of the navy) were leading players in the European Enlightenment.[20] This was partly because their numbers and importance rose so conspicuously in all the major European states after 1740, but it was also because – especially, though not exclusively at officer level – these were people of considerable education who naturally participated in the intellectual curiosities and debates of their day. In France, as Robert Darnton shows, demand for Enlightenment literature in garrison towns like Metz or Montpellier was markedly high, as was the proportion of military subscribers to the *Encyclopédie*. And here, as in other European states, men at arms were sometimes highly active as producers of culture, as well as being avid consumers of it.[21]

Despite their lingering, stereotypical reputation as chinless wonders and/or mindless action men, there is no reason to believe that Britain's military in the eighteenth century, or after, was any less intellectually engaged. As in most other European states, British regular army and naval officers were recruited disproportionately from the younger sons of landed, moneyed, professional and clerical families. This did not necessarily make them intelligent, but it did ensure that most received some education. John Burgoyne, the British general whom we have encountered surrendering at Saratoga, was arguably much more successful as an amateur playwright with close connections to the London theatres, than he was on the battlefield. Nor was Burgoyne at all unique in his interest in the written word. Back in the 1750s, when still a lieutenant-colonel, he made it a rule that all army officers serving under him should be able to speak French, be numerate, spend a portion of each day reading, and write English 'with swiftness and accuracy'.[22]

As this suggests, writing was something that British officers were increasingly expected to do as part of their job. Keeping a journal or a detailed

55. Mrs Louisa Brown in 1841 with the military journal of her son, an officer of the East India Company.

log-book, like writing copious letters, was for men of this profession often a response to orders, and not merely a private, individually chosen pursuit. This was virtually always so in the case of senior officers. When Colonel Adlercron went with a royal regiment to India in 1754, he carried with him instructions to 'keep a regular diary of all your proceedings' from both the king, George II, and the commander-in-chief of the army, the duke of Cumberland. As British imperial ambition widened, the ceaseless hunger for intelligence meant that junior officers too, and occasionally even their men, were expected to observe alien surroundings and encounters closely, and commit their observations to paper. This was emphatically true of India, even though most army officers here were employed by the East India Company and not directly by the British state, and were usually of lower social origins than the generality of regular army officers. 'Those officers are deserving of your notice', the Company's historiographer Robert Orme advised in the 1760s, 'who in their marches through the country, make . . . remarks of whatever is worthy of observation, who in short keep a kind of journal.'[23] Men-at-arms not only fought for empire, they also played a prominent role in describing, analysing, and communicating it on paper.

The growing number of fighters who were also writers in this period was thus partly a function of growing military professionalism, and the demand by states for detailed, on-site reportage of the extra-European world. But men of the sword did not simply write in obedience to their superiors and because it was part of their job. Some also wrote for pleasure, and/or in the hope of making their name or at least making money. As a glance through any British newspaper or periodical from this time will demonstrate, military and naval officers regularly sold stories, memoirs, maps and drawings of European and extra-European campaigns and explorations to the press, as well as publishing discrete volumes on these topics. The young Winston Churchill was thus acting entirely in conformity with British army traditions when he wrote up and published his own imperial and military observations – and captivity experiences – on the north-west frontier and in the Boer War.[24] Just what men in uniform chose to publish or contribute to the press tended at all times to be varied. An officer who had retired from active service, or who nurtured some kind of grievance, might decide to publish controversial or embarrassing material and be damned, but paid for his trouble, rather than confining himself to the official line. As for common soldiers and seamen, the constraints on what they wrote and published could be sparser still. So to say that most Mysore captivity writings were by men in uniform is not to say that these texts were uniform as well. Many of the authors involved had been taught ways of writing and techniques of close observation by their profession. Some were conventional patriots, warriors, and careerists, anxious to serve their country, the East India Company, and the politicians. Others were not. Theirs was a distinctive but also a mixed genre.

Initially, however, most of those who wrote while they were still captives in Mysore did so as a strategy of resistance and survival. There were two reasons why Haidar Ali and Tipu Sultan went to the trouble of taking and feeding large numbers of British prisoners. First, these men and the

56 and 57. Exterior and interior of the officers' dungeon at Seringapatam.

occasional woman were counters in the diplomatic game, means whereby the Company might be brought more quickly to terms, and pressured into yielding up territory and concessions. Second, both Haidar and Tipu viewed select Britons and other Europeans as useful and exploitable. Highly ambitious and expansionist rulers themselves, they were understandably suspicious of the Company's territorial intentions in India. But both men accepted – as Indian rulers had persistently done since the 1500s – that individual Europeans could supply useful skills, and might potentially be incorporated in their state.[25] Consequently, both men sought to divide their British prisoners in order better to control and make use of them.

As a result, there was never one Mysore captivity experience, any more than there was ever a single Barbary or Native American captivity experience. Even when men from the same regiment, company, garrison or ship were seized as a group, Mysore tactics were speedily to fragment them. Captives held in the same fort or city were usually housed in different parts of it. Even now, if you visit the massive, ruined fortress-city of Seringapatam, badly overgrown and crumbling, but still profoundly impressive on its island site on the Cauvery River, your tour guide will probably show you a large vaulted prison where some 300 British officers were reputedly incarcerated in the early 1780s. This particular prison was carefully preserved by Victorian imperialists, and has been rendered and whitewashed so often that it now resembles a rather elegant, subterranean wine-bar, and not a place of pain, squalor, and fear. Break free from the standard tourist route and explore Seringapatam on foot or by bike, however, and you quickly come across other, less well-signposted, less salubrious prison sites where non-commissioned Britons along with Company sepoys and other Indians were detained.[26] Confining the non-commissioned away from their officers was the norm in most, though not all Mysore forts. But both captive officers and captive men could expect to be split up, sometimes repeatedly so, and allotted different kinds of treatment during their detention. James Scurry, a boy serving aboard HMS *Hannibal*, was captured by the French at sea, handed over to Mysore, and taken with his comrades initially to Bangalore. Once there, this batch of captives was split into three. His group was marched to another settlement where it was then further subdivided according to age. Scurry ended up back in Bangalore along with some fifty other British boy soldiers and sailors, the oldest of whom was seventeen years of age, the youngest twelve.[27]

Mysore captivity involved then a deliberate assault on the cohesion of those British individuals experiencing it. It was also physically harsh, though not uniquely so. As we have seen, European writers at this time were agreed that the treatment of prisoners-of-war was a significant measure of a nation's level of civilisation. Yet, as in the American Revolutionary War, peacetime scruples on this score were often abandoned in practice under pressure of actual conflict. The penal reformer, John Howard, claimed it was the 'barbarity' of French treatment of some British prisoners during the Seven Years War that first aroused his interest in prisoner welfare. Conversely, Admiral de Suffren justified handing over British prisoners to Mysore in the early 1780s by reference to the sufferings their countrymen were allegedly inflicting on French POWs in North America and India.[28] Whether in Europe, or outside it, the life of a POW, especially if he came from the lower ranks, was fraught with risk and sometimes very brief. The sufferings of British captives in Mysore were not exceptional, then, so much as of a particular kind.

There was the year-long exposure to southern India's tropical climate, the chill nights followed by burning sunshine, the devastating monsoons, the millions of biting insects, and the persistent disease, made worse in the case of non-commissioned soldiers by their being forced to labour outdoors digging trenches or repairing fortifications. There was the lack of proper medical attention, which meant that those wounded when seized died in very large numbers, or only semi-healed with broken bones or internal organs still protruding from their flesh.[29] There were the 9lb irons and chains linking the captives' ankles, which made anything more than hobbled walking impossible, and deformed some of them for life. There was the regular verbal and sometimes physical abuse of guards, many of whom had no cause at all to love the Company or the British. And there were the humdrum mortifications of having to carry out all bodily functions in public, of rarely or never being able to bathe, of being deprived of adequate or familiar food and the cutlery to eat it with. There was a lack often of books, a lack always of liberty, and a lack too of alcohol. Many British males in India drank to excess. But captives supervised by strict Muslim or Hindu guards might be deprived even of this means of escape. When the British peace commissioners travelled to Mysore in 1784, they came equipped with all kinds of comforts for the captives there, medicines, hats, shoes, preserved meat, familiar British condiments like mustard. But above all they brought along drink: one hundred dozen bottles of Madeira alone.[30]

And as it always does, captivity preyed on minds. One of the reasons why few British POWs in Mysore in the early 1780s attempted to escape was because it was desperately unclear to them at this stage *where* exactly they should try to escape to. Seringapatam was only some 250 miles of harsh terrain away from the Company's stronghold of Madras. But what if Madras itself should fall? The captives knew, none better, that Mysore's armies could be formidable. Cut off and incarcerated, they had no means of telling how far those armies would eventually advance. Mysore captivity narratives testify to the debilitating effect of rumour in this situation. Newly arrived prisoners would pass on reports of fresh British defeats or, even worse, news of British victories that turned out to be false. Sometimes Mysore guards fed prisoners reports designed to sap their morale. Thus on 27 February 1782, officers held at Seringapatam learned that the British commander in southern India, Eyre Coote, was now a captive like them; the next day they were told that '15 Battalions of ours are taken', and that 7000 Frenchmen together with Haidar Ali's forces were laying siege to Madras.[31] None of these reports was true, but British captives could not be certain of this – any more than they could be sure of ultimately being set free. Britons captured by Mysore forces in the early 1780s encountered in its prisons countrymen who had been seized during the 1767–69 Anglo-Mysore wars. 'They have guards over them, and appear quite dejected,' an officer recorded of these veteran captives: 'They are allowed to dress in the European style, but are very dirty.'[32] By this stage, these men had been POWs in Mysore for over a dozen years. So what chance did the rest of them have of ever getting out?

The need to counter the corrosive effects of uncertainty, fear, physical hardship, and being separated from comrades helps to explain why so many of these captives resorted to writing. Not all of them could write. Some British soldiers and sailors held in Mysore were illiterate. Moreover, paper was a sparse and costly commodity in the prison economy. Indian guards and servants had to be bribed to smuggle it in; or a dead officer's few precious books had to be cannibalised for blank pages; or a prisoner had to have enough free time to improvise his own paper and ink from material around him. Captives also needed sufficient time and space to be able to write safely removed from the guards' surveillance. All these things worked against members of the other ranks, who were generally worked harder and held in more crowded cells, keeping prison notebooks during their captivity. Letter-writing, though, was another matter. Writing to each other was what most kept the captives together. Brief, scrawled messages were constantly circulating among them, rolled up and concealed in rice cakes, in cheroots, in bricks, or behind loose tiles. On at least one occasion, a captive officer wrote his message on a tiny strip of paper, and rolled it up tightly so that it would fit into the quill of a pen. The pen and its contents then disappeared into the anus of an Indian servant who walked it out of the fort and to its intended recipient.[33]

This ploy, which manifestly relied on the consent at some level of the messenger, was a particularly dramatic instance of a widespread pattern. In Mysore captivity in the 1780s, as in all other parts of India and at all other times, the British remained profoundly dependent on indigenous auxiliaries. It seems overwhelmingly to have been British captives who wrote messages (though at least one sepoy message survives). But it was Indian servants, washermen, guards and workers who necessarily carried these messages between the different prisons in the various Mysore cities and forts.[34] Their motives for acting in a way that inevitably put their own safety at risk were various. Some of these Indian messengers were bribed. Some were sepoy deserters from the Company's service, who perhaps chose to aid white representatives of their former employer out of residual loyalty, or because they could not know at this stage who would finally triumph in southern India. A few message-carriers may have been Hindus who regarded Haidar and Tipu as Muslim usurpers. And some, on the basis of the accounts we have, simply acted as they did out of charity.

Whatever the motive, these intermediaries have a broader significance. Superficially, the message networks that evolved to service the Mysore captives have an almost *Boys' Own* quality to them. Some later published captivity narratives certainly made the most of how British pluck and ingenuity had overcome Mysore attempts to divide and demoralise. Yet, as we have seen, communication between the captives actually relied substantially on *Indian* pluck and ingenuity. Moreover, not all Mysore attempts to divide and demoralise British captives failed. If some individual Indians crossed religious and racial lines during this captivity crisis and helped the British, the reverse was also true. Some of the latter also crossed the line and helped Mysore.

This was what lay behind some of the incessant message writing and smuggling. British captives in Mysore wrote to each other covertly for various reasons, to send words of comfort, to pass on the latest rumour, to ask for medical advice, to inform each other who among their ranks had died that day, to maintain – if they were officers – some contact with and influence over those of their men imprisoned in other places. But captives also used the message system to establish who among their number was still to be relied on, and who by contrast was showing signs of shifting loyalty.

One of the most extraordinary Mysore captivity narratives to have survived was kept by an Irish Company officer called Cromwell Massey (with that first name, we may safely assume he was a Protestant), imprisoned at Seringapatam from 1780 to 1784. Now in the British Library in London, the original is just over four inches high and barely two inches wide.[35] Massey sewed its makeshift pages together himself, just as he manufactured his own ink, scribbling his daily entries in microscopic script, and concealing the document in his clothing at night. But this tersely written journal, which is partly in code, was not just a personal record. Massey also used some of its pages to write to other captives in different parts of

58. Cromwell Massey's prison journal.

the fort. These miniature letters were then smuggled out and delivered by Indian guards and servants. Replies were smuggled back – also via Indian intermediaries – and then carefully sewn or transcribed into Massey's journal. The end-result is a testament to how protracted, harsh captivity tests and transforms individuals.

At some point in 1781 (Massey's dating is unclear), he and other Seringapatam captives noticed out of their cell windows companies of

Mysore troops being drilled in accordance with British army regulations by white men. Over the months, these white drill-sergeants and other whites in Mysore uniform reached more than a hundred in number.[36] Massey monitored the rot. In October, a sergeant smuggled a letter to him describing how fifteen 'healthy looking young men' from among the British private soldiers confined in the fort had been pressured to join Mysore's armies. On their refusal, they had been 'taken from thence one by one to an apartment', body-shaved, stretched naked on their backs over a large bowl with their legs and arms firmly held down by guards, and then 'circumcised . . . by force'. Massey soon learnt, however, that not every British defector who had undergone this conversion ordeal had been coerced. 'To be candid,' a young officer who had been circumcised wrote to him, 'when the Brahmin came to select young men for their diabolical purposes, I voluntarily offered myself and was accepted.' Massey learnt too that these crossings-over were not confined to Seringapatam. 'Fifty-one boys and young men . . . are now in the fort', wrote an informant from Bangalore, '. . . all circumcised, among them are 5 midshipmen.'[37]

This was perhaps the most dramatic, though not the most important example of overlap between the British on the one hand, and the Mysore of Haidar Ali and Tipu Sultan on the other. Having captured large numbers of officers and men, Mysore's warrior rulers were not only incorporating some of them in their own state, but also experimenting with British styles of military drill. As for the British captives themselves, some of them were voluntarily or involuntarily crossing frontiers of political and religious allegiance and being recruited into Mysore's service, their very bodies becoming marked forever in the process.

Adjusting to defeat

I stress the scale, quality and complexity of Mysore captivities because they are sometimes interpreted as a straightforward propaganda gift to the British, obvious material with which a striving imperial power could vilify a dangerous indigenous opponent. Yet Mysore captivities lent themselves to many kinds of interpretations, by no means all flattering to or convenient for the British. This was the first time since the East India Company's move away from a primarily commercial role that an Indian power had been strong enough to seize large numbers of its white and Indian soldiers, and members of the Crown's forces, and retain them for several years. In this context, captive British bodies easily appeared embarrassing emblems of defeat and disgrace. Especially as – when this war with Mysore ended in 1784 – it was with no triumphant treaty or territorial gain of importance on Britain's part. Those of its captives who were freed simply returned to their duties in India or limped home. 'The Government received us with every mark of inattention and incivility,' wrote a British ensign bitterly of his return to Madras.[38] This man had been captured at Bednur, and subsequently watched over a quarter of the ninety-three officers taken alongside him, die in a Mysore prison. Now he was free again, but found himself unwelcome among his own people, who seemed only to want to forget about former captives like him and what they represented. Not surprisingly, in the short term, none of these released military captives of Mysore published his story. Indeed, no British officer who kept a captivity narrative while being held in Mysore ever subsequently published his text directly and under his own name. When these writings did begin appearing in print, they did so only anonymously or posthumously, and invariably after heavy editing.

Some of the reasons for this initial reluctance to publish Mysore captivity accounts should be apparent. In this emergency, British solidarities had not been comprehensively maintained. According to contemporary estimates, some 1700 British-born male captives remained alive in Mysore in 1784. Almost a quarter of these men were either forced or chose to go over to their captors. That many of these individuals were circumcised only made their defection worse as far as their countrymen were concerned. As some British captives understood, circumcision for Muslims has far more of a social than a sacral significance. It is not one of the Five Pillars of Islam – prayer, the profession of faith, alms-giving, fasting, and the pilgrimage to Mecca – but is rather a practice signifying membership of the group.[39] Consequently, for British captives in Mysore to have undergone circumcision seemed a particularly indelible assault on their identity, an irreversible 'othering'. In the words of one ensign: 'I lost with the foreskin of my yard all those benefits of a Christian and Englishman which were and ever shall be my greatest glory.'[40] This is at once comic, tortured and eloquent. The man insists on his original religion and nationality, but at the same time presents these things as having been irretrievably taken away from him along with a small notch of flesh.

But it was of course the flesh in question that most provoked anger and anxiety. Exactly why the Mysore authorities ordered these circumcisions of British captives is unclear. British attempts at the time to explain them by reference to Tipu's 'bigotry to his religion' were expressions again of those ancient fears of Islam's proselytism by force that had influenced responses to Barbary captive-taking in an earlier period, but they do not convince. Just how strict either Tipu Sultan or Haidar Ali were as Muslims is still a matter of controversy. What is clear is that Tipu, like his father, was a pragmatist, accustomed both to ruling over Hindus, and working with uncircumcised French and Portuguese mercenaries and auxiliaries.[41] There seems little reason to suppose that either he or his officials wanted or expected a few hundred ragged Britons to become genuine co-religionists. In their case, circumcision was probably intended rather as a mark of new ownership, as an indelible symbol of these men's incorporation into the Mysore state. There may also have been an element of humiliation and even punishment involved. In Mysore, it was traditional for convicted felons to be cut in some way, to have their ear lobes removed, or their noses slit as permanent and shameful markers of their crimes. Were some British POWs also cut and marked after a fashion as punishment for perceived crimes? It seems possible.[42]

Certainly the British viewed what had happened to the bodies of some of their number in terms of shame, degradation and terror. As Freud observed, to the unsophisticated whose religion does not involve the practice, circumcision can appear akin to castration. Mysore prison narratives make it clear that the circumcision imposed on some of their number was perceived by British captives not just as a violent affront to who they were in terms of nationality and religion, but also as an assault on their manhood. 'Terribly alarmed this morning for our foreskins,' scribbled Cromwell Massey at one stage.[43] Fear that the Mysore authorities were seeking to unman them may have been sharpened by the fact – subsequently reported in the British press – that Tipu recruited some of the youngest captives, drummers, cabin boys and the like, to serve as *ramzanis* in his court, dancing boys who traditionally wore female costume.[44] In this sense too, then, the British bodies involved in this Mysore captivity panic could be viewed in terms of national humiliation: not just emblems of defeat and lapses in solidarity in India, but of emasculation as well.

Initial British uncertainty about how properly to see the Mysore captives, and how to tell their story, was also a function of there being so many army and naval officers involved, some of whom were of senior rank and considerable social status. Many of the captives examined in this book have been poor, mundane and miscellaneous, or private civilians from only modest backgrounds, merchant seamen, private soldiers, traders, male and female settlers, farmers, stray travellers and the like, typical representatives of the bulk of early modern humanity. The Mysore captives, like British captives in uniform during the American Revolution, were very different. The vast majority were military or naval men who had been captured in action, so what happened to them was a matter of national prestige. Moreover, their leaders viewed themselves as officers and gentlemen, and consequently

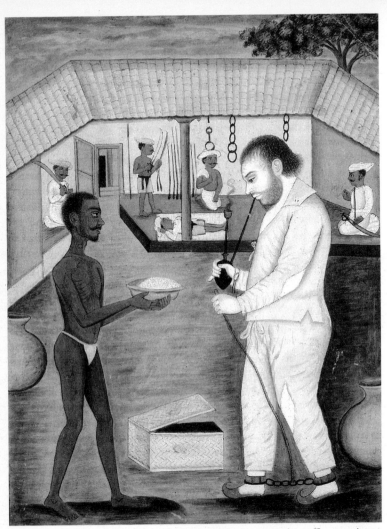

59. A portrait commissioned from an Indian artist by a one-time officer captive at Seringapatam. Is the servant included to offset the shame?

possessed a highly developed sense of individual and professional honour. These were emphatically not men used to posing as victims, or easily or appropriately represented as such in captivity narratives.

For individuals of this type, virtually any protracted captivity experience anywhere would have been a challenge. Accustomed to commanding obedience and prizing physical courage, they now had to learn to obey and submit to insult if they wanted to remain alive. Once men of status with a share of power over others, they now had to accustom themselves to insignificance and powerlessness in an alien society. John Lindsay, an army lieutenant captured at Pollilur when he was just nineteen, recorded being 'much hurt' when a Mysore official asked him if he possessed any skills as a blacksmith. Back home, Lindsay was the son of a Scottish earl: but who cared about that in Seringapatam? Lindsay was also resilient and intelligent, however, and in time came to derive a certain amusement from the metamorphosis that captivity was effecting in him and his fellows:

> Am tormented every day by a parcel of gentlemen coming to the end of my berth to talk politics and smoke cheroots. Advise them rather to think of mending the holes in their old shirts, like me, than trouble themselves about settling the balance of power in India and in Europe.[45]

As Lindsay recognised, these captive warriors could no longer strut upon the world's stage, much less determine how the world turned. They had been reduced to a peculiarly harsh and narrow private sphere, and those captives coped best who occupied themselves busily in the sort of minor, interior pursuits they would normally have consigned to their womenfolk or servants.

In Lindsay's case, this meant regularly dislodging a loose tile high on the outside wall of his prison cell in Seringapatam, and gazing through the resulting chink of light at the Mysore street life from which he was excluded:

> See a vast number of Brahmin girls going down to the river to wash – Four or five hundred horse pass by, guarding a multitude of the Carnatic inhabitants – A Moorman of high family, celebrating his marriage, passes by in great state, and his wife in a covered palanquin – Two old Moorwomen under the house scolding – a crowd of people around them, to whom they are telling their story. Shut my tile, for fear they should look up and observe me.

It was as if he were an inmate of a nunnery or a seraglio, reduced to passivity and enforced seclusion, and only able to sneak stolen glances at life outside that was literally passing him by. But Lindsay was armoured by the optimism of youth, and the confidence of his social class. He made himself take careful note of everything he observed, and then went back to his sewing. As his prison diary shows, he became immensely proud of a newly discovered ability to make and repair clothes.[46] Cromwell Massey, too, who survived his four years' in Seringapatam and lived to be over a hundred, kept fear and boredom at bay by domesticity as well as writing. Anticipating in this regard at least the most famous prisoner of the twentieth century, Nelson Mandela, he found an unwanted patch of ground outside his cell and cultivated a garden. Some British officer-captives however found the transition to captive helplessness at the hands of non-Europeans unbearable. The prison notebooks of Richard Runwa Bowyer, a Royal Navy lieutenant held in Bangalore from late 1781 to 1784, were never published or extracted from, even posthumously.[47] To read them is to understand why. They are an almost unmitigated howl of pain and confusion.

A devout Protestant dissenter from a modest background, and younger even than his years, Bowyer was far more thin-skinned than Lindsay. But the depth of his trauma was primarily due to his being captured at sea off the coast of southern India, on his very first trip from England to the subcontinent. So, at one and the same time, he was obliged to adjust to a country, climate and cultures that he had never been exposed to before, and to the experience of having non-whites and non-Christians exercising absolute power over him, without ever having been in a position himself to exert power over Indians. As a result, Bowyer flailed about in panic, constantly trying to find some firm ground on which to moor his sense of his own religious, national and racial superiority, and frequently failing. The naïvety with which he recorded these struggles makes his narrative one of the rawest documents on cross-cultural shock that I know.

He found the cruder inversions and abuses of captivity – the fact, for instance, that in Bangalore he and his comrades were mustered daily by a 'black' officer armed with a whip – less dismaying than more mundane, seemingly innocuous encounters. He was troubled by the recognition that some of his Mysore captors were kind ('I must own this usage is more Christian-like, than any we experienced from the French'). He was also deeply hurt when some hungry Mysore criminals imprisoned alongside him rejected the food that he, in a conscious display of Christian charity, had offered them ('they would not accept . . . imagining the making use of any thing given them by us would defile them'). Unable himself to hold aloof – captivity, he wrote bitterly, meant being 'entirely dependent on the blacks' – he was never sure how to interact with his captors in such a way as to protect and assert his own precious distinctiveness:

The black people take great pleasure in fighting cocks, and it is become quite modish in our prison. I bought a cock, as did some of my companions, and as the blacks often challenged us, and we in hopes of getting a *fanam* bet with them . . . I was fortunate enough to win 8 shillings by one cock, and after that refrained as I considered it brutish.

Yet, again, Bowyer had got it wrong.

The tensions in his mind emerged most sharply in an encounter that seems so strange, it may have arisen only from his own extreme disorientation. He claimed that in 1783, Bangalore's Muslim governor, with whom Bowyer established a kind of friendship, asked for the loan of some of his Western clothes, so that garments of a similar design could be made for one of Mysore's visiting French allies. 'At night', he writes, 'the Governor, attended by this pretended Frenchman, with music playing and a great concourse of the rabble, came to our prison.' Only then, Bowyer remarks, did he notice that the 'Frenchman's' hands and face were only painted white, and that between the man's new waistcoat and clinging breeches, it was possible to detect 'the genuine black colour of his skin'. Was this all or mainly a creation of Bowyer's tormented imagination, the effect of fear, extreme heat, imprisonment, and assumptions about race, power and virtue coming under strain? Or had Bangalore's governor detected Bowyer's prejudices and deep uneasiness and decided to pluck at them by this masquerade? Back home, Bowyer could easily have seen in the London and provincial theatres white actors playing blacks on the stage. But now he believed himself confronted by a 'black' imitating and mocking his own whiteness, and he could not bear it. Who gets to laugh, and conversely who gets habitually laughed at, are some of the best indicators in any time or place of where power and confidence reside. Those who laughed at Bowyer on this occasion, as he understood all too well, were really laughing at the extreme powerlessness he and his comrades had temporarily been reduced to.[48]

Bowyer was freed in 1784, and almost immediately returned home and sought refuge in the familiar, promptly marrying a woman from his own English county of Hampshire. But he never published his prison story; and neither in the short term did any of his fellow-captives. Their reticence must partly be attributed to the particular nature of this captivity ordeal. It was linked with British defeats in a subcontinent where winning had once appeared easy. It involved physical mutilations that could be interpreted as affronts to British masculinity. Some captives in Mysore had been high-ranking army and navy officers, and looked back at the fear, squalor and compromises involved with embarrassment and shame; and some British captives had defected to Mysore, and were consequently embarrassing and shameful. But the biggest obstacle to writing up these captivities was that few in Britain in the 1780s could feel certain that the military and imperial setbacks they had experienced in India and in other parts of the globe were reversible. Endurance in defeat only becomes something that nations can celebrate once they have regained a measure

60. *The Death of Tippoo or Besieging a Haram!!!* by Thomas Rowlandson.

of confidence and success. Thus returning Vietnam veterans only became *personae gratae* in the United States once its capacity for global intervention and dominion had been effectively reasserted. With the Mysore captives, too, vindication proved elusive until imperial momentum and national confidence revived. Nothing succeeded for them until there was once again evidence of a wider British success.

In the interim – and again just like US veterans of Vietnam – the Mysore captives found themselves castigated not just as losers, but as aggressors complicit in atrocity. In 1783, the year before most of the captives were freed, the *Annual Register*, a periodical associated with Edmund Burke, printed both a flattering obituary of Haidar Ali and a letter from an East India Company ensign accusing his comrades in southern India of pillage, rape and massacre. This letter, which was reprinted in other periodicals in 1784 and 1785, claimed that in just one British attack on a single Mysore settlement, Anantpur, 'four hundred beautiful women' had been killed and injured, '. . . while the private soldiers were committing every kind of outrage'. Other atrocity accusations were levelled against the Company at this time in the French press, and by British politicians intent on prosecuting Warren Hastings, the former governor-general of Bengal, in

Parliament.[49] But it was accusations of an Anantpur massacre against women that critics returned to again and again, and which stuck. As a result, when the earliest Mysore captivity narratives did begin to emerge from the press, their tone was markedly defensive. A bleak, retrospective account written by Harry Oakes, an officer captured at Bednur, came prefaced with an apologetic statement from its London publisher to the effect that Tipu Sultan's treatment of his British captives 'was evidently founded upon principles of retaliation . . . the unjustifiable behaviour of the Company's army goes a considerable way in justification of that of the enemy'.[50] Two years later, in 1787, a group of Company and regular army officers, again including Oakes, dispatched a formal letter from Bombay to East India House in London, insisting that the Anantpur accusations were fabricated, and expressing astonishment that the British press continued to repeat them:

> We will not pretend to assert, that the army was totally immaculate . . . [but] our present aim, is to convince the world, that during our residence in this distant clime, we have not forfeited every title to the feelings of humanity.[51]

The East India Company ordered this letter to be printed, and the House of Commons repeated the order in 1791, but to limited effect. Accusations that Company and regular army officers invading southern India had abused and slaughtered its women continued to be levelled. They surface yet again in a print issued in London in 1799 after the destruction of Tipu Sultan. Marauding Britons, their braid, epaulettes and tricorne hats marking them out as officers, are in every sense invading Tipu's harem. The balloons issuing from the officers' mouths ('Hurrah my Honey: Now for the *Black Joke*') make this undeniably what we would now call a racist print. But such racism as is present here is complex and broadly distributed. The women are shown with brown skins, but also wearing European fashions and features. White plumes ornament their curling hair; white stockings are chastely gartered above their knees. Tipu's bereft womenfolk in this purely imaginary scene become distraught ladies of fashion, undoubtedly so that their plight will more easily attract sympathy from a British audience. But the officers have also been re-imagined in this print, and far less flatteringly so. Their faces are disfigured by lust; their noses in particular are wildly elongated by the artist so as to suggest phallic urgency. Any restraint, like chivalry, is conspicuously absent. One British officer lies helpless beneath his ravished, half-naked Mysore victim, a rapist who has become a captive, and is even ridiculous.

So how did it change? How did these Mysore captivities shift from being emblems of anxiety, defeat and shame to becoming instead a profoundly influential component of British imperial story-telling? Part of the answer has to do with the French Revolution that broke out in 1789, and the world crisis it precipitated, that lasted until the second decade of the nineteenth century. At its outset, this Revolutionary crisis was a libertarian, egalitarian, and in some respects even an anti-imperial force, yet its end-result was paradoxically a strengthening of the power of many nation states, and a conspicuous strengthening too of some – though only some – of the world's overland and maritime empires. The Spanish and Portuguese empires in South America were terminally weakened by this crisis, and the Dutch and ultimately the French empires were also rolled back. But partly as a result of energising themselves so as to cope with the ideological and military ferment that followed on from the French Revolution, other states acquired in the process the momentum, organisation and opportunities to expand their territories at an unprecedented rate. This was true of Russia, which swallowed up Georgia in 1801 and Finland in 1809. It was true, too, of the new empire of the United States, that doubled its size by way of the Louisiana purchase from France in 1803. But, most dramatically, it was true of the British.[52]

After 1789, the British governing and military establishments went on the offensive, not just in terms of warfare on a massive and eventually highly successful scale, but also in terms of political argument and propaganda. India, like other parts of the world, felt the impact. In 1792, after three years of hard fighting, Tipu was forced to concede parts of Mysore's territory to the Company, though not the richest or most important sectors. Seven years and yet more savage fighting later, the walls of his capital Seringapatam shattered, Tipu was killed, and Mysore was restored – on terms – to its former Hindu dynasty, the Wodeyars. As had been the case in its previous conflicts with the British, Mysore received assistance from France. But this time, French aid did more in the end to ensure Tipu's destruction than to damage the British.[53]

True, in the course of the 1790s, French corsairs based in the Isle de France took out thousands of British ships and boats operating in the Indian Ocean; and, in 1798, Napoleon invaded Egypt arguably with the intention of using it as a springboard for a military invasion of India.[54] But this project proved a glamorous distraction, and when Tipu most required substantial French support, it was not available. Cornwallis's invasion of Mysore in the early 1790s was initially neither impressive nor successful.

Had France intervened at that point, it might have proved decisive, but it was still engulfed in its own revolution. Its known connections with Mysore ensured however that when a loyalist reaction emerged in Britain in opposition to the threat from Revolutionary and Napoleonic France, it also became directed against Tipu himself. There could be little sympathy for an Indian state that was linked to the European power planning to invade Britain itself. In the 1790s, as in the 1780s, British propaganda never focused exclusively on Tipu as 'Other', as an Asian prince and a proponent of Islam. It also aligned him with the prime Christian, European enemy. Tipu and Napoleon, in this version, became two sides of the same coin.

Thus despotism was not a characteristic attributed to Tipu solely or even primarily because he was an Indian or Muslim ruler. It was rather – in the British propaganda version – something he shared with Napoleon, yet another usurper.[55] This was just one respect in which the former Mysore captives now became a valuable component of British imperial argument. The harshness with which both captive Britons *and captive sepoys* had reputedly been treated in the 1780s ('worse than the slaves of Barbary') was now, some ten years later, disinterred and used to buttress assertions that Tipu was an oppressor of whites and Indians both. For the first time ever, the British state and the East India Company began orchestrating the writing and publication of captivity narratives about India. The Company now made a point of interviewing all escapees from Mysore imprisonment, both for any information they could provide, and for suitably emotive stories. The best were dispatched to East India House in London which promptly arranged for their publication in the official *London Gazette*. Thus in August 1791, Madras learnt that five British captives had escaped from Seringapatam, including a William Drake, a Royal Navy midshipman. An army officer was promptly instructed to 'collect from them all the information in his power'. Before the end of the year, Madras was able to send London 'a copy of a narrative delivered by Mr William Drake . . . and other prisoners . . . containing an account of the treatment they experienced'. Published the following April in the *London Gazette* (it also featured in the *Calcutta Gazette*), Drake's story was promptly reprinted in the London *Times* and other commercial papers and referred to in editorials on 'the Tyrant Tippoo': 'Perhaps a more interesting narrative than the following never appeared.'[56]

But Tipu, in the British imagination, was not just an Asian Napoleon. He was also – as his own court rituals and chosen symbolism proclaimed – a tiger prince, the personification of all that seemed to the British dangerous and unpredictable about India. And it was partly as a tiger, 'tearing in pieces the helpless victims of his craft, or his rapacity', that British propagandists now began describing him. This was something of a departure. Back in the 1780s, even captive Britons had generally described Tipu in moderate or even respectful terms. 'He bore his success like a man accustomed to victory,' wrote a colonel who had been captured at Tanjore: 'nothing haughty or imperious about him.' 'His manners were easy and affable; his address and behaviour agreeable,' recorded another British officer who was brought face to face with Tipu after the fall of Mangalore.[57] 'Easy', 'affable', 'agreeable': these are the sort of words that Jane Austen employed in her novels to alert readers to one of her more acceptable gentlemanly characters. And the use of code terms denoting an English gentleman in these early British descriptions of Tipu is surely no accident. Nor was it accidental that – like his father – Tipu was often described as pale-skinned. Robert Cameron, an army lieutenant captured at Pollilur in 1780, customarily referred to the guards in his prison as 'blacks'. Brought before Tipu, however, he saw him as 'fair, with a pleasing countenance'. Another Scottish officer-captive of Mysore, Innes Munro, was critical in his narrative of miscegenation in India lest it 'give a sallow tinge to the complexion of Britons', but thought nothing of comparing Haidar Ali approvingly to Frederick the Great of Prussia.[58] Even in 1790, an English observer could liken Tipu to Achilles, with all that this implied in terms of martial valour and classical physique.[59] As would always be the case, non-Europeans of power, rank, and – in the case of Haidar and Tipu proven military success – could deflect and correct a racially hostile European gaze (and *vice versa*).

By the end of the eighteenth century, however, private and public British descriptions of Tipu had darkened in every sense. A senior Scottish army officer who viewed his naked corpse in the ruins of Seringapatam in 1799 remembered it in these terms:

> The outlines of his person had that general shape which is common to the Musselman of India. His bust was corpulent, his thighs rather short . . . *His complexion was swarthy and much darker than that of men of high family in the east.* The colour of his face appeared probably a shade fairer in death . . . A promiscuous intercourse with the [female] sex had left its effects on the Sultan's body.

No longer a powerful southern Indian ruler able to inflict damage on the British, but dead and at their mercy, Tipu here is both blackened and orientalised. His corpse no longer evokes Achilles, but is rather feminised to the extent that it is even given breasts and foreshortened thighs. The fair skin that Cameron had admired back in 1782 is now dark – despite the pallor of death. And the writer's blatant accusation of Tipu's sexual

61. The defensive walls of Seringapatam, drawn by a British artist in 1792.

excesses contains a hint of physical damage, even perhaps of impotence. Yet even this singularly unpleasant passage is a warning against selective quotation and facile assumptions about human consistency. The writer ends by conceding that Tipu's expression in death was 'gentle and contented . . . a tranquil and courteous air for which he was distinguished when alive'. He also concludes by urging that Britain should now consolidate its existing territorial gains in India 'without looking for objects of further aggrandisement'.[60]

The fall of Tipu and Seringapatam in 1799 was undeniably a seismic event, a vital component of Britain's progress towards hegemony in India, and something that attracted mass excitement and attention at home. Yet the surviving evidence confirms what the British government conceded in print at the time: attitudes towards Tipu certainly became more negative, but they remained complex and continued to fluctuate after his death as they had during his life. There was no new consensus either on the desirability or feasibility of continued British advance in India. This did not stop the advance from proceeding, though the scale of its success remained in question until the destruction of the Maratha Confederacy in 1803–4.[61] But British qualms persisted. They surface in high-level correspondence, as in the governor of Bombay's protest at the scale of British violence after the fall of Seringapatam ('a national blot exceeding in turpitude anything that our annals can probably furnish in any part of the world'). They surface too in the early decades of the nineteenth century in all kinds of low-level as well as polite culture. Patriotic parents who purchased *Tippoo Saib; or the storming of Seringapatam* from Hodgson's Juvenile Drama Series for the benefit of their children in the 1820s must have been somewhat taken aback by the opening speech allocated to Tipu himself:

> Tis well, my brave people! I know your loyalty, and dread not the tyrannic power that even now threatens us with destruction!

The argument that oriental despotism, if it ever existed, was now being matched in some respects by the East India Company's military despotism in India was expressed with greater sophistication in other private and public British writings at this time.[62]

And this was where a new generation of Mysore captivity narratives had, for conformists, their greatest value. They helped to humanise Britain's armed forces in the public imagination even as those forces grew in scale and global aggressiveness to an unprecedented degree.

An early but influential work in this regard was William Thomson's *Memoirs of the Late War in Asia* published in 1788, and reissued 'after a rapid sale of a large impression' in amplified form the following year.[63] It was significant that Thomson was not a soldier, but a one-time clergyman turned professional writer. Moreover he was a Scot, and this too was significant. As Tipu himself recognised, the Company and regular army regiments that invaded Mysore in the 1780s and 90s contained a disproportionate number of Scottish officers and men.[64] The government minister responsible at this time for India was also a Scot, Henry Dundas, who had chaired the parliamentary enquiry into Pollilur and other military failures in southern India. For Dundas, India was vital, while the mood of imperial recessional and disillusionment that had followed the lost war with America was anathema. Empire must continue to advance, as he saw it, because Britain's power in general, and Scotland and its talented, hungry males in particular, depended upon its doing so. There is no evidence that Thomson wrote his two-volume work on the Mysore captives on the instructions of the government or the East India Company, but he enjoyed close links with members of the Scottish elite and senior Scottish army officers, and this was crucial to the format of his book.[65]

Despite its title, *Memoirs of the Late War* is less a work of military history than martyrology. As the preface 'To the Reader' declares, it is 'a narrative of what happened to our men under confinement with the barbarians', and as such dwells not on empire or the field of battle but rather on 'the fate of individuals'. Thomson did not shrink from recording British defeats in southern India because he knew how to transmute them into something else. The remnants of the Company's forces after Pollilur became in his prose, for example, the 'gallant remains of our little army', a source of pride. Nor was Thomson afraid of the less dignified aspects of Mysore captivity. Squalor, pain, fear, grief, forcible circumcision, the strains that captivity placed on composure, allegiance and morale were all included in his volumes. As they were bound to be, since he drew heavily – as he admitted – on interviews with former officer-captives and on their prison writings. But by absorbing their stories and memories into his text without at any point naming his sources, he was able to bring out the full agony and pathos of captivity without outraging the masculine, gentlemanly or professional pride of his particular informants. In the process, what was ostensibly a chronicle of imperial warfare became instead:

> A tragedy . . . of *suffering* not of *action* . . . It is hoped that no reader of humanity will be offended at the mention of many facts and circumstances, at first sight of no consideration . . . Violent moral situations tear up and display the passions and powers of the human soul. The sensibility of our captive countrymen . . . The strength of their sympathy with one another; the relief they found under strong agitation, in pouring forth, or in adopting strains of affecting though unpolished poetry.[66]

By means of this literary strategy and highly literary style, Thomson's book began the work of transforming the warriors of the East India Company and the British state into new men or, less anachronistically, into men of feeling. The focus was shifted, quite deliberately, from chronicling military action in southern India with all its controversial episodes and violence, to a moving evocation of British soldiers' emotional stress, torment, and resilience in a situation of extreme pressure.

Thomson was a highly professional hack, but not an original writer. He did not invent this literary method and style, but borrowed it, and his source is very clear: Samuel Richardson's three, immensely influential novels of sentiment, *Pamela* (1740–1), *Clarissa* (1747–8), and *The History of Sir Charles Grandison* (1753–4). Thomson constructed his supposedly factual history, just as Richardson does in his fictions, by linking together letters and narratives by different characters, in his case the writings of various Mysore captives. He also emulated Richardson's immense moral earnestness, his taste for minute detail, and – most of all – his concern with how individuals are tested and redeemed through suffering.

Even before Thomson's book appeared, some of the more educated Mysore captives had recognised the 'fit' between Clarissa Harlowe's predicament as evoked by Richardson, and their own far more distant, masculine ordeals. In the novel, Clarissa is imprisoned in a brothel, persecuted and tested relentlessly, and then drugged so that the villain Lovelace may finally prevail against her closely guarded virginity. But not having consented to her own violation, she retains her essential virtue. She escapes, fades away and embraces her own death, but is posthumously redeemed, while her tormenter is finally destroyed by his own violence. *Clarissa*, in other words, is itself a fictional captivity narrative; and after the appearance of Thomson's book, its influence, and that of other novels of sentiment on the writing of British imperial captivity narratives became increasingly marked.[67] As far as the Mysore captives were concerned, Clarissa's story seemed particularly apt. They too had suffered and been imprisoned; and some of them had been drugged as a prelude to physical violation, in their case circumcision. But, by implication, these men's essential virtue and identity also remained untouched because what had been done to their bodies had been carried out by force and against their will. And now these one-time captive sufferers were free and vindicated, while the chief villain of their story, Tipu Sultan, was set for violent and deserved destruction.

In part, then, because of global war, reviving imperial fortunes, and the emergence of a more conservative brand of British nationalism, but also because of these vital shifts in writing about Mysore captivity, what had previously savoured of humiliation, squalor and defeat came to seem deeply interesting and touched with moral fervour and pathos. One can see this shift at work in many of the Mysore captivity narratives published in the wake of Thomson's bestseller. In 1792, for instance, the Company's press in Calcutta financed the publication of the *Narrative of the Sufferings of James Bristow*. As its preface pointed out, this was designed to be read in conjunction with the *Memoirs of the Late War in Asia*. Thomson's volumes had focused on the British officer class. But Bristow's story was that of a humble Company private soldier captured, forcibly circumcised, and driven into one of Mysore's slave regiments, but who – in this dictated account at least – remains faithful at heart and eventually escapes the clutches of Tipu and returns to his own kind. Again, this was a deeply serious and highly detailed account, which concentrated not on military action or southern India, but on the agonies and determination of an embattled individual. Like Thomson's work, it remains moving to read, and at the time was commercially an immense success, going through at least two London editions in 1793 and a third in 1794, and continuing to be reissued until the 1820s.[68]

What I am suggesting therefore is that to explain British imperial resurgence and successful aggression in India and elsewhere after 1790 in terms of expansion of manpower, military and naval prowess, economic, technological and industrial power, and a hardening of conservative and nationalistic ideologies, is correct up to a point, but also insufficient. Teetering on the verge of unprecedented global intervention, the British then – rather like Americans now – needed to be persuaded that they were not only a superpower, but also a virtuous, striving and devoted people. Successful military machismo and conquests were never enough. Indeed, given the long tradition in Britain of suspicion of standing armies, military machismo by itself could prove immensely unpopular, as the outcry over the Anantpur massacre and other reputed Company excesses in the 1780s clearly demonstrated. Redcoats let loose upon forts, towns and villages in the Indian subcontinent, like those who had ranged themselves against American rebels after 1775, could not be certain of winning support back in Britain just because they were redcoats. They had first to be viewed as good men, and consequently as incapable of bad deeds. The rewriting of Mysore captivity ordeals from the 1780s onwards was one of the ways in which – very much with official sponsorship – the British military overseas was repackaged for improved domestic consumption.[69]

There were other manifestations of the same trend. It is striking, for instance, that – as far as British opinion at home was concerned – the most celebrated incident in these wars with Mysore, apart from the captivities, was Lord Cornwallis's 'kind' reception of two sons of Tipu Sultan, who were taken hostage in 1792 as a guarantee that their father would cede the Company both territory and a substantial cash payment. As Mildred Archer long ago pointed out, this was the most illustrated episode in this series of Mysore wars. There were umpteen paintings, engravings, prints, souvenirs, and even embroideries of it, as well as books, poems, and newspaper accounts. Indeed, almost as much artistic attention was devoted to this episode of apparent British clemency as to Tipu's death and the fall of Seringapatam.[70] In reality, there was of course limited kindness involved in the British taking two young boy children away from their home and father to be used as diplomatic counters. But most of those who recorded this scene in words or images for a domestic audience drew a straightforward moral from it, and one that explicitly contrasted British military virtue with Tipu's reputed systematic cruelty. When the latter had been powerful enough to take thousands of Britons and Company sepoys captive, they pointed out, he had made them suffer. Now, however, the British were not only powerful enough to take Tipu's own sons captive, but also showed their superior humanity by treating the boys well, for indeed these young princes were subsequently cosseted and made much of.

These goings-on can be understood at various levels. One was outlined with spectacular percipience by Edmund Burke in 1784:

> The main drift of their policy was to keep the natives totally out of sight. We might hear enough about what great and illustrious exploits were daily performing on that great conspicuous theatre [India] by Britons. But . . . we were never to hear of any of the natives being actors.[71]

By focusing attention on the incontestable qualities of the British armed forces, their courage, discipline, endurance, self-sacrifice, comradeship and the like, a new generation of military and imperial publicists was effectively distracting attention from the more controversial issue of what these men and their kind were actually doing in India and other parts of the globe. The casualty-levels, pillage, and destruction inevitably attendant on a policy of extending empire by force of arms were sidelined. Instead, Britons were encouraged to concentrate their emotional and moral gaze upon British officers and soldiers in their roles as suffering, valiant, and exemplary men and individuals. Thus when one of John Lindsay's descendants finally published his Mysore prison notebook in 1840, he not only omitted some of its original bleak, mundane and ironic material, but also inserted a preface:

> Deep moral lessons are unconsciously conveyed in every page of this Journal. The eye may be moistened, the heart saddened, but I am sure the reader will rise up a wiser and better man [sic] from its perusal.[72]

But it is also possible to look at these shifts in British representation of empire, armies and captivity in a rather different way. When the unknown Indian artist responsible for the mural of Pollilur in Tipu's palace had sought deliberately to feminise Colonel Baillie's embattled troops, it had obviously been with the intention of mocking and diminishing them. Yet, paradoxically, this successful British repackaging of the military in India and elsewhere also involved an element of feminisation, even to the extent of drawing inspiration from Samuel Richardson's novels of put-upon women. What happened was what Terry Eagleton has called the 'domestication of heroism' in which 'the barbarous values of militarism, naked dominance and male *hauteur*' were concealed or at least offset by the more 'fashionable virtues of . . . sensibility, civility and tendresse'.[73] British imperial warriors in this new and revised version became not just gentlemen, but strangely gentle – at least with each other. 'It is one of the most remarkable and beautiful features of this dreadful captivity', wrote the biographer of General Sir David Baird, a one-time captive in Mysore and subsequently a destroyer of Tipu, in 1832, 'that every man during its continuation seemed more anxious for his fellow-sufferers than for himself.'[74]

This highly effective formula of focusing attention on the emotional and moral development of Westerners caught up in extra-European conflicts has persisted to this day and has long since ceased to be confined to the British. Just think of how many Hollywood films of the Vietnam War, even some critical ones, confine the Vietnamese themselves to the role of extras while placing at their centre the bravery, torment and emotional struggles of all-American heroes. Here, too, in the cinema version of American global ventures, the natives are usually kept firmly out of sight, while the emotional spotlight focuses on the Western intruders. But there were particular reasons why it was the British who pioneered and worked on this shift in representing their armed forces overseas. Increasingly aggressive as the eighteenth century drew to its close, they remained demographically limited, though by now – as we shall see – far less anxiously so. After 1800, as before, British imperial warriors were always going to be at risk of defeat and capture and suffering, because their numbers and the size of their resource base never remotely matched the scale of their global ambitions. It was therefore vital, as far as the British were concerned, to evolve a way of writing about imperial warfare in which sporadic failures and disasters could be represented as being themselves a form of heroic virtue, moral improvement and patriotic service – a victory of sorts.

There is a final point. The East India Company's successive wars with Mysore illuminate the conspicuously shifting fortunes of a small country attempting empire at a faraway distance and on an unprecedented scale. The first and second of these wars, that lasted respectively from 1767 to 1769, and 1779 to 1784, reveal how the East India Company's advance into India became far harder than it had initially anticipated, and the depths of disillusionment and even despair that gripped Britain in the wake of defeat in the subcontinent, in America, and elsewhere. For pessimists, as we have seen, the circumcision inflicted on some British captives in Mysore seemed an ultimate and definitive emblem of national castration and unmanning. Britain, it appeared, was no longer the automatic winner that the Seven Years War had seemed to suggest, but a nation in retreat and an empire in decline. Had an opinion poll been conducted in the 1780s, many Britons, perhaps the majority, would have predicted that the nineteenth century could not possibly be their century. They had peaked, and were now on the way down. In much the same way, but with far less cause, many Americans in the 1980s believed that losing the Vietnam War had demonstrated that their empire too had peaked. The twenty-first century, they allowed themselves for a while to fear, would belong to some other power, not to them. These American pessimists were wrong. So, too, were disconsolate Britons in the 1780s.

For if the first two Mysore Wars, together with the lost American War, taught the British that acquiring overseas territory was not going to be the pushover some of them had foolishly allowed themselves to imagine, the last two Mysore Wars in the 1790s, like the concurrent European wars against Revolutionary France, demonstrated Britain's capacity to reassert and reconfigure itself in the wake of crushing global defeats. The British struck back, more violently than before, and with much more success. As we have seen, this imperial resurgence involved more than an escalation of military effort in India and in other parts of the globe. There was also a vital reconfiguring of both imperial and national ideology. The Mysore captives' transition from figures of national disgrace and embarrassment to gallant heroes whose sacrifice and sufferings exemplified the nation's manhood at its best demonstrates this ideological re-tooling at work. In much the same way, Vietnam veterans in America initially had to contend with the unconcern, embarrassed pity, and even open hostility of their own countrymen. Their subsequent transition to hero status has been so marked that US veteran organisations are now having to cope with an epidemic of American males claiming quite falsely that they saw combat in Vietnam.[75]

In the United States – as in Britain two centuries ago – the will to battle and the will to global dominance have been successfully re-tooled in the aftermath of traumatic defeat. But these comparisons should not be pushed too far. For, however much *in some respects* American empire now echoes earlier British empire, in terms of the size of the imperial metropolis there is an obvious and fundamental divergence. The USA spans a continent, whereas it was the very smallness of Britain's island dimensions that acted simultaneously as a spur to overseas empire, and as a persistent handicap in the process of achieving it. Yet, even in this respect, conflict with Mysore witnessed a significant transition. Initially, the British had been daunted by India's vast population and size, and some of them had also doubted whether the sepoys they necessarily recruited in large numbers to fight for them there would remain reliable under pressure. War with Mysore substantially eased these anxieties. British captives of Haidar Ali and Tipu Sultan were able to persuade individual Indians to take enormous risks carrying messages for them, and although a minority of Company sepoys mutinied or deserted in the wars against Mysore, the majority remained loyal. 'The fortitude and fidelity of our brave sepoys' is a theme touched upon by virtually every British captivity narrative that emerged from these wars.[76] For the British, this proved a vital revelation. They had never been able to recruit and incorporate Native Americans into their imperial war effort to the degree they would have liked, in part because of their relative paucity, and in part because of the objections of their own white settlers. But, in India – the British came to realise – it was very different. Here, they could compensate effectively for their own small numbers by recruiting indigenous manpower on a massive scale. Moreover, and as the Mysore wars demonstrated, men so recruited would in general fight bravely and if necessary die for the cause of Company and British dominion.

A secret memorandum written in 1805 by Lord Wellesley, Governor General of India, was tinged with all kinds of racist assumptions, but was in essence correct:

> As mercenary troops, the natives of India possess obedience, docility and fidelity beyond all others. These qualities are inherent in the people, as they are no less conspicuous in the British service than in that of the powers of the country. . . . [They] have assisted us in retaining their own country in subjection with a fidelity scarce less than our own countrymen.

This was one of the major steps on the British road to imperial resurgence after the lost American war. At the same time that Britain itself was evolving a more powerful and conservative brand of nationalism, its politicians and warriors came to realise as never before that – because of the lack of fully developed national ideologies in the zones where they were advancing – indigenous manpower could be recruited to make up for Britain's own smallness of numbers. The British could indeed capitalise on pre-existing divisions and so rule. By the time Wellesley wrote, there were almost 170,000 sepoys fighting on behalf of the East India Company, while on the other side of the world, black slave regiments were proving equally valuable fighting for the British in the Caribbean.[77]

Yet, for all this, the British still continued to wrestle with the problems posed by their own limitations. For all their growing reliance on indigenous warriors, they still needed a reliable core of their own. In the Mysore captivity panic of the 1780s, almost a quarter of the British troops seized, mostly men from the other ranks, had voluntarily or involuntarily crossed over to the other side. So as Britain entered on a new and far more dangerous and extensive phase of imperial expansion, it had to deal as well with the problems posed by the poor whites who manned its army and navy. How, and how far, could men like this be made into the reliable fodder of imperial legions? Let us see.

TEN

Captives in Uniform

Winning the numbers game

1798, the last full year in Western calendar time of Tipu Sultan's life, saw the publication of one of the most influential texts in imperial terms ever to appear in Britain. The work in question was not a novel, nor a piece of conventional political theory. It was a voluminous, uncompromising tract by a mild intellectual named Thomas Malthus, and its title was *An Essay on the Principle of Population*. Malthus went on to become the first Professor of Political Economy at Haileybury College, set up in 1805 to train civil servants for the East India Company, but his essay was not explicitly concerned with either India or Britain's empire in general. Nor, as an early editor conceded, was it initially widely read or generally understood. But it was one of those rare works that transforms attitudes beyond the bounds of its readership or the intentions of its author. 'When we speak of Mr. Malthus', declared William Hazlitt, who disliked the man and his arguments intensely, 'we mean the *Essay on Population*; and when we mention the *Essay on Population*, we mean a distinct leading proposition, that stands out intelligibly from all trashy pretence, and is a ground on which to fix the levers that may move the world.'[1]

The proposition involved was a blunt one. If left unrestrained, population would increase exponentially in advance of the supply of food: 'the power of population is indefinitely greater than the power in the earth to produce subsistence for man.' The *Essay*'s apocalyptic tone was more a result of Malthus's personal dread of the forces of the French Revolution (and perhaps of the raging toothache gripping him while he wrote it), than of any fear on his part that Britain was already suffering from over-population.[2] None the less, his book changed the terms of contemporary argument. Before this, Britons had often been fearful that their country possessed too few people. After the *Essay*'s publication, however, most came to believe that Britain's population was expanding at an accelerating, even uncontrollable rate. The challenge now appeared to be *too many* people, a revolutionary shift in perception that would be crucial to Britain's growing involvement and investment in empire in the nineteenth century.

For most of the previous century, it had been widely though not unanimously believed that Britain's population was in free-fall. A rise in quantitative research in the second half of the eighteenth century failed to disperse this illusion. Richard Price, the most respected demographer of his day, drew meticulously on urban mortality rates and house tax figures seemingly to prove that the population of England and Wales had declined since 1688 to less than five million in the 1780s. (The real figure for England alone when Price wrote was actually well over seven million.)[3] This pervasive and perverse demographic gloom had profound imperial consequences. British politicians remained for a long time nervous of stationing substantial numbers of troops overseas, or of allowing large-scale emigration by the respectable labouring classes, in case an already diminishing home population became lethally depleted. 'The state of our population was not very flattering,' warned a member of Parliament in 1771, opposing an increase of troops for India: '. . . the species decreased, and . . . we ought to keep as many as possible for the defence of Britain'. As we have seen, such anxieties were reinforced by defeat in America and major setbacks in southern India. Britain, these reverses had seemed to confirm, was just too small and insufficiently populous to generate the taxes and the manpower that were necessary for major imperial conflict, while simultaneously maintaining prosperity at home. Large-scale territorial conquests, as distinct from global commerce, were indulgences the country could not and should not afford.[4] But Malthus's famous book signalled and quickened a transformation in the landscape of ideas.

His *Essay on Population,* as it was widely understood, together with the first ever census in Britain and Ireland in 1801 which showed that their combined population exceeded sixteen million, allowed Britons to feel infinitely more proactive about the demands of empire. Patrick Colquhoun, one of a new breed of political arithmeticians with close links to the government, spelt out the implications in his influential *Treatise on the Wealth, Power and Resources of the British Empire* (1814). His aim was to scotch any lingering 'gloomy apprehensions respecting the resources of the empire'. He printed copious population tables drawn from the second census of 1811, as well as statistics suggesting that the armed forces at Britain's disposal across the globe, including Indian and other foreign troops, now exceeded one million men: 'the most sanguine imagination could not have anticipated such an accession of population, territory and power.' In a suggestive early use of what became a famous phrase, he boasted that 'the sun never sets on the flag', and that successful global war against Napoleon had demonstrated once and for all 'the practicality of conquest'. There need be no more fears of imperial expansion draining Britain's economy and population. Properly regarded, empire was indispensable to both. Every five years, another polemicist suggested in 1817, Britain needed to shed 'at least one million of souls'. The new lands, opportunities, and combat involved in imperial enterprise were exactly the providential outlet required for Malthus's surplus population: 'colonizing . . . can only be looked to as the means of salvation.'[5]

Two other developments contributed to this rising confidence that Britain was now a big enough power for overseas diffusion and destiny: the retention of Ireland and the defeat of Napoleonic France. The year of Malthus's masterwork, 1798, saw a revolt by thousands of Protestant as well as Catholic Irishmen against rule from London. It was bloodily suppressed, and in 1800 an Act of Union brought Ireland into the United Kingdom. Irish manpower, growing at a faster rate even than Britain's own, was now secure, or so it seemed, within the imperial arsenal. This was vital because, without Irishmen, the rampant growth of Britain's empire at this stage would scarcely have been possible. By the 1830s they made up over 40 per cent of its legions. Before the Famine, more than half of all white soldiers in India were Irish: 'the Irish nursery seems inexhaustible', as one East India Company officer purred.[6] The proportion of Irishmen in the British regiments fighting at Waterloo in 1815 was almost as impressive: and this final, conclusive victory over France confirmed an already existing transformation in the scale of Britain's empire, and provided an essential precondition for its further massive growth.

War against Revolutionary and Napoleonic France (1793–1815) increased the number of Britain's colonies from twenty-six to forty-three. The Cape, Sierra Leone, Gambia and the Gold Coast were seized in Africa; Tobago, St Lucia, and Trinidad in the Caribbean; and Malta and the Ionian Islands in the Mediterranean. In addition, vast, additional swathes of Australia and India were conquered or annexed.[7] Dramatic though these new, blood-red splashes on the map were, in one sense the most crucial change in global power politics was within Europe itself. Stress is often laid now on how aggressive Europeans were in the past in relation to other continents. Yet this indictment, understandable though it may be, obscures what has always in fact been the prime focus of European aggression. In every century during the first and second millennium – with only one conspicuous exception – Europeans have devoted more energy to hating, fighting and invading each other, than to hating, fighting and invading peoples outside Europe. The dark continent, as Mark Mazower calls it, has persistently consumed itself, more even than it has encroached on others. The solitary, partial exception before 2000 to this pattern of obsessive intra-European warfare was the hundred years' comparative peace between the European powers from Waterloo to the outbreak of the First World War in 1914, a peace that as far as Britain was concerned was interrupted only briefly by the Crimean War (1854–6).

Victorian Britons would rarely feel completely assured about their continent's unprecedented tranquillity or their own European hegemony. They worried persistently about the old enemy France, about Russia and its possible designs on India, and ultimately about a newly unified Germany. None the less, between Waterloo and 1914, neither Britain nor any other European power experienced conflict on anything like the scale of the Seven Years War or the Napoleonic Wars. And never in this period was Britain confronted with a confederation of Western powers bent on attacking its colonial outposts, as it had been in the American Revolutionary War, and would be again after 1914. The profit and the price of this hundred-year partial European peace was unprecedented Western, and especially British freedom to concentrate on global empire. In 1800, the European powers, together with Russia and the United States, laid claim to some 35 per cent of the globe's total land area. By 1914, in large part because of their reduced tendency after Waterloo to war among themselves, the proportion of the globe claimed by western Europe, Russia and the United States had risen to 84 per cent.[8]

By 1815, therefore, anxiety over what had always been viewed as the main internal obstacles to Britain's indulgence in overseas empire – its demographic limits and its territorial smallness – was receding fast. Yet greater confidence on this score, together with an end to distracting European-wide warfare, and access to unprecedented levels of economic power, did not immediately bring a cessation of Britain's captivity panics. Rather what occurred was a shift in the nature of imperial captivities. Because it felt able to do so, but also because the scale of its empire gave it no choice, the British state now markedly increased the number of its own people who were exiled overseas for long periods of time. Many of these exiles were working-class men and women dispatched to imperial locations and set to labour there under a substantial degree of discipline, and with little say over when or whether they would ever return. In Australia before 1850, the bulk of these white, working-class British exiles were transported convicts. But in Asia, the majority were soldiers, the worker bees of the British empire, yet still men who, after a fashion, were captives of their own state, captives in uniform.

The last half of the eighteenth century and the first third of the nineteenth century witnessed a revolution in the extent and global distribution of British military manpower. In 1740, only three out of the forty-odd

British army regiments had been stationed outside Europe. By the 1770s the position was already changing, and a spell of overseas duty was coming to be part of the normal expectations of every regiment of the line. By 1800, and still more after 1815, the situation was vastly different again. On the eve of Queen Victoria's accession in 1837, more than three-quarters of Britain's one hundred plus regular army regiments were based in the empire.[9] At least twenty of these were garrisoned in India, besides the East India Company's own army that now exceeded 200,000 men, the bulk of whom were sepoys.

These were dramatic transformations. Yet suggestions that they represented the construction of an essentially militarised empire need treating with some care.[10] The British military conspicuously expanded and globalised after 1750: yes. But while this expansion was impressive by previous *British* standards, it was less so when set against some contemporary European and non-European armies. By 1850, Britain's armed forces at home and in all of its overseas 'possessions', barring India, totalled just over 105,000 men. This was less than a third of the size of France's military at that time, less than an eighth of Russia's, and smaller even than the army of Prussia which possessed no colonies at all.[11] True: the East India Company's army needs adding to the equation. But the vast majority of its men were Indian not British; and, as one officer pointed out in 1833 – even here – the disparity between the number of British and Indian imperial troops on the one hand, and the subcontinent's size and population on the other, was a marked one. His estimate was one imperial soldier to every 450 Indian inhabitants. This contrasted poorly, for instance, with the situation in the United States, emphatically a second-rate power at this time, where the ratio of regular and militia troops to population was nearer one to a hundred:

> Casting the eyes over the map of British India, it seems incredible the long line of exposed frontier, frequently without a single regiment of the line, or even a scattered detachment of sepoys.[12]

In other words, the wider global distribution of British forces, and the emergence of a more relaxed domestic attitude towards the export of civilians and military men, were more striking developments in this period than an actual, sustained expansion in the sum-total of British imperial muscle. 'Imperial overstretch' was not something that Britain suddenly began to experience in the late Victorian era.[13] In terms of the gap between its military (and naval) manpower, and the territory it affected to govern, imperial Britain was always overstretched. The thin red line was more accurately anorexic. This helps to explain why, despite undoubted naval paramountcy at this time and a faster-expanding technological gap between the West and the rest, the armies of Victorian Britain continued to experience sporadic, savage humiliations in imperial locations – deaths, defeats, and occasionally conspicuous captivities.

But the shortfall between Britain's overseas manpower and its global pretensions also provided for another kind of overseas captivity. By 1815, virtually every British regular soldier could expect to spend half, and often two-thirds of his career in imperial postings. The persistent limits on the size of the army, and a consequent sparsity of replacement regiments, meant that before the 1850s especially these postings necessarily lasted for long periods of time, for ten, often twenty years without a break. In 1828, Viscount Palmerston, then secretary at war, told Parliament that two British regiments about to be dispatched overseas had, most unusually, been able to spend the previous six years at home. Before that, however, they 'had experienced seventeen years of uninterrupted foreign service, either in the East or West Indies, or at Ceylon'. Such extended periods of banishment meant that soldiers, superficially the most straightforward agents of British empire, became in practice rather more unpredictable actors. As the Army Quartermaster General admitted in 1836:

> Everybody who has seen the nature of colonial service must know . . .
> that it is exceedingly difficult, if not impossible, under the very best
> discipline, to prevent the soldiers acquiring directly, or through their
> wives, *a certain degree of locality*.[14]

From the authorities' perspective, it was the degree of locality that was the rub. Confined for years to non-European locations, without any provision for home leave, how were ordinary British soldiers to be prevented from becoming irremediably changed in the process? And what might follow from such changes? Were troops who spent virtually all their adult lives in other continents at risk of 'going native' to the extent that their original religious, political and national identities became compromised? Might some desert and go over entirely? How could British soldiers operating at vast distances from home, and in regions where communications might well be non-existent, be properly monitored and controlled?

Official anxieties on this score must be understood in the light of European as well as extra-European pressures. The period between 1770 and 1840 was an age of revolution and new republics in France and the Americas, and of accelerated growth in population, urbanisation, means of production, literacy, print culture, and consciousness of social class in

Britain itself. It is now generally accepted that there were parallels between the British state's reactions to this barrage of change at home, and the quality of its imperial exertion overseas. A more conservative and militaristic nationalism, a new emphasis on ceremonial display and religious seriousness, together with a proliferation of barracks and prisons, were cherished and fostered by those governing late Georgian Britain and Ireland; at the same time, a more rigorous policy of control and greater ideological assertiveness was practised by British imperial activists from Canada to the Cape and beyond.[15] Yet there was another side to this connection between accelerating change in Britain, and the quality of British empire at this time. Between the 1770s and the 1840s, Britain's own lower and middling orders became more turbulent, more politicised, more vocal in expressing complaints. In much the same way, and at the same time, those governing Britain's empire also faced growing disorder and protest from below. Not just from the indigenous populations they sought to rule, but also from their own poor whites, the captives in uniform.

These men were obviously not captives of empire in the same straight-forward sense as the individuals we have encountered in earlier chapters. These were ostensibly free men, and they were armed warriors, not obvious victims. Yet the gulf between the growing numbers of British soldiers stationed overseas, sweltering (or freezing) in stinking, unsuitable red woollen uniforms in dingy barracks or insect-infested tents, and white and non-white colonial elites was a very wide one; and – in some respects – these white soldiers overseas shared levels of unfreedom with black slaves. As one British private soldier complained in his shaky grammar:

In India the men of the army generally is looked upon as so many pieces of one great machine that is passive in the hands of the engineer: and as to sense or feeling, that is not thought of, the private soldier is looked upon as the lowest class of animals, and only fit to be ruled with the cat o' nine tails and the Provost Sergeant.[16]

Vulnerable to capture by non-Europeans because of where they worked and fought and what they represented, men like this could also feel in bondage to the British state. They were shipped abroad, often in foul conditions and sometimes against their will. They could be separated from their families, womenfolk and culture of origin for decades, often for ever. If judged disobedient or rebellious, they were likely to be flogged. If they tried to run away, they might be executed; and if they stayed and obeyed orders, they were apt to die prematurely anyway.

62. Depending on the Indian. Robert Clive receives a princely grant to aid the East India Company's poor white troops and their dependents back home: a painting by Edward Penny.

All imperial soldiers had to contend with these severities to some degree, but in India they registered with peculiar acuteness, for military service there and throughout Asia was arduous in particular ways. It was not just that tours of duty were long, and mortality and discomfort rates were high. Unlike British soldiers in Australia, or New Zealand, or Canada, or South Africa, ordinary soldiers in Asia had virtually no hope of being allowed a place to settle, a patch of their own land. Nor could the majority of white troops in India hope to marry while on service, or father children who would survive. But perhaps the biggest challenge they confronted was that, in the eyes of those in charge, these men were at once indispensable and of limited significance. In 1830, the 36,400 white officers and men of the East India Company and the regular army made up 90 per cent of all British males resident in India.[17] None the less, these white troops were outnumbered by Indian sepoys in British service five to one. As far as the Company and the British state were concerned, at least before 1857, the logic of this was clear. In times of pressure, it was the sepoys who most demanded consideration and conciliating, not their own working-class soldiery. It was on the sepoys, it was generally accepted, and not on the white soldiery, that Britain's empire in India perforce had to rely. As a result, and however accurately, British soldiers stationed here often perceived themselves as the lowest of the low. They were captives of an alien environment, captives of their own state, and captives of a situation where their sepoy counterparts were in some respects better treated because they were deemed more important.

Like the slaves some felt themselves to be, however, white imperial soldiers in India are hard to investigate outside of the archives compiled by their masters. Many of these men were unable to write; and there could be marked limits on what even fully literate soldiers were allowed to write, and on what they were prepared to write. But the biggest obstacles to investigating these men are the incuriosity and prejudices of posterity. Black slaves rightly command our retrospective sympathy. They are assumed to have suffered and often to have rebelled: and evidence is looked for accordingly. But, to modern eyes, the British or any other imperial soldiery easily appear uncongenial or at best predictable. It is assumed that they were violent (which they were), and that they were necessarily and inherently conformist (which they were not). Exploring these men, and their multiform experiences of imperial captivity, requires then a discarding of blinkers. Given the sparsity of their own writings, it also means drawing imaginatively on miscellaneous, less than satisfactory evidence, having recourse in Edward Said's words to 'unconventional or neglected sources', so as to construct 'an alternative history' of empire to the official one.[18] We need to probe beneath the lush proconsular and plutocratic chronicles of Indian empire and uncover different, more subterranean, less dignified stories, stories of renegades and deserters, stories told around punishment and resistance, stories of those majority of British soldiers who stayed loyal and outwardly obedient but sometimes with gritted teeth: the subalterns with white faces.

Anyone curious about the last half millennium of global history should visit the National Army Museum in London. Yet few make the journey to Chelsea and walk past its famous hospital and gardens to the squat, charmless 1960s building concealing so much that is controversial, difficult and important. The catalogue of the Museum's library, still indexed on cards, is a painstaking guide through books, pamphlets, prints, maps and manuscripts on virtually every aspect of conflict in five continents in which the British participated as minor or major players. The changing face of battle, the meanings of fear, conquest, and slaughter, the fate of millions of war victims and victors, white and non-white, female and male, all await reconstruction here. Only in a very few areas is the Museum's catalogue stubbornly unrewarding. No amount of searching among its dog-eared cards will turn up references to 'renegades', any more than it will direct you to records of deserters. More even than most states, official Britain does not publicly admit to its warriors having changed sides or opted out.

Yet censorship is less of a problem in this regard than forgetfulness and myths. From the 1810s, at least, the British state compiled lists of known military deserters from all of its colonial outposts. It also published random statistics which confirm that the number of these men could be considerable. In 1815, an estimate based on seriously incomplete returns from India, South Africa, the Mediterranean colonies, and North America, still put the number of British deserters from those areas at 2400.[19] Yet no comprehensive study has been attempted of these figures, or of what they can tell us about the quality and attitudes of Britain's imperial manpower over time. At the height of Britain's cult of empire, it became almost unthinkable that its soldiery should ever have wavered in allegiance. 'A man of British nationality would not be suitable, because presumably he could not be trusted to oppose his own people,' pronounced a one-time governor of Bombay in 1907, introducing a book on white mercenaries in Indian service in the eighteenth and early nineteenth centuries. Thus, he suggested (quite inaccurately), 'the men available would [have been] of Continental origin'.[20] More recent histories can be almost as blinkered as Sir Richard Temple's sturdy Edwardian Euroscepticism. British renegades are either excised from the picture altogether, or treated as picaresque figures, cool, adroit white men on horseback astounding the natives. Yet the majority of renegades on imperial frontiers were more mundane beings. They were also a persistent minority whose experiences illumine more than just themselves.

Most military whites who turned renegade outside Europe did so because, as Braudel wrote of the Spanish troops shipped to North Africa in the sixteenth century, imperial service for the mass of men and women resembled deportation, and this was one variety of escape from it.[21] As far as India was concerned, English and British renegades of different kinds are known to have existed from the earliest commercial contacts, their numbers inversely proportionate to the power and geographical reach of the East India Company. In the seventeenth and early eighteenth centuries, as G.V. Scammell remarks, there is a 'huge fund' of information on renegades in the records of the Company because its position in the subcontinent was so marginal then. Once British soldiers, sailors, merchants and technicians passed beyond its coastal settlements into the rich expanse and employment prospects of Mughal India, they were equally beyond recall and retaliation. Both Charles II in 1680, and James II in 1686, issued proclamations ordering home subjects who had entered indigenous Indian service. Like similar proclamations by Portuguese, Dutch and French sovereigns, these had negligible effect.[22]

Patterns of renegade behaviour began to shift in the 1740s as the French and British became more active in local Indian wars. There was now a growing demand for military and technical manpower from contending white as well as indigenous regimes, and some Britons took advantage of this to change sides not just once, but several times with impunity. In May 1752, a French detachment surrendering to the Company on India's Coromandel coast was found to include thirty-five British deserters. Since healthy white soldiers were a scant resource, these men were pardoned and reabsorbed into the Company's ranks.[23] Indeed, the closer one looks at any military grouping in India in this early period (and much the same was true of armies in Europe), the more it becomes clear that overarching national and ethnic labels are frequently little more than that. Equipped in 1760 with a 'British' force of sepoys, Swiss, Germans, Americans, French, Caribbean blacks, Britons and Irishmen, and about to do battle in southern India with a no less miscellaneous 'French' army, Eyre Coote instructed all his men to wear 'a green branch of the Tamarind tree fixed in their hats and turbans' because this was the only way they could be confidently distinguished from their equally motley opponents. In such a swirling, multi-national, multi-racial military scene, turning renegade might be as simple as plucking a plant from one's hat.[24]

Losing men to other European powers in India remained a minor challenge to the Company until the end of the century. As late as 1785, when thirty of its white soldiers were deserting from Calcutta alone every month, the Company negotiated cartels with the French and the Dutch: British and Irish deserters were to be handed over in return for any French and Dutch nationals who had strayed into Company territory.[25] But it was British desertion to Indian regimes that was always the greatest anxiety. As a military lawyer wrote in 1825:

> When European soldiers desert there [in India], the consequences that may ensue rise in importance, for if they are enabled to conceal their flight, they enter, perhaps, into the service of one of the native princes . . . and thus give intelligence to our enemies.

The space devoted to curbing renegade tendencies in successive army general orders and parliamentary acts for punishing mutiny and desertion in India points to the longevity of official concern on this score. 'Notwithstanding the enemy's promises,' every white and sepoy regiment was pointedly told in 1813, 'those who have been guilty of it [changing sides] are employed only in services of the lowest and most laborious descriptions.'[26] In case such warnings proved insufficient, appeals were made to money, one of the imperial power's undoubted strengths. By 1810, any regular army or Company private or NCO taken prisoner in India lost six pence in pay daily until 'he should actually regain a British corps'. The intention was obviously to discourage soldiers from allowing themselves to be captured, or from remaining captive longer than was necessary. Forty years on, the rules were stricter still. Now, any soldier in British service 'absent as a prisoner of war' in Asia lost all pay and pension rights for the duration. Only if he returned and convinced a court martial he had not 'served with or under or in some manner aided the enemy' could he recover his arrears.[27]

Such legislation was partly aimed at Company sepoys. Yet by the early nineteenth century, desertion was becoming more a characteristic of *white* troops in India; and parliamentary speeches and officers' writings show that these controls were formulated very much with the white soldiery in mind and not just sepoys. The reasons are clear. By the early 1800s, it cost over £100 to recruit a soldier in Britain and ship him to India; training and equipping him cost yet more. So even men deserting with no intention of joining other armies represented a substantial waste of resources. British desertion to indigenous Indian forces was much worse, however, and not just because of the loss of face involved. It bears repeating that the British had cause to be worried about the growing military sophistication of some of the Indian regimes ranged against them, and this remained true after the conquest of Mysore. Hence the threat posed by the renegade. He might, it was believed, transmit to new, indigenous paymasters British military knowledge, information about emerging war technologies, and superior conventions of leadership and discipline.[28]

This was the official nightmare: what of the motives of the renegades themselves? Men who ran away and crossed over on imperial frontiers seldom hung around to tell, much less publish their stories; but on one occasion the British state did it for them. On 18 May 1792, an extraordinary edition of the official *London Gazette* was published, with a six-page account of over 200 Britons, most of them military and naval men, 'yet alive' in Tipu Sultan's Mysore. This information had been collected from a wave of recent British escapees from Tipu's fortresses who had made contact with Cornwallis's advancing armies. One wonders if any contemporaries speculated as to why these men, captive in the main since the early 1780s, had refrained from escaping until their countrymen were closing in on Mysore, for looked at in detail the *Gazette* report was an ambivalent one. It conveyed, as was intended, some of the undoubted horrors of this captivity, naming Britons held in Mysore who had committed suicide in desperation, or gone blind from malnutrition, or been executed. But the *Gazette* also documented how some captives had adapted and settled down. Over sixty were listed under new Muslim as well as their original British names, the confused spellings reflecting the printers' ragged attempts to deal with an unfamiliar language. Thus George Clark, a Madras Company ensign, appeared in the *Gazette* as 'Murtount Khan', while Sergeant James Snelling was listed as 'named in the country Sultaun Beg'. It was made clear too that most of these men were not in prison, but in some kind of paid employment in Mysore, and that some had deserted to Tipu rather than been captured by his armies. Information in the Company's archives, omitted from this published account, shows that officials were also aware that some of these men had assumed Indian dress, settled into relationships with local Hindu and Muslim women, and in some cases forgotten their cradle tongue.[29] What was ostensibly a list of captives of empire, then, serves as well as a guide to the kinds of men likely, if it seemed necessary or advantageous, to turn renegade.

Typically enough, most of them came from the other ranks. Only eleven of the men listed in the *Gazette* were army and naval officers, none of them senior figures. This does not mean that men holding British commissions were always averse to serving Indian employers as freelance warriors. About to launch a decisive assault on the Marathas in 1803, the future duke of Wellington chose first to detach all of their European mercenary officers. Sixty of these turned out to be British or Anglo-Indian.[30] But, as in this case, officer-class males usually felt that they had too much to lose in material and psychological terms to contemplate remaining mercenary if this involved fighting against their own kind. The exceptions to this rule tended to be men in dire financial straits. Company army officers in India were more eclectic in social origin than their counterparts in Britain's regular army, and some came unstuck. Alexander Dempster, who features in several British captivity narratives as one of the more flamboyant renegades in Mysore, clad 'in the Mohammedan dress, with a large red turban', was from 'a very respectable and ancient family'. He was also broke. He had been forced to sell his royal army commission, went to India, and was finally reduced to non-commissioned rank in the Madras artillery. From here he deserted to Mysore which made him an officer again. One of his fellow renegades, a man called Thompson, had also been obliged to sell out. He explained to a British captive in the 1790s how, after marrying a French woman from Pondicherry, he had found it impossible to support them both on half pay, and since 'he preferred a military life, and could not procure a commission in the English army . . . was come to Tipu to look for service'.[31]

Official accounts of British renegades tended to emphasise such mercenary motives as a means of downgrading the individuals involved. Greed or lack of cash were powerful incentives, of course, especially among the sparsely paid lower ranks; and so was a desire to escape the rigours of conventional military discipline. The mass of British private soldiers and ordinary seamen listed in the *Gazette* as having contrived a life for themselves in Mysore were men with low expectations and little hope of rescue, likely to take the easiest path open to them at any particular time, especially if it came strewn with rudimentary comforts. Back in 1783 some British soldiers who had already defected to Mysore, stood outside the walls of the southern Indian fortress of Mangalore, then under siege by their new masters, and harangued their former comrades inside on the compensations of a renegade existence: 'high wages, freedom from the restraints of discipline, food, women, and the means of intoxication'. As a result of these siren calls, at least seventeen more white British troops deserted from Mangalore, including the quarter master sergeant of the 42nd Regiment who slipped out of the city one night having first 'robbed one of the European women of what money she had'.[32]

It is suggestive, too, that many Britons who lingered on in Mysore were very young. In all places, and at all times, it is the young who find it easiest to forget past associations, learn new skills and adapt: the selfsame qualities that are required for successful defection. James Scurry, a former Royal Naval seaman who by his own account did not try escaping Mysore until Cornwallis's troops began closing in, was only sixteen when he was captured; one of his comrades in captivity, William Whiteway, a Company seaman, was just fourteen. Such boy-warriors were not unusual among British forces in India. Almost one in three of the East India Company's recruits in 1779 was sixteen or under. The proportion was much the same at intervals between 1793 and 1815, when once again the demands of warfare on a global scale led to fierce competition for men between the regular British and Company armies and the Royal Navy. Once the supply of qualified, mature recruits ran out, recruiting parties in Britain had no choice but to make do with second, even third best.[33] As so often, one comes back to the problems inescapably inherent in Britain's combination of limited human resources with inflated global ambition. The thin red line was not just anorexic. At certain times, and in certain locations, it was adolescent.

Whiteway's captivity narrative, which was published in London together with Scurry's in 1824, points to yet another reason why men from the lower echelons of Britain's armed and imperial forces might turn renegade: less out of simple greed, than from a desire to better themselves in other, more intangible ways.[34] When captured at sea by the French in 1782, Whiteway was a cabin boy on an East Indiaman. As a result of being handed over to Mysore, he received for the first time in his life an education. He was 'instructed in the Mahratta learning, and in Arabic, as preparatory to acquiring some knowledge of the Persian language . . . Of the masters, Mr Whiteway speaks in terms of high commendation.' This experience seems permanently to have shaped his mind. When he dictated his story in the 1820s, he broke away entirely from conventional imperial narratives. He admitted that the conditions Haidar Ali and Tipu Sultan had inflicted on their British captives were sometimes cruel, but this was 'not a fair criterion by which to estimate their characters', and anyway what could the British expect: 'Aggression provokes retaliation.' As Whiteway chose to remember him, Tipu had been no tyrant merely, but 'comely', 'noble', 'an encourager of learning in all its branches':

> With this view he endeavoured to secure the talents of such Europeans as the fortunes of war threw into his hands, and spared no pains to elicit their natural abilities, and extinguish in their breasts all attachments to their native home. With many of these he succeeded . . . He viewed them as incorporating with his subjects.

Confinement in Mysore seems to have released in Whiteway for the first and only time in his life a sense of wider possibilities: 'I was as happy as I could wish, I wanted for nothing, enjoyed good health, and was beloved by all.' Whether his ten-year renegade career was as unalloyedly fulfilling as this we may choose to doubt, but it is clear why he was desperate in retrospect to invest it with a rosy glow. Driven to escape in the early 1790s, almost certainly out of fright that the invading British would execute him as a traitor, Whiteway eventually returned, not so much home as to Britain. Having worked on an East Indiaman so briefly, he was not entitled to a pension or any arrears of pay. As a special concession, the Company gave him a labouring job in one of its London warehouses where his Persian proved of little use: 'His early acquirements have faded from his recollection, and he can now do little more than make the characters of words with which he was once familiar.'

Whiteway's experience was at one level an unusual though not a unique one, his adolescence burnished by alien captivity, his maturity impoverished by return. Yet his pitiful story also indicates why men such as this are more broadly significant. Renegades were not just marginal folk, idiosyncratic rebels, losers, and deviant careerists. They were usually extreme manifestations of more widespread patterns of weakness and unreliability in the societies and military forces from which they came. Thus the immaturity in terms of age of many Mysore renegades reflected the excessive youthfulness of the East India Company's white legions in general before 1815, which was widely acknowledged to be a source of instability. By the same token, experiences such as Whiteway's vividly confirm what many radicals and military reformers contended in this period: namely, that unreformed Britain's armed forces, both at home and abroad, offered poor chances of advancement or reward to men from the lower ranks.[35] Ordinary, low-grade British warriors with no hope of finding a marshall's baton in their knapsacks, might desert and cross over in imperial locations (or merely decide to remain captives) out of a conviction, justified or no, that the grass could only be greener on the other side.

There is another respect in which renegades and deserters from British forces overseas drew attention to a more broadly significant fracture. Many of them were Irish.

That Irishmen were prone to desert was an Anglophone commonplace in the eighteenth century, and it is easy enough to find seeming anecdotal corroboration as far as India is concerned.[36] Dempster, the Mysore renegade, was Irish. So was George Thomas, whom we will soon encounter, the only British renegade to be accorded a full-scale biography. But until an exhaustive analysis of deserters on this and other British imperial frontiers is attempted, we cannot know how far varieties of Irishmen were more likely to defect than their non-Irish comrades, or how far their prominence among these and other kinds of military trouble-makers merely reflects their preponderance in Britain's armed forces at this time.

Napoleonic France, like Bourbon France, certainly worked on the assumption that Catholic Irishmen in British uniform were potentially a weak link, and these expectations were sometimes validated in European theatres of war, and in colonial locations where the British were confronted by Catholic European forces.[37]

It is not clear, however, whether Catholic Irishmen in British service were less reliable than other groups in locations and contexts where the enemy was non-Christian and non-European. Many officers serving in India judged not. General Charles Napier, for instance, who was part Irish, and sympathised with Catholic Irish grievances, believed that Irish troops in colonial service were actually more tractable than their English or Scottish counterparts. 'There is a promptness to obey, a . . . willingness to act', another officer wrote of the Irish troops he had commanded in India, 'which I have rarely met with in any other body of men.'[38] Certainly, if even a bare majority of Catholic Irishmen in British uniform had rebelled, imperial enterprise in India and elsewhere might have foundered, since their numbers by this stage were so great. All this said, it seems likely that the long tradition, dating back to the Reformation, of Irishmen selling their swords to other powers, including Spain, France, Portugal, the Italian states, and Russia, allowed Irish soldiers who did change sides in colonial locations to inhabit their roles with greater fluency and conviction. This was emphatically the case with George Thomas.

Thomas kept his background deliberately obscure, but he was probably Catholic and born in Tipperary in 1756. He deserted from the Royal Navy in Madras in the early 1780s and went on to forge a successful mercenary career in Northern India. Agile as a verb, he worked in turn for the Poligars, for a remarkable female ruler, Begum Samru, in what is now the Indian district of Meerut, and for the Marathas. Then, 'about the middle of the year 1798', he 'formed the eccentric and arduous design of erecting an independent principality for himself'. Basing himself at Hansi, some ninety miles north-west of Delhi, he claimed overlordship of some 5000 inhabitants 'to whom I allowed every lawful indulgence'. He built fortifications, assembled his own mixed race mercenary army, set up a foundry to cast artillery, and a mint to coin rupees 'which I made current in my army and country'.[39]

At least some of this was true. Samples of Thomas rupees still survive. But Thomas's narrative of his Indian adventures, which he wrote or more likely dictated in 1802, and the biography of him published the following year by William Francklin, reveal not just an extraordinary career, but one that remains in large part concealed, and was ultimately a failure. As Rudyard Kipling's wonderful story makes clear, the white man 'who would

63. George Thomas: the frontispiece of William Francklin's biography.

be king' in a non-Western environment was always at the mercy of events beyond his control and comprehension.[40] Thomas's experiment in government at Hansi lasted barely a year. Then, his troops mutinied for lack of ·pay, his Indian 'subjects' began drifting away, and neighbouring warlords moved in. Early in 1802, 'as the only means of safety and escape from the persecution of numerous and inveterate foes', he crossed back into British-controlled territory. His subsequent narrative was compiled for the benefit of Richard Wellesley, governor general of India. Briefer and much less accomplished than that other apologia by a warrior crossing cultures, T.E. Lawrence's *The Seven Pillars of Wisdom*, Thomas's narrative resembles it in being at once selective and unintentionally revealing.

Desperately anxious to re-establish his credentials with the British, Thomas was unforthcoming about the circumstances of his desertion from the Royal Navy, and about his actions before 1793. It is possible that these included fighting at times against the forces of the East India Company. Instead, he concentrated on supplying Wellesley with erratic, strictly impersonal information about Northern Indian politics and princely armies, and on stressing his loyalty. His entrepreneurship at Hansi, he insisted, had been designed from the start to advance British imperium: 'I wished to put myself in a capacity . . . of planting the British standard on the banks of the Attock.' Since Thomas had deserted the British standard, and worked contentedly under different banners for two decades, this was audacious to say the least. But his rewriting of his renegade career was enormously assisted by Francklin, a lieutenant-colonel in the East India Company, a gifted orientalist and explorer, and a man utterly committed to empire. Francklin met Thomas just before he died at Berhampore in August 1802, and was captivated by the man. In the notes he compiled for his biography, Francklin describes Thomas as 'our friend and hero', 'an ancient Roman', a man, as the subtitle of his book puts it, 'who, by extraordinary talents and enterprise, rose from an obscure situation to the rank of a General'.[41] Francklin went on to place great emphasis on 'the wonderful and uncommon attachment generally exhibited towards his [Thomas's] person . . . by natives'. 'No man, perhaps,' he wrote, 'ever more thoroughly studied or more properly appreciated the Indian character.'[42] Here, in this tale of a charismatic, six-foot Irishman, often dressed in Indian costume, and fluent in Persian and Urdu, is a recognisably early variant of the kinds of legends that would later be constructed around Lawrence of Arabia. Thomas, as Francklin presents him, becomes the white man who knows non-whites better than they know themselves, and who can therefore lead them in battle, while all the time striving on the empire's behalf.

It was a sign of the tightening grip of empire on Britain's culture and self-image that this sort of mythologising of renegade experience was now being attempted, and not just in Thomas's case.[43] In reality, there were strict limits on the extent to which renegade Britons and other Europeans in non-Western environments were able to act as freelances. Thomas's own experiment at political autonomy in North India failed; and even highly valued European mercenary commanders and expert technicians in Indian princely service seem to have been kept on a close rein by their employers.[44] As for white renegade foot soldiers, they might sometimes win more freedom and rewards in indigenous service than were available to them in European armies, but most remained foot soldiers, low-grade human beings in societies that were different from their own but no less hierarchical. A Muslim account exists of the 400-odd Britons still hanging on in Tipu's capital, Seringapatam, in the 1790s. Most were working by then as soldiers in Tipu's *cheyla* or slave battalions, or as weavers making uniforms, or coining money in his mints, or labouring in his armouries and fortifications. For this, they received 'a rupee and a bottle of arrack a day'. Out of charity, whites who were unfit for work got 'an allowance of rice, ghee and curry stuff and fifteen gold fanams, about seven rupees per month', but they were not allowed to go outside the fortress walls.[45] Virtually all of these men were either executed on Tipu's orders as the British made their final advance on Seringapatam in 1799, or lost their lives in the chaos of its fall. It was a long way from the brilliant sagas of audacious white men on horseback ventured by George Thomas and William Francklin, but closer probably to majority white renegade experience in Asia.

Yet, just like T. E. Lawrence, Thomas gave more away than he intended even as he spun his calculated yarns of renegade adventure. For him, as for Lawrence, 'going native' was clearly never an option, but neither was it possible for either of these men to mimic and live within another society without becoming changed in the process:

> The effort for these years to live in the dress of Arabs, and to imitate their mental foundation, quitted me of my English self, and let me look at the West and its conventions with new eyes: they destroyed it all for me. At the same time I could not sincerely take on the Arab skin . . . I had dropped one form and not taken on the other.[46]

Lawrence's assessment of his own resulting schizophrenia and alienation must have applied as well to many earlier, less articulate Britons who crossed over into non-European societies. Only the very young sometimes managed this kind of transition decisively and satisfactorily. Thomas, for all his guts and energy, could not. He failed in the end both to construct the kind of Indian role he wanted for himself, and to reintegrate back into British imperial society, dying almost as soon as he tried to do so. 'What is to prevent the restless Indian from [rising up]', he enquires at one point in his narrative '. . . when a prospect offers of liberating themselves from our yoke?' Quickly, he recovers himself: 'Mr. Thomas observes that he purposely makes use of the word *yoke*, as he knows that the natives of India always consider the government they are under as such.' Perhaps so. But it seems more likely that, at this point in his tale, Thomas lost his narrative footing, and slipped into the crevices between his various identities and agendas. For just a moment, he seems to have faltered between the demands of British empire and self-interest on the one hand, and two decades of Indian coexistence and perhaps his own Irish origins on the other.[47]

George Thomas's fate points to something that was true of virtually all renegades. Superficially, these men were free spirits, rebels who kicked over the traces. Yet in reality their trade made them vulnerable figures who faced enormous risks, sometimes squalid compromises, and constraints. What they could do, and how long they remained alive to do it, always depended on state systems and rulers infinitely more powerful than they. This is why examining such men in the context of imperial frontiers becomes valuable. Far from being mere picturesque individuals, British renegades in India and elsewhere in Asia are a measure of indigenous regimes' ability and will to attract and employ British and other European strays, and of the imperial authorities' changing capacity over time to regulate their own manpower. As the British came closer to achieving hegemony in India, alternative options for white military careers and enterprise there were cut back, and regulations and restrictions increased. It is time to turn from this white renegade minority to the majority of white captives in uniform, the men who were kept in line.

Whipping the legions into line

Joseph Wall was hanged at Newgate on 28 January 1802. As he climbed the scaffold, his clothes were as elegantly understated as ever; and even without them, his six foot four inches of height would have proclaimed an affluent, unfailingly well nourished existence. Himself a former lieutenant-colonel in the East India Company, Wall had married the daughter of a Scottish peer. That money and position were perishing on a site normally given over to executing the underprivileged was, however, less remarkable than the size and behaviour of the crowd on this occasion. It took Wall twenty minutes to die, but the 60,000 spectators in front of Newgate prison and spilling over into the surrounding streets, many of them in red or blue uniforms, did not react with the usual voyeuristic pity, faintings and cries of shame. They howled in triumph and applauded. Yet Wall had been no standard bugbear, no child murderer, no killer or ravisher of helpless females. His chief victim had been a tough army sergeant, while his real crime had been to lay bare some of the more paradoxical captivities and costs involved in the expansion and exercise of British empire.[48]

Twenty years earlier, Wall had been governor of Goree, a slave-trading base on the west coast of Africa seized by the British in the Seven Years

GOVENER WALL.

Published Feb. 1. 1800. by Nuttall, Fisher & Dixon Liverpool.

64. A cheap print of
Joseph Wall; note the
misspelling.

War. Lethal for so many blacks, the place also killed the majority of whites
who were dispatched there. Wall ran the risk of its climate, microbes, and
brutality, only because by this stage a reputation for violent temper, sexual
scandal and duelling to the death debarred him from more eligible imperial postings. Goree's British garrison was made up of 'regiments in
disgrace for mutiny, deserting . . . or some such cause', hard men with no
alternatives and no future. On the penultimate day of Wall's governorship, sixty of these troops advanced on his quarters, demanding arrears
of pay that they claimed were due to them. Wall's response was to arrest
five of the ringleaders and, without a trial, order them 800 lashes apiece.

Three of the men, including a Sergeant Benjamin Armstrong, were
'whipped, not with the ordinary instrument, but with ropes; not by the

ordinary persons, but by black slaves'. The blacks in question, who spoke no English, had been assembled specially, and that day in July 1782 they took turns 'inflicting 25 lashes, till the number of 800 had been inflicted' on each soldier. 'Lay on you black bastards,' Wall called out repeatedly, and pointlessly, as he supervised the punishment, 'or else I will lay upon you!' Long before the end of his own ordeal, Armstrong was shitting and pissing blood, and choking as it flooded his lungs. The garrison's assistant surgeon who watched the man die over the next four days noted with interest that what was left of his back was almost 'as black as a new hat'.

After this episode, Wall went into hiding on the Continent, only returning to London at the beginning of the nineteenth century. He seems to have believed that with the passage of time, the distractions of the Napoleonic wars, and his wife's titled relations, he would be able to secure a pardon. As the Privy Council quickly resolved, this was out of the question. Wall was an embarrassment on every front. Britain was still effectively at war with the ideologies and armies of the French Revolution, and its rulers were desperate to sustain some kind of patriotic, cross-class consensus. Yet Wall was linked to the British aristocracy and guilty of murder and sadism against working-class soldiers. The Abolitionist movement had by now equipped Britons of all classes and both sexes with horrific images of West Indian overseers flogging black slaves. Yet Wall's case revealed how the whip was an integral part of Britain's own military culture. Wall had offended in another respect as well. The Attorney General at his trial, and virtually every published account and woodcut representation of it, dwelt on the point that Armstrong and his fellow-sufferers, white men in British uniform, had been flogged to death by men who were black.

Race and racial stereotypes were crucial and explicit ingredients of the Governor Wall affair. They were no less central to the growing debate at this time over the legitimacy of flogging as a form of discipline in Britain's armed forces. That the whip, the prime emblem of slavery, was deployed with sometimes lethal savagery against them, lay at the very heart of British soldiers' sense of themselves as captives of their own state, as white slaves.[49] These parallels between white soldiers and black slaves were laboured persistently, for their own purposes, by anti-Abolitionists. The polemic was already an established one when Edward Long compiled his unabashedly racialist *History of Jamaica* (1774). 'I need not *again* revive the comparison between them [plantation slaves], and the British sailors and soldiers,' he wrote:

I need not urge that the ordinary punishment inflicted on these poor wretches for the most trivial offences against discipline, would, if inflicted

Governor Wall contemplating on his unhappy Fate in the condemn'd Cell.

65. Joseph Wall awaiting execution.

on a negro in Jamaica be condemned universally as a most detestable act of barbarity.

Similar arguments were sometimes resorted to in courts of law by whites seeking to legitimise physical assaults on non-whites in other parts of the globe. In 1787, for instance, the Hon. Basil Cochrane, a senior East India Company merchant and acting resident at Negapatam in southern India, was put on trial for ordering one of his Indian servants a beating from which the man subsequently died. Cochrane called as witnesses in his defence a string of army officers who testified that in terms of severity this flogging was 'not comparable to the punishments which are constantly inflicted on European soldiers'.[50]

Because such comparisons between floggings of blacks and floggings of white soldiers were regularly employed for contaminated purposes – to minimise the significance and iniquity of slavery and other abuses – they have generally been passed over by serious scholars. The Governor Wall affair, for instance, one of the great *causes célèbres* of class, race and empire, still awaits its historian; so, astonishingly, does corporal punishment and its shifting meanings in British imperial, military and masculine culture.[51] Yet because men like Long were bigots, this does not mean that the parallels they drew attention to were without foundation. As Seymour Drescher argues, one of the consequences of growing agitation over black slavery after 1770 was that discussion of the treatment of working people became globalised in a new way. Growing awareness of the sufferings of enslaved blacks in Britain's colonies worked to illumine as well the plight of its own white multitudes, and not least the plight of its common soldiers and sailors.[52] Those who were most active and risked most in defending and extending the bounds of the British empire – its plebeian warriors – were increasingly represented in this period, and increasingly viewed themselves, as being in some respects comparable to black slaves. The very vehemence with which spokesmen for the British state downplayed such comparisons testifies to their bite. The claim that a 'British soldier [was] . . . in a worse state than an African slave' was appalling, declared a government MP in 1812.[53] Any 'comparison . . . of the soldiers of England to negro slaves' should be met with indignation, Palmerston insisted in the same debate. There was nothing in common, wrote General Charles Napier, 'between the two cases of flogging soldiers and flogging black men'.[54] But, as the Governor Wall affair made damningly clear, there was. In both cases, the whip was deployed out of ruthlessness of control, and because of assumptions about the mentalities and limited worth of those enduring it.

As Robert Southey argued at the time, mass euphoria at Wall's execution was in a vital sense without foundation. Wall was found guilty not because three British soldiers had been flogged to death, but because he had not allowed them a trial first: 'Had he called a drum head court martial, the same sentence might have been inflicted and the same consequences have ensued, with perfect impunity to himself.'[55] Floggings in the British army (and Navy) remained common after 1802, and may even have increased in absolute terms, especially in imperial locations. In 1817, 692 British soldiers stationed in the Windward and Leeward Islands suffered the whip, as did 635 white troops in Jamaica. As these figures make clear, flogging was not reserved for a vicious minority. Like the branding-iron, sometimes inflicted on deserters, it was part and parcel of being in the lower ranks. In just one year, 1822, two out of every five white soldiers stationed in Bermuda suffered the lash.[56] The statistics for punishment in India are less comprehensive, but it seems likely that the Company's forces were no softer than the regular army in this regard, and may have been harsher. In 1836, a Bengal artilleryman claimed that thirty-one white troops in his Company had received on average 380 lashes each in the last six months. By this stage, it was rare for soldiers in the United Kingdom to be sentenced to more than 200 lashes.[57]

Behind these figures, so eagerly accumulated by early Victorian Britain's statisticians, lay the human reality, the scarified flesh, the spraying gobbets of clotted blood and skin, the split muscle, devastated spirits, and sickened stomachs characterising every ritual of military flogging. By 1815, corporal punishment in the armed forces had been abolished in France and the United States, and all but abandoned in Prussia. By the 1820s, even West Indian assemblies were prescribing severe limits, at least on paper, to the number of lashes overseers and owners were allowed to administer to black slaves. Why, then, did such physically violent, mutilating punishments continue to appear acceptable to the British state as a form of discipline against their own whites in military uniform, and especially against white troops in overseas locations?

One of the most common rationalisations would have been familiar as well to slave-owners. As James Walvin remarks, flogging slaves was regularly defended in the Caribbean and American South on the grounds that it was public and therefore exemplary, a means of keeping other blacks 'in awe and order'. This was exactly how the duke of Wellington also defended military flogging. The imprisonment of one of their own number, he argued, made no impact on men in the British ranks. The 'real meaning' of flogging, by contrast, was '. . . example'.[58] Whether it reformed the soldier victim was less important than its wider deterrent effect. There was also agreement that the condition of common soldiers made it hard to punish them effectively except through their own bodies. Like slaves, these men had too little money or property to be effectively subjected to fines. Imprisonment, if it released them from the everyday burdens of labour and discipline, might seem a reward rather than a penalty. Transportation certainly would. 'Was it likely', thundered a Member of Parliament in 1834, 'that a soldier smarting under the broiling sun of Middle India, would object to a trip to the cool and pleasant climate of Sydney.'[59] Australia offered the prospect of land for all and a place to settle, and some British troops stationed in Asia are known to have offended repeatedly in the hope of being dispatched there as convicts. A Private Forbes had to desert from Fort William at Calcutta seven times in 1820 before achieving his transportation; Private Ryder, who also served there, simply struck his sergeant full in the face in 1834, telling him 'it was intended to effect his transportation to New South Wales'.[60]

As this suggests, disorder and protest levels among the white soldiery in India were high. After 1809 – though not before – full-scale mutiny became virtually a monopoly of the Company's Indian soldiers; but less dramatic, everyday disobedience was much more a preserve of white troops. The latter were outnumbered by their sepoy counterparts five to one. Yet, in the 1820s and '30s, charges of desertion were brought against eleven times more white soldiers than against Company sepoys.[61] Although by now the opportunities to turn renegade in India were receding fast, other varieties of escape, be it desertion, absence without leave, self-mutilation as a means of securing discharge from service, and above all drunkenness, were abundantly practised by white captives in uniform. So, as court martial records show with weary regularity, were mutinous conduct, disobedience to superior officers, verbal sedition and riot. For disciplinarians, all this was proof positive of the low moral calibre of Britain's common soldiery, and consequently of the indispensability of the lash. They were 'fine fellows', Sir Henry Hardinge told Parliament smoothly in 1832, but the 'very irregularities' of their lives before recruitment dictated 'that strict degree of discipline which corporal punishment alone can give'.[62] Historians have sometimes acquiesced in this line of reasoning, forgetting perhaps that slave-owners also justified beating black slaves on the grounds that they too were congenitally idle or vicious. In the case of both of these groups, such rationalisations of corporal punishment were more often than not precisely that.

Thanks to the East India Company's own bureaucracy and the painstaking researches of Joel Mokyr and Cormac ó Gráda, we now know that the generality of white soldiers in India were not quasi-criminal, Foreign Legionnaire types, but broadly representative of their age and class cohorts within the home population.[63] Almost 10 per cent of Company recruits between 1802 and 1814, for instance, were weavers; another thousand were carpenters, cordwainers and tailors, standard artisanal trades. Such men were joined as recruits by very large numbers of agricultural and unskilled urban labourers and, in periods of high unemployment, by members of what might be styled the working-class aristocracy: petty clerks, failed printers, low-grade teachers and the like. These men were not in the main hardened desperados when recruited; and neither it seems were most regular army soldiers sent to India, though the latter were less likely to be literate. Granted that these were young, generally barely educated men who had been trained to violence, original sin forms an inadequate explanation as to why they protested and offended at the level and in the fashion that they did.

At least some of the disorder and disobedience that characterised British troops in Asia should rather be understood in terms of their society of origin. What E.P. Thompson styled the making of England's working class occurred much further afield, and not just in Ireland, Scotland and Wales. Because of the dimensions of British empire and emigration, this was a phenomenon acted out on a global scale, and urgently needs investigating as such. Since white soldiers in India were so representative of the British and Irish working populations at large, it was to be expected that their patterns of protest sometimes borrowed from those operating in the United Kingdom itself. In November 1816, for instance, a Corporal Kearnan in the Company's service was charged with 'entering a combination with several men of the horse artillery', administering oaths of secrecy, and then deserting with his weapons. He was caught and shot, and his fate read out to every regiment in India.[64] There were local explanations for this well-publicised punishment (artillery men were precisely the kind of white renegades indigenous rulers in India liked to attract), but there were also political reasons closer to home. Entering combinations, administering secret oaths, and collecting illicit weapons were common tactics in the United Kingdom at this time among illegal trade unions, among Luddites opposed to the new industrial machinery, and among secret societies like the United Irishmen.[65] Corporal Kearnan (who may well have been Irish) was executed in part because – just like these dissidents back home – he challenged the authority of the British state, but on another shore.

Yet customs of protest in common were only part of the story. White soldiers in Asia were also conspicuously unruly because of the particular circumstances of their jobs and lives. The East India Company army still behaved in many respects as a private, autonomous force. It was far more politicised than the regular British army, emphatically middle-class in terms of its officers, and often turbulent. In 1795, the year William Pitt the Younger rushed through parliamentary acts banning 'seditious' meetings of more than fifty people in Britain, Lord Cornwallis, governor-general in Bengal, also banned 'promiscuous meetings' within the Company army. This, be it noted, was a prohibition aimed at the commissioned ranks! As one high-ranking British officer remarked in 1832, when military men regularly met, as Company officers did in India, to 'form committees, appoint delegates, subscribe funds', and talked in terms of 'rights infringed', 'compacts broken', and the 'bad faith' of their rulers, it was 'idle to talk of military subordination' of a conventional kind. It is likely that at least some of the Company soldiery's unruliness and often highly literate protest was fostered by the politicised and sometimes truculent style of their own officers.[66] But both regular army and Company soldiers protested in India, and with reason.

There were, to be sure, compensations for the hardships they endured, enough for some men to be content, and even deeply committed. In wartime, there was pillage, the charge of combat, a reaffirming sense for some perhaps of national and racial superiority; and there was always comradeship, a reasonable certitude of employment and regular pay, the opportunity to see sights most of their compatriots never encountered, and the chance, as far as more literate Company privates were concerned, of promotion to sergeant. Against this, however, there was sporadic danger, unremitting heat and disease, protracted periods of boredom, savage discipline, and a sense often of terrible deracination and personal confinement. 'The irksomeness of the life of the European soldier is truly pitiable,' wrote the governor-general of India in 1834: '. . . his barrack with his check and roll-calls is converted into a sort of prison'.[67] The most demoralising circumstance of all was that these men were at one and the same time bound to stay in India, yet forced to remain in crucial respects rootless there. Until the 1840s, regular army soldiers commonly remained in India for up to twenty years without a break. Company soldiers were allowed to sign on for twelve years, but since they received a pension only after twenty-one years, most signed on for life: or rather death. In the 1830s, white soldiers in Bombay were more than twice as likely to die as soldiers based in Britain. In Madras, the death-rate among this group was over three times as high as among their counterparts in Britain, and in Bengal almost five times as high. Before mid-century, few private soldiers and NCOs in India could hope to live long enough to fulfil their term of service and return to Britain.[68] Yet these men were not allowed to make India their home either.

India was not a colony, and whites were discouraged by the Company from settling there. Those soldiers who did see out their time were promptly shipped back to Britain at the end of it, as were those who became too physically or mentally damaged to be of further service. Some eluded the net, but every official step was taken to gather up the maimed, the worn out, and the retirees, and prevent their establishing an Indian niche for themselves outside of the army. This policy also meant that British soldiers here were discouraged from marriage. Most were too young when recruited already to be married. Those with wives usually had to leave them behind in Britain, and in most cases never saw them again. Even in 1861, by which time the regulations had been much relaxed, only 12 per cent of men in each regiment dispatched to India were permitted to take wives along with them. What awaited these men on arrival in the subcontinent was predictably not celibacy, but close regulation of their sexuality and of any domestic urges they might cherish. This needs stressing, because attempts have sometimes been made to gauge soldiers' racial attitudes from the quality of their relationships with Indian women.[69] Yet these men were not free agents. They might be free to use the *lal bazar*, the regimental brothel. They were only occasionally free to marry Indian women and to have such alliances recognised by the British authorities.

By the 1820s, the East India Company leaned towards the view that 'only . . . Christians are capable of marriage'. Soldiers who married 'half-caste' women brought up in Christian orphanages might, it was thought, legitimately claim exactly half the marriage allowances granted to those few British wives who managed to accompany rank and file males to India, but this was all.[70] By this stage, soldiers' Indian wives and widows received no financial allowance whatsoever. Indian wives were not allowed to accompany soldiers who were sent back to Britain, and nor were any Eurasian children they might have. Indian families of white soldiers might even be forbidden to accompany their men when they were transferred to other postings in Asia. In 1817, for instance, the 66th Regiment was ordered from Bengal to St Helena. It left behind fifty-five unprovided for 'unmarried women' and fifty-one children.[71] Some of the British soldiers involved may have welcomed release from these commitments; others may have been distraught at being torn from the only families they were ever likely to have barring their regiments. As so often, the extant evidence shuts us out from the minds of this kind of men, and still more from the minds of this kind of women. The point is that the British state and the Company allowed these people no choice. The soldiers concerned could not take their non-white families with them to St Helena. They could not break their terms of service and stay on in Bengal. Had they deserted from the army, they would either have been hunted down, or remained precariously on the loose, unpaid, unpensioned, and at risk of starvation. As with slaves, the sexual and familial arrangements of men such as these remained substantially at the mercy of those with authority over them. 'The poorest labourer in England', scrawled a private soldier in India in the 1850s, 'when returning from his daily labour, finds someone to cheer his cares away, and participate in all his doubts and fears.'[72] So too did most of the Company's sepoy troops who could live with their wives while on service in their own accommodation. But the generality of British troops in India were allowed no such comforts.

66. Indian painting of a Company sepoy and his wife in the 1780s. Virtually no portraits exist of their poor white counterparts at this time.

There were some in positions of authority who believed that this was wrong. 'The discouragement to their [the soldiers'] marriage is unjust and impolitic,' a senior officer serving in India told a parliamentary committee in 1832:

> Where the European soldiers form connexions with local native women, and live out of barracks, they are generally remarkable for their good conduct, sobriety and attention to their duties. These women are faithful to them and are serviceable attendants in the field . . . These connexions would have a tendency to break down the prejudices of the European soldiery and would enable them, when superannuated, to become useful settlers.[73]

Yet, as this committee's final report makes clear, such a position as regards British soldiers' possible intermarriage and settlement in India was by this stage emphatically a minority one. The reasons for this hinged on attitudes to race and social class, but also on perceptions of the foundations of British imperial power in India, and the applicability of the lash.

Opposition to intermarriage in India certainly stemmed in part from racially driven xenophobia. It also turned, as so much else did, on a matter of numbers. Both the Company and London were concerned about the rising 'half caste population of India', by this stage larger at 20,000 than the total number of British civilians based there. To allow widespread marriages between white troops and Indian women would inevitably have led to this liminal grouping increasing at a still faster rate, and this – it was thought – might have significant and damaging political repercussions. The 1810s and '20s had witnessed successful creole and mixed-race revolutions in South America against Portuguese and Spanish imperial dominion. Some in Britain may have considered the possibility of a future dangerous alliance between an expanding contingent of Anglo-Indians on the one hand, and its own unruly white soldiery on the other, especially as most white troops in India at this stage were not employed directly by the British state, but by the Company.

Moreover, while some argued that soldiers' intermarriage with Indian women would serve to contaminate and enfeeble British males, at official level the emphasis was often on the reverse point: if allowed to settle and form permanent connections in India, the British soldiery would themselves be a contaminating influence. As Douglas Peers points out, there was a perception among British officers, not statistically impeccable but none the less powerful, that the majority of white common soldiers in India and elsewhere were in origin impoverished labourers, overwhelmingly from urban areas, dissolute, unteachable, godless, brave certainly, but brave because reckless and dangerous. By contrast, sepoys, especially those viewed as high-caste rural peasants, were praised for their zeal, honour, trustworthiness, temperance, physique, and above all for their obedience.[74] 'The moral character of the native', one British colonel told the parliamentary committee of 1832, 'is far superior to the European.' Were retired British common soldiers to be allowed to settle in India, agreed a major-general, it would be detrimental to the country: 'When control would be removed from them, they would become a very bad description of people.' The white soldiery, General, the Hon. Sir Edward Paget judged, were 'very drunken and dissolute people'. Or, as yet another senior officer had pronounced earlier: 'The English soldier exhibits to the natives of India a disgusting specimen.'[75]

Such comments must be understood in part in British domestic terms. Popular agitation in Britain and Ireland in the 1820s, '30s, and early '40s over parliamentary reform, Roman Catholic emancipation, trade unions, and ultimately Chartism inevitably shaped attitudes among the British elite in the empire as well. Expressions of alarm and revulsion by patrician officers and officials about British and Irish underprivileged elements in imperial locations cannot, and should not be disaggregated from similar responses by members of the British ruling order at this time to mass dissidence at home. In both cases, there was a heightened sensitivity to potential threats from those below, and a heightened determination to maintain control and discipline. Indeed, it is partly in this context of growing social polarization at home that one can understand the British state's continuing resort to the whip against its white soldiery. Slaves, observes Michael Bush, can be treated as such because they appear alien in some way.[76] They are black. Or in Islamic slave systems, they are non-Muslim; or they are Jews or gypsies perhaps. Whatever the source of their perceived difference, it allows them to be treated in a different and inferior fashion from individuals within the home society. By the same token, as a private soldier dispatched to fight for the empire complained, large numbers of affluent and powerful Britons did not 'consider a common soldier, as a fellow subject'.[77] And this made it possible for the British state, that prided itself on its superior freedoms, to deploy against these men the lash, the quintessential emblem of unfreedom. To be an effective common soldier, it was widely believed, a man needed to be tough, brutal and unthinking. And since British soldiers were tough, brutal and unthinking – and after a fashion alien – they could and must be whipped into line.

Yet there were also more pragmatic and entirely Indian factors involved here. In 1830, there were an estimated 36,400 British regular army and

Company officers and men stationed in India. But there were almost 190,000 sepoys in Company uniform, and these Indian warriors had proved their indispensability to the British not only in their own subcontinent, but also in the campaign against the French in Egypt in 1800–1, in the expedition to Mauritius and Java in 1810–11, and in other extra-Indian campaigns. The logic of all this was crystal clear to Britain's high command. British empire in India – and in other parts of the world – could never outlast the period of sepoy obedience. But since many Britons in positions of authority idealised the sepoy, they believed – as of course they had to – that a kind of perfect, enduring chemistry could be created between an expert and valiant British officer class and a noble, numerous but ultimately tractable Indian sepoy army. In this chemistry, the mass of ordinary British soldiers in India were seen as having little to do. 'There is no error more common', General Sir John Malcolm told the governor-general of India, Lord William Bentinck, in 1830:

> than that of considering [white troops] as a check upon the Native armies. They never have and never will prove such . . . The necessity of check implies distrust that degrades. It is by complete confidence alone that the Native army of India can be possessed in efficiency and attached to the Government.[78]

It was in absolute conformity to this line of reasoning that in 1835 Bentinck abolished the use of flogging against Indian troops, while permitting the lash to continue to be used on the backs of British troops in India. Indian soldiers, as he explained to Parliament, were much better behaved than the British variety. But, as Bentinck pointed out, there were also far more of them:

> He saw no reason why 150,000 men [sic] should . . . be subjected to corporal punishment in order that 20,000 [sic] other men, who might properly be subjected to the punishment, should not be displeased.[79]

For a small nation like Britain, engaged now in global empire on a scale that was unprecedented in history, numbers mattered and not just race.

Re-envisioning the imperial soldiery

In terms of opinion in Britain, Bentinck's reform proved decisive in a sense that he had not appreciated. A year later, in 1836, the Whig administration of the day conceded a parliamentary enquiry into military flogging. As one politician put it, Bentinck's initiative finally 'upset the system'. It had long been a commonplace that British soldiers were treated in some respects like African slaves. Now, it appeared, they were to fare worse than their Indian counterparts as well. Was there anything, an MP enquired,

> in the character, habits, or disposition, of our fellow-countrymen to render them unworthy the consideration which the noble Lord felt justified in extending to the natives of India.

Or as the Irish radical Daniel O'Connell demanded, with an eye to his countrymen's massive representation in imperial legions, why should the lash be 'applied to the back of a British soldier, when it was discontinued even amongst the black men'.[80]

The racial assumptions behind such interjections are evident. O'Connell's phrasing '*even* amongst the black men' speaks volumes. Yet the paradox he and others identified was a real and jarring one. The early modern British state had never customarily employed the whip against its civilian labouring classes. In the last quarter of the eighteenth century, and the first quarter of the nineteenth century, its politicians and public developed growing qualms about the use of corporal punishment against black slaves. Yet during this same period, there was a growing recourse to the whip to discipline and terrorise Britain's own armed forces. This anomaly often passes unnoticed, perhaps because soldiers, and especially the imperial soldiery, still meet with something like the same condescension and contempt that was often bestowed on them in the past. These were violent, unlettered men. They were whipped. So what? Yet how these men were regarded and treated by their own state is crucial to an understanding of this most violent epoch of British imperial activity.

From the 1750s, but much more from the 1790s, a rising proportion of Britain's armed forces was active overseas transforming the geographical scale of its empire at an unprecedented rate. The political will providing for this later, particularly intense period of global aggression would not have been forthcoming had Britain's population not been expanding fast, and been recognised at the time as expanding fast. For the first time ever, it became widely accepted that Britain possessed a sufficiency of young males, and even a surfeit. War and empire could employ and winnow them, without fear of enfeebling Britain itself. Yet, in practice, it was not as straightforward as that. The United Kingdom was now more demographically buoyant than ever before, but its population and armed forces still remained smaller than those of other leading European powers. In order, therefore, to intrude as decisively into as many global zones as it did, the British state had to have recourse to extraordinary levels of determination and violence, not just with regard to European and non-European opponents, but also with regard to its own manpower. It is a commonplace that the classic era of Britain's pioneering industrialisation, *c.* 1770–*c.* 1840, was characterised by a more ruthless and systematic treatment of labour at home. By the same token, the contemporaneous surge in Britain's overseas empire was characterised by a more calculated, uncompromising and often brutal disciplining of its own white soldiery overseas. A thin red line kept ever more ruthlessly in line, these men were literally whipped to work and win.

They were also frequently looked down upon, denounced, and disapproved of for all their indispensability to the British imperial effort. The experiences of these captives in uniform demonstrates yet again that empire could disrupt racial notions and identities as much as it fostered them. Exposure to non-European otherness never straightforwardly and uniquely accentuated an assurance of British, still less European solidarities. It often served to throw into still sharper relief divisions and tensions already existing among the white incomers themselves. East India Company and British authorities treated Indian sepoys in some respects (and still more India's landed, mercantile and princely elites) more benevolently and more respectfully than they did their own white working-class soldiers, because they could not afford to do otherwise. At the same time, exposure to India, as to other imperial locations, tested, changed and sometimes alienated the white soldiery themselves. A minority turned renegade. More deserted. Still more perceived themselves as slaves, or lashed out in different ways at those with the power to lash them. The anonymous diary of an English private, stationed in India in the 1840s and '50s, devotes far more space to excoriating his own aloof, upper-class countrymen than to downgrading Indians. It was the 'aristocrats of our native isle' whom this man hated, together with Britain's middle-class reformers, 'talking gentlemen' as he called them, who seemed to care more about cruelty to dumb animals than about the treatment of ordinary red-coats like himself.[81]

This kind of anger on the part of discontented imperial soldiers rarely led them in the direction of anything approaching radical politics. Nor did men who thought like this necessarily feel any empathy with the indigenous peoples around them. A white soldier's sense that he was 'less thought of in India than a common *mheter* [sic] who looks after the officer's dogs' might indeed encourage festering racism on his part.[82] British captives in uniform overseas could not vent their fury, frustration and boredom on their own country's aristocracy or its comfortable middle classes, however much they might wish to do so. By contrast, it was all too easy to strike out physically, verbally, or only in their minds at those they presumed to call 'natives'.

Yet one should not fall into the trap of viewing these men in monolithic terms, or of taking on trust the characterisations of them supplied by their superiors. British officers regularly decried the unfortunate racial prejudices of the lower ranks, doubtless justifiably in many cases. But condemning the common soldiers as vulgarly racist was also a function of elite perceptions of these men as unlettered brutes. In this, as in other respects, it is vital to reconstruct the imperial soldiery, like other subalterns, from their own sources as much as possible, and to acknowledge their multiplicity.[83] It is imperative, too, to consider them in tandem with their civilian counterparts back home. Any assessment of the strengths and weaknesses of British empire abroad in the late eighteenth and early nineteenth centuries must take on board the fact that its white soldiers and seamen were recruited from the same social and occupational groupings that were becoming more literate, more disorderly, and in many cases more politically active at home. Controlling its white imperial soldiery was sometimes as troubling to the British state in this era as maintaining order at home, or ruling over indigenous populations overseas.

Yet, by the 1830s, there were signs that the imperial soldiery was coming to be re-envisioned both at home and abroad. A more active concern emerged for these men's physical and spiritual welfare, and there was growing provision of schools for soldiers' children, garrison hospitals, regimental libraries, recreational facilities, army chapels, and (relatively) clean accommodation. By the end of this decade, the mortality rate among British soldiers overseas, even in tropical locations like India, had fallen substantially; and by the late 1840s, limits began to be set on the number of years soldiers could be exiled overseas.[84] And there was another major change. Resort to the lash continued, but its use in the army (and the Royal Navy) much diminished, both overseas and in Britain itself. Back in 1822, two out of every five British soldiers stationed in Bermuda had been whipped. By 1836, the proportion of soldiers being flogged in this part of the empire was less than five in a thousand, and similar dramatic reductions occurred in other British colonies and overseas bases.[85] Despite Bentinck's ruling in 1835, flogging of white troops also declined sharply in India, though less rapidly in some areas than floggings of Company sepoys.

The amelioration in the condition of the British imperial soldiery after 1830, like their conspicuous disorderliness in previous decades, represented in part an extension of domestic social, political, religious and economic changes overseas. There were obvious connections between the growing concern to improve (and regulate) the conditions of the working classes in Britain's own sprawling industrial conurbations at this time, and efforts to improve the welfare (and good order) of its overseas legions. By the 1830s, for instance, the British government was providing annual grants to supply carefully chosen books and newspapers for its soldiers overseas, and so were the East India Company and various philanthropic associations. As a result of this campaign to 'inform their minds and to lessen licentious propensities', ordinary troops in Bengal, Bombay and Madras, and in other regions of British imperial enterprise, secured access to religious tracts in abundance, as well as to texts on geography and natural history, and stirring stories from Britain's past and present. They also received novels like *Robinson Crusoe*, and – as was only fitting – a volume entitled *Perils and Captivity*.[86]

In other respects, too, there were close links between Britain's domestic conditions at this time, and conditions in its empire. The improved living standards of the imperial soldiery evident by the end of the period covered by this book, 1850, owed much to the buoyancy of Britain's economy by that stage, which so transformed the welfare of its own domestic working classes. Now that job opportunities and income levels were rising, railway construction was booming, and large-scale factory production was becoming widespread, it was much harder to tempt labouring men into the armed services. As a result, the British state began to care for its servicemen more, not just because it wanted to, but also because it had no choice. The armed services had to be made more attractive, because civilian blue-collar job opportunities were rising, as was the rate of working-class emigration from the United Kingdom. The Irish Famine of 1845–9 only confirmed this trend. Together with the waves of Irish emigration that followed, this severely reduced – without ever eradicating – those bevies of Irish recruits, Catholic as well as Protestant, on which the imperial armed forces in India and elsewhere had previously been so dependent. Here was another reason why Britain had, perforce, to devote more attention and thought to those legions it still had left.

All of which goes to underline what I have argued throughout this book: namely, that the history of Britain and the histories of its various overseas ventures cannot be adequately approached separately. For good, and for ill, they were interlinked. On the one hand, the treatment of British soldiers in different continents, and indeed of the empire's indigenous troops, was influenced by circumstances within Britain itself. On the other, the working conditions of black slaves in Africa and the Caribbean, and of sepoys in India influenced – as we have seen – debates about Britain's own labouring population, both military and civilian. At plebeian level, as at other social levels, this was now an interconnected world.

It was also a world in which Britain was now the undisputed super-power. In 1839, Queen Victoria's geographer, James Wyld, published a map suggesting that the British empire was almost three million square miles in extent. Its dimensions, he claimed, made it twenty-eight times bigger than Spain's empire, and forty times bigger than the empire of France.[87] These measurements were questionable, and so – even more – was the degree to which a small set of islands could seriously exercise and sustain authority over such a vast expanse of the globe's surface. But the enhanced consciousness of Britain's astonishing imperial reach, of which Wyld's cartographic effort was merely one example, also contributed to the re-envisioning of the imperial soldiery. It now seemed far less appropriate to refer to these men – even casually – as brutes, rogues, immoral outcasts, the scum of the earth, for it was on them that this inflated empire substantially had to rely. Increasingly, as Victoria's reign wore on, Britain's captives in uniform came to be widely re-imagined by their civilian countrymen as 'an almost ostentatiously Christian army', our brave lads abroad.[88]

Yet, as Britons began to relax into a wholly unaccustomed level of global power, many of them nurtured the hope that the time of dangerous, unpredictable conflicts and collisions abroad was passing. They had finally escaped, or so it seemed, from the protracted constraints of their own territorial and demographic smallness. And surely, by now – many of them allowed themselves to believe – Britain was too strong to be seriously challenged, too formidable to be vulnerable anymore to captivity traumas overseas. In this respect, they were both right and wrong.

To Afghanistan and Beyond

More captives, more stories

It proved easy enough that autumn for the world's most powerful state to move against Afghanistan. Moving against Afghanistan usually has been easy. To be sure, the area that now goes under that name is protected by merciless winters that endure from November until April, by the great mountain ranges of the Hindu Kush, and by semi-desert conditions to the north, west and south of its heartland; but these harsh defences of climate and terrain have counted for little over the centuries by comparison with the curse and lure of its location. From the reign of Ashoka the Great, proximity to the subcontinent has exposed this region to the ambitions of successive Indian rulers; while, since the days of Alexander the Great, powers with designs against the Indian peninsula have regularly treated Afghanistan as a gateway and as a staging post for their legions. Poor, dusty, ethnically hybrid, and often startlingly beautiful, this is a place accustomed to invasion, less because of what it is itself, than because of where it is, and who its neighbours are.

The new intruders were a classic case in point. They were not, they insisted, at war with the Afghan people themselves, though thousands still died in the fighting, and from its disruption of food supplies and shelter. Nor, the intruders claimed – with a large measure of truth in this case – did they seek any permanent, large-scale annexation of Afghan territory. Their quarrel was with the current rulers of Kabul who threatened their own interests and security. Once a *coup d'état* had been forced, and new and better men governed securely at Kabul, the invaders would retreat back from whence they had come, well pleased. And so – initially – it came to pass: and the ease and speed with which the revolution was apparently effected only strengthened the invaders' belief that it was popular with the Afghan people at large.

The British had known little of Afghanistan or anywhere else in Central Asia before 1800, but as their grip on India increased, so, predictably, did their curiosity and their anxieties in this direction. During the Napoleonic

347

67. British officers captured in Afghanistan: a romanticised 1844 print based on an earlier Afghan sketch.

Wars, London had worried in case France invaded northern India through Afghanistan and so destabilised the richest and most populous sector of its empire. After Waterloo, British fears of a European rival using Afghanistan as a springboard into India became focused on another power with a far larger army than its own, Russia. In 1837, the year of Queen Victoria's accession, Persia besieged Herat in western Afghanistan with Russian encouragement. This was enough. Late the following year, the governor-general of India, Lord Auckland, ordered an expeditionary force of 21,000 men, the grandly named Army of the Indus, into Afghanistan. Its avowed aim was to restore the former shah, Shuja ul-Mulkh, who had been in exile for thirty years, and drive out the current amir, Dost Muhammad Khan, who was judged to be pro-Russian, or at least insufficiently pro-British. By August 1839, the *coup* had been accomplished, and

Shah Shuja was back in Kabul. Only belatedly was Britain made to realise what others would discover after its empire was dust and memory. Invading Afghanistan was relatively simple. Remaining there for any time, and imposing change was not.[1]

Wanting to cement Shah Shuja's patched-up regime, a portion of the expeditionary force lingered on in Kabul. The Indian troops who made up four-fifths of this force had already been allowed to bring their women and children along with them, though naturally most of the white working-class soldiery had not. Now, many of the British army officers who remained at Kabul, and who had families in India, summoned them to their side, and began making themselves at home. They organised a social calendar, set up a race-track, played cricket, indulged in amateur dramatics, held horticultural competitions, and competed against the locals at cock-fighting. They also constructed a cantonment in the city, but it was a weak and half-hearted affair. Money and manpower were stretched as usual, so fortifications at Kabul were skimped, and the storehouses of food and ammunition were allowed to remain outside the cantonment walls. And why not? From the start of this campaign in 1838, to 1840, just thirty-four British officers had perished in Afghanistan, and of these only five had been killed in action. Elaborate and expensive fortifications appeared superfluous. The invaders' recognised technological superiority, and the hospitality and tribal divisions of the Afghans themselves, seemed defences enough. But, in 1841, things began to change.[2]

What happened then has traditionally been interpreted as an extraordinary British humiliation, as a small imperial war that mushroomed astonishingly and unprecedentedly out of control because of local, individual and idiosyncratic factors.[3] Throughout 1841 relations between the expeditionary force and Afghan tribal groups deteriorated, and ambushes, assassinations and death-rates increased. In November, the month of Ramadan, an insurrection broke out at Kabul. The cantonment was besieged for over sixty days, and as its inadequate defences crumbled, so did the morale and discipline of its Indian and, still more, its British defenders. Late in December, the British capitulated; and in January 1842, some 4500 British and Indian troops and 12,000 camp followers began the 116-mile tramp from Kabul back to Jalalabad. By February, most of these men, women and children were dead, killed by exposure and frostbite, by starvation and disease, and by their desolate, snow-covered route that continually drove them along narrow valleys and ravines where Afghan tribesmen perched high above in the mountains could fire down on them with impunity. But some did not die. Some, famously, were taken captive.

This happened in various ways and at various stages. Having

announced in December 1841 that the British force 'was in their power and that they could completely destroy it whenever they thought fit', victorious Afghan warlords demanded that six of its married army officers and their womenfolk be handed over as hostages. Some of the British officers involved threatened to shoot their wives rather than entrust them to Muslim warriors (and consequently in their minds to the harem), so six bachelor officers were accepted in their stead.[4] Some women and children, both Indian and British, were subsequently snatched on the retreat to Jalalabad and disappeared for ever into various Afghan villages; while some Indian sepoys – and some British males – were seized and sold into slavery in the markets of Kabul.[5] Most dramatically, in terms of opinion in Britain itself, as those retreating through the snow, ice and bullets began to die in large numbers, Afghan proposals that British officers' wives be handed over, together with the husbands involved and some of the wounded, were agreed to, as the only way of possibly ensuring their survival. One Englishwoman subsequently described how she was taken with the rest to a fort:

> Three rooms were cleared out for us, having no outlets except a small door to each; and of course they were dark and dirty. The party to which I belonged consisted of Mrs Trevor and seven children, Lieut. and Mrs Waller and child, Mrs Sturt, Mr Mein, and myself, Mrs Smith and Mrs Burnes, two soldier's wives, and young Stoker, child of a soldier of the 13th, who was saved from people who were carrying him off to the hills, and came in covered, we fear, with his mother's blood . . . The dimensions of our room are at the utmost fourteen feet by ten.

How many captives were seized in total will never be known: but, as far as the British were concerned, thirty-two officers, over fifty soldiers, twenty-one children, and a dozen women remained alive to be handed back to their countrymen in September 1842.[6] Well before that, a remarkably high proportion of these captives had begun to write.

They did so for all the familiar reasons. Some of them wrote because, initially, survival seemed 'very doubtful indeed', and they wanted to leave some trace of themselves behind, as well of course as their own version of events.[7] Like others before them, these captives also wrote because they came from a profoundly Protestant culture that placed a high value on the written word, and that had endowed them with an expectation of peculiar and arduous trials, but also with a belief in ultimate redemption. 'It has pleased God to try us in the furnace of adversity for many years,' scribbled one of them:

68. Florentia Sale in captivity, a turban covering her lice-ridden hair.

But in every cloud that overhung our path, the rainbow of His mercy has shone conspicuously, forbidding us to despair, and reminding us that we are the object of His providential care.[8]

As the year advanced, and another army set out from India to Kabul, bent on rescue and revenge, still more of these captives wrote about their sufferings, emotions, and adventures because a return to Britain and its printing presses now appeared feasible again, and they clutched – as so many others had done – at the prospect of publication and momentary fame.

This was certainly true of Florentia, Lady Sale, wife of General Sir Robert Sale, whose captivity narrative *A Journal of the Disasters in Afghanistan* (1843) became a bestseller, and whose manuscript and printed words were studied by ministers, quoted in Parliament, and pored over by Queen Victoria.[9] She may have begun keeping a diary even before the British cantonment at Kabul came under siege. Once the situation deteriorated, she made notes whenever she could, keeping them in a bag tied around her waist under her clothes. An experienced imperial army wife, and tough as barbed-wire, Florentia Sale at least seems to have been confident that her virtue – and consequently her papers – were likely to remain safe even if she fell into Afghan hands. Her original intention in writing, she subsequently claimed, was to supply her military son-in-law (who died in the retreat) with material for a fully-fledged account of the war. But one suspects that this formidable, courageous, narrowly opinionated and immensely selfish woman, who was impatient of most males outside her family circle, also wanted her voice heard and her moment in the spotlight. To the early Victorian public, Florentia Sale would indeed become a heroine, the first British woman ever to achieve nationwide fame in connection with her own contribution to military action overseas, and as such a precursor of Florence Nightingale. But to her fellow-captives in Afghanistan, Florentia Sale and her relentless pursuit of copy were a pain and something of a joke. 'Lady Sale at Lawrence and the men for more particulars,' groaned Captain William Anderson in June 1842, after her Ladyship had wandered yet again, paper and pencil in hand, from her own loosely guarded room into theirs. 'I gave her a yarn yesterday.'[10]

Behind Anderson's tone lay not just personal exasperation and an element of masculine patronising, but also literary rivalry. Since many of these captives were educated, and since they were mewed up for months in moderately benign though unsanitary conditions, with nothing to do but kill lice, tolerate their own and each other's stench, and, in the case of some of the married women, give birth, writing narratives became a widespread habit amongst them and a highly competitive business. There are references to accounts by at least a dozen British army officers held captive in Afghanistan in 1841–2, though some of these texts seem not to have survived.[11] Anderson himself, like other East India Company men before him, showed how instinctively some imperial fighters turned in leisure or emergency to the business of writing. He had brought a notebook with him to Afghanistan in which he routinely jotted down pieces of information useful for a man of his trade: remedies for cholera and scorpion stings, instructions for preparing embrocation for weary horses, recipes for suet puddings and other nostalgic delicacies. Once captive, Anderson simply turned this home-made self-help manual back to front, wrote 'Private' on the cover, and began to pen his narrative, systematically keeping an illustrated diary on the right-hand pages, while inserting the more impersonal observations he was trained to make on the left-hand pages.

Several female captives, too, and not only Lady Sale, responded with pen, pencil and paper to the rare opportunity, for them, of being at the

69. A sketch of his cell in William Anderson's captivity narrative.

centre of imperial and military action: 'able to judge for themselves the actual state of affairs'. 'Our party', recorded one anonymous woman of those confined with her, 'were seized with a scribbling mania. Every one seemed occupied in composing "The only True and Particular Account" of the Kabul insurrection.' She noted too how some of the writers, like many captivity narrators before them, resorted to different modes of fabrication: 'Diaries were ante-dated, and made to assume the tone and character of memoranda written at the period. Those who had the most retentive memories, or fertile inventions, were likely to prove the most successful in this employment.'[12] The sheer number and variety of texts emerging from this expensive Afghanistan episode, by those in uniform and those not, and by women as well as men, form – at one level – a final, conclusive demonstration of how accustomed the British were by this stage to overseas captivity crises, and how automatically they converted them into different kinds of prose. They had been here before. And amidst all the anger, humiliation, tedium and terror, they knew what to do.

What remained the same, what was different

In some ways, indeed, what happened in Afghanistan was not an aberration in British imperial terms at all. As in every captivity crisis featured in this book, there were particular, contributing factors involved, like the frailties of the British commander, General Elphinstone, dispatched to Kabul in an heroic but on this occasion misconceived blow against ageism. But while such conspicuous idiocies attracted scorching criticism at the time, and have been satirised in novels and histories of this Afghan War ever since, to focus solely upon them is to neglect more significant and enduring problems, failures, and tendencies.

All too evident in this Afghanistan episode were certain constraints on British power that had existed in the 1600s, and could still prove problematic in some contexts a quarter of a millennium later. Even now, in the 1840s, the British could find themselves under pressure *vis-à-vis* numbers and availability of manpower and suffer militarily as a result. Since Afghanistan was landlocked, the Royal Navy's range and firepower signified little, and therefore the onus fell on land troops, Britain's besetting Achilles heel. 'The Russians were said to have an army of hundreds of thousands and untold wealth', a sepoy who fought for the British, Sita Ram, recorded hearing during the lead-up to this crisis. As a result, he wrote, some of his comrades and some of the British themselves anticipated the collapse of the East India Company's dominion: 'the end of the

Sirkar's rule was predicted. For how could they withstand their enemies with only twelve or thirteen regiments of Europeans, which were all that were then in India?'[13]

This was actually an underestimate of the number of white soldiers in India by this stage. But it was certainly the case that, of necessity, most troops in the Army of the Indus were not British at all, but Afghan supporters of Shah Shuja, and above all Indian cavalry and infantry from the Company's legions. When the crisis came, many of these 'loyal Afghans' proved unreliable, while some of the Indian troops succumbed very rapidly to freezing temperatures for which their own background left them utterly unprepared. None of this might have mattered had the British commanded the sort of overwhelming technological superiority still sometimes routinely attributed to nineteenth-century imperialists, but they did not. Afghanistan illustrates yet again what other captivity crises in this book have demonstrated: that before 1850, and in terms of land warfare, a technology gap between highly organised Western states and the rest could not always be relied upon, and – even when present – sometimes turned out not to be decisive. The British emphatically possessed far superior artillery at Kabul in 1841, but this was cancelled out by the Afghans' better rifles, and the fact that the latter were often more accurate shots.[14]

Then, again, the sort of collapse in morale and cohesion that occurred among the British at Kabul cantonment and on the subsequent retreat, would have been familiar to Tangier's reluctant garrison back in the 1670s and '80s. At Kabul, as in Tangier, regimental pay was sometimes badly in arrears, tensions surfaced between some of the English and some of the Irish troops, and some soldiers tried to desert or simply refused to do their job. It should come as no surprise to readers of this book that these defaulters were not in the main Indian troops, but poor British and Irish whites. 'The sepoys alone appear to have behaved steadily to the last,' thundered one English magazine on the Kabul débâcle, '. . . We have abundant evidence of a lamentable want of discipline and proper spirit in the European troops.' 'The native troops in our service', agreed a Scottish journalist, 'often behaved with more gallantry and devotedness than the Europeans.'[15] Afghanistan, indeed, confirmed some among the British political and military elite in the view that 'the brave sepoy . . . [held] a station quite on a par with our own excellent yeomanry', whereas the mass of British and Irish common soldiers were by contrast markedly inferior stock and by no means an invariable imperial asset.[16]

As this suggests, even now, those Britons engaged in implementing empire were far from monolithic. Compensated for their smallness by a remarkably strong state, and by a precocious and ever more assertive

collective national ideology, the British none the less remained characterised by certain internal divisions that found ample expression in their
overseas enterprise. Even now, at the start of the Victorian era, divisions
amongst them, divisions of social class, divisions of religion, divisions of
language and precise national background, and the gender division, proved
sometimes more grating and more obtrusive than differences between Britons
and particular non-Europeans.

In Afghanistan, as in Tangier in the 1680s, or Mysore in the 1780s,
defeat and captivity could lead to these fault lines within the British ranks
gaping open. When Afghan leaders demanded and received the officers'
wives from the sad caravan retreating from Kabul in January 1842, the
husbands concerned seem to have been content to go with them. By so
doing, they left the lower ranks in their care and under their command –
British as well as Indian – to their fate. As one NCO who survived grimly
remembered:

> The men in front then said 'The officers seem to take care for them-
> selves. Let them push on if they like, we will halt till our comrades in
> the rear come up.'[17]

And so these white subalterns waited, and most of them died. Captivity,
and the writings spawned by it, exposed the gulf between imperial Britain's
poor and privileged just as powerfully. Most manuscript and printed
accounts from the time make a point of calling the officers' wives who
were captured 'ladies', while referring to other captive British females as
'women' or merely by their surnames. Some of the other ranks' womenfolk were omitted from the record altogether. We know the names of at
least two soldiers' wives, a Mrs Bourke and a Mrs Cunningham, who were
taken by Afghan tribesmen on the retreat from Kabul and never handed
back. Instead, these women remained in Afghanistan for the rest of their
lives, embracing Islam and new, Afghan, husbands. Their memory endures
in Afghan folklore, and is cherished as a demonstration of the triumph of
Islam – and Afghan masculinity – over infidel invaders. But almost all
British writings of the time (and since) ignore these women, and others
of their sort who shared the same fate.[18]

Yet most contemporary accounts acknowledge how captivity in
Afghanistan – like other captivity crises – sometimes strained and altered
British identities. As always, it was the youngest captives who proved most
susceptible. Captain Anderson and his wife lost their eleven-year-old
daughter, 'Tootsey', to an Afghan family in Kabul for several months in
1841. When restored to the parents whom she now called infidels to their

face, she was reported to have 'totally forgotten English . . . and could only chatter away in Persian'.[19] Some adults involved in these captivities also changed. It is often claimed that the British, and particularly the English, clung stoutly and ostentatiously to their own customs and company when exposed to foreign and imperial climes: stubbornly 'dining in the jungle' on roast beef, in black tie or pearls as it were. Yet this is a late and a very selective piece of national and imperial mythology. As countless episodes in this book have demonstrated, in the seventeenth, eighteenth, and early nineteenth centuries, some Britons reached accommodations with, and occasionally became amalgamated with the various non-European peoples amongst whom they found themselves. The same remained true to a degree in Afghanistan in the 1840s.

It is worth examining in this regard two very different images of captives. One is the work of Emily Eden, the highly intelligent sister and chatelaine of Lord Auckland, governor-general of India. In June 1841, she painted from life portrait heads of Dost Muhammad Khan, the ousted amir of Afghanistan, and three other male members of his family, who were then being held by the British in genteel imprisonment at Barrackpore. Dark-eyed, dignified, and austere, the men wear elaborate white turbans, rich robes and beards; and three of them gaze pointedly away from the unveiled female amateur who is so eagerly and – in terms of their culture – so inappropriately portraying them. These particular Afghan captives (who would soon return home in triumph) manifestly have little intention of adjusting to, or even acknowledging their surroundings, and are reluctant to compromise what they are. Compare this with some of the images of British prisoners in Kabul drawn from life by Lieutenant Vincent Eyre, with the intention (which he survived to carry out) of supplying his captivity narrative with illustrations should it ever reach the press. One heavily bearded British officer lounges cross-legged against a wooden chest, his hair bound up in a turban, a slippered foot protruding from his robe; another officer of the Queen stands barefoot, his long overdress slung over his shoulders, his hair done up in a striped cloth, and with an elaborate hookah in hand and in use. Without knowing, one would scarcely suspect that these men were British, or Christian, or professional agents of empire.

The disparity between these two sets of images was partly one of circumstance. Dost Muhammad Khan and his family were elite captives and ostensibly guests of the governor-general, at Barrackpore, so the conventions were observed. Servants were available to groom and oil their beards; and customary costumes were kept freshly laundered and in repair. British captives in Afghanistan on the other hand were a bedraggled lot coping

70. Emily Eden's water-colour of the four Afghan captives.

71. Captain Bygrave by
Vincent Eyre.

with harsher conditions. Their skin was burnt brown from exposure, they
had few razors or any other grooming aids to hand, and their original
costumes had either rotted on their backs or been lost in the retreat. Yet
the contrast between how these very different captives allowed themselves
to be represented goes deeper than this. Evident in some of the British
subjects drawn by Eyre is an active acceptance of new and different
clothing and bodily postures. It would be wrong to interpret this as the
swagger of confident imperialists moving coolly and assuredly in and out
of different cultures, though Eyre himself may have added an element of
flamboyance to his original drawings before publishing them. When he
made his initial sketches, however, neither he nor his subjects knew if they
would survive, never mind return home; though they did know, all too
well, that they had lost. At some level, at least, these are drawings of individuals submitting to metamorphosis, ruefully adjusting to new surroundings, and in some cases even wilfully blending in. Such candour may have
been one reason why, when Eyre did publish his text and illustrations in

72. Captive and artist: Lieutenant Vincent Eyre back in Britain.

London in 1843, they were roundly condemned by some senior British military figures.[20]

As this book has shown, such flexibility in the face of enforced exposure to alien surroundings had many precedents. Time and time again, British men and women taken captive in the Mediterranean, or in North America, or in India, changed their behaviour, their language, their outward appearance, and even their political and religious allegiance. Often this occurred under pressure and only temporarily; but in some cases it happened permanently and out of a measure of choice. Such adaptability in the face of other cultures was never confined merely to Britons taken captive. The cliché that Britons overseas clung to their peculiar, parochial habits ('Mad dogs and Englishmen go out in the midday sun', etc.) needs examining carefully and sceptically, like every other cliché, in the light of all, and not just some of the evidence. Always sparse in number, the British would scarcely have been able – or wanted – to attempt empire on the scale that they did, or be the avid emigrants that they remain today, had not some of them possessed in fact a markedly chameleon tendency.

In the case of the Britons held in Afghanistan, a measure of adjustment and mimicry may have been easier because their captors were Muslims. In this respect, too, what happened here in 1841 and 1842 was in keeping with other, earlier captivity crises. Once again, and as in Morocco and Mysore, British overseas enterprise was slowed down, embarrassed – and in this case defeated – by an Islamic power. Once again, Islam revealed its capacity to supply non-Western opponents of Western empire with a cohesion that was often otherwise lacking. This said, and as in other regions of the world, events in Afghanistan rarely revealed a clean and unambiguous gulf between Muslims on the one hand and British imperialists on the other. When the British invaded in 1838, they did so in alliance with an exiled Muslim ruler, and with the military support of other Muslims. And, as was usually the case, their own recorded reactions to contact with an Islamic culture were mixed and confused.

Britons caught up in this crisis regularly described the Afghans who fought them, defeated them, and captured them as barbarians, and as 'wild and savage men', cruel, primitive, treacherous, and all too susceptible to 'white-bearded mullahs'.[21] Simultaneously, however, and sometimes in the identical letter, narrative or report, Afghan Muslims were also described as 'gallant' defenders of their freedom, full of 'energy and activity', 'frank, open, and manly . . . brave and industrious', the very same adjectives that early Victorian Britons enjoyed applying to themselves.[22] It helped of course that Afghanistan was a cold, mountainous country full of warriors. It helped even more that it had resisted them successfully. None the less, this captivity crisis demonstrated yet again that, for the British, as for other Europeans, Islamic societies rarely appeared comprehensively and unalloyedly their own backward or malign antithesis. Those attached to the Crescent might often be the enemy; and were certainly often colonised. But they could not easily be merely despised or invariably and unmitigatedly othered, which was one reason why tough, angry and captive British army officers were willing to pose and be represented in Afghan dress.

Yet the most obvious respect in which events in Afghanistan in 1841 and 1842 form a fitting climax to, and summation of the themes treated in this book, is that they underline again just how central captivity was, both to the British experience of imperial conflict in this period, and to how Britons at home understood the business of empire. As critics of the war complained, before the Kabul insurrection in November 1841, Parliament and the media in Britain devoted scant attention to what its

73. Lieutenant Muir
by Vincent Eyre.

troops and their Afghan and Indian auxiliaries were doing in Afghanistan, a place that most Britons would have been hard-pressed to identify on a map. 'A few words written in the cabinet of England are like the sudden removal of a tiny bolt, setting free the complex forces of a great engine!' wrote the Whig colonial administrator and reformer, Henry Lushington:

The vast machinery of oriental war stirs and works; armies march, artillery rolls, lands are wasted, cities are stormed, the thrones of Asia go down, half the human race is shaken with alarm. *And for all this – the nation does not care.*[23]

But the British nation began to care enormously once things went wrong and captives were seized. As had always been the case, Britons taken captive served to personalise overseas and imperial events and emergencies, making them seem far more immediate and engrossing to their countrymen at large. The fate of the captives, judged one British magazine in 1843, had 'excited more interest in the mother country than all the other events of the war'. 'The history of the world', declared the *Illustrated London News,* in an article that same year on the Kabul captives, 'barely contains scenes of more terrific interest.' So great was the public clamour, that the politicians were left with little choice but to act. In the wake of the disaster at Kabul, virtually the whole of British official and military actions became focused, as M.E. Yapp argues, on restoring national prestige and on recovering the captives, policy objectives that were seen as identical.[24]

If all this seems reminiscent of another international crisis over captives, then – in all sorts of ways – it is. The closest recent parallel to the British furore over its Afghan detainees in 1842 was the absorption of the White House and the American public in the fate of the Iranian hostages between 1979 and 1981. Both crises were prompted by the prime Western power of its day becoming linked with support for a highly unpopular Muslim ruler, Shah Shujah in the British case, the deposed Shah of Iran in the American case. And in both cases the number of individuals directly caught up in the hostage crisis was modest by the normal standards of global violence. Yet, for the British in 1842, as for Americans some 140 years later, this proved quite beside the point. Warren Christopher, the US Deputy Secretary of State who organised the release of the Iranian hostages, put it well:

In the long sweep of history, the Iranian hostage crisis may occupy little more than a page. Yet it riveted the attention of the US government for more than fourteen months and preoccupied the country as an event rarely has.[25]

As Part Two of this book demonstrates, Britain, and what is now the United States, have long possessed an influential culture of captivity in common. That culture has usually expressed itself in different ways on the different sides of the Atlantic, but it stems from, and points to, these societies' linked pasts and joint Protestant tradition. This transatlantic culture of captivity arguably also points to a certain shared isolationism and insularity. Rather like the United States is now, Britain in its imperial phase was at once a power with vast global interests and influence, and simultaneously an often inwardly obsessed society whose citizens in general cared little for much of the time about events beyond their own borders. Overseas captivity crises and narratives of different kinds mattered over the centuries as far as imperial Britain was concerned – as they continue to matter in America – in part because of their bridging of the global on the one hand and the national and local on the other. It might be possible to disregard the outside world in normal circumstances, but not when Britons (or Americans) were dramatically caught fast or suffering there.

Yet the most significant parallel between British responses to the catastrophes in Afghanistan in 1842, and American responses to the hostage crisis in Iran in 1979–81, goes deeper than this.

For the British, overseas captivity crises in the seventeeth and eighteenth centuries, and even in the early 1800s, had often called forth more profound anxieties that winning and keeping territorial empire was too dangerous and might be beyond their capacity. Tales of captivity were not generated and scrutinised primarily because they deflected attention from Britons' own aggression, though this was sometimes part of their effect. They were scribbled and pored over as explorations of fear, risk and deeply felt constraints. But the Afghanistan captivity crisis was significantly different. To be sure, there were continuities between some of the weaknesses and divisions displayed in 1841–2 and earlier British imperial débâcles, but in terms of domestic responses there was also a crucial and perceptible change. The premier emotion displayed by the British in 1842 – as by Americans in 1979 – was not anger, or even humiliation, so much as shock and astonishment. By the 1840s, most prosperous Britons no longer expected to fail, or to be seriously constrained on the global stage. The domestic agitation over the Afghan captives, which was of a different and greater volume and scale than anything that had gone before, testified paradoxically to the degree that Victorian Britons had come to take for granted their nation's unique 'character of success'.[26] Like Americans at the time of the Iran crisis and since, they now viewed themselves as the most powerful nation in the world, and were consequently utterly taken aback, traumatised, and obsessed when a comparatively weak opponent damaged them and held their compatriots at its mercy.

To this extent, the Afghanistan captivity crisis marks both a summation of many of the themes treated in this book, and the onset of a different phase of British imperialism and imperial awareness. In the immediate aftermath of the crisis, some writers and politicians did hark back to earlier imperial traumas. British defeat in Afghanistan was occasionally likened to the humiliations of the lost war with Revolutionary America; and references were made to Tipu Sultan's tiger legions and to the captives of Mysore. Yet it is striking how – on this occasion – other, more imperturbable voices rapidly cut in and took charge of the post-mortem. Ancient history, wrote a singularly unexcited Dr Arnold, pondering the lessons of Kabul, was full of examples of individual Roman consuls and their legions being wiped out in stray imperial battles: 'but then the next year another Consul and his legions go out, just as before.' Arnold's use of a Roman parallel was eloquent, and his optimism entirely justified. The famous roll-call by Jack Gallagher and Ronald Robinson makes the point:

> Between 1841 and 1851 Great Britain occupied or annexed New Zealand, the Gold Coast, Labuan, Natal, the Punjab, Sind and Hong Kong. In the next twenty years, British control was asserted over Berar, Oudh, Lower Burma and Kowloon, over Lagos and the neighbourhood of Sierra Leone, over Basutoland, Griqualand and the Transvaal; and new colonies were established in Queensland and British Columbia.[27]

In the wake of a signal imperial and military calamity, the military, commercial, missionary and entrepreneurial legions of Victorian Britain were not simply going out just as before. They were going out faster still and even further.

The lack of sustained, worried introspection in the aftermath of a conspicuous defeat and a major captivity crisis, and the absence after 1841 of even a pause in the rate of Britain's global advance and aggression take us in many respects into a different imperial era. Back in 1600, when our story began, empire for the English had been something that the great Islamic powers, the Chinese, and some Catholic Europeans were adept at, but not them. As far as their own extra-European forays were concerned, reverses were for a long time as conspicuous as successes, and often resulted in definitive retreats. As Joyce Lorimer reminds us, the English frequently devoted far more thought, money and energy in the early decades of the seventeenth century to colonising Guiana, than they did to their settlements on the Atlantic seaboard of North America. But their numerous efforts in the former region miscarried, and they were forced to retire in the face of Dutch competition.[28] Tangier, as we have seen, captured the imagination as well as the unprecedented largesse of the English state. Yet it, too, had to be given up, and thereafter the English, and later the British, made no serious attempt at securing a permanent enclave in North Africa for almost two centuries. Instead, they tolerated for much of the time the existence of Barbary's corsairs, grimly paying ransoms and protection money, as the necessary price for a British presence in Gibraltar and Minorca. Even so, European rivals were still able on two occasions to expel them by force from the latter base.[29]

And while Britain's power expanded enormously both inside and outside Europe in the century after 1689, its politicians and public remained for a long while apprehensive and even incredulous. It still appeared possible that all their novel global reach, wealth and grandeur would vanish as rapidly and as embarrassingly as the Emperor's new clothes. So when a future prime minister, the earl of Shelburne, contemplated Britain's defeat against Revolutionary Americans, he was immediately fearful that this was only the start of the rot. 'Away goes the fishery and 20,000 seamen,' he predicted glumly: 'After this will follow the West Indian islands, and in the process of time, Ireland itself; so that we should not have a single foot of land beyond the limits of this island.'[30] By the same token, the defeats and captivities inflicted on the East India Company by Haidar Ali and Tipu Sultan frightened London into a formal declaration in 1784 that no further advance in India could be contemplated, and led some to predict that Asia, too, was a frontier much too far. It is easy to forget how stubborn such insecurities proved among men and women who naturally lacked our retrospective understanding of the 'Rise of the British Empire'. Even in the early 1800s, there were experienced and sensible soldiers, pundits and politicians, who believed that it was far more likely that Britain itself would soon be conquered and made part of Napoleon's empire in Europe than that its own extra-European empire would endure for very long.[31]

By the 1840s, however, the world looked very different, both to the British, and to those co-existing, competing and contending with them. True, the Afghanistan crisis provoked tremors even at the highest level. 'George', wrote Emily Eden in 1841 of her brother, the governor-general of India, 'wonders every day how we are allowed to keep this country a week.'[32] The perception, even at the acme of their power, that the British were being *allowed* to retain India, as distinct from thoroughly controlling it themselves, is well worth noting. But although expressions of imperial uncertainty and insecurity persisted – and with good reason always would – they were now more easily and quickly drowned out. The more representative British voice was not any more that of Lord Auckland, soon to be dismissed from the governor-generalship in disgrace. The more representative voice belonged to a deservedly obscure poet greeting the rescue by force of the captives in Afghanistan:

> *Io Triumphe*! Afghanistan's won!
> *Io Triumphe*! Our great task is done!
> Captivity!
> Thy thralls are free;
> Britons have nought to do with thee![33]

Yet how true could this be in fact? How and how far had these small islands been able finally to evade their intrinsic constraints?

The domestic underpinnings of Britain's national egotism and imperial reach by 1850 are by now well known, and in some cases have been touched on already. There was – as there had long been – its strong state and fiscal inventiveness. There was its unparalleled navy and merchant fleet, backed by a chain of dockyards and bases around the globe. There were the financial tentacles of the City of London, in which both Britain's older landed elites and its newer plutocrats were involved. There was the knowledge that Britain had formally freed its colonial slaves in 1838, after earlier pulling out of the slave trade, and that its navy and diplomats were actively coercing other powers to do the same. For many, these initiatives crowded out guilt about Britain's earlier, busy slave-trading, and offered irresistible proof that empire, modern liberty, and benevolence were fully compatible. And complementing all these sources of wealth, power and complacency, there was a widespread conviction that Britain was a chosen nation, morally serious and actively reforming, and reserved by God for great things. A striking aspect of the Afghanistan captivity literature is how often the authors involved – unlike many earlier British officer class captives – carefully record their Sunday rituals of worship and moments of private prayer.[34]

In addition, Britain's geographical smallness had paid off in a new and vital way. It was in large part because rich deposits of coal and iron, together with abundant water power, were situated so closely and so conveniently together within its narrow boundaries, that it was able to generate the world's first fully-fledged, mineral-based industrial revolution, although the full impact of this took longer to emerge than once was supposed. Even in 1800, Britain had still trailed behind both China and the Indian subcontinent in terms of its share of world manufacturing output; even then, by some economic criteria, it was possible to think of 'a polycentric world with no dominant centre'.[35] Not so by 1850. By then, a previously unknown level of industrial innovation and productivity, combined with Britain's older financial and commercial riches, had made the business of acquiring, running, and exploiting a vast overseas empire much easier – though never at any time easy.

Industrial and technological advance brought with them more powerful, efficient, and mass-produced weapons of control and coercion. Queen Victoria's iron-clad, steam-driven battleships, boasted Lord Macaulay, could have annihilated the ancient navies of 'Tyre, Athens, Carthage,

Venice and Genoa together' in 'a quarter of an hour'. Industrial and technological advance meant faster, cheaper, and more reliable communications, both within particular imperial zones, and between them and Britain. Trains and telegraphs spanned distances that had previously appeared unmanageable. Emigrants, soldiers, sailors, administrators, exports, and ideas travelled out to imperial destinations at a much faster rate and in far larger quantities; while information, imports and profits flowed back to Britain's shores as never before. 'A most powerful steam flotilla has been . . . created,' purred Sir John Hobhouse to the House of Commons in 1842:

> They have made the communications between India and England regular and quick – they have opened the Indus to British commerce – they have displayed the British flag, for the first time in history, on the Tigris and Euphrates.[36]

As this suggests, industrial and technological advance also fostered arrogance, a sense that Britain was in the vanguard of modernity, and consequently that its invasions overseas were both ineluctable and a motor of global progress. 'I tell them about steam-engines, armies, ships, medicine and all the wonders of Europe,' recorded a Scottish political agent of his interviews with Afghan leaders in the 1830s.[37] This did not save him from being subsequently hacked to pieces, but the assurance was unmistakable.

Better communications also made it easier for British governments to shape and regulate the imperial narrative at home. The English, Welsh, Scots, and (obviously but not exclusively) the Irish had never been unanimous in their reactions to overseas ventures. There had always been disagreements, doubts, and sharply discordant stories – as well as widespread indifference and profound ignorance. The invasion of Afghanistan in 1838, for instance, was condemned by *The Times* and the *Spectator* in London, and some more downmarket papers, as well as by most English-language newspapers in India.[38] The sheer volume and range of Britain's print culture made it almost impossible – at all times – to prevent dissenting voices and occasional, deeply embarrassing disclosures. But the more rapid transmission of information from imperial locations back to London, together with the faster circulation of news within the United Kingdom itself made possible by railways, by macadamed roads, by cheaper newsprint and by growing literacy, gave politicians and imperial officials means and opportunities to lead and shape opinion they had previously lacked.

Back in the 1770s and '80s, American Revolutionaries had sometimes contrived to have their versions of battles and controversies printed and circulated in London before any official British version was available. Compare this lack of grip and censorship with the imperial authorities' meticulous organisation and ordering of information during the Indian rebellion of 1857:

> At weekly or fortnightly intervals, official narratives of the latest occurences were compiled . . . by the Governments of Bengal, the North-Western provinces etc . . . The narratives were forwarded to the Governor-General and copies made and sent to London. In addition, a summary of military intelligence was prepared every fortnight by the Military Department for despatch by each mail steamer.[39]

Now that highly detailed, seemingly authoritative narratives of this sort reached London so much faster, and could be promptly distributed, after appropriate alterations, by way of the new national broadsheets, it became more difficult for men and women to remain uninfluenced by them, and harder too for more idiosyncratic, individual narratives of empire and encounter to find an audience, or even a publisher.

A closer monitoring of imperial writings, and a greater degree of homogeneity among those published, were already apparent during the Afghanistan crisis. The fact that the most successful and well-publicised captivity narrative to emerge from it was written by a woman does not disprove this point, rather the reverse. Waspish enough to entertain and savour of independence, Florentia Sale's was an essentially conformist, imperially zealous text: 'What are *our lives* when compared with the honour of our country?' – which was just what one would have expected from the wife of an army general, a favourite of Queen Victoria, and a correspondent of the prime minister. The fact that the author was female probably also made her tale of captivity and defeat more acceptable to conventional British patriots and imperialists. Any weakness and fear in its pages could be put down to her gender, while passages of self-sacrifice and courage appeared all the more impressive from a member of the weaker sex. There was another respect too in which printed accounts of this Afghanistan crisis revealed a greater conformity. No captivity text seems to have been published on this occasion by anyone outside the officer class. The likes of Sarah Shade, or William Whiteway, or Joseph Pitts, or Thomas Pellow, and certainly George Thomas would find it harder now to set their stories of empire free. Some disgruntled captives in uniform and other poor whites caught out in imperial situations continued to write, but they were less likely after 1850 to publish.[40]

But industrialisation's most crucial contribution to Victorian imperial confidence and aggression was not the factory chimney, or the steamship, or the mechanization of the press, or ultimately the Gatling gun, but its easing of former anxieties about population levels. On the one hand, the new jobs and greater agricultural productivity it made possible allowed Great Britain's population to come close to quadrupling over the nineteenth century, without any of the subsistence crises that Malthus had anticipated. (Though both Ireland's industrial and demographic experience were substantially and terribly different.)[41] On the other hand, this unprecedented population growth enabled Victorian Britons to regard the ceaseless outflow of soldiers, sailors, administrators and emigrants from their shores with greater equanimity. They no longer feared, to the extent that earlier generations had done, that there were far too few of them. Instead, the argument that Patrick Colquhoun had deployed now became a widely current one: that the sheer abundance of Britons rendered overseas empire logical and indispensable. By the late nineteenth century, even America's leading anti-imperialist, Carl Schurz, was allowing himself to think in these terms. '*Nothing could be more natural*', he wrote: 'than that, as the population pressed against its narrow boundaries, Englishmen should have swarmed all over the world.'[42] Before 1800, this version of cause and effect had rarely appeared natural at all.

Indeed, there were important ways in which – for all its new material wealth, technology and physical force by 1850, and the ingenuity of its actors – Britain's empire remained in fact deeply *un*natural, and even downright peculiar. The empire always seemed bitterly unnatural of course to many of the men and women ruled by it, though others supported it, or were simply too caught up in the business of survival to think much about it one way or another. But Britain's empire was also inherently unnatural for the familiar reason: the utter smallness at its core. Recovering the voices embedded in successive captivity crises has revealed – along with many other things – how different Britons coped over time with the challenges of smallness. But for all the expedients, the tremendous rate of change, and the growing, terrible power, Britain's domestic limits were ultimately non-negotiable. To this extent, Queen Victoria was precisely emblematic of her empire. Statues of her (invariably much larger than life and raised high on pedestals) preside over town squares around the world, while her name remains linked even now with huge tracts of land and mighty natural phenomena. Yet the reality behind this global ubiquity and the calculated evocations of tremendous size was actually a dumpy woman less than five feet tall. Victoria the Great was also Victoria the small.

An awareness of the disparities between Britain's domestic dimensions and its grand imperial frontage surfaces in even the most strident imperial propaganda. 'The British empire', explained a former royal geographer, G.H. Johnston, on a map of the world generously picked out in red and published in honour of the Third Imperial Conference in London in 1902:

> is fifty-five times the size of France, fifty-four times the size of Germany, three and a half times the size of the United States of America, with quadruple the population of all the Russias.

The studious number-crunching, like the points of comparison selected – all of them physically bigger powers than the United Kingdom itself – is eloquent both of tremendous pride and a certain trepidation. 'Greater Britain,' Johnston continued, 'that is the possessions of the British people over the sea, is one hundred and twenty-five times the size of Great Britain.'[43] So how was this extraordinary construct conceivably to be retained and kept together?

All empires and great powers suffer from insecurity and a sense of transience. This is the flip side of arrogance and aggression. But as those presiding over it sometimes acknowledged, Britain's imperium was peculiarly conditional upon circumstances beyond its control and auxiliaries outside itself. Much of its territory and influence were owing to the decline of the great eastern empires, and the weakening of the Spanish and Portuguese empires, processes that Britain had sometimes assisted but scarcely initiated. The inception of *Pax Britannica* had been contingent upon the post-Napoleonic exhaustion of France, which had always previously competed furiously for territory, while challenging and de-stabilising Britain's own colonies. *Pax Britannica*'s persistence relied upon the fact that, before 1870, no single German state existed. It relied too upon Russia continuing to concentrate, as China did, on its own internal demons and empire; just as it relied upon the United States not seeking a global role, for all that it was expanding and growing richer every year. Most of all perhaps, British imperium depended on those it ruled in Asia, Africa, the Pacific, North America, and Europe not developing the sort of fierce nationalist ideologies that the British themselves had forged so precociously. As more thoughtful Britons recognised, these external preconditions for their imperial pre-eminence were unlikely to endure for very long.

There was a further vital and vulnerable degree to which Britain's primacy was heavily dependent upon others. Of necessity, the so-called British empire had always been a cross-cultural enterprise in fact, relying in the Mediterranean upon the assistance of North African Islamic powers, drawing on various Native Americans for vital information and military support, and – in America as in the Caribbean – recruiting black soldiers

Lesson 1.—The British Empire, 1.

1. The British Empire is the largest empire on the face of the globe.

(i) The sun never sets on the British Empire, and never rises.

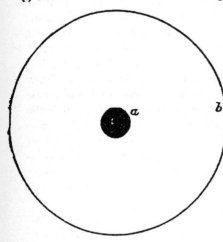

(ii) The British Empire is one hundred times as large as Great Britain. In this diagram, *a* is Great Britain; *b* represents the size of the British Empire.

2. It has an area of over 13,000,000 square miles.

(i) The British Empire is larger than the Russian Empire by above 4 millions of square miles.

(ii) The British Empire has about one-fourth of all the land on the globe.

3. It has a population of about 434,000,000.

(i) The British Empire has about one-fourth of all the people in the world.

(ii) The most thickly peopled part of it is the Valley of the Ganges.

74. Pride and insecurity: a 1913 textbook represents the disparity between British size and British empire.

in times of emergency. But in regard to imperial manpower and the money to pay them, Britain's dependence upon India was on an altogether different scale. To a very considerable degree, it was the Company's Indian troops – and Indian tax-payers – who supplied Britain with 'the rod of order, the shield of defence and the sword for further advance' that it wielded not just in the subcontinent itself, but increasingly as well in other parts of Asia, in the Middle East, and in Africa.[44] Awareness of this had been behind the cult of the brave and trusty Indian sepoy, and underlay much of the horror and hatred with which Britons reacted to the events they termed the Indian Mutiny in 1857–9.

It should come as no surprise by now that one of the most vivid expressions of this panic took the form of a captivity narrative, in this case a fictional one. In December 1857, Charles Dickens published a short story in his periodical *Household Words* entitled 'The Perils of Certain English Prisoners'. The story was set in South America in 1744, but what Dickens had in mind – as his readers recognised – were actually those Britons who had recently been killed, taken prisoner, or otherwise imperilled in the current rebellion in India. The story's hero is a private in the Royal Marines who is captured, along with other men, women and children, in an uprising against an English garrison. The rebels involved are described as 'niggers, savages, and pirates, hideous, filthy and ferocious in the last degree'. This careful selection of deviants (for the echoes of earlier captivity villains, Barbary *pirates* and Native American *savages* are clear) are led of course by a Roman Catholic, 'a hideous little Portuguese monkey'. There is also a spy in the English camp, a black called 'Christian George King', a sepoy-figure in other words, ostentatiously loyal, but secretly treacherous. After many hardships, heroic deeds and painful sacrifices, the marine and his English companions are rescued by 'good blue-jackets and red-coats . . . every man with his face on fire when he saw me, his countryman who had been taken prisoner'.

There are many things that might be said about this unpleasant tale. There is conspicuously its extreme anachronism: the way it reimagines the past to suit mid-Victorian imperial and nationalist expectations. A real-life English private soldier taken captive outside Europe in the eighteenth century (and after) would have had little expectation of a full-scale rescue party being dispatched to save him, and perhaps even little desire to be saved. As various captivity stories in this book suggest, such an individual – had he survived – might have been enslaved by the local population. On the other hand, he might have settled down placidly enough amongst them, abandoned his original identity, and found an indigenous wife. To modern readers, however, it is the overt racism of this tale that jars. 'I have stated myself to be a man of no learning', the marine is made to declare, 'and if I entertain prejudices, I hope allowance may be made . . . I never did like Natives, except in the form of oysters.'[45]

The shock of encountering this sort of language from a novelist normally associated with warm humanity can get in the way of recognising what lay at the root of Dickens's fury. He and many other Britons were certainly appalled by what they read about the 'Mutiny' and its white victims; but they were also more fundamentally dismayed. As they well knew, outside the realm of fiction, imperial Britain could not afford to rely only on 'good blue-jackets and red-coats' to fight on its behalf and rescue it in time of emergency, because there were not enough of these homegrown heroes available in a pre-conscription age. There never had been enough. Britain's own armed forces, and especially its army remained limited in size, absurdly so in terms of the global scale of its empire. Imperial defence, imperial enlargement, and imperial order had therefore to rely substantially on those whom Dickens presumed to style 'Natives'. And what would happen if these men were to prove unreliable like Christian George King, or rebelled *en masse* as tens of thousands of Indians formerly in imperial service were now doing? It was this fundamental manpower quandary – and not merely tales of massacre and rape – that made the British response to the events of 1857–9 so over-charged and emotional. Close, now, to the very apex of their global power and wealth, they thought they felt the cracks that always lay beneath them beginning to shift and widen.

Twenty-first-century issues

Those cracks have long since gaped open, swallowing up the British empire, together with those other European colonial empires it once competed against and ultimately surpassed in size. For many people in Britain now, the empire seems in retrospect embarrassing or anathema, or a subject of mild nostalgia and regret, or simply an irrelevance, in every sense a lost world. Either way, there is usually an assumption that the empire is a known quantity. It was about global power, which the British no longer have. For many people outside Britain, the empire also seems a known quantity. It was about global power, yes. But it was also about oppression, exploitation, violence, arrogance, slavery and racism, as indeed at different times and in different places it often was. For some, what the British and their miscellaneous auxiliaries once did represents no less than an early Holocaust, which demands apology and reparation, but requires no further investigation and no great effort to understand. Once again, the empire gets treated as a known quantity, as something that was uniform in character and *sui generis*.

The British empire is emphatically not a subject where the adage 'to understand all is to excuse all' should apply. But neither – and this must be my conclusion – is it yet sufficiently understood. In all sorts of ways, indeed, Britain's empire remains an unknown quantity. In part, this is a challenge for the historians. We still need to know far more than we do about the perspectives and actions of those whom the British sought to rule. We need to investigate far more thoroughly than we have how Britain's empire compared with other empires, both Western and non-Western, that influenced it throughout, and from which it regularly borrowed techniques and ideas of rule. In addition – and in two different respects – Britain and its overseas empire need approaching far more in tandem, and not separately as they generally have in the past.

At one level – and as writers as diverse as Sir John Seeley and Salman Rushdie have argued – this means treating Britain not as an Olympian initiator of empire elsewhere, but as a society that was itself caught up in, transformed, and sometimes traumatised by the business of empire, though never to the exclusion of other influences.[46] One of my purposes in *Captives* has been to demonstrate how wide and diverse the impress of empire was: how it affected Britain's economy, material life and politics, of course, but how it also impinged on private and public writings, religious and secular culture, polite and plebeian art, and on all sectors of society. Empire was never just the business of gentlemanly (or ungentlemanly) capitalists, of the politically influential, and the imperially grand and famous. As in every other part of the world, empire's impact on Britain and Ireland was directly and disproportionately felt by the unimportant and the poor, by the soldiers and sailors, by voluntary and involuntary emigrants and settlers, by small traders and fishermen, by multitudinous women and very many children. The history of empire has often been reconstructed as a grand and terrible saga of international and intercontinental rivalries, contacts and collisions, of epic initiatives and major acts of destruction and genocide: and it was indeed all of these things. But for the British, as for those they invaded, empire was also critically made up of small stories of small people whose lives were rendered utterly different and sometimes destroyed by it. This book has uncovered some of these individual stories: there are many thousands more, from these islands and beyond, that cry out for recovery and close analysis.

Insisting on the heterogeneity of the British experience of empire is important for more than just the British themselves. For while it is increasingly being argued – and I agree – that the British must come to terms with their imperial past, the logical corollary of this is often missed. The British need to understand more about their one-time empire: yes. But, by the same token, those concerned with this empire's impact on other parts of the world, require an accurate, comprehensive and nuanced understanding of Britain itself, the ways in which it was once powerful, but also the ways in which its power overseas was always constrained and sometimes faltered. In *Captives* I have insisted on complexity, drawing attention to the persistent divisions among 'the British', to the degree to which they were always dependent in their empire on those who were not British at all, and – above all – to the ways in which their limited population, limited geographical size and resources, and limited indigenous military power inflected and distorted their imperial enterprise throughout. My intention has not been to deny their devastating power and impact at particular times and in particular places, but to show how these people were not just warriors, but in different ways captives too.

Acknowledging both the power and the violence of Britain's one-time empire, and the degree to which it was always a miscellaneous and multi-stranded phenomenon, characterised at its core by insecurities and persistent constraints, is important for more than just historians. It is vital for a proper understanding of our twenty-first-century world. This is mani-festly true for the British themselves, but it also applies far more generally.

It is often argued now that the British should learn more about their one-time empire so as to remind themselves of their debts to different parts of the world. Here too I am inclined to agree. But there are selfish reasons, too, why the British could profitably acquaint themselves with what their empire involved in fact, rather than assuming they already know. Acknowledging the degree to which it was not simply global and grasping, but also insecure, patchy, and dependent on others and causes outside itself, might mitigate the sense of decline and nostalgia: the persistent feeling that this empire ended because of some deep-rooted national malaise and a lack of grip. As Paul Kennedy suggests, it is the fact that this empire lasted as long as it did that is remarkable, not its ultimate and entirely predictable demise. British politicians, in particular, might usefully wean themselves away from the notion that a grand and intrinsic national destiny has somehow got lost along the way. Winston Churchill, who knew his geopolitics, once declared that: 'We in this small island have to make a supreme effort to keep our place and status, *the place and status to which our undying genius entitles us.*'[47] Churchill was absolutely right to see in British smallness an inherent challenge and obstacle: but the yearning revealed in his words for a special, global status in the wake of lost empire has sometimes distorted post-war British policy. In particular, it has encour-aged a persistent inclination to pursue empire vicariously by clambering like a mouse on the American eagle's head. That great bird needs no assis-tance, and we should look to our own directions.

Then there is the urgent matter of race. There are those who argue, with the utmost sincerity, that were the British to remind themselves of their empire it would only further incite the racism inextinguishably asso-ciated with it. Others argue, with equal passion, that one of empire's lega-cies has been a rooted racism in Britain that will require massive work to extirpate. Both of these arguments seem to me not so much wrong, as overly simple and pessimistic. Empire, as this book has sought to show, was never a monochrome, predictable entity. British imperialists some-times espoused what we would now regard as fiercely racist ideologies. But the practicalities of running a huge multi-ethnic global construct where they, the British, were so much in the minority, meant that these ideolo-gies were always compromised and qualified in practice. For the British to familiarise themselves now with the racial mix and the ethnic messi-ness of their one-time empire, as well as with its intolerance, might be no bad thing. A wider knowledge, say, that 'British' rule in India relied in fact overwhelmingly on the bayonets of Catholic Irishmen on the one hand, and on Indian troops on the other, might open minds, not close them. To be sure, empire could and did deepen racial and cultural divides. But it also shook them up. Britain's current high level of racial violence *may* at some level be a legacy of empire, but the fact that this country now produces more mixed marriages and equivalent relationships per head of population than almost anywhere else in the world may also in some way be a legacy of empire. Either way, we should not assume that a past expe-rience of global empire of itself makes racism inescapable in Britain. That way lies both complacency and despair.

Looking at the history of this empire questioningly, and with an appre-ciation of how it was impacted on by Britain's own varieties of smallness, is important, however, far more widely. It is important, obviously, for those countries that were formerly colonised by Britain. It is scarcely to be wondered at that their populations sometimes harbour resentment, and even hatred of the British and other past colonisers, and a feeling of debts owed. No one likes to be invaded. But it is possible to exaggerate the power and the durable impact of these one-time colonisers, to make them seem more important and formidable than in fact they were. In some contact situations, colonisers were unquestionably drastic and lethal. Certain Native American peoples, like certain Pacific peoples, were wiped out by the germs English, Welsh, Scottish and Irish intruders carried with them, or subse-quently hunted to death by land-hungry settlers; while Africans transported as slaves across the Atlantic experienced an atrocity that was not peculiar to the British empire, but was certainly fostered by it. In other contexts, however, the impact of empire was more uneven, sometimes very shallow, and far more slow. Environments, economies, customs, power relations and lives were sometimes utterly devastated; but by no means always, because these intruders were frequently limited in number, and dependent often on a measure of indigenous tolerance. Minority languages, for instance, like many other forms of cultural diversity, have vanished at a much faster rate since 1945 than before, despite the disappearance of European empires. The enemy this time has not been arrogant colonial officials, but more insidious and ubiquitous invaders: television, Hollywood, cyberspace, and monster, multi-national corporations.

These are deeply controversial issues that arouse strong emotions, and about which no consensus will ever be possible. But, as this last example suggests, exploring what the British empire, and its European counterparts, were able to do in the past – and what they could not or did not do – matters for more than just academic reasons. We live in a post-colonial world, but we do not yet live in a post-imperial world. All of today's great powers, while eschewing the description 'empire', retain in fact an imperial component and quality, either because they still bear the impress of past European imperialisms, or because they possess an imperial tradition of their own, or both. India, that extraordinary experiment in democracy, none the less treats its Sikh and Kashmiri separatists/freedom-fighters with a ferocity that the Raj would scarcely have exceeded. Indonesia is a large, multi-ethnic polity dominated by the Javanese, whose control has often rested more on military force than on consent. The Chinese Republic rules over provinces that, in some cases, were conquered by former Chinese emperors long after the Spanish and Portuguese conquest of the New World, and – again – does not always do so with the conspicuous consent of the governed.[48] And then there is the United States, a fiercely anti-imperial, fiercely democratic republic that is also an empire like no other. It is an empire in the sense that much of its territory was originally acquired by force, purchase, and migration at the expense of other, weaker peoples. But it also possesses now a string of military bases across the globe, a paramount navy, and an air force that can strike anywhere. 'We are the first empire of the world to establish our sway without legions,' declared the American Reinhold Niebuhr in 1931. 'Our legions are dollars.' The dollar rules still: but now there are legions too.[49]

Is all this dangerous? Not necessarily. The sheer size of these twenty-first-century covert empires means that they are most unlikely to seize overseas territory as the old European empires once did. They have no need. It was Britain's very smallness that helped to drive – as well as constrain – its overseas enterprise, for without other peoples' land and resources it could not be powerful. Small can be aggressive; large can be confident and inward-looking. However, there is another side. Because its core was so constrained, and because it depended on maritime power, Britain's empire was always overstretched, often superficial, and likely to be limited in duration. The current behemoths, being in the main contiguous, land-based empires, are likely to prove far more enduring, and possess weapons of mass destruction of a kind that dead European empires never imagined.

And this is why looking intelligently, questioningly, and – above all – comparatively at Britain's empire is imperative, as is pondering the complex connections between size on the one hand, and levels of power and ambition on the other. The years between 1600 and 1850 saw a set of small islands acquiring astonishingly and at great cost the biggest global empire that the world has ever seen. The twentieth century witnessed this empire, and its fellow European empires, become one with Nineveh and Tyre, and the emergence in their stead of new nations in every continent. One of the challenges of the twenty-first century will be establishing how we can monitor, balance, and keep within bounds the vast, new multi-ethnic giants in our midst, that are both safer and more dangerous than the old maritime empires. Lest we fall captive.

APPENDIX

The Captivity Archive

In the United States, captivity narratives have long been a familiar source for novelists, artists and film-makers, as well as for historians. On the other side of the Atlantic, these texts have been explored and exploited far less. Yet manuscript and published accounts of captivity overseas were produced regularly in England and its adjacent countries, and in other parts of Europe, from at least the sixteenth century, and have remained prolific to this day. As should now be clear, modes of writing about captivity were – and are – many and diverse; and it needs stressing that, as far as Britain was concerned, thousands of captivity narratives were produced over the centuries in response to conflicts *inside* Europe, as well as in response to extra-European encounters outside the three large geographical regions that feature in this book. What follows is therefore a very select list in terms of provenance, chronology, and locations of stories told.

This is also a select list in that it is confined to those prose narratives with a high autobiographical content that are referred to in this book. It omits the innumerable ballads, poems and novels that were produced about captives, as well as the reports of individual experiences to be found in official documents of different kinds, though all of these formed part of a broad culture of captivity. Nor have I included general works, like Increase Mather's *An Essay for the Recording of Illustrious Providences* (1684), which contain factual captivity tales alongside other material. I have also omitted many British narratives about captivity that are very slight in length or content, as well as narratives published only in North America during this period, which were not slight at all, but which attracted only minimal attention on the other side of the Atlantic. Readers curious about the whole range of North American captivity narratives, both before and after 1783, should consult Alden T. Vaughan, *Narratives of North American Indian Captivity: A Selective Bibliography* (New York, 1983), and – better still – the hundreds of modern editions of these narratives published by Garland. Robert C. Doyle's *Voices from Captivity: Interpreting the American POW Narrative*

(Kansas, 1994), takes the story of America's obsession with captives up to the Vietnam War. Those wanting to investigate British captivities in regions other than those covered here, might start with I. J. Niven, L. Russell and K. Schaffer (eds), *Constructions of Colonialism: Perspectives on Eliza Fraser's Shipwreck* (1998), a set of essays on one of the most famous nineteenth-century Australian captivity narratives. For two recent British and Irish narratives (both of which contain references to earlier captivity stories), see John McCarthy and Jill Morrell, *Some Other Rainbow* (1993), and Brian Keenan, *An Evil Cradling* (1992).

In the case of accounts of captivity in my three zones of concentration published between 1600 and 1850, I have given the dates of all British and Irish editions within this period known to me, because the content – and sometimes the title – of these texts often changed significantly over time. Many of these texts went through yet more editions after 1850 and continue to be re-issued even today. In the case of narratives published only in North America, but of broader British imperial significance, I cite the date and place of publication of the first known edition. For narratives that survive in manuscript, I have provided the archival location and reference where available, together with details of any printed edition.

I would be astonished if the manuscript originals of more of the printed text listed below, together with additional writings by English, Irish, Scottish and Welsh men and women who underwent captivity in the Mediterranean region, India and Afghanistan, and North America in this period, did not still await discovery in archives, libraries and private homes throughout the world.

Mediterranean

Anon: 'The manner of the slavish usage suffered by the English in Barbary written by one who by woeful experience endured the same', Bodleian Library, Oxford, MS Rawlinson. c. 695.

Anon: *An Account of South-West Barbary . . . by a Person who had been a Slave there*, 1713.

Hector Black: *A Narrative of the Shipwreck of the British Brig Surprise*, 1817.

Francis Brooks: *Barbarian Cruelty*, 1693, 1700.

Edward Coxere: *Adventures by Sea*, ed. E.H.W. Meyerstein (Oxford, 1945). Includes Coxere's memories of captivity in Tripoli.

Adam Elliott: *A Narrative of my Travels, Captivity and Escape from Salle*, 1682, 1731, 1770.

James Irving: Narrative. Beinecke Library, Yale University, Osborn shelves c. 399; version published in Suzanne Schwarz (ed.), *Slave Captain* (Wrexham, 1995).

Vincent Jukes: *A Recovery from Apostacy set out in a Sermon*, by William Gouge, 1639.

Francis Knight: *A Relation of Seven Years Slavery*, 1640, 1745.

Thomas Lurting: *The Fighting Sailor Turned Peaceable Christian*, 1680, 1710, 1766, 1770, 1813, 1816, 1821, 1832, 1842.

Elizabeth Marsh: 'Narrative of her Captivity in Barbary'. Charles E. Young Research Library, University of California, Los Angeles; version published as *The Female Captive*, 2 vols, 1769.

William Okeley: *Eben-ezer: or, a Small Monument of Great Mercy*, 1675, 1684, 1764.

Thomas Pellow: *The History of the Long Captivity . . . of Thomas Pellow*, 1739?, 1740?, 1751, 1755.

Thomas Phelps: *A True Account of the Captivity of T. Phelps*, 1685, 1745.

Joseph Pitts: *A True and Faithful Account of the Religion and Manners of the Mohammetans . . . with an Account of the Author's Being Taken Captive*, 1704, 1717, 1731, 1778, 1810.

Devereux Spratt: *Autobiography of the Rev. Devereux Spratt* (1886). Includes account of his captivity in Algiers.

James Sutherland: *A Narrative of the Loss of H.M.'s ship The Litchfield*, 1761, 1768, 1788.

Thomas Sweet: *Deare Friends*, 1646. Printed letter narrating his captivity in Algiers, BL, 669.f.11 (3).

T.S.: *Adventures of Mr. T.S. an English Merchant, Taken Prisoner*, 1670, 1707.

Thomas Troughton: *Barbarian Cruelty*, 1751, 1788, 1807.

John Whitehead: Narrative. BL, Sloane MS. 90.

America

Ethan Allen: *A Narrative of Colonel Ethan Allen's Captivity* (Philadelphia, PA, 1779).

Thomas Anburey: *Travels through the Interior Parts of America*, 2 vols, 1789, 1791.

John Blatchford: *Narrative of the Remarkable Occurrences in the Life of John Blatchford* (New London, CT, 1788).

Jonathan Dickenson: *God's Protecting Providence, Man's Surest Help and Defence*, 1700, 1720, 1759, 1787, 1790.

John Dodge: *A Narrative of the Capture and Treatment of John Dodge, by the English* (Philadelphia, PA, 1779); reprinted in *The Remembrancer*, London, 1779.

Ebenezer Fletcher: *Narrative of the Captivity* (Amherst, MA, 1798).

Benjamin Gilbert: *Sufferings of Benjamin Gilbert and his Family*, 1785, 1790.

Henry Grace: *The History of the Life and Sufferings*, 1764, 1765.

John Gyles: 'A Memorial of the Strange Adventures and Signal Deliverances'. New York Public Library; version published as *Memoirs of Odd Adventures, Strange Deliverances* (Boston, MA, 1736).

Elizabeth Hanson, *An Account of the Captivity*, 1760, 1782, 1787, 1791.

Charles Herbert: *A Relic of the Revolution* (Boston, MA, 1847).

Thomas Hughes: *A Journal by Thomas Hughes*, ed. E.A. Benians (Cambridge, 1947).

Susanna Johnson: *The Captive American, or, A Narrative of the Sufferings*, 1797, 1802, 1803.

John Leeth: *A Short Biography . . . with an Account of his Life among the Indians*, ed. R.G. Thwaites (Cleveland, OH, 1904).

Jean Lowry: *A Journal of the Captivity* (Philadelphia, PA, 1760).

Thomas Morris: 'Journal of Captain Thomas Morris', in R.G. Thwaites (ed.), *Early Western Travels 1748–1846* (32 vols, Cleveland, OH, 1904–7), I.

Mary Rowlandson: *A True History of the Captivity and Restoration*, 1682. The first American edition of this narrative is entitled *The Sovereignty and Goodness of God*.

John Rutherfurd: 'Relation of a Captivity among the Indians of North America', National Army Museum, London, Acc 6003/17 (transcript); version published in M.M. Quaife (ed.), *The Siege of Detroit in 1763* (Chicago, IL, 1958).

Captain John Smith: *The General Historie of Virginia* (1624): the first full account by Smith of his capture, and 'rescue' by Pocahontas.

Hannah Swarton: Narrative in Alden T. Vaughan and Edward W. Clark (eds), *Puritans among the Indians: Accounts of Captivity and Redemption 1676–1724* (Cambridge, MA, 1981).

William Widger: 'Diary of William Widger of Marblehead, kept at Mill Prison, England, 1781', *Essex Institute Historical Collections*, LXXIII (1937).

John Williams: *The Redeemed Captive, returning to Zion* (Boston, MA, 1707).

Peter Williamson: *French and Indian Cruelty, Exemplified in the Life and Various Vicissitudes*, 1757, 1758, 1759, 1762, 1766, 1787, 1792, 1794, 1801, 1803, 1806, 1807, 1812, 1826.

India and Afghanistan

Anon: 'Narrative of events following surrender of Bidnanore'. NLS, MS 8432.

Anon: 'The English Captives at Cabul, by One of the Female Prisoners', *Bentley's Miscellany*, XIV (1843).

William Anderson: Narrative. IOL, MSS Eur. c 703.

Henry Becher: *Remarks and Occurences of Mr Henry Becher during his imprisonment*, Bombay, 1793.

Richard Runwa Bowyer: Narrative. IOL, MSS Eur. A94 and MSS Eur. A141.

James Bristow: *A Narrative of the Sufferings of James Bristow*, 1792, 1793, 1794, 1828 (Calcutta).

Donald Campbell: *A Narrative of the Extraordinary Adventures and Sufferings by Shipwreck and Imprisonment*, 1796, 1797, 1798, 1801, 1808.

Robert Cameron: Narrative. Scottish Record Office, Edinburgh, RH/4/34.

Arthur Conolly: Narrative. IOL, MSS Eur. B29.

William Drake: Narrative. *Calcutta Gazette*, 8 December 1791; *Times* (London), 10 April 1792.

Vincent Eyre: Narrative. IOL, MSS Eur. A42. Version published as *The Military Operations at Cabul . . . with a Journal of Imprisonment*, 1843.

Eliza Fay: *Original Letters from India . . . and the Author's Imprisonment at Calicut*, 1817, 1821.

Robert Gordon: 'Narrative or Journal of the Misfortunes of the Army'. NAM, 6409–67–3.

J.Z. Holwell: *A Genuine Narrative of the Deplorable Deaths . . . in the Black Hole*, 1758, 1804.

John Kaye, *History of the War in Afghanistan. From the Unpublished Letters and Journals of Political and Military Officers* (2 vols, 1851). Includes selections from captivity narratives which have not otherwise survived.

John Lindsay: 'Prison Life in Seringapatam, 1780–84'. NLS, Acc 9769 (transcript); versions published in 1840, 1849.

Cromwell Massey: Narrative. IOL, MSS Eur B392; editions published in Bangalore in 1876 and 1912.

Innes Munro: *A Narrative of the Military Operations on the Coromandel Coast*, 1789. Includes references to his captivity in Mysore.

Henry Oakes: *An Authentic Narrative of the Treatment of the English*, 1785.

Francis Robson: *The Life of Hyder Aly* (1786). Includes references to his captivity in Mysore.

Florentia Sale: Narrative. IOL, MSS Eur B275; version published as *A Journal of the Disasters in Afghanistan*, 1843, 1846.

James Scurry: *The Captivity, Sufferings and Escape of James Scurry*, 1824, 1831.

Sarah Shade: *A Narrative of the Life*, 1801.

William Thomson: *Memoirs of the Late War in Asia*, 2 vols., 1788. Compilation of captivity narratives from Mysore.

Edward Arthur Henry Webb: Narrative. IOL, MSS Eur D160. This also
    contains captivity memories by his wife.
William Whiteway: Narrative. Printed in *James Scurry*, 1824.

NOTES

Since the references to each chapter make up what is in effect a running bibliography, I have dispensed – with one exception – with a separate list of further reading. The exception is the Appendix which gives publication and provenance details of all the major captivity narratives drawn on in this volume, together with additional references. In the endnotes that follow, captivity narratives have been referred to throughout by the name of the captive involved: e.g.,. *Edward Coxere*, followed by the relevant page numbers. In the case of published narratives that passed through several editions over time, I have also indicated the date of the edition quoted from in the text: e.g., *Thomas Pellow* (1740?). The endnotes also make clear when I am quoting from a manuscript rather than a published captivity narrative: e.g., *John Lindsay MS*. Interested readers should then turn to the Appendix for the full title reference and bibliographical and archival information on the narrative concerned.

The place of publication in these notes is London unless otherwise stated. The following abbreviations are used throughout:

Add. MS	Additional Manuscript
AHR	*American Historical Review*
BL	British Library, London
CSPD	R. Lemon *et al.* (eds), *Calendar of State Papers: Domestic Series*, 91 vols, (1856–1964)
CSPC	W. Noel Sainsbury *et al.* (eds), *Calendar of State Papers: Colonial Series*, 40 vols, (1860–1939)
DNB	*Dictionary of National Biography*
HMC	Reports of the Royal Commission on Historical Manuscripts
Hansard	*Hansard's Parliamentary Debates*
IOL	India Office Library, British Library, London
JSAHR	*Journal of the Society for Army Historical Research*
MAS	*Modern Asian Studies*
NLS	National Library of Scotland, Edinburgh
OHBE	W.R. Louis *et al.* (eds), *The Oxford History of the British Empire*, (5 vols, Oxford, 1998–9)
I	N. Canny (ed.), *The Origins of Empire*

II	P.J. Marshall (ed.), *The Eighteenth Century*
III	A.N. Porter (ed.), *The Nineteenth Century*
IV	J.M. Brown and W.R. Louis (eds), *The Twentieth Century*
V	R.W. Winks (ed.), *Historiography*
Parl. Hist.	W. Cobbett, *The Parliamentary History of England from the earliest period to 1803* (36 vols, 1806–20)
PP	*Parliamentary Papers*
PRO	Public Record Office, London
RO	Record Office
WMQ	*William and Mary Quarterly*

Introduction

1 Daniel Defoe, *Robinson Crusoe: An Authoritative Text, Contexts, and Criticism*, ed. Michael Shinagel (1994), 15, 100, 174. The quotation from Joyce is at p. 323 of this edition. Defoe's acute sensitivity to captivity stemmed in part, as Sir Leslie Stephen noted, from his own experience of prison.

2 A good modern edition of *Gulliver's Travels*, complete with critical essays and edited by Christopher Fox, was published in 1995.

3 *OHBE* I, 77. The five volumes of this series, though controversial (how could they not be) supply an expert and broad-ranging survey of this extraordinary empire. For an interesting critique, see Dane Kennedy, 'The boundaries of Oxford's empire', *International History Review*, 23 (2001).

4 I have drawn these figures from *Whitaker's Almanac* for 2002.

5 Norman Davies, *Europe: A History* (Oxford, 1996), 1068–9.

6 E.A. Wrigley *et al.*, *English Population History from Family Reconstitution, 1580–1837* (Cambridge, 1997), 547.

7 On British population anxieties in the 1700s, see D.V. Glass, *Numbering the People* (1978).

8 Daniel A. Baugh, *British Naval Administration in the Age of Walpole* (Princeton, NJ, 1965), 147 *seq.*; N.A.M. Rodger, 'Guns and Sails in the First Phase of English Colonization, 1500–1650', and 'Sea-Power and Empire, 1688–1793', in *OHBE*, I, 79–98; II, 169–83.

9 John Brewer, *The Sinews of Power: War, Money and the English State 1688–1783* (1989). As one British politician complained in 1781: 'In every quarter of the world our forces were much more upon paper than they were in the field', *Parl. Hist.*, XII (1781–2), 833.

10 J.A. Houlding, *Fit for Service: The Training of the British Army 1715–1795* (Oxford, 1981), 7–8; Miles Taylor, 'The 1848 revolutions and the British empire', *Past and Present*, 166 (2000), 150–1.

11 On European versus non-European military technology on land and sea, see Michael Adas, *Machines as the Measure of Men: Science, Technology, and Ideologies of Western Dominance* (1989); Douglas M. Peers (ed.), *Warfare and Empires: Contact and Conflict between European and non-European Military and Maritime Forces and Cultures* (Aldershot, 1997).

12 Patrick O'Brien, 'The impact of the Revolutionary and Napoleonic Wars, 1793–1815, on the long-run growth of the British economy', *Review: Fernand Braudel Center*, XII (1989), 367–8.

13 C.W. Pasley, *Essay on the Military Policy and Institutions of the British Empire* (1810), 44; Edward Said, *Culture and Imperialism* (New York, 1993), 11.

14 J.H. Leslie (ed.), 'Letters of Captain Philip Browne, 1737–1746', in *JSAHR*, 5 (1925), 103. For Halifax, see David Armitage, *The Ideological Origins of the British Empire* (Cambridge, 2000), 142–3; Defoe is quoted in Daniel A. Baugh, 'Maritime Strength and Atlantic Commerce' in Lawrence Stone (ed.), *An Imperial State at War: Britain from 1689 to 1815* (1994), 201.

15 J.H. Stocqueler, *The Wellington Manual* (Calcutta, 1840), 195–6; Adam Smith, *An Inquiry into the Nature and Causes of the Wealth of Nations*, ed. R.H. Campbell and A.S. Skinner (2 vols, Oxford, 1976), II, 946.

16 Pasley, *Essay on the Military Policy*, 54.

17 On Britain's early state and national development and its limitations, see my *Britons: Forging the Nation 1707–1837* (1992); Brendan Bradshaw and John Morrill (eds), *The British Problem, c.1534–1707: State Formation in the Atlantic Archipelago* (1996); and Brewer, *Sinews of Power*.

18 I am indebted to Peter Gay for this glance at Adler.

19 Quoted in Jill Lepore, *The Name of War: King Philip's War and the Origins of American Identity* (New York, 1998), 74.

20 Mary Louise Pratt, 'Fieldwork in Common Places', in James Clifford and George E. Marcus (eds), *Writing Culture: The Poetics and Politics of Ethnography* (Los Angeles, CA, 1986), 38.

21 Mike Parker Pearson, 'Reassessing *Robert Drury's Journal* as a historical source for southern Madagascar', *History in Africa*, 23 (1996). I am most grateful to Dr Pearson for sending me this and other material on Drury.

22 *Ibid.*; Mike Parker Pearson *et al.*, *The Androy Project: Fifth Report* (1997), 40.

23 Brian Keenan, *An Evil Cradling* (1993), 58.

24 James S. Amelang, *The Flight of Icarus: Artisan Autobiography in Early Modern Europe* (Stanford, CA, 1998), 37.

25 Dominic Lieven, *Empire: The Russian Empire and its Rivals* (2000), 17; Anthony Pagden, *Peoples and Empires* (New York, 2001), xxi.

1 Cholmley's letter-books and papers, which I have drawn on throughout this chapter, are in the North Yorkshire RO (ZCG). See also *The Memoirs of Sir Hugh Cholmley* (1787). The man deserves a modern biography.

2 On Tangier and the Navy, see Sari R. Hornstein, *The Restoration Navy and English Foreign Trade, 1674–1688* (Aldershot, 1991), a valuable study that neglects, however, the Moroccan contribution to the colony's fate. For Cholmley's contract, see 'A Short Account of the Progress of the Mole at Tangier', in *Tracts on Tangier*, BL, 583.i.3 (1–8); and PRO, CO 279/2, fols 18–19.

3 [Sir Henry Sheeres] *A Discourse touching Tanger* [sic] *in a letter to a person of quality* (1680), 7.

4 Robert Latham and William Matthews (eds), *The Diary of Samuel Pepys* (11 vols, 1970), IV, 299, 319.

5 Julian S. Corbett, *England in the Mediterranean* (2 vols, 1904), II, 17, 137.

6 E.M.G. Routh, *Tangier: England's Lost Atlantic Outpost 1661–1684* (1912), 38; Richard T. Godfrey, *Wenceslaus Hollar: A Bohemian Artist in England* (New Haven, CT, 1994), 27, 159–60.

7 For Tangier's colonial population, see Bodleian Library, MS Rawl. A185; 'A discourse of Tangier', BL, Lansdowne MS 192, fol. 164.

8 For the fabric of colonial life in Tangier, see the volumes of correspondence in PRO, CO 279; and *Memoirs of Sir Hugh Cholmley*, 103–296.

9 Routh, *Tangier*, 365–9; 'Reasons Touching the Demolishing Tangier', Beinecke Library, Yale University, Osborn MS, Fb. 190 vol. 4. The definitive work on English royal income and expenditure in this period – which, however and predictably, gives Tangier only limited attention – is C.D. Chandaman, *The English Public Revenue 1660–1688* (Oxford, 1975).

10 See the plans in PRO, MPH 1; and Cholmley's letter-book, *passim*.

11 Bodleian Library, MS Rawl. A342, fol. 151; MS Rawl. A191, fol. 44; Corbett, *England in the Mediterranean*, II, 137.

12 Frank H. Ellis (ed.), *Poems on Affairs of State: Augustan Satirical Verse, 1660–1714* (7 vols, New Haven, CT, 1975), III, 473–4; Edwin Chappell, *The Tangier Papers of Samuel Pepys* (1935), preface.

13 See *OHBE*, I. Atlanticist bias was already operative in Routh's day, as her subtitle suggests. At the time it was an English colony, Tangier was discussed overwhelmingly in terms of Mediterranean power and trade.

14 *The Mediterranean and the Mediterranean World in the Age of Philip II* (2 vols, 1995 edn), II, 1240. Scholarly interest in the Mediterranean is showing signs of reviving. In particular, the work of Professor Molly Greene of Princeton University promises much.

15 Hornstein, *The Restoration Navy*, 37–8. It bears repeating that England's European and extra-European trading interests were always interconnected. Colonial and extra-European re-exports contributed to its Mediterranean trade. Conversely, Mediterranean profits helped to offset the bullion it paid out for its East Indian commodities.

16 I owe this information on Ottoman population and army size to Professors Virginia Aksan and Sevket Pamuk.

17 I am grateful to Dr Simon Price for this example of Ottoman fiscal zeal.

18 Routh, *Tangier*, 264; P.G. Rogers, *A History of Anglo-Moroccan Relations to 1900* (1970), 232.

19 BL, Lansdowne MS 192, fols 123–9; *A Discourse touching Tanger* [sic] . . . *to which is added The Interest of Tanger, by Another Hand* (1680), 37.

20 *An Exact Journal of the Siege of Tangier* (1680).

21 For a useful discussion on these points, see Ann Laura Stoler, 'Rethinking colonial categories: European communities and the boundaries of rule', *Comparative Studies in Society and History*, 31 (1989).

22 See *OHBE*, I, 280.

23 Bodleian Library, MS Rawl. c. 423, fols 1, 127.

24 'Minutes of Courts Martial at Tangier 1663–67', BL, Sloane MS 1957, fols 45–6.

25 Rogers, *Anglo-Moroccan Relations*, 52–3.

26 See Colonel Percy Kirke's Tangier letter-book, Lewis Walpole Library, Farmington, CT, Hazen 2572.

27 HMC Dartmouth I, 96–7; PRO, CO 279/32, fols 184–9.

28 BL, Lansdowne MS 192, fols. 30 and 132.

2 *The Crescent and the Sea*

1   This was, Professor Shula Marks informs me, a common device for stressing the 'animality' of Hottentot women. It was also used to downgrade other subject or looked down upon females: Jennifer L. Morgan, 'Some could suckle over their shoulder', *WMQ*, 54 (1997).

2   Accounts of the 'Barbary' phenomenon are numerous but vary widely in quality. Some elderly, over-emotive books still contain valuable material: notably Godfrey Fisher, *Barbary Legend* (Oxford, 1957), and R.L. Playfair, *The Scourge of Christendom* (1884). M.S. Anderson, 'Great Britain and the Barbary states in the eighteenth century', *Bulletin of the Institute of Historical Research*, XXIX (1956), is a balanced overview of British diplomatic sources. John B. Wolf, *The Barbary Coast: Algiers under the Turks 1500–1830* (1979), and P.G. Rogers, *A History of Anglo-Moroccan Relations to*

1900 (1970) are useful accounts of the two main North African powers. Many of the best analyses though have come from scholars based in France or writing in French. Fernand Braudel, *The Mediterranean and the Mediterranean World in the Age of Philip II* (2 vols, 1995 edn) is essential. Bartolomé and Lucile Bennassar, *Les chrétiens d'Allah* (Paris, 1989), should be read for the European-wide context of captivity in Barbary. French-language journals like *Les cahiers de Tunisie, Le monde musulman* and *Revue d'histoire maghrebine* regularly contain valuable new research on the corsairs and their victims.

3 Jamil M. Abun-Nasr, *A History of the Maghrib in the Islamic Period* (Cambridge, 1987), 2.

4 Quoted in G.A. Starr, 'Escape from Barbary: a seventeenth-century genre', *Huntington Library Quarterly*, 29 (1965), 35.

5 On Muslim slaves in France and Italy, see Moulay Belhamissi, *Les captifs algériens et l'Europe chrétienne* (Algiers, 1988); Peter Earle, *Corsairs of Malta and Barbary* (1970). Christian corsairs in the Mediterranean – including English ones – also sometimes preyed on their co-religionists.

6 PRO, SP 71/16, fol. 135; Ellen G. Friedman, *Spanish Captives in North Africa in the Early Modern Age* (Madison, WI, 1983).

7 See, for instance, Admiral Herbert's letter-book, Beinecke Library, Yale University, Osborn Shelves, f.b.96.

8 Abdallah Laroui, *The History of the Maghrib: An Interpretive Essay* (Princeton, NJ, 1977), 244.

9 John Brewer, *The Sinews of Power: War, Money and the English State, 1688–1783* (New York, 1989), 198.

10 See David Armitage, *The Ideological Origins of the British Empire* (Cambridge, 2000), 100–24.

11 Russell King *et al.* (eds), *The Mediterranean: Environment and Society* (1997), 10, drawing on Braudel's arguments.

12 The following paragraphs draw heavily on Robert C. Davis, 'Counting European slaves on the Barbary coast', *Past and Present*, 172 (2001).

13 The earliest English language Barbary captivity narratives date from the 1570s: see Nabil Matar, *Turks, Moors and Englishmen in the Age of Discovery* (1999), 181.

14 William Laird Clowes, *The Royal Navy: A History from the Earliest Times to the Present* (7 vols, 1996 repr.), II, 22.

15 David Delison Hebb, *Piracy and the English Government 1616–1642* (Aldershot, 1994); Todd Gray, 'Turkish piracy and early Stuart Devon', *Report and Transactions Devonshire Association*, 121 (1989).

16 *A Relation of the Whole Proceedings concerning the Redemption of the Captives in Algier and Tunis* (1647).

17 Frank H. Ellis (ed.), *Poems on Affairs of State: Augustan Satirical Verse, 1660–1714* (7 vols, New Haven, CT, 1975), VII, 243. For the naval assault on Barbary, see Sari R. Hornstein, *The Restoration Navy and English Foreign Trade. 1674–1688* (Aldershot, 1991).

18 'Navy, state, trade, and empire', in *OHBE*, I, 473; Ralph Davis, *The Rise of the English Shipping Industry* (1962), 15.

19 'List of Ships and Men Taken', PRO, SP 71/18, fol. 25; Dominique Meunier, *Le Consulat anglais à Tétouan sous Anthony Hatfeild* (Tunis, 1980), 36–40.

20 W.E. Minchinton (ed.), *Politics and the Port of Bristol in the Eighteenth Century* (1963), 82–3.

21 Joseph Redington (ed.), *Calendar of Treasury Papers, 1556–1728* (7 vols, 1868–1889), III, 250–1.

22 Anderson, 'Great Britain and the Barbary states', 103.

23 Fisher, *Barbary Legend*, 227; *CSPD*, 1661–2, 285.

24 This is my estimate based on ransoming information scattered throughout the state papers and contemporary printed sources. As set out below, it rests on incomplete information and will err on the conservative side.

25 Meunier, *Le Consulat anglais à Tétouan*, 39.

26 PRO, SP, 102/1, fol. 53; *British and Foreign State Papers 1812–1814* (1841), 357, 363.

27 I am indebted here to Gillian Weiss of Stanford University who allowed me to consult her manuscript 'From Barbary to France: Processions of Redemption and Early Modern Cultural Identity'.

28 PRO, SP 71/16, fol. 256.

29 *An Exhortation to those Redeemed Slaves, who came in a Solemn Procession to St Paul's Cathedral* (1702), 17; *DNB*, 14, p. 775.

30 Gregory King placed seamen at the bottom of England's social structure in the 1680s alongside common soldiers and paupers. See Geoffrey Holmes, 'Gregory King and the social structure of pre-industrial England', *Transactions of the Royal Historical Society*, 27 (1977).

31 *CSPD*, 1700–1702, 470–1.

32 The 1714–19 list is printed in Meunier, *Le Consulat anglais à Tétouan*, 36–40; for the Tripoli estimate, see Michel Fontenay, 'Le maghreb barbaresque et l'esclavage Méditerranéen aux XVIè et XVIIè siècles', *Les cahiers de Tunisie*, XLIV (1991).

33 *John Whitehead*, 4–11; Abun-Nasr, *History of the Maghrib*, 161.

34 References to British captives in other parts of the Ottoman empire can be gleaned from Alfred C. Wood, *A History of the Levant Company* (1964).

35 'Petition of the Poor Seamen Captive in Algiers', 4 March 1641: I am

grateful to Professor Maija Jansson for referring me to this text, which she is editing. For the 1670s appeal, see Guildhall Library, London, Broadside 12.12.

36 Quoted in Christopher Lloyd, *English Corsairs on the Barbary Coast* (1981), 101.

37 For guidance on this inevitably contentious subject, see Joseph C. Miller, 'Muslim slavery and slaving: a bibliography', *Slavery & Abolition*, 13 (1992). I have also found useful J.R.Willis, *Slaves and Slavery in Muslim Africa* (2 vols, 1995); H.A.R. Gibb *et al.* (eds), *The Encyclopaedia of Islam* (8 vols, Leiden, 1960–97 edn): entries for '*Abd, Hab<u>sh</u>ī, Hartini, Ghulām*, and *Ma'dhūn*; Bernard Lewis, *Race and Slavery in the Middle East: An Historical Enquiry* (Oxford, 1990).

38 John Braithwaite, *The History of the Revolutions in the Empire of Morocco* (1969 reprint of 1729 edn), 67.

39 *Thomas Sweet* (1646); Braithwaite, *History of the Revolutions*, 185–6.

40 *Francis Knight* (1640), 29. On galley warfare and slavery, see Jan Glete, *Navies and Nations: Warships, Navies and State Building in Europe and America, 1500–1860* (2 vols, Stockholm, 1993), I, 114–46, 250–2.

41 *The Memoirs of Sir Hugh Cholmley* (1787), 137.

42 See *Thomas Phelps* (1685) for one Briton's involvement in Moulay Ismaïl's building works. For slaves and public works in Algiers, see Ellen G. Friedman, 'Christian captives at "hard labour" in Algiers, 16th–18th centuries', *International Journal of African Historical Studies*, 13 (1980).

43 *Thomas Troughton* (1751), 14–16 and *passim*.

44 See the discussion of these points in Davis, 'Counting European Slaves'.

45 *The Arabian Journey: Danish Connections with the Islamic World over a Thousand Years* (Århus, 1996), 87.

46 Orlando Patterson, *Slavery and Social Death: A Comparative Study* (1982), 7; Seymour Drescher and Stanley L. Engerman (eds), *A Historical Guide to World Slavery* (Oxford, 1998), 284–5.

47 A classic example is Samuel Pepys's account of how he strolled to London's Exchange at noon on February 8 1661 and encountered two former Barbary captives: 'and there we spent till 4 a-clock telling stories of Algier and the manner of the life of slaves there': Robert Latham and William Matthews (eds), *The Diary of Samuel Pepys* (10 vols, 1970–83), II, 33–4.

48 'An account of Mr Russell's Journey from Gibraltar to Sallee [sic]', Bodleian Library, MS Eng.hist.d.153, fol. 1; Proclamation, 12 March 1692, Bristol RO, EP/A/31/4.

49 *Gleanings in Africa . . . with Observations . . . on the State of Slavery* (1806), 149; Morgan Godwyn, *The Negro's & Indian's Advocate* (1680), 28. I am grateful to Professor Dror Wahrman for the former reference.

50 Betton Charity Papers, Guildhall Library, London, MS 17034, bundle 4.

51 Ottoman historiography is in rapid and exciting flux as the archives in Istanbul become better known. Useful guides to current revisionism include Donald Quataert, *The Ottoman Empire, 1700–1922* (Cambridge, 2000); Virginia H. Aksan, 'Locating the Ottomans among early modern empires', *Journal of Early Modern History*, 3 (1999); and Halil Inalcik and Donald Quataert (eds), *An Economic and Social History of the Ottoman Empire. 1300–1914* (Cambridge, 1994).

52 In his *The Perspective of the World* (1984), 467.

53 'The Barbary states', *Quarterly Review*, XV (1816), 151.

54 [Matthew Barton], *An Authentic Narrative of the Loss of His Majesty's Ship the Litchfield* (London, n.d.), 2.

55 Andrew C. Hess, 'The Forgotten Frontier: The Ottoman North African Provinces during the Eighteenth Century', in Thomas Naff and Roger Owen (eds), *Studies in Eighteenth-Century Islamic History* (Carbondale, IL, 1977), 83.

56 Bodleian Library, Rawl. c.145, fol. 21. On Morocco's dynamic military development in the early modern era, see Weston F. Cook, *The Hundred Years War for Morocco* (Boulder, CO, 1994), and Allan Richard Meyers, 'The 'Abid al-Bukhari: Slave Soldiers and Statecraft in Morocco, 1672–1790', Cornell University PhD dissertation, 1974.

57 'Papers regarding the redemption of English captives', Corporation of London RO, Misc. MSS 156.9; Redington, *Calendar of Treasury Papers*, VII, 62.

58 *Mediterranean and the Mediterranean World, passim.*

59 See pp. 126–132.

60 The best studies in English are George Hills, *Rock of Contention: A History of Gibraltar* (1974), and Desmond Gregory, *Minorca: The Illusory Prize* (1990). Anyone interested in the diplomatic, naval and commercial history of the Mediterranean after 1700 should make a point of consulting the copious archives in the Governor's Library at Gibraltar. At present, they are virtually untouched by scholars.

61 Gregory, *Minorca*, 207–9.

62 On this, see Janet Sloss, *A Small Affair: The French Occupation of Minorca during the Seven Years War* (Tetbury, 2000).

63 Paul M. Kennedy, *The Rise and Fall of British Naval Mastery* (1976), 109.

64 J.A. Houlding, *Fit for Service: The Training of the British Army, 1715–1795* (Oxford, 1981).

65 PRO, SP 71/20 Part I, fol. 182.

1   See, for instance, *Francis Brooks* (1693), 7. On the English belief that Barbary corsairs could find them by magic, see Basil Lubbock (ed.), *Barlow's Journal* (2 vols, 1934), II, 55.

2   *Adam Elliot* (1731), xxiii.

3   For the activities of other denominations, see Kenneth L. Carroll, 'Quaker slaves in Algiers, 1679–1688', *Journal of the Friends Historical Society*, 54 (1982), 301–12; and B. Gwynn (ed.), 'Minutes of the Consistory of the French Church of London . . . 1679–92', *Huguenot Society Quarto Series*, 58 (1994), 271, 275, 280 and 342. I am grateful to Randolph Vigne for this latter reference. Charles Henry Hull (ed.), *The Economic Writings of Sir William Petty* (2 vols, 1964 repr.), II, 512.

4   Accounts of money collected, Corporation of London RO, GLMS/284 and 285.

5   On this device, see W.A. Bewes, *Church Briefs, or, Royal Warrants for Collections for Charitable Objects* (1896); and Mark Harris, '"Inky blots and rotten parchment bonds": London, charity briefs and the Guildhall Library', *Historical Research*, LXVI (1993), 98–110.

6   R.N. Worth, *Calendar of the Tavistock Parish Records* (Plymouth, 1887), 56–7.

7   *Ibid.*, 56–63. The prominence of women in these ransoming campaigns, both as donors in church collections, and through clauses in wills, is very marked.

8   For a classic account of the social breadth of British abolitionism after 1780, see Seymour Drescher, *Capitalism and Antislavery: British Mobilization in Comparative Perspective* (1986).

9   Guildhall Library, London, Proc. 23. 20.

10 See for instance the reports of the processions in *Daily Post*, 5 December 1721, and *Daily Journal*, 12 November 1734.

11 *The great blessings of redemption from captivity* (1722), 3 and 22.

12 *Daily Journal*, 12 November 1734; William Sherlock, *An Exhortation to those Redeemed Slaves who Came in a Solemn Procession to St. Paul's Cathedral* (1702), 16.

13 This paragraph draws on an unpublished paper by Gillian Weiss: 'From Barbary to France: processions of redemption and early modern cultural identity'.

14 Joseph Morgan, *Several Voyages to Barbary* (2nd edn, 1736), 142.

15 I have reconstructed Jukes' story from two sources: William Gouge, *A Recovery from Apostacy* (1639); and Richard Gough, *The History of Myddle*, ed. David Hey (New York, 1981), 115. I owe the latter reference to Professor David Underdown.

16 The verses quoted come from a *c.* 1790 version of 'Lord Bateman' called 'Young Baker', Bodleian Library, Harding B 6 (86). The ballad remained sufficiently popular for the young Charles Dickens and the artist George Cruickshank to combine their formidable talents in a new version: *The Loving Ballad of Lord Bateman* (1839).

17 I have found useful the approaches to narrative contained in Lewis P. Hinchman and Sandra K. Hinchman (eds), *Memory, Identity, Community: The Idea of Narrative in the Human Sciences* (Albany, NY, 1997).

18 R.L. Playfair, *The Scourge of Christendom* (1884), 135.

19 I owe this transcription of a destroyed Greenwich Hospital memorial inscription to Barbara Tomlinson of the National Maritime Museum.

20 See the account of his examination, Lancashire RO, QSP 1223/7.

21 See G.E. Hubbard, *The Old Book of Wye: being a record of a Kentish country parish* (Derby, 1951), 130–1: 'For the rest of the seventeenth century and throughout a good part of the eighteenth the Wye churchwardens' accounts are seldom quite free of entries relating to Turkish slaves'.

22 W. Petticrew to Lord Holderness, 2 October 1753, PRO SP 71/19, fols 123–6, enclosing 'A declaration made here by two Moors . . . before the Governor and Chief Justice [sic]'.

23 *Ibid.*, fols 125–6.

24 *Francis Knight* (1640), preface.

25 See *Strange and wonderfull things happened to Richard Hasleton . . . penned as he delivered it from his owne mouth* (1595).

26 Simon Schama, *Dead Certainties, (Unwarranted Speculations)* (1991).

27 *William Okeley* (1676), preface and opening verse.

28 *Thomas Troughton* (1751), 6–8.

29 For an example of an early New England captive seemingly able to take notes while in Barbary, see *Narrative of Joshua Gee of Boston, Mass.* (Hartford, CT, 1943), 26–7; *William Okeley* (1676), 26.

30 *William Okeley* (1676), preface.

31 *Ibid.*, 1764 edn, x–xi.

32 See Lennard Davis, *Factual Fictions: The Origins of the English Novel* (New York, 1983).

33 P.J. Marshall and Glyndwr Williams, *The Great Map of Mankind* (1982), 53; Percy G. Adams, *Travel Literature and the Evolution of the Novel* (Lexington, Kentucky, 1983), 97.

34 For a valuable discussion of these arguments, see the introduction to Stuart B. Schwartz, *Implicit Understandings: Observing, Reporting, and Reflecting on the Encounters between Europeans and Other Peoples in the Early Modern Era* (Cambridge, 1994), 1–23.

35 *Thomas Pellow* (1890), 186; P. Mercer, 'Political and Military Developments

within Morocco during the early Alawi Period', London University PhD dissertation, 1974, 41.

36 Magali Morsy, *La relation de Thomas Pellow: Une lecture du Maroc au 18e siècle* (Paris, 1983).

37 See Daniel Nordman, 'La mémoire d'un captif', *Annales*, xli (1986). It is suggestive that Brian Keenan's modern narrative of his four-year Beirut captivity also reveals a lack of attention to Western calendar time: see *An Evil Cradling* (1992).

38 *Thomas Pellow* (1890), 235; Morsy, *La relation*, 205n.

39 Joan Brady, *The Theory of War* (New York, 1993), 94.

40 *Thomas Pellow* (1740), 385.

4 Confronting Islam

1 On Rich, Covent Garden and *The Beggar's Opera*, see John Brewer, *The Pleasures of the Imagination: English Culture in the Eighteenth Century* (1997), 325–56, 428–44.

2 'English Slaves in Barbary', *Notes and Queries*, March 5 1921, 187. Troughton and his comrades arrived back in London on 22 March 1751.

3 *Poems on Several Occasions* (1734), 271.

4 *Thomas Phelps* (1685), preface; *John Whitehead* MS, 4 and 16.

5 Edward Said, *Orientalism: Western Conceptions of the Orient* (1995 edn), *passim*. Discussions of this rich and suggestive text are now legion. Those I have found most valuable include: Sadiq Jalal al-'Azm, 'Orientalism and Orientalism in Reverse', in Jon Rothschild (ed.), *Forbidden Agendas: Intolerance and Defiance in the Middle East* (1984), and Dennis Porter, '*Orientalism* and its Problems', in Francis Barker *et al.* (eds), *The Politics of Theory* (Colchester, 1983).

6 James Grey Jackson, *An Account of the Empire of Morocco* (3rd edn, 1814), 153. For an excellent discussion of the ubiquity of prejudice at this point, but also its limited impact on contact and collaborations in practice, see Rhoads Murray, 'Bigots or informed observers? A periodization of pre-colonial English and European writing on the Middle East', *Journal of the American Oriental Society*, 110 (1990).

7 Verses by Lord Hervey, quoted in my *Britons: Forging the Nation 1707–1837* (1992), 35.

8 For an elaboration of these points, see K.N. Chaudhuri, 'From the Barbarian and the Civilized to the Dialectics of Colour: An Archaeology of Self-Identities', in Peter Robb (ed.), *Society and Ideology: Essays in South Asian History* (Delhi, 1994).

9   See Nabil Matar, *Islam in Britain 1558–1685* (Cambridge, 1998), 74–86; and
    G.J. Toomer, *Eastern Wisedome and Learning: The Study of Arabic in Seventeenth-Century England* (Oxford, 1996).

10 Matar, *Islam in Britain*, 73–83.

11 *Devereux Spratt*, 25–6; Nabil Matar, *Turks, Moors & Englishmen in the Age of Discovery* (New York, 1999), x, 170.

12 *Sentences of Ali, son-in-law of Mahomet* (1717), preface. Ockley, who merits a
    biography, was anxious to stress the intellectual calibre of 'polite Asiaticks
    (amongst which the Persians do most deservedly claim the preference . . .)'
    even when denouncing Barbary captive-taking: see *An Account of South-West Barbary* (1713), xix.

13 Quoted in Albert Hourani, *Islam in European Thought* (Cambridge, 1991), 10.

14 *The Koran, commonly called the Alcoran of Mohammed* (1734), preface; *The Life of Mahomet, translated from the French* (1731), dedication.

15 *A Compleat History of the Piratical States of Barbary* (1750 edn), v; see, too,
    Morgan's *Mahometanism Fully Explained* (2 vols, 1723–5).

16 'Moors', those one-time Spanish Muslims who had settled in North Africa,
    were usually imagined as dark-skinned, but as Shakespeare's *Othello*
    suggests, in some contrast with sub-Saharan blacks, this was not necessarily seen as evidence of inferiority or lack of power. See Khalid
    Kekkaoui, *Signs of Spectacular Resistance: The Spanish Moor and British Orientalism* (Casablanca, 1998).

17 *John Whitehead* MS, fol. 26; *The Memoirs of Sir Hugh Cholmley* (1787), 137.

18 *Elizabeth Marsh* MS, unfoliated.

19 On British toleration of North African Jewish and Muslim traders on the
    Rock, see George Hills, *Bone of Contention: A History of Gibraltar* (1974).

20 Yale University's Map Library, for instance, holds a late eighteenth-century
    embroidered map which explicitly includes North Africa within an image
    of Europe. *The Adventures of Mr. T.S. an English merchant, taken prisoner by the Turks of Algiers* (1670), 157.

21 Michael Adas, *Machines as the Measure of Men: Science, Technology and Ideologies of Western Dominance* (1989).

22 BL, Add. MS 47995, fols 30 and 39.

23 *A Compleat History*, 255–6. For pre-1750 British instability, see J.H. Plumb,
    The Growth of Political Stability in England, 1675–1725 (1967); and Paul Monod,
    Jacobitism and the English People, 1688–1788 (Cambridge, 1989).

24 *Edward Coxere*, facing p.60.

25 *Devereux Spratt*, 11–13, 33–4.

26 'Islamic Law and Polemics over Race and Slavery in North and West
    Africa', in Shaun E. Marmon (ed.), *Slavery in the Islamic Middle East*
    (Princeton, NJ, 1999), 43.

27 *James Irving* MS, 29; *Elizabeth Marsh* (1769), I, 38–9.

28 N. J. Dawood (ed.), *The Muqaddimah: An Introduction to History* (Princeton, NJ, 1989), 59–60; *Joseph Pitts* (1704), 24.

29 See, for instance, John Braithwaite, *The History of the Revolutions in the Empire of Morocco* (1969 reprint of 1729 edn), 214–15: '[We] were sure to be affronted as we passed the streets, three or four hundred fellows setting up a great scream together, and crying Cursed are the unbelievers. Sometimes the common people would fling stones and brickbats.'

30 *William Okeley* (1684), 12–14.

31 *James Irving* (1995), 128.

32 Said, *Orientalism*, 11.

33 Michelle Burnham, *Captivity and Sentiment: Cultural Exchange in American Literature, 1682–1861* (Hanover, NH, 1997), 2.

34 *William Okeley* (1684), 41, 46–7.

35 *Joseph Pitts* (1704), 142, 156, 158–62, 171.

36 Pierre de Cenival and P. de Cossé Brissac (eds), *Les sources inédites de l'histoire du Maroc: archives et bibliothèques d'Angleterre* (3 vols, Paris, 1918–35), III, 68; *Devereux Spratt*, 26.

37 *Genesis*, 41, v. 52.

38 William Nelson, *Particulars of the hardships and sufferings of William Nelson . . . who was afterwards taken prisoner by an Algerine galley* (Grantham, 1820?). The British Library holds the only copy known to me, but has mislaid it. Not being able to consult it, I cannot say whether it is genuine.

39 See Peter Linebaugh and Marcus Rediker, *The Many-Headed Hydra: Sailors, Slaves, Commoners, and the Hidden History of the Revolutionary Atlantic* (2000); for Saphra, see Thomas Pocock, *The Relief of Captives, especially of our own countrymen* (1720), 10–12.

40 A.R. Meyers, 'The 'Abid al-Bukhari: Slave Soldiers and Statecraft in Morocco, 1672–1790', Cornell University PhD dissertation, 1974, 142–4; *James Irving* (1995), 119; *Thomas Troughton* (1751), 14–16.

41 See Ian Duffield and Paul Edwards, 'Equiano's Turks and Christians: an eighteenth-century African view of Islam', *Journal of African Studies*, 2 (1975–6). For Equiano's likely American birthplace, rather than the African setting he described in his published narrative, see the introduction to Olaudah Equiano, *The Interesting Narrative and Other Writings*, ed. Vincent Caretta (1995).

42 This point should not be over-stressed. There was a wider spectrum of opportunities open to black slaves in North Africa, but the majority seem to have been treated less well than white captives. Moreover, black Britons, like white Britons, reacted to captivity here in different ways. Thomas Saphra, for instance, reputedly a fervent Christian, chose to return to Britain.

43 PRO, SP 71/14, Part Two, fol. 221.

44 For one aspect of this, see Nicholas B.Harding, 'North African piracy, the Hanoverian carrying trade, and the British state, 1728–1828', *Historical Journal*, 43 (2000).

45 Guildhall Library, London, MS 17034, Betton Charity Papers, Bundle 3.

46 Fernand Braudel. *The Mediterranean and the Mediterranean World in the Age of Philip II* (2 vols, 1995 edn), II, 889.

47 For the Butlers, see PRO, FO 113/3, fol. 272.

48 See, for instance, BL, Egerton MS 2528, fol. 97.

49 In the 1710s and '20s, there was a considerable debate in Britain on the overlap between Unitarianism and Islam: see J.A.I. Champion, 'The Pillars of Priestcraft Shaken: The Church of England and its Enemies, 1660–1730', Cambridge University PhD dissertation, 1992.

50 *Joseph Pitts* (1704), 14, 82, 104 and 130.

51 Quoted in F.E. Peters, *The Hajj: The Muslim Pilgrimage to Mecca and the Holy Places* (Princeton, NJ, 1994), 116–17.

52 *Joseph Pitts* (1704), 68, 86, 115, 182–3.

53 See Carlo Ginzburg, *The Cheese and the Worms: The Cosmos of a Sixteenth-Century Miller* (New York, 1982), 50–1.

54 For the Hyde Parker incident, see P.G. Rogers, *A History of Anglo-Moroccan Relations to 1900* (1970), 96–9.

55 John Hughes, *The Siege of Damascus* (London, 1720), 6. For a detailed account of Marsh, see my 'The Narrative of Elizabeth Marsh: Barbary, Sex, and Power', in Felicity Nussbaum (ed.), *The Global Eighteenth Century* (forthcoming, Baltimore, MD, 2003).

56 *Elizabeth Marsh* (1769), II, 18–94.

57 I discuss this point in more detail in 'The Narrative of Elizabeth Marsh'.

58 Maija Jansson (ed.), *Proceedings in Parliament, 1614* (Philadelphia, 1988), 200; 'To the Right Honourable the Commons', Guildhall Library, London, Broadside 12.12.

59 *Francis Knight* (1640), 50; C. R. Pennell, *Piracy and Diplomacy in Seventeenth-Century North Africa* (1989), 62.

60 William Chetwood, *Voyages and Adventures of Captain Robert Boyle* (1726), 34; Paul Rycaut, *The Present State of the Ottoman Empire* (1668), 81. I am indebted for this reading of *Robinson Crusoe* to Ben Holden of Merton College, Oxford.

61 For recent discussions of this point, see Stephen O. Murray and Will Roscoe (eds), *Islamic Homosexualities: Culture, History and Literature* (New York, 1997).

62 One aspect of this was portraiture. Before 1750, high-ranking and ambitious British males, such as Lord Sandwich, sometimes chose to be

portrayed in Turkish costume. After 1760, however, it was overwhelmingly women who were represented in this mode of 'oriental' dress.

63 *Letters from Barbary 1576–1774: Arabic Documents in the Public Record Office*, trans. J.F.P. Hopkins (Oxford, 1982), 84.

64 Piers Mackesy, *British Victory in Egypt, 1801* (1995), 21; for the 1816 bombardment, see Roger Perkins and K.J. Douglas-Morris, *Gunfire in Barbary* (1982).

5 *Different Americans, Different Britons*

1 For Bird and his work, see R. Gunnis, *Dictionary of British Sculptors 1660–1851* (1968 rev. edn), 53.

2 On Britain's imperial power – and its limits – by 1713, see *OHBE*, I, 423–79.

3 For an excellent survey that attempts to get beyond this, see Colin G. Calloway, *New Worlds for All: Indians, Europeans, and the Re-making of Early America* (1997). Readers wanting to explore some of the new work on Native Americans can profitably begin with J.C.H. King, *First Peoples, First Contacts: Native Peoples of North America* (Cambridge, MA, 1999), and Carl Waldman, *Biographical Dictionary of American Indian History to 1900* (New York, 2001 rev. edn), which are both well illustrated, before moving on to periodicals such as *Native Peoples* and *Ethnohistory*. But perhaps the best introduction is through objects and images. The Chase Manhattan Gallery of North America in London's British Museum, and the National Museum of the American Indian, New York, are both excellent.

4 This literature is vast and still growing. Good introductions which reprint sections from the narratives are Alden T. Vaughan and Edward W. Clark (eds), *Puritans among the Indians: Accounts of Captivity and Redemption, 1676–1724* (Cambridge, MA, 1981), and Richard VanDerBeets, *Held Captive by Indians: Selected Narratives, 1642–1836* (Knoxville, Tennessee, 1994). An influential though now disputed attempt to offer a distinctively American interpretation is Richard Slotkin, *Regeneration through Violence: The Mythology of the American Frontier, 1600–1860* (Middletown, CT, 1973). For a recent, expert attempt to breathe new life into (for Americanists) an old source, see John Demos, *The Unredeemed Captive: A Family Story from Early America* (New York, 1994).

5 See K.O. Kupperman (ed.), *Captain John Smith: A Select Edition of his Writings* (1988). It is possible that Smith's life was never in real danger, and that he was rather exposed to a symbolic execution before being reclaimed by Pocahontas as a prelude to rebirth as an Indian.

6 See K.O. Kupperman, *Settling with the Indians: The Meeting of English and*

Indian Cultures in America, 1580–1640 (Totowa, NJ, 1980); James H. Merrell, '"The Customes of our Countrey": Indians and Colonists in Early America', in Bernard Bailyn and Philip D. Morgan (eds), *Strangers within the Realm: Cultural Margins of the First British Empire* (1991).

7   Kupperman, *Captain John Smith*, 72; Anthony McFarlane, *The British in the Americas 1480–1815* (1992), 57.

8   Quoted in the introduction to K. O. Kupperman (ed.), *America in European Consciousness, 1493–1750* (Chapel Hill, NC, 1995), 17; Alden T. Vaughan, 'From White Man to Redskin: changing Anglo-American perceptions of the American Indian', *AHR*, 87 (1982).

9   *CSPC*, V, 97.

10 For a useful survey of how Native Americans adapted to European styles of warfare, see Patrick M. Malone, *The Skulking Way of War* (1991).

11 King, *First Peoples*, 34.

12 *OHBE*, I, 195, 390, and 328–50 *passim*.

13 For a wonderful account, see Jill Lepore, *The Name of War: King Philip's War and the Origins of American Identity* (New York, 1998).

14 *CSPC*, XXXIV, 220–1; *OHBE*, II, 352.

15 On this point, see William Cronon, *Changes in the Land; Indians, Colonists, and the Ecology of New England* (New York, 1983).

16 Infants unable to walk or feed themselves might also be killed because they were too much trouble to take captive: see Demos, *Unredeemed Captive*, 7–27.

17 See Alexander Hamilton's account of how the Indians who captured him and four others at Kennebac River in 1722, on French instructions, were rewarded with food and tobacco: *CSPC*, XXXIII, 407–15.

18 Gregory H. Nobles, *American Frontiers: Cultural Encounters and Continental Conquest* (New York, 1997), 35–6, 74.

19 *Jonathan Dickenson* (1700), 12, 28, 37.

20 *Ibid.*, 40–1, 70.

21 Alden T. Vaughan and Daniel K. Richter, 'Crossing the cultural divide: Indians and New Englanders, 1605–1763', *Proceedings of the American Antiquarian Society*, 90 (1980).

22 Ian K. Steele, 'Surrendering Rites: Prisoners on Colonial North American Frontiers', in Stephen Taylor *et al.*, *Hanoverian Britain and Empire: Essays in Memory of Philip Lawson* (Woodbridge, 1998), 141.

23 *Mary Rowlandson* (1997), 111; Vaughan and Richter, 'Crossing the Cultural Divide', 82.

24 *OHBE*, II, 291; and see Michael Zuckerman, 'Identity in British America: Unease in Eden', in Nicholas Canny and Anthony Pagden (eds), *Colonial Identity in the Atlantic World, 1500–1800* (Princeton, NJ, 1987).

25 For an excellent modern edition, see *The Sovereignty and Goodness of God by Mary Rowlandson*, ed. Neal Salisbury (Boston, MA, 1997).

26 *Ibid.*, 71, 81, 94.

27 As printed in VanDerBeets, *Held Captive by Indians*, 94, 97.

28 On this, see June Namias, *White Captives: Gender and Ethnicity on the American Frontier* (Chapel Hill, NC, 1993).

29 Lepore, *Name of War*, 5.

30 Vaughan and Clark, *Puritans among the Indians*, 153: Hannah's story is reprinted in this volume.

31 Demos, *Unredeemed Captive*, 49.

32 It should be noted however that American colonial captivity narratives were sometimes reprinted as additions to British-authored books. Thus Richard Blome, a London-based publisher with a marked interest in topography and empire, included Quentin Stockwell's narrative in his *The Present State of His Majesties Isles and Territories in America* (1687).

33 On the Deerfield attack, see Demos, *Unredeemed Captive*; L.F. Stock (ed.), *Proceedings and Debates of the British Parliaments respecting North America* (5 vols, Washington, DC, 1924–41), III, 73.

34 *CSPC*, XXV, 73–5.

35 J.H. Elliott, *The Old World and the New 1492–1650* (Cambridge, 1970). R.C. Simmons, *British Imprints Relating to North America 1621–1760* (1996) is a useful guide which demonstrates the surge in publications on this area after 1750. Books printed in Britain on France, Spain and Italy remained however far more numerous throughout.

36 Lepore, *Name of War*, 48–56.

37 See his *Pastoral Letter to the English Captives in Africa* (Boston, MA, 1698); and *The Glory of Goodness* (Boston, MA, 1703).

38 I am sure for instance that one of the reasons for the unusual success of Jonathan Dickenson's narrative, which was repeatedly reissued in Britain throughout the eighteenth century, was that the events recorded in its pages occurred in Florida rather than in New England. Dickenson's text and subtitle also made much of episodes of shipwreck and cannibalism and of one of his fellow captives, a leading English North Country Quaker.

39 Charles Fitz-Geffrey, *Compassion towards Captives, chiefly towards our brethren and country-men who are in miserable bondage in Barbarie* (Oxford, 1637), 2–3.

40 'The British Empire and the Civic Tradition, 1656–1742', Cambridge PhD dissertation, 1992, 35.

41 *Mary Rowlandson* (1997), 64; VanDerBeets, *Held Captive by Indians*, 96.

42 Stock, *Proceedings and Debates*, II, 438. Even the most forceful exponent of the view that British empire in America was military in ethos from the start, describes the regular army presence in the colonies thus: 'The

garrisons were diseased, dispersed, and undisciplined, and their numbers were small. In the seventeenth century there were seldom more than one thousand regular soldiers in the North American continent. Often there were no more than three hundred.' Stephen Saunders Webb, *The Governors-General: The English Army and the Definition of the Empire, 1589–1681* (Chapel Hill, NC, 1979), 454.

43 Stock, *Proceedings and Debates*, II, 435.

44 See Appendix B of J.A. Houlding, *Fit for Service: The Training of the British Army, 1715–1795* (Oxford, 1981), 410–13.

45 Stock, *Proceedings and Debates*, III, 359–60.

46 *Ibid.*, V, 257.

47 Vaughan and Richter, 'Crossing the Cultural Divide', 51.

48 *OHBE*, I, 215.

49 See Lepore, *Name of War*, 173–4.

50 See Eric Hinderaker, 'The "Four Indian Kings" and the imaginative construction of the First British Empire', *WMQ*, 53 (1996); and, for the Verelst and other images of the 'kings': Bruce Robertson, 'The Portraits: An Iconographical Study', in John G. Garratt, *The Four Indian Kings / Les Quatre Rois Indiens* (Ottawa, 1985), 139–49.

51 Hugh Honour, *The Golden Land: European Images of America from the Discoveries to the Present Time* (1976), 125.

52 Richard P. Bond, *Queen Anne's American Kings* (Oxford, 1952), 77; for a classic analysis of cross-cultural relations in North America stressing the 'nexus of relations and transactions' rather than conflict, see Richard White, *The Middle Ground: Indians, Empires, and Republics in the Great Lakes Region, 1650–1815* (Cambridge, 1991).

53 Quoted in P.J. Marshall and Glyndwr Williams, *The Great Map of Mankind* (1982), 195.

6. War and a New World

1 *Susanna Johnson* (1797) *passim*. I have also drawn on *A Narrative of the Captivity of Mrs Johnson* (Lowell, MA., 1834) which includes additional material.

2 *Susanna Johnson* (1797), 65–70.

3 H.V. Bowen, 'British conceptions of global empire, 1756–83', *Journal of Imperial and Commonwealth History* 26 (1998), 6. The best recent accounts of the Seven Years War as American colonists and Britons at home experienced it are Fred Anderson, *Crucible of War* (New York, 2000), and Eliga Gould, *The Persistence of Empire* (2000).

4 *An Inquiry into the Nature and Causes of the Wealth of Nations*, ed. R.H.

Campbell and A.S. Skinner (2 vols, Oxford, 1976), II, 708. For the downturn in Western admiration for China after 1760, see Jonathan Spence, *The Chan's Great Continent* (1998).

5 R.C. Simmons and P.D.G. Thomas (eds), *Proceedings and Debates of the British Parliaments respecting North America 1759–1783* (6 vols, 1982–6), I, 71.

6 See, for instance, *Treaty and Convention for the Sick, Wounded, and Prisoners of War* (1759).

7 *Jean Lowry* (1760), 17; PRO, T1/391.

8 For pre-Revolutionary American visitors to Britain in general, see Susan Lindsey Lively, 'Going Home: Americans in Britain, 1740–1776', Harvard University PhD dissertation, 1997.

9 Richard C. Simmons, 'Americana in British Books, 1621–1760', in Karen Ordahl Kupperman (ed.), *America in European Consciousness 1493–1750* (1995).

10 John Brewer, *Party Ideology and Popular Politics at the Accession of George III* (Cambridge, 1976), 139–60.

11 See, for instance, *Elizabeth Hanson* (1760); [Arthur Young], *The Theatre of the Present War in North America* (1758), iv-v.

12 See *Mary Rowlandson* (1997), 69, 75, 76, 79, 81. For the distinctiveness of colonists' pre-1776 experience: see Jon Butler, *Becoming America* (Cambridge, MA, 2000).

13 *John Rutherfurd* (1958), 233; *Peter Williamson* (1996), 11n; *Henry Grace* (1765), 12.

14 *Thomas Morris* (1904), 315, 318. Morris's initial text was written soon after the events he described, in 1764. A version was sent to George III in 1775, but the narrative was only published in 1791. Since the original manuscript seems not to have survived, we cannot know what – if anything – he added in the interval.

15 For a balanced account of this débâcle, see Daniel J. Beattie, 'The Adaption of the British Army to Wilderness Warfare, 1755–1763', in M. Ultee (ed.), *Adapting to Conditions: War and Society in the Eighteenth Century* (Alabama, 1986); *Thomas Morris* (1904), 316.

16 Anderson, *Crucible of War*, 151–2.

17 See W.J. Eccles, 'The social, economic, and political significance of the military establishment in New France', *Canadian Historical Review*, 52 (1971).

18 See, for instance, John Shy, *Toward Lexington: The Role of the British Army in the Coming of the American Revolution* (Princeton, NJ, 1965), 1–40.

19 NLS, MS 6506, fol. 38.

20 *Gentleman's Magazine* (1758), 259–60; *John Rutherfurd* (1958), 226–7.

21 *Henry Grace* (1765), 47–8; Ian K. Steele, 'Surrendering Rites: Prisoners on Colonial North American Frontiers', in Stephen Taylor *et al.* (eds), *Hanoverian Britain and Empire: Essays in Memory of Philip Lawson* (Woodbridge, Suffolk, 1998), 141.

22 Williams' account of this episode and his own Indian captivity are in Huntington Library, Pasadena, LO 977, box 21, deposition dated 5 Feb. 1757, and LO 5344, box 115, examination dated 5 Jan. 1758.

23 Ian K. Steele, *Betrayals: Fort William Henry and the 'Massacre'* (Oxford, 1990); for an example of British desertion in the face of a possible Indian attack, see Robert R. Rea, 'Military deserters from British West Florida', *Louisiana History*, 9 (1968), 124–5.

24 On these, see Eileen Harris, *The Townshend Album* (1974).

25 Though this was by no means a unanimous view in Britain: see, for instance, [Horace Walpole], *Reflections on the different ideas of the French and English, in regard to cruelty* (1759).

26 See *Proceedings of the Committee . . . for Cloathing French Prisoners of War* (1760); Francis Abell, *Prisoners of War in Britain 1756 to 1815* (1914), 449–50.

27 *The Law of Nations* (2 vols, 1760 edn), Book III, 26, 49–56.

28 PRO, CO/5/50, fols 579 and 611.

29 Beattie, 'The Adaption of the British Army to Wilderness Warfare', 74n; W.A. Gordon, 'The siege of Louisburg', *Journal of the Royal United Service Institution*, LX (1915), 125.

30 The verdict on Amherst is in Michael J. Mullin, 'Sir William Johnson, Indian Relations, and British Policy, 1744 to 1774', University of California, Santa Barbara, 1989 PhD dissertation, 244; Anderson, *Crucible of War*, 546.

31 For Amherst and genocide, see Bernard Knollenberg, 'General Amherst and germ warfare', *Mississippi Valley Historical Review*, XLI (1965); for John Stuart, see J. Norman Heard, *Handbook of the American Frontier: The Southeastern Woodlands* (1987), 344, and James W. Covington, *The British meet the Seminoles: Negotiations between British Authorities in East Florida and the Indians, 1763–8* (Gainesville, FL, 1961).

32 For a British colonist's casual admission of how he and a companion killed and scalped a defenceless Indian woman, see *A Journal of Lieutenant Simon Stevens . . . with an account of his escape from Quebec* (Boston, MA, 1760), 12; and for an example of the ferocity of British regular army warfare in America, see P.G.M. Foster, 'Quebec 1759', *JSAHR*, 64 (1986), 221–2.

33 Quoted in Richard L. Merritt, *Symbols of American Community 1735–1775* (Westport, CT, 1966), 164.

34 *Man of the World* (2 vols, 1773), II, 169–83; Tobias Smollett, *The Expedition of Humphry Clinker* (Oxford, 1966), 192–4.

35 J. Bennett Nolan, 'Peter Williamson in America, a colonial odyssey', *Pennsylvania History*, XXX–XXXI (1963–4), 24–5. Williamson merits a proper biography as a Scottish, imperial and cultural phenomenon. The 1762 version of his narrative was reprinted with a useful introduction by Michael Fry in 1996.

36 *Peter Williamson* (1757), 10, 14, 20, 24.

37 *Peter Williamson* (1996), 14, 87, 89, 92–3, 108 *seq*.

38 *The trial of divorce at the instance of Peter Williamson* (Edinburgh, 1789), xxiii.

39 For his story, which was also made into a (sadly neglected) film with Pierce Brosnan, see Lovat Dickson, *Wilderness Man: The Amazing True Story of Grey Owl* (1999).

40 Some of Rutherfurd's family background and Detroit experiences can be reconstructed from the James Sterling letter-book at the William Clements Library, Ann Arbor.

41 *John Rutherfurd* (1958), 227, 229, 233–43.

42 *Ibid.* (1958), 220–1, 241, 247, 249.

43 Peter Way, 'The Cutting Edge of Culture: British Soldiers Encounter Native Americans in the French and Indian War', in Martin Daunton and Rick Halpern (eds), *Empire and Others: British Encounters with Indigenous Peoples 1600–1850* (1999), 142–3; S.H.A. Hervey (ed.), *Journals of the Hon. William Hervey in America and Europe* (Bury St Edmunds, 1906), 144.

44 Rea, 'Military deserters', 126; James Sullivan (ed.), *The Papers of Sir William Johnson* (14 vols, Albany, NY, 1921–65), IV, 428. For a useful survey of these kind of crossings, see Colin Calloway, 'Neither red nor white: white renegades on the American Indian frontier', *Western Historical Quarterly*, 17 (1986).

45 [William Smith], *An historical account of the expedition against the Ohio Indians* (1766), 27 and *passim*.

46 *Ibid.*, 28.

47 PRO, WO 34/27, fol. 150.

48 On this, see Philip Lawson, *The Imperial Challenge: Quebec and Britain in the Age of the American Revolution* (Montreal, 1989); and Robert L. Gold, *Borderland Empires in Transition: The Triple Nation Transfer of Florida* (Carbondale, IL, 1969).

49 Merritt, *Symbols of American Community*, 119 *seq*; see also T.H. Breen, 'Ideology and nationalism on the eve of the American Revolution: revisions once more in need of revising', *Journal of American History*, 84 (1997).

50 Based on population figures in *OHBE*, II, 100.

51 On this, see Bernard Bailyn, *Voyagers to the West: A Passage in the Peopling of America on the Eve of the Revolution* (New York, 1988), 3–66.

52 John Mitchell, *The Present State of Great Britain and North America* (1767), viii, 114; for Grenville's warning, see L.F. Stock (ed.), *Proceedings and Debates of the British Parliaments respecting North America* (Washington, DC, 5 vols, 1924–41), V, 566–7.

53 R.W. Chapman (ed.), *Boswell Life of Johnson* (Oxford, 1970), 592.

54 The best account of London's thinking on these points is still Jack M.

Sosin, *Whitehall and the Wilderness: The Middle West in British Colonial Policy 1760–1775* (Lincoln, NE, 1961).

55 See Fernand Ouellet, 'The British Army of Occupation in the St Lawrence Valley', in R.A. Prete (ed.), *Armies of Occupation* (Kingston, Ont., 1984), 38–9.

7 Revolutions

1 For André's story and cult, see Horace W. Smith, *Andreana* (Philadelphia, PA, 1865); William Abbatt, *The Crisis of the Revolution: Being the Story of Arnold and André* (New York, 1899); James Thomas Flexner, *The Traitor and the Spy* (New York, 1953).

2 Flexner, *Traitor and Spy*, 146; Abbatt, *Crisis of the Revolution*, 68.

3 Stephen Conway, *The War of American Independence 1775–1783* (1995), 48.

4 *Ibid., passim.*

5 Two valuable studies placing the Thirteen Colonies in a wider imperial context are D.W. Meinig, *The Shaping of America: A Geographical Perspective on 500 Years of History* (1986); and A. J. O'Shaughnessy, *An Empire Divided: The American Revolution and the British Caribbean* (Philadelphia, PA, 2000).

6 Conway, *War of Independence*, 157.

7 George Adams Boyd, *Elias Boudinot, Patriot and Statesman 1740–1821* (Princeton, NJ, 1952), 45. There are many studies of American Revolutionary prisoners of the British, far fewer of their opposite numbers. A rare and useful comparative essay is Betsy Knight, 'Prisoner exchange and parole in the American Revolution', *WMQ*, 48 (1991).

8 PRO, CO5/105, fol. 171.

9 Richard Sampson, *Escape in America: The British Convention Prisoners 1777–1783* (Chippenham, Picton, 1995), 193; BL, Add. MS 38875, fols 74–5.

10 James Lennox Banks, *David Sproat and Naval Prisoners in the War of the Revolution* (New York, 1909), 116.

11 For the Spanish estimate, see PRO, ADM 98/14, fol. 199; Franklin's opinion is cited in PRO, ADM 98/12, fol. 262.

12 Ray Raphael, *A People's History of the American Revolution* (New York, 2001), 114; W.V. Hensel, *Major John André as a Prisoner of War* (Lancaster, PA, 1904), 13.

13 Newberry Library, Chicago, Ayer MS 728, vault box.

14 Charles H. Metzger, *The Prisoner in the American Revolution* (Chicago, IL, 1971), 4; Memorial of John MacGuire, PRO, 30/55/82. The American Revolutionary Terror – and how it impacted on all the protagonists and ethnic groupings involved – still awaits its historian.

15 Larry G. Bowman, *Captive Americans: Prisoners during the American Revolution* (Athens, OH, 1976), 59.

16 [Allan Ramsay], *Letters on the Present Disturbances in Great Britain and her American Provinces* (1777), 20. I owe this reference to Professor Eliga Gould.

17 *William Widger* (1937), 347.

18 *Thomas Hughes* (1947), 17.

19 *Charles Herbert* (1847), 19–20; *John Blatchford* (1788), 9.

20 *Charles Herbert* (1847), 34.

21 Olive Anderson, 'The treatment of prisoners of war in Britain during the American War of Independence', *Bulletin of the Institute of Historical Research*, 28 (1955), 63; *An Authentic Narrative of Facts relating to the Exchange of Prisoners taken at the Cedars* (1777), 5.

22 Howe to Lt.-Col. Walcot, 26 January 1777, PRO, 30/55/4, fol. 388; K.G. Davies (ed.), *Documents of the American Revolution 1770–1783: Vol. XI Transcripts, 1775* (Dublin, 1976), 73.

23 For example, Washington to Howe, 10 February 1778: PRO, CO5/95, fol. 322.

24 See Raphael, *People's History, passim*.

25 Robert John Denn, 'Prison Narratives of the American Revolution', Michigan State University PhD dissertation, 1980, 61–2. For an attempt to reach beyond the propaganda to a more reliable estimate of American casualties in prison and on the battlefield, see Howard H. Peckham, *The Toll of Independence* (Chicago, IL, 1974).

26 *Substance of General Burgoyne's Speeches at a Court Martial . . . at the Trial of Colonel Henley* (Newport, MA, 1778); Boyd, *Elias Boudinot*, 45.

27 Boyd, *Elias Boudinot*, 57.

28 See the evidence assembled in PRO, CO5/105, fols 315 *seq*.

29 *Thomas Anburey* (1791), I, preface.

30 Thus a Resolution of 5 January 1781 accused the British of ignoring 'the practice of civilized nations [and] . . . treating our people prisoners to them with every species of insults', Anderson, 'Treatment of Prisoners of War', 75.

31 Washington to Cornwallis, 18 October 1781, PRO, 30/11/74, fol. 124; Lee Kennett, *The French Forces in America 1780–1783* (1977), 155.

32 Denn, 'Prison Narratives', 28–30.

33 For examples of British atrocity accusations against the Revolutionaries, see [John Lind], *An Answer to the Declaration of the American Congress* (1776), which went through five editions that year. For American propaganda networks: Philip Davidson, *Propaganda and the American Revolution, 1763–1783* (New York, 1973 edn).

34 Catherine M. Prelinger, 'Benjamin Franklin and the American prisoners

of war in England during the American Revolution', *WMQ*, 32 (1975), 264.

35 As Richard Sampson remarks, 'most British military historians appear to have been satisfied to "write off" these men' – and not just military historians: *Escape in America*, xi–xii. *Parl. Hist.*, 19 (1777–8), 1178.

36 Raphael, *People's History*, 135, 332.

37 For Allen, see Raphael, *People's History*, 18–21; Michael A. Bellesiles, *Revolutionary Outlaws: Ethan Allen and the Struggle for Independence on the Early American Frontier* (1995).

38 *Ethan Allen* (1930), 37, 40, 82, 118.

39 Howe to Washington, 1 August 1776, PRO, CO 5/93, fol. 487.

40 For McCrea, see June Namias, *White Captives: Gender and Ethnicity on the American Frontier* (Chapel Hill, NC, 1993), 117 *seq.*; *Parl. Hist.*, 19 (1777–8), 697.

41 BL, Add. MS 32413, fol. 71B.

42 Revd Wheeler Case, *Poems occasioned by . . . the present grand contest of America for liberty* (New Haven, CT, 1778), 37–9.

43 Carl Berger, *Broadsides and Bayonets: The Propaganda War of the American Revolution* (San Raphael, CA, 1976 rev. edn), 199.

44 *John Dodge* (1779), 14; *John Leeth* (1904), 29–30; Neal Salisbury (ed.), *The Sovereignty and Goodness of God by Mary Rowlandson* (1997), 51–5.

45 *Benjamin Gilbert* (1784), 12; *Ebenezer Fletcher* (1798), 6.

46 See Sidney Kaplan and Emma Nogrady Kaplan, *The Black Presence in the Era of the American Revolution* (Amherst, MA, 1989); and Raphael, *People's History*, 177–234.

47 There has been an explosion of published work on these aspects of the Revolution in recent decades. For some of the best, see Kaplan and Kaplan, *Black Presence*; Sylvia R. Frey, *Water from the Rock: Black Resistance in a Revolutionary Age* (Princeton, NJ, 1991); Gary B. Nash, *Race and Revolution* (Madison, 1990); Colin Calloway, *The American Revolution in Indian Country* (Cambridge, 1995); and see Kirk Davis Swinehart's forthcoming Yale University PhD dissertation 'Indians in the House: Empire and Aristocracy in Mohawk Country, 1738–1845'.

48 BL, Add. MS 32413, fol. 73; [Lind], *Answer to the Declaration*, 96, 108.

49 Sidney Kaplan, 'The "Domestic Insurrections" of the Declaration of Independence', *Journal of Negro History*, XLI (1976), 244–5; Benjamin Quarles, 'Lord Dunmore as Liberator', *WMQ*, XV (1958).

50 Quoted in Lester C. Olson, *Emblems of American Community in the Revolutionary Era* (Washington, DC, 1991), 80; Burke quoted in Ronald Hoffman and Peter J. Albert (eds), *Peace and the Peacemakers: the Treaty of 1783* (Charlottesville, VA, 1986), 9–10.

51 James W. St. G Walker, *The Black Loyalists* (1976), 4; Jack M. Sosin, 'The use of Indians in the War of the American Revolution: a reassessment of responsibility', *Canadian Historical Review*, 46 (1965).

52 Raphael, *People's History*, 140.

53 Robert W. Tucker and David C. Hendrickson, *Empire of Liberty: The Statecraft of Thomas Jefferson* (Oxford, 1990), 305.

54 Abbatt, *Crisis of the Revolution*, 83.

8 Another Passage to India

1 See *Sarah Shade* (1801), a 45-page pamphlet that I have drawn on throughout this chapter.

2 See Matthew Stephens, *Hannah Snell: The Secret Life of a Female Marine, 1723–1792* (1997); and Dianne Dugaw (ed.), *The Female Soldier* (Los Angeles, CA, 1989).

3 Like all people operating in a mainly verbal culture, Sarah often mis-remembers dates. Thus her own narrative has her born in 1741, whereas the Stoke Edith parish register reveals that she was baptised on 30 November 1746. But all the characters and major events in her story can be verified. For example, her first husband John Cuff is down on a Madras army muster roll as arriving in India in 1764, five years before Sarah: IOL, L/MIL/11/110. I make these points to stress how possible it is – despite assertions sometimes made to the contrary – to uncover and investigate imperial histories from below.

4 *OHBE*, II, 542.

5 C.W. Pasley, *Essay on the Military Policy and Institutions of the British Empire* (1810), 1–4.

6 IOL, L/MAR/B/272G and L/MAR/B/272S (2).

7 For two expert and colourful evocations of the East India Company's maritime evolution, see John Keay, *The Honourable Company* (1991) and Anthony Farrington, *Trading Places: The East India Company and Asia 1600–1834* (2002). Those interested should visit the National Maritime Museum at Greenwich and ask to be shown the many canvases of East Indiamen, by no means all of which are normally on display.

8 For a succinct and valuable survey, see Philip Lawson, *The East India Company: A History* (1993).

9 Brian Allen, 'The East India Company's Settlement Pictures: George Lambert and Samuel Scott', in Pauline Rohatgi and Pheroza Godrej (eds), *Under the Indian Sun* (Bombay, 1995).

10 *OHBE*, II, 487–507.

11 As the future Lord Macaulay put it: 'After the grant, the Company was not, in form and name, an independent power. It was merely a minister of the court of Delhi.' Its transformation into something very different, was 'effected by degrees, and under disguise': *Hansard*, 3rd ser., 19 (1833), 507.

12 P.J. Marshall, *East India Fortunes: The British in Bengal in the Eighteenth Century* (Oxford, 1976), 217–18.

13 P.J. Marshall (ed.) *The Writings and Speeches of Edmund Burke: Madras and Bengal, 1774–85* (Oxford, 1981), 402. For a powerful evocation of mortality rates, see Theon Wilkinson, *Two Monsoons: The Life and Death of Europeans in India* (1987 edn).

14 William Fullarton, *A View of the English Interests in India* (1788 edn), 49–50.

15 'In calculating the relative power of England over that country [India], we were too apt to commit the fallacy of estimating our own strength in one balance, and placing in the other the resources of 150,000,000 of inhabitants': *Hansard*, 3rd ser., 64 (1842), 449. It is interesting that Disraeli still felt this was a problem at a time when British hegemony in the subcontinent was virtually complete. C.A. Bayly, *Indian Society and the Making of the British Empire* (Cambridge, 1988).

16 Marshall, *East Indian Fortunes*, 43; Om Prakash (ed.), *European Commercial Enterprise in Pre-Colonial India* (Cambridge, 1998); S.Arasaratnam, *Maritime Commerce and English Power: Southeast India, 1750–1800* (Aldershot, 1996), 242.

17 C.A. Bayly (ed.), *The Raj: India and the British 1600–1947* (1991), 130. On the military labour market in India, see D.H.A. Kolff, *Naukar, Rajput and Sepoy* (Cambridge, 1990); and Seema Alavi, *The Sepoys and the Company* (Delhi, 1995).

18 NLS, MS 2958, fol. 77.

19 At least three British civilians caught up in the Patna 'massacre' of 1763 produced captivity narratives, for instance, but none of these was published until the twentieth century: W.K Firminger (ed.), *The Diaries of Three Surgeons of Patna* (Calcutta, 1909).

20 See Kate Teltscher, '"The Fearful Name of the Black Hole": Fashioning an Imperial Myth', in Bart Moore-Gilbert (ed.), *Writing India, 1757–1990* (Manchester, 1996); and S.C. Hill (ed.), *Bengal in 1756–1757* (3 vols, 1905), especially vol. III.

21 Hill, *Bengal*, III, 303 and 388.

22 *Ibid.*, III, 380; Robert Orme, *A History of the Military Transactions* (3 vols, 1803 rev. edn), II, 76.

23 G.J. Bryant, 'The East India Company and its Army 1600–1778', London University PhD dissertation (1975), 36, 247; and his 'Officers of the East India Company's army in the days of Clive and Hastings', *Journal of Imperial and Commonwealth History*, 6 (1978); *OHBE*, II, 202.

24 K. K. Datta *et al.* (eds), *Fort William–India House Correspondence . . . 1748–1800* (21 vols, Delhi, 1949–85) VIII, 287. For nervousness in London about the pace of expansion, see H.V. Bowen, *Revenue and Reform: The Indian Problem in British Politics 1757–1773* (Cambridge, 1991).

25 *British India Analysed* (3 vols, 1793), III, 839.

26 A.N. Gilbert, 'Recruitment and reform in the East India Company army, 1760–1800', *Journal of British Studies*, XV (1975).

27 *Ibid.*, 92; *British India Analysed*, III, 827. Losses at sea virtually every year can be traced in Edward Dodwell and James Miles, *Alphabetical List of the Officers of the Indian Army* (1838).

28 Gilbert, 'Recruitment and reform'.

29 IOL, MSS Eur. D 1146/6, fol. 111; James Forbes's Memoirs, Yale Center for British Art, New Haven, Rare Books and Manuscripts Department, IV, fol. 8.

30 *Proposal for Employing Mallayan or Buggess Troops* (Edinburgh, 1769), 2.

31 *Interesting Historical Events relative to the Provinces of Bengal* (1765), 181.

32 On these trends, see Stewart N. Gordon, 'The slow conquest: administrative integration of Madras into the Maratha empire, 1720–1760', *MAS*, 11 (1977); Burton Stein, 'State formation and economy reconsidered', *MAS*, 19 (1985); Pradeep Barua, 'Military developments in India, 1750–1850', *Journal of Military History*, 58 (1994).

33 BL, Add. MS 29898, fol. 41.

34 Quoted in Randolf G.S. Cooper, 'Wellington and the Marathas in 1803'. *International History Review*, II (1989), 31–2 (my italics); BL, Add. MS 38408, fols 243–4.

35 See Judy Egerton's description of one version of this work in Christie's of London's sales catalogue, *British Pictures*, 8 June 1995, 84–7.

36 For Stubbs and his contemporaries on tigers, see Christopher Lennox-Boyd, Rob Dixon and Tim Clayton, *George Stubbs: The Complete Engraved Works* (1989); Edwin Landseer, *Twenty Engravings of Lions, Tigers, Panthers and Leopards* (1823).

37 Landseer, *Twenty Engravings*, 30.

38 Egerton, sale catalogue entry, 86; Edmund Burke, *A Philosophical Enquiry into the Origin of Our Ideas of the Sublime and Beautiful*, ed. J.T. Boulton (1958), 66 (my italics).

39 Landseer, *Twenty Engravings*, 8.

40 Lennox-Boyd *et al.*, *George Stubbs*; Amal Chatterjee, *Representations of India, 1740–1840* (Basingstoke, 1998), 78.

41 Edmund Burke in 1781: *Parl. Hist.*, 22 (1781–2), 316. For Tipu and his tigers, see Chapter Nine, and Kate Brittlebank, 'Sakti and Barakat: the power of Tipu's Tiger', *MAS*, 29 (1995).

1 For the prominent Scottish presence in this and other Mysore battles, see Anne Buddle *et al.*, *The Tiger and the Thistle* (Edinburgh, 1999). See, too, note 66 for this chapter.

2 NLS, MS 38408, fol. 31. I have benefited from discussing these murals, and many other matters Indian, with Professor Christopher Bayly and Dr Susan Bayly.

3 *Parl. Hist.*, 22 (1781–2), 114; W.S. Lewis *et al.*, *The Yale Edition of Horace Walpole's Correspondence* (48 vols, New Haven, CT, 1937–83), XXIX, 123.

4 See M.D. George, *Catalogue of Prints and Drawings in the British Museum: Political and Personal Satires* (11 vols, 1978 edn), VI, prints 7928, 7929, 7932 and 7939; P.J. Marshall, '"Cornwallis Triumphant": War in India and the British Public in the Late Eighteenth Century', in Lawrence Freedman *et al.*, *War, Strategy, and International Politics* (Oxford, 1992), 65–6.

5 *Narrative of all the Proceedings and Debates . . . on East-India Affairs* (1784), 89.

6 *Parl. Hist.*, 21 (1780–1), 1173; P.J. Marshall, *The Impeachment of Warren Hastings* (Oxford, 1965).

7 For three rather different approaches to these rulers, see Nikhiles Guha, *Pre-British State System in South India: Mysore 1761–1799* (Calcutta, 1985); Burton Stein, 'State formation and economy reconsidered', *MAS*, 19 (1985); and Kate Brittlebank, *Tipu Sultan's Search for Legitimacy* (Delhi, 1997).

8 Pradeep Barua, 'Military developments in India, 1750–1850', *Journal of Military History*, 58 (1994).

9 *Appendix to the Sixth Report from the Committee of Secrecy . . . into the Causes of the War in the Carnatic* (1782), 335, No. 11; C.C. Davies (ed.), *The Private Correspondence of Lord Macartney* (1950), 20; *Descriptive List of Secret Department Records* (8 vols, Delhi, 1960–74), III, 36.

10 Quoted in C.A. Bayly, *Indian Society and the Making of the British Empire* (Cambridge, 1988), 97.

11 For an illuminating account of Haidar by one of his Portuguese mercenaries, see BL, Add. MS 19287.

12 See *Descriptive List of Secret Department Records*, III, 80, 129, 156; K.K. Datta *et al.* (eds), *Fort William–India House Correspondence . . . 1748–1800* (21 vols, Delhi, 1949–85), XV, 541.

13 [Jonathan Scott], *An Historical and Political View of the Decan, South of the Kistnah* (1791), 15–22.

14 *Parl. Hist.*, 21 (1780–1), 1201–2; and see the reasoning of Lord Wellesley in 1799: Edward Ingram (ed.), *Two Views of British India* (Bath, 1970), 189.

15 Contemporary estimates vary. These are taken from an account by a former captive: *Innes Munro* (1789), 351; NLS, MS 13615A, fol. 32.

16 *Robert Cameron MS* (unpaginated).

17 *Innes Munro* (1789), 277.

18 IOL, H/251, fol. 699.

19 Spandrell's damning verdict on his military stepfather in Huxley's novel *Point Counterpoint.*

20 Michel Foucault, *Discipline and Punish: The Birth of the Prison* (1977), 169.

21 Robert Darnton, *The Business of Enlightenment* (1979), 292–3, 297. For army officers as cultural producers in another European power, see László Deme, 'Maria Theresa's Noble Lifeguards and the Rise of Hungarian Enlightenment and Nationalism', Béla K.Király and Walter Scott Dillard (eds), *The East Central European Officer Corps 1740–1920s* (New York, 1988).

22 Lewis Namier and John Brooke (eds), *The House of Commons 1754–1790* (3 vols, 1964), II, 142.

23 'An essay on the art of war', IOL, Orme O.V. 303, fols 109–111; IOL MSS Eur.C.348, fols 1 and 7.

24 See his *The Story of the Malakand Field Force* (1898), and *London to Ladysmith* (1900).

25 See G.V. Scammell, 'European exiles, renegades and outlaws and the maritime economy of Asia *c.* 1500–1750', *MAS*, 26 (1992).

26 Seringapatam/Srirangapatna should be visited and deserves to be a World Heritage site. For an efficient, modern guide in English, see L.N. Swamy, *History of Srirangapatna* (Delhi, 1996).

27 See *James Scurry* (1824), 48–68.

28 John Howard, *The State of the Prisons* (Abingdon, 1977 edn), iii; *Gentleman's Magazine* 54 (1784), 950. For a broader discussion of POW treatment in Europe at this time, see Michael Lewis, *Napoleon and his British Captives* (1962).

29 For the plight of the wounded, see for example BL, Add. MS 41622, fol. 52 *seq.*

30 BL, Add. MS 39857, fols 317–18.

31 *Cromwell Massey* (1912), 24.

32 [William Thomson], *Memoirs of the Late War in Asia* (2 vols, 1788), II, 45.

33 IOL, Eur. MSS E. 330. Indian intermediaries transported messages for whites during the insurrections of 1857 in an identical fashion: see Jane Robinson, *Angels of Albion: Women of the Indian Mutiny* (1996), 81.

34 This emerges in virtually all Mysore captivity narratives, see Thomson, *Memoirs* (1789 edn), I, 122, 179–80.

35 For the details of Massey's text, see Appendix.

36 See also the account of these developments in *John Lindsay MS.*

37 *Cromwell Massey* (1912), 12–30.

38 See *Robert Gordon MS*, fol. 36.

39 Abdelwahab Bouhdiba, *Sexuality in Islam* (1985), 180.

40 *Cromwell Massey* (1912), 18.

41 On Tipu's religious politics, see Brittlebank, *Tipu Sultan's Search for Legitimacy.*

42 I owe this suggestion to Nigel Chancellor of Cambridge University.

43 *Cromwell Massey* (1912), 23; Felix Bryk, *Circumcision in Man and Woman: its History, Psychology and Ethnology* (New York, 1934), 29.

44 Marshall, '"Cornwallis Triumphant"', 70–1.

45 *John Lindsay* MS (unpaginated).

46 *Ibid.*

47 Though there is evidence that he revised his original prison notebook with a view to publication, but then did not go through with it: see IOL, MSS Eur A94, fol. 149.

48 *Ibid.,* fols 41–4, 69, 84, 88, 108, 137.

49 See Kate Teltscher, *India Inscribed: European and British Writing on India 1600–1800* (Delhi, 1997), 157–91, 230–33.

50 *An authentic narrative of the treatment of the English who were taken prisoners . . . by Tippoo Saib* (1785), advertisement and 70.

51 *A Vindication of the Conduct of the English Forces Employed in the Late War* (1787), 34.

52 For a survey of this world crisis, see my 'Yale, America, and the World in 1801', in Paul Kennedy (ed.), *Yale, America and the World* (New Haven, CT, forthcoming).

53 See Marshall, '"Cornwallis Triumphant"'.

54 For a revisionist interpretation of these French ventures, see Maya Jasanoff, 'Collecting and Empire in India and Egypt, 1760–1830', Yale University Ph.D dissertation, 2003.

55 For British notions that Mysore and Revolutionary France were inter-linked, see C.A. Bayly, *Imperial Meridian: the British Empire and the World 1780–1830* (1989), 113–14.

56 *Times,* 10 April 1792; *Fort William–India House Correspondence*, XVI, 422–3; and XVII, 184, 230.

57 NLS, MS 13775, fol. 274; BL, Add. MS 41622, fol. 245.

58 *Innes Munro* (1789), 51, 119; *Robert Cameron* (1931), 19.

59 Anne Buddle, *Tigers round the Throne: The Court of Tipu Sultan* (1990), 11. For a shrewd and subtle British defence of Tipu by an East India Company officer, see Edward Moor, *A Narrative of the Operations of Captain Little's Detachment* (1794), 193 *seq.*

60 NLS, MS 13790, fols 177–9, 355–6.

61 For British official acceptance that the verdict on Tipu was still mixed, see *Copies and Extracts of Advices to and from India relative to the . . . war with the late Tippoo Sultaun* (1800).

62 The British Library copy of this piece of children's drama appears to have been published *c.* 1827. C.H. Philips (ed.), *Correspondence of David Scott Director and Chairman of the East India Company* (2 vols, 1951), II, 372.

63 See the Appendix.

64 'There were two officers with us dressed in the Highland garb who appeared particularly to attract Tippoo's attention. He said he was acquainted with the good qualities of this people as soldiers, and enquired how many men we had of this description.' NLS, MS 13775, fol. 271.

65 For Thomson, see *DNB*, 56, 274–5.

66 *Memoirs* (1st edn), I, iv-v, and *passim*; (2nd edn), 8 *seq.*

67 For Richardson's novels and their impact, see Terry Eagleton, *The Rape of Clarissa: Writing, Sexuality and Class Struggle in Samuel Richardson* (Oxford, 1982).

68 For details of Bristow's narrative, see Appendix.

69 See also my *Britons: Forging the Nation 1707–1837* (1992), 177–93.

70 Mildred Archer, *Tippoo's Tiger* (1983).

71 *Narrative of all the Proceedings and Debates*, 386.

72 *Oriental Miscellanies: Comprising Anecdotes of an Indian Life* (Wigan, 1840), 177.

73 Eagleton, *Rape of Clarissa*, 14–15.

74 Theodore Hook, *The Life of General . . . Sir David Baird* (2 vols, 1832), I, 43.

75 See the article on this phenomenon in the London *Guardian* supplement of 21 August 2001.

76 See, for instance, *Harry Oakes* (1785), 28.

77 NLS, MS 13653, fol. 5; *OHBE*, II, 202–3.

10 Captives in Uniform

1 William Hazlitt, *The Spirit of the Age*, ed. E.D. Mackerness (Plymouth, 1991 edn), 165.

2 *An Essay on the Principle of Population. First edition* (1996 edn), and the introduction by Samuel Hollander. For contemporary reactions, see D.V. Glass (ed.), *Introduction to Malthus* (1953).

3 For an illuminating discussion of the connections between the population debate and Britain's perceptions of its power, see J.E. Cookson, 'Political arithmetic and war in Britain, 1793–1815', *War & Society*, I (1983).

4 *Ibid.*; A.N. Gilbert, 'Recruitment and reform in the East India Company army, 1760–1800', *Journal of British Studies*, XV (1975), 99.

5 Colquhoun, *Treatise*, especially vi, 7, 16 and 196; *Memoir on the Necessity of Colonization at the Present Period* (1817), 1.

6 *PP*, 1831–32, XIII, 319.

7   On this phase of expansion, see *OHBE*, II, 184–207.

8   James D.Tracy (ed.), *The Political Economy of Merchant Empires* (Cambridge, 1991), 163.

9   M.F. Odintz, 'The British Officer Corps 1754–83', Michigan University PhD dissertation, 1988, 45–6; Peter Burroughs, 'The human cost of imperial defence in the early Victorian age', *Victorian Studies*, 24 (1980), 11.

10 See C.A. Bayly, 'Returning the British to South Asian history: the limits of colonial hegemony', *South Asia*, XVII (1994).

11 Miles Taylor, 'The 1848 revolutions and the British empire', *Past and Present*, 166 (2000), 150–1.

12 'Military forces of the civilized world', *East Indian United Service Journal*, I (1833–4), 94–5. The British also employed a growing number of police in India. But, again, these men were overwhelmingly Indian.

13 The term is Paul Kennedy's: see *The Rise and Fall of the Great Powers* (1989).

14 *PP*, 1836, XXII, 8 (my italics); *Hansard*, 2nd ser., 18 (1828), 629.

15 See C.A. Bayly, *Imperial Meridian: The British Empire and the World 1780–1830* (1989); and my *Britons: Forging the Nation 1707–1837* (1992), 147 *seq*.

16 'A grenadier's diary 1842–1856', IOL, MS Photo Eur 97, fol. 40.

17 P.J. Marshall, 'British immigration into India in the nineteenth century', *Itinerario*, 14 (1990), 182.

18 'Foreward', in Ranajit Guha and Gayatri Spivak (eds), *Selected Subaltern Studies* (Oxford, 1988), vi.

19 *PP*, 1806–7, IV, 427; for deserter details, see PRO, WO 25/2935–51.

20 H.G. Keene, *Hindustan under Free Lances, 1770–1820* (1907), xiii; cf. S. Inayat A. Zaidi, 'Structure and organization of the European mercenary armed forces in the second half of eighteenth-century India', *Islamic Culture*, 63 (1989).

21 Braudel is cited in Ellen G. Friedman, *Spanish Captives in North Africa in the Early Modern Age* (Madison, WI, 1983), 46.

22 G.V. Scammell, 'European exiles, renegades and outlaws and the maritime economy of Asia *c*. 1500–1750', *MAS*, 26 (1992).

23 C.S. Srinivasachariar (ed.), *Selections from Orme Manuscripts* (Annamalainagar, 1952), 33.

24 Coote's journal, 21 January 1760, IOL, Orme India VIII. For the miscellaneous composition of the Company's forces before the 1760s, see G.J. Bryant, 'The East India Company and its Army 1600–1778', London university PhD dissertation, 1975, 292–3.

25 K.K. Datta *et al.* (eds), *Fort William–India House Correspondence . . . 1748–1800* (21 vols, Delhi, 1949–85) XV, 507.

26 William Hough, *The Practice of Courts-Martial* (1825), 138; and his *The Practice of Courts-Martial and Other Military Courts* (1834), 74.

27 *Act for punishing mutiny and desertion* (Madras, 1850), 19–20.

28 In London, there was even profound concern about half-pay Company officers advising 'friendly' Indian states, because of the 'extension of the European system of military discipline' it would foster. IOL, L/MIL/5/380, fol. 136.

29 See, for instance, the report in N.B. Kay, *The Allies' War with Tipu Sultan 1790–1793* (Bombay, 1937), 475.

30 John Pemble, 'The Second Maratha War' in Maarten Ultee (ed.), *Adapting to Conditions: War and Society in the Eighteenth Century* (Alabama, 1986), 393.

31 *Henry Becher* (1793), 185, 188; *James Scurry* (1st edn, 1824), 60–2.

32 NLS, MS 13775, fols 193 and 368.

33 Gilbert, 'Recruitment and reform'; *James Scurry* (2nd edn, 1824).

34 This paragraph is based on Whiteway's narrative appended to *James Scurry* (2nd edn, 1824).

35 See for instance Sir Francis Burdett's speech in *Hansard*, 20 (1811), 703.

36 Irish desertion was never only or even mainly a political, anti-British act. Irish-born soldiers appear also to have deserted George Washington's Continental army in disproportionate numbers: see Charles Patrick Neimeyer, 'No Meat, No Soldier: Race, Class and Ethnicity in the Continental Army', Georgetown University PhD dissertation, 1993, 2 vols, I, 101.

37 PRO, WO 90/1: General Courts Martial abroad, entry for 21 November 1796.

38 *Memoirs of the Extraordinary Military Career of John Shipp* (3 vols, 1829), II, 78; Charles J. Napier, *Remarks on Military Law and the Punishment of Flogging* (1837), 127n.

39 For Thomas, see BL, Add. MSS 13579 and 13580; and William Francklin, *Military Memoirs of Mr George Thomas* (Calcutta, 1803).

40 See Rudyard Kipling, *The Man who would be King and Other Stories*, ed. Louis L. Cornell (Oxford, 1987).

41 I am indebted to my former Yale student Eric Weiss for information on William Francklin; BL, Add. MS 13580, fols 117, 144b.

42 *Ibid.*, fol. 145; Francklin, *Military Memoirs*, 250.

43 See, for instance, a similar romanticisation of the wayward, charismatic white leader of 'natives' in the fictional *Narrative of the Singular Activities and Captivity of Thomas Barry among the Monsippi Indians* (Manchester, 179?).

44 See, for instance, the remarkable account by a Portuguese mercenary officer serving Haidar Ali: BL, Add. MS 19287.

45 NLS, MS 8432, fols 116–17.

46 T.E. Lawrence, *Seven Pillars of Wisdom* (New York, 1991), 31–2.

47 BL, Add. MS 13579, fol. 56.

48 The following paragraphs are based on *The Trial of Lieutenant-Colonel Joseph Wall* (1802); and *Genuine and Impartial Memoirs of the life of Governor Wall* (1802).

49 Not least because British deserters were sometimes sentenced to be branded with the letter D; and the brand, like the whip, was known to be inflicted as well on slaves.

50 For Cochrane's case, see NLS, MS 8460, fols 54 and 56; Long's collections for the history of Jamaica, BL, Add. MS 18270, fol. 83.

51 Though see Scott Claver, *Under the Lash* (1954); and J.R. Dinwiddy, 'The Early Nineteenth-century Campaign against Flogging in the Army', in his *Radicalism and Reform in Britain. 1780–1850* (1992).

52 'Free Labor vs Slave Labor: The British and Caribbean Cases', in Seymour Drescher, *From Slavery to Freedom* (1999). Comparisons between black slaves and the white soldiery were made in other European imperial powers at this time: see C.R. Boxer, *The Dutch Seaborne Empire 1600–1800* (1965), 212.

53 *Hansard*, 21 (1812), 1275.

54 *Ibid.*, 1282; Napier, *Remarks on Military Law*, 191–2.

55 *Letters from England*, ed. Jack Simmons (Gloucester, 1984), 64.

56 *Statistical report on the sickness, mortality and invaliding among the troops in the West Indies* (1838), 10, 49; and *Statistical report on . . . the troops in . . . British America* (1839), 10b.

57 Peter Stanley, *White Mutiny: British Military Culture in India, 1825–1875* (1998), 69; Dinwiddy, 'Campaign against flogging', 133.

58 *Ibid.*, 137–8; James Walvin, *Questioning Slavery* (1996), 56.

59 *Hansard*, 3rd ser., 22 (1834), 239.

60 Hough, *Practice of Courts-Martial* (1825), 157–8; *East Indian United Service Journal*, 4 (1834), selections, 76–9.

61 Douglas M. Peers, 'Sepoys, soldiers and the lash: race, caste and army discipline in India, 1820–50', *Journal of Imperial and Commonwealth History*, 23 (1995), 215; for white as well as sepoy mutinies in India, see Alan J. Guy and Peter B. Boyden (eds), *Soldiers of the Raj: The Indian army 1600–1947* (1997), 100–117. It is possible that white deserters were prosecuted more aggressively than sepoys, and this is partly why more charges were brought against the former.

62 *Hansard*, 3rd ser., 11 (1832), 1229–30.

63 See their 'Height and health in the United Kingdom 1815–1860: evidence from the East India Company army', *Explorations in Economic History*, 33 (1996).

64 Hough, *Practice of Courts-Martial* (1825), 154.

65 The classic account is of course E.P. Thompson, *Making of the English Working Class* (1965).

66 *PP,* 1831–2, XIII, 158; *A Narrative of the Grievances and Illegal Treatment Suffered by the British Officers* (1810), 153.

67 C.H. Philips (ed.), *The Correspondence of Lord William Cavendish Bentinck* (2 vols, Oxford, 1977), II, 1351; for a vivid account of the life-styles of the white soldiery in India, see Stanley, *White Mutiny.*

68 Philip D. Curtin, *Death by Migration: Europe's Encounter with the Tropical World in the Nineteenth Century* (Cambridge, 1989), 8.

69 For an interesting attempt, see, Kenneth Ballhatchet, *Race, Sex and Class under the Raj* (1980); P.J. Marshall, 'The white town of Calcutta under the rule of the East India Company', *MAS,* 34 (2000).

70 IOL, L/MIL/5/390, fol. 25.

71 IOL, L/MIL/5/376, fol. 238. Harshness to soldiers' common law wives was not unique to India or necessarily racist in intent. Economy was also a factor. The troops who fought with Arthur Wellesley for years in Spain during the Napoleonic Wars were similarly forced to leave their local partners and children behind them when they left.

72 'A grenadier's diary', 132.

73 *PP,* 1831–32, XIII, 397–8.

74 Douglas M. Peers, '"The habitual nobility of being": British officers and the social construction of the Bengal army in the early nineteenth century', *MAS,* 25 (1991).

75 M. Monier-Williams, *A few remarks on the use of spiritous liquors among the European soldiers* (1823), 6; *PP,* 1831–32, XIII, 82, 172.

76 M.L. Bush (ed.), *Serfdom and Slavery: Studies in Legal Bondage* (1996), introduction, 2.

77 *A Soldier's Journal . . . to which are annexed Observations on the Present State of the Army of Great Britain* (1770), 180–1.

78 IOL, L/MIL/5/397, fols 317–18.

79 *Hansard,* 3rd ser., 32 (1836), 1043.

80 *Ibid.,* 934; *Hansard,* 3rd ser., 31 (1836), 892.

81 'A grenadier's diary', 126, 132–3.

82 *Ibid.,* 141–2.

83 See, for instance, Carolyn Steedman, *The Radical Soldier's Tale* (1988) for how a seemingly conventional and committed soldier in India gained from his experiences there both a knowledge of Indian religions and a critique of the British state.

84 See Hew Strachan, *The Reform of the British Army 1830–54* (Manchester, 1984).

85 *Statistical report on . . . British America,* 10b.

86 *Report . . . into the System of Military Punishments,* 187; IOL, L/MIL/5/384, fols 273–7.

87 *Comparative View of the Extent and Population of the Colonial Possessions of Great Britain and Other Powers* (1839): Wyld's commentary on the map.

88 See Olive Anderson, 'The growth of Christian militarism in mid-Victorian Britain', *English Historical Review*, LXXXVI (1971).

Epilogue: To Afghanistan and Beyond

1   Louis Dupree, *Afghanistan* (Oxford, 1997) is the best introduction to the history of this region in English. For the background to the 1838 invasion, see M.E. Yapp, *Strategies of British India: Britain, Iran and Afghanistan. 1798–1850* (Oxford, 1980); and J.A. Norris, *The First Afghan War, 1838–1842* (Cambridge, 1967).

2   For the British at Kabul, see Patrick Macrory, *Kabul Catastrophe: The Story of the Disastrous Retreat from Kabul* (Oxford, 1986).

3   Today the best known version of this thesis is probably George MacDonald Fraser's, *Flashman* (1969), which draws heavily on the classic Victorian indictment of the campaign by Sir John Kaye.

4   *E.A.H Webb* MS (unfoliated); James Lunt (ed.), *From Sepoy to Subedar: Being the Life and Adventures of Subedar Sita Ram* (1970), 12.

5   Lunt, *From Sepoy to Subedar*, 115 *seq.* This contains a rare example of a sepoy's captivity narrative.

6   Peter Collister, 'Hostage in Afghanistan', IOL, MSS Eur C573, fol. 127; Patrick Macrory (ed.), *Lady Sale: The First Afghan Wars* (1969), 109.

7   *Vincent Eyre* (1843), viii.

8   J.H. Stocqueler, *Memorials of Afghanistan* (Calcutta, 1843), 280.

9   See the information in a modern edition of her captivity narrative: Macrory, *Lady Sale*. Even before it was published in 1843, Lady Sale's letters from her Afghanistan prison to her husband, General Sir Robert Sale, had been passed on to the governor-general of India and sent by him back to the ministers in London. She went on to inspire several celebratory songs and poems, as well as a circus act in her honour at Astley's amphitheatre in London.

10 *William Anderson* MS (unfoliated).

11 Some of these 'lost' captivity narratives are quoted copiously in J.W. Kaye, *History of the War in Afghanistan from the Unpublished Letters and Journals of Political and Military Officers* (2 vols, 1851).

12 'The English Captives at Cabul', *Bentley's Miscellany*, XIV (1843), 9, 159.

13 Lunt, *From Sepoy to Subedar*, 86.

14 Macrory, *Kabul Catastrophe*, 141 and 173.

15 *Tait's Edinburgh Magazine*, X (1843), 458; *Blackwood's Magazine*, 51 (1842),

103, 254. On the inadequacies of men, wages, and ammunition among the British in Afghanistan, see *A Narrative of the Recent War in Afghanistan . . . By an Officer* (1842).

16 *Quarterly Review* (1846), 509.

17 Quoted in Dupree, *Afghanistan*, 391n.

18 Louis Dupree, 'The retreat of the British Army from Kabul to Jalalabad in 1842: history and folklore', *Journal of the Folklore Institute*, IV (1967).

19 'English Captives at Cabul', *Bentley's Miscellany*, XV (1844), 189.

20 Eyre published the revised drawings separately as *Prison Sketches. Comprising Portraits of the Cabul Prisoners* (1843). See, for instance, General Sir Charles James Napier's furious scribbled notes on his copy of Eyre's captivity narrative: 'God forgive me but with the exception of the women you were all a set of sons of bitches . . . I never put much faith in your half and half fellows who pretend to be *moderate* and tell "only what they saw" – if you speak truth your history is not worth a damn.' Napier was at this stage an imperial hero and warrior of a conventional stamp. IOL, MSS Eur B199, fol. 450.

21 *E.A.H. Webb* MS (unfoliated).

22 Stocqueler, *Memorials of Afghanistan*, iii-iv; *Bentley's Miscellany*, XIV (1843), 149.

23 Henry Lushington, *A Great Country's Little Wars* (1844), 9–10.

24 Yapp, *Strategies of British India*, 452 seq.; *Tait's Edinburgh Magazine*, X (1843), 370; *Illustrated London News*, II (1843), 359.

25 Warren Christopher *et al.*, *American Hostages in Iran: The Conduct of a Crisis* (New Haven, CT, 1985), 1.

26 *Report of the East India Committee of the Colonial Society on the Causes and Consequences of the Afghan War* (1842), 29.

27 W.R. Louis (ed.), *Imperialism: The Robinson and Gallagher Controversy* (New York, 1976), 6; Dr Arnold is quoted in William Hough, *A Review of the Operations of the British Force at Cabool* (Calcutta, 1849), 154.

28 'The failure of the English Guiana Ventures 1595–1667 and James I's foreign policy', *Journal of Imperial and Commonwealth History*, XXI (1993).

29 The French drove them out in 1756; while the Spanish expelled them during the American Revolutionary War.

30 Quoted in H.V. Bowen, 'British Conceptions of Global Empire, 1756–83', *Journal of Imperial and Commonwealth History*, 26 (1998), 15.

31 See, for instance, C.W. Pasley, *Essay on the Military Policy and Institutions of the British Empire* (1810).

32 Peter Yapp (ed.), *The Traveller's Dictionary of Quotation* (1983), 457.

33 Charles James Cruttwell, *Io Triumphe! A Song of Victory* (1842).

34 See, for instance, Kaye, *History of the War*, II, 489.

35 Kenneth Pomeranz, *The Great Divergence: China, Europe, and the Making of the Modern World Economy* (Princeton, NJ, 2000), 4; Paul Kennedy, *The Rise and Fall of the Great Powers* (1988), 190.

36 *Hansard*, 3rd ser., 44 (1842), 492; Michael Adas, *Machines as the Measure of Men: Science, Technology and Ideologies of Western Dominance* (1989), 136.

37 Quoted in Macrory, *Kabul Catastrophe*, 48.

38 See George Buist, *Outline of the Operations of the British Troops* (Bombay, 1843), 291.

39 Rosemary Seton, *The Indian 'Mutiny' 1857–58* (1986), xi–xii.

40 For an example of a later 19th-century working man's imperial narrative that remained in manuscript, see Carolyn Steedman, *The Radical Soldier's Tale* (1988).

41 The link between demographic take-off and industrial growth emerges strongly in E.A. Wrigley and R.S. Schofield, *The Population History of England, 1541–1871* (Cambridge, 1981).

42 Frederic Bancroft (ed.), *Speeches, Correspondence and Political Papers of Carl Schurz* (6 vols, New York, 1913), VI, 19–20 (my italics).

43 *The Howard Vincent Map of the British Empire* by G.H. Johnston (7th edn, 1902), 'Explanation'.

44 Ronald Robinson and John Gallagher with Alice Denny, *Africa and the Victorians* (2nd edn, 1981), 11–12.

45 Charles Dickens, *The Perils of Certain English Prisoners* (1890 edn.), 245, 281, 318–20. See Peter Ackroyd, *Dickens* (1990), 799–800, for the circumstances of its composition.

46 See my 'The Significance of the Frontier in British History' in W.R. Louis (ed.), *More Adventures with Britannia* (1998), 15–16.

47 Quoted in Correlli Barnett, *The Verdict of Peace* (2001), 81 (my italics); Paul Kennedy, 'Why did the British empire last so long?' in his *Strategy and Diplomacy 1870–1945* (1983).

48 These points are expanded on in Dominic Lieven, 'The Collapse of the Tsarist and Soviet Empires in Comparative Perspective', in Emil Brix, Klaus Koch and Elisabeth Vyslonzil (eds), *The Decline of Empires* (Vienna, 2001) 100; and see his *Empire* (2000), vii–86, 413–22.

49 Quoted in David Reynolds, 'American Globalism: Mass, Motion and the Multiplier Effect', in A.G. Hopkins (ed.), *Globalization in World History* (2002), 245.

INDEX

Page numbers in *italic* indicate illustrations and captions.

Linda Colley
Britons: Forging the Nation 1707-1837
WINNER OF THE WOLFSON PRIZE

With a New Introduction by the Author

'The most dazzling and comprehensive study of a national identity yet to appear in any language.' Tom Nairn, *Scotsman*

How was Great Britain made? And what does it mean to be British? In this brilliant and wide-ranging book, Linda Colley explains how a new British nation was invented in the wake of the 1707 Act of Union, and how this new national identity was nurtured through war, religion, trade and imperial expansion.

Here too are numerous individual Britons – heroes and politicians like Nelson and Pitt; bourgeois patriots like Thomas Coram and John Wilkes; artists, writers and musicians who helped to forge our image of Britishness; as well as many ordinary men and women whose stories have never previously been told.

Powerful and timely, this lavishly illustrated book is a major contribution to our understanding of Britain's past and to the growing debate about the shape and survival of Britain and its institutions in the future.

'A very fine book . . . challenging, fascinating, enormously well-informed.' John Barrell, *London Review of Books*

'Wise and bracing history . . . which provides an historical context for debate about British citizenship barely begun.' Michael Ratcliffe, *Observer*

'Controversial, entertaining and alarmingly topical . . . a delight to read.' Philip Ziegler, *Daily Telegraph*

'The most original, penetrating and readable volume on the 18th-century published for many a long year.' Tim Blanning, *Independent*, Books of the Year

'Uniting sharp analysis, pungent prose and choice examples, Colley probes beneath the skin and lays bare the anatomy of nationhood.' Roy Porter, *New Statesman & Society*

'A triumph, bold in scope and intellectual range, executed with skill, clarity and understanding.' Jeremy Black, *Times Educational Supplement*

£12.50   0-7126-9785-3

Piers Brendon
The Dark Valley: A Panorama of the 1930s

'Riveting . . . Brendon's canvas is global, and he paints every inch of
it brilliantly . . . leading the reader from one chapter to the next in
such a way that it is hard to put the book down . . . *The Dark Valley* is
scholarly popular history to rank with Norman Davies's history of
Europe or Antony Beevor's *Stalingrad*, and deserves to be equally
successful.' John Campbell, *Independent*

Piers Brendon's magisterial overview of the 1930s is the story of the dark, dishonest
decade, child of one world war and parent of the next, that determined the course
of the twentieth-century. Dealing individually with each of the period's great powers
– the USA, Germany, Italy, France, Britain, Japan, Russia and Spain – Brendon
takes us through the ten years dominated by the Great Depression and political
turmoil, when the giants of unemployment, hardship, strife and fear took hold.
From the concentration camps of Dachau and Kolyma, the Ukraine famine and
the American Dust Bowl, to the Moscow metro, the Empire State Building and the
Paris Exposition, *The Dark Valley* brings the 1930's back to life with meticulous scholarship.

'The best history book I've read since Orlando Figes's *A People's Tragedy* . . . wonderful
and enthralling.' Ruth Rendell, *Daily Telegraph*

'Brilliant, cinematic, utterly illuminating . . . No other historical account I know
can rival this . . . Masterly.' Valentine Cunningham, *Financial Times*

'A delight to read, a literary triumph sparkling with moments of real humour and
compassion, sombre where it needs to be. Brendon is the master of the swift pen
portrait, the telling anecdote, the curious footnotes to history that tell us more than
a page of dusty scholarship.' Richard Overy, *Sunday Telegraph*

'Has any decade in human history been more written about than the 1930s? . . .
Piers Brendon's long book has such brilliance and narrative power, and contains so
much fascinating detail, that reading it has all the excitement of novelty.' John Grigg,
Evening Standard

'Should be read by anyone who wants to understand the terrible harm that world
recession, allied with fanatical ideology in some quarters, and feeble leadership in
others, did then – and could do again.' David Cannadine, *Observer*

'Excellent . . . Brendon tells the story of this enormous and weighty subject with
great skill and good humour.' Antony Beevor, *Mail on Sunday*

£12.50   0-7126-6714-8

Norman Davies
Europe: A History

SHORTLISTED FOR THE 1997 NCR AWARD

From the Ice Age to the Cold War, from Reykjavik to the Volga, from Minos to Margaret Thatcher, Norman Davies here tells the entire story of Europe in a single volume. Chosen ten times as Book of the Year, it is the most ambitious history of the continent ever undertaken.

'Books of real quality and importance are rare. Norman Davies's history of Europe is one of them. It is a brilliant achievement, written with intelligence, lucidity and a breathtaking width of knowledge . . . This is a book everyone should read.' A.C. Grayling, *Financial Times*

'A noble monument of scholarship, and all the more noble because it is so full of surprise and feeling . . . There are superb assessments of vastly daunting subjects.' Jan Morris, *Independent*

'Comprehensive, irreverent and immensely stimulating.' Michael Burleigh, *Independent on Sunday*

'A huge, heroic book . . . After Davies, it will never be possible to write a history of Europe in the old way again.' *London Review of Books*

'It brims with learning, crackles with common sense, coruscates with wit and abounds in good judgement.' Felipe Fernandez-Armesto, *Sunday Times*

'Monumental, authoritative . . . A book for enquiring minds of all ages, it will answer hundreds of enquiries and provoke thousands more.' Noel Malcolm, *Sunday Telegraph*

'One of those great books . . . It deserves the greatest possible readership.' *The Times*

'No history of Europe in the English language has been so even-handed in its treatment of east and west . . . Strong characterisation, vivid detail, trenchant opinions, cogent analysis all make this tremendous reading.' *Times Literary Supplement*

£16.00   0-7126-6633-8

Orlando Figes
A People's Tragedy: The Russian Revolution 1891–1924

WINNER OF THE WOLFSON HISTORY PRIZE

WINNER OF THE W. H. SMITH LITERARY AWARD

WINNER OF THE LONGMAN/*HISTORY TODAY* BOOK
OF THE YEAR AWARD

Vast in scope, based on extensive original research, and written with passion, narrative skill and human sympathy, *A People's Tragedy* is the definitive account of the Russian Revolution for a new generation.

'Profoundly researched, brilliantly written, full of wit, wisdom and humanity. It is by far the best history of the Russian Revolution I have ever read.' Frank McLynn, *Glasgow Herald*

'A memorably good book . . . *A People's Tragedy* combines dramatic power, absorbing narrative and magisterial scholarship . . . A magnificent *tour de force*.' Christopher Andrew, *Sunday Telegraph*

'I doubt if there is anyone in the world who knows the revolution as well as he does.' Norman Stone, *Sunday Times*

'This book is not just a history; it is an item of history . . . Orlando Figes has taken the chance to display the very experience of revolution as it affected millions of ordinary Russians.' Neal Ascherson, *Independent on Sunday*

'It balances big ideas with vivid personal histories and must be the most moving account of the Russian Revolution since *Doctor Zhivago*.' Lucasta Miller, Books of the Year, *Independent*

'Few historians have the courage to attack great subjects, fewer have the grasp to succeed. This is a book that lets the reader look into the face of one of the major social upheavals of history . . . *A People's Tragedy* will do more to help us understand the Russian Revolution than any other book I know.' Eric Hobsbawm, *London Review of Books*

£16.00   0-7126-7327-X

Edited by A. G. Hopkins
Globalization in World History

'This is an excellent volume that offers a great deal to those interested in a historical perspective on globalization'. *Commonwealth Journal of International Affairs.*

'Neither history nor ideology has come to an end. The advocates of capitalism and free trade see globalization as a positive progressive force generating employment and ultimately raising living standards throughout the world. The critics see it as a means of expropriating the resources of poor countries by drawing them into debt, encouraging the use of sweated labour, and accelerating environmental degradation. The protagonists will turn increasingly to history for support. The obligation now falls on historians to ensure that the history cited is based on evidence rather than on honorary facts, and to consider how they can apply arguments about the present to improve out understanding of the past.' From the Introduction by A.G. Hopkins

Globalization was the buzzword of the 1990s; it promises to become even more important in the first decade of the twenty-first century. There is now a flood of literature on the economics, politics and sociology of globalization, and regular commentary in the serious daily and weekly press.

Virtually all of this discussion makes the assumption, and frequently explicit claims, about the novelty of globalization. According to one view, globalization is a new phenomenon that can be dated from the 1980s. A second view holds that globalization has a long history that can be traced to the nineteenth-century, it not earlier. The importance of these themes scarcely needs elaborating. Yet they have still to attract significant attention from historians. This volume is the first by a team of historians to address these issues.

Globalization in World History has two distinctive features. First, it offers a categorization of types and stages of globalization that existed before the twentieth-century. No such taxonomy exists at present. Secondly, it emphasizes a feature that the current debate greatly underestimates: the fact that globalization had non-Western as well as Western origins. Globalization is much more than the 'rise of the West' presented in new terminology. The contributors bring their expertise to bear on themes that give prominence to China, South Asia, Africa and the world of Islam as well as to Europe and the United States, and span the last three centuries while also showing an awareness of more distant antecedents. The result is a coherent and thought-provoking collection of essays. Globalization will become a major theme of historical research during the next decade; this book will help to set the new agenda.

£12.50   0-7126-7740-2

Order more Pimlico books from your local
bookshop, or have them delivered
direct to your door by
BOOKPOST

Linda Colley
Britons: Forging the Nation 1707-1837   0-7126-9785-3   £12.50

Piers Brendon
The Dark Valley: A Panorama of the 1930s   0-7126-6714-8   £12.50

Norman Davies
Europe: A History   0-7126-6633-8   £16.00

Orlando Figes
A People's Tragedy: The Russian Revolution 1891-1924   0-7126-7327-X   £16.00

A. G. Hopkins, Ed.
Globalization in World History   0-7126-7740-2   £12.50

FREE POST AND PACKING
Overseas customers allow £2 per paperback

PHONE: 01624 677237

POST: Random House Books
C/o Bookpost, PO Box 29, Douglas
Isle of Man, IM99 1BQ

FAX: 01624 670923

EMAIL: bookshop@enterprise.net

Cheques (payable to Bookpost) and credit cards accepted

Prices and availability subject to change without notice.
Allow 28 days for delivery
When placing your order, please mention if you do not wish
to receive any additional information

www.randomhouse.co.uk/pimlico

FOR THE THORN:

MY CONSTANT COMPANION. THE RIGHT SHOE FOR MY LEFT FOOT. THE ANDY CARROLL TO MY *Lawrence of Arabia* KEVIN NOLAN. *The Selected Letters* WE WILL ALWAYS HAVE URUK (WE MUST PREACH THE GOSPEL OF HARRY TO THE ARABS). HOPE THIS SERVES AS GOOD INSPIRATION. NOW WRITE THE DAMN BOOK. YOU CAN'T PLAN FOREVER. STORM COMING. YOU KNOW I LOVE YOU. LET'S SU___ LIKE DOLPHINS A___ SOMETIME SOON. S___ ON THE OTHER SIDE, BABY, SHAME ON THE OTHER SIDE. STAY AWAKE. YOURS IN ROMPEN. ADAM.

X

'Ware letter-writing.
It's a bad habit.

T. E. Lawrence to Edward Garnett
7 September 1922

Lawrence of Arabia
The Selected Letters

Edited by Malcolm Brown

This edition published in 2005 by Little Books Ltd,
48 Catherine Place, London SW1E 6HL

10 9 8 7 6 5 4 3 2 1

A CIP catalogue record for this book is available from the British Library.

ISBN: 1 904435 43 2

The author and publisher will be grateful for any information that will assist them
in keeping future editions up-to-date. Although all reasonable care has been taken in the
preparation of this book, neither the publisher, editors nor the author can accept any liability
for any consequences arising from the use thereof, or the information contained therein.

Printed and bound in Great Britain by William Clowes Ltd, Beccles, Suffolk

This is a Big Book from Little Books Ltd.

CONTENTS

FOREWORD

The 2005 Edition

It is important at the outset to state what this book is and what it is not. Essentially it is the collection published by J. M. Dent of London as *The Letters of T .E. Lawrence* in 1988 and by W. W. Norton of New York as *T. E. Lawrence: The Selected Letters* in 1989. Subsequent paperback editions perpetuated the difference: thus the Oxford University Press edition adopted the Dent version, while the Paragon House, New York, edition adopted the variation chosen by Norton.

When early in 2005 the idea of republishing the collection in a new, updated edition and in a new, contemporary format became a serious proposition, it rapidly became apparent that a new title was required. The choice was made somewhat easier in that I was already engaged in acting as consultant to a major exhibition at the Imperial War Museum planned to run from October 2005 to April 2006 under the title *Lawrence of Arabia: The Life, The Legend*, and was simultaneously writing and compiling an illustrated companion volume to the exhibition, similarly titled, to be published by Thames & Hudson. Meanwhile, from the earlier titles I borrowed the word 'selected' as being true to the nature of the book.

There was another factor. In 1988, I instinctively avoided the 'Lawrence of Arabia' formula, not only in the case of the volume of letters but also in relation to the concise biography co-written with Julia Cave, which was published, also by J. M. Dent, earlier in the same year. It was as though the sandstorms emanating from the hugely successful 1962 David Lean spectacular, *Lawrence of Arabia*, with its strikingly flamboyant interpretation of Lawrence by Peter O'Toole, were still blowing across the cultural landscape, obscuring any attempt to look at its subject as a figure of history as opposed to a creation of Hollywood. Avoiding all attempt at glamorization and modestly entitled *A Touch of Genius: The Life of T. E. Lawrence*, the biography clearly struck an appropriate note for the time, receiving many favourable reviews on both sides of the Atlantic and also being nominated for two major non-fiction prizes in Great Britain in 1989. Several reviewers clearly felt a kind of relief, as though they were grateful that we could now get back to looking at a genuine, life-size Lawrence (who was in fact almost a foot shorter than the actor who played him in the film), and assess him as a human being as opposed to a celluloid myth.

The film is still with us, being regularly voted one of the best of all time, but the sandstorms it created are sufficiently distant for us to ignore their far-off rumblings. So I am pleased to use the Lawrence of Arabia formula at the head of this reprint of a book which, I should add on a personal note, was more challenging in its creation than any book I have written or edited before or since, and which yet holds a firm and permanent place in my affections.

An important rider should be added. From the start, the decision was taken by both my publisher and myself that no attempt should be made to reconstruct the book or add significantly to its length. There might be a change of title, but basically there would be no change of content. This was not only because of considerations of time – for a range of reasons the book had to be made ready for the printers as soon as reasonably possible – it was also a matter of common sense. My good friend Clifford H. Irwin, formerly of Chicago but now living in Florida, is still pursuing what has become a more than twenty-year-long task to create a database recording as many of Lawrence's letters as he can trace. His latest conclusion is that, altogether, there are a little over 5,000 letters in existence. By contrast, the number of letters which appeared in the magisterial 1938 compilation edited by David Garnett, in a volume of almost 900 pages, is 583. My own compilation, restricted by my original publishers to rather fewer than 600 pages, includes fewer than 500, not all of them printed at full length. If a new collection of letters were to be created, it would have to be a work of several volumes and with a vastly greater perspective.

So there were in effect two choices. One was to abandon the project entirely, in the hope that eventually an editor, or team of editors, might appear with the time, the scholarship and the financial support to produce a collection in the style of, for example, the collected correspondence of his namesake, D. H. Lawrence, an initiative by Cambridge University Press which runs to eight volumes and which took over twenty years to compile. The other choice was to put back on the shelves a book out of print for over a decade which, as the comments of numerous reviewers and readers have shown, has given many people a great deal of interest, enlightenment and pleasure: a book, too, I believe, which has something of the quality of the autobiography Lawrence never wrote, since essentially its author (with, as it were, continuity notes by myself to help the story on) is T. E. Lawrence himself.

However, having established a virtual law of non-interference in relation to the original collection, I admit to having decided, in certain rare instances, to break it. For one thing, it is important to take account of later developments, and also to avail myself of the opportunity to make corrections. Thus, to give one important example: in 1988 a substantial number of the letters included were drawn from what was then known as the Bodleian Reserve Collection, an assembly of Lawrence documents and papers held under formal embargo until the year 2000. Fully sorted and catalogued by Anna Dunn in 2001, this collection is now integrated into the Bodleian Library, and letters from that source are so credited in the new volume.[1] I am also pleased to be able to correct a number of errors in my editorial matter, some discovered by myself, others pointed out by friends or reviewers – though in a book of such length, dealing with a writer whose range of reference was by any standards very remarkable, there are bound to be mistakes or failures of understanding for which I plead the reader's indulgence.

More significantly, I have added a small, select number of letters that I wished to include for what might seem arbitrary reasons, while pleading that in such cases the editor's decision, or perhaps I should say editor's whim, is final. In 2003, the Imperial War Museum, to which I have been attached as a freelance historian since 1989, purchased at my suggestion two important letters written by Lawrence to the head of the press and publicity branch of the Air Ministry, C. P. Robertson: one in December 1929, shortly after his return from India, and the other in February 1935, just before he left the Royal Air Force. Robertson was a key figure in Lawrence's life at this time, in fact his best defender against the publicity hounds of the press, so that these letters add new insights into the matter of his celebrity, a subject arguably of particular interest to the reading public of today. Additionally I have included another letter written in February 1935, to the then Chief of Air Staff, purchased together with the Robertson letters. Finding space for letters from this hitherto unknown collection (if at the expense of several minor letters or extracts in this area that I have reluctantly deleted), allows me to draw attention to the fact that the Imperial War Museum is itself a far from insignificant source of Lawrence material, whether in terms of works of art, exhibits and artefacts (some of them donated by Lawrence himself), photography (it holds the most comprehensive collection of his war photographs) or documents of various kinds, including a number of autograph letters.

The new version has presented me with a further opportunity. I included in the 1988 compilation a letter written to Lady Astor on 26 November 1934, in which Lawrence referred somewhat dismissively to a married woman well-known to both of them who was apparently troubling him with attentions he

---

1 Entitled *Catalogue of the Papers of T. E. Lawrence and A. W. Lawrence*, c. 1894–1985, University of Oxford, Bodleian Library, by Anna Dunn, © 2001, the document is held in the Bodleian Library's Department of Special Collections and Western Manuscripts.

had come to find unwelcome. I met the person in question myself when working on a BBC television documentary on Lawrence in 1962, and a certain delicacy led me to exclude her name from Lawrence's text. In the present version I have included the name, that of Mrs Clare Sydney Smith, wife of Wing Commander, later Air Commodore Sydney Smith, author of a book of reminiscence entitled *The Golden Reign* (as referred to in my 'General Introduction' page xxx). Readers might be interested to know that I first revealed Mrs Smith's name in an introduction to a reprint of *The Golden Reign*, published in a fine limited edition by Simon Lawrence at The Fleece Press, Upper Denby, South Yorkshire, in 2004. So many years had elapsed since my first edition, and all attempts to trace Mrs Smith's family having failed, there seemed no point in continuing the concealment. As in that volume, so in this. Even so, over forty years after meeting this most charming, and even in comparative old age, undoubtedly beautiful lady, I salute her memory.

Additionally, I have included an essay I wrote not long after publishing this book's first edition on the absorbing but challenging experience of working on a book of letters. This has so far been published only in the *Journal of the T. E. Lawrence Society*, and I am pleased to state that its editors have kindly given me permission to reproduce it here. It appears in the book as an afterword.

T. E. Lawrence – scholar, archaeologist, soldier, diplomat, author, international celebrity (known forever as 'Lawrence of Arabia'), and, under the aliases Ross or Shaw, most extraordinary of ordinary servicemen – wrote to Flight Sergeant H. A. Ford of the Royal Air Force on 18 April 1929: 'I am trying to accustom myself to the truth that probably I'll be talked over for the rest of my life: and after my life, too. There will be a volume of "letters" after I die.'

Shortly after his premature death in 1935, his friend, the novelist E. M. Forster, undertook the task of preparing such a volume, but ill-health and the fear that publication of Lawrence's often outspoken correspondence might result in a spate of libel actions (Forster was caught up in one himself even as the project was being launched) caused him to withdraw. The editorship passed to the critic and novelist David Garnett, whose collection appeared in 1938 as *The Letters of T. E. Lawrence*.

In 1986 the Trustees of the Seven Pillars of Wisdom Trust, of whom the leading member was Lawrence's younger brother A.W. Lawrence, decided to commission a new collection, to include some of the best material already in Garnett's admirable volume, but also, and more importantly, to put into print many of the great number of letters which had come to light or become available for publication since Garnett made his selection. Having had a long acquaintance with the subject since the 1960s and being already engaged in co-writing *A Touch of Genius*, I was asked to undertake the task, a prime condition of acceptance being that the book should be published in Lawrence's centennial year, 1988. This volume in its original format was the product of this commission, now being reissued seventy years after Lawrence's death.

The letters themselves are arranged in seven parts chronologically, each part having its own introduction which gives the necessary biographical background and comments on the main trends and content of Lawrence's letter-writing during the period in question. In general the letters have been left, with some assistance from footnotes, to tell their own story, but occasionally I have intervened with brief explanatory paragraphs to indicate a major development or landmark in Lawrence's career. Many letters are printed in full, but numerous others have been shortened, and in some cases it seemed worth including only key paragraphs. All my omissions are marked with the following unambiguous typographical device [...]. Where a series of dots occurs in the letters without such brackets, they are Lawrence's own — it was his lifelong habit to indicate in this way a pause for thought or a change of direction. I should add that I have also used square brackets to indicate such editorial interjections as an assumed date or address (and for one other important purpose given below). Dates are given on the left and are usually printed as Lawrence wrote them; addresses are on the right and have frequently been shortened, particularly when, as often happened in his service years, he included his number, rank and name.

As already indicated, many letters in this volume were published (or believed to have been published) here for the first time. On the whole the reader can assume letters to be such unless they are followed by the initials *DG* or *HL*. *DG* indicates that the letter was in David Garnett's 1938 volume. *HL* indicates that the letter is in the volume entitled *The Home Letters of T. E. Lawrence and His Brothers*, edited by his elder brother M. R. Lawrence and published in 1954, but for reasons given in the 'General Introduction', this will almost always be followed by the reference 'Bodleian Library', meaning that the text has been checked against the originals held in the library and is printed here as written and not as M. R. Lawrence published it. Where *HL* occurs on its own, the letter or extract is precisely as printed in *The Home Letters*, but this occurs rarely because where M. R. Lawrence did not alter his brother's text, he regularly changed his paragraphing, thus, in my view, interrupting the letters' natural flow. I have restored Lawrence's paragraphs and I believe the letters read much better because of this. Where I have reinstated passages deleted by M. R. Lawrence I have indicated this by enclosing them within square brackets.

Additionally, a handful of other letters included had already been published in the 1963 volume (originally issued as two separate books) entitled *T. E. Lawrence to His Biographers: Robert Graves and Liddell Hart*. These are indicated in the source note by the letters *RGB* or *LHB*. H. Montgomery Hyde's book about Lawrence's postwar service years, *Solitary in the Ranks*, supplied a number of letters to Sir Hugh, later Lord, Trenchard; these are followed by the formula *HMH*.

I must emphasize that certain other letters have appeared, usually in the form of extracts, though some have been printed in full, in Lawrence biographies or articles about him or in other similar works. I have included such information only when it seemed important or relevant to do so, or (since publications about Lawrence are international, multilingual and legion) when it was known to me.

With regard to the matter of footnotes, it seemed important to place them on the appropriate page, but my aim has been to enrich the reader's understanding of the letters without cluttering the pages with too much detail. I have not managed or indeed tried to explain everything: to know all the answers one would have to have a mind as well-stocked as that of the writer himself — and his range of knowledge, reading and experience was formidable.

A personal word is perhaps necessary here. Before becoming a full-time author, I was for many years a producer of historical documentary programmes for BBC Television. Twice in my career I collaborated in the making of major programmes about Lawrence: *T. E. Lawrence 1888-1935* in 1962, and *Lawrence and Arabia* in 1986. In the course of working on those programmes I came to know A. W. Lawrence, and also met a number of others from T. E. Lawrence's wide circle of contemporaries, including Sir Basil Liddell Hart, Sir Alec Kirkbride, Canon E. F. Hall, C. F. C. Beeson, A. H. G. Kerry, H. F. Matthews, Mrs Celandine Kennington, Air Commodore and Mrs Sydney Smith, Jock Chambers, Arthur Russell, Tom Beaumont, Pat Knowles, even Lowell Thomas. Thus when I was asked in 1986 by A. W. Lawrence to undertake the task which has resulted in this present volume, I did not feel entirely disqualified.

I was responsible for its plan and style, but the balance of old and new material was much as he foresaw it, and it was he who encouraged me to include only the essential parts of letters where it seemed appropriate, thereby excluding much material that was routine or repetitious. The choice of letters throughout was mine, and he made no attempt to influence or censor me. He was in fact a most benign patron, and I took the opportunity in the original edition to express my deep gratitude to a remarkable man who was not only a scholar and writer of distinction in his own right — he had, for example, held professorships in archaeology at Cambridge and in Ghana, where he had been director of the Ghana National Museum – but who also, as we do well to remember, for over fifty years had borne with both patience and wisdom the burden of being, as it were, his brother's keeper.

To my thanks to him I added in 1988 my great gratitude to his fellow trustees of the Seven Pillars of Wisdom Trust: Mr Michael Carey and the Hon. H. A. A. Hankey C.M.G., C.V.O. Of these, only Michael Carey is still with us, and I am pleased to be able to thank him, and his fellow trustee, Professor Robin Cormack, former professor of art history at the Courtauld Institute, London, for their support in the making of the present volume.

When the original version of this book was about to appear in what would prove to be its final manifestation, as a paperback under the imprint of Paragon House, New York, published in 1992, I asked if I could add a brief supplementary preface, which seems worthy of being reprinted verbatim here:

'The appearance of this selection in this new edition allows me an opportunity of which I am glad to take advantage to express my thanks to the many people who have corresponded with me following the book's initial appearance in Britain and America. Several have suggested corrections; I have incorporated them gratefully. Others have stated that the book has had, to some degree, an enlarging effect on their lives. One American lady even wrote that it had given her the kind of experience which Lawrence sometimes found in his own reading, as described in the fine last paragraph of the letter of September 1910 printed on pp. 23-4. The credit, of course, is Lawrence's, but such reactions make all the labour of researching and sifting and editing seem worthwhile.

'More down to earth, one or two have asked what was my aim, my strategic plan, in compiling the book – a question to which I had assumed the answer was largely implicit; I apologize to those for whom it was not. In brief, I was searching for the man, the story, the autobiography, as it were, much more than I was seeking, say, the literary views of Lawrence the voracious reader and would-be writer of the 1920s and '30s. David Garnett's 1938 selection has such material in abundance; I made it my prime task to choose letters which seemed to cast light on the remarkable if elusive personality that was T. E. Lawrence/J. H. Ross/T. E. Shaw. To me, therefore, a letter to a Tank Corps private (or to a Tank Corps private's mother) had as much right to bid for inclusion as a letter to a well-known author, or, for that matter, to anyone else in Lawrence's wide circle of famous friends.'

It would be churlish as well as inopportune to conclude this foreword without paying a more extended tribute to A. W. Lawrence, whom I came to know not only during the making of this book, but also – indeed even more so – after its publication.

As time went by I became increasingly impressed with a man who had no shame, or even concern, about the matter of his unusual family background – something which troubled his more famous brother, as this book shows, throughout his life – so much so that he rejoiced in the name 'Lawrence', asking people such as myself to call him such while, for example, calling me by my first name in the normal contemporary style. Formulae such as 'Professor Lawrence' or 'A. W.' were anathema to him – he made no bones about it: 'Call me Lawrence'. It was almost as if he was quietly disowning, though without hint of rebuke, his brother's anguished determination to rid himself of a name he knew was false and which he had come to loathe, and was quietly asserting his own determination to wear the name with pride.

Yet there were obvious scars resulting from his family's troubled past. He was not above admitting that he thought his mother guilty of, to quote T. E.'s words, 'hammering and sapping' into his famous brother's personality in order to make him the person she thought he ought to be. Her attempt to achieve forgiveness for the sins of the parents by saving the souls of the children had left him so disenchanted that he had consciously and deliberately turned his back on religious belief. I have seen him strike a table in anger while uttering with some force the words 'I hate Christianity'. (If readers should wish to explore further the reasons for what might seem so extreme an attitude, as articulated by his more famous brother, they should turn to the letter of 14 April 1927 to Mrs Charlotte Shaw, giving particular attention to its searing final paragraphs on page 345.) Yet he could also declare his position without anger, in subtle, deliberately inoffensive ways. He regularly offered 'going to and fro in the earth and walking up and down in it' as his 'recreation' in his annual entry in *Who's Who?* This should not be taken as implying a fondness for foreign travel or for exploration; it is a quotation from the Book of Job, where we read in Chapter I, verse 7: 'And the Lord said unto Satan, Whence comest thou? Then Satan answered the Lord, and said, From going to and fro in the world, and from walking up and down in it.' Not that he was in any way satanic – far from it; but I sense that, for him, these words represented a gesture against religion and religiosity in a way that might tease, or possibly even affront, the knowledgeable, but in which the majority of people would see nothing sinister or extraordinary.

He was in fact the enemy of excess in all areas, not least in the field (or the desert) where rival forces clashed over T. E. Lawrence's reputation. His attitude was constant and clear: he could not recognize the brother he had known and admired in the saint of the pro-Lawrence faction or the charlatan and *poseur* of the denigrators. He faced numerous difficulties, such as the attack by Richard Aldington in his debunking biography of Lawrence in 1955; the fuss in 1962 over the Spiegel/Lean film *Lawrence of Arabia*, from which he withdrew support at what he saw as a distortion not only of T. E., but also of General Allenby; and the *Sunday Times* revelations in 1968 about his brother's alleged masochism. At the other extreme, he deplored excessive adulation, an attitude he made clear in an interview about his brother in a BBC *Omnibus* film in 1986: if people wished to make a religion of T. E. Lawrence, he had no intention of becoming that religion's St Paul.

This required the building of a defensive cordon. Knowing my book would raise interest and produce letters from people eager not so much to see him for himself but to discuss his brother, he asked me to fend off all correspondence following its publication. I faithfully did so, the only exception being a letter which came to me via my New York publisher from an American living in Denver, Colorado, whose qualification was that, in the 1960s, as a teenager living in a working-class neighbourhood in New York's Bronx district, he had written to A. W. Lawrence in enthusiastic response to the latter's articles on Middle Eastern archaeology in the *Encyclopaedia Britannica*, without realizing that he was the brother of the internationally famous war hero. A. W. had written a kindly letter in reply which had been carefully preserved by its recipient for over twenty-five years. Bringing Ray Kemble to meet A. W. – a widower at this stage and living in quiet seclusion in Devizes, Wiltshire, where he was being graciously looked after by his friend of many years, herself an archaeologist, Peggy Guido – produced a memorable and moving occasion. The meeting of the elderly scholar and the intelligent, personable American, himself with a not undistinguished track-record as actor, theatre manager and, courtesy of the draft, former artillery officer in Vietnam, was heart-warming to both these men, as it was to Peggy Guido and myself as approving observers.

For despite an often austere demeanour, A. W. had a tender core. I remember him almost with tears in his eyes praising a biography of his brother written by an Argentinian writer, Vittoria Ocampo, under the title (quoting his official number in his R.A.F. days) *338171 T. E. Lawrence of Arabia*, published in French in 1947 and in English, in a translation by David Garnett, in 1963. He had described it in a review as 'the most profound and best-balanced of all portraits of my brother'. Why was it so good? Because, he said, 'she loved him'.

He could show an emotional side to his character in most unexpected ways. Once, my wife and I went to see him shortly after the death of a particularly favourite cat. He commented: 'I'm still mourning a cat who died fifty years ago.'

My last meeting with him took place shortly before his death. In 1990 the Imperial War Museum asked me to a contribute a brief introduction to a facsimile reprint of an anthology of T. E. Lawrence's minor writings on the Middle East originally published in 1939, with A. W. Lawrence as editor, under the title *Oriental Assembly*. Permission was sought from Lawrence and his fellow trustees of the Seven Pillars of Wisdom Trust, and the project went ahead.

One of the satisfactions I looked forward to with some eagerness was that of presenting him with a copy of the book when published. As soon as advanced copies became available, my wife and I hurried to visit him in Devizes. It was Good Friday, 29 March 1991, and we had an agreeable hour or two together, the highlight of which was the presentation of the book, which he received with good grace and evident, if characteristically understated, pleasure. We bade him farewell, and went on our way. He died suddenly two days later, on Easter Sunday, at the age of 90.

In retrospect, I see A. W. Lawrence's death (the only other brother to survive into old age, M. R. Lawrence, had died twenty years earlier, in 1971), as the ending of a long, now ancient saga which started in the 1880s when an unhappily married Anglo-Irish aristocrat fell in love with a comely Scottish governess and the train of events began which produced one of the strangest but also one of the most compelling and fascinating personalities of the last century. The name 'Lawrence', legitimate or illegitimate, does not survive. The only extant relatives have other names and, understandably, have moved on elsewhere, committing themselves to other interests. The curtain is down. This is a case where one might genuinely use that well-known catch-phrase without the flippancy often attached to it: end of story.

Except that, one should add, in the case of this remarkable figure of the twentieth century who is still exciting interest, admiration, anger, controversy in the twenty-first, the story might be over, but the aftermath and the consequences are not. The ripples resulting from this extraordinary man's extraordinary life flow on and on.

Malcolm Brown

ACKNOWLEDGEMENTS

In addition to those mentioned in the 'Foreword', I should like to express my thanks to the following:

at the Bodleian Library, Oxford, D. S. Porter (until recently Senior Assistant Librarian), Colin Harris, Serena Surman and the rest of the staff of Room 132; at the Houghton Library of Harvard University, Vicki Denby; at the Harry Ransom Humanities Research Center of the University of Texas at Austin, Cathy Henderson; at the Imperial War Museum, Roderick Suddaby, Keeper of the Department of Documents; at the Ashmolean Museum, Dr Roger Moorey and his secretary Ruth Flanagan; at Jesus College, Oxford, Dr D. A. Rees; at All Souls College, Oxford, Peter S. Lewis and Norma Aubertin-Potter; at Worcester College, Oxford, Lesley Le Claire; at St Antony's College, Oxford, Gillian Grant; at King's College, Cambridge, Dr Michael Halls; at Churchill College, Cambridge, Elizabeth Bennett and Lesley James; at the Department of Archives and Manuscripts, Reading University Library, Michael Bott; at the R.A.F. Museum Hendon, Peter Murton; at Eton College, Michael Meredith; at the BBC Written Archives, Caversham, Geoffrey Walden; also the staffs of the Public Record Office; the British Library; the British Library Newspaper Library, Colindale; the Cambridge University Library; the Fitzwilliam Museum, Cambridge; Kettle's Yard, Cambridge; the Liddell Hart Centre for Military Archives, King's College, London; the Tate Gallery Archives; the Royal Commission on Historical Manuscripts, Quality Court, Chancery Lane, London.

Others whom I should like to thank include Dr John E. Mack of Harvard University (author of the Lawrence biography *A Prince of Our Disorder*); Dr D. C. Sutton, of Reading University, whose *Location Register of Twentieth Century English Literary Manuscripts and Letters* (published 1988) was particularly useful; Christopher Matheson; Ingrid Keith of the T. E. Lawrence Society; and Arthur Russell, fellow soldier with Lawrence in the Royal Tank Corps and later one of his bearers.

I should also like to thank those who helped me in the matter of footnotes, including Doreen Harris, Shirley Seaton, Peter Murton, and, especially, my wife Betty, who also typed many letters and subsequently read and checked the text at all stages from first assembly to completion and finally helped with the indices.

Very specially I must express my gratitude to A. J. Flavell, Assistant Librarian of the Bodleian Library and organizer of the Bodleian's Lawrence Centenary Exhibition, 1988, who read through much of the text and the footnotes and elucidated a number of obscure but important references; and to St John Armitage C.B.E., who subjected my editorial matter, my choice of material and my footnotes to rigorous and helpful examination, and contributed some valuable footnotes as well. I took most but not all the advice I was given and must accept responsibility for any errors or shortcomings the book may contain.

Finally, the Trustees of the Seven Pillars of Wisdom Trust and I should like to thank the original recipients of the letters printed in this book and also, where applicable, their present owners, without whose placing of Lawrence's letters in known and secure sources this centennial collection would not have been possible.

Thus my acknowledgements as printed in the original volume: to them I must add the names of those to whom I am especially grateful for the production of the present one.

Above all I am deeply indebted to Margaret Little, founder of Little Books, who came to me early in 2005 with the idea of reviving the work. Moreover, she proposed to republish it not in facsimile, but in a newly printed edition, thus allowing me the opportunity to correct, improve or add to the work in such ways as might seem appropriate, while offering the extra bonus of re-using in it some of the illustrations included in the first anthology of Lawrence's letters, that edited by David Garnett in 1938. Her enthusiasm and commitment have been shared by her colleagues, among whom I must single out for particular gratitude the book's editorial manager and layout artist, Jamie Elizabeth Ambrose, who has performed with admirable skill, expedition and, I should add, resilient good humour the challenging task of re-making the book in its new format, thus proving that old wine can indeed be successfully put into new bottles. Others who have added their talents to this enterprise include Ian Hughes, Debbie Clement, Helen Nelson and Pru Rowlandson.

I also wish to express my thanks to the present trustees of the Seven Pillars of Wisdom Trust, Michael Carey and Professor Robin Cormack, for their support. Finally, I should like to pay tribute to three people mentioned in the 1988 list who have subsequently passed away, for whom I had, and have, a special regard: Lawrence's ex-Tank Corps comrade, Arthur Russell; Professor John E. Mack; and St John Armitage C.B.E., the last two sadly dying within days of each other in the autumn of 2004.

A NOTE ON THE TEXT

Many letters have been transcribed from the originals or from photocopies of originals, but use has also been made of typed or previously printed transcriptions. Almost all Garnett letters and the majority of 'home letters' have been reproduced as previously published. In the case of letters from the Bodleian Library, most have been taken from collections checked against the originals by E. M. Forster, A. W. Lawrence or David Garnett. I have not thought it necessary to identify the small number which do not come within this category. Like Garnett's, this book contains a mixed economy in the matter of 'and' versus '&'. In his selection, for example, letters to him, his father Edward Garnett and Lionel Curtis are printed with 'and' throughout, whereas the ampersand occurs in letters to D. G. Hogarth, John Buchan and E. M. Forster. Some editors prefer to standardize with 'and' but in my own 'new' letters I have retained the '&', (thus following the practice of such recent collections as the letters of Evelyn Waugh, E. M. Forster and Dylan Thomas). The letters to Mrs Charlotte Shaw are a major exception to this rule, as the typed transcriptions in the possession of the Trustees of the Seven Pillars of Wisdom Trust contained 'and' throughout and I have not attempted to re-ampersand them. It should be added that Lawrence seems to have used both forms interchangeably.

Obvious mistakes have been corrected and names of literary works, periodicals, ships, and some foreign words and phrases, etc., have been italicized, as are many words in the letters Lawrence underlined for emphasis. Postscripts have been uniformly put at the end of letters. All the numbered footnotes in small type are mine; those indicated by asterisks are Lawrence's own.

With regard to the spelling of Arabic names, there being no accepted transliterations from the Arabic, Lawrence and his contemporaries spelt as they wished; I have retained the original spelling in all the letters and reports here reproduced.

For Lawrence's own approach to this problem the reader is recommended to turn to the preface to *Seven Pillars of Wisdom* contributed by A. W. Lawrence.

T. E. LAWRENCE:
BIOGRAPHICAL SUMMARY

Born 1888, 16 August, Tremadoc, North Wales

Oxford City High School, September 1896 to July 1907

    In northern France studying castles, summers of 1906 and 1907

Jesus College, Oxford, October 1907 to June 1910 (1st Class Honours in modern history, 1910)

    In France, studying castles, summer of 1908

    In Syria, studying castles, summer of 1909

    Wrote his thesis, *Crusader Castles*, winter of 1909-10

At Jebail in Syria, studying Arabic, winter of 1910-11

Excavating at Carchemish (Jerablus) under D. G. Hogarth and R. Campbell Thompson, April to July 1911

    Walk through northern Mesopotamia, summer of 1911

Excavating in Egypt under Flinders Petrie, beginning of 1912

Excavating at Carchemish under C. L. Woolley, spring 1912 to spring 1914

    At home in Oxford, summer of 1913

    Survey of Sinai, January to February 1914

At Oxford and London, summer of 1914, completing *The Wilderness of Zin* (archaeological report on Sinai co-written with Woolley), eventually at War Office; commissioned October 1914

In Egypt as Intelligence officer, December 1914 to October 1916

    On special duty in Mesopotamia, March to May 1916

    Journey to Jidda with Ronald Storrs, October 1916

    First meeting with Feisal, October 1916

    Joined Arab Bureau, November 1916

Attached to Arab forces, December 1916 to October 1918

    Akaba expedition, May to July 1917

    Akaba falls, first meeting with General Sir Edmund Allenby, July 1917

    Promoted to major, summer 1917

    Deraa episode, November 1917

    Present at official entry into Jerusalem, December 1917

    Battle of Tafileh, January 1918

    Promoted to lieutenant-colonel, March 1918

Enters Damascus, 1 October, leaves Damascus 4 October 1918
Present at meetings of Eastern Committee of War Cabinet, October to
    November 1918
    With Feisal in France and Britain, November to December 1918
In Paris for Peace Conference, January to October 1919
    Journey by air to Egypt, May to June 1919
    At All Souls College, Oxford (as Fellow), and in London, 1919 to 1921
Adviser to Winston Churchill, Colonial Office, 1921 to 1922
    On missions to Aden, Jidda and Transjordan, August to December 1921
    Resigns from Colonial Office, July 1922
Joins Royal Air Force as John Hume Ross, August 1922 to January 1923
    Discharged following press disclosure of his identity
Private T. E. Shaw, Royal Tank Corps, March 1923 to August 1925
    Acquires cottage at Clouds Hill, near Bovington Camp, Dorset
Aircraftman Shaw, Royal Air Force, from August 1925 to March 1935
    Subscribers' edition of *Seven Pillars of Wisdom* completed 1926
In India, January 1927 to January 1929: *Revolt in the Desert* (popular
    abridgement of *Seven Pillars*) published and later withdrawn; *The Mint*
    completed; brought back to England following press stories claiming he
    was involved in a rebellion in Afghanistan
At various air stations in England, March 1929 to March 1935, working
    principally on high-speed marine craft
Retires to Clouds Hill, spring 1935
Has accident on motorcycle near Clouds Hill, 13 May 1935
Dies in Bovington Military Hospital, 19 May 1935
Funeral at Moreton, Dorset, 21 May 1935

Based on chronological table in *T. E. Lawrence by His Friends*,
edited by A. W. Lawrence, 1937

GENERAL INTRODUCTION

Lawrence wrote and received innumerable letters, but relatively few of those he received have survived. His standard practice was to destroy them. He did this not out of malice or contempt but because he felt that once a letter had been read and understood, its purpose had been fulfilled. For him, a letter was a private communication that should not be hoarded for later scrutiny by strangers. Moreover, throughout his army and air force years – the peak period for his correspondence – he had little more than his own bed space in which to keep his possessions, and other people's letters held a very low priority.

Writing from his R.A.F. base in India on 29 March 1927 to Mrs Charlotte Shaw, his most constant correspondent in the last decade or so of his life, he admitted to her that of late he had 'regretfully destroyed many letters of yours' in spite of their being 'first class, as pictures of today, and historically valuable'. He expanded on the subject – evidently in response to a comment from her – in his letter of 12 May: 'I do not want you to feel that in burning your letters I'm doing anything wanton. It's not that. They are personal documents, and I feel that they belong utterly to me, when they reach me: as though you wrote them only for me, and kept no share in them, after you had posted them. They could not be shown to anybody else, without breach of intimacy between us. [...] Nor can I keep them safely: what place have I where to keep anything? Service men have the privacy of gold-fish in their bowls. The other fellows read my books, and see my pictures, and use my mug and plates, and borrow my clothes, and spend my money, and overhear and oversee every act and word and expressed thought of mine from sunrise to sunset. So what room have I for a private life? [...] So after I have read them I burn them.'

That letters might be seen by other than their intended recipients was bad enough; that they might be published for consumption by the general reader he found even more offensive. One of his very last letters, to his American friend Ralph Isham, written on 10 May 1935, was a cry of protest on hearing that an American university had published a letter of his 'without even attempting to ask my permission first'. He continued: 'As you know, I greatly dislike the publication of private letters (except after very full consideration).' Yet, as is clear from his letter to Flight Sergeant Ford, quoted on page ix, he foresaw the possibility of such treatment and, to his annoyance, that knowledge could sometimes affect his style. He wrote to his publisher friend K. W. Marshall on 6 September 1932: 'My letters ceased being personal seven years ago, when an American magazine advertised a batch as "characteristic products of a remarkable adventurer". That cured me of writing sense.' He even wrote once to Mrs Shaw (19 January 1930), 'Perhaps I am not writing to you, but for my some-day "Life and Letters".' He was aware that she preserved his letters to her as regularly as he destroyed her letters to him.

The existence of not only this new volume but also its predecessor is, of course, a tribute to the fact that fortunately most of Lawrence's recipients followed Mrs Shaw's practice of preserving letters rather than his of destroying them. Doubtless many correspondents kept his letters because they were written by one of the most famous men of the day, but this was surely not the sole reason. His letters had a quality which made them unlikely candidates for the fire or the wastepaper basket. Even when brief, routine or apparently casual, they were consciously and carefully crafted and carried a distinctive hallmark. They were usually very legible (his handwriting generally presents no problem to the transcriber), and though they were not always comfortable reading, being sometimes written in depression and often in self-disparagement, they almost always had pace, vigour and a sense of style.

Though he took pains over his letters he did not believe in re-writing. 'Nobody ever wrote a good letter in a fair copy,' he stated to Charlotte Shaw on 14 April 1927. 'It's the first draft, or none.' But if he was to write a serious letter, the task must be worthily accomplished. He described his letter-writing philosophy to his artist friend Eric Kennington in a letter of 6 August 1934: 'It is very difficult to write a good letter. Mine don't pretend to be good ... but they do actually try very hard to be good. I write them in great batches, on the days when at length (after months, often) the impulse towards them eventually comes. Each tries to direct itself as directly as it can towards my picture of the person I am writing to: and if it does not seem to me (as I write it) that it makes contact – why then I write no more that night.' 'In great batches': one thing that has been interesting to me as an editor assembling material from many sources has been to note how much his mood could vary in letters written on the same day. Determining a possible order of writing has been a considerable problem and I make no claims always to have found a satisfactory solution. I am well-aware that the pack might be shuffled in a number of different ways.

Consciously crafted they might be, but their author was not attempting to achieve through letters the literary success which he came to feel eluded him in the writing of *Seven Pillars of Wisdom* or *The Mint*. He wrote to G. W. M. Dunn, fellow airman and published poet, on 19 July 1934: 'I don't think much of letters as an art form. Not even Fitzgerald, or Keats; or D. H. Lawrence or Gertrude

Bell's. They always have something ragged, domestic, undressed about them.' Yet his letters have attracted many admirers and much has been claimed for them. In the *Dictionary of National Biography*, Sir Ronald Storrs wrote: 'It has indeed been said that he would have survived (as would Edward Fitzgerald without Omar Khayyam) if only as a letter writer.' Similarly Basil Liddell Hart, a great admirer of Lawrence and one of his early biographers, has commented: 'For my own part, I wonder if he may not live longest in literature through his letters.'

Lawrence would certainly have rejected such praise, and not merely because of his veneration for the 'real thing' in literature and art. He also felt that letter-writing was distinctly second-best to a good face-to-face conversation. 'What a whale of a letter,' he commented after writing the quasi-obituary on himself which Robert Graves drew out of him in February 1935: 'Five minutes' talk would have been so much more fun!' He wrote to his friend in Aleppo, E. H. R. Altounyan, doctor and poet, on 7 April 1934: 'I have 1800 other letters to answer, and have spent all this time, and wasted all this ink, on addressing a being 2,000 miles away from me in space, and three weeks in time. Long before you get this note you will be a different creature, and out of reach of all my thoughts. That is the murrain upon correspondence. Five minutes of a meeting, once a blue moon, was worth all the letters that Lord Chesterfield addressed to his son.'

'1800 letters': he was doubtless exaggerating, but certainly from the moment he became famous until his death he was pursued by hordes of correspondents who would never leave him alone. They included admirers, well-wishers, sycophants, cranks, enquirers, would-be suitors, former servicemen who claimed acquaintance on the strength of, say, having trod the deck of the same ship in the Red Sea during 1917 or 1918, or people simply prompted to converse with him because he was a celebrity in the public domain. This was yet another reason why as ordinary serviceman Ross or Shaw he had no compunction in destroying his correspondence. He had little chance of storing it and even less chance of answering it. His 'justifiable percentage' – all he could cope with – was, as he told the Labour M. P. Ernest Thurtle in April 1929, twenty percent. For the rest? He wrote to Sergeant Pugh, with whom he had worked at the R.A.F. Cadet College, Cranwell, from India on 30 June 1927: 'Do you remember how that tray on the table used to get blocked solid: and how then I'd stuff the new-coming letters into those pigeon holes on my left, till they too were tight: and then we'd light the stove, & I'd chuck the time-expired ones by armfulls into the fire, and groan over answering the rest?' Also from India, on 23 March 1928, he wrote to his mother: 'If everybody ceased writing to me from today I could be free of back-correspondence in ten weeks at 16 letters a week. Letters take on the average ¾ of an hour each, if you add in the getting pens & ink out of my box, & the job of getting them to the post office. [...] The letters bore the people who get them as much as their letters bore me, I suppose. Who invented this curse?'

In the same letter he mentioned an idea which he was ultimately to take up seriously in the last weeks of his life. 'I think I shall print a small card "to announce cessation of correspondence" and send it to the 300 or 400 of my regular addresses. After that I shall write not more than one letter per week, & take a holiday once a quarter.' Early in 1935 he had a card specially made bearing the message: 'To tell you that in future I shall write very few letters.' 'I'm sending out dozens of the enclosed', he wrote to a Tank Corps friend on 6 March. 'Good idea?'

There were many people, of course, with whom he was happy to correspond, but he never got the relief he sought from the endless obligation to write letters. He was writing them – often on the backs of his specially printed card – almost to the day of his fatal accident. Yet with all his doubts, disclaimers and apparent contempt for the form, he is nevertheless, I believe, one of the most articulate, consistently interesting and rewarding letter-writers of this century. One reason for this, of course, was the urge born in him to write well, whether he was composing a signal from the desert or a letter to the great and famous. Another reason was that with the challenge of the war years and the political years over, his energy and talent needed to find some kind of outlet at a time when he had deliberately lowered his ambitions – so that although he sometimes raged against letter-writing, it was arguably necessary, indeed vital, to him that he was forced to do so. To quote from a letter sent to me in 1988 by the late St John Armitage, a Middle East specialist with long experience of the area and people and an impressive knowledge and understanding of Lawrence: 'Once Lawrence left the Middle East and government, he had a comparatively empty life or, rather, he had to create his own challenge to make life worthwhile. People, authorities, did not turn to him, he had to turn to them to keep "in the swim". Thus *Seven Pillars* and regular exchanges, such as those with Charlotte Shaw, in particular, were lifelines, and letter-writing in general was his salvation. Without the latter his years in the ranks would have been a total drop-out. Lawrence was a genius who denied himself full expression, and I believe that letters allowed him to unleash his intelligence and intellect, both of which were constrained by the narrowness of his chosen position.'

Yet Lawrence could have his doldrums. He is perhaps especially tedious in his self-disparagement, and in particular his disparagement of *Seven Pillars of Wisdom*, his highly idiosyncratic account of the Arab Revolt, in writing which he consciously attempted to create a major work that would have more value than a mere war memoir. In the now-famous Lyttelton/Hart-Davis correspondence there is a forthright comment on this tendency by George Lyttelton, dated 4 June 1958. 'I took up last week the letters of T. E. Lawrence – which', he tells Rupert Hart-Davis, 'clearly should have been edited by you.[1] You would have eliminated much of the endless jaw about the *Seven Pillars* and his ultimately repellent utterances about its entire worthlessness, which never strike me, at least, as quite sincere. I don't wonder that many of far less venomous spirit than Aldington have been allergic to him, but I expect you have noticed that, like G. B. S., everyone loved him who knew him in person and not only on paper.'

Lawrence resisted equally persuasive arguments against his condemnatory attacks on his book from his admirers and friends. The Cambridge writer and critic F. L. Lucas wrote to him in 1928: 'You are ridiculous about *Seven Pillars* ... You admit you're not qualified to criticise (it's not true; but that's *your* hypothesis); the hardest thing in the world is to judge one's own work; ergo, your opinion that it's bad is worthless; and when I say it's superb, I'm right.' Such arguments were unlikely to shift his view. When his former Oxford friend Vyvyan Richards took him up in 1923 on the same subject, his terse reply was: 'Self-depreciation is a necessity with me.' While understanding the exasperation of both Lucas and Lyttelton, I believe his letters show that his condemnation of what almost everybody else thought was a most distinguished work was not a pose or a ruse to win greater praise but was the result of a genuine conviction that however hard he might try, he was an imitative artist and not a real one. The completion of *Seven Pillars* left him convinced that his hopes of creating a book to stand beside such works as *Moby Dick* or *The Brothers Karamazov* were vain. He felt that there was an uncrossable barrier between himself and the genuine writer. As he wrote to E. M. Forster on 29 November 1925: 'You can rule a line, as hard as this pen-stroke, between the people who are artists & the rest of the world.' Similarly he wrote to John Brophy on 19 November 1929: 'I think I did write better than the average retired military man: but between that and "writing" there is a gulf. I have talked to many whom I think great writers. All of them have a likeness, in that they get some pleasure out of the phrases as they are born. Not the finished work, perhaps. Few look back with pleasure: but there is joy in the creation, and I have never had anything but weariness and dissatisfaction. This I put down to my works being an imitation, made with great care and pains and judgement, of the real thing.' He concluded that he was not quite the professional writer just as he

---

1 Rupert (later Sir Rupert) Hart-Davis had been at Jonathan Cape when Garnett was compiling his 1938 collection and had been responsible for preparing the text for the printers, a contribution which Garnett acknowledged in his preface.

had been not quite the professional soldier or the professional diplomat. Nor was he; what is remarkable, however, is not that he performed so inadequately, as he would have it, but that he did so well in all these fields. I have taken note of Lyttelton's strictures, but I have not excised Lawrence's self-disparagement entirely, for his assaults on himself are part of him, and they are also likely to be eloquently and even wittily expressed.

Most of the quotations used so far in this introduction are from letters believed to be in print here for the first time. But, the question will be asked, what *significant* revelations or insights can be found in this selection of letters that are not available in previous published editions?

A basic difference between this selection and its predecessors is that it is unexpurgated. Garnett felt obliged to omit material that was too frank for the 1930s but which we in the 1980s have no qualms about reading. He also did not have to hand some of the most enduringly interesting and revealing of Lawrence's letters. In the case of M. R. Lawrence, his tactic was to remove anything in his brother's letters that was remotely outspoken or contentious. The passages he excised – almost always without indicating that any deletion had taken place – are often precisely the passages that catch the eye when reading the originals. Bob Lawrence, as M. R. Lawrence was generally known, was the one Lawrence son who fulfilled his mother's ambition by devoting his life to Christianity; he became a medical missionary with the China Inland Mission. When he edited his brother's letters, his mother was still alive. These two factors affected him to the extent that he felt obliged to censor his more brilliant brother. The original text shows, for example, that T. E. Lawrence had forthright, indeed advanced, views about the relation of Britain and other such powers to the emergent nations – views sharpened by thinking about China, where not only his brother but also his mother went to propagate their evangelical Christian beliefs. 'We used to think foreigners were black beetles, and coloured races were heathen,' he wrote to his mother on 16 June 1927, 'whereas now we respect and admire and study their beliefs and manners. It's a revenge of the world upon the civilisation of Europe.' This (and there are other variations on this theme) is an important statement in the light of the fact that he is still thought of in some circles as an almost archetypal imperialist.

On the level of family relations, the original text confirms how correct he was in his often quoted statement to Mrs Charlotte Shaw (8 May 1928) that his mother was always 'hammering and sapping' to break into 'the circle of [his] integrity'. Writing to his mother in China on 28 December 1925, he rebelled against this pressure: 'You talk of "sharing my life" in letters: but that I won't allow. It is only my own business. Nor can anybody turn on or off the tap of "love" so called. I haven't any in me for anything. Once I used to like things (not people) and ideas. Now I don't care for anything at all.' Five years later, writing on 27 September 1933, he felt impelled to defend his younger brother Arnold (A. W. Lawrence), now a married man, from similar maternal encroachments. 'You are inclined to persecute him, you know. People brought up together, when full grown, rather resent their relatives. I think Arnie does not want to see too much of us, and the best treatment for that is to see too little. When he feels safe – sure that we are not trying to "get at" him – he will lose that nervousness. If any of us really needed anything, we would help each other. Till then, do let each manage his own affairs.' M. R. Lawrence had, of course, every right to remove such passages, but there can be no offence in printing them now.

I have also included a great deal of previously unpublished material relating to the war period. I have written at some length on this subject in the introduction to 'Part 2: The War Years', and will therefore simply state here my belief that his letters and reports give little support to the view that he was a military charlatan who later rode to celebrity on the back of Lowell Thomas's publicity machine. That his role was a most important one, and seen as such at the time, is firmly substantiated by the reports and letters of others involved in the campaign, including such men as Colonel Newcombe, Colonel Wilson, Colonel Joyce, Brigadier-General Clayton, Major Buxton, D. G. Hogarth, Lord Lloyd, Field Marshal Lord Wavell and Field Marshal Lord Allenby, and the Arab leader Sherif Feisal, later King Feisal I of Iraq. Lawrence was too unconventional a soldier to win everybody's approval but the overall opinion was that he was the best man for an extremely difficult and important task and that he performed it supremely well.[2]

Some evidence relating to his family background has also emerged (*see* the introduction to 'Part 1: The Early Years'). There are various references in the new material to his illegitimacy – some jocular, some more poignant – but perhaps the most important letter, which I am pleased to be allowed to publish, is that to his solicitor, the Hon. Edward Eliot, dated 16 June 1927, in which he reported his decision to change his name by deed poll to Thomas Edward Shaw and asked Eliot to attend to the necessary legal processes. The letter reveals that he had never seen his birth certificate and was in doubt as to his

---

2 For more on the subject, *see* my *T. E. Lawrence in War and Peace: An Anthology of the Military Writings of Lawrence of Arabia* (Greenhill Books, 2005).

original name – in fact he *was* registered as Lawrence, not, as he thought possible, under his father's family name of Chapman – and implies that he thought Shaw might possibly be an intermediate name only, 'for eventually, I suppose, Chapman it will have to be'. He added: 'there is a lot of land in that name knocking about: and I don't want to chuck it away, as Walter Raleigh, for whom I have a certain regard, gave it to my father's first Irish ancestor. I have a feeling that it should be kept in the line. My father's death [his father had died in 1919] wound up the baronetcy (a union title, of all the rubbish!) and one of my brothers is breeding heirs. So the family looks like continuing, in the illegitimate branch!' The implication is surely that he hoped he might somehow be able in due time to graft the 'Lawrence' branch of the family back into the family tree. His joke to David Garnett that his translation of *The Odyssey* ought to be called *Chapman's Homer* might have had an underlying seriousness.[3] To Sir Ronald Storrs he wrote in January 1935, just before leaving the R.A.F., 'I venture to hope we shall see each other, but I don't know where I shall live, or what do, or how call myself.' There is surely in all this a hint of weariness with his various assumed identities, and an understandable longing, half-romantic, half-realistic, to secure himself to firm and long-established roots.

The book also contains material with a bearing on the much-discussed subject of Lawrence's sexuality. The truth, I believe (in line with almost everyone who knew him personally), is that he was neither heterosexual nor homosexual in practice. Replying on 26 March 1929 to F. L. Lucas, who had been tackling him about the chapter in *The Mint* in which he had quoted the Oxford preacher who had implored his young friends 'not to imperil [their] immortal souls upon a pleasure which, *so I am credibly informed*, lasts less than one and three-quarter minutes', Lawrence wrote: 'the period of enjoyment in sex, seems to me a very doubtful one. I've asked the fellows in this hut (three or four go with women regularly). They are not sure: but they say it's all over in ten minutes: and the preliminaries – which I discounted – take up most of the ten minutes. For myself, I haven't tried it, & hope not to.' Similarly he replied to Robert Graves on 6 November 1928 when discussing the same chapter: 'As I wrote (with some courage, I think: few people admit the damaging ignorance) I haven't ever: and don't much want to.'

On the matter of homosexuality, in a letter of 21 December 1927 to E. M. Forster, after commenting admiringly on Forster's curious homosexual ghost story *Dr. Woolacott*, and adding that it had helped him to come to terms with his own enforced homosexual experience at the hands of the Turks, he stated: 'I

3 *The Familiar Faces* by David Garnett, p. 104.

couldn't ever do it, I believe: the impulse strong enough to make me touch another creature has not yet been born in me.' As if that were not clear enough, when enthusing in September 1929 to Robert Graves about the latter's auto-biographical *Goodbye to All That*, Lawrence wrote of Siegfried Sassoon, fellow officer with Graves in the trenches: 'S. S. comes out very well. I'm glad of that, for I like him; homosex and all.' Not, surely, the remark of someone who thought himself to be homosexual; and it should be added that neither Forster (of whose homosexuality he was well aware) nor Graves nor Lucas was the sort of man to whom he would write with other than complete frankness.

There remains his strong and affectionate relationship with his Arab friend at Carchemish, Dahoum, who has been generally accepted as being, at least in part, the 'S. A.' to whom he dedicated *Seven Pillars*, and later with R. A. M. Guy, a young aircraftman, a number of letters to whom are printed in this book. There is no evidence in either case to suggest any physical relationship. The letter to C. F. Bell in Part I, dated 10 December 1913, shows that both Leonard Woolley (in charge of the Carchemish dig) and Lawrence liked and admired Dahoum, but there is no hint of improper behaviour, rather the tone is that of the standard *badinage* of a scholarly, all-male world. Dahoum was a youth whose potential both men recognized and encouraged; and A. W. Lawrence has told me that the impression he left when he visited Oxford was that 'he was a very nice chap' whom all the family liked. As for Lawrence's letters to Guy, they are basically caring ones calculated to reassure a young man who plainly much admired Lawrence and was grieved to find their friendship interrupted by the senior man's abrupt departure from the R.A.F.; Guy was in any case shortly to be married. Perhaps the one thing which has angered his closest R.A.F. and Tank Corps friends more than anything else as Lawrence's reputation has come under the scrutiny of some of his modern interpreters has been the speculation that he was a homosexual. The discussion had no meaning for them. The idea had never crossed their minds. And these were men living in the same hut and aware of his friendship with such men as Forster and Sassoon – who were, indeed, thanks to the classless conviviality of Lawrence's Dorset cottage, Clouds Hill, friends of theirs, too.

But he was not sexless. 'I'm so funnily made up, sexually,' he wrote to E. M. Forster on 8 September 1927, refusing to read the latter's overtly homosexual unpublished novel *Maurice*.[4] ('Sexually' is correct; not 'sensually', as the letter is transcribed in Garnett.) It has now been acknowledged that he submitted himself to beatings in the last decade or so of his life, which his brother A. W. Lawrence

4 Published in 1971, the year after Forster's death.

believes were in the tradition of the mediaeval flagellants (Lawrence was well-versed in mediaeval history and knew of them) but which have also been interpreted in more modern terms as having a sexual as well as a punitive element; and it is undeniable that there was, as is made clear in *Seven Pillars*, a sexual element in his response to the beating he suffered in 1917 at Deraa. (There is a thorough and sympathetic analysis of this subject in the Pulitzer Prize biography of Lawrence *A Prince of Our Disorder*, by Dr John E. Mack.) By contrast, it was also quite possible for women to feel that he had heterosexual potential.

Indeed, Lady Astor plainly thought him capable of even having an affair and virtually (indeed, almost jealously) accused him of such – *see* his letter to her of 11 December 1933, wittily denying the charge. He later wrote to her (26 November 1934), that there was a particular R.A.F. officer's wife who wrote regularly to him while he rarely wrote back: 'Am I a beast? But she wants something which I want to keep, and she ought to understand it.' (*See* viii-ix) There seems never to have been any actual likelihood of his getting married, but more than a few people close to him thought that he might have done so if circumstances had been appropriate. Precisely what he *was*, in these highly personal terms, is difficult to define and, in the end, is not our business, but there seems to me some value in attempting to use the evidence of his own letters to clarify what he was not.

There is an important statement on this whole subject in a letter by A. W. Lawrence to a Miss Early, an American lady, dated 17 December 1963, of which a copy is held in the Bodleian Library. 'No one who knew him or worked with him ever believed him to be a homosexual. He wasn't, though homosexuality disgusted him far less than the abuse of normal sex and attitude of some of the men in the huts in the R.A.F. or Tank Corps. He had more respect for women as *people* than many men. The circumstances of his life, not his birth, account for much of his ill-ease. We were a family of five boys with little or no contact with girls of our own age or mental interests. He chose to study Near Eastern archaeology and conditions in countries where it was then impossible that young women should travel or work. I, on the other hand, took up Classical archaeology, a subject which many women could take up, and while still a student at the British School of Archaeology in Rome met and married a fellow-student. T. E. had no such opportunities to meet women of his own age and with similar mental interests. After the war it was too late. Dr. Ernest Altounyan, I think and so does my wife, was correct in writing: "Women were to him persons as such to be appraised on their merits (not their sex)... He never married because he never happened to meet the right person; and nothing short of that would do; a bald statement of fact which cannot hope to convince the perverse intricacy of the public mind." Nearly all his friends were married, certainly his most cherished friends, and their wives found no difficulty with him.'

From other letters it is clear that some of the claims made about Lawrence for which he has been much derided are, in fact, true. When researching their biography *The Secret Lives of Lawrence of Arabia*, Phillip Knightley and Colin Simpson decided to check whether Lawrence had been offered, in 1934, the secretaryship of the Bank of England. They wrote to the bank and were informed that no record could be found of his having been offered the secretaryship but that he had once been considered for the post of night porter (as indeed he had, *see* p. 404). They used this reply to support the statement in the opening pages of their book that 'any attempt to take a cool look at the Lawrence legend dissolves into a quicksand of hearsay, rumour and fantasy'. However, in December 1986, clear evidence that such an offer was actually made was put up for sale at Sotheby's in the form of (i) a letter by Lawrence to the Hon. Francis Rodd – Rodd had sounded him out on the Bank's behalf – refusing the offer, (ii) an explanatory note by Rodd describing how the offer came to be made, and (iii) a letter by Sir Leslie O'Brien, former chief cashier of the Bank of England, promising to 'stop saying that the only job he [Lawrence] was ever offered was that of nightwatchman'. (The reader is referred to Lawrence's letter to Rodd dated 23 November 1934, on p. 533; it was printed by Garnett, but with the precise nature of the offer made to Lawrence unfortunately concealed by omissions.)

Similarly Lawrence has been accused of having had the fanciful idea that he might be called by the nation to the task of reorganizing home defence. Lady Astor's last letter to him, fortunately not destroyed but preserved in typed copy form in the Bodleian Library and here quoted as a footnote to his reply, dated 8 May 1935, shows that such an offer was indeed under serious consideration at that time. He was invited by her to come to Cliveden to meet, among other people, Stanley Baldwin, who later that month as Lord President of the Council made a major statement on Britain's air policy producing such headlines as 'R.A.F. at Home to be Trebled'. A few weeks later Baldwin was prime minister. That Lawrence, with his reputation still high in the British establishment, should have been thought capable of contributing in this area makes very good sense: see, for example, his letter to Lionel Curtis of 19 March 1934 (p. 514). His refusal of the invitation to Cliveden, dated 8 May 1935, is the last letter in Garnett's collection. Unfortunately, the context of the letter was not given nor the nature of the job on possible offer. Five days later, Lawrence had his motorcycle accident and six days after that he was dead, leaving much grief among his friends and many unanswerable questions as to how the course of his life, both public and personal, might have developed.

Unanswerable questions certainly, but I believe I have been able to assemble some interesting new material which throws light on Lawrence's state of mind in the last few weeks of his life. Although brief, this seemed an important enough period to be given a separate section of the book. What emerges from these last letters is that he had found no equilibrium in his new situation, in that he wrote at times with vigour and energy and at other times in deep depression and unease. Which mood prevailed when he went on his last motorcycle ride on 13 May 1935 it is impossible to know.

Apart from such specific contributions to what I believe to be a more accurate interpretation of the man, I am also pleased to be able to print letters hitherto unpublished to, among others, Lady Astor, Lord Trenchard, Lord Lloyd, Major-General Alan Dawnay, Sir Ronald Storrs, Peake Pasha, Colonel Newcombe, H. St J. B. Philby, Wilfred Scawen Blunt, Mrs Thomas Hardy, E. M. Forster, Robert Graves, Liddell Hart, Edward and David Garnett, Henry Williamson, Ezra Pound, Noël Coward, Eric Kennington, Augustus John, Ernest Rhys, R. D. Blumenfeld (editor of the *Daily Express*); and to members of 'the rank and file' who served with him, such as H. W. Bailey, T. W. Beaumont and S. C. Rolls from the war period, 'Jock' Chambers, R. A. M. Guy, Dick Knowles and Sergeant Pugh of the R.A.F. and Alec Dixon, 'Posh' Palmer and Arthur Russell of the Tank Corps. If there is a jewel in the crown it is perhaps the extensive usage for the first time of many eloquent, revealing, and at times confessional letters to Charlotte Shaw, overall his most intimate correspondent. As I have said, she denied any use of them to David Garnett, but a year after Garnett published she relented. On 6 March 1939 she wrote to her friend Dorothy Walker (I quote verbatim from Janet Dunbar's biography of Charlotte Shaw, *Mrs G. B. S*): 'I think T. E. meant his letters to be published. He was an inexpressibly complicated person. In a sense he was tragically sincere. But, also, he always had one eye on the limelight. You say you are thankful I do not allow any of my letters to be published. Now I feel this book shows they ought to be published just to show how much better he could be than anything in that [word crossed out].'

Plainly the book referred to is Garnett. Perhaps one can conclude that Charlotte Shaw would have been pleased that at last there was to be a substantial publication of Lawrence's letters to her ('my letters' as she calls them in her comment to Dorothy Walker) and that their author would not have objected too angrily to the decision, first made shortly after his death and repeated now, that some of his many hundreds of letters should be made available to the public.

ABBREVIATIONS

Bodleian Library Letters held in the Bodleian Library, Oxford, including those held until the year 2000 in the collection referred to in the original edition as the Bodleian Reserve; *see* p. viii

DG The Letters of T. E. Lawrence edited by David Garriett (1938)

HL The Home Letters of T. E. Lawrence and His Brothers edited by M. R. Lawrence (1954)

RGB T. E. Lawrence to His Biographers: Robert Graves (1963)

LHB T. E. Lawrence to His Biographers: Liddell Hart (1963)

HMH Solitary in the Ranks by H. Montgomery Hyde (1977)

Harvard University Houghton Library, Harvard University

University of Texas Harry Ransom Humanities Research Center, the University of Texas at Austin

University of Reading Department of Archives and Manuscripts, Reading University Library

TNA: PRO (plus File No.) The National Archives: Public Record Office, Kew, Richmond, Surrey

All other sources are named in full.

Note: As stated in the 'Foreword', the device [...] indicates an editorial omission, while dots within a letter are Lawrence's own. Matter previously omitted from the *Home Letters* is enclosed within square brackets.

The Lawrence brothers, 1910. From left to right: Ned,
Frank, Arnie, Bob and Will

I THE EARLY YEARS
to 1914

In the mid-1880s, an Anglo-Irish landowner called Thomas Chapman, master of South Hill, a country house not far from Dublin, fell in love with the governess whom he had appointed to look after his four daughters. He was approaching forty, and the governess, born illegitimate in County Durham and brought up in Scotland, was fifteen years his junior, but for her he gave up his home and his inheritance (he was heir to a baronetcy) and then proceeded over the next decade and a half to found a second family of five sons. Edith, the abandoned wife, was a severe, sourly religious person with a reputation that won her the nickname of 'the Vinegar Queen', but Sarah, her successor, though attractive, energetic and lively, was far from a free-thinking modern woman; in religious commitment she was Edith's equal. The circumstances of her union with her former employer were always to leave her – and him also, to a lesser extent – with a sense of guilt. Since Edith outlived her husband and had no thought of conceding a divorce, the name they assumed in their new life, Lawrence, would never be other than a convenient alias. Nevertheless, after some years of wandering they successfully set themselves up as what was to all intents and purposes a normal, middle-class family (with just a hint of gentility) in a large semi-detached house at 2 Polstead Road in north Oxford.

They brought up their sons (of whom T. E. Lawrence, born in Tremadoc, north Wales, in 1888, was the second) to be regular attenders at St Aldate's Church, which was presided over by a veteran and much-loved evangelical divine, Canon A. M. W. Christopher. Meanwhile, one by one the Lawrence brothers enrolled at the recently established Oxford City High School, which gave them a sound, classically based education and prepared for acceptance into Oxford University. Montagu Robert ('Bob') and the third son, William George ('Will'), went to St John's College; Thomas Edward (known throughout his boyhood as 'Ned') and the fourth son, Frank Helier (so-named because he was born when the family was residing briefly in St Helier, Jersey), went to Jesus College; Arnold Walter ('Arnie', not born until 1900, the youngest by some years), went to New College.

The mother, in addition to looking after the religious upbringing of the boys, provided stern discipline and a well-run household. The father, who adopted no profession but lived, by his own description, as a gentleman of 'independent means', provided his sons with interests: bicycling, photography, and an awareness of mediaeval history. It was these interests that combined to make the young T. E. Lawrence into a dedicated and enthusiastic traveller, first in England and Wales and then further afield in France, where he visited churches and castles, sketching, photographing, and writing full and regular accounts of his experiences and discoveries in his letters home. In his school and undergraduate years he covered thousands of miles, sometimes with his father or one or other of his brothers, sometimes with school-friends, but more often alone, on his specially built three-speed bicycle. Reading modern history at Jesus College, he decided to offer a thesis which involved the making of detailed comparisons between the castles of western Europe and those of the Middle East built during the Crusades. To research the latter he spent eleven weeks of the summer vacation of 1909 journeying on foot through Syria and Palestine, visiting numerous castles and bringing back many photographs, plans and drawings. The prevailing belief among mediaeval historians was that the castle-builders of the East had been the principal innovators, and that those of the West had been their timid imitators. Lawrence took a diametrically opposed view, arguing his case with much vigour and weighty evidence in a thesis that contributed crucially to his gaining a first-class honours degree.

His examination success and the friendship and patronage of D. G. Hogarth, keeper of the Ashmolean Museum, Oxford, led to the next step forward. He was elected to a four-year 'senior demyship' (postgraduate scholarship) at Hogarth's college, Magdalen, and appointed by the British Museum to an important archaeological dig, of which Hogarth was in charge, at Carchemish on the upper Euphrates: the money accruing from the demyship helped finance him as an archaeologist. An earlier plan to produce a thesis on mediaeval pottery for a bachelor of letters (B. Litt) degree was abandoned. By Christmas that year he had fulfilled a long-held ambition to visit Greece, had also tasted and enjoyed Constantinople and was in Jebail (ancient Byblos) in the Lebanon, at the American mission school which he had discovered on his walking-tour, learning Arabic in the company of a number of women teachers who were to become his firm friends and, in the case of Mrs Rieder and Miss Fareedah el Akle, regular correspondents. Hogarth joined him there in February, and they set off for Carchemish, travelling by way of Haifa, Deraa and Damascus (Lawrence was to know the last two in very different circumstances in the war), and reaching their destination in March.

Lawrence spent the best part of four digging seasons at Carchemish, first under Hogarth and then, from 1912, under Leonard Woolley. These were his most unclouded years. The skills he had first developed as a schoolboy, when he had rubbed brasses and collected archaeological relics for the Ashmolean, provided a useful foundation (he was well-qualified as the expedition's photographer) and the experience of living off the land during his walking-tour had nurtured a natural talent for getting on with the local people, which he now exploited and developed as the expedition's principal employer of labour. When off-duty there was much opportunity for practical jokes; high spirits were often the norm at Carchemish. Between digs he went off on long exploratory journeys, visiting castles, collecting Hittite seals for Hogarth, and pitting himself with relish against the challenges of terrain and climate. A companion on some of these journeys was a young Arab donkey-boy, Dahoum, to whom he became both close friend and mentor and whom he took home to Oxford in 1913, together with the site foreman, Sheikh Hamoudi. The Arabs in their robes created a mild sensation among the towers and spires. C. F. Bell of the Ashmolean commissioned artist Francis Dodd to come down to Oxford to draw Dahoum; an account of the occasion sent to its instigator in Italy, where he had gone on holiday, is one of several amusing and discursive letters to Bell, which have only recently been released from a fifty-year embargo.

It has been suggested that Lawrence and Hogarth were engaged in espionage at this period and that the Carchemish dig was a cover for Intelligence work; the fact that, hard by the British Museum site, the Germans were building a massive bridge across the Euphrates as part of their Berlin-Baghdad railway has been adduced in support. There is nothing in any new material to support this view; his brother A. W. Lawrence has always strongly discounted these allegations, and certainly if Lawrence was so involved, the burden lay lightly on him. However, in early 1914 he and Woolley did provide scholarly respectability for an essentially military survey, requested by Kitchener, of an unmapped part of Turkish-controlled Sinai – 'red herrings, to give an archaeological colour to a political job' was Lawrence's own neat definition of his and Woolley's role (letter to his mother, 4 January 1914). This expedition and the experience of his Carchemish years left him well-prepared for the wartime Intelligence duties in which he would shortly be engaged.

There is such a wealth of previously unused material available from 1914 onwards and this early period has been so well-covered in previous collections that it seemed best to reflect it with a relatively concise anthology – mainly of extracts, though some letters are published in full. From those collections I have taken examples of what seem to me good writing and observation, such as his accounts of Chartres, Athens and Constantinople, or his response to his first sight of the Mediterranean, or (in a letter now correctly dated September 1910) his *rêverie* about the magic of reading. In addition to republished material there are a number of hitherto unpublished letters, most of them in full: to C. F. Bell, as already described; to Miss Fareedah el Akle; to Mrs Rieder; to D. G. Hogarth; to

James Elroy Flecker[1]; as well as one to his mother listing the expenses of his 1909 walking-tour and including the important summarizing comment (it was the last letter of the journey): 'I won't repent this trip. It has been all wonderful, worth three times its cost.'

I have also reinstated some passages suppressed by M. R. Lawrence when he edited his *Home Letters* (*see* 'General Introduction'). This section contains, in a new letter to Fareedah el Akle dated 26 June 1911, a nice description of the contents of his letters to his family as he saw them: 'general affairs, with a dig in the ribs here, and a pin-prick there'. It was a description that would remain apposite throughout his life; small wonder that the sensitive M. R. Lawrence found certain digs and pin-pricks hard to take. One notable passage here restored shows that Lawrence was uncertain about the further development of his career. In the letter to his mother of 11 April 1911, in which he discussed future options and defended the dream he shared at that time with his Jesus College friend, Vyvyan Richards, of founding a William-Morris-style printing-press, he told his mother: 'I am not going to put all my energies into rubbish like writing history, or becoming an archaeologist. I would much rather write a novel even, or become a newspaper correspondent: however there is still hope that Richards may pull the thing through.' The printing-press project was very dear to him and even survived the war years, but Lawrence as archaeologist, novelist and newspaper correspondent was never to be heard of again. The historian did survive, but as a chronicler of his own very personal history. As with so many men of his generation, the war greatly changed the lives of those whom it did not destroy.

Almost all Lawrence's home letters are described here, as elsewhere in the book, as being written to his mother, even when there is no formal greeting to indicate that this is the case. The assumption seems a safe one, however. Such envelopes as have survived are normally addressed to Mrs Lawrence; in his letter of 2 July 1909, he begins: 'Dear Mother (the rest are understood)'; in his letter of 31 January 1911 he refers to her as his 'principal listener'; and the fact that he occasionally addresses a letter specifically to his father or to one of his brothers suggests that he generally assumed that she would be the prime reader of all letters not so assigned. This was to continue; even in his last years, writing to his mother and M. R. ('Bob') Lawrence when the latter was a missionary in China, it was assumed that she was the principal recipient, but that Bob would read the letter in his turn.

---

1 This list originally included E. T. Leeds, but in May 1988 a volume of Lawrence's letters to Leeds, edited by J. M. Wilson, was published by the Whittington Press in a limited edition.

HIS MOTHER
August 13, 1905   *FLEECE HOTEL COLCHESTER*

Dear Mother

[...] We came here from Ipswich over a rather hilly road 18 miles long. Still we took two hours over it; and walked about six hills; a proceeding Father does not like. We are feeding splendidly. Father is much better and has not coughed since Lynn.[1]

I have had to give up Bures. We came by the other road because of the wind; still I hope to get Pebmarsh tomorrow;[2] and I got one yesterday so I'm not altogether mournful. I have sent off all my rubbings to Miss Powell; hope she'll like them. I expect you have Will with you now. Will you please tell him not to let you do more work than is necessary to keep you in condition? Also tickle Arnie when he gets up and when he goes to bed all from me. Tell him there are dozens of butterflies of all sorts about here, some Red Admirals; and a lot of other very queer ones. Ask Beadle[3] to come up here as he has never seen a Death's Head or some such insect. Norwich Museum he would have enjoyed. There was the largest collection of raptorial birds in existence 409 out of 470 species: I wonder if he'll shriek with horror when he hears that I did not look at them but went off and examined the Norman W.C.s. In the hall was a thrilling stuffed group a boa constrictor strangling a tiger. We hope to return to Oxford Wednesday. Kindly take heaps of love from me for yourself; and when you've had enough, divide the remainder into three portions, and give them to the three worms[4] you have with you. I wonder how the Doctor is enjoying Jerry.[5] Don't forget the Canon's birthday next Sunday.[6] We have had one post card from Will, 1 from yourself and one letter from you. Loud snores to all. Love to yourself.

Ned   *HL/Bodleian Library*

1 Lawrence's father suffered from bronchitis.
2 Bures (Suffolk) and Pebmarsh (Essex) were places where Lawrence had planned to make brass rubbings.
3 Beadle: his brother Will.
4 'The three worms you have with you': the other members of the family present at Polstead Road. 'Worms' was also used by Lawrence as a farewell, a salutation (*e.g.* 'accept my best worms'), or, in the singular, to denote the youngest member of the family, Arnold, who was frequently referred to as 'Worm' into his teens. In using the word Lawrence would also have been aware of its archaic meaning: serpent, snake or dragon.
5 Jerry: a dog. The doctor was presumably Dr A. G. Gibson, the Lawrence family physician, who lived nearby in the Banbury Road.
6 Canon Christopher of St Aldate's Church, Oxford: *see* the introduction to this section.

HIS MOTHER
Friday, Aug 4, 1906   *LE CLOS BRIANT* [DINARD]

Dear Mother

I have arrived here quite right after an excellent crossing. The Kerrys almost missed the train at Oxford of course, and came to the boat just with a minute to spare.[1] The journey down to Southampton was uneventful, except for scares about the luggage going wrong. I rode straight to Netley,[2] and caused a spirit of eager enquiry to be manifested by the youth of Southampton. Netley is as fine as if not finer than I had imagined. It is certainly the finest ruin I have seen, and much the most picturesque. I do not think that the Chapter House and guest room can be equalled. [...]

On board the boat I found my berth, and deposited all my spare goods, and then put on the extra thick coat (this information is for Mother). The Moon was full and glorious: Mr. Kerry and I stayed up till about 11.30 looking at it; I cannot say whether the cloud effects or the reflection on the water were the best but the 'ensemble' was perfect and left nothing to be desired. I never before understood properly Tennyson's

'Long glories of the Autumn Moon'[3]

but I see his reasons now for mentioning it so often, it was so different from the pale moon of the land. The moon was out from about seven to four, and there were heavy clouds with continuous lightning in the East. We only had about ½ hour's rain. The sunrise was on the whole a failure, there was nothing so good as the sunset before. About 2 we passed between Sark and Jersey. Tell Chimp[4] I was not much impressed with the latter. It was all too dark and gloomy, for a residence; the only bright spot was the Corbière Light-house. St. Malo was reached before six, but we had to wait till seven before landing. The sea was very choppy and irregular with a strong swell around the Channel Islands. Everyone in the boat appears to have been sick with the exception of four or five, among whom Mr. K[erry] and myself were prominent. I found Mons. Chaignon[5] at the

---

1 The Kerry family were friends and near neighbours of the Lawrences in Oxford.

2 Netley Abbey, a Cistercian house founded from Beaulieu Abbey in the 13th century.

3 From *Idylls of the King: The Passing of Arthur*; but Lawrence was misquoting: Tennyson wrote 'winter moon'.

4 Chimp: his brother Frank, who was born in Jersey.

5 The Lawrences had lived for a time in Brittany in the years before they settled in Oxford and had become particular friends of the Chaignon family, whom Lawrence used as a base and a point of contact during his visits to France.

Douane (?);[6] we recognised each other at the same moment. He has hardly changed at all, if anything he is a trifle stouter. The customs people were chalking all the baggage as fast as it appeared, they do not seem to have opened any: there was a fearful crush; I should think there were 120 bicycles. [...] The Chaignons send all sorts of messages for Bob; it took me nearly ten minutes to explain all about the Brigade to them;[7] it was about the first thing they asked me. They also send dittos to you and the other nippers. Poor Hall[8] is not 1st in Locals after all. Love to yourself. (Don't do any work at all). To Father and to all the other worms down to the smallest. Just off to post. Ta Ta.

HL/Bodleian Library

HIS MOTHER
14 Août, 1906   *HOTEL DU COMMERCE GUINCAMP*

[...] Erquy is a bathing town so called, with enormous quarries of rose-coloured granite. We walked all over the quarry cliffs after eight, and the wind being high we enjoyed ourselves much. The cliffs were about 400 feet high, and commanded a good view. From Erquy, we rode to Château du Guildo, near Ploubalay. At Erquy when returning from bathing, I rode a measured half-kilo. on the sand in 40 seconds exactly. There was a gale behind me, and the sands were perfectly level and very fast, but still 30 miles per hour was distinctly good. I have never gone faster; of course my high gear was the one I rode. Father would like to come to stay at Erquy for a week, to do a little speed-work on the sands; he would not do it anywhere else, for the roads, like most Breton ones, are vile. [...]

[With reference to touring in France. There is no doubt that people would cheat you if possible. When we did not get an accurate statement of accounts we got huge bills (this only happened twice). I have finished up with nearly 39 francs over and have not cashed the sovereign Scroggs[1] brought. If you want an

6 *Douane*: French customs. The question mark is Lawrence's.
7 The Brigade: the Church Lads' Brigade at St Aldate's, of which both Bob and Ned were members.
8 E. F. Hall (1888-1986), a contemporary of Lawrence both at Oxford High School and Jesus College. Later a canon of the Church of England. The 'Locals' were the Oxford local examinations.

1 'Scroggs': nickname of C. F. C. Beeson, friend of Lawrence at the Oxford High School, fellow brass-rubber and amateur archaeologist at home (they collaborated in collecting pottery, glass, coins, etc., at building sites in Oxford and presenting them to the Ashmolean Museum) and occasional companion abroad.

account of the expenditure during the trip, consult S. who kept the books. I thus spent some 61 francs in the eight days and this includes repairs 5 francs, and postcards with stamps, a gigantic item, although I only have about 8 p.c.'s over. We had no troubles, although I must get a new outer cover at once. (p.s. got a puncture today, S's front wheel) & will try a Dunlop Agency in St. Servan.] [...]

HL/Bodleian Library

HIS MOTHER
Friday morning [18 August 1906]   *DINARD*

[...] I see you want notes on the children here.[1] Pierre is rather more refined than the rest, but behaves worse than the baby of an English bargee. He is almost as tall as I am, and is very delicate, having overgrown his strength. Henri is a very boisterous imp, without a spark of delicacy, but what elderly spinsters call 'a thorough boy'. Dédée is very inquisitive, but rather nice. Lucienne is very loving and would be sweet if not so dirty, & Madelaine is terribly spoilt. The others are at present lumps of fat. Mr. Chaignon is short and inclined to stout, and is turning grey: he might be strong, and is not particularly interesting. Mme Chaignon is exceedingly nice, and easily includes in herself all the virtues of the rest of the family. I like her very much. The house is not so large as the stables, but my room is very nice. Yesterday [...] I bought and fixed a repair band over the weak spot in my tyre. I hope it will do for the present. [...]

Bodleian Library

HIS MOTHER
April 1907   *CAERPHILLY*

Dear Mother
Here I am at my last Welsh castle, and, I think, in most respects my best. [...]
    Caerphilly [...] is magnificent. The Horn-work is most interesting, and the outworks could not be excelled, either for preservation or attractiveness.

---

1 *I.e.* the children of the Chaignon family. As no part of this passage appeared in *HL* it is credited only to the Bodleian Library, a practice observed in such cases throughout the book.

There are no good photos to be obtained, and there have been none at any time or at any castle I have visited. The conviction has been continually growing stronger upon me, that I must tour round this part again with a camera. Details which interest me, such as the moulding of a chimney piece, or the shape of the flue, even the vaulting of a room, are always neglected by the professional p.p.c. maker. [...]

[Any person wishing to create an attraction or sensation in Wales may appear without a hat. It is always sure to draw. Yesterday for instance 49 people told me that I had no hat (I thought this was obvious?) 6 told me I belonged to the hatless brigade (there is a strong branch of it at Swansea) hundreds (I counted 254 and then stopped) asked me where my hat was; nearly as many asked me if I had lost it, and streetfuls yelled to me that I hadn't got no 'at. I keep no account of Welsh remarks, but they must have been almost as numerous as the English ones.]

After ten days in Wales I ought to be able to sum up all the character, habits, peculiarities, virtues, vices, and other points of the Welsh people. I am sorry I cannot do this yet. They seem to me to be rather inquisitive, [more dirty, and exceedingly ugly. I am at last discovering where I got my large mouth from. It's a national peculiarity.][1] At the same time they appear honest; I have had no extortionate bills (which reminds me that I have over £3 in hand). I have come to the conclusion that two meals a day with a glass of milk at one o'clock, suit me better than three. At any rate I have always felt fresh in this trip in spite of very hard journeys, and the number of castles has not palled on me; I am fresh for any amount more and could continue for months. I also feel stronger as the day goes on: with my luggage left at home I could do 180 miles in the day with ease. [...]

HL/Bodleian Library

HIS MOTHER
Sunday 11 August 1907   *EVREUX*

Dear Mother
Father is out, and so I am at last writing to you. I would have written before, but was so busy taking photos, etc. at Château Gaillard. Beauvais was a wonderful

---

1 Lawrence rarely thought of himself as in any way Welsh, but he was particularly aware of his Welsh connection at this time in that his birth in Wales had qualified him to apply for the Meyricke Exhibition in History at Jesus College which he had won two months previously.

place, and I left it with great regret for Gisors which was disappointing, (a large castle, but all the towers locked up), from Gisors we came to Petit Andelys. The Château Gaillard was so magnificent, and the post cards so abominable, that I stopped there an extra day, & did nothing but photograph, from 6.0 a.m. to 7.0 p.m. I took ten altogether, and if all are successful, I will have a wonderful series. I will certainly have to start a book. Some of them were very difficult to take, and the whole day was very hard. I think Pt. Andelys would be a good place to stop at. The hotel is cheap, and very pleasant. The Seine runs near the back door, & the bathing is excellent, from a little wooded island in the centre of the river. There are plenty of hills within sight, & many interesting places. Also the scenery all along the river is exceedingly fine. Long strings of barges pulled by a steam-tug pass the hotel occasionally, and the whole place is over-shadowed by the hills with the ruins of the Château. I have talked so much about this to you that you must know it all by heart, so I had better content myself with saying that its plan is marvellous, the execution wonderful, and the situation perfect. The whole construction bears the unmistakable stamp of genius. Richard I must have been a far greater man than we usually consider him: he must have been a great strategist and a great engineer, as well as a great man-at-arms. [...]

HL/Bodleian Library

HIS MOTHER
26 August 1907   *LE MONT ST MICHEL* [1]

Dear Mother
Here I am at last about to spend a night at the Mont. The dream of years is fulfilled. It is a perfect evening; the tide is high, and comes some 20 feet up the street. In addition the stars are out most beautifully, and the moon is, they say, just about to rise. The phosphorescence in the water interests me especially: I have only seen it once or twice before, and never so well as tonight. The whole sea, when oars are dipped into it, seems to blaze, for several feet around.

[1] Fortress, monastery and town poised on top of a tiny precipitous offshore island on the frontier between Normandy and Brittany, Mont-St-Michel was precisely the kind of place to excite Lawrence as historian and photographer. Four of his photographs of it – including a telephoto shot from fifteen miles off – are included in *HL*.

I rode here from Dinan, getting Frank's P.C. in St. Malo on my way. As you do not say you want anything, I will not bring back more than a cider-jug for Arnie. It is just large enough to hold all the cider he will ever want, and is a reddish-brown tint. (This news is for him). I am bringing it because there are none of the stamps which he wanted to be bought.

With Dinan and the Rance I am entirely in love. The Rue de Jersual from the old bridge to the *place*, is perfect: the river is most lovely. Above the town it becomes very quiet and peaceful, like the Thames: lined with Aspens & Lombardy poplars. When you add waterlilies, willows, and an occasional high bank, crowned with a quaint farmhouse or château, you have a fair idea of the characteristics of the stream. With its bathing (excellent they tell me) its boating (they have some of Salter's boats)[2] and its beauty, I think it should suit the entire family. Suppose we transport ourselves thither some Autumn?

Since I left Father (to return somewhat on my travels) I have had a very wonderful time. It began at Fougères, which I saw by moonlight, and a more exquisite sight I have seldom seen. That castle is quite above and beyond words. It pollutes it to mention any but Château Gaillard, Pembroke, and Caerphilly in the same breath, and I am not sure but that Fougères is the finest of them all. The Tour des Gobelins is six stories in height, and circular. It stands on a granite cliff 80 feet high, and in the moonlight had a marvellous effect. It set off the strength of the Melusine, a tower near, with an enormous expanded base. The talus shoots right out like the Keep of Ch. Gaillard. Beyond the Melusine, after a hundred yards of machicolated curtain, come Raoul and Yrienne, two wonderful *chefs-d'oeuvre* of the military architect. They are semi-circular bastions, projecting some 70 feet from the wall, are over 80 feet in diameter, and more than that in height; neither has a window or projection in the face, and over against them leans the Spire of St. Sulpice the most crooked, and the thinnest in Bretagne. I would have given anything to have been able to sketch or paint these things as I saw them. I really must return to Fougères soon, and do justice to the whole. The neglect in which it has been left by the guide-books is abominable.

From Fougères I glided S.E. to Le Mans, to photograph the effigy of Mrs. Richard I., Berengaria, in the cathedral there. The Apse and Nave of the building were splendid: the former especially. From Le Mans I rode to Saumur, via Le Lude, a most splendid Renaissance Château, unhappily private. Saumur itself is still in parts as Balzac painted it in *Eugénie Grandet*, though the main streets have

2 Salter's was and still is the best-known Oxford boat-hire firm.

been rebuilt. The Castle is a military store-house, and the photos of Fontevrault were not as good as I had wished. I slept that night at Angers. On this stretch one of the small nuts holding the bolt that joins the chain fell off and the bolt, fortunately striking the crank & making a noise, was almost falling out.

Angers was a very quaint town, spoilt by electric trams. The exteriors of the castle & of the prefecture were interesting (nothing at all inside), and the cathedral, roofed as it was in domes, was a new style for me in architecture.

From Angers I rode the next day, through Lion D'Angers, where I was asked for my 'permit', to Rennes, and so on to St. Malo & Dinard. The vineyards were quaint but monotonous. At Dinard I tried 5 hotels & all were full. As it was by then 8p.m. I went to the Chaignons, & strolled in whilst they were at dinner. When I spoke & revealed myself there was a most enthusiastic scene: all yelled welcome at once, they insisted on my staying to dinner, & sleeping there, and, whilst sending all sorts of messages to you, told me that I was always a friend there: that I was always welcome & was to come in whenever I could. They were quite upset at the idea of my going off next day. M. Corbeil was with them, & collapsed when he heard where I had come from. I have given them a topic of conversation for a week. *Deux cent cinquante kilomètres, Ah la-la, qu'il est merveilleux. Deux cent cinquante kilomètres.* [...]

HL/Bodleian Library

Lawrence's most challenging, and rewarding, bicycle ride took place in the summer of 1908, when he achieved a two-thousand-mile exploration of France, beginning and ending in Normandy and reaching as far south as the Mediterranean.

HIS MOTHER
Sunday August 2 1908   *AIGUES-MORTES*

Dear Mother
I had better begin from my last letter before Vézélay.[1] This I found superb but rather in sculpture than in proportions.[...] From Vézélay I rode to Nevers, arriving on Friday. It is a quaint rather than beautiful town, with a good

---

1 Vézélay, in Burgundy, was where St Bernard of Clairvaux preached to such effect that he inspired the Second Crusade.

Renaissance ducal palace, & a fine cathedral. I telephoned from here to Dunlop in Paris for a new tyre, which after anxious waiting arrived all right on Monday: since then all has gone like a marriage bell in the way of punctures, and I am generally happy. The cost was however immense: – with telephoning: carriage: fitting etc., it cost nearly 20/–: result is I'm afraid I'll be short later on: in fact I am rather disgusted with my costs to date. The hotels all charge 2 f. for bed, & at least 2 for dinner (I don't like going to any but fairly decent places, alone, with money). My litre of milk staggers them for breakfast, (I always order it the night before, and it is amusing to watch their efforts to convince me I'm mistaken 'Monsieur does not mean a litre: it is too much' etc.), but not sufficiently to persuade them to charge less than 75 c. to 1 f. result 5 f. are gone by the morning: add some fruit or milk in the day, post cards (now total over 100) & postage, repair-bands, solution, tips for show places, an occasional bath etc. and you have a fair 7 f. per day: I had really hoped to do it cheaper. 6/– a day is absurd for one. (I have changed a note[2] quite successfully by the way: pocket proved admirable).

From Nevers I went by Moulins to Le Puy. Tell Father I had a 20 mile hill up into Le Puy. Part of my ride was up a superb gorge, with river foaming in the bottom, & rock & hill on each side: it was the finest scenery I have ever come across: truly the Auvergne is a wondrous district: but *not* one for a cycle: I'll take a walking tour there some day I hope. [...] From Le Puy I rode up for 10 miles more, (oh dear 'twas hot!) consoling myself with the idea that my sufferings were beyond the conception of antiquity, since they were a combination (in a similar climate) of those of Sisyphus who pushed a great weight up hill, of Tantalus who couldn't get anything to drink, or any fruit, and of Theseus who was doomed ever to remain sitting: – I got to the top at last, had 15 miles of up and down to St. Somebody-I-don't-want-to-meet-again, and then a rush down 4,000 feet to the Rhône. 'Twas down a valley, the road carved out of the side of the precipice, & most gloriously exciting: in fact so much so that with that & the heat I felt quite sick when I got to the bottom. I slept that night at Crussol, a fine xii. c. castle on a 500 feet precipice over the Rhône. Next day via Valence to Avignon, glorious with its town walls & papal palace, (Popes lived there 90 years, & built an enormous pile) & passed thence through Tarascon to Beaucaire, which I saluted for the sake of Nicolette,[3] into Arles. [...] From Arles I rode to Les Baux, a queer little ruined & dying town upon a lonely 'olive sandalled'

2 *I.e.* a £5 note.
3 A reference to the thirteenth-century romance *Aucassin et Nicolette*, set in Beaucaire.

mountain. Here I had a most delightful surprise. I was looking from the edge of a precipice down the valley far over the plain, watching the green changing into brown, & the brown into a grey line far away on the horizon, when suddenly the sun leaped from behind a cloud, & a sort of silver shiver passed over the grey: then I understood, & instinctively burst out with a cry of 'Thalassa, Thalassa'[4] that echoed down the valley, & startled an eagle from the opposite hill: it also startled two French tourists who came rushing up hoping to find another of the disgusting murders their papers make such a fuss about I suppose. They were disappointed when they heard it was 'only the Mediterranean'!

From Les Baux I descended to Arles, & thence to St. Gilles – Aigues-Mortes. I reached here late last night, & sent you a pencilled p.c. It is a lovely little place, an old old town, huddled along its old streets, with hardly a house outside its old walls, still absolutely unbroken, & hardly at all restored or in need of it. From it St. Louis started for his crusades, & it has seen innumerable events since. Today it is deserted by the world, & is decaying fast: its drawbacks are mosquitoes, (a new experience for me, curtains on all the beds), and the lack of a cheap hotel. It is however almost on the sea, and exceedingly pleasant, (above all if one could get acclimatised quickly to these brutes, I'm all one huge bite).[5] I bathed today in the sea, the great sea, the greatest in the world: you can imagine my feelings: [...]. I felt that at last I had reached the way to the South, and all the glorious East; Greece, Carthage, Egypt, Tyre, Syria, Italy, Spain, Sicily, Crete ... they were all there, and all within reach ... of me. I fancy I know now better than Keats what Cortes felt like, 'silent upon a peak in Darien'.[6] Oh I must get down here, – farther out – again! Really this getting to the sea has almost overturned my mental balance: I would accept a passage for Greece tomorrow: – and there I am going to Nîmes: – I suppose it cannot be helped: well I am glad to have got so far. [...]

HL/Bodleian Library

---

4 'Thalassa, Thalassa': 'The sea, the sea' – the famous cry of Xenophon's army of the Ten Thousand when, on their journey back to Greece from Mesopotamia in 401 BC, they caught their first glimpse of the Black Sea. Written in Greek on the original letter.
5 He became infected with malaria at this time and was to suffer recurring bouts of the disease throughout his life.
6 From Keats's sonnet *On First Looking into Chapman's Homer*.

HIS MOTHER[1]
28 Août, 1908   *HOTEL DE LA PLACE LAIGLE*

Dear Mother

[...] I expected that Chartres would have been like most French Cathedrals spoilt by restoration, so I slipped out before breakfast to 'do' it. What I found I cannot describe – it is absolutely untouched & unspoilt, in superb preservation, & the noblest building (for Beauvais is only half a one) that I have ever seen, or expect to see. If only you could get an idea of its beauty, of its perfection, without going to look at it! Its date is late xiith & early xiii cent. It is not enormous; but the carvings on its 3 portals are as fine as the best of all Greek work. Till yesterday I would put no sculptors near the Greeks of the vth cent. Today the French of the early middle ages *may* be inferior, but I do not think so: nothing in imagination could be grander than that arrangement of three huge cavernous portals (30 odd feet deep), of gigantic height, with statues everywhere for pillars, bas-reliefs for plain surfaces, statuettes & canopies for mouldings. The whole wall of the cathedral is chased & wrought like a Florentine plaque, and by master hands! You may think the individual figures stiff – the details coarse – everything is hard & narrow I admit, but when you see the whole – when you can conceive at once the frame *and* the picture, then you must admit that nothing could be greater, except it were the Parthenon as it left the hands of Pheidias: it must be one of the noblest works of man, as it is the finest of the middle ages. One cannot describe it in anything but superlatives, and these seem so wretchedly formal that I am half tempted to scratch out everything that I have written: Chartres is Chartres: – that is, a gallery built by the sculptors to enclose a finer collection than the Elgin Marbles. I went in, as I said, before breakfast, & I left when dark: – all the day I was running from one door to another, finding in each something I thought finer than the one I had just left, and then returning to find that the finest was that in front of me – for it is a place absolutely impossible to imagine, or to recollect, at any rate for me: it is overwhelming, and when night came I was absolutely exhausted, drenched to the skin (it had poured all day) and yet with a feeling I had never had before in the same degree – as though I had found a path (a hard one) as far as the gates of Heaven, and had caught a glimpse

---

1 David Garnett thought this, Lawrence's response to a visit to Chartres Cathedral, 'the most beautiful and emotional of his early letters', but was refused permission to print it in his 1938 volume; he did, however, manage to insert it in the 1952 reprint of his *Selected Letters* and it was later published, without cuts, in *HL*. The core of the letter is reproduced here, only the opening paragraph (a brief summary of his travels since his previous letter) being omitted.

of the inside, the gate being ajar. You will understand how I felt though I cannot express myself. Certainly Chartres is the sight of a lifetime, a place truly in which to worship God. The middle ages were truer that way than ourselves, in spite of their narrowness and hardness and ignorance of the truth as we complacently put it: the truth doesn't matter a straw, if men only believe what they say or are willing to show that they do believe something. Chartres besides has the finest late xvi & early xvii bas-reliefs in the world, and is beautiful in its design & its proportions. I have bought all the picture post-cards, but they are of course hardly a ghost of the reality, nothing ever could be, though photography is best for such works. I took a photo myself of Philosophus, a most delightful little statuette, about 18 inches high: if not fogged, (I forgot to lock my camera, & somebody has fiddled with it), it may give one an idea of how the smallest parts of the building are finished with as much care as the centre-posts of the main doorways, and if Philosophus were of Greek marble there would be photographs of him in every album, between the Hermes of Praxiteles & the Sophocles of the Lateran. He is great work. I also tried to take a photo of the masterpiece, the Christ of the south portal, but that cannot be worth looking at. I expect I will burn my photos. of Chartres as soon as they are visible. Yet perhaps with care & time, one would get something worthy from a photograph. We must return there (I would want assistants) and spend a fortnight in pure happiness.

HL/Bodleian Library

Early in 1909, while planning his visit to the crusader castles of the Middle East, he wrote for advice to Charles Doughty, veteran traveller and author of *Arabia Deserta*, a classic work which he much admired. Doughty's reply was not encouraging: 'In July and August the heat is very severe and day and night, even at the altitude of Damascus (over 2000 feet), it is a land of squalor where a European can find evil refreshment .... The distances to be traversed are very great. You would have nothing to draw upon but the slight margin of strength which you bring with you from Europe....' Nevertheless Lawrence persevered and during his summer vacation undertook an 1100-mile walking-tour through Syria and Palestine, in the course of which he visited thirty-six out of some fifty castles on his proposed route and carried out the field research which enabled him to produce his impressive thesis.

HIS MOTHER
August 13 1909   *TRIPOLI (TARABULUS)*

I have quite unexpectedly got an opportunity of sending you a line, so I will take
it though there is nothing special to tell you: still you may be glad to have additional
evidence that I am all right. I did not leave Beyrout till last Friday 6th & then went
N. to the Nahr-el Kelb, the Dog River. [...] Then I went further N. (by the way
I passed the place where S. George killed his dragon) to Jebail, crossing the river
Adonis which at certain seasons runs blood-red. It used to be the centre of the
Adonis worship of Aphica [?] and Byblus. Jebail is of course Byblus,[1] & I stayed there
3 or 4 days with Miss Holmes, the American missionary. She was most exceedingly
kind in feeding me up, & as she had plenty of books & a marble-paved hall,
with water ad lib. and trees (real green ones) in her garden I was very happy. [...]

[Miss Holmes told me one most striking thing — there exists among the
Mohammedans today a secret sort of Christian, organised under a head in
Damascus. She won the confidence of a customs-officer in Jebail, & one day he
showed her a bible: she was astounded, & still more so when some other
prominent members of the town came in, & there was, behind doors, singing of
Christian hymns (*not* translations of European productions, but home-made
chants) and a communion service administered by a layman. They would not tell
her much, but naturally she has been put on the alert, & she has found that the
sect is fairly large. She got an introduction to the head of it in Damascus but he
would not see her: they fight very shy of intercourse with missionaries, on
account of the row there would be. Still I think it is the best sign I have heard
of in the country so far. A native Christian church is so much more likely to win
than a foreign grafting, and with the new toleration the members can become
bolder.[2] Miss Holmes, who is the best Arab linguist in the Mission (she has
been half a lifetime in the country), thinks there are visible signs of the gradual
decay of Islam. If so the American Mission has had the larger share.] [...]

HL/Bodleian Library

1 Byblus, or Byblos: an ancient city of Phoenicia, the traditional birthplace of Adonis. The name
  would have had a special resonance for Lawrence, as it was the sale of Egyptian papyrus by
  Byblos merchants to the Greeks for bookmaking which ultimately gave English such words as
  'bible' and 'bibliography'.
2 Lawrence is showing early signs of the view he was to express with force in later years, when M. R.
  Lawrence was a medical missionary in China, that emergent nations should not be patronized by
  developed ones in the matter of religion and culture but should be left to find their own salvation.

HIS MOTHER
29.8.1909 *LATAKIA*

Dear Mother

Another chance for a note: this time hurried. I wrote last from Tripoli. I went thence to Aarka, & then to Kala'at el Hosn, passing one night on a house roof, & the second in the house of an Arab noble, reputed, as I was told next day, of the highest blood: a young man very lively, & rather wild, living in a house like a fortress on top of a mountain: only approachable on one side, & there a difficult staircase. If you keep this note I can tell you all sorts of amusing things about him later: name Abdul Kerim. He had just bought a Mauser, & blazed at everything with it. His bullets must have caused terror to every villager within a mile around: I think he was a little cracked.

Then I got to Hosn, which is I think the finest castle in the world:[1] certainly the most picturesque I have seen – quite marvellous: I stayed 3 days there, with the Kaimmakam, the governor: a most-civilised-French-speaking-disciple-of-Herbert-Spencer-Free-Masonic-Mohammedan-Young Turk:[2] very comfortable –. He sent an escort with me next day to Safita, *a Norman keep, with* ORIGINAL *battlements*: the like is not in Europe: such a find. Again I slept with Kaimmakam & Co. (Co. here means fleas) and next day I went on again with a huge march, to two more castles, and a bed for the night in a threshing floor, on a pile of tibn, chopped straw, listening to the Arabs beating out their Dhurra[3] in the moonlight: they kept it up all night in relays, till about 2 a.m. when they woke me up, & said they were all exhausted, would I keep watch because there were thieves, & I was a Inglezi & had a pistol: I obliged thinking it was humbug of the usual sort, (every village distrusts its neighbour), but they told me in Tartus next day that there really were not thieves, but *landlords* about! Isn't that charming? These dear people wanted to hide the extent of their harvest. [...]

No smoking yet, though here every man woman & child does: Latakia tobacco, which Father knows all grows here: the peasants dry & smoke their own, all in cigarettes: I will have such difficulty in becoming English again, here I am Arab in habits & slip in talking from English to French & Arabic

1 Usually known as Krak des Chevaliers.
2 Herbert Spencer (1820-1903) had won a wide reputation as a revolutionary philosopher; the Young Turks had carried out an armed, if bloodless, revolution against the Sultan of Turkey just over a year before Lawrence was writing, in July 1908.
3 Indian corn or millet.

unnoticing: yesterday I was 3 hours with an Orleannais, talking French, & he thought at the end I was a 'compatriot'! How's that?

[Worms Love

This goes to Oxford. I expect Jersey is nearly over.]⁴ I may manage a pencil scrawl from Antioch: but you may be happy now all my rough work is finished successfully: & my Thesis is I *think assured. Iradé invaluable.*⁵

DG/HL/Bodleian Library

HIS MOTHER
Sept. 22 1909   *ALEPPO*

After all I am coming home at once, for lack of money. Of course you could send me more but I'd want new clothes, those I wear at present shall be left in Beyrout, I'd never get them past the sanitary inspection at P. Said: — new boots the present being 'porous', I've walked them to bits at any rate, & my feet lately have responded to it. They are all over cuts & chafes & blisters, & the smallest hole in this horrid climate rubs up in no time into a horrible sore. I can't imagine how many times I would have had blood poisoning already if it hadn't been for my boracic: but I want to rest the feet now or there will be something of the sort. To undertake further long walks would be imprudent, for even in new boots these holes would take long to heal. [...]

By the way it is remarkable that all this 3 months on most unaccustomed & most changing food & water my stomach has never been upset. That is the great bugbear of the European traveller in Turkey. I suppose my exercise etc. (I have walked 1100 miles) is responsible for my health.

I find an absurd canard in the Aleppo paper of a week ago: my murder near Aïntab (where I didn't go). I hope it has not been copied. The hotel people received me like a ghost. Mr. Edvard Lovance sounds like me.

Tell Will I have got about 24 Hittite seals & congratulate Arnie on his bicycle his tumbles & his handwriting. The P.O. had my letters here after all.

---

4 His mother had evidently been on a visit to Jersey, birthplace of his brother Frank.
5 *Iradé:* official authorization to travel through Turkish-held territories. Lawrence had applied for his before leaving Oxford through Lord Curzon, at that time chancellor of the university.

They thought no apology necessary for their former mistake; but I got one after a little work. Am glad you are all right, & that Jersey was pleasant. 'So warm' indeed come out here & revel in 106° in the shade. Must finish now. Will spend 3 days Damascus (not a penny to spare) & then leave Beyrout 30th. Miss Holmes has offered me her purse: so I'll borrow if I run short at last. But not if I can help. Salaams.

Ned

HL/Bodleian Library

HIS MOTHER
Saturday 9 Oct [19]09   *R.M.S. OTWAY*

I am afraid I cannot write you any account of Eastern towns:[1] I don't know them well enough yet: but I thought I would send you a copy of the rough account I kept of my expenses, as they have been so great this trip. They are in round figures only, but I think nearly correct. You will see that living expenses in the hotels were enormous – £11.4.0 for 35 days – over 6/– a day. That is because the hotels are built for Europeans & rich merchants only, & are dear: also they have a vile system of 'pension' by which so much is charged whether one takes one's meals inside or not. So I couldn't usually follow my French trick of taking a room only & catering for myself. The usual charges were 8 francs a day.

Now I left Oxford with about £65 –

	£	s	d	
In London	6	0	0	fare from Oxford, 2 maps, a water bottle, & the Mauser pistol
On board		15	0	In tips, a subscription, & stamps at Gibraltar
P. Said	2	10	0	I stayed 5 days, & had extras.
To Beyrout	3	2	0	Steamer fares, & customs, port dues, etc.
In Beyrout	1	0	0	I stayed 3 days.
First tour	6	10	0	Includes a stay at Haifa & steamer fare: about 1 month in all
In Beyrout	3	10	0	I stayed 10 days & bought stamps etc.

1 In a postscript to his previous letter he had written of his hope to spend a week or ten days in Damascus '& work up the details of town life' into an account for his family.

To Aleppo	2	10	0	Second tour: about 5 weeks
In Aleppo	2	10	0	I stayed one week: a very dear place
Aleppo castle	I	0	0	Much formality to see castle & all sorts of officials with me
To Urfa				
carriage	8	0	0	2 men & 3 horses for a fortnight: tips to driver included
Food		4	6	
Tips on	I	0	0	Includes Euphrates boatmen etc.
way				
Camera	I	10	0	Well spent if it is recovered:[2] baksheesh of course
In Aleppo	I	10	0	I stayed 5 days
To Damascus	2	0	0	Railway fare
In Damascus		12	0	I stayed 3 days
To Beyrout	I	6	0	Railway fares
To Port Said	I	2	0	Steamer fare, deck passage
To London	12	0	0	Steamer fare, water rate, but includes Beyrout 12/– hotels
				P. Said hotel expenses 17/– a day
Hittite seals	6	0	0	Some of this I hope to get back
Tripoli	2	8	0	A mission
Urfa	3	3	0	A famine fund
Naples		7	0	A bronze head: too cheap & good to lose
In hand	I	0	0	Tips & train fare

71	8	6

So you see I made £6 0 0

This was from the sale of my Mauser pistol (at a profit) in Beyrout on my departure (£5. 0. 0). The odd £1 is simply due to my crushing figures into the round. You see £11. 8. 0 is unnecessary expense: antiquities & charities: but the seals I came out to get, & the other people will do a lot with the money. I would only have spent it on 2nd class fares on rail (Syrian 3rd is beastly) & 2nd class on board. Still from Beyrout to P. Said is only 3 nights. The real bother was that I had to feed myself that time. The money in hand is just enough – but of course nobody will expect presents: Arnie the worm has had his. The stamps altogether came to 11/6. We will squander anything Mr. Hogarth pays me in riotous living to make up. I can't say when I return: Sat, or Sund they think: but she is a new boat (trial trip)

2 His camera had been stolen.

with speed untried. Tell Will Naples Museum glorious, including bronze footballer. Worms to the rest of the party, & to Father, & yourself.

Ned

[...]
I hope Father found the College authorities agreeable: in any case I won't repent this trip. It has been all wonderful, worth three times its cost.

Supplement for Will
In a bronze foundry in Naples when searching for a 'footballer' (none to be got worthy under £2) I saw a Hypnos head,[3] very good work, but a bad cast, modern naturally. I asked price & tumbled down with it to 8 francs, little more than the value of the metal. You will admire it immensely: and I'll give you minutes to find out the fault in the casting – The bronzes in the Naples museum are beyond words.

Bodleian Library

Lawrence was late back for the Michaelmas term, but he had asked his father to call at Jesus College to make his apologies and he had also written to the college principal, Sir John Rhys, explaining his situation and pleading 'four bouts of malaria when I had only reckoned on two'. A lecturer who was also a family friend described him on his return as 'thinned to the bone by privation'. Towards the end of term he wrote to Doughty informing him that his walking-tour had 'ended happily' and that he had found the castles he had visited 'so intensely interesting that I hope to return to the East for some little time'. Lawrence now settled to work on his thesis (which he entitled *The Influence of the Crusades on European Military Architecture – to the End of the XIIth Century*) and prepare for his final examinations. In the following summer he was one of a handful of students to be awarded a first in history.

3 Hypnos was the Greek god of sleep.

HIS MOTHER
September 1910[1]   *HOTEL BELLEVUE LE PETIT ANDELYS*

[...] The sculptures of Rheims are almost perfect, it is not a Chartres, but wonderful all the same, I have got what PCs I could get: none worthy of course. Gisors I liked: Frank didn't. He is enjoying this place, because it has a river[2] and steam tugs, & an English family: so we will stay over Monday & let him get a little more of it. There is very safe bathing: & some boating in flat tubs of boats. [I took him over Chateau Gaillard this morning, & did my best to reconstruct it for him & make him interested. There were some sloe-bushes he preferred in the outer ward.]

The country here is altogether lovely: & the views more & more necessary: if I stayed very long I would take root. I sat up in the castle this morning a little after Frank went to *dejeuner*, & read below the keep. The colours in the water below me, & the sweep of the river under the cliffs were superb. Is there any chance of Will getting here this year? I can assure him he will find it repay any pains. The view has the same effect on people as a forest or a church: they talk in whispers.

The book I had was *Petit Jehan de Saintré*,[3] a xv Cent. novel of knightly manners – very good: – I have wanted to read it for a long time, but the Union[4] Copy was so badly printed that I had not the heart for it. Now I have found (for I f. 25) a series quite nicely typed on fairly good paper. So far I have only got 4 volumes, because they are rather much to carry: [as for the expense I saved that on food: – only 6 francs (and I reckoned to spend 3 frs a day on it).] It is altogether glorious to have found good French books at last. I can read Molière & Racine & Corneille & Voltaire now: – a whole new world. You know, I think, the joy of getting into a strange country in a book: at home when I have shut my door & the town is in bed – and I know that nothing, not even the dawn – can disturb me in my curtains: only the slow crumbling of the coals in the fire: they get so red & throw such splendid glimmerings on the Hypnos[5] & the brass-work. And it is lovely too, after you have been wandering for hours in the forest with Percivale or Sagramors le

---

1 Dated August 1910 in both *DG* and *HL* but September 1910 in the original.
2 The Seine. *Cf.* his letter of 11 August 1907.
3 By Antoine de la Sale (or Salle), c. 1386-c. 1460.
4 *I.e.* the Oxford Union.
5 The head, bought in Naples, referred to in the previous letter.

desirous[6] to open the door, and from over the Cherwell to look at the sun glowering through the valley-mists. Why does one not like things if there are other people about? Why cannot one make one's books live except in the night, after hours of straining? and you know they have to be your own books too, & you have to read them more than once. I think they take in something of your personality, & your environment also – you know a second hand book sometimes is so much more flesh & blood than a new one. – and it is almost terrible to think that your ideas, yourself in your books may be giving life to generations of readers after you are forgotten. It is that specially which makes one need good books: books that will be worthy of what you are going to put into them. What would you think of a great sculptor who flung away his gifts on modelling clay or sand? Imagination should be put into the most precious caskets, & that is why one can only live in the future or the past, in Utopia, or the wood beyond the World.[7]

Father won't know all this – but if you can get the right book at the right time you taste joys – not only bodily, physical, but spiritual also, which pass one out above and beyond one's miserable self, as it were through a huge air, following the light of another man's thought. And you can never be quite the old self again. You have forgotten a little bit: or rather pushed it out with a little of the inspiration of what is immortal in someone who has gone before you.

Ned

DG/HL/Bodleian Library

6 A reference to Sir Thomas Malory's *Morte d'Arthur*, one of the great influential books of Lawrence's youth; he carried a copy of it with him throughout his wartime campaigns.
7 A reference to William Morris's romance *The Wood Beyond the World* (1894). Morris was a powerful and formative influence in Lawrence's life, as writer, translator, artist and printer of fine books.

E. T. LEEDS[1]

Nov. 2 1910   *GRAND HOTEL DU NORD ROUEN*

[…] It should create a good impression on your mind to know that I am in Rouen looking at Mediaeval Pots: Mr. Bell[2] got me letters from Mr. Salomon Reinach[3] that make me out to be a sort of god: and they all rush about the Museum here offering me keys and cupboards and cups of coffee: the last rather a bore.

Also Mr. Hogarth is going digging: and I am going out to Syria in a fortnight to make plain the valleys and level the mountains for his feet: – also to learn Arabic. The two occupations fit into one another splendidly.

These exhaust all my hopes: except that this wind will die down and give me a quieter crossing than I had yesterday. I was just feeling premonitions of internal crisis when Havre came in sight. I would, tho', not have been alone in my misfortune. *Vale*

.L.

Bodleian Library

Lawrence left for the Middle East in December 1910, his journey being made more enjoyable because the steamer on which he sailed through the Mediterranean, the *S.S. Saghalien*, suffered from persistent engine trouble, thus providing him with the opportunity for leisurely explorations of Naples, Athens and Constantinople. He was to remain in the Middle East for most of the next four years, returning only for occasional visits to England.

1 Edward Thurlow Leeds (1877-1955) was assistant keeper of the Department of Antiquities of the Ashmolean Museum; he succeeded D. G. Hogarth as keeper of the museum in 1928, holding the post until 1945. He had met Lawrence in 1908, and the friendship then begun was to produce a regular correspondence throughout Lawrence's years in the East. A note on the life of Leeds by D. B. Harden is published in the volume of Lawrence to Leeds referred to on p. 4.
2 C. F. Bell, one of Leeds's colleagues at the Ashmolean: *see* letters to him later in this section.
3 An eminent French scholar; he had been *conservateur des Musées Nationaux* since 1886.

HIS MOTHER
Dec. 1910   *ATHENS*

[...] Just as we entered the Piraeus the sun rose, & like magic turned the black bars to gold, a wonderfully vivid gold of pillar and architrave and pediment, against the shadowed slopes of Hymettus. That was the Acropolis from a distance: – a mixture of all the reds & yellows you can think of with white for the high-lights and brown-gold in the shadows. Of course I got ashore at once, & plunged into the intolerable cesspit of the Piraeus: the place is a filthy drain for all the dregs of the capital, its only virtue that it saves it from being a port. Before you reach Athens you pass through green fields & over small streams, that effectually wash away the taste & smell of the sea. The rail lands you in the midst of a very modern looking town of squares & gardens, with a character partly French but not wholly European or Asiatic; too bright for the one & too clean for the other. It was above all things quiet, the quietest town imaginable, with few trams, & those slow ones, no motors or bicycles & very few carts. The streets are usually asphalt-paved, & there seemed hardly any dogs to bark and fight. Even the vegetable-hawkers shouted like men, not like jackals or fog horns. Everywhere were palm trees & mimosa, with green lawns. [...] The quiet was really almost uncanny, as I walked up the shallow valley below Mars hill, & along the processional way to the gateway of the citadel. There were no boys to bother one, no loud bellows'd leather sellers, only a misty sunlight in which all Attica, Phaleron, Salamis, Eleusis, and the distant Peloponnese lay motionless, 'drowned in deep peace', below the rock platform of the Wingless Victory. To get there I had to climb up the white marble staircase of the Propylea within the entrance gate. There were no porters, no guides, no visitors, & so I walked through the doorway of the Parthenon, and on into the inner part of it, without really remembering where or who I was. A heaviness in the air made my eyes swim, & wrapped up my senses: I only knew that I, a stranger, was walking on the floor of the place I had most desired to see, the greatest temple of Athene, the palace of art, and that I was counting her columns, and finding them what I already knew. The building was familiar, not cold as in the drawings, but complex, irregular, alive with curve and subtlety and perfectly preserved. Every line of the mouldings, every minutest refinement in the sculptures were evident in that light, and inevitable in their place. The Parthenon is the protocathedral of the Hellenes. I believe I saw the Erectheum, and I remember coming back to look again at the Propylea, and to stand again beside the Niké Apteros: but then I came down again into the town, & found it modern and a little different. It was as though one had turned from the shades of the ancestors, to mix in the daily vocations of their sons: and so only this about Athens, that there is an intoxication, a power of possession in its ruins, & the memories that inhabit them, which entirely prevents anyone attempting to describe or to estimate them. There will never be a great book on Athens unless it is one by an enemy: no one who knew it could resist its spell, except by a violent attack upon its spirit, and who can attack it now of artists, when Tolstoy[1] is dead? He, and he alone, could have uprooted Greek culture in the world. I am coming back by Athens I think next year to stay a little time. For the present I am only confused with it: I do not know how much was Athens, and how much the colouring of my imagination upon it.

N.

DG/HL

VYVYAN RICHARDS[1]
Dec 15 [1910]   *CONSTANTINOPLE*

[...] Constantinople is as much life as Athens stood for sleep. It is a huge town, crammed with people, who all live and eat, and sleep in the streets apparently. All day the huge Galata bridge, on boats over the Golden Horn is pressed with a multitude of people, all foot-passengers, jostling each other, going all ways apparently. One cannot stand an instant without being hustled all over the road by passers by, or walk forward a yard without dodging to one side or other to avoid a carriage, or a pack of mules, or only a porter, with two asses' burden on his shoulders. The colour and movement in the streets are insurpassable: – Damascus is not within a call of it: – and besides there are glorious-coloured mosques, in blue and

1 Tolstoy, for whom Lawrence expressed the highest admiration, had died on 20 November 1910, aged 82.

1 *See* introduction to this section: Richards was the most serious of three enthusiasts for fine book-printing with whom Lawrence discussed the idea of setting up a printing-press, the other two being C. F. C. Beeson and Leonard Green. He had first met Lawrence when the latter lived, briefly, in rooms at Jesus College, Richards being in his third year and Lawrence in his first. He became greatly attached to Lawrence and later wrote an admiring biography of him – *Portrait of T. E. Lawrence: The Lawrence of The Seven Pillars of Wisdom* – which was published in 1936.

gold and cream and green tiles, and yellow glazed pottery of *exactly the shapes in England in the xivth cent.,* and a street, a whole street, of the most divine copper-ware. The modern stuff is sometimes good, more often polished after making till the hammer marks are ground away, or even machine pressed but in all the shops are the old out of date shapes exchanged for new, the wares of two or three generations back, perfect in shape and workmanship (before the French invasion), some bronze, some copper so heavy & thick, that they are not resold, but melted down, for the mere value of their metal. And I can't buy them, for I don't know Turkish: but I have bought a grammar, and started it: It won't be my fault if the hut is not full of old Turkish & Arab metal ware.

If you could only have seen the bronze water-cistern I saw yesterday.

DG

HIS MOTHER
Dec 31 1910   *JEBAIL*

[…] Miss Holmes is writing to you to say all is well with me: that went off last Tuesday, so you may get it first. She is flourishing, & her school: I came in for great Xmas festivities, which I kept out of mainly: Arabic now, with a little Antiquity: some 5 good flint saws: much prehistoric pottery.

Father should really come out here. Today, mid-winter, has been roasting hot, with a glaring sun, & clouds of flies & mosquitoes. We can pick ripe oranges in the gardens, and roses and violets in Miss Holmes' patch (facing N.): everything is green and flourishing, for there have been two or three showers since I landed. Still the heat, & the perfect calm, and the exquisite twilight effects are nearly equal to summer's. I need a sun-helmet, really. It is very sandy soil, & they say a golf-links is preparing on the seven miles of sand-dunes below Beyrout. I hope he is better in Wales, but it is not much good asking after his health, since all things will have changed before I get the reply: you must wire if it is to be of use.

Seven letters tonight: and some p.c's. […]

HL/Bodleian Library

HIS MOTHER
Jan 24 1911   *JEBAIL*

[...] We[1] both feel (at present) that printing is the best thing we can do, if we do it the best we can. That means though, (as it is an art), that it will be done only when we feel inclined. Very likely sometimes for long periods I will not touch a press at all. Richards, whose other interests are less militant, will probably do the bulk of the work. The losses (if any) will be borne by us both, according as we are in funds (we will approximate to a common purse): the profits will be seized upon as a glorious opportunity to reduce prices.

You will see, I think, that printing is not a business but a craft. We cannot sit down to it for so many hours a day, any more than one could paint a picture on that system. And besides such a scheme would be almost sure to interrupt *The Seven Pillars of Wisdom*[2] or my monumental work on the Crusades. [...]

HL/Bodleian Library

HIS MOTHER
March 11 1911   *CARCHEMISH (JERABLUS)*

We have got here, & this is a hurried note to go off by the returning camelmen. We left Aleppo Thursday: this is Saturday, nothing of note on the journey except the flooded Sadjur: which was easily crossed tho', at a ford. I had no camera ready unfortunately. Mr. Hogarth drove & walked & rode: Thompson[1] rode & walked: I walked, except of course over the river.

Not much yet of course to say about this place. The mounds are enormous: but I'll send you a photo. or drawing later. We only got in about 4 o'clock: and have been unpacking since: eleven baggage horses, ten camels. ...

The head-man of the village, who is also the agent of the Liquorice Company that I ran into last time, has put the Co's house at our disposal. It is a big, stone-built, one storied place, with a court-yard adjoining: the roof

1 Lawrence and Richards.
2 Lawrence planned to use this title for a book he hoped to write about seven eastern cities; when this project failed (he destroyed the manuscript in 1914) he did not abandon the title. For his own account, *see* his letter to Robin Buxton dated 22 September 1923.

1 R. Campbell Thompson (1876-1941), second in command to Hogarth.

will be good for sleeping on later in the year: at present the thermometer is 40° with a gale off those N.W. summits of the Taurus, that, snow-clad, were in view all this afternoon. We have bedding enough, good hap, for a host.

The village is about ¾ of a mile from the site, & the river: on high ground, so there is no possibility of fever in the hot weather, when or if it comes: snow here a few days ago: no skating on the river, worse luck.

As for the place: there is a high plateau in the corner N. of the Sadjur and W. of the Euphrates: this is some 500 feet above the river. We started on that this morning & then dropped gradually from foothill to foothill until we reached this village. It is a little place, of about 40 houses, very clean and fresh-looking, being all quite new, with a very fast-running spring on one side. I thought (and Mr. Hogarth said) that there was nothing but river-water in the place: as it is 'the most delicate fabrics may be washed without damage': the water is quite clear, fairly cool, and good-tasting. Its situation puts it out of the way of defilement.

The mound is about ¾ of a mile N. of the village: the river about ½ mile to the E.: and it bends round until it washes the edge of the great 'Acropolis' hill.

Our unpacking was a lively sight: heaps & heaps of baggage animals of all sorts; horses, mules, donkeys, camels: about a dozen of our men, and perhaps 20 villagers, who swarmed out of their houses when we approached, & as soon as we had approved the house, all turned to under the orders of the little overseer, and cleared it out. It was full of camel-hides, & corn, poplar-poles and lentils. The last were impounded for the benefit of the expedition. I cater to some extent.

I want to go to bed now: we have had two very rough nights, and it is very cold. All quite well: I like the second-man Thompson, very much.

N.

[I think I should say a word about Father's letter: (which is not to hand at present). I do not much concern myself about the exact arrangements (one cannot at this distance): but I would prefer one on which Richards & himself agreed: if not let it be his own arrangement, since it is he who provides the money. Only it is not a gift or loan to Richards, as a person merely. It is an attempt to get started the press we both desire so much; the question whether Richards himself is approved or not does not enter the question hardly at all. I gathered that Florence[1] does not like him: his assumption of intellectual conceit tried her; but remember that people do not usually wear their inside skin out. I think myself that he is quite a heaven-sent partner.] [...]

HL/Bodleian Library

1 Florence Messham, the Lawrence boys' former nurse.

E. T. LEEDS
Mar. 27 [1911]   *CARCHEMISH*

Economy in letter writing! One must write to somebody, (one owes to 3 bodies); wherefore write to the meekest among them, and suggest he carry out commissions: and you know it is really rather a privilege to get a line at all, for we are busy out here.

Concerning digs: we are getting rather bored with bits of Hittite inscriptions that keep on turning up:[1] the only fun is squeezing 'em, which is my particular part of the job. D.G.H. has nobly sacrificed his sponge to help me: and really he didn't want a sponge: it was not as though there was society here. Squeezing is rather good sport:[2] (I forgot to say that D.G.H. has also given up his toothbrush for it: his teeth are mostly false, and so we decided there was least need for his.) Next ... we haven't found anything else, except a rude figure of a female (known as 'the lady') and another broken figure or two: there is a lot of top hamper[3] and late stuff to clear, and so many big stones that we go slow. Very little pottery, and no small objects: (except myself)....

The second point should be the house: it is of stone, with mud floors roof, and from the roof little bits drop all day and all night: and it is full of birds that baptize the bald-heads at their leisure: my hair is still growing, and every day I give thanks that I brought with me a few spare hairpins.

Then there are the cats: Father (who is only suffered, not encouraged); he comes in at the holes in the roof and walls by night, and offends lewdly in our beds. Then D.G.H. throws a boot towards it and hits Thompson, and plants it in the bath, or knocks the light down: and when he has got out and repaired damages he finds the cat in his bed when he lies down again. So much for Father. Mother is plaintive, and rather a bore: she wails aloud for food, usually about 2 a.m.: then she gets it, but in a tin: of late she receives sympathy, in spite of one very irregular night, when she woke me up with her claws over the face, and the rest of the expedition (who sleep together, with piled revolvers) by trying to escape my yells by jumping off the jam-tins through the window. She only knocked the tins down of course, and fell short in the wash-basin. Of late Mother has been in the family way, with Thompson a very

1 Lawrence and his colleagues were bored with Hittite inscriptions because they were incomprehensible at that date.
2 In archaeology to take a squeeze is to make a cast of an inscription or relief by packing it with wet paper, etc. – hence the usefulness of Hogarth's sponge – which subsequently hardens.
3 Top hamper: archaeologically useless overburden.

gallant midwife. Her four kittens are David George (a tab), Gregori (a black), Haj Wahid (ginger),[4] and R. Campbell, a sort of Scots Grey. They make a ghastly noise in the Expeditionary bedroom half the night: I am a tolerable sleeper, but the others get up two or three times each, and draw beads on each other with revolvers. The sanitary arrangements are primitive, and the spring-water distressingly medicinal: so in the various excursions necessary (3 for D.G.H. 2 for R.C.T. and sometimes one for myself) one slides silently past the muzzles of the pistols, and past the sleeping Gregori with a hammer and a pick laid at his bed-side, and past Haj Wahid snoring beside his Martini;[5] then one may slip behind the corner of the house, and so be under cover from the Zaptiehs[6] and their rifles. Some day one of these deadly weapons will go off, and the Expedition will be advertising a vacancy.

The next point should be the baths: but there really isn't much to enlarge upon. Really being in the Euphrates valley makes a canvas bath seem so futile, though D.G.H. conquered this feeling last Sunday and the Sunday but one before. I had a bath one Saturday. Thompson is rather fair-skinned, and shaves regularly, so he has them more often. The personnel is many-sided. I don't think much of its cooking, and ornamentally it is a failure, but it can make mustard, and black paint, and bookshelves, and cigarettes, and salads, and once in a way a jest. It has planted a garden, and hopes for onions and chrysanthemums, and sunflowers and cabbages. The chief of it has evolved a jerry and a clothes-line, and what-not (this latter end is for the conventions and your imagination): It eats rather a lot, but all exes. are paid, and how else are five bottles of cascara and castor oil and croton not to be a sheer waste. Also it enjoys everything except the alarums and excursions of the nights, and the getting up at sunrise: and it is in very excellent health.

Will you assure Mrs. Poole[7] of this? (I mean the last phrase only … don't enter into details.…) If we had some printing paper I would send her some photographs of a Fellow and Demy of Magdalen[8] in difficult situations. […]

Bodleian Library

---

4 Named after Gregori, chief foreman, and Haj Wahid, expedition cook.
5 Martini: the Martini-Henri, a breech-loading rifle.
6 Zaptieh: Turkish gendarme.
7 The wife of Lawrence's Oxford tutor R. L. Poole.
8 *I.e.* Hogarth and Lawrence.

HIS MOTHER
March 31 1911   *JERABLUS*

[...] Today we are moving great stones: the remains of walls & houses are buried about ⅔ of their height in fairly clean earth, but the upper few feet are filled up with rubble, and small rocks, with the ashlar masonry and concrete of the late Roman town. Whenever we break fresh ground dozens of these huge blocks have to be moved. Some of them weigh tons, and we have no blasting powder or stone-hammers with us. As a result they have to be hauled, prehistoric fashion, by brute force of men on ropes, helped to a small extent by crowbars. At this moment something over 60 men are tugging away above, each man yelling Yallah as he pulls: the row is tremendous, but the stones usually come away. Two men out of three presume to direct operations, and no one listens to any of them, they just obey Gregori's orders, and their shouting is only to employ their spare breath. Now they are raising the 'talul', the curiously vibrant, resonant wail of the Bedawi. It is a very penetrating, and very distinct cry; you feel in it some kinship with desert-life, with ghazzus[1] and camel-stampedes. (Meanwhile the stone has slipped & fallen back into the trench, and Gregori's Turkish is deserting him). Whenever he is excited he slips back into Greek in a high falsetto voice, that convulses our hoarse-throated men. [...]

My faculty of making & repairing things has recently demonstrated how to make paint (black & red) for marking antiques, how to render light-tight a dark slide, how to make a camera-obscura, how to re-worm a screw (difficult this without a die), how to refit a plane-table, and replace winding mechanism on a paraffin lamp. Also I have devised a derrick, and a complicated system of human-power jacks (out of poplar poles, & rope, and Arabs) which have succeeded in setting an Ishtar[2] on her legs again. The Romans or Assyrians had broken her off at the knees, and the men could not shift the slabs back again, with any delicacy: so Mr. Hogarth & myself set to, and with our brains, & the aid of 90 men, put all right again. Before this there had been 120 men playing about with the ropes quite ineffectually. [...]

DG/HL

---

1 Tribal raids.
2 Ishtar: goddess of love and fertility worshipped in Syria and Palestine, equivalent to the Greek Aphrodite.

HIS MOTHER
11 April 1911   *JERABLUS*

[...] [Richards has been a little remiss in the business line I expect: of course he has no time to spare for it, with all the interest of type designing, and the annoyance of his schoolwork. I do not think a lease of less than 20 years would be sufficient: my own wishes would be at 30 or 40 to be altogether on the safe side. But I fear very much we will never get it done: in which case I fear my opportunities of doing something good that will count will be very small: at least I am not going to put all my energies into rubbish like writing history, or becoming an archaeologist. I would much rather write a novel even, or become a newspaper correspondent: – however there is still hope that Richards may pull the thing through: I am doing nothing to help out here, while he is going straight ahead through twice as much mess as we have any conception of, with no side interest whatever. There is something really great – and fine – about the man. One feels so selfish enjoying oneself out here when one might be in the fight. It is no laughing matter to be working against the 20th century.]

[...] Poor Father! his sons are not going to support his years by the gain of their professions & trades. One a missionary: one an artist of sorts and a wanderer after sensations; one thinking of lay education work: one in the army, & one too small to think.[1] None of us can ever afford to keep a wife: still the product of fairly healthy brains & tolerable bodies will not be all worthless in this world. One of us must surely get something of the unattainable we are all feeling after. That's a comfort: and we are all going for the same thing under different shapes: Do you know we illustrate the verse about heart, soul, mind, body? Will Arnie prove the strength that will make it all perfect & effective?

Frank's toes can (like other candidates) be operated on. Consult Dr. Gibson[2] if you do anyone. He knows the dodges of the red-tape fence. But let him in any case try for the Scholarship unless Mr. Cave[3] says it is not worth the continued preparation. The ordinary route into the Army is less pleasant than by Oxford & the O.T.C.[4]

Glad you sent Miss Holmes her cheque. She is doing a hard work, under great handicaps. If Will wants a little preliminary breathing time he might do

1 *I.e.* Bob, himself, Will, Frank, Arnold.
2 The family doctor.
3 A. W. Cave, headmaster of the Oxford High School 1888-1925.
4 Officers' Training Corps.

far worse than try his hand at her boys' school. There is such need in Syria for taste, as well as good will. [Those lubberly vulgarians in the American College are undoing with both hands the good the Jesuits of Beyrout are trying to do, and all with the best intentions in the world. The result will be a sort of 'babu'[5] (ask Menon what that is)[6] if they are not checked by better example and better sympathy with the people. Dr. Bliss the President of the College is almost the only one of the Foreign Colony who seems to act on this idea: and he is almost single-handed, with a horrible Yankee staff to fight against. Not that there is any friction.] [...]

Digging is tremendous fun, & most exciting & interesting. The results so far are not nearly enough to justify a second season (I'll write about them soon) but the thing is (as I have said perhaps) like Pandora's box, with Hope in the last spit of earth. I have had some good pottery lately.

Mr. Hogarth returns next week: he hopes to get to Oxford about mid-May, & shortly after will publish interim report in *The Times*. I'll ask him to let you know when. He has been most exceedingly good to me all through: taught me a tremendous lot about everything from digging to Greek erotic verse: He'll help in my Meleager:[7] whom he enjoys also. [Worms & Euphrates fish (closely allied) to all.]

N [...]

HL/Bodleian Library

HIS MOTHER
April 29 1911   *CARCHEMISH*

[...] The most pleasing part of the day is when the breakfast hour gets near: from all the villages below us on the plain there come long lines of red and blue women & children, carrying bread in red-check handkerchiefs, and wooden measures full of *leben*[1] on their heads. The men are not tired then, and the heat

---

5 Term for an Indian clerk writing in English, with only a superficial knowledge of the language.
6 An Indian student friend of his brother Will.
7 Meleager of Gadara, Greek poet of the late 2nd-early 1st century BC. His anthology of epigrams, *The Garland*, provided the core of the *Greek Anthology*.

1 Coagulated sour milk, a staple Arab drink.

is just pleasant, and they chatter about and jest & sing in very delightful style. A few of them bring shepherd's pipes, and make music of their sort. As a rule, they are not talkative: they will sit for minutes together at the house-door without a word: often coming out in the morning we have found 100 men grouped outside, wanting work, and have not heard a sound through the open window just above! The only time they get talkative is when they are about half-a-mile apart. A little companionable chat across Euphrates is a joy — except to one's ears near by, for sound carries tremendously in this region, and they bawl with their raucous voices. However not even Sheisho and Berkawi, two Kurd brothers, and the last in our employ, can talk over the noise of the flood at present: the other men gave up trying some days ago, and so the valley is at peace.

[...] Some of the workmen are rather fine-looking fellows: all of course are thin as sticks: and the majority small: there was no one within an inch of Mr. Hogarth's height: indeed the majority are hardly more than mine. Many shave their heads, others let their hair grow in long plaits, like Hittites. Today, Saturday, is pay day, and we knock off at 4, instead of 5, to give us time to get them paid. Each man, or nearly each man, gets an extra every week, according to the value of his finds. This little gamble appeals to them immensely. [...]

HL/Bodleian Library

HIS MOTHER
23 May 1911   CARCHEMISH

[...] Miss Gertrude Bell[1] called last Sunday, & we showed her all our finds, and she told us all hers. We parted with mutual expressions of esteem: but she told Thompson his ideas of digging were prehistoric: and so we had to squash her with a display of erudition. She was taken (in minutes) over Byzantine, Crusader, Roman, Hittite, & French architecture (my part) and over Greek

---

1 Gertrude Bell (1868-1926): traveller, writer, archaeologist, mountaineer. She was already well-known (and known to Lawrence) through such books as *The Desert and the Sown* (1907), an account of her journey into the Syrian interior. She was the first woman to reach the required standard for a first-class degree in history at Oxford (in 1888, the year of Lawrence's birth), but was not entitled to a degree as no woman could be a member of the university. During the World War I she was a leading figure in military and political circles in Egypt and Mesopotamia. Afterwards she served first with the military administration and then with the government of Iraq under the British Mandate.

folk-lore, Assyrian architecture, & Mesopotamian Ethnology (by Thompson); Prehistoric pottery & telephoto lenses, Bronze Age metal technique, Meredith, Anatole France and the Octobrists (by me): the Young Turk movement, the construct state in Arabic, the price of riding camels, Assyrian burial-customs, and German methods of excavation with the Baghdad railway (by Thompson). This was a kind of hors d'oeuvre: and when it was over (she was getting more respectful) we settled down each to seven or eight subjects & questioned her upon them. She was quite glad to have tea after an hour and a half, & on going told Thompson that he had done wonders in his digging in the time, and that she thought we had got everything out of the place that could possibly have been got: she particularly admired the completeness of our note-books.

So we did for her. She was really too captious at first, coming straight from the German diggings at Kala'at Shirgat, where they lay down gravel paths, wherever they want to prove an ancient floor, & where they pile up their loose stones into walls of palaces. Our digs are I hope more accurate, if less perfect. They involve no 'reconstruction', which ruin all these Teutons. So we showed her that, & left her limp, but impressed. She is pleasant: about 36,[2] not beautiful, (except with a veil on, perhaps). It would have been most annoying if she had denounced our methods in print. I don't think she will. [...]

DG/HL

D. G. HOGARTH[1]
June 8 1911   *CARCHEMISH*

Your letters to Thompson & myself just come: very many thanks on account of the photographic notes: though I packed 16 of my films undeveloped: they may have become lost somehow. Will you send a list of the plate negatives, so that I may know what to take again?

2 She was 43.

1 David George Hogarth (1862-1927) was the most important of Lawrence's Oxford mentors. Educated at Winchester and Magdalen College, Oxford (of which he became a Fellow), he explored Asia Minor 1887-94, was director of the British School at Athens 1897-1900, became keeper of the Ashmolean Museum in 1909 (holding the post until his death) and was appointed president of the Royal Geographical Society in 1925. He was also to be closely associated with Lawrence in the Middle East during the war.

Another matter. Thompson was calculating for another ten days here, and so I have taken 60 photos these last two weeks: all the pottery & small objects: except fragments of inscription & some reliefs. There are only about 4 dozen plates left, and subjects for most of these were booked.

I will have to revise most of these photographs now, for every day we find new things: I will use up the ones I have taken in developing (many thanks for the chemicals, they are admirable) and so will get at the right length of exposure. The results will thus be better: but I will want at least 3, and better 4, dozen of Wratten-Wainwright ½ plates, as last times' [*sic*]. The Binocular camera has plenty still, for there has been little to do with it of late,[2] since I put in most of the day up here at the house, mending pottery, and photographing things. I have plenty of my own films now, for the prolongation of the diggings will take from me all chance of much castle-hunting this season. Small objects I have to take indoors of course. These great winds blow every day & every night, and in the open air a carefully arranged sheet of beads or whorls is sent rolling to the four airts [*sic*]. Even large pots tumble about.

[…] The heat is not bad, and cannot be, as long as the winds stay cool: the idea of digging on is glorious, for there is really hope of several parts of the digs. That is Thompson's department tho! He is not quite at ease in all points: his bi-weekly letters depress him vastly: I expect that affair is not likely to survive this new shock of separation: and he is rather cut up about it,[3] though very determined that digs are better: is eating more than ever: swears that in hot weather one must constrain oneself to eat plenty of meat: we were provident not to throw away the covering stone of the last champagne grave on the mound.

[…] There does not seem to have been any Arab occupation of the site of any importance: but a long Byzantine one, following closely on the Roman, and coming down after 1000 AD. The remains of streets etc. belong to this last period. I don't think the Roman-Hellenist was much of a place.

Has Thompson told you that the arm & shoulder are the ones that fit? I have got 9 fragments all told on the block, which is nearly all there except the head of the back man. No other scrap of the great head has turned up: but it must be somewhere about: if we had a piece of body I think it would go on to the greaved legs.

The two basalt reliefs (the monstrous lion, double-headed, and the slab of bull-legged & lion headed people fighting) in the wall-line trench are the best

2 Lawrence's 'binocular camera' has attracted the interest of those who support the supposition that he was involved in espionage at this time; he was, however, already using a telephoto lens during his travels as an undergraduate in France.

3 Thompson married following this first season at Carchemish and did not return.

we have found on the site: first-class work, as different as day from night compared with the chariots.

Those despised horses (180 now in my stable) are proving interesting: and fellow with them are some little humans of the style of the ruder, high-nosed bronzes, and a number of *females* grasping their breasts. They are all Hittite, I fancy, but what they are all doing I don't know. [...]   *Bodleian Library*

HIS MOTHER
June 18 1911   *CARCHEMISH*

[...] Our people are very curious and very simple, and yet with a fund of directness and child-humour about them that is very fine. I see much of this, for I sleep on the mound and start the work every day at sunrise, and the choosing of new men so falls to my lot. I take great care in the selection, utterly refusing all such as are solemn or over-polite, and yet we are continually bothered by blood feuds, by getting into the same trench men who have killed other's kin or run off with their wives. They at once prepare to settle up the score in kind, and we have to come down amid great shouting, and send one to another pit. There is no desire to kill, and public opinion does not insist on vengeance, if there is 50 feet of earth between the offender and the offended. [...]

HL

Dahoum, date and source unknown

HIS MOTHER
June 24 1911   *CARCHEMISH*

[...] The donkey boy mentioned above (Dahoum)[1] is an interesting character:
he can read a few words (the only man in the district except the liquorice-
king) of Arabic, and altogether has more intelligence than the rank & file. He
talks of going into Aleppo to school with the money he has made out of us.
I will try & keep an eye on him, to see what happens. He would be better in
the country, only for the hideous grind of the continual forced labour, and
the low level of the village minds. Fortunately there is no foreign influence as
yet in the district: if only you had seen the ruination caused by the French
influence, & to a lesser degree by the American, you would never wish it
extended. The perfectly hopeless vulgarity of the half-Europeanised Arab is
appalling. Better a thousand times the Arab untouched. The foreigners come
out here always to teach, whereas they had much better learn, for in everything
but wits and knowledge the Arab is generally the better man of the two.

I am not living in a tent: it is much too hot for that. I am only sleeping on
the top of the mound. The river is swift, but quite pleasant for bathing: I have
been in a few times: but at present it is not really warm (c. 90°). There are
mosquitoes here about the house in plenty: on the top of the mound never,
for the wind drives them off. I have written to the Canon.[2] [...]

HL/Bodleian Library

1 Lawrence's friendship with Dahoum (picture on the previous page) whose real name was
Ahmed) was to be an important one. In a footnote to Lawrence's 1911 *Diary of a Journey
across the Euphrates* (included in *Oriental Assembly*) A. W. Lawrence wrote of him: 'It is believed that
his personality supplied the largest element to the figure of S.A., to whom the *Seven Pillars of
Wisdom* is dedicated.' He went on to quote, however, 'a Note of the Author's', *i.e.* of T.E.L.'s, to
the effect that S.A. was 'An imaginary person of neutral sex'. By contrast when talking to
Liddell Hart (*LHB*, p. 143) Lawrence stated that 'S. and A. were two different things, "S" a
village in Syria, or property in it, and "A" personal.' Granted that Lawrence was not prone to
simple straightforward answers and liked to keep his own counsel it seems likely that
Dahoum was the 'personal', and probably the dominant, part of this equation. *See also*
Lawrence's letters to G. J. Kidston dated 14 November 1919 (p. 168) and to R. A. M. Guy
dated 25 December 1923 (p. 253).
2 Canon Christopher of St Aldate's Church, Oxford.

40

MISS FAREEDAH EL AKLE[1]
June 26 [1911]   *CARCHEMISH*

I think Mrs. Rieder[2] has the big [text unclear] with her: she said, in a very charming little letter she sent me, that you were extremely annoyed with me: your excuse for this most unchristian change of temper was that I had not written to you:

Now

I have twice tried to write to you in Arabic, and each time got as far as the serious part: then I was interrupted. One letter got six lines long, then waited about for weeks, and finally evanished. I am really most extremely sorry for having failed in my promise, if it was a promise, but at present we work 19 hours a day, in the open air mostly, & when we do get to the evening, we are too bothered to do more than write the perfunctory English scribble. I have read no Arabic since our first few weeks here, except your letters, & the last one took me about an hour!

Now

I didn't write to you in English, because you said in a letter of yours (in Arabic & English) that you didn't want a reply: and I always believe what some people say: you and Miss Holmes for some of them. Mrs. Rieder is not that sort. So when you said you didn't want an answer, I supposed you didn't want an answer, and now Mrs. Rieder calls me names! It isn't fair of her at all. Do you know that in England we used to call you the fair sex? Are you horribly ashamed of yourself yet?

Now

I have written almost entirely to Miss Holmes, but my letters have been no more for her than for Noël[3]: they are like my letters home, general affairs, with a dig in the ribs here, and a pin-prick there. (I am talking of my brothers now: Miss Holmes' letters have not been blistering.) I wrote once to Mrs. Rieder in French, which I suppose you wouldn't much admire: at any rate she didn't. She said it wasn't French, but was very like me. If you can find out ask her what I am like.

---

1 A Christian Syrian schoolmistress who taught from 1911-14 in the American Mission School in Jebail and numbered Lawrence among her favourite pupils. Born in 1882, she was corresponding with Dr Mack about Lawrence in the late 1960s.
2 *See* next letter.
3 Mrs Rieder's six-year-old son.

Will you please tell Miss Aseem that I prostrate myself before her overcome by the affluence of her beneficence? That I wish her all the medicines in the world, and the fun of taking them? In fact I send my kind regards.

Now then, are apologies enough? Wouldn't you really be annoyed if you got a letter that did nothing else? It would be like a mutton chop that was all chop and no mutton. [...]

I have some thoughts of coming back to this district for the winter. Thompson & I may buy the site we are digging: it's about as big as Jebail, and the Baghdad railway will cross the river from it, and it's going for £33 — and make it a harbour of refuge for the district. There are a particularly villainous set of *effendis* about here, and we don't want our donkey boys flayed alive, and our workmen plundered while we are away.

It would be rather fun living alone in one of the villages: they are all mud-built you know, and quite pleasant. And the Arabic is such amusing stuff. If I could talk it like Dahoum (by the way what does the name Dahoum mean?)[4] you would never be tired of listening to me. I would say *aitchfa* for enough and *bartchir* for tomorrow: and lots more like that.

[...] Salaams to Miss Holmes, who will get a letter soon. I will be in Aleppo, returning to you, in six weeks from date. Nothing new found.

L.

Bodleian Library

MRS RIEDER[1]   *CARCHEMISH*
July 4 [1911]

[...] I have had quite a success with our donkey-boy,[2] who really is getting a glimmering of what a brain-storm is. He is beginning to use his reason as well as his instinct: He taught himself to read a little, so I had very exceptional material to work on but I made him read & write more than he ever did before. You know you cannot do much with a piece of stick & a scrap of dusty

---

4 'Dahoum' means 'the dark one'. According to Leonard Woolley's *Dead Towns and Living Man* (1920), Dahoum's mother stated that he was very black at birth.

1 Mrs Rieder (or more strictly Mme André Rieder; she married a Frenchman) taught languages at the American School at Jebail.
2 *i.e.* Dahoum.

ground as materials. I am going to ask Miss Fareedah for a few simple books, amusing, for him to begin on. Remember he is to be left a Moslem. If you meet a man worth anything you might be good enough to remember this? A boy of 15 ... I would be vastly obliged.

DG

MRS RIEDER
Am August 11 1911[1]   HOTEL DEUTSCHER HOF BEIRUT

[...] What I wanted for the donkey boy was a history book or a geography which should be readable and yet Arab. I cannot give him such productions as those Miss Holmes uses, since nothing with a taste of 'Frangi'[2] shall enter Jerablus by my means. I have no wish to do more for the boy than give him a chance to help himself: 'education' I have had so much of, & it is such rot: saving your presence! The only stuff worth having is what you work out yourself. With which last heresy please be content a while. I will (probably ...) write from England.

Yours sincerely
T. E. Lawrence

DG

Shortly after returning to Carchemish for his second season, Lawrence, on the recommendation of Hogarth, spent some weeks in Egypt working under Flinders Petrie.

---

1 Presumably Lawrence put the date in German because of the profession of the recipient and his current address.
2 Frangi: a corruption of 'Frankish', hence European.

MRS RIEDER
[Postmark 23.1.12]   *KAFR AMMAR*
                              (WHICH IS 40 MILES S. OF CAIRO, ON THE DESERT)

[...] No one but I would have achieved a letter at all from a Petrie dig.[1] A Petrie dig is a thing with a flavour of its own: tinned kidneys mingle with mummy-corpses and amulets in the soup: my bed is all gritty with prehistoric alabaster jars of unique types – and my feet at night keep the bread-box from the rats. For ten mornings in succession I have seen the sun rise as I breakfasted, and we come home at nightfall after lunching at the bottom of a 50 foot shaft, to draw pottery silhouettes or string bead-necklaces. In fact if I hadn't malaria to-day I could make a pretty story of it all: – only then I wouldn't have time. To begin with the Professor is the great man of the camp – He's about 5' 11" high, white haired, grey bearded, broad and active, with a voice that splits when excited, and a constant feverish speed of speech: he is a man of ideas and systems, from the right way to dig a temple to the only way to clean one's teeth. Also he only is right in all things: all his subs. have to take his number of sugar lumps in their tea, his species of jam with potted tongue, or be dismissed as official bound unprogressists. Further he is easy-tempered, full of humour, and fickle to a degree that makes him delightfully quaint, and a constant source of joy and amusement in his camp. [...]

About the digging: 'we' have stumbled on what is probably the richest and largest prehistoric cemetery in Egypt, and in our first week have dug out about 100 graves: these contain wooden coffins and bedsteads, boxes of alabaster jars, dozens of pots of new and known types, some little ivory, (spoons and gaming pieces and scraps of caskets) a good many bronze implements, axes, adzes, chisels, and other trifles. Also a good many baskets, and the shrouds and cloths in which the bodies were wrapped. We have found very few flints, and those not of the best, since the bronze was in general use. The graves are usually about 5 feet deep, and as all the soil is pure sand, digging is merely child's play. Owing to a hitch in his arrangements the Professor has all his workmen here, and so twice as many graves are found than we can record properly: with plenty of time it would be delightful, whereas now we are swamped with the multitude. We have about 900 pots (complete; – all broken ones are thrown away) about 120 alabasters, and a matter of twenty

---

1 Flinders, later Sir Flinders Petrie (1853-1942), was an eminent British Egyptologist who carried out many important excavations in Egypt from 1884 onwards and held the Edwards Professorship of Egyptology at University College, London, from 1892-1933. He also excavated in Palestine and was the author of many books, both scholarly and popular, based on his work.

bedsteads. Also we have preserved a number of bodies and skeletons complete by soaking them with boiling paraffin wax. These will go to Museums. [...]

DG

JAMES ELROY FLECKER[1]
Feb. 18 [1912][2]   *ALEPPO*

Am still here! Of course when I got to Aleppo I found that the B.M.[3] idiots had sent me orders to buy the site and build the house, and had forgotten to provide the funds. Result, as I arrived with 16 piastres in my pocket, was a visit to Mr. Fontana,[4] and a borrowing of £10. With this I have scoured all Aleppo, buying Hittite seals. Huge sport! However, first of all, I went to Damascus, called on Devey at 10 a.m. and delivered the fish. He was overwhelmed with his sense of obligation to you, and turned out in pyjamas to tell me so. So our interview was short. Cavass, far-seeing man, turned up at the station to see me off. That's all for Damascus, except that I bought my 'lira' cylinder (Hitt.) for 10 frs. and had a little one (also Hitt.) thrown in. Good buying, and good objects.

Next – about things here. Fontana up to the ears in Greek anthology: Erotica of course: has spoken twice of your P. P. Cards of Italy. Have seen him four times. He received your salaams with the stomach of avidity and the bowel of satisfaction. What more could he do?

Have now over 20 Hittite seals: two of them superb Cappadocian-Hittite cylinders: love at first sight, but neither of them too dear. No bronzes, except one Hadad with a dealer, who will not descend below £4 Ottoman. This is causing me acute indigestion. Am sniffing at another glorious Cappadoc-Hitt.

1 James Elroy Flecker (1884-1915), poet and playwright. After reading classics at Oxford he enrolled in the Levant Consular Service, spent two years studying oriental languages at Cambridge and then took up his first consular appointment in Constantinople in 1910. He and Lawrence met when he was in his second and final post as vice-consul at Beirut. His prime ambition was to write; by this time he had already contributed to *Georgian Poetry*, published two volumes of verse and begun the play which was eventually to emerge as *Hassan* (*see* Lawrence's letter to his widow about the first London production of the play, dated November 1923). He was, however, dogged by ill-health; he left the Middle East in 1913 and died of incurable tuberculosis two years later.
2 This letter, dated only 'Feb. 18' by Lawrence, is assigned to 1914 in the documentation of the Houghton Library, Harvard. However, Flecker was no longer in Beirut in 1914; in February 1913 Lawrence was in Sinai, and comparison with other letters shows clearly that it dates from 1912.
3 B.M.: British Museum.
4 R. A. Fontana was the British Consul in Aleppo.

cylinder, aspersing its rarity: have been doing this for a week with a 50% effect so far: if the funds hold off much longer, I'll be begged to take it *belash*.[5] On the whole, to buy antikas is sport, not commerce, and does no violence to one's sense of the instinctive glories of nature and the arts: — though that does not palliate the nature of the weather here, which is brumeginously [*sic*] humid.

There is a most beautiful *Muristan*[6] here, and I have reserved (by appointment) the most eligible-windowed room therein, for my retreat, when I shall have spent the tenth pound, and acquired the last thing Hittite in Aleppo. I look forward to closing there the evening of my days in dignity and retirement. Please tell D. G. Hogarth or C. L. Woolley[7] where they may find me, when they come to Aleppo next: Muristan el Wazir, top floor right on the staircase in the gate, Suk-es-Stamboul, Haleb. Letters care of Fontana. Woolley thinks he knew your son at Oxford, and that you may be useful: wherefore be warned, and don't lean towards altruism. Expect him about March 5, and warn him, if he goes to Jerablus, that he will find no roof to his head. I reserve for him the room beneath mine in my Muristan — and we can accommodate D. G. Hogarth at a pinch. In Albayiehs, with our *narghilehs*,[8] we will posture the wise men of Gotham.

Aleppo is all compact of colour, and sense of line: you inhale Orient in lungloads, and glut your appetite with silks and dyed fantasies of clothes. Today there came in through the busiest vault in the bazaar a long caravan of 100 mules of Baghdad, marching in line rhythmically to the boom of two huge iron bells swinging under the belly of the foremost. Bells nearly two feet high, with wooden clappers, introducing 100 mule-loads of the woven shawls and wine-coloured carpets of Bokhara! such wealth is intoxicating: and intoxicated I went and bought the bells. 'You hear them', said the mukari, 'a half-hour before the sight.' And I marched in triumph home, making the sound of a caravan from Baghdad: 'Oah, Oah', and the crowd parted in the ways before me. Why are you staying in Beyrout? Come up!'[9]

.L.   *Harvard University*

5 *Belash*: for nothing.
6 Or *Maristan*, a Turkish word from the Persian used in Syria and Egypt for a mental hospital.
7 Leonard, later Sir Leonard Woolley (1880-1960), was in charge of the Carchemish dig from 1912-14. He was with Lawrence in the 1914 Sinai survey and served with him in Middle Eastern Intelligence during the war, though he spent the last two years of the war as a prisoner in Turkey. He later became well-known for his excavations at Ur and for his books about his archaeological activities, *e.g. Ur of the Chaldees* and *Digging up the Past*.
8 *Narghile*: oriental tobacco-pipe, hookah.
9 *See* Lawrence's *Note on Flecker* published in *Men in Print*, edited by A. W. Lawrence (Golden Cockerel Press, 1940): 'This strange gawky figure felt the banishment of hot Beyrout...'

HIS MOTHER
April 6, 1912   CARCHEMISH

[...] The Germans are very friendly now, for we are allowing them to clear away our dump-heaps of last year and this year free of charge. As we want to dig under them in the near future we are doing ourselves a good turn as well. The railway is too far away to disturb us.

As for money, I have lots: about £40: in hand: or to be in hand shortly, when Mr. Hogarth pays me for our seals. We have a very splendid collection.

Woolley gets on most excellently here. He is fresh enough from Egypt to see the glory of the country and the people and the customs: I don't think he will ever settle down in Egypt again. The men are as good this year as last: splendid humorists: Bedouin for ever!

N.

HL

A. W. LAWRENCE[1]
July 21, 1912

Ancient beast
It is about a year since we wrote letters to one another: suppose we do it again? It doesn't cost anything but time, and of time, do you know, I have mints just now. This is the first time for years and years that I have been able to sit down and think, and it is so precious a discovery: and one that so many people want to take from you. [...]

I have turned school-master, O tumult, and taught up to 11 times table a class whose average age was about seventeen. Then the house became a hospital, and I put an end to the local education authority. It was sad for they did so want to learn twelve times: It was a very wonderful school: everybody who got a table right got a lump of sugar each time. We finished two large tins! I took a class of four (including our Commissaire) in local history (special subject) and had the mollah of the district to listen to my lecture on geography. They can't make out why, if the world is really round, the people

1 For a biographical note on A. W. Lawrence, *see* p. 397.

on the other side don't fall off. All this is stopped now and the head-master is reduced to writing nonsense to a worm. [...]

Have just been interrupted by a spider as big as a whale's nebula: bottled him in whiskey for you: such hooked teeth and toes: I took him for a crab when he knocked at the door and said 'come in'. Such a fright: Salaams to the world.

N.

DG

HIS MOTHER
22 Feb. 1913   *CARCHEMISH*

[...] [M]y canoe has been 3 weeks in Beyrout, waiting till our agent there can find a spare moment to put it on the train for Aleppo,[1] and I have bought 6 carpets, two 16 feet long, and am short of money therefore and I don't know if we will dig or not this spring, and so I don't know if I will come back or not this summer .... [...]

[At Aleppo I stayed five days more than I need, entertaining two naval officers who became partners in my iniquity of gun-running in Beyrout. The consular need of rifles involved myself, the Consul-General in Beyrout, Flecker, the Admiral at Malta, our Ambassador in Stamboul, two captains, and two lieutenants, besides innumerable cavasses,[2] in one common law-breaking. However Fontana got his stuff, and as he was too ill to entertain the porters, I had to trot them over Aleppo. And we did trot over it all, all day & all night, and out to Jerablus *en prince*, and back laded [?laden] with Babylonian gems, and Greek coins, & Roman bronzes, and Persian carpets and Arab pottery ... all going to a warship, a modern engine of efficiency and destruction ... what will their Captain say to their stuffed bags?][3]

---

1 Lawrence had imported a canoe, equipped with an outboard motor, made by Salter's of Oxford, for use on the Euphrates.

2 Cavasses combined the functions of watchmen, messengers and orderlies at embassies and consulates.

3 The reason for Lawrence's gun-running (his account of which was omitted from *HL*) was that R. A. Fontana, the consul in Aleppo, feared that Aleppo might shortly be under attack from dissident Kurdish tribesmen, in which eventuality the consulate might need means of self-defence. The naval vessel involved was *H.M.S. Medea*.

Now all is peace, and I have been wandering up and down: ... forming a very beautiful collection of Hittite seals ... small but very select, and with some nice pieces of Roman bronze and glazed pottery as sidelines ... also I am in treaty for other carpets in the villages. Meanwhile I am making all day tarpaulin for our roofs, which leak, and repairing the house, and whitewashing, and getting all into trim for a season in a week's time ... and perhaps all quite needlessly! Salaams to Worm from the men ... here they rejoice in his socks, and all wear them themselves ostentatiously.

L.

HL/Bodleian Library

D. G. HOGARTH
End of February [1913]   *CARCHEMISH*

I am getting garrulous, but no matter ... the Ottoman post will correct these faults: and besides I have got more seals, which I packed this evening to send to you: it is a pleasure to pack seals, even when there is no post in view ... and these are very nice seals: at least one is a beauty: button-like (*feu bulla-bead*), red stone, with characters incised ... not big, or sharp, or well cut, but you cannot have everything for your money as a rule .... I cannot even get one of your copper-plate posters from the greedy Leeds – though the number of seals presented by me, through forgetfulness to claim the purchase money, is legion –

Seriously, this last half-dozen, bought by me on the fringe of Abu Galgal, is very good. I rushed back, and have not been down again, because some villains began a dig at Deve Huyuk ... a Hittite cemetery of the last period, with Roman shaft tombs in between. The Hittite graves were full of great bronze spears and axes and swords, that the wretches have broken up and thrown away, because Madame Koch,[1] who is doing the dig, didn't buy such things. I got some good fibulae, which are yours, and not Kenyon's this time at all events ... (18 miles away) much better than the B.M. ones, some bracelets & ear-rings of bronze, a curious pot or two ... and as a sideline, some Roman glazed bottles, with

---

1 Madame Koch was an antiquities dealer – arguably not the most respectable member of her trade – in Aleppo.

associated Greek pottery, and a pleasant little lot of miscellanea ... tomorrow I return there to gather up, I hope, Hittite bronze weapons in sheaves: — unless the police get there first. It is exciting digging: — a plunge down a shaft at night, the smashing of a stone door, and the hasty shovelling of all objects into a bag by lamp-light. One has to pay tolerably highly for glazed pottery, so I will probably buy no more ... glass is found, but very dear ... bronze is thought nothing of....

I found our house filthy with leaking roofs, and have been lighting great fires in all rooms, and rebuilding fallen walls, and whitewashing, and making tarpaulins to mend roofs. You have no idea (unless you too have tried) how hard it is to make three large tarpaulins from one tin of tar and one tin of pitch.

[...] Salaam Dr. Cowley[2] from me: no time for Aramaic yet.

L.

Ashmolean Museum Oxford

D. G. HOGARTH
June 14 [1913]   CARCHEMISH

I wrote to Leeds this afternoon, and thought it enough, but perhaps I'd better write to you as well. We got your letter of joy upon the sculptures of the wall of animals and the King's gate. They are splendid, aren't they. For the photographs are very unsatisfactory so far as making them pretty goes. The carving on the captains is very soft, and delicate. The king & queen are not so good, from my point of view ... a little hard: the children are ugly, but very well done. The slab of dancers, for an archaic piece is also very fine: and there is probably quite a good lot more to find thereabouts.

[...] I'm sorry you didn't like my last lot of seals, those from Marcopoli. Leeds says they arrived without documentation, but I expect that has been set right. I am almost sure they are all genuine, and I thought them rather a nice set. After all three of them are inscribed spheroids, and the cylinder (dated, as it may be in a little) is far and away the best cut of that period that I have ever come across. I'm rather wild at having paid so much for them since they are not up to your mark: and you are short this year. [...]

2 Of the Bodleian Library: *see* letter to him dated 29 October 1914.

I think I had better not buy anything else in Aleppo this season, unless it is something quite necessary to you. In any case, putting the lot together, you have got very good ones from me this year, though very dear also. But when I do come across a very fine one, I feel so disinclined to let it go. I'd much rather give it you half price?

You recommend selectiveness in buying ... for a long time I have not been buying ¼ of the seals offered to me: only if I thought they were very good, or had something not quite regular in their shape or design.

I expect to get back about mid-July, & may bring the Hoja[1] & Dahoum with me: which will shock you!

L.   *Bodleian Library*

Lawrence duly brought his Arab friends Dahoum and Sheikh Hamoudi to Oxford. For their impressions of England, *see* his letter to his mother of 30 September 1913. They in their turn impressed Lawrence's friends, among them C. F. Bell, who arranged for the artist Francis Dodd to paint a portrait (or portraits) of Dahoum.

C. F. BELL[1]
12 Aug. 1913   *2 POLSTEAD ROAD OXFORD*

Dear Mr. Bell
It's rather late, but I think I ought to scribble you a line to tell you of today's happenings.[2] Dodd[3] turned up smiling in the morning, and got to work like a steam engine: — black & white, with little faint lines of colour running up and down in it. No. I was finished by midday, and was splendid: Dahoum sitting down, with his most-interested-possible expression ... he

---

1 The site foreman, Sheikh Hamoudi.

1 Charles Francis Bell (1871-1966) was keeper of the Department of Fine Art at the Ashmolean 1909-31; he was also, like Hogarth, a Fellow of Magdalen College. He was a trustee of the National Portrait Gallery 1910-40.

2 Bell had brought about the 'happenings' here described (the portraits of Dahoum as a present for Lawrence) but was on holiday in Florence when they took place.

3 Francis Dodd (1874-1949) had had an extensive artistic training in Glasgow, Paris and Italy and was becoming known as a portrait painter. He was later an official war artist, one of his notable achievements being a series of portraits of generals of the British Army.

thought it great sport – said he never knew he was so good-looking – and I think he was about right. He had dropped his sulkiness for a patch.

No 2 was almost a failure. Dodd gave it up half-finished.

No 3, standing, was glorious. My brother came to the door with some people, and Dahoum just at the critical moment looked round a little bit annoyed, to see what the dickens the matter was. Dodd got him on the instant, and promptly stopped work in the funk of hurting it. It is an absolute inspiration: no colour, 'cause it was perfect as it was, unfinished.

I raved over it, and Dodd therefore gave No 1 to Dahoum, who in some unknown way had asked him for one of them. I left No 3 – the best, most pleasing though not the most 'pleasant' – with Dodd, to be sent you. Really it's worth looking at.

Dahoum is taking his out to Carchemish to show his people. I think I shall steal it later, since he says with them it will be only a nine-days wonder, and then done with. It's a most splendid thing: – though not so entirely the boy as No 3. Behold there isn't any room left for you![4] Which is a blessing, since I am not good at thanking people politely. It really was most awfully good of you: you got the right man absolutely, and the results are joyful .... How in the world did you ever dream of getting it done.

Good-night!

T.E.L.   *British Library*

HIS MOTHER
30 September 1913   *BARON'S HOTEL ALEPPO*

[...] You are obviously interested to hear what the Arabs think of England. Unfortunately they are too intelligent to be ridiculous about it. They describe it as a garden, empty of villages, with the people crowded into frequent towns. The towns wonderfully peaceful and populous, the houses very high: the tube railways are to them a source of stumbling. They tell the villagers that Syria is a small poor country, very likely to be coveted by us tree-lovers ... and that the Arabs are too few to count in world-politics. All of this is very proper. They also estimate the value and quality of the food they ate in England: ... and feel relieved at their discovery of the true end of the collecting of

4 *I.e.* on the page of notepaper.

antiquities. Concerning ourselves, they praise Will and Arnie ... Mr. Bell and Sir Arthur Evans:[1] in this order.

They were very pleased to see Will[2] again in Jerabîs.[3] Both went with him to Busrawi's camp. [...]

HL

C. F. BELL
Dec. 10 1913   *CARCHEMISH*

I think you would laugh till your 'dome-like stomach' cracked, if you could see us now. Woolley is sitting at a table, dressed in white flannel, not spotless, writing to Basil Blackwell[1] with a photograph of Dahoum propped up against the inkpot to console and inspire him: and I am sitting as close as I can to a fire of olive logs in the fireplace, dressed entirely in black and white with a cloth of gold cloak, writing to you, with a squeeze of a Hittite inscription to inspire *me*. Our room is about 30 feet long, and so between us there is about twenty five feet of very rough mosaic, starred with carpets: one would think we had had a row: but it is only because each of us is so dazzlingly lovely that we put one another out.

I got a letter from you a day or two ago, in which you had survived the little saddle-bag pieces of rug that Dahoum sent you. I am glad you don't object to them over much: and told him so: for really I was afraid that your prolonged silence was due to your difficulty in digesting such hairy morsels.[2] All is well apparently. What is a Zoilist?[3]

1 Sir Arthur Evans (1851-1941), British archaeologist, famous particularly for his excavations in Crete, but also well known in archaeological circles for his reorganization of the Ashmolean Museum, Oxford, of which he was keeper 1884-96, making it into the finest museum in England outside national collections.
2 Will Lawrence was staying for a time with his brother before going on to India to take up a teaching post.
3 *I.e.* Jerablus: Lawrence was using the Arabic form.

1 Woolley was a devoted friend of Basil, later Sir Basil Blackwell, son and successor of the founder of Blackwell's bookshops, Oxford, when the latter was a postmaster (scholar) at Merton College.
2 Far from merely tolerating the 'pieces of rug' sent to him by Dahoum as a present, Bell thought them 'very pretty' and made them into floor cushions which he greatly prized.
3 A zoilist is a malignant or censorious critic; from Zoilus, the grammarian and critic of Homer.

I wrote to you a few days or weeks back, I fancy, which should absolve me the need of writing this time: but it seems it doesn't.

You jeer at our quantities of rugs — but we have not enough even to cover the nakedness of this floor: we have to eke them out with goat-hair tent-cloth.

Digs are finished: we spent two days in Kurd country looking at Hittite monuments, and shivering with cold: and tomorrow we go down to Aleppo to look round about for things Hittite for Hogarth. We have not got the remotest little thing as a present (Xmas) to cheer him up. Please tell him that on Christmas Day I hope to dig Hamman, with Woolley: it will be great fun taking notes in a blizzard, for we have a real winter here.

A stupid letter: obviously a Hittite inscription is not a good inspiration: I'll take away the photo Woolley is gazing at, and send it to you as an appendix. It isn't good, since the drawing is in colour, and under glass: but it will do till I bring the original home: did I tell you that I bought it off Dahoum with a gun and a knife, with great difficulty? He likes it overmuch. Salaam Leeds from me

E. L.

British Library

MISS FAREEDAH EL AKLE
Dec. 10 1913   *CARCHEMISH*

Dear Miss Fareedah
I got your letter two or three days ago — but I had already heard from Mrs. Rieder that you were off to Damascus with Miss Hoel,[1] so it was not such great news. I am sorry you do not like the place. Damascus always seemed to me to have been such a splendid town. Those great mosques and khans and baths are wonderful, and the ruins of the bazaars: also the crowds of people in the town, of all the races of the earth, are rather wonderful too: Don't you think so? or do you want open country and a sea breeze?
      [...]
My brother was in Damascus a month ago: I suppose you didn't see him?

1 Presumably a member of staff at the American Mission School.

Dahoum returns your salaams, with interest: which is forbidden him by his law.
Salaam Miss Hoel from me.

T.E.L.

Bodleian Library

MISS FAREEDAH EL AKLE
Dec. 26. [1913]   *CARCHEMISH*

Dear Miss Fareedah
[...] We[1] are coming down to Beyrout next week, (where you probably are)
and pass straight on to Jaffa, where we land, and go off South, from Gaza to
Petra, with an expedition mapping the country.[2] We end up at Petra, I believe,
and if so will take the Hedjaz line up to Damascus, in the first days of March:
We will not stop more than a couple of days in Damascus, since we are
supposed to begin to dig here in the first week of March. Altogether, you see,
we are rather busy.

Dahoum comes South with us .... So if you do not run away too quickly
from Damascus, you will see us all three together. Miss Hoel thinks Mr.
Woolley is just like me: which saddens me, because I think him ugly.

Salaam me to Miss Hoel: prettily.

Yrs
T. E. Lawrence

Bodleian Library

1 We: Lawrence and Woolley.
2 *See* introduction to this section. The survey of Sinai had been initiated by Lord Kitchener, at
  this time British agent and consul-general in Egypt. Since the territory in question was under
  Turkish rule, it was thought that permission would be the more easily gained if it could be
  described as having an archaeological purpose. The expedition was therefore officially
  sponsored by the Palestine Exploration Fund for which the two archaeologists were
  instructed to produce a report for publication, which duly appeared in 1915 under the title
  The Wilderness of Zin. The director of the survey was Captain Stewart F. Newcombe of the
  Royal Engineers, who was to become Lawrence's lifelong friend and to play a distinguished
  part in the Arabian campaign.

C. F. BELL
Dec. 26 1913   *CARCHEMISH*

Dear Bell

I owe you a letter or two I fancy: at any rate, if I don't you will owe me one which is better.

Woolley got a letter from you yesterday, with a glorious account of the Martyrs Memorial-hat.[1] I sent the extracts to Flecker, who had written to me asking for something cheerful. He is on a hill-top in Switzerland eating sour milk and sleeping in [*sic*] a verandah, being cured of consumption. Which cure usually remains incomplete.

Our Xmas festivities were yesterday: on Xmas Eve Woolley went out into the outer quad, (outer at my request) and sang two short carols, and 'Auld Lang Syne'. The effect was really beautiful, from a little distance: near at hand it was a little strong: there had been 15 pigeons in a house in the quad – and there are now only five, of which the black one has a broken leg. I found the cat groaning about midnight and put it out of its misery. The misery was so great that it ended only at the eleventh bullet.

We are going off tomorrow or the next day, to Jaffa: thence to Gaza and Petra on a P.E.F. survey:[2] it may be fun ... requirements are Arabic and an archaeological eye!

We have for the last week had a horrible time of it at night: after dinner and tea and hot baths we have gone out in a drizzle wrapped in white sheep-skin (Woolley's stinks like it, too) and have repassed charcoal braziers before the face of slabs to dry them (under tents): focused them and photographed them with flash-lights: when it was only a damp drizzle we did not mind it so much: when there was a strong cold wind driving sleet or mist into our faces, and scattering the flash-powder, we didn't like it ... or when it was fine & dry, and freezing hard, with a snow-wind coming off the Taurus so cold that we could hardly turn the screws of the camera.

Why do it? Because D.G.H. is sitting in the Ashmolean, over a coke furnace, and cursing our slowness in getting out those negatives: and here also the sun

1 Bell's notes explain what so delighted Lawrence and Woolley. A Balliol undergraduate had put a chamber pot on the pinnacle just below the cross which tops the Martyrs' Memorial in St Giles, Oxford. Since it was made of enamelled iron, attempts to shoot it off failed and a steeplejack had been brought in to effect its removal. This had been achieved at midday, with all surrounding spaces, including the balconies and windows of the great gallery of the Ashmolean, crowded with cheering spectators.
2 P.E.F.: the Palestine Exploration Fund.

shineth not even at noonday. And we have no coke fire ... only a beaten copper hood and hearth (beaten with a 2 inch hammer) on which flame olive trunks:

Still in a week we will be too warm. Woolley says you will be sending me some snakes .... I clean forgot the Turkish customs ... they will think you did it on purpose ... or that I did. However perhaps they won't open them. Dahoum comes south with Woolley & me ... so that we will not find them till March. No matter.

Do you know Albert de Samain? a Frenchman: Flecker recommends him in a breath with Heredia?[3]

British Library

HIS MOTHER
Jan 4 1914   *AT SEA*

I wrote to you from Aleppo, saying that I would write again when it became possible. Well, we ran down to Beyrout, getting a letter and a telegram on the way, which showed us that we must catch the first steamer to Jaffa, and then run down quickly to Gaza, and after seeing the consul there, go inland to Beersheba, and thence as local advice directed. There are a certain number of R.E.'s[1] thereabouts, beginning the survey. We are obviously only meant as red herrings, to give an archaeological colour to a political job.

[...] We have Dahoum with us, and are warned that we may have to ride camels some of the time: otherwise we are as ignorant of our supposed work as we were at first. I sent off from Beyrout to Mr. Hogarth a little cylinder seal: of prettily veined stone. I hope he will send it up to you and that you, if it seems to you worthless, will hand it on to Mrs. Rieder. It is Persian, about the time of Darius, or a little later perhaps. Now I want to go to sleep. There is no saying when I can write next: certainly not for a week or so.

N.

Got ashore: & going off today at midday for Ashdod.   *HL*

3 Albert Samain (1858-1900) published three volumes of poetry in the 1890s; José-Maria de Hérédia (1842-1905) published three volumes of poetry between 1887 and 1894. Both were, *inter alia*, adept at the dramatic historical sonnet: *cf.* the former's *Cléopâtre* with the latter's *Antoine et Cléopâtre*.

1 Royal Engineers.

E. T. LEEDS
Jan 24 [1914]   *EL AÛGA*

A quaint place to write to you from, this, a little lost Gov. station on the frontier line of Egypt and Syria. Still the spirit moves me.

To appreciate as you should our exploits in getting here, you would have had to follow our steps day by day. That I spare you: over the consequences of much riding of camels I draw thick veils: but take it as a summing up that we are very unhappy: Woolley is the more uncomfortable, since he is a flesh-potter: I can travel on a thistle, and sleep in a cloak on the ground. Woolley can't, or at least, is only learning to, quite slowly.

Our cook can't grasp a word of English, which explains his continued presence with us: after Woolley in a clear tone last Thursday had expressed his desire (in front of the whole camp) to bugger him with a rough stick.

(Don't brag of this to D.G.H. he is too proper: C.F.B. will appreciate the inner meaning of Woolley's apparent wastefulness.)

Our menu is a broad one: we eat bread and eggs: and Turkish delight. Only yesterday we finished the eggs, and the nearest hens are three days journey to the N. If only a camel would start laying we would be in Paradise tomorrow.

We have evolved rather a sporting dinner: Woolley you know likes a many storied edifice.

Hors d'oeuvre

The waiter (Dahoum) brings in on the lid of a petrol box half a dozen squares of Turkish delight,

Soup
Bread soup
Then
Turkish delight on toast
Then until yesterday
Eggs
Then, sweet ...
Turkish delight
Dessert
Turkish delight.

Of course the bread is ad lib. You can see by this the perfectly delirious time we are having out here. It is weeks (or ten days) since we saw an Arab encampment:

and the 'shop' in this place, much looked forward to for the last week, of eatables sells only Turkish Delight. Foul stuff: I don't want much more of it.

However other stores for us may turn up tomorrow:

Not a sign or smell of Israelites wandering about here: only on the old road from Gaza to Akaba did we find two little scraps of early pottery; we are doing the P.E.F. in the eye. Fancy our transforming a hill fort of the Amorites into a Byzantine monastery! Sounds almost impious, doesn't it.

.L.

Bodleian Library

E. T. LEEDS [1]
Feb. 28 [1914]   *HOTEL D'ANGLETERRE DAMAS SYRIE*

Months since I wrote to you, and oceans have passed over my head since then, though alas! all the rest of me yet requires washing. Where was I? Aha ... I got down to Akabah alone and on foot, since my idiot camels went astray. Alone in Arabia! However, it was only a day and a night, but by jove, I was glad to see a tent (not mine) at the end of it. 48hrs later, up came my camels, not smiling in the least.

Kaimmakam of Akaba was a bad man.[2] He had (or said he had) no news of us and our little games: and so he forbade Newcombe to map, and me to photograph or archaeologise. I photographed what I could, I archaeologised everywhere. In especial there was an island, said to be full of meat. The Bay of Akaba is full of sharks, hungry sharks (shivers) and the island was half a mile offshore. So, of course I engaged a boat ... and it never came, for the boatman went to prison at once. That looked to me a chance of a cheap sail, so I carried off the manless boat ... but a squad of police cut me off and robbed me of my treasure. I was alone alas! Well, I sent word to the Kaimmakam that upon his head was the forbidding me to go, and he said yes ... and while his police were carrying our mutual recriminations I puffed a zinc tank full of air, tied to its tail another for Dahoum, and one for a camera and tape and things ... and splashed off for the island with a couple of planks as paddles. The police returning a little later

1 This letter was published in *DG* but with the recipient described as 'A Friend'.
2 The Turkish governor of Akaba.

found my fleet sailing slowly seawards, and they had no boat, and no zinc tanks, and so could only weep while we worked. I had tied Dahoum to my tail, since I felt that any intelligent shark would leave me in the cold, but the whole squadron sailed across safely, saw, judged and condemned the ruins as uninteresting,[3] and splashed homewards, very cold and very tired: there was a most unkind breeze in our teeth, and the return took hours. Kaimmakam was informed of his fate, and cursed my religion: he attached to me in revenge a lieutenant and a half company of soldiers to keep me always in sight. [...] It's a long story ... they had camels, and couldn't walk and couldn't climb as fast as self and Dahoum ... and we walked them out of water, and they were hungry, and we dodged up valleys and slipped their trails; until the desired happened and the last one left us, and I spent a splendid morning all in peace on top of Aaron's tomb in Mount Hor. Perfect peace without ... rather a strained situation within, mitigated partly by a sweet rain-pool, partly by the finding of my tents next afternoon after a two-day absence. I shot a partridge on the hill at dawn, and we cooked it over brushwood, and ate half each. A very good partridge but a small one. The night just under the hill-top was bitterly cold, with a huge wind and blinding squalls of rain. We curled up in a knot under a not-sufficiently-overhanging-rock and packed our sheepskin cloaks under and over and round us, and still were as cold and cross as bears. Not thirsty though, at all.

We had luck, since we found the two great cross-roads through the hills of the Arabah, that serve modern raiding parties entering Sinai, and which served the Israelites a bit earlier. Nobody would show them us, of the Arabs, which accounts for our rather insane wanderings without a guide ... but we did it all well.

[...] Petra, O Leeds, is the most wonderful place in the world, not for the sake of its ruins, which are quite a secondary affair, but for the colour of its rocks, all red and black and grey with streaks of green and blue, in little wriggly lines ... and for the shape of its cliffs and crags and pinnacles, and for the wonderful gorge it has, always running deep in spring-water, full of oleanders, and ivy and ferns, and only just wide enough for a camel at a time, and a couple of miles long. But I have read hosts of most beautifully written accounts of it, and they give one no idea of it at all ... and I am sure I cannot write nearly as nicely as they have ... so you will never know what Petra is like, unless you come out here . ... Only be assured that till you have seen it you have not had the glimmering of an idea how beautiful a place can be. [...]   DG

3 In *The Wilderness of Zin*, however, he described the island as a 'point of capital interest' and gave a detailed account of its fortifications.

The 1914 season at Carchemish was a brief one. Hogarth came to visit the site in May and shortly afterwards Woolley and Lawrence closed down the dig and returned to England to write up their accounts of the Sinai survey. Lawrence was not to return to the place where he had spent the happiest years of his life. On 28 June Archduke Franz Ferdinand of Austria and his wife were assassinated at Sarajevo, and within weeks the First World War had begun.

The Mound of Carchemish, from a drawing by T. E. L.

Lawrence at Wejh, early 1917

2 THE WAR YEARS
1914-18

The outbreak of war in August 1914 found Lawrence in England. There is some confusion as to whether he volunteered for military service and was rejected because of his lack of height; arguably he implied as much to John Buchan in a letter from India in 1927 (*see* p. 356), but when Liddell Hart, researching his 1934 biography of Lawrence, wrote to him asking 'When and where was it you tried unsuccessfully to enlist?' he replied, 'I did not try to enlist.' In the event, it was his connection with Middle Eastern archaeology and with the Sinai survey which led to him finding suitable war work. After he and Woolley had discharged their duty to the Palestine Exploration Fund and to Kitchener by completing *The Wilderness of Zin*, Woolley obtained a commission in the Royal Artillery while Lawrence was enrolled by MO_4: the geographical division of Military Intelligence based in the War Office in London. He began as a civilian but was soon offered a commission, becoming a second lieutenant on the special list (*i.e.* an officer without regimental affiliation) on 26 October 1914.

Turkey became a belligerent, on the side of Germany and the Austro-Hungarian Empire, on 29 October. Before the year was out, Lawrence was in Cairo, a member of a swiftly assembled Intelligence Department, which included not only former colleagues like Newcombe and Woolley (the latter seconded from the artillery), but also other men of calibre such as the Hon. Aubrey Herbert and George Lloyd (both Members of Parliament) and Philip Graves of *The Times*. His principal function was that of map officer, but he was also involved in general Intelligence assessment and became an expert on such subjects as the disposition and strength of Turkish forces. All this was important work, but he was essentially desk-bound; when in 1915 first his brother Frank and then his brother Will lost their lives in France, he began to feel increasingly ill at ease. He wrote to Leeds in November 1915: 'It doesn't seem right, somehow, that I should go on living peacefully in Cairo.'

He was briefly in a war zone in March 1916 when he was sent to Mesopotamia to help in negotiations with the Turks regarding a British force which was trapped by Turkish forces at Kut-el-Amara on the river Tigris. Aubrey Herbert was one of two other partners in this enterprise, of which the purpose was to discuss on what terms the Turks would lift their siege. By the time they reached the enemy lines and met the Turkish commander their task was rather that of trying to achieve the best terms of surrender. On his journey back to Cairo, Lawrence wrote a report condemning British organization and generalship in Mesopotamia which was substantially borne out by the inquiry Herbert won later that year from Parliament. His report was so outspoken that it was thought advisable to have it somewhat doctored before it was shown to the commander-in-chief in Egypt, Sir Archibald Murray. Before any serious repercussions could affect Lawrence's position, the initiation of the Arab Revolt against the Turks by Grand Sherif Hussein of Mecca in June 1916 opened a major new phase in the war, giving Lawrence the opportunity to exchange his Cairo desk for 'field-work' in the desert.

The letters of this early period frequently reflect the mood of frustration bred in him by almost two years of a largely paper war. 'We have no adventures, except with the pen,' he writes to C. F. Bell in April 1915 (in a letter that includes his fullest and most caustic account of his life in Cairo). 'One would be so much happier, I think, in a trench, where one hadn't to worry out politics & informations [*sic*] all the day.' Or again, 'I am going to be in Cairo till I die,' he writes to Mrs Hasluck in February 1916. 'Yesterday I was looking over samples of pyramids at an undertaker's with a view to choosing my style. I like the stepped ones best.' But other letters show him in more buoyant mood, such as the two wide-ranging, light-hearted and even slightly outrageous surveys of the Middle Eastern situation written to George Lloyd while the latter was on active service in Gallipoli. 'Seriously, we were very cut up about getting no news of you,' he writes on 29 June 1915, '& we think the Staff above the rank of Captain are shits.' 'I haven't much right to tell you all this,' he admits on 19 September 1915; 'inform Deedes, if he's trusty, & then use it for bumf or burn it.' Fortunately Lloyd did neither.

Even before the revolt began, he had been much involved in Arabian Intelligence and in early June 1916 he became the first editor of a regular publication, produced to high printing standards, called the *Arab Bulletin*, which was to run to well over a hundred numbers and of which the principal editor was to be D. G. Hogarth. One of its regular features was to be reports, often long and generally very well-written, by the field officers of the Arab Bureau, of which Lawrence was soon to be a distinguished member.[1]

---

1 Hogarth wrote in the 100th edition: 'Since it was as easy to write in decent English as in bad, and much more agreeable, the *Arab Bulletin* had from the first a literary tinge not always present in Intelligence Summaries.'

In October 1916 Lawrence accompanied Ronald Storrs, the oriental secretary of the high commissioner in Egypt, on a visit to Sherif Abdulla, one of the four sons of Grand Sherif Hussein of Mecca, at Jidda in Arabia. (Hussein's sons, Ali, Abdulla, Feisal and Zeid, were his field-commanders in the Arabs' armed struggle against Turkey, now being conducted with the support of Britain and France.) When Storrs returned to Egypt, Lawrence stayed on to assess the situation, and in particular to decide which of the four sons was most likely to succeed as leader, or, as he would put it in *Seven Pillars of Wisdom*, 'the leader who would bring the Arab revolt to full glory'. Having met Abdulla at Jidda and Ali at Rabegh (Zeid at eighteen was scarcely in the running), he rode inland by camel to Wadi Safra, where he met Feisal, by whom he was immediately impressed. He later wrote: 'I felt at first glance that this was the man I had come to Arabia to seek.' The reports, both written and oral, that he made following this crucial meeting with Feisal virtually guaranteed (though that was not his specific intention) that he would be sent back to Arabia to work with Feisal as liaison officer and adviser. He performed this role with significant variations for the rest of the war, gradually assuming more power and independence. The capture in July 1917 of the strategically important port of Akaba by an Arab force led by Sherif Nasir of Medina and veteran Howeitat chief Auda abu Tayi, with Lawrence as accompanying British officer, brought about a major shift in the Arab war and in Lawrence's career. The Arabs would thenceforward conduct their campaign in close alliance with the British, now under the dynamic General Sir Edmund Allenby, as the right wing of an advancing army. When Lawrence, arriving in Cairo with news of the fall of Akaba, was sent to meet the new commander-in-chief, he and Allenby quickly came to an understanding, with the result that Allenby virtually gave Lawrence a free hand in Arabia, while Lawrence worked to harmonize Arab actions with Allenby's overall strategy.

Lawrence wrote very few personal letters in this important second period of the war. There are long gaps between his letters home, and evidently some he sent did not arrive, either because they were censored or, to use his own term, 'submarined'. I have included almost all that have survived, because, though he was restricted in what he could tell his family of his activities, they often convey simply and clearly the gist of what he had been doing and something, though far from all, of his state of mind at the time of writing. (It is the home letters, for example, which produce such quotable sentences as 'I have become a monomaniac about the job in hand', or 'there are few people who have damaged railways as much as I have'; similarly it is there that he produces some nice definitions of his role in the later stages of the war, as when he writes, 'the situation out here is full of surprise turns, and my finger is one of those helping to mix the pie', or when he describes himself, in a throw-away phrase, as 'an Emir of sorts'.) I have also been able to include some letters to E. T. Leeds, of which only a handful were available to Garnett, and then with the recipient's name disguised, which indicate the darker side of his mind, and reveal hints of the sense of guilt at the Allies' ultimate intentions towards the Arabs, which was to ruin his peace of mind throughout most of the campaign. This guilt is shown incontrovertibly in the message which he drafted but did not send to his Intelligence head, Brigadier-General Clayton, printed on p. 117. Yet another mood, that of wistfulness for a lost world ('Very many thanks for writing. It has opened a very precious casement') informs the long and moving letter to Vyvyan Richards of July 1918, reprinted here from Garnett.

However, the most interesting and important war letters published in this book are those he wrote from the field to his friends and masters, letters which necessarily contain obscure military or political references (or, sometimes, a wealth of Arabic names) but which nevertheless communicate because they are hallmarked by Lawrence's accustomed vigour, clarity and forthrightness. These letters – to which I have added extracts from one or two reports which were not intended for or not used by the *Arab Bulletin*[2] – were not in the public domain when Garnett made his selection and, so far as I am aware, apart from occasional sparse quotation have not been published since. Writing to Robert Graves in 1927, when the latter was working on his biography of him, Lawrence wrote: 'All the documents of the Arab Revolt are in the archives of the Foreign Office, and will soon be available to students, who will be able to cross-check my yarns. I expect them to find small errors, and to agree generally with the main current of my narrative.' I believe these letters, patchy as they are and the survivors, I feel sure, of numerous letters lost, go with, rather than against, Lawrence's claim. They certainly throw some considerable light on his grasp of the essentials and the details of the Arab campaign, and indicate what has been called into question by some of his more critical biographers (notably, of course, Richard Aldington), the central importance of his role.

2 In 1988 I wrote: 'There seems no virtue in reprinting any of Lawrence's reports which were published in the *Arab Bulletin*, as they were collected in a fine edition produced by the Golden Cockerel Press in 1939 under the title *Secret Despatches from Arabia*, edited by A. W. Lawrence. More recently the whole of the *Bulletin* has been reissued in facsimile.' Since then I have twice assisted in reprinting Lawrence's wartime reports: first in *Secret Despatches from Arabia, and Other Writings by T. E. Lawrence* (Bellew Publications, 1991) and subsequently in *T. E. Lawrence in War and Peace*, (Greenhill Books, 2005); *see* p. xxvii.

DR. A. C. COWLEY[1]
29 Oct. 1914   [*WAR OFFICE LONDON*]

[...] You ask when I am coming down ... I don't know. You see, there is only the Head of the Department (Col. Hedley)[2] left now, with myself to run errands: and so things are really a little short. Before the war there were six little men to help him, and there's more to do now.

I don't know if one gets days off ... as an exceptional favour I think one can, but I don't like such things. And working all days a week till 7 or 8 p.m. doesn't leave much time for the humanities. I disapprove of London on eighteen counts, of which most are explicit, but they take a long time. London seems curiously unmoved.

Sala'am me to Mrs. Cowley. Please tell her that I also talk French to Belgians, the subject of conversation being lithography.[3] It is very hard to get the hang of their terms: especially as in English I don't very well know what a rotary rubber-bed offset machine really is. [...]

Bodleian Library

E. T. LEEDS
Mond. [16 November 1914]   [*WAR OFFICE LONDON*]

Dear Leeds
I was to have gone to Egypt on Sat last: only the G.O.C. there wired to the W.O. and asked for a road-report on Sinai that they were supposed to have.

Well, of course they hadn't got it – not a bit of it. So they came to me, and said 'write it.'

I thought to kill two or three birds with my stone, so I offered 'em the wilderness of Sin ... they took it and asked for more. So I'm writing a report from the military point of view of a country I don't know, and haven't visited

1 Dr Arthur Cowley (1861-1931) was sub-librarian of the Bodleian Library, Oxford, 1900-19 and librarian 1919-31. He was knighted shortly before his death.
2 Colonel Coote Hedley was head of MO4, the geographical division of Military Intelligence.
3 In the second half of 1914, London was swarming with refugees from Belgium, through which country the Germans had marched in order to attack France in the opening moves of the war.

yet. One of the minor terrors is, that later on I'm to get my own book, and guide myself over the country with it. It will be a lesson in humility, I hope.

It's rather hard luck though, to have devilled my way all over Sinai, and then to have to write two books about it, gratis. And this second one is an awful sweat, for it has to be done against time, and the maps are not yet drawn. So I have to oversee them also, and try and correlate the two. It will not astonish you to hear that I have found a grey hair on my pillow this morning.

The W.O. people are very easily to be deceived into a respect for special knowledge loudly declared aren't they?

I'm to go out on Sat. next, I am told. I don't care, but I'm sure somebody will ask the W.O. for an epic poem on Sinai about next Friday, and I'll be turned on to that, gratis.

No matter....

I hope to see you on Friday, if you aren't ill. You might tell C.F.B. if you see him.

This month up here has been great sport. I reckon that it will take my successor months to get over the effect of my official letters on several occasions. He has gone down to Southampton today to placate the Ordnance Survey over my criticism of their suggested route of the Exodus. They nearly fused the telephone between 'em yesterday.

L.

Bodleian Library

JAMES ELROY FLECKER[1]
Dec. 3 [1914]   [WAR OFFICE LONDON]

Dear Flecker

I should have written very long ago ... but I have been for weeks up at the War Office working day, & half-night, at Sinai and Syria ... maps, & reports: nothing very exciting, but a little grind. Now it is all over, and on Tuesday I start E.[2] Woolley goes on Saturday.

---

1 Flecker (*see* note to letter of 18 February 1912) was terminally ill at Davos in Switzerland at this time. He died on 3 January 1915.
2 E: East.

About your people ... I have lost touch of Oxford. Roberts has enlisted. Cheesman is officer in an infantry regt. – I can't find out which, but will ask further. Beazley can't get anything to do, because he's short-sighted.[3] Not many dons have taken commissions – but 95% of the undergrads. have taken or applied for them. Next term Oxford will come to an end, I think. This term there are about a thousand up.

The war goes well, though too slowly. The Christians in Beyrout have been getting very restive, & the Moslems there are getting out. Quaint business, fighting.

Peaceful poems about willow-lined water-ways, & dreaming spires, and bells, are quite the things. Best war poems are written in peace-time. The converse should be true. Good luck to your pen.

Don't reply to this. I'll write again from Egypt.

In case of need Address TEL. G.H.Q. British Army Occupation Egypt.[4]

Harvard University

Lawrence, together with Newcombe, finally left for Cairo on 9 December 1914.

E. T. LEEDS
24/12/1914   *INTELLIGENCE DEPT WAR OFFICE CAIRO*

You see this is what we are. There wasn't an Intelligence Office, and so we set to, and are going to make them one; today we got the Office, and we all have the Intelligence: it is only a simple process of combining the two. However we have to complicate it by wireless and paid agents (beautiful words) and air reconnaissance and light of nature. All the time you know light of nature would write such a much more beautiful report by himself. But he must hamper himself with greasy Armenians, and unintelligent camel drivers.

---

3 Cyril Roberts, G. L. Cheesman and J. D. Beazley were close friends of Flecker's from his Oxford days, though he had met Roberts earlier. Cheesman joined the Hampshire Regiment on the outbreak of war; he was killed in action at Gallipoli in 1915. Beazley became a brilliant Greek scholar and was later knighted. All these men shared a passion for poetry; *see* Lawrence's letter of May 1927 to Sydney Cockerell (*DG* 309): 'Beazley is a very wonderful fellow, who has written almost the best poems that ever came out of Oxford. [...] If it hadn't been for that accursed Greek art he'd have been a very fine poet.'

2 There is no signature; this line is written at the head of the letter.

Newcombe is Director ... a magnificent but unpaid position. If Maxwell[1] didn't object to Staff we'd all be It: as it is we do the work, much cheaper; ... the Gods alone know what our pay is to be ... for me I'm broke already, so have only a lack-lustre interest in the thing.

Woolley looks after personnel ... is sweet to callers in many tongues, and keeps lists of persons useful or objectionable. One Lloyd who is an M.P. of sorts and otherwise not bad looks after Mesopotamia ... and Aubrey Herbert who is a quaint person looks after Turkish politics:[2] between them in their spare time they locate the Turkish army, which is a job calling for magnifiers. One Hay does the Tripoli side of Egypt ... And I am bottle-washer and office boy pencil-sharpener and pen wiper ... and I think I have more to do than others of the faculty. If we can get somebody to grapple with the telephone (which burbles continuously) I will be as happy and as lazy as I want to be.

Perhaps someday there will be work to do ... but Carchemish seems a most doleful way away.

Salute C. F. B. I'll write to him a letter as soon as I do something ... I don't see any good in fooling him this way. I must write too to D. G. H. If any of our agents show promise I'll give them a card to Marcopoli in Aleppo, and pick him up a few easy spheroids.

Meanwhile – bed.

.L.

Bodleian Library

---

1 General Sir John Maxwell was British commander-in-chief, Egypt, at the outbreak of war.
2 Both George Lloyd (1879-1945) and the Hon. Aubrey Herbert (1880-1923) were Unionist M.P.s, Lloyd for West Staffordshire, Herbert for South Somerset. Lloyd later became governor of Bombay and, as Lord Lloyd, high commissioner for Egypt. Aubrey Herbert, traveller, linguist and a man of powerful if eccentric personality, was John Buchan's model for his upper-class hero Sandy Arbuthnot, Lord Clanroyden – alias 'Greenmantle'. Both Lloyd and Herbert were to become lifelong friends of Lawrence.

HIS MOTHER
12/2/15   *INTELLIGENCE OFFICE CAIRO*

Well, here goes for another empty letter: my bicycle is here: very many thanks for getting it out so quickly: I wish the W.O. would send out maps equally promptly.

You ask about the other people in the Office: well Newcombe and Woolley you have heard of. There is Hough ex-consul at Jaffa ... pleasant and nothing more: there is Lloyd, an M.P. (I should think probably Conservative, but you never know) who is a director of a bank, and used to be Attaché at Constantinople. He is Welsh, but sorry for it: small, dark, very amusing ... speaks Turkish well, and French, German & Italian: some Spanish, Arabic & Hindustani ... also Russian. He is quite pleasant, but exceedingly noisy. Then there is Aubrey Herbert, who is a joke, but a very nice one: he is too short-sighted to read or recognise anyone: speaks Turkish well, Albanian, French, Italian, Arabic, German ... was for a time chairman of the Balkan League, of the Committee of Union and Progress, and of the Albanian Revolution Committee. He fought through the Yemen wars, and the Balkan wars with the Turks, & is friends with them all. Then there is Père Jaussen, a French Dominican monk, of Jerusalem. He speaks Arabic wonderfully well, and preceded us in wanderings in Sinai. We praise his work very highly in *The Wilderness of Zin*. He is very amusing, & very clever: and very useful as interpreter....

There is also Graves, *Times* correspondent,[1] and very learned in the Turkish army organisation. I think that is about all. We meet very few other people, except officers on business ... see a good deal of them, from General Maxwell downwards. He is a very queer person: almost weirdly good-natured, very cheerful, with a mysterious gift of prophesying what will happen, and a marvellous carelessness about what might happen. There couldn't be a better person to command in Egypt. He takes the whole job as a splendid joke.

The Turks are off for the time being. The troops that attacked us last week were from Smyrna (Turks) and from Nablous & Jerusalem & Gaza: there were no men from Aleppo, and very few from Damascus: our prisoners are very comfortable, and very content here: when they have been a few weeks in idleness they will be less pleased.

Lady Evelyn Cobbold turned up, on her usual winter visit to Egypt. I am to have dinner with her tonight.[2]

1 Philip Graves, half-brother of poet Robert Graves.
2 Lawrence had met Lady Evelyn Cobbold at Petra on the last leg of the Sinai survey. She had lent him the money to return by the Hejaz Railway to Damascus.

Dr. Mackinnon[3] is here: he is doing medical work, and Dr. Scrimgeour of Nazareth is looking after the prisoners: Cox[4] is being paid 15/– a day for me: so I hope that my account there will be clear: There are no carpets in Cairo that I want to buy: you don't get good ones under £50 here: so don't expect anything at present ... perhaps when I get back to Carchemish?

N.

HL/Bodleian Library

C. F. BELL

18.4.15   *MILITARY INTELLIGENCE OFFICE WAR OFFICE CAIRO*
          TELEGRAPHIC ADDRESS 'MUKHABARAT' TELEPHONE NO. 996

I know: – it's months since I wrote to Leeds, & so he is cursing: – and it's longer since I wrote to you, and I am like Allan in all respects except colour of hair. But in my case simply I am ashamed to write. Because I sit here all day long, looking like this notepaper. Telephone 996 and 2263 Cairo: Telegraphic address Mukhabarat ... so much for my Intelligence side; I am also officer in charge of Maps: telephones 3621, 3622, 1153, 3647. Telegraphic address Maps, Cairo. There you have it all. Is that anything to be proud of?

We came out here in mid-December: Woolley has now gone off to Port Said, where he runs about in a motor launch, & does exhibition work on hydroplanes and French battleships. He is an authority on prize law, and has taken prisoners.

Newcombe & I remain here. We are made base for the Mediterranean Expedition:– and we are I.O.[1] for Egypt: The first consists in maps, maps, maps, hundreds of thousands of them, to be drawn, & printed, & packed up & sent off: – my job: – also in keeping track of Turkish army movements, which is like hunting an inebriated needle with St. Vitus through whole fields of hay: & for it we send violent & rude telegrams to Sofia, Belgrade, Petrograd, Athens, Basra, & Tiflis. The last sounds rather a decent place. We then file up all these

3 A medical missionary formerly based in Damascus.
4 Cox and Kings were bankers to the army in Egypt.

1 Intelligence Office.

telegrams & our own ideas into a book, called the *Turkish Army Handbook*, now in its fourth edition. A very dull volume, with an extensive circulation (third thousand) [*sic*].

Then we do funny little pamphlets telling our soldiers how to speak to a Greek, & compendia of Turkish manners: and we advise all sorts of people in power on geographical points. The ignorance of these people would give them impossible-ever-to-sit-down-again experiences in a preparatory school. 'Who does Crete belong to?' 'Where is Piraeus?'

We edit a daily newspaper[2], absolutely uncensored, for the edification of 28 generals: the circulation increases automatically as they invent new generals. This paper is my only joy: one can give the Turkish point of view (in imaginary conversations with prisoners) of the proceedings of admirals & generals one dislikes: and I rub it in, in my capacity as editor-in-chief. There is also a weekly letter to 'Mother' (the London W.O.) in which one japes on a grander scale yet. Last week I sent them an extract from a Greek paper of Smyrna, freely translated, which compared our fleet at Smyrna, in its efforts at blocking the harbour, to an excited gentleman – but I don't think this is quite fit for your ears. It was elaborate, & very long.

Well, well, you see we have no adventures, except with the pen, and those one can create in peace time outside an office. Cairo is unutterable things. I took a day off last month, & went & looked at it: no more: – and to think that – this folly apart – one would have been living on that mound in the bend of the Euphrates, in a clean place, with decent people not too far off. I wonder if one will ever settle down again & take interest in proper things. Newcombe – did you meet him – is a most heavenly person. He runs all the spies, & curses all the subordinates who don't do their duty, & takes off the raw edges of generals and things. Without that I should have gone mad, I think. One would be so much happier, I fancy, in a trench, where one hadn't to worry out politics & informations all the day.

TEL.

British Library

2 *I.e.* a daily Intelligence summary.

HIS PARENTS
4.6.15   *MILITARY INTELLIGENCE OFFICE CAIRO*

I haven't written since I got your wire as I was waiting for details.[1] Today I got
Father's two letters. They are very comfortable reading: – and I hope that when
I die there will be nothing more to regret. The only thing I feel a little is, that
there was no need surely to go into mourning for him? I cannot see any cause
at all – in any case to die for one's country is a sort of privilege: Mother &
you will find it more painful & harder to live for it, than he did to die: but I
think that at this time it is one's duty to show no signs that would distress
others: and to appear bereaved is surely under this condemnation.

So please, keep a brave face to the world: we cannot all go fighting: but we
can do that, which is in the same kind.

N.

HL/Bodleian Library

HIS MOTHER
[Undated]   *MILITARY INTELLIGENCE OFFICE CAIRO*

Poor dear mother
I got your letter this morning, & it has grieved me very much. You <u>will</u> never
never understand any of us after we are grown up a little. <u>Don't</u> you ever feel
that we love you without our telling you so? – I feel such a contemptible worm
for having to write this way about things. If you only knew that if one thinks
deeply about anything one would rather die than say anything about it. You
know men do nearly all die laughing, because they know death is very terrible,
& a thing to be forgotten till after it has come.

There, put that aside, & bear a brave face to the world about Frank. In a
time of such fearful stress in our country it is one's duty to watch very carefully
lest one of the weaker ones be offended: and you know we were always the

---

1 Written following the death of his brother Frank, who had been serving in France as a
  second lieutenant of the 1st Gloucesters. He was killed on 9 May by shell-fire when leading
  his men up to the front preparatory to an attack. He was 22.

stronger, & if they see you broken down they will all grow fearful about their ones at the front.

Frank's last letter is a very fine one, & leaves no regret behind it.[1]

Out here we do nothing. There is an official inertia against which one is very powerless. But I don't think we are going to have to wait much longer.

I didn't go to say good-bye to Frank because he would rather I didn't, & I knew there was little chance of my seeing him again; in which case we were better without a parting.

TEL

HL/Bodleian Library

CAPTAIN GEORGE LLOYD
29.6.15   *MILITARY INTELLIGENCE OFFICE WAR OFFICE CAIRO*

Dear Lloyd

Your 'after the storm' letter arrived today with Stepan Effendi. Mine was written at 117° in the shade, & a scirocco blowing, which was stronger than your dust storm, & hotter. Seriously, we were very cut up about getting no news of you, & we think the Staff above the rank of Captain are shits.[1] Now for business. That Bagdad Expedition did a very good thing. It attacked Ruta,[2] & captured 3 field guns, & then sent a gunboat with some officers & 88 men, up river top speed. They overhauled a Turkish gunboat burning palm logs, & so bagged 3 more guns, & then steamed into Amara. There they caused some

---

1 Frank's last letter, begun on 1 May 1915 and updated three times over the following week, contained this passage (expressing attitudes widely held and understood at the time): 'I am writing this letter on the hypothesis that I have been killed, so will treat it in that way. I am glad I have died, not so much for my country, as for all the many wrongs by which the war was mainly commenced and also which it inspired. The purpose for it all I do not think can be seen by us in this life but there is a purpose all the same.'

1 Lloyd was on active service in Gallipoli at this time; hence the anxiety about him expressed in the letter's first paragraph.
2 Ruta Creek on the Tigris, which had been mined by the Turks.

astonishment ashore & bagged another river steamer. Their guns cut off retirement from Amara up the Persian bank, & so the Vali, & Seif el Din, Commandant of the C. P. Fire Brigade[3] surrendered with 1400 merry men, 3 German officers & much machine guns, & a little Field Artillery. The 88 men lay low, & next morning there came in the advance guard (1500 strong) of the army of Mohammud Pasha Daghestani, who had been threatening Ahwaz. Vanguard found itself girt about with machine guns & challenged in English – so surrendered before it counted its opponents. The main Daghestani army unfortunately got warning & went by another road in a terrific hurry.[4]

Ajaimi's tribesmen (who had been flirting with the Turks) came in to make their peace, and offered two gory heads of German officers as a proof of sincerity & repentance. There was a 6th German in Mesopotamia, & he's missing.

Now for Arabia. We have made a quite fit & proper treaty with Idrisi, & Home[5] has ratified it. Only I'm afraid he's not ambitious of anything more than Assir, & a riotous battle with the Imam's tribesmen.[6] I wanted him to have ambitions on the Hedjaz, & to go & do a more than Wahabi purge of the Haramain! no luck there;[7]

Ibn Saoud has made peace with Ibn Rashid:[8] Ibn Rashid promises to be no more impudent, & to look kindly on our progress in Irak. Also to chasten the Ibn Hamad who were against us. Ibn Saoud is now making a treaty with India, the spirit of which is unknown here at present.

Otherwise? Well, we nearly sent a Camel brigade to Sheikh Said to capture it, because some sporting gunner there was having pot-shots at Perim lighthouse. Fortunately K. didn't want it, because Perim lighthouse doesn't really matter as much as a brigade.[9]

3 Constantinople Fire Brigade; the name belied the fact that they were picked troops.
4 The exploit which so excited Lawrence, a foray by a British force up the river Tigris in Mesopotamia in May/June 1915, was to become known as 'Townshend's Regatta', after the name of the senior officer involved, Major-General Charles Townshend.
5 Home: the British Foreign Office.
6 Imam: the ruler of Yemen.
7 A difficult paragraph: Idrisi was a young Arab leader whom Lawrence had seen as leader of an Arab revolt against the Turks. He had signed a treaty with the British Resident in Aden in the previous month. Wahabi: a reference to the fundamentalist Islamic teachings of an 18th-century holy man, Mohammed ibn Abdul Wahab. Haramain: two holy cities, i.e. Mecca and Medina.
8 Abdul Aziz ibn Saud, Emir of Riyadh (now capital of Saudi Arabia), was well-disposed towards the British; ibn Rashid was the head of the pro-Turkish rival house at Hail.
9 K: Kitchener. Perim is an island, at this time a British territory, two miles off the coast of Arabia at the southern end of the Red Sea.

The Canal holds out nervously.[10] It expects an attack every full moon, & when it is dark also: & continually pretends to us that the Turks are coming on. It is divided by us. Fact is 3000 men at Arish, 1000 at Nekhl, 1000 at Beersheba, & the rest behind Jaffa, Haifa & Beyrout. And as the coal of Syria is out they are ruining their engines with lignite & olive logs.

We apostasised from your creed (as a revenge for no news) & planned a gaudy attack on Aleppo. It was to begin at Lattakia, push up the road to Jisr Shogr on the Orontes, & thence raid Aleppo & Hama, & come home by way of Hamman & Beilan: force: — 6000 infantry to hold the Latakia hill-crescent, & 2 divisions of cavalry to do the raiding.

Sat on: lack of cavalry: though someone regretted that it seemed the only chance in this war for good use of horse.

Syria is a horrid wash-out, & we all sit here & cipher & decipher telegrams, & print maps, & wonder when you will push. Apparently you will now, or when your new men come. Which is a new reason for capturing more Asiatic maps & a few of other parts of the world.

By the way, it isn't necessary for G.H.Q. to sit on new maps till it has a set, & then send them all down for *immediate* reproduction. We can draw piecemeal, & so perhaps not work overtime at 110° in the drawing office, & 119° in the Printing Office: as last week. The above paragraph is a grouse.

Incidentally most of the Printing Office are now dead. That is why Cairns, your printer, is wanted back. The photographer is dead also, and one draughtsman.

Oppenheim — damned rat — is in Syria. He will probably cause an anti-German rising if he behaves as usual.[11]

I wish you were back here. One learns so little of what is happening at home & in politics from Newcombe!

I'll come up your way shortly: BORED.

Yrs
TEL.

Churchill College Cambridge

---

10 The Suez Canal.
11 Oppenheim: Baron von Oppenheim, German archaeologist, and chief of the Kaiser's Intelligence Service in the Middle East; known in Cairo as 'The Spy'.

W. G. LAWRENCE
17.7.15   *MILITARY INTELLIGENCE OFFICE WAR OFFICE CAIRO*

[...] Your job – revolver practice sounds pleasant.[1] We live in offices and in railway trains: also interviewing Turkish prisoners, & supplying information on any subject that crops up. No civil work however and much map-drawing & geography, both of which please me.

Frank's death was as you say a shock, because it was so unexpected. I don't think one can regret it overmuch, because it is a very good way to take, after all. The hugeness of this war has made one change one's perspective, I think, and I for one can hardly see details at all. We are a sort of Levant Foreign Office, and can think of nothing else. I wonder when it will all end and peace follow?

All the relief I get [is] in *The Greek Anthology*, Heredia, Morris & a few others! Do you?

DG

CAPTAIN GEORGE LLOYD
19.9.15   *MILITARY INTELLIGENCE OFFICE WAR OFFICE CAIRO*

Dear Lloyd
You don't in the least deserve a pearl such as this letter will prove: – you are perverse, absolutely perverse about that 25th Division. ANZAC never took a prisoner from it, and it was all in Syria till Mid-July. Your suggestion that part was in the Peninsula & went back to C.P.[1] to welcome its friends is an enormity. However let's forget that.[2]

---

1 Will had returned to England from India in March 1915 and was a second lieutenant in the Oxford and Bucks Light Infantry.

1 Constantinople.

2 Lawrence was an expert on the disposition of Turkish forces throughout the Ottoman Empire: hence his bantering tone to Lloyd, who had plainly been in error in regard to the recent moves of the Turkish 25th division. ANZAC is the standard abbreviation for the Australian and New Zealand Army Corps, which won a heroic reputation for its performance at Gallipoli – 'the Peninsula', as Lawrence calls it here. Lloyd was attached at this period to the staff of the ANZAC commander, General Birdwood.

We wire to Basra regularly, & tell them that you want news of them, & they sit on their tails, & won't say a word. All I know beyond the *Bulletin* is, that they say they are advancing against Kut el Amara, & that their Headquarters have moved from Basra to Amara.

Got a wire from you today about Sherif's information. The XIIth A.C. as you should remember (& would had you not left this office – see what you lose!) came to Aleppo as a whole in Nov. December 1914. Fakhri was O.C.[3] Yasin Bey Chief of Staff.

Then in Jan 35th Division was sent to Basra, where we were violating the virginity of Irak … and the 36th a little later went off to Mosul, & thence to Van region.

Fakhri, his staff, & his corps troops stayed behind in Aleppo & Hama, & began to feel lonely.

So they began to raise a new division or two for themselves out of the depots of the 6th A.C., which had gone to Constantinople, & didn't need any depots, as they were completing it from the recruiting areas of A.C. II and A.C. III.

Then the Arab movement became ominous, & Yasin Bey was sent up to Constantinople, where he became C.G.S. XVIIth A.C. There he is now.

Fakhri acted as deputy for Jemal in Aleppo for a time, & has now gone down to Damascus, where his headquarters probably are. He has got a German Staff officer to replace Yasin Bey: and he helps Azmi to curb Jemal's little aspirations. Isn't it heavenly of me to tell you all this?

Now about Sherif. His plans[4] are to slip into the Hedjaz, have a chat about tactics with the Sherif, slip out again, raise the 10 Syrian officers & the 600 rank & file we took on the canal, add to them 50 officers and 2000 men now in India, & drop into the Hedjaz heavily this time. Nuri Shaalan[4] has promised to help him, & can cut telegraph wires, tear up the Hedjaz line, & provide transport, which will enable them to proclaim the Sherif Khalifa,[5] & roll up

---

3 Fakhri Pasha and the XIIth Army Corps were subsequently to move to Medina, where they were to hold out successfully against the Arabs until after the armistice with Turkey in October 1918.

4 'His plans': Lawrence was referring to an Arab officer of the Turkish Army who had just deserted at Gallipoli. A prominent Arab nationalist, he was eager to meet Grand Sherif Hussein in the Hejaz with a view to discussing the practicalities of an Arab rebellion against the Turks. In the event he promised more than he could deliver, but plainly his plans enthused Lawrence and, no doubt, Lloyd.

5 Nuri Shaalan was the paramount chief of the Ruwalla tribe in northern Arabia; he would play an important part in the later stages of the Arabian campaign.

6 Khalifa: civil and religious leader.

Syria (with the help of Syrians) from the tail end. It will come off, if the first landing & attack on Medina succeed. The G.O.C.[7] is shy of it, Clayton is for it: I – but you will guess what I'm at: –

I haven't much right to tell you all this: inform Deedes,[8] if he's trusty, & then use it for bumf, or burn it. The Armenian affair may go through. Our stout men didn't 'see any advantage' in stirring up N. Syria – and so 4 divisions have been added thence to the Dardanelles army. The other 3 or 4 will follow, as soon as they raise scallywags to replace 'em, unless we some day do something. Couldn't your show point it out picturesquely to the G. S.?[9]

The Armenians of Jebel Musa (about 300 fighting men, with shot guns & black powder) put up a fight for about 6 weeks, & slew many Turks. They could have gone on indefinitely with arms & ammunition provided. The women & children of Armenian villages have all been expelled from Cilicia to Mesopotamia & Syria, but the men of fit age [have been] all sent into labour battalions. So N. Syria is full of unarmed battalions of Armenians & Christians, fit men, with no relations or home ties. In addition there are many outlaws, Mohammedan & Christian, in the hills: – all of it good material for a rising backed by us: a few hundred men, a company or two of machine guns, 10,000 rifles, & acceptance of Armenian offers of volunteers arriving daily from America, & we'll have all the Armenians & Cilicia in a horrible tangle. The G.O.C. is willing, & if you'll back up we can carry over the French & have a huge loot. Sherif in rear & Armenians in front: Baron von Oppenheim will hang:[10] –

The last touch is sheer, unmixed, professional, archaeological jealousy: –

Love
T.E.L.

Churchill College Cambridge

---

7 G.O.C.: General Officer Commanding, i.e. Maxwell.
8 Captain Deedes, later Lieutenant-Colonel Sir Wyndham Deedes, was soon to join Military Intelligence in Cairo.
9 G.S.: General Staff.
10 *See* footnote to previous letter to Lloyd dated 29 June 1915 (p. 75).

E. T. LEEDS
16. 11.15   *MILITARY INTELLIGENCE OFFICE CAIRO*

Dear Leeds

I have not written to you for ever so long ... I think really because there was nothing I had to say. It is partly being so busy here, that one's thoughts are all on the jobs one is doing, and one grudges doing anything else, and has no other interests, and partly because I'm rather low because first one and now another of my brothers has been killed.[1] Of course, I've been away a lot from them, & so it doesn't come on one like a shock at all ... but I rather dread Oxford and what it may be like if one comes back. Also they were both younger than I am, and it doesn't seem right, somehow, that I should go on living peacefully in Cairo.

However I haven't any right to treat you to all this.

Salute Bell from me: tell him it is what I have to do to Lieut-Commdr. Hogarth when I first meet him in the morning. It's very good to have him out here, stirring one up to all sorts of other ideas.

I wish one might have an end sometime.

Yours
T E Lawrence

Bodleian Library

---

[1] The brother killed was Will, the one to whom he was closest both in age and interests. Will had transferred to the Royal Flying Corps in August 1915, becoming an observer. He was shot down on 23 October after being less than a week in France. He was officially posted 'Missing', but Lawrence correctly assumed the worst. His death was formally confirmed in the following May. He was 26.

MRS HASLUCK[1]
28.2.16   *ARMY HEADQUARTERS THE FORCE IN EGYPT CAIRO*

Dear Mrs. Hasluck

This is a reply to your letter of December 4! My manners at times astonish even myself.

[...]

We do nothing here except sit & think out harassing schemes of Arabian policy. My hair is getting very thin and grey. I hope you have found some excellent job, which will take all day and be interesting. I'm very sorry you did not come to Alexandria with the main body.

The plum pudding turned up, and was devoured mightily. It came a week late, & so was the only one in Egypt that did not go down with the *Persia*.[2] Many unkind things were said about us, but it was green jealousy only. Very many thanks indeed for the gift.

I am going to be in Cairo till I die. Yesterday I was looking over samples of pyramids at an undertaker's with a view to choosing my style. I like the stepped ones best.

I am a 2nd. Lieutenant ... and a Staff Captain, which explains the riddle. It's much better to use the archaeologist, as the first is cumbrous, and the second abominable.

Remember me to Hasluck if you hear from him: and my sincerest apologies to yourself for my delay in writing to you.

T E Lawrence

Bodleian Library

1 Mrs Hasluck: the wife of F. W. Hasluck, author of, among other works, *Athos and its Monasteries* (1924) and *Christianity and Islam under the Sultans* (1929).
2 The *S.S. Persia*, a troopship en route from England to India, had been torpedoed in the eastern Mediterranean on 30 December 1915 with heavy losses.

The following two letters were written during Lawrence's assignment to Mesopotamia in March to May 1916. The first, to Mrs Rieder, contains information to the effect that the railway bridge at Jerablus, under construction throughout his years at Carchemish, had at last been completed. The second, to his mother, (a letter so long that Lawrence wrote: 'I do not know how the Censor will find it in his heart to pass so Gargantuan a bale of manuscript') was published in *DG* and in full in *HL*. I have therefore reproduced, apart from the beginning and end, only the paragraphs relating to his mission's central purpose: negotiation with the Turkish commander besieging the trapped British force in Kut.

MRS RIEDER
End of March [1916]   *OFF MUSKAT*[1]

Dear Mrs. Rieder
This is a reply to your letter of the beginning of the month. I'm writing on board, with Arabia in view on the left and Persia on the right. Arabia is the better . . . . Persia is all hills and looks wet.

I'm very sorry not to have written to you for so long. It is simply mental inertia. I am written out, and have nothing in my head but Arabian politics, Bagdad Railway, and such like emptinesses. If it was not that you ask me for news of the Railway I doubt whether even after ten days at sea I would have found words.

The old railway is complete from Constantinople to Kara Punar which is about 6 miles South of Bozanti, at the north end of the Cilician Gates. Then comes a stretch of about 20 miles under construction. There are difficult tunnels (35 of them) on this stretch, and it will take about one or two years to finish.

The line then runs from Dorak (about 18 miles N.E. of Tarsus) to Mamourie, which is about 8 miles N.E. of Osmanié, north of Alexandretta.

From Mamourie to Islahie there is another gap, of about 30 miles. This is due to a tunnel of 4882 metres long. It is finished, so far as boring is concerned, and should be open for traffic very shortly.

From Islahie the line runs on to Aleppo (or nearly there: – Aleppo is on a Y line from Muslimie) and from Aleppo out to Jerablus. The bridge there is in order, and finished. The wooden bridge was washed away, too late.

From Jerablus the line works through Tell Abaid (about 10 miles S. of Harran) to Ras el Am, about 210 Kilometres E. of Jerablus. This is railhead, and the Company has no present intention to extend it.

---

1 Lawrence was sailing to Basra on board the Canadian liner *Royal George*.

I'm writing from memory, so I cannot give you the kilometre distance of each section: but you will be able to find most of the above places. One of the best maps (for N. Syria and Mesopotamia) is that in Max von Oppenheim's *Von Mittelmeer zum Tarsische Golf*, which is the best book on the area I know. For the Taurus section of the Railway (Karapunar to Dorak) there is an article by Newcombe in the R.G.S.[2] *Journal* for about September 1914.

The above information is all published in various places: this is for the information of the Censor, who has a tendency to snap up such details, and bore his Intelligence Officers by sending them in for 'information'.

We should get to Basra about Sunday: and I expect this letter will be posted there. I expect to stay ten days or a fortnight, and then return to Egypt. But in the Army one's programme is about as regular as a jumping cracker's.

Very many thanks for an electric torch (which is really the *fons et origo* of this note, and as usually tends to be a postscript; I think I am feminine by instinct). It has been most useful in this unexpected journey, and has probably further duty ahead of it before I see Egypt.

Will you, when next you write make clear to me the sex, name, and address of the sender? It is a relation of yours … a hand-writing that looks prim, but is full of mysteries!

Please remember me to Noël. When I see him next he will be a budding undergraduate, with an incredible ignorance of Arabic, French & German!

Yours sincerely
T E Lawrence

Bodleian Library

HIS MOTHER
May 18 [1916]

We are at sea, somewhere off Aden, I suppose, so before it gets too late I am going to tell you something of what I saw in Mesopotamia. You must excuse the writing, because the ship is vibrating queerly. [...]

Colonel Beach, one of the Mesopotamian Staff, Aubrey Herbert (who was with us in Cairo) and myself were sent up to see the Turkish Commander in Chief,

2 R.G.S.: Royal Geographical Society.

and arrange the release, if possible, of Townshend's wounded. From our front trenches we waved a white flag vigorously: then we scrambled out, and walked about half-way across the 500 yards of deep meadow-grass between our lines & the Turkish trenches. Turkish officers came out to meet us, and we explained what we wanted. They were tired of shooting, so kept us sitting there with our flag as a temporary truce, while they told Halil Pasha we were coming – and eventually in the early afternoon we were taken blindfolded through their lines & about ten miles Westward till within four miles of Kut to his Headquarters. He is a nephew of Enver's, and suffered violent defeat in the Caucasus so they sent him to Mesopotamia as G.O.C. hoping he would make a reputation. He is about 32 or 33, very keen & energetic but not clever or intelligent I thought. He spoke French to us, and was very polite, but of course the cards were all in his hands, and we could not get much out of him. However he let about 1,000 wounded go without any condition but the release of as many Turks – which was all we could hope for.[1]

We spent the night in his camp, and they gave us a most excellent dinner in Turkish style – which was a novelty to Colonel Beach, but pleased Aubrey and myself. Next morning we looked at Kut in the distance, and then came back blindfolded as before. We took with us a couple of young Turkish officers, one the brother-in-law of Jemal Pasha, the other a nephew of Enver, and they afterwards went up to Kut from our camp in the hospital ships which removed the wounded. The ill feeling between Arabs and Turks has grown to such a degree that Halil cannot trust any of his Arabs in the firing line. [...][2] After that there was nothing for us to do, so the Headquarters ship turned round, and came down again to Basra. We got there about the 8th and I spent four or five days settling up things and then came away.

This is an old Leyland liner, now a transport. There is only myself and a General Gillman[3] on board. He is from near Cork and excellent company: we sit on deck and write reports and notes all day, and sleep gigantically at night ...

Hereafter I will again be nailed within that office at Cairo – the most interesting place there is till the Near East settles down. I am very pleased

---

1 Their mission was to no avail. The British force in Kut surrendered while the talks with the Turkish commander, Halil Pasha, were in progress. Seventy per cent of the force perished while being force-marched to Turkey or during subsequent captivity; their commander, Major-General Townshend (of 'Townshend's Regatta' fame; *see* letter to Lloyd, 29 June 1915) spent the rest of the war as a prisoner in Constantinople.
2 Three lines omitted owing to unclear text.
3 General Webb Gillman had been sent by the War Office to investigate and report on the difficulties facing the expeditionary force in Mesopotamia.

though to have had this sight of Mesopotamia in war time. It will be a wonderful country some day, when they regulate the floods, and dig out the irrigation ditches. Yet it will never be a really pleasant country, or a country where Europeans can live a normal life. In these respects, and in the matter of inhabitants, it must yield to the upper river, where we are.

I expect to find letters and papers knee-deep in Cairo when I return. The accumulation of two months business and pleasure will be awful to see – so do not look for immediate news of me.

Would you ask Gillman[4] to make me another pair of brown shoes like the last? Also please ask Arnie to send me out two books by Cunninghame Graham,[5] my Aristophanes, and a Bohn translation of Aristophanes. Latter can probably be bought second-hand from Blackwell. I would like my William of Tyre (*Estoire de Eracles*)[6] if the volumes are not too heavy for the post – and a Lucretius, if I have one. If Arnie likes any of these too well to part with let him send something else choice in their stead.

HL/Bodleian Library

June 1916 saw the launching of the Arab Revolt by Grand Sherif Hussein of Mecca and also the issue of the first edition of the *Arab Bulletin*; the latter event, dated 6 June, preceding the former by three days. Apart from his work on the *Bulletin* Lawrence's most noteworthy achievement in the first months of the revolt was his highly professional contribution to the devising and production of new postage stamps for the grand sherif.

4 Gillman: shoemakers of Oxford.
5 R. B. Cunninghame Graham (1852-1936): Old Harrovian, anarchist, M.P., traveller, travel-writer, story-writer. Probably *Mogreb-el-Acksa* (1898), an account of Cunninghame Graham's attempt to reach the forbidden city of Tarudant in Morocco, was one of the books asked for by Lawrence in this letter. The two men corresponded after the war; there are five letters by Cunninghame Graham in *Letters to T. E. Lawrence*.
6 Guillaume de Tyre (1130-c1186): Frenchman, prelate – he became Archbishop of Tyre in 1175 – and chronicler. His chief work, *Historia Rerum in Partibus Transmarinis Gestarum* (English title, *History of Deeds Done Beyond the Sea*) is one of the main authorities for the study of the Latin kingdom of the East in the twelfth century.

HIS MOTHER
July I [1916]   [*CAIRO*]

Here goes for a letter to you, though there is little to say. The Reuter telegram
on the revolt of the Sherif of Mecca I hope interested you. It has taken a year
and a half to do, but now is going very well. It is so good to have helped a bit
in making a new nation – and I hate the Turks so much that to see their own
people turning on them is very grateful. I hope the movement increases, as it
promises to do. You will understand how impossible it is for me to tell you
what the work we do really consists of, for it is all this sort of thing. This
revolt, if it succeeds will be the biggest thing in the Near East since 1550.

We carry on much as usual in the office, though Clayton has gone back to
England for a couple of weeks, to talk over things with the Foreign Office.
Mr. Hogarth still here, and in charge of Red Sea politics.

Tell Father I received his letter of the 14th of June, and will reply to it
when I have time. The last two weeks we have lived in the middle of a storm
of telegrams and conferences, and excursions, and to consider one's private
affairs is not possible. The money may have come very opportunely, for the
army here are very savage at being left out of the Arabia business, and I may
have to cut adrift of them, which would reduce my pay a good deal.

I have gone out, with Mr. Hogarth, to live with an Irishman called
MacDonnell,[1] who is one of our office. He has a house on the island in the
Nile, where he normally lives with his family. They have gone to Alexandria,
and we have freedom of the house. It is a change from the Hotel, and quiet.

I don't really think there is anything else I can tell you. I feel written out,
for now I have two newspapers (both secret!) to edit,[2] for the information of
Governors and Governments, and besides heaps of writing to do: – and it is
enough. It is a very good thing everything goes on so well. As long as the show
succeeds no very great difficulties will crop up. It is curious though how the
jealousies and interferences of people on your own side give you far more
work and anxiety than the enemy do. I have some very pretty maps in hand,
and am drawing myself one of the country East of Damascus and Aleppo.
Thanks to this war I know an incredible lot about the Near East. Our office
is the clearing house through which every report and item affecting the Near

---

1 According to a letter to his mother not included in this selection, Captain MacDonnell's
   special province in Military Intelligence was Tripolitania.
2 *I.e.* the daily Intelligence reports and the *Arab Bulletin*.

East has to pass ... the mass of Stuff is amazing, and it all fits into itself like a most wonderful puzzle. If we had only begun in peace time there would have been almost nothing we had not known.

Tell Mrs. Rieder that Dieb her coachman has been sentenced to some years imprisonment for insulting the Ottoman Government ... I think he will be only a few weeks there.

N.

HL/Bodleian Library

HIS MOTHER
22.7.16   *[CAIRO]*

I'm afraid there is nothing to say this week either. William of Tyre, Cunninghame Graham and Aristophanes appeared duly. Very many thanks. One does not read them much, but the fact of their being on hand gives one a sense of security. It's like having a balance in books.

Clayton has got back. Everything here is going excellently, though as ever there is enough to do.

Arnie will be glad to hear I am printing stamps for the Sherif of Mecca. I'll send him some when they come out. Of course they are only a provisional issue. It's rather amusing, because one has long had ideas as to what a stamp should look like, and now one can put them roughly into practice. The worst is they can only be little designs, not engraved, so that the finer detail is not possible. I'm going to have flavoured gum on the back, so that one may lick without unpleasantness.

I saw Kerry[1] a day or two ago, for a few minutes. He is at Ismailia, with a post and telegraph company, I fancy or motor cyclist.

They have never heard of Hugh Whitelocke[2] here. I think he must be at Luxor. No news otherwise. N.

1 A. H. G. Kerry was at the Oxford City High School with Lawrence, a boyhood visitor to the Lawrence household and a member of the Kerry family referred to in Lawrence's letter of August 1906. He later became a housemaster at Eton.
2 Hugh Whitelocke: also an Oxonian friend: he served later in the Egyptian Expeditionary Force.

[Please don't give any papers of Will's to Janet,[3] if possible, till I have seen them. There is no hurry about them. N.]

HL/Bodleian Library

HIS MOTHER
10.10.16   *[CAIRO]*

Post out tonight, and as I did not write last week I must this week. I noticed from a recent letter that you had not heard of me for some time. I suppose a post must have dropped out in that sunk French steamer. Anyway I wrote.

I enclose 9 more stamps in this. The half and quarter piastre are not yet on sale.

Have been interrupted eleven times since last sentence. A telephone is useful but a nuisance.

I would like to know if my letters to you are opened? Two interruptions here.

Mr. Hogarth is due here on Friday, which will be pleasant. He is so entirely unprofessional that he acts like a breath of fresh air. (Telephone.) Here is a story for Worm.[1] Storrs,[2] of the British Residency, went down to Jidda lately with the Holy Carpet. When there he wanted to talk to the Sherif. So he went to the telephone, and rang up No. 1. Mecca, and began. In a few minutes he heard other voices on the line, so he told the Sherif that someone was trying to overhear their conversation. Sherif, very angry, rang up the Exchange, and ordered all telephones in the Hejaz to be cut off for half an hour. After which things went splendidly. The Sherif has a sense of humour, and is doing well. His weakness is in military operations. Four interruptions.

---

3 Janet Laurie: a friend of the family whom his brother Will had planned to marry. Lawrence himself had been an admirer of Janet in his undergraduate years and had actually proposed marriage to her himself. She later married Harvey Hallsmith and Lawrence became godfather to her first child.

1 Transcribed as 'Arnie' in *HL*.

2 Ronald, later Sir Ronald Storrs (1881-1955), who was to become a lifelong friend of Lawrence, had been oriental secretary to the British Agency in Egypt since 1909. He had been much involved in negotiations with the Sherif of Mecca about the Arab Revolt.

We have added a new man to our bunch, one Ormsby-Gore, an M.P.[3] ... seems good ... Ismailia come up soon and amalgamate with us. Then we are nearly 40 strong! There ought to be intelligence enough in the bunch to down Turkey – but unfortunately half of them are only door-posts and window frames! Things will go much more smoothly, though, when we are all in touch. (Telephone.) Worm should read Spenser as often as possible: not in large doses (4 more interruptions) but for a few minutes at a time, and frequently. More interruptions – I think I must give this up. It is too hopeless trying to write when soldiers keep on rushing into one's room and throwing fresh papers into one's baskets. I have three baskets now, and three tables, and they are all about knee deep. (Telephone.)

When they get too bad I go out and see somebody somewhere else in the building (this place is nearly as big as the War Office) and come back and tear things up [and generally spiflicate things].[4]

More interruptions. I'm off. (Telephone).

N.

P.S. –This evening is worse than usual.

N.

HL/Bodleian Library

Lawrence arrived in Arabia on 16 October 1916, accompanying Ronald Storrs on his journey to Jidda to meet Sherif Abdulla.[1] Two days later he wrote his first operational report to Brigadier-General Clayton (printed on pp. 92-3), forerunner of many such reports to Clayton and others.

3 William George Ormsby-Gore (1886-1964), later 4th Baron Harlech: Etonian, Unionist M.P. for Denbigh, later for Stafford.
4 The words 'and generally spiflicate things' are omitted in *HL* – one of many curious minor excisions by M. R. Lawrence, in this case because of his abhorrence of slang.

1 Abdulla (1882-1951), second son of the Grand Sherif Hussein, was emir of Transjordan 1921-46 and king of Jordan 1946-51. He was assassinated in the Aqsa Mosque, Jerusalem. The present king of Jordan is his great-grandson.

ERNEST DOWSON[1]
17.10.16   *JIDDA*

Dear Dowson

No point in writing to you: except to prove to you the existence of stamps! They are quite pleasantly received here. Some say that the design is rather out of date, and that a modern style (more like a cigarette picture) would be fitter. However, they are used, and well liked. In fact the half-piastre is sold out, in Jidda, and more than half have been wired for to Mecca.

About the Survey. No progress, I'm afraid. I happened on Jidda at a very unfortunate moment, which I will explain to you at length some day. So Sherif Abdullah (I could not see S. Hussein)[2] could hardly be brought to a very fine point.

I hope to have another go at him tomorrow.

My regards to Mrs. Dowson.

Yours sincerely,
T. E. Lawrence

Bodleian Library

1 Ernest, later Sir Ernest Dowson (1876-1950), was at this time director-general of the survey of Egypt, in which capacity he had been responsible for the printing of the recently issued Hejaz stamps.
2 S. Hussein: the Grand Sherif Hussein of Mecca, Abdulla's father. He had been a presence in the discussions at Jidda in which Lawrence had taken part, but not in person, by telephone. Born in 1853 or 4, he was (by self-proclamation) king of the Hejaz from 1916 until he abdicated in 1924; he died in Amman in 1931.

BRIGADIER-GENERAL GILBERT CLAYTON[1]
18/10/16

General Clayton

We spent about two and a half days at Jidda, about half of which was occupied with discussions with Sherif Abdullah. We got there just as Wilson[2] had received the telegram about the 'final' decision not to land a brigade at Rabegh (suggest you inform H.M.G. there are no 'final' decisions in war time, though I agree with this one!) and he was so taken up with the point that Syria was never mentioned.

Abdullah looks about thirty, and is very quiet in manner: all the same one could see that the decision against a Brigade was a heavy blow (mostly, I think to his ambitions). He was very cut up at first, and tried to get the order changed, as he was afraid to inform his Father of it. I think it was pushing the principle a little too far, when they counter-ordered the aeroplanes! After all, I am going to land at Rabegh, and am just as much 'British troops' as they are.[3] However, that point can be pressed later if necessary. The Turkish planes, if they are handled by Turks will crash pretty soon, and their moral effect will then pass off.

The actual moment when the planes were called back was a particularly unfortunate one. They will never believe that the real reason was other than an excuse, I'm afraid.

I'm getting a few details on the sort of expenditure of Sherif Hussein.

The old man is frightfully jealous of his purse-strings, and keeps his family annoyingly short. I think both Abdullah and Feisal should have allowances. The money question is going, I think, to be decisive: the Turks have been trying to circulate paper lately, which will be the end of them, if persisted in.

Sherif Hussein is obviously, from what everybody says, very clever, rather suspicious, and interferes in everything. But he is such an old dear that they

1 Gilbert, later Sir Gilbert Clayton (1875-1929), was Lawrence's chief at headquarters for most of the war; at this time he was B.G.G.S. (Brigadier-General, General Staff) Hejaz operations, *i.e.* the senior staff officer involved in the Arabian campaign.

2 Lieutenant-Colonel C. E. Wilson, British Resident in Jidda.

3 The debate over the landing of an Allied brigade in Arabia had two aspects: the reluctance of the British commander-in-chief Egypt to commit scarce resources, and the anxiety that the presence of Christian soldiers on sacred Moslem soil might cause a violent anti-Allied reaction in the Arab world and also – very important to the British – in India. Lawrence's impending visit to Rabegh had been agreed the previous day at Jidda during Storrs' conversations with Abdulla: he was to meet Ali, Hussein's eldest son, at Rabegh, and then ride inland to meet the third son, Feisal, at his camp in Wadi Safra. According to *Seven Pillars,* Lawrence transmuted these visits into a mission to find the most promising leader among Hussein's sons; he was to find him in Feisal.

only protest half-comically. He entertains royally, is accessible to everyone, very vigorous physically, and is perfect in all ceremonies. He is too mild to his enemies, but is respected the more by the people. He seems to be getting a little old, and looks upon his sons as boys not quite fit to act independently. Abdullah humours him, and tries to wheedle him round by diplomacy. Feisal[4] is a little impatient sometimes.

Aziz[5] has not taken me into his confidence, but is enormously interested in the Hejaz Railway, <u>North</u> of <u>Maan</u>. I cannot get him worked up to consider the El Ala-Medina stretch at all. All his questions are about the Hauran, Kerak, and the Nebk-Selemich region: even Aleppo sometimes. I fancy he may be trying to get up into the Rualla-Hauran country, not to do very much perhaps, but to sound the people, and cut the line. He will not take troops with him from Hejaz.

However, unless he asks my opinion I needn't take any notice of what I suspect, and indeed a diversion there might aid us in the end of November most powerfully. If he would blow up the Hama bridge, it would be safe to start excavating Beersheba!

Aziz suspects that all idea of an offensive from Medina has been abandoned by the Turks; however, he does not know much more about it than we do.

There is great need of some Intelligence work being done at Jidda. The opportunities are quite good, and at present there is no one to do them. If one stayed there, and worked, one would be able to appreciate the Hejaz situation quite well. There are some personal remarks here about Colonel Wilson which I won't write down. Will you please ask Storrs a few leading questions about him? Cornwallis regards me as prejudiced!

The tone of public opinion at Jidda is rollicking good-humour towards foreigners. It will however be quite a good thing when the French Political Mission goes.[6]

Jidda is a wonderful town, like gimcrack Elizabethan exaggerated. Storrs

---

4 Third son of the Grand Sherif (1883-1933); later principal Arab delegate to the Paris Peace Conference and king of Iraq from 1921 until his death.

5 Aziz Ali el Masri: competent Egyptian officer who soon faded from the Arabian scene but was thought at this stage to be a likely commander of Arab forces in the Hejaz. A pro-German in the Second World War.

6 Lawrence's view on French involvement in the Hejaz was shared by his superiors. The relationship between Lawrence and the head of the French military mission to Jidda, Colonel Edouard Brémond, which was to continue after the war, was never an easy one, though he admired Brémond's military record (he had fought on the Somme) and in an early reference in *Seven Pillars* described him as 'the only real soldier in Hejaz'.

will give you some of the gems of our experience: most of it felt as though Gilbert was editing the Arabian nights, and adding footnotes! The most amusing atmosphere I've ever had.

T.E.L.

Bodleian Library

HIS MOTHER
18.11.16   *ARAB BUREAU SAVOY HOTEL CAIRO*

This is only a scrawl to inform you what I wired: — namely that I have got back to Cairo. I left on October 13 from Cairo, reached Jidda on October 16, left there on October 19, for Rabegh. Left Rabegh on October 21, by camel; went up to Sherif Feisul's H.Q. at a place called Bir Abbas, half-way between Medina and the sea, about 100 miles North of Rabegh. After a few days there returned by road to Yenbo, and embarked on Nov. 1 for Jidda. On November 4 changed ships there, and went across to Port Sudan with Admiral Wemyss.[1] Reached Khartoum on November 7, and stayed with the Sirdar[2] till November 11, when I took train down the Nile to Halfa, then steamer to Asswan, and then by rail to Cairo.

At Asswan Hugh Whitelocke got into my carriage, and we were together as far as Luxor where he intended to stay a day to sightsee.

Since my return I have been extravagantly busy: — so much so that I cannot possibly write to you probably for two or three days yet. The day is one long series of interruptions.

I have now left G.H.Q. and joined the Arab Bureau,[3] which is under the

---

1 Admiral Sir Rosslyn Wemyss: commander-in-chief, East Indies and India, 1916-17, First Sea Lord 1917-19, created Baron 1919.

2 The Sirdar, *i.e.* commander-in-chief, of the Egyptian Army at this time was Sir Reginald Wingate; he was also (1899-1916) governor-general of the Sudan. He was high commissioner of Egypt 1917-19 and G.O.C. Hejaz Operations. Created Baron 1920.

3 The Arab Bureau had been established in February 1916 to deal specifically with Arabian problems and initiatives. It was under the control of the Foreign Office and (to quote Robert Graves, *Lawrence and the Arabs*, Chapter V) 'was run by a small group of men, some of them, like Lloyd and Hogarth, old friends of Lawrence's, who really knew something about the Arabs — and about the Turks'. It acted as a staff and Intelligence office for the Arabian campaign.

Residency here. That is, the Sirdar is in charge of it, or will be very shortly. The atmosphere of being one's own master — or at any rate of being with people whose voices are not drowned by their grinding of axes — is pleasant. All very well.

N.

HL/Bodleian Library

By the time the following letter was written, Lawrence was back in Arabia with the Sherifian forces, with whom he would serve for the rest of the war, though he would also make many visits to General Headquarters (first in Egypt, later in Palestine) and to other places, such as Suez, Jidda, Jerusalem, Beersheba, as occasion required. His appointment to Feisal was originally envisaged as temporary, but it was so successful that there was no thought of removing him. The successful relationship between him and Feisal — welding Arab vision and leadership with British enthusiasm and commitment — was to prove a powerful energizing force throughout most of the campaign. For a clear layman's introduction to the situation in which Lawrence now found himself, the reader is recommended to turn to his letter to his mother dated 12 February 1917.

DIRECTOR, ARAB BUREAU[1]
2.12.16   YENBO

Director Arab Bureau
I got a wire from George Lloyd asking me to meet him at Yenbo. So I stopped till today. I am off now in half an hour to Feisal, who is at Kheif Hussein. No more news of the skirmish at Kheif. I hope to clear up that situation, and expect to be back on Monday night.

Garland[2] takes over my cipher. He is a most excellent man, and has won

---

1 Major, later Sir Kinahan Cornwallis (1883-1959); director of the Arab Bureau 1916-18.
2 Major Herbert Garland, attached to the Egyptian army at this time with the rank of *bimbashi* (equivalent to major). Writer, metallurgist, inventor of the 'Garland' grenade and expert in explosives. Lawrence wrote of him in *Seven Pillars*: '... his knowledge of Arabic and freedom from the theories of the ordinary sapper-school enabled him to teach the art of demolition to unlettered Beduin in a quick and ready way.'

over everybody here. The very man for the place. His pupils seem to have got on well on the Railway on the 29th.

Atmospherics here have been very bad, and so I have not been able to wire much. Lloyd has arrived at the root of the matter, and his report will be worth seeing.[3] Let me know Newcombe's movements.

TEL

Have been wildly rushed all day & yesterday mapping an aeroplane ground here.

TNA: PRO FO 882/7

DIRECTOR, ARAB BUREAU
5.12.16   [*YENBO*]

[…] I had better preface by saying that I rode all Saturday night, had alarms and excursions all Sunday night, and rode again all last night, so my total of sleep is only three hours in the last three nights and I feel rather pessimistic. All the same, things are bad.[1] Henceforward much of the Harb will have to be ruled out. […]

There is nothing now to prevent the Turks going South except Ali's anaemic force at Rabegh itself, the possibility of a recrudescence of the warlike spirit of the Harb in their rear, or the fear of Feisal behind them all. Feisal's position becomes difficult. He is cut off by the Wadi Safra from the Hejaz proper, and his power of cutting the Sultani road becomes remote. He is left with the

---

3 Lloyd shortly produced a long *Report on the Hejas* [*sic*], dated 22 December 1916, covering all aspects of the Arab Revolt, political, military and economic, of which one keynote passage (with which Lawrence would have had full sympathy) reads: 'It must … be realised that whilst the Shereef is undoubtedly fully grateful and sensible for the sympathy and assistance which His Majesty's Government are giving him, he is yet quite acute enough to realise that he on his side is rendering important service to the British in this theatre of war. He recognises that his revolt is immobilising the best part of two Turkish divisions … and that he with his tribesmen has been holding up as large a force as that which is engaged in Sinai… In consequence of this it is scarcely surprising that he feels that his own wishes and views should have weight with H.M.G., if not as an equal yet still as something more than a mere suppliant in receipt of favours.' (*TNA: PRO FO 686/6*)

1 Lawrence had arrived at Feisal's camp to find that he had suffered a severe setback at the hands of the Turks. In a surprise attack they had routed one of the main elements of Feisal's army, the levies of the Harb tribe. They had also set by the heels the smaller force under the command of Feisal's younger brother, Zeid, which had retreated in confusion towards Yenbo.

Juheina only and they are a tribe with the seeds of trouble all present in them, in the jealousy of the Ibn Bedawi family of the hold Feisal is getting over their tribesmen. Feisal is the *beau ideal* of the tribal leader. I heard him address the head of one battalion last night before sending them out to an advanced position over the Turkish camp at Bir Said. He did not say much, no noise about it, but it was all exactly right and the people rushed over one another with joy to kiss his headrope when he finished. He has had a nasty knock in Zeid's retreat, and he realised perfectly well that it was the ruin of all his six months' work up here in the hills tying tribe to tribe and fixing each in its proper area. Yet he took it all in public as a joke, chaffing people on the way they had run away, jeering at them like children, but without in the least hurting their feelings and making the others feel that nothing much had happened that could not be put right. He is magnificent for to me privately he was most horribly cut up. [...]

Another thing, Feisal is out of his area here. He knows little more about Wadi Yenbo than we do. The names of places, sorts of roads and water supply are strange to him. He could still strike north, raise the Billi and Huweitat tribes and develop into South Syria, only he cannot do this while the Turkish force is free to attack Mecca in his absence.

I asked him about the effect on the tribes of the fall of Rabegh and Mecca.[2] It seems both have a great name among the tribes and he was not sure that the warlike feelings of the Juheina would survive the recovery of them by the Turks. Once he thought they would and then he thought they would not. Anyway he himself would not stick in the north and see Mecca fall. He swore he would come down by sea at once with the few Bisha and Hadtheil[3] that could come with him and die in defence of his people. On the other hand he does change his mind, and I estimate his personal prestige among the Arabs so great as to survive everything except actual and direct military disaster. If he loses Wadi Yenbo it will be greatly dimmed and he will go to Wadi Ais as a sort of fugitive and will lose Yenbo.

Feisal received me most cordially and I lived all the time with him in his tent or camp, so I had a very great insight into what he could do at a pinch.[4] If I was not such a physical rag I would tell you all about it.
T. E. Lawrence

2 Lawrence was asking what would happen if Rabegh and Mecca fell; they had not done so.
3 *I.e.* tribesmen from the vicinity of Mecca.
4 It was during this visit that Feisal made the request, to which Lawrence was happy to accede, that he should wear Arab clothes like his own while in his camp; one of the reasons given in *Seven Pillars* is that if so attired he could 'slip in and out of Feisal's tent without making a sensation which he had to explain away each time to strangers'.

P.S. Don't use any of above in bulletin or elsewhere, it is not just – because I am done up.

TNA: PRO FO 882/7

DIRECTOR, ARAB BUREAU
[c. 11 December 1916]

I am going down to Rabegh today to see Colonel Joyce and Major Ross.[1] I want to ask Colonel Joyce why he never sends me any information, and to get him to withdraw the Egyptian contingent, who are only a nuisance to us and the Arabs. I want to talk over the question of satisfactory air reconnaissance with Ross. He has four times tried to send a plane up here, and it has only once got through. That time its observation was a farce, so far as Yenbo was concerned, for he sent it up Wadi Safra from Bedr to near Bir Abbas, and then back to Waset, and up through Jebr to Nujeil, and so down over N. Mubarak to Yenbo. It was the end of a four-hour flight when they reached Yenbo, and the last half hour only was over an area of importance, and during that half-hour the men were too dazed to see anything. Also they only had the old map, and no notes on what places looked like, or what to look for. So they saw nothing, though they passed over Nakhl Mubarak during the battle.

My want them to come to Yenbo straight, and do their local reconnaissance on their way back to Rabegh, when we have primed them with what we want to know. If Ross cannot arrange this then the only thing to do will be to base a plane on Yenbo itself. The seaplanes have been doing yeoman work these last two days, bomb dropping on Bruka, and scouring the country.

My position at Yenbo is a little odd. I wire to Colonel Wilson only, and got a letter from him to say that I was in charge of supplies at Yenbo. That is not possible, for Abd el Kader, as agent of Sherif Feisul, runs the supply question ashore, and our interference would not be welcomed – and is not necessary. Whatever may be the position at Rabegh and Jidda, I can vouch

---

1 Lieutenant-Colonel Pierce Joyce, who had been less than impressed by Lawrence at their first meeting in November 1916 (at Port Sudan when Lawrence was on his way to report to Sir Reginald Wingate in Khartoum), was soon to become his close ally and friend. 'Joyce worked for long beside me' (*Seven Pillars*, Chapter XVI). Major A.J. Ross was the Royal Flying Corps commander in the Hejaz.

that Yenbo is a most efficiently-run show. All that a 'supply officer' has to do is to hand over the way-bills or whatever you call them, to Abd el Kader.[2]

I regard myself as primarily Intelligence officer, or liaison with Feisul. This was all right while Feisul was in the Interior, as they seem settled to have no one but myself in there. Only he is now in Yenbo, half-besieged, and in these circumstances Garland is much more use than I could be. For one thing, he is senior to me, and he is an expert on explosives and machinery. He digs their trenches, repairs their guns, teaches them musketry, machine gun work, signalling; gets on with them exceedingly well, always makes the best of things, and they all like him too. He is quite alive to intelligence work also, though he has not been in contact enough with things or documents to know much outside the immediate area here. Anyway he is the best man for Yenbo, and while he is here, I am wasting my time walking about with him. That is really why I am going down to Joyce, to see if he can suggest anything worth doing.[3]

Communication to & from Yenbo by wireless is very slow, for the naval work takes precedence, and Captain Boyle[4] wires a great deal of naval stuff, as well as intelligence reports, based on notes picked up by his interpreter, and from various telegrams. The interpreter is an Egyptian, and is not good. Feisul has now swung round to the belief in a British force at Rabegh. I have wired this to you, and I see myself that his arguments have force. If Zeid had not been so slack, things would never have got to this pass. [...]

T E Lawrence

Garland has written to you suggesting he have a few days' leave in Egypt. I hope this can be arranged, for he has done most admirable work here, and just at present all that is at a standstill.
.L.

TNA: PRO FO 882/6

2 Abd el Kader el Abdu (described by Lawrence in *Seven Pillars* as 'a well-informed, efficient, quiet and dignified person'), had only recently arrived in Yenbo from Mecca, where he had been postmaster-general of the Hejaz at the time of the Hejaz stamps issue.
3 The problem of the division of labour between Lawrence and Garland was of short duration; Lawrence continued as adviser to Feisal as the latter's army moved north towards Syria, Garland spent much of the next two years carrying out valuable demolition and other work in the Hejaz.
4 Captain (later Admiral) W. E. D. Boyle R.N. was senior naval officer, Red Sea, and the Earl of Cork and Orrery.

HIS MOTHER
14.12.16   *[RABEGH]*

Am in Rabegh – half way between Jidda and Yenbo – tonight, & have just heard that a mail is closing for England. So as I did not write last one here goes this one. I cannot write you details till I reach Egypt, which will not be for some two weeks or so yet. Things very interesting at Yenbo, where is Sherif Feisul, one of the Sons of the Sherif of Mecca. I left there three days ago, and ran down to Jidda, to do a little business: am now going back, to stop a few days. Weather delightful, neither hot nor cold, with beautiful winds.

This letter will probably reach you a little after Christmas. I hope it will not be too wet again. All today I have been discussing Arabian geography & politics, which are the local topics. One has forgotten that there are other wars on.

If that silk headcloth with the silver ducks on it – last used I believe as a table-cloth – still exists, will you send it out to me? Such things are hard to get here now.
N.

This is not a letter: only a substitute for a field post card.
N.

HL/Bodleian Library

COLONEL C. E. WILSON[1]
19th December 1916   *YENBO*

I am taking the opportunity of Mr. Garland's leaving Yenbo for Cairo on leave to send you some notes on local conditions here. I hope it will be arranged that he returns here when his leave expires; his knowledge of tools and arms has been invaluable, and when Feisul is able to restore communication with the Hejaz Railway, it will be possible for him to go up there and direct his explosive parties personally. Everybody ashore likes him.

---

1 As British Resident in Jidda, Wilson had met Lawrence at the time of the Storrs/Abdulla conversations and had not been impressed; he later reported, however, on the 'great value' of his services to the campaign and on his 'pluck and endurance' (official report: 28 May 1917).

[...] Mr Garland will speak to you about the question of guns for the Sherif's troops. I personally feel strongly that the inferior quality of these troops demands a superfine technical equipment. They have not the tactical skill to make an inferior gun, by superior handling, equal to the better gun of their enemies. Unless we can give them weapons in which they have confidence they will not be capable of meeting the Turkish artillery. When with Feisul in November I wrote down to Colonel Parker, and asked for a battery of British field guns, latest pattern, with telescopic sights. The guns supplied to Feisul are two German-made fifteen-pounder guns, very much worn, without telescopic sights or range-tables, with defective fuses and ammunition, and lacking essential parts of elevating gear, etc. I think that a battery of used 18-pounders, with complete equipment, should be supplied to replace them. [...]

I think the Arab forces have made a fair show. The night that Turks were rumoured to be within a few miles the garrison was called out about 10 p.m. by means of criers sent round the streets. The men all turned out without visible excitement, and proceeded to their posts round the town wall without making a noise, or firing a shot. This is in contrast to their usual waste of ammunition without excuse, and shows an intention of rising to an emergency. The sentries have also kept a fairly good watch, and the outpost lines have been maintained steadily by day and night, at considerable distances outside the walls. The attitude towards ourselves of the Syrian and Mesopotamian officers in the army has been good. I have detected no signs of professional or political jealousy, except as regards the Egyptians. [...]

[...] There was a fight three days ago between 300 Ageyl and 400 Hadheyl, over a question of camels. About 1000 rounds were fired, and two men were killed and six wounded. The fight was checked by Feisul himself, who went out bare-headed and bare-footed, as he happened to be, and made peace at once. Some bullets struck the Monitor (M.31) in the harbour, and narrowly missed wounding or killing some of her crew. Sherif Feisul came off, when the matter was pointed out to him by Captain Boyle, and expressed his regret. The prompt quelling of the disturbance gives, I think, a good illustration of his personal prestige among his followers, since the affair was taking large proportions.

Rumours are current on the ships that British rifles can be bought cheaply ashore. I have tried to verify these, but without success and I think they are generally false, though isolated instances of men anxious to get rid of their arms may have occurred. The British rifle is highly prized.

T. E. Lawrence

TNA: PRO FO 882/6

MAJOR KINAHAN CORNWALLIS
27.12.16   [*YENBO*]

Dear K.C.

It has been very good of you to send those two wires about Abd el Kader's son. The old man is more than grateful, and I am sure that he deserves it! He does everything in Yenbo, and is the best disposed person towards us I have struck.[1] I fear I am irregular & bad in reporting things to you. There has been so little worth sending of late.

If I am to stay here I will need all sorts of things. Have you any news of Newcombe? The situation is so interesting that I think I will fail to come back. I want to rub off my British habits & go off with Feisul for a bit. Amusing job, and all new country. When I have someone to take over here from me I'll go off. Wadi Ais is the unknown area of N. Hejaz, and I want to drop up and see it – anything behind Rudhwa will be worth while.

I enclose a file of papers: will you distribute them to the wise and the foolish? The map corrections are filthy, but I got so tired of making copies for everyone that you only get the original – unless the Flying people performed according to their promises and sent you a proper copy. However Dowson will, inshallah, make it out. I want it embodied, not in 3rd. Ed. Medina-Mecca, but in the 1st. Edn. <u>Medina</u> A map showing Wejh and the Railway is an absolute necessity. Hogarth will find you Huber or Wallin – Burton is the other source. Let it be the full size & shape of the final sheet.

The 3rd. Medina-Mecca will then be a future issue, including probably a further revise of the Wadi Yenbo, and the new R.F.C. work Fina-Gaha etc. Ask Dowson to press the drawing of the Medina sheet. It should be very rough, and sketchy.

Am glad Bray[2] is back. I wonder what the next week will bring forth, here and there. Somehow I do not believe in a Turkish advance on Mecca, though they could, if they wished.

Wilson will send you a note on Dhurmish of Akaba. About Faiz, I thought you would try to bag him: he is a very unusual person. Don't get him caught by the Turks as a spy!

Send me a Hejaz Handbook some day, and an *Arab Bulletin* later than 31.

---

1 Abd el Kader el Abdu: *see* p. 99.
2 Captain, later Major N. N. E. Bray, Indian Army. Worked for Arab Bureau 1916. Subsequently emerged as a critic of Lawrence's role in Arabia notably in his book *Shifting Sands*, published in 1934. *See* letter to Mrs Charlotte Shaw December 1934 (headed 'Monday night late'), p. 541.

You know they had no copy of my route-notes in Rabegh. They would have been useful to R.F.C.[3]

Wedgwood Benn of the *Ben-My-Chree*[1] has got 200 negatives of the Muller party murdered near Jidda. They include a lot of Yemen things. Get them, if you can. Limbery gave them to him.

TEL

Will you get from Citadel & send down to Abd el Kader a leather portfolio of E[gyptian] Govt pattern. It should be 3 times as long as the paper is high. Present from me.

TEL

TNA: PRO FO 882/6

The most important development in the Arabian campaign in early 1917 was the advance of Feisal's army from Yenbo to Wejh, 180 miles to the north on the Red Sea coast. The move, closely supported by the Royal Navy, had the twin virtue of taking the war to the enemy and exposing more of the Hejaz Railway to attack; and of providing a vital psychological boost to Arab pride and thus increasing the incentive to tribes not yet involved to rally to the revolt. 'We wanted this march, which would be in its way a closing act of the war in Northern Hejaz, to send a rumour through the length and breadth of Western Arabia. It was to be the biggest action of the Arabs in their memory; dismissing those who saw it to their homes, with a sense that their world had changed indeed; so that there would be no more silly defections and jealousies of clans behind us in future, to cripple us with family politics in the middle of our fighting.' (*Seven Pillars of Wisdom*, Chapter XXII)

Feisal left Yenbo on 3 January and reached Wejh on the 25th.

3 R.F.C.: Royal Flying Corps.

1 William Wedgwood Benn, later Lord Stansgate (1877-1960), father of Anthony Wedgwood Benn (former Labour M.P. Tony Benn). The *Ben-My-Chree* was a seaplane carrier, converted from a cross-channel steamer; she was sunk by Turkish shore batteries in 1917. Wedgwood Benn described his wartime experiences in his book *In the Side Shows*, by Captain Wedgwood Benn D.S.O. D.F.C. M.P., published in 1919.

COLONEL C. E. WILSON[1]

5.1.17   [*YENBO*]

I have just come in from Feisul, and the *Race Fisher*[2] is leaving in half an hour. So I am sending a hurried note on Northern Politics.

As I reported to Captain Bray, Ibn Sheddad, Feisul's self-appointed messenger to the North (he is a Beni Wahab sheikh) left about Nov. 15 for Jauf. He got there in 12 days hard riding, without incident. In Jauf he found Nuri, Nawaf, Fawaz, and Sinaitan.[3] They held a committee meeting & came to the decision that they would break off all relations with the Turkish government at once. They will not however commit themselves to an active policy, until Feisul has established himself at El Ula,[4] and has opened up direct communication with them. This involves his occupying Teima, and blocking out Shammar Ghazzua – which Nawaf will not undertake. Teima is held by Abu Rumman for Ibn Rashid with seven men: – and offers to surrender to 8 – but Nawaf will not move against Ibn Rashid as yet.

The reasons that influence the Aneza sheikhs are those of ammunition (they have Martini & Gras guns) barley, and wheat. Jauf produces enough dates for the tribes, and some over, which are sent to Damascus. El Ula is the first possible point with which they can have direct contact with supplies from the Sherif.

The tone of the messages sent by Nuri and Nawaf to Feisul is excellent. They are quite ready to do their work, as soon as it gives a fair chance of success.

[...]

Feisul will not send ibn Sheddad North again, except from El Ula, when he has reached there himself. Matters stand over till then.

[...]

T E Lawrence

1 The letter is addressed to Colonel Wilson, but with a note by Lawrence at the head of the page: '(Copy sent: this direct Cairo to save time).'
2 The *Race Fisher* was a fleet messenger ship, one of five employed on the East India & Egypt Station.
3 Sheikhs of the Ruwalla tribe.
4 El Ula: a station on the Hejaz Railway, about a hundred miles to the north-east of Wejh.

Feisul asks for

All recommended
by me, and
urgent

{

10	valises & flea-bags (for himself & staff: it is very cold here)
I	Attaché case (a leather case with two locks about 18 inches long, & flat, for confidential papers)
I	sleeping tent, for himself. To be small and double if possible: big enough for a bed, and sitting ground for five or six people round a tray. We all feed in his tent together. The Survey[5] can make this tent, if none are available. Strong ropes, and double set pegs, iron & wood.
3	batteries of Q.F.[6] Mountain Guns.
I	battery of 18 pounders.

Also please send me 4 sets of 1/250000 of Syria, and 1/500000 of Maan etc. (MAPS) Also one R.G.S. 1/200000 Syria Mesopotamia, etc.

TEL

TNA: PRO FO 882/6

5 The Survey of Egypt, headed by Dowson.
6 Q.F.: quick-firing.

His Mother
16.1.17   *Umm Lejj*

I have not written for a fortnight, for at first I was up country hopping about on a camel, and later there was no post-boat. You see we have no mail-steamers, but depend entirely on the Navy for our communications, and they go about their business strictly. However, in any case you know that I am completely well. I have got leave to stay down here a fortnight longer, because things here are interesting, and new. Life in Yenbo was varied, because I lived always on ships, and while there was always a ship, it was sometimes one and sometimes another sort of ship. Some were luxurious, some warlike, & some very plain – but all different. This place you will not find on any map, unless you buy the northern sheets of the Red Sea Admiralty charts (I don't recommend them!): any way, it is about 100 miles North of Yenbo, and is a little group of three villages (about 40 houses in each) on a plain about a mile square under red granite hills. As it is spring just now the valleys and slopes are sprinkled with a pale green, and things are beautiful. The weather is just warm enough to be too hot at midday, but cold at night. I'm on a ship, as usual.

Sherif Feisul (3rd Son of Sherif of Mecca), to whom I am attached, is about 31, tall, slight, lively, well-educated. He is charming towards me, and we get on perfectly together. He has a tremendous reputation in the Arab world as a leader of men, and a diplomat. His strong point is handling tribes: he has the manner that gets on perfectly with tribesmen, and they all love him. At present he is governing a patch of country about as large as Wales, and doing it efficiently. I have taken some good photographs of things here (Arab forces and villages and things), and will send you copies when I can get prints made. That will not be till about the end of the month, when I go to Cairo.

My Arabic is getting quite fluent again! I nearly forgot it in Egypt, where I never spoke for fear of picking up the awful Egyptian accent and vocabulary. A few months more of this, and I'll be a qualified Arabian. I wish I had not to go back to Egypt. Any way I have had a change.

N.

HL/Bodleian Library

LIEUTENANT-COLONEL S. F. NEWCOMBE[1]
17.1.17   [UM LEJJ]

Dear S.F.N.

So I miss you by a day! I'm very sick, but it was either that or miss Wadi
Hamdh, with the foreknowledge that I may never see Wadi Hamdh again, and
that I will certainly see you at Wejh.[2]

I prepared Feisal (who is an absolute ripper) carefully for you, and had him
well wound up to meet you on the morrow – and after all I took Vickery out
with me instead.[3] It won't do, you know, that sort of thing.

This show is splendid: you cannot imagine greater fun for us, greater
vexation and fury for the Turks. We win hands down if we keep the Arabs simple
… to add to them heavy luxuries will only wreck their show, and guerilla does
it. It's a sort of *guerre de course*, with the courses all reversed. But the life and fun
and movement of it are extreme.

I'm awfully glad you have come out … you'll find it as good as I say and
better – especially after you have met me. With which modest – but not
senseless, saying – sleep. Boyle is good … proud of his profession, but white,
and itching for a show.[4] Try and get him a little game at Wejh. I'd like him to
land N. of the town, & work along the sand-hills into the camp.

Vickery had a funny idea that nothing had yet been done out here. It's not true:
may I suggest that by effacing yourself for the first part, and making friends with
the head men before you start pulling them about, you will find your way very much
easier? They tried the forceful game at Rabegh – and have spoiled all the show. After
all, it's an Arab war, and we are only contributing materials – and the Arabs have
the right to go their own way and run things as they please. We are only guests.

Shall look forward to the 23rd beyond measure.[5]

L.   *St Antony's College Oxford*

1 Later that year Colonel Newcombe's camel saddle-bag containing this letter and other
documents was taken by a Turkish officer, Ismet Karadoyan Bey, at Qaleat Al Zumarrad on
the Hejaz Railway after a skirmish between Arab and Turkish patrols. The two officers
corresponded after the war and Newcombe's papers were returned to him.
2 Lawrence was writing during the march to Wejh.
3 Major Charles Vickery was a regular gunnery officer of considerable experience (he had served
in the South African War, spent five years with the Egyptian army and been at Gallipoli) whose
military expertise Lawrence respected but with whom he differed over policy and tactics.
4 Captain Boyle was in charge of the sea-borne force involved in the move to Wejh.
5 In fact Newcombe joined Lawrence in the desert on the 18th, the day after this letter was written.

HIS MOTHER
31.1.17   *ARAB BUREAU SAVOY HOTEL CAIRO*

Am back in Cairo, though only for a few days. Left Yenbo about a fortnight ago, for Um Lejj, by sea. Landed at Um Lejj and came up by land to Wejh, which we took without fighting.[1] A landing party from the ships had practically done the work the day before. I snatched a week's leave, to come up here and buy some things, before going off to Sherif Feisul again.

As I have not had any letters lately (due to my moving about, and the difficulty of posts in the Red Sea) I cannot answer any particular questions. Things in Arabia are very pleasant, though the job I have is rather a responsible one, and sometimes it is a little heavy to see which way one ought to act. I am getting rather old with it all, I think! However it is very nice to be out of the office, with some field work in hand, and the position I have is such a queer one – I do not suppose that any Englishman before ever had such a place.

All of which is rather tantalising reading to you, because I cannot enter into details. I act as a sort of adviser to Sherif Feisul, and as we are on the best of terms, the job is a wide and pleasant one. I live with him, in his tent, so our food and things (if you will continue to be keen on such rubbish!) is as good as the Hejaz can afford. Personally I am more and more convinced that it doesn't matter a straw what you eat or drink, so long as you do not do either oftener than you feel inclined.

It has been very cold down there lately: the thermometer one morning was down to 50° which struck us as rather serious!

The war in Arabia is going on very well: the Arabs are very keen and patriotic, and the Turks are beginning to get really frightened. I hope to write a better letter tomorrow: this is only a scrawl to catch the mail.

N.

HL/Bodleian Library

1 There was no fighting by Feisal's army, but there was by the landing force, which included tribesmen, of whom twenty were killed. A British lieutenant of the Royal Flying Corps also died. Lawrence, who believed Wejh could have been made to surrender without any show of force in a matter of days, was angered by what seemed to him pointless losses, If the whole garrison of Wejh had escaped, 'it would not have mattered the value of an Arab life. We wanted Wejh as a base against the railway and to expand our front; the smashing and the killing in it had been wanton.' (*Seven Pillars*, Chapter XXVII)

HIS MOTHER
12.2.17   *WEJH*

Here I am, back in Wejh again, sitting in our funny house trying to write or think or work. I'm afraid there are too many interruptions for much success.

Newcombe is here, and I hope things are going well. I got a letter from Arnie the other day pleading for more news of what the Sherifian forces are doing. Well you know, it is not my fault. They do a great deal, but some people – not themselves – seem to wish to keep the progress of the campaign a secret. As a matter of fact progress is difficult. The Arabs of the Hejaz are all for the Sherif, some keenly enough to volunteer, others less keen, but all well-wishers. Only, they are tribesmen, and as such are rebellious by instinct. They hate the Turks, but they don't want to obey anyone's orders, and in consequence they turn out only as a mob of snipers or guerilla-fighters. They are wonderfully active, quite intelligent, and do what they do do fairly well. They are however not fit to meet disciplined troops in the open, and it will be a long time before they are.

These details will give you a fair idea of the sort of campaign it is. There is a bunch of about 12,000 Turks in Medina and the neighbourhood, clinging to certain important water-supplies and roads South and West of Medina, and surrounded, on all sides except the Railway, by Arabs. The Turks are also holding the Hejaz Railway, which we now threaten from Tebuk downwards, but not as yet in any force. The Arabs proved incapable of taking Medina, held by its present garrison, and the Medina garrison proved unable to advance through the Arabs against Mecca. So now we have shifted part of our forces North to this place, and the struggle for the Railway will probably be the feature of this second phase of the Hejaz Campaign.

The Arab Movement is a curious thing. It is really very small and weak in its beginning, and anybody who had command of the sea could put an end to it in three or four days. It has however capacity for expansion – in the same degree – over a very wide area. It is as though you imagine a nation or agitation that may be very wide, but never very deep, since all the Arab countries are agricultural or pastoral, and all poor today, as a result of Turkish efforts in the past.

On the other hand the Arab Movement is shallow, not because the Arabs do not care, but because they are few – and in their smallness of number (which is imposed by their poverty of country) lies a good deal of their strength, for they are perhaps the most elusive enemy an army ever had, and inhabit one of the most trying countries in the world for civilised warfare.

So that on the whole you may write me down a reasonable optimist: I hope that the show may go as we wish, and that the Turkish flag may disappear from Arabia. It is indiscreet only to ask what Arabia is. It has an East and a West and a South border – but where or what it is on the top no man knoweth. I fancy myself it is up to the Arabs to find out! Talk about Palestine or Syria or Mesopotamia is not opportune, when these three countries – with every chance – have made no effort towards freedom for themselves.

I wonder what the censor will make of this letter? It may contain news for him, but I'm afraid precious little to the enemy! However you never know what they will do, and there is a 'Hush' policy over the Red Sea and Arabia which causes a good deal of amusement to the Arabs – and to us who are down here.

I hope to be able to send you some photographs of the Sherif and of Feisul and the rest of us shortly. Please wait in peace till then. Incidentally I'm to have no post towards you now for about ten days. Patience!

N.

HL/Bodleian Library

HIS MOTHER
25.2.17   *ARAB BUREAU SAVOY HOTEL CAIRO*

Back in Cairo again for a few days – till the 28th to be exact. One does run about on this show! But as a matter of fact I have only come up to get some mules, and a wireless set, and a few such-like things.

Affairs are going a little slower than I had hoped, but there has been no suspicion of a set-back, and we are all well contented. I enclose a few photographs – as long as they are not published there is no harm in showing them to anyone. I have a lot more, but they have not been printed yet. They will give you an idea of the sort of country (in the oases) and the sort of people we have to do with. It is of course by far the most wonderful time I have had.

I don't know what to write about! What we will do when I get back I don't know exactly – and cannot say any how. Cairo is looking very gay, and everybody dances & goes to races as usual or more so – but after all, there is not, and never has been, war in Egypt.

The weather here is fresh – and in Wejh warmish. [...]

I got the headcloth safely, about a week ago, in Wejh,[1] together with news that Bob had gone to France.[2] As a matter of fact, you know, he will be rather glad afterwards that he has been ... and as it will be easier work, and healthier than his hospital work in London, I do not think that you have much cause to regret. Many thanks for the headcloth. [...]

I have now been made a Captain and Staff Captain again, which is amusing. It doesn't make any difference of course really, as I am never in uniform in Arabia, and nobody cares a straw what rank I hold, except that I am of Sherif Feisul's household.

Can't think of anything else to say, as have become a monomaniac about the job in hand, and have no interest or recollections except Arabian politics just now! It's amusing to think that this will suddenly come to an end one day, and I take up other work.

N.

HL/Bodleian Library

A FELLOW BRITISH OFFICER[1]
22.3.17   *EL AIN IN WADI AIS*

I should have written before but have been ill. However things are quite alright now. Situation on line is stationary. Deserters come in daily and we have got a decent intelligence service with places right down to Medina. [...] The three aeroplanes in Medina have been burnt. I suspect they were bad ones, given up as useless therefore got rid of them and there are wild rumours in the place. Colonel Wilson asks that Ross be informed where we are. El Ain is about 10

1 *See* his letter home of 14.12.16.
2 M. R. Lawrence (Bob) served with the Royal Army Medical Corps in France from 1916-19.

1 This letter was preserved in typescript in a series of files containing papers, mainly carbon copies of letters and signals, apparently accumulated by Colonel Wilson. No addressee is given. The letter is an interesting one, being written on the seventh day of the ten days' illness in Abdulla's camp during which, according to Chapter XXXIII of *Seven Pillars*, Lawrence rethought the whole strategy of the Arab campaign. For Lawrence's account of conditions in Abdulla's camp and the reasons for his being there *see* next letter.

miles West and South of Murubba in W. Ais on the 1/500,000 of Wejh as far as I can see. I did a compass traverse from Wejh but it was a shaky one. The road I came by was awful; hardly possible for camels. Am making headway steadily and hope to have a force of my own shortly. I want here two big railway moveable spanners and two wire cutters. There are supplies of each in the house at Wejh and Sherif Feisal will send them up.

Please see Sidi[2] Feisul for me and tell him I have not been able to do my job here because I have been ill. I hope to go down to the railway tomorrow for a preliminary reconnaissance and after that will be able to say what can be done, but in any case I will stay here a bit as it is most important that the Turks should not be able to concentrate much of their Medina force at El-Ula against him, and I am afraid if I do not stay here not much will be done.

Please beg him not to remain in Wejh unless it is absolutely necessary. The effect both on Arabs and Turks of knowing him to be near the line would be very great, and if he left his heavy baggage in Wejh he could fall back on it in case of need, quickly.

He has aeroplanes now and Wejh is very easy to defend. Also if the Turks pushed West from El-Ula I would get Sidi Abdulla to march up the line towards El-Ula which would have the effect of bringing the Turks back.

In fact I hope most strongly to find him at Jayadah or Ainsheifa soon.

Lawrence

TNA: PRO FO 686/6

---

2 Sidi: the customary honorific title used for the four sons of Grand Sherif Hussein (lit, 'my lord').

COLONEL C. E. WILSON[1]

16.4.17   *WEDJ*

[...] I had to stay in Abdulla's camp from March 15th to March 25th. On the way up I developed boils, which made camel riding uncomfortable, and on top of them first a short attack of dysentery, and then somewhat heavy malaria for about ten days. This combination pulled me down rather, so that I was unable either to walk or ride. I think, however, that even had I been fit I would have been unable to get Sidi Abdulla to take action much sooner than was actually the case.

The conditions in his camp were, I thought, unsatisfactory. He had a force of about 3,000 men, mostly Ateiba. They seem to me very inferior as fighting men, to the Harb and Juheina.[2] [...] Access to the camp is nearly limited to his intimates, and he spends very little time with visiting Sheikhs or deputations. The business arrangements of supplies, equipment, money, accounts, and secretarial work generally are in the hands of Sheikh Othman, a Yemeni scholar, much over-worked and without even a clerk to assist him. Sidi Abdulla exercises little or no supervision and Shakir,[3] though he does a certain amount, hardly replaces him. Abdulla himself spends his time in reading the Arabic newspapers, in eating, and sleeping, and especially in jesting with one Mohamed Hassan, an old Yemeni from Taif, nominally Muedh Dhin[4] in the camp, but whom Abdulla introduced to me as his Karageuz (Punch). Abdulla and his friends spend much of the day and all the evening in playing practical jokes on Mohamed Hassan. These take the form usually of stabbing him with thorns, stoning him, or setting him on fire. The jests are somewhat elaborate: the day before I arrived Abdulla set a coffee pot on his head, and pierced it three times with shots from his rifle at 20 yards. Mohamed Hassan was then given £30 reward for his patience. Sidi Abdulla is fond of rifle practice, and also of Arabic poetry. Reciters from the camp while away much of his time with songs and dances.

---

1 A brief summary of the contents of this report, with some direct quotations, appeared in the *Arab Bulletin* of 23 May, under the title 'In Sherif Abdullah's Camp'. It should be stressed that though Lawrence's account of Abdulla as a military leader was critical, he had been sent out specifically 'to find out why he [Abdulla] had done nothing for two months' (*see Seven Pillars*, Chapter XXXI) and to stimulate him into action; and that he balanced his criticisms by paying tribute to Abdulla as the 'head and cause' of the revolt, he having been the chief Arab negotiator with the British from 1914 onwards.

2 Men of the Harb and Juheina tribes formed a substantial part of Feisal's force at this time.

3 Shenf Shakir ibn Zaid was Abdulla's second-in-command.

4 Caller to prayer.

He takes great interest in the war in Europe, and follows the operations on the Somme, and the general course of European politics most closely. I was surprised to find that he knew the family relationships of the Royal Houses of Europe, and the names and characters of their ministers. He takes little interest in the war in the Hedjaz. He considers the Arab position as assured with Syria and Iraq irrevocably pledged to the Arabs by Great Britain's signed agreements, and for himself looks particularly to the Yemen. He regards this, rather than Syria, as the future basis of strength of the Arab movement, and intends, as soon as set free from the boredom of these Northern operations, to chase Muhieddin out of Ibha, Idrissi out of Arabia and compel the Imam to the position of a feudatory. This sounds a large operation, but Abdulla is convinced of its practicability, and has even worked out the details of his actions. [...]

For the actual work for which I have come to this camp, Sidi Abdulla's attitude was hardly favourable. His Ateiba knew nothing of the country in which they were, – and their Sheikhs are non-entities. He had only a handful of Juheina with him and, led away by Shakir's tastes, scarcely desired more. Of his five machine guns only two were effective for lack [of] armourers or spares; he had no artillery officers, and till Feisal stripped himself of two of his four 2.95 mountain guns in Abdulla's favour, no artillery except 2 small and very uncertain howitzers. His regular troops (70 Syrian deserters, the gunners and machine gunners) lack nearly all equipment, and he had taken no steps to help them. His Ateiba were two months in arrears of pay, simply through *laisser faire*, for the gold was present in the camp to pay them up in full. He understands very little about military operations, and the only officer in the camp, Sidi Raho, the Algerian Captain,[5] is either unable, or unwilling to persuade him to move. Since his arrival in Wadi Ais Sidi Abdulla had not ordered any attack on the railway. [...] As it was impossible to arrange a proper routine of destruction of the railway at once with Sidi Abdulla, I began by some isolated efforts against various points. I give a rough list below, but cannot guarantee the dates since I got mixed up during my stay:

March 24th	Bueir	60 rails dynamited and telegraph cut.
March 25th	Abu el-Naam	25 rails dynamited, water tower, 2 station buildings seriously damaged by shell fire, 7 box-waggons and wood store and tents destroyed by fire, telegraph cut, engine and bogie damaged.

5 Algerian officer in the French Army, a member of the staff of the head of the French mission to the Hejaz, Colonel Edouard Brémond.

March 27th	Istal Antar	15 rails dynamited and telegraph cut.
March 29th	Jedhah	10 rails dynamited, telegraph cut, 5 Turks killed.
March 31st	Bueir	5 rails dynamited, telegraph cut.
April 3rd	Hediah	11 rails dynamited, telegraph cut.
April 5th	Mudahrij	200 railway [sic] blown up, 4-arched bridge destroyed, telegraph cut.
April 6th	Mudahrij	Locomotive mined and put out of action temporarily.
April 6th	Bueir	22 rails cut, culvert blown up, telegraph cut.

The Turks lost about 36 killed and we took some 70 prisoners and deserters during the operations. [...]

The Turks search the line very carefully by daylight before a locomotive passes. A trolley came first, and then an infantry patrol of 11 men, of whom three were each side of the way, looking for tracks and fire on the way itself, walking bent double, scanning the line for signs of disturbance. For this reason tracks should be made through (i.e. both E . and W. of the line as though by a party crossing over) and the burying of the charges and fuse should be done most carefully. The railway is well laid, ballasting ample, and earth work and bridging solid. The rails are very light, and badly worn, and the sleepers (all steel) light in section and shallow. The heads of many bolts have been buried to prevent loosening of the nuts, which makes it impossible to undo them with any ordinary short wrench.

[...] I came back to Wedj on receipt of the pressing letter of Sidi Feisul (attached).[6] He was very annoyed with me for staying so long and is I think in a nervous and exhausted state. This will however right itself as soon as he leaves Wedj which will be shortly. [...]

T. E. Lawrence

I hope that in making the above strictures on Sidi Abdulla's behaviour, I have not given the impression that there is anything between us, he treated me like a Prince, and we parted most excellent friends in spite of my having said some rather

6 Feisal's letter, addressed to 'My Dear affectionate friend' and signed 'Your affectionate friend, Feisal', gives some indication of the importance which the Emir attached to Lawrence: e.g. 'I am waiting for your coming because I have many things to tell you. The destruction of the railway is easy. Major Garland has arrived and we can send him for this purpose.... You are much needed here more than the destruction of the line because I am in a very great complication which I had never expected,' etc.

strong things about the tone of his camp. I had come straight from Feisal's headquarters where one lives in a continual atmosphere of effort and high thinking towards the better conduct of the war — and the contrast with this of Abdulla's pleasure-loving laughing entourage was too great to be pleasant. One must remember however that Abdulla is the head and cause of the Hedjaz revolt and neither his sincerity nor his earnestness can be called in question. I do think, however, that he is incapable as a military commander and unfit to be trusted, alone, with important commissions of an active sort.

He did a great deal for me: — paid up the Ateiba, took an interest in his guns and machine guns, sent out his dynamite parties and began to prepare for a general move towards the line.

[…]

TNA: PRO FO 882/6

Over the next few months Lawrence wrote a number of reports for the *Arab Bulletin* but, apparently, very few letters; in his 'home letters' there is a gap of almost six months, though some may well have gone astray. This lacuna is scarcely surprising, however, as he was much on the move. From leaving Wejh in early May until arriving in Akaba in early July he was deep in the desert, far from any convenient naval transport or fleet messenger ship. He was also much preoccupied with the moral aspects of the campaign in which he was engaged. It was at this time that his sense of guilt at what he saw as British and French duplicity in regard to the political aspirations of the Arabs drove him to write the message, drafted but not sent, which follows. The letters that follow, written after the seizure of Akaba and his crucial meeting with Allenby, show him to all intents and purposes back in total control. In particular his letters to Clayton suggest a man in full grip of the situation, dealing professionally and confidently with everything from strategy to supplies, mindful of the smallest detail which might bring future advantage. His letters home are buoyant and cheerful; the campaign may be the 'maddest' ever run, but it will be 'imperishable fun to look back upon' (27 August). Only to Leeds — as he would also to Vyvyan Richards in the following year — does he present a different face.

BRIGADIER-GENERAL CLAYTON
[June 1917]

Clayton. I've decided to go off alone to Damascus, hoping to get killed on the way: for all sakes try and clear up this show before it goes further. We are calling them to fight for us on a lie, and I can't stand it.[1]

British Library

COLONEL C. E. WILSON
30th July, 1917   *JEDDAH*

On July 29th the Sherif sent a message asking me to come and see him and in the course of a long private conversation he gave me his views of

1 This message, found heavily pencilled over in one of Lawrence's wartime diaries and deciphered under special lighting and magnification, has been previously quoted by J. M. Wilson (who found it) in *Minorities*, p. 33, and John E. Mack, *A Prince of Our Disorder*, p. 182. Lawrence was using an army signal pad at this time to scribble various diary notes and the message is written as though it were a normal signal; second thoughts evidently brought about his attempt to destroy it. It is relevant to two much discussed subjects: first, his sense of guilt arising from his belief that the Arabs were fighting on the basis of promises of independence which the Allies did not intend to keep; and second, the daring reconnaissance journey which he undertook to Damascus through enemy-held territory in June 1917, for which he received the unstinting admiration of his military superiors but about which he afterwards said or wrote very little. The Arab historian Suleiman Mousa considers the journey, and the report which followed it (published as *DG* 97) fabrications. However, none of Lawrence's colleagues at the time saw any reason to doubt his account of the distances he had allegedly covered or the discussions with tribal and other leaders he claimed to have held. This unsent message raises the possibility of a more credible interpretation of his reticence about this disputed journey: that he undertook it in a disturbed state of mind more concerned about his own attitudes than the task in hand. Lawrence refers to the journey in *Seven Pillars of Wisdom*, Chapter XLVIII; the published account omits, however, an important passage which occurs in the draft version of the book printed privately for him by the *Oxford Times*: 'Accordingly on this march I took risks with the set hope of proving myself unworthy to be the Arab assurance of final victory. A bodily wound would have been a grateful vent for my internal perplexities, a mouth through which my troubles might have found relief.'

the Sykes-Picot Mission.[1] The main points were that he had altogether refused to permit any French annexation of Beyrout and the Lebanon. 'They are Arab countries but I will neither take them myself nor permit anyone else to take them. They have deserved independence and it is my duty to see they get it.'

He said that he refused a detailed discussion of boundaries, on the grounds that hostilities between Turkey and the Allies still continue, and all decisions taken now would necessarily have to be modified in accordance with the actual results of military operations, for which he must have an absolutely free hand. 'If advisable we will pursue the Turks to Constantinople and Erzeroum [*sic*] – so why talk about Beyrout, Aleppo, and Hail.'

He is extremely pleased to have trapped M. Picot into the admission that France will be satisfied in Syria with the position Great Britain desires in Iraq. That he says, means a temporary occupation of the country for strategical and political reasons (with probably an annual grant to the Sherif in compensation and recognition) and concessions in the way of public works. 'I was ready without being asked to guard their interests in the existing railways, and assist their schools: but the Hedjaz and Syria are like the palm and fingers of one hand, and I could not have consented to the amputation of any finger or part of a finger without leaving myself a cripple.'

In conclusion the Sherif remarked on the shortness and informality of conversations, the absence of written documents, and the fact that the only change in the situation caused by the meeting, was the French renunciation of the ideas of annexation, permanent occupation, or suzerainty of any part of Syria – 'but this we did not embody in a formal treaty, as the war is not finished. I merely read out my acceptance of the formula "as the British in

---

1 Grand Sherif Hussein, by this time self-proclaimed king of the Hejaz, had just been visited by Sir Mark Sykes and M. Georges Picot, co-devisers of the Sykes-Picot Agreement of 1916, whereby the Allies (including at this stage Russia) secretly colluded over the disposition of the territories of the Ottoman Empire after the war. Included in the agreement was the proposal that France should have a dominant interest in Syria, while Britain had a dominant interest in Mesopotamia (Iraq).

Iraq" proposed to me by M. Picot, since Sir Mark Sykes assured me that it would put a satisfactory conclusion to the discussion.'

T. E. Lawrence, Capt.[2]

TNA: PRO FO 882/12

HIS MOTHER
12.8.17   *ARAB BUREAU SAVOY HOTEL CAIRO*

This is only a note, to catch what I believe is a post. I'm sending some photographs in hope that they will arrive: of course they are not mine, but some R.F.C.[1] people who had taken them sent me copies. I've sent you a lot, one time and another, but I don't suppose many get through. I cannot send any enlargements, for printing paper is scarce.

Went down to Jidda a month ago, and saw Feisul at Wejh, and the Sherif himself at Jidda, and discussed things with them. Results satisfactory on the whole. I had never met the Sherif himself before, and liked him exceedingly: a very simple straightforward old man, clever enough too, but knowing so little. Upon us as a people is the responsibility of having made him a ruling power, and he is pitifully unfit for the rough and tumble of forming a new administration out of the ruins of the Turkish system. We will have to help

2 This report was despatched on the following day to the high commissioner for Egypt, Sir Reginald Wingate, with an accompanying letter by Colonel Wilson, marked SECRET, in which he wrote: 'I have the honour to forward herewith for Your Excellency's information a note by Captain Lawrence on a private conversation he had with the Sherif on July 29th.' What concerned Wilson, rightly as events turned out, was his 'fear of a misunderstanding' on the part of the Sherif 'as to what was, or what was not, agreed upon at the meeting between Sir Mark Sykes, Monsieur Picot and the Sherif'. Certainly the idea that the French would be content with a transient relationship with Syria was an erroneous one; indeed the repercussions of Sykes-Picot were not only to cause much disaffection and dismay to the Arabs later but were in addition crucial in forming Lawrence's ambivalent attitude to the Arab struggle. The report is also a significant pointer to Lawrence's role at this time; the fact that, although only a captain, he was invited to a private conversation with the senior figure on the Arab side suggests that he was seen as the Arabs' best interlocutor among the British officers attached to the revolt, through whom Hussein's words would reach high places.

1 Royal Flying Corps.

him and his sons, and of the sons only Feisul and Zeid will play square to us. Abdulla is an intriguer, and poor Sidi Ali, the eldest son is a religious fanatic, and will be the tool of evil spirits. I do hope we play them fair.

I'm now going back to Akaba to look round at the country there: will start about the 16th from here. The average length of my last five visits to Cairo has been about 5 days! However it is more restful in Arabia, because one feels so nervous of what may happen if one goes away.

I cannot ask for leave, as I know there is so much to do down there, and no one to do it. If I asked I would probably get it, but it would not be right at present. If ever things get safe there, it will be possible to rest. You know there are very few of us on the job.

N.

About writing: – please try to realise that one's thoughts for nearly two years have been fixed on one object. We have realised part of the scheme, & the situation is critical but hopeful. In the circumstances one has become a monomaniac, unable to do or think about anything else – and of the one thing I cannot write to you.

N.

HL/Bodleian Library

BRIGADIER-GENERAL GILBERT CLAYTON
[Undated: ? between 23 and 27 August 1917]   [AKABA]

General Clayton
Please excuse the ink: I'm writing under difficulties.

When we reached Akaba on Aug. 17 I found that one caravan of bombs had already gone to Kuntilla, and a second was just leaving. I arranged with Sherif Nasir[1] to send the balance next day, and on the 21st I went to Kuntilla myself, & saw the dump in position and the landing sign out. Ten Ageyl, under Shawish Daoud are holding the police post there pending the arrival of the aeroplanes.

---

1 Sherif Nasir of Medina, a leading figure on the Arab side, commander of the Akaba expedition and of the Arab entry into Damascus.

On the way to Kuntilla we met 14 parties of Beduins from both sides of the old Turk-Egyptian border, coming in to Akaba to salute Sherif Nasir. I think it all points to a decided move of Sinai opinion towards the Sherif, & away from the Turk. Nasir and Feisul are trying to persuade them that their new orientation involves friendship with the British. The Arabs seem rather prejudiced however.

Please tell Captain G. Lloyd that Jeddua ibn Sufi is being sounded in the sense agreed upon between us.

Sergt. 'Lewis' and Corporal 'Stokes'[2] are doing most excellent work training their Beduin in gun & machine gun work. I think the results will be very good. Would you please inform Major Hulton (O.B. G.H.Q.)[3] that I wish to keep them a little longer, since the training is not complete.

There is no news from the Guwaira area. A Turkish cavalry patrol visited Delagha, but was driven out with some loss by the Bedu, who have recently sent 40 captured mules here. I should not be astonished by a Turk occupation of Delagha, with a view towards Gharandel, to cut us off from W. Musa.

Jaafar Pasha[4] is taking over Akaba defence, which involves the maintenance of posts at Guwaira & Gharandel, Ghadian, etc. This sets free the Abu Tayu for extended raiding.

Please tell Major Lefroy that the Receiving set picks up Cairo easily, using the raised aerial. The ground aerial is not acute enough. The *Humber*[5] also picks up his messages to me. As his code is much safer than any Naval cipher, I would like disguised Y wires sent to me in his code for preference. I will not wire back in it, unless absolutely necessary. W. T.[6] from Akaba to Egypt is not good. The *Humber* cannot call anything in Egypt. I wonder if Major Lefroy

---

2 'Their names may have been Yells and Brooke, but became Lewis and Stokes after their jealously-loved tools.' (*Seven Pillars*, Chapter LX) Yells, who was Australian, was a sergeant-intructor in the Lewis gun: Brook (not Brooke) was an instructor, later also a sergeant, in the Stokes trench-mortar.

3 Ordnance Branch, General Headquarters.

4 Jaafar Pasha was a Baghdadi officer who had served in the German and Turkish armies; captured by the British and on parole in Cairo (following an escape in which he had been injured) he volunteered to serve on the Allied side when he heard of the outbreak of the Arab Revolt. He later served as minister of defence and prime minister under Feisal when the latter was king of Iraq, and was assassinated in 1935.

5 *H.M.S. Humber* was a monitor (*i.e.* a warship built principally for bombardment of enemy shore defences), described by Clayton in a letter to Lieutenant-Colonel Joyce as 'the main defence of the place [*i.e.* Akaba], commanding as she does, with her gun-fire, the whole of the available water' (18 September 1917: *TNA: PRO FO 882/7*).

6 W.T.: Wireless Telegraphy.

could suggest anything. They can work up to 1000 metres length, on a 3 kilowatt power, but have a very low aerial. I have given Lieut. Feilding £2 from my secret service money. He will return this to you in Cairo.

Colonel Wilson arranged with Sherif Feisul to get him an extra £25000 by the first ship, from the £200000 grant. I hope this will be enough for the present. The £1000 bag in Major Cornwallis' safe might be sent as part of this.

Sherif Feisul is anxious to get here the prisoners willing to join his army from the P.O.W. camp in Egypt. He asks for them without equipment or extra training. Nessib el Bekri,[7] going to Egypt on *Hardinge*[8], can bring the draft down. I hope this question may be settled in this way – or that the Bekris after trying the men, may report 'none willing'.

Feisul suggests that the Egyptian Red Crescent might send a commission, or funds, for the relief of Syrians deported to Asia Minor. He has reason to believe that they are badly treated. Do you think it would be possible to arrange this?

Auda abu Tayi wants a set of false teeth.[9] The ship's doctors question their ability to cast his mouth in wax. Could a dental assistant be sent down from Egypt to do what is possible here? For all reasons it is not desirable to let Auda go away to Egypt for long.

T E Lawrence

TNA: PRO FO 882/7

7 Nessib el Bekri (also spelled Nesib or Nasib by Lawrence) is described in *Seven Pillars*, (Chapter XXIV) as 'a Damascene land-owner, and Feisal's host in Syria (*i.e.* during Feisal's stay in Damascus before the Revolt), now exiled from his country with a death-sentence over him'. He served on Feisal's staff. He and Lawrence did not always see eye to eye; they had, for example, clashed over the purpose of the Akaba expedition. *See Seven Pillars*, Chapter XLVIII.

8 *H.M.S. Hardinge* was an armed Royal India Mail steamer attached to the Red Sea Fleet and used to transport troops and supplies.

9 Auda abu Taya, legendary chief of the Howeitat, who had ridden with Lawrence to Akaba, had smashed his previous set of false teeth because they were Turkish. *See Seven Pillars*, Chapter XXXVIII.

His Mother
27.8.17   [AKABA]

This is written in a tent full of flies at Akaba, and the boat is leaving this afternoon. There is as usual nothing to say. I got here on the 17th of August, and found all as I had left it, except that my milk-camel has run dry: a nuisance this, because it will take me time to find another. I have too much to do, little patience to do it with, and yet things are going tolerably well. It is much more facile doing daily work as a cog of a machine, than it is running a campaign by yourself. However it's the maddest campaign ever run, which is saying quite a little lot, and if it ever works out to a conclusion will be imperishable fun to look back upon. For the moment it is heavy and slow, weary work, with no peace for the unfortunate begetter of it anywhere.

Newcombe is in Egypt ill; (nerves mostly). I've lost sight of everybody else. By the way I have returned to the Egypt Expeditionary Force, and should properly have no more to do with the Arab Bureau: but so eccentric a show as ours is doesn't do anything normal. Wherefore please address me as before, and don't put any fancy letters before or after my name. These things are not done by my intention, and therefore one can hardly count them.

I'm very glad you saw Mr. Hogarth. He will have probably given you a better idea than anyone else could give you of what we are really trying at. It consists of making bricks without straw or mud: – all right when it is a hobby, as with me, but vexatious for other people asked to do it as a job. By the way isn't it odd that (bar school), which was part nightmare & part nuisance, everything I've done has been first hobby and then business. It's an odd fortune, which no one else could say, because everybody else plays games. It was a mercy that I broke my leg long ago, and settled to sit down the rest of my days.

Tell Arnie never to use an adjective that does not properly express what he means: slang reduces one to a single note, which is fatal.

N.

Some stamps enclosed.

HL/Bodleian Library

BRIGADIER-GENERAL GILBERT CLAYTON
27.8.17   [*AKABA*]

General Clayton

The *Race Fisher* is leaving for Egypt today, and I am writing to you again, since I may not have another opportunity for post for some time. The situation here has not changed in any way. I have stayed on in Akaba at Feisul's request, since he is altogether overwhelmed by the crowd of visitors, the new conditions, and the local difficulties arising. He is in very poor health, which makes things difficult.

Operations

The Abu Tayi[1] are owed two months' wages. Till they receive this we can hardly ask them to undertake a new job. However they will be the first charge on the funds the *Hardinge* is bringing, and we will then undertake the Railway between Maan and Mudowwara. There are seven waterless stations here, and I have hope that with the Stokes and Lewis guns we may be able to do something fairly serious to the line. If we can make a big break I will do my best to maintain it, since the need for shutting down Wejh altogether is becoming urgent.

As soon as the Railway attack is begun a force of 'regulars' will enter the Shobek-Kerak hills, & try to occupy them.

If these operations are part-successful, the Turkish force at Fuweileh[2] will probably be withdrawn, or reduced, and our position at Akaba then becomes safe. We cannot attack Fuweileh, and its retention in force by the Turks after the rains would be serious. At the same time I have little fear of anything unfortunate happening, since by extended threats on the Railway we can force the Turks to increase their forces there, and I believe that the Hejaz line is already working to full capacity to support the troops now between Deraat and Medain Salih. For this reason I do not think they can at once defend it, & attack Akaba on the necessary scale.

Captain MacIndoe[3] has shown me a report he has written on the local military situation. The facts are, I think, correctly stated, but he appears to overrate the man-power factor in this area. I have found hitherto that questions of Railway capacity, traffic conditions, camels, water and roads count for far more than the

1 *I.e.* Auda's men.
2 A Turkish-held block-house some fifty miles northeast of Akaba, near the important railway strong point of Maan.
3 Captain J. D. MacIndoe, Scots Guards, had been appointed as general staff officer (G.S.O.3), Hejaz Operations, in January 1917.

quantity or quality of troops on each side. To send the Camel Corps down to Akaba at present, and to attack the Railway with it, would, I am convinced, subtract from the Sherif such Beduin as are helping him now, and involve almost a certainty of conflict between the Arabs and our camel corps. One squabble between a trooper and an Arab, or an incident with Beduin women, would bring on general hostilities. An Arab victory next month, or an Arab defeat, might modify their present attitude. In the latter case (as in the Rabegh question) it might be too late to prevent disaster: but I would prefer personally to run this risk rather than incur the certainty of trouble by bringing down Imperial troops now. If Imperial troops are sent, to carry out an offensive against the Railway, sufficient supports must be sent to hold their L. of C.[4] in view of the probability of Beduin raids against them, and the Wadi Itm is not an easy line to guarantee in such case. However I take it that no modification of the policy agreed upon in Cairo will be decided upon, without my being given an opportunity of putting forward my views in detail.[5]

Supplies
This is a very difficult question just now. Feisul is dealing with it as vigorously as possible, and it may be modified by a success in the Kerak hills. It seems however as if we had underrated the local requirements. A list of the inscribed Beduin camel men was brought in yesterday, complete, and amounted to 22000 men. I have not seen a quarter of this total, and the lists are being revised today. I will send the new total if finished before the steamer ~~sails~~ steams. The true number will not be known till pay-day. Besides the men now inscribed there are hundreds (almost thousands) of others coming in daily. The slide of Arabs towards the Sherif was obvious when Nasir was here, and has become immense, almost impossible, since Feisul arrived. He is unable even to see all the head sheikhs of the newcomers. All have to be fed while here, and for the return journey, & the imposition (quite unavoidable) is very serious.

In addition to the rations of the fighting men the Howeitat point out that their families are starving. Feisul tells them to go & buy food for them, & they retort that there is nothing for sale in Akaba. If flour, rice and coffee & sugar were for sale here we could turn over thousands per week: it would save a huge waste of rations and simplify the supply question generally. I know that the transport is a difficulty almost insurmountable, but if by any chance an extraordinary call of

4 L. of C.: Line of Communication.
5 Two companies of the Imperial Camel Corps *were* used for a specific limited operation against the Hejaz Railway a year later in August 1918.

the Khedival line from Jedda could be arranged for Akaba it would be a great relief. Feisul says there are many Jidda merchants with foodstuff for sale who would come here at once. At present, thanks to Nasir's having had to give rations to the Arabs' families there remain in store at Akaba 531 bags of flour, & 812 of rice, only. There is enough coffee and sugar, and 863 bags of barley, which is good – but the flour will hardly last us till the September amounts arrive, unless they arrive punctually. It is now impossible to supply the up-country troops, and in consequence Ibn Nueir, Gasim abu Dumeig, and Mifleh abu Rikeiba, with their Arabs, have had to go in to Maan to surrender to the Turks. They went unwillingly, but it is rather a blow to the Arab prestige up at Guweira.

The August allowance, which was I believe calculated on 10000 heads, proves to have been just right, so far as the Howeitat are concerned. What is breaking down the situation is

(a) the need of keeping a reserve till the September allowance is notified

(b) the arrival here of Sherif Maalla with Shadli Alayan

(c) the visitors from the North.

(a) is unavoidable, till a reserve dump can be established under Captain Goslett[6] here (b) means 2000 extra mouths, (c) is an indefinite and floating quantity, at present in the neighbourhood of 2500 a day, but liable to irregular increase. I am afraid the provision of food on sale, promptly, at Akaba will appear to you too difficult to establish. Its great value, to me, would be that we would have an immediate touchstone to show whether the present apparent need is real or not. The Howeitat swear they are starving, & produce piteous evidences of it: but I suspect a good deal of it is mere begging, as they know that any food that they may extract this way will be gratis. I doubt their spending very much of their wages on food, if it was for sale at a stiff price. There is no doubt though, that the strangers would, since they are in real want.

Jaafar Pasha[7]

Is on the whole fairly sensible, I think, & shows more comprehension of the Arab point of view than any of the other Syrian officers. Captain MacIndoe criticises his force rather bitterly, but their real object is not so much to engage Turkish forces on equal terms, as to stiffen the Beduin resistance, by providing the comforting spectacle of a trained reserve, and to impress the Turks with the

6 Captain, later Major, Raymond Goslett was supply officer at Akaba, having performed a similar function earlier at Wejh: 'the London business man who had made chaotic Wejh so prim'. (*Seven Pillars*, Chapter LVII)

7 *See* previous letter to Clayton, p. 121, footnote 4.

fact that behind the Beduin screen lies an unknown quantity, which must be disposed of before they can conquer Akaba. The Turkish C. in C. cannot risk arriving here with less than 2000 men, because Jaafar has 2000 men: their quality, so long as it is not proved bad by premature action, has of necessity to be estimated by the Turks as good. Of course it would be nice and much simpler for us if the Arab movement emerged from the bluff-and-mountain-pass stage, and became a calculable military problem: but it hasn't yet, & isn't likely to. Jaafar's force is serving its moral purpose admirably, & if he can find reliable officers to handle the men tactfully & improve their discipline, it may become of practical value in the near future. Most of the Syrian officers are such blind prejudiced fools.

I don't think that any appreciation of the Arab situation will be of much use to you, unless its author can see for himself the difference between a national rising and a campaign.

I'm writing to Cornwallis for some trifles for Sherifs & Sheikhs. I have asked for such things before, and will have to again. The cost will never be very large, and even if it was, and I spent say 5% of the Syrian grant on these private supplies, yet I fancy it would pay me. We want the Arabs to keep step with our tune in this next affair, and to do that they must (or their heads must) dance when we pipe. This means being on easy terms with them all. Please explain, if necessary, to E.E.F.[8] that a gold watch may sometimes carry further than a hundred rifles.

T E Lawrence

TNA: PRO FO 882/7

COLONEL C. E. WILSON
2.9.17   [*AKABA*]

The Hejaz show is a quaint one, the like of which has hardly been on earth before, and no one not of it can appreciate how difficult it is to run. However it has gone forward, and history will call it a success: but I hope that the difficulties it has had to contend with will be equally clear. All my memories of it are pleasant (largely due to you,[1] of course, for on the face things should

8 The Egyptian Expeditionary Force: *i.e.* the main Allied army under General Allenby.

1 Notwithstanding the criticism of some of his biographers, Lawrence was always ready to acknowledge the part which others played in the revolt.

not be so), and if ever I can get my book on it out, I'll try to make other people see it.[2] They do not seem always to appreciate that while we hop about the Railway and places smashing things up, and enjoying ourselves, someone else has to sit and stew in Jidda keeping the head of the affair on the rails. You would be glad to hear sometimes how Feisul and the rest speak of you. [...]

DG

HIS PARENTS
5.9.17   *AKABA*

Got a letter of August 9 from you, which shows you never got a letter I sent you some time in July (12th I think) telling you what had happened on the way to Akaba. As a matter of fact it was a poor sort of letter, because I was rather doubtful how much to say. Either I said too much, or the ship sank.

I'm now off for a trip inland, lasting for about 3 weeks I expect, so this is the end of letters for the time being: indeed it's only as camels are late that I can write this anyhow.

Since July 10, when I got to Egypt from Akaba I have been to Wejh, Jidda, Yenbo, Akaba, up country, back to Egypt, to Alexandria, up to Akaba again, up country, back, & am now going up again – So you see it is a mobile sort of life, this.

Tell Mother they asked for that twopenny thing she likes, but fortunately didn't get it.[1] All these letters & things are so many nuisances afterwards, & I'll never wear or use any of them. Please don't, either. My address is simply T.E.L., no titles please.

In reply to Father's query, Yes, I have boils, lots of them. They began in March, & will go on till I have time to get to Egypt and be inoculated. Only I am usually too rushed in Cairo to get anything of my own done. Am very fit and cheerful enough when things are not too hectic. Going up country is always a relief, because then there is only one thing at a time to do.

2 Evidence that Lawrence was already contemplating writing the book which would eventually emerge as *Seven Pillars of Wisdom*.

1 He had been recommended for a Victoria Cross on account of his reconnaissance journey through Syria but was appointed a C.B. (Companion of the Order of the Bath), Military Division, instead.

Is Elsie Hutchins married?[2] I have had a letter signed Elsie, & think it must be from her. Will you get me Janet's address again, I've lost it?[3]

Cheque enclosed for £300. Will you ask Father to invest it for me? I can't do anything out here: Ask him to put it in the most obvious thing, without troubling himself – or keep it, if you want money.

Am off now.

N.

HL/Bodleian Library

HIS MOTHER
Sept. 24 1917   *AKABA*

Writing to you isn't very hopeful, since it is clear that you never get any of my letters. However I'll go on doing it, and some day one may get through. Would you like me to have a weekly telegram sent from Cairo telling you all well? I could arrange it easily enough. It's really a little serious that you should have received no letters between my wires. I sent the second one when I got back to Egypt from a visit to the Hejaz, because I had just had a note to say you had had no letters for two months, or some odd time.

By the way have any of my letters ever been opened by censor?

I'm now back in Akaba, after having had a little trip up country to the Railway, for the last fortnight. We met all sorts of difficulties, mostly political, but in the end bagged two locomotives and blew them up, after driving out the troops behind them. It was the usual Arab show, done at no cost to us, expensive for the Turks, but not decisive in any way, as it is a raid and not a sustained operation.[1]

---

2 Elsie Hutchins had been a near neighbour and playmate of the Lawrence boys in Oxford days: her married name was Ryman.

3 Janet Laurie: *see* letter home of 22.7.16.

---

1 Lawrence's official report describing this 'show' was printed in edition 65 of the *Arab Bulletin* under the title 'The Raid at Haret Ammar'. The *Bulletin* added a footnote on Turkish casualties, to the effect that the Turks admitted losing 27 killed and 42 wounded. The following two letters also include descriptions of the event, that to E. T. Leeds – in peaceful faraway Oxford – being markedly different in tone from the distinctly jaunty account to Stirling.

There are few people alive who have damaged railways as much as I have at any rate. Father may add this to the qualifications that I will possess for employment after the war! However, seriously, do remember that thanks to him I'm now independent, so far as money is concerned, of any employment whatever, and therefore I'll get back on to that printing-press scheme as soon as I am free. After all, you can't say that I haven't seen something of the world by now, and I can honestly say that I have never seen anyone doing anything so useful as the man who prints good books.

So don't worry about my future – and for my present don't put either Major or C.B. or any other letters (past present or future) after my name when writing to me. These sorts of things are only nuisances to a person with £250 a year, & the intention of not having more, and the less they are used the better. I'm sending back all private letters so addressed.

Do you remember a very light dusty-amber silk cloak I brought back with me once from Aleppo? If it is not in use, I would be very glad to have it sent to me. Arab clothes are hard to find now-a-days, with manufacture and transport thrown out of gear.

I got a letter from Bob the other day & news that Arnie has been excused responsions.[2] Also it proves that the anonymous thanks for a carpet was Elsie Hutchins! I'm glad she is married.

Do you know I have not written a private letter to anyone but you for over a year? It is a wonderful thing to have kept so free of everything. Here am I at thirty with no label and no profession and perfectly quiet. I'm more grateful to Father than I can say.

N.

HL/Bodleian Library

2. Responsions: qualifying examinations for entry into Oxford University.

E. T. LEEDS[1]
Sept 24. '17   *AKABA*

Dear Leeds

I'm sorry, but I felt the usual abrupt beginning would be too much for your nerves, and that you would fall exhausted on to the floor of your gallery, without even a Turkish carpet to break the shock of my writing at last. What can have happened? I was pondering last night how for a year I had written no private letter (except to my people, and those don't count, for my mails are sunk or censored!) and today I go and break the habit. Perhaps it's because it was a habit, and I'm getting old and stiff (not to say tired, for every year out in Arabia counts ten) and habits must be nipped in their shells.

I'm in Akaba for two days – that for me spells civilisation, though it doesn't mean other than Arab togs and food, but it means you lunch where you dined, and not further on – and therefore happy. The last stunt has been a few days on the Hejaz Railway, in which I potted a train with two engines (oh, the Gods were kind) and we killed superior numbers, and I got a good Baluch prayer-rug and lost all my kit, and nearly my little self.

I'm not going to last out this game much longer: nerves going and temper wearing thin, and one wants an unlimited account of both. However while it lasts it's a show between Gilbert and Carroll, and one can retire on it, with that feeling of repletion that comes after a hearty meal. By the way hearty meals are like the chopped snow that one scatters over one's bowl of grapes in Damascus at midsummer. Ripping, to write about –

This letter isn't going to do you much good, for the amount of information it contains would go on a pin's head and roll about. However it's not a correspondence, but a discourse held with the only person to whom I have ever written regularly, and one whom I have shamefully ill-used by not writing to more frequently. On a show so narrow and voracious as this one loses one's past and one's balance, and becomes hopelessly self-centred. I don't think I ever think except about shop, and I'm quite certain I never do anything else. That must be my excuse for dropping everyone, and I hope when the nightmare ends that I will wake up and become alive again. This killing and killing of Turks is horrible. When you charge in at the finish and find them all over the place in bits, and still alive many of them, and know that you have done hundreds in the same way before and must do hundreds more if you can. [...]
DG

1 Published in *DG* but without disclosing Leeds's name: he was described as 'A Friend'.

MAJOR W. F. STIRLING[1]
25 September 1917   *AKABA*

Dear Stirling

Very many thanks! Though I think people are prone to ascribe to me what the Arabs do (very efficiently, if oddly) on their own. I have a heavenly temper, great natural modesty, and the art of window-dressing (the last sentence is composed for the benefit of Holdich.[2] Please read it to him, and ask him who is meant!)

Seriously, the Arabs put up a surprisingly good show, and as the only Englishman and historian, I get more than my share of notoriety. I don't think it my fault. One must send in a report, and what more is to be done?

The report you ask to see. As a matter of fact I handed it to Clayton whose eyebrows went high (some of it was comic, some scurrilous, some betrayed horrible secrets) and who sat on it. I don't think anyone in the Savoy[3] ever saw it, whole. It certainly never went to H.C. or W.O. or F.O.,[4] and I'm too tender-hearted to ask after it now. It was a MS document of three pages, and compressed two months march into it: rather dull, except to one who knew Syrian politics.[5] A note I scribbled in the train on a mounted scrap we had, near Maan, appeared (with cuts) in the *Arab Bulletin*, about No. 57, or 58. I haven't it by me, but old Cornwallis would show it to you if you ever got to Cairo: or G. Lloyd, or Nugent.

It is all ancient history now. The last stunt was the hold up of a train. It had two locomotives, and we gutted one with an electric mine. This rather jumbled up the trucks, which were full of Turks shooting at us. We had a Lewis, and flung bullets through the sides. So they hopped out and took cover

---

1 Stirling was about to join the Sherifian forces in the desert, his principal task, to quote his autobiography *Safety Last*, being that of building 'a proper Arab Army, a force composed of Iraqis, Palestinians and Syrians, most of whom were released prisoners of war'. Stirling was to be chief staff officer. He remained in the Arabian war-theatre for the rest of the war and entered Damascus with Lawrence in October 1918.

2 Lieutenant-Colonel G. W. Holdich: a staff officer in Cairo with whom Lawrence did not see eye to eye. *See Seven Pillars*, Chapter VII.

3 The Hotel Savoy, Cairo, housed British Military Headquarters.

4 H. C., W. O., F. O.: High Commissioner, War Office, Foreign Office.

5 The report referred to is that describing the Akaba expedition and Lawrence's reconnaissance journey into northern Syria in June 1917. It is printed in *DG*, and also in Garnett's *Selected Letters* and his *Essential T. E. Lawrence*. A typed copy of the original is held in The National Archives (formerly the Public Record Office) in *FO 882/16*.

behind the embankment, and shot at us between the wheels, at 50 yards. Then we tried a Stokes gun, and two beautiful shots dropped right in the middle of them. They couldn't stand that (12 died on the spot) and bolted away to the East across a 100 yard belt of open sand into some scrub. Unfortunately for them the Lewis covered the open stretch. The whole job took ten minutes, and they lost 70 killed, 30 wounded, 80 prisoners and about 25 got away. Of my hundred Howeitat and two British NCO's there was one (Arab) killed, and four (Arabs) wounded.

The Turks then nearly cut us off as we looted the train, and I lost some baggage, and nearly myself. My loot is a superfine red Baluch prayer-rug.

I hope this sounds the fun it is. The only pity is the sweat to work them up, and the wild scramble while it lasts. It's the most amateurish, Buffalo Billy sort of performance, and the only people who do it well are the Bedouin. Only you will think it heaven, because there aren't any returns, or orders, or superiors, or inferiors; no doctors, no accounts, no meals, and no drinks.

Yours ever
T. E. Lawrence

Give my salaams to Holdich, and tell him to sprint, or we'll be in Damascus first.

J. M. Wilson/University of Texas

The following letter to Clayton was written as Lawrence was about to set off on one of his most important operations: a raid deep into enemy territory, the principal purpose of which was, at Allenby's request, to blow up a key bridge in the Yarmuk Valley (just east of the Sea of Galilee) which carried the railway line linking the Hejaz Railway with the Palestinian coast. The attempt, on the night of 8 November, did not succeed, as the subsequent letter to Colonel Joyce makes clear; but the letter does not make clear the extent of his disappointment at letting down his chief. *See Seven Pillars,* Chapter LXXVI in which the page describing the *débâcle* is headed 'THE CUP SLIPS' and which ends with the statement: 'Our minds were sick with failure, and our bodies tired after nearly a hundred miles over bad country in bad conditions, between sunset and sunset, without halt or food.' After compensating for this major setback with attacks on the railway, the raiding force retired to Azrak, the ancient Arab fort and oasis in the desert to the east of Amman.

BRIGADIER-GENERAL GILBERT CLAYTON
24.10.17   *AKABA*

Dear General Clayton

A hurried note because I leave today at 2 p.m. and everything is still undone.

About Arab Legion.[1] Feisal will believe himself let down if they do not come by *Hardinge*. Their training is not so important as the prevention of this. Also the cholera trouble is a new reason for putting into Akaba at once as many reinforcements as you can.

The same applies to the Armoured Cars.[2] Even if everything is unfinished about them, something should come down in the *Hardinge*. They will be a great comfort here, and there are probably going to be panics and attacks by the Arabs from here soon.

Please send Izzet el Mukaddam to Akaba by *Hardinge*. He is wanted in the North.

I asked for nine exploders: only four have been sent, so I have had to rearrange plans somewhat. If others are available, they would be very useful. Also about the cable. I received at first 400 yards thick single cable (doubled this makes 200 yards of line) and after using it wired for 1000 yards light twin cable. You sent 500 yards of the old thick single in reply. Then I came up to G.H.Q. and saw you & Gen. Manifold, chose two good light wires, & asked for 4000 yards of them. In reply you have sent 650 yards of the old thick single line. The total length received is therefore only 1500 yards (750 when doubled) which is not enough for the 6 exploders in Akaba, or for the five more on order when they arrive: – and this thick single cable really hampers one seriously. Of course if there is no other we will make it do.

Then about Indian mountain guns. The two for Nuri[3] were never sent. Please send four now, for Feisul. We can use them on Bedouin raids, and so keep our remaining E.A.Q.F. guns for the regulars. I hope they may be put on the *Hardinge*.

The remainder of the special grant will no doubt have been sent off before this letter comes. Nasir & Zeid[4] (when he gets to Akaba – Colonel Wilson

---

1 The Arab Legion was a force raised from Arab prisoners-of-war who had been members of the Turkish Army.

2 The (British) Hejaz Armoured Car Company was to play an important part in the campaign in 1918; its members were listed by name in Appendix I of *Seven Pillars*.

3 Nuri Said was chief of staff to General Jaafar, the commander of Feisal's regular force. He was later to serve as prime minister of Iraq no fewer than fourteen times and to lose his life when Feisal's grandson, Feisal II, was overthrown in 1958.

4 Zeid: King Hussein's youngest son.

misreading a telegram from Cairo thought Akaba was blockaded & no one might land!) will bring it North with them on the 31st.

Colonel Wilson is writing to you about the £25,000 Wejh money taken off by Feisul at Akaba. The sight of £45,000 going into Wejh that month, to pay the Billi, was too much for us. I think we made better use of the £25,000 here!

I am taking Lieut. Wood, R. E. with me up country: It makes for insurance in case of accident on the job.

It's not my job – but I hope that Basset's appointment in Jedda is only temporary. G. L. will be back soon, & will give you all news we have.[5]

Yours sincerely
T. E. Lawrence

HL/Bodleian Library

COLONEL PIERCE JOYCE[1]
13.11.17   [*AZRAK*]

Dear Joyce
Please tell Feisul we rode to El Jefer, and found Zaal and the Abu Tayi afraid to come with us. Sherif Ali[2] and Auda did their best to work them up, but they were not for it. The Abu Tayi have almost revolted against Auda, and I doubt whether we shall see much more good from them: they have seen too much good from us.

---

5 G. L. was George Lloyd. For new light on the first part of this expedition, *see Lord Lloyd and the Decline of the British Empire* by John Charmley, 1987, Chapter 9. Lloyd left on 29 October; however, as he noted in a diary of his journey, 'Lawrence said definitely that he thought it was useless and that although he did not pretend that he would not like me to come he felt that any additional individual who was not an expert at the actual demolition only added to the risk. He would like me best to go home to England for he felt that there was a risk that all his work could be ruined politically in Whitehall and he thought I could save this; failing this he would like me to rejoin him either in the north or in Kerah as soon as the bridge job was over, but he wanted me to tell Clayton that he did not want anyone else with him.'

1 Pierce Joyce was a regular officer of the Connaught Rangers; he was now based at Akaba and he and Lawrence were collaborating in organizing the Arabian campaign. Lawrence wrote later: 'It was Joyce who ran the main line of the Revolt, while I was off on raids.'

2 Sherif Ali: Ali ibn Hussein el Harith (or el Harthi), Arab commander of the expedition and close friend of Lawrence; portrayed by Omar Sharif in the film *Lawrence of Arabia*.

Thence we went to Bair, where we found Mifleh ibn Zebn. He with Fahad and Adhub ibn Zebn went with us, and did most splendidly. I think them three of the best Arab sheikhs I have met. Fahad was badly hit in the face in the train scrimmage, but will, I hope, recover.

From Bair we rode to Azrak where we met the Serahin. Sheikh Mifleh ibn Bali rode with us to the bridge, and did his best, but he and his tribe are not in it with the Beni Sakhr.

Emir Abd el Kadir came with us to Azrak, where we made the plan of attack on the bridge at Tell el Shehab. He said he would come with us, and we had no idea anything was wrong, but the same day he rode off (without warning either Ali or myself or the Arabs with us) to Salkhad, where he is still sitting. Tell Feisul I think he was afraid: much talk, and little doing, in his way. Neither Ali nor myself gave him any offence.

Tell el Shehab[3] is a splendid bridge to destroy, but those Serahin threw away all my explosive when the firing began, & so I can do nothing – If the Turks have not increased their guard we can do it later: but I am very sick at losing it so stupidly. The Bedu cannot take the bridge, but can reach it: the Indians can take it, but cannot reach it!

From Tell el Shehab we turned back to the Railway south of Deraa, and destroyed two locomotives. We must have killed about 100 Turks too. It was a most risky performance but came off all right. Little Ali is a very plucky youth, and came to my rescue on each occasion very dashingly. He will certainly get himself killed unless he continues to travel with a person as skilful and cautious as myself. Besides being in the thick of it when anything happens he keeps very good control of the Arabs on the march, and has been very decent to me – I think he is quite in the front rank of Sherifs – but he really must go easy with himself, or I will want a successor to travel with!

Please give Feisul (& Snagge)[4] any extracts you like from the report to Clayton enclosed.[5] Tell him the whole country of the Hauran fellahin is slipping towards him, and they only require arms, money and a shock to get all moving together. We can get no news of what happened at Gaza.

---

3 Tell el Shehab: the bridge in the Yarmuk Valley which was the special target of the raid. Its destruction had been requested by Allenby, so that the failure to achieve this was a deep blow to Lawrence's professionalism and pride.
4 Snagge: Captain A. L. Snagge R.N., naval commander at Akaba.
5 The report referred to was published in the *Arab Bulletin* of 16 December under the title 'A Raid'.

I think the attached might go to the Press.[6] Ali deserves a mention, for he is a very uncommon youth. My personal requests in another paper.[7]

Yours
T E Lawrence

DG

HIS MOTHER
14.11.17   *AZRAK*[1]

I wonder if you can find this place: – it's out in the desert between Deraat and Amman – and if you do find it you will think it a most improbable place to live at.

Living however is quite easy and comfortable here. We are in an old fort with stone roofs and floors, and stone doors of the sort they used in Bashan. It is a bit out of repair, but is improving in that respect every day.[2]

I do not know what its postal arrangements are like: at least they begin with about ten days on a camel of mine, and after that the ordinary risks of letters now-a-days. Your chances of getting it are therefore a little thin, it seems to me.

I go on writing and writing and it has no effect: every letter I get from you says that you have not heard from me since last time: very disheartening, since

6 The attached was a brief report, as follows: 'On November the eleventh a detachment of the Northern Army of Sherif Feisul, under the command of Sherif Ali ibn Hussein el Harith, attacked the Railway and troop trains between Deraat and Amman. Two locomotives and some coaches were completely destroyed, and a bridge blown up. The Turks lost heavily in killed and wounded. The Arabs lost seven men.'
7 Lawrence's 'personal requests' were for explosives, detonators, fuses and guns.

1 *Azrak* in Arabic means blue, doubtless a reference to the colour of its numerous lakes and pools under a clear sky.
2 For a somewhat more eloquent description of Azrak – which plainly caught Lawrence's imagination – *see Seven Pillars*, Chapter LXXV. 'Of Azrak, as of Rumm, one said *Numen inest* ['Divinity is here']. Both were magically haunted: but whereas Rumm was vast and echoing and God-like, Azrak's unfathomable silence was steeped in knowledge of wandering poets, champions, lost kingdoms, all the crime and chivalry and dead magnificence of Hira and Ghassan. Each stone or blade of it was radiant with half-memory of the luminous silky Eden, which had passed so long ago.'

writing is always a risk (if our friends get this letter they will pay me a visit) and often difficult. Meanwhile it is restful. I am staying here a few days; resting my camels, and then will have another fling. Last 'fling' was two railway engines. One burst into fragments, & the other fell on the first. Quite a successful moment!

If you see a note in print saying that 'A detachment of the N. army of Sherif Feisul etc.' Then that's me ... the rest is anonymous.

In case my last three letters have fallen through, please tell Arnie that his plan is excellent. I told the people concerned in Cairo, and either Mr. Hogarth or myself can get it arranged quite easily if the time comes. Personally I don't expect it will, but I always was an optimist.

I wonder if Gillman could make me another pair of brown shoes? There may be regulations against export, so he should find out first. I do not often wear shoes, but they come in handy sometimes in reserve. I sent you a cheque for £300 some weeks ago, and asked for Janet's address. Did you get them and if not will you let me know?

There, this letter has been 3 days in writing, & I have done all the rest of the work meanwhile.

T. E. Lawrence

HL/Bodleian Library

On 20-21 November 1917 Lawrence underwent the ordeal that was to affect him for the rest of his life: his capture, beating and rape at Deraa (as described in Chapter LXXX of *Seven Pillars*). There appears to be no wartime reference to this episode. It is, however, summarized in a report written after the war during his visit to Cairo in June 1919 (*see* Part 3, p. 174) and it is touched on, if sparingly, in his later letters: *e.g.* to Edward Garnett, 22 August 1922; to Charlotte Shaw, 26 March 1924 and 26 December 1925; to E. M. Forster, 21 December 1927. Three weeks after Deraa he was present at the official entry into Jerusalem, which was seized from the Turks in early December. His letter to Leeds after this event (15 December 1917) shows that he was beginning to realize that the war had changed his life irrevocably: 'after being a sort of king-maker one will not be allowed to go digging quietly again. Nuisance.'

HIS PARENTS
14.12.17   *THE RESIDENCY CAIRO*

Well here I am in Cairo again, for two nights, coming from Akaba via Jerusalem. I was in fortune, getting to Jerusalem just in time for the official entry of General Allenby.[1] It was impressive in its way – no show, but an accompaniment of machine gun & anti-aircraft fire, with aeroplanes circling over us continually. Jerusalem has not been taken for so long: nor has it ever fallen so tamely before. These modern wars of large armies and long-range weapons are quite unfitted for the historic battlefields.

I wrote to you last from Azrak, about the time we blew up Jemal Pasha, and let him slip away from us. After that I stayed for ten days or so there, and then rode down to Akaba in 3 days: good going, tell Arnie: none of his old horses would do so much as my old camel. At Akaba I had a few days motoring, prospecting the hills and valleys for a way Eastward for our cars: and then came up to H.Q. to see the authorities and learn the news-to-be.

Tomorrow I go off again to Akaba, for a run towards Jauf, if you know where that is. Mother will be amused to learn that they are going to send me to England for a few days in the spring, if all works well till then: this is my last trip, possibly. Don't bank on it, as the situation out here is full of surprise turns, and my finger is one of those helping to mix the pie. An odd life, but it pleases me, on the whole.

I got that little cloak all well – many thanks; the Near East used to make all these wonderful things, but the interruption of trade routes and the call of military service hamper it now, and one's needs are every day more and more difficult to meet. I'm an Emir of sorts, and have to live up to the title.

I see A[2] is getting slowly up the obstacles of many exams. They are silly things, terrible to the conscientious, but profitable to the one who can display his goods to effect, without leaving holes visible. As real tests they are illusory. So long as you can read good books in the languages they affect, that's enough for education: but it adds greatly to your pleasure if you have memory enough to remember the why & wherefore of the waxing and waning of peoples, and to trace the slow

1 Jerusalem fell to Allenby on 9 December 1917 and the official entry took place on the 11th. Lawrence's participation in the latter event was due to Allenby, who, according to *Seven Pillars*, 'was good enough, although I had done nothing for the success, to let Clayton take me along as staff officer of the day. The personal Staff tricked me out in their spare clothes till I looked like a Major of the British Army.' Lawrence appears fleetingly in the newsreel film of the occasion, a diminutive, distant but clearly recognizable figure.
2 Arnold Lawrence.

washing up & down of event upon event. In that way I think history is the only knowledge of the easy man. It seems to me that is enough of didactic.

Mr. Hogarth is here in Cairo, acting as our base of information. He is one of the people whom the Arabs would have great difficulty in doing without. The blank in knowledge when he goes back to England is always great. Pirie-Gordon[3] is coming out, to write popular articles on the Arab war for the home papers – so soon you will know all about it. Secrecy was necessary while the fight was a life and death one in the Hejaz: but since the opening of Akaba the stress has been eased, and today we are as comfortable as any front. As public sympathy is desirable, we must try and enlist on our side a favourable press. A. will be content, but must take it as said that it was quite impossible before. This show of ours began with all against it, and has had first to make itself acceptable to the elect. They converted, we can afford to appeal to a wider circle. It is not much use trying, with a J pen, to tell you how we are going to do it.

Many thanks to Father for investing that cheque of mine. When I stay out in Arabia for months on end I spend comparatively little, for the Government buys my camels, & the Sherif pays the men. I have only cloth (cheap things Arab clothes) and personal presents to pay for. On the other hand, when I get to Cairo I have many commissions, from Arab sheikhs, for things they want – and if they have been useful, or will be useful, they get them free of charge! My acquaintances are legion, or the whole population from Rabegh to Deraa, and the burden correspondingly heavy. However they have just raised my pay, by pushing me up the roll of Staff appointments. I'm now called a G.S.O.2.[4] The French Government has stuck another medal on to me: a *croix de guerre* this time. I wish they would not bother, but they never consult one before doing these things. At least I have never accepted one, and will never wear one or allow one to be conferred on me openly. One cannot do more, for these notices are published in the Press first thing, and to counter-announce that one refused it would create more publicity than the award itself. I am afraid you will be rather disgusted, but it is not my fault, and by lying low and simply not taking the things when given me, I avoid ever really getting them.

This letter should get to you about Christmas time, I suppose, as few mails have been sunk of late. That will mean that you are getting at least fortnightly letters from me, which should put off any anxiety you might otherwise feel. Mr. Hogarth of course hears of me every few days, so that his information is much fuller than anything I can ever give you.

3 C. H. C. Pirie-Gordon was an archaeologist friend from Lawrence's university days.
4 General Staff Officer, grade 2.

I'm in the proud position of having kept a diary all the year 1917. To date, it is rather a brief one, consisting only of the name of the place where I sleep the night of each day: and the best thing about it is the disclosure that ten successive nights in one place is the maximum stop in the 12 months, and the roll of places slept in is about 200. This makes it not astonishing that my Arabic is nomadic! I hope A. is getting on with his army subjects. It would be a useful thing to know how to drive a car, but judging from the papers there must be fewer cars in Oxford than in Akaba.

He should keep an eye on the illustrated papers soon. They are going to get an occasional photograph from us, to help keep the Sherif (and Feisul above all) before the public eye. The Arab Bureau have about 500 excellent prints, and so the selection may be a good one. Some of them you will probably have already had, as I remember sending you some of the best.

I'm also sending you a sheet of Hejaz 1 piastre stamps. You said you had not received any of this value. These are of course 1st edition, and are worth a good deal more than you would expect! Lady Wingate gave them to me, for of course it is impossible to find them anywhere for sale.

Here endeth this letter.

N.

HL/Bodleian Library

E. T. LEEDS
15.12.17   *THE RESIDENCY CAIRO [ERASED]*

I suppose it was because your pen was a thin one: anyhow your letter gave me an impression of London in gloom. It's what all the papers say, and is terrible.[1] I hope you are bearing up.

About stuff here. Jerusalem cheered all of us mightily. Casualties were so few, and the booty so immense. I was in the official entry, and going up there we found the whole countryside strewn with the old store-heaps

---

1 Late 1917 had been a bad time for war news: huge casualties and little territorial gain in Flanders, the Central Powers successful in Italy, Russia out of the war following the Bolshevik Revolution. The best news was from the Middle East, where the British had seized Baghdad and Jerusalem.

of the Turks. Twenty million rounds of SAA,[2] and uncounted shells. Also there are thousands of deserters, and God knows what amount of stuff looted by the villagers before we came. It is the loss of the accumulated stores of two years to them: and it will take them six months to pile up such another lot, if they can concentrate all their efforts on the job. In actual prisoners, and in killed and wounded the show was not over great – but then there were not many Turks to begin with – and very few to end with.

Commend me to ffoulkes. I heard of his Tower catalogue. I've got a trophy he would like for his War Museum.[3] The Turks took four of the short Lee Enfield rifles taken at Gallipoli, and engraved them in gold on the chamber 'Part of our booty in the battles for the Dardanelles' in a most beautiful Turkish script. Deeply cut by hand, and then gold wire beaten in. Four of these rifles were sent, one to each of the sons of the Sherif of Mecca. I carry Feisul's, which he gave me (it's a 1st Essex gun) and I'm trying to get Zeid's, which I'll send C.J.ff if I win. They form admirable gifts, tell him. Ali has one, but Abdulla's has been given to Ronald Storrs, oriental secretary to the Residency here.

The idea seemed so good that I'm doing some Turkish rifles, with inscriptions in Arabic, presents from Feisul to R.N. officers who have helped him. There will be seven of these, in all, if I complete my programme.

It's very good of you to go on helping the brutal and licentious after the B. and L. way they have treated you. I don't know why we should do things in that sort of way. Give an Easterner who is not a hereditary grandee, power, and he is a tyrant in a week. Are we the same, or is it only our stupidity? Bad men, or bad manners?

It's very nice to hear about sack-bottles and tokens again, for one is getting terribly bound up in Eastern politics, and must keep free. I've never been labelled yet, and yet I fear that they are going to call me an Arabian now. As soon as war ends I'm going to build a railway in S. America, or dig up a S. African gold-field, to emancipate myself. Carchemish will either be hostile (Turks will never let me in again) or friendly (Arab), and after being a sort of king-maker one will not

2 SAA: small arms ammunition.
3 Charles John ffoulkes (1868-1947), one-time lecturer on armour and mediaeval subjects at Oxford, was curator of the armouries of the Tower of London from 1913-35 and first curator and secretary of the Imperial War Museum (founded March 1917) from 1917-33. His 'Tower catalogue' was doubtless his *Survey and Inventory of the Tower of London*, published 1917.

be allowed to go digging quietly again. Nuisance. However the war isn't over yet, and perhaps one needn't worry one's head too soon about it.

Saw D.G.H. yesterday. All well here and there.

.L.

Bodleian Library

'Don't expect any letter from me for a time now,' he wrote to his mother on 8 January 1918. 'I'll be very busy, and quite away from touch with Egypt.' It is a keynote statement for the last year of the war, which would include his one conventional battle at Tafileh in January (fought in the hills to the south of the Dead Sea during an attempt, later abandoned, to link with Allenby's forces in the Jordan Valley); his promotion to lieutenant-colonel in March; his first encounters with Lowell Thomas, the American publicist who would ultimately convert him into 'Lawrence of Arabia' (there are, however, no references to Thomas in his war letters); and finally (the climax of two years of strenuous effort) the advance on Damascus in September-October in collaboration with Allenby's northward thrust through Palestine.

Only seven home letters have survived (he managed only one brief message between the end of March and mid-July) and his letters relating to the war are equally few and far between, though they include some of great interest. There are two important ones to Clayton, particularly that of 12 February, which is very illuminating on the matter of his perception of the nature of his role in the revolt ('I do my best to keep in the background, but cannot', etc.); and which also shows that it was he who assumed the task of persuading the most effective of all the Arab leaders, Feisal, to go along 'for the duration of the war at least' with Britain's pro-Zionist Balfour Declaration of November 1917. There are three letters to, and carefully preserved by, the governor of Beersheba, Mr A. F. Nayton, given to Lawrence's brother in 1946. In addition, there is Lawrence's only known letter written in Arabic, dated 'Ramadan 17, 1336–June 25, 1918', to none other than King Hussein of the Hejaz himself, encouraging him to continue his support and informing him: 'Had it not been for your courage in ordering Sidi Feisal to leave Medina and proceed to Wejh and Akaba, the Arab movement would not have been as completely successful as it is today.' Finally, there are two despatches from the last phase of the campaign.

HIS MOTHER
8.1.18   *AKABA*

In this country one's movements never work out as planned: in proof of that, here I am in Akaba again after quite a short excursion up country. I wrote to you last from Cairo, I fancy, and prophesied that I would be a long time away! Tomorrow perhaps we will get off about midday, to go up towards the Dead Sea, on the East side. It is beautiful country, but too hilly for pleasure. Today I'm busy buying some new riding camels, and saddles and saddle-bags.

I looked through the last few letters received, but I don't think there is anything requiring answer. Newcombe, about whom you asked, has been taken prisoner, and is now probably in Asia Minor. He was working with the army in Palestine when he was caught.[1]

Posts have been a little disorganized lately, for the last letters from England are dated November 9: however one knows that had there been anything wrong there would have been telegrams about. It is only good news which is not worth spending money on: you hear the bad too soon.

This Akaba is a curious climate. On the coast we have a typical Red Sea winter, which at its worst is like a fine October day, and at its best is like summer weather. No rain to speak of, not much wind, and persistent sunshine. If you go thirty miles up country at once you get into cold wet weather; with white frosts at night. If you go 20 miles further East you find yourself in miserable snow-drifts, and a wind sharp enough to blow through a sheepskin. Next day you are in Akaba again, and thoroughly warm.

I'm sending you a photograph or two with this letter: none of them are very interesting, but some day we may be glad of them. The Arab Bureau, to which Mr. Hogarth belongs, has a wonderful collection of Arabian photographs, of which I want a few published in the *Illustrated London News*. They include a rather impressive snap of Feisul himself, getting into a car at Wejh, and some of his bodyguard, taken by me from the saddle, as I was riding in Wadi Yenbo with them and him. It would take a great painter, of course, to do justice to the astonishing life and movement of the Bedouin armies, because half the virtue of them lies in the colours of the clothes and

---

1 Newcombe had been captured in early November 1917 when a scratch camel force under his command, with which he had been harassing the Turks in southern Palestine, was attacked by no fewer than six Turkish battalions. His force held out resolutely, only surrendering after sustaining heavy casualties and having exhausted all its ammunition. He was taken as a prisoner of war to Turkey but later escaped.

saddle trappings. The best saddle-bags are made in the Persian Gulf, on the Eastern shore of Arabia, and are as vivid and barbaric as you please.

One of the prints to appear, showing the Sherifian camp at dawn, in Wadi Yenbo, was taken by me at 6a.m. in January last, and is a very beautiful picture. Most sunrise pictures are taken at sunset, but this one is really a success.

There, I have an article to write for an Intelligence Report published in Egypt, and much else to do. Don't expect any letter from me for a time now. I'll be very busy, and quite away from touch with Egypt.

N.

HL/Bodleian Library

MILITARY GOVERNOR, BEERSHEBA[1]
22.1.18   *TAFILEH*

Commandant Beersheba
The bearer of this letter, [2] Sheikh Jeddua el Sufi, is the nephew of Hamad el Sufi, the former head sheikh of Beersheba district, and now one of the adherents of Sherif Feisul. I have asked Jeddua to go in to you with the letter enclosed, for General Clayton, and assured him that he will be well treated in

---

1 Behind this letter lay the problem, faced throughout the campaign by Lawrence, of finding the necessary gold to keep the Arab armies in the field. The sequel to it is described in a note by the recipient, Mr A. F. Nayton, Military Governor Beersheba District in 1918, to A. W. Lawrence, dated 9 January 1946: 'I did not consider Jeddua to be a safe enough messenger to carry a large amount of gold and informed T. E. L. accordingly. As a result your brother himself came across to Beersheba and spent a couple of nights with me there. He travelled, as usual, with some twenty of his personal bodyguard, a queer mixture of "toughs" from numerous tribes, all beautifully mounted on first-class riding camels. As you know the Turks had put a high price on T. E. L.'s head and in the first place your brother considered it safer to camp in the midst of his guard at some distance from my headquarters. He was persuaded, however, to stay in our mess and seemed to enjoy the somewhat primitive amenities which enabled him to have a hot bath and some English food! Once we had overcome his shyness he entertained us for hours with accounts of his varied experiences with our Arab allies.

'He collected his gold and rode off "into the blue" far too soon for our liking. Of T. E. L.'s so many admirable qualities the one that has always appealed to me most was the infinite patience with which he handled the Arabs, notwithstanding the many disappointments and the innumerable times he was "let down" by them.'
2 *See* next letter, to Brigadier-General Clayton.

Beersheba, and given supplies, if necessary, for himself, his men, and his animals, so long as he remains. In the letter to General Clayton I have asked him to get G.H.Q. to telephone you to this effect. Until that confirmation arrives I hope you will be able to provide him with what is necessary, on your own authority. I have asked General Clayton, in the letter enclosed, for £30000 in gold, which Jeddua will bring back to me here; (he is quite trustworthy); but to get the necessary authority, and to send the money to Beersheba from Cairo, will, I expect take at least five days. Jeddua should return here as soon as it arrives, and I would suggest that if possible he retain his arms, while waiting. You will find him on his best behaviour.

T E Lawrence

I would be most obliged if the letter to General Clayton could be sent forward as quickly as possible, and that he be advised by telephone or telegraph, of the arrival of Jeddua with a letter from me for him. I do not think that Jeddua himself need go up to G.H.Q. in any case, though that of course would be for General Clayton himself to decide.

[On back of envelope containing letter] The specie, when it arrives, please divide up into its bags of £1000 each, and put each into a camel sack of the type enclosed. The wooden cases are too heavy for transport by the Kurnub roads. The sacks can be made in Beersheba, I expect.

Bodleian Library

BRIGADIER-GENERAL GILBERT CLAYTON
22/1/18   *TAFILEH*

General Clayton
I am sending this letter in to you by Jeddua el Sufi, to Beersheba. Will you please as soon as it arrives, get G.H.Q. to telephone to the O.C. there to treat him well. He will have about 15 men and animals with him, and should be given supplies by us for them as long as he has to remain there. I am asking the Commandant to do this temporarily, till your approval reaches him.
    Affairs are in rather a curious state here. The place surrendered (after two false reports and a little fighting at the last) on the 15th. The local people are

divided into two very bitterly opposed factions, and are therefore terrified of each other and of us. There is shooting up and down the streets every night, and general tension.

[…] Zeid is rather distressed by the packet of troubles we are come in for (amongst other things a colony of besieged Moors and a swarm of destitute, but very well fed, Armenians) and is pulled here and there by all sorts of eager new-comers all intriguing against one another like cats.

I am really sending in Jeddua for money. The figures of tribal wages given Zeid at Guweira prove rather inadequate (*i.e.* the Sakhur get £22000, and not £6000) and we are going to be out of funds perhaps before we take Kerak, even. Can you send me, via Jeddua £30000 special grant? This will be quicker than fetching from Akaba, even if there was the money at Akaba.

As for operations: Jaafar Pasha was up here, wanting the Beduin all to go from here to the Railway, and 'cut it'. Which is all very well, but not possible in the present state of affairs. We have sent Sherif Abdulla, with Hamad el Sufi, and locals, to El Mezraa, to block any leakage of supplies from Kerak, Westward, and Mastur goes today to Wadi el Hesa, to block it on the South. The Sakhur left this morning for Bair, to move slowly up to just N.E. of Katrane, and thence dash at Madeba as soon as Kerak falls, or we get to Hamman el Zerka. Which plan we adopt depends on the reply of the Kerak people to messengers sent them yesterday. Rifaifan, the head of the Majaili, is pro-Turk, and will, I hope, hop it. Hussein el Tura, the other headlight, is secretly pro-Sherif and may call up enough courage to take a visible plunge. If so, Kerak should fall in about 4 days time and Madeba almost simultaneously. If not, there will be a delay. We can enlist 500 Tafileh men, and move up the East coast of the Dead Sea to Hamman el Zerka, and then call in the Sukhur to help. I would prefer the first course. For the second the extra £30000 is necessary and that will take, I calculate, 10 days to reach us.

[…]

T. E. Lawrence

TNA: PRO FO 882/7

HIS MOTHER
Feb. 6, 1918   *[GUWEIRA]*

Excuse a scrawl: this is only to say that I am here and quite fit: in Guweira, a place 35 miles NE of Akaba. I have come down for a night to see Feisul, from Tafileh, where I have been for the last few days.

No news from you for a long time, and no opportunity, I expect, of hearing from you for some time yet. General Clayton has, I believe, wired for Arnie – but I do not know in what terms, why, or what the answer has been. If I hear of him in Cairo, I'll try to cut across for a day or two and fix things up with him. He must spend at least some months there.

We had a fight north of Tafileh the other day – the Turks attacked us and we annihilated them. Took 23 machine guns & two guns, all in working order. Our loss 20 killed, theirs about 400.[1] I am now off again, buying camels in the Eastern desert, round Wadi Sirhan and Jauf.

Weather bitterly cold, with persistent snow and rain, but not likely to endure much longer. The coast & Dead Sea are warm, but our work lies on the plateau, 4,000 or 5,000 feet up.
N.

Stamps enclosed are part of Tafileh post office, all surcharged Peninsula of Sinai!

HL/Bodleian Library

BRIGADIER-GENERAL GILBERT CLAYTON
12th February 1918   *TAFILEH*

Dear General Clayton
I found your letter last night when I arrived from Guweira. The gold had already reached there when I got there, and is on the way up.[1] The roads are

---

1 The Battle of Tafileh took place on 25 January. Lawrence was far more disturbed about the battle, which he felt was an unnecessary one, with unnecessary casualties, than this letter suggests. *See Seven Pillars*, Chapters LXXXV-LXXXVI.

1 Lawrence had been to Guweira to organize a subsidy of £30,000 in gold sovereigns for Zeid's army (Zeid had been the nominal commander at the Battle of Tafileh), travelling each way through appalling wintry weather.

awful – mud, snow and slush – and of the 19 riders who left, only 7 got through. The others will come in gradually as the conditions improve. One must reckon on ten days now, from Guweira to Tafileh. I have numbered your paragraphs, for convenience.

(1) Your sending back Jeddua so well pleased with us, has had an excellent effect. I am very glad he went. [...]

(2) [...] The I.C.C. could not work across W. Arabia unless they could do without supply columns, or feed from Akaba. I am still against their use, except as last resort if the Arabs fail, and I think they would have to be re-modelled (*e.g.* put on graze feed) in any case, before they came across.[2] I have given Deedes' officer[3] a few summary notes, but I know they will not be considered enough. If Intelligence still press, get them to send an officer to look. I'll send any escort he wants, to Hebron or Beersheba.

(3) I'm very glad X (I can't remember his name) came. I enclose a letter to Deedes, about his scheme. If you agree, please send it on.

(4) Zeid hummed and hawed, and threw away his chance of making profit from it. He had the country from Madeba at his feet. These Arabs are the most ghastly material to build into a design.

[...]

(6) This £30,000 will last the N. tribes this month, and leave enough over to carry us on into the middle of March.[4] The Sukhur cost £26,000 a month, Ibn Jazi £4,000, Abu Tayi £7,000, Howeitat oddments £3500. Cost of living for regular soldier in Tafileh about £1 a week. If the situation does not change Zeid will spend about £45,000 a month and Feisul about £50,000, for the next two months. If we take Madeba, add about £4,000 a month. I hope to spend

---

2 I.C.C.: Imperial Camel Corps. Two companies of them were used, with Lawrence's agreement and support, for a specific brief operation in the desert in the summer of 1918.

3 'Deedes' officer', or X (*see* next paragraph), was Lieutenant Alec Kirkbride, Royal Engineers, later Sir Alec Kirkbride, British Resident in Transjordan. He had been sent by Lieutenant-Colonel (later Sir Wyndham) Deedes to investigate the possibility of supplying some of the needs of the Arab armies direct from Palestine instead of the normal route through Suez and Akaba. He was with Lawrence in the final advance on, and occupation of, Damascus.

4 This was an incorrect prediction. When Lawrence returned to Tafileh a week later after a reconnaissance towards the Jordan Valley, he found that Zeid had disposed of all the gold for past services and had none for future ones. There was thus no possibility of continuing with the next stage of Arab operations as agreed between himself and Allenby. For Lawrence's reaction to this development *see* p. 152.

about £15,000 on camels, shortly, extra, as agreed with Dawnay[5] in Guweira: otherwise we are wasting about £20,000 a month on an unemployable regular army. The Azrak camel contract will be extra, and by then I hope the railway will be cut, and £16,000 a month saved in wages. However, I have prophesied many times, and each time wrongly, so am getting shy. If the Arabs had any common spirit, they would have been in Damascus last autumn.

[…]

(8) Zeid having lost his frontal chance, I am stirring up the Sukhur to cut across the line by Ziza, and raise Cain about Madeba, W. Sirr, Chor el Riba. If I get them to taste I'll ride with them, but I am getting shy of adventures. I'm in an extraordinary position just now, *vis à vis* the Sherifs and the tribes, and sooner or later must go bust. I do my best to keep in the background, but cannot, and some day everybody will combine and down me. It is impossible for a foreigner to run another people of their own free will, indefinitely, and my innings has been a fairly long one.

[…]

(12) For the Jews, when I see Feisul next I'll talk to him, and the Arab attitude shall be sympathetic, for the duration of the war at least.[6] Only please remember that he is under the old man, and cannot involve the Arab kingdom by himself. If we get Madeba he will come to Jerusalem and all the Jews there will report him friendly. That will probably do all you need, without public commitment, which is rather beyond my province. […]

L.

TNA: PRO FO 882/7

5 Colonel Alan Dawnay (1888-1938) Old Etonian and officer of the Coldstream Guards, served with Lawrence in the desert in 1918. *See Seven Pillars*, Chapter XCII: 'Dawnay was Allenby's greatest gift to us – greater than thousands of baggage camels.' The two men became friends and, later, regular correspondents.

6 The Balfour Declaration of November 1917 had stated that the British Government viewed with favour the establishment of a Jewish national home in Palestine, provided the rights of people already living there (mostly Arabs) were not infringed – an impossible equation, as history would show. Lawrence's task was to ensure that concern about this new development should not affect the Arabs', or more particularly, Feisal's, war effort.

MILITARY GOVERNOR, BEERSHEBA DISTRICT
16.2.18   *EL GHOR EL SAFIYE*

Commander Bir Seba

Please inform G.H.Q. (General Clayton) that the Turks sent a launch to Mezraa, towed the broken launch and dhows into deep water, and sank them. Mezraa remains in our hands. Sherif Abdulla is camped (10 tents) near some ruins in a garden bearing 326 from the N. point of Jebel Usdum and one mile from the E. beach of the Dead Sea. He has 100 Ageyl, 150 Ghawirneh, 100 Audat, and western details with him: also two machine guns. The fighting men with him are Ibrahim abu Irgeyig (very good), Jeddua el Sufi and Mohammed Gabbua of the Dhullam. The Audat sheikhs are second rank. Please inform Colonel Parker that the horse is a matter of some difficulty. Sherif Feisul gave it to one of his officers. Does he require that horse, particularly, or would another of the Sherif's animals do? They are at his disposal, but not very good, I'm afraid. One Juma abu Seneima went to Khan Yunus with a letter from the Sherif, and has been arrested. Jeddua el Sufi is interceding for him. Could you push on his affair, and get him finished?[1]

Bearer Mohammed Ferhan is buying camels for the Sherifian forces. If you can help him in any way, without troubling yourself, please do. Our lack of transport would be comic if it was not such a nuisance.

Please inform Colonel Deedes that his officer,[2] with letters for General Clayton and himself, has gone to Akaba, and should reach there about Feb 18. Any messages for me may be sent by any decent Terabin Arab, c/o Sherif Abdulla ibn Hamza. Hamad and Jeddua are both with him, and so access is easy. Tafileh is only hours further. I return to Tafileh tomorrow, and expect to move E from there a day later.

T. E. Lawrence

Bodleian Library

1 In late January, urged by Lawrence, Sherif Abdulla el Fair (not to be confused with Abdulla, son of Hussein) had attacked and taken the little Dead Sea port of Mezraa (or El Mezra) capturing ten tons of grain and sixty prisoners; the launch and (six) dhows referred to, which they had found at anchor, had been scuttled — which explains why the Turks, having retrieved them, sank them. Liddell Hart in '*T. E. Lawrence*' in Arabia and After wrote (p. 277) that this 'interruption of the Turks' lines of supply pleased Lawrence far more than his own tactical victory' — *i.e.* Tafileh. The Turks had been lightering food supplies up the Dead Sea and the disruption of this traffic had been assigned to Lawrence by Allenby as an important objective.
2 Kirkbride.

MILITARY GOVERNOR, BEERSHEBA DISTRICT
18.2.18   *TAFILEH*

Governor Beersheba

The air attack on Katraneh[1] is reported to have been carried out by eleven aeroplanes, and to have caused great damage. Jemal Pasha, with the governor of Kerak rode thither at once with 500 cavalry, and none of them have yet returned. Hundreds of Kerak Arabs (including Faris, the head of the Butush) have come in to us in consequence, and things have greatly improved. If the raid could be repeated, we would profit still more, and if the castle at Kerak is a good mark bombs dropped there would probably bring over the Majalli, who are wavering.

A Sherifian ambush day before yesterday captured and killed a Turkish patrol of 10 cavalry and 16 mule M.I. on the northern bank of Seil el Hesa. Above for General Clayton, by post, please.

T. E. Lawrence

Please send following to Colonel Parker.

If possible please send to Sherif Abdulla ibn Hamza two Terabin Arabs, Mohammed abu Mughasib, and Nassar Gelaidan, at present imprisoned in S. Palestine. They will take service with the Arab forces. If Nassar's camel can be released with him, it will be good.

T. E. Lawrence

Bodleian Library

Taken aback by Zeid's disclosure that he had no gold left to finance any further operations (*see* letter to Clayton dated 12 February 1918, footnote 4), Lawrence decided to place his future in Allenby's hands and rode to Beersheba to ask to be relieved of his duties. However, under persuasion by Hogarth and Clayton, and hearing that General Smuts, a member of Lloyd George's War Cabinet, had come from London to expound important new plans, he relented and agreed to continue. He had no further dealings with Zeid, returning to his collaboration with Feisal, with whom he worked in more or less close association for the rest of the campaign.

1 A station on the Hejaz Railway.

HIS MOTHER
8.3.18   *CAIRO*

Here I am in Cairo again. At Tafileh I had a difference of opinion with Sherif Zeid, the 4th son of the old man of Mecca, and left him for Beersheba. This was about the 22nd. I then went to Jerusalem, Ramleh, Jerusalem, Beersheba, Ismailia, Cairo, Suez, Akaba, Guweira, Akaba, Suez, and got back here last night. I hope to be here four nights.

This year promises to be more of a run about than last year even!

As for coming back – no, not possible now. The situation has changed since I came over, and I'm to go back till June at least. One rather expected that, I'm afraid.

I thought I had told you that Newcombe had left the Sherifian forces before he was captured? He never came to Akaba at all, but went to Palestine with the British.

No letters from you lately, except a November unit which I picked up at Akaba. By the way after this note don't expect any other from me till about the middle of April, for I'm going up country for a month, on an inspection trip.

They have now given me a D.S.O.[1] It's a pity all this good stuff is not sent to someone who would use it! Also apparently I'm a colonel of sorts.[2] Don't make any change in my address of course.

I wonder if you remember Young,[3] an Indian Army officer who came to Carchemish while Will was there? He has just come over to help our thing forward, I hope. He should be the right sort of man: the work is curious, and demands a sort of twisted tact, which many people do not seem to possess. We are very short-handed, and it will make things much easier if he fits in well.

Hugh Whitelocke has just joined the Egyptian Army I hear. They say he is somewhere in Cairo, so I may see him, but it is only a chance, as on these flying visits I rush about all day and do very little ordinary speech. It will be a comfort when this gipsy mode of life comes to an end. However thank goodness the worst of the winter is over. I had one very bad night out in the hills when my camel broke down in the snow drifts, and I had to dig a path out for it and lead it for miles down slippery snow-slopes. One's usual airy sort of white shirt and bare feet are better in summer than in winter. Of

---

1 Distinguished Service Order, for his conduct at the Battle of Tafileh.
2 He was officially promoted from temporary major to temporary lieutenant-colonel on 12 March.
3 Major, later Sir Hubert Young.

course the hill country east of the Dead Sea is very high, and one gets what frost and snow there is, anyhow.

There, I can't think of anything else cheerful to tell you about – except perhaps that three of my camels have had babies in the last few weeks. That makes me about thirty riding camels of my own, but then my bodyguard of servants is about 25, so there are not so many spare. I never have any baggage camels with me ... we carry what we need on our own animals.

Here by good fortune are some new photographs just to hand.

N.   *HL/Bodleian Library*

HIS MOTHER
28.3.18   *AKABA*

Well, I foretold a long trip, when I was in Cairo a few days ago, and here I am back in Akaba for two nights. Various things happened to delay my start – and indeed I may have one more chance of writing about a week hence, from further North.

News? none. We have lost so much by frost and snow and rain that movement has become difficult, and very unpleasant. There is however hope that the spring is coming. Yesterday was warm, but then Akaba always is.

About A. General Clayton asked me about him last time I was in Palestine. They did not wire for him, after all, as another man turned up, who will do for the present, and I knew he would rather not hurry things too much. As soon as I hear from you that he is ready to come out they will make an application for him to the War Office. For it to be successful he must be in the army, and an infantry regiment will be the easiest place, unless he gets a special list commission, which may not be still possible. I do not think there will be any difficulty about it at all, so long as he keeps up with his Arabic.

I saw Kerry the other day, and Hugh Whitelocke – the only people from Oxford seen for some little time. No matter: after four years of this sort of thing I am become altogether dried up, and till the business ends I can't do anything else either here or there. It will be a great comfort when one can lie down & sleep without having to think about things; and speak without having one's every word reported in half a hundred camps. This is a job too big for me.

N.

HL/Bodleian Library

HIS MOTHER
12.5.18
ARAB BUREAU SAVOY HOTEL CAIRO

I sent you a wire a week ago, as I passed through Cairo on my way up to Palestine. Since then I have been travelling at red hot speed, but tonight have finished. Tonight I am going to spend in Cairo, and I got here last night. It is the first time for six weeks that I have spent two nights running in one place.

I'll get letters from you tomorrow, and answer them at my leisure, because I expect I'll be here a week.

This is only a scrawl meanwhile. All is very well, and while we have not done all we want, we have done all that we could do by ourselves, and it is not at all bad.

N.

HL/Bodleian Library

KING HUSSEIN OF THE HEJAZ[1]
Ramadan 17, 1336–June 25, 1918

His Majesty King Hussein
Probably, I am afraid, I told you some things uncertain about the Northern Army. I intend now to give you a brief account in order to eliminate any inconvenience which may have been caused by my repeated demand for assistance.

At Present
There are now 4,000 Turkish soldiers at Ma'an entrenched in strong fortifications with cement machine gun points and many guns. There is a good supply of water and sufficient food for three months. Against this force stands Sidi Faisal's regular army of 3,500 with guns stronger than the Turks. The big guns are all placed opposite Ma'an supported by 700 infantry soldiers at Wahida about two hours from Ma'an, 800 at Jerdun and 600 at Jurf al-Darawish.

The Turkish force at Jerdun is made up of 150, about 500 at Anaza and 400 at Jurf. The railway has been cut off to the south of Ma'an and between

[1] Written in Arabic, this letter eventually became the property of the king's youngest son, Emir Zeid.

all the stations from Ma'an to Fareifra. The enemy can repair the railway between Ma'an and Fareifra within three weeks, but that between Ma'an and Mudawwara could not be repaired until after peace. No Turkish force could move through the destroyed sections.

Your Majesty will conclude from the above details the following:
(1) Feisal's force of 3,500 will not be able to occupy Ma'an in direct assault. No commander could attack nowadays an entrenched force if he has not under him at least twice or three times the surrounded force.
(2) Feisal cannot gather all his forces against Ma'an. The Turks want to lift the siege from Ma'an after the pilgrimage and on that account they moved a month ago their force from Jurf and Anaza in order to repair the railway but they were stopped and surrounded by the Arabs.
No doubt your Majesty will recognise that your small Northern Army has:
(1) Cut the railway between Syria and Hejaz permanently.
(2) Surrounded a superior force for three months at Ma'an.
(3) Stopped and surrounded the reinforcements of the enemy estimated at half the strength of your army for six weeks at Jurf al-Darawish.

All this has been achieved by the 3,500 regular soldiers under the command of Ja'afar Pasha. The bedouins are no good for a continued siege and would not attack fortifications. The Huweitat, Beni Sakhr and other tribes which are under the command of Sidi Feisal did not participate in the operations of Ma'an.

The British General Staff is of the opinion that rarely has an army accomplished what Ja'afar's army has, under the command of Emir Feisal and the British Officers (Col. Joyce, Major Maynard and myself) who helped to organize it. All the above mentioned are satisfied with their work but we are a little afraid of the future.

The Future
The first Turkish force was surrounded by Feisal at Jurf. The Turks are bound to lift the siege upon Jurf as well as upon Ma'an within the next two months. The strength of the Turkish army at Amman is estimated at 8,000 and it is possible that the German General Staff would send a third of it from Katraneh to Ma'an.

Sidi Feisal's army is now doing so much more than any other army equal in strength would do. When Katraneh forces advance, Feisal will be bound to assemble his forces at Waheida, while the enemy is engaged in repairing the railway between Fareifra and Ma'an. Sherif Nasir has now at Hesa 70 regulars and 400 bedouins and has done admirably well on your side, but he cannot stand alone against 3,000 Turkish regulars.

After the railway to Ma'an is repaired, the Turks will be able to reinforce Ma'an by infantry and means of transportation and then they will attack Abu al-Lissan. The Arab fortifications there are in good condition and therefore your army will probably be able to defend itself. Otherwise the army should retreat to Guweira, a well fortified position which the Turks will not be able to attack. Moreover they can neither attack Akaba nor be able to repair the railway to Mudawwara.

As to Arab plans I can say nothing now but I must state that there will be no successful results from a direct attack at the vanguard of the enemy. Had it not been for your courage in ordering Sidi Feisal last year to leave Medina and proceed to Wejh and Akaba, the Arab movement would not have been completely successful as it is today.

In war it is more profitable for the Arabs to adopt the daring plan which the enemy does not anticipate.

I have submitted to Sidi Feisal a plan which General Allenby might help us in implementing. If this plan succeeds, Ma'an and its garrison of 14,000 Turks is now locked in with no hope of escape to north, south, east or west.

I beg you Sir to burn this letter after reading it, because I am writing to you about matters which I should have disclosed to you orally.

I conclude begging you to be so kind as to accept my sincere respect and best wishes.

T. E. Lawrence[2]

British Library

2 Signature both in Arabic and English.

VYVYAN RICHARDS[1]
15.VII.18   *[CAIRO]*

Well, it was wonderful to see your writing again, and very difficult to read it: also pleasant to have a letter which doesn't begin 'Reference your F.S. 102487 b of the 45th inst.' Army prose is bad, and one has so much of it that one fears contamination.

I cannot write to anyone just now. Your letter came to me in Aba Lissan, a little hill-fort on the plateau of Arabia S.E. of the Dead Sea and I carried it with me down to Akaba, to Jidda and then here to answer. Yet with all that I have had it only a month and you wrote it three months ago. This letter will be submarined and then it is all over for another three years.

It always seemed to me that your eyes would prevent service for you, and that in consequence you might preserve your continuity. For myself, I have been so violently uprooted and plunged so deeply into a job too big for me, that everything feels unreal. I have dropped all I ever did, and live only as a thief of opportunity, snatching chances of the moment when and where I see them. My people have probably told you that the job is to foment an Arab rebellion against Turkey, and for that I have to try and hide my frankish exterior, and be as little out of the Arab picture as I can. So it's a kind of foreign stage, on which one plays day and night, in fancy dress, in a strange language with the price of failure on one's head if the part is not well filled.

You guessed rightly that the Arab appealed to my imagination. It is the old old civilisation, which has refound itself clear of household gods and half the trappings which ours hastens to assume. The gospel of bareness in materials is a good one, and it involves apparently a sort of moral bareness too. They think for the moment and endeavour to slip through life without turning corners or climbing hills. In part it is a mental and moral fatigue, a race trained out: and to avoid difficulties they have to jettison so much that we think honourable and brave: and yet without in any way sharing their point of view I think I can understand it enough to look at myself and other foreigners from their direction, and without condemning it. I know I'm a stranger to them, and always will be: but I cannot believe them worse, any more than I could change to their ways.

---

1 When Richards showed Lawrence this letter seven years later (in much changed circumstances), Lawrence found it interesting enough to copy for himself. He subsequently sent his copy to Charlotte Shaw apparently believing it to be the only surviving letter of his 'Arab period'. *See* letter to Charlotte Shaw, 29 March 1927, p. 340.

This is a very long porch to explain why I'm always trying to blow up Railway trains and bridges instead of looking for the well at the world's end.[2] Anyway these years of detachment have cured me of any desire ever to do anything for myself. When they untie my bonds I will not find in me any spur to action. Though actually one never thinks of afterwards: the time from the beginning is like one of those dreams, seeming to last for aeons, out of which you wake up with a start, and find that it has left nothing in the mind. Only the different thing about this dream is that so many people do not wake up in life again.

I cannot imagine what my people can have told you. Until now we have only been preparing the groundwork and bases of our Revolt, and do not yet stand on the brink of action. Whether we are going to win or lose, when we do strike, I cannot ever persuade myself. The whole thing is such a play, and one cannot put conviction into one's day-dreams. If we succeed I will have done well with the materials given me, and that disposes of your 'lime-light'. If we fail and they have patience, then I suppose we will go on digging foundations. Achievement, if it comes, will be a great disillusionment, but not great enough to wake one up.

Your mind has evidently moved far since 1914. That is a privilege you have won by being kept out of the mist for so long. You'll find the rest of us aged undergraduates, possibly still not conscious of our unfitting grey hair. For that reason I cannot follow or return your steps. A house with no action entailed upon one, quiet, and liberty to think and abstain as one wills, yes, I think abstention, the leaving everything alone and watching the others still going past, is what I would choose today, if they ceased driving me. This may be only the reaction from four years opportunism, and is not worth trying to resolve into terms of geography and employment.

Of course the ideal is that of the lords who are still certainly expected but the certainty is not for us, I'm afraid. Also for very few would the joy be so perfect as to be silent. Those words peace, silence, rest, take on a vividness amid noise and worry and weariness, like a lighted window in the dark. Yet what on earth is the good of a lighted window? and perhaps it is only because one is overborne and tired. You know when one marches across an interminable plain, a hill (which is still the worst hill on earth) is a banquet, and after searing heat, cold water takes on a quality (what would they have said without this word before?) impossible in the eyes of a fen-farmer. Probably I'm only a sensitised film, turned black or white by the objects

2 A reference, which Richards would have appreciated, to William Morris's romance *The Well at the World's End*.

projected on me: and if so what hope is there that next week or year, or tomorrow, can be prepared for today?

This is an idiot letter, and amounts to nothing except a cry for further change; which is idiocy, for I change my abode every day, and my job every two days, and my language every three days, and still remain always unsatisfied. I hate being in front, and I hate being back, and I don't like responsibility and I don't obey orders. Altogether no good just now. A long quiet like a purge, and then a contemplation and decision of future roads, that is what is to look forward to.

You want apparently some vivid colouring of an Arab's costume, or of a flying Turk, and we have it all, for that is part of the *mise en scene* of the successful raider, and hitherto I am that. My bodyguard of fifty Arab tribesmen, picked rioters from the young men of the deserts, are more splendid than a tulip-garden, and we ride like lunatics and with our Beduins pounce on unsuspecting Turks and destroy them in heaps: and it is all very gory and nasty after we close grips. I love the preparation and the journey, and loathe the physical fighting. Disguises and prices on one's head, and fancy exploits are all part of the pose. How to reconcile it with the Oxford pose I know not. Were we flamboyant there?

If you reply – you will perceive I have matting of the brain and your thoughts are in control, please tell me of Berry, and if possible Winkworth.[3] He was the man for all these things, because he would take a berserk beery pleasure in physical outposts.

Very many thanks for writing. It has opened a very precious casement.

L.

DG/British Library

HIS MOTHER
15.7.18   *CAIRO*

Well, this has been a long interruption of writing. I went off to Jidda, after the last letter, as soon as I had been to Alexandria (to see the High Commissioner) and to Palestine, to see General Allenby. At Jidda I had to stay several days, before I could get a boat back to Suez. It was an unprofitable journey, and I was not able to get anything done of my hopes. There were a great many local things however, which I saw, and which rather changed the outlook.

---

3 Friends of their undergraduate days.

Then from Jidda we dashed up to Wejh, and thence to Suez: a bad trip, in a small boat, against a strong head wind. Took us days. From Suez I came here for a night, then Alexandria, then Palestine, and have now come to anchor here for perhaps a week. It is very nice to have finished one part of the show. We begin something fresh next month, and the change will be a pleasant one.

Having said that much, that is all, I think, that I have got to say. You know I have nothing doing or to do which does not actually concern Feisul's campaign, and that I make a rule to write nothing about. I cannot talk about books because I don't read any, or about people, because I only meet the Staff who deal with our operations, or places, because most of them are not to be made public property. So there you are –

I'm in the middle of the show, I have to be more careful than anybody else. Mr. Hogarth is coming back to England about the middle of August, and hopes to see you and explain something of how we get on. The communiqués in the press contain the least part of the truth. The two Sherifs down by Medina, Abdulla and Ali, allow their fancy very free play with their achievements, and keep on reporting that they have broken thousands of rails and bridges. The bridges are tiny culverts, and the breaks in the rails only shorten them a few inches. Besides they break usually only 10% of their published figures. The communiqués of Feisul's army are written by ourselves, or at least checked by us, and are more truthful.

One thing they have not brought out, I fancy, and which I can tell you, is that from Maan southward for 100 kilometres there are no Turks, and the 8 stations and all the rails and bridges have been smashed to atoms by us. This makes a break that I am sure they will not be able to repair so long as the war lasts, and thanks to it the very large body of troops from there to Medina are cut off from Turkey, as much as the little garrisons of Turks in South Arabia. Medina is a holy city, and the Arabs do not attack it: it has huge gardens and palm groves, and is quite self-supporting so far as food goes, so there is no definite reason why the troops there should ever surrender. We are not in any hurry about it, anyway, though the capture of the place might be a political gain to the Sherif.

There, I think that is enough talk. If I could think of anything more to say I would prolong it. The W.O. reply to our application for A. should arrive any day, and when it comes I will write again. We left it purposely till the vac.

N.

HL/Bodleian Library

Lawrence's war ended in a flurry of military and political action, as the Turks, heavily defeated by Allenby west of the Jordan and severely harassed by Feisal's Arab forces to the east, retreated in disarray, leaving Damascus open to capture. He was one of the first to enter the city on 1 October, becoming briefly its 'de facto Governor' (his own phrase), his purpose being to set up an Arab administration strong enough to survive the inevitable crises that followed liberation. One of his first actions in Damascus was to throw out a provisional government set up when the Turks left by two usurping Algerian brothers, Mohammed Said and Abd el Kadir, whom he saw as evil geniuses and betrayers of the revolt.[1] The following documents are from this final phase: a despatch written as the advance gained momentum and his last campaign despatch, written on the day of his entry into Damascus.

GENERAL STAFF, G.H.Q.
24.9.18
UM EL SURAB[1]

The Turks have given up the repair of the line, and are streaming up the Haj road to Deraa. In consequence we have closed down here. Sherif Feisal returns at once to Azrak. Saad El Skaini goes west with Rafa El Khoraisha to the Irbid district. Sherif Nasir and Nuri Shalaan move to Umtaiye, Taibe, Tafas, Sheikh Saad to place the army there, and get into contact with the British by way of the new El Al, Kefr Harib road.

The Turks are entrenching Deraa, but the country is such that they will inevitably be cut off there, if they delay, by your cavalry if they issue either by Beisan, Irbid or by Semakh – El Al roads. If we can get El Al quickly, we will secure you the latter at least.

We spend to-night in Umtaiye, and would cross the railway near Tell Arar to-morrow night (25-26), if all goes well.

Will you please try and arrange the evacuation of the aerodrome here to-morrow. There are 2 mechanics, and some kit, and little or no petrol. We will leave the cars here till the planes leave. Till mid-day, therefore, the Bristols[2] here will do us. If it is possible, after mid-day on the 25th and throughout the 26th, we would like a continuous patrol of Deraa, dropping bombs as is possible, and if there is an important concentration of enemy on the line

---

1 On this subject *see* Lawrence's report to D.C.P.O., 28 June 1919 (p. 174).

1 On the road from Azrak to Deraa.
2 *i.e.* Bristol F2B fighter aircraft.

between Deraa and Ghazale, dropping a message to that effect on us. Our position will be between Umtaiye and Naeime, and we will lay out an H on the ground when we see a machine over us. We will put out the same sign at Sh. Saad next day if you like to send out to find us.

Please get £10,000 in gold to Ramleh to be drawn on by us in case of urgency. It can be replaced from the £100,000 in Akaba.

In case of need please communicate with Sherif Feisal at Azrak.

T. E. Lawrence

TNA: PRO WO 157/738

GENERAL STAFF, G.H.Q.

1.10.18

DAMASCUS

Please forward following to Hedjaz Operations.

An Arab force left Deraa on September 29th under Sherif Nasir and Nuri Bey Said, following up the 4th Cavalry Division on the right flank. We marched up the Hedjaz Railway, and in the morning of September 30th came in contact with an enemy column of 2000 men with 4 guns retiring from Deraa. Our mounted men kept up a running fight with these till 4 p.m. when Sherif Nasir galloped ahead of them with 30 horse and threw himself into Khiara Chiftlik, South of Kiswe, to delay the enemy, as General Gregory's Brigade was just marching into Kham Denun. The Turks showed some fight but were shelled effectively by the British, and taken on the head and west flank by the British, while the Arabs hung on to their tail. The Arabs took about 600 prisoners, 14 machine guns and 3 guns.

From Kiswe the Sherif sent a mounted force forward to get contact with his followers in the gardens east of Damascus, to find that his local committee had hoisted the Arab flag and proclaimed the Emirate of Hussein of Mecca at 2.30 P. M.

Sherif Nasir with Major Stirling and myself moved into Damascus at 9a.m. on October 1st amid scenes of extraordinary enthusiasm on the part of the local people. The streets were nearly impassable with the crowds, who yelled themselves hoarse, danced, cut themselves with swords and daggers and fired volleys into the air. Nasir, Nuri Shalaan, Auda abu Tayi and myself were cheered by name, covered with flowers, kissed indefinitely, and splashed with attar of roses from the house-tops.

On arrival at the Serai Shukri Pasha el Ayoubi was appointed Arab Military Governor, as all former civil employes [*sic*] had left with Jemal Pasha[1] on the previous day. Martial law was proclaimed, police organised, and the town picketed. The Rualla are behaving very well, but the Druses are troublesome.

I have no orders as to what .political arrangements should be made in Damascus and will carry on as before till I hear further from you. If Arab military assistance is not required in further operations of the Desert Corps, I would like to return to Palestine as I feel that if I remain here longer, it will be very difficult for my successor.

T. E. Lawrence

G.O.C., Desert Mounted Corps has seen above, and agrees with my carrying on with the town administration until further instructions.

T.E.L.

The Arab Army since September 26th have taken 8000 prisoners and 120 machine guns.

TNA: PRO WO 157/738[2]

On 3 October the principals on the Allied side, Allenby and Feisal, reached Damascus. Lawrence asked Allenby's permission to go, which was granted. On the 4th he left, first for Egypt and then home. 'The old war is closing, and my use is gone,' he wrote from Cairo to the Base Commandant at Akaba, Major R. H. Scott, adding: 'We were an odd little set, and we have, I expect, changed History in the near East. I wonder how the Powers will let the Arabs get on.'[1]

1 The Turkish commander in Syria.
2 Published in *Allenby's Final Triumph*, by W.T. Massey (Constable, 1920).

1 Letter of 14 October 1918: published in *DG*.

T. E. Lawrence (*left*) in major's uniform, with D. G. Hogarth as a commander,
Royal Navy Volunteer Reserve, and Colonel Alan Dawnay, Cairo, 1918

Colonel Lawrence. Taken in Paris in 1919, this photograph was issued by an
American agency – an indication of the rapid spread of his fame

3 THE POLITICAL YEARS
1918-22

Following the triumphal entry into Damascus, Lawrence returned home to England, exchanging the military for the political arena. Before the end of October he was arguing the Arabs' case before the Eastern Committee of the War Cabinet, at the same table as, among others, Lord Curzon (who was chairman), General Smuts, Lord Robert Cecil (assistant foreign secretary), Edwin Montagu (secretary of state for India) and Sir Mark Sykes. His reputation had gone before him, so that if there was a certain naïveté about the solutions he proposed for the problems of the Middle East, he was nevertheless listened to with both respect and admiration. In early November, even before the official end of hostilities, he telegraphed with Foreign Office approval to King Hussein of the Hejaz urging that Feisal should be despatched to Paris as his representative at the peace talks which would soon follow. The French government cavilled about Feisal's precise status but eventually he was allowed to sail for Europe. Lawrence was present as he stepped ashore from *H.M.S. Gloucester* at Marseilles on 26 November to be met by senior French officials, and the party was joined by Colonel Brémond, former head of the French military mission to the Hejaz, on arrival at Lyons. Subsequently, after Feisal had been taken on a brief tour of the French battlefields without Lawrence (as a 'foreign hanger-on' – his own phrase – he was not made welcome), the two men spent much of December together in Britain. Notable meetings took place with the king and with the Zionist leader Chaim Weizmann, a meeting at which it seemed possible that Jewish and Arab aspirations might be reasonably harmonized.

In January 1919, Feisal and Lawrence went to Paris. Lawrence found that no seats had been assigned to Arab delegates but his intervention speedily produced the two necessary tickets. Frequently seen wearing an Arab headdress with his British uniform, he was a public relations success – Gertrude Bell called him 'the most picturesque' figure at the conference – but French determination combined with Lloyd George's *realpolitik* gave the Arabs little chance. Woodrow Wilson's doctrine of 'self-determination' seemed to offer encouragement, but Arab aspirations were inevitably low in the pecking order of international concern after a war which had seen so massive a blood-letting in Europe. France, having suffered not only a huge loss of manpower but also four years of partial territorial occupation, needed to reassure herself by annexations elsewhere, and Syria, which she had long coveted, was the necessary consolation prize. Feisal's removal from Damascus, where he briefly set himself up as a *de facto* ruler, was merely a matter of time. Lawrence found himself increasingly isolated and his pro-Arabism more and more unacceptable as British pragmatism and French determination found their inevitable accommodation. For much of 1919 and 1920 he waged an eloquent and hard-hitting campaign through letters and articles in the press, using his public reputation to gain publicity for his attacks on establishment policy and decisions.

Meanwhile, other factors were at work which complicated a psychological condition already overwrought after four years of war, two years of which he had lived at almost white heat. Early in 1919 he embarked on the long, draining task of writing and re-writing his account of the Arab campaign, the book which was to emerge as *Seven Pillars of Wisdom*; the work would occupy him on and off until 1926. Oxford gave him a base and a sanctuary by electing him to a research fellowship at All Souls College, but he was not at ease in an academic environment and found it more congenial to write in a garret room in Barton Street, Westminster, loaned to him by his architect friend Herbert Baker; there he often wrote for hours at a time, taking only minimal nourishment and refreshing himself with solitary walks through the London streets.

In mid-1919, American publicist Lowell Thomas, after a successful season in New York, launched at the Royal Opera House, Covent Garden, his 'illustrated travelogue' about the Middle Eastern war which turned Lawrence almost overnight into a show-business celebrity. He would thenceforward always be known as 'Lawrence of Arabia'. Churchill brought him back into positive political work in 1921 and he spent some months in the Middle East helping to devise a settlement sufficiently fair to the Arabs for him to feel that he could leave the political milieu, which he had never found to his liking, with clean hands. Feisal was given a kingship, though of Iraq, not Syria, while his brother Abdulla was installed as emir in Transjordan. Later in 1921 Lawrence was again in the Middle East as chief political representative in Transjordan before handing over to H. St J. B. Philby. He then returned to England where, his duty to Churchill discharged, he retired not only from politics, but also from normal life. To the amazement and dismay of many of his friends, in the summer of 1922 he enlisted under an assumed name, John Hume Ross, in the ranks of the Royal Air Force. He would never again hold any high office or play any important military or political role.

Compared with the years ahead this was a period when he wrote relatively few letters. Much of his energy went into verbal argument or in articles or memoranda

– and he was, of course, writing *Seven Pillars*. There are only four known letters to his family (though he was frequently in Oxford, he was also much away from it): one from Paris in 1919, two from Cairo in 1921, one from London in 1922. I have included all of these (if not all at full length) and I have reproduced a number of the personal letters of this period printed in Garnett; the political ones to newspapers, available not only in Garnett but also in Stanley and Rodelle Weintraub's *Evolution of a Revolt*, seemed less worthy of repetition. I have, however, tried to cast new light on his political activities by including three of the numerous forthright minutes written by him at the peace conference and most of the long and often eloquent cables he sent from Jidda in August and September 1921, when he was engaged in the difficult, indeed impossible, task of trying to persuade King Hussein of the Hejaz to accept Churchill's Middle Eastern settlement. 'This is the beastliest trip ever I had,' he wrote to Eric Kennington from Aden at this time.

Among other letters, some of them new, some republished, there are two to Fareedah el Akle, in which he writes interestingly if disenchantedly about the war, the Middle East and Lowell Thomas; one to Sir Archibald Murray, Allenby's predecessor as commander-in-chief in Cairo, in which he makes one of his rare approving comments about *Seven Pillars*: 'the story is in parts very odd and exciting [...] for it is not badly written, and is authoritative, in so far as it concerns myself'; and two to Ezra Pound about his hopes and fears as a writer, the second of which includes a dismissive reference to the poetry of his future critic-in-chief Richard Aldington. I have also printed the letter to the Foreign Office official G.J. Kidston, to whom he wrote outspokenly about his secret war aims, first published in *The Sunday Times* in 1968. In addition I have included a number of letters which he wrote when he was trying to persuade certain former participants in the Arab war to sit for the artists whom he had asked to collaborate in the production of his lavish subscribers' edition of his book. They show him apparently buoyant, even jesting, at a time when he was about to take his plunge into social and personal obscurity.

Other recipients represented here who were not featured in Garnett include Geoffrey Dawson, then editor of *The Times*; the artist Augustus John; the veteran traveller, poet and political radical Wilfred Scawen Blunt; and, already mentioned above, H. St J. B. Philby. There are also a number of letters to Sir Hugh Trenchard, chief of the air staff, written on the eve of enlisting in the air force. Among the last letters in this section, previously published but certainly worthy of being re-used, are two to George Bernard Shaw that initiated the relationship with the Shaws which was to produce numerous letters to G. B. S. and, much more significantly, the intimate, long-sustained correspondence with his wife Charlotte.

GEOFFREY DAWSON[1]
Sunday [?17 November 1918]   *CARLTON HOTEL PALL MALL LONDON*

I'm afraid this is really meant by providence for the *Daily Mail*. I found I couldn't give you the original MSS and was kept busy till last night, and then wrote this at a sitting. It's a pity, because it begins decently, & drivels off into incidents. Please burn it.[2]

Feisul will probably be in London on Thursday and then I'll try and arrange you something useful.

The points that strike me are that the Arabs came into the war without making a previous treaty with us, and have consistently refused to listen to the temptations of other powers. They have never had a press agent, or tried to make themselves out a case, but fought as hard as they could (I'll swear to that) and suffered hardships in their three campaigns and losses that would break up seasoned troops. They fought with ropes round their necks (Feisul had £20000 alive & £10000 dead on him. I the same: Nasir £10000 alive, & Ali el Harith £8000) and did it without, I believe any other very strong motive than a desire to see the Arabs free. It was rather an ordeal for as very venerable a person as Hussein to rebel, for he was at once most violently abused by the Moslem press in India & Turkey, on religious grounds.

Hussein took the headship of the Arabs because he was invited to, by all the Arab secret societies, as the one man whose pre-eminence was founded on an arbitrary reason – birth.

England spent about £10,000,000 in all on the Arabs, and two of the British staff were killed over it. More should have been but there were only about 20 of us all told.

The actual value of Arab alliances is a matter of opinion (posterity's opinion, probably) but the East has been rather impressed by our having taken the most unlikely material in the world, and pushed it to undreamed of success. And we have done it all without losing a grain of its good will!

There is a private matter which I would like to tell you – not for action. Sir Henry MacMahon [*sic*] did all the spadework of the entry of the Sherif

---

1 Geoffrey Dawson (1874-1944), born Robinson (he changed his name by Royal Licence in 1917) was editor of *The Times*, 1912-19 and 1923-41.

2 This paragraph refers to an account of the Arab Revolt which subsequently appeared in *The Times* as three articles on 26, 27, and 28 November, under the authorship of 'A Correspondent' attached to the Arab forces. These are reprinted in my *T. E. Lawrence in War and Peace*, p. xxviii.

into the war, and was sacked (largely for it) when things got bad in the early days of the rising. Now Wingate says he did it. It was really MacMahon advised by Storrs, Clayton, & perhaps myself.

The Sherifian solution for the Near East is Irak (Bagdad to us) like Egypt, under the British, with nominal Arab prince: Jezireh (Mosul to Diarbehir & Birejek) Arab-Kurd province of Irak, under separate constitution, with nominal Arab prince: Syria (port of Tripoli) independent under Feisul: it has fought for it, and deserves preferential treatment. Palestine British protectorate, with some scope for Jewish expansion. They would like the French to take over the business of the Armenians (Cilicia, & the six vilayets.)[3]

The old Sherif wants to be prayed for in Mosques on Friday. He is, already, in Syria, and in parts of Mesopotamia, and will be generally if we leave things alone.

T. E. Lawrence

Bodleian Library

HIS MOTHER
30.1.19   *HOTEL MAJESTIC PARIS*

I got your letter yesterday, and will answer it this morning, while waiting up here for breakfast. I'm living at the Continental, which is half an hour's walk from the Majestic and Astoria, the British quarters, and this morning I found a taxi, which is a rare thing. In consequence I have ten unexpected minutes.

About work – it is going on well. I have seen 10 American newspaper men, and given them all interviews, which went a long way. Also President Wilson, and the other people who have influence. The affair is nearly over, I suspect. Another fortnight, perhaps.

Everybody seems to be here, and of course it is a busy time. I have had, personally, one meal in my hotel since I got to Paris! That was with Newcombe, who turned up unexpectedly.

3 The old Turkish provinces.

Bliss, of the Beyrout College is here,[1] and proving a very valuable assistant of the Arab cause. Tell A.[2] I haven't seen a bookshop yet. I cannot come to England to meet Bob, but if he came to Paris could see him. I'm always in my room (98, at the Continental) before 10a.m. (unless out at breakfast as today) and after 11.30 p.m.

N.[3]

HL/Bodleian Library

SIR LOUIS MALLET[1]

22.4.19 *[PARIS]*

Sherif Feisal asks me to tell you that some of his Mesopotamian officers will wish shortly to return home. These men are mostly convinced that Abdulla should become Emir of Bagdad, and will inevitably say so on their return.[2] Feisal will not of course send with them, or make, any expression of his own opinion on the matter. He cannot on the other hand instruct them to keep silent on the point. They are officers who have served us and him very well, and are mostly very pro-British. He cannot without suspicion keep them in Syria indefinitely, but he does not want them to go back to Mesopotamia without our knowing of them, and of their opinions and probable course of action on arrival. Indeed he would be glad to have our assurance that they will not be hindered so long as their behaviour is reasonable – and that their beliefs will not be considered seditious.

1 Dr Howard S. Bliss, president of the American University at Beirut, whom Lawrence had met before the war (*see* his letter home of 11 April 1911), had been officially invited by the United States to produce evidence on the Syrian question.
2 A.: Arnold Lawrence.
3 This was the last letter home written to both his parents. His father died in early April, victim of the great influenza epidemic of 1918-19. His mother was to outlive his father by 40 years, dying in November 1959, aged 98.

1 Sir Louis Mallet was a senior member of the British delegation to the peace conference. Lawrence's memorandum evidently failed to reach its destination as swiftly as he intended, for it carries the footnote: 'I saw this for the first time on June 1, 19 L Mallet.'
2 Lawrence was still campaigning at this time for the political solution which he had put to Lord Curzon's cabinet committee in October 1918: namely that Feisal should be ruler of Syria and Abdulla ruler of Mesopotamia – a scheme which had aroused much hostility in the India Office and was becoming equally unpopular with the Foreign Office.

I need hardly say that they all expect and want a British mandate in Mesopotamia.

T E Lawrence

TNA: PRO FO 608/92

FROM A PEACE CONFERENCE MEMORANDUM
3.5.19   *[PARIS]*

In a nutshell, nothing has passed.[1] Clemenceau tried to make a bargain with Feisal, to acknowledge the independence of Syria in return for Feisal's statement that France was the only qualified mandatory.

Feisal refused. He said first that it wasn't true. France hardly understood the mandatory system. Secondly, if he said so he would only have to go away to Mecca, since he could not make his people agree with him. The French had now, by means of the commission, to deal with the people, not with him.[2]

Thirdly, that a statement that the French refused to admit the independence of Syria would help him. They had admitted it in the declaration of Nov 1918: in the Sykes-Picot, and it was the first clause of the mandate they were hoping for. Therefore it was not worth paying a lie for.

TEL

TNA: PRO FO 608/93

1 From a memorandum headed 'Relations between Emir Feisal and the French Govt' containing a request to Lawrence to clarify 'what did actually pass' in the recent conversations and correspondence between Feisal and M. Clemenceau, the French Premier, about the future of Syria. Basically neither Feisal nor Lawrence trusted French intentions and Feisal had returned to Syria on 23 April without having arrived at any understanding.
2 The Inter-Allied Commission proposed by President Woodrow Wilson to ascertain the wishes of the local inhabitants in those areas of the Middle East which were in dispute. The commission that went out consisted of just two Americans (Messrs King and Crane) and its findings were ignored.

In May 1919 Lawrence joined an experimental flight of Handley Page bombers bound for Egypt, intending to visit Cairo to collect his wartime reports and personal effects. His aircraft crashed at Rome during a night landing. The two pilots were killed; Lawrence received minor injuries but was able shortly to continue his journey. He was helped out of the wreckage by Aircraftman Daw, a letter of gratitude to whom is printed on p. 176. In Cairo he wrote the important report that follows about the two Algerian brothers he deposed in Damascus, one of whom he held in part responsible for his ill-treatment at Deraa (*see* p. 162).

DEPUTY CHIEF POLITICAL OFFICER, CAIRO[1]

June 28 1919   *GRAND CONTINENTAL HOTEL CAIRO*

D.C.P.O.

I want to begin at the beginning about this as to do so will probably put the question at rest for good.

These brothers Mohammed Said and Abd el Kadir were judged insane in 1911, but escaped detention in asylums by free use of their wealth. Mohammed Said holds a world's record for three successive fatal pistol accidents. He accompanied the propaganda mission of FROBENIUS[2] to the Red Sea for the Sudan in 1915, but turned back from Kunfida as Frobenius did not treat him with sufficient dignity. He was then removed to Brusa with his brothers, and kept under loose surveillance. The Ottoman Government soon decided that they might be useful, and Abd el Kadir offered to run a counter-Sherifian Arab propaganda under Abbas Hilmi against the British in Egypt. He was accordingly released from Brusa and sent down to Damascus. Thence he made a sham escape to Feisal, and went on to Mecca (in October 1917). He persuaded Hussein that he was a man of first importance in Syria, and was commended by him to Feisal. He returned to Akaba in the end of October 1917, and was sent up by Feisal with Ali ibn Hussein and me, to try and cut the Deraa bridges behind von Kress during Allenby's Jerusalem push.

Abd el Kadir was a fanatical Moslem, and had been much annoyed by the Sherifs' friendship with the British. He tried to persuade Ali & me to base ourselves in his Jaulan villages to cut the line, promising us the help of the

---

1 This post had been held since earlier in the year by Lawrence's wartime colleague, Major W. F. Stirling.

2 Frobenius had been head of a German military mission in the Middle East.

Algerian peasantry. We refused this plan (he intended to betray us) and he pretended to be annoyed, and deserted one night from Azrak. He rode into Jebel Druse, to Salkhad where Feisal had an adherent in Hussein el Atrash. Abd el Kadir stayed with him for three days, talking bombastic rot about the Turks, and trying to provoke Hussein el Atrash to rise. He intended to denounce him when he did so. Hussein was too wily to be taken in, and Abd el Kadir slipped away from his house one night, and rode in to the Turks at Deraa. He told them the results of his mission, and especially that Ali & I were going for the Yarmuk bridge that week. The Turks ordered out cavalry to intercept us, but we made our attempt that very night, failed, and slipped back before the Turkish cordon was complete. Abd el Kadir then went to Damascus. I went in to Deraa in disguise to spy out the defences, was caught, and identified by Hajim Bey the Governor by virtue of Abd el Kadir's descriptions of me. (I learnt all about his treachery from Hajim's conversation, and from my guards.) Hajim was an ardent paederast and took a fancy to me. So he kept me under guard till night, and then tried to have me. I was unwilling, and prevailed after some difficulty. Hajim sent me to the hospital, and I escaped before dawn, being not as hurt as he thought. He was so ashamed of the muddle he had made that he hushed the whole thing up, and never reported my capture & escape. I got back to Azrak very annoyed with Abd el Kadir, and rode down to Akaba. Mohammed Said now came across to Feisal with false friendly letters from Jemal[3] in answer to some Feisal had sent to him with my approval. Just before he came Ali Riza sent a note to Feisal to say that Mohammed Said was coming to make anti-Arab propaganda among the officers of the Arab army. So we isolated him, and in disgust he only stayed two days in the camp.

Abd el Kadir now became Jemal's confidential adviser on Arab questions and raised volunteers for him. These fought the British in the first & second Amman raids, and did well for the Turks.

When September 1918 came, and Feisal's flying column attacked Deraa district, Abd el Kadir at once transferred his volunteers to the Hauran, and garrisoned the Railway against us. We captured a lot of them, and they told us of all his efforts against us. When the Turkish débâcle came Abd el Kadir ran away quickly to Damascus, and as soon as the Turks had gone, took forcible control of the local government, in virtue of the remains of his Algerian volunteers.

When Nasr & I arrived Abd el Kadir & Mohammed Said were sitting in the Serail with their armed servants. Feisal had begged me to get rid of them,

3 See p. 164 note I.

so I told them to go, and that Shukri el Ayubi would be military governor till Ali Riza returned. Abd el Kadir refused to go, and tried to stab me in the council chamber. Auda knocked him down, & Nuri Shaalan offered me the help of the Rualla to put him out. Mohammed Said & Abd el Kadir then went away, breathing vengeance against me as a Christian. I thought they would be quiet, but that night they called a secret meeting of their Algerians & the Druses, & begged them to strike one blow for the faith before the British arrived. I heard of this, warned General Nuri Said, and borrowed the Rualla from Nuri Shaalan. With the latter I rushed Abd el Kadir's house, and took him, while Nuri Said cleared the Druses out of the streets. I meant to shoot the two brothers, so interned Abd el Kadir in the Town Hall till I should have caught Mohammed Said. Before I had done so Feisal arrived, and said that like a new Sultan he would issue a general amnesty. So Abd el Kadir escaped again. He got some of his men to shoot at me that same day, but I won.

(Later on Abd el Kadir broke out again, and went for Feisal's house, & was shot, I believe by one of the sentries. This was after I left.)

If ever two people deserved hanging or shooting in Syria they were these two brothers, and I very much regret that Mohammed Said has been given so much rope. Feisal has asked several times for his internment. He is the only real pan-Islamist in Damascus, and in his insanity is capable of any folly or crime against us.

T. E.Lawrence

University of Texas

FREDERICK J. DAW
5.7.[19]19   *[CAIRO]*

Dear Dawes [*sic*]
Will you buy yourself some trifle to remind you of our rather rough landing together at Rome? I was not at all comfortable hanging up in the wreck, and felt very grateful to you for digging me out.[1]

Yours sincerely
T E Lawrence   *Bodleian Library*

I Daw was an Aircraftman of the R.A.F. The letter was accompanied by a cheque for £10.

FROM A PEACE CONFERENCE MEMORANDUM[1]
[18 or 19 July 1919]   [PARIS]

Some of these officers are resigning' from the Arab Army, and in that case they will presumably return to Mesopotamia as private citizens. As they are all the men in Mesopotamia who had the courage to fight for their country, I regret that they are apparently going to be driven into opposition to our administration there. It is curious that men useful (indeed necessary) to Allenby in Syria should be 'spreaders of undesirable propaganda' in Mesopotamia. I prefer the terms of Lord Curzon's letter of June 16.[2]

TEL

TNA: PRO FO 608/92

VYVYAN RICHARDS
I. Sept. [1919]   *2 POLSTEAD ROAD [OXFORD]*

[...] I'm out of the army today: and today I have paid for 5 acres 2 rods 30 poles of Pole Hill:[1] that is the whole upper field, down to the rudimentary hedge. I haven't yet got the conveyance, so am not yet the legal owner, but they cannot draw back from the bargain, and as far as I'm concerned it's finished. I feel years more settled in mind, and hope that we will acquire merit there together. When we meet next (or even before) we'll have to make up our serious minds how to tackle Gardiner. I have not yet been able to buy the

1 This is Lawrence's note on a memorandum circulated for comment entitled 'Return of Feisal's Officers to Mesopotamia', dated 18 July, which quoted a Foreign Office telegram of 17 July stating 'that it is inadvisable to give official countenance to the spread of undesirable propaganda in Mesopotamia'. Lawrence had already made clear his thoughts on this subject in his note to Sir Louis Mallet dated 22 April 1919 (*see* p. 172).
2 The 'letter of June 16' giving Lord Curzon's views stated that 'his Lordship would deprecate any appearance on the part of His Majesty's Government of putting obstacles in the way of the return to their native country of men who have volunteered for service in the Allied cause and have been of such assistance to the Allied operation in Syria'.

1 Pole Hill was a property in Essex where he planned to set up a printing press with Vyvyan Richards.

hedge from the Chingford Estate, and am so short of funds temporarily that I am not pressing them vigorously.

I hope to have about £300 more in six weeks time, and we must then interview builders. The anti-aircraft station fate is still uncertain. The Air Ministry and the War Office cannot decide who is in charge of London air defence. I just thought I'd write and tell you of the Hill: and also that I've borrowed your Bradley.[2] I'm not studying it, but find gobbets (*e.g.* the discussion of space) most stimulating and suggestive. How pleased Bradley would be if he knew I approved of it. *a rivederci.*

L.

DG

G.J. KIDSTON[1]
[14 November 1919][2]

Dear Kidston
You asked me 'Why' today, and I'm going to tell you exactly what my motives in the Arab affair were, in order of strength:

(i) Personal. I liked a particular Arab very much, and I thought that freedom for the race would be an acceptable present.[3]

(ii) Patriotic. I wanted to help win the war, and Arab help reduced Allenby's losses by thousands.

(iii) Intellectual curiosity. I wanted to feel what it was like to be the mainspring of a national movement, and to have some millions of people expressing themselves through me: and being a half-poet, I don't value material

---

2 F. H. Bradley, brother of the noted Shakespearian scholar A. C. Bradley, was the author of several influential works on metaphysics and logic.

1 A member of the Eastern Section of the Foreign Office who had asked Lawrence about his motives during the war.
2 I have retained the date given in *The Sunday Times* of 16 June 1968 in which this letter was first published, but internal evidence suggests that it was probably written much earlier in 1919. It is also published in Knightley and Simpson's *The Secret Lives of Lawrence of Arabia*.
3 Presumably a reference to Dahoum.

things much. Sensation and mind seem to me much greater, and the ideal, such a thing as the impulse that took us into Damascus, the only thing worth doing.

(iv) Ambition. You know how Lionel Curtis[4] has made his conception of the Empire — a Commonwealth of free peoples – generally accepted. I wanted to widen that idea beyond the Anglo-Saxon shape, and form a new nation of thinking people, all acclaiming our freedom, and demanding admittance into our Empire. There is, to my eyes, no other road for Egypt and India in the end, and I would have made their path easier, by creating an Arab Dominion in the Empire.

I don't think there are any other reasons. You are sufficiently Scotch to understand my analysing my own mind so formally. The process intended was to take Damascus, and run it (as anyone fully knowing the East and West could run it), as an independent ally of G[reat] B[ritain]. Then to turn on Hejaz and conquer it: then to project the semi-educated Syrians on Yemen, and build that up quickly (without Yemen there is no re-birth for the Arabs) and finally to receive Mesopotamia into the block so made: all this could be done in thirty years directed effort, and without impairing British holdings. It is only the substitute of a 999 years' lease for a complete sale.[5]

Now look what happened when we took Damascus: —

Motive (i) I found had died some weeks before: so my gift was wasted, and my future doings indifferent on that count.

Motive (ii). This was achieved, for Turkey was broken, and the central powers were so unified that to break one was to break all.

Motive (iii). This was romantic mainly, and one never repeats a sensation. When I rode into Damascus the whole country-side was on fire with enthusiasm, and in the town a hundred thousand people shouted my name. Success always kills hope by surfeit.

---

4 Lionel Curtis (1872-1955): fellow of All Souls College, lecturer in colonial history, former member of the Transvaal Legislative Council, barrister, civil servant, editor and author. From 1923 one of Lawrence's most constant correspondents.

5 The previous paragraph suggests a vision of the British Empire not unlike the present British Commonwealth; compare his letter to Lord Curzon of 27 September 1919 (in *DG*, not reprinted here) in which he wrote: 'My own ambition is that the Arabs should be our first brown dominion, and not our last brown colony.' This paragraph appears to suggest that such a dominion should be formed by conquest; but again see the letter to Curzon which makes the same point but less dramatically: 'It seems to me inevitable that the next stage of the Arab Movement will be the transfer of the Hejaz towns to Damascus in the same relation as they formerly stood to Turkey.' For other variations on this theme, *see* the last page of *Seven Pillars* and the famous passage beginning 'All men dream...' in the introductory chapter.

Motive (iv). This remained, but it was not strong enough to make me stay. I asked Allenby for leave, and when he gave it me, came straight home. It's the dying remains of this weakest of all my reasons which made me put up a half-fight for Feisal in Paris and elsewhere, and which occasionally drives me into your room to jest about what might be done.

If you want to make me work again you would have to re-create motives (ii) and (iii). As you are not God, Motive (i) is beyond your power.

I'm not conscious of having done a crooked thing to anyone since I began to push the Arab Movement, though I prostituted myself in Arab Service. For an Englishman to put himself at the disposal of a red race is to sell himself to a brute, like Swift's Houyhnhnms.[6] However my body and soul were my own, and no one can reproach me for what I do to them: and to all the rest of you I'm clean. When you have got as far as this, please burn it all. I've never told anyone before, and may not again, because it isn't nice to open oneself out. I laugh at myself because giving up has made me look so futile.

T.E.L.

Bodleian Library[7]

6 In the fourth part of *Gulliver's Travels*, the Houyhnhnms, a race of noble and rational horses, are contrasted with the Yahoos, who are human-shaped but brutish in their behaviour. *See* 'Chapter I' of *Seven Pillars*, where the same idea occurs: 'A man who gives himself to be a possession of aliens leads a Yahoo life, having bartered his soul to a brute-master.'
7 Published in *The Sunday Times* on 16 June 1968; also in Knightley and Simpson's *The Secret Lives of Lawrence of Arabia* (Nelson, 1969).

ST J. B. PHILBY[1]
21.11.19   [ALL SOULS COLLEGE OXFORD]

Dear Philby

I'll drop in on Monday evening about 5.30: if you don't put me off meanwhile. Please do so like a shot if anything turns up, for I have ample leisure.

Yours sincerely

T E Lawrence

Also please don't call me Colonel. That folly died months ago.

L.

Then the ostrich egg. That's another remissness. I'll call for it next time I'm up. For the moment an economy fit is on me, and so I sit here and glower through my window at the quad: (you would call it a court).[2]

TEL

St Antony's College Oxford

SIR ARCHIBALD MURRAY[1]
10.1.20   2 POLSTEAD ROAD OXFORD

Dear Sir Archibald Murray

I am painfully aware of what Mr. Lowell Thomas is doing. He came out to Egypt on behalf of the American Government, spent a fortnight in Arabia (I saw him twice in that time) and there he seems to have realised my 'star' value on the film.

1 Harry St John Bridger Philby (1885-1960): explorer, orientalist, member of the Indian Civil Service, father of the spy, Kim Philby. Philby had led the British political mission to central Arabia in 1917-18, but the two men did not meet until June 1919, when Lawrence reached Crete during his prolonged flight to Egypt; it was in Philby's aircraft that he finally reached Cairo.
2 Oxford quadrangle is Cambridge court; Philby had been at Trinity College, Cambridge.

1 Sir Archibald Murray (1860-1945) was the commander-in-chief Egyptian Expeditionary Force from early 1916 to mid-1917, when he was succeeded by General Allenby.

Anyway since he has been lecturing in America & London, & has written a series of six articles about me, for American & English publication. They are as rank as possible, and are making life very difficult for me, as I have neither the money nor the wish to maintain my constant character as the mountebank he makes me.

He has a lot of correct information, & fills it out with stories picked up from officers, & by imagination. In your case you are saddled with what Holdich[2] did (when I went to Arabia I had never seen you, & I don't suppose you had ever heard of me: we first met in Cairo when I came back from Yenbo) and I wish I could escape so lightly. My impressions when I saw General Allenby were mixed, for after considerable difficulties (you may remember a conference in Ismailia, when you were not very kind!) what we had done & said had persuaded you & General Lynden Bell,[3] and you had sent a report to London supporting the Arab affair warmly. Then you were recalled, & I wondered how Allenby would look on us. As a matter of fact he was magnificent.

Lowell Thomas asked me to correct his proofs: but this I decided was impossible, since I could not possibly pass one tenth of it, & he was making his living out of it. He then asked me what view I would take about misstatements, & I said that I would confirm or deny nothing in public. The stuff was to me too obvious journalism to weigh very deep with anyone serious. If you wish I will write to him and correct the remarks about you: but I would point out that I am sitting still while he calls me an Irishman, and a Prince of Mecca and other beastlinesses, and it seems hardly possible to begin putting it straight.

I am very glad you wrote to me, because I have been wondering for some time about writing to you. I put on paper my account of what happened to me in Arabia some time ago, but had it stolen from me, and am therefore doing it again, rather differently.[4] It seems to me unfit for publication, but if published

---

2 Colonel Holdich: *see* p. 132 note 2.

3 General Lynden Bell had been Murray's chief-of-staff.

4 The first version of *Seven Pillars* was lost at Reading Station (between London and Oxford) in November 1919. *See* Liddell Hart's notes on a conversation with Lawrence dated 1 August 1933: 'Details of loss of 1st [version]: On train journey from London to Oxford. Went into refreshment room at Reading and put bag under table. Left it. Phoned up from Oxford an hour later, but no sign of missing bag – it was a bank messenger's bag, the "thing they carried gold in" (It was manuscript – on loose-leaf ledger; blank sheets, not ruled. Only wrote one side of page. None of it was ever typed.) T. E. wonders – Did fancy (involuntarily) play with it?' (*T. E. Lawrence to His Biographers* Part II, p. 145) 'Surely an invitation to theft' was Dr Mack's comment. However, A. W. Lawrence refutes any suggestion that he deliberately put the manuscript at risk: 'To me it is inconceivable that the bag can have been lost "accidentally on purpose".' (Letter to me, 29 November 1987).

it will have some success (for the story is in parts very odd and exciting – there were many strange things) and will probably last a long time, & influence other accounts in the future, for it is not badly written, & is authoritative, in so far as it concerns myself.

You are mentioned inevitably, by name five or six times, (not always perhaps just as you would have put things, but to my information, correctly) and I wondered whether you would agree to look it over in MSS. The labour would not be great, for I could mark the places concerning you, and I rather want everybody mentioned to see it, in case of accident. It sounds like blackmail, but I fear there is nothing worth paying for, and I do not think there is anything that will annoy you too much. If there was, and it was possible, I would knock it out.[5]

As I said, the first draft was stolen, & the second is not finished, so this letter is a little too soon: but if you will be so kind as to allow me to send it to you, then there need be no delay when it is ready.

Please write to me if you want [the] Lowell Thomas thing altered (it will probably come out in book form, & I suppose in French & Arabic & Chinese & Esperanto also), and I will see that it is done at once. I don't pay him ... but I could kick his card-house down if I got annoyed, & so he has to be polite. As a matter of fact he is a very decent fellow – but an American journalist, scooping.

Yours sincerely
T E Lawrence

Please address Mr. now. My colonel days are over!

Harvard University

---

5 I am not aware that Murray took up Lawrence's offer, but if he had done so he might have been less than pleased. *See* letter to C. E. Wilson dated 19 February 1926: 'I've shortened the new edition [...] by [...] making two words do for six. Where Archie Murray was described as "jealous, spiteful, bad-tempered, vicious, clever, quick & narrow" he is now called "feminine & feline".'

MISS FAREEDAH EL AKLE
Feb. 16 [1920]

Dear Miss Faridah

Of course I'll write to you: why did you ever think I wouldn't? It was only bad
manners for the man to begin the correspondence with the lady.[1]

I was very glad to have your news at last. Mrs Rieder told me you were alive
& well, and this was good news after all the horrors of the war in Syria. At
any rate, however bad things are now they were worse then.

Please thank the Jabail people from me: though I fear I did very little, &
that little has been misunderstood.

[...] Feisal is a very nice fellow, much too good for the horrible trade of
politics, and too weak to do the right thing just now. However we are going
to do our duty in Mesopotamia, so if you live out your proper life (this is, I
believe, if you eat a lot and work a little) you will see everything come true. It
is going to take many years.

For myself, I have stopped all my work, and am just wandering about
London thinking. It sounds rather silly, but in reality it is a very happy
business. I hope you will be able to come to England some day, as we always
talked about. You would find it so odd, so small & so crowded.

If you want to write to me, you will be wisest to write to Oxford. Better
not write politics, because they may look at your letters.

There is no book [title in Arabic]: an American has told a lot of lies about
me, that's all. And I'm afraid I can't ever come to Syria again. Because I failed.[2]
L.

Bodleian Library

1 Miss el Akle wrote in reply to Lawrence's opening gambit: 'So you expect the lady to start
   the correspondence! And what if she happens to be an oriental being, whose customs and
   ways are just the reverse of yours???'
2 Miss el Akle replied: 'You say "you failed". Is it meekness on your part to say that? After
   all that you have achieved, you may have failed in letting others see what you think is right.
   The failure, therefore, is on *their* side, and not *yours*.'

COLONEL S. F. NEWCOMBE
16.2.20

Dear S.F.

I owe you five letters! At first it wasn't worth while for you were reported to me in one week as at Aleppo, Azrak, Bagdad & Cairo: and then it became a habit.

However the arrival of a smaller (I hope not cheaper) edition[1] is an occasion for a bookworm like myself. The *editio princeps* always has a special value: but in some cases (Shakespeare folios *e.g.*) new matter is embodied in the reprints, which gives them a market reputation little, if any, less than original. At the same time collectors, and especially collectors of sentiment, always prefer the genuine article.

However Mrs. Newcombe will regard the graft as the first. These things, as Solomon quoted from Adam's table-talk, depend on the point of view. Please give her my heartiest congratulations.

Then about business. Of course Lawrence may have been the name of your absolutely favourite cousin or aunt, (observe my adroitness in sex), and if so I will be dropping an immodest brick by blushing – but if it isn't, aren't you handicapping 'it'? In the history of the world (cheap edition) I'm a sublimated Aladdin, the thousand and second Knight, a *Strand-Magazine* strummer. In the eyes of 'those who know'[2] I failed badly in attempting a piece of work which a little more resolution would have pushed through, or left un-touched. So either case it is bad for the sprig, unless, as I said, there is a really decent aunt.

As for god-fathering him, I asked two or three people what it meant, & their words were ribald. Perhaps it is because people near me lose that sense of mystery which distance gives. Or else it was because they didn't know it was you – or at least yours. Anyhow I can't find out what it means, and so I shall be delighted to take it on. Everybody agrees it means a silver mug – but tell me first if his complexion is red or white: I wouldn't commit a colour-discord.

Give Rose my ~~love~~ you will know what to say … something neat, & not too Newcomian. As for the rugs, please take any that seem worthy to you.

---

1 Colonel Newcombe's son, Stewart Lawrence Newcombe just been born.
2 'Those who know': Garnett presumed that Lawrence was quoting Dante (*Inferno*, Canto IV) on Aristotle: *Il maestro di color che sanno* – 'The master of those that know'; but as a great reader of Tennyson Lawrence might well have had in mind the latter's description of Francis Bacon in *The Palace of Art*: 'as large-browed Verulam/The first of those who know'. Very probably he was consciously echoing both these sources.

There were two Afghans in the Arab Bureau, & a big (and not bad but thin) Shiraz, in the Savoy.

I have abandoned Oxford, & wander about town from a bedroom in Pimlico, (temporary, for Bethnal Green is nicer to the nose) looking at the stars. It is nicer than looking at Lord Curzon.

Please give Mrs. Newcombe my very best regards. How odd it must be having married you. Tell her my letter wasn't fit for her to see.

L.

Hogarth sends his warmest congrats. to all three.

Seriously I am changing my own name, to be more quiet, and wish I could change my face, to be more lovely, & beloved!

DG

AUGUSTUS JOHN[1]
19.3.20

Dear John

Really I'm hotter stuff than I thought: the wrathful portrait went off at top speed for a thousand to a Duke! That puts me for the moment easily at the head of the field in your selling plate. Of course I know you will naturally think the glory is yours – but I believe it's due to the exceeding beauty of my face.

---

1 Augustus John (1878-1961) had been an official artist at the Paris Peace Conference and it was there that he had met Lawrence. This letter was a response to John's exhibition entitled *Types* which had opened at the Alpine Club Art Gallery, London, in early March 1920. Among the 'types' were portraits of the father of the modern British Navy Lord Fisher, the assistant foreign secretary Lord Robert Cecil, and George Bernard Shaw; and there were two portraits of Lawrence and two of Feisal. The so-called 'wrathful portrait' (*see* first paragraph) was bought by the Duke of Westminster, who later in 1920 presented it to the Tate Gallery. It was reproduced in black and white on p. 126 of the 1935 edition of *Seven Pillars of Wisdom*. A copy of it hangs in the Hall of Jesus College, Oxford.

May I write to Orpen[2] and say what a pity I think it that you troubled to paint 38 other people? It means of course a pity from the commercial point of view only, for there is no doubt the others set me off! What do artists' models of the best sort fetch per hour (or perhaps per job, for I might fall on a Cezanne, and I don't want to get rich)? It seems to me that I have a future.

I went to your show last Thursday, with Lionel Curtis. We were admiring me, and a person with a military moustache joined us, and blurted out to us: 'Looks a bloody sort of creature doesn't he?' Curtis with some verve said 'Yes'. I looked very pink.

Yours
TEL

Tate Gallery Archives London[3]

F. N. DOUBLEDAY[1]
29.3.20

[...] Unless I am starving (involuntary) there will be no London publisher. My whole object is to make the money in U.S.A. and so avoid the notoriety of being on sale in England. One gets, inshallah, the goods without the publicity.

Please thank Mrs. Doubleday for her letter: and assure her that I would have answered it by cable, only that she called me Colonel, which is an antique, red-faced, shrivelled man, with a white moustache: quite horrible.

Yours sincerely
T.E. Lawrence

Bodleian Library

2 Sir William Orpen (1878-1931) had been a war artist on the Western Front and had also been present at the Paris Peace Conference, where he had met and portrayed Lawrence. Robert Graves saw in Orpen's portrait 'a sort of street urchin furtiveness' which he recognized and endorsed, but Lawrence much preferred John's interpretation of him to Orpen's.
3 Microfiche TAM 21G (64/67).

1 Frank Nelson Doubleday was head of the American publishing house which would eventually publish *Seven Pillars*. He and Lawrence had met at a dinner party in London in December 1918 and subsequently at the Paris Peace Conference.

ROBERT GRAVES[1]

15.IV.20   *[ALL SOULS COLLEGE OXFORD]*

Dear Graves

I am settled in All Souls for five or six weeks: and owe you a letter and many thanks for your blue booklet:[2] do look me up when you first can: I'd like to see you any time day or night, though we won't dine in College – too heavy that for my taste.

If you could warn me before you come it would be prudent, since my movements are as odd as my manners. Suppose you begin with a lunch any day except the 21st?

Yours ever

T E Lawrence

(No longer a Colonel, please!)

Harvard University

---

1 Robert Graves (1895-1985): poet, novelist, writer of one of the undisputed classics of the Great War *Goodbye to All That*, and, in 1927, author of the first popular biography of Lawrence by a British author, *Lawrence and the Arabs* (Cape, 1927). At this time, although 24 and married, he was an Oxford undergraduate at St John's College. The two men had met at a guest-night at All Souls in the course of which, during a discussion about Greek poetry, Lawrence had said: 'You must be Graves the poet? I read a book of yours in Egypt in 1917 and thought it pretty good.' This was the start of a long though not always untroubled friendship.
2 Graves's book of poems *Country Sentiment*, published by Martin Secker in England and by Knopf in America in March 1920.

EZRA POUND [1]
Sunday [April 1920]   *ALL SOULS COLLEGE OXFORD*

Dear Pound

Your letter has confused me. I'd very much like to write, especially to make money, (regretting exceedingly that it must be prose which is only half-price), but there are difficulties.

First of all I haven't even a wish to feel the existence of a vortex – if I had one I'd try to get it cut out: – and so I fear that my writing would not be to your standard. Of course *The Dial* may be ordinary, but I haven't seen it, and so it is likely to resemble *Blast*.[2]

That leads up to difficulty the second. You'll say you don't care a — what I write, so long as I sign it by my name, which has a certain value as advertisement.

True, but I won't use it therefore.[3] Here in Oxford I'm still Lawrence (not Colonel, please), but in London I've changed it, for peace and cleanliness, and I couldn't dream of printing anything over it.

Wherefore it seems to me I'm no good to you. The cinema doesn't in the least represent the truth, and what I do truly, must therefore sail under other than cinema colours.

---

1 Ezra Pound, controversial American poet (1885-1972), had been long prominent in English literary circles, though he was shortly to move to Paris and then to settle more or less permanently in Italy. He was co-founder of the Imagist school of poetry (with Richard Aldington and Hilda Doolittle), and author of the *Cantos* and other volumes of poetry. Lawrence was writing in reply to a letter by Pound dated 20 April 1920 (addressed in characteristic style to 'My dear Hadji ben Abt el Bakshish, Prince de Meque, Two-Sworded Samurai', etc.) in which the subject of Lawrence's contributing to the American literary magazine *The Dial*, famous for publishing many of the most distinguished writers of the day, was discussed.
2 In referring to 'a vortex' and to *Blast*, Lawrence was alluding to the aggressive literary movement known as Vorticism of which Pound was a leading member and which had expressed its literary philosophy in a magazine entitled *Blast*, edited by Pound and Wyndham Lewis.
3 On the matter of his wish to write anonymously, Pound had commented: 'Also I don't care a saffron ... whether you use your name or not; only if you don't you will be under the shameful and ignominious necessity of writing something which will interest the editor.' He added: 'In sending copy to America, let me caution you to use an incognito as well as a pseudonym ... My bright compatriots are quite capable of printing an article by Mr Smith, and then printing a leetle note at the end of the number saying "The article by Mr Smith is really written by the distinguished Sheik-tamer and Tiger-baiter etc who for reasons of modesty has concealed himself 'neath the name of Smith-Yapper' *See also* Lawrence's letter to Pound dated 20 August 1920.

I came down here (penniless!) last Thursday after a six months' very pleasant loaf in London: and here I'll stay till quarter-day (June) and then back to London. They give me credit in this establishment.

Congratulations on going to Italy. You'll be a millionaire there on small outgoings and it's going to be beautifully warm. I wish I could leave England for a long spell. No such luck.

Yours sincerely
T E Lawrence

Bodleian Library[4]

H. ST J. B. PHILBY
21 May [1920]   *ALL SOULS*

Dear Philby
A word of explanation about this. It happens to be – politically – the right moment for pressure towards a new Middle East Department, since some re-shuffling of spheres is certain to happen quite soon: and the enclosed is a step taken under advice, to add pressure from outside, to what is going on inside.

They have asked me to get your name on the list: other 'experts' invited are Hogarth, Curtis, Toynbee, & myself. I have no doubt you will agree, so I won't bother to argue. It is a step necessary before a new policy can be put in force, and when we get it through, then we'll have to open up a battery of advice on the new men.

There are five peers in it (*pour encourager...*) and two or three of each H. of C. group – Maclean & Benn: Lord R. Cecil & Aubrey Herbert: Hoare & Elliott: Yate & Glyn: Clynes & Barnes: all chosen for 'weight' reasons in the present balance of power.

4 This and a later letter to Pound (p. 192) were published in the literary magazine *Nine* in 1950.

Curzon is of course the enemy: but he's not a very bold enemy, & won't like a rift in his family showing up: I have good hopes of it.[1]

Yours
E.L.

I called on Wed: but vainly: will try again next week.

St Antony's College Oxford

WILFRED SCAWEN BLUNT[1]
10.8.20   *ALL SOULS COLLEGE OXFORD*

Dear Mr. Blunt
This letter is so long delayed that it is very hard to write: but I felt for a long time that it would be butting in on you, and then when I saw the note you sent to Philby, I felt I might risk it.

Unfortunately I have been driven down into Oxford (here I live on credit: elsewhere I need cash!) and will be here probably for another month. I'd very

1 Philby joined Lawrence's distinguished lobby, which duly approached Lord Curzon, who was foreign secretary. Elizabeth Monroe's biography of Philby gives the background to this initiative: 'Delay over framing a peace treaty with Turkey, caused partly by President Wilson's stroke, and consequent uncertainty over American intentions in the Middle East, gave scope for much amateur planning of the Arab future. Philby, always ready to join campaigns that interested him, found himself in demand on committees and deputations ... He joined a deputation collected by T. E. Lawrence to rescue the Middle East from the "pernicious grasp" of the India Office and Foreign Office. This group asked Curzon for a "semi-diplomatic, semi-administrative clearing house" that would put an end to clashes over British policy in the Arab world between rival political governments. With Lord Robert Cecil, D. G. Hogarth, Lionel Curtis, Arnold Toynbee, T. E. Lawrence, Aubrey Herbert and politicians of all three political parties "chosen for weight reasons", Philby called at the Foreign Office to lobby for this change, only to be defeated by Curzon's "Indian outlook".' (*Philby of Arabia*, 1973, p. 103) However, the defeat was not total in that Middle East affairs were transferred from the Foreign and India offices in 1921, but not to a separate department; they went to the Colonial Office under Churchill as colonial secretary, where he asked Lawrence to join him.

1 Wilfred Scawen Blunt (1840-1922) was a man of many parts: famous traveller, anti-imperialist, supporter of Egyptian nationalism and Irish home rule (he was briefly imprisoned in 1888 while agitating for the latter cause), poet, historian, biographer, and diarist. At this time a veteran of 80, he was living in retirement at Newbuildings Place, Southwater, Sussex.

much like to come down and see you, and if you'll let me write again when it is possible for me to say what time, I'll be very much obliged.

Yours sincerely
T E Lawrence[2]

Fitzwilliam Museum Cambridge

EZRA POUND[1]
20.8.20   *ALL SOULS COLLEGE OXFORD*

0 E–P!

For twenty days I have been faced by your letter: each day I read a new name of a contributor to *The Dial*: but there is surely no place for me in that galaxy? Of course Joyce can write (and does, just occasionally): you can write (and do): T. S. Eliot ... perhaps: but the people I like are so different, Hodgson; Sassoon: D. H. Lawrence: Manning: Conrad: [...] but do you see the point? I'm academic idyllic, romantic: you breathe commas and exclamation marks. We ought not to exist together on one earth, but the earth is so broad-minded that she doesn't care.

I've written in the *Round Table*: in *The Times*: in the *Daily Herald*: in the *Army Quarterly* (all anonymous). I've never read any Fritz Vanderpyl: I don't feel as though I must: where can I see *The Dial* free of charge because I'm broke to the world, and can't buy it: surely R. Aldington[2] and W. B. Yeats[3] are no good?

E.L.

Bodleian Library

2 Blunt replied: 'Any one who can talk to me of Arabia & the desert life finds a free seat at my coffee hearth & you especially who know so much.' Blunt's reply is printed in full in *Letters to T. E. Lawrence*, edited by A. W. Lawrence.

I *See* previous letter to Pound of April 1920, p. 189.
2 An interesting comment on the poet and novelist who was to become, thirty-five years later, Lawrence's bitterest critic.
3 For a later, different view of Yeats *see* p. 497.

WILLIAM ROTHENSTEIN[1]
27.9.20 *ALL SOULS COLLEGE OXFORD*

Dear Rothenstein

I've behaved rottenly in not answering your first card: only I made a vow not to write before I'd finished a job I was doing – and I have not finished it yet.

On the same account I can't come up to London till next month – October 1 or 2 probably, but then I'll be there for some weeks, and that will give you a tremendous chance. I'm sorry for the delay ... but it is beyond my power to alter for the moment.

The world is still running on top-gear, apparently, and that makes quietists like myself nearly breathless: however, perhaps it's better than being dull. Only (*ridiculus mus*) it breaks up my work horribly!

Yours sincerely
T.E.L.

I have about a thousand unanswered letters: so instead of cursing my slowness, you should be singing for joy of getting even a fortnight-old word.

L.

Bodleian Library

CHARLES DOUGHTY
October 4 1920 *ALL SOULS COLLEGE OXFORD*

Dear Mr. Doughty

I'm very glad that *Arabia Deserta* is being pushed so fast. It will be a great thing

---

1 Later Sir William Rothenstein (1872-1945: knighted 1931): artist, trained at the Slade School London and later in Paris, where he knew Degas and Toulouse-Lautrec; official war artist with British and Canadian Forces in the First World War. He and Lawrence met in London in the autumn of 1920 and shortly afterwards Rothenstein began a painting of him in Arab dress. The letter is about the arrangements for the necessary sittings. Rothenstein wrote of him in *Lawrence by His Friends*: 'Generous with his time, he never seemed to object to standing for hours together.'

to have it on the market once more: though I regret the price, which seems terribly high.[1]

It is good that you should look over the proofs: the first edition had singularly few misprints, and it will be a pity if the second falls below it in accuracy.

Your preface will add very much to the understanding of the book, and I look forward to reading it.

I wish I could say the same about my miserable effort. They asked me for 5000 words, and I managed it at last: but it was as difficult a thing as I have tackled, and the whole affair is in shocking taste. Of course *Arabia Deserta* cannot be prefaced by anyone but the author. The Medici people were interested only in their American sales, in which my name will be useful, for I have had better advertisements there than you have had: but the people who like *Arabia* will find my thing a blemish, and will be annoyed with me for writing it, and with you for letting me write it!

However time will cure all these things: and I'll make sure that my note appears only in the second edition!

Yours sincerely
T. E. Lawrence

If possible I will come down to Eastbourne and see you at the end of next term. October and November are very busy months for me.

L.

Bodleian Library

---

1 Lawrence had been for many years an admirer of Doughty's classic work, *Travels in Arabia Deserta*, which he had read avidly as a boy and had found of considerable value during the war. However, it had long been out of print and he had therefore launched a personal campaign to have it republished. His first thought was to have this done by the Egyptian Survey Department which had printed the *Arab Bulletin*, but in the end it was published more effectively and nearer home by the Medici Society in association with Jonathan Cape. The price of his achieving this ambition was that he was required to write an introduction – the 'miserable effort' referred to in the fourth paragraph.

MISS FAREEDAH EL AKLE
January 3 [1921]

Dear Miss Fareedah

I wonder how many letters from you to me have gone astray? You mention one in April. I don't know when it was, but long ago I got one, and answered it! I distinctly remember that, as I was proud of it, for I very seldom write letters.
[...]
Don't take what is said in *Asia* too accurately.[1] L. Thomas was never up country with me at all (and only ten days in Arabia, far behind the front) and his stories of fighting & riding are second-hand. The Arab war was not nearly as silly as he makes out: and I was not in charge of it, or even very prominent. Only I was in fancy dress, & so I made a good 'star' for his film. Dahoum died some years ago, during the war, of fever.[2]

No, I don't see Mrs. Rieder nowadays, & I haven't seen Noel since he was in Jebail. I expect he's grown up now. Mrs. Rieder lives in London I think. I saw her once in Paris in 1919.

I didn't see Miss Holmes' book. You know I'm busy at book-printing now, and read very little. Also I've forgotten all the Arabic I ever knew – reading or writing, that is: probably I could still talk it, if I ever met an Arab, but I haven't seen one since July 1919 – which you remember was not very much: not as much as it should have been, in view of the excellence of my teachers.

My best address is All Souls College Oxford and I'm Mr. Lawrence now! There is no reason why the post should be bad.

I've long given up politics.

Yours sincerely
TEL

Bodleian Library

1 *Asia*: journal of the American Asiatic Society of New York, which had published articles by Lowell Thomas about Lawrence.
2 Miss el Akle had asked for information about Dahoum.

Lawrence had found a friend and admirer in the former war artist Eric Kennington, whom he had invited to help with the provision of illustrations for his book, and the two men had planned a visit to the Middle East, so that Kennington could meet and draw portraits of some of Lawrence's Arab comrades-in-arms. In the end, however, Kennington went on his own while Lawrence, persuaded by Churchill to join him at the Colonial Office, travelled with his new chief to Egypt for the Cairo Peace Conference.

WILFRED SCAWEN BLUNT
2.3.21

Dear Mr. Blunt
It's very good of you to have written to me. I'm only sorry that the short time will not let me come & see you, or write to you properly[1]. We start tomorrow, or rather this morning for Cairo, for that odd conference, where I'll either get my way or resign – or even do both things!

It's the Colonial Office: Winston is a new and very keen mind on the Middle East business, & I hope will take it the right way. It's a very great chance given me.

Yours sincerely
T E Lawrence

Fitzwilliam Museum Cambridge

HIS MOTHER
March 20, 1921   *SEMIRAMIS HOTEL CAIRO*

We got here about a fortnight ago: and it has been one of the longest fortnights I ever lived: started about March 3, & went via Marseilles & Alexandria. Eight days out.

---

1 Blunt had written to him on 26 February 1921: 'A line to congratulate you on having forced your policy on the Foreign (or is it the Colonial) Office & I should be glad to have another talk with you before you leave England again for the East.' (*Letters to T. E. Lawrence*, edited by A. W. Lawrence)

Here we live in a marble & bronze hotel, very expensive & luxurious: horrible place: makes me Bolshevik. Everybody Middle East is here, except Joyce & Hogarth. We have done a lot of work, which is almost finished. Day after tomorrow we go to Jerusalem for a week: after that don't know: perhaps home: perhaps I return to Egypt for a further fortnight.

Kennington has gone to Damascus.

Can't tell you anything else. Have seen Allenby several times, he's very fit: Kennington drew him, & Ironside[1] & me: wanted to draw Gertrude,[2] but hadn't time.

We're a very happy family: agreed upon everything important: and the trifles are laughed at.

Hope A is better.

N.

HL/Bodleian Library

HIS MOTHER
April 12 [1921]   *GRAND CONTINENTAL HOTEL CAIRO*

Back here in Cairo for two days: have been moving rapidly since I last wrote. We went from Cairo about March 25 to Jerusalem, stopping at Gaza on the way. Two days later I was driven over by car to Salt, across Jordan, where I met Abdulla, Feisal's brother, who drove back to Jerusalem with me. It was an amusing performance, for the people of Salt & Jerusalem were very enthusiastic & excited, & nearly mobbed the car in their anxiety to welcome Abdulla.

From Jerusalem I went, on the 31st back to Amman by car, through Salt. The country across Jordan is all in spring, and the grass & flowers are beautiful. On this side of Jordan the rains have not been very good, & things are too dry already.

Spent eight days in Amman, living with Abdulla in his camp. It was rather like the life in war time, with hundreds of Bedouin coming & going, & a general atmosphere of newness in the air. However the difference was that now everybody is trying to be peaceful.

1 General Sir Edmund Ironside.
2 Gertrude Bell.

On Saturday last I ran back to Jerusalem by car (it takes six hours from Amman) & on Sunday I went down to Ramleh, on the coast plain near Jaffa, where our aerodrome is, & flew with four machines to Amman. Abdulla had been longing for aeroplanes, & gave us a great reception & a large lunch. Then we went back to Ramleh, & I went up to Jerusalem to dinner.

Next morning they drove me down to Ramleh, where another four machines took me in to Egypt: and here I have been yesterday and today.

Tonight I'm off to Jerusalem again, and after three days there to Amman, with Sir H. Samuel,[1] who is going over to call on Abdulla, & who will probably stay two nights. Some of his party want to see Petra, so perhaps after that I'll go down there for a night or two to show them round. That ought to finish my jobs out here. I'll be very glad to get back. Would you tell Hogarth of my movements? I haven't written to anyone since I left, & he may be back by now.

N
I am trying to buy him some bronze weapons from tombs on Philistine plain, axes and daggers. *HL/Bodleian Library*

Lawrence came home for some weeks in the early spring and summer of 1921, returning east in early July having been appointed a plenipotentiary under the great seal of England for his next mission: to the Hejaz.

MRS RIEDER
7.7.21 COLONIAL OFFICE

Dear Mrs. Rieder
Tonight when I was clearing up my papers before leaving for the East, out popped your letter. It's two months old, so has no doubt settled itself meanwhile. I rejoice that Noel is snatched from science, though only late in life: but it might have been too late. As for modern languages, there's only one worth studying: English: that I am aware of: but it's better than science: even if he learns French.

Apropos of France: I'm not anti-French any more. Feisal has swept Mesopotamia, & that is amends for his scurvy treatment in Paris. Do you know

---

1 Sir Herbert Samuel (1870-1963), later Lord Samuel, was at this time British high commissioner for Palestine.

that proverb about when you need a long spoon? I laugh every now & then in Whitehall, and the Whitehalled think me mad.

Very sorry for the delay: but my advice never was worth anything.

Yours
E.L.

Bodleian Library

WILFRED SCAWEN BLUNT
7-7-21   *COLONIAL OFFICE*

Dear Mr. Blunt
I kept your letter for some days, in the hopes that I would have a free time, or that the train service would get better. Unfortunately neither happened, & I have to start tomorrow. I'm exceedingly sorry. I go straight to Jidda, to see King Hussein, & then perhaps to Yemen: return probably in two months, & will then call. Very many more apologies

Yours sincerely
T E Lawrence

The last ten days I've been a shuttle cock, tossed between the Colonial & Foreign Offices, & much distracted & annoyed by it all. Please forgive my apparent rudeness.

Fitzwilliam Museum Cambridge

Lawrence spent much of August/September 1921 in Jidda, trying to persuade King Hussein of the Hejaz to accept the political settlement proposed at Cairo and already accepted by Feisal and Abdulla – the problems of which are clear from the following cables. He later told a Tank Corps colleague 'that the mental strain to which he was subjected during the negotiations had been worse than anything he had known during the campaign', *i.e.* during the war. His performance at this time has not endeared him to Arab historians, even though the new settlement coincided far more with Arab aspirations than that which had emerged from the hard-headed negotiations in Paris. Hussein was ousted by Ibn Saud in 1924 and spent the rest of his life in exile.

CABLE TO FOREIGN OFFICE
2.8.1921

LAWRENCE, JEDDAH, TO PRODROME, LONDON

Have had several meetings with King, who has not referred[1] to the draft treaty since he saw it. He urged his claims to Kingship of Mesopotamia, but collapsed and gave up idea when I discussed practical effect of move. He has announced his abandonment of position founded on McMahon letters,[2] but raises absurd new ideas daily. Old man is conceited to a degree, greedy, and stupid, but very friendly, and protests devotion to our interests. His entourage are anti-British, except for Fuad el Khatib and Zeid,[3] who are helping us continually, and all sorts of interests are begging him not to conclude any treaty. However he shows such reluctance to quarrel with me that I suspect his own mind to be divided: but until he introduces subject of Treaty again I cannot say whether there is any hope of it. If he could be kept here for a month he would become biddable: but he will go off the rails as soon as he is back in Mecca. He has suggested my returning after the pilgrimage.[4] I will not do so unless he accepts the principle of a treaty now.

TNA: PRO FO 686/93

CABLE TO FOREIGN OFFICE
4.8.1921

LAWRENCE, JEDDAH, TO PRODROME, LONDON

Have had more conversations with the King. He was only playing with me so I changed tactics and forced him to make exact statements. After some questions he made clear that he refused absolutely all notion of making a treaty but expected acknowledgement of his kingship in Mesopotamia and Palestine, priority over all rulers in Arabia who were to be confined to their pre-war boundaries, and cession to himself of Asir and Hodeida. His ambitions are as large as his conceit, and he showed unpleasant jealousy of his sons.

1 'Refused' in original text.
2 Sir Henry McMahon, then high commissioner for Egypt, had corresponded with Hussein in 1915; his most important letter, dated 24 October 1915, stated that Britain, subject to certain reservations, was 'prepared to recognise and support the independence of the Arabs'. The McMahon-Hussein understandings had been superseded by the Sykes-Picot agreement.
3 Hussein's youngest son.
4 *I.e.* the annual pilgrimage to Mecca.

I gave him my candid opinion of his character and capacity. There was a scene, remarkable to me in that not only the Foreign Secretary but the King also burst into tears. I walked out with parting remarks which brought Zeid to me last night with a rough draft of a treaty based on ours for my consideration.

The King is weaker than I thought, and could, I think, be bullied into nearly complete surrender. Reason is entirely wasted on him since he believes himself all-wise and all-competent, and is flattered by his entourage in every idiotic thing he does. The difficulties of using force are the short time, and the fear that if I hurt him too much he will sulk in Mecca. I will not be able to finish anything before the pilgrimage, but his draft, if he submits it formally to me today, will give me grounds for returning here at the end of the month.

TNA: PRO FO 686/93

CABLE TO BRITISH HIGH COMMISSIONER, BAGHDAD
8.8.1921
LAWRENCE, JEDDAH, TO HIGHCOM, BAGHDAD
Hussein's telegram may now be delivered with message from me that King is gradually coming round to our point of view, and has been provisionally paid a month's subsidy in consequence. The negotiations have been difficult.

TNA: PRO FO 686/93

ERIC KENNINGTON[1]
25.8.21   *ADEN*

Dear Kennington
After all the mail delayed two days: but there was no profit for you in them. I had to go up country, and could not write your note any better than it was.

---

1 Eric Henri Kennington (1888-1960): artist and sculptor, official war artist 1916-19 and 1940-3.

This is muck:[2] but it has the advantage either

(i) Of getting home a week early, and so giving you time to get someone proper to write an alternative

or (ii) Of being four times too long, and so giving you room to select the least bad.

It's altogether yours, to reject, shorten, cut about, add to, rearrange, correct. There's no good in it: and I'll be glad if you kill it. However if I remember the Leicester they only put about three lines in front of the catalogue of names: and there are three not good, but harmless lines in this: I'd cut it down to that myself, but I'm bothered if I know which three they are. I hope to be back soon: with Abdulla: news to you later.

E.L.

This is the beastliest trip ever I had: but thank the Lord I took no dress clothes.

Bodleian Library

CABLE TO FOREIGN OFFICE
7.9.1921
LAWRENCE, JEDDAH, TO PRODROME, LONDON

On my return King went back on his decision and demanded

(1) Return of all states in Arabia except his to their pre-war boundaries.
(2) Cession to him of all areas so vacated.
(3) Right to appoint all Cadis and Muftis[1] in Arabia, Mesopotamia, Palestine.
(4) Recognition of his supremacy over all Arab rulers everywhere.

2 Lawrence enclosed with the letter his introduction to the catalogue of Kennington's Arab portraits being shown at the Leicester Galleries. Written while he was engaged in a dispiriting struggle with their leader, he shows in it a great affection for the individual Arab warriors with whom he fought: *e.g.* '[T]he desert is full of legends and songs of their fighting [...] and personally I am very content to have had a share in causing to be made these records of their faces while the knowledge of what they did is fresh in men's minds.' The full text is in *The Essential T. E. Lawrence*, edited by David Garnett.

1 Cadis: civil judges. Muftis: expounders of Islamic law.

My reply made him send for a dagger and swear to abdicate and kill himself. I said we would continue negotiations with his successor. Ali then took a strong line, and formed a committee of himself, Zeid, Haddad, and Fuad, to discuss with me. Things are now going in most friendly and rational way. King is not formally superseded but has certainly lost much of his power. The sons report to him and the Queen, who is of our party, lectures him at night. I look upon the assumption of responsibility by Ali as a most happy event and am taking the opportunity to get his ideas on paper concerning all outstanding Arab questions without committing either side in any way. We will go on with Treaty in two or three days. [...]

TNA: PRO FO 686/93

CABLE TO FOREIGN OFFICE
22.9.1921
LAWRENCE, JEDDAH, TO PRODROME, LONDON
King Hussein had approved each clause of Treaty and announced publicly his forthcoming signature of it. When Ali presented him text for ratification he shouted and struck at him, and then sent us eight contradictory sets of prior conditions and stipulations all unacceptable. Ali says the old man is mad, and is preparing with Zeid to obtain his formal abdication. Ali and Zeid have behaved splendidly, and they may change things in the next weeks. Have left Marshall[1] text of Treaty, and if King climbs down he will receive his signature: but meanwhile, or till I reach England and report I suggest that no changes or new lines of policy be taken by you. Have asked King to return the eighty thousand rupees paid him in advance of subsidy on his promise to sign.

TNA: PRO FO 686/93

---

1 W. E. Marshall, British minister at Jidda; he had served with Lawrence as a doctor in the Arab campaign.

ERIC KENNINGTON
1 October [1921]   *GRAND CONTINENTAL HOTEL CAIRO*

[...] The reasons for stopping work are three. I don't know their order of magnitude. A lump of money I was expecting has not (probably will not) come. My house in Epping has been burnt down. In the leisure hours of this trip I have read the manuscript of my book; and condemned it. Not good enough to publish, because it's not as good as I can make it (unless I deceive myself). [...]

What more? Nothing. I'm bored stiff: and very tired, and a little ill, and sorry to see how mean some people I wanted to respect have grown. The War was good by drawing over our depths that hot surface wish to do or win something. So the cargo of the ship was unseen, and not thought of. This life goes on till February 28 next year. Au revoir.

TL   *Liddell Hart Centre for Military Studies, King's College London*

SIR HUGH TRENCHARD[1]
[January 1922]

You know I'm trying to leave Winston on March the first. Then I want about two months to myself, and then I'd like to join the R.A.F. – in the ranks, of course.[2]

I can't do this without your help. I'm 33 and not skilled in the senses you want. Probably I couldn't pass your medical. It's odd being too old for the job I want when hitherto I've always been too young for the job I did. However my health is good: I'm always in physical and mental training, and I don't personally believe that I'd be below the average of your recruits in either respect. If you think so that will end it.

You'll wonder what I'm at. The matter is that since I was 16 I've been writing: never satisfying myself technically but steadily getting better. My last book on Arabia is nearly good. I see the sort of subject I need in the beginning of your Force ... and the best place to see a thing from is the ground. It wouldn't 'write' from the officer level.

---

1 Hugh Montague Trenchard (1873-1956), the acknowledged 'father' of the Royal Air Force, was to be a considerable benefactor to Lawrence from this time forward. He was created a baronet in 1919 and raised to the peerage in 1930.
2 Lawrence had met Trenchard at the Cairo conference and had already broached the idea of his joining the air force as an ordinary airman at some future time.

I haven't told anyone, till I know your opinion; and probably not then, for the newspapers used to run after me and I like being private. People wouldn't understand.

It's an odd request this, hardly proper perhaps, but it may be one of the exceptions you make sometimes. It is asking you to use your influence to get me past the Recruiting Officer!

Apologies for making it: if you say no I'll be more amused than hurt.

Yours sincerely
T.E. Lawrence

R.A.F. Museum Hendon

HIS MOTHER
15 February 1922   [*14 BARTON STREET LONDON*]¹

[…] [About the ring, don't worry. Nothing mankind has yet made is worth any regret. If you need another send me word, & I'll send you some. There are thousands in London and their newness doesn't matter: for when you lose a thing there is no rhyme or reason in losing its associations also. You can transfer them to your finger itself, or to something else, for your imagination made them, & is all powerful over them & you.]

[…] I'm perfectly well, & very comfortable in Barton Street which is quite beautiful. The quiet of so little a place in the middle of a great mess has to be experienced a thousand times before it is properly felt. I will be very sorry to leave, when I have to leave, but it's altogether too pleasant to be allowed to go on too long. […]

My own plans are still doubtful. I asked Winston to let me go, and he was not very willing: indeed he didn't want it. I told him I was open to hold on for a little till his first difficulties were over (there are new things happening just now), but not in a formal appointment. Probably I'll get leave on the first of March, & not go back again, unless that Paris idea comes further: or some other odd notion. There was a question of me for Egypt, if Allenby came away: but

1 Herbert Baker's house in Westminster: *see* p. 168.

that of course I wouldn't accept. I don't think ever again to govern anything.[2]

If I get away finally from the Colonial Office about May my plans are to do nothing for a little, & then perhaps to consider the Air Force. Of course I'm too old to join it, but I think that the life & the odd mind (or lack of mind) there, might give me a subject to write about. This long-drawn-out battle over my narrative of the campaigns of Feisal has put an ink fever into me. I find myself always going about trying to fit words to the sights & sounds in the world outside me.

However all this remains uncertain, and will remain uncertain for me till I do it. That's a new course I have: of trying to prevent myself making up my mind till afterwards, when the need of action is over.

Let me know what you yourselves do, please, now & then. It's odd you know how impossible it is to be altogether alone. It's the one experience that humanity has never really worked towards: and I'm quite sure that we can only manage it in a crowded place. The difficulty is to keep oneself untouched in a crowd: so many people try to speak to you or touch you: and you're like electricity, in that one touch discharges all the virtue you have stored up.

However these things don't really matter.

N.

I'm afraid this letter's very scrappy: but I've answered the points in your last as they arose.

HL/Bodleian Library

---

2 This hint that he had been thought of as a successor to Allenby as high commissioner of Egypt was ridiculed by Richard Aldington but Lawrence certainly believed this to be the case. When Allenby's successor, Lord Lloyd, was forced to resign in 1929, Lawrence wrote to Lady Astor: "There but for the grace of God", say I.' (29 July 1929: not printed in this book).

SIR HUGH TRENCHARD
July 2 1922   *COLONIAL OFFICE*

Dear Sir Hugh Trenchard
Winston has agreed to let me go after next Tuesday. I have not told him what
I want to do next, as since I first wrote to you Geddes[1] has happened, and may
make impossible for you what you then thought possible.

 If there is still a chance of it may I come and see you?[2]

Yours sincerely
T.E. Lawrence

R.A.F. Museum Hendon

ERIC KENNINGTON
Monday [10 July 1922]

Dear Kennington
It's abnormally good of you to offer the cottage. A month ago I'd have leaped
at it. On Saturday a man offered to help me to a job which I have wanted to
do since 1919. I don't know if it will come off yet or not: but I think it will:
and in that case it will hold me in London for at least a year. No money in it,
but keep, and very interesting work.[1]

 So I'll refuse yours on the chance of this other thing's coming my way. Very
many thanks indeed.

 The cuttings are very good. Why did no one curse you?

E.L.   *Bodleian Library*

---

1 Sir Eric Geddes had presided over a committee on government expenditure which had
  reported in February 1922, proposing swingeing cuts in, *inter alia*, education, public health
  and the armed services.
2 Trenchard invited Lawrence to stay the night with him at his home at Barnet in Hertfordshire
  so that they could talk the matter over with no one else present apart from Lady Trenchard.
  Trenchard later told A. W. Lawrence that he tried to persuade T.E.L. that he could achieve more
  in the R.A.F. in a more responsible position, 'but he was so insistent that I eventually agreed'.

1 Doubtless a reference to his impending enlistment.

SIR HUGH TRENCHARD
21.VII.22   *14 BARTON STREET S.W.1*

Dear Sir Hugh
Winston very agreeable. I hope your lord was the same.[1] In which case – about
August 9?

Yours sincerely
T.E. Lawrence

R.A.F. Museum Hendon

Events proceeded at a somewhat slower pace than that envisaged by Lawrence
in the preceding letter to Trenchard. He and Trenchard met at the Air Ministry
on 14 August, when he was informed that his enlistment would be arranged by
Air Vice-Marshal Sir Oliver Swann, member of the Air Council for Personnel.
Swann shortly afterwards nominated 21 August as the day for this to take
place; the date was subsequently changed to 30 August at Lawrence's request.

COLONEL S. F. NEWCOMBE
22.7.22   *14 BARTON STREET S.W.1*

I found a wingless angel called Macintosh (tears in Heaven over that!) who
offers to forward your letters.

This is to say that I've started a collection of heads of Englishmen of
character, connected with the Arab Revolt.

Vickery is not in it:[1] you are. But I haven't got your head. Will you let me get it?

There's a young cubist artist called Roberts.[2] Very gifted & good. He'll
make it look like a problem in Euclid. You'll love it. So'll I. He's in London: &

1 The air minister – Trenchard's 'lord' – was Captain F. E. Guest.

1 He had clashed with Vickery at the time of Feisal's advance to Wejh, as Newcombe would
  have recalled. *See* p. 107 note 3.
2 William Roberts served as an artist in the two World Wars. When Lawrence invited him to
  contribute to *Seven Pillars* he was a struggling 27-year-old.

will draw you when you can give him two hours. Line only: no paint or colour.

I'm aiming at 12 heads: all different men, all different artists: all schools except the Royal Academy. A huge joke. Eventual illustrations for my eventual book.

Mrs. N. will hate it (the drawing) but wives & mothers always do. She shouldn't interfere: it's not her baby (or b.b.) who's to suffer.

Are you willing? 'Cause if so please tell me when you'll be next in London: & I'll fix up Roberts or another to meet you: lunch; & off with your head.

E.L.

Bodleian Library

WILFRED SCAWEN BLUNT
23.7.22   *14 BARTON STREET WESTMINSTER*

Dear Mr. Blunt

Yes, I got away, later than I intended, but I liked Winston so much, and have such respect for him that I was determined to leave only with his good-will: – and he took a long time to persuade! Otherwise I would have been free in February.[1] I'd like to see you again, and hope that you are now more comfortable in yourself than when I came down last. It can only be a day visit, I'm afraid. Would next Friday, by the 10.26 at Southwater, suit you? If not, then any day of the following week.

Yours sincerely
T E Lawrence

Fitzwilliam Museum Cambridge

1 Blunt had written to Lawrence, on reading his letter of resignation in the *Morning Post*: 'I congratulate you on having been true to your word and broken your official bondage. Liberty is the only thing worth a wise man's fighting for in public life.' (*Letters to T. E. Lawrence*, edited by A. W. Lawrence) Blunt was unwell at this time; he died some weeks later, on 10 September 1922.

COLONEL S. F. NEWCOMBE
Sunday [?August 1922]

Munificence
He made a great drawing of it: it's a very splendid work of art: better so than as portrait: because he's turned you from flesh into metal, & made you so fierce & warlike that my blood runs cold to see it. It's uncannily like, & yet so much harder. Perhaps it's the being drawn which drew you so much together: or else it's family cares. Any way time will make your face like that, & will leave the hair only a regretted memory. Who brushed it?

[…] It's hard for a youngster to be so great an artist, & to know it, & to be unable to sell anything. However his head of you marks a step in advance of anything he's done to date. It ought to go to the Tate Gallery. I suppose you don't mind it's bearing your name if shown? I took it to Kennington, who wondered at it. I'll get Roberts to do two or three others: because by itself it would look too pointedly excellent.

Do you hate it? and did Mrs N.? Some day I'll have prints of it for you.

T.E.L.

Do tell Boyle when he comes back, what he's missed: & say that if he'll let you know dates, I'll send someone down later to have a dab at him.

However it won't be as good as yours.
Bodleian Library

BRIGADIER-GENERAL SIR GILBERT CLAYTON
15-8-22   *14 BARTON STREET WESTMINSTER*

Dear General Clayton
I wrote a book about that dog-fight of ours in Arabia. It is not for present publication, partly because it's too human a document for me to disclose, partly because of the personalities in it, partly because it is not good enough to fit my conceit of myself. The last is a weak point, but the first in my mind: though it is difficult to judge of one's own work. Hogarth is reading it, as an insurance against inaccuracies.

You come into it: not very much, not as much as you should, but the thing is only a narrative of my private accidents. However, you had a share in them, & that's why I am writing to you. I want a drawing of you for one of the illustrations. Decent pictures will cover up a multitude of faults in their book: so I'm rather putting myself about to collect some. Kennington went East for me, & did about twenty Arabs: and I want about a dozen Englishmen. to balance them.

English people all look alike, in dress anyway: so to make an extra variety I'm out to have the dozen drawn by different artists. They include Newcombe, Alan Dawnay, Hogarth, Boyle (R.N.), Brodie, Bartholomew, & that sort of person.

The best man I think to do you, if you agree to sit, will be William Nicholson,[1] of Apple Tree Yard, between Jermyn Street & St. James Square. He's a very subtle & very talented person. I've talked to him about you, & he thinks you sound good for a wood-cut. These he has done many of, & is famous for. He suggests September as the best time for it. It would probably take two sittings, I expect, about 2 hours each. You would find it boring, but the result would be interesting. I hope you will agree to it. If you do, I'll put Nicholson in touch with you when the month comes. I am going away myself.

Yours sincerely
T E Lawrence

By the way, the wood-block would of course be my property: but I think there is no chance of its being published for years, so that the publicity will be nil. Lady Clayton will be amused to have a few proofs pulled of it: after which I'd have it stored away.

E.L.

Bodleian Library

---

1 William, later Sir William Nicholson, illustrator, poster designer, even costume-designer (*e.g.* for the first production of]. M. Barrie's *Peter Pan*), won his principal reputation as a portrait painter. He duly produced a portrait of Clayton for *Seven Pillars*. He was the father of the noted abstract painter Ben Nicholson and father-in-law of Robert Graves.

BERNARD SHAW[1]

17.VIII.22   *14 BARTON STREET WESTMINSTER*

Dear Mr. Shaw

You will be puzzled at my writing to you: but Cockerell some months ago took me round to you and introduced me, and you did not talk too formidably.[2]

I want to ask you two questions: the first one, 'Do you still read books?', doesn't require an answer. If you still go on reading I'm going to put the second question: if you don't, then please skip the two inside pages of this note and carry over to my signature at the end, and burn it all without replying. I hate letter-writing as much as I can, and so, probably, do you.

My real wish is to ask if you will read, or try to read, a book which I have written. It's about the war, which will put you off, to start with, and there are technical unpleasantnesses about it. For instance it is very long: about 300,000 words I suspect, though I have not counted them. I have very little money and do not wish to publish it: however it had to be printed, so I got it done on a lino. press, in a newspaper office.[3] That means it's beastly to look at, two columns on a quarto page, small newspaper type which hurts your eyes, and dozens of misprints, corrected roughly in ink: for only five copies exist, and I could not afford a proof. The punctuation is entirely the compositor's fancy: and he had an odd fancy, especially on Mondays.

That's the worst to be said on the material side. So far as concerns myself you must be told, before you commit yourself to saying 'yes', that I'm not a writer, and successfully passed the age of 30 without having wanted to write anything. I was brought up as a professional historian, which means the worship of original documents. To my astonishment, after peace came I found I was myself the sole person who knew what had happened in Arabia during the war: and the only

1 George Bernard Shaw (1856-1950): Irish-born playwright, critic, Socialist thinker, personality and wit. At this time 67 with a reputation as a successful dramatist going back to the 1890s.

2 Sydney Cockerell, curator of the Fitzwilliam Museum, Cambridge, had introduced Lawrence to Shaw earlier in the year following a lunch at which Lawrence and Cockerell discussed how they could help Charles Doughty, author of *Arabia Deserta*, who was in financial difficulties. Cockerell was due to call at Shaw's home in Adelphi Terrace to pick up a portrait of Shaw for his museum and suggested Lawrence accompany him. Lawrence demurred but consented when Cockerel pointed out that it being Saturday the Shaws would almost certainly be away at their country retreat at Ayot St Lawrence. The Shaws, however, were home. It was on the strength of this casual encounter that Lawrence decided to ask Shaw to read *Seven Pillars*.

3 The newspaper office was that of the *Oxford Times*; the text thus produced became known as the 'Oxford' version. Eight copies were printed, of which five were bound for circulation to friends and a sixth was given to Edward Garnett for his proposed abridgement.

literate person in the Arab Army. So it became a professional duty to record what happened. I started out to do it plainly and simply, much as a baby thinks it's easy to talk: and then I found myself bogged in a confusion of ways of saying the easiest things, and unable to describe the plainest places: and then problems of conduct came along, and the people with me had to be characterised: – in fact I got fairly into it, and the job became too much for me. Your first book was not perfect, though it was a subject you had chosen for yourself, and you had an itch to write!

In my case, I have, I believe, taken refuge in second-hand words: I mean, I think I've borrowed expressions and adjectives and ideas from everybody I have ever read, and cut them down to my own size, and stitched them together again. My tastes are daily mailish, so there's enough piffle and romance and wooliness to make a realist sick. There's a lot of half-baked thinking, some cheap disgust and complaint (the fighting fronts were mainly hysterical, you know, where they weren't professional, and I'm not the least a proper soldier): in fact all the sham stuff you have spent your life trying to prick. If you read my thing, it will show you that your prefaces have been written in vain, if I'm a fair sample of my generation. This might make you laugh, if the thing was amusingly written: but it's long-winded, and pretentious, and dull to the point where I can no longer bear to look at it myself. I chose that moment to have it printed!

You'll wonder, why if all this is true (and I think it is) I want any decent person still more a person like yourself* to read it. Well, it's because it is history, and I'm shamed for ever if I am the sole chronicler of an event, and fail to chronicle it: and yet unless what I've written can be made better I'll burn it. My own disgust with it is so great that I no longer believe it worth trying to improve (or possible to improve). If you read it or part of it and came to the same conclusion, you would give me courage to strike the match: whereas now I distrust my own judgement, and it seems cruel to destroy a thing on which I have worked my hardest for three years. While if you said that parts were rubbish, and other parts not so bad, and parts of it possible, (and distinguished those parts variously) then your standards might enable me to clear up mine, and give me energy enough to tackle the job again. (If you say it is all possible then I will reluctantly get rid of your own books from my shelves.)

All this is very unfair – or would be, if you knew me: but deleting that twenty minutes with Cockerell we are utter strangers, and likely to remain so, and therefore there is no pressure on you to answer this letter at all. I won't be in the least astonished (indeed I'll write another of the same sort to a man called Orage[4] whom

4 A. R. Orage (1875-1934), editor of *The New Age*. *See also* note to letter to Ezra Pound dated December 1934 (p. 539)

I have never met, but whose criticism I enjoy): and my opinion of you will go up.

Yours with many apologies
T E Lawrence

Incidentally: I don't want people to know that the book exists. So whether you reply or not, I hope you will not talk of it.

*ambiguous: but I wanted to avoid expressing my liking for your work.

DG

EDWARD GARNETT[1]
22.VIII.22   *[POSTMARKED LONDON S.W.1]*

I should have warned you before I sent it (only it seemed so remote a contingency) that if your opinion was favourable it would be wasted on me. Perhaps as you haven't yet finished it, this is still not too rude to say. The thing is spotted in nearly every line with blemishes of style, and while my critical sense doesn't reach as far as subject matter and construction, I judge them equally bad, by analogy.

So please don't consider the point of publication. That never came into my mind when writing it: indeed I don't know for whom I wrote it, unless it was for myself. When it came to the point of printing it, several passages had to come out, for fear of the compositor, and I cannot imagine showing it except to a few minds (like yours) already prejudged to kindness.

If that Deraa incident whose treatment you call severe and serene (the second sounds like a quaint failure to get my impressions across, but I know what you feel) had happened to yourself you would not have recorded it. I have a face of brass perhaps, but I put it into print very reluctantly, last of all the pages I sent to the press. For weeks I wanted to burn it in the manuscript: because I could not tell the story face to face with anyone, and I think I'll feel sorry, when I next meet you, that you know it. The sort of man I have always mixed with doesn't so give himself away.

I Edward Garnett (1868-1936): father of David Garnett. A novelist and critic, he was most famous as a publisher's reader (notably for Jonathan Cape) and encourager of important writers, among them E. M. Forster, Joseph Conrad and D. H. Lawrence. T. E. Lawrence summed up something of Garnett's gift in his last letter to him in 1934: 'Your criticisms have always gone personally from you to the artist, instead of being exhibition pieces to catch the public eye on the way.'

I shall hope for help from your pencilled notes, and am very grateful for your goodness in reading it, and for what praise you have given it: only please don't do more, because it only underlines what I know to be my failure. Hitherto I've always managed, usually without trying my hardest, to do anything I wanted in life: and it has bumped me down, rather, to have gone wrong in this thing, after three or four years top-effort. That shows the difference between mere brick-laying and creative work. It's what I told Nicholson and yourself that day in Piccadilly: there's no absolute in the imaginative world, and so journeymen like myself are confused and miserable in it.

I'm afraid this is a very affected note: but your letter has upset me. Sorry. E.L.

The other passage you mention, where the tommies went wrong.[2] – I may be in order exhibiting myself: but how can I give them away? They were such decent fellows, and we treated them so poorly.

When you have had enough of it I'd like to come down and ask you some technical questions. *DG*

BERNARD SHAW
27.VIII.22   *14 BARTON ST WESTMINSTER*

[...] I'd like you to read it [...] partly because you are you: partly because I may profit by your reading it, if I have a chance to talk to you soon after, before you have got over it. You see the war was, for us who were in it, an overwrought time, in which we lost our normal footing. I wrote this thing in the war atmosphere, and believe that it is stinking with it. Also there is a good deal of cruelty, and some excitement. All these things, in a beginner's hands, tend to force him over the edge, and I suspect there is much over-writing. You have the finest cure for flatulence, and I have great hopes that you will laugh at parts of what I meant to be solemn: and if I can get at you before you have forgotten which they are, then I'll have a chance to make it better.

You'll be amused at my amateur method of getting help: and at my having a standard of work: but it's the only book I'll write, and so I want it to be tolerable. [...]
DG

2 A reference to a passage which Lawrence decided to delete describing the punishment of a British soldier and an Arab who had been arrested for having homosexual relations.

Tuesday 6-4-26

Your letter has interested me much: though you vitiate your thinking by the assumption that books are meant to be read. They are to be written only.

The abridgement is better than the complete text. Half a calamity is better than a whole one. By excising heights & depths I have made a balanced thing: & yet I share your difficulty of seeing the shorter version's real shape across the gaps.

Specific points
. (i) The ending. I was overpersuaded to stop on page 644. The natural place is after "Sun," on line 35 of page 635. It fulfils your demands for balance & reflection and sordidness among the triumphs. Pages 632 and 633 are the philosophic climax of the narrative;

If you will consider anew, & approve this new Finis, will you then please so amend your text, and also cross out "a" before "pearl" in the last line of the revised version.

Your statement that the hospital passage would be a joke in the eye of 19 readers out of 20 puts it out of court, as I put it. This abridgement is to be fit for girl guides.

[ii] To include the death of Farraj meant the restoration of many pages, to explain it. The "private delectation" of 115 people is better than the public delectation of 10.000. My men are not to walk the common street.

Me to write again? God forbid. I do not bear another mis-shaped child. Last finis. If only I'd had the courage to destroy this one in time.

yours
TES.

Left handwriting constrains to brevity

A letter from T. E. Lawrence, written with his left hand in 1926

4 FIRST YEARS IN THE RANKS
1922-26

Lawrence joined the Royal Air Force as 352087 Aircraftman John Hume Ross on 30 August 1922. During his basic training at Uxbridge he compiled the notes and observations that were to form the core of his second famous literary work, *The Mint*. Early in November he was sent to the R.A.F. School of Photography at Farnborough. On 27 December, the fact that a 'Famous War Hero' was lurking in the ranks under an assumed name was revealed on the front page of the *Daily Express*. On 23 January 1923, he became a civilian again, dismissed, as he wrote a week later to the editor of *The Observer,* J. L. Garvin, 'for possessing too large a publicity factor to be decent in an A.C.2'. Yet by March he was in the ranks again, this time as a private in the army, and with a new alias, T. E. Shaw.

He was posted to the Tank Corps Training School at Bovington in Dorset, where he remained for over two years, frequently railing at army life and campaigning throughout to return to the air force, even at one time hinting at suicide unless he got his way. Without Bovington, however, he would not have forged some of his most important friendships, with Tank Corps men on the one hand or, for example, Mr and Mrs Thomas Hardy on the other. Without Bovington, too, there would have been no Clouds Hill, the half-derelict cottage a mile and a half from the camp which was to be his home and sanctuary for the rest of his life. Clouds Hill soon became a venue where people from a wide range of backgrounds gathered; writers and artists mingled easily with men in khaki or air force blue, with rankers as likely as the aesthetes to be curled up with a book of poems or a literary novel. 'What was Clouds' Hill?' Lawrence wrote to Mrs Shaw on 31 August 1924: 'A sort of mixed grill, I fancy: but very good. Everybody is beginning to fall in love with it. The air of it is peaceful: and the fire burns so well.'

All this, however, was not enough to reconcile him to life in a service for which he felt no affection. He punctuated his Tank Corps years with pleas to the chief of the air staff, Sir Hugh Trenchard: 'February is "supplication month" ...' he wrote in early 1925, 'so for the third time of asking – Have I no chance of re-enlistment in the R.A.F., or transfer? It remains my only hope and ambition, dreamed of every week, nearly every day.' At last in August he was readmitted to the R.A.F. and sent to the cadet college at Cranwell in Lincolnshire – though not, as a cadet, but as an ordinary aircraftman. He stayed there until late 1926, when he sailed by troopship for India. Throughout this period he was working intermittently on *Seven Pillars of Wisdom*; by the time he left for India his lavishly printed and illustrated subscribers' edition was completed and the popular abridgement, entitled *Revolt in the Desert*, was awaiting publication. That this latter event would inevitably lead to another upsurge of publicity and myth-making led to his request to be posted abroad.

This is an important period for letters: the beginning of the high tide that only subsided, and that far from completely, in the last weeks of his life. The circulation of the 'Oxford' text of *Seven Pillars* inevitably prompted many exchanges; two letters worth singling out are an undated letter to Vyvyan Richards, written early in 1923, and a letter to Colonel Wavell dated 11 May 1923. The Charlotte Shaw correspondence – candid, confessional, written with a sense of style and ranging widely over life and literature – began shortly after he reached Bovington. Bovington also produced a series to Lionel Curtis between March and June 1923, which David Garnett described as 'the most revealing letters of Lawrence's I know'. While it is true that Garnett could not compare them with those to Charlotte Shaw, being denied access, he was right in making high claims for them: not only are they remarkable pieces of writing, but they are also a most vivid portrait of a mind on the edge of despair. Lawrence began almost lightly, proposing a series of letters 'more splendid' than Daudet's *Lettres de Mon Moulin*; by the time they ended they had become a composite statement more comparable in tone to Wilde's *De Profundis*. They are all reprinted here (one somewhat shortened), though whereas Garnett ran them as a complete sequence I have interleaved them with letters to other recipients.

There are many new letters, too: outspoken to R. D. Blumenfeld of the *Daily Express*, frank and depressed to Alan Dawnay, affectionate to R. A. M. Guy. There are also some revealing letters to E. M. Forster and one to Vyvyan Richards, dated 26 June 1924, in which he writes on a subject with which he deals rarely: his beliefs. The period also includes a long letter written in a mood of such unhappiness and disillusion that it has been fittingly described as the bitterest letter he ever wrote: his letter to Charlotte Shaw sent from Cranwell after his meeting with Lord Winterton and King Feisal of Iraq (*see* p. 306).

Although not evident from his letters, it was during his Bovington years that, according to revelations made in *The Sunday Times* in 1968, he first submitted himself to beatings from a young Scotsman, John Bruce. Bruce is mentioned in only two letters in this collection: one to Charlotte Shaw dated 19 July 1924, and one to American publisher F. N. Doubleday dated 18 September 1930, republished here from Garnett (in Part 6), in which he is referred to as 'Jock, the roughest diamond of our Tank Corps hut in 1923'.

AIR VICE-MARSHAL SIR OLIVER SWANN[1]

1.IX.22   *[R.A.F. UXBRIDGE]*

Dear Swann

I can't ask the corporal how an aircraft hand addresses an air-vice-marshal: – so please take this letter as a work of my late existence! I hadn't meant to write, except when I changed station, but the mess I made of Henrietta St.[2] demands an apology. I thought I was fitter: but when it came to the point, walked up and down the street in a blue funk, and finally went in with my nerves dithering, and my heart dancing. My teeth never were any good, so the doctors threw me straight downstairs again. There Dexter[3] caught me, and lent me what was no doubt his right hand to steer me past the medical, and through other rocks of square roots and essays and decimals. However I was obviously incapable of getting through on my own, so he got another chit from you, and that did the trick satisfactorily. If I'd known I was such a wreck I'd have gone off and recovered before [join]ing up: now the cure and the experiment must proceed together. I'm not very certain of myself, for the crudities, which aren't as bad as I expected, worry me far more than I expected: and physically I can only just scrape through the days. However they are a cheerful crowd; and the N.C.O.s behave with extraordinary gentleness to us (there's no other word fits their tone – except on the square, from which good Lord deliver us!) and I enjoy usually one hour of the sixteen, and often laugh in bed after lights out. If I can get able to sleep, and to eat the food, and to go through the P.T.[4] I'll be all right. The present worry is 90% nerves.

Would you tell the C.A.S.[5] that he's given me the completest change any mortal has had since Nebuchadnezzar: and that so far as I'm concerned it's to go on? Fortunately I told him I wasn't sure how long I could stick it, so that there is always a bridge – but it isn't required yet, and I hope won't be: only it's a comforting thought for the fifteen bad hours.

---

1 Swann, as already indicated on p. 208, had been instructed by Trenchard to arrange Lawrence's entry into the R.A.F. but he had done so without enthusiasm ('I disliked the whole business, with its secrecy and subterfuge') and had met Lawrence once only at the Air Ministry. He was therefore somewhat surprised at the tone of this and several other letters which Lawrence subsequently wrote to him from which, Swann told Garnett, 'one would think ... that I was a close correspondent of Lawrence's, possibly even a friend of his'.
2 Henrietta Street was the site of the R.A.F. recruiting office where Lawrence enlisted; his enlistment is described in the opening chapter of *The Mint*.
3 A Flight Lieutenant to whom Lawrence had been instructed to report.
4 P.T.: Physical Training.
5 C.A.S.: Chief of Air Staff, *i.e.* Trenchard.

As for the special reason for which I came in – there's masses of gorgeous stuff lying about: but the scale of it is heart-rending. I found the Arab Revolt too big to write about, and chose this as a smaller subject to write about: but you'd have to be a man and a half to tackle it at all decently.

I must say you have an amazing good crowd in the ranks: as a new force it ought to be pretty alive: but its keenness and life is better than I dreamed of.

In case I'm wanted by the Colonial Office I'll send you a note as often as I change station: but not more unless I want something, which will be a sad event. Less than two years won't do what I planned, in my present opinion: and they all say that things are easier outside Uxbridge. Also I'll have got used to being a dog's body.

Please tell the C.A.S. that I'm delighted, and most grateful to him and to you for what you have done. Don't bother to keep an eye on what happens to me.

Yours sincerely
T E Lawrence

I've re-read this letter: it gives too dismal an impression. It's only the sudden change from independence to dish-washing, and from mental to physical living which has been too much for my strength. And I'd harmed my health more than I thought by these three years trying to write a war book. It's hard to squeeze the last drop out of your memories of two years, and I sweated myself blind trying to make it as good as possible. Result that I leap into the air when spoken to unexpectedly, and can't reply a word: only stand there shivering! And it's hard not to give oneself away at such moments. The actual conditions are better than I thought.

E.L.   DG

EDWARD GARNETT
Monday 9.X.22   [R.A.F. UXBRIDGE]

[…] It's good of you to (or rather that you should) like my effort more on the re-reading. My test for a book is that one should finish it each time with a mind to read it again – some day. It's particularly interesting that the last fifty pages seem to you alive: I've never been able to see them at all: always by the time I have got so far my eyes have carried forward to the end, and I've gone through the last fighting like a dream. Those pages have been worked at very hard, but I've never got them in perspective: and I've always had a lurking fear that they were flatter than the VIth and VIIth parts (the failure of the bridge and the winter war) and formed an anticlimax – a weak ending. It was impossible for me to last out so long a writing with my wits about me: and I've feared that there would be found no reader long-winded enough to get there either. Your judgment that the book is in excess, as regards lengths, is also, I judge, true as regards intensity and breadth. I've had no pity on myself writing it – nor on my readers reading it. There's a clamour of force in it which deafens. A better artist would have given the effect of a *fortissimo* with less instrumentality. It's unskilled craftsmen who are profuse.

What you say about the oddity of my brain doesn't surprise me – but it helps to explain the apartness of myself here in this noisy barrack room. I might be one dragon-fly in a world of wasps – or one wasp among the dragon-flies! It's not a comfortable place: but if the oddity of my standing produces a fresh-feeling book, I suppose I shouldn't grouse about my luck.

The personal chapter clearly bothers you.[1] A man (a metaphysician by nature, who was at Oxford with me and knows me very well)[2] read it, and told me that it stood out as the finest chapter in the book. I tend more to your opinion: it's not meant for the ordinary intelligences, and must mislead them: but to set it out in plain English would be very painful. However six months away from it, and then a fresh approach may work a change in my feeling towards it: may even give me energy to re-write it. At present nothing sounds less probable. I don't even feel capable (though I'd love to) of writing a fresh book on this place. I've made some rather poor notes, which show me how hard it would be to bring off a picture of the R.A.F. Depot.

I wonder how the reduction seems to you now.[3] If you get it to 150,000 and satisfy yourself, and then I take out 20,000 or so, that should do the trick. What an odd book it will be! It's over-good of you to attempt such a business. I decided yesterday in church (church-parade!) that I ought to publish nothing. Today I feel inclined to publish. Am I neurasthenic or just feeble-willed?

I'm afraid I can't come away, even for a day.

E. L.

(Glad you like Auda, I did!)

DG

1 Chapter CIII: 'Myself'.
2 Vyvyan Richards.
3 Edward Garnett had offered to produce an abridged version of *Seven Pillars*.

R.D. BLUMENFELD[1]

II.XI.22   *14 BARTON STREET SW1*

Dear Blumenfeld

This letter has got to be indiscreet – shockingly so, when one thinks how the *Daily Mail* gave away the poison in the chocolates – please keep it as a personal one, from me to you.

When Winston at last let me go – it took four months work to make him: I refused salary, & begged for release each time I saw him, etc. – I found I was quite on the rocks: and so I enlisted, as a quick and easy way of keeping alive, and alive I am, in the ranks, & not always miserable. It's a varied life, often very bad, but with spots of light, very exciting and full of freshness. You know I was always odd, & my tastes my own. Also the only way I could escape politics entirely was to cut myself sharply off from my former way of living: and making a living with one's fingers is joyful work, & as clean as possible, after politics – to which not even the *Express* shall drag me back!

No reflection on Winston, who's a great man, & for whom I have not merely admiration, but a very great liking. If we get out of the Middle East Mandates with credit, it will be by Winston's bridge. The man's as brave as six, as good-humoured, shrewd, self-confident, & considerate as a statesman can be: & several times I've seen him chuck the statesmanlike course and do the honest thing instead.

I use Barton Street as an address, & either call there, or have my letters sent away to barracks for me. You will understand that I'm no more master of my time, & can't come up: nor can I write very much down here: nor have I the will to write much. I wore my nerves into a mop, finishing my war journal of events in Arabia. It ended as a very long book, indiscreet in the personal, political, & military spheres, & a complete picture of myself! Anyway it shan't be published in its entirety: but I'm tired of having written so much, & prefer to play about with rifles meanwhile.

---

1 Born in the U.S.A., R. D. Blumenfeld (1864-1948) was editor of the *Daily Express* from 1902-32. Lawrence had written two articles for the *Express* in May 1920 for which he refused to accept payment, whereupon Blumenfeld sent him a rare copy of the *Arabian Nights*. Lawrence thanked him but explained that he felt uncomfortable about Blumenfeld's generosity, since by publishing his articles the *Express* had 'achieved some things I wanted very much, and I am still therefore deeply in your debt'. He added: 'Unfortunately I cannot pay my side of it with beautiful books – but please let me know any time I can be of use to you.' Blumenfeld had at last taken up Lawrence's offer, only to find that the latter was no longer in either a position or a frame of mind to accept any journalistic commission.

Do keep this news to yourself. No one in camp knows who I am, & I don't want them to.

Yours sincerely
T E Lawrence

Bodleian Library

WINSTON CHURCHILL
18 November 22

Dear Mr Churchill
This is a difficult letter to write – because it follows on many unwritten ones. First I wanted to say how sorry I was when you fell ill, and again when you had to have an operation. Then I should have written to say I was sorry when the Government resigned. I meant to write & congratulate you on getting better: but before I could do that you were in Dundee and making speeches. Lastly I should write to say that I'm sorry the poll went against you[1] but I want to wash out all these lost opportunities, & to give you instead my hope that you will rest a little: six months perhaps. There is that book of memoirs to be made not merely worth £30,000, but of permanent value. Your life of Lord Randolph shows what you could do with memoirs. Then there is the painting to work at, but I feel that you are sure to do that anyhow: but the first essential seems to me a holiday for you. It sounds like preaching from a younger to an elder (and is worse still when the younger is an airman-recruit!) but you have the advantage of twenty years over nearly all your political rivals: and physically you are as strong as any three of them (do you remember your camel-trotting at Giza, when you wore out all your escort, except myself, & I'm not a fair competitor at that!) and in guts and power and speech you can roll over anyone bar Lloyd George: so that you can (or should) really not be in any hurry.

Of course I know that your fighting sense is urging you to get back into the scrimmage at the first moment: but it would be better for your forces to rest & rearrange them: & not bad tactics to disengage a little. The public won't forget you soon, & you will be in a position to choose your new position and

1 Churchill had lost his seat at Dundee in the general election of 15 November.

line of action more freely, for an interval. I needn't say that I'm at your disposal when you need me – or rather if ever you do.[2] I've had lots of chiefs in my time, but never one before who really was my chief. The others have needed help at all times: you only when you want it: – and let me say that if your tools in the rest of your career to date had been of my temper you would have been now too big, probably, for the country to employ! That's a modest estimate of myself, but you know it doubles the good of a subordinate to feel that his chief is better than himself.

Yours sincerely
T. E. Lawrence

By the way, I've got keen on the RAF and propose to stick to it for the present.

Churchill Papers[3]

R. D. BLUMENFELD
24.XI.22   [*FARNBOROUGH*]

Dear Blumenfeld
Your offer is a generous and very kind one: and you will think me quixotic in refusing it: but I ran away here partly to escape the responsibility of head-work: and the *Daily Express* would expect me to take it up again.

Had I fewer wits I would have been a merrier person. My best thanks all the same.

No, please don't publish my eclipse. It will be common news one day, but the later the better for my peace in the ranks:[1] and I'd be sorry to have to render reasons for it. As you say, it reads like cheap melodrama, and my life so

2 In a letter of 17 July 1922 Churchill had written to Lawrence stating he very much regretted his departure from the Colonial Office and adding 'Still, I feel I can count upon you at any time when a need may arise.'

3 Printed in *Winston S. Churchill* by Martin Gilbert, Companion Part 3 to Volume IV.

1 It was the *Daily Express* which did publish Lawrence's 'eclipse', just over a month later while Blumenfeld was away ill.

far has been that, nearly since the odd circumstances of my birth. Some day I'll tell you stories about myself – if you will hear them.

Meanwhile I'm excogitating a new book – in no way personal – on the spirit of the Air Force;[2] a most remarkable body: and am hoping to take advantage of my obscurity to produce an abridgement of my old war-book on Arabia. This latter book I printed privately (5 copies) a while ago: and if the abridgement is approved by a publisher I'll find myself rich – according to my standard. Whether I'll continue in the R.A.F. then, or return to London life – I don't know.

I hope the nursing home (now half over, I suppose, for my post comes spasmodically, with long delays) will go prosperously for you. It's beastly, the being in any way ill. By the way don't you think it's good for me at my great age, after a ragged life, after seven bad air-crashes, after nine war-wounds, and many peace-ones, to be able to enlist and hold my own with a lusty crowd? I'm contented with myself.

Yours ever
T. E. Lawrence

Bodleian Library

2 The 'new book' would eventually emerge as *The Mint.*

BERNARD SHAW
30.XI.22   *14 BARTON STREET*

Dear Mr. Shaw
I'm afraid you are either making a labour of it,[1] or you don't want to tell me
that it's rubbish. I don't want to bore you (nice of me!) and if you say it's rot
I'll agree with you & cackle with pleasure at finding my judgement doubled.
    Please laugh & chuck it![2]

Yours sincerely
T. E. Lawrence   *Jesus College Oxford*

BERNARD SHAW
27.XII.22   *[R.A.F. FARNBOROUGH]*

Dear Mr. Shaw
Your letter reached me on Christmas day, and has interested me immensely —
especially one phrase. No doubt it was used to help me with Constable's[1]
(gratitude etc.) and it's immodest of me to refer to it — but you say that it's a
great book. Physically, yes: in subject, yes: an outsider seeing the inside of a
national movement is given an enormous subject: but is it good in treatment? I
care very much for this, as it's been my ambition all my life to write something
intrinsically good. I can't believe that I've done it, for it's the hardest thing in
the world, and I've had such success in other lines that it's greedy to expect
goodness in so technical a matter. However your phrase makes me hope a bit:

1 In an annotation to this letter dated 7 July 1940 G.B.S. wrote: '"it" is the *Seven Pillars*: one of
  the early copies that he got printed in double columns at a newspaper office. I had to cut out
  or rewrite several passages that were outrageously libellous. He showed these passages, with
  my revisions, to the victims, and expected them to be amused!' *See* for example Lawrence's
  letter to Sir Archibald Murray dated 10 January 1920 (p. 181) and footnote 5, p. 183
2 Shaw replied on 1 December: 'Patience, patience: do not again shoot your willing camel
  through the head' (Lawrence had killed his own camel in the excitement of action at Aba
  el Lissan just before the seizure of Akaba) adding that he had not read *Seven Pillars* yet but
  that his wife had 'ploughed through it from Alpha to Omega'. For the text of this and other
  letters by G.B.S. to Lawrence *see Letters to T.E. Lawrence*, edited by A.W. Lawrence.

1 Constable's: Bernard Shaw's publisher.

will you let me know your honest opinion as to whether it is well done or not? When I was actually writing it I got worked up and wrote hardly: but in the between-spells the whole performance seemed miserable, and when I finished it I nearly burned the whole thing for the third time. The contrast between what I meant and felt I could do, and the truth of what my weakness had let me do was so pitiful. You see, there's that feeling at the back of my mind that if I really tried, sat down and wrung my mind out, the result would be on an altogether higher plane. I funk this extreme effort, for I half-killed myself as it was, doing the present draft: and I'd willingly dodge out of it. Isn't it treated wrongly? I mean, shouldn't it be objective, without the first-person-singular? And is there any style in my writing at all? Anything recognisably individual?

Apologies for bothering your eminence with 'prentice questions: but I'm mad-keen to know, even if it's to know the worst.[...]

You ask for details of what I'm doing in the R.A.F. Today I scrubbed the kitchen out in the morning, and loafed all the afternoon, and spent the evening writing to G. B. S. Yesterday I washed up the dishes in the sergeants' mess in the morning (messy feeders, sergeants: plates were all butter and tomato sauce, and the washing water was cold) and rode to Oxford in the afternoon on my motor-bike, and called on Hogarth to discuss the abridgement of the Arabian book. It being Christmas we do fatigues in the morning, and holiday in the afternoon. Normally I'm an 'aerial photographer, under training': it doesn't mean flying, but developing the officers' negatives after they land: and the 'under-training' part means that I'm a recruit, and therefore liable to all sorts of mis-employment. For three weeks I was an errand-boy. I've also been dustman, and clerk, and pig-stye-cleaner, and housemaid, and scullion, and camp-cinema-attendant. Anything does for airmen recruits: but the life isn't so bad, when the first crudeness works off. We have a bed each, and suffer all sorts of penalties unless they are 25 inches apart: twelve of us in a room. Life is very common, besides being daily. Much good humour, very little wit, but a great friendliness. They treat my past as a joke, and forgive it me lightly. The officers fight shy of me: but I behave demurely, and give no trouble.

Yours sincerely
T E Lawrence

DG

The preceding letter to Bernard Shaw was written on the day on which the *Daily Express* disclosed Lawrence's presence in the air force in a story headlined 'UNCROWNED KING' AS PRIVATE SOLDIER. There was more in the centre pages and more again on the following day under such headlines as PRINCE OF MECCA ON RIFLE PARADE. The press came down to look for Lawrence at Farnborough, where, to quote David Garnett, he was 'valiantly protected' by his friends in the ranks. The ultimate result of this sudden outburst of publicity was to be his expulsion from the R.A.F., but its more immediate consequence was his decision to stop the proposed publication of the abridged version of *Seven Pillars of Wisdom*.

BERNARD SHAW
2.1.23   FARNBOROUGH

Dear Mr. Shaw
Our letters crossed. I'm sorry.

It's most good of you to wish to help me, & I'm afraid I'm rather a difficult person to help. The publication of the whole book seemed to me an impossible business, for personal reasons. So I agreed to the abridgement, which, as a censored article, was in essence dishonest. Then, the *Daily Express* blew out that rubbish (not Cape's fault: it was written by one of the officers here) & I felt that to publish anything now might look as though I were using the R.A.F as an advertising stunt. So I've cancelled Cape's contract (fortunately not completed, & so I hope there will be no damages to pay) and have told him that nothing is to appear this year.

About Doughty. It was a book which owing to its length (longer than my effort) and its Arabic, & its cuts, was very expensive to re-set, and its prospect of selling seemed problematical to all publishers, till Cape (then with Lee-Warner) said that he would risk a 500 edition, at a price to cover costs, if I'd write a preface.[1]

I hate introductions to masterpieces (puff-introductions by pygmies: it's like tourists cutting their names on the walls of Kenilworth) but there seemed little chance of getting the book out without an effort by me in that direction. I consulted Doughty, who very nobly agreed to suffer it: & then I pieced together pages from my *Seven Pillars*, with some few lines written expressly, & put asterisks where the separate fragments seemed to jar together.

---

1 The successful republication of Charles Doughty's masterpiece *Arabia Deserta*, with Lawrence's introduction, was a major factor in establishing Jonathan Cape as a publishing house.

Cape got his reward, for the 500 copies sold in about three months. Doughty got £300 or so: everybody was satisfied: and I withdrew the puff, which I hope will soon be decently forgotten. It's unpardonable, for the lesser to praise the greater, & *Arabia Deserta* is a far greater book than the *Seven Pillars*.

Cape has since printed off another 500 *Arabia Desertas*, & they are selling slowly. Moulds have been made, & the book won't again be unprocurable. That's a pious work to have done, & condones my offence of taste. This long explanation is for Mrs. Shaw's benefit, as she is interested. If I had an *A.D.* with my preface I'd send it: but I haven't!

The cancellation of my book means that I stay in the R.A.F. for the time being: and my address here (this isn't a tout for another letter!) is

I'm going to wash out that old name, which has too many war associations to please me: and which isn't my real name, any more than Ross!	352087 A.C.ii Ross B.3. Block School of Photography R.A.F. S. Farnborough Hants.

TEL.

University of Texas

RAYMOND SAVAGE [1]

7.1.23   *R.A.F. S FARNBOROUGH*

Dear Savage

I came up yesterday and saw Cape and Garvin,[2] and made up my mind (is it final? The beastly thing has wobbled so that I despair of its remaining fixed for life) not to publish anything whatever: neither abridgement nor serial, nor full story: at least this year: and probably not so long as I remain in the R.A.F. I've written to Cape with this and told him. I needn't say how much I am

---

1 Lawrence's literary agent. During the war he had served on Allenby's staff; he later wrote a biography of his former chief under the title *Allenby of Armageddon*, published 1925.

2 J. L. Garvin, editor of the *Observer*, who had hoped to serialize the abridged *Seven Pillars*. *See* letter to him dated 30 January 1923 (p. 233).

ashamed of the trouble everyone has had, and will have, as a result of this decision: but it's the only one I can make.

You will probably want to say something, on your own account, to clear up the matter. I'd suggest, if so, your writing that 'Mr. Lawrence wrote his narrative in 1919: and later printed privately an edition of eight copies, which have been circulated among the people concerned; and that while he has no intention of publishing this version, he did recently agree provisionally, to the publication of an abridgement (one third of the original matter) by Mr. Jonathan Cape.'

The next stage is more difficult. You can either say, bluntly, that afterwards I withdrew from the negotiations: or that my service in the R.A.F. in my opinion precludes me from publication meanwhile: or that I'm too fed up with the *Daily Express* to endure the thought of giving away the remainder of myself to them.

Anyway, invent something, if you will, and if you want to: and let me see it before you publish it; and meanwhile tear up those contracts, and accept my very deepest apologies for the whole miserable business.

Yours ever
T. E. Lawrence   *Bodleian Library*

MRS CHARLOTTE SHAW[1]
8.1.23   *R.A.F.*

Dear 'Mrs. G.B.S.'
It's a wonderful letter, that of yours, and I've liked it beyond measure: [2] though my doubts as to the virtues of the *Seven Pillars* remain: indeed I'd be an insufferable creature if I was sure of it, for to me a good book is the best thing that can be done. However I'd been thinking it possibly a bad book, and your

1 Charlotte Payne-Townsend (later -Townshend) married Bernard Shaw in 1898; though their marriage was solely one of companionship, it endured until her death in 1943. Over thirty years Lawrence's senior, the two shared an Irish background, mother-dominated childhoods and a predisposition to celibacy; they wrote to each other with a remarkable and sustained intimacy. Strictly she should be named 'Mrs Bernard Shaw', but she is so frequently referred to as 'Mrs Charlotte Shaw' in the Lawrencian context that I have adopted this form throughout.
2 In a letter dated 31 December 1922 Charlotte Shaw had written: 'Now is it conceivable, imaginable, that a man who could write the *Seven Pillars* could have any doubts about it? ... I devoured the book from cover to cover as soon as I got hold of it. I drove G.B.S. almost mad by insisting on reading him special bits when he was deep in something else.... [I]t is one of the most amazingly individual documents that has ever been written ...' etc.

praise of it makes me more hopeful. At the same time, you know, it's more a storehouse than a book – has no unity, is too discursive, dispersed, heterogeneous. I've shot into it, as a builder into his yard, all the odds and ends of ideas which came to me during those years: indeed I suspect that it's a summary of myself to February 1920, and that people who read it will know me better than I know myself.

Since 1920 I've had new experiences, and it's partly that newness today which makes the *Seven Pillars* seem to me so inadequate to their theme. This last adventure in the R.A.F. is a chapter in itself. It would be hard to remain inhuman while jostling all days and nights in a crowd of clean and simple men. There is something here which in my life before I'd never met – had hardly dreamed of.

I explained my action with the Doughty preface in a letter to G.B.S. last week:[3] and have told him also that I've refused to sign my contract for any part of the *Seven Pillars*, to Cape or anyone else. I'd like to publish the whole, but that's as improbable as that I'd walk naked down Piccadilly: not that I'd like that either, but the whole is the only honest thing.

I showed my Mother your letter. She likes you now, because you praised my work, and mothers have (privately) an inordinate pride in sons. The horrors of the book strike her painfully, and she hates my having noted, or seen, such things.

Meinertzhagen saw his description, and laughed over it, not in any way annoyed.[4] There is an astonishing power in that man.

It's very good of you and G.B.S. to offer me your help. It would be invaluable if I was publishing: but today I feel that I won't. It was only lack of food which frightened me into consenting: and in the R.A.F. they give us quantities of food.

Yours sincerely
T. E. Lawrence

British Library

3 *See* letter to G.B.S. dated 2 January 1923 (p. 228).
4 Colonel Richard Meinertzhagen had served with Lawrence in the Middle East and also in Paris. He later presented a somewhat unflattering account of Lawrence in his *Middle East Diary 1917-1956*, published in 1959, but in his *Army Diary*, published in 1960, he wrote of him: 'I respected him, admired him and was devoted to him.'

The following letter shows that when his air force career had been put at risk by the *Daily Express* disclosures, Lawrence briefly contemplated the idea, put to him by Robert Graves, of going to live with Graves and his wife Nancy Nicholson in Nepal. Five days after refusing the offer he was discharged from the R.A.F.

ROBERT GRAVES
18.1.23

Dear R.G.
I've delayed, thinking about it: and thinking is slow in B block because people talk more readily. Now there is a sort of riot happening over by the fire: and so writing is made difficult.

The conclusion is that probably I won't.[1] The escape from what is nearly squalor here was attractive: and Nepal is out of the world (by the way passports won't be difficult: the I.O. will do that much for my sake. Lord Winterton was 'one of us' in Hejaz): but partly I came in here to eat dirt, till its taste is normal to me; and partly to avoid the current of other men's thinking; and in your hill-court there will be high thinking. My brain nearly went in Barton St. with the weariness of writing and re-writing that horrible book of mine: and I still am nervous & easily made frantic.

So I think I'm going to stay on in the R.A.F. which has the one great merit of showing me humanity very clear & clean. I've never lived commonly before, & I think to run away from the stress of it would be a failing.

I owe you a word about that book. It may be printed privately, in a limited subscription edition, next year. A sort of 15 guinea book, almost unprocurable. I hovered for a while this year with the notion of a censored version: but that seems dishonest, until the whole story is available.

I'm glad you're feeling easier. In mechanical jargon you've been 'revving' yourself too high for the last eighteen months. Such forced running means a very heavy fuel consumption, & is not true economy. Your 'philosopher' period

1 The background to this letter is explained in *RGB*, though with the name of the country in question (Nepal) omitted. Graves wrote: 'I was troubled about his [Lawrence's] life in the ranks and felt that he ought to be rescued. Then I, and my family, had an invitation from the Foreign Minister of a certain remote Eastern principality to go there and live at the Government's expense: the invitation was extended to Lawrence. If he went, we went.' Lawrence's refusal meant that Graves and his family did not go, either. 'The I.O.' was the India Office, at which Lord Winterton was under-secretary of state.

as a poet is worth taking care for, since its product will surpass your lyrical.

Many thanks to Malik.[2] I very nearly came, but I wanted to too much for it to be a wholesome wish.

E.L. *Harvard University/RGB*

J. L. GARVIN[1]
30.1.23 *14 BARTON ST S.W.1*

Dear Garvin

I sent you the *Seven Pillars* from Farnborough last week: but within half an hour of that I'd got my dismissal from the R.A.F. for possessing too large a publicity factor to be decent in an A.C.2. Wherefore I've sent to Savage, who was the long-suffering man acting as my agent, & told him that the proposed publication again falls through.

You'll remember that after sleeping over my talk with you I cancelled all idea of publishing an abridgement. It seemed too dishonest a white-washing of the ugly side of the Arab business. Cape was miserable about it, so to comfort him I offered him the proceeds of serial publication with you. He countered with ideas of a limited subscription edition of the entire work, & I had provisionally accepted this, & was turning over the draft contract in my ruminant mind – when the new blow fell, & I wired to say that it was all over again. Since then I've been wandering about, rather address-less, but sooner or later I'll blow into Barton St, where Herbert Baker anyway will receive anything for me: so the *Seven Pillars* may well go there till I want them. You don't know any serious person who would like to buy one of the five copies of that inordinate work? Going very dear!

I hope that your eyes have refused to attempt the strain of its horrible print, & consequently that you haven't read it. If my marching order had come an hour earlier you wouldn't have been bothered.

2 Malik (*sic*): Basanta Mallik, a graduate of Calcutta University and of Exeter College, Oxford, and later a postgraduate student at Balliol College, was the initiator of the invitation to Nepal.

1 James Louis Garvin (1868-1947) was editor of *The Observer* 1908-42. He was one of the most influential journalists of his time. He was made a Companion of Honour in 1941.

What an unending nuisance being known is! I'm beginning to despair of ever getting away from my past.

Yours
T E Lawrence

University of Texas

H. W. BAILEY[1]
4.2.23   *24 BARTON STREET WESTMINSTER*

Dear Bailey
You must have given up hopes of me! But as a matter of fact, when that newspaper shriek about me came out, the Air Ministry got angry and gave me the sack, and I've been dodging about since after jobs.

My letters lay in a neglected heap at Farnborough for a long while, and were finally sent on to me by the Air Ministry. The idiot Press said that I'd enlisted in order to write a book about the War – but this was written three years ago and lies in a cupboard. The truth was that I was a little short of cash and still am, though things are looking better.

The address above will find me always (even if I go abroad in the near future as I expect), and I'd very much like to hear how you are and what you are doing. Please send me a line if you have time for it. Do you know by any chance, where Rolls, the tender-driver, is?[2]

I hear occasionally from most of the officers who were on our show, but very seldom from any of you; when we got to Damascus I hopped off like a scalded cat and swore that I'd never go back, so couldn't get any addresses. Lately they have been offering me command of armoured car units in Palestine; but I feel somehow that I don't want any more commissions. It was very good of you to write to me.

Yours ever
J. H. Ross

1 H.W. Bailey is listed in Appendix I of *Seven Pillars of Wisdom,* as being a member of the Machine Gun Corps in the Hejaz Armoured Car Company.
2 S. C. Rolls: *see* letter to him dated 10 June 1931 (p. 485).

People would bore me by calling me 'Colonel' Lawrence. So I changed it in 1920.

Marshall	The 'Doc' is British Minister to Hejaz. Lives at Jeddah.
Joyce	is in Bagdad, military adviser to Feisal.
Goslett	is in business in London.
Gilman	I last heard of married and an engineer in France.
Stirling	is in Palestine.
Young	is in the Colonial Office, London.
Kirkbride	is in Palestine.
Junor	the flying man up at Azrak with us, was with me at Farnborough lately.
Wade and Dowsett	I haven't heard of for a long while.

Bodleian Library

VYVYAN RICHARDS
Thursday [early 1923]

The seal in which I bound the S.P. must have died of a surfeit of tomatoes. Isn't it a glorious colour.

I've been thinking over your letter: its praise is very welcome, because my feelings towards the *Seven Pillars* are mixed. Relatively it's a bad book, & gives me no pleasure. That's why your enjoyment of parts or elements of it gratifies me, as a sign that others can find in it something of what I failed to put into it in full measure. Positively I know that it's a good book: in the sense that it's better than most which have been written lately: but this only makes me yet sorrier that it isn't as good as my book should have been.

If you dig malevolently behind these last sentences you will realise that I have a tolerable opinion of myself. The criticisms of the book miss their aim in me, partly because I have made them all (& many others) in a far stronger sense, to myself: and the reason why the book isn't different is because my will-power to persevere with it failed. I don't know if it will return. A book dropped behind a man is so soon left behind.

Now for your points: —

<u>You are intoxicated with the splendour of the story.</u> That's as it should be. The story I have to tell is one of the most splendid ever given a man for writing.

<u>Some things mar it for you.</u> Please mark them marginally & I'll discuss them at leisure. You should not need so long to acquire my angle or need to acquire it at all.

<u>Plain lapses.</u> I can't have written hurtled. Wasn't it only hustled or something? and a misprint? Any way, please mark such points. In so long a book my head must sometimes have nodded.

<u>Black marks on white paper.</u> Deliberate, I'm afraid. We will discuss the fitness together.

<u>Self-depreciation</u> is a necessity with me.

<u>More critic than artist.</u> That's the analytic vein in me. Ineradicable. A critic in conscious creation is of course an artist. Ditto a blacksmith or a playwright. A critic is no more barred from creation than any other being. I'll say even that there's creative criticism: not literary nor artistic, but personal (biography) or ethical (Pater's *Imaginary Portraits*). To have an excess of creative over critical sense produces a Swinburne. To be excessively critical is to be like Rupert Brooke. The perfect artist is half-critic & half-creator.

<u>Written history has never yet so nearly approached the unity of a work of art.</u> Written history is inevitably long & must be judged by the standard of epic rather than lyric. *The Iliad* has only a fictitious unity. Gibbon at least as much. I suppose the *Peloponnesian War* has more unity than the average drama. Only perhaps you'd call it not true. I'll admit that modern history has seldom been 'composed' in the artistic sense. Trevelyan's Italian efforts perhaps. But modern history tries to be a science, not an art.

<u>Your intelligence seems to limit instinctive experience before it is part of you.</u> It at least tried to do this. I could have written a simple story, but only fraudulently, since by nature, & education & environment I'm complex. So I tried to make my reactions to experience as compound as they were in reality. I don't agree with your implied hint that simplicity is ethically better (when it would be false): or in any circumstances more artistic. A twice-swallowed oyster would be a double profit to the consumer.

<u>The fine choice of adjective is a perpetual delight.</u> I'm most glad of this, for I took great care with them: there's a fault or two however in every paragraph, but not other than I can correct in a week's care. These stylistic changes are easy & pleasant to make.

<u>The purple passages even when they are meant to be purple.</u> I suspect every purple passage is intentional. In my experience purple things are a conscious straining upward of the mind. Yes, too, it was & is very hard to write about oneself in action. I'm proposing to flatten off a good deal of the personal doing – and to eliminate (it comes easy) five out of six of the 'I's'. The book will gain in power by that much restraint. Already there's a lot, but I'm ambitious after power & want to knock my readers down with it.

<u>Cut out all suggestions of self-depreciation.</u> But I really do cut myself in all sincerity. I've been & am absurdly over-estimated. There are no supermen & I'm quite ordinary, & will say so whatever the artistic results. In that point I'm one of the few people who tell the truth about myself.

<u>I might make it the perfect lyrical triumph.</u> Yes but that was only the superficial aspect of the campaign, & it would be superficial to write it as a triumph. The word on my title page is ironic.[1]

<u>The making of a great tragedy in its being not really my triumph.</u> I tried to bring this out, just this side of egotism, as a second note running through the book after Chapter V, & increasing slowly towards the close. But it would be a fault in scale to represent the Arab Revolt mainly as a personal tragedy to me.

<u>The stillness of absolute works of art.</u> <u>You admire these most.</u> Which are they? Isn't it that you admire more than the category of history & biography, the category of whatever it is. I don't want to rack my head (in barrack room with the other 46 making a noise) to think of what they are. But honestly I doubt whether stillness is an 'absolute' element in works of supreme art. It seems to me a manner like another. My big books Rabelais, *Moby Dick*, *Karamazov*, leave their readers in a sweat. *Zarathustra* has his stillness. Of the poems there's no stillness in the *Cenci* (exhaustion rather) or in the *Oresteia*: or in *Lear*. Of the priests who serve one stands still, & eight move about & work for him: and there are religions full of movement. I think you are mistaking a preference for a principle.

1 *Seven Pillars* is sub-titled *A Triumph*.

There is a danger where one savours too much, of creating what one has found savoury in others. Have I done this? or do you suspect it too frequently? If so, please mark the spots.

I think Brooke's technique as good as Keats, but his sense of the taste of words was less fine: and his native irony restrained him from the sugary... pictures of Keats. It restrained him too much, so that it was seldom musical: whereas Keats when his self-criticism held back from the sugar, had almost no likely fault to avoid. Art Creation is avoidance as much as it is presentation. And it's interesting to see Keats's growth in force (& decline in sweetness) from *Endymion* to *Hyperion*.

I agree that the *Seven Pillars* is too big for me: too big for most writers, I think. It's rather in the Titan class: books written at tiptoe, with a strain that dislocates the writer, & exhausts the reader out of sympathy. Such can't help being failures, because the graceful things are always those within our force: but as you conclude their cracks & imperfections serve an artistic end in themselves: a perfect-picture of a real man would be unreadable.

We ought to talk over the S. P. I'm coming up to London on Saturday next (2 p.m. in the hall of Charing Cross Underground probably). Your Sundays are busy, so you probably can't come: and perhaps I can't. If so I'll wire on Saturday saying No go. Don't bother to reply to this meanwhile. After Charing X I go on to Barton St. till about 7 p.m. If you come bring the book with you.

E.L.

Bodleian Library / University of Texas

Forbidden the air force, there was always the army. Again Lawrence's connections in high places provided the solution to his dilemma. General Sir Philip Chetwode (later Field Marshal Chetwode) had commanded under Allenby and was now adjutant-general to the forces at the War Office. Apparently at the prompting of Colonel Alan Dawnay, close comrade of Lawrence in the last year of the war, Chetwode approached the commandant of the Tank Corps, Colonel Sir Hugh Elles, who saw no difficulty in accepting Lawrence into his training centre at Bovington Camp, Dorset. Lawrence was allowed to enlist in the Tank Corps on a seven-year engagement, was given the number, rank and name of 7875698 Private T. E. Shaw and was posted to A Company of the Royal Tank Corps depot at Bovington with effect from 12 March 1923.

LIONEL CURTIS
19.3.23   *[BOVINGTON CAMP]*

Lorde

My mind moves me this morning to write you a whole series of letters, to be more splendid than the *Lettres de Mon Moulin*.[1] Nothing will come of it, but meanwhile this page grows blacker with the preliminaries.

What should the preliminaries be? A telling why I joined? As you know I don't know! Explaining it to Dawnay I said 'Mind-suicide': but that's only because I'm an incorrigible phraser. Do you, in reading my complete works, notice that tendency to do up small packets of words foppishly?

At the same time there's the reason why I have twice enlisted, in those same complete works: on my last night in Barton Street I read chapters 113 to 118, and saw implicit in them my late course. The months of politics with Winston were abnormal, and the R.A.F. and Army are natural. The Army (which I despise with all my mind) is more natural than the R.A.F.: for at Farnborough I grew suddenly on fire with the glory which the air should be, and set to work full steam to make the others vibrate to it like myself. I was winning too, when they chucked me out: indeed I rather suspect I was chucked out for that. It hurt the upper story that the ground-floor was grown too keen.

The Army seems safe against enthusiasm. It's a horrible life, and the other fellows fit it. I said to one 'They're the sort who instinctively fling stones at cats' ... and he said 'Why what do you throw?' You perceive that I'm not yet in the picture: but I will be in time. Seven years of this will make me impossible for anyone to suggest for a responsible position, and that self-degradation is my aim. I haven't the impulse and the conviction to fit what I know to be my power of moulding men and things: and so I always regret what I've created, when the leisure after creation lets me look back and see that the idea was secondhand.

This is a pompous start, and it should be a portentous series of letters: but there is excuse for it, since time moves slower here than elsewhere: and a man has only himself to think about. At reveille I feel like Adam, after a night's pondering: and my mind has malice enough rather to enjoy putting Adam through it.

---

1 Lawrence's letters to Lionel Curtis between March and June 1923 are among his most powerful. *See introduction* to this section and Lawrence's letter to Charlotte Shaw dated 18 August 1927 (p. 365). For Lionel Curtis *see* note to letter to G.J. Kidston dated 14 November 1919. *Lettres de Mon Moulin*, a book of sketches of life in Provence, is one of the most famous works of nineteenth-century French writer Alphonse Daudet.

Don't take seriously what I wrote about the other men, above. It's only at first that certain sides of them strike a little crudely. In time I'll join, concerning them, in Blake's astonishing cry 'Everything that is, is holy!' It seems to me one of the best words ever said. Philip Kerr[2] would agree with it (one of the engaging things about Philip is his agreement with my absence), but not many other reflective men come to the same conclusion without a web of mysticism to help them.

I'm not sure either that what I've said about my creations is quite true.

I feel confident that Arabia and Trans-Jordan and Mesopotamia, *with what they will breed*, are nearly monumental enough for the seven years' labour of one head: because I knew what I was at, and the others only worked on instinct: and my other creation, that odd and interminable book . . ., do you know I'm absolutely hungry to know what people think of it – not when they are telling me, but what they tell to one another. Should I be in this secret case if I really thought it pernicious?

There again, perhaps there's a solution to be found in multiple personality. It's my reason which condemns the book and the revolt, and the new nationalities: because the only rational conclusion to human argument is pessimism such as Hardy's, a pessimism which is very much like the wintry heath, of bog and withered plants and stripped trees, about us. Our camp on its swelling in this desolation feels pustular, and we (all brown-bodied, with yellow spots down our front belly-line), must seem like the swarming germs of its fermentation. That's feeling, exterior-bred feeling, with reason harmonising it into a picture: but there's a deeper sense which remembers other landscapes, and the changes which summer will bring to this one: and to that sense nothing can be changeless: whereas the rational preference or advantage of pessimism is its finality, the eternity in which it ends: and if there isn't an eternity there cannot be a pessimism pure.

Lorde what a fog of words! What I would say is that reason proves there is no hope, and we therefore hope on, so to speak, on one leg of our minds: a dot and go one progress, which takes me Tuesday Thursday and Saturday and leaves me authentic on the other days. *Quelle vie.*

DG/All Souls College Oxford

---

2 Sir Philip Kerr (1882-1940), later 11th Marquess of Lothian, was a friend of Lionel Curtis, with whom he had worked in South Africa after the Boer War in what became known as Milner's 'Kindergarten', *i.e.* the group of young admirers assisting Lord Milner when the latter was governor of the Transvaal and the Orange Colony. Ambassador to the U.S.A. 1939-40.

ROBERT GRAVES
20.3.23   *14 BARTON STREET*

Dear R.G.

I've been some while wanting to write, & your note (which came to hand yesterday) is the last straw to weigh down my mind.

Sorry to have missed you in London: but my movings have been eccentric of late. The R.A.F. threw me out, eventually. Crime of too great publicity. Stainless character. I took the latter to the W.O. and persuaded them to let me enlist with them. So I'm now a recruit in the Tank Corps. Conditions tough, companions rough, self becoming rough too. However there is a certainty and a contentment in bed-rock.

I wanted to ask you ... we are near Dorchester, & I run about Dorset on wheels (when they take their eyes off us) ... do you think old Hardy would let me look at him? He's a proper poet & a fair novelist, in my judgment, & it would give me a feeling of another mile-stone passed if I might meet him. Yet to blow in upon him in khaki would not be an introduction. You know the old thing, don't you? What are my hopes?[1]

Youuurs
T.E.?[2]

Harvard University/RGB

1 Graves duly wrote to Thomas Hardy on Lawrence's behalf, and the latter soon became a favourite visitor at Hardy's Dorchester home, Max Gate.
2 I have followed Graves's transcription 'T.E.?', but the original signature is an almost indecipherable scrawl of which the first letter looks rather more like R than T, as though he had begun to write 'Ross' or, more simply, 'R' (as in his letter to Lionel Curtis on the following day).

A. E. (JOCK) CHAMBERS[1]
21.3.23   [BOVINGTON CAMP]

I liked B.iii and the R.A.F. and this army life feels very drab in comparison. Also you know we really were a decent crowd: and the present lot with me are the sort who'd always throw something at any cat they saw. It's a moral difference, I feel, and unless I can get over it I'll find myself solitary again.

The camp is beautifully put – a wide heath, of flint & sand, with pines & oak-trees, & much rhododendron coming slowly into bloom. When the heather flowers in a few weeks there will be enough to please me.

One of my sorrows is the recruits' course (new name, naturally, new age, no previous service) & a consequent imprisonment in the camp for a month, being damnably shouted at. [...]

Regard me to B3. My only present likeness to it is another corner bed!

Yours
R.   DG

R.A.M. GUY[1]
21.3.23   BOVINGTON CAMP

My rabbit
I do no good here. Out upon the army & all its clothes and food & words and works. You in the R. A. F. are as lucky as I thought myself in the old days, & as I used to tell you.

They give us great leisure. Five hours work a day on Monday and Thursday. Tuesday is an afternoon for sports. Wednesday is a half-day. On Friday our work is drawing pay, & wondering afterwards why they, out of all

---

1 Jock Chambers had been the orderly of Lawrence's hut (B3) at Farnborough, where the two became close friends. He had served in the navy and army before joining the air force. He contributed to *T. E. Lawrence by His Friends* and remained a lifelong admirer and disciple, defending him against all detractors.

1 Robert (Bob) Guy was a young aircraftman with whom Lawrence developed an especially close friendship. See particularly his letter to Guy written on Christmas Day 1923 (p. 266).

the possible payments in the world, should have given us just that little or that much. Saturday, needless to say, is Saturday: and Sunday is Sunday.

I'm going to dazzle you, if ever I see you again, with the perfection of my salute: while at slow marching! I march slower and slower: the whole camp agrees that my slow marching is slow. Though some idiots this afternoon were arguing as to whether it was marching. God help them, they are fools, & myself the solitary wise man in Dorset.

'Easter leave' did you say, in your exquisite letter? I get none. They dazzle us with the prospect of eight days' leave in August: but to win that we must have done eighteen weeks upon the square, & must have reached, as a squad, the standard of finished squads. Horrors & horrors piled upon one another! Thanks be to God that I require no leave. Only, rabbit, I'm sorry, since that summer holiday in Oxford would have been perhaps a pleasure to you. There are no rabbits here (or at least no imitation ones) and it would give me contentment to see your queer but jolly face again. There are men from Brum, but their accent isn't like yours (except when they miss an h) and their wishes are ordinary.

My attack upon you in the last letter was presumably a bad joke. I envy everyone who doesn't think continually.

Brough[2] is in London, & myself confined to camp.
R.

Tell Jock that soldiers are men like Jimmy Carr, & that I can't do the weight. I might sham A.C.II-ship, but this is too difficult.

I wasn't in Farnborough on Monday. Depot.

Bodleian Reserve

---

2 *I.e.* his motorcycle: *see* p. 266n.

MRS THOMAS HARDY[1]

25.3.23   [BOVINGTON CAMP]

Dear Mrs. Hardy

A letter from Robert Graves (to whom I had written) tells me that I'm to get into communication with you. It feels rather barefaced, because I haven't any qualifications to justify my seeing Mr. Hardy: only I'd very much like to. *The Dynasts* & the other poems are so wholly good to my taste.

It adds to my hesitation that I'm a private in the Tank Corps, at Wool, and would have to come across in uniform. You may have feelings against soldiers. Also I'm therefore not master of my own time. They let us off on Wednesdays, Saturdays, and Sundays at noon: and I have a motor cycle so that getting over to Dorchester is only a matter of minutes. I must be in camp again at 9.30 p.m: but between that & noon on any one of those three days for the next three months I should be free, if you are good enough to offer me a time.

The deepest apologies. I'm suggesting that you take a great deal of quite unwarrantable trouble.

Yours sincerely
T E Lawrence

In case you like R. G. enough to reply, please address me
7875698 Pte T. E. Shaw Hut F12 B Company 1st Depot Battalion Tank Corps Bovington Camp Wool
I dropped the 'Lawrence' part of me six months ago.

Bodleian Library

---

1 Florence Hardy, *née* Dugdale (1879-1937), was Thomas Hardy's second wife; they had married in 1914, two years after his first wife's death. She met Hardy in 1907 when she volunteered to help him with the checking and revision of his verse-drama *The Dynasts*. Lawrence's relationship with the Hardys was to become not dissimilar to that with the Shaws — in each case he was seen to some extent as a kind of surrogate son. In each case, too, Lawrence's correspondent was the wife, not the husband. Lawrence invited himself through Graves into the Hardy home (Max Gate on the edge of Dorchester), but this was not seen in any way as an imposition. Both Hardys became very fond of Lawrence, who also gained the reputation of being one of the few visitors to Max Gate who could cope with their terrifying dog, Wessex.

LIONEL CURTIS
27.3.23   [BOVINGTON CAMP]

It seems to continue itself today, because I've been wondering about the other
fellows in the hut. A main feeling they give me is of difference from the R.A.F.
men. They were excited about our coming service. We talked and wondered of
the future, almost exclusively. There was a constant recourse to imagination,
and a constant rewarding of ourselves therefore. The fellows were decent, but
so wrought up by hope that they were carried out of themselves, and I could
not see them mattly. There was a sparkle round the squad.

Here every man has joined because he was down and out: and no one talks
of the Army or of promotion, or of trades and accomplishments. We are all
here unavoidably, in a last resort, and we assume this world's failure in one-
another, so that pretence would not be merely laughed at, but as near an
impossibility as anything human. We are social bed-rock, those unfit for life-by-
competition: and each of us values the rest as cheap as he knows himself to be.

I suspect that this low estimation is very much the truth. There cannot be
classes in England much more raw, more free of all that the upbringing of a
lifetime has plastered over you and me. Can there be profit, or truth, in all
these modes and sciences and arts of ours? The leisured world for hundreds,
or perhaps thousands of years has been jealously working and recording the
advance of each generation for the starting-point of the next – and here these
masses are as animal, as carnal as were their ancestors before Plato and Christ
and Shelley and Dostoevsky taught and thought. In this crowd it's made
startlingly clear how short is the range of knowledge, and what poor
conductors of it ordinary humans are. You and I know: you have tried (Round
Tabling[1] and by mouth) to tell all whom you can reach: and the end is here, a
cimmerian darkness with bog-lights flitting wrongly through its gas.

The pity of it is, that you've got to take this black core of things in camp,
this animality, on trust. It's a feeling, a spirit which colours every word and
action, and I believe every thought, passing in Hut 12. Your mind is like a
many-storied building, and you, its sole tenant, flit from floor to floor, from
room to room, at the whim of your spirit's moment. (Not that the spirit has
moments, but let it pass for the metaphor's sake). At will you can be gross,
and enjoy coffee or a sardine, or rarefy yourself till the diaphancité [sic] of
pure mathematics, or of a fluent design in line, is enough to feed you. Here –

1 Lionel Curtis was editor of *The Round Table*, a quarterly review of British Commonwealth politics.

I can't write it, because in literature such things haven't ever been, and can't be. To record the acts of Hut 12 would produce a moral-medical case-book, not a work of art but a document. It isn't the filth of it which hurts me, because you can't call filthy the pursuit of a bitch by a dog, or the mating of birds in springtime; and it's man's misfortune that he hasn't a mating season, but spreads his emotions and excitements through the year but I lie in bed night after night with this cat-calling carnality seething up and down the hut, fed by streams of fresh matter from twenty lecherous mouths ... and my mind aches with the rawness of it, knowing that it will cease only when the slow bugle calls for 'lights out' an hour or so hence and the waiting is so slow.

However the call comes always in the end, and suddenly at last, like God's providence, a dewfall of peace upon the camp ... but surely the world would be more clean if we were dead or mindless? We are all guilty alike, you know. You wouldn't exist, I wouldn't exist, without this carnality. Everything with flesh in its mixture is the achievement of a moment when the lusty thought of Hut 12 has passed to action and conceived: and isn't it true that the fault of birth rests somewhat on the child? I believe it's we who led our parents on to bear us, and it's our unborn children who make our flesh itch.

A filthy business all of it, and yet Hut 12 shows me the truth behind Freud. Sex is an integer in all of us, and the nearer nature we are, the more constantly, the more completely a product of that integer. These fellows are the reality, and you and I, the selves who used to meet in London and talk of fleshless things, are only the outward wrappings of a core like these fellows. They let light and air play always upon their selves, and consequently have grown very lustily, but have at the same time achieved health and strength in their growing. Whereas our wrappings and bandages have stunted and deformed ourselves, and hardened them to an apparent insensitiveness ... but it's a callousness, a crippling, only to be yea-said by aesthetes who prefer clothes to bodies, surfaces to intentions.

These fellows have roots, which in us are rudimentary, or long cut off. Before I came I never visualised England except as an organism, an entity but these fellows are local, territorial. They all use dialects, and could be placed by their dialects, if necessary. However it isn't necessary, because each talks of his district, praises it, boasts of it, lives in the memory of it. We call each other 'Brum' or 'Coventry' or 'Cambridge', and the man who hasn't a 'place' is an outsider. They wrangle and fight over the virtues of their homes. Of solidarity, of a nation, of something ideal comprehending their familiar streets in itself – they haven't a notion.

Well, the conclusion of the first letter was that man, being a civil war, could not be harmonised or made logically whole ... and the end of this is that man, or mankind, being organic, a natural growth, is unreachable: cannot depart from his first grain and colour, nor exceed flesh, nor put forth anything not mortal and fleshly.

I fear not even my absence would reconcile Ph.K.[2] to this.

E.L.

DG/All Souls College Oxford

COLONEL A. P. WAVELL[1]

11.v.23   *[BOVINGTON CAMP]*

Dear Wavell

Many thanks for your letter: it pleased me, for though (as of a son) I can see and say no good of my book, yet I'm glad when others praise it. I hate it & like it by turns, & know that it's a good bit of writing, and often wish it wasn't. If I'd aimed less high I'd have hit my mark squarer, & made a better little thing of it. As it stands it's a great failure (lacking architecture, the balance of parts, coherence, stream-lining): and oddly enough among my favourite books are the other great failures – *Moby Dick, Also sprach Zarathustra, Pantagruel,* – books where the authors went up like a shoot of rockets, and burst.[2] I don't mean to put mine into that degree of the class: but it is to me as *Zarathustra* was to Nietzsche, something bigger than I could do.

Apart from literature, how does it strike you as history? It's hard to see another man's campaign – but you ~~say~~ as much of mine as I saw of yours... does my record of mine stand up, so to speak, upon its military feet? I've never posed as a soldier, & feel that the campaign side of the book may be

2 Ph.K.: Philip Kerr (*see* note to letter of 19 March 1923, p. 240).

1 Colonel A.P. Wavell, later Field Marshal Earl Wavell of Cyrenaica (1883-1950), had been chief of staff of XXth Corps in Allenby's Palestine and Syria campaigns and was at this time assistant adjutant-general at the War Office. He and Lawrence met in December 1917 on the occasion of the official entry into Jerusalem. *See* his contribution to *T.E. Lawrence by His Friends*, with its keynote statement: 'He [Lawrence] will always have his detractors ….. They knew not the man.'
2 *Moby Dick* was by Herman Melville, *Also sprach Zarathustra* was by Friedrich Wilhelm Nietzsche, *Pantagruel* was by François Rabelais.

technically weak. That's why I was glad you asked to read it, because I hope you'll have an opinion (critical not laudatory) on your professional side. Bartholomew made no comment. That's the worst of writing too long a book … it gets beyond criticism, by being too ~~rich~~ abounding in weak & strong points. Keep it a little longer if you wish, but not too long please, for a friend of mine (who wants it eagerly), has been waiting quite a while for a spare copy. Another fault of a long book: it circulates so slowly. There are only six copies, & three of them are on permanent loan to Hogarth, Alan Dawnay, & Kennington, the artist, who did some forty or fifty drawings of its contents for me. As for holding it private – well I've suffered more than I can bear of public discussion & praise, & the insufficiency & obliquity of it are like a nightmare of memory. To publish the whole book might cause a new clamour, for I don't hide from myself that it might be a successful book, as sales went. To censor it would mean practical re-writing, & I'm weary of the work put into it already: also it feels a little dishonest to hide parts of the truth. Further I remind myself that the feelings of some English, some French & some Arabs might be hurt by some of the things I tell of. Against these ~~feelings~~ instincts you have to set the vanity of an amateur who's tried to write, & would like to be in print as an author: and my need of money to live quietly upon. It's a nice calculation, with the balance just against, & so I bury all my talents!

When you have finished with it will you post it me? I'm now

   Pte. T. E. Shaw. 7875698

    Hut F. 12

     B. Coy.

      1st Depot Batt. Tank Corps

       Bovington Camp

       Wool

       Dorset.

 A horribly long address I'm afraid, but not my fault, though the coming here was: however I was decided not to touch politics again, & my untrained hands & wits failed to earn me a certain living: so after the R.A.F. chucked me out I got Chetwode to let me into the army, where the work is so little & so dull that all my mind's time is my own. Of course it gives me no chance of coming to London. Don't tell people.

Yours ever

T.E.L.

                  Bodleian Library

LIONEL CURTIS
14.V.23   *TANKTOWN*

I should have written before, but a split thumb, and the sudden discovery of the authorities that I belonged to a criminal class, have put me out of the mood for subjective writing: – and since politics passed out of me the only theme between us is myself.

There was one injustice in your letter. My crying-out here was not at the foul talk. To me it's meaningless, unobjectionable, on a par with heedless fair-talk. The R.A.F. was foul-mouthed, and the cleanest little mob of fellows. These are foul-mouthed, and behind their mouths is a pervading animality of spirit, whose unmixed bestiality frightens me and hurts me. There is no criticism, indeed it's taken for granted as natural, that you should job a woman's body, or hire out yourself, or abuse yourself in any way. I cried out against it, partly in self-pity because I've condemned myself to grow like them, and partly in premonition of failure, for my masochism remains and will remain, only moral. Physically I can't do it: indeed I get in denial the gratification they get in indulgence. I react against their example into an abstention even more rigorous than of old. Everything bodily is now hateful to me (and in my case hateful is the same as impossible). In the sports lately (they vex us with set exercises) I was put down to jump, and refused because it was an activity of the flesh. Afterwards to myself I wondered if that was the reason, or was I afraid of failing ridiculously: so I went down alone and privily cleared over twenty feet, and was sick of mind at having tried because I was glad to find I still could jump. It's on a par with the music for which I'm hungry. Henry Lamb[1] is in Poole, and will play wonderfully to me if I go over: and I won't go, though I'm so starved for rhythm that even a soldier's stumbling through a song on the piano makes my blood run smooth (I refuse to hear it with my head).

This sort of thing must be madness, and sometimes I wonder how far mad I am, and if a mad-house would not be my next (and merciful) stage.

Merciful compared with this place, which hurts me, body and soul. It's terrible to hold myself voluntarily here: and yet I want to stay here till it no longer hurts me: till the burnt child no longer feels the fire. Do you think there have been many lay monks of my persuasion? One used to think that such frames of mind would have perished with the age of religion: and yet here they rise up, purely secular. It's a lurid flash into the Nitrian desert: seems almost to strip the sainthood from Anthony. How about Teresa?

---

1 Henry Lamb (1883-1960): artist, served as doctor in the Palestine campaign, contributed two illustrations to *Seven Pillars of Wisdom*.

I consume the day (and myself) brooding, and making phrases and reading and thinking again, galloping mentally down twenty divergent roads at once, as apart and alone as in Barton Street in my attic. I sleep less than ever, for the quietness of night imposes thinking on me: I eat breakfast only, and refuse every possible distraction and employment and exercise. When my mood gets too hot and I find myself wandering beyond control I pull out my motor-bike and hurl it top-speed through these unfit roads for hour after hour. My nerves are jaded and gone near dead, so that nothing less than hours of voluntary danger will prick them into life: and the 'life' they reach then is a melancholy joy at risking something worth exactly 2/9 a day.

It's odd, again, that craving for real risk: because in the gymnasium I funk jumping the horse, more than poison. That is physical, which is why it is: I'm ashamed of doing it and of not doing it, unwilling to do it: and most of all ashamed (afraid) of doing it well.

A nice, neurotic letter! What you've done to deserve its receipt God knows. … perhaps you have listened to me too friendly-like at earlier times.

Sorry, and all that. You are a kind of safety-valve perhaps. I wish you were an alienist, and could tell me where or how this ferment will end. It makes me miserable on top of all the curiosity and determination: and sets me so much aside that I hardly blame the powers for jumping on me with their dull punishments.

L.   *DG/All Souls College Oxford*

MRS THOMAS HARDY
21.V.23

Dear Mrs. Hardy

I'm afraid I'll come on Saturday next at tea-time! De la Mare is known to me only by his books – but he should be delightful, if he lives up to them:[1] and most good people are better than their books.

It sounds greedy, always to come when you ask me: but your house is so wonderfully unlike this noisy room that it is difficult to resist, even for its own

---

1 Poet and story-writer Walter de la Mare (1873-1956) was by this time well into the literary career which would bring him such honours as the C. H. (Companion of Honour), the O. M. (Order of Merit) and burial in St Paul's Cathedral.

sake: and then there is Mr. Hardy, though you mustn't tell him so, for the thrill is too one-sided. He has seen so much of human-kind that he must be very tired of them: whereas for me he's Hardy, & I'd go a long way even to see the place where he had lived, let alone him living in it.

There, you will think me absurd: but still I'll arrive on Saturday!

Yours sincerely
T E Shaw

DG

COLONEL A. P. WAVELL
21.V.23   [*BOVINGTON CAMP*]

Dear Wavell

Many thanks for the book (which has gone forward to its next) and for your long letter. It's exactly the sort of thing which I wanted to read.

No, I don't feel confident militarily. All the while we fought I felt like a conjuror trying an insufficiently-rehearsed trick – surprised when it came out right. A succession of such chances gave me the feeling I was apt at the business: that's all. [...]

As for the reply to raiding tactics. As you say, it's greater mobility than the attack. This needn't mean large drafts from the harassed G.O.C. If the Turks had put machine guns on three or four of their touring cars, & driven them on weekly patrol over the admirable going of the desert E. of Amman & Maan they would have put an absolute stop to our camel-parties, & so to our rebellion. It wouldn't have cost them 20 men or £20,000 ... rightly applied. They scraped up cavalry & armoured trains & camel corps & block-houses against us: because they didn't think hard enough. [...]

There is one other thing of which every rebellion is mortally afraid – treachery. If instead of counter-propaganda (never effective on the conservative side) the money had been put into buying the few venial men always to be found in a big movement, then they would have crippled us. We could only dare these intricate raids because we felt sure and safe. One well-informed traitor will spoil a national rising.

Bombing tribes is ineffective. I fancy that air-power may be effective against elaborate armies: but against irregulars it has no more than moral value. The

Turks had plenty [of] machines, & used them freely against us – and never hurt us till the last phase, when we had brought 1000 of our regulars on the raid against Deraa. Guerrilla tactics are a complete muffing of air-force.

.L.

DG

LIONEL CURTIS
30.V.23

[...] You say my friends feel the absence of me – but personality (which it is my gift to you to exhibit) is of a short range, and in my experience has not touched more than ten or twelve friends at a time: and here I live with twenty very barren men, who feel my being with them. The hut is changed from what it used to be, and unlike what it would be (will be?) if I left. This isn't conceit, but a plain statement; for there would be a change if any one of us twenty was taken away: and I am richer and wider and more experienced than any of the others here. More of the world has passed over me in my 35 years than over all their twenties put together: and your gain, if you did gain by my return, would be their loss. It seems to me that the environment does not matter. Your circle does not draw from me (except superficially) more than theirs: indeed perhaps caenobite man influences as much as man social, for example is eternal, and the rings of its extending influence infinite.

For myself there are consolations. The perfect beauty of this place becomes tremendous, by its contrast with the life we lead, and the squalid huts we live in, and the noisy bullying authority of all our daily unloveliness. The nearly intolerable meanness of man is set in a circle of quiet heath, and budding trees, with the firm level bar of the Purbeck hills behind. The two worlds shout their difference in my ears. Then there is the irresponsibility: I have to answer here only for my cleanness of skin, cleanness of clothes, and a certain mechanical neatness of physical evolution upon the barrack-square. There has not been presented to me, since I have been here, a single choice: everything is ordained – except that harrowing choice of going away from here the moment my will to stay breaks down. With this exception it would be determinism complete – and perhaps in determinism complete there lies the perfect peace I have so longed for. Free-will I've tried, and rejected: authority

I've rejected (not obedience, for that is my present effort, to find equality only in subordination. It is dominion whose taste I have been cloyed with): action I've rejected: and the intellectual life: and the receptive senses: and the battle of wits. They were all failures, and my reason tells me therefore that obedience, nescience, will also fail, since the roots of common failure must lie in myself – and yet in spite of reason I am trying it.[…]

DG

ERIC KENNINGTON
27.VI.23   [BOVINGTON CAMP]

Dear Kennington
I'm a worm, a peccant worm: should have written months ago. […]
    I'm very glad you are helping Roberts. He makes help difficult sometimes, and yet I feel that I would like the oyster if I had any tool strong enough to pry it open. Tell me some time what you think of his considered effort at me. He painted with astonishing certainty: not like John who put a new expression in [my] eyes and mouth on each sitting: but as though there was a fixity in my appearance and mood.[1]
    Do I go further now? No, I don't think there is anything more to say. The army is loathsome: Dorsetshire beautiful: the work very light. So I can carry on here.

T.E.

Bodleian Library

LIONEL CURTIS
27.VI.22 [really 23]

Old thing. This correspondence nearly died: might have died if you had not asked whether I did not join for the sake of the others here. Of course I didn't: things are done in answer to a private urge – not one of altruism.

---

1 Roberts's portrait of Lawrence, done in 1922 in oils and depicting him in air force uniform, is now in the possession of the Ashmolean Museum, Oxford.

You've been talking to Hogarth about my discomfort in the Tank Corps: but you know I joined partly to make myself unemployable, or rather impossible, in my old trade: and the burning out of freewill and self-respect and delicacy from a nature as violent as mine is bound to hurt a bit. If I was firmer I wouldn't cry about it.

It isn't all misery here either. There is the famous motor-bike as a temporary escape. Last Sunday was fine, and another day-slave and myself went off with it after church-parade. Wells we got to, and very beautiful it was: – a grey sober town, stiffly built of prim houses, but with nothing of the artificial in it. Everything is used and lived in; and to make the XVth century habitable today they have put in sash-windows everywhere.

One 'close', the Vicar's close, was nearly the best, it was so cloistered off (even from its quietest of streets): and so grey and green: for the local limestone has turned very sad with time, and has crannied, so that its angles are living with flowers of many sorts: and each of the 'cells' in this close has a little grass-plot between it and the common path down the centre: and on these plots poppies stood in groups like women at a garden party. There was sunshine over it, and a still air, so that all the essence of the place was drawn out and condensed about our heads. It was a college-like place, and looked good to live in: so for a while the camp waiting here for me became an ungrateful thought. Hogarth had written, hoping to get me back into the R.A.F. and the prospect of such happiness had made the Army nearly intolerable. However that's over, easily, for I was only hoping against the knowledge that it wouldn't be possible.

Afterwards I trailed into the cathedral precinct, and lay there on the grass, and watched its huge west front, covered over with bad sculpture, but very correct and proper still, in the manner of the town. There is a remoteness about cathedrals now-a-days –: they are things I could not contribute to, if they were still a-building: and in front of Wells today there was a white-frocked child playing with a ball; the child was quite unconscious of the cathedral (feeling only the pleasure of smooth grass) but from my distance she was so small that she looked no more than a tumbling daisy at the tower-foot: I knew of course that she was animal: and I began in my hatred of animals to balance her against the cathedral: and knew then that I'd destroy the building to save her. That's as irrational as what happened on our coming here, when I swerved Snowy Wallis and myself at 60 m.p.h. on to the grass by the roadside, trying vainly to save a bird which dashed out its life against my side-car. And yet had the world been mine I'd have left out animal life upon it.

An old thing (it pleased me to call him Canon) doddered over and sat by me on the grass, and gave me a penny for my thoughts: and I told him (reading

Huysmans[1] lately) that I was pondering over the contrasts of English and French cathedrals. Ours set in closes so tree-bound and stately and primly-kept that they serve as a narthex to the shrine: a narthex at Wells grander and more religious than the building proper. Whereas French cathedrals have their feet in market places, and booths and chimneys and placards and noise hem them in: so that in France you step from your workshop into the aisle, and in England you cannot even enter till the lawns have swept the street-dust from your feet. The old clergyman gave me another penny to read him the riddle and I did it crab-wise, by a quote from du Bellay,[2] and that Christchurch poem about Our Sovereign Lord the King.[3] He was a book-worm too, and we talked Verhaeren and Melville and Lucretius[4] together, with great pleasure on my part, and the vulgar relish that I was making a cockshy of his assurance that khaki covered nothing but primitive instincts.

He took me round the bishop's palace-garden, pumping me to learn how I endured camp life (living promiscuous seemed to his imagination horrible, and he by profession a shepherd of sheep!), and I hinted at the value of contrast which made all Wells crying-precious to me: and then we leaned over the wall and saw the fish in the moat, and it came upon me very hardly how excellent was their life. Fish are free of mankind you know, and are always perfectly suspended, without ache or activity of nerves, in their sheltering element.

We can get it, of course, when we earth-in our bodies, but it seems to me that we can only do that when they are worn out. It's a failure to kill them out of misery, for if there isn't any good or evil but only activity, and no pain or joy, only sensation: then we can't kill ourselves while we can yet feel. However I'd rather be the fish (did you ever read Rupert Brooke's 'And there shall be no earth in heaven', said fish' [*sic*])[5] or the little bird which had killed itself against me that morning.

There, my letters always end in tears!

E.

DG / All Souls College Oxford

---

1 Joris Karl Huysmans was the author of an epic work on Chartres called *La Cathédrale* (1898); earlier he had won a reputation as a 'decadent' novelist and as such had exercised an important influence on Oscar Wilde.

2 Joachim du Bellay: 16th-century French poet.

3 A reference to the anonymous poem *Preparations* ('Yet if His Majesty, our sovereign lord …'), found in a manuscript of Christ Church, Oxford, and printed in *The Oxford Book of English Verse*.

4 Emile Verhaeren, Belgian poet who published, in French, between 1883 and 1911; Herman Melville, American poet and novelist and author of one of Lawrence's favourite works *Moby Dick*; Lucretius, Roman poet and philosopher of the 1st century BC.

5 A reference to the last two lines of Rupert Brooke's *Heaven*: 'And in that Heaven of all their wish, There shall be no more land, say fish.'

EDMUND BLUNDEN[1]
17.VII.23[2]

Dear Blunden

It's a mirage, of course. I wrote my beastly thing in 1919: & by 1921 had summoned up enough courage to print it (in an edition of six copies, run off on an Oxford newspaper press). That is as far as it has gone, except that something like a dozen people have read it. I have no intention of publishing it: there has been far too much talk already. That poor purblind Lowell Thomas creature imagined by talking that he was doing me no harm (and making his fortune). The second possibility forced me to let him continue: and he drove me out of sight, that I might avoid the disgust of being the vulgar creature of his invention. Then I lost what little money I ever had, & cut the two knots together by enlisting under another name. The Army is not a rose-bed, but at any rate one is obscure in it: & here I propose to stay.

These details aren't for publication: but they will inform your discretion of what to say if there is more chat. My respect for your work (and regret that its excessive goodness drives you into shifts to earn food) is the cause of my writing to you.

Yours sincerely
T E Lawrence

Lowell Thomas' story is a myth, built up on a very small foundation of official information, & padded with gossip. He came out to Egypt on a semi-official mission, & was allowed to see & hear things.

.L.

University of Texas

1 Edmund Blunden (1896-1974): poet, biographer and later, professor, both in Tokyo and Oxford. His reputation depended at this stage largely on his early volumes of poetry; his most famous work, *Undertones of War*, a distillation of his experiences as a trench-officer on the Western Front in the First World War, was to appear in 1928.
2 Lawrence actually dated this letter '17.VII.22', but the reference to his being in the Army makes clear that this is a mistake.

A. E. (JOCK) CHAMBERS
17.IX.23   [BOVINGTON CAMP]

Dear Jock
I'm no writer: can't write: wish I could see you: am home-sick for the R.A.F.
The army is more beastly than anything else which the wit of man has made.
Only of course it wasn't his wit that made it: it came suddenly from him at
midnight one moonless time, when he was taken short.

God be merciful to us sinners.

R.

Bodleian Library

R. A. M. GUY
17.IX.23

Rabbit, son
It's true I don't write: can't write: am suffering from dryness of the brain & decay
of the natural affections: but I'm in the Army as a penance to kill old Adam: so
the more I neglect duties the deeper my satisfaction at my increasing beastliness.

They have stopped chasing me. I exist only for fatigues, which I perform
with a dull thoroughness; hardly Brough at all (it rusts in a shed): write
nothing of my own: but have translated two French novels lately, for gold.[1]

Gold means paper. The second one, just finished, was done on your
account, for I had the ambition to send you a trifle for your birthday. My
pleasure in the R.A.F. was partly, largely, due to the pleasure I got from your
blue & yellow self: and I owe you a deep debt for many happy times.

Now you tell me Birmingham is not going well, so I'm sending it enclosed
in this, hoping that you won't take offence. I made it in less than a month, so
that it is no great gift which I offer you.

---

[1] The translation he was completing at this time was that of the novel *Le Gigantesque* by Adrien le
Corbeau, pseudonym of the Romanian-born writer Rudolf Bernhardt, which was published by
Cape the following year as *The Forest Giant*. He refers to two novels, however, presumably because
he had agreed in the first instance to translate Mardrus's *Arabian Nights*, but another publisher had
announced a forthcoming translation, with the result that the project had been abandoned.

I wish we could meet again: though every R.A.F. uniform I see makes me heart-sick.

R. *Harvard University*

ROBIN BUXTON[1]
22.IX.23

Dear Robin,

Glad you are reading the thing. Please don't inhibit yourself from scribbling comments of an insulting sort in the margins, made especially wide for the purpose. Your praise makes my stomach warm: but your criticisms are really helpful: whether in the field of morality; *belles-lettres*, tactics, or just manners. Down with them while you can!

The 'Seven Pillars of Wisdom' is a quotation from Proverbs[2]: it is used as title out of sentiment: for I wrote a youthful indiscretion-book, so called, in 1913 and burned it (as immature) in '14 when I enlisted. It recounted adventures in seven type-cities of the East (Cairo, Bagdad, Damascus etc) & arranged their characters into a descending cadence: a moral symphony. It was a queer book, upon whose difficulties I look back with a not ungrateful wryness: and in memory of it I named the new book, which will probably be the only one I ever write, & which sums up & exhausts me to the date of 1919.

S.A. was a person, now dead, regard for whom lay beneath my regard for the Arabic peoples. I don't propose to go into further detail thereupon.[3]

[...] Have you read my account of the I.C.C. march? Please say honestly what parts of it, or of its tone, hurt your feelings. I was wrapped up in my burden in Arabia, & saw things only through its distorting prism: & so did third parties wrong. It wasn't meant: just the inevitable distraction of a commander whose spirit was at civil war within himself.

DG

1 Major Robin Buxton had commanded the two companies of the Imperial Camel Corps (the I.C.C. of the final paragraph) which had carried out a special mission in the desert in association with Lawrence in August 1918. He was now a banker with Martins Bank and Lawrence's financial adviser.
2 Proverbs 9, I: 'Wisdom hath builded her house, she hath hewn out her seven pillars.'
3 *See* the dedicatory poem 'To S. A.' at the beginning of *Seven Pillars*.

LORD WINTERTON[1]

27.X.23   *[BOVINGTON CAMP]*

Dear Winterton

Sorry to have appeared to make mysteries: I didn't mean it: it's only that I'm not again returning to decent life, & feel a little less than proud of myself & my state. My constant address (as Lawrence – did you know that wasn't my real name?) is at 14 Barton St. Westminster, the house of Herbert Baker, one of the Delhi architects, & a supremely decent person. I used to live there, & his Staff still send my stuff on.

If you want to write to me directly you will have to call me

    7875698 Pte. T. E. Shaw
       B. Company
          1st Depot Battn.
             Tank Corps
                Bovington Camp
                   Wool
                      Dorset

and that's so complicated an address that few people use it. After the R.A.F. slung me out I didn't much care what happened: (the Air I was very keen on, & was enjoying more than anything I've ever done): so finally when broken in cash I enlisted, & have been quietly in Dorset since. Can't & don't pretend to like it, but it's better than the Colonial Office anyhow: for if I'm not making the world better (an immodest ambition of you politicals!) at least I'm not making it worse, as I used to do.

There is a sporting chance of my getting on a draft to India, armoured cars, which would deliver me from mud. I prefer sand & sun, even with scorpion-sauce.

You are lucky to get flying again. The very sight of a plane or of an airman makes me sort of homesick. If Hoare dies horribly some day you will know it's my bad wishes dogging him.[2]

This letter doesn't sound cheerful. Actually things aren't bad (when it's not raining, as now) for I've got an extravagant motor-bike, as fast as a hurricane,

---

1 Edward, 6th Earl Winterton (1883-1962), at this time under-secretary of state for India, had served with Lawrence in the last phase of the Arab war.

2 Sir Samuel Hoare, later Lord Templewood (1880-1959), was at this time secretary of state for air. He was to prove the principal obstacle to Lawrence's readmission to the R.A.F.

& hurl over S. W. England on it, pleasing myself at every sharp bend & bad place ... and to be anonymous & out-of-sight & very speedy isn't a bad estate.

Curtis is trying to get printed that fantastic book of mine: a privately subscribed edition, at a huge price. Don't buy one, unless you are suddenly enriched-I'll lend you mine, if it comes off. Your portrait by Roberts will be a decoration of it. He is having a show next month I believe, in Chelsea somewhere.

Yours ever
TE?

Bodleian Library

SIR HUGH TRENCHARD
2.XI.23   *BOVINGTON*

Dear Sir Hugh
I'd like to,[1] very much: but there are two difficulties already in my view: –
  (a) It is armistice day, and I do not know if leave will be given.
  (b) I have a decent suit, but no dress clothes at all.
The leave I will ask for, but till Thursday next (Nov. 8) there will be no answer to the application. The clothes are beyond my power to provide: and I fear that Lady Trenchard might not approve a lounge suit at dinner. It depends on the other company probably. Please ask her before you reply. [...]

The Army and Navy Club at six or six-thirty would suit me excellently and I hope it may come off. Undiluted Tank Corps is a disease. It is very good of you to ask me.

Yours sincerely
T.E.?[2]

R.A.F. Museum Hendon/HMH

1 *I.e.* go to dinner with Trenchard at his club.
2 Lawrence was told that it would be in order to wear his private's uniform so the invitation was accepted.

LORD WINTERTON
5.XI.23

[BOVINGTON CAMP]

Dear Winterton

Thanks for wanting the book. There are some irreverencies in it concerning yourself. I don't know of course if the reprint idea will actually take shape.

As for coming to the I.O.[1] – you know I'm in khaki, & can't show up in that. The 'bike is often being laid up, since it is a costly item: and the railway return fare is rather steep. However next time I reach London I'll ring you up – if it's a week-day – and talk. The mischief is that they only let us off on Sat, afternoon, till Sunday night ... and you don't (God be thanked!) go to office in those hours.

Yes, I remain as cheerful as possible, & am very well: but it isn't a good life. However perhaps Hoare will be thrown out next election. Get the Air for yourself if so. Good job, as big as its holder, & the only one with growth unlimited.

Yours ever
TE?

Bodleian Library

MRS HELLÉ FLECKER[1]
5.XI.23

Dear Mrs. Flecker

Well at last I saw *Hassan*, standing one week-end night behind the dress-circle, where one could both see and hear. I liked the seeing best ... but it is extraordinarily hard to write to you about the play. When that brute intoned

I I.O.: India Office.

I Mrs Hellé Flecker was the Greek-born widow of James Elroy Flecker. Lawrence had been to the first production in English of Flecker's play *Hassan* at the Haymarket Theatre, London. (It had been performed earlier in the year in German at Darmstadt.) The play was produced by Basil Dean, the costumes and design were by George W. Harris and the incidental music was by Frederick Delius. Opening on 20 September 1923, *Hassan* was a considerable success, running for 281 performances.

the Yasmin ghazel I wanted to kill him:[2] and he butchered the prose just as horribly, and the others had no sense of style, and their voices were false – all but Ishak's[3] – and it was cruelty to all those lovely lines and yet, and yet, the play came over and held not merely me but everybody else about me – everyone in the theatre, I think. It was a conquest of mind over matter ... and made me very proud of Flecker's strength.

The settings were beautiful. The man Harris who made the designs and Dean who I suppose oversaw the whole, have done splendidly: nothing in it tawdry, except perhaps the fountain in the court. The closing chant of Samarkand was fine, and Delius throughout superfine.

There hasn't I suppose been such a play in London before: and will not be again: and it is a very proud sight to have seen. Yet it's murder, complete murder.

I hope one more thing – a most important thing – that the job will pay. They have spent enormously upon it ... and I hope will reap as they deserve, and that some of their grains will fall by your wayside. Flecker would have liked that – would have cursed mightily if it hadn't come off – and would have wanted it even more in the actual circumstances.

My joining up was quite direct and plain. I hate the semi-politics to which my Eastern efforts in the war had seemed to doom me: and to break away from them, to make myself quite independent of them and their glamour, I changed my name, and had consequently to begin rather low down. I'm not worth much money apart from Arabia: and to that I'll not return. I won't even make money by publishing my beastly book upon the war-period, because that's all of a piece with it.

Wherefore I'm an oppressed private, hating the army and quite out of place in it: but growing more into my place and company, daily.

Yours sincerely
TEL

Bodleian Library

2 The 'brute [who] intoned the Yasmin ghazel' (a 'ghazel' is a piece of oriental love poetry) was the distinguished actor Henry Ainley, playing Hassan. Yasmin was played by Cathleen Nesbitt. 'Yasmin, A ghazel' had earlier appeared in Flecker's 1913 collection *The Golden Journey to Samarkand*.
3 Ishak (minstrel to the Caliph of Bagdad) was played by Leon Quartermaine.

A. E. (JOCK) CHAMBERS
5.XI.23   [BOVINGTON CAMP]

Dear Mahomet

[...] I'm not wholly resourceless in Bovington: found a ruined cottage near camp
(a mile out) & took it for 2/6 a week.[1] Have roofed it & and am flooring it. At
present one chair & a table there. Am hoping for a book case this week, & a bed
next week but cash isn't too plentiful & needs are many. I'll let you know for week
after next it might do you to stay in. There is firewood & you are good at bed-
making. No floor-scrubbing.[2] Scruffy place. About a dozen good books already.
    Too many people talking to me can't write.

R.

Bodleian Library

HIS MOTHER
22.II.23   [BOVINGTON CAMP]

A month has passed. This is going to Paoing.[1] You told me to write to Vancouver,
which I did, no doubt too late to overtake you. Shanghai you did not mention,
& I haven't written there. If I had, it would no doubt have been too late also.
    You are fortunate to miss this November. It has been colder than any other
in my memory. No news here or elsewhere. I sent you a Doughty by post the
other day: & hope you get it. The postage was dear, & the book is rare, in that
edition. Now Cape has brought out a £3.3.0 edition, of the complete book,
on quite good paper. The identical print of course.
    I am doing a little work for Cape, to fill up my odd moments: and Buxton
(the banker) is looking for 100 subscribers of 30 guineas each, to make
possible a private reprint of my book on Arabia. Hardy praised it, & makes

1 Clouds Hill.
2 At their first meeting at R.A.F. Farnborough, Chambers as hut-orderly had immediately
    ordered Lawrence to scrub his own bed-space.

1 In west China, to which Mrs Lawrence was travelling in order to live with her eldest son Bob,
    who had joined the China Inland Mission in 1921 and was serving as a medical missionary.

me feel justified in giving it so much distribution. Of course there would be no reviews, no copies for public sale, & no profits.

I still see Hardy occasionally. John has painted (at my request) a very beautiful portrait of him. The old man is delighted, & Mrs. Hardy also. It is seldom that an artist is so fortunate in his sitter's eyes.

I've taken a little cottage (half ruinous) a mile from camp, & water-tighted it to act as a work-room for myself. There I hope in future to do my writing, which is becoming more & more a habit. No original stuff, of course: just translations. I hope not again to do anything of my own. It is not good for man to make things.

Nothing else I can think of to write.

I hope the journey is not still wearisome to you: but you must be looking forward to its end: yet, you know, these journeys don't really end, till we do.

N.

HL/Bodleian Library

Eric Kennington
13.12.23

Dear Kennington

At a meeting last Sunday Hogarth, Dawnay, Curtis, and I decided to produce 100 copies of the *Seven Pillars*, at 30 guineas a copy, if so many subscribers can be found.

I am to be solely responsible (that the law of libel, civil or criminal, may fall blunted on my penniless status as a private soldier), will pay all bills, and sign all papers and copies. Hogarth will help edit my proofs: you, edit my pictures (I hope).

Production to start as soon as £200 has been subscribed: ('starting' means sending four Arab pastels to W. & G.).[1]

1 Whittingham & Griggs, The Chiswick Press, London.

Intending subscribers are to write to me (under any name), to
    Clouds' Hill[2]
      Moreton,
        Dorset
for details and conditions. I'll reply personally to each.

If you know any unco' rich please try and pillage them.

I estimate the job might take a year at the shortest, two at the longest.

<u>As for printer.</u>

Aforesaid copyright act and law of libel will make advisable my being a nominal partner in the printing firm. To retire as soon as job is completed.

I want it done monotype, in eleven point or fourteen point, of a type approximating to O.F. Caslon, unleaded: with side-headings in side margin: no top-heading, lines not long, but print-panel taller than usual in quartos. The size of the page you know (it's the Ghalib[2] proof, anyway. I forget the dimensions).

Paper to be a *thin* decent rag brand, hand-made or machine-made of similar quality. Not perfectly bleached: — a tone of yellow or mud in it.

Book will run between 300,000 and 330,000 words: preferably the lesser number.

Matter will be sent in in sheets of the book you have, hand-corrected (scissors and paste). So it will be a very legible M.S. to set up from.

Will you ask your printer how this proposition appeals to him ... what sample experimental type-panels and margins he would set up: how long he would be before he could start the job: how many words per week he would be prepared to set up: how many sheets he would be prepared to hold in type, what he would charge per thousand words? (I can't say per folio, because we haven't yet set up a dummy page).

I would interfere with the sample pages a good deal, with the accepted format very little. Author's corrections almost nil. Matter sent in regularly.

I've printed enough to have a conscience and regard for type-matter.

Yours
T.E.

Bodleian Library

2 For Lawrence's views on the variant spellings of his cottage's name, *see* p. 295, footnote 2.
3 Ghalib: one of Kennington's Arabs', *i.e.* one of his Arab portraits done for *Seven Pillars*.

MRS THOMAS HARDY
22.XII.23   [*BOVINGTON CAMP*]

Dear Mrs. Hardy

I waited to see if I could: and I'm afraid I can't. It's a good thing because it would feel intrusive to go to lunch on Christmas day. However I would probably have fallen to it, only that I'm without transport. The ancient & splendid bicycle was borrowed (without leave) by a villain, who rode her ignorantly, & left her, ruined, in a ditch.[1] It saved me the pang of selling the poor beast: but also it shuts me unhealthily close into camp: – and so I'm trying to persuade the maker of it to supply me with another!

I'll hope to see you and Mr. Hardy soon.

Yours sincerely
T E Shaw

Bodleian Library

R. A. M. GUY
25.XII.23   *CLOUDS HILL MORETON DORSET*

Dear Poppet

Xmas, – spent alone in my new-old cottage – has been a quiet time of simple thinking. It seems to me that I've climbed down very far, from two years ago: and a little from a year ago. I was in the guard-room of Farnborough that night, & next day the newspapers blew up and destroyed my peace. So it's a bad anniversary, for me.

Yes, Trenchard writes to me sometimes, but it won't be to have me back. Baldwin, the Prime Minister, tried to persuade him, & failed. Trenchard is a very

---

1 The second of seven Brough motorcycles Lawrence owned between 1922 and 1935; an eighth was on order at the time of his death; the first was badly damaged on 31 March 1923 during a return journey from London to Bovington. George Brough, their 'maker' as Lawrence calls him here, had been manufacturing motor-cycles since 1910; Lawrence called his machines George I, George II, etc. in tribute to him. The two men did not meet until 1925, after which date they corresponded regularly. Lawrence was dubbed 'Broughy' Shaw by his fellow soldiers because of his addiction to Brough Superiors.

great man, & makes up his mind only once. In my case I think he was wrong, & I think he knows it. My fault, if I was at fault in my conduct at Farnborough, was not a big one, & I've paid for it in these ten months of misery here. However you will be tired of my dwelling so much on the same subject: the excuse is that my mind dwells on it every day, & many nights, for the R.A.F. is my best memory.

I'm glad you got your fortnight at home. You are become almost a sailor now, & such feel lost when their service ends, or when their leave-money is all spent. Try to be civil as well as naval and aerial. It's easier to be three things than two, because the intensity of each is less.

I'm seeing Bernard Shaw tomorrow, which will be a treat for me. You saw Russell[1] – well, he's the best fellow I can find in camp, and he's decent in suffering my fancies patiently: but I long for something a little hotter & stronger at times, something which goes further along my road & extends my mind a little. Brain-men like Hardy & Shaw do me that service, and therefore I love meeting them.

When I said 'This is the last' I meant that again for an overwhelming time we were going to be apart. Letters don't work, nor do casual meetings, for the shadow of the near end lies over them, so that the gaiety is forced & the talk foolish. You & me, we're very unmatched, & it took some process as slow & kindly as the barrack-room communion to weld us comfortably together. People aren't friends till they have said all they can say, and are able to sit together, at work or rest, hour-long without speaking.

We never got quite to that, but were nearer it daily ... and since S.A. died I haven't experienced any risk of that's happening.

That added an extra regret when Trenchard so firmly cut my vital cord.

Back on the old subject you see.

I hope you will enjoy the cruise & be contented some day with your job. Believe me, you're lucky.

Yours
R.

Harvard University

---

1 Private Arthur Russell, a young man from Coventry, was one of Lawrence's roommates at Bovington and a frequent visitor to Clouds Hill. *See* next letter, to Russell's mother.

MRS RUSSELL
25.XII.23   CAMP[1]

Dear Mrs. Russell

Does it feel queer to be Arthur's mother? Sometimes, I expect. He is rather an uncommon person.

I don't know, of course, what stories he has told you about me. The truth is that he gives up a good deal of his spare time to showing me about: and in return for his kindness I try to be as little tiresome to him as I can. The debt is all mine, to him.

Many thanks for your Xmas present. It was the only one I had, as it happened, and the cigarettes were very successful. They made me break my rule, or rather my habit, of not smoking. Years ago in France we used to get nothing but those 'Caporal' cigarettes, & so they brought back memories with them.

We have been, (Arthur & I) all day up here in a little cottage I have near camp, doing nothing but sitting still & talking. The Christmas in the other place was a bit too merry for our tastes. A sober man feels such a fool when all the world around him is tipsy.

It's started raining now, which is hard luck on the others… and on me, for I've got to walk home a mile through it. Arthur's going to sleep here by himself, on the floor or the sofa; he says it'll be all right: anyway it is better than the guardroom where he has to doze away a night a week. He'll keep the fire going, & old Bill, my tenant, will snore away in the kitchen downstairs.

As for coming to Coventry – yes we mean to do that one week-end next year, when the evenings get longer and the roads drier. We'll come up by Brough, & that means you will hear us long before you see us. As he says I like a bike with a good healthy exhaust.

Again with many thanks

Believe me

Yours very sincerely

'Brough'

It's as good a name as any. I haven't a proper one. We call him 'Bullet' (his head) 'Cov' (his native town) 'Imp' (his manner) 'Infant' (his appearance). I once heard him called Russell, too.   *University of Texas*

---

1 *I.e.* Bovington. Though Lawrence gave 'Camp' as his address the letter was obviously written from Clouds Hill.

MRS THOMAS HARDY
31.1.24 *[CLOUDS HILL]*

Dear Mrs. Hardy

I'm very sorry, but I cannot manage to get over by train: my fault I expect, though the army standard of conduct does ask too much of us.

. If I had a bicycle I'd have managed it: and I'm getting one soon. The maker of the old marvel is sending me (on loan) one of his latest. So in a fortnight or so I'll again be blessed with the freedom of Dorset (not to mention Hants, Devon, Somerset, Wiltshire, and others). A pity that a fortnight is so long as fifteen days.

Till then it's Clouds Hill for me on my spare afternoons. If you or the Asquiths ('and' the Asquiths, rather, though I don't know them)[1] are at a loss for an excursion, and the day is lovely, then do take them over the great Heath, & call at the cottage going or coming. Some of the fellows are making it their habit to drop in: but mostly they are quiet men, & if they irked you I could drive them out, temporarily. You see the cottage is unlike camp, & it gives them a sense of healthy change to visit me, and I like them to like coming.

Yours sincerely
T E Shaw   *Bodleian Library*

---

1 Presumably Herbert Asquith (son of H. H. Asquith, prime minister 1908-16) and his wife Lady Cynthia Asquith, friends of the Hardys. Lady Cynthia was also secretary to author J. M. Barrie.

E. M. FORSTER[1]
20.2.24

I've been transferred from B. Company: so a man brought your letter over to me two nights ago just after I had gone to bed with a bout of malaria: and a miracle happened: the fever left me and I sat up in bed and read it all! This book is my only one, & I have a longing (which I seldom admit) to hear what men say of it.

In your case it is wonderful. Writers & painters aren't like other men. The meeting them intoxicates me with a strangeness which shows me how very far from being one of them I am. Of your work I only know *Howards End* & *Siren & Pharos*:[2] but that's enough to put you among the elect ... and yet you bother to write to me whole pages about my effort. No one else has done that for me;[3] and I'm abnormally grateful. Grateful even to the point of wishing for more – not written of course, but to ask you of some of the difficulties I've met. However you will be spared this probably. The army does not let me off at practical times.

Your division of books into the active and the passive pleased me. The fluid ones are those written by writers: and the static ones are those (the many more) written by imitators like me. The second have no justification of being, except the scarcity of the real thing ... and the need of books which shall be tools, ancillary. Works of art have their own life, and so aren't best fitted to be railway timetables, or dictionaries, or histories.

My thing was forced from me not as a poem, but as a complete narrative of what actually happened in the Arab Revolt. I didn't think of it till all was over, and it was compiled out of memory (squeezing the poor organ with

1 Lawrence's friendship with the well-known novelist E. M. Forster (1879-1970) was of great importance to him; he saw him as an established writer with that hallmark of creativity which he feared he did not have himself. They met briefly in 1921 at a lunch for Feisal at a Mayfair hotel, from which Forster took away the impression of a 'small fair-haired boy' who 'rapped out encouraging words about the Middle East'. They had now been brought together through their mutual friendship with Siegfried Sassoon, who had lent Forster a copy of *Seven Pillars*. If Lawrence valued Forster's comments on his book, Forster for his part found *Seven Pillars* a valuable aid to the task he was then engaged in: attempting to finish his most famous and successful novel, *A Passage to India*. See P. N. Furbank, *E. M. Forster: A Life*, vol. II, p. 120: 'The book [*Seven Pillars*] affected him not only as a man but as a writer. He wrote the two final chapters of *A Passage to India* under its influence, completing them, and the novel, in a burst of confident energy.' Forster then wrote to Lawrence the detailed letter of criticism to which this letter was his reply. The full text is in *DG*.
2 *The Story of the Siren* and *Pharos and Pharillon*. *Howards End* (1910) had been very influential in establishing Forster's reputation.
3 In a footnote on this letter, David Garnett remarked, 'Edward Garnett alone had been writing about *Seven Pillars of Wisdom* for months', but his loyalty to his father seems to have blinded him to the difference between general praise (Edward Garnett's) and detailed criticism (Forster).

both hands, to force from it even the little lively detail that there is). If I invent one thing I'll spoil its *raison d'être*: and if there are invented conversations, or conversations reconstructed after five years, where will it be?

Also, you know, I feel profoundly dejected over it all. It reads to me inferior to nearly every book which I have found patience to read ... and that is many. If it is the best I can do with a pen, then it's better for me to hump a rifle or spade about; and I fear it's the best I can write. It went through four versions in the four years I struggled with it, and I gave it all my nights and days till I was nearly blind and mad. The failure of it was mainly what broke my nerve, and sent me into the R.A.F. ... where I found six months of full contentment. The Army is a sad substitute. However I'm off the point.

War and Peace is almost the largest book in the world. I've carried it whenever I had the transport, and ever wished it longer. But then Tolstoi was an enormous genius. While I was trying to write I analysed most of you, and found out, so far as it was within my fineness to see, what were your tricks of effect, the little reserves & omissions which gave you power to convey more than the print says. But it is hopeless to grapple with Tolstoi. The man is like yesterday's east wind, which brought tears when you faced it and numbed you meanwhile.

Your goodness in writing to me with such care shows that you think (or makes me think that you think) there's some hope in my writing. Yet the revise I'm going to give the *Seven Pillars* in the next ten months can be one of detail only: for the adventure is dead in me: and I think it is the only thing I'll ever try to write. The Army is a great assoiler ... and my two years of it has nearly cured me of the desire to work gratuitously. This means 'without self-satisfaction or money': the first I only get out of hot speed on a motor-bike. The second I never get. My own writing has brought me in eleven pounds since 1914. A scruple (absurd in view of the obliquity of the whole movement) prevented my taking pay while I was East: and prevents my taking profits on any part of the record of the adventure. I can make a little translating foreign novels: but it's not much, and painful work. The army is assured bread & butter ... and that feels better than a gamble outside. Also I feel disinclined to struggle again for a living. If I can't keep alive without much pain then I won't bother to do so at all.

I wonder why I'm writing all this to you. I think perhaps because you are a stranger, and have been interested in my addled egg. It was an extraordinary experience for me, the reading of your letter.

DG

SIR HUGH TRENCHARD
1.3.24

Dear Sir Hugh

Forgive me this letter. I'm ashamed of it already, since I know that you sacked me for good, and it's perverse of me not to take it so. Yet the hope of getting back into the R.A.F. is the main reason of my staying in the Army. I feel eligible, there, for transfer or re-enlistment. You once took over some Tank Corps fellows: and lately the change of Ministry heartened me: and I've served exactly a year in the Army now, & been found amenable to discipline. Don't say that the Army can more easily digest an oddity than can the R.A.F. It isn't true. The Air has twice the vitality with good reason.

Whenever I get one of your letters I open it excitedly to see if your mind has changed. It seems to me so plain that the presence in the ranks of a man as keen on the Air as myself must be generally beneficial. Yesterday however you told me plainly, for the first time, that it was my gaiety which got me into trouble at Farnborough. I didn't know of it, & doubt it yet. Guilfoyle's neurasthenia made him imagine things.[1] He didn't amuse me – rather he made me sick and sorry. I don't like saying so (since part of the game is to take what happens in C.O.s) but I fancy he injured me out of deliberate fear. It wouldn't happen again, for not one in a hundred of your Squadron-Leaders is a nerve-wreck.

However on the whole I was happy at Farnborough, and so perhaps I did, unawares, walk about smiling. Surely not a great fault, & one easily put right. The superiors have lots of power over the ranks, in every service, including yours, and Guilfoyle could have made me cry (if he'd wished) by some sentence less than indefinite years in the Army. I don't mind the present discomfort (as long as I can hope to reach the R.A.F. at the end): but the filth is a pity, for no fellow can live so long in it & keep quite clean. I feel I'm not worth so much to your people as I was a year ago ... but as I said before, I'm still worth having. It was a stimulant to the other A.C.s to have a man, relatively as experienced as me, content among them: and I liked them, which shows that it was all right. I still hear from many of them.

It's all difficult to write. If you'd been a stranger I could have persuaded you: but my liking for your Force and its maker make it impossible for me to

---

1 Guilfoyle: Lawrence's C.O. at Farnborough, whom he blamed for giving him away to the press.

plead properly. Do think of the many hiding-holes there are (India, Egypt and Mespot and seaplane-ships) before you tear this up![2]

Yours sincerely
TEL

R.A.F. Museum Hendon/HMH

MRS CHARLOTTE SHAW
16.3.24   *CLOUDS HILL MORETON DORSET*

Dear Mrs. Shaw

I've read *Joan, St. Joan* ... and want to say straight out that it is one of his best writings.[1] Don't take me as a play-judge. I know nothing of the stage, and don't care very much for it: a play to me is only a particular art-form like a sonnet: but as writing *Joan* is magnificent.

Some sea-change has come over G.B.S. in the last ten years. Perhaps it isn't new that he should be on the side of the angels – even when they are undisguised angels – but surely it's new that every one of his characters should be honest and kindly and even-minded? I like it, and find it essentially true, the more I see of men (almost I'm able to think gently of some sergeants ... they mean less than appears ... their official style has to be subtracted before you measure the manner and matter of their delivery): but people don't usually feel fair towards humanity till they are old and successful and ready to retire ... and G.B.S. isn't the third, and probably will never be the first ... just as I'll never be the second.

Seriously, it's done his art and heart good to get the doctrine of *Methuselah* off his breathing-works:[2] and the poet in him is now going to have a little dance. Did you note the balance of prose in the fighting parts of *Joan?* Take

2 Air Vice-Marshal Philip Game, successor to Swann as the Air Council member for personnel, minuted favourably on Lawrence's plea to Trenchard, who took it up with Air Minister Sir Samuel Hoare, but Hoare rejected it out of hand.

1 *Saint Joan* was first produced just ten days later on 26 March 1924 at the New Theatre, London, with Sybil Thorndike in the title-role.

2 *Back to Methuselah* was Shaw's previous play. A gigantic work taking three nights to perform, it was Shaw's favourite play – an opinion not widely shared.

care: he may yet write an epic of blood-lust. All things are possible with a delivered evangelical.

Wonderful lines in *Joan* were on p. 26, where the Archb[ishop] rebukes the lap-dogs. Oh, I'd like to hear de Rais stamp out his desperate sane-face from that!

I shrink from Joan's very little dialect. It seems to me a literary manner, like italics: unworthy of an artist with Mr. Shaw's cut and sweep of spoken word. He gives Joan a loud simplicity without it … and I'm a detester and despiser of bumpkins. The best men in the ranks aren't the bumpkin-spoken. A fellow worth listening to isn't the tyro, but the man who is trying once more, on top of ten thousand failures, to phrase precisely what his mind feels.

I found pp. 66-95 intolerable. The shadow of the tragedy at the end lay over the first pages, and made the so accurate historical 'placing' of the men a horror. Over these pages I galloped, to reach the crisis. Joan came in, and held her own, indeed increased her nobility. It was good to make her sign that confession … and then she died, 'off'. I have a prejudice against the writer who leaves the reader to make his top-scene for him. *Hounds of Banba*[3] does it, in the story of the burning of the village … but faces the struggle in the story of the man's funeral. I funked it, in the death of Farraj, my man:[4] faced it, in the plain narrative of my mishaps in Deraa the night I was captured.[5] Here in *St. Joan* the climax will be red light shining from the fire into the courtyard. Authors feel they aren't up to writing about so tremendous a thing, and so they put a row of dots, or swallow silently, and leave the poor reader to stuff up their gap with his cherished and grudged emotion. It's indirect art and direct shirking.

Of course if he'd dipped his pen in all his strength and written straight forward the play could never have been presented: but the more honour so. It would have cleaned us all to have seen Joan die.

The fifth act is pure genius. I wouldn't have a thought of it otherwise than written: I'm most thankful to you for letting me read it.

E. S.

[…] My bike will probably let me see one of its nights, if it goes properly. S. Thorndyke [*sic*] doesn't look like St. Joan, you know!

3 A novel by the Irish writer Daniel Corkery, published in 1920.
4 *See Seven Pillars*, Chapter XCIII.
5 *See also* Lawrence to Mrs Shaw, 26 March 1924 (p. 275, opposite).

It was my fault that I didn't see you during *Methuselah*: but I was innocent of the ringing up. The grime and oiliness of those dark 150-mile dashes sandwiched in between laborious days were thick on me when I twice called: and the guardians of your entanglement couldn't pierce through them to see the harmless softness of my face: nor was my brogue strong enough. They were firm that neither you nor he ever saw anyone without appointment.

When G.B.S. scoffs at my fear of publicity he should go down the first half-flight of stairs and look at that gate and imagine himself without it ... imagine himself day-tenant of one-twentieth of a barrack-floor, and owner of the handkerchief and money in the pocket of his government suit!

T.E.S.   *British Library*

MRS CHARLOTTE SHAW
26.3.24   *CLOUDS HILL*

O dear. I've gone and done it. Very very sorry. This 'to-be-envied' camplife makes me rebound too high at times. Explanations.

(i) Barrie. You justify him as a man. My attack is upon the artist. He writes with an eye upon the box-office, with an ear to please the very many. He succeeds: but must pay the price of annoying the few. It infuriates me when a line writer (or painter) deliberately does the not-quite best. I don't mind dead silence. I can't stand Peter Panning or Arnold Bennetting.

(ii) Belloc. Great gifts: *Path to Rome* a delightful saucy book. His historical work impudence. Half-truths or calculated lies, served out to the public brilliantly. It's like putting a fine sauce over diseased ill-cooked meat. Done for money. Caddish, I call that.

(iii) Lowell Thomas. Not to be condemned like B & B & B.[1] He's a born vulgarian, who does the best that is in him. If his victim was other than myself I'd praise him. But it rankles in my mind to be called proud names for qualities which I'd hate to possess... or for acts of which I'm heartily ashamed. Would you like to be known only by your inferior work?

(iv) Hogarth. A very kind, very wise, very lovable man, now in failing health. I'd put him high among the really estimable human beings. All my opportunities all those I've wasted, came directly or indirectly, out of his trust in me.

1 *I.e.* Barrie, Bennett and Belloc.

(v) Style. I make it a tin god, because I'm in need of the help of that god. People like Belloc and G.B.S. despise him, since they are endowed with the very utmost of his gifts.

(vi) Contempt. Of course we don't really. A man gets carried away and says brave things... but if you take him away into a quiet place and lend him your pocket mirror he will recant. Yet, if it were possible to man, it would be a lawful emotion. We can indulge it only of ourselves. Its counterfeiting holds much of envy. I'm sorry to have overstepped.

(vii) The trial scene in *Joan*. Poor Joan, I was thinking of her as a person, not as a moral lesson. The pain meant more to her than the example. You instance my night in Deraa. Well, I'm always afraid of being hurt: and to me, while I live, the force of that night will lie in the agony which broke me, and made me surrender. It's the individual view. You can't share it.

About that night. I shouldn't tell you, because decent men don't talk about such things. I wanted to put it plain in the book, and wrestled for days with my self-respect... which wouldn't, hasn't, let me. For fear of being hurt, or rather to earn five minutes respite from a pain which drove me mad, I gave away the only possession we are born into the world with — our bodily integrity. It's an unforgivable matter, an irrecoverable position: and it's that which has made me forswear decent living, and the exercise of my not-contemptible wits and talents.

You may call this morbid: but think of the offence, and the intensity of my brooding over it for these years. It will hang about me while I live and afterwards if our personality survives. Consider wandering among the decent ghosts hereafter, crying 'Unclean unclean!'[2]

The sting of the burning was very big in *Joan*: and G.B.S. would have made his play impossible by portraying it. Yet if the play was to be not a morality but life itself, he would have given the physical its place above the moral.

In *Methuselah* his human-kind ended in the supremacy of mind. The army has taught me that our race is running towards a supremacy of body. The criteria of camp, in sensation, in mind, in spirit, in conduct, are sensual, are sexual simply: and since I'm shut out from that I live among them as an oddity.

You speak of submissive admirers ... but that hurts them and me. I'll write you pictures of the two most concerned some day, and will try to show you

---

2 A. W. Lawrence has suggested to me that his brother very probably had in mind Leviticus 13:45 'And the leper in whom the plague is, his clothes shall be rent, and his head bare, and he shall put a covering upon his upper lip, and shall cry Unclean, unclean.'

how far from an object of admiration I must be to them. And the contrary? Do I admire them? There's not a clean human being into whose shape I would not willingly creep. They may not have been Colonel Lawrence ... but I know the reverse of that medal, and hate its false face so utterly that I struggle like a trapped rabbit to be it no longer.

What a mixed metaphor. Excess of emotion always ends in carelessness of style.

If you hadn't sent me the Brieux plays I couldn't have sent you this letter.[3] Probably I shouldn't have, anyhow. But it will a little explain my half-heartedness before my blessings. I dodge G.B.S. reading part of *Joan* to me, partly because he's great and I'm worthless: partly because it's my part to shun pleasures ... through lack of desert. There's expiation to be made: and the weak spirit is only too ready to lunch with you, or to enjoy a book, or to hide a quiet while in a cloud-defended cottage: any alleviation of the necessary penalty of living on.

T.E.S.

You will perceive that my mixture of flu and malaria is over: all but the weariness after. Tonight you triumph. Congrats.

British Library

E. M. FORSTER
6.4.24   *CLOUDS HILL*

Your coming here was a very great pleasure to myself: and a very great profit, I hope, to that difficult book I'm engaged in. You, being by nature a writer, won't realise how lost I feel in attempting to see whole, & improve what was more an experience than a creation of my seeking. The compulsion of circumstance upon me to write it removed it from the normal category of welten things.

Any other time you feel moved to come & see, not me but us, (for Palmer

3 Mrs Shaw had been much impressed by the contemporary French playwright Eugène Brieux and had translated two of his plays. It was doubtless their explicit sexual subject matter which prompted Lawrence's comment.

& Russell[1] gained from you as much or more than I did) please send word & come. You will be extremely welcome. Any stranger is, almost: but men who write or draw come nearer to my taste than others.

The prospect of reading your book in two months or so is a pleasant one. Time goes quickly here. I hope it will satisfy your standard when you see it in form.

I'd like, very much indeed, to see the unpublishable stuff. any of it you feel able to show me. It shall be safely kept, & returned quickly.

'Unpublishable' is a relative, even a passing qualification. The *Seven Pillars* earned it two or three years ago: and have lost it in that little time. [...]

Bodleian Library

E. M. FORSTER
9.v.24

Wonderful you should wish my book back again. Certainly it shall be sent when Doughty is finished with it. I'm glad you are reading the old man. To me, and to nearly all people who have had even a slight taste of the desert, that book brings a clear impression of it. It seems to me impossible but that you should enjoy it.

Your return to Clouds' Hill (which now has a bed in it, for hardy campers who like a solitary sleeping place) will be red-letter. Such interruptions to our ordinary smooth living are a joy. In camp there is so little daily change that we are like figures sitting deep in still water: so still, by reason of the clatter of senseless living about us, that often I fancy I hear time dragging slowly past me, like an endless snake. Do you remember how Sigurd lay in a pit in the way, while Fafnir crawled slowly down to water?[1] Something like that, is the feeling.

I Palmer and Russell were fellow privates of the Tank Corps who became Lawrence's special friends (*see* letters to R. A. M. Guy and Mrs Russell, Christmas Day 1923). Palmer – usually known as 'Posh' – worked with him in the quartermaster's stores. Russell was eventually to be one of Lawrence's pall-bearers.

I Any reference to Sigurd by Lawrence is likely to be the product of his enthusiasm for William Morris, whose *Story of Sigurd the Volsung* was for him a book of seminal importance.

I don't seem to have put my remarks on your story[2] very well. That's good, because my mind has never cleared upon it. I agree with S.S.[3] as to its excellence: my memory is still concerned, not with its parts, but with its general impression: for anything to last with me three weeks is unusual and this preoccupation is a daily one, almost. You have conveyed something, very powerfully: but it feels like a something quite foreign·from the impression of the details, which I criticised. As though your two and two, put together, had made not four, but a prime number of some sort.

Technically, as writing, as a story, I don't think it quite so good as very much else of your writing: but what comes through is very strong. To try another metaphor ... as if it were a fine stone, finer than most, but your cutting of it were not quite finished ... or quite exact, anyway.

Why make it over-ripe? or cynical? That seems to me grievous; the thing is so healthy as it stands, in its meaning, that it seems a pity to taint any detail of it.

The writing which disgusts me is stuff aimed deliberately below the belt: Barrie: Belloc: much of Chesterton: they could write so well, & are too cheap in grain to wish to try. Your efforts are always so patent, that no one could ever be troubled by them. It isn't a subject which can give offence, but its treatment. Imagine the bawdiness if Kipling or Elinor Glyn or Aldous Huxley had tried to write *The Life to Come*!

Don't take my criticisms seriously. I have dabbled in writing, but have no vocation, & therefore no technical standard on which to base a judgement. Only I thought you might be interested to know that my absorption in the stream of your main idea was broken into sometimes by a detail, whose foreignness I took to be unessential to the story: but which quite probably you inserted deliberately. It's these conscious variations, flaws, in the rhythm of ideas which mark the artist like the irregularities in Shakespeare's blank verse, I suppose.

Yournn
T.E.S.

Bodleian Library

---

2 The story in question was *The Life to Come*, one of Forster's 'unpublishable' stories (because of its homosexual content) which did not appear in print until after Forster death. *See also* Lawrence's comments on *Dr Woolacott* in his letter to Forster dated 21 December 1927 (p. 382).
3 Siegfried Sassoon.

HARLEY GRANVILLE-BARKER[1]
9.V.24   [CLOUDS HILL]

Many thanks for the page. I've decided to make it 14-point, after all, since that reads easier, to my eye, & to the eyes of four out of five of the men in Hut G.25. Quaint, isn't it, to submit such an affair to such judgement? But it's seldom one can get such an approach to 'the man in the street'.

Netherton leaves me always with a feeling that camp is a horrible place, & that's a silly feeling, because I've chosen to make my living here, & to fuss about its inessentials is very near self-pity. The perfection of your surface strikes sharper, I expect, on a visitor than it does to the lord & mistress of the place: for one thing, we don't have to deal with a fire or two per week.

Do tell me what your insurance people say. Their faces must be worth a good deal of smiling.

My genuine, birth-day, initials are T.E.C. The C. became L. when I was quite young: & as L. I went to Oxford & through the war. After the war it became a legend: & to dodge its load of legendary inaccuracy I changed it to R. In due course R. became too hot to hold. So now I'm Shaw: but to me there seems no virtue in one name more than another. Any one can be used by anyone, & I'll

---

1 Harley Granville-Barker (1877-1946) (the hyphen was added halfway through his career) won distinction as an actor, a theatre director, a playwright and, from 1923 onwards, as the author of the much admired *Prefaces to Shakespeare*. He and Lawrence had met at the Hardys' Dorchester home, Max Gate. Granville-Barker and his second wife, were living some thirty miles to the west of Dorchester at Netherton Hall in Devon, and were thus, thanks to Lawrence's Broughs, virtual neighbours. Until his divorce, Granville-Barker had been very close to the Shaws (he had done much to establish G. B. S.'s reputation) and it has been suggested that Lawrence took over the vacancy left by Granville-Barker's fall from favour (for more on this subject, *see* particularly *Private Show and Public Shaw* by Stanley Weintraub, Cape, 1963). He and Lawrence never became intimate friends, but there was, writes his American biographer Eric Salmon, 'an immediate and spontaneous attraction between them which comes out very clearly in [their] letters' (*Granville Barker and His Correspondents*, Wayne State University Press, Detroit, 1987). Salmon's book prints their entire surviving correspondence, consisting of eight letters by Lawrence and two by Granville-Barker. Earlier the latter had published Lawrence's letters to him in 1939 in a privately printed edition, limited to fifty copies, entitled *Eight Letters from T. E. L.* One letter was printed in *DG*. I have included two in the present collection. The one printed here is valuable mainly for Lawrence's discussions of his variant initials; he was, however, wrong in stating that his birthday initials were T.E.C; his birth certificate gives both his and his parents' name as Lawrence. Lawrence and Granville-Barker had evidently been discussing the typeface to be used in the subscribers' edition of *Seven Pillars*. The decision recorded here held; the book was printed in Caslon Old Face, with the main text of the book set in 14 point.

answer to it: while the postman delivers to my cottage anything with Clouds Hill on the envelope. He did say, once, quite early on, that my name seemed to be Legion, but that it wasn't his affair. As he's a Salvationist, the New Testament comes naturally to his lips.[2]

Consequently you may tell anyone anything you like about me & my book ... but please don't put yourself about. I don't want you to start working on my behalf ... but thought that perhaps you might some day meet a quaint rich person, one who would welcome a new curio for his gallery ... and one who would be grateful to you for the chance of picking up my confessions.

I see that in discussing Netherton, above, I forgot to add that therefore I wouldn't come down again for a while: not till I've ceased to be envious of your state. Many thanks, none the less, for your suggestion of an early return.

Yours sincerely
TES

Bodleian Library

D. G. HOGARTH
9.v.24

Yes, that was it. I took thought for a night, & then declined. The job[1] is a hazardous one (T. wants a 'literary' history, the C.I.D.[2] a 'technical) attractive, very, to me by reason of its subject. The terms (three years) compare unfavourably with the six which the Army offers: and the responsibility is one which I'd regret as soon as I had shouldered it. Also it's no use, having gone through the grind of climbing down to crowd-level, at once to give it up for three years decent living. It would leave me older, less strung up to make another effort at poor living. If I can complete my seven years in the Army I

---

1 *See* Mark 5:9, Jesus to the Gadarene demoniac: 'And he asked him, What is thy name? And he answered, saying, My name is Legion: for we are many.' Lawrence used the word 'Legion' to describe himself when writing to Liddell Hart in 1933 (*LHB*, p.79).

1 Lawrence had been asked to write the official history of the Royal Flying Corps and Royal Air Force in the Great War.
2 Trenchard and the Committee of Imperial Defence.

should be able to slip quietly into a job of some sort at the end. There is a garage near here which might take me on.

I hope you are fit again: much of the illness which you have had lately I put down to the plague of that ungrateful book. You must feel like a reprieved prisoner.

Here at Bovington I seem to sit still: so still that often I fancy the slow passing of time about me can be heard. Isn't it rare for a person, who has been as unsparing as myself, to be purged quite suddenly of all desire? Even the longing or regret for the R.A.F. sleeps now, except when I come suddenly at a turn in the road, on its uniform. That was another bar to the job: because I'd have had to visit aerodromes, & each time the home-sickness would have made itself felt afresh.

Writing to people I have known is becoming difficult for me. Wherefore ...

T.E.S.

DG

MRS CHARLOTTE SHAW
10.VI.24   *CLOUDS HILL*

I'm letter after letter behind, but have been nursing a broken rib, and awaiting a moment when I felt inclined. Bank Holiday was a camp orgy, and after it there is a little silence. I fear it will rain again this afternoon why do I always feel the weather so keenly in Clouds' Hill? ... The cottage is nearly closed in with mountains of rhododendron bloom, of the screaming blue-pink which I used to dislike: now that they are my plants I love them. Isn't it greedy to give such undue favour to one's own?

The important thing to answer is about *Cock Robin*[1] ... and I've been puzzling over it. You expected it to be difficult for me. That radiance thrown over the fact of birth... it's at odds with my own mind and desire.

It seems to me so sorry and squalid an accident – the beginning of a hazardous career fittingly closed by death: and of the two accidents death

---

1 Mrs Shaw had sent Lawrence an article entitled *Who Killed Cock Robin?*, published in two parts in a quarterly review called *The Quest* (January and April 1924); the author was John Hancock, a poet and artist who had died in 1918, aged 22. In the July 1924 edition of the same review Hancock was described as a 'prophet-artist' and compared to William Blake.

seems the greater, because it has causes and birth only has effects. I can't believe in that edifice he builds up, of pre-natal effort and consciousness on the part of the child-to-be. Nor that it could be so petty as to wish that its parents be deliberate in conceiving it. Why if fathers and mothers took thought before bringing children into this misery of a world, only the monsters among them would dare to go through with it. The motive which brings the sexes together is 99% sensual pleasure, and only 1% the desire of children, in men, so far as I can learn. As I told you, I haven't ever been carried away in that sense, so that I'm a bad subject to treat of it. Perhaps the possibility of a child relieves sometimes what otherwise must seem an unbearable humiliation to the woman: – for I presume it's unbearable. However here I'm trenching on dangerous ground, with my own ache coming to life again.

I hate and detest this animal side – and I can't find comfort in your compartmenting up our personalities. Mind, spirit, soul, body, sense and consciousness – angles of one identity, seen from different points of the compass.

Hancock is a very powerful fellow: his presentation of his case reeks with character: and with a rare wistfulness too. A man who could so sublimate birth, naturally hurried himself into death. For me there isn't such a course. It seems too serious a treatment. I think I'm sorry I was brought into the world. I think I'll be glad when I go: but meanwhile I can't associate myself with the process in any effort to end or mend it. It's like measles, or the broken rib I've been nursing the last fortnight: you wait, and it's a memory, and even some memories fade with time.

British Library

VYVYAN RICHARDS
26.VI.24   CLOUDS HILL

They bewilder me, rather, these very earnest men. Somehow in their survey
the senses and sensual aspect of art seem forgotten: – and to me they are the
most important.[1] Perhaps that's because I live a beast-life among my fellow-
beasts; in the army inevitably life becomes physical, & we go about only by
feel, by the feels of things & persons. They stall us worse than oxen or
carriage-horses, feed us by rote, dress us by rule: and we respond as best we
can to their prompting & become more animal than savages, less individual
(because more fearful of opinion) than dogs.

Poof: –

I showed the aesthetics to Forster, a novelist of some standing & friend, while
at Cambridge, to this group. He liked their illustrations, but not their attitude. It
interested me, as it did him: but there seems to me no salvation down this road.

My new feeling (a dreaded conviction is looming up in the near distance)
is that the basis of life, the *raison d'être* of us, the springs of our actions, our
ideals, ambitions, hopes are carnal as our lusts: & that the appositions of mind
& body, of flesh & spirit, are delusions of our timid selves.

Your lease enclosed: sorry for its delay. Life slips over me here, in a quality
of dull forgetfulness which endears the camp to me. Never before have I lived
so quickly & so barrenly.

Au revoir some day ... but why not come down here? A bed, tinned food,
bread butter & jam: a quiet cottage, very lovely. Any day after July 4. Wool
station. Razor & tooth-brush & pyjamas not provided.

T.E.S.

Bodleian Library

1 Vyvyan Richards and Lawrence had presumably been engaged in a discussion of the move-
ment in the study of art and in literary criticism associated with his namesake, I. A.
Richards, fellow of Magdalene College, Cambridge – an important figure in the Cambridge
English faculty at this time. The book referred to in the third paragraph is probably *The
Foundations of Aesthetics*, by Richards and C. K. Ogden, with J. Wood, published in 1922.
Richards also published his influential *Principles of Literary Criticism* in 1924. In his view,
irony and complexity in poetry were virtues, while vagueness and sentimentality were not.
For evidence that Forster seems to have largely shared Lawrence's attitude, *see* his letter (to
an unidentified recipient) of 13 August 1930, (*Selected Letters of E. M. Forster*, Vol. II, p.94).

MRS CHARLOTTE SHAW
19.VII.24   CLOUDS HILL

[...] *Kreutzer Sonata* being played by Bruce (a Scotsman, inarticulate excessively uncomfortable).[1] He comes up here often on Sundays, will enter only if I'm alone, glares and glowers at me till I put some Beethoven on the gramophone, and then sits solid, with a heroic aura of solidity about him: my room after four hours of Bruce feels like a block of granite, with myself a squashed door-mat of fossilised bones, between two layers. Good, perhaps, to feel like a prehistoric animal, extinct, and dead, and useless: but wounding also.

I can't write this afternoon. Can I ever?

TES.

British Library

ALAN DAWNAY
27.VII.24   CLOUDS HILL

Lord help us: did I write miserably?[1] Learn the unworthy reasons
    (a): being choked off by the Adjutant for impertinence – to wit, passing an officer at more than twice his speed, while motor-cycling.
    (b): having my face damaged and my lately-broken rib re-broken (I think) by four drunks after lights-out in the hut. An epidemic of drinking lately in A. Company.
    (c): my inability to help one of the few really decent fellows here, he having lately fallen into rather a bad mess, with much worse inevitably to follow.
    Normally I preserve a decent balance, and try not to bother other people with my self-inflicted troubles. I'm not coming out of the Tank Corps (unless a sudden heat-wave melts Trenchard, whom I've annoyed lately by refusing to

1 One of the very few references in Lawrence's letters to John Bruce, the man he paid to inflict the numerous beatings which he suffered from 1923 onwards. *See* introduction to this section.

1 In a letter to Dawnay of 11 July, Lawrence had described himself as 'over-worked: tired, woollen- and wooden-headed' and stated that 'things have been a bit rough lately. (b – rough ... b– brutal ... b ... n^2)': *i.e.* bloody to the nth degree squared.

write the R.A.F. war-history). Nor am I going to be respectable ever any more. Why should you worry about my slow climbing down the social ladder?

There comes a sudden impatience over me at times, when the ordinariness Of ordinary people for one instant seems unbearable. If I were almighty, I'd blast them then: but instead I do something silly, which recoils on my own humble head: and being abnormally sensitive (not a raging terrible lion, as some people, including Trenchard, seem to think) I distress myself for days over a fault which may have been too slight for outward reproof. Then too I'm always, even now, trying to influence others beyond their capacity, and grieving when they return to type.

Lately the job of proof-correcting has made the war-memories very vivid to me, so that they have been coming back as night-terrors to shorten my already few hours regular sleep. When I'd woken up the other fellows five nights running they gave me a sort of barrack-court-martial, to keep me quiet. This was humiliating, and rather painful.

'Humiliating' … and just above I've called myself humble. There's a fine consistency, when one soldier resents being man-handled by other soldiers! However I am humble too, in spite of that.

Yes, Sales go well. The 100 will be up long before the book is ready.

Cheers for everybody who has helped it.

Thanks for Barty's[2] address. I've written to him.

I'm old-fashioned enough to expect 75% of the world's lavatory basins and 30-guinea books not to coincide.

Shall run up to Oxford one Saturday or Sunday, if you are free ever.

T.E.S.

Bodleian Library

---

1 *I.e.* General Sir William Henry Bartholomew, who as Allenby's brigadier-general general staff in 1918 had planned the operations for the advance from Jerusalem to Damascus.

MRS CHARLOTTE SHAW
31.VIII.24

The proofs are not coming so soon. Pike, the printer, is taking a holiday in Cornwall, and meanwhile the work halts for our joint reflections.[1]

I want you to realise, even before you see his work, that Pike is an artist of great severity and carefulness, and that his pages are made as beautifully as he can compass them. To him the balances of lines and paragraphs and passages are vital: they are the elements of which the physical book is made up.

I have no share in this aspect of the book: my work has been only to write the hand-draft of it. The translation from manuscript to metal is his work, and is as difficult as mine. My paragraphs and prose have to be arranged as well, in metal, as they will go.

He is fortunate in having found a living author: for it makes his work much easier, often, to leave out a few words, or a few lines, to make a new paragraph begin here or there, to telescope two chapters: – and I've given him *carte blanche* to cut and change the text as he pleases (only refusing to let him add anything): this is fair, for words are as elastic as ideas, and type-metal isn't elastic at all. He has the harder job.

Neither Pike nor myself are proof-readers: we try to grasp paragraphs entire, and the mis-spelt word escapes us. Even sometimes we let words drop our, unknowing. So you will find many glaring errors in the pages.

And what form should your corrections take? Any you please. My pleasure is bounded only by your pains. Do as much, in each batch, as comes easy to you, avoiding laborious drudgery. In fact, read the thing as long as you can do so without boredom: without intolerable boredom. The wide margins make marking pretty easy.

As the hesitant nervous author I'll value most such corrections as affect the manner and matter of the expression of ideas: because they will tend to make the book better, and I dread strangers seeing the thing in its existing unworthy clumsy form. Surely I can't be so bad a writer as these pages seem to me to declare: and yet I've done almost my best at them. Their failure lies in my insufficiency, not in any sparing of effort.

My spelling is good, originally, and any errors in it, or in the grammar, will be frank misprints and therefore negligible or nearly so. However for other

---

1 Manning Pike was an American whose only experience in printing before taking on *Seven Pillars* had been in a small firm of commercial printers. Lawrence described him in a letter to the American book-designer Bruce Rogers in October 1927 as 'a difficult man, but a fine workman, and ingenious engineer and artist'. Pike worked on the book at two addresses in west London.

people's sake I'll be grateful for any corrected misprints: but the sense of the book is the thing. Do please try and knock out redundant paragraphs. My judgement has left me again, now it is a question of detail. I leave in the bad places, since I'm afraid that it's fear, not good taste, which prompts me to excise them.

What a pother about a trifle! G.B.S. has brought forth twenty books; and I'm in a mess over one. The first no doubt is hardest, but the difference must lie between us. Of course his genius makes him feel sure what is important, and what isn't, and my blundering imitation confounds essentials and inessentials. Also, you know, it's the only book I'll write, and it's an apology for my first thirty years, and the explanation of the renunciation which followed on them....

I'm writing on a fine afternoon, after a broken morning. They gave me a pass, and I slept last night on the floor of the sitting room in Clouds Hill, while one of the R.A.F. who shared Farnborough Camp with me slept in the bedroom. They have found me here, and come down for week-ends of books and music. We ran over to Corfe, in the rain, for breakfast (and a hot bath too: luxury) in the little Hotel: and you'd have laughed to hear me reconstruct the Castle there in all its periods. Once I wrote a book on 'Medieval Military Architecture in Europe, and its modifications in the light of the Crusades'.[2] Lord Curzon was pleased to commend it. Now...

However that passed the fore-noon, and since then we have played a tinned version of the 7th Symphony, and all sorts of quartette snippets: and last night till 2 a.m. the Choral Symphony ground itself out in sections between tea-drinkings, to keep us awake. Whenever there was an interval Chambers (the R.A.F.) read *Methuselah*. What was Clouds' Hill? A sort of mixed grill, I fancy: but very good. Everybody is beginning to fall in love with it. The air of it is peaceful: and the fire burns so well. I'm the only fortunate in camp. The rest burn coal.

This is a silly hotch-potch letter: but the Air Force fellows are like Oxford undergraduates in their second term ... buds just opening after the restraint of school and home. Their first questioning, their first doubt of an established convention or law or practice, opens a flood-gate in their minds for if one thing is doubtful all things are doubtful: the world to them has been a concrete, founded, polished thing: and the first crack is portentous. So the Farnborough fellows used to come to me there, after 'lights out' and sit on the box by my bed, and ask questions about every rule of conduct and experience, and about mind and soul and body: and I, since I was lying on my back, could answer succinctly and with illumination. Those who seek me out down here are the keenest ones, and they

2 His university thesis. Lord Curzon was chancellor of Oxford University when it was submitted.

have been following up the chase of the great Why themselves, since I disappeared: and the books they can get hold of are so mixed and dithering that they feel the question marks more than the progress.

Methuselah is a prime card to play in their case. It puts one side quite quintessentially. G.B.S. would laugh to see himself, the prime reaction against the carnality of barrack-life ... but that's the way it goes. You get a reinforced masculinity by herding men together and segregating them for 20 hours of the 24 ... and reinforced masculinity is a way of describing an animalism which is not the less bestial for being happy and deliberate.

There is no harm in colouring the other side to these fellows. They wouldn't come so far to live on tea and bully beef if they hadn't felt it already: and the best cure for feeling is to feel as quickly and as hard as possible. After all they go back to barracks tomorrow morning. So do I.

A letter yesterday, and one today. What a spate of words! *Meistersinger* just starting. Help!

British Library

MRS CHARLOTTE SHAW
15.x.24

You know, you talk about stinking fish, but when adventuring among you great planets I feel like a burned out cracked electric globe. Never more than 15 C.p. when new, requiring the current of cataclysmic events to chafe into me any sparkle of light, and now only fit for the outer darkness. That's why I can't say anything when G.B.S. works over my proof as if it was worth while. I know it isn't ... and it's such an overwhelming compliment. When a V.C. (a decoration given for a heedless act of physical valour) passes an army guard-room the guard turn out and salute: the poor shy soldier wearing it isn't thereby puffed up to believe himself very brave. He convicts himself of fraudulence. It's like pricking the swelling frog. [...]

Ten million pities that G.B.S. didn't raise the Arab Revolt and write the history of it. There is a book of books gone to waste, because nobody made him a Brigadier-General! It's easy to be wise afterwards, I suppose. If I'm Prime Minister for the next war, all independent commands shall be given to the finest writers of the generation. We may lose the war ... but think of the glories to be published as the Peace rolls on!

T.E.S.   *British Library*

LIEUTENANT-COLONEL W. F. STIRLING
15.X.24   *CLOUDS HILL MORETON DORSET*

Dear F. S.

The book arrived a while ago. Very good of you to read it so quickly and to give me your notes upon it. I'm particularly glad you found few errors of magnitude. The thing is an effort of memory, and I have, after sad experience, a grave distrust of my accuracy after the event.

'The lack of climax'. Yes, I'm afraid that is partly intentional. The book was the record of me in the Arab movement: and before the end I was very weary, and moved in a haze, hardly knowing what I did. Up to Deraa, perhaps, I fought: after that clearly the crisis was solved in our favour, and the last advance and entry into Damascus were almost formalities ... things which had to be passed through, but which required no grip or preparation. Didn't you notice that I was three-parts vacant then?

The same with Nasir's pursuit-battle. I wasn't in it, and so I wrote not of it. That was the rule of the book. So far as it could be, it reproduced the sight of my eyes, and the evidence of my senses and feelings. If people read it as a history: – then they mistake it. I'll strengthen my warning against such a line: but to reboil the final crisis to get it hotter and fitter to the dramatic demands of the Revolt: – no, that I can't do, since day by day, as the years pass, I hate and despise myself more and more for the part I played in it. Today my wish is to strip off from the yarn all the little decorations and tricks and ornaments with which I have made it ever-so-little exciting: so that the core of it should stand out as a disenchanting, rather squalid, experience. That's today: and the book is being printed today for the final time. If I waited till tomorrow probably I'd give effect to this wish, and gut the whole yarn of its adventitiousness: and then all would cry out that I'd spoiled it. So the way of least resistance is to let it, generally, alone.

My memory of the entry into Damascus was of a quietness and emptiness of street, and of myself crying like a baby with eventual thankfulness, in the Blue Mist[1] by your side. It seemed to me that the frenzy of welcome came later, when we drove up and down in inspection. Am I right or wrong? I'll alter this, on receipt of your reply, for you had more leisure to remember than I had. In the book there are two welcomes set out, first a silent one, second a burst of popular excitement. It will be easy, if necessary, to make one only. Simplification is a virtue too.

'The falseness of Storrs'.... Oh yes, I saw it: but because I knew it, and he knew that I knew it, it had no share in our relations, which were between the real Storrs and the real me. Storrs could retort about the falseness of me ... and there wasn't less or more in use. Each of us was a complete dramatic actor, as dressed in appropriate sentiments as in clothes.

The 'emollient' shall come out: but your gentleness and tact and the diversions by which you kept the peace between war-worn Young, Joyce and myself, and the professional competence of yourself which fed my whims and cured Young's wants ... these shall be forcibly acknowledged, in a less ambiguous word or phrase. You were an astonishing comfort to the close of the adventure. What a foul job it was. I don't want readers to 'enjoy' the book.

In girding at discipline and servitudes I seek mainly to condemn myself. My life has been service, and I hate it ... service to an ideal of scholarship, to the nation-building demand of nationality, and now service in the ranks. As you say in such surrender there lies a happiness ... but this seems to me an immoral feeling, like an overdraft on our account of life. We shouldn't be happy: and I think I've dodged that sin successfully! The Tank Corps is a hefty penance for too rich and full a youth!

H. G.'s verdict is extraordinarily interesting:[2] I wish he would tell me what were the worst places, so that I could cut them out. The book is over-long, and I don't like it, any part of it, much.

Do tell me about the Damascus business, so far as it hangs in your memory ... and at the same time check any other falsities which occur to you when thinking it over.

Yours ever
T.E.S.

British Library

1 'The Blue Mist' was Lawrence's Rolls-Royce tender.
2 H. G. Wells.

SIR HUGH TRENCHARD
6.II.25   *CLOUDS HILL MORETON DORSET*

Dear Sir Hugh

February is 'supplication month' ... so for the third time of asking – Have I no chance of re-enlistment in the R.A.F., or transfer? It remains my only hope & ambition, dreamed of every week, nearly every day. If I bother you only yearly it's because I hate pestering you on a private affair.

Last year I said all I could in my favour, & have no eloquence left. My history hasn't changed. Clean conduct sheet since then, which (in a depot) shows that I have been lucky as well as discreet. I've kept my job as storeman in the recruits' clothing store, except for intervals of clerking (for the Q.M.), a Rolls-Royce Armoured Car Course, and a month in Company store. Official character (from the Q.M. who is good to me) 'Exceptionally intelligent, very reliable, and works well.' A descending scale, you will note: but I so loathe the Army that I might not work at all. Even in better days I was not laborious. 'Intelligent' was because I got 93% on my Rolls course: the highest marks ever given. 'Reliable' because when a company stores went wrong they borrowed me to enquire, check, make new ledgers, and wangle deficiencies.

I've lived carefully, & am in clean trim, mind & body. No worse value, as an Aircraft Hand, than I was. Last Sunday, I rode to Yorkshire & back, averaging 44 m.p.h. just for fun. The war-worry & middle-east are finished: and I'd be peaceful and moderately happy, if I weren't always seeing the R.A.F. just out of reach.

Please don't turn me down just because you did so last year and the year before. Time has changed us both, & the R.A.F., since then. I could easily get other people to help me appeal to you: only it doesn't seem fair, and I don't really believe that you will go on refusing me for ever. People who want a thing as long and as badly as I want the R.A.F. must get it some time. I only fear that my turn won't come till I'm too old to enjoy it.

That's why I keep on writing.

Yours very apologetically

T E Shaw
Ex. TEL)
JHR)

R.A.F. Museum Hendon/HMH

MRS CHARLOTTE SHAW
26.3.25   *[CLOUDS HILL]*

[…] The Air Ministry are considering my transfer from the Army to the Royal
Air Force. Such a thing would push me up into the seventh level of happiness.
May is to be the month of decision. Perhaps a good thing may at last happen!

Yours
TES

British Library

DR C. HAGBERG WRIGHT[1]
12.IV.25   *CLOUDS HILL MORETON DORSET*

Dear Dr. Wright,
I saw General Wright yesterday and he told me that you still wanted a copy
of my very expensive book. He has read it, & is naturally interested in the
special subject. I doubt whether its appeal will be general enough to appeal
to you: and I doubt whether it is to be advised as an investment. Thirty
guineas is so high a first price, that I doubt there ever being any
appreciation.[2] I hope to deliver the copies to subscribers towards the end of
this year: but I am in the Army, & soldiers' lives are irregularly lived. So I
promise nothing. There may be 130 copies, (if so many subscribers present
themselves) since my aim is to sell enough (at 30 guineas each) to cover the
total printing bills.
   I don't want the book reviewed, or put in public libraries: none are going
to B. M. Bodleian etc: nor should one go to the London Library. There will

1 Dr Charles Hagberg Wright (1862-1940) was secretary and librarian of the London
  Library 1893-1940. He was knighted in 1934. His elder brother, noted physician and
  pathologist Sir Almroth Wright (knighted in 1906), was the originator of anti-typhoid
  injections and other medical improvements. General Wright (*see* first sentence) was his
  younger brother, Major-General Henry Hagstromer Wright (1864-1948), who had been
  engineer-in-chief, Egyptian Expeditionary Force, from 1916-19.
2 In 1988, the going rate for a copy of the subscribers' edition was £18,000, according to
  the London bookseller, Henry Sotheran.

be an abridgement, in 1927, at a guinea, for public consumption. I suppose all this is agreeable to you?

Subscribers have to put a cheque for £15 15 0[1] to
Manager
   Bank of Liverpool & Martins'
      68 Lombard St
         EC3

Cheque to be made out to T. E. Lawrence & marked 'Seven Pillars Acct'.

Will you let me know if you do finally decide to subscribe. I warn you that the book is long, detailed, discursive, technical: and that it contains no political disclosures whatever.

Yours
T E Shaw

London Library

1 *I.e.* 15 guineas.

LIONEL CURTIS
Undated[1]   *CLOUD'S HILL MORETON DORSET*

This was Pike's first effort: please delete the apostrophe in your mind.

R.A.F. said – that the question of my transfer would be put up to Sir S. Hoare[2] on his return, which will be tomorrow. If any good comes my way I will write. So don't expect to hear from me!

Having you down here was a delight. The reason why I behaved so clumsily was because of the rarity of such occasions. George Lloyd (ex-Bombay)[3] has been here since.

T.E.S.

John Buchan: do you ever see him? Could I? Without seeming to wish to? Naturally, in other words.

All Souls College Oxford

MRS CHARLOTTE SHAW
16.V.25   *[CLOUDS HILL]*

I'm very sorry to hear that you and G.B.S. are ill. Influenza is becoming a perfect curse to everyone but myself whom it unaccountably misses. I called last Wednesday, on the chance that you might be in, but was unfortunate. The R.A.F. after chopping and changing (nautical phrases which refer to a sailing wind) definitely turned me down. I have the feeling in my bones that this time the decision is final. Am I a pessimist? Not too quickly, anyway, for it has been nearly three years since my rejections began. Odd, to have tried so many ways

1 Early May 1925. The address is printed on a correspondence card. Lawrence sometimes wrote Cloud's, sometimes Clouds' and sometimes Clouds: this letter suggests his own preference was 'Clouds Hill' – the version now universally used.

2 *Cf.* footnote 2 on p. 259. Sir Samuel Hoare was strongly opposed to the proposal that Lawrence should be readmitted to the air force and duly vetoed it on his return to Whitehall. The postscript suggests that Lawrence, already anticipating Hoare's refusal, was thinking of the 'chance' meeting with John Buchan to enlist his support which took place shortly afterwards – *see* next letter but one – and which began the process which would eventually get him what he wanted.

3 His former wartime colleague had been Governor of Bombay from 1918-23.

of living, to have found only one of them thinkable as a permanency, to have endeavoured for seven years consistently to follow it, and to have achieved it for exactly six months in those seven years. Exactly what effect the disappearance of my last ambition will have upon my course I can't say yet, since for the rest of the year all my attention must be upon finishing the revise of the *Seven Pillars*. About Xmas I will have to make up this very veering and fickle mind, afresh.

T.E.S.

I will come up and see you as and when I can: but to make an appointment! No good. My mobility depends on Boanerges,[1] and the weather, and my energy: three variables.

British Library

JOHN BUCHAN[1]
19.V.25   *CLOUDS HILL MORETON DORSET*

Dear Buchan

I don't know by what right I made that appeal to you on Sunday.[2] It happened on the spur of the moment. You see, for seven years it's been my ambition to get into the Air Force, (and for six months in 1922 I realised the ambition), and I can't get the longing for it out of my mind for an hour. Consequently I talk of it to most of the people I meet.

They often ask 'Why the R.A.F.?' and I don't know. Only I have tried it, & I liked it as much after trying it as I did before. The difference between Army

---

1 *Le.* his motor-cycle. Lawrence took the name from St Mark's gospel, chapter 3, verse 17, in which Mark writes that Jesus surnamed his disciples James and John 'Boanerges', meaning 'The sons of thunder'. The name was transferred from machine to machine.

1 John Buchan (1875-1940), 1st Baron Tweedsmuir, combined the career of a prolific novelist and biographer with a distinguished career in public life, which culminated with his appointment as governor-general of Canada. During the war he had been with the Department of Information with responsibility for propaganda in the Empire and foreign countries and in this capacity had facilitated Lowell Thomas's trip to Arabia. For a fine account of Lawrence's character and achievements, *see* Buchan's *Memory-Hold-The-Door* (1940), Ch. VIII.

2 Lawrence had, apparently, successfully contrived to meet Buchan in the street and had spoken of his desire to return to the R.A.F.

& Air is that between earth & air: no less. I only came into the army in the hope of earning my restoration to the R.A.F. and now the third year is running on, and I'm as far away as ever. It must be the ranks, for I'm afraid of being loose or independent. The rails, & rules & necessary subordination are so many comforts. Impossible is a long word in human dealings: but it feels to me impossible that I should ever assume responsibility or authority again. No doubt any great crisis would change my mind: but certainly the necessity of living won't. I'd rather be dead than hire out my wits to anyone importantly.

The Air Ministry have offered me jobs: a commission, & the writing of their history. These are refinements of cruelty: for my longing to be in the RA.F. is a homesickness which attacks me at the most casual sight of their name in the papers, or their uniform in the street: & to spend years with them as officer or historian, knowing that I was debarring myself from ever being one of them, would be intolerable. Here in the Tank Corps I can at least cherish the hope that I may some day justify my return. Please understand (anyone here will confirm it) that the Battalion authorities are perfectly content with me. Nothing in my character or conduct makes me in any way unsuitable to the ranks: and I'm fitter & tougher than most people.

There, it's a shame to bother you with all this rant: but the business is vital to me: & if you can help to straighten it out, the profit to me will far outweigh, in my eyes, any inconvenience to which you put yourself!

I think this last sentence is the best one to end on,

Yours sincerely
T E Shaw

DG

EDWARD GARNETT
13.VI.25

[...] Trenchard withdrew his objection to my rejoining the Air Force. I got seventh-heaven for two weeks: but then Sam Hoare came back from Mespot and refused to entertain the idea. That, and the closer acquaintance with the *Seven Pillars* (which I now know better than anyone ever will) have together convinced me that I'm no bloody good on earth. So I'm going to quit: but in my usual comic fashion I'm going to finish the reprint and square up with Cape before I hop it! There is nothing like deliberation, order and regularity in these things.

I shall bequeath you my notes on life in the recruits camp of the R.A.F. They will disappoint you.

Yours
T.E.S.

Post Office closed. So the stamps are put on at a venture.

DG

The hint of suicide in this letter so alarmed Garnett that he wrote at once to Bernard Shaw who promptly sent Garnett's letter to Prime Minister Stanley Baldwin, suggesting the possibility of an 'appalling scandal' unless something was done. Buchan also appealed forcefully on Lawrence's behalf. Baldwin decided to intervene and overrule the objections of Sir Samuel Hoare. Whether the suicide threat was a real possibility or whether it was a dramatic gesture to force the issue is impossible to say. Trenchard for example, to whom Lawrence had made similar hints, did not take them seriously. (*See Trenchard* by Andrew Boyle, pp. 515-16) Lawrence's move was, however, undoubtedly an effective one.

E. M. FORSTER
17.VI.25   *CLOUDS HILL MORETON DORSET*

I'm very glad to see that you're in the land of the Angles, again. It seemed impossible to write to you abroad, though Aries and Avignon and St. Rémi, Aigues Mortes, St. Gilles and Beaucaire are symphonies of names. I hope you went to Les Baux, & Mont Majeur?

Clouds' Hill is proud, at this moment, with rhododendrons ... and the brake is full of birds' nests. Posh[1] asks me to tell you that the scarlet of your marsh-pimpernel is getting less. Perhaps its long season is ending.

The Isle of Wight? Don't like it: except a part, a muddy flat, called New Hampstead on the Newtown river, & that was many years ago.[2] An interesting

---

1 Private Palmer.
2 Among other places the Lawrence family had lived briefly in the Isle of Wight before they settled in Oxford.

woman (very E.M.F. character-like … early novels) Mrs. Fontana, lives intensely at Brading, with two children.

Did I ever tell you how very much I liked *The Longest Journey*?[3] It struck me as more from the heart than any other of your work: and the characters were all three-dimensional, that rarest of (unintentional) creations. They keep on coming back to me, as people; not in virtue of any particular thing they say.

At this point the pen-nib was changed. I would not have you think the spluttering of the old one was rage. They are the mapping pens with which I correct proofs: and proofs are all about me as I write. The original text is finished correcting. What I am now doing is adjusting the elastic text to fit the inelastic type & page.

The Lowell Thomas review is an excellent idea, & should be great fun.[4] I resent him: but am disarmed by his good intentions. He is as vulgar as they make them: believes he is doing me a great turn by bringing my virtue into the public air:

He came out to Allenby as an American official correspondent, saw a scoop in our side-show, & came to Akaba (1918) for ten days. I saw him there, for the second time, but went up country to do some other work. He bored the others, so they packed him off by Ford car to Petra, & thence back to Egypt by sea. His spare credulity they packed with stories about me. He was shown copies of my official reports, & made long extracts or summaries of them. Of course he was never in the Arab firing line, nor did he ever see an operation or ride with me. I met him occasionally afterwards in London in 1920.

So much for his basis. The rest of his book is either invention or gossip. Some of the invention is deliberate, though much that he put into his American magazine articles (red-hot lying it was) has been left out of the American edition of his book.[5] I've not seen the English edition. I thought the American version so disjointed & broken-backed as to be nearly unintelligible, as a history of me in Arabia or of the Arab Campaign above my head! However perhaps I am biassed.

His details are commonly wrong. My family isn't Irish from Galway (*we were an Elizabethan plantation from Leicestershire in Meath without a drop of Irish blood in us, ever) … and they hadn't any ancestors called Lawrence (*which is a very recent assumption, no better based than Shaw or Ross or any

3 An early novel by Forster, published in 1907.
4 Forster had been asked to review Lowell Thomas's *With Lawrence in Arabia*, which been published in 1924 in the United States, and was published in Britain in 1925.
5 Lawrence was doubtless referring to Lowell Thomas's articles in *Asia* of which he had written disparagingly to Fareedah el Akle in his letter of 13 January 1921 (*see* p.183).

other of my names.) His school & college yarns are rubbish: ditto his story that I was medically unfit, or a child when war began. I was employed in the Geographical Section of the General Staff in the War Office till December 1914.

I was never disguised as an Arab (though I once got off as a Circassian:[6] & nearly got on as a veiled woman!)

My height is 5′ 5½″! Weight ten stone. Complexion scarlet. I have not been pursued by Italian Countesses.

You are at liberty to say, if you wish, that

(a) I'm not going East again

(b) Am not at All Souls

(c) Am not breeding cows in Epping Forest

(d) Am not writing books: and did not enlist to do so,

but

(a) Am still serving in the ranks, as was widely published in 1922 (this leaves it ambiguous whether R.A.F. or Army)

*Private information. It conceals a family mess.

(b) am distributing some private copies of my war book, which was written in 1919, & privately printed years ago, to my friends & their friends, with an undertaking not to reprint it in my lifetime

(c) am proposing to publish in U.K. and U.S.A. an abridgement of ⅓ of the above, for public sale, in 1927

(d) and do please, above all, say that the Arab Revolt was a pretty scabious business, in which none of the principals can take any pride or satisfaction: and that my disgust with it expresses itself in my refusal to profit in any way by the spurious reputation I (most unjustly) won in it.

T.E.S.

In pp. 3 & 4 I write your review. Do please do something quite different. Have I deserved a Lowell Thomas?

King's College Cambridge

---

6 Possibly a reference to his escape from Deraa in November 1917: *see Seven Pillars of Wisdom* Chapter LXXX.

ROBERT GRAVES
25.VI.25

Dear R.G.

You underestimate *Poetic Unreason*.[1] It isn't a bit over-worked: *au contraire*: one of the freshest things ever written on poetics. And the matter is as good as the manner. The only place where I cavilled was the treatment of *The Tempest*. God knows each of us have our own fancy pictures of W.S. ... and my fancy is to have no picture of him. There was a man who hid behind his works, with great pains and consistency. Ergo he had something to hide: some privy reason for hiding. He Being a most admirable fellow, I hope he hides successfully. [...]

The *Viva* must have been an appalling affair for your judges. If I'd been there the door would have been locked (against rules, no doubt) and I'd have produced a Thermos & some salted almonds, and said 'Mr Graves, for appearance sake we have to pass 20 minutes in here. Can you do with a cup of coffee?' [...]

Harvard University

MRS CHARLOTTE SHAW
Saturday 4.VII.25   *CLOUDS HILL*

[...] About the R.A.F. John Buchan seems to have worked the oracle: anyway Trenchard and Hoare have agreed to let me back into the ranks, in any terms I please: and the matter will be put in hand straight away and completed – some time before October. I think Mr Baldwin said something to Hoare.

This has made the world feel very funny. The first effect was like a sunset – something very quiet and slow as if all the fuss and trouble of the day was over. Now I feel inclined to lie down and rest, as if there was never going to be any more voyaging. I suppose it is something like a ship getting into harbour at last.

The impulse to get that book finished by Christmas is over. I may be living on for years now, and so why hurry it? Also there isn't any longer any need for

1 Graves's *Poetic Unreason*, published in 1925, was an attempt to interpret poetry in terms of the psychological process underlying its creation. It has been described as his 'most overtly "Freudian" book'. Although it was already published, Graves was allowed to submit it for a B. Litt degree at Oxford: hence the reference to the *Viva* (*i.e. viva voce* examination) in paragraph 2.

the book. I was consciously tidying up loose ends, and rounding the oddments off… and now it seems there aren't any loose ends or oddments.

Don't get worried over this: a few days will see me square again, and I'll realise that it will be as well to finish all the consequences of the Arabian business before pushing off into the R.A.F. You see, if I can clean up the Arab mess, and get it away, behind my mind, then I can be like the other fellows in the crowd. Perhaps my mind can go to sleep: anyway I should be more ordinary than I have been of late. The relief it will be, to have the fretting ended.

In making this fresh start I'll be very careful to give people no grounds for thinking me in any way unlike, or in different circumstances to, the rest.

British Library

JOHN BUCHAN
5.VII.25   *CLOUDS HILL MORETON DORSET*

Dear Buchan
The oracle responded nobly. I was sent for by Trenchard on Wednesday last (horribly inconvenient, for my revolver course did not finish till Saturday, yesterday) and was told that I was acceptable as a recruit.

The immediate effect of this news was to put me lazily and smoothly asleep: and asleep I've been ever since. It's like a sudden port, after a voyage all out of reckoning.

I owe you the very deepest thanks. I've been hoping for this for so many years, and had my hopes turned down so regularly, that my patience was completely exhausted: and I'd begun wondering if it had ever been worth waiting and hoping for. Odd, that the Air Force should seem to me (after trial too!) as the only way of getting across middle age. I wish I could make you some sort of return.

Formalities will take some weeks: but I should change skins in September at latest.

Please inform your family that the bike (Boanerges is his name) did 108 miles an hour with me on Wednesday afternoon. I think the news of my transfer has gone to its heads: (cylinder heads, of course).

More thanks,

Yours ever
T E Shaw   DG

On 16 July 1925 Trenchard signed the order approving Lawrence's transfer back to the R.A.F. He was instructed to put in an application for transfer through his commanding officer at Bovington.

R. D. BLUMENFELD[1]

4.VIII.25

CLOUDS' HILL MORETON DORSET

Dear Blumenfeld

God forbid. I will never come up again, least of all now. Do you remember in 1922 'featuring' my Air Force stage? They gave me a night to clear out. Since then I've been wandering in the night of the Tank Corps, hoping to justify my return to the R.A.F. (the only life I covet) by decent conduct & obscurity. It seems to have worked: my application for transfer lies at this moment in the Air Ministry, & is being favourably, if slowly considered.

One word from you and I'm in outer darkness again. So for the Lord's sake keep calm.

Do you know I so hate that Arabian business that I'd give all the world (if it were mine) to wipe the record of it off my slate? The only consolation is that I've never made a half-penny out of it. Nor will I, rumours of profitable publication to the contrary.

So there you are: publicity (*quorum pars magna estis*)[2] has taken away

(i) My pre-war job

(ii) " " " name

(iii) My All Souls' Fellowship

(iv) All the poor opportunity I had of a fresh start to make a living and you suggest more of it!

Hoots!

Yours ever

T E Shaw

Not feeling at all miserable, because the R.A.F. is again opening its arms. Hoots again.

Bodleian Library

1 Editor, *Daily Express*.

2 *Quorum pars magna estis*: 'of which you are a substantial part'.

HIS MOTHER
18.VIII.25   *CLOUDS HILL*

It is so long since I wrote. Some day, you know, I will sit down & close everything: and never after write a letter or go to see a person or speak. Each day I find the satisfying of life's claims harder and harder. Existence is the heaviest burden we bear.[1]

Also your letters have stopped. Perhaps you feel it too. Or is it this Chinese nationality which has cut the road? I am delighted, of course, (except in so far as it may trouble you) to see such signs that the last, & politically the most degraded nation on earth is beginning to live. In time, if the western powers go on long enough, China will realise her own character & throw off all presumption to control her.

My last letter was to suggest that you might find it necessary to retire out of your place southward or westward. Inevitably the awakening of China will be in the East, & will spread inland.

Today I leave Bovington, probably for Uxbridge, since I am again to join the R.A.F. That is a satisfaction to me.

Arnie & his wife are in Clouds Hill. They do not seem to me to understand the rarity & beauty of the place. They eat in it! In my day there was no cooking allowed. However they seem quiet & happy. I saw them only last week, when they were off to Weymouth for the day. I'll try & see them today before I go.

No other news.

Ned

Bodleian Library

Lawrence was sent first to R.A.F. West Drayton to be processed as a recruit, then after a brief spell back in Uxbridge, where he had begun his R.A.F. career three years earlier, he was posted to the cadet college at Cranwell, Lincolnshire, arriving 24 August. He would remain for the rest of his service years 338171 Aircraftman Shaw.

---

1 This letter was not reproduced in *Home Letters*. Its despairing tone is all the more remarkable in that it was written (*see* paragraph four) on the day towards which he had been working ever since his ejection from the air force two and a half years earlier.

MRS THOMAS HARDY
26.VIII.25   *R.A.F. CADETS' COLLEGE CRANWELL LINCS.*

Dear Mrs. Hardy

You see, it has happened! Quite suddenly at the end: so that I was spared a visit of farewell. It is best to go off abruptly, if at all.

I never expected the move to be so drastic. Cranwell is not really near anywhere (nor is it anything in itself): and the disorder of falling into a new station is yet upon me. The R.A.F. is a home to me: but it is puzzling to find the home all full of strangers who look upon me as strange. My known past always rouses curiosity in a new station. Probably in a few days things will be comfortable.

Alas for Clouds Hill, & the Heath, & the people I had learned in the two years of Dorset!

Please remember me to Mr. Hardy, who is no doubt wholly taken up now in *Tess*. You have a good actress.[1] I hope it will seem fitting both to you & the public. It is hard to please two masters.

You said to me that I might see that work of yours again, some time.

Please don't forget that: though I can't seem either to read or to write in this noise!

Yours sincerely
T E Shaw

DG

COLONEL A. P. WAVELL
29.VIII.25   *R.A.F. CADETS COLLEGE CRANWELL LINCS.*

Dear Wavell

Your letter has followed me up here. I have changed my skin, & love the new one: though the job is less good, & the pay less, & the aspect of the countryside very bleak. However: if things were twenty times worse I would still do it with contentment, for the R.A.F. is a show of my own.

---

1 Gwen Ffrangcon-Davies (b. 1891) was to play in a dramatized version of Hardy's *Tess of the D'Urbervilles.*

The book halts, staggers, for the moment. When I am settled, & can make leisure for myself, it will move on again.

Yours sincerely
T. E. Shaw   *Bodleian Library*

MRS CHARLOTTE SHAW
28.IX.25   *R.A.F. CRANWELL*

Do you know what it is when you see, suddenly, that your life is all a ruin? Tonight it is cold, and the hut is dark and empty, with all the fellows out somewhere. Every day I haunt their company, because the noise stops me thinking. Thinking drives me mad, because of the invisible ties about me which limit my moving, my wishing, my imagining. All these bonds I have tied myself, deliberately, wishing to tie myself down beyond the hope or power of movement. And this deliberation, this intention, rests. It is stronger than anything else in me, than everything else put together. So long as there is breath in my body my strength will be exerted to keep my soul in prison, since nowhere else can it exist in safety. The terror of being run away with, in the liberty of power, lies at the back of these many renunciations of my later life. I am afraid of myself. Is this madness?

The trouble tonight is the reaction against yesterday, when I went mad: — rode down to London, spent a night in a solitary bed, in a furnished bedroom, with an old woman to look after the house about me: and called in the morning on Feisal, whom I found lively, happy to see me, friendly, curious. He was due for lunch at Winterton's (Winterton, with me during the war, is now US of S. for India).[1] We drove there together and had lunch in Winterton's lovely house[2], a place of which I'm splendidly fond, because it has been his for hundreds of years, and is so old, so carelessly cared for. Winterton of course had to talk of

1 Lord Winterton was under-secretary of state for India from 1922-4 and again from November 1924-9. In his autobiographical volume *Fifty Tumultuous Years*, published in 1955, he paid handsome tribute to Lawrence's genius and the range and fertility of his mind and also admitted to hero-worship of him.
2 Winterton's 'lovely house' was Shillinglee Park, Chiddingfold, Surrey. The venue was of special significance to all three of them, in that it was at Shillinglee Park in 1921 that Lawrence and Winterton, together with Lord Harlech and Lord Moyne, had persuaded Feisal, in the course of a discussion lasting five hours and ending at 3am., to put his disappointment at his ejection from Syria behind him and accept the kingship of Iraq.

old times, taking me for a companion of his again, as though we were once again advancing on Damascus. And I had to talk back, keeping my end up, as though the R.A.F. clothes were a skin that I could slough off at any while with a laugh.

But all the while I knew I couldn't. I've changed, and the Lawrence who used to go about and be friendly and familiar with that sort of people is dead. He's worse than dead. He is a stranger I once knew. From henceforward my way will lie with these fellows here, degrading myself (for in their eyes and your eyes and Winterton's eyes I see that it is degradation) in the hope that some day I will really feel degraded, be degraded to their level. I long for people to look down upon me and despise me, and I'm too shy to take the filthy steps which would publicly shame me, and put me into their contempt. I want to dirty myself outwardly, so that my person may properly reflect the dirtiness which it conceals ... and I shrink from dirtying the outside, while I've eaten, avidly eaten, every filthy morsel which chance threw in my way.

I'm too shy to go looking for dirt. I'd be afraid of seeming a novice in it when I found it. That's why I can't go off stewing into the Lincoln or Navenby brothels with the fellows. They think it's because I'm superior: proud, or peculiar, or 'posh', as they say: and it's because I wouldn't know what to do, how to carry myself, where to stop. Fear again: fear everywhere.

Garnett said once that I was two people, in my book: one wanting to go on, the other wanting to go back. That is not right. Normally the very strong one, saying 'No', the Puritan, is in firm charge, and the other poor little vicious fellow, can't get a word in, for fear of him. My reason tells me all the while, dins into me day and night, a sense of how I've crashed my life and self and gone hopelessly wrong: and hopelessly it is, for I'm never coming back, and I want to:

O dear O dear, what a coil.

Here come the rest: so here endeth this wail. No more thinking for a while.

I'm pitching it straight away to you as written, because in an hour I'll burn it, if I can get my hands on it.

British Library

HON. FRANCIS RODD[1]

6.XI.25   *CRANWELL*

Dear F. R.

Your offer of the flat is uncommonly kind: & hits me close: but my affairs don't point to my being able to use it much. Week-ends at Cranwell are only alternate Saturday nights. Pleasant: but hardly justifies a flat in town. Christmas leave ... well, I ought to get a fortnight: but it was a privilege to be granted to 'airmen in their first year at a station only if their Commanding Officer signifies that they are of good character and satisfactory'. Do you think I will pass this test? I have grave doubts. They will not tell us till December 15. Christmas leave, if it comes, will be pleasant, like the week-ends. But it seems hardly to justify a flat in town.

So do try & find another tenant, of the shadow-loving sort. I'd have jumped at the chance, had I been free: had I had a decent certainty of using it for a month, even: but a fortnight, plus two potential week-ends. It wouldn't keep the place warm.

Concerning the book. The reprint differs, in many ways, from the 'Oxford' text, which is that which Childs had. I do not want to leave bibliophiles of the twenty-first century two variants, to spend useful hours comparing & cross-checking: so I propose to cause the six copies of the Oxford edition to disappear.

You shall have, since you want it, a copy of the new text: but it will be one of the plain texts, complete in every way as regards the letterpress, but short in the illustrations. Most people will regard them as no loss. It will be a handier book to move from one dwelling to another. The complete edition will be so very large & heavy.

These plain texts have been produced for the fellows who shared in the Arab business, and who are not rich enough to spend thirty guineas on a memento of [text unclear]. You come well under that category. They are paid for by the subscribers (the ultra-rich, the Haslamians[2] etc.) and so virtue is served: *i.e.* they are distributed gratis.

---

1 Hon Francis Rodd (1895-1978: later 2nd Baron Rennell) had met Lawrence while serving in Intelligence in Egypt and Palestine and again following Lawrence's crash in Rome in 1919, when he had been staying with his father, James Rennell Rodd (later 1st Baron Rennell), at that time the British ambassador to Italy. Rodd was himself a distinguished traveller and explorer.
2 Haslam was a friend or associate of Rodd's: *see* letter to Rodd dated 28 January 1926 (p. 316).

Do not expect it before March. (For how many Marches have I not said this to the subscribers! But each year the thing is never finished!)

Again many thanks for the flat notion. It was exceedingly kind of you.

Yours ever
T.E.S.

Bodleian Library

MRS THOMAS HARDY
9.XI.25

Dear Mrs. Hardy

[...] I'm in Lincolnshire now: very far off Dorset: very cold, very bare, the land all brown or green fields, with low dry walls of oolite dividing them. No hedges, no trees, no hills. It feels almost like a fen country, though Cranwell is high up. The churches are all spired, and very beautiful and large. That is fen-like, of course.

Once I got to Bovington, late on Saturday. They put me up in the camp, and I set off again at midday on the Sunday to return. It is a little too far for a winter ride, with the probability of wet roads under the wheels. When summer comes I'll hope to come more often, & will then call.

They tell me that *Tess* is very good, at Barnes. If it runs much longer I will be able to see it, for our cadets go home at Christmas, & that sets us, their slaves, free for long week-ends. I'm very glad it has gone so well. Are you and Mr. Hardy pleased? Or has it been modified to catch the many, & yourselves annoyed?

Don't bother answering these questions. *Tess* was out of your hands when the actors took hold, & you have no more liability than the composers whose jigs go on the barrel organs. It's only that I'm rather by myself, up here, & I had so nearly taken root in Bovington that I can't help thinking of it.

Please give Mr. Hardy my very best regards. I've promised myself to call as soon as I have the chance. It's a solidity, to be sure that he will be in Max Gate whenever I can come.

Yours sincerely
T.E. Shaw

Bodleian Library

HON. FRANCIS RODD
21.XI.25   *CRANWELL*

Excuse the pencil. It is being written in the hangar. Life has been a rush at
Cranwell for the last week: & will be a rush till Dec 15, when the Cadets term
ends. I've got the keys. My very best of thanks. I'll do my best to use them – but
you realise that I'm a man under authority. I've put in for the leave they will give
me. Good luck in U.S.A. I must see your father's book.[1] Sounds interesting!

T.E.S.

A bell just ringing for me. Let it ring: till I've addressed this.

Bodleian Library

EDWARD MARSH[1]
21.XI.25   *[R.A.F. CRANWELL]*

Dear E. M.
The red foot-note on page 257 is the only reference later than 1919, in my
war-book. I haven't of intention said enough: because I feared that people
might say that in praising him I was praising myself. And there is a limit to
the disclaimers & protestations that a man can make.
    Yet I don't think that he'll object to the briefness or the purport of the
note. It's only going to you to make sure.

---

1 Rodd's father, James Rennell Rodd, wrote three volumes of autobiography under the title
Social and Diplomatic Memories and was also a published poet. In his youth he had been for a
time a close associate of Oscar Wilde.

1 Sir Edward Marsh (1872-1953) was a notable man of letters (editor of five volumes of
Georgian Poetry, author of a memoir of Rupert Brooke and a translator of Horace and La
Fontaine) and also private secretary to two great politicians: Asquith from 1915-16, and
Churchill from 1917-22. Lawrence was writing to him in this last capacity: the 'him' in the
opening paragraph is Churchill. The footnote referred to by Lawrence (to be found on p.
283 of modern popular editions of *Seven Pillars*) pays tribute to Churchill's settlement of the
Middle East at the Cairo conference.

A miracle, (called Baldwin, I believe, in the directory, but surely a thing with wings & a white robe and golden harp)[2] put me back suddenly into the R.A.F., when I had completely lost hope. And now I'm a ludicrously contented airman: it's like the old ship *Argo*, on the beach after all her wanderings, happily dropping to pieces.

Let me have the proof back. S. v. p.

Yours ever
T.E.S.

Bodleian Library

LIONEL CURTIS
24.XI.25   *R.A.F. CADET COLLEGE CRANWELL*

My lord
Your address was perhaps not the most exact possible: but it reached me. The above is better. I'm not a private now, but an Aircraftman, 2nd class. There is unfortunately no 3rd class, or I'd be that. I'm foolishly happy, and propose to stay 'put' till I'm ninety years old.

Yes. I will come & see you: but not for some while: three weeks perhaps: & then it will be a short quick visit.

Canada and the U.S. You deserve a little peace after such an ordeal. By good chance, Kidlington is peaceful: and Hales Croft very beautiful.[1] I like to know people with beautiful houses, for then I can go round the year touting for beautiful beds, & getting them. What a mercy it is to be small, & easily fitted in, whatever the crush.

2 Stanley Baldwin, prime minister. *See* Lawrence's letter to him dated 27 August 1931 (p. 488).

1 Hales Croft was Lionel Curtis's home at Kidlington, Oxford.

The sweater is a great kindness. I hope you have not overdone it. A.C.II's are, as a class, almost immeasurably humble. They beg leave, each morning, of their flight sergeants, to live. I'm the juniorest A.C.II in Cranwell.

Yours
T.E.S.

All Souls College Oxford

E. M. FORSTER
Sunday 29.XI.25   *[R.A.F. CRANWELL]*

I have secured my pass for next week end: have been to church the last four Sundays, to make my claim to Dec 6. incontestable. Also I have read D'Indy's book, & *The Magic Flute* — and the *Prisoners of War*. So my conscience feels there is nothing left undone to prepare me for the occasion.[1]

I'm looking forward to it immensely: and am at your disposal any part of the day from 11 a.m. onward. Only I hope it isn't cold. The snow & frost up here have been unbroken for days & days: and I am dying of it.

The D'Indy book is the best I've ever read on music.[2] Of course he must be a considerable musician himself. That is what makes the technical side of the book understanding & interesting even to a person who doesn't like me know the difference between Major & Minor.

I'm sending the D'Indy back so soon as the paper & string come conveniently to hand. This weather seems to close up every pore of activity. The writing this letter has been lying on my conscience as a hard lump since yesterday morning.

We have a gramophone here now, & I got the Polidor *Fruhlings Sonata* [*sic*].[3] So that has nerved me. The rest of the hut play dance music: some of which is good fun.

---

1 The 'occasion' was a visit to Cambridge during which Lawrence would have the opportunity to meet some of Forster's literary friends.
2 The French composer Vincent D'Indy (1851-1931) was the author of *A Treatise on Composition*, based on his lessons at the Schola Cantorum in Paris, which he had founded in 1896.
3 The *Frühlingssonate* ('Spring Sonata') is Beethoven's *Sonata in F* for piano and violin (*Opus 24*). The trade-name of the record company, misspelt by Lawrence, is Polydor.

The Magic Flute was intensely interesting, for its argument.[4] I suppose the somewhat irritating form has its uses, by conducting the ideas in smooth order before you? I don't like allegory unless it is opaque, so that it's only long afterwards that the slower brains begin to suspect that there was something behind the form. Have you read *They Went*, by Norman Douglas?[5]

Ackerley's play[6] was first rate psychology. The people in it were our very selves. I liked it exceedingly. It is too purely real for literature... or rather it is the sort of literature of which very gifted characters can produce one sample, for each life they live. Ackerley will not write anything more that's good. That's the way with human documents.

Lowes Dickinson, being Intelligence with a capital letter, should be more durably useful as a companion than the 'instinctive' people. Yet I can't help itching for the latter. There is always in my mind the thought that I'm perhaps going to meet a miracle at last. Which is why I've bothered you to know more about Lucas.[7] You can rule a line, as hard as this pen-stroke, between the people who are artists & the rest of the world.

About Sunday: send me a line to say where & when I'm to meet you: & fix up anything, anywhere you like, for the rest. Only, if possible, not too late. If the road is dirty it will take me two hours to get back: and 9.30 p.m. is the camp limit.

If the road is still snow-bound & ice-coated I'll come by train: which on Sundays will be even worse: slower, I mean.

Yours
T.E.S.

4 *The Magic Flute* was a pacifist allegory by Goldsworthy Lowes Dickinson (1861-1932), fellow of King's College, Cambridge. Forster, himself to be later a fellow of King's, was to write Lowes Dickinson's biography (published 1934).
5 Norman Douglas (1868-1952), expatriate novelist and essayist, most famous for his travel books and his novel, *South Wind*.
6 Ackerley's play: *Prisoners of War*, referred to in the opening paragraph, by Forster's friend J. R. Ackerley (1896-1967), had grown out of its author's experience as a junior officer in the First World War, in the course of which he had been wounded and taken prisoner, and had subsequently been interned in Switzerland. Written in 1919, it had at last been staged in 1925. Later Ackerley was to become well-known as a novelist, autobiographer, and literary editor of *The Listener*.
7 F. L. Lucas (1894-1967), poet and critic, also a fellow of King's, was to become a friend and correspondent of Lawrence and a great admirer of him as a writer.

Your kindness is taken for granted, above; and my gratitude hides between the lines.

King's College Cambridge

MRS. CHARLOTTE SHAW
26.XII.25

I haven't any ink in the hut, which is empty now, except for myself. So I'm writing, very languidly, since I have been working all day at my proofs. Book VI has been sent off in penultimate form to Pike: or rather, will go off on Monday morning, when the post-office opens. That is the 'bad' book, with the Deraa chapter. Working on it always makes me sick. The two impulses fight so upon it. Self-respect would close it: self-expression seeks to open it. It's a case in which you can't let yourself write as well as you could. [...]

Christmas? I don't know what to say of it. The camp has come down to 40 men. They live in the wet bar, mostly. The hangars are locked up. I have been transferred as runner (*i.e.* orderly and charman), to the Accounting Section. A row of eight dirty offices, in a corridor. The old charman, (on leave) did not do them very well. So I've been going down there in the holidays, when the place is empty, and scrubbing or sweeping or window-cleaning. It passes the time, and I can lock myself in. The other fellows are all happy and friendly: but a drunk man is such a fool that he wears my patience to shreds in a few hours. It is only bad at night. Yes, I would call it a happy Christmas, on the whole. Mankind punishes himself with such festivals.

This book of mine is too ambitious – I wrote it too hard and big (G.B.S. will grit his teeth: – hardly and bigly – but that isn't modern enough). I've printed it too elaborately: illustrated it too richly. The final effect will be like a scrofulous peacock.

Don't worry that this letter is silly. You know what rot people talk of at night-time, round the fire. That's all it is: not a letter at all but yawny gossip. The world is dripping, outside: a thaw at last. The roads have been icebound, and Boanerges rusts in his stall. Did I tell you how I damaged him, and myself, three weeks ago, when the first snow fell? He is mended. My arm is cured. My knee nearly so. Till my leg can bend again I'll not ride him: and it is good to ride him. Chases off the broody feeling.

Falmouth. Did they give you a high seaward room, looking over the decayed green bones of the German submarines, like dead mackerel on the rocks? I hope not. The other side is rather jolly. Across the Fal you have St. Just, in Roseland, which is a good style for a new peer: and a beautiful place – or was. 1906, was it? I was a garrison gunner for a little in the old castle.[1] My mind was not so peaceful then, for I had not tried everything and made a final choice of the least ill.

Does my writing the word GUNTER[2] wake any guilty feeling in your mind? They disappeared like snow on the desert's face. My year (1917) was unlucky for snow. It lay for six weeks. The chocolates did not.[3]

British Library

HIS MOTHER
28.XII.25   [*CRANWELL*]

[Clouds Hill is very beautiful, & suits me. Though I will not live there till I have been as long in the Air Force as pleases me. You know I always wanted to be in the R.A.F.] [...]

I've sent you a Blackwood article, in which Candler, an Indian journalist,[1] has written some butter & sugar stuff about me. Don't worry about that – or me – or anything. People are solitary things (myself especially so) and as long as it isn't true, I don't care what praise or blame I get. [You talk of 'sharing my life' in letters: but that I won't allow. It is only my own business. Nor can anybody turn

I This is an important reference to a much-discussed episode of Lawrence's schooldays, namely his enlistment in the artillery, having left home 'at the urge of some private difficulty' (*LHB*, p.81: the phrase occurs in Lawrence's rewriting of Liddell Hart's draft for the opening chapter of his *T.E. Lawrence in Arabia and After*). He was apparently bought out by his father. It has been argued that the story was invented but he was away from home for several months early in 1906 and this letter lends substance to his claim. The nature of the private difficulty has not been resolved.

2 Gunter's of Berkeley Square was a firm well-known for the excellence of its confectionery and ices.

3 Letter annotated by Mrs Shaw at end: 'We were in Falmouth at Xmas and at Port Elliott after on a visit.'

I Edmund Candler: official 'Eye Witness' with the Indian Expeditionary Force during the Mesopotamian campaign and author of *The Long Road to Baghdad*, published in 1919.

on or off the tap of 'love' so called. I haven't any in me, for anything. Once I used to like <u>things</u> (not people) and <u>ideas</u>. Now I don't care for anything at all.]²

HL/Bod!eian Reserve

HON. FRANCIS RODD
28.1.26

Dear F. R.
The 23rd, so Haslam said, was your day of return. I left my keys with him: and he was going to leave them with his housekeeper, if he went to Mexico. All this going is terrible.

I hope you are back, & over the first emptiness of return. I've got to thank you for four exceedingly good nights in London. Four, you will say, is too few to justify my holding those keys all the weeks: but consider the quality of those nights. The place so quiet, so absolutely mine, and the door locked downstairs, so that it was really mine. Why there isn't a lock in my power at Cranwell, not even on the shit-house door! The happiness & security of those nights were very keen.

I didn't read many books: but I worked the bath-machine over-time. The best of thanks possible.

Yours ever
T.E.S.

DG

2 For a comment on his mother which sheds light on his determination to keep clear of her influence, *see* his letter to Mrs Charlotte Shaw, 14 April 1927 (p. 343): 'I have a terror of (mother] knowing anything about my feelings, or convictions, or way of life. If she knew they would be damaged, violated, no longer mine.' In A. W. Lawrence's view he was emotionally damaged by her despite his best efforts to retain his own integrity.

COLONEL C. E. WILSON
19.2.26   *R.A.F. CADET COLLEGE CRANWELL*

Dear Colonel Wilson

I held your letter up a while, hoping that the two present holders of my Oxford text would send them back to me. They haven't. You shall have whichever reaches me first. It will reach you in a week or so.

[...] I've shortened the new edition, shortened it considerably, by letting out wind, & making two words do for six. Where Archie Murray was described as 'jealous, spiteful, bad-tempered, vicious, clever, quick & narrow' he is now called 'feminine & feline'. Don't tell Mrs. Wilson of this improvement! They are improvements, though!

I apologise for the print of the Oxford text. It was not meant to circulate. The new one is decently done. It will follow in May perhaps. Proof-correcting is not a suitable activity for the barrack!

Yours ever
T.E.S.

Bodleian Library

MRS CHARLOTTE SHAW
22.2.26

I'm glad you are better. 'Flu is dangerous, for its possible consequences. The fellows here get chills on top of it and then become wholly sick. However, Ayot is a warm and comfortable home.

Mrs. Warren's Profession[1] is being welcomed in B. Flight. Three have already finished it and praise it. A fourth is dealing with it. *Stalky*[2] and *Mrs. Warren* at present dispute the field. I'm afraid G.B.S. will have a very difficult time dealing with Mrs. W.

---

1 *Mrs Warren's Profession*, Bernard Shaw's third play, had been written in 1893 but had long been banned and, though it had been performed privately, had only recently (28 September 1925) had its first public performance.
2 *Stalky & Co.*, by Rudyard Kipling.

Measles is a gift – though it has left me, personally, very tired and heavy-headed. Everybody in camp is getting it: so yesterday they cancelled Church parade. That obliterated the one real grudge an airman has against a weekend in Cranwell. I had ridden hard on the Saturday, to Barton on Humber: that road (from Lincoln) includes a stretch of seventeen miles: which I did in seventeen minutes, and felt better for. So on Sunday I sat about the morning in the hut, and played bits of gramophone records to myself. The others were skylarking, and playing rummy, a noisy card-game. So the Beethoven didn't disturb them. Nor did they disturb Beethoven.

The afternoon was fine-grey, heavy-clouded, windy: so I took Boanerges over to Nottingham, his birthplace, for a stroll. The roads were not fit for going fast, so we turned into by-roads and idled through Newark and Southwell. Nottingham is one of those 'Sunday' places – the market square deserted: dust and fog blowing unchecked along the empty streets. The crowds were going to a Wesleyan Mission in their Albert Hall (a hopeless name, Albert. It is ruined for a hundred years). I went instead to a Lyons shop, and ordered tea. The other people were amusing. They hadn't come from my planet, I think. The only friendly person was a black cat, who sat beside me and was exceedingly insistent upon the point of food. I bought an eclair and split it open down its length, like two little dug-out canoes. The cat flung itself upon them, and hollowed out all the pith with its grating tongue. When it got down to the brown shell, it sat back on its hind legs and licked its face lovingly. A Jew merchant-looking man on the opposite seat, also had cream on his cheek and tried horribly hard to lick it. Only his tongue was too short. Not really short, you know: only for that ... The cat was a very excellent animal. The human beings were gross, noisy, vulgar: they did the same things as the cat, but in a clumsy blatant way.

T.E.S.

Heaven knows why I've bothered to write you this nonsense. The moral spoils it. I should have put it into a preface.

British Library

LIONEL CURTIS
8.3.26

Dear Prophet

I owe you – help! is it three letters, or four. I don't know where I am.

Last night, at 10 p.m. I finished correcting the text of the *Seven Pillars*.
Gibbon at Lausanne: etc. etc.[1] Soft music off.

Lowell Thomas' book. Burn it please. No, don't: books are very hard to
burn. Use it (them) to strengthen the embankment on the river front of
Halescroft. No, don't. The swans haven't deserved that. Give it to Oman.[2]

Very sorry about your health. To be convalescent for months is a terrible
business. I'm nearly over my measles, which have been pretty bad.

Major Marriott I've never heard of before. There are lots of these lunatics.

In 1918 & 1919 Allenby got a library of gnostic pamphlets: & I've had a
good many.

Your remark about ancestry, for which you apologised, I've entirely
forgotten! So what can it have been? Bars sinister are rather jolly ornaments.[3]
You feel so like a flea in the legitimate prince's bed!

All Souls College Oxford

F. L. LUCAS[1]
14.3.26   *R.A.F. CADET COLLEGE CRANWELL LINCS*

Of course it has to be answered: but not easily. I told E.M.F., a week before
that your opinion of my book would be important, since you were the best
critic just now writing. Then your 'Authors' came along, & confirmed what,
after all, was a hasty judgement, since I don't often see the weekly papers. I

---

1 A reference to Edward Gibbon's eloquent description of the sense of freedom mixed with
melancholy which he experienced when he finally completed his masterpiece *The Decline and
Fall of the Roman Empire* and thus took 'an everlasting leave of an old and agreeable companion'.

2 Sir Charles Oman (1860-1946) was the mediaeval historian whose views Lawrence had
vigorously attacked in *Crusader Castles*.

3 In heraldry a bar or bend sinister is an indication of illegitimacy.

1 Fellow of King's College, Cambridge, whom Lawrence had met during the visit to Cambridge
arranged by E. M. Forster the previous November. *See* letter to E. M. Forster dated 29 November
1925 (pp. 312-13).

meant to write to you about your book, comparing your promising plantation of young trees with my builders'-yard of second-hand materials and the next step is your finding my thing good!

It puzzles me, and shakes my conviction that it is rotten: of course I'll come back to my own position, afterwards, when the shock of your judgement has died past. Surely you can see that the effective scenes in the book are made effective by writing 'tricks'? I always had the ambition to write something good & when the Revolt gave me a subject I tried to make up for what I felt to be my lack of instinct by taking immense pains: by studying how other people got their effects, & using their experience.

So I built an enormous mass of second-hand ornaments into my skeleton and completely hid the skeleton under them. At least I think I spoiled it, though I notice you detect a certain unity, where S. S. found a lack of his 'architectonics'.[2]

It sounds very conceited, that I should go on believing the book rotten, when you have written in the contrary sense. S. S. also called it epical (though an epic hasn't yet been built on the feelings, as aside from the actions, of men): and I've lived down his praise. So there isn't much hope for your downing me. Yet I admit it is a knock, all the harder because I was sure that your classical spirit would condemn me outright. It is also awfully good of you to have written at such length.[3]

Bodleian Library

Mrs Charlotte Shaw
17.6.26

I have offended. I'm sorry. Things arise from differences in point-of-view. 'Dram-drinking', I said, thinking of the effect on me. A 'whisky bottle' said you, looking at G.B.S. with new eyes. Yet if I had called him stimulating no harm would have been done. I thought of 'drinking', you thought of 'dram'.

He is stimulating. He stimulates his household. That is why Ayot will never be my good toast-and-water. I can only keep happy in the R.A.F. by holding myself a little below par: if it's much below I mizzle: grow sorry for myself.

2 S. S.: Siegfried Sassoon.
3 For a sample of Lucas's opinion of *Seven Pillars* see 'General Introduction', p. xxv.

This happens if I get hurt, or am crazed overmuch by some N.C.O. with a grievance to hand on. If I grow excited, then I chafe at the tightness of uniformed life. When I'm at Ayot the serenity of the sky overhead, and the keen air and the intellectual delight of fencing with a real swordsman intoxicate me. Then I go back to Cranwell, and the policeman in the guard room makes me stand to attention while he checks my clothes and attitude. The contrasts are too great: G.B.S. talks to me as if I were one of his crowd: the policeman as if I were one of his crowd: and I get flustered and sorrowful. Hut 105 is balm to this: for there we are all on the same footing: it is compulsory intimacy: not of mind, but of existence. Everybody sees everybody in his shirt daily. Equality exists only under compulsion, among the bullied.

All this I've said before. I tried (All Souls and elsewhere) to live with decent people; and couldn't. There is too much liberty up aloft. I was able to avoid others all day long: and there is no goodness in being a recluse. So I wrote myself down a failure, socially: and I believed (I still believe) that I'd failed in my ambition to become an artist, at book-writing, by taking thought. Creative work isn't achieved by dint of pains. Consequently rather than be a half and half, a Cherry Garrard[1] or Stephens[2] or Stanley Baldwin, I backed out of the race and sat down among the people who were not racing. Racing, in these modern and specialised days, is a pursuit limited to thoroughbreds and detached observers sometimes wonder whether these over-tensioned, super-charged delicate creatures are bred really to improve the race, or just to give pleasure to men-fanciers.

However, that is another story altogether. I'm sorry I called it dram-drinking. What I wanted was a tipple the contrary, the converse of Lethe: the water (G.B.S. principles are sacred) of memory. My mythology breaks down. What are the waters of remembrance? Swinburne has a wonderful chorus of them in *Atalanta*. Is that squared up? When in the Tank Corps I so distrusted my fortitude that I would not take the leaves in my power. Now, at Cranwell, I am not afraid of the temptations to desert: but the equilibrium between conditions and expectations of life is so fine that I shun all disturbances. Happiness lies in maintaining this balance of opportunity and desire.

And also, like a cat, I love firesides, and rugs and quietude: and these things are outside the power of a serviceman. You and G.B.S. having them, will find a yearning for them contemptible. But it isn't really. People only feel little

---

1 Apsley Cherry Garrard: polar explorer and author of *The Worst Journey in the World* (Constable, 1922).
2 James Stephens, Irish poet and story-writer.

things (like me, the throb of my right wrist) when their bodies are at rest: and there is a world of importance in the little things.

Is this a sermon? It was meant to be an apology.

T.E.S.

British Library

MRS CHARLOTTE SHAW
22.8.1926   *GEORGE HOTEL EDINBURGH*

The George Hotel – that's that – and outside it I walk down Bernard Terrace, and feel as though I am about to be entertained at Ayot. Only 'Shaw' here still means a snuffy local lawyer-chap. The Scotch haven't yet, the dear provincials, tumbled to the fact that G.B.S. has pre-empted his name for the future, and assumed its past.

You know, as time passes, the number of names for a man ambitious to write, is drawn in. Take my case. I wanted to make books. Lawrence was impossible, since there is a very great but very strange man writing book after book as D.H.L. I can smell the genius in him: excess of genius makes his last book sickening: and perhaps some day the genius will burst through the darkness of his prose and take the world by the throat. He is very violent, is D.H.L.: violent and dark, with a darkness which only grows deeper as he writes on. The revelation of his greatness, if it comes, will be because the public grow able to see through his dark thinking … because the public begin to be dark-thoughted themselves. D.H.L. can't make himself clear: he can't use the idiom of you and me. So often you find men like that, and sometimes the world grows up to them and salutes them as 'kings-before-their-time' … and sometimes nobody ever bothers about them at all, afterwards.

However, I'm off the point: but nobody with any sporting sense of D.H.L.'s fine struggle to say something would make it more difficult for him by using the same name while his fate yet hung balanced: so I took 'Ross' as a yet unreserved name: and then I lost the hope of writing, and here I am.

Not literally here. My purpose in Edinburgh is to see Bartholomew, the map-making firm which is adapting a War Office map to the illumination of the *Seven Pillars*. Tomorrow morning I will see them and tomorrow afternoon I will be in Cranwell. It takes 7 hours, Boanerges, going respectably. The respectability is mine. Boanerges would go madly, if I would. Alas, surely I grow old. Again and again, this morning, when we came to a piece of road which invited ninety, I patted his tank and murmured 'Seventy only, old thing', and kept to it. The excuse I gave myself was that Edinburgh was a long way and that there must be no full-open throttle on a long journey. Indeed that was once my maxim: but today I kept the maxim without being vexed thereby: and that is significant. Or is it only that I have ridden too many hundreds of miles this last week. My time in England draws short: and I'm not yet surfeited, but want to be. That appetite of the well-fed for more food.

News? None. The colour printers are proving their last three prints. One has 23 colours upon it. Lord save us! Kelman, a Constable partner, was admiring some of the prints at Chiswick and said to the printer ... 'Now why shouldn't you give *us* some work of that quality?' 'We will', said Newberry, if you'll pay 10/– a print!' Exit K.

Bookbinding... October. Distribution... November. Deportation ... December.

I hope you and G.B.S. are well, fiercely active, hot and happy.

T.E.S.

British Library

MRS CHARLOTTE SHAW
24.8.1926   *[LONDON]*

[...]At Cranwell I got your letter, doubting whether I liked your writing to me. I posted my Edinburgh note there, and came on here, wondering how I was to answer you: for therein lies the crux of the matter. It isn't any good my telling you that I look forward to your letters and enjoy them ... for you will not believe that unless I answer them in kind ... and I can't do that. It is easy when we are working together on a book: that gives me a peg to hang a letter on: but upon thin air! I can't. Candler said that I was essentially an unclubbable man: meaning one who took everything, and returned nothing. I like your letters: they are the only 'general' letters I ever get, for no one but yourself has persevered in writing to me: but though I like them as much as I do, I can't send the same sort of things back, any more than I can play any other game on earth. You know, I've never, since I was able to think, played any game through to the end. At school they used to stick me into football or cricket teams, and always I would trickle away from the field before the match ended.

The same apparently with letters. It isn't a Belfast-nonconformist-conscience: because I haven't any convictions or disbeliefs – except the one that there is no 'is'. You can go about the earth being interested in itself, for its own sake, because you believe in many things. Whereas I can't be interested in Durham, even, or in Boanerges, except I wish to interest another person in them.[1] Also I hate talking about the involutions and convolutions of my insanely-rational mind! By the way, you'll laugh at the in-keeping of my ride up to Edinburgh. I did a thirty-mile return-around, because my road came to a toll-bridge, and I never pay tolls! 'When a thing is inevitable, provoke it as instantly and fully as possible' said the *Seven Pillars*. My matter of fact ancestry compels me to carry my impulses into action. Imagine a person utterly lacking in common-sense, but with every other quality normal.

At Cranwell I greeted B. Flight, who came out and stroked Boanerges lovingly, and then fled again wildly down the Great North to London. It seemed harsh to roar through Codicote, though. When you come back I want to drop in, suddenly, again. A night is too long. One short sharp drink, and back, soberly, in the saddle.

It is altogether too late. Westminster has just struck a half-hour, which must be half-past one. It's only after midnight that I can write such rubbish.

T.E.S.

British Library

SIR HUGH TRENCHARD
20.II.26

Dear Sir Hugh

It is good of you to give me the option of going overseas or staying at home: but I volunteered to go, deliberately, for the reason that I am publishing a book (about myself in Arabia) on March 3, 1927: and experience taught me in Farnborough in 1922 that neither good-will on the part of those above me, nor correct behaviour on my part can prevent my being a nuisance in any camp where the daily press can get at me.

1 He had just ridden south from Edinburgh and explored Durham on the way.

Overseas they will be harmless, & therefore I must go overseas for a while & dodge them. After a few years the bubble will be either burst or deflated, & I can serve again at home. England seems to me much the best place to be, anyway.

I'm sorry you should have been unnecessarily troubled. It had been my ambition that you shouldn't hear of or from me, after my readmission to the R.A.F. I'm perfectly happy in it on the ordinary terms: and if the other fellows knew that I used to know you, my character would be ruined.

Yours sincerely
T E Shaw

R.A.F. Museum Hendon/HMH

HON. FRANCIS RODD
3.XII.26   *[R.A.F. UXBRIDGE]*

I had an awful month: real hard labour upon my old-man-of-the-sea: final printings, plates, collection, collation, issue to binders, correction of subscribers' lists, allotment of copies. Yet though I sweated at it every possible hour of the day & night, seeing no-one and doing nothing else, even now it is not finished. About 20 copies have gone out, & most of the rest will go out about Christmas time: but the very special copies will hang on till the new year. I think my experience is almost a conclusive demonstration that publishing is not a suitable hobby for an airman.

I've crashed my bike & sold the bits, & am not good company for the world. They inspect us very often in the depot here, & on Tuesday morning we sail for Southampton. Karachi next stop, though only temporary. I'll write to you after I come to rest finally, and ask you how you like the massive volume. Amateur writers, & one-book-men always write at exhausting length. [...]

I spent one week-end in a house with your Sahara book, & liked it,[1] though it is written to instruct, & my reading is for amusement. I'm awfully glad you took such care in the style & the arrangement. If every modern traveller ... however, enough said. A good book. My own is more ambitious, aimed, if I

---

1 Rodd had crossed the Sahara and published a book about his experiences and observations of the Touareg tribe under the title *People of the Veil* (Macmillan, 1926).

may say so, for a more remote star and falls proportionately shorter than yours. A case of over-vaulting.

Well, that's that. I'd have liked to have seen you, & did ring up three nights, when unexpectedly I found that my proper work had come to a temporary standstill ... but each time there was no reply. These things do not really matter, of course, but I should have liked it.

Yours
T.E.S.

Bodleian Library

DICK KNOWLES[1]
3.XII.26

Dear Dick

I'm sitting in a very poor hut at Uxbridge, writing the same thing to dozens of people. On arriving in London for my 28 days leave I found the book not nearly ready for the binders. I put in a months hard work on it: have got all of it out to binders, and nearly half of its copies bound. Some 20 have been sent out already.

In doing this I spent the whole of my leave, seeing no one, & going to no concerts: not one single scrap of public music all that while: though by the goodness of my dentist,[2] I twice heard Harold Samuel play in his house.

I managed to squeeze out an hour in Clouds Hill: and an hour at the Hardys. I had meant to come to you last Sunday, & started about 7.30a.m but Islington streets were greasy (I had to see G.B.S. on my way) & I got into a trough in the wood paving, & fell heavily, doing in the off footrest, kickstart, brake levers, handlebar, & oil pump. Also my already experienced knee-cap learnt another little trick. Alb Bennett took the wreck for £100. I limp rather picturesquely.

So that is that. It's an explanation, for I've apologised too often today on paper to repeat it again.

1 Dick Knowles was one of the three sons of Sergeant W. A. Knowles, Lawrence's across-the-road neighbour at Clouds Hill. He followed Lawrence into the ranks of the R.A.F.
2 W. Warwick James, senior dental surgeon at the Middlesex Hospital and music enthusiast: he contributed an article on Lawrence's interest in music to *Lawrence by His Friends*.

I sent you a set of the largest possible proofs: the dirty old "'B" Flight Manual' which circulated to so many people at Cranwell. Some squadron leader or other re-covered it!

The final book came out not so badly: the printing is lovely, some of the tail-pieces beautiful, some curious, some amusing: some otherwise: and the binding is being well done. Of course it is very large: too large but that I knew long ago, & was prepared to be shocked at. There were not quite enough copies, after all, so that I've not been able to give away many to the fellows who helped the Arab Show forward.

It is a strangely empty feeling to have finished with it, after all these nine years. Now comes the voyage east in the *Derbyshire*, a pause in being: and then will come a need to find enough interests in my reach to busy me henceforward. I'll write from India, when I've been posted somewhere permanently, and tell you how it feels like to be poor and finished!

Yours
T.E.S.

DG/Bodleian Library[3]

---

3 First three paragraphs published in part in *DG*.

Aircraftman T. E. Shaw, Miranshah, India, 1928

5 THE YEARS IN INDIA
1927-29

Lawrence went east without enthusiasm. 'I squat on deck with Smith, C.J.,' he wrote on 16 December 1926 from the *S. S. Derbyshire* to his R.A.F. friend Sergeant Pugh, 'lamenting Cranwell and England, and all good things.' When the long, unpleasant voyage was over he found himself in an R.A.F. camp at Drigh Road, just outside Karachi. 'The Depot is dreary to a degree,' he commented to Charlotte Shaw on 28 January, adding: 'its background makes me shiver.' To his American friend Colonel Ralph Isham (10 August 1927) he was even more outspoken: 'I hate the East. It holds bad memories for me.' However, to his old wartime comrade Lieutenant-Colonel F. G. Peake, now commanding the Arab Legion in Transjordan, he wrote wistfully (20 October 1927) of that 'delectable land. I am often hungry for another sight of its hills. Rum, too [*i.e.* Wadi Rumm]. If only ... Drigh Road, this place, is dismal.' But this was written at a time when he had been stirred to think warmly of his wartime past by a letter from Mrs Shaw, who had just met Feisal and had, apparently, aired the idea when writing to Lawrence that Feisal might not be averse to their working together again. Lawrence was taken with the possibility but swiftly rejected it. 'I don't think he wants me, really,' he told her on 18 October 1927. 'When with him I am an omnipotent adviser: and while that is very well in the field, it is derogatory to a monarch.'

He made no attempt to relieve the monotony by getting to know India; throughout his year and a half at Drigh Road he never once visited Karachi. Similarly at his second posting, Miranshah (in Waziristan, near the Afghan border), to which he transferred in June 1928, he never went beyond the confines of the camp. Though he found much to dislike about his exile from home and friends, he appreciated that it gave him, or at any rate appeared to give him, freedom from publicity. Writing to Mrs Shaw on 29 March 1927, he described himself as 'killing time there [*i.e.* at his R.A.F. depot] till my books are forgotten'. A distant Fleet Street seemed to offer little threat. 'The English Press [...] feels so old, after the three weeks and the journey.'

His work was undemanding and he had much free time, which he filled with reading, occasional writing for publication (*see* his letters to Evelyn Wrench and Francis Yeats-Brown) and with correspondence. At home there was the prospect of meeting his friends; as he wrote to Charlotte Shaw on 29 March 1927: 'In England there was a current of life round me, and I swam in it [...] and now my physical radius is cut down to a mile, my company to eleven airmen [...]' Without the prospect of seeing his peers, letters offered the only method of contact. He received so many that he could answer only a small proportion of them, but to those he wished to write, he gave generous measure; his letters to Charlotte Shaw, E. M. Forster, Robert Graves, Sir Hugh Trenchard and Sergeant Pugh are often many pages long. This is also the period of some of his most frank and revealing letters: to Charlotte Shaw about his family background and his parents (particularly his mother); to Graves and Forster about his sexuality; to his mother about the attitude of the West to China and about the missionary movement. It was also at this period that he took the decision to change his name by deed poll to T. E. Shaw; *see* his letter to the Hon. Edward Eliot, dated 16 June 1927.

Ironically, it was his chosen remoteness from civilization which, in January 1929, abruptly brought his stay in India to an end. Some months after arriving in Karachi, he had been offered a two-year plain-clothes engagement as a clerk to the British attaché in Kabul, and had turned it down because, among other reasons, as he told Mrs Shaw in a letter of 1 June 1927, 'Probably the British military attaché in Cabul [*sic*] is only a glorified kind of spy. [...] Safety first, as they say in 'busses [*i.e.* aircraft]. Better the camp you know ... and Drigh Road is as hidden a place as any in the world.' He had thought himself equally hidden in Miranshah, but now the news of a revolution in nearby Afghanistan combined with the fact that he was based only ten miles from the Afghan frontier led to sensational stories in the British press claiming that he was actively involved. In the *Daily Herald* report which broke the story (5 January 1929), he was referred to as 'the arch spy of the world'. At the time his most important extracurricular activity was the task to which he had just been contracted by American book-designer Bruce Rogers of producing a new prose translation of Homer's *Odyssey*. Moreover, this disturbance of his peace came only weeks after he had made a particular point of writing in gratitude to the daily paper of Lahore, the *Civil & Military Gazette*, which had taken the 'Home papers' of Britain to task for their obsession with Lawrence's whereabouts, stating, 'His station is known to us, but we see no reason for interfering with his desire for freedom from publicity.' Lawrence had told the editor (29 October 1928): 'I have not done anything, for many years now, to deserve publicity: and I will do my best not to deserve publicity in future.' All this was scarcely the stuff of sedition, but to Fleet Street the fact that a rebellion had happened so near to where Lawrence of Arabia was now based was enough; soon there were questions in the House of Commons while anti-imperialists burnt him in effigy on Tower Hill. The Air Ministry, despite its own reservations, acceded to the request of the government of India that he should be removed from the subcontinent as soon as possible. Trenchard was prepared to offer him a posting in Aden or Somaliland, but he also insisted that Lawrence himself should be consulted. Lawrence opted to come home.

SERGEANT A. PUGH[1]
16.XII.26   [ON BOARD THE TROOPSHIP DERBYSHIRE]

Dear Sergt.

Your letter to Uxbridge pleased me so that I repent the thinness of this reply to it: but we live on board in a clotted and organised misery which takes me out of the little inclination I ever had to write letters. Today is the tenth day at sea. Tomorrow is Port Said, where this letter can be posted. From the Canal is 21 days to Karachi, and land. Twenty-three times have I crossed this Mediterranean – twenty three times too many for my happiness. I squat on deck with Smith, C.J. lamenting Cranwell and England, and all good things. Smith asks you to distribute his best wishes among the Flight.

[...] I don't start in fit order to smile at the discomfort of a trooper, because of the tangle of my affairs behind me, some private troubles, and my regret that I've got to go abroad again, when I'd been hoping to lie quietly in England for the duration. The combination of these things makes me drizzle softly about myself. Please remember me to Mrs. Pugh, & tell the fellows I'll send a decent scrawl, after they have fixed me somewhere in India for good.

Yours ever
T E S.

It's quite true about my being overseas. In London I saw Trenchard, who very nicely gave me the choice of going or staying, on Winston's initiative. I had to choose to go, of course, damn it. I'm always hurting myself or my interests. T. says that he might let me sign on again, in 1930, if I was fit & wished it. If so I shall not be back till 1932, a whole age away.

Bodleian Library

1 A member of Lawrence's flight at Cranwell. His reminiscences of Lawrence in the R.A.F., written for Robert Graves, are to be found in Chapter 31 of the latter's *Lawrence and the Arabs*.

MRS CHARLOTTE SHAW
11.I.27

This is one of a flock of letters which say to everyone,

My address is

Room 2 out of a block of
8. The letters stand for
Engine Repair Section –
the mechanical shops – in
which I'm a messenger clerk.

> 338171 AC$_2$ Shaw
> Room 2. E.R.S.
> R.A.F. Depot
> Drigh Road
> Karachi
> India

I'd very much like that book of yours, for I have leisure, or shall have, to read it here, and the Indian atmosphere should be congenial to its philosophy.[1] Not that there is much of India about these stone built palaces in the sand. We are housed like hospital patients, sumptuously and barely.

The voyage out was better from Port Said to Basra (where I did not land), and overcrowded again from Basra to Karachi: so I am glad to stop here, only six miles from the port. Enough of travelling. Only one moment on the boat delighted me, as we steamed down the river from Basra for the sea, in early morning. The sun, not a third up its quadrant, was shining faintly against us through a mist. It cast our shadows on the deckhouse behind – a pale shadow only half our height; but across the shoulders of this shadow-body danced a blacker shadowed pair of legs: very strong and sharp these legs, with a curious shuttle-weaving play across their colour. I looked for the second illuminant, and saw that it was the projection of the sun from its image in the river: and the watering of the shadow-texture was a reproduction of the burnished ripples which sat firmly across the oiled water, dented into it, like hammer marks.

On the road out I read *War and Peace* (still good: very good: but not more-than-human, as I first thought) and all Pepys' *Diary* (Sub-human that! What a poor earth-bound lack lustre purblind worm). That, with Ecclesiastes and Synge's *Aran Islands*[2] represents all my recent food. Books are very dear here, owing to a duty which is charged on all imports, so please mark the value of

1 *See* letter to Mrs Shaw dated 24 February 1927 (p. 337).
2 J. M. Synge's *The Aran Islands* (1907), an account of the way of life of the fishermen and peasants of the Aran Islands off the west coast of Ireland, was based on his experience of living among them.

the books you send me upon a modest scale. The *Seven Pillars* is not 'worth' 30 guineas to me!

I suppose I should tell you something of this place but I cannot. There is five years yet for talk upon paper between us.

By the way Synge said apropos of Aran Islanders,

'There is hardly an hour I am with them that I do not feel the shock of some inconceivable idea, and then again the shock of some vague emotion that is familiar to them and to me. On some days the island is my perfect home and resting place: on other days I am a waif among the people. I can feel more with them than they can feel with me, and while I wander among them they like me sometimes, and laugh at me sometimes, yet never know what I am doing.'

That is not very finely said (the first sentence being clumsy), but finely felt, I fancy. One feels it whenever one is again amongst strangers.

T.E.S.

British Library

ERIC KENNINGTON
11.I.27

[…] My opinion of Karachi? None, as yet. We are seven miles away from it, and on the way here saw only squalid back-yards from the carriage-windows. I'm going to mope about camp in my spare time, and avoid pleasuring in the town, so far as I can avoid it. Housed well, and fed well, in a blinding wilderness of sand.

It seems years ago since I sat to you. How did the bust please you after all? It seemed to me, on that last sitting, not to be quite finished, but to be magnificent. I hope the magnificence did not depart when the finish came.[1]

[…]

Bodleian Library

1 Kennington had been working on the bust of Lawrence which is now in St Paul's Cathedral.

HIS MOTHER
11.1.27   *R.A.F. DEPOT DRIGH ROAD KARACHI*

I've only just got here, and cannot yet say what I think of the place. It is comfortable, almost magnificently-built, and cool. I am in room two, with fourteen fellows. It seems a quiet place, though the stone floors & high ceilings are noisy and distant, hospital-like, after the homeliness of Cranwell....

Before leaving England I got my *Seven Pillars* finished, & sent out the early copies to specially privileged subscribers. You will laugh at me to hear that the first went to the King: but he wanted one, & I amused myself by treating him well! Arnie has your copy, to keep till you instruct him to the contrary. Its completion takes a load off my mind.

[Chinese politics do not improve much, though I'm glad to see their anti-foreign bias.[1] Salvation comes from within a nation, & China cannot be on the right road till, like Russia, she closes her eyes & ears to teaching & follows her own instincts to their logical and absurd limits. So long as she permits outsiders to teach or preach in her boundaries, so surely is she an inferior nation. You must see that. People can take from one another, but cannot give to one another.

It seems to me that the inevitable victory of the Canton party may be delayed yet a long while, & that the disorder is nearly bound to spread up the river till it reaches you. The journey is unwholesomely long, even in peaceful conditions. In war conditions it might be very hard, even if not dangerous to you – and I have noticed that there are no foreign casualties in all this unrest – and therefore I'd urge strongly that it's Bob's business to get you out before you are both compelled to go. There cannot be any conception of duty to urge him to stay. In olden days doctors & medicine were respectable mysteries: but science is rather out of fashion now: and it seems to me that the fate of everyone upon earth is only their own concern. It is no merit to prolong life, or alleviate suffering: – any more than it is a merit to shorten life or inflict suffering. These details are supremely unimportant.

---

1 Lawrence was writing at a time of much upheaval in China, where a united front of Nationalists and Communists, strongly motivated by anti-imperialism and an opposition to Western ideas (hence his reference to 'anti-foreign bias') and actively supported by Soviet Russia, was engaged in a military 'Northern Expedition' (so-called because they were moving north from their original power base at Canton) to take over the country. Lawrence's concern at his mother's and brother's vulnerable, and in his view untenable, position in China was a regular theme in his 'home letters' from now onwards.

Of course you will do as you like: remembering always that you are the guests of China, & that guests should leave their hosts before the hosts are replete, so that their leaving shall be yet regretted.] [...]

N

Bodleian Library

MISS FAREEDAH EL AKLE
28.I.27   *R.A.F. DEPOT DRIGH ROAD KARACHI*

[...] This country, India, is not good. Its people seem to feel themselves mean. They walk about in a subdued, repressed way, also it is squalid, with much of the dirty industrialism of Europe, with all its native things decaying, or being forcibly adjusted to Western conditions. I shall be happy only when they send me home again, (which may not be till 1932). [...]

Bodleian Library

MRS CHARLOTTE SHAW
28.I.27   *[R.A.F. KARACHI]*

Work here ends each day at 1 p.m., except on Thursdays and Sundays, when it never begins. We get up at 6. The hours from 1 p.m. till ten at night are for ourselves to fill. [...]

The Depot is dreary, to a degree, and its background makes me shiver. It is a desert very like Arabia: and all sorts of haunting likenesses (pack-donkeys, the colour and cut of men's clothes, an oleander bush in flower in the valley, camel-saddles, tamarisk) try to remind me of what I've been for eight years desperately fighting out of my mind. Even I began to doubt if the coming out here was wise. However there wasn't much chance, and it must be made to do. It will do, as a matter of fact, easily.

The home papers seem to be yapping about me, a little. I believe *The Times* started them off, though I have not seen its article. The troops blushingly lay before me snippets of *The People* or *Tit-Bits*, which represent me as a marvellous rifle-shot or a master of back-chat. Odd that my ordinary present should breed that type of story.

Two letters, this makes, in three weeks, while you haven't an address! Not fair; but it's my fear that later on our letters may peter out. Space and time are as real, or unreal, as us, and will affect us.

By the way, on that last walk in London (its quietude a very blessed memory) as we crossed Maiden Lane you betrayed that it was your hand which each Christmas deflected a share of Fortnum and Masons' wealth to the little crowd of us in camp. I'd narrowed the probability of it to three or four people but couldn't tax them, for fear of getting three or four helpings the next year. The goods were enjoyed as you would have wished. My curious taste delights in exotic things (exotic in the Services means food rarer than beef or potatoes): and the other fellows, who perhaps hadn't lived in the wider world, loved the luxurious 'adventures' of peach-fed ham or foie-gras. Dispensing the bounty made me feel quite the patron. If you had been more patient of thanks I'd have given you a picture of the surprised delight of Clouds Hill when the first case arrived. However, enough said.

The weather is smoothly fine, with a warm sun at mid-day; but the dark mornings are very cold, and the evenings too. I shall be glad when the winter ends, and real heat comes along. Dust-storms come, however, in spring, nearly every afternoon, they say: and as all this Sind desert is sand, dust-storms they will be! Still it's worth putting up with that for the sake of being warm.

T. E. S.

British Library

MRS CHARLOTTE SHAW
24.II.27

[...] (vii) I've made a beginning on your little book.[1] A slow beginning, as throughout it will be slow progress, for my mind is inert, rather than curious or contemplative. Only abrupt contact with some flinty edge of actuality will strike a thought out of me. If I strive to dwell upon pure idea, my brain gets quickly moidered,[2] and wanders dreamily away down the broader problems of conduct. Conduct (doing) is really so much larger a subject than existence – not larger, perhaps, in the sense of feet and inches, but – well, you can explore Arabia, whereas we speculate vainly about Mars. To do a day's work, as I do, is only possible by taking for granted that we exist, a white lie which discourages us from being abstract-minded. Christianity has handicapped itself with a growing proportion of people since 1600 by apparently assuming (i) that we exist, (ii) that man is the centre of his universe, and (iii) that God is, more or less, analogous to man. When you say 'not proven' to (i), 'impossible' to (ii) and 'ridiculous' to (iii), then you lose patience with a crowd which fusses over details like transubstantiation. However your little book isn't so interested in super-structure as to neglect the foundations, so I have a better chance of liking it, than of liking S. Thomas Aquinas, who feels to me more like the founder of European dogmatic Christianity than its rather pitiful eponym. Also in this colourless place I have more time for speculation than ever before in my life. It's most severely colourless, except for the red roofs of the blocks and the red lamp on the top of the wireless masts at night. I do not like it much. Karachi town is seven miles off, and most of it, they say, out of bounds to us. I have not yet been out of camp, and feel no urge to go out, specially.

T.E.S.

British Library

1 The 'little book' was a pamphlet entitled *Knowledge is the Door*, written by Charlotte Shaw and published in 1914. It was a study of the views on life, faith, spiritual healing, etc., of American writer and lecturer Dr James Porter Mills, whom she met through the actress Lena Ashwell and by whose philosophy she had been deeply impressed.
2 *I.e.* bothered or fatigued.

ROBIN BUXTON
4.III.27   [KARACHI]

Dear Robin

It was good of you to send me that huge letter. This is a reply to it, *seriatim*.

1) Karachi will do as a place of exile. The C.O. is light-headed, & gives us too much drill. The work hours are too few. The country round is without form or colour. The natives are poor gruel-feeding mean-bodied things. Our rooms are comfortable, & the atmosphere of the camp friendly. I'm reduced to reading Greek for some wanton employment of my spare time. The voyage out was worse than anything I expected ... and my standards of living aren't high.

[...]

4) Kennington's bust of me seemed to me very good. K. is a very fine artist, I fancy. He will want a lot of money for each copy of it, probably. The papers say the *S.P.* is up to £150: perhaps, in rare instances: but I doubt whether it stays there. The public imagine there are only 100 copies. Actually no one but myself knows how many there were: 128 were more or less subscribed for: and I gave away half as many, some complete & some incomplete. If I'd put a decent inscription into the copy you are selling I could have raised its value: but in the rush of that last week I left undone all the little things I might have done. I'm glad you like the second copy. Sell them both if you get bored with possession!

[...]

6) Anything you can reasonably do to keep Pike afloat is a good deed. I respect the man, & am very sorry for him. I hope he has finished the distribution to subscribers. By my letters I judge he has nearly finished.

7) 'tempt you to divulge your feelings about your life'. Well: I feel that the complication is past: & with it the last vestige of responsibility for what I did in Arabia. Under Winston I put in order the actual situation in the Middle East, to my full content. In the *S.P.* I've put on record my 'why' and 'how'. So now that is all over, and I'm again a private person, and an insignificant one.

It remains for me to do something with the rest of my life. Having tried the big things & collapsed under them, I must manage something small. The R.A.F. in England suits me perfectly. If I could be always fit and at home and not grow old I'd stay in it for ever. India is exile, endured for a specific purpose, to let the book-fuss pass over. After India I may be still fit enough for a little more service in the R.A.F. at home. When my health drives me out of it (or Trenchard drives me out!) I'll try & get some quiet job, near London, which is the place I like. A night-watchman, door-porter, or else something like a chauffeur: though I will soon be too old for anything exposed. Perfection would be to do nothing: to have something like a pound a day from investments, & live on it, as I very well could. I've learnt a lot about living in the last five years: and have a curious confidence that I need not worry at all. Desires and ambitions & hopes and envy … do you know I haven't any more of these things now in me, for as deep down as I can reach? I am happy when I'm sitting still, in complete emptiness of mind. This may sound to you very selfish … but the other fellows find me human, & manage to live with me all right. I like so much the being left alone that I tend to leave other people alone, too.

Yours ever
T.E.S.

[…]

Bodleian Library

MRS CHARLOTTE SHAW
4.III.27

[…] Allenby sent me a very pleasant letter: talking of our co-operation, and enclosing a message from Lady Allenby, who was always friendly. This relieves me, for it has been a fear of mine that his sense of proportion (a very sober and stern quality in him) somehow associated my person with the ridiculous reputation raised about it by the vulgar. You see, my campaign and fighting efforts were entirely negligible, in his eyes. All he required of us was a turn-over of native opinion from the Turk to the British: and I took advantage of that need of his, to make him the step-father of the Arab national movement: a movement which he did not understand, and for whose success his instinct had little sympathy. He is a very large, downright and splendid person, and the being publicly yoked with a counter-jumping opportunist like me must often gall him deeply. You and G. B. S. live so much with poets and politicians and artists that human oddness attracts you, almost as much as it repels. Whereas with the senior officers of the British army conduct is a very grave matter.
   […]

British Library

ERIC KENNINGTON
25.III.27

[...] So you feel old sometimes! Here in Karachi I not merely feel old, but am old. And you want to create: whereas I've bust all my head's blood vessels in an abortive effort to create, and am condemned not to exert myself in future. What would you do in such a case? Say ha ha and blow your brains out? Too messy.

If only it were all over.

Yours
T.E.S.

Bodleian Library

MRS CHARLOTTE SHAW
29.3.27   *DRIGH ROAD KARACHI INDIA*

Your expectation of a fat letter will be roused by the fat envelope: but it is not so much after all. I write a day early, because of the probability that I may be on guard in a day or two. Your last letter was written from bed, ill: and it was depressed: partly because you thought I resented the preface of G. B. S.: whereas it gave me several readings of pure joy – (after the first, I didn't trust him for that, and dashed through it heart in mouth, wondering what would happen. Only he was discretion itself, considering all he knew. I take it as the greatest compliment I'll ever be paid) – and I've sent it on to China reluctantly. This Chinese business is looking very bad. I try not to dwell on it. Mother is old, and not well: and adamant.

I hope it was only because you were yourself depressed. I sent you the Indian cutting to show you how G.B.S. reaches all over the world: and round it wrote a true account of All Souls, because I thought he had not done that well-meaning club justice. He does not like Oxford (Oxford is heaven from 18-21 years old, and spoils its natives for after life) but Oxford is a great love of mine, into which I only wish I could fit, and I don't want him to think that I have a grouse against it, or the British Government. Both have been generous to me.

Your mention of Richards' rushing into print amuses me. I hadn't heard of it. He is an unworldly sincere, ill-mannered Welsh philosopher, who makes a living out of candidates for Sandhurst or the Consular Service by coaching them in special subjects. We were at Jesus together and at Chingford for a few days. My books are at his house (3 Loudoun Road) in St. Johns Wood. An interesting man. I dug out this letter I wrote him in 1918 to send you: partly because I have nothing of my own to say this week, partly because it may interest you, despite its slightness and carelessness, as the only war-letter of mine which has survived, to my knowledge.[1] He kept it, oddly and I found it interesting enough, in 1925, to copy for myself at Clouds' Hill, where he brought it to show me. Indeed I suspect it has a value, as my only side light of the Arab period. I don't think Hogarth has any letters of that date: if indeed he keeps them. I've never yet begun to wonder about that question of letters. Of course somebody will want to write a life of me some day, and his only source will be such letters as chance has preserved. Had they been all kept, there would be a pretty complete history of events since 1910: volumes of stuff enough to discourage any historian: but chance will winnow his pile down. Lately I have, regretfully, destroyed many letters of yours: with a feeling that you would not like them shown to strangers: yet they are first class, as pictures of today, and historically valuable. It's vandalism to burn them, and yet, wouldn't you rather choose to be unknown, if you had the choice? There isn't any question either, of waste, or buried talents: for everything has existed and will exist everywhere and for ever, after all.

Now I should say something about your illness. Flu probably: and if so your second attack this winter. You will probably say more about it when you write next: and by today it will be over. Bother that three-weekly gap between your speech and my ear. However in a fortnight we will have a fortnightly air mail, which should bring down the 17 day journey to 10 days: that means a very great deal to me.

As you say, I'm not really in India. I'm careful not to be. I am at Karachi, in the R.A.F. Depot, killing time there, till my books are forgotten, and I return to England. The time killing is on a heroic scale. I wonder if peace is really worth so many years of life. No doubt it is: but it is so complete a peace I can hardly realise that in England people must have talked quite a bit about myself and books. Not a whisper of it reaches here except in your letters, and in an occasional faded paragraph of the *Daily Sketch*, which is the reading-room paper. The English Press – in bulk, feels so old, after the three weeks and the journey. Whereas your cuttings do not date themselves. Odd, that is. It is good of you to send them: but I like them with a guilty conscience. You must spend too much of your very scanty leisure on them. Please do not over-do them, for my self respect's sake.

1 Letter to Richards dated 15 July 1918: *see* p. 162.

G. B. S. also sent me a letter last week. I wrote to him lately so we have crossed: and I won't write again yet. I have a feeling that letters to him must somehow be remarkable. It doesn't seem as though one could offer him any pearl less good than one's best: and when the pearl fishing is having a thin season there doesn't seem anything fit for him. I'd like to describe my oyster beds as exhausted. You cannot conceive how empty, uprooted, withering, I feel out here. It is really a case of having come to a stand. In England there was a current of life round me, and I swam in it: meeting people like you, reading many things, working at my book-printing, flying up and down the country on my Brough. And now my physical radius is cut down to a mile, my company to eleven airmen (two of my own draft from England, nine of previous drafts) all in the same uprooted state: with behind me the knowledge that I have finished the little show of activity which the revision of the *Seven Pillars* provided, and with a sense that this sense of having finished is really a conviction – a final certainty. There is not a germ of desire left inside my frame.

G. B. S. has tackled Baldwin again, apparently, on my behalf.[2] It is good of him, but he cannot play providence. Nor need he. The R.A.F. will not eject me again, at short notice. I give no one any offence out here: and in three years or five, when I come back, my books will have been forgotten, and will have taken all the sparkle out of my supposed romantic character, by having been forgotten. *Revolt in the Desert*, after the appetite excited by Lowell Thomas, comes as a dose of bromide, an anti-climax. Cape sent me a copy and I've looked through it and two of the fellows in the room have read it. They (spontaneously) confessed that it was a 'binder' (indigestible) through which only their knowledge of me had sustained them. You will find that the popular view, and all the people annoyed with my late reputation will now have their chance. So I calculate that I shall not be deprived of my living in the R.A.F. for at least the next seven years, by when I shall be 45, and approaching infirmity of body. Not really infirm, but too stiff and brittle to keep my place in the ranks: perhaps to want to keep it It is a hard life, even for a man with my history of privations. I'll leave with a good character, and that will enable such friends as Robin Buxton to recommend me for a London job. My aim is something like night-watchman in a bank or city office – a very quiet style of living, not physically arduous, nor much sought-after. To work at night and sleep by day is not the life for everybody: but it will suit me well enough, for I am solitary by nature, now, and will grow more so, in time, since my friends are nearly all much older than myself.

2 G.B.S. had been campaigning for Lawrence to be offered a pension for his services to the nation.

It is not like G. B. S.' programme for me, of £1000 a year, and a dispensary of patronage (Patronage! — and I'm like a squeezed orange, now being sun-dried) but it is likelier to be the real event. Do please suggest it to him, some day when he is in a smooth, receptive mood. It is hard for him, with all that inherent force and courage, to credit a man's being worn out at thirty-five. I feel as though the slow black oxen of the verse had been trampling their heavy way up and down my prostrate self, until there was not a whole bone or serviceable sinew left.

Apologies for so much introspection. But it represents no more than my life out here. [. . .]

British Library

MRS CHARLOTTE SHAW
14.IV.27   *DRIGH ROAD KARACHI INDIA*

Two letters, really, last week. One, convalescent from the shelter on a fine day (all days here are fine, though the weather is still too cold, for my pleasure. Not once, since arrival have I felt that rich sticky hotness all over me. However it is mid April, now, and if they ever have any warmth in this ramshackle country, it must soon declare itself), all full of sunshine and spring winds. Very good. The second letter from London (obviously you are really better) discussing Winston and Plato, in that order.

And I am facing a blank. No sensations, feelings or desires since I wrote to you last. And even in books not much to say, for lately I've mooned about the camp or aerodrome in my spare time (which is now not as much as it was, because I have two jobs together) hardly opening a page. No Greek at all. I think the book reviews of *Revolt in the Desert* have worried me. You say you have seen some common notes in them. I've only been jarred by the improbabilities they spray out. 'Genius' comes once in each, ten times in some. Who are they to judge genius? I haven't the slightest awareness of any in myself. Talent, yes, a divinity of talent: but not the other quality which dispenses with talent and walks by its own light.

'Modesty' recurs: whereas I *meant* the abridgement to feel modest. Anything loud was excised, and little odd bits left in, as it were accidentally, to show the readers that, though not stressed, I was really in the middle of things. And if the modesty is deliberate or even conscious, then it's really a clever man's improvement upon pride. The reviewers have none of them given me credit for being a bag of tricks — too rich and full a bag for them to control. Nor have they seen (Col. Pope-Hennessy, whom I don't know, and haven't heard of before, least of all seen) that the Arabs were, as individuals, magnificent fighters. Used in single-man battles, as I used them each was equal to three Turks: the issue of the campaign would have been the same, but quicker and easier for me, if the enemy had been British troops. We'd have gone through them like brown paper.

At the same time your Colonel has seen the intellectual basis of my lack of race feeling. It's because men are all puppets – but not, as he thinks, my puppets – God's, whatever every person means by the word God.

It's odd that I should pay attention to these cuttings, when I would not, probably, pay any attention to the reviewers' opinion if I met them in the flesh. I take it as a sign that perhaps my mind is not sound on the belief that my writing is no good at all. My appetite for action would be wild with delight if the rest of me could be brought to believe that its productions had an absolute value: but if you want to believe a thing very badly, it's a good reason for believing the contrary. Yet I like reading Mr. Robert Lynd and Mr. Ralph Straus and the rest of them *Ita sunt avidae et capaces meae aures*[1] ... that was Cicero's confession, I remember. I don't think that Cicero had much to plume himself on. An eloquence which died with him, like an actor's art; a policy which was doomed before he had enunciated it; some unreadable speeches; some dressed-up letters. Nobody ever wrote a good letter in a fair copy. It's the first draft, or none. Believe me, who write the worst imaginable letters to everyone except yourself, and to yourself too! Only I'm so dazzled at our success in keeping the game going (three or four letters in the air at once) that I refuse to confess the total failure of my share. You know, to no one else can I, or do I, write anything at all. My mother hears from me about 4 times a year, and banalities only. I would like you, if you agreed (it is to take a risk) to see her if she comes to England now that China has closed itself to her. Mother is rather wonderful: but very exciting. She is so set, so assured in mind. I think she 'set' many years ago; perhaps before I was born. I have a terror of her knowing anything about my feelings, or convictions, or way of life. If she knew they would be damaged, violated, no longer mine. You see, she would not hesitate to understand them: and I do not understand them, and do not want to. Nor has she ever seen any of us growing, because I think she has not grown since we began. She was wholly wrapped up in my father, whom she had carried away jealously from his former life and country, against great odds, and whom she kept as her trophy of power. Also she was a fanatical housewife, who would rather do her own work than not, to the total neglect of herself.

1 'So keen and receptive are my ears.'

And now two of my brothers are dead, and Arnie (the youngest) and I have left her, and avoid her as our first rule of existence: while my eldest brother is hardly her peer or natural companion. It is a dreadful position for her, and yet I see no alternative. While she remains herself, and I remain myself it must happen. In all her letters she tells me she is old and lonely, and loves only us; and she begs us to love her, back again, and points us to Christ, in whom, she says, is the only happiness and truth. Not that she finds happiness, herself.

Of course I shouldn't tell you all this, but she makes Arnie and me profoundly unhappy. We are so helpless; we feel we would never give any other human being the pain she gives us, by her impossible demands, and yet we give her the pain, because we cannot turn on love to her in our letters, like a water-tap; and Christ to us is not a symbol, but a personality spoiled by the accretions of such believers as herself. If you saw her, you whose mind has not grown a shell-case, perhaps you could show her the other sides and things of which she does not dream. If only she would be content to loose hold of us.

My father was on the large scale, tolerant, experienced, grand, rash, humoursome, skilled to speak, and naturally lord-like. He had been 35 years in the larger life, and a spend-thrift, a sportsman, and a hard rider and drinker. My mother, brought up as a child of sin in the Island of Skye by a bible-thinking Presbyterian, then a nurse-maid, then 'guilty' (in her own judgement) of taking my father from his wife.... To justify herself she remodelled my father, making him a teetotaller, a domestic man, a careful spender of pence. They had us five children, and never more than £400 a year: and such pride against gain, and such pride in saving, as you cannot imagine. Father had, to keep with mother, to drop all his old life, and all his friends. She by dint of will raised herself to be his companion: social things meant much to him: but they never went calling, or on visits, together. They thought always that they were living in sin, and that we would some day find it out. Whereas I knew it before I was ten, and they never told me; till after my father's death something I said showed Mother that I knew, and didn't care a straw.

One of the real reasons (there are three or four) why I am in the service is so that I may live by myself. She has given me a terror of families and inquisitions. And yet you'll understand she is my mother and an extraordinary person. Knowledge of her will prevent my ever making any woman a mother, and the cause of children. I think she suspects this: but she does not know that the inner conflict which makes me ·a standing civil war, is the inevitable issue of the discordant natures of herself and my father, and the inflammation of strength and weakness which followed the uprooting of their lives and principles. They should not have borne children.

There, that's too much I expect. You have the formative mind and will understand better than I do, or can. Or else you will not understand and will leave her alone. Don't let's, any way, discuss it again. It leads only to a general unhappiness.

T.E.S.

British Library

H. H. BANBURY[1]
20.4.27

[...] 'T. E. L.' Well, I'm 'T. E. S.' now, and may be T. E. anything shortly, for only the first two are authentic names. Original family began with 'C', but is not to be used, because the authentic family does not approve of me. [...]

Bodleian Library[2]

STEWART LAWRENCE NEWCOMBE[1]
27.IV.27

Dear Monster

Life rolls on. Soon you will be lucky, and will go to England. I will not.

Thank you ever so for the huge tin of caramels. The Post Office here nearly fell in love with me, out of greediness. It was very brilliant of you to choose a tin as large and as heavy as that monstrous book of mine. It's a good thing we are both monsters: otherwise books & tins like that would give us aches in the lower part of our chests. Life, as I said before, rolls on. I wish the blessed thing had a decent top gear.

Moascar is hot.[2] You lucky creature. India is a land of shivers and storms. I haven't been once decently warm since we landed.

---

1 Regimental Sergeant-Major, Royal Tank Corps; at this time also serving in India.
2 The remainder of this letter, mainly concerned with answering questions about the press reaction to *Revolt in the Desert*, is printed in *DG*. This revealing paragraph was omitted.

1 Son of Colonel Newcombe, named after Lawrence: born 1920.
2 Near Ismailia, Egypt.

I enclose you some grains of the Sind desert. We eat them here nearly every day.

Love and tickles
T.E.S.

Bodleian Library

EVELYN WRENCH[1]
5.V.27   *KARACHI*

Dear Wrench
Your letter arrived duly, and has been thought over, but I can't imagine what
sort of a reception you'd give to the only sort of stuff I'd consider writing. I'll
never again use the name Lawrence, nor allow anything I write to be connected
in any way with the reputation I have made as Lawrence. Nor will I ever write
upon the Middle East, nor upon any political subject. Nor upon archaeology.

   If you want poems reviewed, anonymously, or literature (biography, criticism,
novels of the XXth Cent., sort of Forsters, Joyces, D. H. Lawrences, etc.) at an
interval of three months from the fountain head: – but of course you don't....

   Probably you didn't think at the time that I was 5,000 miles off, and had
finished with my Arabian incarnation.

   Best of luck to *The Spectator*, in your hands.

Yours ever,

If despite time and space, you still feel charitable, why I'll be delighted! I'm
not ambitious, financially (my pay, and sole resource is the R.A.F. 22/– a
week), and not proud, critically, for I've never imagined that my writing was
any good. So I'll do the very smallest stuff, gladly.

Bodleian Library

---

1 Evelyn Wrench (1882-1966) was founder of the English-Speaking Union and editor of *The
   Spectator* from 1925-32. He was knighted in 1932. He and Lawrence met through Lord
   Winterton shortly after the armistice of 1918. It was he who gave theatrical producer Percy
   Burton permission to stage Lowell Thomas's illustrated travelogues in London under the
   auspices of the English-Speaking Union.

MRS CHARLOTTE SHAW
12.V.27   *DRIGH ROAD KARACHI INDIA*

The languor deepens – not because of the climate, which remains, to my taste, on the cold side; with however, some beautiful warm nights, when it is a pleasure to lie still thinking: – but for some other mysterious reason. It may be old age, coming on: you know, I've had more sustained and fiercer physical ordeals than almost any man I've ever met: and always I watch myself for signs of a sudden breaking-down: one leg falling off, and white hair or baldness, and a mouthful of shed teeth as I wake at dawn. Well, it may be the approach of that which makes me so slowly contented now with leaving undone the things I ought to do: not my R.A.F. work: that I do punctiliously. Which reminds me of something I've forgotten this morning.

Right, I have now swept out two rooms, which is my daily duty. I do that while the others go on parade, and thence to work. So most people call it 'a scrounge': that is, an expedient to avoid the parade. I'm delighted to miss the parade, of course: and in gratitude I sweep the rooms properly and conduct long careful hunts of mosquitoes, flies, ants, beetles, and bugs. The bugs are our chief trouble here. They live in the crevices of the iron beds and wooden fittings of the rooms, and plague us: but with creosote I've got them nearly extinct. Not quite because the sanitary section has now run out of creosote. However, with patience all things can be arranged. The room job also gets me off church on Sundays, a very great benefit. So in thankfulness for that I sweep and spray out my rooms on Sunday, which is considered extravagantly dutiful by my fellow-room-orderlies. There are five of us. We do it for the first hour every day. After that we go on to our proper jobs: in my case the keeping a record of all the little changes and defects and replacements of the engines as they pass through the shop on overhaul. [...]

Now, to your last letter from Malvern. [...]

(ix) I do not want you to feel that in burning your letters I'm doing anything wanton. It's not that. They are personal documents, and I feel that they belong utterly to me, when they reach me: as though you wrote them only for me, and kept no share in them after you had posted them. They could not be shown to anybody else, without breach of intimacy between us. They change with time, like ourselves. I do not want to meet my past, round some future turn of the road. It does not do to live at all in memory. Nor can I keep them safely: what place have I where to keep anything? Service men have the privacy of gold-fish in their bowls. The other fellows read my books, and see my pictures, and use my mug and plates, and borrow my clothes, and spend my money, and overhear and oversee every act and word and expressed thought of mine from sunrise to sunrise. So what room have I for a private life? To be sociable we must live only on our surfaces, and keep underground any elements in us which would be strange or uncommon in the room. Every room of troops has its key, like a broken scrap of music, and we tune ourselves to it. My past, and my outside life (which I used to lead in England on week-ends when I went off from camp solitarily on Boanerges, the lonely ride before and after separating world and service) are now done with, except in so far as your letters and books draw them out: they are my week-ends: and I do not want the others to share in what I feel about them. So after I have read them I burn them: (not the books: they go round, all of them, except your note-book, and the *Seven Pillars*, which are hidden in my box, and looked at by stealth).

(x) 'No man liveth to himself, and no man dieth to himself.' No: that's right: but don't you see that in choosing the services for a way of life I chose the first part of your saying, in its extreme and bitterest degree? and that the second part is a mystery, if it means anything? I suspect it of being only a sounding mask of words, in apposition to the first part, to round off the rhythm of the phrase. Living is dying, really. You sometimes are in a room, with your door shut. I, never: and by making public everything that was in me (in the *Seven Pillars*) I have robbed the grave of the chance of holding secret anything which had been mine.

T.E.S.

British Library

DR A. E. COWLEY[1]
19.V.27   *R.A.F. DEPOT DRIGH ROAD KARACHI INDIA*

Dear Dr. Cowley
Someone has muddled the sending of the *Seven Pillars* to you. It should have been preceded by the same list of conditions as Kenyon's copy
   i) That for two years it was the personal property of the Librarian.
   ii) That it was to be returned to D. G. Hogarth if the Library

---

1 Head of the Bodleian Library, Oxford (*see* letter of 29 October 1914, p. 68). The original of this letter is pasted inside the Bodleian copy of the subscribers' edition of *Seven Pillars*.

received another copy from any other source in the two years.

iii) That after the two years it might be transferred to the Library, but that it be made available only to [people *erased*] readers moved by some other motive than personal curiosity: and that this [condition *erased*] restriction remain in force till the book is republished after my death.

There, do you think I make an absurd fuss over a trifle? Perhaps; but a fellow doesn't feel his own private feelings to be a trifle: and mine, I fancy, is a book which would never have been written by anyone properly imbued with the public school [feelings *erased*] spirit.

Also I justify myself in making conditions on the grounds that the book is rare and valuable!

You'll have to index it under Shaw, that being my initials in it. God help the catalogue with me, some day, for not even Lawrence is the correct and authentic name which I will eventually have to resume. I've published as Lawrence, as Shaw, as Ross: and will, probably eventually publish as C². What a life!

Your letter came to me four days ago, with the last mail, to Karachi, where I languish for my sins in publishing a little bit of the *Seven Pillars* called *Revolt in the Desert*. I'm due to stay here till Jan. 1932, worse luck. I've put my address on the top of this scrawl: but Hogarth keeps in touch with me, & will forward anything you want to send him.

I hope your fortunes, & Bodley's grow no less. Increase isn't a thing to wish, blindly

Yours
T E Shaw

Bodleian Library

MRS CHARLOTTE SHAW
I.VI.27

[...] My brother tells me that mother has suffered a lot by her stay in China. I hope England will put her right again. She has been too long in unwholesome surroundings and ways of thinking. [...]

---

2 One of several hints that he hoped ultimately to assume his father's name of Chapman (*see* 'General Introduction', p. xxviii).

A surprise last week: the adjutant sent for me (our first meeting) and asked if I'd like myself recommended as clerk to the British Attaché in Kabul: a two-year plain-clothes engagement. I was taken by surprise: but explained that I wasn't a clerk, and couldn't undertake to make myself one at short notice. It seems to me that I'd better stick as tight to Karachi as I can: or to Drigh Road rather. Karachi remains seven miles away, so far as I'm concerned: and if it wants to see me, it must come up here: for voluntarily I will not pass the camp limits. I think that's a good rule. So I can be five years in India, and never see India or any part of India. Drigh Road is R.A.F. only, and might be any one of a hundred camps.

Please do not make public this offer of the adjutant's: the affair is to be confidential, I think. Probably the British military attaché in Cabul [*sic*] is only a glorified kind of spy. It would have been interesting to have seen the whole of the Khyber Pass: and I might have liked Afghanistan. However, it won't be. Safety first, as they say in 'busses [*i.e.* aircraft]. Better the camp you know… and Drigh Road is as hidden a place as any in the world. All Government land about it, and no residents or private houses or visitors. It's practically impossible for an outsider to meet me, against my wish.

T.E.S.

British Library

EUGEN MILLINGTON-DRAKE[1]
10.VI.27   *KARACHI*

Dear Mr. Millington-Drake
I haven't, yet, signed any copy of *Revolt in the Desert*: and do not expect to. Whereas I signed every copy of the English edition of the *Seven Pillars*.

This difference of treatment of the two books is evidence, I think, of the different regards I have for them. The little book is a mere pot-boiler, intended to pay for the big one: and will lose any temporary interest it may have when the big one is reprinted after my death. So I'd suggest that it isn't worth including in your collection?

---

[1] Eugen Millington-Drake (1889-1972) was educated at Eton and Magdalen College, Oxford, and became a distinguished career diplomat. He was at the Paris Peace Conference, was knighted (K.C.M.G.) in 1938 and was ambassador to Uruguay during the *Graf Spee* affair in 1939.

Headlam, of Eton,[2] has a copy of the full text, which he probably makes available to the few people in his neighbourhood who may be interested in the side issues of the war. You will realise that the Arab revival is in no sense a consequence of the war. It merely took advantage of it.

Yours sincerely
T E Shaw

If I do change my mind and autograph copies, I'll let you know. Improbable, though.

Eton College

H. S. EDE[1]
16.VI.27   *DRIGH ROAD KARACHI INDIA*

Dear Ede
I feel nervous. I'm an entirely ordinary person: nearly everybody is. There are 14 fellows in this room with me, and we are all, at once, of a muchness, and different. If you were here you would be 15th (and an unlucky fifteenth, for there are only 14 beds!) and that's all there would be to it.

When I wrote that book of mine I was trying very hard to do a thing for which I am totally unfitted by nature: – to produce a work of creative imagination – and all the strain of the unnatural effort came into the print, and affects people. At least that's the only explanation I can give: for the book, as writing, is entirely contemptible. A bag of tricks, quite unconvincing.

2 G. W. Headlam was a housemaster at Eton College.

1 Usually known as Jim Ede: at this time an assistant at the Tate Gallery, later the author of *Savage Messiah* (1931), a biography of the French sculptor Henri Gaudier-Brzeska, and the founder, in 1957, of Kettle's Yard, Cambridge, where twentieth-century objects and works of art are laid out in an environment which, in its deviser's words, is 'a refuge of place and order, of the visual arts and of music'. He had visited the exhibition of *Seven Pillars* pictures at the Leicester Gallery in May 1927 thinking that Lawrence was 'just another War Lord' but had been much taken by the tone and style of Lawrence's introduction to the catalogue; he then read *Revolt in the Desert*, and thereafter, even more impressed, began a correspondence which lasted till Lawrence's death and which he subsequently published in a limited edition under the title *Shaw-Ede: T. E. Lawrence's Letters to H. S. Ede 1927-35* (Golden Cockerel Press, 1942). All Ede letters in this book have, however, been credited to the Bodleian Library collection, which holds copies of them.

And you are judging by a fragment only. The whole affair is quite unlike *Revolt in the Desert*. May I suggest you develop your acquaintance with Kennington (or with Augustus John) and borrow from one or other of them the complete work? That gives the game away, and will destroy what I feel sure is an illusion which some accident of an unrelated remark on some page of mine has created in you. I couldn't have lived all these years with myself and not have seen I was a remarkable person, if I was.*

Yours ever
T E Shaw

*Perhaps you can see what I wanted to say. My syntax seems to have collapsed. Will you remember me to Aitken,[2] some day you see him? I used to plague him with offerings of small undesirable pictures.

Bodleian Library

HON. EDWARD ELIOT[1]   *DRIGH ROAD KARACHI INDIA*
16.VI.27

Dear Eliot
Yes, I want to change my name formally. Will you try and do it as quietly and inexpensively as it can be done? I'd better be
                    Thomas Edward Shaw
in future. Of Pole Hill, Chingford, Essex, if they require an address.

I'm in some doubt as to my previous name, for I've never seen my birth certificate. I fancy I was registered as born on August 15, 1888 (which was not the real date, however!)[2] at Tremadoc, in Carnarvon County, N. Wales. My father and mother, who were not married: – or rather he was, but not to her – called themselves Lawrence, at least from 1892 onwards. I do not know whether they did so when I was born or not.[3] He died in 1919. She is still alive. I believe Lawrence

2 Also on the staff of the Tate Gallery.

1 Lawrence's solicitor and a trustee of the Revolt in the Desert Fund.
2 He was actually born in the early hours of 16 August.
3 Both parents are named Lawrence in T. E.'s birth certificate.

was the name of her supposed father: but her mother (called Jenner) was not married to the original Lawrence. My father was a younger son of an Irish family called Chapman, of Killua, in Co. Meath. His own place was called Southhill, also in Meath. His widow, Lady Chapman, and her daughters still live there: but Killua has been sold. Debrett, I fancy, shows him as still alive: but actually, as I say, he lived with my mother elsewhere than in Ireland, from 1885 onwards, and died in Oxford in 1919 as T. R. Lawrence. Whether he changed his name formally or not I don't know. I suppose not, or his widow would have changed too, wouldn't she? They were not divorced: there isn't much divorce in Ireland.

I suppose we were an odd family, because it never struck me to ask him the facts of the name of Lawrence. His will might solve the question.

Perhaps, though, you won't require parents' names, for my deed-poll. Better not, if possible, for I don't want anyone to know about it, while my mother and step-mother are both alive. There are two or three skeletons, besides this, in the last generation's history.

Of course if Father registered me as Chapman, that will do, and there's no need to have the intermediate stage of Shaw, between Lawrence and it: for eventually, I suppose, Chapman it will have to be. There is a lot of land in that name knocking about: and I don't want to chuck it away, as Walter Raleigh, for whom I have a certain regard, gave it to my father's first Irish ancestor. I have a feeling that it should be kept in the line. My father's death wound up the baronetcy (a union title, of all the rubbish!) and one of my brothers is breeding heirs. So the family looks like continuing, in the illegitimate branch![4]

I'm sorry to give you all this rigmarole: but my complete ignorance of deed-polls leaves me in the dark as to what facts you require. I've tried to give you

   (i) my present name and address
  (ii) my since-birth name
 (iii) my father's name & address (he was a British, & not a Free-State subject: rather a hot unionist, too!)
 (iv) my mother's name
  (v) my date & place of birth.

4 Arnold Lawrence had one daughter.

I can't think of anything else they may want: except description or occupation. I'm an airman, now: and as 'Lawrence' was last employed in the Colonial Office as a temporary civil servant. I gave up the use of L. in August 1922.

Apologies again
Yours
T E Shaw

The Trustees of the Seven Pillars of Wisdom Trust

HIS MOTHER
16.VI.27   [*DRIGH ROAD KARACHI INDIA*]

I was glad to get your letter at last. I'm sorry you tried to write to me before, but hope there was nothing in the letters which the man who got them shouldn't read. [Airmen, you know, dislike mention of love and God because they care about these things and people should never talk or write about what is important. Intercourse, and particularly social intercourse should be limited to trivial things.]
[...]
I wonder what you and Bob will do. Low blood pressure is a good thing in reason: but he is probably tired, and will want a rest. He has been away so long that England will have become strange to him; and that is a pity, for there will be of course no question of his going back to China. [The civil wars will last for a while yet, and after that a violently national Government will want to restore Manchuria and Korea. So for a long time China will look after herself: indeed I think there will not be much missionary work done anywhere in future. The time has passed. We used to think foreigners were black beetles, and coloured races were heathen: whereas now we respect and admire and study their beliefs and manners.

It's a revenge of the world upon the civilisation of Europe.]

N.

HL/Bodleian Library

JOHN BUCHAN
20.VI.27   *DRIGH ROAD KARACHI INDIA*

Dear Buchan

(For I suppose you have dropped the Colonel. The label is a hindrance in politics, and a while ago I saw you in the Press, triumphing among the Scotch Universities.) Cape has just sent me a copy of the American edition of my *Revolt in the Desert*, and they tell me the introduction to it is by you. In which case I owe you many thanks. It is tactful, & interesting, and gives nothing away)[1]. So it pleases me, and it must have pleased America, for they say 120,000 copies of the U.S.A. edition have been sold. Cape has sold 30,000 in England, too: so my debt is paid off in lordly fashion, and I have nothing burdensome on my mind. In a few weeks, I hope, the English edition will run out of print, and be let die. Then Things will be quiet, by the time I'm due for home: though that may not be till the winter of 1931, probably.

The reference to the Tank Corps makes me think you probably did write it: it is a most excellent red-herring. Probably some of the other statements are also herrings: – as the ascription of the abridgement to Edward Garnett (the friendly man of letters!). Cape would not lend me Garnett's text, to edit: so I had make a new abridgement of my own, unaided except by two airmen from Cranwell. We did the whole thing in two evenings!

I wasn't rejected in 1914 for physical reasons. The W.O. were then glutted with men, and were only taking six-footers. As a fact I was then unusually strong. The *Seven Pillars* doesn't perhaps bring out clearly enough that I was wounded in nine different scraps (sometimes two or three damages at once: I have about 50 scars tallied on me) and had two attacks of dysentery, besides a touch of typhoid, blackwater, and much malaria. not to mention five broken bones. Also, I fancy I over-exerted myself during parts of the campaign, for I've never felt much good since. Yet in 1922, 1923, and 1925 the wreckage of my body was minutely gone over in recruiting offices, and each time I was passed fit for general service. So pre-war I must have been quite fit.

---

1 Buchan replied immediately to Lawrence's letter: '... alas! you are thanking me for something I did not do. I would not have dared to write an introduction to a book of yours, and certainly not without your permission.' Buchan added in relation to *Seven Pillars* 'When you do not get inundated with adjectives you are the best living writer of English prose.' (*Letters to T. E. Lawrence*, ed. A. W. Lawrence, 1962)

'Lawrence' like 'Shaw' was an assumption. My father's people were merchants in the Middle Ages: then squires in Leicestershire. In Tudor times they had promoted themselves to soldiering, and had married with a Devon family: by favour of one of these cousins (Sir Walter Raleigh) they got a huge grant of County Meath in Ireland, from Queen Elizabeth: and there they lived till the Irish Land Acts did away with most of the estate. My father had other troubles too, which made him change his name, & live abroad, in Wales and England, the latter half of his life. So there weren't any Lawrence ancestors or relations: but it's not my line to say so, since the fiction is less trouble than the truth.

My 'two-year expedition in native dress' is also fiction. All my walking tours in Syria were done in European clothes: and four months was the longest. I only wore Arab kit on one or two short treks after forbidden antiquities.

The three destroyed copies of my 'Oxford' proofs are accountable for: One was cut up to make Garnett's abridgement: and I needed two to make my own, more detailed, new text for Pike's printing. There are still the five bound copies in my hands: or rather, belonging to me, and stored with Hogarth, Kennington, Alan Dawnay, Mrs. Bernard Shaw, and E. M. Forster. I think of destroying them, eventually, so that only a single text shall survive to posterity! The *Seven Pillars*, as you know it, is a condensation, not an abridgement, of the Oxford text: and I think it is technically much better.

There, you probably know all this and more, & were throwing dust in the public's eyes. Serve them right, though I haven't the art to do it myself.

It will amuse you to know that my satisfaction with R.A.F. life keeps me contented in this dismal station and country. We spend much of our time playing infantry-games! However it is only for a term of years: and my appetite for England will grow & grow & grow, till, upon return, I'll lie down in the Strand and start eating the pavement in hungry delight. With any luck I'll have three years more to serve, after I get home. They will be great years.

Yours ever
T. E. Shaw

This letter is designed so as not to require an answer. It is written because I think you have again put me in your debt. I hope your copy of the *Seven Pillars* was a sumptuous one. I gave that order, but could not stay to see it done.

Bodleian Library

FRANCIS YEATS-BROWN[1]

23.VI.27   *R.A.F. DRIGH ROAD KARACHI*

Dear Yeats-Brown

[...] Did I say I'd review for you, or *try* to review? I'm not a writer by instinct, you know, & things come to me slowly with immense difficulty: and the quality of the things doesn't impress me, any more than the way I put them.

However I'm going to have another try. My last two employers cast me away very firmly, after a trial. I'm expecting you to do the same.

The books you mention in your letter of June I have not turned up. Book-post is quick; parcel post twice as long. Any way India is far off, so you must choose me subjects which, like Stilton, are the better for a little keeping.

D. H. Lawrence I'll be delighted to have a try at. I've read all his stuff since *The White Peacock*.

Hakluyt is only a name to me.[2] So on that you'll get the reflection of a fresh mind: if it does reflect anything.

The Koran is barred. Nothing Arabian or related. Besides it's a proper mess of a book. A mixture of Bradshaw and major prophet and police news.

Balzac: perhaps. I like him, like Shakespeare, at times.

Guedalla I had the misfortune to meet at Oxford.[3]

Disraeli's novels: no: I think not. I got through two of them. It was nearly as sad stuff as Chesterton's.

I'll do you the best I can: and will trust in you to turn it down at once if it doesn't reach *Spectator* level. Wrench suggests a pseudonym. Colindale was the last Tube Station I entered.[4] How's that? Split in halves? There's an American novelist called Dale Collins: but I can't think of anyone called Colin Dale.

Yours

T E Shaw

Bodleian Library

1 Major Francis Yeats-Brown (1886-1944), soldier and writer (notable for *Bengal Lancer*, published in 1930) was the literary editor of *The Spectator*. He had written to Lawrence following the latter's favourable response to the approach of his editor, Evelyn Wrench, who was also his cousin.

2 Richard Hakluyt (1552-1616), geographer, historian and publicist of English explorations in the New World.

3 Philip Guedalla (1889-1944): Balliol-educated popular biographer and historian.

4 Presumably because it is the nearest station to R.A.F. Hendon on the London Underground.

SERGEANT A. PUGH
30.VI.27   *KARACHI*

Dear Sgt

Another letter! Really I'm getting a marvellous good writer. Do you remember
how that tray on the table used to get blocked solid: and how then I'd stuff
the new-coming letters into those pigeon holes on my left, till they too were
tight: and then we'd light the stove, & I'd chuck the time-expired ones by
armfulls into the fire, and groan over answering the rest?

Yet it was easy in 'B' Flight. *Here, I have to do all my letters in my own time.*
Terrible: or it would be if we worked eight instead of five hours a day: and if
I had the proofs of a book to correct in my evenings, and tarred roads and a
Brough for my spare afternoons. But there aren't any of these things. I write
no more: there is only one road (from Drigh Road to Karachi) and no motor-
bike. Indeed, I keep clean my record of having not yet been outside camp
bounds. Imagine an airman six months at Cranwell without going out!

We were all very sad here when Carr did not get here, the first time: and
we all said 'Bad show' when he didn't get here the second time.[1] The first try
was such a very good one, that the failure of the second machine came as a
shock. I hope the R.A.F. will go on till they get the record, now, if they lose
every H.H.[2] in the service whilst trying.

Karachi Depot will not rival Cranwell in such efforts. The R.A.F. here is
distinguished only when it turns out in infantry order for royal birthdays or
Vice regal visits. On Nov. 3 I am going, in my person, to line a little bit of the
street in honour of the second personage.[3] Usually on these occasions a group
of six-foot people take station behind my back, and use me as a convenient low
shelf for leaning on to view the procession. Street-liners should be as tall as
lamp-posts and as wide as pillar-boxes.

Life here is definitely better. They pay me full-up now: so I have plenty of
cash for stamps, and an occasional record (the Room gramophone is quite
good, though harsher than I like them). If you came past our door you would
hear Wagner & Mozart & Beethoven at all hours of the off-days. The other

---

1 Flight Lieutenant (later Air Marshal) C. Roderick Carr made two attempts to fly non-stop
from Britain – in fact from Cranwell to India: one in May, one in June. On the first he
ditched in the Persian Gulf; on the second he had to return almost immediately.

2 H.H.: Hawker Horsley, the aircraft used by Carr in his attempts.

3 The viceroy of India at this time was Lord Irwin, better known by his later name, Lord Halifax.

fellows prefer Layton & Johnson:[4] and some of them like jazz. However it is a happy enough family, and we pull together fairly.

You wouldn't expect an ERS,[5] 190 strong, to be as decent a unit as a flight, anyhow, would you. The great point of B Flight was that we worked together, & slept together, & could live together, too, if we wanted. It put everybody keen to play up to the others.

I've had one piece of very good news: in the shape of a friendly letter from a very big noise.[6] He gives me to understand that I'm not to be five years in India. Probably not more than three. God be praised, though I don't know whether it's quite good form to want to scrounge out of part of my overseas tour. Only I've spent now nearly 15 years of my life away from England, in spite of a tremendous desire to get fixed into England so firmly that nothing but death would get me out of it. People always want to do what they aren't supposed to do.

My little book has sold 30,000 copies in England, and 120,000 in the States. So all my debts are most royally paid off, and my trustees will have a small balance to get rid of, in addition. I am taking steps to close down the sale of the English edition, which is a stage forward towards my return home. At the same time my American publisher has gone one step in the other direction, by deciding to commission a 'life' of me, for the autumn. Hard luck, for I haven't I fancy, finished my life yet. However there is no holding these wild Yanks. So my friends conspired to put the commission into the hands of Robert Graves, a very good modern poet, and recent friend of mine. He will write something quite good, and not at all cheap: probably it won't suit the Yanks at all: but that will not grieve me. Graves will do his best to play the game by me. If he comes to Cranwell, be nice to him. He is absolutely to be trusted.

Give my regards to Mrs. Pugh, and to the flight, or rather so much of it as is still there!

Is Cranwell still decent? No trumpeters? no guards? no roll-calls? no general nonsense? Has the band stopped playing the Lincolnshire poacher? Does the hot water still work? Particularly I want to know if it's decently warm at reveille. Dusty will know. I used to bribe the stoker to do our fire first, in the mornings.

---

4 Layton and Johnstone (not Johnson) were a black singing duo who were later to make a popular hit in Britain by their recording of 'Happy Days are Here Again'.
5 E.R.S.: Engine Repair Section.
6 The 'big noise' was doubtless Trenchard, who had recently written to Lawrence.

I heard last post that Nigger is the complete clerk. Does he carry an indelible behind one ear & a pen behind the other? Warn him that I'm keeping my hand in. I do as much logging of repairs & overhauls every week here as he does in six months: and we get 12 gross of split pins per week. Help. Help.

T.E.S.

Bodleian Library

FRANCIS YEATS-BROWN
8.VII.27   *KARACHI*

Dear Y-B

There, I've got down to initials in which I feel more comfortable: because I don't know if you are man or woman. One never does these days – or any day really. Birth is such a toss-up. Till the child actually gets into the daylight it doesn't know its sex: and (except at tennis) there doesn't seem, later, much distinction in their performance.

This preliminary paragraph conveys the personal note. So your secretary (bound to be female, this one, at least) will lay this note before yourself. As I'm to write under a pseudonym I'd better be told how to address my contributions. The fewer people aware of C. D. in your team the better. For if talk began about that person I should cut his throat.

'If talk began'. I'm being more optimistic than I believe: but before starting a journey one should look where the road might eventually lead. I enclose you a note on D.H.L. Your books (taking 5 weeks by parcel post – book post is eighteen days) came to me on Wednesday (6/7/27). I read the three D.H.L.'s on Thursday, & have written this today. Too quickly, no doubt, but I did not want to keep you longer without a sample: besides I've been reading him since before the war, so that my mind was made up before this week.

As for the note, of course it's no good. By nature I wasn't meant to write. The job comes very hard to me. I can't do it without trying my very best: and if I've ever in my past written decently it was under the dire command of some mastering need to put on paper a case, or a relation, or an explanation, of something I cared about. I don't see that happening with literature and so I don't expect you to like what I write.[1]

I've signed it C.D. because it's the first, if you do print it, after all. I'd suggest the first five or six things worth signing be restrained to their initials. If the miracle continues after that (surely either your forbearance or my endeavour will break down) we might climb so far as Colin D., keeping the full truth about the D till it was certain that the fellow could write and had a character. In my heart I know he hasn't. People have been led away by his retinue of extraneous accidents.

Commend me to Wrench. Thank him for all your books. I'll try now to say something about Hakluyt, & Gerhardi, and some one new to me of the batch in hand.

TES.

Special apologies for the scruffy manuscript: but I have no typewriter.

Bodleian Library

EDWARD GARNETT
I.VIII.27

The slow months begin to total respectably. When I got here it was 7/1/27: and now I'm past the half year. Did ever free agent so long to be three years older?

This is a reply to your letter of June 27, which ended up with a well-introduced remark about my Uxbridge notes. I write this on the back of one, to show you that the not sending them as they are is only kindness to you. I wrote them pell-mell, as the spirit took me, on one piece of paper or another. Then I cut them into their sections, and shuffled them, as Joyce is supposed to have shuffled *Ulysses*, with the idea of curing you of any delusion you might be persuaded by the

---

I Lawrence's review of the novels of D. H. Lawrence was published in *The Spectator* on 6 August 1927. It is reprinted in David Garnett's *The Essential T. E. Lawrence* (Cape, 1951) and in *Men in Print: Essays in Literary Criticism by T. E. Lawrence* (Golden Cockerel Press, 1940), edited by A. W. Lawrence, which also reprints a review by Lawrence of the short stories of H. G. Wells. In addition, he wrote two other pieces which were printed and a third, about the works of Walter Savage Landor, which was not – however, both Garnett and A. W. Lawrence included this in their respective publications.

chorus of critical England to entertain of me as a person of literary promise or capacity – where was I? – Ah yes: to disillusion you as to my literary ability – where was I? Ah yes: – to show you that I can't write for toffee, I decided to send them you. You would have thought them the raw material of a paper-chase. I began at Clouds Hill to stick each class in some sort of order on to sheets of paper, meaning to have them stitched for you. But that did not work, for the sections were too intertwined.

So I am copying them *seriatim* into a notebook, as a Christmas (which Christmas?) gift for you. It is a posh manuscript, in my most copper-plated hand. It will be bound, and gilt-edged. Can I do more? (or less.) Please regard it as an expensive gift. Copying my old notes is like eating yesterday's vomit. I add nothing but take away repetitions, where vain. I 'did' three Church parades for example: and I believe they can be boiled to two: or even to one, which would be the quint-essence and exemplar of all my church parades.

Enough of this stuff. Do not expect it for ever so long. It is done against the grain. About a third of it is done. Am I making a fool of myself? Would you rather keep your illusion? There are sixty sheets like this. You understand they are not emotions remembered in tranquility: but the actual fighting stuff. Photographic, not artistic. All were in pencil. It's better than the *Seven Pillars*, in its class: as like as butter and cheese: that is, not like at all: but equally rotten. The *S.P.* showed that I could not ratiocinate: this that I can't observe.

DG

RALPH H. ISHAM[1]
10.VIII.27   *DRIGH ROAD KARACHI INDIA*

Dear Isham
Last week and this week your two very good letters came to me. It is most kind of you. I'll comment on the second: – [...]

My de-luxe edition was financed by a banker friend of mine, to whom I gave security of its original pictures, its subscriptions, and the title deeds of some land I have in Essex. (Annual value of land £50 a year, which mostly goes in rates:

I Lieutenant-Colonel Ralph H. Isham was an American who had served as a British officer in France and had been awarded the C.B.E. He had met Lawrence through Ronald Storrs in 1919. A contributor to *Lawrence by His Friends*.

capital value £3000 or more, as building land. I do not want it built over.) Total cost of the *Seven Pillars* was £13,500 of which £6,500 was covered as above. Balance of £7,000 has been met by the sale of *Revolt in the Desert* through Doran and Cape. The whole liability is now discharged, & I owe nobody anything.

Yes, I hate the East. It holds bad memories for me: and I am old enough to grudge my spending more years away from England, where only I feel at home. This is my fifteenth year abroad. Yet I had to ask the R.A.F. to put me on foreign draft, since the personal publicity unavoidable in connection with the sale of *Revolt in the Desert* would have rendered my life intolerable, and my presence a cursed nuisance to my C.O., in any camp in England. I am exiled, therefore, until the fuss of my books has died down in the Press. The R.A.F. will let me come in 1930 and it will not be safe for me to return before. So actually I'd be no better off as a free agent.

In England I found life in the R.A.F. not at all bad, after I got used to the rather bare conditions, and the excessive number of rules. When this foreign spell is ended, and I get home again I shall be quite happy.

Revolt in the Desert has sold enormously, and made a small fortune. I executed a deed by which its first receipts paid off my debts, and the balance is to go to a charity[2] in which I am interested. Did I tell you (I did not go about explaining myself) that I consider what I did in Arabia morally indefensible? So I refused pay & decorations while it lasted, and will not take any personal profit out of it: neither from a book about it; nor will I take any position which depends on my war-reputation. 'Arabia barred'.

Publishers would pay money for any article I wrote as 'Lawrence': but I have finished with that name, and printed all I mean to print about my war activity. I write occasionally under other names, but my stuff has no commercial value. I review books, and get myself free copies of books that way. There is no money in anonymous work. I can't write a novel, & if I did it would not be a good novel, probably. And I don't feel ambitious as a writer. I do not like the idea of struggling for 20 years, with a pen, pot-boiling, with the risk always of running dry. I can't, of course, write about Arabia. That is covered by the self-denying ordinance.

So you see the case is pretty hopeless. I have an excellent private intelligence, and have looked at myself and my prospects from every angle: and can see no way of bettering myself. I propose to stay in the R.A.F. as long as I can, it being the line of least resistance: and when it rejects me, to get a job as

2 The R.A.F Memorial Fund, re-named R.A.F. Benevolent Fund in 1933.

night-watchman at some Bank or block of offices in the City. You realise that I have no trade I can work at.

Lowell Thomas was 10 days in Arabia. He saw me for two of those, and again one day in Jerusalem: and afterwards I breakfasted with him once or twice in London. His book is silly and inaccurate: sometimes deliberately inaccurate. He meant well.

No, I have written nothing else of any interest: a little archaeology, some translations from the French: some reviews of books.

My father's name (& therefore mine) was neither Shaw nor Lawrence. But the other day I adopted Shaw as my legal name. So it will be that till further notice. It is a short simple name, easily pronounced and spelt.

There, in answering your letter I have written mine. It is exceedingly good of you to want to help me so much, and I'd not hesitate to take advantage of it if my sense of fitness would allow me to profit by you. But experience has taught me that I will inevitably turn down every job I'm given the chance of getting – the truth being, I fancy, that the service has become a second nature to me, and that I'll feel lost if (or when) it chucks me out.

My regards to Mrs. Isham, the *incognita*. Please tell her that the odds against my visiting America are huge. But after 1930, if ever you come to London (and all good bankers do) then we will be able to see each other. Let's hope for that.

Yours very gratefully
T. E. Shaw

Bodleian Library

MRS CHARLOTTE SHAW
18.VIII.27

DRIGH ROAD KARACHI INDIA

[...] I've not written any letters of this sort to anyone else, since I was born. No trust ever existed between my mother and myself. Each of us jealously guarded his or her own individuality, whenever we came together. I always felt that she was laying siege to me, and would conquer, if I left a chink unguarded. So when Graves asked me about letters[1] I told him that only you (for the recent period) and Lionel Curtis (for the Tank Corps period) held anything illuminating. Curtis' letters are

1 Robert Graves was writing, with Lawrence's help, a popular biography which was published later in 1927 by Cape under the title *Lawrence and the Arabs*.

essays in misery, for I felt like Lucifer just after his forced landing, at that stage of my career. Yours are — well I don't know — you know more of them than I do, for they are thrown off quickly, and never dwell in my mind. But I never have to be conscious of an audience in writing to you. We misunderstand one another only over my book-writing, which I think is putrid rubbish, and you think is good. I'd like to go further, and say that we'd agree in the fundamental point that it fully represented the author's character and spirit! But do you think any man could sincerely write himself down as putrid rubbish? Even the clearest sighted person will cherish somewhere a reservation — that he cannot be so poor as the stuff he creates. I think my books do me an injustice. Therefore I wish I hadn't written anything. I wish I'd burned them, after I'd written them, when I saw their shortcoming: and whenever I come across an old letter, I wish the owner had burned that, too. We would be happiest if we left no trace behind. [...]

British Library

F. N. DOUBLEDAY
25.VIII.27   *KARACHI*

[...] *Revolt in the Desert* now belongs entirely to a small Trust, of three decent people I know, who own all its present and future direct or derived rights, and have the obligation (after their expenses are paid) of applying all its profits to such charitable objects as meet with their approval. The not making any profit for myself out of what happened in Arabia (which I consider to have been a dirty show) has been a cardinal point with me since 1917. I've carried my scruple too far: to the point of having lost money over it. Today I'm much worse off than I was in 1916. But that is my own fault.

So you see the name 'Lawrence' bars itself. It is worth a lot of money, because of Arabia: whereas my father chose it for me because it meant nothing, to his family. The only authentic part of my name is the initials T. E. (they do not, I believe, translate into Thomas Edward ... but that's no matter) and most people who know me write to me as Dear T. E.! They feel safe at that. There aren't many things safe about what are beautifully called 'natural' children! [...]

Bodleian Library

H. S. EDE
1.9.27

Dear Ede

I cannot write fluent letters: indeed letter-writing is very grievously hard in camp.

Your criticism of the *Seven Pillars* interests me very much. You are the first person to come to it, after *Revolt*. The people who have read the *S. P.* find *Revolt* unreadable.

Your criticism hits the mark most justly. In the *S. P.* I started out to write a history of the Arab Revolt: and the first third of the book is an elaborate building up of the atmosphere and personality of the Revolt. After the capture of Akaba things in the field changed so much that I was no longer a witness of the Revolt, but a protagonist in the Revolt. So the latter third of the *S. P.* is a narrative of my personal activity. If I were going to re-write the book tomorrow I could hardly do it differently. The interests of truth and form differ, there as generally.

In making *Revolt* out of the longer book I had no preoccupation with history or truth. It was necessary only to make a book, by the use of scissors. So I produced a thing which has some design and unity, and is by so much less honest and real than the *S. P.* for these 'selected' designs which rule Art today are not quite true, ever; though aesthetically they give greater contentment. Only, when it comes to a choice (as it may come to each man once or twice) you know aesthetic goes to the wall, always.

I've got fever on me, so will stop writing what my eyes are too staring to read.

Yours
T.E.S.   *Bodleian Library*

E. M. FORSTER
8.IX.27   *KARACHI*

You get my first letter this week: anyway. Nearly I gave you my last letter of last week: but I had dysentery, and the flesh, being weak, suspected that the head was weak also. So I gave it a few days to settle down. All is very well now.

Your booklet (such a little one!) on *The Novel*[1] is superb. No other word fits it because there's a complete lack of superbity about the manner & matter of

---

1 *Aspects of the Novel* (Arnold, 1927), the text of Forster's Clark Lectures at Cambridge.

it. So that the total effect is superb shows that the novel really belongs to you. It's like sitting at the feet of Adam, while he lectures to a University Extension Society about the growth and development of gardens. As soon as it came I rolled it out flat, and galloped through it: the names of some of the books & people I liked or disliked were in it, all right. Two days later I galloped across it again, seeing more of them: and this week, if my stretching and shrinking eyes will hold themselves to a page for an hour – this week I'm going to begin to digest it. There's a curious difference in tone, between you and Lubbock.[2] One treats the novel rather like the glazed unapproachable pictures in a public gallery. The other talks of novels as though they were things one writes. I expect you will find it one of the best-selling of your works.

[...] By the way you called your novel-book 'a saucerful of last week's grapenuts'. And I called the *Seven Pillars* a 'builder's yard'. We do well in decrying our goods. Only you have the inestimable sauce of wit to make your seriousness tasty. The other day someone (disappointed) sent me a *Revolt in the Desert* to autograph. Before returning it I read some of it. Punk, of course: but better, so far as form & unity and speed and compactness went, than the *Seven Pillars*. Should I have mightily abridged the *Seven Pillars* before issuing it to subscribers? Say to a half? However I trust much to your collation. Robert Graves says he likes the Oxford text better. Its faults make it less chilly than the *S.P.*, to his diaphragm.

I'm sorry your short story isn't publishable. As you said, the other one wouldn't do for general circulation. Not that there was a wrong thing in it: but the wrong people would run about enlarging their mouths over you. It is a pity such creatures must exist. *The Royal Geographical Journal*, and *Journal of the Central Asian Society*, two learned societies, both found *Revolt in the Desert* indecent. It seems almost incredible.

I wanted to read your long novel,[3] & was afraid to. It was like your last keep, I felt: and if I read it I had you: and supposing I hadn't liked it? I'm so funnily made up, sexually.[4] At present you are in all respects right, in my eyes: that's because you reserve so very much, as I do. If you knew all about me (perhaps you do: your subtlety is very great: shall I put it 'if I knew that you knew . . .'?) you'd think very little of me. And I wouldn't like to feel that I was

2 *The Craft of Fiction*, by Percy Lubbock.

3 *Maurice*, Forster's overtly homosexual novel, written in 1913-14 but not published until 1971, the year after Forster's death.

4 Mistranscribed as 'sensually' in *DG*.

on the way to being able to know about you. However perhaps the unpublished novel isn't all that. You may have kept ever so much out of it. Everywhere else you write far within your strength. [...]

T.E.S.

DG/King's College, Cambridge

MRS CHARLOTTE SHAW
18.X.27

I'm writing in the Shop, in working hours, which is clean contrary to my habit, and wish: for I give the R.A.F., usually, a very honest day's work. But if they give me overtime, then I must fit my private affairs into their hours. Not that there are really any hours, of course: we are paid for 24 hours a day for seven years: but trade union habit makes everyone regard eight hours as a unit of working – so there we are!

Which exordium, and this letter, is called forth by your letter of meeting Feisal. Yes, that is a surprise. I'm awfully glad you liked him. For so long he was only my duckling: and I crow secretly with delight when he gets another inch forward on his road. When you think of the harrassed and distant figure of Wadi Safra in 1916 and then to the Hotel Regina Palace in 1927: why it is very wonderful.

After your letter came I lay awake all the Sunday night, arguing my position (in Arabic: how much of it I have forgotten!) with an imaginary Feisal. I made a distinct impression on him, and completely convinced myself. I don't think he wants me, really. Not even the nicest man on earth can feel wholly unembarrassed before a fellow to whom he owes too much. Feisal owed me Damascus first of all, and Bagdad second: and between those stages most of his education in kingcraft and affairs. When with him I am an omnipotent adviser: and while that is very well in the field, it is derogatory to a monarch: especially a monarch who is not entirely constitutional. Feisal often has to lead his people: which is seldom the conduct of G. R.[1]

Also peoples are like people. They teach themselves to walk and to balance, mainly by dint of trying and falling down. Irak did a good deal of falling between 1916 and 1921: and since 1921, under Feisal's guidance has done

1 George Rex, *i.e.* King George V.

much good trying and no falling. But I don't think it yet walks very well. Nor can any hand save it from making its messes: there is a point where coddling becomes wicked. All my experience of the Arabs was in the god-father role: and I think they have outgrown that. If they are to make good as a modern state (how large an 'if') then it must be by virtue of their own desire and excellence.

So that I remain unrepentant. I was right to work for Arab self-government through 1919 and 1920: and my methods then, though not beyond criticism, were I think reasonably justifiable. The settlement which Winston put through in 1921 and 1922 (mainly because my advocacy supplied him with all the technical advice and arguments necessary) was, I think, the best possible settlement which Great Britain, alone, could achieve at the time. Had we waited for the French to come to their right mind and co-operate in a complete settlement, we would be waiting yet. And after June 1922 my job was done. I had repaired, so far as it lay in English power to repair it, the damage done to the Arab Movement by the signing of the Armistice in Nov. 1918.

The people who want me to go on keeping my hand on the plough are either unfair to the existing ploughmen, or unfair to the plough. The class of work I was doing is finished. Had I continued to be connected with Arab affairs I should have had to change my style and subject and status. I thought it easier – no I thought it imperative, to change roles altogether. Hence the clean break with my past which the R.A.F. represents.

It's because I've chosen the R.A.F. that people make a fuss of my abdication from Arab affairs. If I'd accepted a Governorship – of Cyprus, or Jamaica, or Borneo, they would have taken for granted my leaving the Arab sphere. And their sense of proportion seems to me all wrong. It's as good to serve in the R.A.F. as it is to govern Ceylon: I'd say that it was much better. You may condemn all service life, by holding a pacificist view: and if so you'll regard all soldiers and sailors and airmen as more or less brute beasts: but I have no such views – indeed few views of any sort: and no feeling that one sort or class or profession of man is better or worse than another.

So much for the side of it which affects myself. For what affects Feisal, I'm happy, indeed, that you liked him. He is one of the best people I know. Your remarks about his tenacity interested me. He is both tenacious and weak: perhaps these qualities always go together. It is easy to swing him off his point: and when released he tends to swing back to it. Therefore the French called him treacherous. He was (and perhaps is) still quite weak: but, I agree, tenacious. Very gentle, you know, and very kind, and very considerate, and outrageously generous to friends, and mild to his enemies, and cleanly and honest and intelligent: and full of wild freakish humour: though I suppose that is a little overlaid with kingliness, now. He has been king for six years, which is a deep experience. I wish you could have known him as I did, when he was Feisal, just. One of the most attractive human beings I have ever met.

What you say about his looking young and happy and peaceful pleases me. Of course he has won great credit for himself: and that brings a man to flower. And in 1919 when John painted him he was up against very terrible conditions in Paris. No man could have looked other than broken with worry. Those five months in Paris were the worst I have lived through: and they were worse for Feisal. However, he learnt the whole art of politics, from them. Perhaps I did, too!

Feisal has been painted –

(i) By Aug. John. At Manchester Art Gallery.

(ii) ”　　　” In Kennington's house (TES. property)

(iii) By Orpen

(iv) By Laszlo

Sculpted –

(v) By Mestrovic (Victoria and Albert)

(vi) By Fudora Pleichen (in Bagdad)

There may be more. These I know. (ii) and (v) belong to me.

You know, without my telling you, how much I liked him. I talk of him always in the past tense, for it will be a long time before we meet again. Indeed I hope sometimes we never will, for it would mean that he was in trouble. I've promised myself to help him, if ever that happens.

As for Irak ... well, some day they will be fit for self-government, and then they will not want a king: but whether 7 or 70 or 700 years hence, God knows. Meanwhile Feisal is serving his race as no Arab has served it for many hundred years. He is my very great pride: and it's been my privilege to have helped him to his supremacy, out there, and to have made him a person, for the English-reading races. Gertrude has nobly supported him in this last effort. Her Bagdad letters give a splendid idea of him in action as a ruler.

Don't you think he looks the part, perfectly? Was there ever a more graceful walk than his? G. B. S. probably (being an emperor, himself) thinks poorly of kings: but he'd admit that I'd made a good one.

A very distinguished Person – to me in Nov. 1918,

'This is a bad time for Kings: seven new republics were proclaimed yesterday'.

me, cheerfully,

'Courage, Sir. I have made three new Kings in the East'.

Very distinguished Person 'I thought the remark was not in the best taste'.

Health absolutely as usual. Busy to death. A letter some day: post after next, probably.

British Library

LIEUTENANT-COLONEL F. G. PEAKE[1]
2.X.27   *R.A.F. DEPOT DRIGH ROAD KARACHI INDIA*

Dear Peake

Apologies, should this reach you, for invading your peace. One of our 'lads' called De Pellette (yes, I know it sounds bad: but actually he is a Glasgow Scot) asked me yesterday did I know anyone military in Palestine? I thought at once of you, and provisionally said 'Yes'. He then disclosed that his idea of a life and profession when he left the R.A.F. was in the Palestine Special Police. Are these what we used to call the Gendarmerie? He says they are mostly in Trans Jordan, and that they go out, when they speak Arabic, as Sergeants in charge of districts.

I told him that, possibly, if I worried you, you'd give me a verdict of the excellence of the force, and the methods of its recruitment and its terms. He is about 28: and will not be free for over a year. By trade a fitter, and says he knows any make of car-engine. Used to be engineer on motor-yacht. Learnt some Arabic in Mesopotamia, and is learning more. A very solid, silent, not-sociable person: his drink is beer: but not extravagantly. Never even unsteady. Alas: he's married. A plague of women. By the way, do read Gertrude Bell's letters. They are splendid.

I wonder if you still ride up and down that delectable land. I am often hungry for another sight of its hills. Rum, too. If only... Drigh Road, this place, is dismal. But in 1930 I am due for home, and then I'll be very happy.

Give my regards to the Emir[2] : if he remembers me.

Yours ever
T. E. Shaw.   *Imperial War Museum*

---

1 'Peake Pasha', commander of the Arab Legion in Transjordan, which he founded in 1920 and continued to command until his retirement in 1939. He fought with Lawrence in the final stages of the Arab war, and had a high regard for Lawrence's leadership and political vision.
2 *I.e.* Emir Abdulla of Transjordan.

E. M. FORSTER
27.X.27   KARACHI

Now I have your short story.[1] It's the most powerful thing I ever read. Nearly made me ill: and I haven't yet summoned up the courage to read it again. Someday I'll write you properly about it. A great privilege, it is, to get a thing like that.

Virginia obviously hadn't seen it: or she wouldn't have put so much piffle in her note on you.[2] Which note also holds some very good stuff. I liked it: but she has only met the public side of you, apparently. Or else she doesn't know the difference between skin and bone.

I say, I hope you know what a wonderful thing *Dr. Woolacott* is. It is more charged with the real high explosive than anything I've ever met yet.

And the odd, extraordinary thing is that you go about talking quite carefully to us ordinary people. How on earth....

However more later
T. E. S.

It is also very beautiful. I nearly cried, too.

King's College, Cambridge / Bodleian Library

1 *Dr. Woolacott*, a homosexual ghost story first published in 1972, after Forster's death, in a collection entitled *The Life to Come*. For further comment on the story, *see* Lawrence's letter to Forster of 21 December 1927 (p. 382).
2 In 1927 Virginia Woolf wrote an article on Forster, which was shown to him in draft and which did not please him. 'Part of the trouble', comments his biographer P. N. Furbank, 'though he didn't tell her so, was that he neither wanted to show her *Maurice* [his homosexual novel] nor to have his work summed up without it.' The article was later published in *The Saturday Review of Literature*, 17 December 1927.

SIR HUGH BELL[1]
4.XI.27   *INDIA*

Dear Sir Hugh

You will probably remember me as Lawrence, my war-time name: we met several times in Cairo when Gertrude and myself were playing a tune on the political conference there in 1921. I've just been reading the 'Letters' which Mrs. Bernard Shaw sent me, and they have been so great a pleasure to me that I felt I must write to you and thank you for letting them come out. Until they were announced I hadn't realised that Gertrude was dead; after the Cairo business had finished my war-work so honourably and completely I left politics and enlisted in the R.A.F., with whom I am now near Karachi in India. I don't write much to people, and each service is a world of its own, which talks nothing, and reads little, of the worlds outside. So my not knowing that is usual.

I think she was very happy in her death, for her political work – one of the biggest things a woman has ever had to do – was as finished as mine. That Irak state is a fine monument; even if it only lasts a few more years as I often fear and sometimes hope. It seems such a very doubtful benefit – government – to give a people who have long done without. Of course it is you who are unhappy, not having Gertrude any more; but there – she wasn't yours really, though she did give you so much.

Her letters are exactly herself – eager, interested, almost excited, always about her company and the day's events. She kept an everlasting freshness; or at least, however tired she was, she could always get up enough interest to match that of anyone who came to see her. I don't think I ever met anyone more entirely civilised, in the sense of her width of intellectual sympathy. And she was exciting too, for you never knew how far she would leap out in any direction, under the stimulus of some powerful expert who had engaged her mind in his direction. She and I used to have a private laugh over that: – because I kept two of her letters, one describing me as an angel, and the other accusing me of being possessed by the devil, – and I'd show her first one and then another, begging her to be charitable towards her present objects of dislike.

---

1 The father of Gertrude Bell, who had died in Baghdad on 12 July 1926. A two-volume edition of her letters, selected and edited by her stepmother, Lady Bell, D.B.E., was published by Benn in 1927 (re-issued by Penguin, 1987).

However, you won't want to know what I think; her loss must be nearly unbearable, but I'm so grateful to you for giving so much of her personality to the world. [...]

Yours sincerely,
T. E. Shaw.

Bodleian Library

MRS CHARLOTTE SHAW
10.XI.27

Yesterday Buxton wired me that Hogarth is dead: and that means that the background of my life before I enlisted has gone. Hogarth sponsored my first tramps in Syria – then put me on the staff for Carchemish, which was a golden place – then moved me to Sinai, which led to the War Office: which sent me to Cairo on the Staff and there we worked together on the Arab business, until the War ended: and since then whenever I was in a dangerous position I used to make up my mind after coming away from his advice.[1] He was very wise for others, and very understanding, and comfortable, for he knew all the world's vices and tricks, and shifts and evasions and pretexts, and was kindly towards them all. If I might so put it, he had no knowledge of evil: because everything to him was fit to be looked at, or to touch. Yet he had his own position and principles, and was unmovable on them. Till I joined up he did everything for me. It was the first thing I did entirely on my own. So lately I have seen little of him: but I always felt that if ever I went back to living I'd be able to link up with him again.

Tomorrow the Viceroy, and this horrible celebration of an armistice of long ago.

T.E.S.

British Library

[1] Lawrence's special relationship with Hogarth was known to his friends. On hearing of Hogarth's death, Alan Dawnay wrote to Robert Graves: 'His will be a loss that I fear T. E. will feel tremendously. I always placed him an easy first in T. E.'s friendships and a good choice it was.'

LIONEL CURTIS
17.XI.27   [DRIGH ROAD KARACHI INDIA]

My Lord

Hogarth's death (not unexpected, from the tenor of his last letter to me) puts me out of action, temporarily. He always seemed to me the ripest man I'd met.

Call this not a letter but my answer to your note about Zimmern's *Who's Who*. Of course write anything you please: so long as you don't give away

(i) my original family

(ii) my present address.

I'd be grateful if you'd make it quite clear that in Winston's 1922 settlement of the Middle East the Arabs obtained all that in my opinion they had been promised by Great Britain, in any sphere in which we were free to act; and that my retirement from politics upon that, to me, happy event was necessarily final and absolute.

That is, if the biographies are such as to call for details. If it's only 'b. 1888 m. Eliza daughter of S. Dooly Esq. D.C.L. J.P. 2s. 3d. d. 1922' then so much the better. Do not give anything which could look like an address.

I believe D. G. H. wrote the *Encyc. Brit.* article. I have not seen it.

Who's Who pleased themselves over their note on me. They are a tiresome silly publication. Zimmern should have more sense.

Yours
T.E.S.

All Souls College Oxford

MRS CHARLOTTE SHAW
17.XI.27

[...] This week I send you a book. I've been trying to look at it with your realising its shabbiness and dirtiness, outside and inside, after seven years of keeping me company. I found that not even the *Oxford Book of English Verse* quite fitted my whim. So I took to copying, carelessly, in a little Morrell-bound notebook (a decent plain binding, once) the minor poems I wanted. Some are the small poems of big men: others the better poems of small men. One necessary qualification was that they should be in a minor key: another that they should sing a little bit. So you will find no sonnets here.

The worst is you do not like minor poetry: so that perhaps the weakness of spirit in this collection will only anger you: and then my notebook will not be a fair return for your notebook. In my eyes it is: for I'm not so intellectual as to put brain-work above feeling: indeed as you know, I don't like these subdivisions of that essential unity, man. It's like trying to pretend that our left hand and our right hand are hands as well as being ours. It's only our fancy to call them hands.

The book had only three or four empty pages when I sailed from Southampton and these I filled with a Wolfe poem and a scrap of Blake. In this last year I have slowly copied it into another book (with a few more blank pages) which will last me for another seven years.

You live always within touch of shelves, and can keep so many poets on tap that you won't feel how necessary a friend is such a notebook as this. Its poems have each of them had a day with me. That little hackneyed Clough, for instance, about light coming up in the west also: I read that at Umtaiye, when the Deraa expedition was panicking and in misery: and it closely fitted my trust in Allenby, out of sight beyond the hills. There's all that sort of thing, for me, behind the simple words.[1]

T.E.S.   *British Library*

B. H. LIDDELL HART[1]
17.XI.27   *DRIGH ROAD*

Dear Captain Liddell Hart
I'm putting this down to your innocent account: it must have been your letter to me which gave the perfectly damnable business side of the *Encyclopedia* my address. It's one of the world's worst firms: they used to send (indeed probably they still send) to me at All Souls, as to every fellow on its books, pages of

---

I The book affectionately described in these paragraphs, to which he gave the name *Minorities* and which contained 112 poems, was published by Cape in 1971, with an introduction and notes by J. M. Wilson. The 'little hackneyed Clough' is the famous poem by Arthur Hugh Clough beginning 'Say not the struggle naught availeth'.

I Captain Basil (later Sir Basil) Liddell Hart (1895-1970): distinguished, and frequently controversial, military historian and thinker, and future biographer of Lawrence.

frantic adjuration to buy something or other from them for 30/– as a final and unique chance! My prejudice against their method (they were clearing off the old stock before producing a new edition) became so strong that I feel a slight irritation at the mere sight of the *Encyc. Brit.*

Now, if they address me with two names, by the public post, they will do me a good deal of harm. Will you do me the favour of going to the business branch, and rooting out of their card catalogue every trace of my being, either as Shaw or Lawrence? It's a mockery to expect a fellow with a net income of below a pound a week to buy such a whale of information, as they sell. And If I had ten pounds a week I wouldn't buy it. Information isn't a thing I go hungry for.

I hope you'll manage this, reasonably soon: otherwise they'll sell my address to other advertising firms, and my already cumbrous mail will become impossible. Also perhaps they'd go on putting all the names and titles I'm doing my best to live down on the envelopes.

Yours sincerely
T. E. Shaw[2]

Liddell Hart Centre for Military Studies, King's College London

2 Liddell Hart commented:
'He enclosed with the letter a printed post-card addressed to:
Col. Lawrence, 338171. A.C.2. Shaw,
Room 2, E.R.S., R.A.F. Depot,
Drigh Road,
Kaveehi. India.
If this address was a grotesque example of clerical error, obviously inconvenient, the card itself bore nothing more serious than a notification, sent out to all contributors, that the offices of the *Encyclopedia Britannica* were being moved to Regent Street.' The story behind this curious exchange with Liddell Hart is an interesting one. Asked to contribute an article to the fourteenth edition of the *Encyclopaedia Britannica* (to be published in 1929), on guerrilla warfare, a subject of which he was deemed to be a leading, if not *the* leading, British expert, Lawrence refused. Ultimately, however, he agreed that the task should be undertaken on his behalf by Liddell Hart, who was, in fact, the encyclopaedia's military editor. Liddell Hart set to with a will and produced a highly readable article out of Lawrence's various writings which is an excellent summation of Lawrence's strategical views. The article is published, with a full explanation of its provenance, in my anthology of Lawrence's military writings, *T. E. Lawrence in War and Peace*.

DAVID GARNETT[1]
30.II.27

Dear Garnett

That was a very pleasant letter to get: the *Seven Pillars* interests me so much, because I nearly burst myself trying to write it, and when I'd finished it, seemed rotten to my judgement. It still does. I'd meant something so much more and different, while doing it.

[...] Your praise of certain (not named) paragraphs of the *Seven Pillars* is probably just. It is not difficult to write a good paragraph, I think. But it is enormously difficult to write a good book. The balance of parts, the movement of the whole frame along the ground, the architectonics, as SS[2] calls them: — those are the real things. An architect does not call his plan good till it suggests the elevation: nor the elevation good till it suggests the rooms behind. The decent paragraph is only the carving of an ornament on one stone of the house, & is as easy in a bad house as in a good one, so long as the workman likes it. Your saying that my tale moves, like us, on Damascus, is the best news I could have had. But it does not move as surely as we did; and the reality of the men who rode with me has somehow evaporated from my ink. I am not so sure I was lucky in my subject; it was recalcitrant to a degree, and I went over it 20 times to shape it somewhat. If only I could have invented! In the Irish Revolt Figgis[3] had a similar subject, though, to my judgement, an easier one; yet it has defeated him, as signally as mine did me. Indeed I'm not sure that my book isn't the better of the two.

[...] You say it is odd as the only book by a man of action interested in motive; but surely it makes clear that I am not a man of action. I only filled

---

1 David Garnett (1892-1981), son of Edward and Constance Garnett and grandson of Richard Garnett, was a novelist, critic, biographer (of Pocohontas), autobiographer (in three volumes, *The Golden Echo*, *The Flowers of the Forest* and *The Familiar Faces*), and an associate of the Bloomsbury group. He was a conscientious objector in the First World War but served in the R.A.F. in the Second. As well as editing the letters of Lawrence, he edited the novels of Thomas Love Peacock and his own correspondence with T. H. White. He was sometimes referred to by Lawrence as Garnett iii. At this stage the two men had not met. Garnett began their correspondence; the above paragraphs are from the extremely long letter which Lawrence wrote in reply.

2 SS: Siegfried Sassoon.

3 Darrel Figgis, Irish writer and nationalist, who had been involved in 1914 with Erskine Childers in the gun-running to Howth and had been a prominent member of Sinn Fein throughout the Irish troubles, had recently (1927) published his *Recollections of the Irish War*.

the place of one, because none was available. I'm much better at writing than at soldiering and as I don't think my writing any good, you'll realise where I put my military capacity. […]

Bodleian Library

C. F. BELL   *KARACHI*
14.XII.27

Dear C. F. B.

I sent you a wire (laconic, because I had only 5 rupees free to spend on it) last pay-day, withdrawing my trustees' offer of the John portrait of D. G. H. I hope it will be clear enough to enable you to take action. Will you return it to Colonel R. V. Buxton

c/o Martins' Bank
68 Lombard Street.

   I'm sorry: because I liked the little drawing, as a portrait. I know I don't understand art enough to appraise it, that way: but two or three experts told me it was good. It was very like D. G. H., too. I knew he didn't like it: but I like none of my portraits, which are sixteen in number![1]

   However, there it is. I shall be glad to have it, myself, if I ever have a place where I can put it. In barracks its life would be too uncertain. Also they do not encourage us to put up pictures!

---

1 The portrait of Hogarth in question was drawn for, and was included in, the subscribers' edition of *Seven Pillars of Wisdom*; it was also included in *Revolt in the Desert* and the 1935 *Seven Pillars*. It was not, however, popular with its subject or his friends. Bell's explanatory note preserved with this letter gives the background: 'At Lawrence's request Hogarth spent a morning in [Augustus] John's studio. Hogarth described the artist's *modus operandi* with much humour. John made some five or six sketches in block chalk or charcoal and threw them on the floor as they were finished, and children and dogs ran about over them. At the end of the morning John picked out that which he thought best, or was least damaged, and said that was the portrait to be kept. Later on Lawrence suggested giving it to the Ashmolean and handed it over to Hogarth who brought it to me, asking what could be done with it as he couldn't bear it hanging in the Museum. I suggested that it should be removed from the frame and put away. This was done. I think everybody but Lawrence thought it a brutal libel, not even a caricature. After Hogarth's death Mrs. Hogarth particularly desired that it should not remain in Oxford as an acceptable likeness of her husband and asked me to withdraw it. I wrote to him [Lawrence] and a telegram and this letter were his replies.' As it happens the final resolution of the problem caused by this portrait is the subject of Lawrence's last known letter; *see* p. 579.

The death of D. G. H. seems to have flattened me out, rather. He was like a reserve, always there behind me; if I got flustered or puzzled. And I have no confidences.

I do hope that you & Leeds will be allowed to carry on the Museum as it should go: but I see the temptations before the Trustees: and archaeologists seldom love and admire one another. Leeds has done such selfless and splendid work that he should be unassailable: but he never dined often enough at high table. And you cannot help him, socially, because you never stood for much of that sort of thing yourself.2

I shall be afraid to come to Oxford now. Still, by 1930 all that may have changed.

Your letter gave me the impression that you were getting better. I hope so.3 Ominously you gave no report of your own feelings.

I wish I'd been strong enough to stick to my resolution not to pass that book round. It has led by slow steps to *Revolt in the Desert*, and now to Robert Graves' life of me ... [with] God knows what more to follow: & myself made ridiculous by all this notice. A weary world, it is.

Yours
T.E.S.

British Library

2 Leeds duly became Hogarth's successor, remaining keeper of the museum until 1945.
3 Bell had been ill in hospital

E. M. FORSTER
21.12.27   [KARACHI]

Do not regard this as a letter. I got your note about *Dr. Woolacott*, and am going to read it page by page, and send you my untouched commentary:[1] and as I've been firing my course of rifle-shooting this morning I am tired: and my head aches and I am very miserable. But the post goes tomorrow and last week also I did not write. I do not know what is the matter with me. I fancy it's the loss of Hogarth, for whom I had long cared very greatly.

I Par ii of page I. 'Convalescence ....' This would have been very good if 'Farm hands...' had not begun the first paragraph. Your first par. is so good. It sets exactly the note, in 8 lines, of *all* you want to say. [...][2]

III 'Disease knows its harmonies'. You are wonderful in these phrases. They are like the notes of tenor bells. The conversation with disease is grandly true. [...]
    The car lights are wonderful. I'd got frightened here, wondering how you would get out of it, and beginning to doubt you had skill to end what you had begun.
    The rest is marvellous. There is no other word for it. It bruises my spirit. I did not know there could be such writing.
    Is the mechanism of the ring necessary?
    There is a strange cleansing beauty about the whole piece of writing. So passionate, of course; so indecent, some people might say: but I must confess that it has made me change my point of view. I had not before believed that

1 This is the fuller comment on Forster's story *Dr. Woolacott* foreshadowed in Lawrence's letter of 27 October. Forster appreciated Lawrence's observations and adopted some of his recommendations. ('Replying to your note has excited me a good deal,' he wrote. 'There you were time after time on the spot, seeing me through.') But the note is less interesting for its views on Forster's story than for the light it casts on the much discussed subject of Lawrence's sexual nature, indicating clearly that what happened when Lawrence was captured by the Turks at Deraa in November 1917 (the experience in which, to quote *Seven Pillars*, 'the citadel of my integrity was irrecoverably lost') was enforced homosexual intercourse – male rape. It also suggests that Forster's story helped him to come to terms with his 'whimpering' reaction to that event. Moreover, it helped him to recognize that homosexuality could be presented in writing in terms that were – even if unpublishable – 'cleansing' and 'beautiful'. The note surely confirms that of his own volition he had not had, and did not contemplate having, any physical homosexual relations himself; just as his letter to Robert Graves of 6 November 1928 (*see* p. 412) confirms that he had had no heterosexual relations. *See* 'General Introduction', p. xxviii.
2 [...] Over fifty lines of close textual comment have been omitted.

such a thing could be so presented and so credited. I suppose you will not print it? Not that it anywhere says too much: but it shows far more than it says: and these things are mysteries. The Turks, as you probably know (or have guessed, through the reticences of the *Seven Pillars*) did it to me, by force: and since then I have gone about whimpering to myself Unclean, unclean. Now I don't know. Perhaps there is another side, your side, to the story. I couldn't ever do it, I believe: the impulse strong enough to make me touch another creature has not yet been born in me: but perhaps in surrender to such a figure as your Death[3] there might be a greater realisation – and thereby a more final destruction – of the body than any loneliness can reach.

Meanwhile I am in your debt for an experience of such strength & sweetness and bitterness and hope as seldom comes to anyone. I wish my account of it were not so vaguely inadequate: and I cannot suggest 'more when we meet' for it will be hard to speak of these things without dragging our conduct and bodies into the argument: and that's too late, in my case.

T.E.S.

King's College Cambridge

EDWARD GARNETT
23/12/27   *KARACHI*

[...] Graves has indeed pulled the thing together since the typescript[1]. Yet I do not call it good. The truth is so much less flattering than the rumour. And he follows the old fault of regarding my war trouble as the biggest part of the show. Whereas my effort at construction with Winston after the War was a harder and better effort. And in the distant future, if the distant F. deigns to consider my insignificance, I shall be appraised rather as a man of letters than as a man of action. You know my opinion well enough to acquit me of conceit

---

3 Death is virtually a persona in the story in that the central character, Clesant, a young, ailing country squire, dies following what purports to be an impulsive homosexual encounter with an attractive employee from his estate, who is really the ghost of a soldier fatally wounded in the Great War. The soldier had died refusing the ministrations of the same doctor – the Dr Woolacott of the title – who is notably failing to cure the doomed Clesant.

1 *Lawrence and the Arabs.*

in saying this: you know I think myself a contemptible writer, a bag of tricks. Best-selling tricks, I grant: but tricks that no man with his one eye on the truth would have time for.

By the way I never heard how Cape regarded the stopping of *Revolt*. I hope he had realised from the first that if I had my way its sale would not pass the point of necessity. Had I been in London the stoppage would have come some three thousand pounds earlier. As it is I am most grateful to my Trustees for killing their golden goose. They showed a superb disregard for charity. I believe the R.A.F. Fund is £4,000 better off by me. Cape must see that this was a game which could not go on; each sold copy was so much more trouble for me ... and always there was the prospect of a cheap edition to make me desperate. How hard the lives of publishers would be, if their authors did not write for profit! I hope he regards rather the lump of money he did make out of *Revolt* than the little more he might have made out of it, in the duration. It is a common gag to call me unbusinesslike – and indeed there are things I care for more than money; but I do try to keep in mind that the people I have to do with are out for money, and I have tried my best to ensure their getting what they like. He has only to remember the percentage I insisted on getting for his firm on the contract with Doran, to be convinced of my attempt to deal fairly with him. I remain of course still mindful of my bond to offer him my second book, and I will set this right between us by sending him the text (for publication *in extenso*) of my R.A.F. notes; and then all will be as it ever was.*2 [...]

*This reads cryptic: I mean he will see they are not publishable, and will refuse them, thus acquitting me of any need to write anything else to get clear of promises.

Bodleian Library

2 Lawrence did not send his 'second book' – *i.e. The Mint* – to Jonathan Cape as suggested here, but to Garnett himself some weeks later; *see* footnote 1 p. 392.

Ralph Isham
2/1/28   KARACHI

Dear Isham

Forgive the office typewriter, and my botching of its keys. It's in case I need a copy of what I say to answer your letter about Homer's *Odyssey*. It has knocked me out temporarily.[1] Why should you be so much better to me than I am to myself? The money suggested is wonderful,[2] but that only shows how well they expect it to be done: and I have no trust whatever in my writing. Agreed the reviewers spoke highly of it, when *Revolt* came out: but they speak as well of seventy percent of the books they notice, so one discounts that: and in my case they were astonished that a practical man could write at all. 'So clever of him, my dear, to be able to sit up' – as they'd say of a toy dog.

When your letter came I took *The Odyssey* down from the shelf (it goes with me, always, to every camp, for I love it), and tried to see myself translating it, freely, into English. Honestly, it would be most difficult to do. I have the rhythm of the Greek so in my mind that it would not come readily into straight English. Nor am I a scholar; I read it only for pleasure, and have to keep a dictionary within reach. I thought of the other translators, and agreed that there was not a first-rate one. Butcher & Lang – too antique. Samuel Butler – too little dignified, tho' better. Morris – too literary. That only shows the job it is. Why should my doing be any better than these efforts of the bigger men?

Bruce Rogers' dressing of the book will make it glorious, so that even an inferior version would pass muster. You are fortunate to be able to dine with him. I have for years admired him from ground level, and have even been able at intervals to buy books of his production; of course I've never met him: but you know, and he knows, that he's the ideal of all those who have tried to produce

1 The background to this approach to Lawrence to translate *The Odyssey* is described in the introduction to the book from which this letter is taken: *Letters from T. E. Shaw to Bruce Rogers*, of which 200 copies were published in a private edition in 1933. Rogers, a distinguished American book-designer whose reputation was well-known to Lawrence, explained that it was while reading *Seven Pillars of Wisdom* in 1927 that it occurred to him that its author was 'the very man to translate *The Odyssey* anew.... Here at last was a man who could make Homer live again – a man of action who was also a scholar & could write swift and graphic English. But where was he? At that time he was to me a half-legendary person and I knew only that somewhere east of Suez was an air-craftsman who had legally changed his name to Shaw. I casually mentioned my project & my perplexity to Col. Ralph Isham, who startled me by exclaiming, "The very thing for Shaw to do! I'll write to him tomorrow – he's in Karachi".'
2 £800.

books. Or perhaps I should say, of all who have gone far enough in the direction of producing books to know what a job it is. It would be an awful thing if my share in the Homer did not justify its setting, in my own judgement.

So let me make stiff terms, in the hope of being refused an honour which I feel too great to carry off successfully. I can not refuse so profitable an offer bluntly.

1. I should need two years in which to complete the translation, after I began work on it.

2. I do not feel capable of doing it as well as Homer would have liked; and shall feel unhappy if it turns out botched.

3. I could not sign it with any one of my hitherto names. It must go out blank, or with a virgin name on it.

4. I would do the first book within six months of having concluded the agreement with the publishers; and if they were not satisfied with it I would agree to let the contract go, upon their paying me a fraction of the fee which the first book bears to the whole.

Notes on above:

1. Because it is long, and difficult. Probably I'd write it twice or three times before it felt right. Also I can't begin right off. I must get several of the older translations by me, to compare with.

3. And they would have to promise to respect this privacy. I hope never again to be the victim of the press.

4. Six months, because the writing of the first ten pages or so fixes the style of all the rest, and it is the hardest part. And I do not want to do it for nothing. Fifteen or twenty pounds would see me nicely through it.

My strongest advice to you is to get someone better, to do you a more certain performance: I am nothing like good enough for so great a work of art as *The Odyssey*. Nor, incidentally, to be printed by B. R.

Your kindness remains overwhelming. Do realise that I have no confidence in myself, and what I'd like is some little job, unquestionably within my strength and my leisure hours in the R.A.F.[3]

Yours ever
T. E. Shaw

Letters to Bruce Rogers

3 Despite his initial reluctance, Lawrence finally agreed to Rogers' proposal, beginning his work on the translation in the spring of 1928.

HIS MOTHER
4.1.28

[KARACHI]

That is much better: when we do not write so rapidly, our letters have time to reach their destinations and answer their questions: so that we do not need to repeat everything many times. It is not as though I had much to say. Life with me is much the same, from week to week, or from year to year: in camp at Farnborough, or at Bovington, or at Cranwell, or at Drigh Road. One room is like another, in barracks, and one airman is like another airman. We do not have changes or adventures. We stay still, and are physically taken care of, like stock cattle.

[...]

[Good thing you left China. Everything points to the slow development of its internal politics ... in a century or so everyone there will have points of view: and then foreigners will be able to learn things. The generation which tried to teach them is finished. Bob must prepare for some other walk in life than that. I hope very much it will be in England this time.

N]

HL/Bodleian Library

MRS THOMAS HARDY
15.1.28

KARACHI

Dear Mrs Hardy

This is a Sunday, and an hour ago I was on my bed, listening to Beethoven's last quartet: when one of the fellows came in and said that T. H. is dead. We finished the quartet, because all at once it felt like him: and now I am faced with writing something for you to receive three weeks too late.

I was waiting for it, almost. After your letter came at Christmas I wanted to reply: but a paragraph in the papers said that he was ill. Then I held my breath, knowing the tenuous balance of his life, which one cold wind would finish. For years he has been transparent with frailty. You, living with him, grew too used to it perhaps to notice it. It was only you who kept him alive all these years: you to whom I, amongst so many others, owed the privilege of having known him.

And now, when I should grieve, for him and for you, almost it feels like a triumph[1]. That day we reached Damascus, I cried, against all my control, for the triumphant thing achieved at last, fitly: and so the passing of T. H. touches me. He had finished and was so full a man. Each time I left Max Gate, having seen that, I used to blame myself for intruding upon a presence which had done with things like me and mine. I would half-determine not to trouble his peace again. But as you know I always came back the next chance I had. I think I'd have tried to come even if you had not been good to me: while you were very good: and T. H.

So, actually, in his death I find myself thinking more of you. I am well having known him: you have given up so much of your own life and richness to a service of self-sacrifice. I think it is good, for the general, that one should do for the others what you have done for us all: but it is hard for you, who cannot see as clearly as we can how gloriously you succeeded, and be sure how worth while it was. T. H. was infinitely bigger than the man who died three days back – and you were one of the architects. In the years since *The Dynasts* the Hardy of stress has faded, and T. H took his unchallenged – unchallengeable – place. Though as once I told you, after a year of adulation the pack will run over where he stood, crying 'There is no T. H. and never was'. A generation will pass before the sky will be perfectly clear of clouds for his shining. However, what's a generation to a sun? He is secure. How little that word meant to him.

This is not the letter I'd like to write. You saw, though, how I looked on him, and guessed, perhaps, how I'd have tried to think of him, if my thinking had had the compass to contain his image.

Oh, you will be miserably troubled now, with jackal things that don't matter: You who have helped so many people, and whom therefore no one can help. I am so sorry.

T E Shaw

DG

---

1 Hardy had died on 11 January. Mrs Hardy replied (15.3.28): 'You say the news struck you as a triumph. When I saw him after he had been laid out I was spell bound [*sic*]. On his face was a radiant look of triumph. Never on any other face have I ever seen such a look, nor could ever have believed it possible....' She also told Lawrence: 'He was devoted to you. Somehow I think he might have lived had you been here.... You seem nearer to him, somehow, than any one else, certainly more akin.'

ALAN DAWNAY
20.1.28   [*R.A.F. DRIGH ROAD KARACHI*]

I try now to answer letters on the flash – or not at all: and always on this paper, which rots in two years. So I'll cheat the fellow who tries to write 'my life and letters', out of some of his materials, anyway.

Graves' book is enough for a lifetime. I like it, because it puts paid, I think, to Lowell Thomas: who will now have to take his stuff from Graves' book or shut up. I like it because he has played the game most honourably with my likes and dislikes, and spared me all the unpleasantness he could. But it remains a horrid thing to happen to a fellow. My instinct told me it would be that: but I thought it worth going through with, because the effect of yet another book on me will be to surfeit the British Public. They will write me down, now, just as a person who wants to advertise himself for some end which they can't see, and therefore will be all the more suspicious of. That should put me out of court as a public subject: and in the quietness which will follow I can come home and live unnoticed. When, depends a little on Cape, to whom I must write and ask intentions as to further editions, if any, of the Graves book.

Yes, Hogarth's going was a bad knock to me. I relied on him, always, to know where I was at, and why, without being told: and, for his existence there, I like Oxford. Now he has gone: and Hardy has gone since. If G. B. S. and Forster go, I'll have no writing friends left, anywhere. It's a misfortune, perhaps, to be so much older than one's generation.

I had Christmas in the Guardroom, where I took turns, with three others, in patrolling a verandah. Don't ask me why! All camps do it, and will do till some General asks 'Why'. When you are C.I.G.S. I shall hope for you to do it: and will remind you of this letter.

Au revoir...? 1930.
TES

Bodleian Library

DAVID GARNETT
16.2.28

Dear Garnett

You are over-imagining the importance of my Uxbridge notes. I call them a book only in derision. They were written, as the basis for a projected book, night by night in 1922. The book hasn't come off: and will never come off: for I now like the R.A.F. too well, despite its faults, to put out a true account of it to a public which would not understand: which would read blame, where I'd written praise. They are artlessly photographic: interesting, perhaps, as documents.

Not to regard my conviction that I'm not a writer, and that my *Seven Pillars*, if it is any good, achieves it without any concurrence! [*sic*] Perhaps it was a very good subject, though I found it too large. However it was, the *Seven Pillars* is not going to have a successor: and my only motive in suggesting that you should read the R.A.F. notes was to cure you of the lingering suspicion that I could write, if I tried. I've tried once, very hard: and got these notes ready for another try, and that's all. You talk of my writing a story. Why I've never invented anything in my life!

To like Drigh Road: – now that would be an unhealthy sign. We agree there. I want to be in England, where there are clean blue roads, and people who think themselves as good as me in the streets. Of course I'm R.A.F. still, after I get home: till about 1935, probably. It is not as good as a monastery because it turns you out when you get old or ill. Otherwise it would be my vocation, as you say. Too late!

There are no Holy Men, conscious or unconscious, real or pretendant, in the R.A.F. or the Army or the Navy. The ultimate intention of these three great institutions is non-Christian, which is anti-Christian: and every service man knows that his religion can't get any deeper than his lips. So few think it worth while to profess any. We get hot, instead, on football, or flying, or motor-biking.

Sorry you don't like Caesar's *Gallic War*. I call it a miracle of self-suppression: one of the most impressive things in print. My *Seven Pillars* is nearer Xenophon, a much less ambitious ancient.[1] Hats off to Caesar, though, for really pulling off the impersonal thing, and.yet leaving his stuff palpitant with excitement.

Rough edges my preference? I like a rough texture, which is not the same thing. After correcting each paragraph of the *Seven Pillars* I used to forget what

---

1 A reference to Xenophon's *Anabasis*, an account in seven books of the expedition of Cyrus against his brother Artaxerxes II, king of Persia, in 401 BC; Xenophon was a leading participant as well as chronicler.

came before and after it: just see it for a moment as a single piece of writing: and watch through it for a high point: some idea or single phrase or single word which stung me awake. If it hadn't that, it was deleted, or improved. If it had that, O.K. If it had two or more, out came all but one, usually. [...]

I don't think, despite my patchy pleasure in French poetry since 1500, and French prose since 1890, I can be properly called Anti-French. A fellow must pick and choose in foreign literature. For instance I loathe Horace and love Virgil: a remark which would discredit a Roman's judgement: but is only a foible with an Englishman. These Aldingtons who have a spiritual home in France – they have only a physical home in England surely?

We seem to differ about E. M. F. and D. H. L.[2] I call the form of *The Plumed Serpent* very shapely and satisfying: and the architecture of most of his novels excellent. Of course his prose stammers often. Somebody said he was trying to make the solar plexus talk plain English.

E. M. F.'s crises are the crises of a super-sensitive mind: storms in tea-cups, I called 'em once: that is except the Pan solutions:[3] and Pan to him means physical excitement, I fancy. His best Pan-stuff is unwriteable, I fancy: but in his mind, very surely and succinctly. His social work (*The Longest Journey*, most significant of all) seems to me great ... just great, without qualification. It hangs permanently in my memory, as if it were stuck there: it's like rolling on a fly-paper, which I've seen a hairy lap-dog do. E. M. F.'s stuff clings. [...]

Bodleian Library

SIR HUGH TRENCHARD
17.3.28   *R.A.F. DRIGH ROAD KARACHI*

Dear Sir Hugh
I've been wondering, since the sea-mail left, if I'm forsworn. In 1922, when you let me enlist, I promised that the C.A.S. should see, first, any book I wrote

2 E. M. Forster and D. H. Lawrence.

3 Pan reverence and neo-paganism were popular literary themes at this period, and writers such as Robert Graves, W .B. Yeats, and D. H. Lawrence explored distinctly magical/paganistic themes and the revival of 'old gods'. So also did E. M. Forster, who, in his first novel, *The Longest Journey*, published in 1907, has his anti-hero write a story about a modern man falling in love with a dryad, the title of which was *Pan Pipes*. Lawrence's attitude in this context seems somewhat guarded: aware of Forster's 'Pan solutions', but more at ease with his 'social work'.

on the R.A.F. I don't think it's a book: — but I posted something rather like one yesterday to Edward Garnett: and you'd better hear about it.[1]

In those days I hoped to turn as much of me as had survived the war into a writer; and I thought the R.A.F. was a subject. So I made full and careful notes of Uxbridge. Afterwards, at Farnborough in 1923, I had a look at the printed *Seven Pillars* and realised I should never write well. So pop went that ambition; and the notes popped into my kit-box.

In the midst of that misery I was kicked out of what had become my profession: and so re-met Garnett, whose name you probably know as a critic of genius. Of course he's more than that; but that's only his reputation. I explained to him that the reason had fallen out of my existence — and so there wouldn't be another book. He remained curious. If not a book, what of the notes? I sort of grinned, and said 'I'll give 'em you, for keeps'. But they'd been left at S.O.P.[2] in one of the fellows' lockers; and they banged about the earth for years, occasionally coming into my hands. They felt bearably vivid and meaningful to me, like a part of myself (for private reasons) and I didn't want to lose them: but at last you let me back again, and then I cared for them no more.

Garnett used to hint at his unfulfilled present, from time to time. So in Karachi I took them up, at last, to send him: but time had blurred their original pencil into unintelligibility, except for me. They'd been written nightly, in bed! So they had to be fair-copied; and I sweated on them for months, till they were all out straightly in a little note-book of 176 pages (70,000 Words) called *The Mint*. *The Mint*, because we were all being stamped after your image and superscription.

This note-book it was which I posted yesterday. Last night I made a lovely bonfire of the originals. Up came the orderly sergeant, and asked silly questions: wanted to know what I was burning. 'My past' said I. But suddenly I thought – perhaps they'll say I've written another book. Do you think so? If you care to see it you may. This letter will catch up, and I am sending Garnett a copy to show him it's your right to see it. That will explain the typing of an A.C.H.,[3] afraid to type well for fear they promote him into a soft-boiled clerk.

1 Lawrence was writing two days after sending a fair copy of his 'R.A.F. notes' (*i.e. The Mint*) to Edward Garnett. In his accompanying letter (printed as *DG* 344) he wrote: 'I want it offered to Cape, for publication, *in extenso*, without one word excised or moderated [...] and I want him to refuse it, so as to free me from the clause in his contract of the *Revolt of the Desert*, tying me to offer him another book.'
2 S.O.P.: School of Photography, Farnborough.
3 Aircraft Hand.

It also shows devotion to duty, to send two Air-Mail letters in one week. Twelve annas gone west.

Garnett will not hawk the thing about; only his son will read it. After I'm dead someone may censor out of it an edition for publication. I shall not care, being dead; and the R.A.F. will be different and indifferent. Quite wrong of it: doesn't know its mercies: may be years before it has another A/C like me.

I don't advise even Garnett to read it; much less a man of action. 170 pages of my handwriting. It's a worm's eye view of the R.A.F. – a scrappy uncomfortable thing. I've been an uncomfortable thing while I wrote it. The ranks, even of your incomparable force, don't make for easy living or writing. Every word of this has been done in barracks. Any word used in barrack rooms has been judged good enough to go in; wherefore Scotland Yard would like to lock up the author. The general public might be puzzled, and think I didn't like the R.A.F. whereas I find it the only life worth living for its own sake. Though not the Depot. Uxbridge was bad, and I'd have written and told you so, only that it seemed implicit, in your letting me join, that I should take my stuff quietly.

You'll please yourself, after all this. Garnett's address is No. 19 Pond Place, Chelsea, S.W.3.

T.E.S.

There's a laugh in the beast's tail. Gifts are lousy things, anyhow: and the sole copy of a second book by a best-selling author is about as seasonable a gift as a full-grown alligator. And I meant to please Garnett, who has been very good to me. He won't know whether to insure it, or burn it, or poke it in the British Museum.

Bodleian Library/HMH

MRS CHARLOTTE SHAW
20.3.28

[…] What you say about the Uxbridge notes, and their effect on you, delights me.[1] When you asked me for them I had to send them you. If you had not asked I should not have. Such intimate meats aren't meant to be hawked about. But if anyone of the qualified ones wants them: why then, upon their own head! I was not really very fearful of your head being bowed under them: though it is a test, rather. There never was, I fancy, such stuff put on paper before – or is this the vanity of every author? It's so hard to see that one's own intimacies may be other people's commonplaces of exchange. Parts of the notes shocked me: as much as the original experiences they try to mirror, though I tried very hard not to look shocked or sound shocked. But you take them exactly as I'd like everybody to (and as I fear hardly anybody would). I was very nervous after I'd posted them: and the second part is worse than the first. I think the third part, the Cranwell part, is sunny. […]

I've told you in a letter crossing yours[2] (how can one explain across five thousand miles, and six weeks?) that the hardness and bareness are the square and the barrack-room: and the tightness is our discipline and uniform. The serviceman's life is cribbed, amazingly. We never get out of bonds. Only we see freedom about us in the trees and birds, and stars. That is why you'll sometimes find little landscape snatches – parts of the notes. The sight of nature sometimes reaches our notice, and tells us that we are not natural: – or rather, that our way of life is not. No more natural than a box-tree trimmed into a peacock: you don't call that a tree. The services are things of their own sort: a slavery of the spirit, I sometimes think.

I've tried not to remember back: not to introduce one idea or sentence or adjective which had not found place in my original notes. The temptation to

1 Lawrence had sent a rough copy of his 'Uxbridge notes' to Mrs Shaw some weeks earlier. He wrote on 2 January 1928: 'So soon as I found, at the end of your letter, your request for the Uxbridge notes (collected as *The Mint*) I unlocked my box, thrust the rough copy into an envelope, & took them to the post. It was a matter of minutes only, before I could think it over.' He had added the caution: 'Please regard yourself (in reading it) as being in an equivocal position, eavesdropping in a man's barrack.'
2 In 'the letter crossing yours' (dated 1.3.28) Lawrence had written: 'What you & G. B. S. think about the tightness & spareness of it pleases me more than pages of praise. Think of the tightness and spareness of our uniform: and for its bare severity look at the barrack-room. That is the scene, this the manner, those the figures. Service life is not freedom. It can be a contented slavery though.'

write the book for which these were meant to provide the foundation, – that temptation died out years ago. The R.A.F. is now my very own service, and I learn to fit in, slowly: to give up my rights to personality.

[…]

T.E.S.

The permitted readers of them are: – (i) Mrs. Shaw. (2) Trenchard (if he wants) (3) Edward Garnett and David Garnett (if they want) (4) perhaps, I don't know: EMF. (5) D. G. H. if he had not died.[3]

British Library

HIS MOTHER
23.3.28   [KARACHI]

There, I have sorted out, in the last three days, my recent letters. There are 132 business letters which I must answer: 26 letters from people I once used to feel with, & whose friendliness has gone on past our separation. I would like to drop them, but am too soft-hearted: and I have thrown away two boxes-full of stuff that did not matter.

My average mail is 20 letters a week: of which perhaps six or seven are of no importance. That just balances my maximum reply-capacity. I can afford two rupees (3/–) for stamps every week, & the little extra which envelopes & paper cost. So if everybody ceased writing to me from today I could be free of back-correspondence in ten weeks at 16 letters a week. Letters take on the average ¾ of an hour each, if you add in the getting pens & ink out of my box, & the job of getting them to the post office. So 12 hours a week (2 a day) for the next ten weeks would see me quit. Only each week there arrive more letters than I can answer. So the problem remains impossible. Also I refuse to waste all my leisure on letter-writing. The letters bore the people who get them as much as their letters bore me, I suppose. Who invented this curse?

3 Written in the margin against the paragraph about his 'Uxbridge notes'.

I think I shall print a small card 'to announce cessation of correspondence' and send it to the 300 or 400 of my regular addresses. After that I shall write not more than one letter per week, & take a holiday once a quarter.

All of which nonsense has well filled these pages, & conceals the fact that nothing has happened here since I wrote to you last. All well. Hope Bob's better, & settling down.

N.

HL

SERGEANT A. PUGH
13.4.28

[...] I seem never to have answered your query re Miss Brown of Purley who wanted a photo of me. Let her cut one out of the *Daily Mail*. These flappers!

Hoots.

A publisher wrote & asked if I had any little poems I'd let him publish (a hen might as well lay cabbages as me write poetry) because if so he'd send me the latest Brough Superiors for the years 1928-29-30-31-32.

I told him
  a) That I had no poems
  b) That Karachi had no roads.
     Hoots again.

TES

Bodleian Library

A. W. LAWRENCE[1]
2.5.28

Dear A

I am leaving Karachi soon, for some squadron up-country: and shall not regret going on the whole.[2] Will let you know my new address, when I have it.

They are nibbling again at the *Odyssey* idea. Hope it comes off.

Do you remember my telling you that you were my heir? There'll be about four pounds to inherit in cash, and £18 in the Bank, and some books, and Clouds Hill (perhaps). Not Pole Hill, which goes to Richards.

Also my copyrights which now no longer include *Revolt in the Desert*: but you will be O.C. the *Seven Pillars*, and the greater controls the less: so that should make up for the disappointment of the preceding paragraph.

I'm not consciously dying yet: I'm detailing these past facts to add a present fact to it. I have written out a clean copy of some notes I made in 1923 at Uxbridge, on a recruit's life in the R.A.F. of the time. They total some 80,000 words, and therefore amount, pretty well, to another book. Edward Garnett, of 19 Pond Place, Chelsea is the owner of the Manuscript, at present the sole copy. If he has it typed, which he may do, for security's sake, I'll have a copy sent to you. Garnett's son David will presumably inherit from his father, eventually.

The copyright of this M.S. of course remains mine, for life: and passes to my heirs, for the statutory period, which I believe is 40 years after death. I will not publish these notes (whose present name is *The Mint*) in my day. And I hope that you will not (without the permission of the Chief of Staff of the R.A.F. for the time being) publish them, if the option is yours, before 1950. They are very obscene.

Regard these things as possible windfalls for your child. They will not profit you much. What else? You know that John Snow, of Mallam's, the Solicitors, in St. Giles, Oxford, has my will: and that Eliot and Robin Buxton (R.B. c/o

---

1 Arnold Walter Lawrence (1900-91), T.E.L.'s youngest brother. Professor of classical archaeology, Cambridge University, 1944-51; professor of archaeology, University College of Ghana, and director, National Museum of Ghana, 1951-7. Author of books on Greek sculpture and architecture, editor of Herodotus, etc. T.E.L.'s literary executor.

2 The move from Karachi was at Lawrence's request. His immediate C.O. was content to have him among his team but, as he told Robin Buxton in a letter of 10 May 1928 (*see DG*, p. 607) 'higher up they panic, over my mere existence in the camp'. Miranshah, his second posting, was the smallest and most remote R.A.F. station in India. (N.B. Both Karachi and Miranshah are in what is now Pakistan.)

Martins Bank, 68 Lombard St. and the Hon. E. Eliot, c/o Kennedy, Ponsonby & Ryde, of Guildhall Chambers, Bishopsgate St.) are trustees and owners of *Revolt in the Desert*: and that Eliot has my Power of Attorney, to look after the *Seven Pillars*: and that Richards (V.W.) of 3 Loudoun Road, St. John's Wood, N.W.8 has my books, & can explain the situation of Pole Hill.

There, I think all those things are clear. As I say, I'm not conscious of dying: but while I'm informing you of the existence of *The Mint* I'd better put you again exactly informed of the other arrangements. Handy-like, to have it in a nut-shell.

TES

Bodleian Library

MRS CHARLOTTE SHAW
17.5.28

There we will forget *The Mint*. It is dead and buried. I am still tired: and in addition have a Nunc Dimittis feeling again. All the loose ends of my life have now been so tidied up. The Arab Campaign: fought, won, recorded, the political settlement, following on it, finished so far as my eyes can see. The things of Ibn Saud and the things of Irak go well. Palestine is not a country, but a religious museum or laboratory. Syria: that has been beyond man's wit for very long.

So there's the public part finished: and the private part is finished too. The causes that led me into the Air Force have come to their full consequence, and are dead, like the Arab business, probably: at least I have felt strong enough to put them out on paper. *The Mint* has been impossible to write all these years: for six years I have had its pieces in my bag, and it was not till England was away behind me that I could take it up and work on it. It is not easy, either, in this place and climate, and in service conditions, to write seriously. You'd have laughed, I think, if you'd seen me working away with a pencil, as I sprawled on my bed, afternoons and evenings, while the crowd chattered and wrangled over my head.

All this finishing and finishing for ten years without the faintest desire or stirring to begin anything anywhere again. I have no more notes for books in my bag: and no urge to join the boy scouts or the House of Commons. The R.A.F. seems natural somehow, as a way of living: and no other life seems

natural: or is it that no energy to attempt any new life remains? Nunc Dimittis
... if I had a Lord, and he were a decent fellow, he would tell his servant to go
to sleep, in reward for having worked 'over-time', and very hard, for forty years:
or I think he would. It is what his servant (if profitable) would ask as reward.

Of course G. B. S. at forty was just beginning to get in his stride, with
plays: but between the power and courage of G. B. S., and my weariness, how
great a gap! And when I think of lives for which I am very grateful: for poor
Dowson, who wrote ten lovely poems, and died; for Rossetti, who wrote a few
more, and died; for Coleridge, who wrote for two years, and then ran dry; why
surely duration and bulk aren't the first considerations? It seems to me that the
Arab Revolt, of activities of the body: and the *Seven Pillars* and *Mint*, of
activities of the mind, may be all that my tissues can do. Certainly for the
moment, it is all. I just labour, grudgingly, through the daily duty the R.A.F.
compels from me: and lie restlessly on my bed (restlessly for the flies and
prickings of external difficulty) during the other, very long, hours of this
interminable day. It will be so good to be free of Drigh Road. On the 23rd, my
move is: to Peshawar,[1] to No. 20 Squadron R.A.F. But I will write from there
(no letter next week: I shall be in the train, seeing half India) and tell you just
what my address will be, and how the new conditions first strike me. Drigh
Road has been dreary and even a little dangerous for me, lately: though now-a-
days perhaps I grow too easily apprehensive of risk. I clutch my place in the
R.A.F. like a life-buoy, because if it went from me I would sink straight away. I
hope *The Mint* will not make Trenchard hate me. He is so very kind and large:
but it offends against his tradition of loyalty, and perhaps he will think me a
scab for betraying my service. I wish you knew Trenchard. It would explain a
good deal to you. Now D. G. H. has gone, he's the man whose opinion I shall
be sorriest to lose. Of course he is not civilised, like D. G. H.; but he is larger.

A doleful letter, this, it seems to me, re-reading it in the dull light of early
Thursday morning. My first daily job is to open the workshops, half an hour
before the crowd come, so that the open doors and fans may air them. It gives
me twenty minutes calm each day. You can safely ascribe the half of the above
to the coming shadow of my move. I was meant for a stay-at-home, and the
adventure of every new camp frightens me in advance.

[...] You will be seeing my mother, perhaps, soon. [...] I wonder how
you and she will get on. Well, I expect, for my mother is very unusual and

1 Capital of North West Frontier Province; Lawrence stayed there only briefly – by early June
he was at Miranshah.

remarkable. Remember that she was brought up as a charity child in the Island of Skye, and then had to fend for herself: and compare that with her present: and you'll be astonished.

Too many interruptions. I cannot do anything while people talk at and to me every minute. More, later, from Peshawar, about ten or 12 days hence, or whatever their mail-day is. It will be the usual scramble: sending off 20 letters to 20 people, saying where I now am.

T.E.S.

British Library

SERGEANT A. PUGH
9/6/28   *R.A.F. DETACHMENT MIRANSHAH*

Dear Sergt.

This is more like 'B' Flight, only as it happens their number is 'A'. Out on the drome they are just running up the engines (the same old Bifs[1]) for some practice flying: and I am sitting in the Office with lots to do, and not doing it. Instead I shall get busy on the typewriter, and knock you out a letter. A poor typewriter, for every now and then it stammers, and misses a few spaces. Cause unknown, but suspected to be old age and general debility. Poor devil, I feel for it, being near to that case myself... but we are lucky to have a typewriter of any kind here, in the ends of the earth; and if it stutters, why it's up to me to mend it, in my spare time.

Miranshah is an advanced station of the R.A.F., and lies ten miles from the Afghan border. In shape it is a mud and brick fort, about four hundred yards each way. The garrison are an irregular corps of Indian Scouts, who live in one compound, while we twenty five R.A.F. live in another compound. They are out of bounds to us, and we are out of bounds to them. A sociable arrangement, which makes for quietude. This Miranshah is almost the quietest place I have struck, in Stations.

The permanent Staff are three, a storekeeper, a wireless Corp. and a clerk, who will be me, I hope, if my filing and letter-writing and reliability of character and conduct earn me the privilege. At present I am lucky, for there is nobody

1 Bristol fighters.

else running for the job. The place is so remote that not many people have heard of it; I suppose that is why there is no rush to get the privilege of permanence here. It will be a scoop for the ACH class, if I carry it off.

No permanent Officer, but the three or four squadrons who are nearest detach a flight in rotation, to stay here for two months, and work from here up and down the tribal country which borders on the legal border. The Flight Lieutenant commanding this flight is the C.O. of the Station, during his spell of duty: – so I get a change of C.O. every few weeks. That is part profit, and part loss. At Cranwell, it would have been a dead loss. At Karachi it would have been gain. (I apologise, again, for somebody's typewriter; what sex is a typewriter? this is a dog of a one)

Being clerk is not so much fun as ACH in a flight, but in India there are coolies to do the washing down and donkey work, so the poor ACH loses most of his livelihood. Nearly all of us do paper work of some sort, here. And, to tell you the truth, it is rather messy, pulling busses[2] about, in this climate: – doesn't do you any harm, but you want a bath and change of clothes after half an hour of it: and the water is sure to be turned off, just then, and we can't afford new clothes weekly.

I have two years, or nearly, to do out here now, and if I am continually lucky, they will be done in Miranshah. You can hardly conceive the quiet of the tiny place. At night they shut it all up with barbed wire, and by day we are not allowed to go out beyond the edge of the aerodrome without an escort: not that the tribes are now unfriendly, but it is an old tradition that they ought to be, and so strict precautions are the rule in all these forts. Even by day, when the fort gates are open, there is an unbroken peace over us. We lie in a plain, some miles wide, and are ringed by a wall of mountains, sharp mountains, quite clear and clean in line; and these seem to keep off wind and access. I feel as though I had slipped over the edge of the world a little way, and landed on some ledge a few feet down the far side. We get few posts, and slow ones; have no shops or visitors or news; in fact it is like a little bit of Heaven; a perfect home from home. I have been looking for a place like this for years, with little hope that such a thing existed.

There is no luck about this letter, which has been four times on or off the machine already. Really, you know, the mornings are fairly busy. Of course we are not supposed to work in the afternoons; and as a fact there is then little to do; but I have a post to meet, or get off, and the arrear of the morning correspondence to finish up, so I make the job lengthen itself pretty well until

2 *I.e.* aircraft.

the evening. Evenings are a bit dull, for I have no gramophone or records, yet, and no books, nor are my eyes quite up to reading in the half-light which is all the rooms allow us. But if I get the job for keeps, as I hope, then I will produce from some hat the price of a musical box; and records are waiting for me in Karachi to order up; and as Sergt. Williams used to discover, there are ways I have of bettering the lighting scheme laid down by the Works and Buildings Office. So soon after you get this letter there will be great changes in Miranshah. If Mrs Shaw and the others send me out, to here, as many books as they used to send to Cranwell, why then the local library will not hold them all, and I shall have to go round the departing Flights, saying 'Please do not go without helping yourself to at least two books'. It got like that at Karachi, where I received over 250 books, and mustered only 100 of them, when I left. That hundred were what the irks called the 'Binders', but which to my odd taste, included most of the attractive books to arrive. So I am pleased at the course of natural selection, and so (let's hope) were they. If they give me Miranshah for good, then I'll get those 100 sent up in a case by rail.

Anything else? Yes, of course, I should ask kindly after Mrs Pugh, and Miss Pugh, and Tug and Dusty (though Dusty will now have left you); it does not seem any good thinking about home, here. We are too far off and too cut off. It really feels as though things beyond those mountains did not exist. Perhaps that feeling will yield to time, and the arrival of letters from England: – but if it does not, then take fair notice that I am becoming an Afghan. I feel it, in the bones, this week.

Incidentally, we are 3000 feet up, and as cool as cool can be. Nearly midsummer, and the temperature probably not over 100. We do not know for certain as we have no thermometer. Happy Miranshah. But in winter we may be as cold as Cranwell. Heaven forbid. They say however that there is no snow, ever, on the ground: but rain in buckets, and the hills about all snow-tipped, and cold winds and other horrors. [...]

Enough Rot
Au revoir.
T.E.S.

Bodleian Library

MRS CHARLOTTE SHAW
11.6.28   *MIRANSHAH*

[...] This place I think is good: At least we are let alone, out of working hours, to do as we please. That inestimable boon was denied the Depot at Karachi. So I greatly hope that in a few weeks Miranshah will fit me like a suit that has been long worn. Long worn, indeed: it is only a fortnight since we came, and it feels like years. There has been the difficulty of learning the new job (I am really a clerk now, except in name and trade) which has meant overtime: of breaking myself tactfully to the new fellows: of getting used to high mud and brick walls as my view, with towers at intervals, and a frieze of the heads and shoulders of mountains, a few miles off, peeping over the wall-tops, very mistily. Weather thunderous: close, breathless, with occasional half-hearted showers of rain. Neither cold nor hot – just over the hundred, I think: but the fort has no thermometer. Afghanistan – did I tell you? – is about ten miles off. The people are friendly, but on guard: which represents our manner, too. An armed guard. [...]

Your books here will be like water in the desert. The fellows are too few to play games, and so they go very short of amusement. Only tennis, I think. One of the officers has a little gramophone, which he has lent us twice. It did the Elgar Symphony for me, but only like a ghost of the Karachi box, which was a good one. Still: this is Miranshah, and *The Odyssey* has been eating up my spare time. [...]

British Library

HIS MOTHER
10.7.28   *MIRANSHAH WAZIRISTAN INDIA*

[...] I'm glad you've met Mrs. Shaw. It's very hard to be a great man's wife. She succeeds with it. I like her. Hope you'll meet G. B. S. some time. He is like a tonic, and very kind. A most sensible, vigorous old man. [...]

HL

SIR HERBERT BAKER[1]
17.7.28

Dear H. B.

This is most gorgeous news: do please accept my most relieved thanks. The shadow in front of everyone in the Services is always the day of discharge: and now I'll be happier about mine: though I expect all the same sorry to leave. The Bank of England: that does sound magnificently splendid. Apolaustic:[2]

I cannot tell when it is. If Trenchard is displeased with me, it will be in 1930 (March). If he is not displeased, he can let me alone till 1935 (March). I hope, of course, for the later date, but fear the earlier. He may have left before 1930, himself, in which case I may put up a fight for my extension. Fighting him is profitless, for I like and respect him so much that it's like having my hands tied behind my back.

Will you thank the Prophet, too? It is most good of you both. Please assure him and the Governor, if you see either of them while the matter is fresh in your (now very burdened) mind, that there are no seeds germinating in my bosom, to be brought out by jobs of any kind.[3] I'll do my bodily best in the job they give me, and be honest: that is all. To tell them that the volcano is not extinct is untrue, for one thing, and may well frighten them, on the other. There never was an orange drier squeezed than myself. Not a kick in the entire body. I will write nothing else, I'm sure, and do nothing else. Of course a sane man can never foretell his future: but it will be miraculous if any activity ever revives in me. No one can ever have felt so high and dry as myself, after 1922, since the ship *Argo* was drawn up by Jason after the Fleece quest, and excused further voyaging. I may look and sound cheerful, and I am cheerful: but that's a long way from growth.

1 Sir Herbert Baker (1862-1946, knighted 1926) had provided, and would do so again, the garret sanctuary in Barton Street, Westminster, where Lawrence wrote much of *Seven Pillars* and many of his letters. He was an architect of considerable distinction – creator of many buildings in South Africa, the Rhodes Memorial on Table Mountain, Rhodes House, Oxford, India House and South Africa House, London, and the Indian and South African Memorials in northern France at Neuve Chapelle and Delville Wood, respectively. He had also been associated with Sir Edwin Lutyens in the planning of New Delhi. At this time he was engaged in reconstructing the Bank of England and Glyn Mills Bank in Lombard Street.

2 Baker had been lobbying at the Bank of England on Lawrence's behalf; the nature of the employment which might possibly be offered him is made clear in the following letter to Bernard Shaw.

3 The Prophet and the Governor (*i.e.* of the Bank of England): Lionel Curtis and Sir Montague Norman, respectively.

They used to tell me that it was just tiredness, and that time would make me dissatisfied with standing aside. How much time, I ask them, now? This is 1928, and I am 40; surely the rush is over. I have dug, and studied, fought a campaign, fought a political campaign, carried out a settlement, written two books – all by the time I was 34. Now I'm finished. If I forced myself to attempt more, against my conviction, it would be bad work I'd produce: & I am so tired.

Your difficulty in Lombard Street is a tiring one. Inform Buxton's neighbours that you are rebuilding Martins': and beg to enclose plans, specifications and estimates for the new premises which they will find necessary when their present buildings fall into *your* hole. Point out that their prompt acceptance of your scheme will save them cost and delay and disorganisation. With any luck you will rebuild half the street. It will be better than the Quadrant.

Miranshah is a fort, of the sort you saw: but its towers are square, with battlemented parapets, & machicolations for machine guns & search-lights: also iron gates, arched over, and all the rest of the mediaeval apparatus. To reach it from Peshawar we drove through Kohat and Bannu. I like it very much: but we are not allowed outside the barbed wire round the walls. So do not ask me about Waziristan, or Wazirs.

MORE THANKS
T.E.S.

Bodleian Library

BERNARD SHAW
9.7.28   *MIRANSHAH*

[…] No I am not adjutant, to this camp. Just typist, and i/c files, and duty rolls. I do what I am told to do, and rewrite the drafts given to me, meekly. The officers would need to be better than they feel themselves to be, for me to safely exceed the normal rank of R.A.F. clerk. Also, I'm not much good as a clerk; though I type a bit better than this, in the daylight.

You ask what is my expectation of life, when I'm discharged. I can tell you, without many 'ifs'. If Trenchard is displeased with me over *The Mint*, (those notes on the R.A.F. which you saw, and he has seen) he will make me leave the R.A.F. in February, 1930. If he does not bear me any grudge, he will leave me alone here, and at some camp in England, till 1935. Or Trenchard may himself leave the Air Force, and I find kinder treatment from his successor. However, in 1930 or in 1935, I will have to go out. My notion, if I have then a secured income of a pound a day, is to settle at Clouds Hill, in my cottage, and be quiet.

If I have to earn my bread and butter, I shall try for a job in London. The sort of job will depend on my health. My body has been knocked to pieces, now and then, and often overworked, in the past: so I do not feel sure of lasting very well. I have thought of a night-watchman job, in some City Bank or block of offices. The only qualification for these is Service experience; and honesty is the necessity which bars very many ex-service men from getting them. I can get good references, from people bankers will trust, so I have good hope of getting placed. Better than that, almost; for Sir Herbert Baker, the architect, who is building the new Bank of England, has spoken of me to the Council which runs it, and they have put a minute in their book that my application is to be considered as favourably as possible, if or when I apply.

You see, I have no trade to take up, and am old to learn, and tired of learning things. So I must look for an unskilled job; and I want an indoor job, if possible, in case I am not very fit. And I like London. And I'd like to work by myself. It is not easy to get on terms with people. On night work nobody would meet me, or hear of me, much.

I have been thinking hard for the last two or three years of what I should go for, if the R.A.F. came to a sudden end (you see, it is precarious: I depend on the favour of Hoare and Trenchard, and am the sort of fellow on whom people hang tales and believe anything, though I do my honest best to worm along inoffensively) and I have listened or joined myself to the other fellows whenever they have discussed civvy jobs: – and of everything I have heard, this night-watchman job sounds the most likely for me to be allowed to hold for good. You see, there is no more demanded of you than that the safe should be unbroken the next morning. You come on duty as the last clerk goes, and the door is locked. You come off duty when the first comer opens the door in the morning. No others ever hear of you, as an individual.

Thanks to Baker speaking to the Bank Committee, with whom he is in weekly touch, my way to the job seems to have been made suddenly easy. His letter telling me only reached me here, so you see it is recent news.

I hope you will not tell anyone about it. The Bank Committee will not. The rest of the formalities would be done by their Staff-man. I will not have to see any of the big noises. The Bank of England is rather more than I had hoped for (or wanted) as it is really too good. Also the smaller Banks let their night men sleep in. Of course the new Bank building will have more room in it. A gorgeous place to live in, don't you think? But that is a trifle, anyhow. A single man can live anywhere, if his tastes are quite plain. Mine are getting plain. Up here I have begun to think with pleasure of the idea of eating ... once or twice.

Please do not laugh at this sketch of my intentions. What I have wanted and tried to do has always come off, more or less, except when it was trying to write; and then, despite all the good you have said of my books, I am assured of failure. Not complete failure, perhaps. I explain yours and my different judgements of my writing by my knowledge of the standard at which I was aiming, and your astonishment that 'a man of action' should be able to do it at all. A relative failure, let's call it. My aim may have been too high for anybody; it was too high for me. But I think one says just 'too high', not 'immodestly high'. I do not think aims are things modest or immodest, just possible and impossible.

Your ever
T. E. Shaw

I haven't answered your last line 'What is your game *really?*' Do you never do things because you know you must? Without wishing or daring to ask too deeply of yourself why you must? I just can't help it. You see, I'm all smash, inside: and I don't want to look prosperous or be prosperous, while I know that. And on the easy level of the other fellows in the R.A.F. I feel safe: and often I forget that I've ever been different. As time passes that war and post-war time grows less and less probable, in my judgment. If I'd been as accomplished as they say, surely I wouldn't be in the ranks now? Only please don't think it is a game, just because I laugh at myself and everybody else. That's Irish, or an attempt to keep sane. It would be so easy and so restful just to let sanity go and drop into the dark: but that can't happen while I work and meet simple-hearted people all day long. However, if you don't see it, I can't explain it. You could write a good play, over a room-full of Sydney Webbs and Cockerells asking me 'why'.

DG

E. M. FORSTER
28/8/28

[...] Of course the *Seven Pillars* is bigger than *The Mint*. I let myself go in the *S.P.* and gave away all the entrails I had in me. It was an orgy of exhibitionism. Never again. Yet for its restraint, & dignity, and form, & craftsmanship, *The Mint* may well be better. By that I don't mean that *The Mint* has no emotion, or the *Seven Pillars* no balance: only comparatively it's so. E. Garnett, curiously enough, calls the *S.P.* reticent, and *The Mint* a giving away of myself. Why, so far as myself is concerned, I wouldn't hesitate to publish *The Mint* tomorrow!

In truth however, the publication isn't in my hands. Trenchard is not the primary obstacle: though for him I have an admiration almost unlimited. He's a very great man. I think he over-estimates the harm which *The Mint* would do the R.A.F.: but what really holds me back is the horror the fellows with me in the force would feel at my giving them away, at their 'off' moments, with both hands. To be photographed, they put on what they call 'best' clothes, & brush their hair, & wash. To be portrayed, as in my book, unadorned would break their hearts. You must remember that *The Mint* is photographically exact: many of them have their real names! No hut-full could trust itself to live openly together, if there was a risk of their communion becoming public copy, in a few years time.

So *The Mint* shall not be circulated before 1950. By then the characters will not matter. Poor old Stuffy is keeping a hotel in Essex now. He'll be dead, & Trenchard, & perhaps myself: (dead or aged 62, the last item. What a quaint performance *The Mint* will seem to a white-beard of 62!) [...]

DG

BRIGADIER-GENERAL SIR GILBERT CLAYTON
9.X.28   *MIRANSHAH*

Dear Clayton
I wanted to put Sir Gilbert: but it became Clayton, irresistibly. We always used to call you Clayton, amongst ourselves, in 15....

When the wireless fellow here brought me the notice about Irak which he'd overheard in the air, the first thing I said was 'too late to do him justice' – because you should have had it years ago: and the second thing thought was 'how very lucky for Irak, that he's been delayed until he's really wanted.[1] It's ever so good an appointment, from the point of view, and in the interests of, everyone but yourself. Bagdad requires the diplomatic, so much more than the administrative understanding. So I congratulate the whole show on their belated common-sense, and am sure that you'll take this view of it and smile at the past.

As I get further and further away from things the more completely do I feel that our efforts during the war have justified themselves and are proving happier and better than I'd ever hoped. And some of this good progress is surely due to my keeping out of an area that I care too much for?

Give Feisal my regards, when you see him. Tell him that I thought a great deal of him during the war: and that I think far more of him now. He has lasted splendidly. He won't find this familiarity, from a person who stands right away from competition!

I laughed when I read of his instituting the Order of the Two Rivers. The Euphrates is my very old friend; and the Tigris isn't at all a bad river. I nearly wrote and asked him for one of his stars, to put on my hitherto empty coat. After all, I'm almost a foundation-member of his kingdom if he can remember our talks of old days in Winterton's house, and in Mr. Churchill's house, and in the Suez Canal? Of course he has had so much to do, since all that, that perhaps he's forgotten with what difficulty against what prejudice we began. By 'we', I mean him & me. The Kingdom of Irak depended on such slender causes: & I'm so proud of it, now.

Anyway, give him my best regards, and guard your own head, against him & everybody. The only essential is that the show should go along its proper road, after all. So long as that happens the personalities it uses or breaks are trifles.

I'm awfully glad you've got up into the real saddle again.

Yours
T E Shaw

Bodleian Library

1 Clayton had just been appointed British high commissioner and commander-in-chief for Iraq.

HERBERT BAKER
29.X.28   *MIRANSHAH*

Dear H. B.

I seem to trouble everybody I meet. Why should you and the Elizabethan magnate[1] be put to work, for my continued existence? or Trenchard 'waste' an hour of his time: though waste does not properly apply there, I fancy: meeting you is a pleasure, and meeting Trenchard a privilege, and the conjunction ought to have been ambrosial and nectary.

I burble: but didn't you like Trenchard? He is as simply built as Stonehenge, and serves equally as well for a temple, or a public meeting-place or monument. Altogether one of my admirations: though I fear he cannot follow the wimbling and wambling of my career. I puzzle Trenchard, and he misunderstands me, often. Not that any such tiny detail could distress him; or blot his greatness, in my eyes.

I have asked the R.A.F. to prolong my service to the limit of my engagement – till 1935, that is. We sign on for 7 years active, and 5 reserve: and a proportion of us are allowed to convert the reserve years into active. If the Air Ministry says Yes to my petition, they will please me, for I like the R.A.F. beyond measure.

It will seem to you improvident of me, to risk losing a permanency in the Bank for a transitory five years more of pleasure: but indeed I worked hard for this pleasure, and I want to have it while I am still fit enough to feel physical pleasure. My rackety life makes me expect an old age full of aches and ailments, so that I must enjoy myself while I can: and always there's a feeling that perhaps I'll miss old age by some happy accident.

So April 1930 will see me out of the R.A.F., if the Air Ministry refuse me: and April 1935 if they accept me. I shall not know till early next year. I think I have said this to you in a previous letter, and apologise for being no more definite. Will you present my respects to the Elizabethan, and explain that he hasn't given me (or you) any promise to which anyone would wish to hold him: that when I'm out of the service I shall try and get a night-job, somewhere in the City: and that for what he has done, and you have done, I am deeply grateful? I hope I do not sound ungrateful, for clinging to the R.A.F. for as long as it will support me. I like it better than anything I have ever done: though it is England, and not India, wherein I dream myself, every night. I hope to come home early in 1930, anyhow. [...]

Bodleian Library

I Sir Montague Norman, governor of the Bank of England: *see* Lawrence to Hon. Francis Rodd, 23 November 1934, where Norman is similarly described (p. 533).

EDITOR, CIVIL & MILITARY GAZETTE

29.X.28   *338171 A/C SHAW R.A.F. MIRANSHAH FORT WAZIRISTAN*

Dear Sir

I have just been shown a very considerate paragraph in the *C. & M. Gazette*, dealing with my supposed whereabouts:[1] if I remember rightly, there was a similar instance some months ago, when I became the subject of other unfortunate rumours.

I send you this note, partly to thank you for promoting me to L.A.C. (a rank I will never reach, unless I can develop enough humour to work up square roots & vulgar fractions again, to pass an educational test which reminds me too unpleasantly of school-days for me to face it) and partly to assure you that I appreciate the different standpoint & manners of the *C&M* (and also *The Times*, of London, & other decent papers) as contrasted with *The Evening News* & the *Sunday Express* (also, unfortunately, of London).

A firm in England is making a film of *Revolt in the Desert*: much against my will, but I have no control or ownership or copyright of the Arab Revolt, as it happened to be an event, & not a fiction: and I fancy this desire to keep my name in the Press may be to boost their production. I have not done anything, for many years now, to deserve publicity: and I will do my best not to deserve publicity, in future. It displeases me.

So I hope if you read, next week, that I've gone to the South Pole, or to Jericho, or been made President of the United States, or written something sensationally unpublishable, that you'll go on believing me peaceably content in the R.A.F. It is a restful existence, though I prefer it to be in England, whither I hope to go in April 1930.

Believe me
Yours very gratefully
T E Shaw   *University of Texas*

---

1 The *Civil & Military Gazette* was the daily paper of Lahore, in what is now Pakistan. On 27 October 1928, in its regular feature 'By the Way', it had printed an item under the heading 'Lawrence of Arabia', of which the key sentences were as follows: 'The Home papers seem to be very intrigued over the whereabouts and activities of Colonel Lawrence, now in the R.A.F. as Leading Aircraftman Shaw. He has been variously reported in Afghanistan, Amritsar, the Gulf, Australia and Singapore.... We can only say that there is no particular mystery about the location of L.A.C. Shaw *alias* Lawrence of Arabia. His station is known to us, but we see no reason for interfering with his desire for freedom from publicity.' Small wonder the subject of the article was grateful and expressed himself accordingly; ironically it was only a few weeks later that the said 'Home papers', or some of them, found the sensational story they were hoping for.

ROBERT GRAVES
6.XI.28   *MIRANSHAH*

Dear R.G

This is two excellent letters you have given me about *The Mint.* The poor little
thing interests me: because it's my only effort at really writing something
about nothing. *Seven Pillars* was a historical necessity: I don't call it an option:
but *The Mint* was a pure wantonness. I went to Uxbridge with the deliberate
intention of writing something about service life: and I put down those notes
evening after evening in the hut, with the blankets to my chin, writing on the
support of my drawn-up knees. They are the perfect exemplar of journalism,
in its antique sense: & it interests me very much to find that you & Garnett &
Forster (three very different people) all see something in them. It shows that
the daily record needn't be as transient as, for example, the *Daily Mail.* A fellow
can't read (even at Miranshah) a month-old *Daily Mail.*

About printing *The Mint* as you suggested: — thanks very much, but no.
'They' would hear of it, and say I'd written another book: and *The Mint* is 1922
and not a book. It's better left just as a manuscript diary. Diaries exist in
thousands and are thought no harm of.

Your second (and unpublishable!) letter gave me a lot of keenly improper
laughter. It was a good effort: though it would have shocked Squad IV.

Your remarks on Form & Style tickled me, particularly: also the instances. I
wrote 'penis & scrotum' deliberately; not knowing in English any word for the latter.
You call it 'bag of tricks': but I don't like periphrasis. 'Prick' is first rate: 'balls' is like
calling the belly a stomach: putting the inside before the outside. Is there an English
word, (still alive, I mean) for scrotum? Bothered if I know. The Latin alternatives
appealed, just there, to my old fashioned sense of the incongruous. They still do!

'Resides not in drill'.[1] That, you say, is style. I like style, I fancy. The
anticipation of an antithesis, which is not fulfilled is good. Old Asquith's speeches
were intolerably boring because all the anticipations were bitterly fulfilled. 'All there
is to be done is to write with ink on paper'. Alas, that is the last & easy stage. It's
the balancing your subject before you begin on it: the scheming proportion for it,

---

[1] In his commentary on this letter in *RGB*, Graves wrote of *The Mint* that 'in the main I liked it
very much, better than *Seven Pillars* because it had been written straight off, not brooded over',
but that he believed it contained some examples of what its author evidently thought was 'style'
which he saw as 'bad taste in language — pseudo-poetic ornament'; he had passed his views to
Lawrence instancing such phrases as 'resides not in drill' and (*see* next page) 'pencillings of light'.

the adding wings and features to carry all your prepared ideas, fitly: and the spacing the few ornamental ideas each of us have, so as to relieve the monotony of the plain surfaces: – that's all got to be done before the easy ink on paper stage.

I know you didn't mean the remark to be taken so literally. You fell foul of my ornament, not because it is ornamental, but because it isn't, and you're sure right there. It comes in the wrong places, and it is clumsy. Yet the 'pencillings of light' were just as clear (are just as clear) to me as the sweat and swear-words. Only they are so much harder to put down. Anybody can catch the ugly to the life: but to make the smoothly beautiful at once beautiful and not sticky – aha, that's where the poet scores. Look at the *Memoirs of a Foxhunting Man*,[2] to see how magically simple things, like birds, come to life again, on paper, specially for Sassoon, without any twisting of words, or strange words. A man's a great writer when he can use plain words, without baldness. See how bald Theodore Powys[3] is, despite all his power to write ... It's because he's not big enough.

If a fellow isn't big enough he must do the other thing: – what you call style: – surface his work. It is a mode, too. The *War-and-Peace* plainness is better, perhaps: but one is fonder, often, of the rather less big work. It feels more homelike. That's the reward of secondary writers. They don't knock-out: but by their very smallness, or middle-size, they become good companions for ordinary people.

Lately I've been reading *The Odyssey* a great deal: & when I get tired of it I take up *The Aeneid*: and it is like stretching out in bed after a hard day: like stretching out in my bed is going to be, in half an hour, when I come off sentry: for it is half past two in the morning, and I'm sitting on a box under the pilot-light beside the arms-rack, scribbling away. We have to guard the beastly rifles, in memory of 1919 when the Mahouds used to try to steal them.

So I am quite unrepentant about 'resides not': 'resideth not' is Wardour Street: 'does not reside in' is too loose. 'There is no something-or-other-in' is too bald: had I used the last my statement would have been seen through. 'Resides not' carried you on to expect more and you found a full stop, & forgot the argument. So So.

Drill may be beautiful:[4] but beauty is not perceptible when you are expecting a punishment every moment for not doing it well-enough. Dancing is beautiful: – because it's the same sort of thing, without the sergeant-major and the 'office'. Drill in the R.A.F is always punitive: – it is always practice-drill, never exercise-

2 Graves had just sent him (*see* end of letter) Siegfried Sassoon's *Memoirs of a Foxhunting Man*, the first part of his George Sherston trilogy, which had just been published.

3 T. F. Powys: allegorical novelist, one of the three Powys brothers, all of whom were well-known writers publishing regularly in the 20s and 30s.

4 Graves had objected to Lawrence's running down of arms-drill.

drill or performance-drill. Airmen haven't the time to learn combined rhythm. If they did learn it, their (necessarily) individual work with screwdrivers & spanners would suffer. Rhythm takes months to acquire, & years to lose.

No I will never be an eminent literary man. Yet theirs are not the only hyaena-dens[5]. There is a hyaena coughing just outside the fort now: and in many barracks you get very near the den stage. I think literary men are probably not really different from you & me.

Thanks for *Ar Hyd y Nos*:[6] but I don't suppose I'll ever see the MS again: I gave it Garnett for keeps: and it probably won't ever be published.

Your last page, about fucking, defeats me wholly. As I wrote (with some courage, I think: few people admit the damaging ignorance) I haven't ever: and don't much want to. 1¾ minutes was the Bishop's remark.[7] Judging from the way people talk it's transient, if 2¾ or 3¾ or 3 hours & ¾s. So I don't feel I miss much: and it must leave a dirty feeling, too. However I don't want to convert you, or you to convert me: only in the circumstances your positive, comparative, superlative (we make it fucking good, bastard good, fucking bastard good) are meaningless to me. Wherefore I, instead, 'keep literature going', because I can understand these other adjectives, and not the airmen's one. Only you call the one lot inferior, & the others superior. That's because you have a standard, & it enables you to be censorious. I only see what's better than my *performance* (quite different to a mental standard, that) and so I admire & enjoy Wells, & Bennett, & Forster, & Sir Thomas Browne, & Rossetti, and Morris and everybody who deliberately tries to better his every-day speech (which is my definition of style). Not a bettering of speech, mind you: but an effort to better it. It's the trace of effort which warms my diaphragm: – beg pardon, cockles of my heart – whatever are cockles?

Ever so many thanks for the Foxhunter. It is a *book*.

TES

Harvard University/RGB[8]

5 Graves had told Lawrence that writers who pursued style 'ended up as Eminent Literary Men, like old Saintsbury, whom I had recently visited (accidentally) in Bath, where he lived in a hyena-den filled with old books, medicine bottles and second-rate statuary'. Professor George Saintsbury had been an influential historian of literature around the turn of the century.
6 Graves had corrected Lawrence's Welsh.
7 *See* 'General Introduction', p. xxvi, and Lawrence's letter to F. L. Lucas, 26 March 1929 p. xxviii.
8 The version of this letter in *RGB* is much edited.

MRS CHARLOTTE SHAW
20.XI.28

This will be a single line scrawl: you would not know my quiet little place today. There are ninety of us, crammed into every hole and corner. I am the only typist. Senior officers rain on us out of the air like monsoons The excuse for it all, is the destroying those poor few villages. I feel a disproportion of means: but no one has been hurt on either side, and the 'enemy' have yielded, and come in, and promised to be good: and so our bombs and house-breaking have saved a war, next spring. Therefore we can flatter ourselves with having saved some hundreds of tribal and military lives. So it has been worth while, probably.[1]

My sympathies, in such shows, are always with the weaker side. That's partly, perhaps, why I was able to help the Arabs whole-heartedly (Was it whole-hearted? Perhaps: but often I think that it's only in trying to write that my whole heart has ever been engaged: and then not for very long).

No more. Your D.G.H.-Doughty book came.[2] I have just caressed its pages. I wish D. G. H. could have lived for ever. You don't know how good he was to talk to, and to hear talk.

The 70 odd men will leave here in a day or two, and then I'll try and go easy for a few days. It has been difficult to lodge and feed them.

T.E.S.

British Library

---

1 In an earlier letter Lawrence had told Mrs Shaw that a clan in the area had turned on its neighbours, the neighbours had asked for government help, and 'Government had warned the offenders that air action would follow if they persist for 96 hours more.' He had added the comment: 'Each time we bomb, or soldiers shoot, it is a sign that the political officers have failed in their job.'

2 *The Life of C. M. Doughty* by D. G. Hogarth, published 1928.

SIR HUGH TRENCHARD
21/XII/28   *MIRANSHAH*

Dear Sir Hugh

This morning I was in the cabin at broadcasting time, and the message came through that you had resigned. So it's all over, and I can't tell you how sorry I am.[1] Of course I know it's your wisest move, and you have finished and all that: but here I've just been able to take on for five more*[2], as you go out. You'll feel it hard: for you have never really been in the R A F. at all. You've made it; and that means that you're not in it. People can't make things bigger than themselves: not bigger enough to get into. I'm sorry, because it feels nice, to be in it, like I am.

I think you have finished the job. A man would be slow, who couldn't exhaust all of himself into a thing in ten years. You were lucky to have the chance for ten years. No other man has been given a blank sheet, and told to make a Service, from the ground up. Neither the Army nor the Navy have a father, in the sense of the R.A.F. Now you'll see the child tumbling down and hurting its knees, and getting up again. Don't worry, more than you need. It's a very healthy, and tolerably happy child. A C.A.S. with leisure would make it happier: only your successor will be pretty hard-worked, I expect, like yourself. However your resignation means that the child is on its own, and sooner or later it'll make itself happier.

You'll feel exceedingly lonely and tired for a long time: and I wonder what you'll do: for you aren't old enough to settle down. Perhaps you'll go and govern somewhere. That will be only the shadow of power, after what you've had: but shadows are comfortable, after too fierce a light. So possibly you will be contented.

You'll be rather shocked to find that three weeks after you've gone (about the time you're reading this) your past services haven't any interest or value in the Government's eyes. It's what we can do, yet, which makes us regarded.

I've said to you, before, that in my eyes (very experienced eyes, and judgematical eyes) you have done the biggest and best thing of our generation: and I'd take off my hat to you, only that at Miranshah I do not wear one. There'll never be another King like you in the R.A.F., and I'll feel smaller under whoever it is takes your place. Allenby, Winston, and you: that's my gallery of chiefs, to date. Now there'll be a come down.

1 Trenchard's resignation from the air force had been accepted but it was not to take effect until December 1929.
2 *I.e.* five more years.

You know that I'm at your disposal (except in disposing of my body) at all times and circumstances.

Yours
T. E. Shaw

* Salmond sent me on your message, yesterday. I needn't say I'm grateful. As for the people who want me elsewhere ... let 'em want. I know my own mind.

Bodleian Library

MRS CHARLOTTE SHAW
31.XII.28 & I.I.29

[...]Your letter of 10th Dec. is, politically, all wrong. Waziristan is utterly peaceful. Some of our people the other day visited the clan we bombed (they have moved into the low-lands for the winter) and found them eager to talk over the ups and downs of life: laughing heartily at their well behaved neighbours, on one of whose bullocks a stray bomb fell! They say the war cost them £1200 in damages: and they won't do it again. They have paid for the people they murdered, and let their wretched prisoners go.

The Afghan business[1] is over the border, and behind high hills. While it remains civil war in Afghanistan it will hurt us no more than de Valera hurt Sussex. Only if the new king of Afghanistan (*if* there is a new king) declared war on India, to distract his subjects' minds from internal politics – then there would be a disturbance in N.W. India. Yet not much of N.W. India wants to become Afghan – as it would not go very far with good-will.
[...]

British Library

1 *I.e.* the rebellion against King Amanullah of Afghanistan which inspired some sections of the British press to absurd speculations as to Lawrence's involvement.

They are monologues, too, like conversations with our dear good Queen.

13 Bermingham Street
Southampton
11 · XII · 33

Mi Vykowniess

Let me qualify the "any retired Colonel". I should now say "any Colonel who has retired into the R.A.F."

I cannot answer your letters because I cannot read them all! Only by grace of the headed notepaper do I know whence they come. I cannot answer your wires, because often I am not a shilling to spare. Your wires are gloriously legible.

"A very tall dark woman". Let me think over my recent past. I have never met Lady Londonderry. He is very tall, but not dark, I think. Mrs Guldby (not at Lympne) is dark and a woman: but not very tall, judged by myself: and you are little smaller than me. Mrs Lionel Curtis is tall, but always makes a brown impression on me. Mrs Scott-Paine (wife of the boat-builder with whom I work here) is tall: but I don't know what colour she would wash to. The present outward decoration is magenta and cream. Who else was there? Ah! a Lady Juliet Duff, relic of a generation before your own. She is very tall, but white: and there is the Mrs Siegfried Sassoon-to-be. I think she was dark, but ,I seldom photograph women: nor do I know her name. Probably it's her you are after. She lived near Christchurch with her mother, in an Edwardian-Gothic house. Do not suspect us of an affair. Siegfried is a better man than me, and she was honestly in love with me, and in terror of her life of proving inadequate. I tried to cheer her up, without being foolishly optimistic. I liked the foolhardy creature. Fancy trying on S.S.

Letter from Lawrence to Lady Astor, 11 July 1933

6 LAST YEARS IN THE RAF
1929-35

'The Afghan business is over the border, and behind high hills,' Lawrence had written to Mrs Shaw in his letter of 31 December 1928 – 1 January 1929. 'While it remains civil war in Afghanistan it will hurt us no more than de Valera hurt Sussex.' But thanks to the British press (*see* the introduction to Part 5) he became a casualty of the war himself, and on 12 January 1929 he embarked at Bombay on the P&O liner *S.S. Rajputana*, bound for Tilbury in the Port of London. At Port Said he was not allowed ashore, not only to his annoyance but also to that of the British high commissioner for Egypt, his old friend of wartime days, George, now Lord, Lloyd. The first letter in this section was written to Lloyd as his ship steamed westward across the Mediterranean. 'Your police', he wrote, [...] 'peeved me a little, for deportation from India (to curry the favour of Amanullah and the Soviets) has not made me, yet, feel criminal. Nor would my stepping ashore for an hour at Port Said have harmed Egypt.' However, if he was unable to see Lloyd, the latter's son was on the ship going home to Eton and Lawrence went to talk to him in his cabin. 'I wish kids didn't have to grow up,' he told Lloyd. 'They are so beautiful, unfinished.' Lawrence was always benign to the children of his friends.

It was decided that he should be taken off the ship at her first landfall, Plymouth, but even there the press was lying in wait and the R.A.F. had to resort to evasive measures to enable him to escape to London. He was afraid (as it turned out, unnecessarily) that the Air Ministry might decide to be rid of him, because of the activities of the press and the questions raised about him in Parliament; and in order to grasp the latter difficulty he visited the House of Commons to argue his case with two Labour MPs who had challenged his serving in the forces under the 'false' name of Shaw. He managed to persuade them of his good intentions, but his action did not endear him to the Air Ministry. His letter of 8 February 1929 in which he vigorously defended his actions to Trenchard – and then apologized in a much less aggressive postscript – must be virtually unique in exchanges between an ordinary serviceman and his chief. But these difficulties and the disruption of his service life weighed heavily on him, as seems clear from a number of short staccato letters he wrote to various friends at this time. They include a repeated metaphor that he was to use again just before his death, in his last message to Lady Astor some six years later. In several letters written on 28 February he used with minor variations the phrase 'Something's gone wrong with the works'; adding in Newcombe's case 'I can't wind myself up to meet people: instead I moon about, longing to get into Camp again', and concluding, 'I am sorry. Do you think my pipes are frozen?' Earlier on 22 February he had written to Trenchard's former private secretary, T. B. Marson: 'For the moment I wander about London with my eyes on the pavement, like a man who's dropped sixpence, and can't remember in which street it was.' He continued: 'On March 8 I move to Cattewater (Plymouth) which is to be my next camp. I hope it will prove a homely place.'

R.A.F. Cattewater (the name was later changed, largely on his initiative, to Mount Batten) was to prove a homelier place than he could have imagined. Its commanding officer was Wing Commander (later Air Commodore) Sydney Smith, whom Lawrence had first met at the Cairo Peace Conference and who had been in charge of the operation to spirit him off the *Rajputana*. C.O. and aircraftman became close friends, and Lawrence was made especially welcome by Smith's family, which consisted of his wife, Clare (who was to become a great admirer and write a book about this period under the title – the phrase was Lawrence's – *The Golden Reign*), their daughter Maureen (known as 'Squeak') and several dogs. He was soon able to write to E. M. Forster (1 April 1929): 'I feel just like a plant taking root after a transplantation.' In July he was relaxed enough to write that having 'made fools of themselves over me and Afghanistan' the newspapers 'will not readily invent another yarn'. His optimism, as events turned out, was premature. On the cusp of the new year, 30 December, he awoke to find himself the subject of another newspaper absurdity: the canard that he was behind a rebellion that had broken out in Persia. He turned for help to the head of the press and publicity branch of the Air Ministry, Charles Pennycook Robertson, who was effectively Lawrence's public relations manager at this period, worried yet again that his RAF superiors might react as they had back in 1923 and eject him from the service. His letter also contained a notable rebuff which he asked Robertson to transmit to an American journalist who had asked to be granted an interview with him to discuss his dealings with the Arabs during the desert war: 'Do tell your sportsman that he is out of date. It was about ten or twelve years ago and I've forgotten all about it. You handle Arabs, I think, as you handle Englishmen, or Laplanders or Czechoslovaks: cautiously, at first, and kindly always.'

Such temporary hazards apart, Lawrence was to find his final period in the air force a comparatively calm and productive one. In his first year back in England he was one of the R.A.F. support team involved in the races for the Schneider Cup. Yet for most of his final air force years, the work to which he applied his not inconsiderable talents as a mechanic (a talent about which he had cheerfully boasted to his family back in Carchemish days) was to do with boats: fast, modern boats with air-sea rescue as their major role. They were to supersede the naval craft previously in use which had been found to be far too cumbersome and slow. As an increasingly valuable member of the research team assigned by the R.A.F. to develop its own specialized vessels, Lawrence moved between a number of air force and marine establishments over the next few years (Plymouth, Southampton, Cowes in the Isle of Wight, Felixstowe, Bridlington), spent much time in tests and trials, and even wrote an operational textbook. When the first boats were finished and ready to show their paces he invoked his friendship with the editor of *The Times*, Geoffrey Dawson, to get press coverage of quality for an enterprise of which he was proud to be part, the proviso being that his own connection with it was not divulged; his letter to Dawson of 22 March 1932 describing what he and his colleagues were about not only puts the whole matter in a nutshell but also has something of the vigour of his wartime dispatches. Significantly, he did not disparage his mechanical achievements as he did his literary efforts. In September 1934, a few months before his discharge, he wrote to Lord Lloyd: 'My boat work for the R.A.F. (now extending to the Army and the Navy) has been successful, and lets me out of the Service with some distinction, I think. After having dabbled in revolt and politics it is rather nice to have been mechanically useful!' He was aware of an important personal benefit in all this. 'I think many of us go wrong by being too exclusively cerebral,' he wrote to Ezra Pound in December of the same year. 'I've spent the last twelve years in the ranks of the Air Force. My own job has been producing motor boats: and I fancy that each concrete thing I launched took away some of my bile.'

Apart from his time at Carchemish and to a lesser extent at Cranwell, these were, on the whole, his happiest years. But he was never a man for simple contentment across the board. His letters inevitably vary widely in mood. 'If you are to go on knowing me', he wrote to H. S. Ede on 28 November 1929, 'you must allow for – expect – these sort of sulks.' In that particular case he was riding his regular hobby-horse of the inadequacy of letters as distinct from personal contact, but there were 'sulks' on other subjects, too. When, in April 1929, *John Bull* divulged to its substantial readership that 'your old friend "Lawrence of Arabia"' was planning to publish a translation of *The Odyssey* anonymously in the United States, his anger at yet another act of perfidy by the press spilled over into several letters and he almost withdrew from his contract. The military historian Major Archibald Becke, eager to discuss the 1918 Battle of Tafileh for the purposes of the official history of the war, was told (28 December 1929): 'Your letter sits here on my table in the office, and I have been cursing it at intervals. Why on earth should anybody bother about that old war any longer?' T. C. Griffin of Montreal, claiming a tenuous acquaintance going back to the war period, was told (17 April 1931): 'I hope you will pardon my not remembering one of you more than another. It was – how long ago? Nearly fifteen years, wasn't it? I am so old now, and it feels a lifetime away.' He added: 'Nine years ago I enlisted, and have not thought about the Middle East since. The Air Force life suits me, and I'm happy in it.'

He was also happy in extending the circle of his friends. One important friend of this period was Lady Astor, to whom he wrote over forty letters between 1929 and 1935, many of them breezy and witty, others serious and frank. At times, indeed, he wrote to her almost with the intimate confessional tone normally reserved for Mrs Shaw. Other new intimates were the writers Henry Williamson and Frederic Manning, the playwright Noël Coward, and the politician Ernest Thurtle, one of the Labour MPs whom he met when he stormed the Houses of Parliament, with whose views on military reform and such subjects as the abolition of the death penalty for cowardice in war he had much sympathy. Meanwhile, his friends of the barrack room, not discarded as he moved from station to station or even from service to service, were still regular recipients of his letters, written not out of duty but because of his genuine affection for them. If they were in trouble he was always prepared to take great pains to help them.

Throughout this period he worked when he could on the improvement of Clouds Hill. In a letter of 18 May 1934, he wrote to Mrs Shaw: 'My cottage is finished, inside and out, so far as alien hands can finish it – and I feel rooted now.' It was the same expression which he had used to Forster in 1929; but though he was happy at putting down roots at Clouds Hill, his roots in the R.A.F. were under threat and he knew that the day was rapidly approaching when he would have to leave the service which he had come to love. In a letter to E. H. R. Altounyan in April 1934, he wrote that he was looking forward to the 'unbounded leisure' that would soon be his, but this did not represent his general attitude; on the whole, the prospect of his exit from the air force hung like a shadow over these years, growing ever more substantial as the months went by. In the letter to Lord Lloyd of September 1934 (quoted on p. 423) he wrote: 'In March I leave the R.A.F. and it feels like the end of living. [...] How does one pass the fag-end of life?' He expressed the same idea to Sir Ronald Storrs on the last day of January 1935, with under a month to go: 'After my discharge I have somehow to pick up a new life and occupy myself – but beforehand it looks and feels like an utterly blank wall.'

Three letters are included from Lawrence's last weeks in uniform: what has become known as his own obituary, a letter written in reply to a request from Robert Graves; a second letter of protest to Charles Pennycook Robertson reflecting on his ever-troubled relations with the press, all the more worrying to him because he would so soon lose the services of his 'Publicity Deflector'; and a warm letter of gratitude to the chief of air staff, Sir Edward Ellington, reflecting on his twelve years of service, admitting his sadness at going and concluding with the memorable statement: 'The R.A.F. has been much more than my profession.'

LORD LLOYD[1]
22.1.29   [S.S *RAJPUTANA*]

Dear G. L.

I have, imaginatively, written you books and books of letters: but in our camps nothing happens big enough to engage the attention of a High Commissioner. It is only as now, when my past has intervened and spoilt my present, that there comes any cause of writing, really. You must be sure that always you have my best wishes and willingness.

As for telling you that I was coming! Well, your police knew that. They peeved me a little, for deportation from India (to curry the favour of Amanullah and the Soviets) has not made me, yet, feel criminal Nor would my stepping ashore for an hour at Port Said have harmed Egypt.[2] However as I'm English, more or less, they are almost bound to let me land there. It would please me to see the Government of India drowning in a ditch. Positively I would not cross the road to push them under.

For David, I have seen him: and, I hope, not spoilt his digestion.[3] A bit grim for the kid, to be inspected by his father's friends. I told him what you were really like, which was news to him, for there is a divinity which hedges heads of families. A nice kid, you have produced. He is more ornamental than ever you were, and less truculent. Of course he has a father to fight his battles. Perhaps his mouth will harden after he leaves home: do you think we should

1 Lawrence's former wartime colleague George Lloyd, now Lord Lloyd of Dolobran and high commissioner for Egypt, a post he had held since 1925. He had previously (1918-23) been governor of Bombay.

2 'At Port Said, last stop, they picketed the quay-side to prevent my going ashore. I'd like to say something with a B in it about the India Government': Lawrence to Aircraftman H. G. Hayter at Miranshah. *See DG*, pp. 639-40.

3 David Lloyd, Lord Lloyd's only son (1912-85), was returning to England after a holiday with his parents in Egypt.

all fight our own courses? Since I changed ways, and learned to run and hide, life has been far happier. These days I am very meek and obedient. Indeed the officers begin to like me, here & there. A doormat. However, back to David. He was very embarrassed by me. Have you been stuffing the poor child with Lowell-Thomas tales? The contrast between my person & my reputation is grotesque. I wonder if such shyness as his is one of your secret vices. It makes him very nice. The (apparent) lack of it does not injure your central goodness. It would have been a freak of nature if the child of you two had been nasty.

We compared you with Lord Curzon and talked of Mussolini, and of Lenin, my preference. I tried to make him see the grandeur of Lenin. So you will see that our company in his little deck-cabin was mainly of your peers. (I apologise for dragging in poor Curzon).

On the way down from Lahore my pilot (who was sorry for my being so rudely deported) circled about Sukkur,[4] at my request, and explored the hundreds of miles of canals which begin to spin outwards from the unfinished dam. You have written your name across a country as big as the south of England.

At Bombay I tried to see your dredger: but she was invisible. They told me that she (?he) had not been given a peerage when you went up. That's the sort of ungraciousness the Indian authorities are delighted in. [*sic*]

Up to Port Said I had been counting over the people I would see in England. One was to be your father-in-law, whose staunchness of mind made him a great experience.[5] At Port Said I picked up a *Truth* which told of his death. Please tell Lady Lloyd that I am, in my degree, very sorry. Half of the people I have liked in my time are now dead. Aubrey, you know: & Hogarth, & Thomas Hardy. Please go on living, for a while yet. David is only a sketch: beautifully begun, but shaped by others so far; we will see, later, how he shapes himself. I wish kids didn't have to grow up. They are so beautiful, unfinished.

Finished the paper: finished my letter. I hope for you three years more in Egypt, as prosperous as these: and then translation.... but after that there is nothing except an inner life in which to steep yourself.

T.E.S.

Churchill College Cambridge

4 As governor of Bombay Lloyd had been responsible for launching a vast irrigation scheme of which the central feature was a dam at Sukkur; he had also (*see* next paragraph) carried through a scheme for reclaiming land in Bombay harbour.
5 Lloyd's father-in-law was Commander the Hon. Frederick Lascelles R.N. Retd.

SIR HUGH TRENCHARD
5/2/29   *14 BARTON STREET WESTMINSTER*

Dear Sir Hugh

May I have 36 days overseas leave? and leave the 28 extension of service leave*
till the difficulties pass by? I shall be glad to be safe in camp again.

Some anonymous people have bought and sent to me a motor-bike, the
current model of the great things I used to ride. Its cost is three years of my
pay: and I feel rather pauperised: but I will try to pay it back to them, in time.[1]
I mention it only because it restores my liberty of action: and so I can report
to Cattewater, easily, any time you like.

I want to tell you, too, that I have explained to Mr Thurtle,[2] privately, the
marriage tangles of my father (*you* probably know of them: *he* didn't, and is
asking questions which might have dragged the whole story into the light) and
I hope he will respect my confidence, and stop asking questions in the House.
Probably an airman shouldn't discuss his family tree with an M.P.: but I can
hardly ask the Secretary of State to intervene and save me from curiosity.

Yours ever
T. E. Shaw

* Which has no limit, before which it must be taken: we can have it anytime.

Bodleian Library

SIR HUGH TRENCHARD
8/2/29   *14 BARTON STREET WESTMINSTER*

Dear Sir Hugh
I will come in about Wednesday next, if you do not want me early, for any
reason. Tomorrow I hope to go out into the country for four days, to stay with
my mother. (Address: – T. E. Shaw, Holly Copse, Goring Heath, Oxon.)

---

1 The donors were Mrs Shaw and a number of close friends,
2 Ernest Thurtle had been asking questions in Parliament about Lawrence's alleged involvement
   in Afghanistan: Lawrence had 'explained' to him at the House of Commons: conduct
   considered unbecoming by the Air Ministry, hence the next letter to Trenchard. *See* p. 427.

As for the House of Commons raid, I think I was right. Mr. Thurtle was enquiring into what was very much my private business. In explaining this I explained practically the whole affair, and probably the Labour Group will ask you no more questions on my account. In that case, I shall expect you to feel sorry that I did not go sooner to the House!

As for Blumenfeld,[1] whom I tried to see, and for whom I left a message, he is a very old friend of mine, who never publishes any account of my vagaries. What advice he gave as to ending newspaper talk was therefore disinterested, and he knows more of Fleet Street than we do. He can hardly have told you that I was meaning to make any statement: I would not do so without your very specific order:– and perhaps not even then without an argument.

However I have finished Thurtle, and will not visit Blumenfeld (or any other newspaper office) without your future leave.

Will you please shut up the *Daily News*? It goes on chattering, and a word from you to Sir Herbert Samuel, saying that it was my wish, would do the business. A silly rag of a paper.

Many thanks for the leave arrangements, and for the Cattewater posting. I shall breathe quieter when I get into camp again. Am still in uniform, and have not once been recognised in the street, though I walk about all day.

Yours sincerely
T. E. Shaw

I'm afraid the above reads too stiffly. That is the worst of type. I am very sorry to have annoyed you by my slight activity, and will be very patient henceforward. The trouble is that I know too much of Government Offices to have proper confidence in them. They are manned by people just the same as myself, or rather less so: and anything outside their files scares them! However you know them too.

Perhaps I should report that Sir P. Sassoon[2] has asked me to lunch on Thursday next; and that I'll go, unless you say no, meanwhile.

T.E.S.

Bodleian Library/HMH

2 Editor of the *Daily Express*.
1 Sir Philip Sassoon (1888–1939) was under-secretary of state for air.

ERNEST THURTLE[1]

9/2/29   *14 BARTON STREET WESTMINSTER*

Dear Mr Thurtle

I doubt whether you properly observed the street's name or the number of the house, the other night. Will you hand it on, please, to whoever will return my books – and please remind them to be uncommonly discreet over *The Mint*, the R.A.F. book; for I have been told by the Powers that my visit to the House was not approved: told very distinctly, I'm afraid.

It was very pleasant for me that you were so reasonable, that night. You will realise that I can't spend an hour with everybody, explaining that there is no mystery: and I'm delighted to have had the chance, by lending you those two books, to give myself away to you completely. If Mr Maxton[2] will read some of them, he'll never be nervous about me, either, again.

Yours sincerely
T. E. Shaw

DG

---

1 Ernest Thurtle (1884-1954), Labour MP for Shoreditch, had served in the First World War first in the ranks and later as an officer and had been severely wounded at Cambrai in 1917. He had taken up a cause with which Lawrence was to be later associated when in 1924 he published a pamphlet titled *Shooting at Dawn: The Army Death Penalty at Work*, the purpose of which was to establish that executions during the war for cowardice and desertion were miscarriages of justice. He and Lawrence were regular correspondents between 1929 and 1935.
2 James Maxton (1885-1946) was leader of the Independent Labour Party from 1926-46 and MP for Bridgeton, Glasgow. He had been a pacifist and a conscientious objector in the First World War. He had been with Thurtle during Lawrence's House of Commons visit.

T. B. MARSON[1]
22.2.29
14 BARTON STREET WESTMINSTER

Dear Marson

Indeed I am back: and not too quietly, as your letter remarked. Nearly got the sack again, I think. What a life.

There will be another crisis and spasm about August, when a film of my supposed adventures falls due. Hell.

What next?

For the moment I wander about London with my eyes on the pavement, like a man who's dropped sixpence, and can't remember in which street it was. Also it is more cold than I ever thought possible.

On March 8 I move to Cattewater (Plymouth) which is to be my next camp. I hope it will prove a homely place.

Thanks for the offer of hospitality. If it gets warmer, later on in the year, I'll ask if I may come then. I have got a month's re-engagement leave in reserve, to be taken when the film is released. Perhaps then?

Yours
T. E. Shaw.

I've put Wing Commander on the envelope. I hope that is so.

Bodleian Library

I T. B. Marson served in the ranks in the Boer War, joined up again in the First World War, lost a leg at Gallipoli and subsequently transferred to the Royal Flying Corps, where he served under Trenchard. Until his retirement in 1926, he had been Trenchard's private secretary. Lawrence later helped him get his autobiography, *Scarlet and Khaki*, published by Jonathan Cape.

HENRY WILLIAMSON[1]

22/2/29 *14 BARTON STREET WESTMINSTER*

Dear H.W.

They have posted me to Plymouth: so if ever the frost breaks (Brrrr ... Ughhhh) a motor-bike will disturb Skirr Cottage[2]. A horrible bike: but so beautiful in its owner's eyes & heart!

It will be comic, our meeting: I am icy cold, & very English, & correct. Sober as judges used to be. However, all the more reason for meeting a wild man.

At least your reputation won't scare me off. *A bas* all the Hawthorndens. Hawthorn, forsooth! Den, forsooth!

It will not be for a while. A new camp takes learning: especially for me, who am always uneasy with a new crowd. But it will be 1929, & not 1930.

Praise God!

T E Shaw
Bodleian Library

COLONEL S. F. NEWCOMBE

22/2/29

Dear S.F.

I am in London, rather distractedly & jerkily, with one suit of plain clothes, & two suits of uniform, & a motor-bike: I see hardly anyone, & don't know

---

1 Henry Williamson (1895-1977) had recently won popular and critical acclaim as the writer of the classic work *Tarka the Otter*, published in 1927, for which (*see* paragraph 3) he was awarded the Hawthornden Prize in 1928. He and Lawrence had become acquainted through Edward Garnett, to whom Lawrence had sent an immensely long and detailed critique of *Tarka*, which Garnett had forwarded to Williamson. They subsequently opened correspondence. Williamson later wrote a warm appreciation of their relationship in *Genius of Friendship: 'T. E. Lawrence'*, (Faber and Faber 1941). In addition to writing novels based on observations of nature, he also wrote a series of fifteen novels of contemporary life called *Chronicle of Ancient Sunlight*. His fascination with Fascism was to lead to his internment for a time in the Second World War and to some clouding of his reputation as a writer. All letters to Williamson in this selection are printed in whole or in part in *Genius of Friendship*.

2 At Georgeham in North Devon, where Williamson had moved after some years in Fleet Street to live a modest country life. Tarka's river, the Taw, flows into the sea at nearby Barnstaple.

what to say to them, when I do see them. On March 10 R.A.F. life begins again – at Cattewater, which is Plymouth. It will be a blessed relief. Now, it's like being lost.

My regards to N. the Second: and to Mrs. Newcombe, whom I shall hope to see, some time.

Yours
T.E.S.

Bodleian Library

ALAN DAWNAY
28.2.29   *14 BARTON STREET WESTMINSTER*

I am frozen in to London. The bike is at Nottingham,[1] and the roads all ice and snow: so she cannot travel them. The first day of melting I will go up there, by train, and ride her down. But will it ever melt?

If God is good, I'll try and call in at Aldershot on my way down to Plymouth:– about March 8. If only it were tomorrow! I do not think I shall ever go on leave, for pleasure: only to dodge publicity is the misery justified. Something's gone wrong with the works, and I find myself breaking every engagement, and avoiding everyone.

They tell me your child is ill. I am so sorry.

TES

Bodleian Library

1 The Brough motor-cycle factory was in Nottingham.

DAVID GARNETT
28.2.29   *14 BARTON STREET WESTMINSTER*

Something seems to have gone wrong with my works: and I find myself breaking every engagement, and seeing nobody.

This warns you, therefore, not to be frantic if I perjure myself next Wednesday. Do I call at the Nonesuch about 7.30?[1] I shall,* unless you say 'no'.

Yours
T. E. Shaw.

    * Subject to reservation in 2nd paragraph.

Bodleian Library

COLONEL S. F. NEWCOMBE
28/2/29   *[14 BARTON STREET WESTMINSTER]*

Dear S. F.
Please apologise humbly for me to Mrs. S. F. Something has gone wrong with the works: and I can't wind myself up to meet people: instead I moon about, longing to get into Camp again – on March 8, thank goodness.

Please remember me to Jimmy,[1] when next you see him or write to him.

I am sorry. Do you think my pipes are frozen?

T.E.S.

Bodleian Library

1 David Garnett was editing Shakespeare for the Nonesuch Press.

1 Newcombe's son Stewart was usually known as Jimmy.

MRS CHARLOTTE SHAW
12/3/29

This is only to report progress. My address is
        338171 A/c Shaw
        R.A.F. Cattewater
        Plymouth.
    It is a tiny station, on a rocky peninsula, projecting into the Sound. From my
bed the sea lies 30 yards to the South (at high tide:– beach all rock) and 60 yards
to the North. The whole peninsula, with its quays and breakwaters, is R.A.F.
There are about 100 of us living on the rock, in six huts. Today I had a hot bath.
The airmen all praise the camp and its conditions, but complain that it is hard
and slow to reach the town of Plymouth, from it. This will not distress me.
    My job? Not settled. For a fortnight I 'mark time' in the Headquarters
Office: and then they give me to the Workshop's Officer, to employ clerically
or on his motor boats. It seems to me that there are very few disagreeables
here. The food is excellent: the place is comfortable: restrictions very slight,
and those sensible. The Commanding Officer, of course, I know and like.
    In the hut are two gramophones, and a wireless set with very loud speakers.
It will not be easy to work, here, at first: but probably after a week my ears
will be as deaf to hut noises, as to the wash of the sea (which now transports
me!) and the mooing, like strained cows, of the liners groping for the Sound's
entrance in the foggy mornings.
    The beauty of the camp's setting is quite beyond my eyes to see, wholly.
The weather is misted sunshine, and there is a subdued sparkle everywhere. In
summer it will be blazing-bright. The promontory is like a fossil lizard
stretched out into the Sound, with its head towards Plymouth, and its root in
golf-links, which are a cascade of green lawns falling towards the sea.
    The Air Ministry had notified the camp a month ago that I was coming
to it: and so no one took any interest in my actual arrival. It was old news.
    As for the reading:[1] – I write tonight to Lady Astor saying that I will do
my best to come: but I shall not know, till the Friday night, whether they will
let me go or not. The usual week end is only 'after duty Saturday' (1 p.m.) till
midnight Sunday. I cannot get up and down on that: but I am owed four days'
leave, and shall try to get two of them for the 23rd and 24th.
    The bicycle is a heavenly machine. My ride down here was a golden occasion.

1 *See* next letter.

So you must understand that all is very well. After I've written these 20 or so letters, I shall try Homer again!

T.E.S.

Oh, I'm sorry. On the way down I saw John Buchan, who said he had heard (? from Trenchard) of *The Mint*, and wanted to read it.

Now it's been lent to F. L. Lucas: and John Buchan is a busy man, a great benefactor to me. It would not be right to put him to the pain of reading that illegible little MS. Its handwriting is shocking. Of course there is a decent explanation: but I cannot tell that to anyone I meet.

So I told him that you had a typed copy. If he bothers you for it, you'll probably have to lend it him, and then will hate me! Blame, partly, the R.A.F. manner, which holds all property as common.

T.E.S.   *British Library*

LADY ASTOR[I]
12/3/29   *R.A.F. CATTEWATER PLYMOUTH*

Dear Lady Astor

I'd immensely appreciate hearing that G.B.S. reading, and if I can possibly wangle leave for Saturday and Sunday I will attend (probably in uniform, but I shan't mind your being differently dressed!) on the 23rd.

If I do not turn up, then please blame the R.A.F. rather than my expectant self.

Your sincerely
T E Shaw.

Bodleian Library

I Viscountess Astor (1879-1964), born Nancy Witcher Langhorne in Virginia, U.S.A., was the wife of Waldorf, 2nd Viscount Astor of Cliveden. When her husband, who had been a Unionist MP for Plymouth from 1910-19, went to the House of Lords on his father's death in 1919, Lady Astor succeeded to his constituency, holding it until 1945. She was the first woman MP to take her seat in the House of Commons (but not the first to be elected; Countess Markiewicz had been elected in 1918, but as a Sinn Feiner had refused to sit). This letter was apparently the first in their long and lively correspondence.

F. L. LUCAS
26.3.29   *R.A.F. CATTEWATER PLYMOUTH*

I don't want to write tonight, but I must. I'm on Fire Pickets all this week (*i.e.*
distracted & oppressed) and can't settle down to read or write. However, if I
don't write you'll wonder what's the matter.

Your letter about *The Mint* delights me because it is really useful. Detailed
criticism is the only useful kind. Ever so many thanks. Now I'll run through
it & see if there are notes to reply.

About my writing more – No: if ever I had to write again, by such necessity
as made me write the *Seven Pillars*, of course I'd do it: but it's not a thing to be
undertaken wantonly. I have nothing now to tell anyone: nothing to preach:
nothing believed. Wherefore I cannot go on writing, can I?

Of course *The Mint* is a cherrystone compared to the *S.P.* but I think it is
a better piece of work: smaller in its faults (and in its virtues) but more like a
work of art, as a whole. The *S.P.* was an afterthought, after the Revolt had
ended. *The Mint* was meant to be written – and these are the notes which were
to guide my writing, some day. I really think, too, that the *book* would have
been written if my R.A.F. career had not been suddenly interrupted.

It interests me that you should feel the R.A.F. less 'big' than the Arab
Revolt. Of course it isn't: Damascus and Cranwell are different, but if Cranwell
feels less, then that's because it is less well conceived and written down.

I thought Cummings had made a very good thing of *The Enormous Room*.[1]

Others besides yourself have been troubled by the gap between Depot and
Cadet College. I was very unhappy at Farnborough, & decided not to put it
on record. A mean C.O.: and a bad show, Farnborough was. After it I had 2½
years Tank Corps, which is a different subject, & would I think only confuse
the R.A.F. picture. From the Tanks I returned for three days to Uxbridge, the
R.A.F. Depot, *& went thence to Cranwell*, as I describe. That gave me the chance
to carry the story straight through. Do you think I ought to expand the
'explanation' into greater length, & detail the Farnborough & Tank Corps
digressions? I have some raw notes: but they are pretty grim reading.

My bowels have twice or thrice destroyed my poise of stoical indifference,
which is proper to a man of action! A bit of a handicap, is funk: to people of the
V.C. class, in which reputation would put me! Of course I know, in myself, that
I'm not a brave person: and am not sorry. Most brave people aren't attractive.

1 *See* p. 467, footnote 3.

In 'Last Post' the all clear signal I handed down the hut was that Corporal Abbinett was again in Bed! Sorry. Too much compression there, apparently.

I do think that conscious, deliberate exercise is an evil thing: but I didn't class 'prostitution' as important. There are so many prostitutions that one can't take them tragically.

The period of enjoyment, in sex, seems to me a very doubtful one. I've asked the fellows in this hut (three or four go with women regularly). They are not sure: but they say it's all over in ten minutes: and the preliminaries – which I discounted – take up most of the ten minutes. For myself, I haven't tried it, & hope not to. I doubt if any man could time his excitement without a stop-watch: and that's a cold-blooded sort of notion.[2]

I would like to say more about Trenchard some day. A very noble and unusual person.

We do regard flying as a sort of ritual: more an art than a science, it is. Unreasonable to expect other people to feel like that, of course: but it is not an unpresentable Crusade: compared with the Lord's Sepulchre.

You don't like my saying that the old Depot is reformed away: and wish for a moral. But I tried not to moralise or condemn more than the instruments through whom the system worked. As a victim I have hardly the right to condemn.

I am glad you feel the difference between Cadet College & Depot. E.M.F. said that Cadet College didn't 'come through' as a happy place. I re-read said MS before it went to you, & was inclined to disagree with him.

It seemed to me to contain better 'bits' than the first two parts. No doubt they are too 'bitty': a whole Cadet College would be longer than Depot. [...]

Of course one is always apart & intact: but to see another airman in the street is (for me) like one ship sighting another at sea. The sea becomes not lonely, all at once.

Yes, I would like the dedication of your novel:[3] everybody would. You are a very good writer. Your poems (of which I'll write to you when I feel less unworthy of them) prove it. They are a delight.

Yours
T.E.S.

DG/Bodleian Library

2 See 'General Introduction' p. xxviii and letter to Graves of 6 November 1928 (p. 412).
3 Lucas dedicated his novel *Cécile*, published in 1930, to Lawrence.

HERBERT READ[1]
26.3.29   *R.A.F. CATTEWATER PLYMOUTH*

Dear Read

Excuse pencil. I have no ink for the moment. *All Quiet* is a most interesting work. Your judgment 'distilled bitterness of the generation shot to pieces by the war' is exactly fitting. Incidentally it would have been a bigger book without that bias. The railing against our elders of p. 19 is not worthy of a man. Our elders are only ourselves: there is no difference between one generation & another – nor, in war (or in that war) between class & class. The war-fever in England rose from bottom to top, & forced our unwilling government's hand. It was the young (youth) & the ignorant (age) who, as usual, made the war. Wars are made in hot blood, not in cold blood. Of course Cramer[2] suffered so much that one must excuse him. Lots of people lose their balance when they have suffered painfully. Yet the war was all our faults.

It's surely well written – and I expect the goodness is in the German as well as in the translation. The dying man's voice 'like ashes': lots of phrases like that. It is over-written sometimes, the killing of Duval in the crater – that should have been short: so should the shelling in the graveyard. He squeezed his orange too dry there.

He does his pathos wonderfully – the death of Kemmerich: the wounded horses (one of the highlights of the book): the chapter of going home on leave (the highest light of all, I think). Only the pathetic stop is like the organ's *vox humana*. It's too easy. That point also makes me think Cramer not so much strong as sensitive. [...] He revolts too much, usually, against his horrors: but he was only a lad, & it's quite likely he has some Jew in him. The point of view is hardly that of a German amongst Germans. The care with which he inserts the daily coarseness & carnality of army life feels foreign too. I suspect him of not being pure German. Not that it matters what he is. The book is international.

I've seen nothing in English war novels so good as this, and I have read very many of them. [...]

University of Victoria, British Columbia

---

1 Herbert, later Sir Herbert Read (1893-1968), poet, critic and former wartime soldier; he had sent Lawrence a copy of *All Quiet on the Western Front*, by the German writer Erich Maria Remarque, which had just been published in English.
2 As written: Lawrence had apparently mis-remembered the writer's name.

Ernest Thurtle
1.4.29   *Cattewater Plymouth*

Dear Thurtle (This sounds very familiar)
I have read your little bomb. It would modify all subsequent wars.[1] I do not see it coming off: but I think the death penalty will cease pretty soon. The debates on it in the House make my blood boil. I wish I could talk to some of the old stagers for a few minutes, about funk & courage. They are the same quality, you know. A man who can run away is a potential V.C.

A possible modification of the enlistment regulations *might* be brought in by some progressive government: to allow service men to give notice (a month, 3 months, six months: even a year: plus such money penalty as seems equitable) & leave the service in peace time. At present to buy yourself out is difficult. The application is usually refused. Anyway the permission is an act of grace: whereas it should be a right. I think the knowledge that their men could leave the service would effect a revolution in the attitude of officers & N.C.Os towards us. It would modify discipline profoundly, for the good, by making it voluntary: something we could help, if we wished. We would become responsible, then, for our behaviour. At present we are like parcels in the post. It is the peace-army & navy & air force which is the concern of parliament. War is a madness, for which no legislation will suffice. If you damage the efficiency of war, by act of Parliament, then when the madness comes Parliament will first of all repeal its damaging acts. Wars, in England, well up from below: from the ignorant: till they carry away the (reluctant) Cabinet.

Graves' book isn't apocrypha: but it is not to be taken seriously. I eat anything except oysters & parsnips. I live in barracks (*i.e.* we dog-fight promiscuously). What is handshaking? The reason I had no overcoat was financial. It seemed a wicked waste of 3 or 4 pounds, for a mere month.* When I felt cold I changed into uniform. G.B.S. lent me his second overcoat: but it was too gigantic a cloak for my normal wear. If it rained: yes: or late at night. Our evening was not too chilly. I'm very susceptible to cold: in England I'm always getting into hot baths, whenever they are available: because then only I am warm enough. Yet I never get what they call 'a chill'. Odd: because usually I get all the infections going!

Please don't get the public feeling that I'm different from the crowd. By experience in many camps I have assured myself (so certainly that all the print in the world won't shake my conviction) that I'm a very normal sort of Anglo-Irishman.

1 Probably a reference to Thurtle's *Military Discipline and Democracy*, published 1920.

Women? I like some women. I don't like their sex: any more than I like the monstrous regiment of men. Some men. There is no difference that I can feel between a woman & a man. They look different, granted: but if you work with them there doesn't seem any difference at all. I can't understand all the fuss about sex. It's as obvious as red hair: and as little fundamental, I fancy. I will try & call at Temple Fortune Hill, & pay my respects: but I will make no promise. London's centre holds so many pleasures for one who has wasted 20 years abroad: and I'm selfish enough to go walking by myself usually. A sense of social duty does sometimes overcome me, & while it lasts I pay calls, & try to recall my manners. Only so often (especially in new houses) I feel like a Zoo beast without bars to defend me. There are all these absurd stories, with, in my fancy, people watching to confirm them, or make new ones. I know that is absurd: but you can write it down as a nervous affliction. The wearing a false reputation is as itchy a job as a false beard. Mine drives me crazy.

Yes, I get a huge correspondence: and the answering the justifiable percentage (20%) makes an inroad on my time. Also there is a Yankee dealer who pays £20 for my letters. Would you write, *ever*, if that happened to you?

If ever you come to the far west, by all means let me know, & if I can we'll meet somewhere: but my bike has no pillion: so you are safe not to break the speed law on my tail. Airmen are not allowed to carry pillion riders, or ride pillion. Another injustice! Poor troops. Yet I wouldn't change with any civilian.

Yours
T E Shaw.

Cattewater is shaping well. I shall like it, in the warm weather (if any).
* I daren't spend my little reserve of cash. Any moment press chatter may extrude from the R.A.F. & I've got to live while trying to find a rumour-proof job.

DG/Bodleian Library

E. M. FORSTER
1.4.29   *R.A.F. CATTEWATER PLYMOUTH*

Dear E.M.F.

There we are! It is a decent little camp, quiet & easy. Very beautifully placed in Plymouth Sound. A spine of rocks & grass, like a fossil lizard, swimming out from the Devon shore towards the Hoe. Our hut is just above sea level, & has the open Sound 30 yrds to the S: and the Cattewater (harbour) to the N. about 70 yards away. In summer it should be a heaven, when the sun shines. Now it is chillish: not bad.

There are 150 of us in the station, of whom 50 live in Plymouth.

They are not generous about week-ends: after duty Saturday till midnight Sunday: so I will not be able to come up to see people except rarely. Perhaps when summer time comes.

I have not settled in, properly, so have not done any of my *Odyssey* job, bar the three days of this Easter holiday, when I have stuck tight to it, & done the 9th book, in rough draft.

Nowt else to say, alas. I feel just like a plant taking root after a transplantation.

TES.

Called in at Clouds Hill on my way down. It looked so beautiful.

Bodleian Library

MRS CHARLOTTE SHAW
Monday 8/4/29

I am sorry for you:[1] which is the only language that English provides for any occasion of loss: and so I suppose we are not built by the nature of our race to do or think more than that. Yet it feels inadequate.*

She being now beyond your care, it remains to think about yourself and G.B.S. and I am very glad that you hope to leave next Sunday. The effect of death, in my experience, is gradual and cumulative. You will find yourself

1 Mrs Shaw's sister had just died.

more miserable a month after it (if your sister has counted in your life's background) than a day after it. So I'd like you to be away, and in a strange climate, which makes other demands on your mind and body. Also G.B.S. is tired. Probably it is much harder to write plays at 70 than at 40: and he has been ill, which perhaps was not (like the play) his fault. Anyway, he should be taken beyond reach of Miss Patch[2] and the papers. [...]

T.E.S.

* If our feelings could speak, they wouldn't speak English, would they?

British Library

SIR HUGH TRENCHARD
16 IV.29   *R.A.F. CATTEWATER PLYMOUTH*

Dear Sir Hugh

I hope you realised that my not writing meant that all was well. Cattewater is in a lovely place, and will be perfection if the weather and water get hot. The camp is a good one: comfortably laid-out, compact and small, and we are a happy family: or two families: one of H.Q. the other of 204 Squadron. Mine is H.Q.: we are *quite* happy. The Squadron will be happier when it has machines, as you remark. It is hard for its technical people to sit here without jobs or tools. For the H.Q. people this lull before work is a god-send: it means that routine can be got running before the strain begins. Routine matters quite a lot in sections like Stores and Transport and Workshops. Now I am workshops. They put me into a bare room, in an empty shop (no machinery or benches!) and said 'Start a workshop routine'. I *did* reply that I was an A.C.H.[1]

There are other things to do, also. Too much paper work, and too few clerks. So for a while I typed D.R.Os.[2] Then someone (everyone, almost) felt that there must be Station Standing Orders. So I was put on to compile the 'general' parts of those. God be praised that the technical orders didn't come my way!

2 Blanche Patch was G.B.S.'s secretary.

I Aircraft Hand.
2 Daily Routine Orders.

John Bull (a weekly paper) has just announced that I do no duties.[3] Hard: very hard. Nine of my first twenty days here I was on fire-picquet.

The bike is magnificent. It has taken me twice to London (fastest time 4 hrs. 44 minutes. *The Cornish Riviera* train is 13 minutes better than that: but it does not start at Hyde Park Corner and finish at Cattewater).[4]

I heard about your lecture. My officer, who is of the sporting type, a fine pilot, and lover of fast cars, liked what you said. He called it the most *severely* practical speech he ever heard. So if you'd tried to be Winstonianly eloquent, you didn't succeed! Winston's speaking is never severe. To collect all the officers was a great idea. Twice, I think, you've done that. Uxbridge must have been blue from end to end. I wish everybody could meet you.

The R.A.F. would be happier as it knew your aims better. It is supremely hard, in a big show, to get through to the rank and file a clear knowledge of where they are going. You've got a lot through: but not enough to satisfy me, your very particular subordinate.

I enclose a separate sheet, of pure pearls.[5] If you find them too pure and pearly for your Deportment Department, then put them in the fire. They are trifles. It is the trifles that irritate and do most harm.

I hope you will come down. The more abruptly the better, for then our agony of preparing for you will be short. Sharp it must be, but make it short. Choose a fine day. Today the world is weeping, and Cattewater feels as dismal as the sky and sea.

Wing Commander Smith is a trump.*

Yours,
T. E. Shaw.

*This, as you said, is 'only for you'! A/Cs shouldn't have opinions upon Wing Commanders. *Bodleian Library/HMH*

3 The magazine *John Bull* had published on 13 April an editorial paragraph titled 'Still in the Air', in which it was stated that 'Aircraftsman [*sic*] T. E. Shaw – your old friend "Lawrence of Arabia"' had signed on for a further five years in the R.A.F., where he was 'not much troubled with duties' and divided his time between '"leave of absence" in London, tinkering with a "super-sports" motor-bicycle, and literary work. The last takes the form of translating Homer's "Odyssey" into English. His version will be published anonymously in America in the autumn book-season this year.'
4 The *Cornish Riviera Express* started at Paddington and finished, travelling via Plymouth, at Penzance.
5 A list of irritating service practices which Lawrence thought should be abolished, such as the wearing of bayonets, particularly at church parades, or the carrying of 'the silly little stick we have to carry when we walk out', etc. In the event, all his proposed reforms were put into effect. *See also* letter to Liddell Hart, pp. 451-2.

H. A. FORD[1]
18.IV.29   *CATTEWATER PLYMOUTH*

Dear Flight

Here we are: and as for choking off the Press – he will be my friend for life who finds how to do that. I do nothing – and they talk. I do something – and they talk. Now I am trying to accustom myself to the truth that probably I'll be talked over for the rest of my life: and after my life, too. There will be a volume of 'letters' after I die & probably some witty fellow will write another life of me. In fact there is a Frenchman trying to write a 'critical study' of me, now. They make me retch – and that's neither comfortable nor wholesome. I have thought of everything, I think: to join a newspaper (they do not eat each other, the dogs) – but what a remedy for the disease: to emigrate – but those colonies are as raw as wood alcohol: to commit some disgraceful crime & be put away: – but I have some people whose respect I struggle to keep. I don't know.

Meanwhile here we are. Cattewater treats me very kindly, & I have work enough to keep me pre-occupied: and in the evening a musical box to discourse Beethoven & Elgar; Oh, a super-box, like a W/T[2] set inside, with an exquisite smoothness and fullness of tone. I assure you, it is good.

I read your 9th Symphony score very often, trying to keep pace with the records. Music, alas, is very difficult. So are all the decencies of life.

In August I may be in Malvern. They are doing G.B.S.' new play[3] there on Aug 19th.21.27. & 31. and *Heartbreak House*, a marvellous work of art, on 23. & 28. and I'd like to hear them. It is not sure, for the Schneider Cup may make me very busy about that time. But if possible I'll be there. Any chance of you? It is near Shrewsbury: perhaps I might come over one night?

Yours
T. E. Shaw

1 Flight Sergeant, R.A.F.
2 Wireless Telegraph.
3 *The Apple Cart.*

That snobbery 'He does not associate with the other airmen, except a few of the more intellectual' – God, it's poisonous. If I could get that reporter by the neck he would want a new one in 5 minutes.

DG

B. E. LEESON[1]
18.4.29   *R.A.F. CATTEWATER PLYMOUTH*

Dear Leeson
We'll have to meet in London probably, unless I ever get to Nottingham again. That is as near as I am likely to get to Manchester. And when? God knows: not till after the Schneider Cup race, for which I'm a cross between clerk and deck-hand on a R.A.F. Motor Boat.

You do well to distrust the newspaper stories of me. Gods, what a foul imagination they do conjure up! Because I don't drink or smoke or dance, all things can be invented. Please believe that I don't either love or hate the entire sex of women. There are good ones and bad ones, I find: much the same as men and dogs and motor bicycles.

It will be after September, as I said.

Yours
T.E.S.

Bodleian Library

---

1 Leeson: a former Royal Flying Corps officer who had served briefly with Lawrence in 1917.

MRS CHARLOTTE SHAW
27.IV.29

This cannot be more than a line, for there is little to say. In fact my only news is of a meeting – here – with Lady Astor. I was in Plymouth, paying a reluctant call, when a pea-hen voice screamed 'Aircraftman' from a car: and it was her. Next day she rang up the Wing Commander, and was allowed all over the station. We sparred verbally at each other. She got on my motor cycle: I drove with her and Michael[1] to her housing estate, to her house (supper), a children's club she runs in Plymouth. It has since been in the papers. Serves me right for walking about with a talkie sky-sign.

She was very nice: at her swiftest and kindest: one of the most naturally impulsive and impulsively natural people. Like G.B.S., more a cocktail than a wholesome diet.

There: you see that that's that. (Hooray: 3 thats in a row). Life is fairly good. The flaw is that *John Bull* has announced that I do no work in camp, but tinker with my motor-bike and translate *The Odyssey*, and since that note appeared I've not been able to touch *The Odyssey*. I must think out what to do about it now. The sensible thing would be to give it up: the next-best thing to sign it T. E. Shaw. Either move is difficult. I will ask Bruce Rogers, and see what he thinks.

Nancy's seat at Plymouth should be pretty safe.[2] She seems to hold the town in her fingers – they are all friends and enemies, and none neutral. The R.A.F. is wholly hers, of course.

This is written under difficulties, and is no more than a note. I owe G.B.S. a letter, for the proof-preface of *Immaturity*[3] came, and is wonderful reading. If this collected edition is going to be illuminated by such historical notes, it will be very valuable.

Only I won't start on that now, while I'm in a trough of the waves. Up and down it is, always.

Weather here dry, mostly, and cold always. I am glad you get some sunlight: but beware of the bora. I have had them. They kill people who are taken unawares.

TES.

British Library

1 Lady Astor's son, born 1916.
2 *I.e.* in the general election, which took place on 30 May. It was safe, though nationally the Labour Party won 288 seats to the Conservatives' 260.
3 Shaw's early novel, written in 1879, rejected by numerous publishers, finally published in 1930.

A. E. (JOCK) CHAMBERS
27.IV.29   *CATTEWATER PLYMOUTH*

Dear Jock

So there you are. One said dead, one deserted, one signed on: and all the while
you sort letters in the Post Office. Such a nice job, sorter. If you send the
Glasgow letters to Costa Rica nobody can trace it to you: and the *Daily Mirror*
makes a snappy paragraph & *Punch* ditto.

I am now at Cattewater, & very seldom stir out of camp: so we can't hope
to meet till my leave comes, if come it does. I hoard that month, against the
dread day that a film about me may be released. *If* it comes I take the month,
& hide somewhere.

Clouds Hill is still there. I saw it for an hour in February. It is lovely as
ever: only chimney-pots are added as a monument of the new tenants' taste.
Jock, the old tenants were 'some' people. You & me, & Guy, of the R.A.F. and
the brothers Salmond, (Marshals of sorts) Hardy, Graves, Siegfried Sassoon,
poets: Forster, Tomlinson, Garnett, prose-writers. Spencer & John, artists. It
was a good place while it lasted. I wish there was a Clouds Hill in every camp,
assigned for the use of aircraft hands. [. . .]

Jock, I'm very weary of being stared at and discussed and praised. What
can one do to be forgotten? After I'm dead they'll rattle my bones about, in
their curiosity.

Au revoir
T. E. S.

[. . .] *DG*

BRUCE ROGERS
1/5/29   *R.A.F. PLYMOUTH*

Dear B. R.

Today I had meant to send you Book VII & VIII: instead of which I must tell
you of my worries. It's been published (in *John Bull*, of all the world's press!) that
I'm doing an *Odyssey*: and since that day I haven't done a stroke. Up till then I'd
been trying to get on with it. Seven is complete, all but the last look-over. Eight

is having its third revise. Nine is started: but that was all March work: and since, as I say, there has been nothing.

I'm wondering all the time what to do. (i) If I were free to do so, I'd like to return you your payment and cancel the whole business: but I am aware that this cannot be done without your consent. It would be the best solution, in my own interests. Other alternatives are

    (ii)   To acknowledge the work: which I will not do.

    (iii) To find a ghost who will put his or her name to it, and accept the public responsibility for it.

I had not expected this trouble, before publication: *After*, yes: but somehow that didn't matter. You'll realize, I hope, that I can't carry on as it is.

Will you see Walker and Merton,[1] and present them the difficulties, as they stand? I want to be as reasonable and helpful as possible, and only hope that their more sober experiences may find a road out of what seems, to me, rather a deep hole.

I return Book I & II. W. (whom I do not know personally) has been very light with them. This is a relief. I seem to have made no howlers. Comments are attached to the sheets, where necessary.

Please believe that I'm very sorry about this. I've been racking my head for a way out for about three weeks, now, and cannot achieve anything.[2]

Yours
T E Shaw

I'm glad you doubted the Dorsetshire rumours. I have not been out of camp (except to Plymouth on business) for a month.

Letters to Bruce Rogers

1 Sir Emery Walker, the eminent printer and process engraver, who had helped William Morris to establish his Kelmscott Press, was contracted to publish the limited British edition of Lawrence's *Odyssey*; Wilfred Merton was his associate.

2 As will be seen from later letters, Lawrence overcame his doubts and continued his work of translation.

MRS CHARLOTTE SHAW
1.5.29   *338171 A/C SHAW R.A.F. CATTEWATER PLYMOUTH*

I had a nice word, quite accidentally, from F. L. Lucas, an exquisite Cambridge
don: he said (apropos of nothing, or of *The Mint*, rather) that reading the *Seven
Pillars* had been one of the experiences of his life. And he has read everything.
I wonder if there's something in it, after all. Only I can't believe that there's
anything in me rare enough to make my work rare. You see, I'm so exactly like
the other fellows in the hut. [...]

British Library

MRS CHARLOTTE SHAW
22.V.29   [*R.A.F. CATTEWATER PLYMOUTH*]

Today came your telegram saying Venice: so here goes, though there is little
yet to say, and I'm yet unfixed in feeling.
      Whitsun gave me an unexpected holiday: so I went to Granville Barker. He
looked older and softer. She seemed less tragic. In fact, I liked them both
better than before. Much good talk about books. He is a high-brow, but very
intelligent: and has read enormously. They have been in Arizona, and the
Indians there have caught their fancy. Justly so, too.
      Thence to Max Gate. Mrs. Hardy was troubled, because the locals want a
T. H. memorial, and want her to put up most of the funds for it, without
having her will as to its form. Cockerell isn't behaving well.
      Thence to Cambridge, where I saw Lucas (F. L) and Forster. We talked
rather like Aldous Huxley characters: froth: thence to London, where I saw
Laura Riding. She has broken her pelvis, and three bones of her spine, but will
recover, they say, in six months. For love of an Irishman, Geoffrey Phibbs
(who did not love her any more) she had thrown herself down four stories
into Graves' area at Chiswick. R.G. jumped after her, but was not hurt.[1]

1 Laura Riding, American writer and divorcée (b. 1901), lived with Robert Graves and his wife
   Nancy Nicholson in a *ménage à trois* she described as a 'wonderful Trinity'. Their flat at 35A St
   Peter's Square, Hammersmith, was known, according to Graves, as 'Free Love Corner'. Geoffrey
   Phibbs was a Norfolk-born Anglo-Irish poet who had fallen in love with Riding, then
   departed, after which Riding tried to commit suicide by jumping from No. 35A, with Robert
   Graves following suit. Expert medical help saved her from being permanently crippled.

Nancy, Robert's wife, has now gone to live with Phibbs. Phibbs' wife lives every six months or so with David Garnett (*Lady into Fox*).² They are mad-house minds: no, not so much minds as appetites. I think the mess has mainly solved the difficulties of Robert. He has now been delivered from Nancy, and is confirmed towards Laura, whom he will have the job of supporting (with Nancy's four children) on next-to-no-money. Poor R.G. He is a most excellent and truthful person, drowning in a quagmire.

[...] The election is hotly on, I believe. They say there have been rowdy meetings at Plymouth. Nancy³ provokes them, and then does not secretly like the row: though outwardly she revels. I got another letter from her, which I must answer somehow. I'm afraid, a little, of her impulses.

TES.

British Library

LADY ASTOR
6.VI.29   *338171 A/C SHAW R.A.F. CATTEWATER PLYMOUTH*

Dear Lady Astor

How often we write to one another! It is an affecting spectacle.

So there you are, M.P. for again a while. Not so long a while as usual, I fancy. However you'll have more fun while it lasts. My chief regret at the passing of the Government is that Sir Philip Sassoon loses the US. of S. for Air! Winston will be happier in opposition, & may make friends with his party now. For the rest, I'd do the lot up in a bundle (the very splendid Prime Minister of course not included)¹ and sell them for 2d. if 2d. was bid. Winterton & Ormsby Gore excluded from the sale catalogue, because I like them.

I apologise for keeping the G.B.S. letter for so long. I wanted to offer it to Gabriel Wells (a book-seller) who would have given me the price of a Rolls Royce for it. The R.R. I should have driven to Cliveden & handed over to you, or to Michael, if you refused the bargain. It is a gem of a letter.

2 *Lady into Fox*: a novel by David Garnett which Lawrence much admired.
3 Lady Astor.

I Stanley Baldwin.

Alas, I can't come to Cliveden. Nor will I see Elliot Turner. Thank you all the same. The best way to be content in the service is to stick close to it, taking only such reliefs as one's own pocket affords. The helplessness of money: that's a very often forgotten point.

Some day, if you revisit Plymouth quietly, ring up 1634, and we'll brighten the life of the Exchange girls, again.

Yours sincerely
T. E. Shaw

University of Reading

DICK KNOWLES
5.7.29   *[R.A.F. CATTEWATER PLYMOUTH]*

[…] Today we flew to Calshot, and went on to Portsmouth, for a Schneider Cup Committee. I'm a spare-part clerk, in that business. Nearly got to Lee, only the wind and sea were too S.W. I'd hoped to see you.

The wish of people to see Clouds Hill will soon fade: if only the press will leave me alone now, then all the trouble will be forgotten. The papers feel sore at having made fools of themselves over me and Afghanistan: and will not readily invent another yarn. That film project is dead, too, I think. In fact, all's looking well for my peaceful old age.

The new Brough is good: but this is June and she has done only 3500 miles. Something very wrong. However I have to go to London on Saturday, and on Saturday week. So if those days are fine, it will be 4500 miles. Brough will disown me, if I ride so little.

Congs. on your L.A.C. Not the honour: but the cash![1]

Yours,
T.E.S.

Bodleian Library

1 Knowles had been promoted to the rank of leading aircraftman.

MRS CHARLOTTE SHAW
10.VII.29   [*R.A.F. CATTEWATER PLYMOUTH*]

This immense letter of yours shames me. You have so much to do. So have I: and I neglect writing because of it. Today I asked the Wing Commander to find me an understudy. That's the first time, I think, that I've ever asked for help in the R.A.F.: or in anything else, possibly.

Lady Astor was very nice, and almost quiet, at moments, when I saw her a week ago. I think she will be very nice when her legs get tired of running. She leaves me breathless. I told her she was a cocktail of a woman, and about as companionable as a typhoon. That shocked her: so I explained that G.B.S. was a cocktail too, and that you were not. You were habitable: but you are rather like the Semitic God, of whom it is easy to say what isn't, but impossible what is. I have never tried to describe you in words. Did I tell her that the blend of you and G.B.S. was a symphony of smooth and sharp, like bacon and eggs? Possibly. Conjoined you would be complete humanity. Whereas poor Nancy is only a whirling atom.

If they give me an assistant soon I will try and do some *Odyssey*: today I am just exhausted.

Malvern:[1] the fog of doubt hangs as thick as ever over August, and will hang till at least July 24, when a meeting at the Air Ministry may throw us all out of our jobs, as incompetents. So I'll cast a shot at a venture: book me for August 27th night please. I will try and stick to that. If I fail I'll arrange to sleep in some haystack.

As for feeling 'at home' with you: that is not the word. I do not wish to feel at home. You are more completely restful than anyone I know, and that is surely better? Homes are ties, and with you I am quite free, somehow.

Yours
T.E.S.

British Library

---

1 Lawrence had promised to go to the Malvern Festival (started by Sir Barry Jackson mainly as a festival for plays by Bernard Shaw) where *The Apple Cart* was to be performed. The Shaws went there every year unless on one of their frequent journeys abroad.

LADY ASTOR
12.7.29   *R.A.F. CATTEWATER PLYMOUTH*

Dear Lady Astor

That was a beautiful letter you sent me: – but you & I ought to be too busy to write beautiful letters. The Wing Commander sends for me and says – 'Shaw, just write a nice letter for me to this' & back comes a thing like this. That is that. We are lavish with thisses and thattes tonight.

I do like the woods of Cliveden; and if ever I get good enough to play pilot to that Moth, it'll come to rest there or at Sandwich, some day. By all other sorts of transports you are too far. As for the merit of work, study the ant's contribution to animal happiness and then be lazy, like me. I have time to hear & see & smell the unlikenesses of every-day things. So I am never short of attentions. And I cling to camp because there I feel I belong. Belonging is a good feeling.

Yours ever
SHAW.

There I beat the W/C. He cannot type his own name.   *University of Reading*

B. H. LIDDELL HART[1]
14.VII.29   *CORFE*

I'm here, temporarily settling some problems concerning my Dorsetshire cottage. Going back this afternoon. I hope this letter will arrive in time. Your wire was sent on to me.

I. Directly, the C.A.S. might abolish, by a word, bayonets and walking-out canes. Bayonets because they are costly (16/– each), take long to maintain (about I hr. per month, except where a buffing-wheel is available), ugly, and useless. I'd call them dangerous, for there was an idiot Squadron Leader who used to practice open-order attack, in France: waving a sword himself. A fool like that might easily throw away a squadron. Aircraft are a long-distance weapon, and bayonets are out of place in them.

I Letter written following a discussion with Liddell Hart about certain practices current in the R.A.F. which Lawrence feared might inhibit recruitment. Liddell Hart offered to bring them to notice in official quarters privately. *See also* p. 441.

2. The walking-out cane I can leave to common sense. You saw mine: and saw that it's a silly bodkin of a thing, no use as stick or weapon, and no ornament. It was designed, I believe, to keep troops hands out of their pockets: but R.A.F. tunics and breeches have inaccessible pockets, in which no man can keep his hands. Whereas hands and stick both go into our overcoat pockets.

The C.A.S. (Trenchard) has already done two or three of the reforms I urged on him, and repeated to you. So the job is lightened.

3. Kit inspection is another bore. It's supposed to be held monthly, and troops have to show all their kit. This is ridiculous. Our working dress is inspected daily, our walking-out dress weekly, in the normal course of duty. All that is required (besides these two suits, in case of active service which is the justification of kit inspection) is spare socks, spare shirts, pants. Instead of laying everything, which confuses the eye of the Inspecting Officer, and involves everything being very tightly folded, to be got on the bed, troops should (once a quarter) leave out on their beds their spare underclothing, and go off to work. And the inspection should be done by the Flight Officer and his N.C.O., at leisure. It shouldn't be a parade, or a beauty show: but an inspection to make sure that our normally-invisible kit was serviceable and complete. There is no need for us standing by. That makes us hot and ashamed, and the decent officers feel like nosey-Parkers, and avoid looking at us.

4. The last thing is a very small point. In the navy, an officer or N.C.O entering the men's mess takes his hat off, whether on duty or not. The airmen would like this to become the general rule in the R.A.F. It is in some stations, where the C.O. is ex-navy.

There were many other things I'd like to talk about: marriage-establishment rosters, overseas-rosters, posting of airmen in England to the stations most convenient to them (a Scotchman in Plymouth: home fare – £5: an Englishman in Leuchars: ditto). Pillion-riding on motor cycles (airmen are the only people in England forbidden it: not soldiers, not sailors. It's rather an insult to what we fondly hope is the most dangerous service). The week-end pass (I'd make after duty Saturday till Reveille Monday free for all men not warned for duty. Every station keeps a duty crew). I'd make an Air Ministry regulation about plain clothes. At present one C.O. allows them, and another restricts them. Chaos and irritation. It is a very valued privilege, I'm sorry to say. Church parade. This is the most annoying parade of the week. Couldn't it be made voluntary? I think I could get the consent of the two archbishops to that, if the Air Ministry is shy of the C. of E.

DG/LHB

T. B. MARSON
23.VIII.29   *R.A.F. CATTEWATER PLYMOUTH*

Dear Marson

I saw Boom today:[1] he inspected Cattewater, and spoke to me: gently telling me off as usual!

Do you know, he is looking old? His moustache is going white, and he looks nearly his real age. I am sorry. You know he is finally resigning at the end of this year, and John Salmond[2] comes in. It's the end of an epoch, in my life and judgement. I shan't feel as I do about the R.A.F. after he has gone. One takes a pride in being under Boom.

You've been very nice in asking me to see you, at your place, this autumn. I'm of the Schneider Cup party, and tomorrow we move to Calshot, for three weeks at that worst of stations. Alas.

After the Cup (the Italians are asking tonight to have it postponed: alas again!) perhaps they will give me leave: and then I shall try to persuade my bike of bikes into Gloucestershire. Time is so short: people I want to see, would like to see, so many. Alas again. Life just fizzes past, and after it perhaps things do not greatly matter. I should have written to you before. Desperate venture, farming now-a-days. I hope you show up all the others at it. The big men make money, I'm told: but you aren't rich, yet, probably.

Yours
T.E.S

Bodleian Library

HENRY WILLIAMSON
23.VIII.29

Dear H.W.

I have orders to move to Calshot tomorrow – & the Italians are asking to have the race postponed! Such is life.

1 'Boom' was Trenchard's nickname.
2 Sir John Salmond was Trenchard's successor as chief of air staff.

The last three weeks have been one great rush. I hope the Race isn't postponed, & that all the rush will be over by Sept 12. I want some peace: badly.

It was very pleasant to see you, & Mrs Williamson: & the kid; I'm always a bit sorry for children.[1] We've had a hell of a bad time: so'll they, I suppose.

Among my 100 leave plans is a night or two with you in the new place:[2] don't be alarmed. I can sleep on the doorstep, & your food is luxury itself, after the R.A.F. In 48 hours we could tear to pieces all contemporary books, & begin English literature with a new clean sheet!

In this camp one is always on duty: and I want to be able to look at and listen to trees & running water, at my leisure, with no whistles or parades to keep on interrupting.

There's an interesting book coming out next year: a life of Gaudier Brzeska: the French sculptor: by Jim Ede, of the Tate Gallery.[3] <u>Good</u>.

Yours
T.E.S.

Bodleian Library

ROBERT GRAVES
3.IX.29

CALSHOT

Dear R.G.

There should, I feel, have been more to say about this section: but there is not.[1] Except for the epilogue (which is good, appetising, rather curiosity-exciting stuff, and with a falling-close about its paragraphs that makes its genial effect a little sorrowful) the writing is not distinguished, like the first part. I have missed the middle, I fear. They must have kept it at Cattewater. I have written to the Post Corporal, and asked him to trace it and send

---

1 Lawrence's visit to Williamson had taken place some weeks earlier in late July. For an account of this visit and Williamson's reaction to meeting Lawrence in the flesh, *see Genius of Friendship*, p. 29: 'He knew what I was going to say before I said it ... His reflexes were extraordinarily quick and sensitive: quicksilver .... I felt ... for the first time in my life, I was becoming real and strong.' Williamson also described Lawrence's remarkable impact on him and his family in his contribution to *T. E. Lawrence by His Friends*: 'We felt like otters, or Arabs', etc.
2 The Williamsons had moved to another house in Georgeham.
3 *Savage Messiah*, by H. S. Ede, published 1931.

1 Lawrence had been reading part of Graves's classic work *Goodbye to All That*, which was shortly to be published.

on. This Calshot is the hell of a place for mails. We get nothing through.

I've toned my letter down, in the first sentences: and suggested slight cuts later.[2] Is it moral to cut out parts of letters already written & sent? Or should they appear whole. I do not know: but if you can modify this one as I suggest, then it will be kinder to Egypt. One says more to a man's back than to his face.

Nowt els. A good book, this one of yours will be, I think: and you were quite right to cut short the events of 1929. You have had a bad year of it. I hope the weather will be calmer for you now. Please congratulate L.[3] on walking round the table. Not enough, but much. I'll hope to see you, if you are still in England when I am free: – if I am ever free. We work from seven in the morning till eleven at night here. I hope it will end soon.[4]

T.E.S.   *Harvard University*

ROBERT GRAVES
13/IX/29   *CATTEWATER*

Dear R.G.
A rush to read this today & to get it off to you. Ouf! I'm glad that Schneider Cup is over. Too much like work.

This is very good.[1] The war is the best part (terrible idea: is the war always going to be the thing we do best?) and completely carries on & up the excitement of the opening chapters. Most excellent. Your pictures of wounds & nerves are exactly as they should be: sane, decent, *right*.

S.S.[2] comes out very well. I'm glad of that, for I like him: homosex and all. He's a fighting man, & generous. Hates his family millionaires.[3]

---

2 Some paragraphs of a letter by Lawrence to Graves about Egypt appear in chapter 31 of Graves's book. The letter is printed in full in *RGB* (21 October 1925).
3 Laura Riding.
4 Lawrence drew a long arrow down the page from the first sentence to the last two sentences and wrote in the margin: 'This is why'.

1 This: *Goodbye to All That*: *see* previous letter.
2 Siegfried Sassoon. For an important comment on this sentence, *see* 'General Introduction' p.xxix.
3 Sassoon became a Socialist after the war; in the 1918 election he campaigned for Philip Snowden and inveighed against the idle rich: a category in which he included his millionaire cousins.

I'm glad, too, that there is so much humour, so little unalloyed spleen, in the book. You have had enough lately to embitter a saint – and the saint laughs, a little wryly.

No corrections or changes to make, on the point of taste or prose. It's very good writing, and the characters are so alive. A very good book. The rise & fall is noticeably planned, & excellent.

TES

Harvard University

B. E. LEESON
11.X.29.   *14 BARTON STREET S.W.1*

Dear Leeson

Your maid guessed correctly. I was trying a new thing for George Brough, and its engine had run so remarkably that I was half an hour in advance of schedule. So I said 'Manchester, Ha: Victoria Park' (I knew V.P. in the B.C. period) and swirled off there to pass the time of day with you, if you had happened to be lunching at home. Only, of course, you were not. It is often like that in a grey world. Put it to the credit of Manchester that (despite appearance and temptation) it was not raining on that day.

Life otherwise is rather accidented. I have met many hard looks and bad words from the great men of the R.A.F. lately. My head is bowed and not bloody.

Commend me to the maid. You are a plutocrat. I have no maid: nor even a wife: whereas you have two women to look after you. Mohammedan!

Yours
T.E.S.

Bodleian Library

MRS CHARLOTTE SHAW

26.X.29 *SATURDAY NIGHT, LATER*

The sun shone, frostily I admit, but shone. So I could not throw in my present liberty. In fine weather tramps have an ideal life. Therefore I hope to go off a.m. on Sunday into Wales, or Norfolk, or Yorkshire (probably it will be Kent, after all) and eat more smooth miles of road.

Today I went to Chingford, and said good-bye to Pole Hill.[1] It was marvellously beautiful. Our oak 'cloister' has settled into the hill-side, and grown moss, and dignity. My poor trees have added three feet to their stature since a year ago, all except the cypresses, which were to have been an avenue, for my walking when I felt sad; but the drought has browned three of them to death. However they are not wanted: I will not be there when they (and myself) become old: and for the sadness, it was very present with me this afternoon, in the knowledge that I had lost these fields. I wonder why we get so fond of fields? Commonplace fields, you might call these, only that no common place could afford so proud a view. Today it was perfection, for the mist and the cold air held all the smoke of all the chimneys, so that every ridge was sharpened at the top by the waves of grey vapour rising from the next valley. All the sky-lines were remote, and lovely, and it would have been enough for the rest of my day's thinking just to have sat there till dark and watched everything blurr into one blackness, starred with lamps. Only of course I couldn't stop, for the place won't be mine next month: and all the tenants came to me, so sorry for themselves, but telling me not to care, as the forest was the proper owner of the hill. In process of years the tenants have weeded themselves of the unfit, until today there is not one who doesn't often sit still in enjoyment of the view. The police sergeant who has reared his family there in six years says that he's trying to persuade himself that he can be happy in a semi-detached street-house, without four acres of wild garden: but that it'll be like a cell after liberty. He took me down to the bottom field, to see the peep over the lake that he thinks the most beautiful of all the vistas. 'There isn't a house or man-made stick in view' he said: and it was just that which I found lacking to the perfection. It is selfish, isn't it, to take delight in not seeing neighbours? Pole Hill seemed to come nearer to me today than ever before: always, then, I was going to hold it, or held it: and today I had agreed to let it go. Epping Forest will be very good to it,

---

1 Lawrence's selling of Pole Hill marks the end of his long-held ambition to found a private printing press. His intended partner, Vyvyan Richards, had meanwhile helped Robert Graves and Laura Riding to set up the Seizin Press in their flat in St Peter's Square, Hammersmith.

of course: a better master than I have been. Only no corporation can like a place quite as much as the owner who'd saved to buy it, yard by yard, for years.

Enough of all that sob-stuff. I'm off early tomorrow, if it is bright: and I'll stay every night with some ex-fellow of the Tanks or R.A.F.; and after the weather breaks, or I'm broke, or the leave is ended, I'll make for Plymouth, trying to call at Whitehall or Ayot on the way.

O'Casey was *good*.[2]

TES.

British Library

ALAN DAWNAY
31.X.29   *UNION JACK CLUB 91 WATERLOO ROAD LONDON*

Dear ACD
Lady Clayton's income will be made up to about £1000 by Government.[1] This seems to me (and I hope to you) satisfactory. Do not yet give the news any extended currency, as people dislike having their good deeds anticipated: but please see that MacEwen, or other person in touch with her, warns you for me if there is any later hitch in the business.

And don't whisper my name, anyhow, please. The Air Ministry would chalk a new black mark against me, if they heard I'd been interested. One has to be so cursed careful.

Yours
T.E.S.

Bodleian Library

2 Lawrence had seen O'Casey's anti-war play *The Silver Tassie* at the Apollo Theatre, London.

1 Sir Gilbert Clayton had died on 11 September. It was characteristic that Lawrence should have interested himself in the financial welfare of his former chief's widow; he showed a similar concern for the dependants of deceased fellow servicemen.

JOHN BROPHY[1]

19.XI.29   *R.A.F. MOUNT BATTEN PLYMOUTH*[2]

Dear Brophy

Don't let's 'Mr' each other. My past reputation can balance your present social superiority, and make us quits!

I'm sorry about the essay. I have decided – in 1922 I decided – not to try to go on writing. Agreed that with my name on, it sells like tripe: but I've posted it anonymously to this editor & that, and got it all back again. Perhaps the emotion (in solution) in it made the *Seven Pillars* much better than the rest of my writing. Anyway they would not buy it, and I have had seven years without trying to write, and am all the easier for being spared the labour. I think I did write better than the average retired military man: but between that and 'writing' there is a gulf. I have talked to many whom I think great writers. All of them have a likeness, in that they get some pleasure out of the phrases as they are born. Not the finished work, perhaps. Few look back with pleasure: but there is joy in the creation, and I had never anything but weariness and dissatisfaction. This I put down to my works being an imitation, made with great care and pains and judgement, of the real thing.

So I gave it up, I hope finally. Not without having tried it well, you know. 1st book burned:[3] 2nd (*Seven Pillars*) published privately: 3rd still in manuscript. God forbid there being a fourth. It is true that I do translations. My style is easy and correct, and the publishers pay me well for unsigned or pseudonymous versions of French books, and an occasional Greek, such as I am at now. The proceeds very usefully supplement my R.A.F. pay, which isn't enough for my motor bike's costs, and they involve no publicity at all.

Bodleian Library

1 Writer, co-editor with Eric Partridge of *Songs and Slang of the British Soldier, 1914-1918* contributor to *Lawrence by His Friends*.
2 R.A.F. Cattewater had been renamed R.A.F. Mount Batten as from 1 October 1929.
3 The first *Seven Pillars of Wisdom*, written but not completed before the war.

H. S. EDE
28.XI.29   *338171 A/C SHAW R.A.F. MOUNT BATTEN PLYMOUTH*

Dear Ede

Peccavi: and still I go on sinning: this is not a letter, but an apology for not writing: and why I don't write I can't say. To meet you, now, would be a delight: I'd ride two hundred miles, with you at the end of it, if I might: only I must not: and if I can't meet, I won't have the paper-business which is so second-best. If you are to go on knowing me you must allow for – expect – these sort of sulks.

I had a leave while you did – and wandered twice or thrice round the Tate, seeing nothing so exciting as your fish. I did see Aitken, who told me of your coming 'board'. I hope you defeated it. I laughed and laughed over your sun-bath letter: you sound well: you look well: so don't blame the poor board which has more ears and eyes than heads.

I'm glad Heinemann are taken with G-B.[1]

I assure you that it's a really good book: of course de luxe is best: but it wouldn't fall dead in paper covers, broché, at 6d! I hope it comes out soon and sells like – *Revolt in the Desert*!!!

Yours
T.E.S.
                                                          Bodleian Library

MAJOR ARCHIBALD BECKE[1]
28.XII.29   *R.A.F. MOUNT BATTEN PLYMOUTH*

Your letter sits here on my table in the office, and I have been cursing it at intervals. Why on earth should anybody bother about that old war any longer? One does not learn hints for the next one from details of engagements: after a fight starts the rest is common sense and ingenuity. Strategy, the great lines

---

1 Ede's biography of Gaudier-Brzeska, *Savage Messiah*.

1 Major A. F. Becke, RA (Retd), was a military historian employed by the historical section of the Committee of Imperial Defence. He was engaged in compiling the maps for the volume of the *History of the Great War* dealing with military operations in Egypt and Palestine from June 1917 to the end of the war, authored by Captain Cyril Falls. It was published in 1930.

of approach, may be learned from books and maps – not tactics. That silly book of Henderson's did our staff such harm.[2]

As for the scrap at Seil el Hesa, wasn't it rather an indecent show?[3] I haven't copies of either of my books here, but I meant to make it plain in them that the fight was an exception to my practice, undertaken in bad temper as a sardonic jest – whose poor taste I saw later, when the casualties came home. Throughout it I was quoting to myself absurd tags of Foch and the other blood-fighters, and in every movement I was parodying the sort of thing they recommended, but exaggerating just enough to make it ridiculous. The account I wrote of the fight afterwards was in the same vein: a parody of a proper dispatch. The Palestine Staff took it seriously: I hope your section is not going to follow their mistake.

You want me to check the affair now, on my twelve-year-old memories, against air photos of the ground. Isn't that overdoing what was originally meant (as I told you) to be a joke? You've only got to put yourself in my place as I then was to see how hopelessly out of key Seil el Hesa was with all my other conduct. Tafila wasn't worth the men to us: killing Turks was no part of our business. The whole thing's absurd.

So I hope you'll give up the idea of presenting any 'study' of this so-called battle. Battles are usually the last refuge of fools in open war: and I'm very sorry I ever fought this one.

Yours sincerely
T E Shaw

(If you go on with the grisly dissection of my trifle, I suggest that this note be printed as its postscript. It would restore the thing to scale!)

University of Texas

2 'That silly book of Henderson's': a reference to *The Science of War* by Colonel G. F. R. Henderson (1854-1903), edited by Neill Malcolm and published in 1906. Its intention, in its author's words, was to provide 'a clear insight into the innumerable problems connected with the organisation and command of an armed force'; it was also the author's hope that his book would help to 'train the judgement of young officers so that when left to themselves they may do the right thing'.
3 Seil el Hesa: also known, as Lawrence implies later in the letter, as the Battle of Tafila, or Tafileh, 25 January 1918. Lawrence's attitude to the action as given here is much in line with his account in chapters LXXXV and LXXXVI of *Seven Pillars of Wisdom*.

C. P. ROBERTSON[1]

30.XII.29   *R.A.F. MOUNT BATTEN PLYMOUTH*

Dear Robertson

Mugs these papers are. They mean 'Rowanding' [?]: yet, as you guessed, I am still in the same place. It has changed its name, however, from Cattewater to Mount Batten.

I saw your 'dementi'[2] in the Press, and wondered to what new yarn it gave the lie. I'm afraid it's partly true that these public notices amuse me. I sit in camp, busy (more or less) on some ghastly scrounge, and read that I'm making a rebellion in Persia. It's only human to smile broadly: and there'd be nothing but fun in it if my chiefs were not so sensitive. As it is, after my laugh I have to wonder if Lord T. will get peevish. In some ways, the more of these rumours that crop up the better: they keep him accustomed to the sensation of having me somewhere or other unusual. When there's been a year or two of peace, and then a bust-up, the strangeness strikes 'em all of a heap.

Your new gods are unknown to me. I know Sir Geoffrey Salmond very well but have only met Sir John twice, casually. Webb-Bowen I have not seen, except from one side (the safe side) of a wall while he inspected the other. I am hoping that Sir John Salmond will not be old-fashioned. Trenchard was a very great man, and my friend always: but rather a Roman friend, who would be sorry while he cut one's head off, but wouldn't let sentiment interfere with duty. However I felt safer with him than I do now.

My saviour last time was Ramsay: and the time before that Baldwin.[3] No use going higher while a P.M. will do. That is a good motto, incidentally, for the New Year, which I hope will be prosperous, in your case; and will leave me where it finds me, and as it finds me, for myself. Why shouldn't a man wish himself his own New Year wish? I am often wanting time to stand still – though not at the moment, for it rains terribly just now in Plymouth.

The worst part of your job is that the Press is like the beast poor Hercules had a fight with: it has too many heads, & for each one you knock off, two grow.

1 Charles Pennycook ('Robbie') Robertson was head of the press and publicity branch of the Air Ministry, and thus Lawrence's shield and adviser in the matter of approaches to the RAF's most eccentric 'other rank' by the press. Lawrence clearly felt free to share with him his concern that another burst of unsought publicity might produce an adverse reaction in the higher echelons of the air force. 'Lord T.' is Lord Thomson, secretary of state for air at the time, and not a supporter of Lawrence's presence in the R.A.F.; he died in October 1930 in the crash in northern France of the airship R101 during its ill-fated attempt to fly to India.

2 *Démenti*: official denial of a rumour.

3 Two successive prime ministers: Stanley Baldiwn (1924-9) and Ramsay MacDonald 1929-31.

I am not alluding here to Mr Harrison, but to the job of 'telling' the Press where I'm not. It never ends: I was safest at Calshot, where about 1 per cent of the active journalists of England saw me daily. They knew I wasn't anybody other than I looked: but today ... well, they'll be thinking that perhaps there is something in it. 'Queer chap', 'might be doing something' etc. It only shows what a fool a fellow is to make a reputation if he isn't ambitious for himself.

No, my Calshot sorrows came upon me because Lord T. had a row with the R.A.F. people there, and Bullock was snubbed by an Air Vice Marshal. So they decided that the Schneider business was a rotten show: and so were its promoters. Let us hope there will be no more heard of it. Your press behaved like gentlemen. Not even Bewsher fired off an article after your back was turned. I give them full marks: and more than that to you for handling them so gently.

The 'Devonian Magazine' idea puts me cold. I'm not 'prepared to grant an interview' for publication on any subject on earth. In fact, I have orders not to. Nor is there any subject on earth I want to air a view upon. As for the Arabs, do tell your sportsman that he is out of date. It was about ten or twelve years ago, and I've forgotten all about it. You handle Arabs, I think, as you handle Englishmen, or Laplanders or Czechoslovaks: cautiously, at first, and kindly always.[4] Nor can any half-wit 'assure the world' through a number of some ephemeral and unimportant magazine, of anything.

Therefore you are in order if you tell all and sundry that I'm a charming and simple creature, in the R.A.F. and forbidden therefore by King's Regulation No. so & so to talk for publication: but if they are just curious souls, and come to Plymouth, I'll give them tea and a bun in the Canteen and show them round. I'm not in the least shy, but the Air Ministry is.

It is very good of you to let me write to you, privately, if I'm ever in press trouble. I will be, and will do. My literary friends aren't practical wanglers, you see.

I have not written anything with an idea of publication behind it since 1927: my patience wore out about then. I do not think I will ever write any

---

4 The 'sportsman' to whom Lawrence purveyed this remarkably eloquent and thought-provoking one-liner was apparently an American journalist who wanted to ask him the standard basic question 'What it was like?' to work with peoples of a different culture in time of war. It is perhaps noteworthy that one of the nationalities included in Lawrence's rejoinder was Czechoslovakia, a new creation of the peace settlement of 1918-19 which, sadly, was to become a victim of the machinations of Nazi Germany just ten years later. Arguably his feelings for that young and therefore vulnerable country in the heart of Europe paralleled those he held for the new countries in the Middle East which he had helped to create: Feisal's Iraq and Abdullah's Transjordan.

more, as I have found that I can make money easily by translation, anonymously, and that suits better and pays better than original stuff. Lately I've been doing *The Odyssey* of Homer into english prose for an American printer: have got about ½ way, & hope to finish next year. That will be pocket-money for 1930-31. For 'pocket' read 'petrol'.

You will notice that the 'Mr' has disappeared. I agree: nasty word.

Yours
TES

Imperial War Museum

MAJOR ARCHIBALD BECKE
31.XII.29

Dear Major Becke

I've cut about the larger print a bit: substantially your map appears to square with my memories, but the main Turkish effort was along the ridge afterwards cleared by the men of Aisna.

Perhaps your conventions do not distinguish between machine guns & automatics. Our party had at least one Vickers (I remember putting up its sights eventually to 3000 and spraying the retreat) but mostly Hotchkiss automatics: the Turkish captured guns were mainly that little air-cooled thing they fitted into their two-seater aircraft: I can't recall if they had any Maxims or not. I rather think they had: – sledge-guns, probably.

There were present Emir Zeid, G.O.C.[1] the Arabs, and Jaafar Pasha (then a Major Gen. Arab Army, & Brig. Gen. Turkish Army) his adviser. So I do not quite know on what rule you go, in putting my Majority on the ridge!

Sorry I can't help about the *Crusader Castles*. The thesis was not for publication, & I have no idea what happened to it; I lent it to Lord Curzon about 1919: and don't remember it since:* a typescript, it was, with plans & photos.[2]

The Syrian castles are very interesting. The first Crusaders put up their standard square keeps: later they divided into two schools: what I call the

1 G.O.C.: General Officer Commanding.
2 This copy of the thesis is in the possession of Jesus College, Oxford.

'Hospital' took their inspiration from France, & kept on building Frenchified castles all over the hills: and the 'Temple' school put up colourable Byzantine buildings. At least so I concluded after examining about 50 of the ruins out there. Of course features of machicolation etc. developed better out East, because there was no timber for hourds.[3] My general conclusion was that Europe affected Syria rather than Syria Europe.

The entrance to Krak is 'a long way after' Rum Kalaat (Hromgl of Walther von der Vogelweide) near Samsat on the upper Euphrates – a most interesting fort.

Yours
T E Shaw

* Except for a half-notion that he gave it me back & I bound it: but I don't remember this well enough to swear to it. It was only a thesis – a first study. Not worth printing.

University of Texas

MRS CHARLOTTE SHAW
Sunday 19/1/30   *MOUNT BATTEN*

I have been Homering all morning and afternoon, and must not delay for long: only there is so much I should say to you: first of all thanks for reading that XIth Book. I am afraid it is very difficult. I have been over it three or four times since it came back, and have managed about 100 minor alterations. That is for the good. I changed, so far as I could, all the places you had marked. It is very difficult.

What you say about it is about what I feel: a sense of effort, of hard work: of course there must be this. I never wrote (for printing) an easy line in my life. All my stuff is tenth-thoughts or twentieth-thoughts, before it gets out. Nice phrases in letters to you? Perhaps: only the difference between nice phrases in a letter (where one nice phrase will carry the thing) and an *Odyssey* where one phrase not-nice will spoil it all, is too great to carry a comparison.

How like a book all the above sentences! Perhaps I am not writing to you, but for my some-day 'Life and Letters'. If you think so, then burn the thing, and prevent (as Homer would say) the day of its returning.   *British Library*

3 Machicolations: openings for dropping missiles. Hourds: screens.

MRS CHARLOTTE SHAW
6.2.30

I hope it will be all right, a fortnight hence, when they break the plaster corselet: Laura Riding (Graves' No. ii) is recovering. She did the same hurt to herself. So there is hope. If only the bones have set straight.

My work did not end on Friday. So I got another day from W/Cmdr. Smith, and finished on Saturday at noon, just in time to see Wilson in the shop before it shut.[1] I said to him 'who wrote *Her Privates We* – (that being a superb lovable book, what *The Mint* ought to have been) – for I know his touch?'. He said 'I think it begins with M ... and rang up Peter Davies.[2] That let a flood of light in: So to P. D. I said 'You haven't heard of me, my name is Shaw: but perhaps you've read a thing called *Revolt in the Desert* which I published as Lawrence. Did the author of *Scenes & Portraits* write *Her Privates We*?[3] He was flabbergasted, having promised not to give it away. In the sequel Peter Davies, Wilson and your servant lunched at Barrie's and talked much shop. (Barrie in excellent wit: likened George Moore to a decayed gold-fish!).

Scenes & Portraits, which John Murray probably published, has been one of my friends since undergraduate days, so of course *Her Privates We* is bound to make me happy. I wonder if you will like it. It is a war book, of course, but with a difference. There is so much laughter and happiness in it: and it is beautiful. The troops in it are real, at last. Manning is a very exquisite person. So queer. A great friend of Galton, while Galton lived.

It was a very good holiday, and has finally demoralised me. Not a word of Greek this week!

T.E.S.

British Library

1 J. G. Wilson of Bumpus the bookseller.
2 Peter Davies was a distinguished London publisher. He was one of the five Llewellyn Davies brothers who were befriended by J. M. Barrie and for whom Barrie wrote *Peter Pan*. Davies committed suicide in 1960, aged 63.
3 *Scenes and Portraits*, published in 1909, was by the Australian-born writer Frederic Manning (1882-1935), poet, short-story writer, and reviewer before the war for *The Spectator* (*see* next letter). He had served with a British regiment as a private in the war, taking part in the Battle of the Somme. *Her Privates We* (1930) was his fictionalized account of this experience, published under the name 'Private 19022'·

FREDERIC MANNING
25/2/30   *MOUNT BATTEN PLYMOUTH*

Dear Manning

No, it wasn't Rothenstein[1]: and I cannot get up to London this week. Now-a-days I'm lucky to fetch London once in three months, and it is only a month since I was there. As for the authorship of the book – the preface gives it away. It is pure *Scenes & Portraits*. How long, I wonder, before everybody knows? You need not worry at their knowing. It is a book everyone would have been proud and happy to have written.

Of course I'm ridiculously partial to it, for since 1922 my home has been in the ranks, and Bourne[2] says and thinks lots of the things I wanted to have said. But don't imagine that I'm anything like so much of a lad as he was. The R.A.F. is as gentle as a girls' school, and none of us drink.

I have read too many war books. They are like drams, and I cannot leave them alone, though I think I really hate them. Yours, however, and Cummings' *Enormous Room* and *War Birds*[3] seem to me worth while. *War Birds* is not literature but a raw sharp life. You and Cummings have produced love-poems of a sort, and yours is the most wonderful, because there is no strain anywhere in the writing. Just sometimes you seem to mix up the 'one's' and 'his's': but for that, it is classically perfect stuff. The picture about ⅔ through of the fellows sliding down the bank and falling in preparatory to going up for the attack, with the C.O.'s voice and the mist – that is the best of writing.

I have read *Her Privates We* twice, and *The Middle Parts of Fortune*[4] once, and am now deliberately leaving them alone for a while, before reading them again. The airmen are reading the *Privates*, avidly: and E. M. Forster (who sent me a paean about the *Privates*) has *The Middle Parts*. Everyone to whom I write is loudly delighted with the *Privates*. I hope the sales will do you good.

Peter Davies is trying to use my dregs of reputation as one more lever in the sales. Do not let that worry you. Adventitious sales and adventitious

---

1 Manning had written (11 February 1930): 'Was it some uncanny *flair*, that led you to me; or did Will Rothenstein tell you that he has some letters from me with my regimental number on them, 19022?' (*Letters to T. E. Lawrence*, which includes twelve letters by Manning).
2 Private Bourne was the hero of *Her Privates We*.
3 *The Enormous Room*, by E. E. Cummings, was a brilliantly written account of a three-month detention in France in 1917; *War Birds* was written by Elliott Springs, an American who had served as an officer with the Royal Flying Corps and Royal Air Force in 1917-18.
4 The original unexpurgated version of *Her Privates We*, published in a limited edition in 1929.

advertisements are very soon forgotten: the cash will remain with you, and your book be famous for as long as the war is cared for – and perhaps longer, for there is more than soldiering in it. You have been exactly fair to everyone, of all ranks: and all your people are alive.

This is not a very sensible letter. I am very tired, and this weather gets me down: only I owed it to you to thank you for the best book I have read for a very long time. I shall hope to meet you some day and say more – and bore you by saying it – for what is so dead as a book one has written?

Yours
T. E. Shaw

DG

MRS CHARLOTTE SHAW
25/2/30   *RAE MOUNT BATTEN PLYMOUTH*

I am a little sad that you do not like *Her Privates We*. In that is the reality of the common Englishman: and Bourne, the educated little cock-sparrow, is the commonest and most human-like of them all. I think it more of a love-book than a war-book, and have read it three times, without satisfying myself.

I agree with your weariness against all ordinary war books: but for those who fought they are like dram-drinking, and cannot be refused, however one may hate them. Books about ourselves, you know. I cannot help scanning (even if it is always in disgust) anything that appears in print about myself. There is a fascination – a longing to get it over and *know*. *Her Privates We*, however, did not disgust me. I liked it.

[...]

Poor Boanerges has rusted all over, and I only rub more grease over him, instead of going out for a long fast run. How can I, with the long-suffering Odysseus sitting on my neck all the while? It will be all better, when this cold passes, and things get happy again.

.S.

British Library

ROBIN BUXTON
25/2/30   *R.A.F. MOUNT BATTEN PLYMOUTH*

Dear Robin

Have you got my bawdy book – *The Mint*, I mean? Somehow I fancy that Herbert Baker lent it you: because I have need of a copy of it – or shall have need of it in 3 weeks time, to lend an interested person.

I apologise for inflicting such a thing on you: or no: I didn't inflict it on you. I created the horrid thing, & you have brought it on yourself. It is Vol II of my life, all the same. A bit of a come down after the *Seven Pillars*.

T.E.S.

Bodleian Library

MRS CHARLOTTE SHAW
27.3.30

[...] My St. Andrews-degree trouble is easily over: Barrie & Buchan[1] played up and freed me from it. I think the public occasion would have been unbearable. A reaction from publicity, which began in me about 1919 has grown stronger since year by year. I like to see my name in the papers – no: when I see it I get a snatch of horrified interest – and I hate anybody telling me they have seen it.

[...]

British Library

---

1 Lawrence had been invited to accept the degree of doctor of laws at St Andrews University, and had written to John Buchan, who had been behind the offer, begging him to get it withdrawn.

HENRY WILLIAMSON
3.V.30

It has been behind my eyes, in my head, for weeks to answer: but it seemed necessary to send some *Odyssey* too: and now you are ill: or are you just back, & feeling convalescent?

The Village Book[1] sounds good: and I'll look forward to reading it. Your prose is a very conscious & beautiful thing.

These *Odyssey* pages aren't sent for criticism: but to show you that no one can help in them. Translations aren't books, for in them there is no inevitable word: the whole is approximation, a feeling towards what the author would have said: and as Homer wasn't like me the version goes wrong whenever I let myself into it. Consequently the thing is a pot-boiler only, a second-best: and I do not have page-proofs. Bruce Rogers does all the printing part. I send him a typed copy of my stuff, and that is the end of it. These are actual printed sheets, and the few pencil corrections on them are my reading comments.

The work is not meant to interest you: the Homer who wrote *The Odyssey* was an antiquarian, a tame-cat, a book-worm: not a great poet, but a most charming novelist. A Thornton Wilder of his time.[2] My version, and every version, is inevitably small.

Will I ever get to your place again? This Greek eats and drinks all my leisure hours. However I have bought my Dorset cottage out of its profits, as provision for my years when the R.A.F.will not have me any more: so probably it is worth while.

I hope W. III is a successful & howlingly successful infant.

TES

Bodleian Library

1 A book of stories of village life, first published in 1930.
2 American writer, particularly well-known for his novel *The Bridge of San Luis Rey*, and for his play *Our Town*.

MRS CHARLOTTE SHAW
15.VIII.30

[…] On Wednesday I lunched with Philip Sassoon, with whom came Noël
Coward. He is not deep but remarkable. A hasty kind of genius. I wonder
what his origin is? His prose is quick, balanced, alive: like Congreve, probably,
in its day. He dignifies slang when he admits it. I liked him: and suspected that
you probably do not. Both of us are right.

Thence here, all last night in the train. Head like a boiled apple. Tomorrow
I am to fly across into Kent and back on Monday. Meanwhile *The People* has
discovered me at Filton, near Bristol, and the German Press is confident I am
in Kurdistan. […]

S.

British Library

NOËL COWARD[1]
15.VIII.30   *338171 A/C SHAW R.A.F. MOUNT BATTEN PLYMOUTH*

Dear N. C.

Here are your R.A.F. notes. After looking at them you will agree with me that
such tense and twisted prose cannot be admirable. It lacks health. Obscenity
is *vieux jeu*, too: but in 1922 I was not copying the fashion!

Don't be too hard on them, though. They were meant, not for reading, but
to afford me raw material for an introductory chapter to my mag. op. on an
airman's life. Unluckily I survived the Depot only to be sacked when on the
point of being posted to a Squadron, the real flying unit. There followed a
long spell of army life, wasting the novelty of barracks, till I broadened out
into the present common-place and lasting contentment.

Obviously these notes libel our general R.A.F. life by being too violently
true to an odd & insignificant part of it. So out of my head & with no formal

1 The eminent actor, dramatist and composer (1899-1973, knighted 1970), famous for a
string of successes on both stage and screen. Nineteen-thirty was the year of his play *Private
Lives*, to a rehearsal of which (*see* fourth paragraph) Lawrence had been invited. He was later
present at its second performance.

notes I attempted a Part III to show the happiness that came after the bullying. Only happiness is such a beast to put on paper.

Meeting you was such a surprise and pleasure to me. I had often (and quite inadequately) wondered what you were like. Now I'll try to work the rehearsal you suggested into some later raid upon London. The going-round of wheels fascinates me. So I found Wednesday wholly delightful.

Yours
T E Shaw

Please do not keep them longer than you can help — or I shall forget where they are, and be troubled!   *Bodleian Library*

HENRY WILLIAMSON
6.IX.30   *R.A.F. MOUNT BATTEN PLYMOUTH*

Dear H W
It is even as you say: autumnal weather. I wish I knew what was the matter with me. Some unformed impulse keeps me in camp. I am always putting in passes, and saying 'I will go out this week-end': and when the time comes I cannot get into breeches & puttees, so the bike rusts in the garage and I moon about the water's edge in camp, dreaming or dipping inconsequentially into books.

It has come to this, that I feel afraid and hesitant outside. The camp itself is like a defence to me, and I can't leave it. I think I have only been outside three times this summer. [...] I am like a clock whose spring has run down.

I hope you will not hate the U.S.A.[1] So many people do, whereas it all sounds to me so strong and good. Canada less so, but then I like towns because only by contrast with cities do trees feel homelike, or seas look happy.

Will they send this rot on? Probably not. Have patience with me, when you come back, and sooner or later we will meet and talk, without the bike waiting on the kerb outside. [...]

Yours
T.E.S.   *Bodleian Library*

1 Williamson had written to say that he was going to America on an extended visit.

NOËL COWARD
6.IX.30   *MOUNT BATTEN PLYMOUTH*

Dear N.C.

It is very good to laugh: and I laughed so much, and made so many people laugh over your 'may I call you 338'[1] that I became too busy and happy to acknowledge your letter.

I hope Liverpool went off well. Edinburgh – so the press said, but how they lie – went into fits over your mixed grill. I fancied you were coming thence direct to London, but clearly not. It must be very hard and uphill work winning province after province before attacking the headquarters: and London is likely to be your easiest conquest, too. The bits I saw[2] went so swingingly.

Your praise of my R.A.F. notes pleases me, of course, more than it puzzles me. I'm damned if I can see any good in them. Some artifice – yes: some skill – yes: they even come off, here and there: but the general impression on me is dry bones. Your work is like sword-play; as quick as light. Mine a slow painful mosaic of hard words stiffly cemented together. However it is usually opposites that fall in love. At any rate I propose to go on looking forward, keenly, to seeing more of your works and work, and perhaps of yourself, if a kind fate lets me run into you when you are not better engaged.

I'm hoping to get to London some time in October, for a week-end perhaps.

Yours
T E Shaw

DG

1 Noël Coward had begun a letter to Lawrence written on 25 August 1930, 'Dear 338171 (May I call you 338?), I am tremendously grateful to you for letting me read your R.A.F. notes.'
2 Of *Private Lives*.

F. N. DOUBLEDAY[1]

18.IX.30   *[COLLIESTON NEAR ABERDEEN SCOTLAND]*

Effendim

Rotten pen and foul paper, but here on the North East edge of Scotland I've just heard that you are 'out of the wood'. So much to be thankful for, yet no more than is fitting. Understand, that yourself and illness do not go together! I think of you always as part pirate, like Kidd, part buccaneer like Morgan, with moments of legitimacy like Farragut. It is unthinkable to think of an Effendi incapable of bearing arms. So please recover quickly that we may laugh again. Meanwhile come on leave with me for ten days!

Come northward many miles above Aberdeen, and then strike towards the sea across the links, which are sand-tussocked desolations of charred heather and wiry reeds, harbouring grouse to whirr up alarmingly sideways from under-foot, and rabbits so lazy that they will hardly scuttle their snow-white little tail-flags from the path. Add a choir of larks and a thin high wind piping over the dunes or thrumming down the harsh stems of heather.

They are three miles wide, these links, and ever so desolate, till they end abruptly in a rough field whose far side is set on edge with a broken line of cottages. Behind their roofs seems to be pure sky, but when you near them it becomes sea – for the cottages have [been] built round all the crest of the grassy sea-cliff and down it too, cunningly wedging their places into its face wherever there was a flat of land as wide as two rooms. Almost to the beach the cottages fall. Beach, did I say? It is a creek of sand, cemented along one side in a grey quay-wall from which and from the opposing rocks up run the grass-grown cliffs in heart-comforting bastions to the houses fringed against the sky. The creek's a fishing port. You could find room to play a game of tennis in it, perhaps, if the tide went dry. So there are no bigger boats than dinghies and no room for any: nor heart for any with the jaws of greycold reefs champing white seas outside, all day and night.

---

1 Of this letter to Doubleday (frequently addressed as Effendi or Effendim because of his initials) John Buchan wrote: 'he [Lawrence] never wrote better prose than his description of the bleak sea coast of Buchan' (*Memory Hold-The-Door* p. 217). From Knightley and Simpson's *The Secret Lives of Lawrence of Arabia* (pp. 199-200) it appears that the holiday was arranged mainly so that he could submit himself to a harsh physical regime which included not only horse riding and swimming in cold seas but also birching by John Bruce. Bruce later commented (*ibid*, p. 200); 'Here is a man subjecting himself almost beyond human endeavour, willingly, and in the midst of it all he writes a four-page letter in the gayest possible manner.'

Imagine whole systems of slate-like slabby rocks, flung flat-wise and acres square, thrusting out into the maddened North Sea which heaves and foams over them in deafening surges. The North-Easter, full of rain and so misted that our smarting eyes can peer only two or three hunched yards into it, is lifting the waves bodily into the air and smashing them upon the rocks. There is such sound and movement out there in the haze that our eyes keep staring into its blindness to see the white walls rolling in. The concealed sun makes all white things half-luminous, so that the gulls become silvered whenever they dip suddenly to turn a knife-edged cartwheel in the spray: and the thunder of the seas enforces a deafened silence on all other things, so that we feel as much as see the energy let loose. Each big wave makes the air quiver and sends a shading reverberation across the shore about our bodies.

That is the fighting of the sea against the land: and the sea's casualties have filled the port, around the elbow that the jetty makes. There the water is stifled and heaves sickly under a mat of sea-suds one foot thick. You know the creamed and bubbly foam that blows up a beach when the wind rises and the sea, together? Well, that flocculent stuff is all impounded in our bay, filling it so full that black water and jetty and steps and rocks and beach are all invisible, buried under it like a corpse in a blanket.

'Curse the fellow and his seascape,' you are saying. 'Am I paid to read his manuscript?' Peace, Mrs. Doubleday will take it away and burn it, so soon as you roar in anger.

What are we doing here? Nothing, practically. There are 3 of us – Jimmy who used to work in Canada but came home in 1914 and was a gunner for four years in France: now he jobs horses in Aberdeen: – Jock, the roughest diamond of our Tank Corps hut in 1923; – and me. We have Mrs. Ross' cottage lent to us and reluctantly in turn sweep its floor and fetch the water and coal. For meals thrice a day we spread our coats to the wind and fly to the cliff-top, where the Mrs. Baker-and-Butcher feeds us in her parlour. Then heavy inside, we slide down hill to the cottage again in the cove: for ours is the nearest hovel to the high-tide mark. That is good in fair weather and exciting today. Great flocks of surf beat tattoos on the roof till the tide turned.

But what do we do? Why nothing, as I said. Jimmy has his horses to groom and feed and exercise. Sometimes we do the last for him. Jock fishes: boys bring him mussels and he waves a pole from the quay at the wild wild waves. Once up came a codling from the yeasty deep, the poor orphan taking pity on him. He brought it us in silent manly pride, and we made him clean it. Scrape scrape his knife went, like a man cleaning a flower-pot. We helped him eat it, too.

Most of our food is fish, I remember. There is a local industry, called sperling. Cut open a round fish, flatten it, dry him bone-white for days on a rock of wire netting, smoke him, boil him in milk. Not bad, tasting like dull veal. The local people are lovers of sperling, though, and taste more in them than I do. Then there are baby soles, four-inch things too small for sale in the city with the adult soles. They are fried and delicious. Down with great soles henceforward.

The cottage has 3 rooms. Jock took the middle one with big bed and fire-place. Ours open from it and are cold. So we make his our sitting room, and have pushed the bed into the corner, farthest from the fire where I sit and think all day, while turning over the swimming suits to dry. Also I eat pounds of peppermints (pan-drops they call them: Aberdeen and excellent) or read H. G. Wells' *History* in a dollar edition lately produced as you may have heard, by a young and pushing publisher in the States. I wish I had a dozen copies to give away: but only one ran the customs gauntlet to do Cassells out of his English rights. Believe me, it's a good book. 8/6d in England and a dollar in the almighty-dear States.

I tried to get Heinemann's elephant book *Novels Today* in Aberdeen but they had it not. Distribution faulty, for Lady Eleanor Smith and Strong are both first-class. The book-shop lady tried to work off on me a thing called *Angel Pavement*,[2] also by Heinemann. She said everybody was buying it. 'Not quite everybody', I protested politely. 'This very man' she said 'wrote *Good Companions*'. 'Dreary artificial sob-stuffed thing' I snorted, having luckily read *Good Companions*. 'You are hard to please' she grumbled, offering me *The Boy's Book of Colonel Lawrence*[3] at a reduction, seeing I was in uniform and he now in the R.A.F. I told her I knew the fellow, and he was a wash-out: then I bought a *Daily Express* and escaped the shop. Alas, for I wanted to read *Dewar Rides*[4] again.

Effendi, what folly makes me want to talk rot to you when I hear you are ill? The whole man is a gladiator: who demands tall talk? Why babble when he is (temporarily) hurt? God knows. Ask Mrs. Doubleday to take the nasty thing away again.

Our tea-time now. The winds have stopped, but the waves increase. They are so big that only two roll in to the minute now. I wish you could hear the constancy and fresh repetition of their thunder, and the sharpness and loneliness of the gulls questing through the spume. The poor gulls are hungry from the storm and beset our roof for the food-scraps we throw away. They have the saddest, most cold, disembodied voices in the world.

1 By J. B. Priestley.
2 By Lowell Thomas.
3 By L. A. G. Strong.

Evening now. I must go up the shop for oil for the lamp. The shop is the post office and I'll then send this off, before its length frightens me and makes me burn it.

Au revoir, Effendim, soon, let's hope.

T.E.S.

P.S. for Mrs. D-D – Make it London next summer too! and we will get to Kipling this time.[4]

DG

MRS CHARLOTTE SHAW
5.XII.30   [*PLYMOUTH*]

I am working on Book XX now mostly, with an occasional glance at 18 or 19 to try and better them in detail, before fair-copying. One grinds again and again over each passage till the corrections begin to restore former readings. Then it is finished.

As you say 1930 has been a bad year for you. And for me? No. I have nearly finished the Greek and it has been a quiet year, of no publicity at all. This has been the first year for ten years to leave me quite at peace. I think that is very good. One or two more, and my existence will be taken for granted.

So that is to my credit: and so is *The Odyssey*: and so is the speed-boat. And I have read several books which delighted me. In music I have been less fortunate, having got to hear no new thing of great moment to me. Only I hear so little music that perhaps I should not expect it. A Delius cello sonata, an Elgar Symphony, a Brahms Double Concerto: one cannot go on hoping for wonders indefinitely. These were my three years' joys.

I am sensibly older, with more aches and pains, and a lesser inclination to extend myself. That perhaps is the worst sign. Only a strong man can live heedlessly, as I wish to do. A single man who is poor has difficulty when he is old. Only I am not old yet: just older.

4 Lawrence and the Doubledays had planned to visit Rudyard Kipling at his country home, Batemans, in Sussex.

I have not met, this year, people I much wish to meet again. Noël Coward perhaps. But I have seen Manning after some years, and Siegfried Sassoon. You remain the solitary woman who lets me feel at ease with her, in spite of all the benefits you heap on me. Usually I am a very grudging taker, too.

I have flown only once this year, against 100 times last year. That was Lord Thomson's doing, and he seems to have frightened me off flying, for I have not been up since he died.

Tell me, before next Thursday, please, what your plans are for December 20. I have to come up for Lady Astor, and I thought perhaps I might push on to Ayot or Whitehall, for an hour or two, if you would be seen at either. I must spend Saturday night at Cliveden, and be here on Sunday night, so there is not much time: only the morning of Saturday. We have not met since your hurt.

Manning has republished *Scenes & Portraits*, with a very touching little note to me. I like the graces of that book. Also the Gregynog has printed the *Stealing of the Mare*,[1] which I am liking to read again. It is not good, nor authentic desert: but true something-or-other.

Cakes & Ale, that Somerset Maugham, made my flesh creep: It was wrong to do that. Those who did not know him will see Hardy there.[2]

Bed-time – long ago.
T.E.S.

British Library

---

1 The Gregynog Press was a publishing firm specializing in rare and finely printed books. The *Stealing of the Mare* was by Wilfred Scawen Blunt, originally published in 1892.

2 *Cakes and Ale*, published 1930, portrayed the widow of a recently deceased Grand Old Man of Letters, Edward Driffield, whom many people took to be based on Thomas Hardy. In character Rosie Driffield was quite unlike Mrs Hardy, but, according to *The Second Mrs Hardy*, by Robert Gittings and Jo Manton, 'the outward circumstances of her life as Hardy's wife and widow were satirized with such uncanny insight that she herself saw the likenesses, and shrank from doing anything that might "give colour" to them, after she had read the book.' (Chapter 15, p. 131) Gittings and Manton also state that though in many ways Driffield was unlike Hardy, the book contained 'biting parodies which could only apply to the novels of Hardy, and to those of no other writer'. Hence Lawrence's strong reaction.

LADY ASTOR
31.XII.30 *R.A.F. MOUNT BATTEN*

[…] I feel inclined to send a postcard to Sandwich, explaining how much I enjoyed that night at Cliveden, and what an excellent ride back I had (including a race across the Plain with a sports Bentley: well, not so much a race as a procession for the Bent. which did only 88. I wished I had had a peeress or two on my flapper bracket!) […]

University of Reading

MRS CHARLOTTE SHAW
6.2.31

You will have seen the news of our crash here, in the papers. It was due to bad piloting, on the part of a man who (as we all know) should never have flown with passengers. He would not be convinced of that. Fortunately he died with the rest.·[1]

It was horrible to see a huge Flying Boat so cast away by incompetence. I happened to be standing by the sea watching it come in to alight. So that is going to involve me in Enquiries and Inquests. At the Enquiry (which is an R.A.F. affair, not open to the Press) I propose to say just what I saw, and what it meant, in the endeavour to bring the responsibility home upon an Air Marshal Webb-Bowen at the Air Ministry, who refused to listen to reports made him on 3 separate occasions regarding this officer's unfitness to fly. I shall try to do it without getting myself into trouble if I can. If not – well, I think such a case had better not happen again, and I have facts enough to prevent its happening again, if I publish them.

You will not expect me to write again till this is over – a week at least. […]

T.E.S.

British Library

1 The crash, of an Iris III seaplane, had taken place on 4 February within sight of R.A.F. Mount Batten and with Lawrence and Clare Sydney Smith as spectators. For a full account of the occasion and of Lawrence's organizing of the subsequent attempts at rescue (even though his commanding officer was present) *see* Clare Sydney Smith's *The Golden Reign* (Cassell, 1940), Ch. XXII.

MRS CHARLOTTE SHAW
16.2.31

Not a letter

The talks still go on. Perhaps the inquest will end on Wednesday and that will be all.

I was made clerk for the Air Ministry Court of Inquiry, and was able to approve and agree with its findings. G.B.S. will laugh at that.

Please thank him for his letter. When all is over I shall be so relieved.

I think all goes well with what I wanted. Saw Nancy lately. She told me of your new chill. Do you think you should get out of England for two months? With G.B.S.? Only don't ask me where. I think the people of Palm Beach would welcome him, and he could go via Bermuda and so miss the States: or there is Cape-Town: or the Dutch East Indies. Java is lovely they say.

I should suggest going or returning via Plymouth, selfishly!

T.E.S.

British Library

HENRY T. RUSSELL[1]
16.11.31   *R.A.F. MOUNT BATTEN PLYMOUTH*

Dear Mr Russell

Savage[2] has sent me on your letter, and I'm writing to say that my so-called 'seclusion' is a myth. I live in barracks, which is about as public a life as any human being can live. If I do not give interviews or write to the papers every week, it is only because I have nothing I want said. You are up against a contented being, who is perfectly willing to see you or anyone else – but will not put himself to the expense & toil of coming up to London except when absolutely compelled.

As for the Arab business: I had a hateful war: and after it 2½ years of a dog-fight with the British Cabinet to secure the fulfilment of the promises to which they had made me an unwilling and *post-facto* accessory. When Winston Churchill

1 Henry T. Russell was a United Press correspondent.
2 Raymond Savage: Lawrence's literary agent.

fulfilled all that was humanly attainable of those promises I was free to quit events and return to the class & mode of life that I belong to & feel happy in.

Revolt in the Desert is now withdrawn from circulation, and the whole business of my work & myself is over and done with. No value or significance can lie in unrelated episodes. My reputation which still persists in the cheaper newspapers is only founded on what I didn't do or am not, and so long as no truth comes out I am not harmed by it. The last thing I desire is to be 'put across' correctly. Truth hurts!

So while, as I said, I haven't the smallest objection to seeing you, the result, on your side, will be nil. There are no wrongs to put right, no remorse or agony. Only a very ordinary and pleased creature whose position in the R.A.F. forbids him to give interviews for publication.

Forgive this long egotistical letter: but you asked for it —

Yours ever
T. E. Shaw

University of Texas

EDWARD MARSH
10th March 1931   *MOUNT BATTEN PLYMOUTH*

Dear E.M.
This letter, typed more or less ill, is for your owner,[1] please. May your polish and style support its bluntness, in his eyes!

A namesake of his, Bertram Thomas, our Agent at Muscat, has just crossed the Empty Quarter, that great desert of southern Arabia. It remained the only unknown corner of the world, and it is the end of the history of exploration. Thomas did it by camel, at his own expense. Every explorer for generations has dreamed of it. Its difficulty can best be put by my saying that no Arab, so far as we know, has ever crossed it.

Now something good must be done for this most quiet and decent fellow, in the Birthday Honours, if not sooner. It may be all arranged; but if not I

---

1 J. H. Thomas, then secretary of state for the colonies. Marsh was his private secretary.

beg you see to it. Do not let the swag be all carried off by the Rositas[2] and Lawrences of the vulgar Press. Here is one of your own men doing a marvel.

Give him a K.[3] will you? Well, it's a mouldy sort of thing, but as a civil servant he cannot refuse. So it would do: but your sense of fitness, which o-emmned Henry J.[4] (now I address E.M. & not J.H.T.) might prefer a C.H.,[5] or some other honour of which I know nothing.

Properly he should be India Office; but his success decorates England. K.C.S. eyes or ees would be unfitting. Better a Michael & George.

I trust the imagination of J.H.T. to understand your enthusiasm & mine for what is the finest geographical feat since Shackleton and to persuade his colleagues into action and unanimity. It will be a welcome change for them all.[6]

Will you also say that his *Seven Pillars* is not forgotten? This is not bribery of a Cabinet Minister, but the paying of a forgotten debt. The only available copies are of the U.S.A. edition, and it may be weeks yet before I have the chance to get it brought safely through our Customs. Yours constantly (but not too often!)

T. E. Shaw.   *DG*

T. C. GRIFFIN[1]
17.IV.31   *R.A.F. MOUNT BATTEN PLYMOUTH*

Dear Griffin

The *Hardinge* was very good to us – and to me – but she was also a great ship, crowded with people, and I was preoccupied with cares & weariness in those two war-years. So I hope you will pardon my not remembering one of you more than another. It was – how long ago? Nearly fifteen years, wasn't it? I am so old now, and it feels a lifetime away. Nine years ago I enlisted, and have not thought about the Middle East since. The Air Force life suits me and I'm happy in it.

2 A reference to Rosita Forbes (1893-1967), the well-known traveller and travel-writer.
3 *I.e.* a knighthood.
4 Henry James had been given an O. M. (Order of Merit).
5 Companion of Honour.
6 Thomas was not honoured as Lawrence had suggested but he received the Founder's Medal of the Royal Geographical Society, the Burton Memorial Medal of the Royal Asiatic Society, and gold medals from the Geographical Societies of Antwerp and America.

1 A correspondent writing from Montreal who claimed to have met Lawrence when he was a temporary naval officer on board *H.M.S. Hardinge*, during the Hejaz campaign. This letter was printed in facsimile in the *Montreal Daily Star* on 20 May 1935.

So I cannot tell you anything about what happens now in the Red Sea. I don't write there, nor do they write to me. It wasn't a good time, and I like to forget it.

Seven Pillars, that book of mine? One copy did go to Canada, I think. Was it to a Colonel Leonard, at Montreal? I have no copy of my own, and have not seen the book for years. It's rather long, and I fancy dull. All the story part went into a popular version called *Revolt in the Desert*: but that's had its day, too!

I hope your affairs aren't bad. Most people's are, alas.

Yours
T E Shaw

Bodleian Library

ROBERT GRAVES
21.IV.31

Dear R.G.
I have been trying to write to you for months, but couldn't. All manner of jobs have descended on me, for the Air Ministry (after we had been campaigning for two years) suddenly decided to have a try at new types of marine craft for the R.A.F.: and with poetic justice pitched on me to conduct the trials. So imagine me as mainly a mechanic, and tester, oilskin-covered, urging speed-boats up & down Southampton water through the rain & wind at noisy rates. In your sunshiny warmth a pleasant picture: here it is wintry-weather, and I am frozen and soaked, but interested. A job quite worth doing. Very difficult, engrossing, and very exhausting.

It paralyses all my hope of finishing that beastly *Odyssey* to time, nor can I read anything. By evening my eyes are raw with salt-water and rheumy with wind, & I go to bed. So I can only acknowledge receipt of your Heinemann & other poems, Laura's: and Len Lye's.[1] I have looked at them: skimmed them even, unworthily, and descended to *Titbits* and the *Happy Magazine*, which seem to go with speed-testing and water-sports.

I Graves and Laura Riding, now living together in Majorca (hence Lawrence's postscript), had transported their press with them and had produced several books of their own writings and also a collection of letters by their friend Len Lye, a New Zealander of lively and original mind whom they had come to know in London.

All that you have promised me has come: and many letters from you both. I am an ingrate: yet I cannot help. Only in sheer necessity can I put pen to paper, except to report engine-performance, consumption, and hull design modifications.

Fortunately your last night's letter (I am in lodgings at Hythe, near Southampton, and shall be here till some time in May) provided such a necessity. On the back are notes for a Jules Verne aircraft of about 1980 A.D.[2] Too long for your need: rather technical perhaps. Only a rag, of course. Your letter did not give the date of your hero. If he is to be alive tomorrow, then perhaps his aircraft is a bit too advanced for him. If so make the motors petrol-electric. Cut up blade protrusion to .5 mm., double the landing speeds: reduce ceiling to 12000m. make his speed what you think fit (I aim at sound: about 800 feet a second say 900 k.p.m.). This machine would have to be oxygenated at full speed & height, of course. The designer should be a Spanish lady, I think; the aircraft trade being by 2000 A.D. entirely in the hands of the modistes: or is your hero a strong silent man?

If the skit is too Verney, then cut out the technical terms till the paragraphs run: and delete the antennae like cat's whiskers and the rotor propulsion.

In great haste: just going down to try an entirely new *British* marine motor: something designed to challenge the U.S.A. predominance.

Yours
T.E.S.

What should I call you on an envelope? Señor?

Harvard University/RGB

2 Graves and Riding were attempting to write together a novel devised specifically to catch the attention of Hollywood in the hope that it would be made into a successful – and lucrative – film, and Graves had written to Lawrence asking him to supply 'an autogyro of the future'. Lawrence obliged, as indicated here, providing the machine with, *inter alia* 'beam-antennae' which would signal the presence of anybody within 300 metres: virtually an anticipation of radar. The book was published in 1932 under the title *No Decency Left* and with the distinguished authors disguised under the pseudonym 'Barbara Rich'. It was, however, a commercial failure and was not published in America.

S. C. ROLLS[1]
10.VI.31

Dear Rolls

I've been away for two months more, testing and tuning speed-boats for the R.A.F. We are getting a type of our own, with twin 'Invicta' engines: does 30 m.p.h. and is a good sea-boat.

Because of this work, I've been on day and night, pretty well, and haven't had letters sent after me: so your letter turned up on Saturday, when I came 'home' for a few days.

Your Northampton offer sounds good: only I have so little free time. I shall try and blow into you all the same somehow, this autumn, if only I get a month off, and the weather is possible. Last year I spent the whole month working on a foreign book-translation, money making: because it rained every day, and so I never got past London.

So prepare Mrs Rolls not to bang the door on an undersized object in scruffy blue uniform, if it arrives some odd autumn day, suddenly.

Yours
T. E. Shaw

Bodleian Library

LADY ASTOR
10.VI.31   *PLYMOUTH*

Dear Peeress

Indeed and I was asleep & abed. How good of the Corporal to tell you! We had a hard 7½ hours run down from Southampton here in our motor-boat, got in before 7p.m., ate, made down our beds, & slept nobly till Sunday morning.

Now I hope to be at Mount Batten for a month. Ring me up (before 10 p.m., if possible) and we will meet.

1 S. C. Rolls had been Lawrence's driver in the last year of the Arabian campaign; he later described his experiences in *Steel Chariots in the Desert* (Cape, 1937), which includes a highly favourable account of Lawrence, whom he much admired. At the time of this letter he was governing director of the Imperial Autocar Company, Northampton, and proprietor of the Rolls Motor Company, Northampton.

No pillion. The new Traffic Act puts pillion-affording beyond modest means, and forces the love-sick to screw nasty iron-spring-things to their back mudguards.

No speed-boat either, now. I have much testing of the R.A.F. boat still and cannot put my own pet in the water till that is all done.

So you will have to make do with my undistinguished person, unaided except by an anglo-irish tongue.

Au revoir
T.E.S.

University of Reading

MR & MRS ERIC KENNINGTON
10.VI.31   *PLYMOUTH*

Dear Celandine and K.
I've been away for months, testing and tuning speed-boats in Southampton Water: but got back on Sunday to find the Hardy photographs waiting on my bed.[1]

It is superb: and better than that, fine. It holds somehow that strange effect of living within himself that always Hardy gave me. In bronze, when the over-statement of those excavated eyeballs will be corrected, the figure will be beautiful as well as a memorial.

I am so glad, for I liked old T. H. beyond reason, and the commission came to E.H.K. partly by my fault, and it was a terrible grind for him, and I felt sad about it: but now all ends for the best, with everybody.[2]

Excellent: excellent: excellent.

T.E.S.

Bodleian Library

---

1 *I.e.* photographs of Kennington's statue of Thomas Hardy which stands – or, more correctly, sits – at the top of the town in Dorchester, Dorset. It was unveiled by Sir James Barrie on 2 September 1935.
2 Kennington wrote at the side of the letter: 'No need for grief. I enjoyed the work enormously. E.H.K.'

MRS CHARLOTTE SHAW
26/VI/31

A point about Pte. Meek occurred to me last night, driving back from Torquay as guide to an R.A.F. car: (or is it Meake?).[1] He wouldn't have told the Colonel that he was his Intelligence Officer. He might have said 'I do the Intelligence work' or more likely 'I am also your Intelligence Staff Sir' ... to which the Colonel would have responded by dwelling on the Staff, probably, and forgetting the Intelligence. The Meeks of the world are shy of describing themselves as officers.

It is so hard to judge by just one act of a play. Who could deduce *The Apple Cart* from its 2nd Act? But I liked this new thing. It should get home.

Rifles at the ready: stand by – with the maroons: sights up to 2000, over their heads, no hitting: contact. Charge your magazines (or cut-outs open, if magazines were already charged). Ten rounds rapid fire ... something like that.

Meek wouldn't have said illiterate ... at least he doesn't. His difficulty is having not passed the educational exam, for promotion. He would probably have said that he hadn't got his educational certificate. 'Not educationally qualified' is written on my half-yearly return for promotion!

These squalid accuracies should not affect G.B.S. He must write so that the audiences will comprehend.

Yesterday I launched my own boat and went off to Polperro, in Cornwall, a 25 mile run. It was pleasant, sparkling sun and sea, out: and soft rain with a choppy sea, home. The poor boat's first run for months. The other thing has been smashed in two places (not irreparably) by her barbarian new owners. A pity: she was such a good boat. Photo herewith.

I've had to promise *The Odyssey* in August, if possible. So that means a month of leave upon it. If it goes well we shall be able to meet several times. If not – then I shan't deserve privileges.

It was so good to see you restored: for that was what I felt. I had been fearing that all this illness might have sapped you.

---

1 Bernard Shaw had included a caricature figure in the Lawrence mould in his most recent play *Too True To Be Good*, under the name of Private Napoleon Alexander Trotsky Meek. Lawrence happily acted as adviser to G.B.S. in order to ensure the correct use of military vocabulary.

The Cadet College at Cranwell wanted G.B.S. to lecture to them! How reputations change. Imagine him before a Service audience twenty years ago. I laughed![2]

T.E.S.
British Library

STANLEY BALDWIN[1]
27.VIII.31

Dear Mr. Baldwin

I am not quick at saying the right thing on staircases – and yesterday I was thinking instead of how well Ronald Storrs would run Egypt. So I fear I let you imagine that the giving to you of a paltry book counterbalanced the years of pleasure you have given me. Six years to date, and nearly four more to run, I hope, before my time expires. The mouse is very much indebted to his lion, and feels it.

No acknowledgement please …

Yours sincerely
T E Shaw

Cambridge University Library

2 G.B.S. had been a vigorous opponent of the First World War and had incurred much unpopularity at the time, to the extent that his plays were no longer performed and he lost numerous friends.

1 Rt Hon. Stanley Baldwin (later Earl Baldwin of Bewdley) (1867-1947) had already been Prime Minister twice (1923, 1924-29) and would be prime minister again (1935-37). In 1925 he had personally sanctioned Lawrence's return to the air force (*see* p. 298) hence the latter's profound gratitude to him, in recognition of which Lawrence had forwarded a copy of *Seven Pillars* to him through John Buchan in December 1926. The place and occasion of their apparently chance meeting on the day before this letter was written is difficult to establish, but by date it happened just two days after the formation of the 1931 national government under Ramsay MacDonald in which Baldwin took the post of lord president of the council. If Lawrence sought to procure the appointment of Sir Ronald Storrs as high commissioner for Egypt, he did not succeed; Storrs, at this time governor of Cyprus, was appointed governor of northern Rhodesia in 1932.

MRS CHARLOTTE SHAW
14.X.31   *MOUNT BATTEN*

Oh, I've got so many letters to do, all in a hurry. It seems a shame to begin
with you, but unless I do, perhaps I won't reach the end and leisure for days
yet: and you have waited a long time for a reply. I didn't have letters sent on
to me, in doubt as to my movements, and hoping to get back soon.

I think it is going to be all right. The routine has stiffened, with the going
of Group Captain Smith, and I, at least, feel less secure: but the present C.O.
(Wing Commander Burling) shapes well. He will do, I fancy. I'm going to
keep more to myself this time, as with the last C.O. I had too much to do.

Now I have nothing: nothing at all, except a very occasional proof from
Emery Walker's (Sir E. is improving: gets into the garden!) and the typescript
of Bertram Thomas' story of his trip across the Ruba el Khali of Arabia,
which I am reading for him, trying to make marginal hints like yours in the
Seven Pillars. So I hope to be able to read a lot this winter, and hear some
gramophone music, and ride the bike, and drive the boat: it is rather fine to
be owner of all one's 24 hours daily again.

About Hugo Wolf: you cannot have heard the right songs, or there must
be some flaw in your singer. Schubert and water! Wolf seems to me far finer
and rarer as a song-writer than anyone else I have ever heard. He has good
poems to set, and sets them marvellously. I should very much like to hear all
the records that H.M.V. do of him: and your subscription will be a great joy:
but do please perfect it by yourself hearing these records, and enjoying them.
I am sure Wolf is good, and you are bound to like him.

I'm hoping to get up to my cottage for this week-end. There are many good
records, and I intend to hear some Handel. There was a good *Judas* on the
wireless last night, from the Continent somewhere: and it reminded me of *The
Messiah* at Miranshah.

Do you remember F/Lt. Smetham, our queer kindly officer at Miranshah?
On Friday in London I met him. He is at the Air Ministry. He told me he has
many of the Miranshah records with him, still. He bought them from the irks
there, by exchanging for them such tunes as 'Do shrimps make good mothers?'
which the irks preferred.

It is going to be so good, being on my own this winter. I hope there will
be good books published. Are the G.B.S. musical and book-review volumes
out yet? I am going to ask you for the loan of them, when possible. I can keep
them in the office only, and therefore clean.

Last summer feels years ago: how is G.B.S.? And is there any news of *Too True To Be Good?*

(On Friday I was on the embankment near the Temple, just after seeing F/Lt. Smetham. A little bare-headed man rushed up and said 'Colonel Lawrence?' 'Used to be', I replied. 'I want to photograph you'. 'But who are you?' I asked. 'My name is Howard Coster'.[1] 'A professional?' I asked. 'Yes but this is for myself. I don't want to sell it or show it. You and Gandhi are the two people I want to take'. So I went along, for the joke of it, and he put me on a little chair, made me take my tunic off, and photographed me about a dozen times. A little shop in Essex Street. Rather a nice little stammering man, I thought. Works for *Vogue!* Had chased me for minutes, afraid to speak!).

T. E.

British Library

BERTRAM THOMAS [1]
7.XII.31   *HYTHE*

Dear Thomas

I got your doubled letter, via Plymouth and direct, and wired back that I'd get something done by the end of last week: and did. I hope you have had it.

A poor, lame thing: but the only reaction stirred in me by your book was a sense of thankfulness that it was alright. Misery, anger, indignation, discomfort – those conditions produce literature. Contentment never. So there you are.

It will need your censorship: and the proper spelling of all the people's names: and anyhow it is a poor thing. But it will save Jonathan's face, at least.

I am sorry: but what writing ambitions and faculties I did possess have flickered out. Yet they told me yesterday, from London, that my last report on

---

1 Howard Coster, was a leading photographer; he had opened a studio in London in 1926, Specializing in men's portraiture. He had served in the First World War in the photographic section of the R.A.F.

2 *See* letter to Edward Marsh of 10 March 1931, p. 481. Lawrence had written a foreword to Thomas's book *Arabia Felix*, which was published by Jonathan Cape.

the 8/28 dinghy engine we are testing was altogether the goods. So I am consoled. The bow still has a string.

Yours sincerely
T.E.S.

We probably stay here another week – but everything is very uncertain

Bodleian Library

HON. EDWARD ELIOT
7.XII.31   *HYTHE SOUTHAMPTON*

Dear Eliot
I have been meaning for months to write to you, but some ghost stood between us. Probably it was fear of a talk to your girls' school. How would I dare not refuse that? To one person I can talk honestly. To two with some circumspection. To three only from behind a mask. To four hesitatingly. To five in words of one syllable. To six only yes or no. Seven means silence.

How many are the daughters? If it is less than seven may I, in apology, come along one afternoon and tell them that I cannot talk, have never tried to talk, will not, I hope, ever try to talk? Hang it all, I am a contented being, wanting nothing for myself or anybody else, & contentment is uncreative. It is a little folding of the hands for sleep.

As I wrote that paragraph I grew aware that I do want something. One F/Sgt. Hutchinson of Mount Batten fell overboard one night between us & Plymouth and was drowned. As the accident was in his own time, not on duty, the R.A.F. disclaimed responsibility: which is all very well, but did not un-widow him, or get rid of Mrs H's two, young daughters. We subscribed about £30, which has helped. We appealed to the R.A.F. Memorial Fund, which sent her £5 in two helpings. She has a widow's pension of 18/– a week from the Free State Government. (She lives in Dublin): but that is great penury, in Dublin. A decent woman.

We want her to get about £20 a year for the next ten years, by when her children will be grown. I saw Col. Birch, who is secretary to the R.A.F. Memorial Fund: and he says he can't make a regular grant: but would, if his

Dublin branch would apply regularly, & if we would find him £20 a year, subscribed to his general fund.

Would it inconvenience the Trust to pay £20 each year into the general fund? I do not know how it would square with your discretion and the deed. Will you let me know? Mount Batten have squared the matter for 1931, all right: but it is a small station, and we cannot go on much longer finding funds.

I am sorry to trouble you. I had expected old Birch to agree, but he says his income is overdrawn: and was shocked when I said that all the best people and countries were drawing on capital, now-a-days.

Yours
T.E.S.

This letter goes to Robin,[1] as I cannot remember more than the 2nd. & 3rd. names of your firm as it used to be before you moved. I am in Hythe for a while yet, testing a new R.A.F. motor boat & engine, but shall be back at Plymouth before Christmas.

Bodleian Library

GEOFFREY DAWSON
22nd March 1932   *MYRTLE COTTAGE HYTHE SOUTHAMPTON*

Dear G.D.
Are you still editing the national newspaper?[1] I think so, from a copy I saw some weeks ago. It felt correct.

Today it struck me that as editor you might be interested in the new type of motor boat that we have been producing lately for the R.A.F. I'm partly the guilty cause of them — after a big crash a year ago in Plymouth Sound, which showed me convincingly that we had nothing in the Service fit to help marine aircraft in difficulties. Nor could the Navy supply even an idea of the type of craft we needed. The Navy is rather Nelsonic in its motor-boats. I suppose it knows something about steam. I don't, anyway, so I give them credit for it. In

1 Robin Buxton.

1 *The Times.*

petrol engines they are a wash-out: and they are not yet aware of what the States and Italy have done to improve the breed of fast motor-boat-hulls.

So the R.A.F. (partly, as I confessed above, at my prompting) went into the science of it, and have had produced for them, by the Power Boat works of Hythe, here, an entirely new type of seaplane tender. They are 37ft. boats, twin engined, doing 30 m.p.h. in all weathers, handy, safe and very cheap. Many of their features are unique. They cost less than any boats we have ever bought before.

All this has been done through the admiralty, in the teeth of its protests and traditions. Now the boats are finished, the sailors are beginning to take notice, & wonder if there isn't something in it.

Why don't you send your marine man down to see them? On Tuesday and Wednesday next (29 & 30) we have ten to a dozen of them cavorting about Southampton water all day. If he rang me up at the British Power Boat Works (Hythe 102) I would have him picked up at Southampton, and given a show. My name, of course, not to be mentioned. Robertson, the publicity king of the Air Ministry, is prepared for the publication of details. The ordinary press is only looking for stunts: but these boats are novel, and really interesting. Their performance is extraordinary. What about it? It deserves notice and serious criticism.[2]

It's short notice: but on Thursday 31st March we distribute the fleet to all our coastal stations. I hope to take the furthest of them, to Scotland, myself. A four-day cruise: which is my reward for a year's hard work.

Yours...
T E Shaw

Bodleian Library

ARTHUR HALL[1]
15.IV.32   *MYRTLE COTTAGE HYTHE SOUTHAMPTON*

Dear Brum
It is too late, now, for your kid's christening. The poor little creature will be fixed and named. Poor little beast.

---

2 Dawson accepted Lawrence's suggestion and sent down not his marine but his aeronautical
   correspondent to cover the trials. *See* Lawrence's letter of thanks to Dawson, next page.

1 Former aircraftman, R.A.F.: from Birmingham, hence 'Brum'.

I have been away for many weeks. These boats were finished and had to go out to Coastal stations, and I went with one and another of them, showing the new crews how they worked. In the end I got as far as Donibristle in Scotland, near the Firth of Forth bridge. 700 miles of a journey, it was, and very rough weather. They are good boats. At Donibristle they kept me another fortnight, explaining things, and then I came back by train. There are two more sorts of boats to get built.

How is the kid? and Mrs. Hall? I hope all well. I couldn't have been a god father [*sic*] anyhow, for I'm no child-maker. Life isn't very gay, I fancy, and I shouldn't like to feel that I'd brought anyone else into the world to have such times as I've had, and still have. You are happier, perhaps: I have found nothing to justify my staying on, and yet one can't go. It's a sad state – but a fellow ought to keep his troubles to himself, I suppose.

Best of luck
Yours Shaw

Bodleian Library

GEOFFREY DAWSON
21.IV.32   *HYTHE SOUTHAMPTON*

Dear G.D.
Your aeronautical expert, Shepherd, wrote for us two quite admirable articles – or at least I thought them quite admirable. I hope they have not got you into trouble with anyone. The boats are good and deserved notices. They have had them, good measure and good stuff, and that's over. I am most grateful to you for your interest.

I wonder just how S. did his writing, because he seemed to take no notes, just looked calmly at them & listened easily – yet all the stuff came out in print, admirably expressed and arranged. It struck me as a little better than most reporting I've met.

You said 'pay a visit if in London': and I did: but the chair was empty, and *The Times* being commanded from one of its flanks. I'm a seldom visitor but will try again.

Yours
T E Shaw   *Bodleian Library*

SIR WILLIAM ROTHENSTEIN
22.4.32   *MYRTLE COTTAGE HYTHE SOUTHAMPTON*

Dear Sir William? (a)[1]
Dear Rothenstein? (b)
(a) Too stiff, surely.
(b) Too familiar, from an airman to a Civil Servant.

I'm very sorry that your letter got no answer. I never got it, either.* I've been in Hythe now for nearly a year, testing motor boats or watching over their being built. A difficult, occupying job; that I am glad to do, for it needed doing and no-one else in the R.A.F. had my experience to do it. But I should prefer less of it.

As for letters, by all means use them as you wish, tempering your freedom with discretion. One doesn't write letters for publication, and so uses more licence in speech than is polite. If I call poor Orpen a squirt of a painter, for instance, then forgive it and suppress it. I can rely on you for anything of the sort. It is good of you to write and ask. Most people do not bother! I'm sure your writing will have style.

Books have not lain much in my way, lately. We work in the boat-yard all the daylight hours, and when dark comes I am tired, more inclined to read the *Happy Magazine* than Plato. So I compromise by reading neither, and am the better mechanic therefor.

Homer? a pot boiler, long ago done with. When, or if, it will be published is not my concern. The Greek isn't very good, I fancy: and my version is frankly poor. Thin, arty, self-conscious stuff, *The Odyssey*. I believe *The Iliad* to be a great poem – or to have fragments of a great poem embedded in it, rather. But *The Odyssey* is pastiche and face powder.

Yours,
T. E. Shaw.

* I suspect there being a packing case of letters awaiting me in Plymouth, to which I may return in July.

Bodleian Library

1 Rothenstein had been knighted in 1931.

K. W. MARSHALL[1]
6.IX.32   *MOUNT BATTEN PLYMOUTH*

[...] I had no letters sent on to me. So when I got back there was a mound of them on the table waiting. Into that I have dug a little. I hope there are no more of yours to find: for already I have 30 to answer – and God knows when I'll finish, if ever.

Don't worry about the fate of an odd letter or two. My letters ceased being personal seven years ago, when an American magazine advertised a batch as 'characteristic products of a remarkable adventurer.' That cured me of writing sense.

I have not read anything except the *Happy Magazine* for months: but in Plymouth I may have time, again. That will be noble. [...]   *Bodleian Library*

HENRY WILLIAMSON
6.IX.32   *MYRTLE COTTAGE HYTHE SOUTHAMPTON*

Dear H.W.
Another year gone, and us still wide apart, despite
    one perfectly good Silver Eagle Alvis, and one
         "   "   Brough.

I spend my days & nights working on motor boats, still, and chase all round the English coast after them or in them. Web-footed now, and quack before meal times.

I have not written to anyone till tonight for months. Now I have written sixteen letters. That is not correspondence but massacre, and I am ashamed. Likewise I have read almost nothing: and only by the pile of letters awaiting reply can I gauge how far I lag behind human decency. As for books, there stand two shelves of them. How can I ever get a free mind again.

As for writing books, myself: I have done one. 'Handbook to the Class of 37 ft 6 ins. RAF. Motor Boat', 30,000 words of the packiest stodge. It will not be included in my collected works.

I hope you are not more penniless than the rest of us: nor unhappy.

Yours
T E Shaw   *Bodleian Library*

---

1 A bookseller whom Lawrence befriended and who occasionally stayed at Clouds Hill. Later a member of the publishing house of Boriswood Ltd.

MRS CHARLOTTE SHAW
16.IX.32   *PLYMOUTH*

There: I am 'home' again – but for the moment only. Tomorrow I go on leave and shall get to London in a few days: and then call on you. *Very* tired again.

About W. B. Yeats' letter. You know, it staggers me that I should seriously be considered in such company.[1] All the best Irish, except AE, I fancy: and many of the not-so-good, too. I don't think any other country of the size would produce such a list.

I would like it, because it is a gesture on my part, that I am Irish: and I would like to think that. My work from the *Seven Pillars* onward, probably does not justify my joining that company. My reputation probably does. So on the whole I ought to say Yes to W. B. and to thank him for a unexpected and extraordinary compliment. Will you write for me?[2] I should be troubled in writing to him: for I have regarded him always as an exquisite and unattainable poet. He passes the test of the bigger people that his later work is more interesting, if less melodious, than his early work. Those *Tower* poems were splendid.[3]

It feels so odd that he should think of me as a writer. Disturbing: for I felt so sure, as time passed without any impulse to write: that I was right in thinking those books more or less accident. I know, of course, that I have the art of stringing words, and all the tricks of writing: but there is nothing to say. And while there is so much to do, it seems stupid to shut one's hands to that, and go on staring about to find something to write.

I am good at doing, too: despite their sending me away from Hythe. Merit did not enter into the question. Today I put right a boat here.

It will be good to see you in London again. Let us do another *Too good* and take *The Odyssey* Ms. to Wilson.

T.E.S.   *British Library*

---

1 The leading Irish poet and playwright W. B. Yeats (1865-1939) had written to Lawrence to inform him that he had been nominated to the new Irish Academy of Letters, by virtue of being the son of an Irishman.

2 Mrs Shaw duly wrote for him, and Lawrence shortly afterwards received the following reply: 'Your acceptance of our nomination has given me great pleasure, for you are among my chief of men, being one of the few charming and gallant figures of our time, & as considerable in intellect as in gallantry & charm. I thank you/Yours/W. B. Yeats.' (*Letters to T. E. Lawrence*, p. 213)

3 *The Tower* was a collection of poems published in 1928.

GEOFFREY CUMBERLEGE[1]

12.X.32   *R.A.F. MOUNT BATTEN PLYMOUTH*

Dear Mr. Cumberledge [*sic*]

Since your letter came I have seen Bruce Rogers – seen him twice in his last days here, for he has sailed for the States – and we have discussed generally the American edition of *The Odyssey*. Incidentally he showed me a suggested page of it.

I am aware of the importance of the money side of it to B.R. and will allow anything to be done to favour it – short of having an English public edition. Books are miseries, and if I could, there would be no more of them. I hope never to put out anything in England again. The States don't matter to me: I do not care what they do or say. Nor will there be any blow-back on this side. English booksellers are stiff-necked. They do not import American books: and if they do, the public refuse them. So unless someone actually advertises the thing over here, there will be no demand: and imports can be checked by Walker's, as an infringement of his copyright!

I have dealt with the royalty question direct with B.R. as you suggested. He bought out Colonel Isham's interest, which was a good act: but not immediately profitable to me, for had the burden been Isham's there would have been no name of translator on your edition! In my contract for doing the english version I secured myself expressly against all association with any edition of the book.

So I want you to realise that in accepting the use of my name upon your edition I am sacrificing what I regard as very important. I do not want you or anyone to imagine that I have let B.R. down. He understood from the beginning that I was opposed to any mention of myself. Had the version been done in my two years in India, and promptly printed, no curiosity about it would ever have arisen.

I shall be much more careful and exacting upon any future occasion – unless this experience teaches me to prevent future occasions!

Yours
T E Shaw

Worcester College Oxford

3 Geoffrey Cumberlege (1891-1979) was then managing director of the New York branch of the Oxford University Press, which published an unlimited edition of *The Odyssey* in the United States.

SIR EDWARD ELGAR
12.X.32   *MOUNT BATTEN PLYMOUTH*

Dear Sir Edward
In the one week I have had letters from you and from W. B. Yeats – and it is
a little difficult for an ordinary mortal to say the happy things when public
monuments around him come suddenly to speech. I have liked most of your
music – or most that I have heard – for many years: and your 2nd Symphony
hits me between wind and water. It is exactly the mode that I most desire, and
so it moves me more than anything else – of music – that I have heard. But
thousands of people share my liking for your music, and with better reason
for they know more about it than I do: so this doesn't justify the kindness of
the Shaws in bringing me with them that afternoon[1]. The chance of meeting
you is just another of the benefits that have accrued to me from knowing
G.B.S., who is a great adventure.

There are fleas of all grades; and so I have felt the awkward feeling of
having smaller creatures than myself admiring me. I was so sorry to put you to
that awkwardness: but it was inevitable. You have had a lifetime of achievement,
and I was a flash in the pan. However I'm a very happy flash, and I am
continually winning moments of great enjoyment. That Menuhin-Concerto is
going to be a pleasure to me for years: and the news of your 3rd Symphony
was like a week's sunlight. I do hope you will have enough enthusiasm left to
finish it. There are crowds of us waiting to hear it again and again.

Probably it feels quaint to you to hear that the mere setting eyes upon you
is a privilege: but by that standard I want to show you how good an afternoon
it was for me, in your house.

Yours sincerely
T. E. Shaw

DG

---

1 On 2 September 1932 Lawrence had gone with the Shaws to Elgar's home in Worcester to
  hear the test pressings of the recording of Elgar's *Violin Concerto*, with the 15-year-old Yehudi
  Menuhin as soloist.

E. M. FORSTER
22.X.32   *PLYMOUTH*

Dear E.M.F.
I am sorry about this. I cannot send you a copy of the Emery-Walker printed *Odyssey*[1] that I translated. I know it is only a pot boiler, and *The Odyssey* is not much good, anyhow: but it felt right to give it you.

And now I can't. The things cost twelve guineas, and I got only a handful of them: and the people to disappoint are those who know enough to forgive a slight.

If it had had anything of mine in it, you would have had it necessarily: but this second-hand English is no more personal than the filling in of an income-tax form.

I hope you are afloat and engaged. Lately my hull has been not too fortunate. A dose of fever and cold: and a sense of exhaustion. Give me a few weeks and I will be well again.

Lately I was sent the D.H.L. letters.[2] His ungenerousness astonishes me. I can hardly believe that any 800 pages of my writing would fail to include at least a half-word of satisfaction at something someone had written or done.

I am so sorry about that *Odyssey*: but I just can't put down so much money, now.

Yours
T.E.S.

Bodleian Library

MRS THOMAS HARDY
3.XII.32   *MOUNT BATTEN PLYMOUTH*

Dear Mrs. Hardy
I am sorry that your copy[1] should have got muddled, somehow. One has now gone direct to Max Gate, and you should find it there as soon as you return.

It is not in any way a remarkable work. As translation it is faithful within the limits I lay down in a little postscript to the book. The English is very

1 Lawrence was referring to the English limited edition of *The Odyssey* of 530 copies.
2 *The Letters of D. H. Lawrence*, edited by Aldous Huxley, published 1932.

1 Of *The Odyssey*.

schoolmastery – by which I mean that relative clauses, prepositions and particles are correctly placed. There is too much inversion – twisting of sentences to compress the English into little more space than the much more concise Greek. There are some colloquialisms: no slang, I hope; if we call slang those colloquialisms which not everybody yet understands and uses.

As production the book is a fine example of its kind: and you will like it, if you like the kind. I am rather neutral towards the whole effort. Everybody dislikes his last book, of course: but this is only a pot-boiler, and little intensity went to it. I did it as well as I could, of course, but did not feel like signing it. So I have not marked your copy. I will, if you particularly wish it, of course.

The money is being useful. There were wood-beetles eating the roof of Clouds Hill: and it is now being doctored and sprayed. That is the first object. Then the kitchen downstairs is to be cemented and turned into a book-room, with shelves. I may ask your Parsons expert (I have lost his name & address!) to do the shelving. The third object, if the money lasts, will be a bath and hot-water boiler. How tickled old Homer would have been! He used to enjoy his hot baths, anyway.

I am sorry they went to China: but it was inevitable. They are best there, while they feel it is a duty. I wish they could grow out of that: for my mother, at least, is not fitted for overseas living. Also they were happy in the cottage. Perhaps they will come back?

Yours sincerely
T E Shaw

University of Texas

HARLEY GRANVILLE-BARKER
23.XII.32   *PLYMOUTH*

Paris is pleasant, you say. My longest experience of it was in 1919, during the Peace Conference. So I shall not ever think of it as pleasant.

And I can't come to your *Place* and place there,[1] because the Air Force prevents, and the last time (1921) I wanted to cross France they refused me a visa. It is unfortunate to have the name of a spy!

1 A pun on the Granville-Barkers' Paris address: the Place des Etats-Unis.

Don't read *The Odyssey* aloud to Mrs. G.B., please. She would die of it, and both of us suffer a sense of loss, as Homer would say. It must have been nice to live in a literary period when even a platitude was a discovery, and clichés were waiting to be made. He was very successful in both these ways, I think.

The Odyssey to me represents – a bath, a hot-water plant and bookshelves in my cottage. So I have no regrets: but it is not one of my collected works.

You were unwise to buy it.

I'm glad to hear that Shakespeare approaches vol. iii[2] and finality. What will you do afterwards? After having had a period of acting, one of production, one of play-writing, one of criticism ... what next?

And me? Oh, I'm going to retire to Dorsetshire, to my cottage, and neglect its garden.

Yours
T. E. Shaw

Bodleian Library [3]

E. H. R. ALTOUNYAN[1]
9.I.33   *MOUNT BATTEN*

Dear E.A.,
Your letter (I'm glad you are still in England: to save me reproaches for keeping your article too long) is the sort that the most gratified writer alive would yet thank you for: and I don't feel very proud of my writing. So you can imagine how it pleased me. By all means keep the fat book so long as it suits you. That copy is a collection of spoiled sheets, cut and pressed into smallness, and usually it belongs to Mrs. Bernard Shaw – but she is away on a world cruise with G.B.S.

2 Volume III of Granville-Barker's *Prefaces to Shakespeare.*
3 Also published in Granville-Barker's *Eight Letters from T.E.L.* (1939) and in *Granville-Barker and His Correspondents* (1987).

1 Ernest Altounyan, who had first met Lawrence in his Carchemish days, was a doctor in Aleppo where his father had founded the Altounyan Hospital which was famous throughout the Levant. He was a great admirer of Lawence and later wrote a poetic work, *Ornament of Honour*, in his memory.

What the muezzin said was, I fancy – and after fifteen years it is probably fancy – *Wa el besharra*[2] ... No English word or phrase even would translate it, so I paraphrased in his spirit rather than his letter. I only wish that *ya ahl el Sham* had been better rendered than by 'people of Damascus'. The Arabic *ahl* is a fine word. The worst of being a habitual translator is that one gets in the way of trying to squeeze every sponge dry – and so few authors really *intend* all the contents of their sponges. Words get richer every time they are deliberately used ... but only when deliberately used: and it is hard to be conscious of each single word, and yet not at the same time self-conscious.

I mustn't slip again into the technique of writing. Writing has been my inmost self all my life, and I can never put my full strength into anything else. Yet the same force, I know, put into action upon material things would move them, make me famous and effective. The everlasting effort to write is like trying to fight a feather-bed. In letters there is no room for strength.

Am I morbid? Only with people inclined to it, I fancy. By myself I do not brood at all, having so much to do. That vision of the wholeness of life is not a visitor to me, but always there, like a background to the diggings and the war and the R.A.F. Wherefore I get a sense of the sameness and smallness of everything, including us: and so I would not voluntarily put another into my place. Too much glory or none? Why I think the nones, who eat and drink and chase their appetites, are wholesomer. And I like cats and camels, therefore.

This is a silly letter. So was yours. I liked it, too. English people don't write about the verities as a rule, for the good reason that such subjects exceed us, and we look foolish in their shadow.

The two studies of the Euphrates valley are exactly in place in my cottage, and perfect there. I cannot choose between them, or consider sending one back. Call them lost to you, both! I am most glad to have them, for Carchemish was a happy place, and they form a link.

Would you be so interested in me as a writer – not a visioner of life, but just a penman – as to wade through my next-after-the-*Seven-Pillars* book? It has remained in typescript, and is a study of the R.A.F. recruiting depot. Not much glory, but life, in its way. It is short, rather mannered also but better, as writing, than the earlier book, I think.

Yours
T.E.S.

DG

2 *See Seven Pillars of Wisdom*, Chap. CXX.

H. LIDDELL HART
Whitmonday' 33[1]

Dear L-H

I have read this twice, once to get its idea, and once with a pencil in hand.[2] It has been a queer experience – like going back, in memory, to school – for by myself (though with far less knowledge, and hesitatingly) I had trodden all this road before the war. It is a very good little book: modest, witty and convincing. You realise, of course, that you are swinging the pendulum and that by 1960 it will have swung too far!

So far as I can see strategy is eternal, & the same and true: but tactics is the ever-changing language through which it speaks. A general can learn as much from Belisarius as from Haig – but not a soldier.[3] Soldiers have to know their means.

I can't write an introduction: none is necessary. Your sub-title should be 'a tract for the times.'

Yours
TES

Fitzwilliam Museum Cambridge

1 Whit Monday was 5 June in 1933.
2 Lawrence was referring to Liddell Hart's book *The Ghost of Napoleon*.
3 Belisarius was a Byzantine general who had achieved success by employing hit-and-run tactics involving small units at small cost; Sir Douglas Haig (later Earl Haig of Bemersyde), British commander-in-chief in the First World War from December 1915, had won (eventual) success by the use of massed forces at high cost.

ALAN DAWNAY[1]
16.VI.33   *119 CLARENCE ROAD EAST COWES I. OF W.*

Extravagant person. Your letter tore across the Solent in a speed-boat from Hythe, and I was 'phoned to meet and collect. Fortunately the Post Office is next the landing stage, so you had a quick answer.

Only one thing tempted me. 'They will require the manuscript ...' I saw myself approach the mike and mellifluously say 'The B.B.C. caused me to deposit with them the text of my possible delivery upon Feisal tonight. I have forgotten that stupidity. Here goes for what I really think.' And then the red light would pop out and the announcer would say 'Now we will have a short programme of gramophone records...'

That would have been worth fifteen guineas, but not the sack from the R.A.F. Remember that I am *not* (yet) a private person: but when I am, my hat, I'll be private.

Upon withdrawal to Clouds Hill I will go through my address book and to each name send a printed card 'To announce cessation of correspondence'. That will also be worth fifteen guineas.

I hope you do the Feisal touch. If you see the dear man remember me very kindly to him. Say I am very proud of having helped his beginning.

Yours
T.E.S.

Bodleian Library

---

1 The background to this letter is that King Feisal of Iraq was about to pay an official visit to Britain, and Alan Dawnay had just been appointed controller of programmes at the BBC, though he had not yet taken up his post. The BBC archives have no record of any formal approach being made to Lawrence at this time, so it is very possible that Dawnay himself decided to sound out whether Lawrence would be prepared to commemorate the event with a radio talk.

ALAN DAWNAY
30.VI.33   *119 CLARENCE ROAD EAST COWES ISLE OF WIGHT*

How did Feisal-broadcast go? Did you do it? I hope so. They say he is clean-shaven now: that must make a difference.[1]

Reason for writing 'Do you recall anyone named B. Ley Roberts on our staff in Arabia?' I don't. I have asked Goslett, too. Gent is now in business in Cairo and boasts his connection as a reference.

Daily Mail states that I have left the R.A.F. Improbable!

Yours
T.E.S.

Sorry for bothering you: a card saying 'Never heard of him' would be sufficient answer, if true.

Bodleian Library

MRS CHARLOTTE SHAW
23.VIII.33   *13 BIRMINGHAM ST SOUTHAMPTON*

There, I have worked here and watched August slipping away, often saying to myself 'It will be easier soon' – and instead the work piles up. We are in arrears now, and by the end of September we are to finish the first twelve boats.

Of course the work is good, and I lose myself in it, for the while: but not always. If I had a magic carpet and could instantly move myself – but even when time permits it, the twin enemy, space, contains my gross body. They sent me to Kent the first week-end, to talk boats with Sir Philip Sassoon – half an hour of business in two days of a visit – and I must go to him again this week-end. Once I went to London. Five days in Bridlington. One at Farnham ... so it lengthens out.

It is, perhaps, a little excuse that there is no real play: nothing that wants any of the audience to do anything after they go out. But the plays never

---

1 Apparently there was no broadcast about Feisal at this time. There was, however, a broadcast later that year on 8 September, a brief obituary of him by Lord Allenby, Feisal having died in Switzerland at the age of 50.

mattered at Malvern: it was the hills, and the quiet light across that great plain towards the river, and something uplifted in the spirits of yourself and G.B.S. Also this year you talked of Elgar, and the newspapers said that he was ill.

If you see him will you present my constant pleasure in his music, whether human rendered or from my box? Nobody who makes sounds gets so inside my defences as he does, with his 2nd Symphony and Violin Concerto. Say that if the 3rd Symphony has gone forward from those, it will be a thrill to ever so many of us. He was inclined to grumble that the rewards of making music were not big, in the bank-book sense: but by now he should be seeing that bank-books will not interest him much longer. I feel more and more, as I grow older, the inclination to throw everything away and live on air. We all allow ourselves to need too much.

[...]

Liddell Hart has (in haste) finished his book on me.[1] Cape spoilt it, by asking for less military consideration and more life. So he only tells again the three-times-told story, and I am sick of my divagations. When one acts, one has a reason, or instinct, and is privately satisfied. But the past gets all snailed over when these others try to explain it.

I hope Malvern has been good. This has been the best summer weather of my memory: an abiding marvel, the way the sun has shone and the wind blown warm. I have loved all the background of my days, and swum often, and worked hard. Is G.B.S. still at work revising that playlet and play? Will he play them, or just print them and let the stage go hang? It is a problem, to be an elder dramatist.

I met H. G. Wells in the train three weeks ago. 'You' I said rashly 'probably want to write no more stories now'. He replied 'I dare not: my reputation is too great to risk a failure: and one writes a good story only by writing three or four bad ones, and till the public has read them the good does not appear from the bad. So I can only afford to write histories and things'. There is something behind that: probably an excuse for having grown up.

I hope you are well and happy.

T.E.S.

British Library

[1] Published by Cape in 1934 as *'T. E. Lawrence' in Arabia and After.*

MRS CHARLOTTE SHAW
31.VIII.33   *13 BIRMINGHAM ST SOUTHAMPTON*

Yesterday was a DAY. At 1.45 p.m. water, driven by the smallest ram ever installed anywhere, began to flow into my cottage at Clouds Hill. The pipes are a hundred yards long: the ram was turned on at 10a.m. without public ceremony: it worked steadily for hour after hour: and at 1.45, as I have said the water arrived at its destination. The single, oldest and only inhabitant of Clouds Hill took off his R.A.F. cap with a simple gesture (to avoid knocking it against the roof-beam) and collected the first pint in a pint mug. It arrived in four minutes, and the S.O. and O. inhabitant then drank it. The taste was of red lead and galvanised iron: but the quality was wet, indubitably: and they say that in four weeks the taste will be unalloyed water. I hope so: for otherwise my drinking water will come from the spring by bucket![1]

If a pint in four minutes seems to you little, reflect that it works all day and all night at that rate. It is copious; excessive. Indeed I have laid down a spill-pipe, which will feed the kitchen of my neighbour, Mrs. Knowles, with my surplus. Both of us are henceforward endowed with running water. We feel so rich and happy.

Now for the bath.[2] It has arrived, but must wait for fixing till its boiler, cistern and burner are in order. Some date in October, I hope, there will be the sound of a hot bath at Clouds Hill. I shall feel like telegraphing you the news. Imagine that a mere translation of *The Odyssey* does me all this good!

News of my mother, after a long interval. Well, and gently busy with her house and living. My brother better in health and not overworked. The country round about not peaceful enough for anybody's liking. I hope they are not put to anxiety or hardship.

Please tell G.B.S. of my house-wetting. It is an achievement, to have made so small a ram. The parent spring only gives half a gallon a minute: so a quarter of pint per minute is an excellent product. Nice things, rams.

T.E.S.

British Library

1 David Garnett described the ram as 'one of the most admirable of the ingenuities of Clouds Hill'.
2 The manufacturer of the bath was the former supply and ordnance officer at Akaba, Raymond Goslett.

HIS MOTHER
27.IX.33   *SOUTHAMPTON*

[Poor Arnie. You are inclined to persecute him, you know. People brought up together, when full grown, rather resent their relatives. I think Arnie does not want to see too much of us, and the best treatment for that is to see too little. When he feels safe-sure that we are not trying to 'get at' him — he will lose that nervousness. If any of us really needed anything, we would help each other. Till then, do let each manage his own affairs!

I saw Mrs Fontana[1] a few times during this summer. She was made unhappy by Guido's death,[2] for it was a hidden consumption, that she had never suspected. Her daughter Tacita still exists, and has gone to London to study art. Guido was married and had lately lived in S. America. Mrs Fontana has just enough to live on, but is not employing herself well, and feels aimless. A nervous, shrinking person, not easy to help. She sent messages to you, remembering you distinctly.]

Bodliean Reserve

MRS CHARLOTTE SHAW
9.XII.33   *13 BIRMINGHAM ST SOUTHAMPTON*

I wish it were not so cold: I can only hold the pen sideways in my fingers, and that makes sprawly writing. Also the Indian Ink is frozen. I hope you are still warm in London. This goes there, on the chance.

Nancy says you are better: not much, I fancy, in this weather. The English are a tough people, but England kills them off. By the way, what are people to do if the Free State cuts away from England? If only de Valera was an admirable man; but that underhung jaw and the fishy eyes repel me.

I hope *On the Rocks*[1] still marches strongly. Next week, about Thursday night, I am half-promised a visit to London. This week was half-promised,

1 Widow of the former British consul in Aleppo, R. A. Fontana. (*See* p. 538)
2 Guido: her son.

1 G.B.S.'s latest play.

too, but failed. Is there any difficulty of getting a seat? You know that I like to provide for myself.

The real motive of this letter, however, isn't altruism: something happened to me last night when I lay awake till 5. You know I have been moody or broody for years, wondering what I was at in the R.A.F., but unable to let go – well last night I suddenly understood that it was to write a book called 'Confession of Faith', beginning in the cloaca at Covent Garden, and embodying *The Mint* and much that has happened to me before and since as regards the air. Not the conquest of the air, but our entry into the reserved element, 'as lords that are expected, yet with a silent joy in our arrival'. It would include a word on Miranshah and Karachi, and the meaning of speed, on land and water and air. I see the plan of it. It will take long to do. Clouds Hill, I think. In this next and last R.A.F. year I can collect feelings for it. The thread of the book will only come because it spins through my head: there cannot be any objective continuity – but I think I can make it whole enough to do. *The Mint*, you know, was meant as notes for something (smaller) of the sort. I wonder if it will come off. The purpose of my generation, that's really it.

Anyway I shall tell no one else: so Liddell Hart will not get after it! Three years hence we'll know.

T.E.S.

British Library

LADY ASTOR
11.XII.33   *13 BIRMINGHAM STREET SOUTHAMPTON*

Mi Vykowntess
Let me qualify the 'any retired Colonel'.[1] I should have said 'any Colonel who has retired into the R.A.F.'

I cannot answer your letters because I cannot read them all! They are monologues, too, like conversations with our dear good Queen. Only by grace

---

1 In a letter to Lady Astor dated 1 June 1933, Lawrence had described himself as pottering about Clouds Hill 'like any other retired Colonel'.

of the headed notepaper do I know whence they come. I cannot answer your wires, because often I have not a shilling to spare. Your wires are <u>gloriously legible</u>.

'A very tall dark woman'. Let me think over my recent past. I have never met Lady Londonderry. He is very tall, but not dark, I think. Mrs. Gubbay (met at Lympne) is dark and a woman: but not very tall, judged by myself: and you are little smaller than me. Mrs. Lionel Curtis is tall, but always makes a brown impression on me. Mrs. Scott-Paine (wife of the boat-builder with whom I work here) is tall: but I don't know what colour she would wash to. The present outward decoration is magenta and cream. Who else was there? Ah! a Lady Juliet Duff, relic of a generation before your own. She is very tall, but white: and there is the Mrs. Siegfried Sassoon-to-be[2]. I think she was dark, but, I seldom photograph women: nor do I know her name. Probably it's her you are after. She lives near Christchurch with her mother, in an Edwardian-Gothic house. Do not suspect us of an affair. Siegfried is a better man than me, and she was honestly in love with him, and in terror of her life of proving inadequate. I tried to cheer her up, without being foolishly optimistic. I liked the foolhardy creature. Fancy taking on S. S.

Overleaf you talk of the tall dark woman with her shiny broad mouth, and hope that she will make me happy. I hope so, too, if it has to be — but only a walrus has such a mouth, I think. May I postpone the swimming lessons till next summer? Warn me when she comes! And warm me!

I saw Mrs. Shaw a fortnight ago. She has since been ill. So be glad I did not call and find you in.

I hope the play will go well. They were hurt by *Too True*'s short run. Odd how men like repeating their successes — and women their failures!

Your last page contains the word Plymouth — but I never get there now. Southampton always. I also see the word 'Bobbie' twice.[3] Him I 'have yet to meet. I hope he is well and open again.

Your last ominous sentence is 'How <u>much</u> do you see of this tall d- woman?' That might be more happily expressed, perhaps. Awful thought. Does 'd-' mean what it usually does? Is she Lady Portarlington?[4] Help!

T.E.S.   *University of Reading*

2 Siegfried Sassoon married Hester, daughter of Sir Stephen Herbert Gatty, a week after this letter was written 8 December 1933. Lawrence was one of the guests.
3 Bobbie: Robert Gould Shaw III, Lady Astor's son by her first marriage to Robert Gould Shaw II.
4 Lady Portarlington: the mother of Lawrence's friend Lord Carlow.

ALEC DIXON[1]
21.XII.33   *13 BIRMINGHAM STREET SOUTHAMPTON*

Ahoy! Still there? Perhaps. Indeed I am a hot correspondent.

Boats, boats, boats: that is my life. And yours? Not so regular, I hope.

Permanent address Clouds Hill, Moreton, Dorset. In 14 months they give me my lounge suit, and there I am, fixed. The cottage has now water, a bath, bookshelves. No bed. One sleeps where one can. No kitchen. One feeds in Bovington. No drains. One – under any bush, beyond sight of the windows!

No good writing more elaborately, till I hear if you are in the South Seas or where not.

By the way. I have never seen any of your books. What about it?

Yours
T. E. Shaw

I flew over Maidstone (at 2000 feet) last summer!

Bodleian Library

SIR EDWARD ELGAR
22.XII.33   *CLOUDS HILL MORETON DORSET*

Dear Sir Edward,

This is from my cottage and we have just been playing your 2nd Symphony. Three of us, a sailor,[1] a Tank Corps soldier, and myself. So there are all the Services present: and we agreed that you must be written to and told (if you are well enough to be bothered) that this Symphony gets further under our skins than anything else in the record library at Clouds Hill. We have the Violin Concerto, too; so that says quite a lot. Generally we play the Symphony last of all, towards the middle of the night, because nothing comes off very well after it. One seems to stop there.

1 Dixon had been a Tank Corps corporal at Bovington. He subsequently served (1926–31) as a detective-inspector in the Straits Settlements police. He was the author of two books, *Extreme Occasion* and *Singapore Patrol*.

1 Jock Chambers, who had served in the navy before joining the air force.

You would laugh at my cottage, which has one room upstairs (gramophone and records) and one room downstairs (books): but there is also a bath, and we sleep anywhere we feel inclined. So it suits me. A one-man house, I think.

The three of us assemble here nearly every week-end I can get to the cottage and we wanted to say 'thank you' for the Symphony ever so long ago; but we were lazy, first: and then you were desperately ill, and even now we are afraid you are too ill, probably, to be thinking of anything except yourself: but we are hoping that you are really getting stronger and will soon be able to deal with people again.[2]

There is a selfish side to our concern: we want your Symphony III: if it is wiser and wider and deeper than II we shall very sadly dethrone our present friend, and play it last of the evening. Until it comes, we shall always stand in doubt if the best has really yet happened.

Imagine yourself girt about by a mob of young pelicans, asking for III and please be generous to us, again!

Yours sincerely,
T. E. Shaw

DG[3]

LADY ASTOR
31.XII.33   *13 BIRMINGHAM STREET SOUTHAMPTON*

[...] One day last week (Wednesday I think it must have been) I came to London and registered my motor-bike for 1934. Also I asked after Sir Herbert Baker, who is going on well, regaining himself: and then a memory of a half-deciphered sentence in your last letter caused me to ring up St. James' Square. You were reported absent. I felt glad that you had better things to do.

I am sorry about the dark lady, and rather frightened. Where is safety, if I am rumoured to have lost my heart to a lady of sixty, upon once visiting her after lunch to apologise for not lunching? A lady whom I had met for the first time at Lympne in the summer? It is rather hard, I think. Probably it would be wholesome for me to lose my heart – if that monstrous piece of machinery is capable of losing itself: for till now it has never cared for anyone, though

2 Elgar was suffering from inoperable cancer; he died 23 February 1934.
3 This letter is now in the possession of the Elgar Birthplace Museum, Worcestershire.

much for places and things. Indeed I doubt these words of 'hearts'. People seem to my judgement to lose their heads rather than their hearts. Over the Christmas season two men and four women have sent me fervent messages of love. Love carnal, not love rarefied, you know: and I am uncomfortable towards six more of the people I meet, therefore. It's a form of lunacy, I believe, to fancy that all comers are one's lovers: but what am I to make of it when they write it in black on white? If only one might never come nearer to people than in the street. Miss Garbo[1] sounds a really sympathetic woman! The poor soul. I feel for her.

I would now like to turn to happier things, and be brisk for a last paragraph: but no use. Those two in China have been silent for a month which means lost letters or uncivil unrest across their line of communications. They were wrong to court martyrdom thus inaccessibly. [...]   *DG*

LIONEL CURTIS
19.3.34   *UNION JACK CLUB LONDON S.E.1*

My Lord Prophet
Your letter and Philip's wire met me on Sunday in Southampton, as I got back from Birmingham.[1] So this morning I wired to him that I was sympathetic but sorry — and tonight (ordered to London suddenly for an inspection tomorrow at Brentford of a searchlight) I failed to find him in his lordly burrow of St. James.

The defence question is full of snags and is being ineptly handled by Lords Rothermere & Beaverbrook. I agree that the balance of expenditure on Navy, Army and R.A.F. is wrong: but I do not want R.A.F. expenditure increased. Our present squadrons could deal very summarily with France. When Germany wings herself — ah; that will be another matter, and our signal to reinforce: for the German kites will be new and formidable, not like that sorry French junk.

All we now need is to keep in ourselves the capacity to expand the R.A.F. usefully, when the times make it necessary. For this we must have:—

1 Greta Garbo (b. 1905), legendary Swedish film actress, famous for her remark 'I want to be alone', originally spoken in the film *Grand Hotel* in 1932. She ultimately solved the problem of being the focus of much publicity by retiring into private life in her mid-thirties; her last film, *Ninotchka*, was made in 1939.

1 Curtis had written to tell him that the *Round Table* was to publish an article arguing that a large part of the money currently being spent on the navy should be spent on the air force; Philip Kerr, Lord Lothian, had wired him to ask for a meeting to discuss the subject.

(1) Aerodromes enough, sited in the useful places.

(2) Aircraft firms well equipped, with up-to-date designers, designs, and plant.

(3) Brains enough inside our brass hats to employ 1 and 2.

(1) Easy – but means another 15 Aerodromes, each costing £20,000: they take about three years to bring into being.

(2) In hand; excellent; but hampered by

(3) The direction of R.A.F. and Air Ministry. Our air-marshals are rather wooden headed, and some of the civilian A.I.D.[2] inspectors and technicians who handle design are hopeless. Consequently our military aircraft are like christmas trees, all hung with protruding gadgets, our flying boats are a bad joke, our civil aircraft are (almost) the world's slowest; and air tactics and strategy are infantile.

More money should be spent at once on (1) above: and research made into flying boat development (after sacking the present authorities) and wireless-controlled aircraft. Also to develop the art of sound-ranging, and anti-aircraft gunnery. If I had my way, I would constitute a new Flying Boat department of Air Ministry, and have in a dozen good naval men to give it a start.

Upon the Navy I have views also. Our air bombs are not going to sink capital ships; but will render them useless as fighting platforms, and probably uninhabitable. This in only three or four years time. The defence of surface craft against aircraft will be found in manoeuvre: – in being able to turn quicker on the water than the plane can in the air – not difficult, with small ships, as water gives you a firmer rudder. So I expect to see the surface ships of navies, in future, limited to small, high-speed, manouvrable mosquito craft, none larger than the destroyers of today.

There are controversial points in the above, and to argue them one must consider smoke-screens, the one-pounder pom-pom, trajectories, dive-arcs, b-bombs; all sorts of technical things. But I am prepared to maintain my thesis in most company. Do not, however, take this exposition of it as exhaustive or even fair. To deal with imponderables, layer upon layer of imponderables, more resembles faith than argument.

I wish I could have run through your Round Table argument and talked it over with you.

Accordingly
T.E.S.

Off to Southampton tomorrow p.m. after a meeting in Air Ministry.   *DG*

2 Air Inspection Department.

E. H. R. ALTOUNYAN
7 April 34

[...] I have another 12 months of the R.A.F. and after that the prospect of unbounded leisure. I wait for this to happen, with great longing. Work no longer excites me; for more than a short spasm. Tired, I think: and probably getting old, without having physically adjusted myself to the restrictions of age.
[...]
Your poem – essentially it is one, a poetic history – is so long, so interwoven, so exhausting, that it demands full attention.[1] Don't be hurt by the word exhausting. I do not mean wearisome but wearying. It is a strenuous exercise to reach much of it. Like boxing, which is a severe art, whereas golf is easy. You are a muscular poet, and few readers will ever grapple with you competently.

This tax upon your readers is physical. It is possible that intellectually you may make an equal demand. Your metaphysic, your physiology, your philosophy may be as articulated and articulate as [the] forcefulness of your writing. My mind slides over what it fails to understand, and is not troubled at having such depths under its keel. So I do not weary my brain as I read your poems. If your subsequent readers do, why then more of them will fall by the wayside. Be merciful to the reading public! It is not a merit to write, like Blake in his prophetic books, for the very few. The very few are not so useful as the very many. To imagine ourselves – because we are freaks – to be therefore rare and admirable creations is to deceive ourselves. Two-headed chickens and Siamese twins are rare and unfortunate. Generally they are bottled young.
[...]
I have 1800 other letters to answer, and have spent all this time, and wasted all this ink, on addressing a being 2000 miles away from me in space, and three weeks in time. Long before you get this note you will be a different creature, and out of reach of all my thoughts. That is the murrain upon correspondence. Five minutes of a meeting, once a blue moon, was worth all the letters that Lord Chesterfield addressed to his son. [...]

DG/Bodleian Library

1 Altounyan had asked Lawrence to read his poetic writings; he had set down his thoughts in a flood of poems of wide variety both in subject and quality. He regarded Lawrence as 'the only person who understands me'.

B. H. LIDDELL HART[1]
Sunday 7 April '34   *13 BIRMINGHAM STREET SOUTHAMPTON*

Yes, we blew and rolled about the sea, and made Devonport after some interesting days. Thence I returned to the old job. 'Here' is getting precarious, I fancy: a gent, describing himself as the French Consul, rang the bell this morning and then produced a *News Chronicle* card. If it develops I shall have to move.

I am dead against any further publication of the Arab Revolt, and would refuse to permit any of my photographs to be reproduced for the purpose – either here or in the States. So that hamstrings Dodd, Mead, I fancy![1] There has been far too much said already about the affair, which I devoutly wish had never happened: or do I wish that Newcombe, Joyce and Vickery had pushed it to a successful conclusion?

Anyway, I shall not move another turn towards ventilating it again. [. . .]

LHB

GEORGE BROUGH
3 May 1934   *13 BIRMINGHAM STREET SOUTHAMPTON*

Dear G. B.

I was in Wolverhampton for a while, looking at some engines of Henry Meadows – and at Lincoln before that. So I took the chance of passing near Nottingham to look in (during a beastly wet day, of course) and see the new marvel being born.

It looks most promising – and most expensive. I shall be broke but happy. Please take your time over it. The old hack has done only 20,000 miles, and is running splendidly. My breaking the speedometer drive has had the curious effect of putting up my average nearly six miles an hour! My last two long rides have been at 49 and 51 m.p.h. respectively. It looks as though I might yet break my neck on a B.S.[1] [. . .]

Yours ever
T.E.S.   *Bodleian Library*

1 Liddell Hart had had a letter from American publisher Dodd, Mead and Co., stating that the examples of Lawrence's photographs published in his biography had suggested to them the idea of a pictorial history of the Arab Revolt, with photographs and accompanying text by Lawrence. Liddell Hart had passed on the idea in the 'faint hope', as he put it, that Lawrence might relax his rule of taking no profit from his part in the revolt.

1 B.S.: Brough Superior.

LINCOLN KIRSTEIN[1]
11 May 1934   *13 BIRMINGHAM STREET SOUTHAMPTON*

[...] Your review of Liddell-Hart's book does, as you said, succinctly convey
your position. I'm rather regretting L-H's surrender to my 'charm'. Had he
maintained his critical distance and examined my war-time strategy and tactics
with a cool head, the results would have been interesting – to me, at any rate!
He is a good military thinker. But instead there comes only Panegyric III, and
I'm rather sick of my virtues. The worst of being oneself is that one knows all
one's vices, too! And honestly it isn't fair to keep on harping on the credit side.

I suggested a meeting out of sheer altruism. If we ever come together you
will see that I am human. There ain't any such super-creatures as you would
fain see: or if there are, I haven't been lucky enough to meet one.

Your favourable judgment of *The Mint* would give me unqualified delight,
had you flavoured your remarks upon me with some salt. I took a lot of
trouble, in writing *The Mint*, to ram it full of all the feeling I could muster. The
R.A.F. was a huge and gorgeous subject. Oh, I meant to make a whale of a
book. What came into being was hardly its introduction – and now I don't
feel that I'll ever write anything again. It is hard to have learnt so hard how to
write – and then to have nothing to write about.

Don't forget to let me know if you do ever get across. Ede or Garnett will
know my address. A meeting will be good for you.

Yours
T. E. Shaw

Bodleian Library

---

1 Dancer, writer and promoter of the School of American Ballet. He had conceived an
enormous admiration for Lawrence and had written a favourable review of Liddell Hart's
biography. An earlier letter to Kirstein is included in *DG*.

LADY ASTOR
11 May 1934   *13 BIRMINGHAM ST SOUTHAMPTON*

Mi Ladi

Useless for me to promise to come to Cliveden for a week-end or a night, or a visit. I should only break tryst. One does not come: or go: anywhere, now a days: The rare exceptions are to the two or three people who would be hurt by my refusal. You are more or less a man of my own size, and above courtesy.

My mother and brother are still in their C.M.S. Hospital at Mienchu in Szechuan, a rich province far up the Yangtse in China. They are running it, while the staff doctor has a year's home leave. After that year – well who knows? They are well, they say – but the place is so remote that news is months old, and my mother is old, and her letters are exactly those she would write from anywhere she was. So I cannot visualise them there.

It always seems to me that contact, to be real, must be physical. We can only pretend to understand and keep company with those far off. Minds change nearly as quickly as bodies, and these scrappy, old and inadequate letters convey nothing from one to the other. Sometimes the sham seems hardly worth the keeping up – but my mother will never feel that. She writes often and at length, and cries out for letters as when at home she cries out for our love… as if it could be turned on in a tap. Don't play the mother too long to your kids, please! If you are interesting enough they will keep in touch. If not – why don't wish it!

Yours
T.E.S.

An airman for very little longer, alas!

University of Reading

HENRY WILLIAMSON

14.V.34   *13 BIRMINGHAM STREET SOUTHAMPTON*

This is a splendid surprise. I had somehow imagined you settled in America for months. The letter, the cotton-bale, the excellent nuts[1], (I eat one per week, ritually, as I visit my cottage where they are stored) had all confirmed me in that feeling of your being gone.

I dislike people going very far away. They seem to lose their actuality, their roots. I fancy that contact with plain men, one's equals, is a necessity for mental health. They 'place' us.

Sorry about the book – or, rather, about the U.S.A. verdict upon its prospects. I expect the *Falcon*[2] has frightened the publishers over there. You handled them too freely, perhaps.

If you can become objective again, for a spell, it will give us something deeper and more exciting than what you have written before, I hope. The subjective stuff is wonderful exercise, but temporary in its value: or temporal rather, for its significance seems to ebb and flow with the times. Good for now, rotten in 20 years, interesting again after sixty years. Whereas the objective stuff does not date.

However you have the gift of twisting surprises out of ordinary words and situations and happenings: so none of your writing can fail to give at least technical pleasure. Sometimes I would wish you one skin more, for daily wear, however. Your writing costs you too much.

I should like to come to your valley-country: but there are five target boats to put through their paces now in close succession: and after them six dinghies: and in any hours that I can snatch between the boats I must visit my cottage, for that half-ruin and wholly unfinished place must be cleaned up enough, by this winter, to act 'home' to me in the spring. March next; exit of T.E.S. from the Air Force: very sad, I think, this freedom will be at first: but then it should be a safe feeling, to have the house to live in, without rule. (I have never had any sort of house of my own before) and there are so many things I have not yet done, that I can hardly be lonely or bored.

1 Williamson had sent Lawrence a bag of pecans from Augusta, Georgia.
2 *The Cold Falcon*, which Williamson had published, anonymously, in 1933.

I'm not, I think, a lonely person; though often and generally alone. There is a distinction. I like your hypothesis to explain my character[3], by the way. It has experience behind it, I fancy. For myself, I do not know. I measure myself against the fellows I meet and work with, and find myself ordinary company, but bright and sensible. Almost I would say popular!

We will find ourselves together soon!

T.E.S.   *Bodleian Library*

MRS CHARLOTTE SHAW
18.V.34   *13 BIRMINGHAM ST SOUTHAMPTON*

You will think it queer, but I have been looking and longing for this news to appear in the Papers. Your return makes England seem furnished, somehow. I so seldom call: yet my two visits to London while you were away found the place barren: and I came back here sooner than was necessary because there seemed no point in wandering about.

So apparently you are a focus.

I hope the trip has left you satisfied and well. You were so ill when you went that I was afraid for you: and New Zealand may have been too like England for a change.

G.B.S. of course flourishes. I do hope you are.

Boats, boats, boats since you left, and yet more to do. But my cottage is finished, inside and out, so far as alien hands can finish it – and I feel rooted now, whenever I pass its door. Such a lovely little place, and so plain. It is ingenious, comfortable, bare and restful: and cheap to maintain. I do hope you'll be able to see it with me some time soon.

I'm ever so glad you are here.

T.E.S.

We were too late for that Third Symphony after all. He sent me a note about it, just before he died.

British Library

3 Having read Liddell Hart's biography of Lawrence in the U.S.A. Williamson had used this pretext to offer him a lengthy analysis of his character.

HON. EDWARD ELIOT
24 May 1934   *13 BIRMINGHAM ST SOUTHAMPTON*

Dear Eliot

Two events lately. A splurge in the *Daily Mail*, talking of a film to be made around my squalid past. I wonder how much it is true? The article talked glibly of the *Seven Pillars*; so I imagine it is mostly the perfervid imagining of one of the horde of publicity men who afflict the film world.[1]

The second happening was an alarm by Liddell Hart, offering me proofs that I was being personated in London.[2] I took it coldly, and declined his proofs, for never a week passes without my receiving a letter from some poor woman or other, distraught with the fancy that the airman she walked out with in 1920 or 1930 something was me. Clearly personation is a common event – but as a sop to L-H, who is sincere and serious, I suggested he should try to interest you in his tale. Please take it very calmly. If I don't call myself TELawrence, I see no reason why others shouldn't.

Life is all motor-boats still – so far as the Daily Press permit me to be active. In March begins the leisure of leisures. After March how we shall sleep.

Tell your film negotiators that I'll be a very awkward pebble in the rock of their progress!

Yours
T E Shaw

Bodleian Library

1 The impresario behind this latest attempt to make a film out of Lawrence's wartime exploits was the famous Sir Alexander Korda.
2 Lawrence was being impersonated by one George Henry Rogers, who had emigrated to Canada in 1924, returned penniless and had conned a number of businessmen into accepting his advice and supporting him financially on the strength of his being Colonel Lawrence of Arabia. He had apparently shown considerable knowledge both of Arabian affairs and of mechanics.

ROBIN BUXTON
7.VI.34   *13 BIRMINGHAM ST SOUTHAMPTON*

Dear Robin

[...] I saw Alan D. ten days back ... persuaded him and E.[1] to drive me over to my cottage between them: and we talked all the way there and back. He takes the B.B.C. as seriously as a profession, and worries over it. I, alas, never worry over anything. Alan D. worries over the cost of children, and what-not. Very bad for him. I do not think he is really ill, or badly broken down: they have got him in time. Only nerves take so long to cure.

Savage is a nuisance with his film-greediness; but I suspect that Korda will not play. I am too recent to make a good subject – too much alive, in fact. I warned Eliot that the Film Company might be ceded his and your rights in *Revolt in the Desert* ... but that I doubted if that would give them the power to put a lot of living people on the stage. They might be able to reproduce me ... but you and Alan D. and Joyce and Feisal and all the Arabs ... to each man his own right, I fancy. Better wait till we are all dead. Tell the Inland Revenue that too. You have given them already more than they deserve, morally.

We have done our best to safeguard the cottage from heath fires, by open spaces. Two sides (E and S) are safe; but I wish there was rain. My pool holds only 2000 gallons at the moment, but slowly increases. Seven thousand is its capacity. Let's hope for rain, all together!

Yours
T. E. Shaw

Bodleian Library

HON. EDWARD ELIOT
8.VI.34   *13 BIRMINGHAM ST SOUTHAMPTON*

Dear Eliot

I suppose there is no help for it, but coming up.[1] When isn't so easy. We are in the midst of a batch of target boats, and busy from morning to night.

1 Hon. Edward Eliot.

1 To confront his impersonator.

523

However: any day this coming week, except Saturday, can be made free. Send me a wire to this address, or write well beforehand. The Post Office in Southampton is quaint. It hands out letters only about 9 a.m. and I go to work at 8.30. So I never get my mail till 7 p.m. when I get back once more.

I quite see that it ought to be stopped. If this next week won't do, then I can come up any day after June 24 ... but from June 16 to June 24 I am provisionally booked for a coast trip round the S and E coasts, with this batch of boats.

This is kind of you. I hope it has not been a care and trouble. Do not take it too seriously. If only the poor wretch *could* take my war name and all that it connotes!

Yours
T E Shaw

Bodleian Library

HON. EDWARD ELIOT[1]
26.VI.34   *13 BIRMINGHAM ST SOUTHAMPTON*

Dear Eliot

I have been away cruising in some of our boats ... hence the delay. Back last night.

First of all, I have to thank you for so admirably handling that business in London. It was one of my queerest experiences. I feel that I took advantage of your kindness most unwarrantably. That you should be the King Pin of the City Solicitors makes it all the worse. However we could hardly leave the little man alone.

I am returning Mr. Jenny his 'horoscope' with thanks ... and being entirely non-committal about his inventions. The poor child.

As for telling Rogers' father ... I agree, but suggest that it ought to be done as it were in confidence. I gathered that his father was not very fond of him: and it would do the thing no good to get Rogers chucked out of his home. If the father could keep a careful eye on him, as a result of a tactful warning,

---

1 Lawrence and Eliot had met the impostor George Henry Rogers in Eliot's office and Rogers had signed an undertaking that he would never use Lawrence's name again; he had also apologized for any trouble or inconvenience caused. Mr Jenny (third paragraph) was one of the businessmen taken in by Rogers' imposture.

without going to extremities? I feel that in bothering Rogers Père we extend the circle of unhappiness.

Your letter dissuading Jenny from publicity is admirable, and will properly scare him off it.

Remains the Directorship. Do you know, that sounds almost exactly right? I have a good deal of book-trade practical experience, and would probably (even on such occasional terms) be able to pull my weight. As for writing of my own – I couldn't promise anything. It is very unlikely that I will ever (after this long interval) write anything again.

But it must wait. Robin holds the key to the future. If by manipulating my investments he can produce me the full £100 a year, then I am quit of any need for a job. By so much as he fails, do I need a supplement. Our accounting will be in the middle of March, 1935. After that, may I try you again – it being understood meanwhile that nobody is bound, and no offers held open?

There, I think everything is cleared up, and I hope you will see it as I do. 'Imitation', so the proverb says 'is the sincerest form of flattery.' Decidedly I dislike flattery. The poor little worm. What a hole he finds himself in, now. I wish he hadn't done it. I'll encounter repercussions of it, probably, years hence.

If only it would rain: for six days, so they write me, the heath has been blazing round my cottage, and some of my bushes have been burnt. I wish I could get there to see how hurt it is. If that little place goes I'll be properly up against it.

Yours
T E Shaw

Bodleian Library

ROBIN BUXTON
14.VII.34   *13 BIRMINGHAM ST SOUTHAMPTON*

Dear Robin
Well, if they want to film the rotten book, they must. Will you please try and arrange for the scenario to be shown you ... and for me to see it, before it is used? And then for the film (before any showing to Press or Trade) to be shown to you? I am so desirous of keeping the flesh they cut to its exact poundage ... and to give as little offence as possible.

Stirling – yes, I suppose he would be the best of our party: more *savoir commerce!* The poor little man will delight in a job.

As for the actor to play me ... well, Walter Hudd was magnificent but perhaps Leslie Howard might be more unlike, which would be an advantage![1]

Our Grocery speculation fell a bit flat, didn't it? Or are we on the right side? I couldn't quite see from the published account!

This thing came.... will you bestow it on the correct individual amongst the multitude that stand behind grills?

Yours
T. E. Shaw   *Bodleian Library*

LADY ASTOR
27.VII.34   *13 BIRMINGHAM ST SOUTHAMPTON*

Peeress
You accuse me, with superficial reason – but a dry orange cannot be expected to utter juice. My fault is to myself in going dry, and the causes for that are innate. One can be poised, busy and content while engrossed in some loved toy: but when a man lifts his head and looks round him, he grows terrified instanter. How can one even try to rationalise the life outside one's skin?

Mrs. Shaw told me, in no more words than this, that you were troubled but bearing your troubles. Well, that's (I suspect) almost the universal experience. When we are young we hope, when we are old we have given up hoping: but the between-times are hard. If you ever feel you must talk to somebody, will you send for the collected Poems of Cecil Day Lewis[1] and read them? It is not much (only four or five slim volumettes) but sincere, intelligent, grimly-good

---

I Walter Hudd had played Private Meek in *Too True To Be Good.* Leslie Howard, an actor with a considerable reputation on both stage and screen, had just starred with Bette Davis in the film adaptation of Somerset Maugham's novel, *Of Human Bondage.* He was later to appear with much acclaim in such films as *The Scarlet Pimpernel,* which was screened in 1941, just two years before he died in a wartime air crash (shot down by the Germans) in 1943. Arguably Howard was a more apposite casting for Lawrence than his ultimate screen impersonator, Peter O'Toole.

I Cecil Day-Lewis (1904-72), Irish-born Oxford-educated poet and writer; associate of W. H. Auden and Stephen Spender. Poet Laureate 1968-72. He wrote as C. Day Lewis, and also, in a second career as a detective novelist, under the pseudonym Nicholas Blake.

and of today. *The Observer's* fatuous literary gent said last Sunday that he had never heard of Day Lewis. I wrote an indignant protest to Garvin. Day Lewis does me good, you see; and in our way we are not unlike, so you might gain from him too. *Beechen Vigil*,[2] his first poems, are his most musical. He is a famous poet, of some five years ago, and probably not yet exhausted. A schoolmaster, I believe.

I fear that this return to China has not been a great pleasure to my Mother. She writes already, as it were, longingly, of 'coming home in eighteen months'. Eighteen months must seem a long time to give away, at 70: and my brother is 50. I only hope they will have the courage to come home, instead of persisting in an outworn 'call'. I feel that the spirit of the day is against the missionary profession. We do not feel confident enough in our selves to preach or inculcate.

Their coming home will be a problem, too, of course. My brother must do some altruistic work, in doctoring, to content his conscience. If he can do it in a decent place, where my mother can live with him? He is capable of slumming, or fever-hospitalling, or other impossibility. Mother needs a little garden, for flowers, and somewhere to walk in; and a house (not too big) which she can polish with her own hands. 'How unlike Cliveden', you say! Well, well. But my mother has never learned our lesson of giving in, and of doubting our own competence universally. She is fitted only to dictate in a *small* world. That trusting the other fellow (which is laziness on the debit side, and sunshine on the credit side) is beyond her grasp. It is also the secret of bigness, I believe.

In a recent letter she told me how useful your parting gift to her of rugs had been. They have great cold winter journeys. I am sure she would be hurt if I did not take a chance which offers and repeat her gratitude to you. My mother does not encourage kindness, in her brisk utility: but when she receives it, she is touched. No wonder all her children are queer. With such a father (you did not know him, I expect ... before your time) and such a mother, we have no chance of being useful citizens of this great country. If only they sold single tickets to the Moon, now! I think they would elect me President, there.

And talking of those who favour the Moon, how is James Stephens,[3] whom I met, twice and only, at your house or houses? Do you still see him? A small and rare artist, who has written about five good books. I re-read him ever so often. Yes, a moon-dweller, assuredly. But I suppose your days and rooms are full now of American tennis champions. Five and a half times better than cricket, is tennis, for only two need join together to play it. Indeed,

2 Published in 1925.
3 The Irish poet and story-writer.

I'm not sure that 22 are not necessary for cricket. No wonder the noise of cricket rolls across the land like a battle.

Milady, I am tired. I lie on my back at noon, in my hired bed-room in Southampton. They have given me the day off, and I take it recumbently. I do not really want to write to anyone: but if I put it off for a day, the post of tomorrow will cover the past letters with its new leaves ... and then tomorrow and tomorrow and tomorrow, till in despair I slide the heap into a box and post it to my cottage, where it awaits March 1935.

In March 1935 the R.A.F. takes away from me the right to serve it longer, and I relapse into self-supporting life. My cottage, 35/– a week, 24 hours a day. I am so tired that it feels like heaven drawing near: only there are people who whisper that heaven will bore me. When they tell me that I almost wish I were dead for I have done everything in life except rest, and if rest is to prove no refuge, then what is left?

So, you see, the issue of it all is, that I do better not to write and trouble people with my ideas till I can blow a confident tune again and hearten them. Some tune like the Purcell *Trumpet Voluntary* on the Columbia Record. Next day a lot of pessimists obscure your great hall at Cliveden with their 'crisis-talk', just you put the *Trumpet Voluntary* on the gramophone, and blow their cobwebs back to Hades. Bless you.

T.E.S.

University of Reading

ERIC KENNINGTON
6.VIII.34.   *13 BIRMINGHAM ST SOUTHAMPTON*

Oh yes, I take my time; indeed I take time to answer any letter. Why? Well, I think it is mainly laziness. There is my R.A.F. work which has to be done to schedule, willy nilly: so what is not compulsory is told to wait on the mood. And letter-writing, being difficult, is seldom the mood.

For it is very difficult to write a good letter. Mine don't pretend to be good ... but they do actually try very hard to be good. I write them in great batches, on the days when at length (after months, often) the impulse towards them eventually comes. Each tries to direct itself as directly as I can towards my picture of the person I am writing to: and if it does not seem to me (as I write it) that it makes contact – why then I write no more that night.

Yet, as you would say if I was there to hear you, the letters as they actually depart from me are not worthy of this strained feeling. At the far end they appear ordinary. Yes, that is because I'm not writer enough to put enough of myself into any work. Or better, because there is not enough of myself to share out and go round. There has been, upon occasion. Both the *Seven Pillars* and *The Mint* (but *The Mint* especially) stink of personality. Where has it gone? Don't know. I'm always tired now, and I fritter myself away month after month on pursuits that I know to be petty, and yet must pursue, *faute de mieux*.

'What the hell's the matter with the chap' you'll be asking. You send me a sensible working-man of a letter, reporting progress – or at least continuity – and I burble back in this unconscionable way. I think it is in part because I am sorry to be dropping out. One of the sorest things in life is to come to realise that one is just not good enough. Better perhaps than some, than many, almost – but I do not care for relatives, for matching myself against my kind. There is an ideal standard somewhere and only that matters: and I cannot find it. Hence this aimlessness.

It is a pity, rather, that I took so many years teaching myself this and that and everything: for now that I'm full enough to weigh a lot, I've nowhere in which I want to use that weight. If I'd cared less about learning and more about doing things, the story would have been different. It's a common way in the world. The fuller the cask, the less active the damned thing seems to be.

Let's come down to earth. You still carve. I still build R.A.F. boats. On March 11th next that office comes to an end. Out I go. Clouds Hill awaits me, as home (address will be Shaw, Clouds Hill, Moreton, Dorset) and I have nearly £2 a week of an income. So I mean to digest all the leisure I can enjoy: and if I find that doing nothing is not worse than this present futile being busy about what doesn't matter – why then, I shall go on doing nothing. But if doing nothing is not good – why then, I shall cast loose again and see where I bring up.

Is C. well? And Xto?[1] Say that I hope to come and see you some day please.

Yours
T.E.S.

DG

1 Celandine Kennington and her son Christopher.

LORD LLOYD
26 Sept 1934   *13 BIRMINGHAM STREET SOUTHAMPTON*

Dear G.L.

Yes, I know: for once your strictures upon my failure to answer letters have a basis. Your Vol. II came to me months ago.[1] I read it at once, admiringly; it being so much more vivid than No I. Now it sits beside its brother on the 'history' shelf of my cottage, with inside its back cover (I hope, still) the half-page of notes which I scribbled there as I read it, so that when I thanked you for the gift I might have something more (or less, perhaps) than mere gratitude to say.

I <u>may</u> be able to get to my cottage this week-end: it is 45 miles from here and I go when I can, but rarely, all the same. If I do, I will pull out that slip and repeat it to you.

I haven't any valid reason for not writing: just the works are running down. In March I leave the R.A.F. and it feels like the end of living – so close that nothing between now and then can count. Afterwards – well, I don't know. How does one pass the fag-end of life? If there was any thing which I wanted to do, or thought worth doing, or seeing, or trying, or preventing even ... but I'm facing a vacancy. Indeed, yes, the machine is run down. Time's revenge.[2]

It was a lively decent book: but I will not anticipate my tiny collection of notes. Next week, if I'm lucky to be free this Saturday afternoon – but I very much fear our new Diesel craft will want testing again. My boat work for the R.A.F. (now extending to the Army and the Navy) has been successful, and lets me out of the Service with some distinction, I think. After having dabbled in revolt and politics it is rather nice to have been mechanically useful!

Yours with apology and remorse
T.E.S.

Churchill College Cambridge / Bodleian Library

1 Lord Lloyd had sent Lawrence the two volumes of his book *Egypt since Cromer*.
2 Lloyd's and Lawrence's lives took vastly different courses, but their mutual respect and affection remained strong. When shortly after Lawrence's death Lloyd bought a house in the country for his wife, at Offley, near Hitchin, he named it Clouds Hill in Lawrence's memory.

MRS CHARLOTTE SHAW
16.XI.34   *OZONE HOTEL BRIDLINGTON YORKS*

Long-overdue, indeed, my visit to you; and this heading will show why I will add to its length. Only, set against that the twice lately that I have drawn Whitehall Court and found – no, I must abandon my metaphor. G.B.S. is as un-foxed as you are vixenless. 'Ozone Hotel'. It was named, I think, for summer time. The R.A.F occupy it each season, but the last of them went yesterday. I felt him go with a pang, like foretasting myself on February 28th next. I wish the world did not change. This blue protective coating has meant so much to me. I go back to the self of 1920 and 1921, a crazy pelican feeding not its young but its spirit-creations upon its bodily strength. I had hoped, all these years, that I was not going to be alone again. [...]

My history is uneventful. That film is going to fall through, I think: a relief, for the film world only lives by publicity. Somebody called Bray, they say, has lately published a book which proves that I was a dud, in the war[1]. Do you know, I'd be almost glad to think so: but he has very rudely not sent me a copy of his book, and I don't feel that it would be decent of me to buy one. I wonder who he is, and what he is trying to do, so late in the day? It is too late to bury John Brown. [...]

China – all well. They are looking forward to return here twelve months hence. For good, I hope.

T.E.S.

British Library

FREDERIC MANNING
16.XI.34   *OZONE HOTEL BRIDLINGTON*

Alas, you see, it never came off.[1] My visits to Cranwell and Nottingham were postponed – and then came a sudden transfer to the unfashionable winter resort. I wander about a large garage and watch ten R.A.F. boats being reconditioned.

1 *See* further comment in letter to Mrs Shaw dated 'Monday night late' (p. 541) and accompanying footnote.

1 Lawrence had hoped to visit Manning at his home at Bourne, Lincolnshire.

A tricky unsatisfying job, for however done, they could be done better.

My motor bike remains in far-off Dorsetshire, as Homer would say.

Peter Davies wrote to me that you were still consumed with a longing to write that old book which has so often refused to come to you. I beg of you don't. Copy the poise and equal mind of E. M. Forster, whose every book is acclaimed by the highbrowed as a masterpiece, and who yet refrains successfully from ever deliberately achieving another. There are so many books, and you have written two of the best of them. To covet a third is greedy. Don't be a book-hog. Read something instead, and (if you find anything good to read) please benefit me by sending me its name: this person is always hungry to read.

March approaches. In March I put on flannel trousers (after taking off blue breeches and puttees) and retire to my cottage in Dorsetshire, where I shall own the whole twenty-four hours of my day, even as you do, and have the responsibility, even as you have, of filling them. Candidly, the prospect of unalloyed leisure terrifies me, for I shall not have enough money to kill time with travel and motor cars and calls and meals. There will be only about 25/– a week, for all purposes.

I wish you could see my cottage. It pleases and tickles me. No kitchen, no food, no cooking equipment, no bed, no drains, no sanitation. No water even, while this drought-in-the-deep-springs persists. There are two rooms, one book-lined the other slenderly furnished with a gramophone and records. Upstairs is one chair, downstairs one chair. A bath and boiler, in cupboards: two sleeping bags, zipp-fastened and labelled in embroidery MEUM and TUUM. When night falls the cottager takes up his bag, unfolds it on the piece of floor he momently prefers, and sleeps. No good for your infirmity, but I've hitherto been always uncouthly well. The village, a mile off, provides meals. I forgot to describe the large garage and swimming tank in the garden, if an untended wilderness of brushwood can be called garden. A bas gardens, I cry, if one has to care for them oneself.

Enough rubbish for one time: but please don't do violence to yourself for some fancied reader's sake. You have your spacious and upholstered niche in our literature. Rest in it.

Yours
T.E.S.

Michell Library, Sydney, N.S.W.

HON. FRANCIS RODD
23.XI.34   *OZONE HOTEL BRIDLINGTON YORKSHIRE*

Dear F.R.

By the accident that a friend of mine was passing my old lodgings in Southampton as my older landlady was handing your letter back to the postman, it reaches me here, only ten days late. I expect to work in Bridlington (on the ten Air Force boats that are refitting for next season) till the end of February when the R.A.F. goes on its way without me.

I shall feel unutterably lost without my blue covering. Twelve years it has been, of engrossing work with a very happy companionship for the off-duty hours. Few war-relics have been so fortunate as I in the aftermath.

I've even saved money and Robin Buxton has invested it for me until it brings in more than 25/– a week. So if you bogeymen[1] (I read the *New English Weekly!*) don't crash the solar system shortly I should be able to live at peace in my cottage, with all the twenty four hours of the day to myself. Forty-six I am, and never yet had a whole week of leisure. What will 'for ever' feel like, and can I use it all?

Please note its address from March onwards – Clouds Hill, Moreton, Dorset – and visit it, sometime, if you still stravage the roads of England in a great car. The cottage has two rooms; one, upstairs, for music (a gramophone and records) and one downstairs for books. There is a bath, in a demi-cupboard. For food one goes a mile, to Bovington (near the Tank Corps Depot) and at sleep-time I take my great sleeping bag, embroidered MEUM, and spread it on what seems the nicest bit of floor. There is a second bag, embroidered TUUM, for guests.

The cottage looks simple, outside, and does no hurt to its setting which is twenty miles of broken heath and a river valley filled with rhododendrons run wild. I think everything, inside and outside my place, approaches perfection.

Now to business. That enclosed message ought to have been instantly dealt with, by a plain Yes or No. Will you please say No, for me, but not a plain No. Make it a coloured No, for the Elizabethan of Herbert Baker's naming has given

---

1 For 'bogeymen' read 'bankers', a profession to which both Rodd and Buxton belonged.

me a moment of very rare pleasure which I shall not tell to anyone, nor forget.[2]

Please explain how by accident it only came to me tonight, when I got back after work, too late to catch the evening mail from this petty seaboard town.

These newspaper praises lead a fellow to write himself down as a proper fraud – and then along comes a real man to stake himself on the contrary opinion. It is heartening and I am more than grateful.

There – please work all that into your 'NO': explain that I have a chance (if only I have the guts to take it) of next year possessing all my time.

Yours ever
T E Shaw.

DG/Sotheby's

LADY ASTOR
26.XI.34   *OZONE HOTEL BRIDLINGTON YORKS*

Bad of you, Viscountess, thoroughly bad. I had written you my 1934 letter ... and you'll admit it was a beauty. Black ink, white paper, firm if crabby handwriting: well punctuated (*lavishly* punctuated) neatly paragraphed: signed even. That's a letter for which at the Anderson Galleries in New York you could have got several dollars.

2 The 'Elizabethan of Herbert Baker's naming' was the governor of the Bank of England, Sir Montague Norman, and the message to which Lawrence was saying no was the offer of the secretaryship of the Bank of England, transmitted to Lawrence through Francis Rodd, who had been a foreign adviser to Norman before joining the bankers Morgan Grenfell. See 'General Introduction', page xxi, where this offer is discussed; evidence to confirm that it took place was made public in a Sotheby's Catalogue for 18 December 1986, in which Lawrence's letter appeared as lot 163, together with Rodd's explanation of the circumstances in which the proposal was made. As Sotheby's catalogue writers put it, 'Although, of course, Lawrence lacked business experience, he was believed to have had sufficient qualities and stature to fill the post of Secretary, who was not only keeper of the records of the Court of Governors, but their legal persona representing the Bank.' The letter is reprinted here from Garnett, with the difference that Herbert Baker's name is given where Garnett omitted it, thus leaving out the vital clue to the nature of the offer made, in that Baker, who had apparently sponsored Lawrence for the post, was the Bank of England's architect. Garnett evidently considered the matter as being still one of confidence, referring to Lawrence's refusal of 'an extremely important position in the City of London'.

In return, instead of the gracious silence, or the 'Rest Harrow' single-sheet of arabesques ending in a lightning sketch of the Hampton Court maze, I get a six pages of legibility, in which I cannot even pretend to misunderstand a word: with an 'Astor' in *Roman* characters on the last page (only proof of femininity a couple of postscripts) … and, cruellest stroke of all, an enclosed letter from a Queen (you know what I think of even English Queens, and this one is Balkan) 'to be returned'.

Serpent. You knew my sense of duty would compel me to return it: and my punctilious sense of the proper and kindly would not let me return it in silence.

Hence I must spoil the 1934 letter with a sequel!

You are universal when you say of Day Lewis 'I couldn't understand all of it or him – or you'. We all say that, except when we are treating of half-wits. I read *The Observer* again yesterday, but forgot to read the leader. I hope it wasn't Philip (Lothian) again. That old man writes too much. (Tell him I said this: it strikes me as one of the most improbable statements even I have ever made.)

I'm very romantic, they say: I often think of it over my evening fish and chips. As for Miss Cohen,[1] she is apparently romantic too. I heard long ago that she wanted to marry me: but Harriet is not one of my pet names, and there is no piano at my cottage, and I like her gramophone records. Yet I cannot imagine playing one's wife to oneself on the gramophone. Can you? Would you like a Waldorf speech on a record for Christmas? Would he like one of yours?

December 18th.? Now you know that in my R.A.F. embodiment I never decide 24 hours ahead. Probably I shall be at Bridlington still. If not, I would like to reach my Dorset cottage, for my neighbour and tenant, Mrs. Knowles who was a great friend, dropped dead suddenly last week – or rather she was found dead on the floor, having apparently fainted and hurt herself falling. That strands me, rather. I have very much I should see to. So please forget me, for this year. After March I have too much time, alas.

Yes, we cannot help trying to do something, again and again. We are fools, but there it is. Might as well try to stop sleeping.

Mrs. Smith[2] wrote to me ever so often at first. I have sent two notes back. Am I a beast? But she wants something which I want to keep, and she ought to understand it. There are Untouchables, thank Heaven, still, despite the

---

1 Harriet Cohen (1895-1967), the internationally famous concert pianist.

2 Mrs Clare Sydney Smith, wife of Wing Commander, later Air Commodore Sydney Smith, author of a book of reminiscence entitled *The Golden Reign*, as referred to in my 'General Introduction' page xxi. *See also* 'Foreword', pages viii-ix

Ghandi's of this world. Or is it Gandhi? Philip (either) will know.

Neat introduction of my next subject, again. Philip (Lothian) has a plan for me? Why, I have a plan for myself, which is to cease from all plans. People absurdly over-estimate my capacity. I get offered job after job, in which I should make a colossal fool of myself. Fortunately I know better. Only last week I received a shocking offer, which I'd blush to repeat. The bigger they are, the less I'm tempted.

That room idea ... do you know I almost dally with it? Only tubs should stand on their own bottoms. I shall leave the R.A.F. with 25/– a week, which is all right for my cottage, but will not keep me for long in London. Yet to live on you would be either charity or a confession of failure to keep myself. I think I won't. I hope I won't. It would be a hole in my armour. Of course I lose the Union Jack Club when I leave the Service.

No, I don't know Sir K. Wood. A Postmaster, I think.[3] I want all the telegraph and telephone poles taken away and their wires put below ground, just to add spaciousness to our roads: and beauty, too. At night the wires look lovely in approaching headlights – but it is too high a price to pay for their daylight ugliness.

My Mother and Brother were together again (she had spent 2 months on holiday in the hills, against the heat: and I read harm into that. I think she must have been ill to agree to live away from him) and in their Hospital Compound. They talk already (looking forward – again a disquieting sign) to coming home next winter, when their replacement comes. I hope that is return for good. I cannot see her wandering again: and I am going to ask everybody who is charitable to try to find some do-good medical job in England which might ensnare him. He is incurably other-seeking, you know. Like some Peeresses.

My poor bike. It is laid up in my cottage, and when I next ride it, it is only to the maker's, to hand it back. Here I go about, less splendidly, on a push-bike.

I do hope O'Casey will make enough out of New York to establish him finally. It was a fine play: though that 2nd Act of the *Silver Tassie* sticks in my memory as the best stage thing I ever saw. I saw it and saw it and saw it, too!

G.B.S. and 'Charlotte' have both been ill. The Yank Admirals cannot have agreed with them. I suggest you ask the Yanks and the Japs to meet .... if you are insured

Yourrrrrrs
T.E.S.
[...]   *University of Reading*

3 Sir Kingsley Wood (1881-1943) was postmaster-general at the time, and later chancellor of the exchequer in Churchill's wartime government.

MLLE SCHNÉEGANS[1]
26.XI.34   *R.A.F. FELIXSTOWE*

Dear M. Schnéegans

I hope you will pardon my replying in English. Though I can read French easily, I never gained the power of speaking or writing it.

Those who have allowed themselves to produce lives of me (amongst them my friend Mr Graves) have availed themselves, I fear, of much artistic licence, in giving me abundance of qualities and accomplishments which actually I possess only in very small degree, if at all. Thus my knowledge of history and social manners was never great and is twenty years in desuetude.

The point you raise about the Schnéeganz is curious. I think it improbable that any family name of the Rhineland can go back even into the early Middle Ages, much less to the epoch of St. Columba, who was a Celt, and a religious, as were his companions. I do not think they are likely to have had acknowledged descendants, and I do not remember that their mission was accompanied by any movement of families from Celtic Ireland to Middle-Europe.

Would you not be content to establish a claim to descent from one of those famous later 'Wild geese' as Europe called them, the Irish legitimists and loyalists who left this country by edict of our King William of Orange, and fought for their exiled King James II under the banner of your Louis XIV? Some few were Protestants, most Catholics; and their military prowess was one of the main obstacles that faced the Duke of Marlborough in his campaigns. They were very famous as Wild Geese, in five languages, and I can conceive nothing more likely than that one of them, settling in Strasbourg, should have lost some difficult Irish name and been known by the title of his Legion.

I am sorry to give you only a hypothesis: and to give it after six months. It was rather astonishing that your letter to that address should have found me at all!

I envy you a residence in Cahors. It is so long since I followed the Lot from its hills down almost to Bordeaux, but I vividly recall the beauty of its swift reaches: and your bridge is superb. The town was full of interest to me as an

---

I *Schneeganz* means 'snow-goose' in German. Mlle Schnéegans (not *Monsieur* as above) was anxious to discover the origin of her name and had been inspired to write to Lawrence by admiring references by his biographers to his vast historical knowledge. His reply is of particular interest in that it was the one letter from Lawrence's later life included by E. M. Forster in his unfinished selection, which only covered the pre-war archaeological phase: it appealed to Forster as an echo of those long-lost days; *see* p. ix

archaeologist. It is unfortunate that I cannot come back. The best part of France, to my mind, is from Limoges to Albi: and the most historical.

It would have pleased me to have been of service to you: but alas, you need a real cyclopaedia – and I am out of date.

Yours sincerely
T E Shaw

Jesus College Oxford

MRS WINIFRED FONTANA[1]
28.XI.34

OZONE HOTEL BRIDLINGTON YORKS

You see, I am no longer in the Temperate Zone. Here are ten R.A.F. boats in dire need of overhaul and here am I watching (on behalf of Air Ministry) a contractor do the work. Bridlington in winter is a silent place, where cats and landladies' husbands walk gently down the middles of the streets. I prefer it to the bustle of summer, because my February-looming discharge from the Air Force makes me low-toned. It is like a hermit-crab losing his twelve-year-old shell, and I hate the pleasure that my service has been, coming thus to an arbitrary end.

Probably I shall be here till the end, and then my plan is to move to Clouds Hill, Moreton, Dorset (the cottage) and stay there till I feel I can stay there no more: there being a hope behind my heart that perhaps I shall like it and not wish to come away. My savings come out poorly, I fear, amounting to just 25/– a week. I had hoped for more, so as to live easily. However...

[...]

E.A.[2] is depressed. He says he faces bankruptcy (I fear his fevers may have put the patients to fright: they may feel that he cannot succeed his father) and the flush has gone from his writings. Poor E. I wish he could be helped. I read in the great poem-sequence often: it is and it isn't. How tell him?

Vale atque salve.... when I'm free, I hope.

Yours
T.E.S.

[...] *Bodleian Library*

1 The widow of the former British Consul at Aleppo; *cf.* letter to Lawrence's mother on p. 509.
2 Ernest Altounyan. The 'great poem-sequence' is referred to on p. 516.

EZRA POUND

7.XII.34   *OZONE HOTEL BRIDLINGTON YORKSHIRE (ENG.)*

Dear E.P.

Indeed, indeed I've written to you: three times or more, and with hard-earned postage stamps. However at long last ...

I laughed over your letter. You were so hot about something. Now in England (good) the most telling style is understatement. To say that 'you fear some of your adversary's premises may be not well founded' is damaging. To call him a canting nit-wit only provokes a smile. You'd say 'cunting', I fear; there are six shits in your letter. If that happens to me more than once a day, I know that some recent meal is disagreeing with me. More peace to your stomach!

I'm sorry, as I said, about Orage.[1] He is a real loss. For another to continue *The New Age* would not console me any more than if Henry Newbolt (after your premature demise) should in pious memory utter a Canto.[2] It is Orage who mattered: not what he believed or bit. We admire the spirit of the bull-terrier, without endorsing its action in biting the postman's trousers. To my mind both Guild Socialism and Social Credit were levities to engross the mind of Orage.

Your sheet of questions – they don't matter, either. I don't care a hoot for economics, or our money system, or the organisation of society. Such growths are like our stature; what time I have for thinking (not enough, I agree) goes, or tries to go, upon themes within my governance. A fig for financiers.

Of course I know that economics is the fashionable theme, today. A fad almost. Everybody talks and writes about production and exchange and distribution and consumption. Twenty years ago science was *the* subject that we all let off hot air about. It was going to do what the lads fancy political economy will do now. Ah well; I'm 46, and if I live another 20 years there may be a prevalent fashion less dull than economics, and perhaps I'll join in that.

I fancy much of this superior sort of sniffing at today is a result of bad education. By that I don't mean lack of Oxford.... I left a fellowship at Oxford to join the Air Force, so I've stated in very clear implication what I think of Oxford for grown-ups. It's a worse ignorance than that. A lovely example is

1 A. R. Orage, who had just died, had been editor of the influential periodical *The New Age* from 1907-22, and after nine years away from London, spent partly in Fontainebleau and partly in New York, had edited *The New English Weekly* (referred to as *N. E.* in this letter) from 1931 to his death.

2 Pound had been writing his masterwork, the *Cantos*, since 1917; he was to continue doing so until 1970.

quoted by you in the current *N. E.* where some American sneers that Wilson lost his better in sacking Lansing. Lansing was a fourth-grade clerk. The fellow who wrote that had never met the two men – except with a prejudice: and from things you yourself have said I deduced that you'd never met Montague Norman. 'Bogeymen', in my travels in Arabia, were always the tribe beyond the next. You have to be ignorant of a thing to fear it or hate it, if it's a man-made thing.

I think many of us go wrong by being too exclusively cerebral. I've spent the last twelve years in the ranks of the Air Force; and nobody so in daily contact with people who work at crafts could get so heated as the *N. E.* does about the regimentation of the world. My own job has been producing motor boats: and I fancy that each concrete thing I launched took away some of my bile. Whereas the uttering of a poem only increases it. Old Gandhi would prescribe for you a daily wrestle with the spinning wheel, to grow contentment. The English working men are another creation from us. Abstract ideas are another name for maggots of the brain. Heads are happy when they employ hands, not when they earn idleness for them.

Dear me, how sententious I get! Only some instinct tells me that the people who fuss about the money of the world are on the wrong tack. Money only serves to keep us alive: and people like you and me wouldn't impair the usefulness of the world if we went down. I incline to resent our presuming to tell our physical betters what ought to be done. Disposing of other people's minds is an infectious activity.

Let's get down to ground. I'm time-expired, almost, and in two months must return to civil life. My address will be Clouds Hill, Moreton, Dorset, a tiny cottage in four acres of heath land. I've put by enough to bring me in 25/– a week, and have faith enough in the stability of the City to risk retiring on it. Leisure is the only thing I've never had, and always liked the look of. I think I can use spare time with gladness, ad infinitum: or rather for 24 years, which is my 'expectation.'

Will you never come back? The States, England, even Paris? Time-lag forsooth! Rapallo is years away from Texas, as Texas from Rapallo.[3] Who dare put one before the other? Not dunne, O E. P.!

yours
T.E.S.

Bodleian Library

3 Pound had lived in Rapallo, Italy, since 1925.

MRS CHARLOTTE SHAW
Monday night, late[1]

[…] Your chill troubles me, rather. Annually you have them, now (before going round the world) and again, soon after you get back. As G.B.S. has gone to Ayot, he presumably thinks it 'only a cold'. But it sounds uncomfortable.

Casement. Yes, I still hanker after the thought of writing a short book on him. As I see it, his was a heroic nature. I should like to write upon him subtly, so that his enemies would think I was with them till they finished my book and rose from reading it to call him a hero. He had the appeal of a broken archangel. But unless the P.M. will release the 'diary' material, nobody can write of him. Do you know who the next Labour P.M. might be? In advance he might pledge himself, and I am only 46, able, probably, to wait for years: and very determined to make England ashamed of itself, if I can.

Shifting Sands[2] came and I have read it, not perhaps too well. Akaba beach could have been taken by ship's gunfire, like the beach of Gallipoli. What I wanted was the 50 miles of mountain defiles behind the beach, which could (I still think) only have been taken by us from inland. The Arabs are not good at military attack, and Bray's instances are all made in ignorance. His warfare knowledge is very poor, apparently.

As for Damascus, I did wait till Allenby's troops came up: but what Bray means is that his 'two Divisions of Arab Legion' should have been formed, and made into a common front with the British Army: with a civilised Arab Army, the French would have had poorer grounds of complaint. This is true: but the Arab Legion never exceeded 600 men. It could never have been made into even a Battalion: not even one battalion could have been fed and moved along our line of march. He could as reasonably have maintained that a great Arab fleet in the Mediterranean might have made France pause! One of my minor qualities is always to accept (in lieu of the whole loaf) just so many ounces of bread as providence makes possible.

I remember Bray now. He suffered from persecution-delusions and was a very honourable Indian Army Captain, who threw up his job under the Arab

---

1 Mid-December 1934.

2 *Shifting Sands* by Major N. N. E. Bray (Unicorn Press, 1934). Bray accused Lawrence of frittering away 'material, money, time and lives' on secondary objects such as attacks on the Hejaz Railway when all efforts should have been directed to achieving a major Arab military success. Bray was an Indian Army officer who was attached to the Hejaz operation in its early months only.

Bureau on some point of principle. I was not concerned (it was early on, before I joined the great) and don't know what it was. This book isn't of any critical value: I'm sorry, for there is a real book to write, some day, on the difference between the politics of the Desert and the Sown. That was my problem, and none of these sharpshooters will face it. Bray hasn't enough head, of course.

His picture of Leachman[3] chimes with what I saw: but it rather astonishes me that Bray forgives our tearing down all that organised colony-government that A. T. Wilson[4] built in Irak. I expected him to criticise that, the biggest decision I ever took. Instead he appears to approve, though without mentioning my part in the change.

I don't suppose anybody will ever trouble to dig out the Foreign Office Archives about Rabegh and Hussein's claims upon us, and Ibn Saud's part during the war. Better for Bray if they don't!

As soon as you are better, please tell me by a postcard, at least. [...]

T.E.S.

British Library

B. H. LIDDELL HART
[31 December 1934]   *OZONE HOTEL BRIDLINGTON*

Returned to find your note, upon which warmest congratulations.... I am sure that you will be able to correlate the three Defences and Offences to the general benefit.[1]

So I can only wind up by hoping that you are as pleased as myself. I implore you ... to use your new enlargement for some unprofitable but worthy book. Give us some reflections upon the relations of density to type of war: working out the influences of much or little land-room upon tactics....

3 Lieutenant-Colonel Gerard Leachman was an Indian Army officer well known for his pre-war travels and his work as a political officer during the Mesopotamian campaign and after. He was murdered by an Iraqi tribal chief in 1920. Bray was a great admirer and wrote his biography, *Paladin of Arabia* (1936).
4 Sir Arnold Wilson (1884-1940) had been Acting Civil Commissioner in the Persian Gulf 1918-20. Lawrence had been highly critical of the policies with which he was associated.

1 Liddell Hart had just been appointed military correspondent of *The Times*.

For myself, I am going to taste the flavour of true leisure. For 46 years have I worked and been worked. Remaineth 23 years (of expectancy). May they be like Flecker's

'a great Sunday that goes on and on'.[2]

If I like this leisure when it comes, do me the favour of hoping that I may be able to afford its prolongation for ever and ever.

So these are our joint and separate wishes for 1935 and all that.

LHB

Mrs Charlotte Shaw
31.XII.34   *Ozone Hotel Bridlington Yorks*

My last letter for this year. Next year I am going to draw in my ink-horns: for this year I have tried – vainly! – not to spend more than 2/– a week on post. After February my total means will be 25/– a week, and I shall not spend more than three pence weekly upon post; After the first week, when I have to warn people that I am ceasing to write.

These reflections continue my mood of last Friday night. It was pouring with rain as I left London and rode up the Great North Road. At the crest of that rise towards Welwyn I had to pull my front forks back into the main road: they had turned off towards Ayot. If it had been finer, then I might have indulged my appetite: but as old age comes forward my strength of purpose goes. Had I called at Ayot that night and found you both there, no power but yourselves would have set me again into the night and the rain northward: and I felt that you might press me to stop. Such a dog's night, it was.

Instead the Brough purred smoothly, to Royston and Biggleswade and Stamford and Grantham and Bawtry and Goole and Bridlington. Even the rain ceased after a while, and I got in warm and dry. Today I have cleaned the good servant till it shines again. All the last two months it has been stored at Clouds Hill, until I felt that it almost shared my unhappiness in our separation.

---

2 Lawrence was recalling the prologue to *The Golden Journey to Samarkand* by James Elroy Flecker:
> When the great markets by the sea shut fast
> All that calm Sunday that goes on and on:
> When even lovers find their peace at last,
> And Earth is but a star, that once had shone.'

Your news of health makes me feel a little unquiet. A young man overstrains in some race or game and falls exhausted. Half an hour later he is happily eating a meal. So was I, till I got to Uxbridge and tried to keep pace with the other fellows in the Hut. Then I found that I was fagged out for hours after their recoveries. As for G.B.S. he is as old again as I was; the strain of that collapse will hang behind his eyes for weeks. Beg him to be careful: or perhaps better not, for he is wilful enough to react against advice. Better, I suppose, to break than to rust away: but how I hate both choices.

I hope you get securely and well on to your *Reina del Pacfico*, and I hope the cruise is a success. I have always had a picture of Magellan in my mind, and would like to see his Straits. They were dangerous for sail, but today all such narrows are easy water. I saw your ship once. She was good to look at.

When you come back my great change will have happened. I wonder … I wonder how it will be with me. Twelve years ago I thought that the question of an 'after' to the Service would never happen: the twelve years felt as though they would be enough for me. Yet here I am still strong and trenchant-minded, but with nothing in my hand. I have learned only the word NO in 46 years, it seems. However, I suppose myself is my own business and I should not trouble others with it. At least you will find me very different, after this.

I spent Christmas at my cottage. Mrs. Knowles, my tenant across the road, had suddenly died a few days before, and it was necessary to talk leases and arrangements. Fortunately her eldest son, who I like, is hovering on the edge of marriage and wishes to settle there after it. So the peace of Clouds Hill continues. Mrs. Knowles and I were friends.

Between paragraphs I have eaten one of your chocolates. That is why there are so many short paragraphs. Thank you. I wish I could have seen you last Friday, and yet got here to time. They kept me till afternoon at Air Ministry.

I do hope that voyage is excellent. When you come back, Time will mean nothing to me: Then we can meet and not write.

T.E.S.

British Library

H. S. EDE
3.I.35   *OZONE HOTEL BRIDLINGTON YORKS.*

No: the address is not spoof. I have been here for some months doing my last R.A.F. job, overseeing the refit often of our boats in a great garage in the (empty) town. A summer seaside resort is an uncanny place in midwinter.

The refit is due to be completed by the end of February; and early in March I 'get my ticket'. It's like a blank wall beyond which I cannot even imagine. Exactly what leisure is like, whether it will madden me or suit me, what it means to wake up every day and know there is no compulsion to get out of bed ... it's no good. When it comes, I shall try to deal with it; but now, beforehand, I can only say that I wish it had not to be.

The assets are my cottage in Dorsetshire (Clouds Hill, Moreton, Dorset ... you have the address just right) 25/– a week, a bike. If to that I find myself in possession of a quiet mind, then I shall be fortunate. I think I have to 'draw' this mind when I draw my discharge; and dare only hope to find it full and quiet. I do not often confess it to people, but I am always aware that madness lies very near me, always. The R.A.F's solidity and routine have been anchors holding me to life and the world. I wish they had not to be cut. [...]

Bodleian Library

ARTHUR RUSSELL
3.I.35   *OZONE HOTEL BRIDLINGTON YORKS*

Dear Russ

I spent three nights at Clouds Hill, liking the place, but not easy in mind, for Mrs Knowles died suddenly a few weeks ago, and her son, Pat, wants to take on her place and is puzzled how to do it. So we camped there, he in her house and I in mine, and ate a chicken for Christmas and wondered how we were going to work out.

How are you? Do you still drive your bus and swim every morning and think about things? My time in the R.A.F. ends two months from now, and I have not a plan or a notion in my head, for the future. I often think of you as a person to whom I could perhaps come for a while, until I can see better what I want. I am old now, and there seems to be nothing that I care to do. I have a little money (enough to bring me in about 25/– a week) and a Brough (which has to go back to George next month) and a push-bike. Do you think, if I came to Coventry, that you could find me some quiet place in which to settle for a little time, to make up my mind? Nothing definite to be fixed yet: perhaps when March comes I won't need it: but I may want to get away from myself, somewhere where I will not be talked about or known. I think you are the only Coventry chap I know, so it might be a good place. I thought of getting a room, or a bed, anyway, with some working family; till I can pull myself together. I hate leaving the R.A.F. and feel like a snail whose shell is being pulled off him!

Don't let this worry you; and don't fix anything up: but as you go round, just keep one eye open for a backwater in which I could be quiet (and cheap) for a spell. I don't want to do anything: just to moon about and think!

Clouds Hill is charming, now, I think. I hope to live there, after the change has happened and been forgotten: but I don't want to go there till then. I might get to dislike it, you see.

Do send a line here (I am overseeing the refit of ten Air Force boats at Brid. and shall be here till the end of Feb.) and tell me if you are prosperous or not.

Yours
T E Shaw

University of Texas

A. S. FRERE REEVES[1]
7.1.35   *OZONE HOTEL BRIDLINGTON YORKS*

Dear F.-R.

What good books Heinemann's (sometimes) publish! I have just been reading Ford Madox Ford's *It was the nightingale*, and it seems to me that at last he has risen to his full height.[2] He was always a figure – if you remember his *English Review* you remember the most heartening uprush of English Literature in our generation –

---

1 Publisher; a director of Messrs Heinemann, London.

2 Ford Madox Ford, formerly Ford Hermann Hueffer (1873-1939); his autobiographical volume *It was the nightingale* (one of several) had been published in 1933. He had founded *The English Review* in 1908 and edited it for fifteen months. The 'war tetralogy' referred to by Lawrence was a sequence of novels published between 1924 and 1928 now known as *Parade's End*; Christopher Tietjens was its central character.

and he has written now delicately and now greatly … greatly is it; I wonder. I was thinking of the war tetralogy. That uncomfortably-named Tietjens, that flux and flourish of characters all devoid of charm, that refusal of each paragraph of every volume to be set on fire. Yes, I think it is probably a great book, though how it can be, without charm, Heaven only knows. Why doesn't your firm collect its bits from Duckworth (wasn't it Duckworth) and re-set it in one fat volume?

However there's been a shelf of Hueffers and Fords … and at the last he mellows and produces a book of enchantment. The ichor[3] lies in his having now drawn himself at full length. Nobody he meets keeps an aura; but he makes himself more charming, because more full and human, as the pages go on. I like the humour, the pride, the fastidiousness, the folly (even the prejudices of ignorance, where he tries to blacken Lloyd George and Hitler – far be it from me to defend those two great ones.[4] They can forget people like him and me); and most of all I enjoy the superb technical competence. He laughs so well at himself, and never overdraws a mood.

Never? Well, I'm not sure. About six times he tells us how adeptly he handles the time-switch, and about 500 times he does handle it adeptly. I could have done either without the praise, or without the example. By insisting on both we are led too much to see the wheels going round. And he didn't correct the last draft enough after it got into type. At least five sentences fail to parse correctly (five? what's that to the five thousand in *Eimi*, which also Heinemann's should publish in England. Sell 500 copies, I think, and lose £50, but what a credit to your taste. *Eimi*, by E. E. Cummings.[5] The U.S.A. publishers are called Covia and Friede: 'und' I suppose) and not five sentences but nearly the 500 this time are disfigured by a plethora of 'thats', thats conjunctive, relative, demonstrative. In one nasty sentence there lay four of them.

I suppose I'm hypercritical of prepositions and link-words; they trip my ear but not my eye nor my mind. The book as a whole and in all its parts is

---

3 In Greek mythology, ichor was the ethereal fluid supposed to flow in the veins of the gods.

4 That Lawrence saw Hitler as 'great' does not imply approval of his regime or its policies. *Cf.* Winston Churchill: 'Although no subsequent political action can condone wrong deeds, history is replete with examples of men who have risen to power by employing stern, grim, and even frightful methods, but who, nevertheless, when their life is revealed as a whole, have been regarded as great figures whose lives have enriched the story of mankind. So may it be with Hitler.' (*Great Contemporaries*, 1937)

5 *Eimi* (1933) has been described as 'a typographically difficult but enthralling journal of a trip to Russia'.

ravishing. It also told us the proper story of the review and of Pound, and of Quinn. Lately I've had a letter or two from Pound who (misled perhaps by his name into thinking himself a born economist) seems to have run off on a new hobby-horse of financial theory. I think perhaps my art of boat-building is now the only one the silly ass has not tried and done fairly well. It wouldn't matter, but that all the time we are missing a full-sized poet, thereby. Still, he might have died young, and that would have come to the same thing, except to himself. Always angry, is Ezra P.

I hope F.M.F. feels, now he has done it, that he has done it, for good? It seems to me almost perfect as writing, quite perfect in taste, and lovely in matter. He has twice before tried to draw himself: or perhaps I have only come across two of several tries; but this time he has succeeded and made his success seem effortlessly easy. It *is* a good book. I am writing to you in the hope that perhaps you have not read it word for word. I began by tossing through its first pages, but soon stopped and went back and digested them one by one. The thing is beautifully fine-knit, and has not a spare word in it – except that swarm of nasty thats, of course!

Do give yourself a day off-duty and bribe her Reeveship to keep your door against callers and read it end for end. There is no youth or promise to excite you – but fulfilment, fulfilment. Ever so good.

Yours
T. E. Shaw

University of Texas

ARTHUR RUSSELL
18.1.35   *OZONE HOTEL BRIDLINGTON YORKS*

Dear R.
That is kind of you. I shall come, either for a look-see, or for a stay-put-for-a-while. The losing of the R.A.F. is going to hit me quite hard.

I'm glad it's a coach, and not a bus. A bus is dull. In the coach you ought to get variety. I shall volunteer to punch your tickets, if any.

My Brough still goes like unholy smoke, when I turn its taps on. But I have a feeling that it will have to go soon. Did you ever see my little motor boat?

It was a gem. They have it now at Felixstowe (Officers Mess toy) and I only hope they get from it a tenth of the fun I had.[1]

Yes, you must see Clouds Hill this year, if things permit. I have all my books and records there, and love it.

Don't come to Bridlington. I work all day at the boat-shed, and have to visit York, Sheffield and London frequently, at irregular times. Even if I had promised to be here, I mightn't be able to keep it. Patience. March is very near, <u>alas!</u>

Regards to No 96.

Yours
T.E.S.

University of Texas

MRS CHARLOTTE SHAW
26.I.35   *OZONE HOTEL BRIDLINGTON*

Miss Patch will send it on. I hope you are right out of the path of this storm, which is starring all the black windows with wild hail at the moment. It is westerly, an off-shore wind for Bridlington and a great gale which beats the sea down to flatness, and puckers and purfles the running gutters and pavements of the town. Indeed I hope you are not in a ship near it.

This is not a letter, but to report that last Monday Eliot and I lunched with Alexander Korda, the film king. He was quite unexpectedly sensitive, for a king; seemed to understand at once when I put to him the inconveniences his proposed film of *Revolt* would set in my path ... and ended the discussion by agreeing that it should not be attempted without my consent. He will not announce its abandonment, because while he has it on his list other producers will avoid thought of it. But it will not be done. You can imagine how this gladdens me. Eliot took it like a dear.

Thereafter I sat to John for two days, twice each day; and he painted with great ease and surety (a new John, this) a little head-and-shoulders of me in oil,

---

1 The 'little motor boat' was the *Biscuit*, a small speedboat which had been given to him and which he had restored to working order during his posting to R.A.F. Cattewater/Mount Batten; he had had many outings in it, with, among others, Mrs Sydney Smith and Lady Astor.

R.A.F. uniform, with cap on head. I think it much the best thing of me he has ever done. It sparkles with life, is gay-coloured and probably not unlike my real face when thinking. So lively and clean. He himself agreed that it had come off and was comforted, as lately he has found it hard to finish anything. In his pleasure he went on to do two charcoal drawings of me, three-quarter lengths, standing – and then gave me the better of them. I have put it with Merton, who took over the business from Emery Walker, and have asked him to copy it, for safety. A fine swagger drawing: small head, thin body and big knees!

That's a good budget of news. May you and G.B.S. be prospering, wherever your ship is. Voyaging is like flying: whatever the drawbacks, everybody who is not at sea or in the air wishes he was! But what a night! A harbour-night, for sure.

T.E.S.

British Library

BERNARD SHAW

31.1.35   *OZONE HOTEL BRIDLINGTON YORKS*

Dear G.B.S.

This is very bad news. I had been imagining you both off safely for South America, acquiring your winter dose of sunlight. I am so sorry.[1]

You say she is making ground, which is so far good; but that return of blood poison may be very severe on the heart. How Arthurian it sounds, to have an old wound re-open! Please, when she is better, say how very much I'd like to come and see her, though this job is now beginning to accelerate towards its finish (on March 1) and I am likely to be rushed off my feet as the weeks pass. March 1 is my sad date, when I go: and it is also the date for the completion of these ten boats' refitting.

Too True made an awful lot of talk. Bridlington in winter is a large village only, and I'm a known character. So I funked going to see the play. They would have cheered or jeered, probably: cheered, I'm afraid; so I funked it. Sorry. They also did it at Oxford! In London people don't worry, having full-

---

1 The Shaws went on their travels later in the year and were in South Africa at the time of Lawrence's fatal accident in May.

sized affairs daily; but here in these provinces any reputation is rare: and *Too True* surprised them with its immediacy. 'It isn't really entertainment at all' said one foreman. 'It means something'.

I won't write, because you'll have worry enough as it is: but do take care of yourself. You aren't used to the English winter, either ... not of late, anyhow.

Yours
T.E. Shaw

British Library

T. W. BEAUMONT[1]
31.1.35   *OZONE HOTEL BRIDLINGTON*

Dear Beaumont
I vary between my cottage (Clouds Hill, Moreton, Dorset: my only permanent address) and this place, where I'm watching ten boats under repair for the R.A.F. Very fully engaged, and always dodging about, like a flea with a bad conscience.

My time runs out a month hence, and I shall be very sorry. The work passes my time, and the last twelve years would have been long, without it. Yes, I shall be really sorry.

Someone (Mrs Bernard Shaw, I think it was) sent me a copy of Major Bray's book. It wasn't as silly as the Sunday Papers tried to make out: but there wasn't anything to it. Bray is a quite honest but not very wise fellow, who was in Jeddah for a while right at the beginning of the Arab business, and then went to Mesopotamia. I have not heard from him for years, but there was nothing in the book to which one could object.

No, Clouds Hill wouldn't look right with a valet! It is a cottage in the middle of a great heath, of bracken and heather. Two rooms; no bed and no kitchen, and no drains, but a spring in the garden, and a feeling of utter peace. I may go there for a while after my discharge.

Yours
T E Shaw

1 T. W. (Tom) Beaumont served with Lawrence in 1918: his name is listed in Appendix I of *Seven Pillars of Wisdom* as a member of the Hejaz Armoured Car Company.

You ask me for my foot size ... it's six, usually! But don't go and bust your firm, pinching slippers off them. I hope it prospers, and yourself.

I'd meant to try and see you, but am so busy when here, and so often in the South, that I can't either find time to get to you, or security to make an engagement. Let us leave it till after March 1.

Bodleian Library

SIR RONALD STORRS
31.1.35   *OZONE HOTEL BRIDLINGTON*

Dear R.S.
No; alas, Hythe will know me no more. I have only a month to do in the R.A.F. and will spend it up here, overseeing the refit of ten R.A.F. boats in a local garage. The name of the Hotel is real.[1] So, I think, is the ozone, or is it the fishmarket that smells? It is empty, cold, and rather nice. [...]

I hope you are restoring yourself to the former trim, now that that has become your primary duty. Your best excuse for retiring is to benefit thereby in health. Your handwriting retains its vigour.

Alas, I have nothing to say at the moment. After my discharge I have somehow to pick up a new life and occupy myself – but beforehand it looks and feels like an utterly blank wall. Old age coming, I suppose; at any rate I can admit to being quite a bit afraid for myself, which is a new feeling. Up till now I've never come to the end of anything.

Ah well. We shall see after the Kalends of March. Indeed, I venture to hope we shall see each other, but I don't know where I shall live, or what do, or how call myself.[2]

Postal address? Here till Feb. 28 and thereafter the only suggestion is to write to T. E. Shaw, at Clouds Hill, Moreton, Dorset, which is my tiny cottage. If I don't stay there, I shall at least visit it sometimes.

Please regard me to Lady Storrs: and please make yourself again into fighting trim: or, perhaps you are now. Good.

Yours
TES   *Bodleian Library*

1 Storrs had suggested that 'Ozone Hotel' was an alibi.
2 *See* 'General Introduction', pp. xxvii–xxviii.

ROBERT GRAVES[1]

4.2.35   *OZONE HOTEL BRIDLINGTON YORKS*

Dear R.G.

I have been – by lack of thought – guilty of a great fault in taste, and I am so sorry about it.[2] Please believe it was neither conscious nor subconscious. When I told you that I might be short of money at Clouds Hill I had completely forgotten – as for years I have forgotten it – how long ago I was able to help you when you were in difficulties. I was stupidly thinking aloud. Long ago I found out what income I needed for retirement and set it aside, invested. The rest – what I had and what I made – I spent on friends and books and pictures and motor-bikes and joys of sorts. Five years ago I found I needed more, to spend on improving my cottage; so I did that *Odyssey* translation, and put in bath and heater of my own choosing or designing, always secure in the knowledge that the income was safe and intact ... and then down goes the rate of interest and the income shrinks. It is enough to make a saint swear, for had I foreseen it, I would have reserved more. Now when I wanted to be at ease (I have a deep sense that my life, in the real sense, my Life, is over) I have to make about £700 more.

It is very good of you to offer to share the job with me ... but needless. I can easily make that. Easier still could I make ten times that; it's the stopping short that is skilful. I blame not circumstances but my own bad calculating. I pride myself on being knowing and did not foresee the Treasury-induced spell of cheap money. Another eight or nine years and the rates will bound up. Meanwhile my peace must be mixed with effort. Damn.

I had guessed that you would be running short, and had wanted to tell you how my time of spending was over and so I couldn't help you any more. Then

---

1 Graves had been invited by a London daily newspaper to write an obituary of Lawrence to be filed away in its 'morgue', whereupon he had written to Lawrence enquiring 'rather jokingly' what he was to do about the request, and asking 'whether he [Lawrence] would like to take on the job himself and, like the Aztecs, leave nothing to chance' (*RGB*, p. 179). This was Lawrence's reply. An abridged and adapted version of the letter was published as the lead story (headlined MYSELF – BY LAWRENCE) in the *Evening Standard* on 20 May 1935 – the day before Lawrence's funeral – with an introductory article by Graves. Subsequently it was published in *DG* (apart from the opening section) and *RGB*. The text in both these books shows evidence of substantial rewriting, particularly in the final paragraphs.

2 In a letter not printed here (*RGB*: 13 January 1935) Lawrence had written about the modest financial prospects facing him on retirement, whereupon Graves had offered 'to help him with his cottage troubles' (*RGB*, p. 179).

the *Claudius* big noise came along and I saw that you were safe. Safe, I think, now for quite a while. Your next book will be bought on the merits of your last, always supposing it is not poetry! That is a comfortable state … but less comfortable than mine, for I am safe now, and only need another slight effort to be comfortable for all time. You may not ever look to cease work, wholly: though I am glad to hear that the Balearics are cheap for living. I had feared their prices would rise with their popularity. If you hear that I have done something else, you will be able to put the motive to it. I shall be rounding off my capital. You will be a reserve, only if ever I get meshed (like you at Boar's Hill) and unable to help myself; which will be bad management, with my notoriety to help me!

New page, new subject. I saw Alexander Korda last month. I had not taken seriously the rumours that he meant to make a film of me, but they were persistent, so at last I asked for a meeting and explained that I was inflexibly opposed to the whole notion. He was most decent and understanding and has agreed to put it off till I die or welcome it. Is it age coming on, or what? But I loathe the notion of being celluloided. My rare visits to cinemas always deepen in me a sense of their superficial falsity … vulgarity, I would have said, only I like the vulgarity that means common man, and the badness of films seems to me like an edited and below-the-belt speciousness. Yet the news-theatres, as they call them (little cinemas here and there that present fact, photographed and current fact only), delight me. The camera seems wholly in place as journalism: but when it tries to re-create it boobs and sets my teeth on edge. So there won't be a film of me. Korda is like an oil-company which has drilled often and found two or three gushers, and has prudently invested some of its proceeds in buying options over more sites. Some he may develop and others not. Oil is a transient business.

Money explained, films considered. Let us now pass to the epitaph.

Yes, Hogarth did the morgue-men a first sketch of me in 1920, and they are right to overhaul their stocks. Rather you than Liddell Hart, who seems to have no critical sense in my regard. I won't touch it myself, but if you do, don't give too much importance to what I did in Arabia during the war. I feel that the Middle Eastern settlement put through by Winston Churchill and Young and me in 1921 (which stands in every particular … if only the other Peace Treaties did!) should weigh more than fighting. And I feel too that this settlement should weigh less than my life since 1922, for the conquest of the last element, the air, seems to me the only major task of our generation; and I have convinced myself that progress to-day is made not by the single genius, but by the common effort. To me it is the multitude of rough transport drivers filling all the roads of England every night, who make this the mechanical age. And it is the airmen, the mechanics, who are overcoming the air, not the Mollisons and Orlebars. The genius raids, but the common people occupy and possess. Wherefore I stayed in the ranks and served to the best of my ability, much influencing my fellow airmen towards a pride in themselves and their inarticulate duty. I tried to make them see — with some success.

That for eight years, and now for the last four I have been so curiously fortunate as to share in a little revolution we have made in boat design. People have thought we were at finality there, for since 1850 ships have merely got bigger. When I went into R.A.F. boats in 1929, every type was an Admiralty design. All were round-bottomed, derived from the first hollow tree, with only a fin, called a keel, to delay their rolling about and over. They progressed by pushing their own bulk of water aside. Now (1935) not one type of R.A.F. boat in production is naval. . . . We have found, chosen, selected or derived our own sorts: they have (power for power) three times the speed of their predecessors, less weight, less cost, more room, more safety, more seaworthiness. As their speed increases, they rise out of the water and run over its face. They cannot roll, nor pitch, having no pendulum nor period, but a subtly modelled planing bottom and sharp edges.

Now I do not claim to have made these boats. They have grown out of the joint experience, skill and imaginations of many men. But I can (secretly) feel that they owe to me their opportunity and their acceptance. The pundits met them with a fierce hostility: all the R.A.F. sailors, and all the Navy, said that they would break, sink, wear out, be unmanageable. To-day we are advising the War Office in refitting the coast defences entirely with boats of our model, and the Admiralty has specified them for the modernised battleships: while the German, Chinese, Spanish and Portuguese Governments have adopted them! In inventing them we have had to make new engines, new auxiliaries, use new timbers, new metals, new materials. It has been five years of intense and co-ordinated progress. Nothing now hinders the application of our design to big ships — except the conservatism of man, of course. Patience. It cannot be stopped now.

All this boasting is not to glorify myself, but to explain; and here enters my last subject for this letter, your strictures upon the changes I have made in myself since the time we felt so much together at Oxford. You're quite right about the change. I was then trying to write; to be perhaps an artist (for the *Seven Pillars* had pretensions towards design, and was written with great pains as prose) or to be at least cerebral. My head was aiming to create intangible things. That's not well put: all creation is tangible. What I was trying to do, I suppose, was to carry a superstructure of ideas upon or above anything I made.

Well, I failed in that. By measuring myself against such people as yourself and Augustus John, I could feel that I was not made out of the same stuff. Artists excite me and attract me; seduce me. Almost I could be an artist, but there is a core that puts on the brake. If I knew what it was I would tell you, or become one of you. Only I can't.

So I changed direction, right, and went into the R.A.F. after straightening out that Eastern tangle with Winston, a duty that fell to me, I having been partly the cause of the tangle. How well the Middle East has done: it, more than any part of the world, has gained from that war.

However, as I said, I went into the R.A.F. to serve a mechanical purpose, not as leader but as a cog of the machine. The key-word, I think, is machine. I have been mechanical since, and a good mechanic, for my self-training to become an artist has greatly widened my field of view. I leave it to others to say whether I chose well or not: one of the benefits of being part of the machine is that one learns that one doesn't matter!

If you remember the history you will see that Laura and I never met. Nancy and I met, definitely, at Oxford. Laura saw me too late, after I had changed my direction. She is, was, absolutely right to avoid communication with me. There is no woman in the machines, in any machines. You are different. I do not pretend to classify or rank; but you can understand a mechanic serving his bits-and-pieces, whereas she could not. I do not know or care if you are better, or she: it is merely that I like your work, and you could (*mutatis mutandis*) have done as I have done. Whereas she and I could never have changed places. The bar between us was not her artistry, but her self and mine: and quite likely her sex and mine.

All this reads like a paragraph of D.H.L., my step-namesake. I do not think for a moment that I have got it right, but I hope from it your sense of character will show you that there are no faults on either side, but common sense, the recognition of a difficulty too arduous to be worth the effort of surmounting, when there are so many other more rewarding activities within reach. Don't worry or regret or desire me to change the face of nature. We are lucky to have proportion and toleration to pad our bones.

Yours
T.E.S.

What a whale of a letter! I apologise. Five minutes talk would have been so much more fun! Let's hope he does do *Claudius* and you have to help. I told him *No Decency*[1] was a pretty good film-subject, too!

DG/RGB/Sotheby's[2]

C. P. ROBERTSON [1]

13.2.35   *OZONE HOTEL BRIDLINGTON*

Dear C. P.

Damn the Press. I feared they might: and when I'm 'out', one of my greatest losses will be that of my 'Publicity Deflector': *per contra*, when you lose me, it will be like another half-day a week for your Department – or like a rise in pay! Less work, same pay.

My movements – 'Out' on March 11th, I believe; and with discharge leave and things, I ought to have gone after duty today. Unfortunately I'm not quite finished up here: the first of the ten boats I have been overhauling completes on Monday, for launching: and the last launches on Feb. 26.

I want to see the job through, more or less: not the final tidying, but the essence of it. So I have suggested that my successor Corporal Bradbury (more efficient than myself, but lucky in having less news value) come up here about

---

1 *I.e. No Decency Left*, written by Robert Graves and Laura Riding under the pseudonym 'Barbara Rich'. *See* letter to Graves dated 21 April 1931 (p. 483).

2 The letter was given by Graves to Sir Alec Guinness (who had played Lawrence on the stage in Terence Rattigan's *Ross* and *Feisal* in the Sam Spiegel/David Lean film *Lawrence of Arabia*). Guinness sold it in December 1987 at Sotheby's on behalf of Brompton Oratory. It is now in the United States.

1 This letter represents another plea to 'Robbie' Robertson, head of the press and publicity branch of the Air Ministry, apparently after another press attempt to procure an interview: *see* the earlier letter to him dated 30 December 1929. Possibly this is Lawrence's most outspoken comment on the newspaper harassment from which he suffered as his R.A.F. career approached its end, his reaction being doubtless intensified by the fact that he would soon be without his 'Publicity Deflector', *i.e.* Robertson, and would henceforward have to fend on his own. Clearly his state of mind worried Robertson: note in the penultimate paragraph the request to Lawrence to 'look in when [he] was next in town'. He did call at the Air Ministry on 19 March 1935, when on the run from the press and about to appeal for help to Winston Churchill. However, that was their last contact. The Lawrence-Robertson correspondence remained unknown until 2002, when two of the five letters to him put up for sale at Christie's were purchased by the Imperial War Museum; the remainder were purchased by a private bidder.

Feb 19. Handing over might be 3 or 4 days. Then I shall get on my push-bike one fine morning and slide out for Cambridge and eventually my Dorset cottage, which is entitled Clouds Hill, Moreton, Dorset. Your letters to Shaw there will find me, whenever I happen to call: but I shall be there only incidentally, and shall hope to avoid the Press, in course of time; when they have tried sundry times and not found me in. It's a lonely cottage, and I have a young and excitable neighbour. If he and I do find a reporter in the undergrowth, we will knock him on the head and inter the body, safely.

My nominal station is Felixstowe, and they have the problem of filling up my character, references, etc. in my discharge papers. For the moment, of course, I wear blue clothes and 'dig' with the other airmen in their billets in the Ozone. You are probably safe in deflecting the Press bloodhounds to Felixstowe. I shall not tell Felixstowe exactly what day I go, until I've gone.

'What line I wish you to take'! I wish, like Nero, that the Press had but one neck, and that you would squeeze it. I wish.... what do I wish? I wish I were dead, I think. These endings of careers are hurtful things, and I haven't an idea beyond my discharge, and only 25/– a week, and no courage to take another job, because these news-hounds would smell it out and bay about it. Damn them, as I said. The only way to avoid mention is to join their number, and I'd see them all boiled in paraffin wax first.

'Look in when I'm next in town'? Yes, if I can: but I have no plans, beyond that of lying doggo for a while. That might be best done in Hackney, I agree. Alas and alas: why must good things end and one grow old? I don't want to be old .... ever.

Give the *News Chronicle* my detestations, whenever they call!

Yours
T E Shaw

Imperial War Museum

SIR EDWARD ELLINGTON[1]

25.2.35   *BRIDLINGTON, YORKS*

Dear Sir Edward

Not many airmen, fortunately, write to their Chief of Staff upon discharge; but I was admitted by the first C.A.S. so hesitantly that perhaps it is in order for me to thank his successor for the forbearance which has let me complete the twelve years.

I've been at home in the ranks, and well and happy: consequently I leave with a sense of obligation, though always I have tried in return to everything that the rules – or my chiefs – would allow.

So if you still keep that old file about me, will you please close it with this note which says how sadly I am going? The R.A.F. has been much more than my profession.

Yours sincerely,
T. E. Shaw

Imperial War Museum

---

1 Sir Edward Ellington (1877-1967) was chief of air staff from 1933-37. Earlier, after distinguished service in the First World War, he had commanded the Royal Air Force in the Middle East from 1922-23, in India from 1923-25 and in Iraq from 1926-28. He later became a marshal of the R.A.F.

Leaving the air force, Bridlington, February 1935

7 THE FINAL WEEKS
February-May 1935

On 26 February 1935 Lawrence bicycled south from Bridlington, an airman no longer, on his way home to Clouds Hill. His arrival was delayed by the knowledge that journalists were besieging the cottage, and even after he reached it, their presence drove him away. Eventually, having appealed for help to Churchill and arranged a truce with senior members of the press, he was left alone.

'Next year', he had written to Charlotte Shaw on New Year's Eve 1934, 'I am going to draw in my ink-horns [...] and I shall not spend more than three pence weekly upon post.' The principal weapon in this attempt to reduce the volume of his correspondence was a specially printed card bearing the message: 'To tell you that in future I shall write very few letters' – the realization of the idea which had first occurred to him in India. By including a copy of this card with every letter he sent, he hoped to discourage replies and at last stem the tidal flow.

Nevertheless, during these last weeks between his leaving the air force and his premature death he wrote numerous letters, though some were little more than brief notes on the back of the specially printed card. At times he wrote almost in protest: 'What ails me', he complained to Robin Buxton on 13 April, 'is this odd sense of being laid aside before being worn out'. However, many – perhaps the majority – of his notes and letters from this period have a world-weary tone, suggesting a reversion to his 1929 mood of 'something broken in the works' – a phrase which he used in his last communication with Lady Astor, written on 8 May. A note to her three days earlier implies that the passage of time had brought no sense of improvement in his general psychological condition: 'something is finished with my leaving the R.A.F. It gets worse instead of healing over.' 'There's such a blank, afterwards,' he told two R.A.F. officer friends that same day, 5 May, while on the following day he wrote to Bruce Rogers, 'I'm "out" now, of the R.A.F. and sitting in my cottage rather puzzled to find out what has happened to me, is happening and will happen. At present the feeling is mere bewilderment. I imagine leaves must feel like this after they have fallen from their tree and until they die.' The 'fallen leaf' metaphor also occurs in a letter written on 6 May, to Eric Kennington, a letter which ends with what almost has the ring of a valediction: 'Peace to everybody.'

Yet on other occasions he wrote eloquently and at length, showing that his statement to Mrs Shaw in his letter of New Year's Eve 1934 that he was still 'strong and trenchant-minded' was no empty claim. Indeed, several of the letters of the last few days before his accident are most vigorously written; that to Ralph Isham on 10 May, in anger at hearing that an American university had published a letter of his without seeking permission was particularly forthright. The letter to 'Posh' Palmer of the same date shows him offering lively encouragement to an old friend who, apparently, was in a state of near-suicidal depression, telling him that the gas oven offered no solution and inviting – indeed, virtually commanding – him to visit Clouds Hill. The last letter of all, to Karl Parker, the newly appointed keeper of the fine art department of the Ashmolean Museum, Oxford, dated 12 May, is generally brisk and business-like, though it contains the sentence: 'At present I'm sitting in my cottage and getting used to an empty life.' He looks forward, however, to the time when this 'spell' is over and 'I begin to go about again'.

PETER DAVIES
Thursday, 28 Feb 35

Dear P. D.
On Tuesday I took my discharge from the R.A.F. and started southward by road, meaning to call at Bourne and see Manning: but to-day I turned eastward, instead, hearing that he was dead.[1]

It seems queer news, for the <u>books</u>* are so much more intense than ever he was, and his dying doesn't, cannot, affect them. Therefore what has died really? Our hopes of having more from him – but that is greed. The writing them was such pain – and pains – to him. Of late I had devoutly wished him to cease trying to write. He had done enough; <u>two</u> <u>wonderful</u> <u>works</u>,*[2] full-sized: four lesser things. A man who can produce one decent book is a fortunate man, surely?

Some friends of mine, in dying, have robbed me; Hogarth and Aubrey Herbert are two empty places which no one and nothing can ever fill. Whereas Doughty and Hardy and Manning had earned their release. Yet his going takes away a person of great kindness, exquisite and pathetic. It means one rare thing the less in our setting. You will be very sad.

1 Manning had been one of Peter Davies's authors.
2 The asterisks are Lawrence's: the two 'wonderful works' were *Her Privates We* and *Scenes and Portraits. See* earlier letter to Manning on p. 467 and footnote 1.

My losing the R.A.F. numbs me, so that I haven't much feeling to spare for the while. In fact I find myself wishing all the time that my own curtain would fall. It seems as if I had finished, now. Strange to think how Manning, sick, poor, fastidious, worked like a slave for year after year, not on the concrete and palpable boats or engines of my ambition, but on stringing words together to shape his ideas and reasonings. That's what being a born writer means, I suppose. And to-day it is all over and nobody ever heard of him. If he had been famous in his day he would have liked it, I think; liked it deprecatingly. As for fame-after-death, it's a thing to spit at; the only minds worth winning are the warm ones about us. If we miss those we are failures. I suppose his being not really English, and so generally ill, barred him from his fellows.[1] Only not in *Her Privates We* which is hot-blooded and familiar. It is puzzling. How I wish, for my own sake, that he hadn't slipped away in this fashion; but how like him. He was too shy to let anyone tell him how good he was.

Yours ever
T.E.Shaw

DG/Mitchell Library, Sydney, NSW

ARTHUR RUSSELL
6.III.35   [*LONDON*]

Dear Russ
Thank you: you are a comfort. When I come, I'll suggest my doubling up with you, and so I'll be able to pay my shot to your people more easily.

It will not be just yet. The newspaper men are besieging Clouds Hill, and till they ease off I'm going to keep gently on the move. First I have business in London, with my Bank to find out what my means will be after I straighten everything up. Then I have a long call to make in Scotland, before the summer visitors get there. But I promise myself a rest at Coventry, with a nice sort of safe feeling. You shall have fair warning, too. I don't want to come till this restless 'lost' feeling I now have has gone dull. The R.A.F. meant a lot to me.

Yours
S.
                                                                    University of Texas

3 Manning had been born in Sydney and was a chronic asthmatic.

HON. FRANCIS RODD
6.III.35

Thank you very much. I feel lost, now, but everything passes.

Don't look for me in Dorset till the summer is passing: the Press lay siege to my cottage and I must keep away. Going to the Midlands, I think: but we shall certainly meet somehow soon.

TES

Bodleian Library

ALEC DIXON
6.III.35

It is a feeling of aimless unrest: and of course I am sorry, while knowing it had to be.

Clouds Hill is beset by pressmen, and because of them I stay momently in London, with an idea of wandering in the Midlands, perhaps, for a while.

After they tire, the cottage should be a peaceful place. Pat Knowles, the Sergeant's eldest son, hopes to marry and settle on that side of the road. He and I get on easily.

I hope the book goes. What an ache of a profession writing is! Yet there must be at least a craving in it, for here you are at *Tinned Soldier* before the other is accepted. I shall not object to anything you may say: but I prefer sauce to butter, if one has to choose between overdoses of condiment!

I wish I wasn't too old to carry on!

Yours
T.E.S.

I'm sending out dozens of the enclosed.[1] Good idea?

Bodleian Library

1 *I.e.* his specially printed card.

WINSTON CHURCHILL[1]
19 March 1935   C/O SIR HERBERT BAKER 2 SMITH SQUARE WESTMINSTER

Dear Winston,

I wonder if you can help me? My R.A.F.discharge happened about three weeks ago, and I've since had to run three times from my cottage in Dorset (where I want to live) through pressure from newspaper men. Each time I've taken refuge in London, but life here is expensive, and I cannot go on moving about indefinitely.

My plan is to try and persuade the press people, the big noises, to leave me alone. If they agree to that the free-lancers find no market for their activities.

What I am hoping from you is a means of approach to Esmond Harmsworth, who is the new Chairman of the Newspaper Proprietors Association. He used to know me in Paris, 16 years ago, but will have forgotten. If you could tell him I exist, and very much want to see him, I could put my case before him in ten minutes and get a Yes or No.

I am writing to you because I fancy, from something you once said, that you are (or were) on good terms with Esmond – who anyway used to be a decent person. If you can get in touch with him, without embarrassing yourself, I would be most grateful.

I'll see Sir Herbert Baker tomorrow and get him to keep for me any message that may arrive during this week. I believe his Smith Square house is on the telephone, if that simplifies things: though it usually is more trouble than it is worth.

I'm sorry to appeal in this way; but they have got me properly on the run. I blacked the eye of one photographer last Sunday and had to escape over the back of the hedge!

Yours
T. E. Shaw

Churchill Papers[2]

---

1 Churchill, who retained a great admiration for Lawrence despite his 'hiding his talent in a napkin while the Empire needed its best' (*T. E. Lawrence by His Friends*, p. 201), invited him to visit Chartwell on the following Sunday. Lawrence arrived on his push-bike for what was to prove their last meeting.
2 Printed in *Winston S. Churchill* by Martin Gilbert, Companion Part 2 to Volume V (Heinemann, 1981).

EDWARD W. DAVIES[1]
27/3/35   *CLOUDS HILL*

Dear Mr. Davies

I hurl another autograph recklessly towards you, in thanks for your letter of the 21st which I found waiting for me here last night. Will you please, when you find a good chance, thank Mr. Gleave for his good offices? By degrees peace will become ensured!

Since I saw you I have seen several Directors and Owners of Agencies (can one own an agency?) and made working arrangements with most of them. I also saw Mr. Esmond Harmsworth, and have at his request written him a letter to lay before the N.P.A.[2] If they do not rear up and fall over backwards with rage at it, then I am likely to be ignored by the entire London Press hereafter.

If you have opportunity in the future, please do your best always to suppress me. I am most grateful for what you have already done.[3]

Yours sincerely
T. E. Shaw

Bodleian Library

1 Of the Newspaper Society, to which Lawrence had turned for help because of press harassment.
2 Newspaper Proprietors Association; *see* previous letter. A draft of Lawrence's letter to Harmsworth is printed as *DG* 569.
3 Davies was plainly delighted to have come to the aid of so distinguished a figure as Lawrence and wrote back by return: 'Thank you for your letter of yesterday. I suppose Liddell Hart could write an admirable chapter on my strategy in extracting a further sample of your writing, but he would be wrong again, as my letter was prompted by the vanity of wanting to let you know that I had done something. Even in fable, I believe the mouse doesn't help the lion more than once in a lifetime; still, if the chance should ever arise again, it will be my pleasure no less than my duty.'

SIR EVELYN WRENCH
1 April 1935   *CLOUDS HILL MORETON DORSET*

Dear E.W.

Yes, Mrs. Hardy knew my H.Q. and here your note waited till I came. I have been owing you a letter for so long – ever since I read *Uphill*,[1] which had a poignant directness of impact that I found somehow very gracious.

Need I be in the new one? Often I wish I had known at the beginning the weary lag that any sudden reputation brings. I should have refrained from doing even the little that I did; and now I would be left alone and able to live as I chose. To have news value is to have a tin can tied to one's tail. However what you say will not be vulgar: and therefore it may serve to correct (at least in my own esteem) some of what others have said.

I cannot say about London: my income is a 'country' one and therefore my town visits will not be frequent. I was there a fortnight ago, to see Esmond Harmsworth and enlist his aid with the Press to leave me alone. Now I am hoping to stay here quite a while, finishing off my cottage after my own liking. There is pleasure (and engrossment) in arranging and fixing one's surroundings. I find I spend nearly the whole day, beginning job after job and laying them aside, part-done. The sense of infinite time, all my own, is so new.

I've thought out the enclosed card idea, to ease the labour of answering letters. Good, don't you think?

Will it do if I come up in the summer? Or do you ever travel (not that I can put anybody up: I camp out amidst the ruins!) or can we do it on paper? I would like to be useful to you, any way I can ...

Yours
T. E. Shaw

Bodleian Library

1 *Uphill*, published in 1934, was the first volume of Wrench's autobiography; he had written to Lawrence asking for permission to write about him in the second volume, *Struggle*, which appeared later in 1935.

GEORGE BROUGH
5.IV.35   *CLOUDS HILL MORETON DORSET*

[…] I've only ridden the ancient-of-days twice this year. It goes like a shell, and seems as good as new.[1] The push-bike is a reality, though. I came down here from Yorkshire on it and have toured much of the S. of England on it in the last three weeks. It is dull hard work when the wind is against: but in lanes, and sheltered places and in calms or before winds, wholly delightful. So quiet: one hears all the country noises. Cheap — very! not tiring, up to 60 or 70 miles a day, which is all that I achieve, with sightseeing: and very clean on a wet road.

The loss of my R.A.F. job halves my income, so that my motor cycling would have been much reduced for the future, even without this 30 m.p.h. limit idea. I had half-thoughts of a touring sidecar, for long jaunts, with the push-bike for leisured local trips, but we shall see. The old bike goes so well that I do not greatly long for its successor. If only I had not given up my stainless tank and panier bags and seen that rolling stand! But for those gadgets my old 'un would still be the best bike in the S. of England. Good luck with your fan!

Yours
T E Shaw

DG

LADY ASTOR
Friday 10.IV.35   *CLOUDS HILL*

The pressmen came here again. There was a brawl, and one of them got hurt. I applied to the Newspaper Proprietors Association against the nuisance: and life has since been easier.

The place is natural, somehow: and I feel as if I might stay in it always: if only they will go on forgetting me. There are enough pottering-about jobs to

1 Lawrence had just re-licensed his motor-cycle.

fill a whole working day. I still wish it was the R.A.F. ... but that is wasting my time. I am sorry not to have used the room.[1]

T.E.S.

University of Reading

ROBIN BUXTON
13.IV.35   *Clouds Hill Moreton Dorset*

Dear Robin

The Press have not troubled me for two weeks: nor in that time have I looked at a newspaper. So we are quits, I think.

Life here is pottery;[1] I think in time I will get used to the feeling that nobody wants me to do anything today. For the moment it is a lost sort of life. [...]

I do not like civil life, nor leisure.

Thank you for sending the Hogarth portrait so swift to Oxford. I hope they will like it, this time. Things point that way, I think, but I shall hear for certain in ten days or a fortnight.

My little cottage is charming, I think, for what it is. What ails me is this odd sense of being laid aside before being worn out. However I mustn't bore you with that, and Time is on my side.

Yours
T.E.S.

Here is a cheque for my mother: which please fling into the overdraft!

Bodleian Library

1 Lady Astor had given him a key to her house in Plymouth and offered him the use of a room whenever he wished it.

1 *I.e.* Pottering: *cf.* previous letter.

ROBIN WHITE[1]

13.IV.35   *CLOUDS HILL MORETON DORSET*

You will think this is a voice from the dead: and that is almost what it is. I left the RAF (time expired) a month ago, and feel like a lost dog.

Actually that hasn't driven me to letter writing: I find it a worse task than ever. When one has nothing to do, the idea of writing becomes wholly repellent. But for two years I have been carrying about with me a letter on *Antelope*-headed notepaper, meaning to answer it, and the blunted conscience was at last rasped into life by meeting four days ago a little man (name unknown: certainly a naval officer: probably Fleet Air Arm: doing a course at the RAF School of Photography at Farnborough, now; and destined for the *Leander* soon. Can you place him from that?) who told me you were still on or in the *Antelope*. Two years in one ship sounds so incredibly persistent that I feel I must snatch the moment and communicate with you. I hope it is true. The *Antelope*, as a folder from Messrs. Turner and Newall on my table tells me, has their asbestos lagging on her steam pipes. She looks like a destroyer, otherwise: but the photograph is mostly bow-wave and smoke.

You will have forgotten your letter. It was mostly about the Bruce Rogers *Odyssey*, then a recent acquisition. I have my grave doubts about that book. The translation is too unfaithful: too deliberately unfaithful. The print too delicate. The roundels neither true Greek nor new. Bruce Rogers got the ideas from books of drawings from Greek Vases, and adapted freely. However there it is. The cheap edition has sold well in the States: and the dear edition (for England) is nearly all sold. The crash in the U.S.A. meant that none of the expensive copies went there at all, though 250 had been so earmarked. Consequently poor England was asked to absorb the lot.

There are about 50 still unsold, I believe; but they are going.

It was a pot-boiler, almost literally. The heater of my bath, and the bath itself, depended on it. All works well. [...]

You mention my R.A.F. boats. The Navy Controller, an Admiral called Henderson, is ordering them by the dozen for all ships. *Warspite*[2] is to have her complete equipment hard-chined: and every destroyer is to have a 16 foot 18-knot dinghy. The War Office are equipping themselves with them too. I have

---

1 A lieutenant in the Royal Navy. There is an earlier letter to him, dated 10 June 1931, in *DG*.
2 *H.M.S. Warspite* was one of the navy's leading battleships. Completed in 1915, she took part in the Battle of Jutland, was reconstructed 1934-7 and served throughout the Second World War.

great development plans, which I have left to my successors – and there is no successor yet. Our latest boat does 48 m.p.h. 'Our' I say: poor fool. It's all over.

This is permanent (and only) address.

Yours ever
T. E. Shaw

Why is a destroyer a bad design? – because it has too much length for its beam. Beyond four beams to the length one loses speed – in planing boats: and destroyers to be clean and fast should plane. By fast I mean 70 knots with the present machinery – or h.p.

Bodleian Library

G. W. M. DUNN[1]
5.V.35   *CLOUDS HILL*

I hope your signing on came off. Alas, If I were only 10 years less old. Something has gone dead inside me, now.

John[2] likes Gore[3], Cezanne and Epstein. Is rather deaf and quite formidable. He usually gets £50 for a drawing. If I see him before you do, I shall prepare him for canteen prices, instead. He is a great figure. Poor John.

If you come as far as that, come a little further[5] and sleep on my settee for a night (or more, if your poor bones allow).

T.E.S.
Bodleian Library

1 G.W.M. Dunn had been in the R.A.F. with Lawrence as an aircraftman. He was also, thanks largely to Lawrence, a published poet; his *Poems – Group One* was published by Cape in 1934.
2 Augustus John.
3 Transcribed as 'Grew' in the Bodleian copy, but almost certainly Spencer Frederick Gore (1878-1914), an artist whom John greatly admired and who had been a fellow member of the Camden Town Group.
5 John's home at Fordingbridge, Hampshire, was only some twenty-five miles from Clouds Hill.

FLIGHT LIEUTENANTS W.E.G. BEAUFORTE-GREENWOOD
AND H. NORRINGTON
5.V.35   *CLOUDS HILL*

Dear BG-and-N
They look lovely ... in exact keeping with their upper room.[1] By day they sit
on a brown oak mantel shelf above a S.S. fender. By night they move to my
writing table (as at present) or to my reading chair. They clean easily; stand
solidly and feel good. I only wish that they had not been possible – in other
words that our association had not ended. I try to cure myself of the habit of
saying 'we' when I mean the air.

Life here is quiet and good enough, but a very second best. I advise you all to
hang on as long as you feel the job is in your power. There's such a blank, afterwards.

Very many thanks for a very comforting action.

Yours
Shaw

University of Texas[2]

ERNEST RHYS[3]
5.V.35   CLOUDS HILL

Dear Sir Ernest,
I hope it is Sir Ernest ... these Kings are sometimes so remiss in doing their
duty ... or would it go against the grain to decorate an editor who had
swallowed up a poet and celtic scholar?

1 Beauforte-Greenwood and Norrington, with whom Lawrence had worked on the
development of R.A.F. speed boats, had lunched with him at Hythe in late April and
presented him with two hand-made stainless-steel candlesticks as a personal memento of
their association. The candlesticks are still at Clouds Hill.
2 This letter is included in Beauforte-Greenwood's contribution to *T. E. Lawrence by His Friends.*

3 Ernest (not Sir Ernest) Rhys (1859-1946), founding editor of J. M. Dent's famous Everyman's Library, launched in 1906 with the intention of providing a comprehensive library
of representative works of all time. Rhys had written to Lawrence asking for permission to
add *Revolt in the Desert* to his title list.

Anyhow, about *Revolt in the Desert*. I ought not to speak for it, as I parted with all rights in it before publication. It was a financial expedient, rather than a book, and of it I am heartily ashamed. Its present owner is a lawyer, the Hon. Edward Eliot, of Ingram House, Fenchurch Street. You may write to him, if you please: but I think it will be vain, for I own the master-copyrights of the *Seven Pillars* (from which text the *Revolt* was extracted) and am inflexibly opposed to any reprint. If I could have my way and live for ever, neither of them would ever again appear; but mortmain is not a pretty custom, so in my will I am not making any disposition of the *Seven Pillars* rights, other than letting them pass with what other property I may die in possession of, to my heirs.

The heirs may republish if they will: but I am in hopes that it will not be in your time.

We needn't regret this, artistically, for it would do your Everyman no good to descend to such popular lines. Advertisement sells a poor thing as easily as a good one, I'm afraid … and better

Yours
T.E. Shaw

Bodleian Library

LADY ASTOR
5 May 1935

It is quiet here now, and I feel as though I were fixed in my cottage for good. It is as I thought … something is finished with my leaving the R.A.F. It gets worse instead of healing over.

When I see the little latch-key in my pocket I get sorry for having troubled you without cause. Am I to send it back? I am most sorry.

T.E.S.

Bodleian Library

BRUCE ROGERS
6.V.35   *CLOUDS HILL*

Dear B.R.

Very welcome back! *Back* you will notice, with a smile. You seem right, somehow, on this side.

I'm 'out' now, of the R.A.F. and sitting in my cottage rather puzzled to find out what has happened to me, is happening and will happen. At present the feeling is mere bewilderment. I imagine leaves must feel like this after they have fallen from their tree and until they die. Let's hope that will not be my continuing state.

Money is very short, and this is the only spot, apparently, where I can afford to live: but it is too soon to judge of that. In a few months time I will know for sure if my savings are enough, or not. Meanwhile I am practising a not un-amusing penury – or parsimony, rather. Also I work enough at wood-cutting and gathering, pipe-laying and building to tire me out thoroughly by each early afternoon ... and then follows a heavenly laze, in the sun, if available, or by my fires if not.

But on the whole I think I prefer engrossment to comfort. Perhaps comfort is an acquired taste which grows with its indulgence?

We must meet: and I cannot put you up. My activities have reduced the cottage to chaos and almost forbid me to sleep in it! So tell me where and when you will be somewhere (London and Oxford are equidistant from here) and I shall do my best to arrive.

Your Melville book might be of great value. Clarel was not wholly good. His notes for it (which these must be, I think) will afford a very valuable check on how he wrote. As for the Bible ... if you find a spoiled sheet, may I have it? Those I had at Plymouth got too soiled to be fair. Dirty places, R.A.F. workshops.

Yours
T.E.S.

More Letters to Bruce Rogers

ERIC KENNINGTON
6.V.35   *CLOUDS HILL MORETON DORSET*

Dear K.

All over bonfires, the beautiful Dorset, to-night. Twenty six, I think, so far, from my window. Ah well, poor George![1]

Don't bother about those drawings. Leave it a little while till I revive my humanities and come up to see you. I plan a raid on Holly Copse, to stay with you for a night or two ... possible? At your discretion, absolutely: but I do not want to interfere with your development as a nurse. What is the illness? I do hope (by your light hearted reference to it) that it's either over or safe.

The tympanum sounds good. I wonder what it is in. Stone goes out of date slowly, I think.

'You wonder what I am doing'? Well, so do I, in truth. Days seem to dawn, suns to shine, evenings to follow, and then I sleep. What I have done, what I am doing, what I am going to do, puzzle me and bewilder me. Have you ever been a leaf and fallen from your tree in autumn and been really puzzled about it? That's the feeling.

The cottage is all right for me ... but how on earth I'll ever be able to put anyone up baffles me. There cannot ever be a bed, a cooking vessel, or a drain in it – and I ask you are not such things essential to life necessities? Peace to everybody.

T.E.S.

DG

---

1 The bonfires were in celebration of the Silver Jubilee of King George V.

LADY ASTOR[1]

8.V.35   [*CLOUDS HILL*]

No: wild mares would not at present take me away from Clouds Hill. It is an earthly paradise and I am staying here till I feel qualified for it. Also there is something broken in the works, as I told you: my will, I think. In this mood I would not take on any job at all. So do not commit yourself to advocating me, lest I prove a non-starter.

Am well, well-fed, full of company, laborious and innocent-customed. News from China – NIL. Their area now a centre of disturbance.

TES

DG/University of Reading

G.W.M. DUNN

10.V.35   *CLOUDS HILL MORETON DORSET*

Dear Dunn

Not yet, please: everything here is ready for you, and the country beautiful but E. M. Forster (novelist, humanist and critic) has written to suggest himself for some time 'about the 20th'. I cannot do two people together ... and it is as well so, for it would be to waste one of them. There are the physical limitations of the house ... the tiny cottage of two rooms ... to consider.

I will write to you again as soon as E.M.F.'s plans have precised themselves.

For coming ... Wool at 4 miles is the nearest station, Dorchester is 12. Train service to Wool is poor, but I have no time table. Apply Waterloo perhaps. If time presses, use the good service to Bournemouth, and send me word (not by telegram, for that takes 2 days and comes eventually by post) by letter a little while beforehand. Letters come every morning early by sidecar from Dorchester. So even that takes time. But if you notify me in time I can meet you in Bournemouth by Brough and bring you the wretched journey here

---

1 *See* 'General Introduction', p. xxxi Lady Astor had written: 'I believe when the Government reorganizes you will be asked to help reorganize the Defence Forces. If you will come to Cliveden Saturday, the last Saturday in May .... you will never regret it.'

(22 miles) on the carrier. Bournemouth has many more trains than Wool, and it might just make the difference between possibility and impossibility.

E.M.F. will not probably stay more than four or five days, but once he endured a fortnight. The cottage was more comfortable then, however. He is a dear and delightful person.

Nothing more till I can give you a sure date.

Yours
Shaw

Bodleian Library

RALPH ISHAM
10.V.35   *CLOUDS HILL*

Dear Isham
Merton, like the wholly gentle and decent man that he is, was delighted to hear that I had repaired in his name the Firm's involuntary omission to send you one of the Limited *Odysseys*. He has written to confirm you in my forecast. Excellent ending to a *malentendu*.

New subject. The enclosed. Who or what is this self-styled 'University' and where are its manners? They have apparently bought somewhere a letter from me to someone, and have published it without even attempting to ask my permission first.[1] As you know, I greatly dislike the publication of private letters (except after very full consideration) and therefore the insult is greater than the injury. Yet the injury is not negligible. My writing does command a certain market price, and they have stolen it.

As soon as I was sent the column, my mind turned to you. You must be learned in U.S.A. law: you may know a really good hard bad-tempered blackmailing lawyer. When the Anderson galleries published that letter which accompanied your proof of the *Seven Pillars*, I wrote to Nelson Doubleday and

---

I The note 'Leland Stanford', not in Lawrence's hand, in the margin of the Bodleian Library's photostat copy of this letter suggests Stanford University, California (founded in 1885 by Leland Stanford, governor of California), as the offending institution. However a search kindly undertaken at my request by the Stanford University Library failed to locate the letter in question.

suggested that as my American publisher he might be able to twist their tails. He didn't, or couldn't. I do not know how copyright stands in the States: but the bad manners of this effort, at least, seems to me so flagrant that if the University has my refutation, it could be made to squirm.

A caution, though. My total income is now less than 30/– a week, and all of it must go on necessaries. So please don't involve me in any expense greater than the income of one week ... say seven dollars the limit. But if your lawman can squeeze anything from the purse of the pirates, then he will be welcome to it for himself. I want to hear a squeal from them, to teach them manners (or if that is too much, prudence) in the hereafter.

Yours
T E Shaw

Bodleian Library

E. 'POSH' PALMER
10.V.35   *CLOUDS HILL*

Many people oh excellent P, would like to make a complete break with the past – but pasts are unavoidable facts. You can (by the aid of a gas oven) make a complete break with your future ... but that's all![1]

And at Clouds Hill there are no gas ovens, so I shall look forward to seeing you this summer as soon as all the plants have been watered. Pat Knowles and I are the sole inhabitants – two funny little creatures each on his side of the roadway, but meeting often and friendlily.

And ten days hence we expect E.M.[2] for a short stay. The place is not very comfortable, I fear (and the wish for comfort is not yet strong in me. Frankly I do not aim at it!) and so he cannot dare stay long.

You will be a marvellously welcome person as and when you please to come. You will be an abused and conscience haunted major if you fail to come soon.

Beethoven's Violin Concerto in D Major (Op 61) we had and have, it is 'it'.

1 'Posh' Palmer had apparently been suffering from both financial and marital troubles.
2 E. M. Forster.

HHB[3] was here two days before your letter and has returned to Perham Down. He leaves the Army in January next, is jerky but not much altered in face or mind.

Eddington and Jeans are only pen pushers out to make their public atone. Be at complete peace and forget them.[4] But DON'T MISS CLOUDS HILL.

TES

I put an S on the envelope to show how seriously I intend you to visit the Hill this summer. Bring your worst clothes and few of them, I'm as scruffy as ever.[5]

Christopher Matheson

K.T. PARKER[1]
12.V.35   *CLOUDS HILL MORETON DORSET*

Dear Parker

I am delighted that your expert scrutiny has passed the John. To me it has always seemed a powerful and characteristic drawing: but ownership blinds the judgment, and then I liked both Hogarth and John as people. So I couldn't trust myself. However if it is a decent drawing, there is only one fit home for it, and that's in your place. Hogarth was so much the Ashmolean, for his last years.

In my letter to Leeds I asked that it should be classed as a drawing, not hung on the back-stairs among the former Keepers. This is in accordance with a wish of Mrs. Hogarth's. She dislikes it as a portrait – which is the side that most pleased me! I will also ask you to see that its label does not

3 Regimental Sergeant-Major H. H. Banbury.
4 Sir Arthur Eddington and Sir James Jeans were well-known scientists with a talent for writing hugely popular (and at times philosophically contentious) books about contemporary science and astronomy.
5 The envelope was addressed to E. S. Palmer: perhaps a more formal style than usual?

1 Keeper of the department of fine art, Ashmolean Museum, and of the Hope Collection of Engraved Portraits from 1934-62 and keeper of the museum from 1945-62. He was knighted in 1960.

carry either my current or my obsolete name! That's a habit we had long ago when Woolley and I were adding a hundred objects a year to the Collection. It looks all wrong to star oneself all over the cases and screens!

At present I'm sitting in my cottage and getting used to an empty life. When that spell is over and I begin to go about again, I shall see what John thinks of the Ashmolean as a home for some really joyful drawings things done out of delight for himself.

Yours
T E Shaw[1]

Bodleian Library / The Essential T. E. Lawrence

[1] This was probably Lawrence's last letter. He had given the original of Augustus John's drawing of Hogarth (*see* p. 380 on this subject) to the Ashmolean, but it was not liked either by Hogarth or Hogarth's wife or by C. F. Bell. Following Hogarth's death he had cabled from Karachi to the effect that the drawing should be withdrawn. His proposal to Leeds, referred to here, that it should be held as a work of art worthy of retention rather than as a portrait of a former keeper for public display, together with Parker's favourable response to it, seems to have resolved a long-standing difficulty.

On 13 May Lawrence received a letter from Henry Williamson proposing a visit to Clouds Hill, so he rode to Bovington Post Office on his motor-cycle and sent Williamson a telegram with the message: 'Lunch Tuesday wet fine cottage one mile north Bovington Camp SHAW.' On his way back he came upon two errand boys on bicycles riding towards Clouds Hill and in attempting to avoid them clipped the wheel of the rear bicycle. He crashed, flying over the handlebars and suffering severe head injuries as he hit the road. He died on 19 May in the Bovington Military Hospital without having recovered consciousness. He was aged 46.

His funeral took place two days later at the nearby parish church of Moreton. Among the mourners were Mr and Mrs Winston Churchill, Lord Lloyd, Lady Astor, General Wavell, Augustus John and Siegfried Sassoon; the pallbearers were Sir Ronald Storrs, Eric Kennington, Colonel Newcombe, Corporal Bradbury, Private Russell and Pat Knowles. A. W. Lawrence was the only close relation present as his mother and elder brother were returning home from China. The body was not buried in the churchyard proper but in a small graveyard a few hundred yards down the road. A bust by Eric Kennington was subsequently placed in St Paul's Cathedral, London, where other famous Britons such as Nelson, Wellington and Gordon of Khartoum are commemorated. Perhaps the most striking memorial, however, also by Kennington, is a sculpture in Portland stone depicting Lawrence recumbent in Arab clothes, in the tiny church of St Martin in Wareham, a few miles across the heath from Clouds Hill.

T. E. Lawrence, Bridlington, February 1935

AFTERWORD

Editing the letters of a historical character for publication is a curious experience. He ceases to be a project and becomes a person in your life. His letters cease being documents to be assessed for their biographical or literary value and become a voice in your ear. You attune to his varying moods. You become involved, excited, and nervous, even, as to what you might find — or won't find. As you open another packet of photocopies or sift through another collection of originals, it's as though you had hurried to the door as they dropped through the letter-box, eager to snatch them as soon as possible from the hand of the intended recipient. You get a distinct sense of looking over the shoulder, of 'my turn next'. This might not have happened in the case of a plodding or mediocre letter-writer, but T. E. Lawrence was never that. He wrote fluently, often outspokenly, and always with style. Above all, he wrote *fast*. Only rarely did I find him boring.

Letters-editing is no easy ride, however. While there can be great satisfactions, there will also be anxieties, and not a little sweat. Deadlines loom like icebergs bearing down on the *Titanic* and there are so many more collections to assess. Partly you're delighted at finding a new letter offering an unexpected aspect or a lively piece of description; partly you're afraid that it might disturb the pattern of a section you had thought rounded and complete. In that case it's like the arrival of an unexpected guest in the middle of a dinner party: you find yourself shuffling the chairs and the table mats just when you thought you could bring in the coffee. And there's that other constant snare threatening you: the reference you failed to identify, or identified wrongly, on which, inevitably, some reviewer or other will delightedly pounce. Pounce, and, all too often, denounce. 'Mr. So-and-so's unawareness of such-and-such leaves one in the gravest doubts as to the quality of his editorship overall.' 'Connoisseurs of the writings of X still await an interpreter with the necessary scholarship.' You almost feel you're reading one of your old school reports. 'Requires more application.' 'Must do better next term.'

The trouble is you resent being found wanting but know your critic is probably right. Yet what you can't say in reply is, 'Look at the footnote on such-and-such a page. That reference took weeks to trace and needed the wit of Hercule Poirot, plus the help of half the brains in the Bodleian Library to find the answer. That note has added to the sum of human knowledge.' There was such a footnote in my book, though I didn't need all the Bodleian staff — just one, to whom I shall be ever grateful for finding the vital clue in an extremely obscure magazine of the early 1920s. The problem is that your readers can't see the work behind those lines in minuscule print at the bottom of the page; they simply glance at them (or not, as the case may be) and move on. They expect the explanation to be there, and would be offended if it wasn't.

Of course, there's the Christopher Isherwood trick, which I hadn't the courage to play. In introducing an edition of Baudelaire's *Intimate Journals*, Isherwood wrote: 'After some thought, I have decided not to attempt annotation. … What does it matter to the average reader who Moun was, or Castagnary, or Rabbe? Read this book as you might read an old diary found in the drawer of a desk in a deserted house.' I call that masterful. It might also be called a cop-out. While half-envying Isherwood's boldness, I took a different, more dangerous road. When the book was finally committed to the printers, I felt like the man in Bunyan when the burden fell from his back. There'd been quite a bit of Hill Difficulty, not to mention Slough of Despond, and, as happens to walkers when they take off a heavy pack, there was a feeling almost of dizzy levitation. For a number of reasons publication followed almost at once – far too soon to get any sense of perspective on the two years' effort which the book had entailed. My principal pleasure was in simply having got the thing done.

There is, however, if one is reasonably fortunate, a happier event in due course: the appearance of the book in later editions. This is a birth without pain: indeed, if you're reasonably satisfied with the look and style of the new volume, it is one with positive pleasure. In my case this allowed me to look back benignly on the making of the book and to sense the better aspects of the task, and the ones which I am sure will be enduring.

I can now recognize how rewarding the work was for so much of the time. I'd done the documentaries, co-worked the biography, but the letters opened all sorts of new doors. I hadn't quite expected, for example, to find Lawrence fun. In many ways his story is tragic: the genuine wartime performer turned into the Beau Geste matinée idol from which half-real, half-invented persona he retreated into aliases, an obscure life in the ranks, and an early, wasteful death. Shakespeare might have made something of it – or at least put the story in his pending file. But though Lawrence can sometimes sound like Lear on the heath, or, as he put it himself, Lucifer after his forced landing, much of his correspondence is upbeat, buoyant.

Take his letters to former wartime colleagues or servicemen who were his comrades in the R.A.F. and Tank Corps: letters quite as well-written in their brisk and often bantering way as those to literati like Robert Graves or Bernard Shaw. 'Is Cranwell still decent?' he writes from India in 1927 to

Sergeant Pugh, whom he had met at the R.A.F. Cadet College at Cranwell, Lincolnshire: 'No trumpeters, no guards? no roll calls? no general nonsense? Has the band stopped playing the Lincolnshire poacher? Does the hot water still work? Particularly I want to know if it's decently warm at reveille. Dusty will know. I used to bribe the stoker to do our fire first, in the mornings.' To an ex-Royal Flying Corps friend, B. E. Leeson, married, in business in Manchester, but away from home when he chanced to call, he writes in 1929: 'Commend me to your maid. You are a plutocrat. I have no maid: nor even a wife: whereas you have two women to look after you. Mohammedan!'

He can be sharp too, with a razor edge like Oscar Wilde's. Also to Leeson, and also on the subject of women, he writes: 'You do well to distrust the newspaper stories of me. Gods, what a foul imagination of me they do conjure up! Because I don't drink or smoke or dance, all things can be invented. Please believe that I don't either love or hate the entire sex of women. There are good ones and bad ones, I find: much the same as men and dogs and motor bicycles.'

One other thing that struck me again and again was his sheer genius for friendship: not a public-relations skill cultivated like that of a general determined to show he knows his men, but a talent as natural as spring water. And his service friends received at least as much genuine concern as his friends among the glitterati and the nobs. Almost his last letter, written only three days before his fatal motorcycle accident, was to his former Tank Corps comrade, 'Posh' Palmer, whose life was in disarray and who had hinted at suicide. 'Many people oh excellent P. would like to make a complete break with the past – but pasts are unavoidable facts. You can (by the aid of a gas oven) make a complete break with your future – but that's all. And at Clouds Hill there are no gas ovens, so I shall look forward to seeing you this summer as soon as the plants have been watered … You will be a marvellously welcome person as and when you please to come.'

Lawrence was much given to analyzing his own personality and problems as well as those of others. In this area his principal confidante and confessor was someone many years older than he: Bernard Shaw's wife, Charlotte. Like Lawrence she was Anglo-Irish, had suffered under a formidable and domineering mother and had no intention of ever adding to the world's population. He wrote over three hundred letters to her between 1923 and 1935 (enough to fill a volume almost the size of *War and Peace*), of which I found space in my book for, either in whole or in part, about sixty. Here are the most moving references to his beating and rape by the Turks at Deraa in 1917, or to the conflict of identity between himself as ordinary serviceman Ross or Shaw and the high-flying Colonel Lawrence he had once been. Emotionally he was content with his decision to lose himself in the ranks, but constantly undermining his contentment was his reason, which, he wrote to her in September 1925, 'tells me all the while, dins into me day and night, a sense of how I've crashed my life and self and gone hopelessly wrong: and hopelessly it is, for I'm never coming back, and I want to. O dear O dear, what a coil.'

As well as the *de profundis* note, however, he can strike happier ones. His letters teem with much lively discussion of plays and books, and deft descriptions of people whom he had met. This of the playwright and wit Noël Coward in 1930, in a letter to Mrs Shaw: 'He is not deep but remarkable. A hasty kind of genius. I wonder what his origin is? His prose is quick, balanced, alive: like Congreve probably, in its day. He dignifies slang when he admits it. I liked him: and suspected that you probably do not. Both of us are right.' He took to Coward and even went once to one of his play rehearsals. But his admiration for Coward's verbal dexterity brought out another self-undermining trait: that sense of inadequacy about his own writing which never left him. He wrote to him: 'Your work is like sword-play; as quick as light. Mine a slow painful mosaic of hard words stiffly cemented together.'

If he is ever boring, it is perhaps in this persistent denigration of his efforts as a writer. He will not accept anybody else's good opinion of his books *Seven Pillars of Wisdom* or *The Mint*. His rebuttals are excessive; by no standards are these works 'putrid rubbish'. Bernard Shaw, Mrs Shaw, E. M. Forster, F. L. Lucas, all beat against his self-depreciation in vain. In the light of the denigration to which he was later subjected, this genuine wariness at overpraise by his friends is worth stressing.

He was also not happy with any of the books written about him. Of Liddell Hart's biography, published in 1934, he wrote to an American admirer: 'I'm rather regretting L-H's surrender to my "charm". Had he maintained his critical distance and examined my war-time strategy and tactics with a cool head, the results would have been interesting – to me, at any rate! He is a good military thinker. But instead there comes only Panegyric III –' Panegyrics I and II being the earlier biographies by Lowell Thomas and Robert Graves. I don't think he deplored panegyrics because they might lead to subsequent critical onslaughts; he simply wanted his part in events put into a reasonable and fair perspective.

One reason why it has been difficult to achieve such a perspective on Lawrence is that, when in the 1950s the battle was joined over his reputation by Richard Aldington and others, the papers relating to his wartime role were still embargoed under what was then the fifty-year rule. The jury was out, with much of the real evidence unavailable. Perhaps the greatest excitement of my research was to go through the relevant files now available to any visitor to the nation's archives at Kew and find not only a mass of documents relating to Lawrence and his activities but also many letters by him, some copy-typed at headquarters but not a few written in his own hand. These 'new' letters show an officer playing an important, indeed a key role in a complex and difficult war situation – the vital nature of his work as adviser to the principal Arab field commander Prince Feisal being well-understood among his colleagues and superiors. From these letters I pick out one dated 12 February 1918, written after his ordeal at Deraa, a brutally cold winter, much achievement but also many setbacks. 'I'm in an extraordinary position just now,' he informs his boss in Cairo, Brigadier-General Clayton, '*vis-à-vis* the Sherifs and the tribes, and sooner or later must go bust. I do my best to keep in the background, but cannot, and some day everybody will combine and down me. It is impossible for a foreigner to run another people of their own free will, indefinitely, and my innings has been a fairly long one.' In the same letter he agreed that he would see to it, a pretty high-grade mission to be given to a mere 'hostilities only' major not yet thirty, that the Arabs would not be deterred in their war effort by the recently released news of the Balfour Declaration: 'For the Jews, when I see Feisul [*sic*] next, I'll talk to him, and the Arab attitude shall be sympathetic, for the duration of the war at least.' (Look at the Middle East today and we realize these were deep waters indeed which he was obliged to stir.) He achieved this and much else, and, as everybody knows, his 'innings' continued until the Turkish collapse in October 1918. His war ends with a flurry of signals informing Allenby's G.H.Q. about the last stages of the Arab campaign and the seizure of Damascus.

Lawrence once wrote, 'I don't think much of letters as an art form. Not even Fitzgerald, or Keats, or D. H. Lawrence or Gertrude Bell's. They always have something ragged, domestic, undressed about them.' Others, such as Liddell Hart, have claimed that he is assured of a place in literature just through his letters, but he made no such claim himself. It is perhaps precisely because he was not attempting to make literature that his letters, written uninhibitedly, with scarcely any corrections, often at length and to a remarkably wide range of people, shed so much light on so many aspects of his life, and make him seem so much more of a human being than the figure that emerges from the mass of analysis and psychological dissection to which he has been subjected over the years. I found it good to get to know him.

Do not have any anticipations. I will not pull
off another accident.

1. VIII. 27

The slow months begin to total respectably. When I got here it
was 7/1/27: and now I'm past the half year. Did ever
poor agent so long toil three years older?

This is a reply to your letter of Jan 27, which ended up with a well-
introduced remark about my Uxbridge notes. I write this on the back of
one, to show you that the not sending them as they are is only kindness
to you. I wrote them pell-mell, as the spirit took me, on one
piece of paper or another. Then I cut them into their sections, &
shuffled them, as Joyce is supposed to have shuffled Ulysses. With the
idea of curing you of any delusion you might be persuaded by the chorus
of critical England to entertain of me as a person of literary promise
& capacity — who was I? — ah yes: to disillusion you as to
my literary ability — where was I? ah yes: — to show
you that I can't write for toffee, I decided to send them you. You
would have thought them the raw material of a paper-chase. So I
began; to attach each class in some sort of order on to sheets of
paper, meaning to have them stitched for you. But that did
not work, for the sections were too interthronged.

So I am copying them seriatim into a note-book, as
a Christmas (which Christmas?) gift for you. It is a posh
manuscript in my most copper-plated hand. It will be
bound, + gilt-edged. Can I do more? (or less). Please
regard it as an expensive gift. Copying my old notes
is like eating my yesterday's vomit. (I add nothing,)
but take away repetitions, where vain. I "did" three
church parades for example: and I believe they can be
boiled to two: or even to one, which would be the
quint-essence + exemplar of all my church parades.

Enough of this stuff. Do not expect it for ever so
long. It is done against the grain. About a third of it is
done. Am I making a fool of myself? Would you rather
keep your "illusion"? There are sixty sheets like this. You
understand they are not emotions remembered in tranquillity: but
the actual fighting stuff. Photographic, not artistic. All were in
pencil. It's better than the Seven Pillars, in its class: as like
as butter and cheese: that is, not like at all: but equally rotten
The S.P. showed that I could not ratiocinate: this that I can't observe

Letter to Edward Garnett written on the back of a pasted-up page of *The Mint*

Index of Recipients

Note: A biographical footnote has been supplied for most recipients, usually on the same page as their first letter. Where this is not the case the page on which the appropriate information appears is indicated in brackets after the name.

PICTURE CREDITS

Cover: *T. E. Lawrence*, pencil portrait of T. E. Lawrence by Augustus John, 1919, courtesy of National Portrait Gallery. Photographs on pages xxxiv, 166 and 328 courtesy of the Bodleian Library, Oxford. Photographs on pages 39, 61, 216 and 587: David Garnett, *The Letters of T. E. Lawrence.* Photographs on pages 62, 165 courtesy of Imperial War Museum (T. E. Lawrence Collection). Photograph on page 418 courtesy of Reading University (Lady Astor Collection). Photographs on pages 560 and 581 Squadron Leader J. R. Sims.